THE FINANCIAL TIMES

HANDBOOK

— OF —

MANAGEMENT

Editor

STUART CRAINER

FT
PITMAN
PUBLISHING

PITMAN PUBLISHING
128 Long Acre, London WC2E 9AN

A Division of Pearson Professional Limited

First published in Great Britain 1995

© Stuart Crainer 1995

British Library Cataloguing in Publication Data
A CIP catalogue record for this book can be obtained
from the British Library.

ISBN 0 273 60694 8

3 5 7 9 10 8 6 4 2

Typeset by PanTek Arts, Maidstone, Kent.
Printed and bound in Great Britain by
Clays Ltd, St Ives plc

*The Publishers' policy is to use paper manufactured
from sustainable forests.*

For Ro – without whom this book would have been an impossible task and with whom everything is possible – with love.

CONTENTS

Foreword *Gary Hamel*   xiii

Acknowledgements   xxi

Introduction *Stuart Crainer*   xxiii

Part 1 FOUNDATIONS OF MANAGEMENT

The Changing Nature of Organizations

Overview *Christopher Lorenz*   4

INTERNATIONAL PRACTICE: Asea Brown Boveri   13

THINKERS: Rosabeth Moss Kanter   21

Managing Change *Ian Cunningham*   25

THINKERS: Tom Peters   34

Building the Entrepreneurial Corporation *Sumantra Ghoshal and
   Christopher A Bartlett*   39

The Changing Nature of Managerial Work

Overview *David W Birchall*   65

THINKERS: Henri Fayol   85

The Virtual Organization *Laurence S Lyons*   87

THINKERS: Charles Handy   95

Leadership

Overview *Stuart Crainer*   100

THINKERS: Warren Bennis   105

The Work of the Leader *Donald L Laurie*   108

INTERNATIONAL PRACTICE: British Petroleum   120

Strategic Management

Overview *Costas Markides*   126

THINKERS: Igor Ansoff   136

Mission, Vision and Strategy Development *Andrew Campbell*   139

Corporate Value Creation: implementing value-based management
  Neil Monnery, Thomas Lewis and Eric Olsen   150

Creativity in the Search for Strategy *Simon Majaro*   164

The Role of Project Management in Implementing Strategy
  Eddie Obeng   178

Quality and Beyond

Overview *Tim Dickson*   195

THINKERS: W Edwards Deming   201

Total Quality *Owen Bull*   205

Customer Service *Brian Moores*   214

Re-engineering

Overview *Stuart Crainer and Eddie Obeng*   231

THINKERS: F W Taylor   242

Re-engineering in Practice *Colin J Coulson-Thomas*   245

Human Resource Management

Overview *Shaun Tyson*   258

THINKERS: Richard Pascale   268

Recruitment and Selection *Elizabeth Hartley and Patricia Marshall*   273

Appraisal *Brian Watling*   283

Managing High-Fliers *Philip Sadler*   290

Women in Management *Valerie Hammond*   299

Reward and Remuneration *Doug Crawford and Vicky Wright*   309

Career Management *Peter Herriot and Carole Pemberton*   325

Creating High Performance Work Organizations *Edward E Lawler*   338

Empowerment *D Quinn Mills and G Bruce Friesen*   345

INTERNATIONAL PRACTICE: Semco   358

Making the Organization Work

Overview *Stuart Crainer*   362

Manufacturing Strategy *Jay S Kim*   369

Logistics Management *Douglas Macbeth*   385

Outsourcing *Hilary Cropper*   394

Building Customer–Supplier Relationships *Kenneth Cherrett*   402

Research and Development as a Business Resource *Michael Kenward*   409

Managing Marketing *Robert Smith*   415

Managing a Salesforce *Ken Langdon*   421

Design Management *Raymond Turner*   434

Managing Corporate Identity *Terry Tyrrell*   442

Education, Development and Training

Overview *Theresa Barnett*   451

The Role of Business Schools *Arnoud de Meyer*   463

Top Management Development *Robert Sharrock*   470

Evaluating Training Effectiveness: The Stakeholder Model
  Mark Easterby-Smith   482

Outdoor Management Development *Nicola Phillips*   494

Part 2 MANAGEMENT TOOLS AND TECHNIQUES

Managing the Management Tools

Overview *Darrell K Rigby and Crawford S Gillies*   506

THINKERS: Henry Mintzberg   513

Financial Management

Overview *Steve Robinson*   520

Management Accounting *Sydney Howell*   527

Managing the Finance Function *Charles Colman* 535

Managing Long-Term Investment Decisions *Eddie McLaney* 544

Managing Financial Risk *John Heptonstall* 554

Marketing

Overview *Patrick Barwise* 568

Brand Management *Chris Styles and Tim Ambler* 581

INTERNATIONAL PRACTICE: Anheuser-Busch 594

The Europeanization of brands: beyond the global/local dichotomy
Jean-Noël Kapferer 598

Relationship Marketing Strategy *Adrian Payne* 615

Database Marketing *Patrick Forsyth* 623

Competitor Analysis and Benchmarking *Tony Bendell and Roger Penson* 632

Utilizing Technology

Overview *Chris Yapp* 643

IT Management *Veronica Janas* 653

Multimedia *Peter Chatterton* 664

Learning

Overview *Jane Cranwell-Ward* 676

THINKERS: Chris Argyris 687

The Learning Organization *Phil Hodgson* 691

Self-Managed Learning *Andrew Constable* 701

Coaching and Mentoring *Joanna Howard* 714

Project-based Learning *Bob Dodds and Bryan Smith* 723

Using Consultants *Mark Pinder and Stuart McAdam* 735

Communication

Overview *Heinz Goldmann* 747

Communicating with Employees *Brenda McAll* 750

Internal Marketing *Kevin Thomson*   759

Negotiating *Jane Hodgson*   766

Networking *Vivien Whitaker*   776

Managing International Public Relations *John Graham*   785

Government and Parliamentary Relations *Patrick Law*   796

Teamworking *Graeme Leith*   802

Crisis Management *Lex van Gunsteren*   812

Part 3 MANAGING INTERNATIONALLY

The Transformation of the International Economy

Overview *Bruce McKern*   832

Achieving Global Competitiveness *Hans Wüthrich*   850

THINKERS: Michael Porter   868

Cultural Factors of International Management *Fons Trompenaars*   871

Identifying and Developing International Management Competence
Kevin Barham and Claudia Heimer   881

Training the International Manager *Bruno Dufour*   900

Managing the Global Company from the Centre
Robin Buchanan and Richard Sands   905

Managing the Global Company *Paul Evans*   920

The Evolution of Mergers and Acquisitions in Europe *Didier Pène*   930

International Joint Ventures *Peter Lorange*   939

Japanese Management *Jacques Gravereau*   947

Part 4 NEW ELEMENTS IN MANAGEMENT

The Third Industrial Revolution

Overview *Tom Cannon*   964

THINKERS: Peter Drucker   979

Public Service Management *Catherine Fitzmaurice*   982

Managing the Small Business *Panikkos Poutziouris*   989

Corporate Responsibility

Overview *Peter Spooner*   1002

The Role of Ethics in Contemporary Management *Thomas Kerr*   1011

INTERNATIONAL PRACTICE: Levi Strauss & Co   1020

Company, Community and Competitive Advantage *David Grayson*   1027

Managing the Environment *Kit Sadgrove*   1039

Corporate Governance

Overview *Nigel N. Graham Maw*   1052

The Role of Non-Executive Directors in Corporate Governance
  Adrian Cadbury   1061

Creating an Effective Board *Colin J Coulson-Thomas*   1070

Part 5 GLOSSARY

Glossary   1081

Index

Index   1165

FOREWORD
Managing Out of Bounds
Gary Hamel

One searches a handbook for answers, and this is a handbook of answers for managers. One thousand, two hundred and sixteen pages is a lot of answers. With so many answers, it seems only right to begin by posing a few questions – questions about the changing world and work of management. Though we are all quite fed up with being reminded of the fact, it is nonetheless true that we are moving inexorably from the machine age to the information age. The closer we get to the information age, the more questionable become the traditional practices and precepts of Management. (In most companies management still comes with a capital 'M'.)

With the machine age came a technocratic view of management. From Frederick Winslow Taylor's 'scientific management' to the disciplines of operations research to the current fad for business re-engineering, managers have seen themselves as engineers more than artisans. Managers were analysts – left brain people. A manager's job was to reduce the imponderable to the calculable. ('Given a price inelasticity coefficient of 0.81, we believe this new pricing formula should take our market share to 27 per cent over the next thirty-six months.)

In the machine age a manager was a professional (the AMA refers not only to the American Medical Association, but to the American Management Association as well). Managers were given credentials (certified accountant, MBA, or an alumni of Harvard's Advanced Management Program). A manager was an analyst (value chain analysis, segmentation analysis, cost structure analysis).

The act of management took place within the boundaries of industry convention, company tradition, vested authority, national context, functional specialization, the demonstrably feasible, and the here and now. Management was by the rules, by the numbers and by the book. That was then, this is now. The boundaries are gone. The game has changed. The rule book is out of date. Consider:

● **The shifting boundaries of authority**

Traditionally, authority was vested top-down, from shareholders to corporate officers, from officers to managers and then to staff. Levels of authority were delineated in terms of discretionary spending limits and the scope for autonomous action. Practical power derived from the control over resources, the proprietary information one possessed, and the sanctions one could impose.

That was then, this is now.

In the knowledge economy, the only employees that are worth having are those with many other choices of employment. They bore easily if not challenged. They look for work that is consonant with their own interests. The most capable knowledge workers are less inclined to think of themselves as loyal soldiers and more inclined to view themselves as sought after faculty members. It's not HQ any more, it's the corporate 'campus'. So, a few questions: *How effective are sanctions in a world of 'independent labour contractors'? How does one exercise authority in the absence of dependency?* For the brightest and the best, 'take this job and shove it', is not a country & western song, it's an option.

Occasionally authority can command compliance, but it can never command commitment. Beavis and Butt-head aren't the only ones who have a problem with authority – try winning the fealty of a whip-smart 32 year-old bond-trader or brand manager on the basis of raw, positional power. It can't be done. The generation entering the workforce at the end of the 20th century is as unconvinced by authority as any generation in history. *In the absence of positional authority, how does one build legitimacy around decisions? How does one actually 'get things done'?*

Personal computers, networks and corporate-wide E-mail systems are creating, in many companies, something close to an information democracy. The information boundaries that delineate corporate authority are more permeable than ever. *If every decision can be previewed, if relevant facts are broadly accessible, can't every decision be challenged? What is the meaning of authority if authority can never be idiosyncratic, can never be capricious?* 'Just do it!' may be a great advertising slogan, but it doesn't carry much weight when employees are in possession of all the facts, are capable of making their own judgements, and more than willing to challenge the judgement of those they work for.

● The blurring boundaries of control

In the machine age, control was everything. Managers were allergic to surprises. The results of that obsession were painfully detailed reporting systems, endless review meetings, brusque phone calls when budget variances were spotted, a temptation to second guess operating managers, and a seemingly unquenchable thirst on the part of HQ for more data.

There was an equally strong tendency for managers to try and bring all the resources important to success within their direct control. Business unit boundaries were defined to minimize resource interdependencies across the portfolio. Companies integrated backward to gain control of critical inputs. Joint ventures were okay so long as you ended up with 51 per cent of the equity. If you ran a big national subsidiary in a multi-national company, you worked damn hard to get critical development resources located in your country.

That was then, this is now.

Control is often illusory. To measure is not to control, as every weatherman knows. In our fast forward world, product life cycles can be shorter than accounting cycles. Accounting data is great for autopsies, but lousy for direction. And it's not just a question of timeliness, it's also a question of appropriateness. Do control systems actually measure the right things: competitors' intentions?

emerging market needs? subtle regulatory shifts? Typically, no. *Where are the dials, and what are the controls that give management the ability to anticipate and proactively respond to incipient crises and opportunities?* What is needed is over-the-horizon radar. And where anticipation is impossible, flexibility must be built in. *Shouldn't managers work as hard to make things flexible as they do to make things controllable?*

Speed and unpredictability are not the only enemies of control. In the emerging world of networked, global organizations, it is inevitable that more and more of the resources critical to the success of the firm will lie outside the direct control of the firm's managers. The hierarchy is giving way to the network. De-integration brings greater dependence on suppliers. The scale of R&D investment demands risk sharing with alliance partners. New opportunities transcend business unit boundaries. Geographic specialization leaves national subsidiaries dependent on far distant affiliates. As the boundaries of the firm become more imprecise, so do the boundaries of managerial control. *How can managers 'control' resources when those resources lie outside their firm or business unit? How can a manager be asked to take responsibility for that which he or she doesn't control? Is it managers that are needed or influencers?*

- **The shifting boundaries of loyalty and affiliation**

It was once the case that unless you were caught with your hand in the till, or publicly slandered your boss, you could count on a job for life in many large companies. Loyalty was valued more than capability, and there was always a musty corner where mediocrity could hide. Entitlement produced a reasonably malleable workforce, and dependency enforced a begrudging kind of loyalty.

That was then, this is now.

Managers have gleefully abrogated the social contract between the firm and its employees. The entitlement culture is dead. A job for life? You must be kidding! Employees are asked to be flexible, to retrain, to bring their brains to work, to take responsibility for their own development, to enlarge their jobs. In one sense, large companies are asking employees to take on the same responsibilities, and risks, they would take on in a start-up, but are denied the corresponding entrepreneurial freedom. No wonder many bright young things are turning their noses up at big company jobs. In all the talk about the new responsibilities of employees, there is little talk about the new responsibilities of managers. Talk all you like about building a high commitment organization, but isn't commitment reciprocal? No wonder loyalty ain't what it used to be.

Many managers will avow that 'people are our most important resource', but how many employees actually *feel* this to be true? The fact is that most employees feel like they are the company's most expendable resource. Substituting the word associate for employee, or redrawing the organizational pyramid with top management at the bottom is a vapid exercise if employees still feel they are treated as simply one more item of variable cost.

Employees today are urged to love customers, to have a passion for quality, to work ceaselessly for the benefit of shareholders – all laudable goals.

But it's unlikely their commitment to these goals will exceed the commitment shown to them by the company and its executives. Hence the real costs of diminished commitment are likely to be seen not just in plummeting employee satisfaction measures, but in anaemic customer satisfaction measures as well. In a world of downsizing, rightsizing and re-engineering, what should be the nature of management's commitment to employees? If a job for life breeds lethargy, what kind of commitment will breed excitement? Managers know how to re-engineer, do they know how to re-energize?

Extraordinary effort springs from a deep sense of affiliation with an organization and its goals, whether the organization is Greenpeace, Save the Children or an evangelical church. Yet much of what managers have been doing over the last several years has been weakening, rather than strengthening the bonds of affiliation between employee and employer. Of course companies should be intolerant of mediocrity; of course there should be no room for slackers. While a church may be a hospital for sinners, a company cannot afford to be a haven for under-performers. *But is it possible to build a sense of affiliation and belonging in an organization that relentlessly prunes away the under-performers? If so, how?*

● **Beyond the boundaries of experience**

Experience brings authority. A young mountain climber has much to learn from a veteran who has led an expedition up and down Everest. The assumption has been that the same is true in companies. Hierarchical superiority rests on a supposition that people at the top 'know more' than people at lower levels, that two or three decades of industry experience makes one wise.

Of course, experience is of value only to the extent that the future is, more or less, like the past. Historically, industry boundaries were relatively stable, as were the rules of competition within any particular industry. Soft drinks were soft drinks, not fancy foreign waters and exotic flavoured teas. Individuals were savers, not investors, and certainly not international investors. Telecommunications meant universal service brought to you by a monopolist, not value-added services delivered by an up-start. The regulatory environment could be taken as a given. Oligopolists had little to fear from interlopers. Barriers to entry seemed absolute. In the machine age precedents were guideposts, not millstones. There was little to devalue a manager's experience base from year to year, or even from decade to decade.

That was then, this is now.

In industry after industry the terrain is changing so fast as to make experience irrelevant, or dangerous. Do the recipes that guaranteed success a decade ago in retailing, banking, telecommunications, or airlines still bring success today? The people at the top may know more, but what do they know more about? Too often, it's the past.

It is ironic that it is often those managers who have the greatest emotional equity in the past – those with the greatest seniority – that possess the most formal authority. On the other hand, those that live closest to the future – the young people – are expected to acquiesce to the accumulated wisdom of older and wiser heads. Companies seldom miss the future because the future is unknowable, they miss the future because experience blinds them to new opportunities. Those that are most blind typically have most power. *Shouldn't authority be as much a function of foresight as hindsight? In a world of discontinuous change, shouldn't authority rest not only on experience, but also on the capacity to learn and adapt?*

Industry boundaries are in a state of flux. The utilities industry is undergoing the same cataclysmic changes that rent the telecommunications industry into myriad pieces. The boundary line between computers and consumer electronics is fast disappearing as computers become lifestyle appliances. Cosmetics and pharmaceuticals are being wed into 'cosmeceuticals'. Retailing, banking, and publishing are all going on line. It is what the head of one (in)famous software company has termed the convergence of everything. A telephone network operator must understand the world of video games. A computer company must enter the world of strategy consulting. A Japanese gadget maker must come to terms with Hollywood. *In such an environment, what is the value of experience gained solely within one industry context?* As industry boundaries converge, industry specialization may be a handicap. *Might the capacity to think across industry boundaries – to spot opportunities at the juncture of two or more industries; to draw relevant analogies from seemingly unrelated industries – be as valuable as deep experience in a single sector? If so, how does one breed managers with the capacity to escape the conventions of the past and build entirely new industries?*

● Beyond national boundaries

Multinational companies were traditionally build around countries – the German subsidiary, the Italian operation, the outpost in Australia. The basic organizational unit was the national subsidiary. Typically, the home market was assumed to be the 'lead' market – the source of innovation and executive leadership. This was true for Japanese consumer electronics companies, for American computer companies, for European chemical companies, and so on.

Not surprisingly, most managers operated in a largely national context. An American manager on a two year assignment in Paris was still an American manager. And his company, wherever he operated in the world, was still an American company. A Japanese manager starting up a factory in Thailand was still unmistakably Japanese in outlook and demeanour. And while a 'European' manager might feel equally at home in London, Amsterdam and Frankfurt, he or she would have been hard pressed to understand the business culture in Silicon Valley or Osaka.

That was then, this is now.

To a geriatric multinational, suffering from a fifty year legacy of strong and fiercely independent national subsidiaries, 'global' means 'transnational'; it means trying to catch up with the forces of economic and market integration. To a young start-up, 'global' means 'supranational'; it means being a driver of economic and market integration not a bystander. Nike, Sega, Acer, MTV and many others are defining what 'global' means; they are welding together a generation of global consumers; they are linking capabilities across the globe to produce unique products and services. For these and other supranationals, there is no single 'lead' market. The most sophisticated customers may be in one country, the fastest growing market in yet another, key development resources in another, preferred suppliers in another, and critical alliance partners in yet another.

Whatever the rhetoric, there are few managers, and even fewer companies that approach opportunities with anything close to a global point of view. It's not enough to put a global 'patina' on a manager who spent the first 20 years of his or her career in a single country, or looked upon an overseas assignment as a mildly interesting, but lateral career move. It's not enough to create a global business team where members come as representatives of their particular geography. It's not enough to develop cultural chameleons who adapt easily to national traditions. The goal must be to create managers with the capacity to transcend culture, to find the universals and build multi-billion dollar businesses around them.

The task for tomorrow's supranationals is not simply to share learning within an extant network of national subsidiaries, but to access and integrate a set of differentiated national skill sets. The challenge is to access Asia's mass manufacturing capabilities, borrow technology and software skills from US partners, tap into under-utilized talent pools in India and other developing countries, and leverage Europe's aesthetics and world class design capabilities. The most successful managers in the 21st century may well be those that carry the least national baggage. More questions: *How does one create a globalist? What will the new supranational organizations look like? How does one discover transcendent general solutions when presented with competing national solutions?*

● **The changing boundaries between the physical and the intellectual**

The machine age was a physical world. It consisted of things. Companies made and distributed things (physical products). Management allocated things (capital budgets); management measured things (the balance sheet); management invested in things (plant and equipment). The language of accounting is a language of things. In the machine age, people were ancillary, things were central.

That was then, this is now.

In the information age, things are ancillary, knowledge is central. For more and more companies, the ratio of market value to book value is a multiple of three, five, ten or more. A company's value derives not from things, but from knowledge, know-how, intellectual assets, competencies – all of it embodied in people. And none of it's on the balance sheet.

Let the economists and public policy makers debate whether it is somehow more honest, and rewarding, to make and sell things than to make and sell knowledge. The debate is irrelevant. The transition from a world of atoms to a world of ideas, captured and distributed in bits and bytes, is unstoppable. Madonna may have been the material girl, but it was her immaterial assets – copyrights, royalty agreements, digitized images and sounds – that allowed her to satisfy her material appetites. Another, not unimportant point is that while making too many things will destroy the planet; making too much knowledge won't.

So, a few questions: *Companies have spent years perfecting capital allocation; but what about competence allocation? How can a company be certain that its best talent is lined up behind its biggest opportunities, and not stuck in some moribund division? Intellectual assets don't appear on the balance sheet, there's no funds flow statement for knowledge, but shouldn't management, and shareholders, know whether intellectual capital is being created or destroyed? One can secure things (a padlock on a warehouse), but how do you protect knowledge assets? How do you do an inventory of knowledge?* A hoe or horse-drawn plough is useless on a factory floor. Perhaps management tools developed in the machine age may turn out to be as ill-suited to the information age, as were agrarian tools to the machine age.

● **The changing boundaries between present and future**

Few managers are visionaries. Look up the synonyms for management and you will discover administration, supervision, governance and their kin. Managers live in the here and now. The long-term is someone else's problem (an understandable view when one's expected tenure is two or three years and then on to the next job). Making the numbers is more important than making a vision. Doing counts for more than thinking. Managers are, above all, operators.

And why should one bother looking further out? No one can predict the future, can they? After all, the challenge is a bit more difficult than asking what will happen if the price of oil hits $12 a barrel. In a world of discontinuous change and relentless pressure for enhanced efficiency, one can hardly be asked to spend time star gazing. It is not surprising that over the past decade many companies blew up their strategic planning departments; nor that strategy consulting companies refocused their efforts on operational improvement.

That was then, this is now.

Why was it CNN and not the BBC that envisioned a world of global television news? Why was it IBM and Compaq that understood the significance of the personal computer and not DEC or Unisys? Why was it Viacom that created MTV and not CBS or Bertlesmann? The problem is not one of prediction, it is one of imagination. There is not one future; there are as many potential futures as companies. But any company that can't imagine the future is unlikely to be around to enjoy it. Living in the here and now, caught inside industry conventions, and concerned only about the next quarter, many managers fail miserably at the task of imagining the future.

Many are unwilling to invest the enormous energy required to delve deeply into the emerging trends in technology, lifestyle, regulation, demographics and globalization that point to new opportunities. But unless one has built a unique and compelling view of the future, one will be caught within the orthodoxies of the past. If the goal is to shape the future, rather than be its victim, one must live in the future. It must be as real and tangible as the present.

The present and the future don't abut each other. They are not neatly divided between the five year plan and the great unknown beyond. The present and the future are intertwined. Every company is in the process of becoming – of becoming something anachronistic and irrelevant to the future, or of becoming the harbinger of the future. The long-term is not something that happens someday, it is what every company is building, or forfeiting by a myriad of day-to-day decisions.

Even when it's well understood, the future takes time to assemble. Interactive television, video telephony, home banking, electronic publishing, intelligent vehicle and highway systems – as concepts, all these have been around for decades. And in each case it may well be another decade before they become part of the fabric of our life. But any company that has not been working assiduously for years to build the needed competencies, understand the exact needs, and assemble the required partnerships is unlikely to have a share of the spoils when these opportunities finally blossom into mega-markets. Getting to the future first is more like a marathon than a sprint. You can't enter at mile 25 and hope to win. One's view of the future will be imperfect, but a view one must have.

More questions: *How to create an organization that really, truly lives in the future, and then interprets today's decisions in that context? How does one unleash corporate imagination? How does one turn technicians into dreamers? Is there no recourse except to sit back and wait for a visionary to emerge?* Planning may be discredited, and strategists on the run, but managers must not shirk from the responsibility of leading their organizations to the future.

In the out of bounds world of the information economy, the past doesn't have to be an anchor; industry doesn't have to be destiny; borders don't have to be boundaries; employment doesn't have to be servitude; and loyalty doesn't have to be acquiescence. The language, tools, roles and responsibilities of management in this new world are only now being invented.

Our experience, and our answers, rest in the machine age. Our future, and our questions lie in the information age. When you find answers in these pages, and there are plenty, rejoice. When answers seem lacking, search for fresh perspective. And when even perspective seems elusive, seek to improve the quality of your questions. After all, leadership is not about repeating someone else's answers, it is about discovering answers to questions others have yet to contemplate.

GARY HAMEL

Palo Alto, California
March, 1995

Gary Hamel is Visiting Professor of Strategic and International Management at London Business School.

ACKNOWLEDGEMENTS

Grateful acknowledgement is made to the following individuals, companies and organizations for permission to quote from their works. Every effort has been made to ascertain copyright and seek permission. Any omissions will be rectified in future editions of the *Handbook*.

Accountancy Books, publishers for the Institute of Chartered Accountants in England and Wales, for permission to reproduce the 'Customer Contact Spectrum' chart from the *Accountants Digest on Database Marketing*.

Allyn and Bacon, part of the Paramount Publishing Group, for permission to use a diagram from *Making Vocational Choices* (2nd edn) by John L Holland (1985).

H Igor Ansoff for permission to quote extracts from his work *Strategic Management* (Macmillan, London, 1979) and Milestones in Management vol. 5, Schaffer Poeschel, Switzerland, 1994.

Warren Bennis for permission to quote extracts from 'Managing the dream' and *An Invented Life*, Addison-Wesley, Reading, Mass, 1993.

Elsevier Science Ltd, Pergamon Imprint, Oxford, UK for permission to print an extract from 'Mission, Vision and Fusion' by S Cummings and J Davies from *Long Range Planning*, vol. 27, No. 6.

HarperCollins Publishers for permission to reproduce extracts from *Global Embrace*, H Wendt (1993) and *The Practice of Management*, PF Drucker, 1954.

Harvard Business Review: Excerpts from:

'Creativity is not enough' by T Levitt, *Harvard Business Review*, vol. 41, 1963. Copyright © 1963 by the President and Fellows of Harvard College; all rights reserved.

'From competitive advantage to competitive strategy' by M Porter, *Harvard Business Review*, May–June, 1987. Copyright © 1987 by the President and Fellows of Harvard College; all rights reserved.

'What the hell is market oriented?' by B. Shapiro, *Harvard Business Review*, November–December, 1988. Copyright © 1988 by the President and Fellows of Harvard College; all rights reserved.

'The logic of global business: an interview with ABB's Percy Barnevik' by W Taylor, *Harvard Business Review*, March–April 1991. Copyright © 1991 by the President and Fellows of Harvard College; all rights reserved.

'The new productivity challenge' by PF Drucker, *Harvard Business Review*, November–December 1991. Copyright © 1991 by the President and Fellows of Harvard Business College; all rights reserved.

Kogan Page for permission to reproduce a figure from *Transforming the Company* by C Coulson-Thomas; and extracts from *Euromanagement*, H Bloom and P de Woot.

KPMG for permission to use diagrams © KPMG in Owen Bull's 'Total Quality'.

McBer and Company and David Kolb, for permission to reproduce the diagram of David Kolb's 'Learning Cycle' © Experience-Based Learning Inc., 1976, revised 1985. Developed by David A Kolb. Reprinted with permission from McBer and Company Inc, 116 Huntington Avenue, Boston, MA 02116. 617-425-4500.

McGraw Hill Book Company for permission to reproduce extracts from *The Learning Company* by M Pedler, J Burgoyne and T Boydell (1991) and from *The Creative Gap: Managing Ideas for Profit*, S Majaro (1988).

McGraw Hill Inc for permission to reproduce an excerpt from *Techno Vision*, C Wang and O Rothkopf, 1994.

MCI for permission to reproduce 'The functional model' and 'The personal competence model' from *The Senior Management Standards and Personal Competences*, MCI, London, 1995.

OTR Consultants for permission to reproduce diagrams © OTR in Veronica Janas's 'IT management'.

Richard Pascale for permission to quote extracts from *Managing on the Edge*, Penguin, London, 1991.

Kit Sadgrove's 'Managing the environment' is © Kit Sadgrove 1994, anthology rights to *The Financial Times Handbook of Management*.

Edgar H Schein for permission to use the table 'Schein's career anchors' from *Career Anchors: Discovering your Real Values*, Pfeiffer, San Diego, CA, 1990.

Simon & Schuster for permission to adapt an extract from *How to Build a Corporation's Identity and Project its Image* by Thomas F Garbett, Copyright © 1988 by Lexington Books, an imprint of The Free Press, a division of Simon & Schuster Inc; and for permission to reprint a diagram from *The PIMS Principles* by Robert D Buzzell and Bradley T Gale, Copyright © 1987 by The Free Press, a division of Simon & Schuster Inc.

John Wiley and Sons for permission to reproduce extracts from *The Competent Manager*, RE Boyatzis, Copyright © 1982 John Wiley and Sons.

INTRODUCTION

The names of the professions were once written in tablets of stone: the military; the church; the law; medicine and education. Success in your career involved entering a profession. Progression up the professional ladder could safely be assumed, as only the truly incompetent failed to move steadily forward. Of course, there were many other jobs, but their allure lacked lustre.

Conspicuously absent from the hallowed selection of professions was management. Management was an indifferent occupation, associated with the grimy mechanics of manufacturing and the slightly disreputable practice of money-making. Going into 'trade' was for many a step down.

Over many decades, and even centuries, management has had a bad press. And yet, as Peter Drucker pointed out in his masterly celebration of the art of management, *Management: Tasks, Responsibilities, Practices*,[1] it is an ancient discipline which has been practised and thought about throughout the history of civilization. The builders of the great monuments of the past from the pyramids to the Great Wall of China were involved in undertakings which demanded management to succeed. The military leaders whose names litter history were similarly concerned with managing the people and the resources at their disposal to achieve clear objectives.

While management has been a fundamental activity throughout history, the recognition and study of management as a discipline and profession is a thoroughly modern phenomenon. Only in the 20th century has management come of age, gaining respectability and credence. Even now, the study of management is still in a fledgling state. In Europe, France's European Institute of Business Administration (INSEAD) offered an MBA (Master of Business Administration) for the first time in 1959. It was not until 1965 that the UK's first two public business schools (at Manchester and London) were opened.

Elsewhere, management has been seriously studied (at least in academic terms) for a longer period. In the US, Chicago University's business school was founded in 1898; Amos Tuck at Dartmouth College, New Hampshire – founded in 1900 – was the first graduate school of management in the world; and Harvard offered its first MBA as long ago as 1908 and established its graduate business school in 1919.

Of course, these statistics pale into insignificance when set against the centuries spent educating lawyers, clerics, soldiers, teachers and doctors in formal, recognized institutions. But, during this century, management has begun to claw back the ground lost during past centuries. The result is that people are now aware of the importance of management. The modern architectural feats are triumphs of engineering, but they are also triumphs of management and are recognized as such. We celebrate the fact that it is possible to build a tunnel under the English Channel, and that it is possible to manage such a feat.

Recognition of the central role of management has not been helped by the fact that what managers do, who they are and what they stand for continues to be deeply bedded in, what could politely be called, vagueness. Even in the 1990s, for all the MBAs in the boardroom, management remains as open to constant re-definition as ever.

Interestingly, in the global business environment there is little concensus as to what makes a manager, who is a manager or what management involves. Travelling from country to country you quickly uncover differences in attitude and perception. In France, managers are usually referred to as *cadres* – a term founded on social class and education rather than managerial expertise or corporate standing. In Germany, engineers rather than managers run businesses. 'In the UK managers are very proud to be managers; in Sweden they are apologetic; and in Germany, managers see themselves as highly qualified specialists,' says leading management thinker Henry Mintzberg.[2] German managers emphasize their technical knowledge and competence. This, they believe, invests authority in them rather than an elevated position in the corporate hierarchy. In contrast, UK managers emphasize their executive rather than their technical skills. In an age of global business and internationalization, such fundamental differences in outlook and practice provide enormous challenges for the organizations of the future and those who manage them.

In the past, a preoccupation with status and hierarchy has enabled managers to explain away some of the inconsistencies. Grand-sounding titles have hidden a multitude of confusion. Unable to provide a concise answer when asked what they do, managers have preferred to explain who they are in the organizational hierarchy. In the 1990s, however, with hierarchies stripped away in many organizations, managers are being forced to confront the exact nature of their role and the new first principles of management.

What do managers do?

Debate rages over what it is that managers actually do. A great deal of research has been carried out into the activities of a wide range of managers in many different types of business. There is always a feeling that the research would like to report that managers spend a lot of time contemplating and creating; thinking and brainstorming. Unfortunately, they do not. Indeed, research repeatedly suggests that managers flit from subject to subject barely sparing more than a few minutes for any one issue. They are creatures driven by deadlines, continual interruptions and a rush of information.

Confusion over what managers should and should not do has many repercussions. If we don't know what managers should do, how can we measure their success or failure? How can we train them adequately or suitably? The vagaries of management confuse apparently simply issues. For example, how can managers be fairly rewarded? Recent years have seen an upsurge of media interest in financial measurements of managerial success and failure. The link between performance and rewards can seem illogical and is certainly inconsistent. The basic issue of rewarding people for how well they do their job continues to be a surprisingly troublesome task.

In fact, all the work on what managers actually do presents rather depressing reading for theorists in love with neat formulae or addicted to acronyms. Henry Mintzberg's groundbreaking, *The Nature of Managerial Work*,[3] for example, blew away much of the mystique of tidy in-trays and concentrated periods of attention focused on a particular task. Mintzberg spent time with a number of chief executives and simply observed. To the constrained world of management theory Mintzberg's conclusions seemed revolutionary. He found that managers shifted from one task to another, that they did not concentrate on any one subject for very long and that they were continually peppered with information and a variety of calls on their time.

Other examinations of the activities of managers reveal similar patterns of chaotic communication and apparent lack of focus. Phil Hodgson of Ashridge Management College in the UK spent time tracking the activities of a number of senior managers. He found that the managers had very little idea of dates and events from the fairly recent past. This was not altogether surprising – they were busy people. But, three weeks earlier the managers had been able to state categorically the four or five major items on their agenda and could put them in order of importance with dates of meetings and decisions. Only a few weeks later, and having lived through the events, they couldn't say what had happened without desperately searching through their diaries.

'The tendency to spend short periods of time on any one subject makes it even more unlikely that managers can gain a profitable perspective on the past,' writes Hodgson. 'This exposes the fallibility of the traditional case study method of management education. Case studies make management appear tidy and logical. Yet, in reality the thought processes are complex and jumbled. Finding a way through is as practical as unravelling a plate of spaghetti.'[4]

Traditionally, the glib answer to the question of what managers do has been the unspeakable acronym POSDCORB – Planning, Organising, Staffing, Directing, Co-ordinating, Reporting and Budgeting. It cannot be denied that this covers many of the tasks which managers find themselves carrying out. The trouble is that they do many more activities, and even when they are directing or reporting they are often only doing so for very brief periods of time before the next activity begins. Management is wider in its range, more spontaneous, more personal and more dynamic than POSDCORB suggests.

The truth is that research suggests managers find themselves involved in an increasingly impossible balancing act. Management is strewn with paradoxes such as order and chaos; the short- and the long-term; and a host of others battle for attention. Day-to-day management is vague, immediate, intuitive, personal, complex and chaotic. And within these elements lies much of the attraction. It is human and wide ranging. Managers touch on economics, sociology, psychology, morality and politics every day of their working week. Such a range defies systems and dry classification.

Yet, the quest for professional status insists that management should be more clear-cut and clinical. While managers may be attracted to structuring and formalising what they know and how they manage, they are also likely to find great satisfaction in the spontaneous, human and intuitive elements in their work.

There is now more management and more to management than ever before. 'Business, we know, is now so complex and difficult, the survival of firms so hazardous in an environment increasingly unpredictable, competitive and fraught with danger, that their continued existence depends on the day-to-day mobilization of every ounce of intelligence,' Konosuke Matsushita, founder of Matsushita Electric, once observed.[5]

As management becomes ever more critical to social and economic success, more professional and systematized, the elements which make it exciting cannot be ignored. Management is surrounded by the mythology of instinct and intuition. Managers continually talk of gut feeling, hunches and instinct, but not in the board-room. Here rationality takes over and inspiration is hidden away.

A Franciscan friar, Luca Pacioli, born in the middle of the fifteenth century in an obscure Italian town, is credited with being the father of the accountancy profession. Management has no such past to fall back on. Instead, it has invented a colourful Hall of Fame filled with business people who struck lucky with one great idea. Indeed, in the 1980s the intuitive and spontaneous manager became an aspirational figure. The entrepreneur was one of the icons of the decade – ambitious, technologically adept, confident and more interested in figures than people. The stereotypical entrepreneur was a throwback to the time when management was not thought of as a profession, but as an amateur calling.

While the amateurs enjoyed their brief glory, their legacy was a reminder that management is the art of the moment. Unlike other professions it is not backward looking. It cannot afford to be. The rules of yesterday rarely apply. It is not a static art. Instead, its very nature is shiftless and dynamic. It is little wonder that managers appear to have an unquenchable thirst for knowledge and insight into their own profession. Managers buy books like Kenneth Blanchard's *The One Minute Manager* in their millions. Would lawyers buy *The One Minute Barrister*? We know the answer. They would not, because they would see it as demeaning and inappropriate – mastering the legal profession takes many years of study and practice.

Management is elusive and ambiguous. Years of study and practice can, as many have experienced, lead to the bankruptcy court. Bill Gates of Microsoft has observed: 'The art of management is to promote people without making them managers.' It is as if by becoming recognized as managers, managers lose their intuitive and immediate ability to manage. The vacuum of status consumes the innate managerial skills which ensured their promotion in the first place.

The secret of success

Management's credibility has not been helped by its continual shift from fashion to fashion. There is still an air of desperation in the way that managers cling to new ideas, approaches and techniques.

The problem is that the very best management practice often precedes the neatly packaged theory. Isolated but excellent practice then has to be converted into a generic management theory backed with data and research. The practice is at the leading edge – but it also has to work as a theory.

Research at the Massachusetts Institute of Technology suggests that management fads follow a regular life cycle. This starts with academic discovery. The new idea is then formulated into a technique and published in an academic publication. It is then more widely promoted as a means of increasing productivity, reducing costs or whatever is currently exercising managerial minds. Consultants then pick the idea up and treat it as the universal panacea. After practical attempts fail to deliver the impressive results promised, there is realization of how difficult it is to convert the bright idea into sustainable practice. Finally, there follows committed exploitation by a small number of companies.

Ironically, blame for this obsession with the latest trend can partly be attributed to the professionalization of management. Once management became regarded as a profession, it was assumed that there was a number of skills and ideas which needed to be mastered before someone could proclaim themselves a professional manager. The skills of management were regarded like a bag of golf clubs. When the occasion demanded a particular skill it was extracted from the bag and put to work. New skills could occasionally be added to the managerial bag of tricks when, and if, required.

Unfortunately, managerial life is no longer so straightforward; to carry on the analogy, the manager of the 1990s is liable to need a very large golf bag to contain all the necessary clubs and will have to employ many simultaneously. Typically, work by the UK's Management Charter Initiative to identify standard competencies for all middle managers emerged with several hundred.

Despite this, the faddishness of managers continues as they seek out new skills and new solutions to perennial problems. 'It has become professionally legitimate in the United States to accept and utilize ideas without an in-depth grasp of their underlying foundation, and without the commitment necessary to sustain them,' observes Richard Pascale in *Managing on the Edge*.[6]

The search for the secret of management has taken managers and organizations through bewildering loops and has spawned an entirely new vocabulary. Managers have embraced brainstorming as a useful tool; they have explored Douglas McGregor's 'Theory X and Theory Y'; negotiated Blake and Mouton's 'Managerial Grid'; been driven on by 'Management by Objectives'; discovered strategic management through Igor Ansoff in the late 1960s; been converted by Tom Peters and Robert Waterman's *In Search of Excellence*; and have, no doubt, also tried their hand with quality circles and various forms of Total Quality Management. And yet, there is no single best way to manage – simply a rag-bag of shared experiences, short-lived best practice and high expectations.

The new nature of management

In *The Practice of Management*, published in 1954, Peter Drucker identified what he believed would be the seven tasks of the manager of the future. He or she:[7]

1. Must manage by objectives.
2. Must take more risks and for a longer period ahead. And risk-taking decisions will have to be made at lower levels in the organization.
3. Must be able to make strategic decisions.
4. Must be able to build an integrated team, each member of which is capable of managing and of measuring his or her own performance and results in relation to the common objectives.
5. Will have to be able to communicate information fast and clearly. He or she will have to be able to motivate people. He or she must be able to obtain the responsible participation of other managers, of the professional specialists, and of all other workers.
6. Must be able to see the business as a whole and to integrate his or her function with it.
7. Will have to be able to relate the product and industry to the total environment, to find what is significant in it and what to take into account in his or her decisions and actions. And increasingly, the field of vision of tomorrow's manager will have to take in developments outside his or her own market and country. Increasingly, he or she will have to learn to see economic, political and social developments on a worldwide scale and to integrate worldwide trends into his or her own decisions.

Forty years on, these ideas resonate with many modern perceptions of what managers need to do to add value to their organizations. The management sage, Drucker, appears once again to have been ahead of his time.

To some extent, the 1990s have seen a sea-change away from the desperate search for the latest big idea. Already high expectations have become even higher. The range of the debate and the nature of the challenge has expanded considerably. Managers in the 1980s were preoccupied with making incremental improvements to existing practice. The emphasis was on improving the quality of their products and services; performing the same activities faster and more reliably; achieving illusory excellence. It is increasingly recognized, in the 1990s, that incremental improvement is no longer enough. Instead, the emphasis is on 'transformation', 'breakthroughs', and 're-engineering'.

The vocabulary sounds distressingly similar to management fads and fashions of the last 30 years. But behind the hype of consultants and commentators, there is concensus. Change has become the mantra of our time.

Richard Pascale has persuasively mapped out the new agenda:

'The incremental approach to change is effective when what you want is more of what you've already got. Historically, that has been sufficient because our advantages of plentiful resources, geographical isolation, and absence of serious global competition defined a league in which we

competed with ourselves and everyone played by the same rules. Campaigns to become "more automated", "more productive", "more participative", "more dedicated to quality", made sense and, in aggregate, yielded some improvement. For over one hundred years we grew accustomed to improving things without having to alter the mindset upon which the improvements were predicated. It is not surprising that organizational theorists and managers who observed and practised during this era came to regard the assumptions that undergird our success as fundamental truths that no longer warranted questioning and re-examination.'[8]

For managers change is nothing new. Organizations have always experienced the ebb and flow of success and failure. They have always been prone to the cyclical sweeps of economics. Today, however, the force and speed of change means that it is becoming increasingly more difficult for organizations to hold their own, let alone prosper. Between 1955 and 1980 only 238 companies fell out of the *Fortune 500* rankings. Between 1985 and 1990, however, 143 dropped out.[9] From the 12 companies which made up the Dow Jones Industrial index in 1900, a single one – General Electric – remains an industrial giant.[10] Companies are no longer reassuring presences, permanent fixtures in our towns and cities offering jobs for life and constantly-sustained growth. Instead, they are fragile, impermanent and far from reassuring.

As a result, identifying companies as successes, or worthy of emulation, is a risky activity. The management bestseller of the 1980s, *In Search of Excellence,* by Tom Peters and Robert Waterman, for example, identified 43 companies which the authors had identified as 'excellent'. Some of the selections seemed safe choices – at the beginning of the 1980s IBM's place among the elite could not be questioned. Only a few years later, IBM and some of the other 43 companies were in trouble. If they had been asked to identify excellent companies five years on from *In Search of Excellence,* it is likely that Peters and Waterman would have selected substantially different names. Opening his sequel, Tom Peters noted with brutal honesty: 'Excellence RIP'.[11]

The pace of change and its fundamental nature cannot be under-estimated. Over the last decade the very essence of management has been transformed. This transformation has come through the convergence of a number of trends and developments.

First, in many substantial organizations hierarchies have been severely pruned. This has wide-ranging implications. The command and control philosophy rests at the traditional heart of management. The accepted wisdom was that top managers lay down strategies for those on the corporate equivalent of the front line. While managers commanded; others climbed manfully over the ramparts. This model produced layer upon layer of hierarchy and ridiculously complex organizational structures – in the 1970s the cumbersome British Steel had a management chart which filled the entire wall of a moderately-sized room. The size of its management was eventually matched by the size of its losses.

Hierarchies encouraged bureaucracy. Huge numbers of managers were sustained in work because of the hierarchy rather than because they added value to the organization's performance or effectiveness.

Destroying hierarchical layers brings managers closer to the rest of the organization, and *vice versa*. Between 1981, when new chief exective Jack Welch took over, and 1990, GE in the United States cut the average number of layers between the chief executive and the front line from nine to four. At the same time as making huge cuts in managerial numbers and throughout the company GE increased its revenues from $27 billion to $60 billion.[12] Similarly, at Chrysler there are now 50 workers to every manager. In the 1980s there were 20; soon the ratio will be 1 to 100.[13]

The realization that needless hierarchical layers should be removed was prompted by intensifying competition and the rapid emergence of Information Technology (IT) as a key business tool. IT seemed to provide a ready solution to the problems created through employing excessive numbers of managers.

Despite huge investments, there is growing realization that IT's business potential has yet to be fully realized. More effective usage will give added impetus to the revolution in management. The end-result may well be the one mapped out by Charles Handy, one of the most far-sighted of management thinkers. Handy anticipates that the future of work will involve half as many people being paid twice as much to produce three times as much.

This may be as ambitious as the talk of the leisure age in the 1970s. What can be said is that the scale of these changes affects all aspects of management. Management in the 1990s is radically different from anything that has gone before. New demands and expectations of managers require new managerial skills, perspectives and definitions of best practice.

Such a revolution is never going to be easy. 'It's difficult to unlearn behaviours that made us successful in the past,' says Robert Haas, Levi Strauss chairman and chief executive. 'Speaking rather than listening. Valuing people like yourself over people of another gender or from different cultures. Doing things on your own rather than collaborating. Making the decision yourself instead of asking different people for their perspectives. There's a whole range of behaviours that were highly functional in the old hierarchical organization that are dead wrong in the flatter, more responsive organization that we're seeking to become.'[14]

Managers now need to learn to work *with* people from within and outside their own organization. 'Fundamental to the new logic is the belief that value can be added at all levels of the organization. In the conventional logic, the assumption is that organizations, if structured properly, add value primarily at the top,' observes Edward Lawler of the University of Southern California School of Business.[15]

So, the new managers must ensure that value is added throughout the organization rather than in isolated pockets. Ideas that enhance performance need to be utilized whether they come from lathe operators or professional strategists.

Rather than narrowly-defined functional specialists, the new managers are more likely to be generalists able to function in isolation or as members of cross-functional teams. 'Managers are increasingly using multi-disciplinary project teams to identify problems and to plan and recommend solutions,' observes Henry Wendt, SmithKline Beecham chairman. 'Vested with the authority to make decisions, teams that are multilevel and multicultural, as well as multidisciplinary, enable a faster response and more sensitive understanding of important local and global nuances. Their widespread use contributes to reductions in levels of management. Teams can be created and redeployed quickly. Most of all, they are splendid environments for organizational learning and for re-directing patterns of behaviour. In technology-intensive organizations, especially in research and development, team-oriented management structures have become the norm.'[16]

Research by the Institute of Management, *Management Development to the Millennium*, surveyed over 1,200 managers on what skills they thought would be required in the future. In order of popularity, the skills were:

- strategic thinking (eg longer term, broader perspective, anticipating) responding to and managing change
- an orientation towards total quality and customer satisfaction
- financial management (eg role and impact of key financial indicators)
- facilitating others to contribute
- understanding the role of information and IT
- verbal communication (eg coherent, persuasive)
- organizational sensitivity (eg cross-functional understanding)
- risk assessment in decision making.

This represents a fundamental shift in emphasis. Management was once about supervision, of motivating factory-floor workers to produce more goods or to provide services more effectively. Increasingly the emphasis is now on raising productivity and motivation throughout the organization.

Yet again, it is a shift shrewdly predicted and understood by Peter Drucker. In a 1991 *Harvard Business Review* article he mapped out the new challenge to managers for the 1990s and beyond: 'The single greatest challenge facing managers in the developed countries of the world is to raise the productivity of knowledge and service works. This challenge, which will dominate the management agenda for the next several decades, will ultimately determine the competitive performance of companies. Even more important, it will determine the very fabric of society and the quality of life in every industrialized nation.'[17]

The Handbook

Ambitiously entitled a *Handbook of Management*, this book offers no immediate solutions to the problems which confront individual managers in unique situations. It can, however, act as a starting point, leading into complex subjects, such as the changing nature of organizations. It brings together a cornucopia of ideas, practices and thinking. Not all of it may be immediately relevant to a manager's work today, but in all likelihood a career in management will draw on virtually every subject covered in this book.

The subjects lend themselves to four main areas which, in the *Handbook*, are in numbered Parts entitled:

1: Foundations of Management
2: Management Tools and Techniques
3: Managing Internationally
4: New Elements in Management

Individual sections, numbered sub-chapters, are relatively short and major areas, the main chapters, start with an introductory overview to draw out major trends. All are followed by details of further and related reading. Throughout the book there are introductions to the ideas and work of major management thinkers and writers – from the nineteenth century's Frederick Taylor to Rosabeth Moss Kanter. There are also similarly accessible articles from practising business people analysing international best practice in particular areas.

The book does not provide any easy answers. If ever there were any, they have long since ceased to exist. Management in the 1990s is perplexing and challenging, more complex than ever before and, for millions of managers throughout the world, a constant source of learning, stress, excitement, disappointment and achievement.

STUART CRAINER, 1995

References

[1] Drucker, P, *Management: Tasks, Responsibilities, Practices*, Heinemann, London, 1974.
[2] Interview with Henry Mintzberg, 1 March 1994.
[3] Mintzberg, H, *The Nature of Managerial Work*, Harper & Row, New York, 1973.
[4] Hodgson, P, and Crainer, S, *What do High Performance Managers Really Do?*, FT/Pitman, London, 1993.
[5] Pascale, R, *Managing on the Edge*, Penguin, London, 1991.
[6] *Ibid.*
[7] Drucker, P, *The Practice of Management*, Harper & Row, New York, 1954.
[8] Pascale, R, *Managing on the Edge*, Penguin, London, 1991.
[9] Newport, JP, 'A new era of rapid rise and ruin', *Fortune*, 24 April 1989.
[10] Lorenz, C, 'Quantum leaps in a dangerous game', *Financial Times*, 22 September 1993.
[11] Peters, T and Austin, N, *A Passion for Excellence*, Collins, London, 1985.
[12] Dickson, T, Lorenz, C and Kellaway, L, 'Bosses find it's a snip at the top', *Financial Times*, 19/20 March 1994.
[13] Griffith, V, 'Blue-collar team, white-collar wise', *Financial Times*, 11 May 1994.
[14] Bennis, W, *An Invented Life*, Addison-Wesley, Reading, Mass, 1993.
[15] Lawler, E, 'New logic is here to stay', *Financial Times*, 28 January 1994.
[16] Wendt, H, *Global Embrace*, Harper, New York, 1993.
[17] Drucker, P, 'The New Productivity Challenge', *Harvard Business Review*, November-December 1991.

PART

1

FOUNDATIONS

OF

MANAGEMENT

The Changing Nature of Organizations

1

'Tomorrow's effective organisation will be conjured up anew each day.'   *Tom Peters*[1]

'The greatest personal skill needed for this decade will be to manage radical change. There is unlikely to be any business or institution which will escape radical change in the nineties and the choices before us are to manage it ourselves or to have change forced upon us.'   *Sir John Harvey-Jones*[2]

'Organisations are a system of co-operative activities – and their co-ordination requires something intangible and personal that is largely a matter of relationships.'   *Chester Barnard*[3]

[1] Peters, T, *Liberation Management*, Knopf, New York, 1992
[2] Harvey-Jones, J, *Managing to Survive*, Heinemann, London, 1993
[3] Barnard, C, *Functions of the Executive*, Harvard University Press, Cambridge, Mass, 1938

OVERVIEW

Christopher Lorenz

Boundaryless, virtual, horizontal, flat, shamrock- or starburst-shaped, clustered, concentric, circular. Managers are constantly bombarded with these images of the sort of organization their companies must become if they are to survive the change, complexity and chaos of the late 1990s and beyond.

As if one set of such epithets was not enough, executives are assured by gurus and academics that these structures will create the type of customer-facing, value- and process-driven, rapid-response, high-performance, self-managed, team-based enterprises needed to compete in the markets of the future. In an overworked but powerful phrase, they are advised that this is the 'new management paradigm'.

To work successfully in such organizations, managers are told they must abandon their traditional behaviour, and instead learn to become empowering 'coaches'. They must develop their powers of visionary leadership, but at the same time they must become open, trusting, listening, co-operative and supportive 'enablers' of their subordinates – or, in the new *lingua franca* of management, of their 'colleagues' and 'associates'.

All this demands unprecedented proficiency, versatility and performance. Yet, knowingly or otherwise, most are still – in a graphic phrase coined by professors Christopher Bartlett and Sumantra Ghoshal – 'first-generation managers trying in second-generation organizations to operate third-generation strategies.' The mismatch is obvious, painful and dangerous.

What this implies for organizations and those working within them is stark and simple: revolution.

The nature of this revolution is far-reaching – transforming the way organizations do business, the way they are structured, and the relationships between managers and employees – and it is far from over. To repeat an apt if well-worn cliché, one of the few certainties for managers today is that change and uncertainty are here to stay.

Dismantling command and control

The true nature of the revolution under way is shown in stark relief if one considers the traditional structure of organizations. Throughout the twentieth century, large organizations have been structured on the time-hallowed military principle of 'command and control'. So has most management language. Top managers at 'headquarters' – the brains of the organization – set the

4

'strategy', and tell senior 'subordinates' how to implement it. Strategy is then translated into 'operations' by senior managers, who tell their 'direct reports' in various specialist departments – or 'functions' – what to do. The cascade process continues down the corporate hierarchy until the message reaches the 'front line': factory workers, shop assistants and other sales staff.

The hierarchy's role in the reverse direction has been to pass intelligence back up, level by level, from the bottom and from the outside world. As Peter Drucker has argued, many middle management jobs are really about filtering information.

The command and control model has been modified in various ways in past decades, as organizations became too large and complex to be managed entirely from the top. But since the early 1980s the system has broken down under a string of pressures:

- **Cost.** Management has become unacceptably bloated, not just at head office, but also at every level between it and the front line. In some companies this still means more than 10 hierarchical tiers.

- **Competition/shorter product cycles.** Hierarchies have slowed down companies' speed of response. This did not matter in the 1960s, when growth was sure and predictable, and competition mainly limited to other companies from the same country, or at most the same region. Since the late 1970s, competition in one industry after another has rapidly become international in nature. The new onus is on speed of delivery, reducing time to market and competing aggressively in hyper-competitive markets.

- **Information technology.** This has been a crucial influence, rendering many management jobs obsolete, especially since the late 1980s. IT has cut the cost of automated information transfer and processing, making it possible for top management to communicate cheaply direct with the front line. It has also improved immeasurably the ability of people at every level and in every specialist department within an organization to communicate across it, without going through department heads.

- **Horizontal structures.** The pressure for faster results has forced companies to cut the amount of vertical communication. Whole tiers of high-level committees have been replaced by task forces and project teams spanning departmental boundaries. This 'cross-functional' drive has been reinforced by the fashion for 're-engineering' the processes by which organizations do their work – at least in the front line. It has also encouraged 'empowerment', the word consultants and academics use to describe how companies have been trying to give more authority to employees lower down the ladder who are closer to customers and markets. (Perhaps more usefully, Robert Waterman calls this 'directed autonomy'.) In so doing, of course, they effectively by-pass tiers of middle managers and, increasingly, senior executives as well.

- **Economic recession.** All the above pressures were reinforced by the slow-down which gripped western economies in the early 1990s.

The revolution in practice: confronting the corporate death cycle

Long before most large European companies began to confront the need for revolution, America's GE was demonstrating the stark reality of managerial change. Led – some would say frog-marched – by a bombastic new chief executive, Jack Welch, the company tore up its structure, shape and ways of doing business. Between his arrival in 1981 and the end of the decade, GE cut the average number of management layers between Welch and the very front line from nine to four. Its headquarters was slashed from 2,100 people to fewer than 1,000. The number of senior executives across the company was cut, first from 700 to 500, and between 1990 and 1994 by another 100. The overall workforce was almost halved, from 404,000 to 220,000. Yet GE's revenues more than doubled through this period, from $27 billion to $60 billion.

For managers still inside GE, however, the real 'story' is the revolution which has occurred in relationships across and down the organization. Here, the most important concept is what used to be described – in true military manner – as 'the span of control': the number of people who reported to each manager. When Welch arrived, GE was running at a conventional five or six per manager. By the late 1980s its average had doubled, and at the time of writing is at about 14 – with some units pushing 25 or more.

With that change has come a transformation in the way employees relate to 'their' managers, and in the nature of the management process itself. Since the only way for a single person to 'manage' two dozen people is to allow them more independence, management at GE really has changed from being a 'command and control' function to one of mainly 'coaching' people, and – providing their type of task allows it – unleashing their initiative as completely as possible.

Several GE factories now have only one level of management, and a few claim to have none at all – just a collection of self-managing work teams which, within prescribed limits, make all their own decisions, from recruitment to purchasing and production levels.

Few mature large companies have much hope of emulating GE's rebirth – or, at least equally impressive, that of Motorola. This is not for want of trying. Vast numbers of western companies are undergoing drastic change, or are about to do so. They are attempting to escape what has become an unusually intense phase of the natural cycle of birth, life and death which large companies have experienced since the nineteenth century. Of the 1970 *Fortune 500*, 60 per cent have gone – either acquired or out of business. Between 1980 and 1990 alone, almost 40 per cent ceased to exist.

As one senior executive with a US multinational puts it: 'Very few organizations last the lifetime of an individual and still fewer lead their industry for more than 20 or 30 years.'

He is understating the problem. The average corporate survival rate for large companies in the early 1980s was only about half as long as the life of a human being, according to a well-publicised study by the Shell oil giant. It has since accelerated. Yet some companies last well over 75 years.

6

The phenomenon of rapid corporate decline and fall has two traditional explanations: first, the inability of most companies to 'learn', and adapt at least as rapidly as their environment changes; and second, the tendency of companies in certain industries to be disrupted severely by technological change. When an innovator attacks their market, most incumbents fail to react effectively. Within a few years, even months in some unstable sectors, they are toppled from their perch – Kodak by Fuji; GM by Ford, Toyota, Honda and Nissan; and IBM by the combined forces of clones, workstations, personal computers and Microsoft. A related example is Wang, which dominated word processing until PCs almost sank it.

The popular explanation for this phenomenon is the 'fat and lazy' syndrome: a company grows over-confident, careless and sluggish, and either fails to spot the significance of an innovation or cannot stir itself to take remedial action until it is too late. In the post-war years most steam locomotive makers fell into this trap when they finally perceived the challenge from diesel-electrics was serious.

Rebecca Henderson of the Massachusetts Institute of Technology suggests the fundamental problem is what she calls the power of 'embedded architecture'. As successful companies learn more and more about their existing products, services and ways of operating, she says this knowledge becomes deeply embedded within them: in their communications channels, information and accounting systems, strategies, structures and cultures. As a result, they have difficulty recognising the innovative threat, and take too long to launch remedial action. Companies, no matter what their business, can no longer afford to be so laggardly.

Since the Shell study was done in the 1980s, the pace of change in the business environment has accelerated on every front. Consequently, many large companies are experiencing unprecedented pressure. In these circumstances, the old 'success strategy' of continuously improving performance is no longer adequate. Instead, companies in all sectors must focus on becoming not only better but radically different.

The quest for re-invention

Under intensive pressure, far too many companies focus almost exclusively on better management of their existing assets. This response takes the form of 'restructuring' (through downsizing and delayering) and the 're-engineering' of processes, such as product development and order fulfilment. But, these are only two of four overlapping steps necessary for the complete regeneration of a company. The other two, in the jargon of two influential thinkers, are 'reinventing strategy' (Gary Hamel) and 'reinventing the organization' (Richard Pascale).

'Restructuring is necessary, since it makes companies smaller', says Hamel. So is re-engineering – it makes them better. But, without the reinvention of strategy, they will not become different. By the mid-1990s, Westinghouse had become smaller but not better, and Xerox better but not different. In contrast, their main respective rivals, General Electric and Canon, had become better and different.

In mathematical terms, companies are constantly encouraged by investors to improve the efficiency of their current operations and resources – 'to attack the denominator'. They are not being stimulated to 'increase the nominator': to create new products, markets and even industries.

As a result 'more and more clusters of unimaginative, denominator-focused competitors are engaged in successive rounds of downsizing,' says Hamel. 'We have an epidemic of corporate anorexia.' The only way a company can get ahead is to foresee the next round of competitive advantage and evolution in its industry, and to create it. Hamel continues: 'The biggest rewards ultimately go to companies which transform their industries, change the rules of the game, redraw industry boundaries and establish fundamentally new competitive parameters.'

Thus the primary goal must be to become the architect of an industry's transformation – not just once, like Canon, CNN, Intel or Virgin, but repeatedly, like 3M and HP. To do that, as Hamel points out, companies have to challenge not just the orthodoxies of the incumbents in an industry, but also their own – which is far harder.

Traditionally, organizations have been notoriously inept at challenging, questioning and re-inventing their own ways of working and thinking. Today, argues Richard Pascale, organizations must initiate a constant state of reinvention.

'Reinvention is not changing what is, but creating what isn't,' says Pascale, lamenting that precious few large companies measure up to his definition of 'reinvention' and 'transformation'. The reasons for the scarcity of 'reinvention' cases are not hard to find. Pascale often enthuses a company's top managers into embracing the gospel of transformation, only to find them backing off when they discover how conflict-ridden and wrenching the shift can be, especially for themselves.

In order to reinvent itself, a company must alter what academics call the 'organizational context' – the underlying assumptions and invisible premises on which its decisions and actions are based. Rather than just concerning itself with new types of 'doing', Pascale warns, a company must alter its 'being' – its inner nature.

Faced with the painful need to reinvent who they and their companies are rather than just what they do, it is not surprising that most senior executives decide to take the seemingly easier route of incremental change. This involves what Pascale calls 'trying harder', and going 'back to basics', and searching for 'improvement' techniques. Although continuous improvement and reinvention are not mutually exclusive, the first seldom leads automatically to the second.

Mobilizing management

In trying to confront this dilemma, top managers must face the harshest of facts: that most of them are indulging in a convenient but simplistic fiction when they repeat the standard mantra that the biggest barrier to radical change in their organizations is front-line employees or, more often, middle management. The reality is frequently much more painful: that the most intransigent group is top management itself.

In a few high-profile cases over recent years, this has become so obvious that outside directors or institutional shareholders have been forced to have the top man removed. Notable examples include Digital, General Motors, IBM and Kodak in the US, and Midland Bank in the UK.

But, in almost all these instances, action was taken long after the top man had caused serious damage in one of several ways: by allowing the first sparks of the company's strategic crisis to develop into what experts in change call a fully-fledged 'burning platform'; by failing to douse flames which were already burning when he took over; or by failing to change the top team – whether literally or figuratively.

Consultant Don Laurie has undertaken research into what he calls the changing 'work of a leader' in improving the customer-responsiveness of organizations. Unlike the usual wide-eyed studies of leaders' characteristics, Laurie concentrates on the actions they actually take. He focuses mainly on the top, although he also deals with the need for 'distributed leadership' at all levels of an organization.

Effective modern leadership is very different from the traditional exercise of authority and power, and the handing-down of detailed, 'technical' solutions, Laurie concludes. Instead it consists of mobilising the people in an organization to confront difficult problems themselves, and the challenges and uncertainty which arise as a result. This can only be done by communal learning from mistakes, which requires real openness and considerable argument – the lack of which, Laurie says, is a further cause of resistance at the top. Without this openness, companies can never become 'learning organizations' – which is a prerequisite for being able to adapt to environmental changes – and pre-empt them.

Evolving change

There could hardly be a clearer contrast between a lame management and a sprightly one than the ways in which Eastman Kodak and ABB have grasped the cactus of transformational change.

Until George Fisher's arrival at Kodak from Motorola, the two companies' attitudes to the management of change were coincidentally analogous to the nature of their core businesses: on the one hand, a specialist in static images, on the other a maker of flywheels of power. To Kodak, change was once a stop-start series of isolated, intermittent initiatives. But to ABB, since its creation in 1988 out of sprightly Asea and lumbering Brown Boveri, change has been a continuously evolving process which companies must anticipate and shape before their rivals do it for them, even more painfully.

There are no prizes for guessing which approach is more necessary or effective in today's business climate. Companies of all shapes, sizes and nationalities may, like Kodak, yearn for the comfortable days when change could be an intermittent process, in which one project or initiative could be completed before the next began. But all sorts of radical changes now need to be initiated in quick succession, and run either in parallel or as an integrated whole.

This point was forcefully highlighted by a survey on 'change management' published in 1993 by KPMG Management Consulting, an arm of KPMG. Most of its corporate respondents were running four or more different types of cross-functional change programmes. With ample justification, KPMG doubted whether many of them were being properly integrated.

Contrast this with the approach of ABB, which has run co-ordinated programmes on TQM, 'customer focus' (as it calls it), business process redesign, culture change and employee empowerment almost since the company's formation, and expects them to continue indefinitely. Thanks to ABB's careful integration of its programmes, and the restless, change-minded culture which is has bred, it has suffered less than other companies from 'change fatigue'. This is almost certainly not the case for many of the companies in KPMG's sample – over a quarter of the total – which claimed to have undertaken 10 or more change initiatives in just three years.

A forceful and appropriate comment comes from the Boston Consulting Group. Warning of 'the danger of doing too much', BCG reported that many large US companies now had up to 15 'process improvement' initiatives under way, but that these seldom added up to a coherent programme.

In such cases, warned BCG, employees become so overloaded that they gravitate towards easily resolvable problems, and avoid the big ones. Tough cross-functional issues are ignored, and sacred cows continue to fatten. General managers grow increasingly sceptical, failing to see a link between the growing number of improvement programmes and the bottom line.

People and the revolution

The final change dilemma concerns the organization's changing relationship with that most crucial 'group of stakeholders' – its employees.

The message from ABB, Kodak IBM and a plethora of other big organizations could not be more clear. Jobs in almost any type of western company, at any level, are no longer secure in today's brutally competitive global marketplace. What is less well understood is the need for companies to replace naked insecurity among their workforce with a redefined set of relationships to motivate those employees whom they wish to retain. The nature of those relationships, explicit and especially implicit, will dictate each company's productivity, flexibility, creativity and competitiveness.

The pressures to cut, cut and cut again have become irresistible in certain industries and companies – and not just those, like IBM, which have taken far too long to adjust their corporate strategies to the new realities of their particular marketplaces.

Leading executives – such as IBM chairman Lou Gerstner – have mostly been right to wield their hatchets repeatedly. But this is not a sustainable way to run a company over time. Academic research has shown consistently that, while fear may motivate in the short term, prolonged uncertainty creates a fall in employee morale and productivity which is hard to halt, let alone reverse. Many of the best employees leave, while the rest are inclined to put their heads down and cease to give their all.

Companies which take this approach are practising the antithesis of the adage that 'our employees are our greatest asset' – a claim which, in today's business environment, needs increasingly to accord with reality. Their behaviour contrasts starkly with the continued striving of large Japanese companies, even in the straitened circumstances of the 1990s, to hold on to the employees in which they have invested so much. Many have done so by 'insourcing', pulling work back in from their suppliers.

For an organization to remove insecurity from its employees and re-motivate them, while retaining the flexibility to adjust its size as necessary, it must first involve them more effectively in decision-making, even if it does not wish to move to extreme decentralization and fully-fledged 'self-managing' teams. If people feel at least in partial control of their affairs, they are better able to accept that change has become a way of life.

Just as necessary is a re-definition of the type or types of relationship, formal and implicit, which the organization wishes to have with the people who work for it – not all of whom will remain as internal employees. There are plenty of models to choose from. One of the best-known is Charles Handy's 'shamrock', with its three leaves: 'core professionals', 'the contractual fringe' and 'part-time or temporary workers'.

Three characteristics, in particular, are common to all the organizational models. First, the need for many people to develop 'sideways' careers and a 'portfolio' approach, instead of expecting to climb steadily within a single company and remain with it throughout their working life. Second, the consequential need for each employer to provide everyone with the time, opportunity and resources for continuous professional development – 'lifelong learning' – so that their skills remain up-to-date and tradeable. Third, the need for all kinds of flexible working arrangements to be encouraged within each category.

None of this is mere theory. In California's Silicon Valley companies have been applying various elements of it for some time, as have some architectural practices since recession forced them to slash their permanent staffs. One of the most striking examples is the external 'managed contracts' under which Manpower, the employment services company, provides staff for various companies, including IBM.

11

Whatever their future structure – formal and informal – all organizations need their employees' commitment, and must take steps to re-engage it. That – especially in multinationals which are structurally, socially and strategically complex – requires leadership of a new kind, and of a very high order indeed.

Christopher Lorenz is the *Financial Times'* Management Editor. He is co-editor of *The Financial Times on Management,* author of *The Design Dimension* and co-editor of *The Uneasy Alliance: Managing the Productivity-Technology Dilemma.*

Further Reading

Barker, J, *Discovering the Future: The Business of Paradigms*, ILI Press, St Paul, Minn, 1985.

Chandler, AD, *Strategy as Structure*, MIT Press, Cambridge, Mass, 1962.

March, JG, and Simon, HA, *Organizations*, John Wiley, New York, 1958.

Pugh, DS, (ed.) *Organization Theory, Selected Readings*, Penguin, London, 1990.

Waterman, R, *The Frontiers of Excellence*, Nicholas Brealey, London, 1994.

Weber, M, *The Theory of Social and Economic Organization*, Oxford University Press, New York, 1947.

INTERNATIONAL PRACTICE

Asea Brown Boveri

Manfred Kets de Vries

Percy Barnevik, chief executive of the Swedish engineering group, ASEA, surprised the business community in 1987 by announcing the creation of the world's largest cross-border merger between ASEA and Brown Boveri, a Swiss company in the same field. By adding 70 more companies in Europe and the US, a $30 billion giant was created with a portfolio covering global markets for electric power generation and transmission equipment, high speed trains, automation and robots, and environmental control systems.

During its short life span ABB has made an enormous impact on the business community. It has been hailed as the organizational form of the future. In *Nikkei Business*, the managing director of the power plant division at Mitsubishi stated: 'Our greatest rival is no longer the US firm General Electric. The one we have to be most on guard against is ABB.'[1]

The roots of this transformation can be traced back to 1979 when Barnevik became chief executive of ASEA. In 1979, ASEA was slow-growing but respected, one of the ten largest electrical engineering companies in the world and technically a world-class company with some 40,000 employees, 30,000 of them in Sweden. Economically and financially, however, ASEA was in bad shape. There was excess capacity in its markets, demand was weakening and profits were falling steadily. In addition to these external factors, the company had a centralized, bureaucratic internal structure, and serious problems of morale.

ASEA had a long tradition and history as an engineering company. It afforded its employees secure employment, took care of them in a patriarchal way, and selected and promoted its managers on the basis of their technical competence, rather than their business acumen. No personnel had been discharged since the 1930s, a policy which had been assiduously maintained even through the difficult years of the late 1970s. However, it did have leading-edge products in a number of areas that were both growing and profitable.

Barnevik knew, when he assumed his new position, that gradual change would have no effect. ASEA needed a radical shake-up to shock the company into action. Neither did he want the process to be dragged out and create too much uncertainty, preventing the company from refocusing quickly. Doing this was difficult but he made two fundamental structural changes.

The first was to delayer the organization and reorganize it into a global matrix once the company had expanded internationally; the second was to get rid of the bureaucracy of the corporate head office. In doing this he used a simple rule of thumb – the 30 per cent rule. He passionately believed that bureaucracy generates waste and, for that reason, he broke it down by assuming that 30 per cent of central staff could be spun off into separate and independent profit centres, another 30 per cent could be transferred to the operational companies as part of their overhead, another 30 per cent could be eliminated as superfluous to requirements and the remaining 10 per cent could be kept on as the minimum required. He was driven by the conviction that what was needed were business units that were self-contained and situated as close as possible to the end consumer. His radical surgery at head office reduced the number of employees from 2,000 to 200.

Barnevik was fortunate in that because of the poor economic situation, the climate in the company was more open to change than in the past. There was a greater willingness to accept that the old way of doing things was no longer workable. During the seven years he spent as chief executive of ASEA, the company's turnover quadrupled, its earnings rose eight-fold and its market capitalization multiplied twenty times.

However, Barnevik did not stop there. Looking at market trends, he believed strongly that there would be a shake-out in the electrical engineering industry and that ASEA had to become more international. Only companies with a certain critical mass would be able to survive and benefit from the upturn he predicted. He knew that ASEA needed to expand radically and internationally, and that the only way to do so was through acquisitions.

Barnevik's decision to talk to the Swiss company Brown, Boveri & Company (BBC), was based on the pure logic of the fit between the two companies. ASEA operated in geographic areas and in some product spheres that on the whole complemented rather than competed with those of BBC. In some areas, like power transmission, there was a major overlap, but, if properly restructured, the joint company would have a clear lead in size and competitiveness. A merger would add value to both companies. Both companies were staid, traditional mainstays of their local environment, which, if they remained isolated, would sooner or later have either to allow themselves to be bought out, or shut down. In addition, there were similarities between the Swiss and the Swedes: there would not be major temperamental fireworks. Both groups of executives came from small nations and had had sufficient international exposure to know that they were dependent on the rest of the world for the survival of their companies. This would help to avoid any kind of ethnocentrism in their behaviour. (The biggest BBC country, Germany, was another story. The Germans didn't like being dominated by either the Swiss or the Swedes.) Most importantly, though, the timing was right.

An important factor was that BBC was four times the size of ASEA in 1980, but by 1987 they were equal. A 50/50 merger required equality. In fact, since ASEA in 1987 was the more profitable of the two, it became difficult to create a 50/50 venture.

When the merger was announced on 10 August, 1987, at simultaneous news conferences in Stockholm and Baden, Switzerland, it came as a total surprize. Business analysts had expected that something was going to happen, because Barnevik had been on the look-out for suitable acquisitions for quite some time. But he managed to side-step them all by the sheer magnitude of the undertaking. Confidentiality had been maintained by the inner circles of the two companies during the negotiations. He had insisted on secrecy all along. Nobody outside knew anything about the merger. Rapid closure of the deal had been facilitated by the fact that Barnevik had the support of the dominant shareholders of the two companies. Given that they supported the spirit and rationale behind the merger, it was just a matter of time before the merger was finalized. Barnevik managed to complete the whole process in six weeks. He suspended all but the most basic aspects of due diligence exercises, a highly risky move in any circumstances, but he felt the risk to be minimal and the potential returns disproportionately large.

The integration of ASEA and Brown Boveri

Speed was a very important factor both before and after the merger. Barnevik wanted to get the integration process over and done with as quickly as possible, because he felt it was better to avoid confusion and loss of market share[2] and he believed that it was 'better to move swiftly and correct an error here and there afterwards, rather than leave people hanging in the air, uncertain about the future'.[3]

As he had done when he joined ASEA, Barnevik set out to identify key executives who would play the role of his trusted lieutenants to make the new corporation work. He decided that these global executives had to be – among a host of other characteristics – 'people capable of becoming superstars – tough-skinned individuals, who were fast on their feet, had good technical and commercial backgrounds and had demonstrated the ability to lead others'.[4]

At the same time he considered thousands of global managers unnecessary. He believed that in order to work well ABB needed 250 or so global managers, people who were internationally-minded, and who were also comfortable with their nation of origin.[5]

Barnevik personally conducted around 500 interviews to find the right people for his senior team. With these in place, he felt that he needed to share his vision of the company with his people and give them a framework within which to do business. Just five months after the merger, he invited 250 of them to Cannes for a three-day seminar during which he laid out his way of looking at ABB, as the new company was to be called. He explained the principles upon which the merged company would operate, introducing a twenty-one page corporate policy bible and requesting his audience to transmit all of what he had told them to the next layer of management, 30,000 of them worldwide, within the following 60 days. He believed that open communication was the key to successful business.

His next task was to streamline ABB. Just as he had done at ASEA, he set out to reduce head count at corporate headquarters, using the same 30 per cent rule, and began decentralizing the operations of most of the subsidiaries into independent profit centres. Barnevik implemented a radical redeployment of human, technological and financial resources by making them the responsibility of the front-line companies. For example, instead of having centralized corporate laboratories for the development of technology, centres of excellence were created which were closely linked to operating companies that excelled in specific technological developments. The outcome of technological innovation was then leveraged throughout the organization. Only 150 people remained at head office.

A great deal of work had to be done, however, to make this cross-border mega-merger work. Probably the most far-reaching change Barnevik implemented in the newly merged company was to introduce the global matrix he had already used at ASEA. ABB now had a cadre of 250 'global' executives (including 136 country managers and 50 business area managers) leading 210,000 employees in 1,300 companies which were divided into 5,000 profit centres located in almost 150 countries around the world and in at least seven different business segments (later rationalized to four product segments plus one financial services segment). In a sense, it turned ABB into a federation of companies. Barnevik himself, and twelve executive vice-presidents (later reduced to seven), formed the company's supreme decision-making body, the *Konzernleitung*. On a macro-level, they negotiated broad targets (defined in terms of growth, profit and return on capital employed) for each business and geographic area. In addition, they created the Top Management Forum which consists of approximately 400 managers from country and operation regions, and, since 1993, the Top Management Council, made up of 70 senior managers who meet three times a year.

To control this gigantic operation, Barnevik required from each profit centre a dollar-based monthly profit and loss and balance sheets, to be delivered to head office on the tenth of each month. To reduce time spent on decision making, each region had its own control headquarters. The most important matters, however, were referred to Zurich. Every three weeks there was a Konzernleitung meeting during which an entire day was devoted to strategic and operational issues.

The matrix could be viewed as a spreadsheet. On the spreadsheet the column headings were the 'business segments', which were further subdivided into business areas (BAs). At the top of each segment sat a Konzernleitung member, who reported on the performance of this segment as if it were a separate entity (for example, the member responsible for the power generation segment would report on the worldwide performance of that segment). Similarly, each individual business area regarded itself as a worldwide business and reported in that manner. The horizontal axis listed the various country companies. The world was divided up into regions (the Americas, Asia, Europe) or groupings of countries at the head of which sat a Konzernleitung member. A company in a country, a motor company for example, would report both to a global manager for motors and to the country manager. The important thing was that the global business area manager and the country manager should understand their complementary and different roles. The BA manager set the framework: who would develop and produce what, what export markets would be allocated to each company, and so on. He also watched the global quality and standards, safeguarded cross-border transfer of technologies and best practices. The country manager supervised the day-to-day business and would be supportive in domestic market networking, recruitment, union matters, and the like. Sometimes the two managers would have different opinions as, for example, when the company ran into trouble. It was important, therefore, to train people in how to manager the conflict inherent in this situation. To limit the possibility of conflict, all major issues had to be discussed by the BA manager and the country manager.

In spite of this potential for conflict, Barnevik felt that the matrix was a relatively simple model and believed the inherent contradictions within the company could easily be resolved. In his model, top executives spell out broad policy guidelines and challenge the status quo, middle management integrates strategy horizontally, leverages technology and transfers best practices, while front-line executives take on an entrepreneurial role. He explained to the *Harvard Business Review*:

> 'ABB is an organization with three internal contradictions. We want to be global and local, big and small, and radically decentralized with centralized reporting and control. If we resolve these contradictions we create real organizational advantage.'[6]

There was a major flaw in the matrix structure Barnevik used. For the people who were 'at an intersection', reporting to two bosses, each of whom might have different objectives, the matrix could be traumatic. For some, it was never completely clear what the criteria were for success in the job, nor which of the bosses had precedence over the other. Realising that organizations can only be as good as the people working in them, ABB has addressed this problem by going out of its way to clarify different roles and make the mechanism of resolving conflicts work.

Maintaining such a matrix involves substantial effort – there is always a tendency for some executives to transgress the rules of the matrix, and to do something advantageous for their own unit at the expense of somebody else's.

Nevertheless, Barnevik created an organization that was not only lean and flexible and decentralized enough to operate anywhere in the world (thanks to the ABACUS information system that provided data to the front-line operations and helped group management evaluate performance), but that could also benefit from the economies of scale of looking at the world as a single market.

Running ABB

Now, in the mid-1990s, top executives at ABB firmly believe that there is going to be an upturn in the electrical engineering market after the recession in the industrialized world, but that in order to capitalize upon it a company will have to be situated throughout the world with the same market presence and the same commitment to the customer in every area. Because of the global nature of ABB, top executives feel they have succeeded in spreading the risk and reducing the economic set-backs which may occur in any one country or region.

To be present in all areas of the world ABB has accumulated around 150 companies. Once a company has been bought it is integrated into the ABB network as quickly and efficiently as possible. Wherever it can, ABB obtains a majority shareholding.

Internally, Barnevik has continued to insist on a process of constant change. This embraces the entire organization. In 1993, the Konzernleitung was rationalized in a move to strengthen ABB's competitiveness and help the company adjust to the increase in regional trading blocks. Membership of the new Konzernleitung was cut from twelve to eight, and the six operating divisions were reduced to four. Three directors have regional responsibilities, and four have divisional responsibilities; more tasks are pushed down to the next layer of management. Barnevik has changed the responsibilities of each member on the Konzernleitung at least once and has added or withdrawn names from the list of members making up the Konzernleitung. He believes that if people at all levels of the organization are kept on their toes, the organization as a whole is encouraged to be flexible.

The running of ABB now centres around the operation of two dynamics – expansion, and maintaining the momentum of the existing company, which depends on a culture of permanent revolution. This produces very particular problems. It is difficult to maintain a sense of excitement and standards of peak performance when people feel insecure, as they inevitably do in a company which is in a constant state of change, leaving little time for the process of integration and the formation of a stable culture To a certain extent the problems of this second dynamic are resolved by the first: ABB's new ventures into Poland and China, and its commitment to tackling environmental problems in the old Eastern Bloc, are a real source of pride and motivation for employees. Nevertheless, there are equally real difficulties encountered in working for ABB, and Barnevik's legendary emphasis on speed is reponsible for many of them.

Has his vision been properly assimilated? Has a sense of commitment been transmitted? Moulding acquired companies into a cultural whole takes time – and Barnevik has made no secret of his preference for speed over other factors in the process of acquisition.

Barnevik's answer to these difficulties might be to stress his belief in the importance of communication. That was the motivation behind the Cannes conference, where he defined the five core values of the company and initiated the procedure intended to transmit them to all levels of management. The ABB values – meeting customer needs, decentralization, taking action, respecting an ethic, and co-operating – are reinforced through intensive in-house programmes of executive education, in which Barnevik and other members of the

Konzernleitung invest a great deal of time. The prime values, from Barnevik's point of view, are meeting customer needs and decentralization. The first of these emphasizes that the customer always comes first and that everyone in the company has a responsibilitiy to satisfy the customer's wishes. Each employee has to meet customers, even if this is not an obvious part of an individual job description. Decentralization Barnevik sees as the only way to defeat bureaucracy, to which he has always had a deep aversion. By this means, responsibility is passed down the line to more junior people, to motivate them and to provide for the most efficient use of resources at the level where they are required. It is vital that this process is combined with efficient communication and proper supervision.

Taking action is perhaps the most personally motivated of the five basic values: prepare thoroughly; do not get bogged down in detail; do not investigate things to death; and above all, *be fast*. This effectively rules out management by committee. Committees are an extremely rare commodity inside ABB.

The way Barnevik usually defines respecting an ethic is '(to be) regarded as reliable, standing by your word, not trying to be smart and cheat people, whether we talk about internal dealings or we talk about customers'. It might be idealistic to expect everybody to operate according to a sense of honour and honesty but, in fact, the principle works. Co-operation is the value most frequently cited whenever change is imposed on the organization. Barnevik maintains that it does not really matter where somebody operates as long as that individual talent remains within the ABB group. It is the application of this value that causes a tremendous amount of paper to be transferred between people's desk. There is tendency for the principle to be taken too literally, with people scrupulously informing everybody about everything. The operation can be counter-productive; when drenched with information, people tend to stop reading. A massive investment in an electronic network for communication is one way of reducing the paper problem.

Barnevik might hope that the principle of communication established at Cannes will evolve into the glue that will bind the company together. It still has to be tested: will the glue hold against the tensions necessarily accompanying expansion, change, constantly-increasing performance targets, and the inherent contradictions in the company's operational structure?

Barnevik has the satisfaction of knowing that he has shaken the complacency of rival companies, even though ABB shows current profit levels significantly below the best in the industry. When asked if shareholders have got enough returns in the 15 years he has been running ASEA and ABB, Barnevik answers that the value of ASEA stock has gone up 41 times since 1979, or 30.5 per cent per year, which is almost three times the stock index.

Despite ABB's worldwide presence, some critics still wonder whether the sum really is larger than the parts or whether it would not be more valuable to break up the organization. The complexity of the company's matrix structure draws criticism from its own employees as well as outsiders – many feel that they no longer understand how the company functions. Is the 'multidomestic' federalist design really the best way to structure the organization? Also, in a conglomerate of this size, how can an executive committeee be certain that messages filter accurately through to the lower layers of the organization? And how can they know how well they are received? Do the professed synergies between front-line companies really take place? After all, lateral communication is easier said than done. Some critics are concerned about the process of managing change. They say that ABB has had more than its fair share of this and note that transformational processes tend to run out of steam. Are there ways, however, to institutionalize the process of change?

Finally, and most importantly, the complexity of the organization is staggering: what are the implications of running a company that does not really have a national identity?

Percy Barnevik's response to such concerns is straightforward. 'The environment, the competitors, the customers are changing. Thus in order to survive we have to change. You know the expression, "When you are through changing, you are through".'[7]

Manfred Kets de Vries is Raoul de Vitry d'Avaucourt Professor of Human Resource Management at INSEAD. Previously he held professorships at McGill University, the Ecole de Hautes Etudes Commerciales, Montreal, and Harvard Business School.

References

[1] *Nikkei Business*, 1994, no. 1, pp. 19–22.

[2] Florin, M, Frenkel, H and Wilke, B, Vi tvingades att bortse fran alla lik i lasten, Veckans Affarer, August 20 1987, p. 62.

[3] Arbose, Jules, 'ABB: The new International Powerhouse', *International Management*, June 1988, 43(6), p. 27.

[4] Ibid, p. 27.

[5] Taylor, W, 'The logic of global business: an interview with Percy Barnevik', *Harvard Business Review*, March-April 1991, p. 94.

[6] Ibid, p. 95.

[7] Interview with Manfred Kets de Vries.

THINKERS

Rosabeth Moss Kanter

Born 1943: educator and consultant

In the perennial search to pigeon-hole mangement thinkers under a suitable title or specialism, Rosabeth Moss Kanter has proved determinedly elusive. She is not an evangelist in the Tom Peters mould, but nor is she an unworldly academic. She travels the world consulting and lecturing, but remains a Professor at Harvard Business School (and, from 1989 to 1992, editor of the *Harvard Business Review*). 'Seminars are a performance. But I'm not on the circuit; I have a job,' she insists. 'I am interested in being a player, a participant, not just a bystander; perhaps a bystander close to power.'[1] Her books are tightly and rigorously researched, yet have a clear populist element and appeal. Their subject matter evades neat classification ranging increasingly widely, geographically and theoretically.

Her early work was concerned with Utopian communities, such as the Shakers. ('In the 1970s I compared IBM to a Utopian culture,' she now admits.) This interest perhaps can be identified as the thread which runs through her central trilogy of publications – *Men and Women of the Corporation* (1977), *The Change Masters* (1983) and *When Giants Learn to Dance* (1989). 'Kanter-the-guru still studies her subject with a sociologist's eye, treating the corporation not so much as a micro-economy, concerned with turning inputs into outputs, but as a mini-society, bent on shaping individuals to collective ends,' observed *The Economist*.[2]

'I don't fit easily into different slots. I see myself as a thought leader, a developer of ideas,' she says. 'I am idealistic and it was the idealistic entrepreneurs of the 1960s and 1970s who changed things so that business became a great arena for experimentation. I am always interested in positive models and positive change. Business became increasingly interesting to me because it is so pivotal. It is the bedrock.'

Kanter's idealism has also led her into politics. She was involved in Michael Dukakis' presidential bid – writing a book with him along the way. Dukakis' revival of Massachusetts'

Education: Bryn Mawr, PhD at the University of Michigan.
Career: Associate Professor of sociology, Brandeis University; joined Harvard 1973; 1977–1986 taught at Yale and MIT; returned to Harvard as Professor of Business Administration; editor of the *Harvard Business Review* 1989–92; runs her own consultancy company, Goodmeasure.

economic fortunes briefly appeared to offer an example of idealism, entrepreneurism and commercialism in partnership. 'I learned a lot working with Dukakis,' says Kanter. 'He was interested in harnessing the entrepreneurial spirit.'

Given this strain of idealism, it is ironic that Kanter's first major book, *Men and Women of the Corporation*, proved more likely to dash any idealism than to nurture it. It was an intense examination of a bureaucratic organization and, in effect, marked the demise of comfortable corporate America. Among its generally depressing findings was that the central characteristic expected of a manager was 'dependability'. Undaunted by her examination of the limitations and restrictions of the contemporary corporation, Kanter turned her mind to creating the new organizational models. The book which forged her reputation was *The Change Masters*.

This book sought out antidotes to the corporate malaise identified in *Men and Women of the Corporation*. It succeeded in propelling empowerment and greater employee involvement onto the corporate agenda. These issues are developed throughout Kanter's work: 'By empowering others, a leader does not decrease his power, instead, he may increase it – especially if the whole organization performs better,' she says.

Change Masters discovered the corporate world in an awkward state of flux – unwilling to disengage itself from the last vestiges of corporatism and unable or fearful of what to do next. Its vision remained solidly American. Its success, however, allowed Kanter's gaze to move further afield. '*Change Masters* opened doors for me, as a result I've globalized myself in the last decade,' she says. 'At the same time, however, a lot of the romance with Japanese companies went away. Instead, there emerged a belief that the source of much managerial wisdom emanates from the US.'

The wisdom she encountered on her increasing travels was distilled into her next book, *When Giants Learn to Dance*. Describing the process she goes through in writing a book, Kanter says: 'Ideas are, to start off, very vague but, gradually things develop. I say things and if people look blank, I continue. Then I become immersed. I am inductive, not deductive. I need data and experience in front of me. As the book progresses there is a lot of back and forth, checking, questioning and developing.' She is keen to emphasize that her works are not simply pot-boilers full of unsubstantiated or unworkable ideas. 'I reject the term *guru* because it is associated with pandering to the masses, providing inspiration without substance. There is a little bit of the shaman in a guru. I have scholarly standards. My books are dense and theoretical. They have footnotes.'

When Giants Learn to Dance marks the corporate transformation from slumbering behemoth to nimble new creation, what Kanter labelled 'the post-entrepreneurial firm'. *When Giants Learn to Dance* predicts that as companies recognize and focus on their core capabilities, expansion will tend to occur through strategic alliances, and peripheral activities be taken over by specialist service providers. The burgeoning of the service sector in the developed economies is evidence of the kind of structural changes which Kanter describes. On the other hand, global companies harnessing economies of scale will create the need for managers with the ability to manage across cultural boundaries.

'The post-entrepreneurial corporation represents a triumph of process over structure. That is, relationships and communication and the flexibility to temporarily combine resources are more important than the "formal" channels and reporting relationships represented on an organizational chart,' writes Kanter. 'The post-entrepreneurial corporation is created by a three-part mix: by the context set at the top, the values and goals emanating from top management; by the channels, forums, programmes and relationships designed in the middle to support those values and goals; and by the project ideas bubbling up from below – ideas for new ventures or technological innovations or better ways to serve customers.'

Kanter's argument is that businesses need to be flexible but not free-wheeling – she points to the fact that small businesses often suffer from too little organization while larger ones suffer from the reverse problem.

The origins of many of her ideas can be traced back to the work of Elton Mayo in the 1930s and Douglas Maegor in the 1950s. They, too, tried to come to terms with the imponderables of motivation and the relationship between individuals and large corporations.

In *When Giants Learn to Dance*, Kanter identifies seven 'skills and sensibilities' essential for managers if they are to become what she labels 'business athletes'. These are:

- learning to operate without the might of the hierarchy behind them
- knowing how to 'compete' in a way that enhances rather than undercuts co-operation
- operating with the highest ethical standards
- having a dose of humility
- developing a process focus
- being multi-faceted and ambidextrous
- gaining satisfaction from results.

Kanter's work has highlighted people-related issues which were long ignored by the world's top businesses. 'I am increasingly encouraged by the progress some organizations are making in areas like empowerment, but wish they were further along,' she says. 'The real emergent issue is what will people do with their time if they are not working? Job dislocation is now the coming problem.'

In an era of relentless cost-cutting and downsizing, the human side of enterprise has been easily neglected. Indeed, Kanter's idealism is now pragmatic. 'Consulting is a way to create. It is practical and I learn. My education comes from the application of my academic knowledge on the job. I hope that things might happen in organizations which I have helped to create. It is highly satisfying when chief executives use words or phrases, such as infrastructure for collaboration, which I introduced them to, sometimes I invented them,' she says. 'It is a question of continually broadening the context. There is a halo affect. For some audiences what I say has a great deal of credibility. This brings with it a sense of responsibility. But, I am now doing it for myself rather than for a particular audience.'

STUART CRAINER

Further Reading

Rosabeth Moss Kanter:
Men and Women of the Corporation, Basic Books, New York, 1977.
The Change Masters, Allen & Unwin, London, 1984.
When Giants Learn to Dance, Simon & Schuster, London, 1989.

References

[1] Interview with Stuart Crainer, 20 April 1994.
[2] 'Moss Kanter, corporate sociologist', *The Economist*, 15 October 1994.

MANAGING CHANGE

Ian Cunningham

Change is the driving force behind many of the modern foundations of management practice and theory. Strategy is fundamentally concerned with managing change; issues such as Business Process Re-engineering and Total Quality Management are particular change arenas; leadership is crucially about the role of individuals in leading change; communication is a key dimension in managing change. Almost every aspect of management includes some explicit or implicit managing of change.

Even so, managing change is much misunderstood. Practice and theory rarely coincide. This can partly be attributed to extreme rather than pragmatic approaches to managing change; and the tendency to treat change as a thing rather than a process.

Yet, managing change is at the core of real managing and leadership. If someone is only maintaining the status quo in an era of rapid, continuous change they are doing the equivalent of an administrative or clerical job. Managing change is fundamental to the nature and practice of management.

Managing change has become the omnipresent management theme of the 1990s. Organizations are more aware than ever before of the need both to cope with change and to manage the process of change. However, there is considerable confusion about what managing change is and how best to do it.

Such is the pace of change – technological, organizational, managerial and personal – that it produces a tendency to seek solace in universal panaceas, unclear thinking, and decision-making which is often unreliable. There are many theories about how change should be managed but, as is often the case, theory and practice exist in a relationship of mutual disappointment. In order to improve both, theory and practice need to be more effectively juxtaposed.

All managers have theories about managing change: the issue is how to develop, improve and learn from them. For example, some claim that it is not possible to get fundamental change without having a crisis; people will not change dramatically unless they have to. A rival theory is that you can achieve significant change through having compelling visions which will inspire people to change. A scientific attitude, where these theories are tested in practice, shows that both can work: it is not necessary to hold an either/or attitude. A better theory might be that both strategies can be used – and, indeed, there are a number of chief executives who have been successful with an approach which begins with a shock and then is quickly followed by an inspiring vision of the future.

This approach tends to start with a crisis or major issue for the organization to contend with. The chief executive is able to scare people with the potential outcome of such a situation and people are, therefore, in a mood to support change. One chief executive used the now famous quote from Japanese industrialist Matsushita that Japan was going to win and the West lose as Japanese managers had a superior mind-set. Other top managers of companies in a genuine crisis have merely needed to point to the options of accepting and putting into practice radical change or watching as the company goes under. However the shock is administered, the next stage is to show the glowing possibilities of a change, while not denying the tough actions necessary to achieve such a change.

In order for someone to use this sequential approach they need to have a 'mental map' which encompasses both modes. There is evidence to support the view that the richer a person's mental maps the better equipped they are to manage change, because a wider range of choices of action are available to them. But having rich mental maps is not enough – there are other prime requirements (as well as ways in which mental maps may be enriched).

Managing change is not an optional extra

Many organizations in the 1980s concluded that managing change was a vital ingredient in their future success. As a result, they dispensed with whole levels of so-called middle managers who they realized were not adding value to the managerial process. Indeed many of the them were standing in the way of necessary change. Their supposed co-ordinating and supervising roles merely increased bureaucracy and enhanced blockages to change.

This does not mean that in general people will resist change. This latter assumption has led to a great many change management programmes which provide a generalized formula for dealing with resistance to change. If people see improvements through change they will support such change. If employees are offered a pay rise ahead of their expectations they will welcome it. The delayerings already mentioned have often been supported by the remaining employees, with shop floor workers favouring a structure which gives them better access to senior management.

Managing change is a process not a thing

There is a problem in the academic and consulting worlds of creating new pseudo-disciplines. It is good for business – though not necessarily good for clients who may be asked to pay for something that does not warrant being a 'thing'. Change Management is in danger of becoming relegated to this status. The advent of a new discipline is often marked by making a process into a thing by changing verbs to nouns and by using capital letters to denote its promotion from idea to discipline.

While 'Change Management' is often used as a term, I prefer to talk about managing change (verb). When managers talk about 'making a change' we have to be clear what this means. Change is not a thing that can be 'made', like a table or a chair. A noun stands for a person, place or thing; change is none of these. This may appear a pedantic diversion from the central issue, but how we conceive of the process of change influences our actions.

Those who favour a noun, or discipline, approach seem more likely to see change as a time-bounded activity. They set up projects or programmes to apply 'Change Management' methodology to a specific change. This may be linked to a consultant's report in order to implement its recommendations. The base assumptions may be tied to Kurt Lewin's model of managing change, namely 'unfreeze-change-refreeze'. This model, in its original form, was more process oriented, but it has become rigidified in the last forty years. So now, when used as a strategy to implement a proposed change, such as restructuring, it is used to justify an approach which says 'Get rid of the old structure; put in a new one; then *fix* the new one in place'.

In an age of continuous change, the Lewin model no longer applies. If we take the example of a restructuring, it is not something that can be locked in or 'refrozen'. Structures continue to evolve and change even if their original architects do not mean them to: roles evolve due to a range of pressures such as new technology, customer requirements, competitor activity, TQM, and many more. Organization charts cannot represent a fluid evolving world.

Change is not all one process

Much of the literature of Change Management assumes that change is one activity. It is as though changing your stationery supplier is the same process as changing fundamental values in the organization. However, there are those who do recognize the difference and there are various ways in which such differences are articulated. Some identify a distinction between fine-tuning and transformative change or between incremental change and quantum leaps. These distinctions show that an approach to managing a small change probably requires different technology from other kinds of change. Other dichotomies indicate different distinctions. Three are outlined below in order to exemplify the issues. I have not tried to be comprehensive in what follows; my objective is only to establish the value of looking at alternative maps of the field.

1. In *Steps to an Ecology of Mind* (1973) Gregory Bateson suggests that there is a key contrast between first and second order change. First order change occurs within accepted frameworks and ways of thinking; second order change takes you outside these – it requires a mental shift into new habits and patterns. An example of first order change would be revising the standard pyramid structure of the organization; second order change would be eliminating the pyramid and devising a new kind of structure. Achieving the latter requires a totally different way of thinking about the nature of the organization. Other writers label this a *paradigm shift* – a major shift in the collective mind-set.

2. In *Lila: An Inquiry into Morals* (1991), Robert Pirsig makes a fascinating distinction between 'dynamic' and 'static' processes. The former correlate with creative leaps into new modes of operating; the latter with what I prefer to call 'systematic' procedures. In the quality arena (which Pirsig addresses specifically) systematic change is exemplified by the use of quality standards such as ISO 9000; there is change in the organization in order to put procedures in place. However, we know that such a change on its own does not guarantee improvements in quality. The dynamic dimension is related to the wider changes argued for by quality gurus such as Deming.

3. In *The Challenge of Organizational Change*, Rosabeth Moss Kanter and her colleagues suggest two counter posed strategies: bold strokes and long marches. This is similar to other writers' distinctions between big bang change and incremental change. Some TQM proponents argue that one should go for a continuous improvement approach which is based on getting lots of small (incremental) changes which add up over time. Other writers push for large scale (big bang) change, indicating that they do not believe organizations have the time to wait for the impact of incremental change.

The kind of debates that these dichotomies throw up are often quite unhelpful. In reality most organizations seem to need to consider a both/and rather than an either/or approach. For instance, the argument between change driven from the top down or bottom up is wasteful: effective large-scale change often has elements of both. The Brazilian company Semco was revolutionized as a result both of Ricardo Semler's drive as chief executive and the actions of shop-floor workers. It was both a top-down and bottom-up process.

Change is not a clean uncluttered process. The past is not reinvented. There are a number of obvious, though often forgotten, precepts involved in managing change:

1. **Some things do not change.** Indeed it is desirable that they do not. Change needs balancing with conservation. The environment is an obvious example of where such a balance needs to be struck. Even the most widespread change in organizations will leave many things intact – people will still walk about, talk to each other, drink, eat and so on.

2. **Only some changes are possible.** This is predicted by Chaos Theory as well as being obvious common sense. Humans are not infinitely plastic and can only do what is humanly possible (though some managers seem to forget this). In their books the South American academics Humberto Maturana and Francisco Varela, drawing on biological evidence, suggest that there are only certain 'viable trajectories' for organisms. This idea could fruitfully be used in organizations to consider what strategic trajectories are 'viable'.

28

3. Some changes do not stick. Instead, they are reversed over time. A charismatic leader may introduce changes which are reversed when the person leaves and is replaced by a more passive leader. While managers may use the analogy that you cannot make an omelette without breaking the eggs (to justify painful change), it is clear that many changes are not of the omelette-making variety. The latter is irreversible change but a better analogy for some changes would be pendulum swinging. A number of organizations have oscillated between high centralization and high decentralization over a number of years: it creates an illusion of significant change but, in reality, a pendulum simply oscillates from a fixed point.

4. Managing change does not mean controlling it. Outcomes are not the same as goals. With minor change it may be possible to achieve what you set out to do, but the kinds of change requiring real managing are often unpredictable in outcomes. This does not absolve us of responsibility, but it does change the nature of such responsibility. We cannot be responsible *for* the totality of outcomes but we need to be responsible *to* customers, colleagues and the community for our actions. Such responsibility includes developing ourselves to be capable of managing change and having the wisdom to make good decisions.

5. Some changes are not worth attempting. If a product has outlived its usefulness it is not worth trying to change it, yet many senior managers are poor at having the courage to pull out of products or whole markets. Even more difficult for some is the need to accept that some people will not change to accommodate new modes of working. Again to refer to Semco, chief executive Ricardo Semler fired 60 per cent of his senior managers when he took over the company because he could see that the changes he wanted would otherwise be blocked.

Change in context

A further problem in thinking about change in organizations is simply focusing on the organization as the unit of analysis. Much of the literature on strategic change, cultural change, etc, ignores other levels of investigation.

In the early history of the human race change occurred at the level of the person or at the level of the group or team. Individuals and groups changed as they learned new technology, new ways of working together and so on. Over time human society became more complex: organizations and communities came into being. Change at these levels had to be considered. Eventually we had the growth of nation states and then the development of a global perspective.

To return to the issue of change in organizations, we can see that they contain within them individuals and groups/teams and in turn they are contained within communities, nation states and, increasingly, a global arena of action. This is represented diagrammatically in Figure 1. The analogy can be drawn with the rings of a tree which show its development over time.

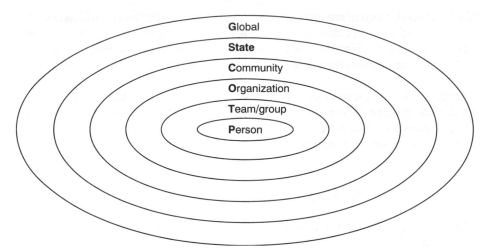

Fig. 1 The tree-ring metaphor of change levels

It is impossible to consider major change issues in organizations without looking at these other levels. If top managers are considering a strategic/cultural change then all these levels must come into the analysis. In the late 1980s a major US-based computer company wanted to make a strategic change which would balance its strength in hardware and its growing capability in software with the ability to provide consultancy services. Its failure to change appropriately and speedily was related to its inability to work at all these levels:

Person level. There was little attention paid to the individual level. People felt under stress by the attempts to continually fix problems; they grew increasingly alienated and detached. The company found it difficult to switch to recruiting different kinds of people to suit the new strategy, and its training programmes were designed to fit people for the world which the company wanted to move away from.

Group/team level. The organization was rife with politics and power play. Teams protected their territory, and the engineers carried on believing that technology could continue to drive the business irrespective of market changes. There was a high degree of disconnection between head office and the field. The latter was not listened to – even when senior managers were presented with well-researched evidence of people's concerns.

Community level. The company recruited from communities with differing cultures, yet it assumed homogeneity in its recruits. It was proud of what it saw as its unique organizational culture and assumed that people would easily absorb the company values. This increasingly did not happen, especially as the company grew larger. In some communities the company was a major employer and when it was forced to shed staff this had a significant adverse effect on these communities.

National level. Despite attempts to get other countries to fit in with US norms the company had to accept that there were different ways of doing things in different parts of the world. However, it continued to believe that the US way was best and did not utilize well the talents and ideas of employees in other countries.

Global level. The global market changed away from the computers the company was making. These global changes were quite visible and obvious. But the company failed to act early enough on this market information – and it did not assimilate these considerations into its strategic decisions.

Working with different levels

There are numerous texts that provide analytical frameworks for considering these levels. Psychologists offer advice at the individual level, such as dealing with the stress of change; social psychologists cover the working of groups and teams and provide rich material on the issues of change; sociologists and economists give their (often conflicting) perspectives on change at the level of organizations and societies; anthropologists provide insights into how communities and cultures change; and so on. The problem for managers is dealing with this vast literature in a sensible way. Much of it is irrelevant or unreadable – or both.

The metaphor of a tree can help to link the levels with theory. The various subject disciplines can be likened to the roots of a tree. The roots are hidden below ground but provide a source of nourishment and a secure base for the trunk (rings) already mentioned. This metaphor is shown in Fig. 2. The figure shows how the roots connect to the rings; there is ideally no separation. Senior managers draw on the roots to develop the trunk (their ability to integrate levels) and the visible outcome of this is the flowering of activity. The flowers mature into fruits of their work – the end-results of change activity. Except that it is not an end in the normal sense of the word. The fruits provide the basis for new trees – new growth and change.

The metaphor (like all metaphors) is not a truth, and it can appear pretentious stated baldy as I have done. But it can show a way into this field, and one that goes beyond generalized hints and tips.

Change and learning

At the current time the major interest in improving the managing of change is in developing learning organizations. Such an organization is seen to be one which can learn and change continually. The emphasis has shifted from changing an organization from one state to another (eg, centralized to de-centralized) towards creating organizations which are able continuously to transform themselves through learning. Of equal importance is the problem of individual managers learning to manage change.

OUTCOMES OF ACTIVITY

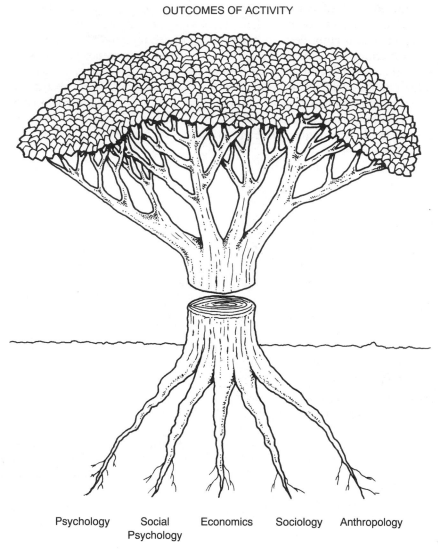

| Psychology | Social Psychology | Economics | Sociology | Anthropology |

Fig. 2 Tree roots nourish the trunk (manager's ability to integrate levels)

There is no change in organizations without people learning. Change is impossible without learning. The difficulty has been that senior managers have often assumed that it is others who need to learn rather than themselves. Yet it is arguable that managers need to be capable of managing their own change (through learning) if they are to manage others successfully.

Research and personal experience suggests that managers become more effective at managing change not through studying what other people have done (eg through case studies) but from having to make change happen in real, live situations. Typically they report that the key things they learn are such qualities as 'self confidence', 'wisdom', etc. They value the analytical, cognitive learning, but only as part of a more integrated development which includes increased emotional sophistication. While the content of their learning is important, it is the process that makes the difference. By having to manage their own learning, managers have to take a strategic look at their own lives and face the need for sometimes significant personal change.

It is through learning that managers really find out what a process such as managing change is all about. Getting managers to test the limits of their capabilities through learning new ways of operating not only pays off for the managers themselves but also for their organizations. A learning-based approach also overcomes the problem of the potential obsolescence of improving tools and techniques, as such tools and techniques are rooted in the world of today. And if we know anything about the world of tomorrow it is that it will not be like today. Learning how to learn more effectively has to be the key to future success in managing change. Or, as Ashleigh Brilliant observes: 'Your own common sense should tell you that common sense alone is not enough.'[1]

Ian Cunningham is chairman of Metacommunications Ltd and chairman of the Centre for Self-Managed Learning. Formerly chief executive of Roffey Park Management Institute, he is the author of *The Wisdom of Strategic Learning* (1994). He is a consultant to organizations in Europe, North America and Australia specialising in strategic and cultural change, learning-based approaches, and the development of self-managing organizations.

Further Reading

Bateson, G, *Steps to an Ecology of Mind*, Paladin, 1973.
Bennis, W, Benne K D, and Chin, R, *The Planning of Change* (2nd edn), Holt, Rinehart and Winston 1970.
Cunningham, I, *The Wisdom of Strategic Learning*, McGraw Hill, Maidenhead, 1994.
Kanter, R M, Stein, B, and Jick, T D, *The Challenge of Organizational Change*, Free Press, New York, 1992.
Vaill, P, *Managing as a Performing Art*, Jossey-Bass, San Francisco, CA, 1990.
Watzlawick, P, Weakland, J H, and Fisch, R, *Change: Principles of Problem Formation and Problem Resolution*, Norton, New York, 1974.

References

[1] Brilliant, A, *All I want is a warm bed and a kind word and unlimited power*, Woodbridge, 1985.

THINKERS

Tom Peters

Born 1942; consultant

There is little doubt that Tom Peters is the pre-eminent contemporary management guru. His books sell in their millions, his seminars fill auditoriums and his syndicated newspaper column is avidly read throughout the world. His message is passionately expressed – describing his presentational style, *The Economist* observed: 'Striding urgently back and forth, bellowing and bantering, he nearly achieves the difficult feat of making management seem exciting.'[1]

Unquestionably, management *is* exciting to Peters. Even the titles of his books are exhortations (they have been called 'charismatic shockers') – *Liberation Management, A Passion for Excellence, Thriving on Chaos* and, most famously, *In Search of Excellence*. The latter book, co-written with Robert Waterman, is the best-selling management book of all time, having sold over five million copies across the world.

In Search of Excellence marked an important development in management publishing as well as management thinking. Its popularity has fuelled a massive increase in the management book market. Its influence on the practice of management, of course, remains immeasurable. Peters has always insisted that the book's massive popularity should not disguise the fact that very few of the buyers actually read the book – and fewer still converted its pot-pourri of best practice into managerial reality.

The book emerged from work carried out by Peters and Waterman with their then employer, the consultancy McKinsey. Their research identified 43 successful companies and went on to identify the characteristics which were common to their success. The selection was based on six financial measurements: 20-year averages of compound asset growth; compound equity growth; ratio of market value to book value; return on capital; return on equity; and return on sales.

There was nothing earth shattering in this technique. Indeed, the conclusion was largely that the excellent companies managed to exercise common sense, keeping an obsessive eye on the business basics. The book's

Education: Masters in civil engineering from Cornell; MBA at Stanford
Career: Worked in the Pentagon; served in Vietnam; Office of Management and Budget in Washington; consultant with McKinsey & Co.; author and consultant with his own diverse company, the Tom Peters Group.

success was secured by the fact that it accentuated the positive at a time of unmitigated gloom – it was published in 1982. As managers lurched from crisis to crisis, and one bright new management theory to another, Peters and Waterman drew out what made successful companies tick and they did so in an approachable way.

As part of their research, Peters and Waterman (along with Richard Pascale and Anthony Athos) produced the Seven S Framework, a kind of instant guide to issues and topics which occupy managerial minds.

The Seven S Framework

Strategy Plan or course of action leading to the allocation of a firm's scarce resources, over time, to reach identified goals.

Structure Salient features of the organization chart (ie functional, decentralized, etc) and how the separate entities of an organization are tied together.

Systems Procedualized reports and routinized processes (such as meeting formats), etc.

Staff 'Demographics' description of important personnel categories within the firm (ie engineers, entrepreneurs, MBAs, etc). 'Staff' is not meant in line-staff terms.

Style Characterization of how key managers behave in achieving the organizations' goals; also the cultural style of the organization.

Shared values The significant meanings or guiding concepts that an organization imbues in its members.

Skills Distinctive capabilities of key personnel and the firm as a whole.

The distillation of the lengthy research carried out by Peters and Waterman, was that excellent companies:

- had a bias for action
- were close to the customer
- had autonomy and entrepreneurship
- believed in productivity through people
- were hands-on and value driven
- stuck to the knitting
- had a simple form and a lean staff
- had simultaneous loose-tight properties.

The messages which emerged from *In Search of Excellence* have now largely entered into the language and practice of management. In one way or another, Peters and Waterman anticipated the future interest in empowerment, core businesses, customer focus, balancing centralization and decentralization, the lean organization and the dismantling of hierarchies.

Over the years since its publication, *In Search of Excellence*'s reputation has taken a good deal of criticism. In particular, commentators quickly latched on to the fact that the 43 excellent companies did not necessarily remain so. Indeed, the fortunes of some of the chosen few plummeted dramatically – the airline People's Express was a notable casualty as was the computer company, Wang. IBM, an unquestioned choice at the time, has since experienced an unprecedented period of decline.

The failure of 'excellent' companies to last the course has encouraged Peters to address the problem of how organizations can sustain success and cope with increasingly competitive and chaotic markets. In *Thriving on Chaos* he begins with the line: 'There are no excellent companies.' It reiterates many of the central ideas of *In Search of Excellence*. It has five basic themes:

- obsession with responsiveness to customers
- constant innovation in all areas of the firm, with risk and some failures encouraged
- partnership
- leadership which loves change and shares an inspiring vision
- control by means of simple support systems aimed at measuring the right things.

In *Thriving on Chaos*, Peters launched a crusade against management hierarchies. He contends that Drucker's suggestion in the 1950s that there should be a maximum of seven layers in an organization is now outdated. 'I insist on five layers as the maximum,' insisted Peters, pointing somewhat suprisingly to the Catholic church's structure as a good example. 'In fact, even the five-layer limit should apply only to very complex organizations such as multi-division firms. Three layers – supervisor (with the job redefined to deal with a span of control no smaller than one supervisor for 25 to 75 people), department head and unit boss – should be tops for any single facility.'

Thriving on Chaos proved a stepping stone to the more dramatic vision of Peters' *Liberation Management*. This is a huge sprawling book – 'Mr Peters has not extended his passion for downsizing to his own prose,' noted *The Economist*.[2] Undoubtedly it is rambling and lacking in focus but, behind its folksy stories of service excellence, it possesses a fervent purpose. It celebrates the death of middle management – 'Middle Management, as we have known it since the railroads invented it right after the Civil War, is dead. Therefore, middle managers as we have known them are cooked geese.' The phraseology is colourful, but eulogizes about the successes of people in a way few other management books have ever contemplated. Peters seeks to put people, creativity, technology, and speed of thought and action at centre stage.

While challenging for readers to negotiate, *Liberation Management* proved highly successful. Once again Peters' timing and ability to identify trends cannot be questioned. *In Search of Excellence* came out as US unemployment headed to 10 per cent; *Thriving on Chaos* came out on the day Wall Street fell by 20 per cent; *Liberation Management* emerged as the world was coming out of recession and organizations were becoming aware of the need to understand new ways of working which utilize technology more productively.

Liberation Management noted the trend towards what Peters labels as 'fashion': 'The definition of every product and service is changing. Going soft, softer, softest. Going fickle, ephemeral, fashion. An explosion of new competitors, a rising standard of living in the developed world, and the ever-present...new technologies are leading the way. No corner of the world is exempt from the frenzy.'

Amid the frenzy emerge the 'excellent' organizations of the 1990s – companies like CNN, Body Shop, ABB and many others which espouse organizational liberalism through their commitment to speedy decisions, free-flowing organization and individual ability. Unlike its predecessors, *Liberation Management* does not provide a recipe for success. Instead, the recipe is an apparently random, unique stew of best practice. Peters' message is more pragmatic – if it is a good idea, make it work for you.

Sceptics suggest that Peters has a flair for marketing and self-publicity. This is undoubtedly true. Rather like a nineteenth century travelling preacher, he has a plentiful supply of colourful slogans – 'the nanosecond nineties', 'crazy times call for crazy organizations'. But, what is eye-catching about *Liberation Management* is Peters' intimate knowledge of some of the world's most advanced and innovative corporations. He has a knack of getting under organizational skins – he may interview the chief executive but is just as likely to focus on the chief executive's chauffeur. Among others, *Liberation Management* is dedicated to two workers in a heavy manufacturing company who have revolutionized the way they work. Peters' message is that corporate revolution is not simply about doing away with parking spaces for directors, but is real and touches everyone.

It is this willinginess to grapple with human nature which goes some way to explaining Peters' popularity. He is interested in what motivates people and the reality of their day-to-day work. Paradoxically, this sort of down-to-earth realism is set against his evangelical idealism.

Peters' work is an antidote to the dry analysis of strategy or the focus on how companies are organized. Yes, he says, these things are important, but people are the driving force. In an effort to understand people his reading and references are increasingly broad ranging – as likely to include Zen Buddhism as baseball. He recently wrote that he would like his epitaph to be: 'He was curious to the end.'[3]

While Peters has cut an eye-catching swathe, Waterman's career has continued at a more leisurely pace. 'Where Peters is the Savonarola of his cause, Waterman is a gentler prophet,' observes Robert Heller.[4] His books, *The Renewal Factor, Adhocracy: The Power to Change* and *The Frontiers of Excellence* have fared less well than Peters'. They are, nevertheless, as perceptive.

In *The Frontiers of Excellence*, Waterman argues that companies which succeed pay primary attention to employees and customers rather than shareholders. Waterman provides a four-point plan to sustaining excellence: small, fairly autonomous units; 'downward' rather than 'upward' organization; effective 'adhocracy' (groups cuttings across functional lines) as well as bureaucracy; 'sheer staying power and the will to commit to long-term plans'.

STUART CRAINER

Further Reading

Tom Peters and Robert Waterman:
*In Search of Excellence, Harper & Row, New York and London, 1982.

Tom Peters:
A Passion for Excellence (with Nancy Austin), Collins, London, 1985.
Thriving on Chaos, Macmillan, London, 1988.
*Liberation Management, Alfred Knopf, New York, 1992.

Robert Waterman:
The Renewal Factor, Bantam, New York, 1987.
*The Frontiers of Excellence, Nicholas Brealey, London, 1994.

* Recommended reading

References

[1] 'Take me to your leader', *The Economist*, 25 December–7 January 1994.
[2] 'Tom Peters, performance artist', *The Economist*, 24 September 1994.
[3] Peters, T, Foreward to Bennis, W, *An Invented Life*, Addison-Wesley, Reading, Mass, 1993.
[4] Heller, R, 'In pursuit of paragons', *Management Today*, May 1994.

BUILDING THE ENTREPRENEURIAL CORPORATION

Sumantra Ghoshal
and Christopher A Bartlett

By the mid-1980s over 85 per cent of large corporations had adopted the multidivisional structure. From its origins in General Motors under Alfred P Sloan, the multidivisional form evolved to become the accepted *modus operandi* of most large business organizations; the concept became elevated to an unquestioned doctrine.

With its advantages over functional organization, multidivisional organization fuelled growth. It did so, however, on the basis of constrained capital and high growth in world markets. In the 1990s these conditions no longer exist. In a world of converging technologies, global brands and solution selling, the multidivisional company has no means of achieving the pervasive interdependence the world now demands.

In its place is emerging a new model of the entrepreneurial corporation. This is a not single clear-cut model but one which embraces three processes: the entrepreneurial process, the integration process and the renewal process.

Around the world, large diversified companies are in a state of turmoil. In the United States, IBM, General Motors and Eastman Kodak have collectively wasted over a hundred billion dollars of their shareholders' money over the 1980s.[1] Others, like Digital Equipment Corporation and Westinghouse, are shell-shocked by the sheer speed of their fall from grace. Yet, they may well have better chances of ultimately regaining control over their destinies than the many more who are creeping along in a state of satisfactory underperformance. Managers in these companies are clearly aware of a progressive decay in their companies' competitive advantage, but are continuously lowering their standards and expectations so as to avoid confronting manifest performance problems.

The situation is no better in Europe. There too, once revered names like Philips, ICI and Olivetti have had their turns at the surgeon's table while others like Daimler-Benz, Air France and Unilever have made headlines more as problem cases than as role models.

In Japan, many of the companies venerated by the West in the 1980s have faltered. Toshiba, Komatsu and many others, such as Sony, Nissan, Sharp and Hitachi have experienced a sharp decline in their fortunes. Elsewhere, organizations such as Korea's Samsung, Australia's Rio Tinto Zinc and India's the house of Tata are in the midst of intense conflict.

Why are all these companies, around the world, in so much trouble at the same time?

A God that failed

There is an idiosyncratic story behind each of these cases of corporate decline. General Motors' inability to adjust to changing market conditions in the automobile industry was caused by unique circumstances different from those responsible for Matsushita's inability to reduce its dependence on VCR sales and profits; and different still was Bull's failure in foreseeing and responding to changing customer requirements in the information technology business.

Yet, there is one common overarching reason behind the difficulties being faced by these companies. And that reason lies in the way they are organized and managed. Over the last four decades, each of these companies, together with a vast majority of large diversified firms around the world, had come to adopt a common organizational doctrine: the multidivisional enterprise. We call it a doctrine because it is more than a mere specification of the organization structure: it also describes the roles and responsibilities of corporate, divisional and business-unit-level managers; it describes relative status and norms of behaviour of staff and line functionaries; machinisms and processes for allocation of resources; and, in general, sets 'the rules of the game' inside the company. Over the last ten years, a variety of changes in market, technological and competitive contexts has rendered this doctrine obsolete and the problems large corporations are facing stem, at least in part, from sticking to this past success formula well beyond the limit of its usefulness.

The multidivisional doctrine

Fashioned in the 1920s by business leaders like Alfred Sloan and Pierre du Pont, and refined over the next five decades in industrial groups such as Westinghouse, Siemens, Matsushita and, above all, General Electric, the multidivisional organization was perhaps the single most important administrative innovation that helped companies grow in size and diversity far beyond the limits of the functional organization it replaced.

General Motors represents not just one of the earliest companies to develop and adopt this new organizational form, but is also one of the best illustrations of the broader management doctrine of which this form was a part. Implemented by Alfred Sloan in the face of an acute financial crisis that had led to the removal of GM's founder chief executive, the new organization played a central role in helping GM raise its US market share from 18 per cent in the early 1920s to over 45 per cent by the late 1970s as the company grew to become the largest automobile company in the world. The three core characteristics of the GM organization built by Sloan, as described by business historian Alfred Chandler,[2] have since become the norm for large diversified companies around the world.

First, Sloan divided the businesses of GM into a set of semi-autonomous operating units, with each unit being allocated the responsibility of maintaining market share and profits in a single business or market. The way the operating units were constructed varied from business to business. Structuring of these operating units was guided by the fundamental principle that 'the responsibility attached to the chief executive of each operation shall in no way be limited. Each such organization headed by its chief executive shall be complete in every necessary function and able to exercise its full initiative and logical development'.[3]

Second, Sloan assigned two key responsibilities to the group of headquarters executives he headed.[4] 'One was entrepreneurial, that is, to determine strategies to utilize for the long term the firm's organizational skills, facilities and capital and to allocate resources – capital and product-specific technical and managerial skills – to pursue these strategies.' The second was more administrative. It was 'to monitor the performance of the operating divisions; to check on the use of resources allocated; and, when necessary, redefine the product lines of the divisions so as to continue to use effectively the firm's organizational capabilities.'

Third, to support these headquarters functions, Sloan created two distinct management groups. The various business divisions were clustered into groups based on 'common problems', and were placed under the executive responsibility of group vice presidents. To protect the autonomy of divisional managers, these group-level executives had no day-to-day operating responsibilities. Instead, they provided advice and support to the corporate management team.

The second management group consisted of staff specialists in areas such as research and development, finance and accounting, engineering, purchase and personnel. The performance monitoring function of the headquarters required accurate, uniform data on costs, production, inventory, income and so forth, which these staff groups were expected to provide.

While the basic structure in its actual operation, both within GM and in the numerous other companies that adopted Sloan's design of the multidivisional enterprise, remained more or less the same over the next five decades, the roles and tasks of the different management groups evolved. For example, the purely advisory role of the group executives was found to be untenable. Over time, in most companies including GM, the group executive became a distinct third layer of management, between the corporate headquarters and the division or business unit, with supervisory line authority and overall performance responsibility for the divisions he or she supervised. Similar changes also had to be made in the roles and functions of corporate staff. Confronted with repeated conflicts between divisional managers and the R&D staff, Sloan created a set of interdivisional committees to co-ordinate functional work across different units. By the mid-1930s, the influence of the general staff at GM was further enhanced when the interdivisional committees were replaced by Policy Groups consisting of line and staff managers at the corporate level. Through these policy groups, the staff continued to co-ordinate interdivisional functions but also came to play an expanded role in policy making.[5]

These expanded influence and substantive roles of group executives and corporate staff also changed the roles of the divisional managers and the corporate top management. As the policy groups assumed greater and greater responsibility for strategic decisions, the divisional managers became responsible for tactical and operating decisions only. At the same time, the growing distance between top management and the divisions increasingly isolated the former from the operating realities of the company's businesses. As a result, their entrepreneurial function became focused on a portfolio model of resource allocation, based on pre-specified roles of divisions and exercised on the basis of purely financial analysis.[6]

Compared to the functionally departmentalized structure that preceded it, this multidivisional organizational form presented a number of advantages, the first and foremost of which was to free up top management time. Freed from the need of day-to-day operational co-ordination, top-level managers in the multidivisional firm had both the time and the psychological freedom to concentrate on broad strategic matters.

At the same time, delegation of operating responsibilities to divisional managers brought these decisions closer to where effective market, competitive and technological information resided, and thus improved both the speed and the quality of the company's response to immediate business issues. Finally, the intermediate and staff managers provided enhanced capacity for information gathering and analysis as well as a reservoir of specialized skills that could be used across the various businesses, capturing economies of both scale and scope.

The failure of success

Yet, as is true of many success formulae, the seeds of its eventual failure lay embedded in the same features of the multidivisional organization that were responsible for its amazing success and worldwide diffusion over the last five decades. Inherent within the organizational form designed by Sloan lay a set of forces that would inexorably lead the companies that adopted this structure first to a state of mediocrity and finally to crisis.

Sloan's organization was designed to overcome the limitations of the functional structure in managing large, established businesses. While it did this quite well, at least for a while, it proved incapable of creating and developing new businesses internally. This inability to manage organic expansion into new areas was caused by many factors. With primarily operating responsibilities and guided by a measurement system that focused on profit and market share performance in served markets, the front-line business unit managers in the divisionalized corporation were neither expected to, nor could, scout for new opportunities breaking around the boxes in the organization chart that defined their product or geographic scope. Besides, small new ventures, as organic developments tended to be at the start of their lives, could not absorb the large central overheads and yet return the profits needed to justify the financial and human investments.

On the other hand, at the corporate level, where visibility of an issue needed large price tags, the entrepreneurship game could only be played for home runs, not singles. As a result, in such companies, entrepreneurial growth could be achieved primarily in two ways: expansions in existing businesses, driven off the benefits of scale, scope, and the power of financial muscle, or entering new businesses through acquisitions. This was not a constraint in the benevolent and high-growth environment in the four decades after the Second World War. In the slow-growth 1990s, however, overcapacity is the norm in most businesses: 40 per cent in automobiles, 100 per cent in bulk chemicals, 50 per cent in steel, and 140 per cent in computers, for example. Both technological progress and customer needs are driving towards smaller lot sizes and higher variety.

Large scale acquisitions, the second growth option for these companies, also appears to have run its course. This, too, was a resource game that played to the strengths of large divisionalized corporations. But, while paying for acquisitions was easy, managing them has proved to be far more difficult. Also, in search of growth at almost any cost, many companies have diversified too far afield, driven by the availability of acquisition candidates rather than by consideration of strategic logics, shared capabilities or commonalities in management processes, thereby exceeding the level of complexity that can be managed under a common corporate umbrella. Finally, competing in this game with other resource-rich large companies, financial strength has ceased to provide any advantage and has instead only raised acquisition premiums to astronomical levels. As a result, by the early 1990s, the M&A balloon has burst, bringing to a halt the second growth process for the hierarchical, divisionalized corporation.

Also obsolete in the 1990s is the assumption of independence among different businesses, technologies and geographic markets that is central to the design of most divisionalized corporations.

In an environment in which different products and services of a company must draw on diverse capabilities and must, in turn, be offered as integrated 'systems' to solve customers' problems, this assumption of independence across units is preventing these companies from integrating their diverse research, engineering, production and marketing resources into a coherent system for value delivery.

Adjustment within the doctrine of the multidivisional enterprise cannot solve the problem, as the failure of the matrix has shown. The multidivisional enterprise is as much a management mindset as it is a formal structure, and horizontal interdependence simply cannot be a part of this mindset.

Besides, the matrix was invented to manage the complexity of integrating organizational resources and aligning corporate initiatives across two dimensions: those of businesses and functions. As companies expanded globally, a third dimension – that of geography – was added to the list. In the 1990s, however, companies are facing the need to link and leverage their capabilities not only across businesses, functions and geographical territories, but also along core processes such as those of new product creation and the make-to-market logistics chain, for specific customers identified as global accounts, by end-user industries and distribution channels, and a host of other such dimensions. The logic of the divisionalized corporation requires the addition of a specialized management group to co-ordinate each dimension of integration and managers, recognizing the complexity that integration across all these dimensions would cause, have no option but to ignore these integration needs for the sake of organizational simplicity.

Finally, the multidivisional doctrine was also premised on the assumption of relative stability. Environmental changes were assumed to be linear and incremental. For such environments, this organization was and still remains almost a perfect and complete design, one that only an engineer could create. But, in an environment of discontinuities and often turbulent and unpredictable change, this very completeness has become its Achilles heel, for it is only capable of operational refinement, not strategic renewal.

The hierarchical relationship between corporate, group and business unit managers is the trunk around which the tree of the multidivisional company functions. Information processing in the company is structured around this fundamental hierarchy. The business units provide data. This data is analyzed, at both business unit and group levels, into usable information that can be leveraged by the businesses. In the multidivisional organization, mechanisms and routines are formed for managing these different information processing tasks. This efficiency in information processing is a key strength of the divisionalized enterprise as it incrementally builds its organizational knowledge and leverages that knowledge to refine operational processes in existing activities.

What these companies lack, however, is the antithesis of this sequential and incremental knowledge building process that is necessary for strategic renewal. They have no process through which institutionalized wisdoms can be challenged, existing knowledge bases can be overturned, and the sources of the data can be reconfigured. In the absence of this challenge, these companies gradually become immobilized by conventional wisdoms that have ossified as sacred cows, and become constrained by outmoded knowledge and expertise that are out of touch with their rapidly changing realities.

The ritual of denial

These problems are not new, and most Western companies are intensely familiar with them, having spent most of the 1980s trying to deny their existence.

As growth slowed, instead of focusing on the factors that impeded their ability to pursue the new kind of opportunities, most of these companies directed their energies to finding temporary band-aids to protect profits by cost reduction. First, they shifted activities offshore. Then they closed many of them altogether under the new slogan of outsourcing. They slashed their capital investments and R&D budgets. Finally, they squeezed whatever they could from their workers, cutting headcounts and demanding wage renegotiation.

Unable to create successful new products through their regular product creation processes, managers threw small amounts of resources at mavericks, calling them skunkworks or new venture groups, and then closed their eyes and prayed for magic. When these efforts failed, they rushed into alliances, again hoping that others would help them hide the organizational problems that they themselves could not overcome.

By the late 1980s, however, the underlying organizational and management problems had become too visible to ignore. After rounds of belt tightening on all other costs, large central overheads stuck out like a sore thumb and an embarrassed top management was forced to take the axe to the layers of middle management and the bloated staff groups that had long been the safe sanctuaries of the corporate world.

In the slash and burn that has followed, the real problem has ultimately become clear. Delayering and destaffing, like all the earlier actions, do not by themselves provide durable solutions to the performance problems these companies have been facing. Reduction of corporate overheads provides one-time relief and buys some time, but the inexorable forces of competition and change catch up again with companies that restructure but do not revitalize; that cut people but do not fundamentally alter their ways of working. From the experiences of such companies has emerged the new, if somewhat cynical, rule that the best predictor of the companies that will restructure in any one year is the list of companies that restructured four years ago.

An emerging management model

But, as always in corporate history, a few companies appear to have broken through these barriers. In General Electric, Jack Welch has spearheaded a revolution that has seen sales increase from $27 billion in 1980 to $58 billion in 1990, accompanied by a profit growth from $1.5 billion to $4.3 billion and a sky-rocketing of stock value from $12 billion to $65 billion, making GE the second largest company in the United States, behind Exxon, up from the eleventh position in 1980. Undergirding this impressive improvement in performance lay a fundamental shift in the organizational doctrine that has been described, perhaps with only slight exaggeration, as 'one of the biggest planned efforts to alter people's behaviors since the cultural revolution'. Across the Atlantic, Percy Barnevik at ABB has wrought a similar revolution in this amalgam of two traditional Swiss and Swedish companies, rapidly expanding the company's global reach through an organization that violates every principle of the multidivisional doctrine. And across the Pacific, the Japanese car giant Toyota has undergone, more quietly but equally vigorously, a similar change that has eliminated three of the seven layers in its management structure, dramatically changed the roles of the section chiefs and division heads, and decoupled salary of middle managers from their titles and linked remuneration to their roles and tasks instead, thereby creating a flat and fluid organization completely different from the one that had been so successful over the past three decades. Similar experiments to overcome the limitations of the multidivisional doctrine are now underway at Intel and Corning, at Matsushita and Toshiba, at Philips and Alcatel, guided by a group of visionary chief executives like Andy Grove, Jimmy Houghton, Akio Taani and Jan Timmer.

While all these experiments may not be successful, business historians in the next decade will find them to have been as revolutionary in ushering in a new model of the entrepreneurial corporation as those in GM, Dupont, Philips and other companies in the 1920s and 1930s that laid the foundation of the multidivisional enterprise . The emerging management philosophy does not imply a single, ubiquitous structural form. It stipulates, instead, a set of key management processes and the roles and tasks of managers at different levels to make these processes effective. The actual configuration of the processes themselves, and the structural shell within which they are embedded, can be very different, depending on the businesses and the heritage of each company.

Three core processes lie at the heart of this new management approach. The *entrepreneurial process* drives the opportunity-seeking, externally-focused ability of the organization to create new businesses. The *integration process* allows it to link and leverage its dispersed resources and competencies to build a successful company. The *renewal process* maintains its capacity to challenge its own beliefs and practices and to continuously revitalize itself so as to develop an enduring institution. Each of these processes requires certain organizational infrastructures and mechanisms; managing all three processes simultaneously requires a management mindset that is fundamentally different from the one that has been shaped so firmly over the last five decades by the doctrine of the multidivisional enterprise .[7]

The entrepreneurial process: supporting and aligning initiatives

Building the entrepreneurial corporation does not require the creation of a society of independent entrepreneurs held together by a top management acting as a combination of a bank and a venture fund. It demands instead the shaping of a strong entrepreneurial process to drive the company's opportunity-seeking externally-focused ability to create and exploit avenues for profitable growth. It is this integrated entrepreneurial process that brings the large company advantages to the front-line entrepreneurs and distinguishes the entrepreneurial corporation from the myths of internal venturing and 'intrapreneurship' that have already been debunked in practice. The large entrepreneurial corporation is not a hierarchical organization with a few less layers of management and a few scattered skunk works or genius awards: it is a company built around a core entrepreneurial process that drives everybody, and everything the company does.

The entrepreneurial process requires a close interplay among three key management roles. The front-line *entrepreneurs* are the spearheads of the company, and it is their responsibility to create and pursue new growth opportunities. The *coaches* in middle and senior management positions play a pivotal role in reviewing, developing and supporting the front-line initiatives. Corporate *leaders* at the top of the organization establish the overall strategic mission of the company that defines the boundary within which the entrepreneurial initiatives must be contained, and also sets the highly demanding performance standards that these initiatives must meet (see Fig. 1). Just as the structural units of corporate, divisional and operating-unit-level management groups were the fundamental building blocks of the multidivisional organization, the three management roles of entrepreneurs, coaches and leaders and their interelationships are the core building blocks of the entrepreneurial corporation. The recent reorganization of a large American computer company provides an example of how such a management process can be structured.

Confronted with the challenge of rapidly changing customer demands and the constraints of a traditional matrix organization that impeded the company's ability to marshal its own formidable technological resources to help its customers solve ever-more complex problems, the company decided to restructure itself to create 'a network of entrepreneurs in a global corporation'. As described by top management, the objective was to create a management approach 'which starts with *opportunity* and capitalizes upon the *innovation*, *creativity* and *excellence* of people to secure the future of the company'. This

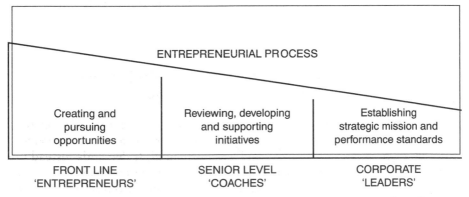

Fig. 1 The entrepreneurial process: management roles and tasks

objective was enshrined in the vision statement: to build 'a global IT service company based on people who are enthusiastic about coming to work every day knowing that they are highly valued, encouraged to grow and increase their knowledge and are individually motivated to make a positive difference.'

To achieve this vision, the company restructured itself into a large number of relatively small units, each unit being headed by a person formally designated as an entrepreneur. There were different kinds of entrepreneurial units, corresponding to different tasks such as product creation, field sales and support, or industry marketing.

All shared a common mandate, however, 'to think and act as heads of companies in a networked holding': pursuit of opportunities was defined as their key challenge. Each entrepreneur was assured significant support and the top management collectively declared that 'everyone in the company works for the entrepreneurs'. At the same time, it was emphasized that no one could afford to own or control all the expertise, resources or services necessary for achieving his or her objectives and independent judgement and action had to reflect this pervasive interdependence so as to effectively leverage the network of resources available in a global corporation.

As part of the reorganization, senior regional, divisional and functional managers were relieved of their normal consolidation and control tasks and were instead regrouped as a pool of coaches. The label of coach highlighted that they should not play in the actual game. Yet, the metaphor was that of a football coach who bore overall responsibility for the team's success, had the expertise to improve the players' skills, possessed the experience to guide the team's strategy, and the authority to change players when the need arose.

In operational terms, each entrepreneur was allotted a specific coach to support him or her, but also a separate 'board' which had formal responsibility to 'review and question the validity of the entrepreneur's strategy and plan, provide feedback, monitor performance, encourage, stimulate, support and, via the chairperson, propose rewards or change of the entrepreneur' (see Fig. 2).

In his or her individual capacity, the coach's main task was defined as helping the entrepreneur to succeed, both through personal guidance and support on

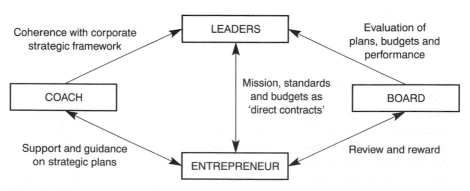

Fig. 2 The operational structure

strategic plans and also by acting as a link between the entrepreneur and all others in the company whose resources the entrepreneur might need. An active role in the entrepreneur's personal development including planning of training inputs and new assignments was identified as an essential part of the coach's role.

The board, to be chaired by the coach, was designed to act in a manner not dissimilar from regular corporate boards. While the chairperson would be nominated by the top management, other members would be selected by the entrepreneur, in consultation with the chairperson, from the company's pool of coaches. In selecting her board members, the entrepreneur was expected to look for specific technological, industry or administrative expertise and, if the desired skills were not available within the company, she could appoint out-siders such as customer representatives, professors in technical or management schools, or even one of the employees within her unit.

While the coach, in his personal capacity, would be responsible for develop-ing and supporting the entrepreneurial initiatives, the board was designed to serve as the company's key instrument for maintaining rigorous and disci-plined financial control. The board's key tasks would be to challenge the entrepreneur's plans, review her budget proposals, monitor performance against budgets, and to continuously advise top management on resource allocation decisions. Budgets were seen as sacrosanct both ways: once pro-posed and approved, the entrepreneur had to achieve the budget and would be expected to take personal responsibility for initiating any changes in plans that might become necessary because of unforeseen developments. Similarly, no one in the company could tamper with an approved budget except in response to the entrepreneur's demonstrated inability in living up to the contract.

Achievement of budgets would be the trigger for release of the next set of resources, and managing this multi-staged resource allocation process would be a key responsibility of the boards. The separation of the development and control responsibilities was designed to prevent both the entrepreneur and the coach from lapsing back into the familiar boss-subordinate role structure and was, therefore, seen as key to protecting the integrity of the system.

While the uniform financial control system was expected to embed rigour and discipline in the exercise of bottom-up entrepreneurship, top management of the company also recognized the need for a clear statement of strategic mis-sion to provide direction and coherence to the entrepreneurial process. In contrast to the company's historical focus on proprietary products, the mis-sion statement unambiguously described the need for refocusing on customer service and on providing and integrating multi-vendor products and services. Further elaboration of the mission highlighted particular industry sectors and specific services for priority attention. The simple, yet unambiguous, statement was explained and debated throughout the company over a six-month period to ensure not only intellectual understanding but also emotional commitment on the part of all employees.

Just the statement and its elaboration was, however, not enough. The process of discussion and debate revealed the need for clear performance standards and norms to link the mission with specific projects and plans. In response, top management articulated five key performance parameters – each clearly linked to the mission statement – and set specific overall goals against each parameter. For example, 'increase market share faster than competition' or 'profit above local competitors' was translated onto tangible but differentiated objectives for the different entrepreneurial units and approval of plans were linked to these objectives.

This is just one example, but a number of key attributes appear to be common to companies that are able to capture the creative energy of their people to develop new growth opportunities.

First, they build their organizations around relatively small units. Matsushita had proliferated the world with its National, Panasonic, Quasar, Technic and other branded consumer electronic products on the strength of its 'one product-one division' concept: as soon as an existing division came out with a successful new product, it was split up as a separate division. ABB is not a $30 billion behemoth: it is a network of 1,300 separate companies, each a legal entity with its own balance sheet and profit and loss statement, with an average of 200 employees per company. One can observe the same practice in companies as diverse as 3M, Johnson and Johnson and Bartelsmann: to maintain the entrepreneurial spirit, each unit must be restricted in size so as to create the strong sense of identity and commitment that is all so common in small companies.

To build such small units, these companies have abandoned the notion of functionally complete 'strategic business units' which had to have ownership of all key resources so as to be in full control of their performance. Instead, they have structured incomplete 'performance units' that are interdependent and must use each other's resources to achieve their own goals. In contrast to the arbitrary and conflict-generating distinctions between cost centres, revenue centres and profit centres, the performance centres are not differentiated based on their activities. Whether they sell to customers, or produce for internal customers, or work to build new technologies, all performance centres are treated similarly in the planning, budgeting and control systems.

Second, they create a multi-stage resource allocation process instead of up-front commitment to a clearly articulated long-term plan. Any employee can propose to start a new business at 3M and 'a single coherent sentence can often suffice as a starting plan'. But, at each stage of developing the proposal, from the initial idea to product development, prototyping, technical and market testing and commercialization, the proposer must present a specific budget and clearly quantified mileposts, and all approvals are subject to satisfactory performance against the earlier commitments. As 3M managers grudgingly admit, 'we spend all out time preparing budgets, but it seems to help'.

Third, they tend to adopt a highly structured and rigorously implemented financial control system. At 3M, for example, such financial discipline is maintained through a standardized management reporting system that is applied uniformly to all operating units which are forbidden by a central directive from creating their own systems. Similarly, at Matsushita, a new division receives start-up capital from the corporate headquarters, and loans, when justified, under normal commercial conditions. It pays interest on the loans to the corporate 'bank' at regular market rates, together with 60 per cent of pre-tax profits as dividend. Performance expectations are uniform across all divisions, regardless of the maturity of the market or the company's competitive position, and divisions in which operating profits fall below four per cent of sales for two successive years have their divisional managers replaced.

An essential corollary of such rigorous financial control is the sanctity of the budget of each entrepreneurial unit. In entrepreneurial companies, the budget of any unit is not changed except in response to variances in the unit's own performance. There is neither a cascading down of budget approvals nor an aggregation up of budget achievements: the budget of each unit is approved separately and its performance is monitored individually right up to the very top of corporate management.

And finally, all these companies have a clearly articulated and widely understood and shared definition of the 'opportunity horizon' that provides a lightning rod to direct organizational aspirations and energy into cohesive corporate development. The boundaries of the opportunity horizon tend to be precise enough to clearly rule out activities that do not support the company's strategic mission, and yet broad enough to prevent undue constraints on the creativity and opportunism of front-line managers. Without such a clearly defined strategic mission, front-line managers have no basis for selecting among the diverse opportunities they might confront, and bottom-up entrepreneurship soon degenerates into a frustrating guessing game. The actual definition of the boundaries may be stated in very different terms – a strong technology focus in Canon or 3M or around specific customer groups in SAS or Cartier, for example – but it provides a basis for strategic choice among different initiatives and serves as a guideline for the entrepreneurs themselves to focus their own creative energy.

The integration process: linking and leveraging competencies

In this world of converging technologies, category management and global competition, the entrepreneurial process alone is not sufficient for effective corporate entrepreneurship: the new management approach also requires the creation of a strong integration process to link the company's diverse assets and resources into corporate competencies, and to leverage these competencies to pursue new opportunities. In the absence of such an integration process, decentralized entrepreneurship may lead to some temporary performance improvement as existing slack is harnessed, but long-term development of new capabilities or businesses are seriously impeded. Many highly decentralized companies, including Matsushita, have recently experienced this problem. But integration can co-exist with and, indeed, complement entrepreneurship, as the following example will demonstrate.

Nikkei Business recently ranked Kao as the third in its list of Japan's most creative companies, well ahead of other local superstars such as NEC, Toyota, Seibu and Canon. The company had earned this distinction because of its outstanding record of introducing innovative, high quality products to beat back not only domestic rivals, such as Lion, but also its giant global competitors such as Procter & Gamble and Unilever. Technological and design innovations in Merries – Kao's brand of disposable diapers – reduced P&G's market share in Japan from nearly 90 per cent to less than ten. Similarly, Attack, Kao's condensed laundry detergent, has seen the company's domestic market share surge from 33 to 48 per cent, while that of Lion declined from 31 to 23 per cent. In the 1980s, this innovative capability allowed this traditional soap company to expand successfully into personal care products where it established Sofina as the largest selling cosmetics brand in Japan, and into floppy disks in which it has already risen to be the second largest player in North America.

A powerful entrepreneurial process lies at the heart of Kao's innovative ability. It practices all the elements of the entrepreneurial process: small, functionally incomplete units driven by aggressive targets, rigorous financial discipline, a structured new product creation process supported by a flexible and multi-stage resource allocation system, and a clear definition of its strategic mission in terms of utilizing its technological strengths to develop products with superior functionality. However, the wellspring behind this entrepreneurial process has been what Dr Yoshio Maruta, the chairman of Kao, describes as 'biological self-control'. As the body reacts to pain by sending help from all quarters, 'if anything goes wrong in one part of the company, all other parts should know automatically and help without having to be asked.' A company-wide integration process has allowed Kao to link and leverage its core competencies in research, manufacturing and marketing not only to solve problems but also to create and exploit new opportunities. And this integration process in Kao, like the entrepreneurial process we have described, is built on some well-defined roles, tasks and value added, on the part of the front-line entrepreneurs, the senior level coaches and the corporate leaders (see Fig. 3).

The small and relatively autonomous work units of the entrepreneurial corporation create an enormous centrifugal force which, in the absence of a countervailing centripetal force, can overwhelm the company with inconsistencies, conflicts and fragmentation. The first task in integration, therefore, is to create a glue to hold the different parts together and to align their initiatives. A set of clear and motivating organizational values often provides the basis for such normative integration, and developing, nurturing and embedding these values becomes a key task of the management group we have described as corporate leaders.

The organizational processes of Kao are designed to foster the spirit of harmony and social integration based on the principle of absolute equality of human beings, individual initiative and the rejection of authoritarianism. 'Free

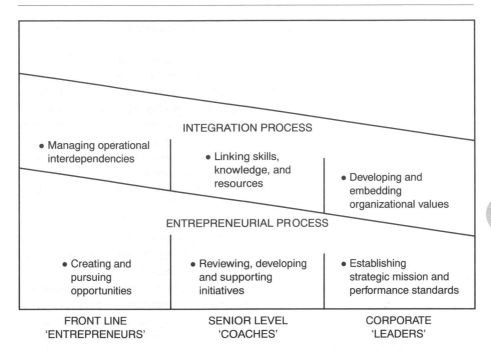

Fig. 3 The integration process: management roles and tasks

access of everyone to all information' serves as the core value and the guiding principle of what Dr Maruta describes as Kao's 'paperweight organization': a flat structure, with a small handle of a few senior people in the middle, in which all information is shared horizontally and not filtered vertically.

These core values of human equality and free sharing of all information are embedded throughout the organization not only through continuous articulation and emphasis by Dr Maruta and other members of the top management team but also through their own behaviours and a set of institutionalized practices.

For example, Dr Maruta and his top management colleagues share the tenth floor of Kao's head office building, together with a pool of secretaries. A large part of this floor is open space, with conference tables, overhead projectors and lounging chairs spread around. This is known as 'Decision Space', where all discussions with and among the top management take place. Anyone passing, including the chairman, can sit down and join in any discussion, on any topic, and they frequently do. The executive vice-president in charge of a particular business or a specific territory can, therefore, be engaged in a debate on a topic that he has no formal responsibility for. The same layout and norm are duplicated in the other floors, in the laboratories, and in workshops. Workplaces look like large rooms: there are no partitions, only tables and chairs and empty spaces for spontaneous or planned discussions in which everyone has free access and can contribute as equals.

Every director of the company and most salesmen have a fax machine in their homes to receive results and news, and a bi-weekly Kao newspaper keeps every employee informed about competitors' moves, new product launches, overseas developments, and key meetings. Terminals installed throughout the company ensure that all employees can, if they wish, retrieve data on sales records of any product from any of Kao's numerous outlets, or product development at their own or other branches. The latest findings from each of Kao's research laboratories are available for all to see, as are the details of the previous days' production and inventory at every Kao plant. 'They can even,' says Dr Maruta, 'check up on the president's expense account.' The benefits from this open sharing of data outweighs the risk of leaks, the company believes and, anyway, 'leaked information instantly becomes obsolete'.

While the corporate leaders carry the principal responsibility for developing and embedding the corporate values that provide the context for integration, it is the front-line entrepreneurs who must integrate the day-to-day activities of the company by managing the operational interdependencies across the different product, functional and geographic units. This requires certain attitudes, some specific skills, but also some facilitating infrastructures and processes.

In Kao, information technology is a key element of the infrastructure and its own extensive value added networks (Kao VANs) provide the anchors for operational integration. Fully integrated information systems link the company's marketing, production and research units, controlling the flows of materials, products and ideas from new product development, to production planning involving over 1,500 types of raw materials, to distribution of over 550 types of final products to about 300,000 retail stores.

Kao's logistics information system (LIS) links the corporate headquarters, all the factories, the independent wholesalers and the logistics centres through a network that includes a sales planning system, an inventory control system, and an online supply system. Kao's marketing intelligence system (MIS) monitors sales by product, region and market segment. Artificial intelligence tools are used extensively on this system to develop new approaches to advertising and media planning, sales promotion, market research and statistical analysis. Another sophisticated computerized system, ECHO, codes all on-line telephone queries and complaints about Kao's products. Linked to MIS, ECHO is an invaluable 'window on the customer's mind' that allows the company to fine-tune formulations, labelling and packaging and also to develop new product ideas.

These extensive IT networks provide the tools for the front-line managers to carry much of the burden of day-to-day operational co-ordination and integration which, in most companies, are the key tasks of middle and senior management. But, these IT networks are not seen as a replacement for face-to-face meetings. Indeed the company has one of the most extensive systems of intra-functional, inter-functional and inter-business meetings to facilitate exchanges of ideas and joint development of new initiatives and projects. Top management, marketers and research scientists meet at regular conferences. 'Open space' meetings are offered every week by different units, and people from any part of the organization can participate in such meetings. Within the R&D organization, the life blood of Kao's innovations, monthly conferences are hosted, in turn, by different laboratories, to bring junior researchers together.

But, while the leaders create the context of integration and the front-line managers link and align operational activites, it is the group of coaches in senior management level who serve as the engine for linking the diverse skills, expertise and resources in different research, manufacturing and marketing units to launch the strategic thrusts of Kao and maintain their momentum over time. If the entrepreneurs are the linchpins for the entrepreneurial process, the coaches are the pivots for the integration process.

A company-wide 'Total Creative Revolution' project (TCR) serves as the main vehicle for the senior managers in Kao to constantly pull together teams and task forces from different parts of the company to find creative responses to emerging problems or new opportunities. The fourth phase in a two-decade long programme that started its life in 1971 as an organization-wide computer-ization initiative (the 'CCR' movement), evolved into a 'Total Quality Control' programme (TQC) in 1974 and Total Cost Reduction effort (TCR) in 1986. Total creative revolution is aimed at making 'innovation through collaborative learning' the centrepiece of Kao's strategic thrust into the 1990s. According to Dr Maruta: 'Kao must be like an educational institution – a company that has learnt how to learn.' And senior managers are formally expected to be 'the priests' – the teachers who must facilitate this process of shared learning.

Thus, when a small and distant foreign subsidiary faced a problem, it is one of these constantly travelling senior managers who helped the local manage-ment team identify the appropriate expert in Japan and sponsored a task force to find a creative solution. Similarly, when some factory employees were made redundant following the installation of new equipment, one of these coaches sponsored five of them to form a team to support a factory in the United States to install and commission a plant imported from Japan. Over time, this group became a highly valued flying squad available to help new production units get over their teething troubles.

The success of Sofina was the result of a very similar process, albeit on a much larger scale. Sensing an opportunity to create a high quality, reasonably priced range of cosmetics that would leverage Kao's technological strengths and emphasize the functionality of 'skin care' rather than 'image', the top management of Kao presented it as a corporate challenge. To create such a product and to market it successfully, Kao would need to integrate its capabil-ities both within specific functions, such as diverse technologies in emulsifiers, moisturizers and skin diagnosis lodged in different laboratories, and across functions including R&D, corporate marketing and sales, production, and market research.

Instead of trying to create one gigantic team involving all the people who would need to contribute to the project, a few senior managers including the head of the Tokyo Research Laboratory, the director of marketing research and a director of marketing formed thermselves into a small team to co-ordi-nate the project. They created small task forces, as required, to address specific problems – such as developing a new emulsifier – but kept the lateral co-ordi-nation tasks among the operating managers at the simplest possible level.

When the new emulsifier created some problems of skin irritation, a different group was established to develop a moisturizer and a chemical to reduce irritation. Similarly, when the Sofina foundation cream was found to be sticky on application, they set it up as a challenge for a marketing team who helped position the product as 'the longest lasting foundation that does not disappear with sweat', converting the stickiness into a strength. This group of senior managers continued to play this integrating and co-ordinating role, for over a decade, as the project evolved from a vision in the early 1970s to a nationwide success in the mid-1980s.

The renewal process: managing rationalization and revitalization

In the last two decades, many books have been written about 'excellent' companies. Typically, it has proven to be dangerous for any company to be featured in such books whose publications have often uncannily coincided with the beginning of the company's performance decline. Failure of success is a widespread phenomenon in every walk of life and the corporate world is no exception. Success breeds momentum and, therefore, inertia. Nothing stagnates as spectacularly as companies that stagnate with spectacular pasts.

To overcome this pervasive failure of success and to protect this spirit of entrepreneurship on an on-going basis, the emerging management approach also requires the development of a renewal process: in some ways, an antithesis of the integration process. To remain successful over time, companies must establish mechanisms in which internalized wisdoms and established ways of thinking and working are continuously challenged. If the integration process links and leverages existing capabilities to defend and advance current strategies, the renewal process continuously questions those strategies and the assumptions underlying them and inspires the creation of new competencies to prepare the ground for the very different competitive battles a company is likely to confront in the future.

The renewal process is built on two symbiotic components. It consists, on the one hand, of an ongoing pressure for rationalization and restructuring of existing businesses to achieve continuous improvement of operational performance. This rationalization component focuses on resource use – the effectiveness with which existing assets are deployed – and strives for continuous productivity growth. This part of the renewal process aims to refine existing operations incrementally to achieve ever-improving current results. Rigorous benchmarking against best-in-class competitors provides the scorecard on concrete operational measures such as value added per employee, contributions per unit of fixed and working capital, time to market for new products, and customer satisfaction to surface performance gaps and focus organizational energy on closing those gaps.

The other part of renewal is revitalization – the creation of new competencies and new businesses, the challenging and changing of existing rules of the game, and the leap-frogging of competition through quantum leaps. Driven by dreams and the power of ideas, it focuses on 'business not as usual' to create breakthroughs that would take the company to the next stages of its ambition. Revitalization may involve fast paced small bets to take the company into new business domains – as Canon is trying in the field of semiconductors – or big 'bet the company' moves to transform industries as AT&T is trying to do in the emerging field of 'infocom'.

As with entrepreneurship and integration, rationalization and revitalization are also often viewed in mutually exclusive terms. Some managers complain of the insatiable appetite of the stock market for short-term results which forces them to focus on rationalization rather than revitalization. Others justify poor operating results as the evidence of long-term investments. The renewal process, in contrast, emphasizes the essential symbiosis between the present and the future: there is no long-term success without short-term performance just as short-term results mean little unless they contribute to building the long-term ambition. Rationalization provides the resources needed for revitalization – not just money and people, but also legitimacy and credibility – while revitalization creates the hope and the energy needed for rationalization.

Amid the general bloodbath that has characterized the semiconductor business, Intel has been among the few players to have achieved steady growth together with satisfactory financial returns. While its fortunes have turned with the tide – from spectacular successes in the 1970s when it introduced, in quick succession, the 1130 DRAM, the 1702 EPROM and the 8086 microprocessor, to heavy losses in the mid-1980s when the company was forced to exit the DRAM and SRAM businesses and cut 30 per cent of its workforce, to phenomenal success again with the 80386 32-bit microprocessor in the late 1980s – Intel has so far taken most of the correct turns as it hit the forks on the road, avoiding hitting the dividers, as many of its competitors have done.

In this process, the company has continuously renewed itself, changing its products and strategies and adopting its organization and culture, to respond to the dramatic changes in its business environment. From the 'self-evident truth' that Intel was a 'jellybean' memory company, it changed itself into a logic devices company, selling boards, and then to a systems house, providing solutions in boxes. From a heritage of manufacturing inefficiency that was almost celebrated as the evidence of creativity in product development, Intel has now become almost cost-competitive *vis-à-vis* its Japanese rivals. Its marketing focus has evolved too, from selling product features in the early 1970s, to benefits-oriented marketing in the late 1970s, to positioning-oriented marketing in the 1980s, emphasizing compatibility with end-user standards, to full-fledged end-user marketing in the 1990s in direct partnership with the final customers of the company's microprocessors. To support these changes, Intel has also transformed its culture. From an organization of and for 'bright, talkative, opinionated, rude, arrogant, impatient and very informal macho men interested only in results and not in niceties', the company has evolved into a better balance between task focus and concern for a friendly work environment in which 'people don't have to be Milky the milk biscuit to get their work done, but then, they don't have to be Atilla the Hun either'.

Intel's ability to stay one step ahead of competition – which is all that separates the winners from the losers in the semiconductor business – has been built on some demanding roles and contributions of managers at all levels of the company (see Fig. 4). But, if the front-line entrepreneurs drive the entrepreunarial process and the senior level coaches anchor the integration process, it is the corporate level leaders who inspire and energize the renewal process. It is they who create and manage the tensions between short-term performance and long-term ambition, challenging the organization continuously to higher levels of operational and strategic performance.

Until the demise of Noyce in 1990, Intel has been led by the trio of Gordon Moore as chairman, Robert Noyce as vice chairman and Andy Grove as president who, collectively, formed the company's executive committee. Of these, while Noyce looked after external relations, it was Moore and Grove who guided the company internally: Moore in the role of the technology genius and architect of long-term strategy, and Grove as the detail-oriented resident pragmatist. Moore has been the quiet, long-term oriented, philosophical champion of revitalization. Grove, on the other hand, has served as the vocal, aggressive and demanding driver of rationalization. When Motorola's competitive micro-

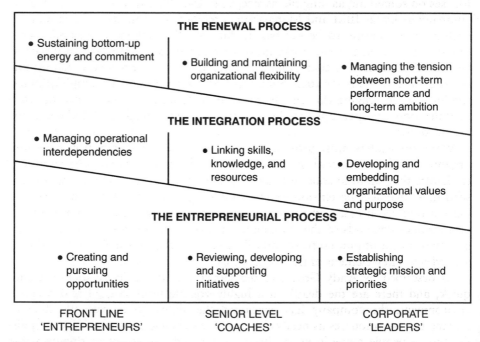

Fig. 4 The renewal process: management roles and tasks

processor gained momentum at the cost of Intel's 16 bit 8086 chip, it was Grove who initiated 'operation crush', an 'all-out combat' plan, complete with war rooms and SWAT teams, to make 8086 the industry standard. But it was Moore who built the company's long-range planning process and provided the blueprint for technological evolution. In essence, the two have divided the renewal responsibility between them in a way that was originally serendipitous but has since been institutionalized within the company as an unusual management concept: the 2-in-a-box. It has become normal in Intel for two executives with complementary skills to share the responsibilities of one role.

Whether through a combination of more than one person, creating and managing this tension between the short term and the long term, between current performance and future ambition – between restructuring and revitalization – is a key part of the leader's role in the emerging model of corporate management. In this role, the leader is the challenger – the one who is constantly upping the ante, and creating the energy and the enthusiasm necessary for the organization to accept the perpetual stretch that such challenging implies.

Personal credibility within and outside the organization is a prerequisite for the corporate leader to play this role, but it is not enough. Charisma sustains momentum for short periods but fatigue ultimately overtakes the organization that depends on individual charisma alone for its energy. To inspire self-renewal, companies must develop an inspiring corporate ambition – a shared dream about the future and the company's role in that future – and must embed that ambition throughout the organization. Whether the ambition focuses on something as tangible as size, as in Canon's expressed desire to be a company as big as IBM and Matsushita combined, or something less tangible such as Intel's desire 'to be the best in the world', what matters is the emotional commitment the leader can build around the dream. Ultimately, it is this emotional commitment that unleashes the human energy required to sustain the organization's ability to continuously renew itself. And developing, marshalling and leveraging this energy is key to simultaneous rationalization and revitalization, and perhaps the single most important challenge for the corporate leaders.[8]

While the leaders must provide the challenge and the stretch necessary for organizational self-renewal, it is the coaches who must mediate the complex trade-offs that simultaneous restructuring and revitalization implies. It is they who must manage the tension between building new capabilities and stretching existing resources, and the conflict inherent in the high and unrelenting performance demands of the company. This requires enormous flexibility and an environment of mutual trust and tolerance, and creating such processes and attitudes is a key element of the coach's role.

As described by Andy Grove, in the semiconductor business 'there are the quick, and there are the dead'. In a highly volatile technological and market environment, the company has developed the ability to be very flexible in moving human resources as needs change. Levels change up or down at Intel all the time – people move in every direction, upwards, sideways or downwards.

Careers advance not by moving up the organization but by individuals filling corporate needs. Official rank, decision making authority and remuneration – highly correlated in most companies – are treated separately and this separation, among different kinds of rewards, lies at the core of its organizational flexibility.

But such a system is also susceptible to gaming, and needs a high level of both discipline and transparency in decision-making processes and mutual trust and tolerance among people to be effective. Flexibility requires not only that the organization acts fairly but also that it is seen to be acting fairly, and creating and protecting such fairness – necessary in any winning team – is again a key task for the coaches.

While Intel's action-oriented and direct, if somewhat confrontational, management style has evolved in Grove's mould of aggressive brilliance, it is the senior management group heading different operating divisions and corporate functions who have embedded the norms of transparency and openness at all levels of the company. Key decisions at Intel are typically taken in open meetings, all of which have pre-announced agendas and inevitably close with action plans and deadlines. During a meeting, participants are encouraged to debate the pros and cons of a subject aggressively through what is described as 'constructive confrontation'. But once something has been decided on, Intel has the philosophy: 'agree or disagree, but commit'. As a result, everyone has the opportunity to influence key decisions relevant to themselves and to openly advocate their perspectives and views and are party to the final decisions, even though the decisions may not always conform to their preferences. The opportunity for such active participation, on equal basis, in open and transparent decision processes, coupled with the norm of disciplined and fast implementation once a decision has been taken, create the environment of trust which, in turn, is key to the operational and strategic flexibility of the company.

Ultimately, the ability of a company to continuously renew itself depends on the ability of its front-line managers to generate and maintain the energy and commitment of people within their units. The battles for efficiency and integration, for rationalization and revitalization, are finally fought at the level of the salesperson in the field, the operator in the plant, and the individual research scientist or engineer in the laboratory. While the energising ambition personified by the top management and the open and transparent decision-making processes orchestrated by the senior managers provide the anchors for the grass-root level commitment at Intel, two other elements of its organizational philosophy and practices also contribute a great deal in maintaining the enthusiasm of its front-line teams.

First, at Intel, there is not only fairness in management processes but there is also fairness in organizational outcomes. In contrast to companies that cut front-line jobs at the first sight of performance problems, Intel adopted the '125 per cent solution' to deal with the industry-wide recession in the early 1980s. Instead of retrenching people, this solution required that all salaried workers, including the chairman, work an extra 10 hours per week without extra compensation. This additional effort was directed to expediting the development of a new generation of microprocessors to revitalize growth. When the recession continued in 1982, still unwilling to lay off large numbers of people, the company proposed a 10 per cent pay cut on top of the 125 per cent solution. As the economy pulled out of the recession, returning the company to profitability, the pay cuts were first restored in June, 1983 and, by November 1983, the employees who had accepted pay cuts received special bonuses. Similarly, in 1986, when the memory product bloodbath finally forced the company to reduce its workforce by 30 per cent, the cuts were distributed across all levels of the company, instead of being concentrated at the lowest ranks.

Second, at Intel, it is legitimate to own up to one's personal mistakes and to change one's mind. Gordon Moore regretfully, but openly, acknowledges his personal role in missing the engineering workstation revolution, even though the company was among the pioneers for this opportunity. Such open acknowledgement of errors and acceptance of alternatives one has personally opposed, creates an environment in which failures are tolerated and changes in strategy do not automatically create winners and losers. It is this overall environment that, in turn, co-opts the front-line managers into the corporate ambition and allows them to sustain energy and commitment at the lowest levels of the organization.

A theory for practice

Over the last decade, many observers of large corporations have highlighted some of the vulnerabilities of the divisionalized organization we have described. The specific prescriptions of needing to build entrepreneurship, integration and renewal capabilities are also not new. Academics, consultants and managers themselves have long recognized these needs to respond to a variety of changing environmental demands.

Typically, however, these changing external demands and the consequent need for new internal capabilities have been observed in a piecemeal fashion, triggering ad-hoc responses. Facing slowing economic growth and increasingly sophisticated customer demands, companies have attempted to decentralize resources and authority to capture the creative energy and entrepreneurship of front-line managers. But prescriptions of creating and managing chaos have ignored the need for clarity of strategy and the discipline of centralized financial control to channel bottom-up energy into a coherent corporate direction. Companies that have attempted such radical decentralization without a centrally managed strategic framework have soon lost their focus and their ability to leverage resources effectively and have been forced to retreat to the known devil of their old ways.

Observing the ever-increasing pace of globalization of markets and the rising cost, complexity and convergence of technologies, managers have recognized the need to consolidate and integrate their diverse organizational capabilities. But, presented typically with examples of high-tech and highly centralized Japanese companies, they have confused capabilities with technologies, and integration with centralization.

Similarly, faced with the rapid enhancement of the skills and resources of once distant competitors and the changing norms and expectations in the many societies in which they operate, companies have realized the limits of incremental improvements and the need for dramatic change. Yet guided by prescriptions of creating dream-like long-term ambitions, they have allowed short-term performance to slip, thereby abandoning the long-term too because of increasing resource scarcity.

In contrast to these fragmented and often contradictory prescriptions, we have presented a broad model encompassing the key capabilities companies must develop to respond to the environmental demands of the 1990s. Nothing needs a theory more than practice, and the lack of an integrated theory of the new organization, we believe, has prevented companies from abandoning the old divisional model even though they have long recognized its constraints. Our model, in that sense, is aimed to provide such a theory for practice.

The real challenge in the implementation task lies in building the different management roles we have described. The metamorphosis of front-line managers, from being operational implementers to becoming aggressive entrepreneurs, will require some very different attitudes and skills. Similarly, the transformation of the senior management role from that of administrative controllers to that of inspiring coaches, will represent a traumatic change. But the management group that will be most severely challenged in the new organization will be the one currently at the apex of the hierarchy. Not only will the top management have to change their own role from that of resource allocators and political arbitrators to that of institutional leaders, they will also have to create the infrastructures and the contexts for the new roles of others in their companies. The managers who can build the attitudes and skills appropriate to these new roles, and the companies that can develop and retain such managers, are likely to be the winners of tomorrow.

Sumantra Ghoshal is Robert P Bauman Professor of Strategic Leadership at London Business School. Christopher A Bartlett is Professor of Business Administration at Harvard Business School. They are the authors of *Managing Across Borders* (1989).

Further Reading

Bartlett, CA, and Ghoshal, S, *Managing Across Borders*, Harvard Business School Press, Cambridge, Mass, 1989
Ohmae, K, *The Borderless World*, Collins, London, 1990
Wendt, H, *Global Embrace*, HarperCollins, New York, 1993

References

[1] Jensen, MC, 'The modern industrial revolution, exit, and the failure of internal control systems', *The Journal of Finance*, July 1993, pp. 831-880.

2 Chandler, AD, *Strategy and Structure*, Doubleday, New York, 1966 (originally published by MIT Press, 1962).

3 *Ibid*, p. 162.

4 *Ibid*, p. 173.

5 *Ibid*, pp. 168–199.

6 For a rich discussion of this gradual evolution see Haspeslagh, P, 'Portfolio planning approaches and the strategic management process in diversified industrial companies', unpublished dissertation, Harvard Business School, 1983.

7 For a more literature-grounded analysis see Bartlett, CA, and Ghoshal, S, 'Beyond the M-form: Toward a Managerial Theory of the Firm', *Strategic Management Journal*, vol. 14, 23–46, 1993.

8 Gary Hamel and CK Prahalad have highlighted the importance of shared corporate ambition in driving the renewal process – see 'Strategic intent', *Harvard Business Review*, Vol. 67, 1989, and 'Strategy as stretch and leverage', *Harvard Business Review*, 1993.

1

The Changing Nature of Managerial Work

'The mad rush to improve performance and to pursue excellence has multiplied the number of demands on executives and managers. These demands come from every part of business and personal life, and they increasingly seem incompatible and impossible.'   *Rosabeth Moss Kanter*[1]

'The way we are doing things is not the best way. The micro-division of labour has fostered a basic distrust of human beings. People weren't allowed to put the whole puzzle together. Instead they were given small parts because companies feared what people would do if they knew and saw the whole puzzle. Human assets shouldn't be misused. Brains are becoming the core of organizations – other activities can be contracted out.'   *Charles Handy*[2]

[1] Kanter, RM, *When Giants Learn to Dance*, Simon & Schuster, London, 1989
[2] Interview with Stuart Crainer, 1 February 1994

OVERVIEW

David W Birchall

Throughout the twentieth century researchers and observers have been eager to know more about what managers actually do in their work. There is an assumption that if we can establish what particularly successful managers do, we can then encourage managers to emulate this behaviour, also to train others to be more effective as managers. Even now, on the threshold of the twenty-first century, solutions to the managerial imponderables are difficult to find – despite decades of intensive research and observation. In fact, the legacy of early management thinkers remains deeply embedded in many of our organizations and managerial practices. For all its high-technology and modernness, management today owes much to the work of people at the end of the nineteenth century.

Their classical studies of management were based more on observation and reflection than research. Frederick Taylor (1856-1917) was one of the first to write about management work, advocating what was then termed a 'scientific approach' to management. Taylor's book *Principles of Scientific Management* was published in 1911.[1] Its contribution to management thinking and practice has to be put in the context of the industrial times in which Taylor lived. Much of the labour entering the newly established factories was untrained and unused to any form of industrial work. He advocated the subdivision of work so that the masses were given simple jobs to perform and management then devoted its energies to understanding how best to do the primary tasks, the scientific selection and training of the worker, motivating the worker to perform in accordance with management's principles and then planning and controlling the productive activity. His pioneering work focused on the level of supervisor and foreman rather than more senior levels of management. Recognized as the 'father of work study' Taylor's principles have been widely adopted and, even now, are still applied in many organizations involved in mass production or mass processing of paperwork.

The Frenchman, Henri Fayol (1841-1925) took another approach. In *Industrial and General Adminstration* (1916)[2] Fayol enunciated five elements and 15 principles of administrative management. The five basic management functions identified by Fayol comprise planning, organising, co-ordinating, commanding and controlling. These elements have been widely disseminated to generations of managers. They have also formed the basis of later writings – in 1937 Luther Gulick modified the list to include staffing, reporting and budgeting.[3] In a 1931 study of the State, the Roman Catholic Church, the military and industry, Mooney and Reiley advocated four major principles:[4]

1. The co-ordination principle, which directed attention to the unity of action towards a common purpose.
2. The scalar principle, which defined the hierarchical flow of authority and the definite assignment of duties to sub-units of an organization.
3. The functional principle, which stressed the need for specialization of duties.
4. The staff principle, which answered the need for advice and ideas by line executives.

These ideas very much reflected the times in which the writers lived and worked. Dominant in their thinking was a strong expectation of respect for authority among the management classes, a lack of training and development for the workforce, the influence of a bureaucratic model of organization, and the relatively inward-looking nature of the role. Generally operating in a suppliers' market, the supplier was not under great pressure to change other than to improve profitability for shareholders by carefully planned productivity improvement. Labour was also in plentiful supply and there was little government intervention regulating the employment contract, enabling employers to hire and fire workers at will.

As a result, it would be easy for today's managers to dismiss the theories and work of people like Taylor and Fayol. Indeed, Taylor in particular has been routinely abused for many years. Their world of paper-pushing bureaucracy and harsh manual labour is far removed from modern reality. But, although the context has changed, many of the ideas of scientific management remain in place. Taylorism lives on in highly functionalized organizations intent on relentless supervision rather than empowerment.

During the post-war period greater emphasis has tended to be placed on the human aspects of the managerial role and on leading rather than commanding. For example, the American political scientist Mary Parker Follett (1868–1933) believed that in a democratic society the primary task of management is to create a situation where people readily contribute of their own accord. She repeatedly emphasized the need for managers to learn from their own experience by systematically observing experiences, recording them and relating these experiences to the total situation. She saw the manager as responsible for integrating the contributions of specialists such as marketing, production, cost accountants and industrial relations so that they contributed effectively for the benefit of all.

Sponsored by the National Industrial Conference Board in the US, Louis Allen commenced research in 1953. He was charged with investigating what management methods were most effective, which new management techniques had proved most effective, and what companies should do to manage more effectively. This is the managerial equivalent of seeking the Holy Grail. He continued the original research over a 15-year period and in his 1973 book, *Professional Management*, put forward four functions of management based on a belief that managers think and act rationally – planning, organizing, leading and controlling.[5] He broke these functions down into 19 management activities:

1. **planning function** – forecasting, developing objectives, programming, scheduling, budgeting, developing procedures and developing policies;
2. **organizing function** – developing organization structure, delegating, developing relationships;
3. **leading function** – decision-making, communicating, motivating, selecting and developing people;
4. **controlling function** – developing performance standards, measuring, evaluating and correcting performance.

These and similar ideas about the nature of managerial work have been influential on later researchers but more importantly on those actually managing organizations whether business or not-for-profit. However, these formulations of management work are not without their critics. Generally they are seen as focusing on a rational view of organization which tends to omit the human and political side. Also, in the main, they lack support from empirical studies. They attempt to produce a general theory of management work disregarding the diversity of management work in different types of organization and in different functions, such as marketing compared to production and finance. They are based on observations wedded into a particular society which is greatly different from many societies in which we now live. Probably most importantly, they focus on what it was believed managers *should* do rather than what they *actually* do and they fail to give any priority to the various roles and to relate them to superior performance. Despite these limitations, the propositions may still have some validity in certain types of organization, though interpretation of meaning and translation into action is probably very different from that intended by the original authors.

In recent years, studies have rigorously attempted to research what managers actually do by undertaking empirical work. Just as the early writings of management theorists have inherent weaknesses, so do later studies of management work. Even so, several research approaches have merit. Many studies have relied upon questionnaires asking managers about their work and the emphasis placed upon various activities. Other studies have relied upon managers completing diaries detailing their activities. Yet others have used direct observation with the researcher present throughout the manager's working day. These observation studies have used a variety of approaches – activity sampling, critical incident, sequence of episodes, unstructured and structured observations.

Questionnaire studies are always limited by the model, explicit or implicit, and used by the investigator to underpin the design of the research study. So if the investigator was influenced by the classical management theory the survey instrument would reflect the functions and activities of these writers and the questioning would be focused on these areas. Diaries, while useful in giving an impression of the work carried out, suffer from the unreliability of managers when recording activities, and the difficulties in then classifying their records. Observational studies are usually confined to a small sample which cannot claim to be representative of management generally. In the case of observation it is not always possible to see what a manager is doing because so much activity is cerebral and it is particularly difficult to interpret the purpose of much of the observed activity.

Many of these studies have contributed more to our understanding of the characteristics of managerial work than to the actual content of the manager's job. They have revealed that much management time is spent with other people – in 1964 an early study of this type reported that 20 per cent of managers' time was spent with superiors, 33 per cent with peers and 50 per cent with subordinates; 50 per cent of the activities were planning or programming activities, 20 per cent were dealing with technical matters and 10 per cent with personnel administration.[6]

Probably the most influential and widely cited observational study is that of five chief executives in the US undertaken by Henry Mintzberg. In *The Nature of Managerial Work*, published in 1973, Mintzberg claimed:

1. A similarity in managerial work whether carried out by the company president, the health service administrator or the general foreman. He categorized it into 10 basic roles and six sets of work characteristics.
2. While differences exist arising from functional or hierarchical level they can be described largely in common roles and characteristics.
3. The managerial job is made up of regular and programmed duties as well as non-programmed activities.
4. The manager is both a generalist and a specialist.
5. The manager is reliant on information particularly that which has been verbally received.
6. Work activities are characterized by brevity, variety and fragmentation.
7. Management work is more an art than a science, reliant on intuitive and non-explicit processes.
8. Management work is increasingly complex.[7]

Mintzberg's model of managerial work identified three overall categories and specific roles within each:

1. **interpersonal category**
   (a) the figurehead role where the manager performs symbolic duties as head of the organization;
   (b) the leader role where he/she establishes the work atmosphere and motivates subordinates to achieve organizational goals;
   (c) the liaison role where the manager develops and maintains webs of contacts outside the organization.
2. **informational category**
   (a) the monitor role where the manager collects all types of information relevant and useful to the organization;
   (b) the disseminator role where the manager transmits information from the outside to members inside the organization;
   (c) the spokesman role where he/she transmits information from inside the organization to outsiders.

3. **decisional category**
   (a) the entrepreneur role where the manager initiates controlled change in his/her organization to adapt to the changing environment;
   (b) the disturbance handler role where the manager deals with unexpected changes;
   (c) the resource allocator role where he/she makes decisions on the use of organizational resources;
   (d) the negotiator role where the manager deals with other organizations and individuals.

Though it proved highly influential, this research is also not without its critics. Later researchers have experienced difficulties in categorizing their observations according to the Mintzberg framework. A focus on individual activities is also criticized for the likelihood of a failure to understand the big picture. Other descriptors are seen as equally valid – later in the 1970s researchers carried out a factor analysis of data collected against the Mintzberg framework and derived six factors:

1. managing organizational environment and its resources;
2. organizing and co-ordinating;
3. information handling;
4. providing for growth and development;
5. motivation and conflict handling;
6. strategic problem-solving.[8]

This research went on to study managerial effectiveness in two organizations. It reported that the managerial behaviour that resulted in effectiveness varied between the two organizations, suggesting that the context in which managers are working will determine the work activities required for success.

While much of this early research has been influential in how managers view their role within the context of organization design, it is based on observation of organizations which were operating in an environment much removed from the present situation facing many businesses. Numerous studies were undertaken in the US at a time when the US was the most powerful manufacturing country. The threat of the Japanese manufacture and service industry had not dawned on the average American. Customer focus, total quality management, just-in-time, distributed computing, empowerment, key organizational competencies, partnership sourcing and continuous change and improvement were not yet articulated as concepts. Strategy formulation was still the exclusive domain of executive management, and execution the province of middle management. Much of the research was based on observing the way managers function in their real world rather than looking at changes taking place and seeing how they might impact on the way management might be carried out in future.

Management work in the modern organization

Over 700 managers, in a variety of organizations and at all levels of management, were surveyed at the Singapore Institute of Management at the beginning of the 1990s. From factor analysis, five 'mega-components' of management work were identified:

1. Goal setting and review.
2. Creating an environment conducive to working.
3. Managing quality.
4. Relating to and managing the external environment.
5. Managing performance.[9]

The strongest contributing factor to the mega-components was 'managing organizational climate' which focused on encouraging and supporting employee involvement and contribution. The second most dominant was 'organizational work control' which combined into mega-component number five and dealt with the importance of policies and procedures in ensuring the smooth functioning of the work organization. The strategic aspects of the work are reflected in analysis of the external environment and of goal setting and review.

Clearly there are differences in management practices in Singapore from those in Western management. However, the expressions used to describe the components reflect the current management agenda, including quality and performance management, and the underlying factors bear similarity to those identified by earlier researchers such as Mintzberg.

Work recently researching the nature of senior management roles can be seen in the senior management standards produced for the UK's Management Charter Initiative. This is the result of a critical incident and questionnaire survey of successful senior managers in UK organizations. The key purpose of senior management was reported as being: 'To develop and implement strategies and provide leadership to further the organization's mission and achieve the objectives.' The functional analysis resulting is outlined in Fig. 1.

This model represents the work of senior managers by reference to the process of strategy formulation into action.

How do managers do what they do?

Clearly, understanding what managers do is important when trying to understand how organizations function and how one might go about training managers to achieve high performance levels. However, these various studies tell us little about the attributes needed for superior performance. More recent research has focused on the key competencies required for superior managerial job performance.

The roots for much of this work can be traced back to the extensive work done by Richard Boyatzis for the American Management Association.[10] The

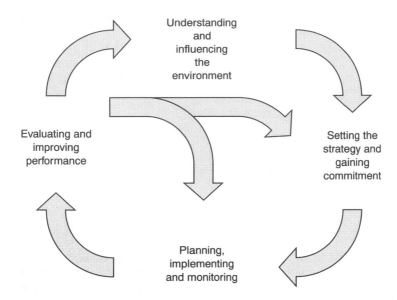

Fig. 1 The functional model

Source: MCI, *The Draft Senior Management Standards and Personal Competences*, MCI, London, 1993

study, published in 1982, involved over 2,000 managers who held 41 different jobs in 12 different public and private organizations. The researchers set out to develop a generic model of managerial competencies applicable in different contexts and organization types.

Boyatzis defined job competency as an underlying characteristic of a person which results in effective and/or superior performance in a job. The underlying characteristic may be a motive, trait, skill, aspect of one's self-image or a social role but it is manifest in an observable skill. The resulting model comprises 12 competencies in six clusters.

Recent work investigating the competencies of successful senior managers carried out by the Northern Regional Management Centre for the Management Charter Initiative developed the personal competence model shown in Fig. 2. Each competence is made up of key behaviours demonstrated by managers through a process of 'behavioural event interviewing', a technique used earlier by Boyatzis. In their report to the MCI, the researchers emphasized that one particular competence may be dominant in any one particular situation or event, but that it will usually be supported by other competencies. They also point out that effective managers will be those who use judgement to apply the appropriate competence at the right time.

Competence in itself does not result in high performance. The theory of motivation evinced by Porter and Lawler in their 1968 book *Managerial Attitudes and Performance*[11] suggests that performance will only result where the person has both the opportunities to perform and the motivation to do so, in addition to the skills (or competencies) required by the job. Also, if the

71

Table 1 The competencies of management

Cluster	Competency	Threshold competency
Goal and action management	• *concern with impact* • *diagnostic use of concepts* • *efficiency orientation* • *proactivity*	
Leadership	• *conceptualization* • *self-confidence* • *use of oral presentations*	• logical thought
Human resource	• *managing group process* • use of socialized power	• accurate self-assessment • positive regard
Directing subordinates		• *developing others* • spontaneity • use of unilateral power
Focus on others	• *perceptual objectivity* • self-control (trait) • stamina and adaptability (trait)	
Specialized knowledge		• specialized knowledge

Note: italics show competencies that are most relevant to executive levels of management; self-control is a competency for entry level jobs only.

Source: Boyatzis R E, *The Competent Manager: a model for effective performance*, John Wiley, New York, 1982 (Table 12.1 'Summary of Competency Results')

goals for the task are not clear, the combination of motivation, opportunities and competencies will still not result in high performance levels.

Rosemary Stewart in *Managers and their Jobs*[12] found that managers with the same job requirements will use their time and energies differently. Given each person's unique combination of competencies, knowledge, understanding and aspirations, it is not surprising that managers operate differently in seeking to achieve the same organizational goals. Each will accommodate to the job as well as modify the job to suit him/herself.

The benefit of competence models is as much to assist managers in self-assessment and the identification of development needs as in recruitment and allocation of managers to organizational roles.

Fig. 2 The personal competence model

Source: MCI, *The Senior Management Standards*, MCI, London, 1993

The research available gives some idea of the work carried out by managers as well as the personal competencies required for effective performance at senior levels. Yet, it has become clear that there is no one best theory of management work and managerial competencies. Applied to any one organization the models inevitably appear deficient. In attempting to develop a universal theory the investigators have had to compromise and overlook industry or organization-specific requirements.

Additionally, much of the research is based on current practice and may well not reflect what managers will be doing, nor how they will be doing it, in five years' time.

The changing world of organizations and the impact on management

The last five years has probably seen as dramatic a change in the organization and management of work as any period since the emergence of the large corporate entity. Depending on the background of the commentator, the explanations for radical change will differ. There is no doubt that factors such as global competition, the emergence and convergence of information and communications technology, recession in most Western economies, the emergence of customer power and changing political philosophy, have all contributed to the changes.

As a consequence, it is clear that much of the work undertaken by middle management no longer requires the considerable number of layers of management which were for so long a feature of the large organization. In part this results from a recognition that front-line employees, with proper training and support, may be capable of dealing directly with the customer and responding on behalf of the organization to the specific needs of that customer. If one accepts that there is much unrecognized talent at the point of contact with the customer, and that empowerment is an appropriate strategy, then it follows that there is less need for immediate supervision. The queries and decisions previously taken by that level are now taken by the employee dealing directly with the customer. In many situations information to support decision-making can also be collected directly from the customer interface, again by using IT effectively. A task taking up much management time in hierarchical structures is now possible with minimal intervention from any of the former levels of management. The effect of modern technology on lower and middle managers can be compared to the effects of the introduction of automated production processes on shop-floor workers. In both cases progress removed the need for a large proportion of the workforce.

Many organizations, when in the process of empowering their front-line staff, have reassessed the role of first-line management. Rather than the traditional supervisory role of allocating work, determining how it shall be done and ensuring progress, the first-line manager has become a facilitator. In this role the manager is in more of a support role, assisting staff in meeting customer needs, training and developing staff and counselling them.

Another change impacting on management has come about because the complexity of design of many products and services is increasing, pressures are growing to compress the time from concept to market and in many industries the costs of developing new products is proving beyond the capability of any one organization. Companies previously in competition are having to combine resources in order to share the costs and risks of new product development. In many cases duplication of effort in the various organizations has been eliminated with resulting reductions in employee and management numbers.

Many companies which previously adopted a policy of vertical integration to control the production processes through to market, are changing their approach to one of specialization in areas within their supply chains where the potential for added value is greatest. Companies are forming new relationships with suppliers and customers in order to protect their position and develop strategic advantage through the supply network or constellation which is unique to that one organization. Concentration on core activities has led organizations to divest of those parts not seen as central to the strategy. This very reduction in size has itself led to the need for fewer managers particularly in support functions. Then, as these support functions have themselves been reviewed and deemed no longer central to the strategy, they in turn have been outsourced.

Work previously undertaken in functional departments has become too complex and specialized for organizations to carry the numbers of technical specialists needed to deal with the business problems encountered. So there is a strong move towards the use of consultants, whether legal practitioners or practitioners of marketing or management. The use of external consultants may well be more cost-effective than retaining in-house staff and, in addition, allows companies to choose the most appropriate available. It also gives the prospect of appointing someone whose knowledge-base is up-to-date through exposure to the way similar problems have been tackled in a variety of situations and organizations. This broad exposure can have additional benefits to organizations in preventing insularity. This again reduces the need for managers, particularly in functional departments.

Much work now being carried out in organizations is of a project nature. Some industries, such as the construction industries, have for many years used subcontracting as the basis of project resourcing. Other sectors have been slow to adopt this approach but many are increasingly doing so. Projects are perhaps managed internally and sourced from a range of outside providers, or alternatively by appointing an outside contractor to manage the total project on a turnkey basis. Again this policy enables the organization to appoint the most suitable resources rather than carrying internal staff with less specialized expertise to do such work. In many areas of technical complexity it would not be feasible to carry all the necessary resources in the organization on a permanent basis. But, increasingly, organizations are using the services of external specialist project managers to oversee the work.

By concentrating on a focused core activity, and keeping employment levels to a minimum, the organization is able to manage its direct employees more effectively because of their reduced numbers. Given the greater dependence upon this group of key personnel – sometimes called 'gold collar' employees – they are likely to be well rewarded and well trained. If this is not the case they are likely to see the alternative of being a contract employee as financially rather more attractive and no more risky than being employed directly.

Companies are seeking ways of maintaining commitment and contribution without any guarantee to employees of a job for life. With no long-term security, employee expectations of immediate rewards are higher than they would have been in the large bureaucracies of the 1970s and 1980s with their 'jobs for life' policy, and good, sound pension provisions. Despite continuing high levels of unemployment, there is still a shortage of first class personnel in many professional areas, including management. Numerous managers who have left the umbrella and safety of large corporate companies have found that their new life-style has not left them disadvantaged, financially or otherwise. Their example serves to unsettle the corporate man or woman committed to the organization but who realizes that the organization has dispensed with the services of a large number of their colleagues.

As business becomes more global, the economics of sourcing activities change. Certain types of work traditionally carried out in developed countries can easily be transferred to areas where labour costs are significantly lower. Other work is transferred for political reasons; for example, to appease local governments concerned about lack of investment of the multi-nationals in developing economies. The economics of production may be distorted by inducements such as tax breaks and other financial incentives. As companies increasingly think on a global scale they need their managers to have a range of new skills and aspirations. Some will not be able to adjust. Additionally, some will have to make way for managers from other national backgrounds who have to be given the opportunity to progress up the corporate ladder in order to achieve the organization's desire to become truly international.

As organizations attempt to become more customer-facing they depend increasingly on the performance of their front-line staff for the provision of high levels of customer service. However, these front-line staff are also proba-bly the richest source of information about the changing customer needs and the impact of competition in the marketplace. Organizations need to tap this rich source of information in their strategic planning process. Partly as a result of this change, the role of senior executives is also changing. Rather than having sole responsibility for determining mission and strategy and transmitting this throughout the organization, the process has been turned on its head. Executives now need to involve people at all levels in the organiza-tion to ensure that they themselves remain in touch with the real and changing needs of the customer. They also need to win the commitment of staff to the mission and strategy. The approaches to corporate planning of the 1970s and 1980s are having to be rethought. The executive role in conse-quence has also changed, more emphasis being put upon the ability to gather views from a wider range of stakeholders and integrate them into a shared vision, mission and strategy. Then the emphasis shifts to the strategic leader-ship role, translating strategy into action and developing strong core values. Just as the emphasis at lower levels of management has moved more towards counselling, senior executives are also having to put much more emphasis on the development of their successors and the creation of a learning culture and a learning organization.

Probably the greatest contributory factor in the reduction of management in organizations is the realization that managers are a highly expensive resource. Generally, the more senior the greater the cost. Not only are these staff paid well but they have expenses associated with the work, they often enjoy additional perks, they have secretaries also occupying separate offices, and they may enjoy profit-related bonuses. Savings on headcount come off the bottom line, not just in the current year but annually. Therefore, many organizations have recognized that they can have greater control over their costs if they employ consultants as and when necessary to carry out special assignments, previously undertaken by in-house management, without the on-going expensive overhead of the employee. In a fast changing world flexible employment contracts are attractive to employers for work which is non-standard and not core activity.

New roles for a new era

We are seeing the realization of what Charles Handy describes as the 'Shamrock Organization'.[13] This comprises a central core with a lean organization supported by a network of suppliers for non-core activities, and a network of peripheral staff brought in to carry out specialist and project-based activity.

Despite all these changes, the general principles of management espoused by the early thinkers still seem remarkably robust. However, three vital differences are apparent in how the work is undertaken. First, management is no longer the sole prerogative of an elite group formerly called 'managers'. The functions of management are now being much more widely shared within the enterprise. Second, while goals and a clear sense of direction are as vital today as they were to the early thinkers, the emphases in the goals of organizations – who decides and agrees them and the strategies for implementation – are very different from those in earlier times. Third, organizations still need leadership and direction but the style of approach required is changing as organizations become much more open and responsive to customer needs.

Nevertheless, there is still the need for management and a role for managers. These are likely to fall within two broad categories:

1. Those managing within the smaller corporate structure or in organizations servicing the corporate. Some of the latter will have been created specifically for the purpose and, in seeking to widen the base of their business, they will probably be highly entrepreneurial.
2. The independent or networked managers providing specific services to both of the other groups.

Those managers wishing to stay within the larger corporate structure will have to be prepared for constant change – at an organizational and personal level. In order to have continuing utility to the organization they will have to adapt quickly to the changed needs of the business. The more successful managers will be those who anticipate the direction of changes and prepare themselves for new roles and ways of working. Personal development will be high on the agenda of these managers. Also, given the uncertainties attached to corporate life, these managers will be concerned not only with development opportunities in line with the needs of the business, but also with personal development to ensure their own marketability outside the business. Rewards will have to be commensurate with risks. With increasing length of service alternative employment is more difficult to obtain so companies may have to pay a premium to retain these people. Organizations will have to be prepared to invest more resources in the development of key managers. However, managers will also have to be more proactive in demanding and using opportunities for personal development.

Much learning may well come through non-conventional methods such as distance learning, mentored on-the-job learning, secondments and project assignments. Distance learning will become available 'on-tap' for many more managers at a time and place to suit their personal needs. Consequently much development will be delivered on a 'just-in-time' basis, when managers have a particular problem confronting them. Technology will give access to training materials in the same way that it will make available information services in the home for the consumer market. Managers will also put emphasis on gaining qualifications to demonstrate their competence. So the qualifications deemed important will reflect capability rather than academic achievement.

These managers will have to develop new frameworks to guide their actions in this rapidly changing business environment. For example, the emphasis on core activities and outsourcing requires those managers involved to exercise rather different skills from those required in the effective management of direct employees. Managing contractors and contract staff in the new-style partnership arrangements requires a different framework or conceptual model to the old adversarial management of contractors. Getting the best out of suppliers depends upon more subtle approaches to relationship building and management as well as to high-level commercial skills. Managers will have to be capable of developing these new models, internalizing them and adjusting their behaviour appropriately.

For entrants into the management career ladder there are new problems. Careers in large organizations are no longer for life. Additionally, delayering and the introduction of budgetary responsibility, even for junior managers, has resulted in the opportunity for considerable levels of responsibility at a relatively young age and with relatively limited prior experience. In order that new entrants can cope with the new demands, more far-sighted companies are investing considerable resources in training these people. However, organizations can no longer demonstrate likely career paths from junior levels to executive responsibility. The traditional route of working one's way through the hierarchy has disappeared with delayering. The promotion funnel is narrow and short with much competition at the base level to enter the neck. For these new entrants it is important that they aim to get a breadth of experience at an early stage, probably by transferring laterally between functions or product divisions, and gaining experiences in many different types of organization. By doing this they can prepare themselves for more senior levels or, alternatively, a career as a consultant. Traditionally, the latter has been used as a route to senior positions in organizations and it may well prove the ideal route for many aspiring executives.

Many managers will find themselves managing people who spend much of their time outside the office. Many mobile workers will be equipped with technology to enable them to work more effectively, including long periods remote from the office. Organizations will help meet the costs of these changes by reducing the office overheads through introducing hot-desking and similar schemes for sharing office space. Many managers will find themselves working in open plan facilities, hot-desking and spending more time on client premises. Employers will accept more flexible ways of working for managers and their staff, and be concerned more with work outputs than the management of the input. Such work arrangements are based on trust, performance measurement and individual appraisal. Managers will have to adjust both their ways of thinking and of working in order to make these new arrangements work.

Those managers in the peripheral workforce will have to spend considerable time in networking. They will no longer have to concern themselves about playing the internal political games of the large organization in order to promote their own career. However, they will have to maintain many contacts in order to generate consultancy assignments. They may well have to develop networking skills as well as competence in marketing and sales. They are likely to make use of professional associations and other networks such as Chambers of Commerce. They will also use facilities such as one-stop-information services and the resources of business/tele-centres with their specialist skills in data handling and desktop publishing, also offering video conferencing services which will be one means of maintaining effective communications with sophisticated clients located in any part of the world.

The nature of many assignments will be political. The consultant needs to be able to enter an organization and quickly assess the sources of power and influence and how they might impact on the outcome of the assignment. The skills required may well be different from those which enabled a reasonably successful career in a large organization.

These consultants will spend part of their time as interim managers, standing in when managers leave their organizations before replacements are found, or covering for illness. Others will specialize in turn-rounds, spending relatively short periods of time in any one business.

The consultant may be called upon to carry out specific investigative work though many organizations are equally concerned about implementation. In such cases the assignment may well be much broader than simply investigative work. It may include the development of a strategy for implementation and then a contribution to the process, for example through running training and development programmes. Again, the skills needed to design and deliver a development programme are outside the range of experience of most corporate managers.

Much of the time of the independent manager will have to be devoted to updating and self-development. This will be achieved partly through experience on assignments of different types and in varying contexts. It will also require a determined effort to read widely in order to maintain understanding of broad business developments as well as the specialist areas of expertise being offered to clients. Research skills will be important in order to maintain a position of added value for clients so that they recognize the value of the contribution that is being made. The choice of clients will be important to the consultant as the key to his/her future success will be an impressive client list along with personal recommendation resulting from high quality delivery.

The independent manager also has to manage his or her personal affairs such as tax returns, insurance and pensions. Clients have to be invoiced and accounts kept. Such tasks for the corporate manager are handled by others in the organization. The self-employed have to recognize the importance of what previously may have been thought of as mundane activities and devote the necessary time to developing skills and carrying out functions. Time management and good organization become very important in enabling the consultant to juggle many balls at the same time.

In order to deliver the assignments required by a client, the newly independent manager may have to develop a range of skills not required in previous roles within organizations. The most successful independents are likely to be those who also master the use of technology to improve their personal effectiveness. However, this will also apply to the manager employed by any large organization.

The new generation of manager – the all-rounder

One thing is certain about the new style of manager – he or she will be much more competent in a broader range of activities than managers of the previous generation. The new style manager will be well trained with a broad understanding of business principles and a range of competencies that include some at high level.

Particular among the new attributes needed will be an understanding of how technology can be applied to move the business forward, as well as personal competence in the use of technology to aid managerial effectiveness. It will be less important for the manager to have computer literacy skills than competence in recognizing how IT can be used to aid the management process, and then deploying it effectively. This will require managers to develop a new set of competencies so that they can use the information available, processed by the computer in ways with which they were previously unfamiliar.

So how will IT change the way managers work? We have already seen widespread adoption of tools such as spreadsheets. Most managers are now used to using data generated by spreadsheet. They are probably less familiar with the use of the spreadsheet as a tool for modelling. However, in many ways the spreadsheet is fairly unsophisticated. Expert systems will be used increasingly in executive decision-making. This will create problems for those who have difficulty understanding not only the opportunities expert systems offer, but also their limitations. As they become increasingly influential in executive decision-making the need to understand expert systems will increase. Managers will be required to develop conceptual models so as to make the best possible use of the systems available. Tools will help in this process, but it does represent a different way of thinking from that currently practised by many managers.

These tools will be widely adopted by consultants for assisting organizations in vital decision areas, also in training and development. Again, there will be a need for better understanding than that required for purely superficial mechanical application.

Increasingly, managers at all levels will be required to do much more than just implement the plans put in place at higher levels. They will be expected to define the problems facing their organizations in the rapidly changing and increasingly complex world in which their businesses operate and communicate this to the executive level. Information search and interpretation will be key skills. Here, again, technology will assist. One of the fastest growing activities in recent times has been accessing international networks for information and networking. Managers will make more use of international data sources to aid in decision-making. For the consultant with a particular expertise these electronic networks will facilitate the selling and provision of services globally. They will also enable managers to keep in touch with the latest thinking in their area of expertise, something vital to the success of the independent consultant. However, electronic information-searching for problem-solving and personal update will also be essential to the corporate manager who wants to keep ahead of the demands of the job and seeks to build reputation and career.

Probably the fastest growing application at present is that of groupware. Using electronic networks groupware has been designed to enable teams of people to work more effectively – particularly where they are separated by time and distance. It can facilitate the working of the distributed team and, what is now labelled, the virtual organization, whether for a specific project or for an on-going business venture. The potential is considerable, though the barriers to making its application effective are equally considerable. For many, this way of working will always remain uncomfortable and for some it will be unacceptable. However, those organizations that are successful in utilizing such tools will be able to generate an advantage over competitors. The same will apply to managers who develop skills in using the technology to enhance their own personal performance. New skills in electronic communication are needed, and these go well beyond the skills in manipulating the keyboard.

Electronic communication is a new art form and managers currently have a clear preference for face-to-face meetings rather than remote communication. This is largely because they can pick up cues from body language and other non-verbal signals. They also use these opportunities to pick up other information peripheral to the meeting, but vital to their role and position in the company. Electronic meetings preclude much of this information. Managers without this source of information often feel naked and politically exposed. The reality is that the technology is now here to stay and managers will have to adjust. If they need this other form of information they will have to find new ways of obtaining it. If it is not essential it may well be that managers will have more time to concentrate on their main purpose – that of establishing goals and managing complex organizations to achieve them.

Groupware will be of considerable assistance to the consultant. It will facilitate networking; provide tools for group decision-making for which organizations will look to consultants for facilitation; and aid in formulating creative solutions. It is likely that as new software developments take place there will be an expanding market for the management consultant in aiding implementation.

Possibly the greatest potential for improving many organizations is still that of releasing their creative capacity. Traditional bureaucracy has not welcomed creativity. Ted Levitt in a classic 1963 article in the *Harvard Business Review* wrote: 'One of the collateral purposes of an organization is to be inhospitable to a great and constant flow of ideas and creativity ... The organization exists to restrict and channel the range of individual actions and behaviour into a predictable and knowable routine. Without organization there would be chaos and decay. Organization exists in order to create that amount and kind of inflexibility that is necessary to get the most pressingly intended job done efficiently and on time.'[14] Many companies are still working to this model but those which are moving towards being customer focused are endeavouring to harness the creativity of all stakeholders including all employees as well as those in interfacing organizations, such as customers and suppliers. Managers have a key role to play in this process by fostering an innovative climate and encouraging risk taking.

The competencies defined in the various studies are still needed for the effective management of organizations. However, there are other competencies that managers will need as we move more into the information age. The competencies will be needed by the independent consultant as well as the internal manager. Those skills needed to operate as a consultant, such as facilitation, investigation and analysis, and training/development will be increasingly important to the corporate manager as well. We will see an increase in the extent to which managers move in and out of employment and for some, how they combine work in one organization, on a part-time basis, with consultancy work for others. One obvious point is that managers will have to put considerable energy into planning their own careers and ensuring that they actively manage their personal development to achieve their own aims.

Probably the greatest stimulus for change is crisis. When chief executives find themselves with their backs against the wall they have justification for the introduction of major change and will take the opportunity to act in many areas where for some time they have longed to see developments but experienced difficulties in their introduction during better times.

Those companies that will be successful into the next century are those which innovate in order to get ahead of their competitors. They will be innovating in a number of areas including:

- challenging existing business definition in order to identify those customers and products/services they most want to have;
- product/service improvement;
- new products and services;
- identifying, attracting and looking after external and internal customers more effectively;
- doing whatever they can to increase efficiency and/or reduce costs.

The key will be innovation. Research at Henley Management College has led to the formulation of eight working hypotheses which form the basis of critical success factors leading to the innovative organization:[15]

- situational empowerment;
- remuneration systems that reward trials and errors;

- clear understanding of customers' needs and external changes, well articulated within the organization;
- a mixture of training for innovation and change as well as specific skills – the 'hard' and 'soft';
- internal focus of control of top executives should be such that executives are convinced of their own ability to influence the situation in which they find themselves;
- an innovation fund that at least matches that of competitors;
- explicit targets for innovation;
- high quality managers.

Executive management has to create a vision of where it wants the organization to go and then agree an appropriate strategy for getting there. In doing this there is little doubt that for many it will lead to a streamlining of the organization in order to increase its focus and long-term profitability. Middle management, in particular, will be a continuing target for change. In the more successful organizations of tomorrow they may well have already introduced the type of changes in the way management is undertaken that are identified above. Many organizations have yet to follow and this will inevitably bring about the kind of changes in the way managers work which have been outlined above. The primary stimulus will be corporations rather than governments or individuals. But these corporations will be responding to market pressures, reacting to global competition and seeking ways of doing what they can best do, but doing it much better.

Professor David W Birchall is director of research at Henley Management College. He is co-author of *Creating Tomorrow's Organization, Financial Times*/**Pitman Publishing, 1995.**

Further Reading

Handy, C, *The Future of Work*, Blackwell, Oxford, 1984.
Schwartz, P, *The Art of the Long View*, Doubleday, New York, 1991.

References

1 Taylor, FW, *Principles of Scientific Management*, Harper, New York, 1911.
2 Fayol, H, *Industrial and General Administration*, Pitman, London, 1916.
3 Gulick, LH, and Urwick, LF (eds), 'Notes on the theory of organizations' in *Papers on the Science of Administration*, Columbia University Press, New York, 1937.
4 Mooney, JD, and Reiley, AC, *Onward industry: the principles of organizations and their significance to modern industry*, Harper, New York, 1931.
5 Allen, LA, *Professional Management: new concepts and proven practices*, McGraw Hill, Maidenhead, 1973.
6 Kelly, J, 'The study of executive behaviour by activity sampling', *Human Relations*, 17, 1964.
7 Mintzberg, H, *The Nature of Managerial Work*, Prentice Hall, New Jersey, 1973.

[8] Morse, JJ, and Wagner, FR, 'Measuring the process of managerial effectiveness', *Academy of Management Journal*, 21, 1978.

[9] Tan, JH, 'Management work in Singapore: developing a factor model', Henley Management College/Brunel University, 1994.

[10] Boyatzis, RE, *The Competent Manager: a model for effective performance*, John Wiley, New York, 1982.

[11] Porter, LW, and Lawler, EE, *Managerial Attitudes and Performance*, Irwin Dorsey, Homewood, Illinois, 1968.

[12] Stewart, R, *Managers and their Jobs: a study of the similarities and the differences in the way managers spend their time*, Macmillan, London, 1967.

[13] Handy, C, *The Age of Unreason*, Business Books, London, 1989.

[14] Levitt, T, 'Creativity is not enough', *Harvard Business Review*, vol. 41, 1963.

[15] Birchall, DW, Swords, S, Brown, M and Swords, DF, *Growth and Innovation*, Henley Management College, 1993.

THINKERS

Henri Fayol

1841–1925; mining engineer and manager

The Frenchman Henri Fayol continues to be an under-estimated figure in the fledgling years of management theorizing. While the American Frederick Taylor gained attention (and later notoriety) for his 'scientific management', Fayol's work is generally forgotten. Yet, Fayol pursued a much broader path than Taylor and his codification of what he thought management involved remains valuable.

In his *General and Industrial Management*, published in 1916, Fayol laid down 14 principles of management. These were:

1. *Division of work:* tasks should be divided up and employees should specialize in a limited set of tasks so that expertise is developed and productivity increased.
2. *Authority and responsibility:* authority is the right to give orders and entails the responsibility for enforcing them with rewards and penalties; authority should be matched with corresponding responsibility.
3. *Discipline:* is essential for the smooth running of business and is dependent on good leadership, clear and fair arguments, and the judicious application of penalties.
4. *Unity of command:* for any action whatsoever, an employee should receive orders from one superior only; otherwise authority, discipline, order and stability are threatened.
5. *Unity of direction:* a group of activities concerned with a single objective should be co-ordinated by a single plan under one head.
6. *Subordination of individual interest to general interest:* individual or group goals must not be allowed to override those of the business.
7. *Remuneration of personnel:* may be achieved by various methods and the choice is important; it should be fair, encourage effort, and not lead to overpayment.
8. *Centralization:* the extent to which orders should be issued only from the top of the organization is a problem which should take into account its characteristics, such as size and the capabilities of the personnel.
9. *Scalar chain (line of authority):* communications should normally flow up and down the line of authority running from the top to the bottom of the organization, but sideways communication between those of equivalent rank in different departments can be desirable so long as superiors are kept informed.

10. *Order:* both materials and personnel must always be in their proper place; people must be suited to their posts so there must be careful organization of work and selection of personnel.
11. *Equity:* personnel must be treated with kindliness and justice.
12. *Stability of tenure of personnel:* rapid turnover of personnel should be avoided because of the time required for the development of expertise.
13. *Initiative:* all employees should be encouraged to exercise initiative within the limits imposed by the requirements of authority and discipline.
14. *Esprit de corps:* efforts must be made to promote harmony within the organization and prevent dissension and divisiveness.

Fayol – unlike Taylor – recognized that *esprit de corps* is a vital ingredient in any organization.

Fayol also devised a commercial organization's activities into six basic elements: technical; commercial; financial; security; accounting; and management. The management function, Fayol believed, consisted of planning, organizing, commanding, co-ordinating and controlling. It is likely that many practising managers, even today, would identify similar elements as the core of their activities.

STUART CRAINER

Further Reading

General and Industrial Management, Pitman, London, 1949.

THE VIRTUAL ORGANIZATION

Laurence S Lyons

The physical manifestation of a company once centred around the office. Technology now enables organizations to provide a more dynamic and flexible approach to the traditional office and how people work within it. Indeed, the office may cease to exist as work is undertaken elsewhere and the organization becomes increasingly diffuse and intangible: the virtual organization.

Pause a moment, and carry out a simple mind experiment: imagine your worst competitor. What does it look like? Perhaps it has unusually small capital requirements. Undoubtedly, it always has the optimum number of people working for it, exactly as and when it needs them. It is both flexible and adaptive. It is readily able to change its tactics at high speed. If it should so wish, it enters or even creates new markets at a moment's notice; and, in addition to all these advantages, it is also enormously productive.

It is present anywhere and everywhere it wants to be. It is stealthy. Yesterday, it was unnoticeable, unobtrusive and silent. But, today, it is in your market. It appeared instantly and unexpectedly, as if by magic. It has violated all those comfortable assumptions in your plans that held fast to the idea that you had impervious entry barriers. You thought no one could touch you. At least, not a completely unknown outsider. Now you realize that those barriers do not exist any more – perhaps they never did. In any event, you now see them shattered. Years, if not decades, of proprietary investment have evaporated overnight.

This new competitor beats your important figures on all fronts. It seems impossible for you to catch it or to match it.

This is the commercial equivalent of alchemy, the ability to conjure gold from base metals. The new competitor has taken the elements of production and transmuted them into organizational gold. For it, fixed costs have become variable; unavoidable costs have become avoidable; tangible assets (and the very significant costs of servicing them), have become less-costly virtual assets.

Virtual assets do the same work as tangible assets, only they are not physically where you normally expect them to be. They are also completely 'scaleable', appearing – albeit at odd times and in unusual places – exactly as and when they are needed. They also disappear when they are no longer needed – incurring no cost to switch.

The new competition is populated with people who have contracts that are both flexible and meaningful. The competitor's contracts define units of productive service and measurable beneficial output, rather than a commitment to complete or exceed a certain number of hours sitting behind an employer's desk. The competitor's people may not even work in an office. Some may work from home. Many others will utilize the various new kinds of workplace that are neither within the confines of the traditional office, nor are they inconveniently force-fitted into the residential home. It is quite possible that your competitor's office work will not even be performed in your country. With all the benefits from cost-effective computer networks and time-zone-shifting, your hypothetical competitor may even be able to complete some work in what seems to be no time at all.

This new competitor is your worst nightmare. It is called the virtual organization. Once it has arrived, it can be seen. It also can be felt. But you cannot fight it because it is not really there. It presents no real target. It is populated with virtual employees, who are located in virtual offices, and who work in virtual time. It has virtual assets that are managed rather than owned, having all the benefits of being variable, scaleable, and moveable. It is a dynamic, resourceful yet minimalist instance of your own organization. It is truly unbeatable.

From image to reality

The image of such a competitor is a nightmarish one. It is, however, increasingly true. Of course, there are a few caveats and cavils surrounding this assertion. But if, like many organizations, your costs of labour, together with those associated with the acquisition, servicing, retention and disposal of buildings, are towards the top of your ranked expense items, your business may indeed have the potential to become a virtual organization. It is almost certain to qualify if many of the business activities attracting these costs are in knowledge-intensive or information-intensive work, or if they are clerical or administrative.

What has happened to make the virtual organization a possibility and even a threat?

Over the last decade we have seen the emergence of new working practices that have been brought about through the growing maturity of information technology.

Given this, it is not surprising that technologically advanced companies have taken the lead in creating the virtual organization. One such multinational company, for example, had an internationally distributed project team at work in the late 1980s. It worked all the way from marketing concept through design and development, and into manufacturing. One third of the team was situated just outside Boston, US. The remainder was located in Reading, England. At that time there was a demographic wall in Boston – there were not enough skilled engineers locally who could work on the project, so the group in Reading was set up. The primary manufacturing plant was located in Clonmel, Ireland. Another corporate manufacturing site in Augusta, US, was nominated to second-source the product.

In the team, use of the most modern electronic mail and on-line conference facilities supplemented frequent face-to-face contacts. Design changes were implemented by electronic communication between sites. Most impressively, the actual engineering blueprints could be modified, and production changes implemented, abroad without people having to walk out of the UK research laboratory.

Such means of working were once the preserve of IT companies or those with apparently inexhaustible budgets. The difference today is that similar facilities are more and more accessible to smaller companies and individuals. With lowered costs and lowered entry barriers, ten years later we now find that there are few businesses or people who are not enfranchised to work in this way.

IT-enabled work practices allow work to move around the world. They shatter all our entrenched beliefs about the location and timing of work. These practices pose both an opportunity and a threat.

Thinking strategically

The competitive attractions of IT-enabled work practices are persuasive and managers will immediately want to know how to apply the principles in their own organizations. When looked at in this strategic context (for example by examining, as we have briefly, the scenario of the worst competitor) I refer to this emerging topic as *future work*. It aims to uncover new technological and work-practice possibilities, and marshals these to *advise the business strategy, so that informed decisions can be made.*

One of the biggest problems that people and companies face when thinking about strategy is that very often it involves little more than responding to the initiatives of competitors. But to continue to think in this reactive way is to face certain oblivion during the dawn of an emerging era. The virtual corporation is the prototype of a new organizational structure. Time is no longer on your side. To do nothing but await the virtual competitor can be a very high-risk strategy indeed. Some companies will awaken to find that their worst nightmare has materialized, with the strategic high ground already fully occupied.

If strategic reaction is indeed too risky, how should organizations plan? How do people and organizations discipline themselves to start to think *pro*-actively, rather than *re*-actively?

They need to think the unthinkable, challenge the unchallengeable, think laterally and consider all the principles and possibilities of *future work*. Consider again that virtual competitor: Where is it based? How is it organized? What unrealized aspirations are there within *your* business that it would make the focus of its own attention? What prospective customers do you only wish you could be servicing, that it might now reach out towards and satisfy? What hidden flexible suppliers can it tap into? Where will it be strong and you remain weak? Where will it invest? Who will be its allies?

Then ask how much room is left in the industry which remains. Although a scan of your environment can provide a rich source of inspiration, so too can your present choices about your existing organization of work. Suppose you had the chance to restructure any way you chose.

So now, imagine *your* organization. Free it from today's constraints of place and time. What else can you now achieve?

As another mind experiment, knowing what you now know, take your chief executive and put him or her in a shed in the car park. Then get him or her to justify, from that point, every single item of significant past capital investment all over again. Question what work is done, where it is done, and why it is done there? What are the alternatives? Then get the rest of the board to justify everything, right up to the point where they end up back in the boardroom.

Do you think they will get back there? I doubt it, and most probably so, too, do you.

If you could re-invent your entire organization, and you were fully aware of *future work* possibilities, would you simply re-create what you have today? Or would there be a gap of missed opportunity? Could the ideas of *future work* help to change the unchangeable – could this gap be filled?

The concept of the virtual organization as competitor, is nothing other than a zero-based method of thinking about the organization's architecture in the light of the new possibilities of *future work*. By using the ideal concept of a virtual organization – externally and then internally – senior managers can start to think with the interests of their organizations uppermost. They can enrich their strategy. And, most importantly, they can reduce risk by shifting their locus of approach from followers to become the intellectual leaders. In the 1990s and beyond, the smart organization is the one that survives.

It is my experience that companies who have been successful in *future work* often do not really talk about it. Because working virtually (how close this is to working virtuously) is a natural way of being more efficient. It is, therefore, a source of competitive advantage. By any conventional standard *future work* organizations can be highly profitable. Additionally, the position they take within the industries they chose to enter or create is very strong, if not unassailable. Thus they are profitable, sustainable, and very quiet about it.

Another important, yet different form, is the stealthy transparent competitor – to be found on the other side of the coin to the virtual competitor. The term 'virtual' means that it is apparent, although the substance seems intangible. There is absolutely no doubt, on the other hand, that 'transparent' organizations exist in substance, yet cannot easily be seen. That is until they surface, when they become highly visible and very real indeed.

Through chance or planning, transparent competitors build up strategic assets in a totally unrelated industry to yours. Then they reorganize those assets into a new mix. They emerge from nowhere as a very concrete and powerful competitor. They, too, break all the supposedly insurmountable entry barriers of the industries into which they intrude.

Some of these magical companies are household names. Think for a moment about what business General Motors is in? Obviously it makes millions of vehicles. But, today, it is also in the credit card business.

Dana Corporation is also in the automotive business. But one of its outstanding divisions is in commercial credit – running leasing programmes for computer companies such as Apple and Compaq. Its typical customer leases only one or two systems, yet Dana has turned this into a highly profitable business.

Supermarket chains Tesco and Sainsbury are in the food business. But who would have expected just a few years ago that BP would be regarding them as major competitors in the petrol business?

If your competitors could move their work around the world, without incurring prohibitive charges, to wherever it was either cheapest or most conveniently carried out, you would be worried. Especially if you were not also doing the same. In fact, there is one kind of work that carries almost trivial transport costs – anything that requires intellectual work can be moved very cheaply indeed.

There are more live examples of this in practice than most of managers or organizations would suppose. Among the most well-known is the insurance company, New York Life. It was increasing its volume of business and needed more claims processing people to handle it. Then it hit a demographic snag. People who live in New York and who are capable with figures, could earn far more on Wall Street than any insurance company would ever pay. But, by using modern communications, the company was able to shift the work to where it could find a proficient English-speaking workforce – it went to Ireland.

The lesson for managers? Knowledge workers can work anywhere. For them work has shifted from hand to head, and where it is done hardly matters any more. Ideas are the most easily exported commodity in the world. That's why several large companies are having computer software written in India. They gain the benefits of highly educated and skilled people for a fraction of what they would pay in Western Europe or North America.

The same applies to that other new icon of the modern way of doing business – the help desk. Ring into any of the major IT software companies and your call could be put through to almost anywhere: USA, Ireland, the Netherlands. It has now become economically viable to provide a similar 24-hour facility for any service sector.

The idea could be attractive, for example, to motoring organizations – they simply do not need to have their control rooms in a particular country any more. Direct banking accounts, open 24 hours a day, could also be run worldwide from two or three centres in different time zones. In each of these examples the person you would be talking to would have instant up-to-date information available.

One new axis of work spans New York, Barbados, County Kerry, the Highlands and Islands of Scotland, Bombay, Singapore and beyond. Another, places Martinique, Guadeloupe, and Paris within the same domain. In the emerging global world of *future work*, it is language rather than national boundary that defines where work is done. There are messages in this that are as important for politicians as well as for managers.

Ask yourself: 'Is the present location of work sensible?'

But then ask the even more fundamental question: 'Is the very idea of an office appropriate any more?' Originally *office* meant *officer,* as in a job or a role. But in the last century it became corrupted in normal usage into meaning a place where a job is done. This semantic shift has constrained our thinking about doing work. It is another constraint waiting to be broken.

Recession has focused thinking on the downsides of property, especially its inflexibility and solid over-permanence. Office buildings tend to be comparatively simple to obtain, but disposed of with difficulty, and often in chunks. As a result, the traditional organization finds itself exposed to a growing and sprawling portfolio of buildings. Amusingly, many companies have woken up and found themselves in the property business. When the retail chain Woolworth renamed itself Kingfisher, it quickly declared that one of its major divisions would be the property side of the business.

Many companies have mistakenly confused the solidity of their premises with the solidity of the business, and proudly engraved their logos into the concrete of their pristine new corporate head offices. All this achieves is slightly to reduce the value of the building to the next tenant or purchaser.

It is also worth bearing in mind that even when you introduce new work practices, it is very unlikely that there will be any contribution to the bottom line until you can dispose of a whole building.

Have you recently considered the ROCE of your offices? Research has shown that a maximum of only five to ten per cent of an office building yields any return at all.[1] Often the real return is about one third of this figure. Independent calculations from large organizations come to the same conclusion. Based on a total possible utilization of 365 days a year, the figure is arrived at after making allowance for a 5-day week; an 8-hour day; holidays, sickness, late arrivals and early departures. The time utilization of office space clearly represents an appalling return on capital employed.

The true figures are probably even worse than this when space utilization is also accounted for. Large portions of office buildings are often taken up with expansive reception areas. Many contain offices that remain constantly unused. It is probably fair to say that the real utilization of office space must often be in the region of single figure percentages. However, it is refreshing to see that with a little innovative thought and simple technology, some companies have successfully set up highly productive facilities that require less than half the conventional floor space.

The tele-conundrum

Teleworking has been receiving increasing publicity for some years. In 1988, Francis Kinsman in uncovering some macro-economic issues commented: 'Teleworking has the potential for relieving the seemingly insoluble problems of road and rail congestion.' Today, teleworking can offer real bottom-line benefits as well as opportunities to businesses – when managed properly. It can also make a major contribution to any company's social responsibility charter.

Successful teleworking usually requires the working week to be multiplexed – typically involving two to three days in a more traditional office and the rest of the time spent perhaps on the road or working from home. Iain Vallance, chief executive of British Telecom has mused that a teleworker is a person 'who travels to work, not down the Piccadilly line, but down the telephone line and who arrives at the office without actually leaving home'.

But there are other non-office, non-home work locations emerging. One is the *telecottage*, which originated in Sweden where a lot of people for practical reasons could not work from home. Yet, there is a substantial gap between supply and demand. Many people would like to work this way. But big organizations have not yet discovered how to unlock the outsourcing conundrum to make use of them – or migrate their own staff to the alternative model. Research sponsored by BT and carried out at Henley Management College's Future Work Forum has identified middle-manager resistance as a major barrier to change. Behind all the rationalization is the fact that many managers do not trust their own staff. Yet, practically every study has repeatedly found that when it is allowed, teleworking is more productive than conventional office work.

One company in the US did a very simple but revealing exercise. It compiled a list of all its personnel together with their ZIP (post) codes. It discovered that 60 per cent were commuting one hour each way from the same neighbourhood. The solution? A plan to convert a condominium in that area and provide data links to the existing office building. Studies have shown that typically some 80 per cent of the hours saved each day are spent on company business.

Future work is re-casting the very basis of competition. There are already sufficient case studies to prove the point. If your organization has not yet surveyed and staked out its place on the *future work* stage, then its destiny is exposed to others outside.

In the world of business we can be sure of precious few things. Among these is a belief that the economic imperative will somehow find a way to determine who the winners of tomorrow will be. If you wish to be among their number, the time is ripe to conduct a reassessment that takes into account these new opportunities and threats.

One of the biggest challenges is the need to re-think the business. The kind of thinking that is now needed goes beyond the normal strategic planning cycle. The standard question: 'Where do we want to get to tomorrow?' must be asked again and again, each time with the rider: 'And where even-better, taking into account *future work* possibilities?'

An excellent way to jolt thinking into this new world is to confront your worst nightmare. The sure way to prevent the spectre from materializing is first to recognize the likelihood that a virtual competitor is lurking somewhere close by. Is it? What is the worst it could it do? How?

And when you truly and fully understand the answers to these questions you will know your virtual competitor as well as you know your own organization. As a by-product, you will also have completed your strategic *future work* plan which must be simply to become that virtual organization.

Dr Laurence S Lyons is the Principal of Metacorp Management Consulting which specializes in advising large organizations on business strategy and organizational development. Dr Lyons is a member of the associate faculty at Henley Management College where he is co-founder and Director of Research of the Future Work Forum – a sponsored research initiative of blue-chip private and public sector organizations. He is co-author of *Creating Tomorrow's Organization: Unlocking the Benefits of Future Work* (1995) and a director of the Centre for Strategic Cell Development, an organization specializing in director development.

Further Reading

Birchall, D and Lyons, L, *Creating Tomorrow's Organization: Unlocking the Benefits of Future Work*, FT/Pitman, London, 1995.

Reference

[1] Lloyd, B, 'Office productivity – time for a revolution', *Long Range Planning*, vol. 23, no. 1, 1990.

THINKERS

Charles Handy

Born 1932; educator

N ot many European management thinkers have been elevated to the heady status of guru. Charles Handy is undoubtedly one of the chosen few. The publication of *The Age of Unreason* (1989) and *The Empty Raincoat* (1994) have cemented his reputation, gaining worldwide attention. His work is increasingly philosophical rather than restricted to the confines of management or organizational behaviour. It is marked by a humane disaffection with how organizations are run and managed. Handy argues that the very nature of organizations and of managerial work needs to be radically altered if organizations and people are to prosper and develop in the future.

Charles Handy's reputation has grown throughout a career which has taken him from Shell International to London Business School and now as a freelance luminary, writing and thinking, occasionally being heard on commercial radio and on BBC Radio Four's 'Thought for the Day'. 'Most of the things I have learnt were not learned formally but through accidents and failure. I learned from small catastrophes,' he says. Unlike other leading business and management thinkers, he is not a consultant. 'A consultant solves other people's problems,' he says, 'I could never do that. I want to help other people solve their own problems.'

After leaving university Handy became an oil executive for Shell International based in Malaysia. Returning to London he became disillusioned with corporate bureaucracy and, after a time working for Anglo-American, joined MIT's Sloan Management Programme. Here, he came into contact with leading management thinkers such as Warren Bennis, Chris Argyris and Ed Schein. This proved to be the turning point in Handy's career. He

Education: Oxford University (studied 'Greats' – a combination of classics, history and philosophy); Massachusetts Institute of Technology
Career: Joined Shell International and became the company's South-East Asia economist; worked for a short time for the Anglo-American Corporation; MIT Sloan School of Management (graduated 1967); helped launch and then directed London Business School's Sloan Programme; Professor at LBS; Warden of St George's House, Windsor Castle (a study centre for ethics and social policy) 1977-1981; now Fellow of LBS.

returned to the UK to play a leading role in the early days of London Business School and the creation of its Sloan Programme.

Handy's first book was *Understanding Organizations* (1976), a densely-packed pot-boiler which has become required reading for many managers. It is a comprehensive and thought-provoking exploration of organizations. For Handy it was, to a large extent, a process of self-education and discovery, putting down on paper the things he had learned and believed in. It remains a highly relevant and comprehensive text book. His other books, though radically different, all retain this impression of Handy developing his own ideas. 'My books aren't based on an immense amount of statistics. I am struggling with the reality of organizational life as I see it and trying to make sense of it,' he admits. 'I am more interested in the questions than the answers, but bystanders often see things more clearly.' He tests his ideas out on small groups of managers as he travels the world – 'This helps me to crystallise my thinking. They don't have to agree with my solutions; I want them to agree with my diagnosis.'

Perhaps the most idiosyncratic of Handy's books is his second, *Gods of Management* (1979) which explores corporate culture through an elaborate analogy. The four gods of the title are: Zeus (power and patri-archy); Apollo (order, reason and bureaucracy); Athena (expertise and meritocracy); and Dionysus (individualism). This creative approach sig-nalled the beginning of a process of rigorous questioning which marks Handy's more recent work which has become progressively more per-sonal. In *Gods of Management* he observes: 'Management is more fun, more creative, more personal, more political and more intuitive than any textbook. Nevertheless, while every organization is different, there are patterns which can be discerned, models to be imitated and some guidelines which can be followed.'

The cornerstones of Handy's thinking are laid out most powerfully in *The Age of Unreason* and *The Empty Raincoat*. (The latter entitled *The Age of Paradox* in the US.) In both he argues that fundamental and rev-olutionary changes are required in our perceptions of organizations and managers within them. 'The way we are doing things is not the best way,' argues Handy, calling on organizations to recognize that their single most important asset is their people. 'The micro-division of labour has fostered a basic distrust of human beings. People weren't allowed to put the whole puzzle together. Instead they were given small parts because companies feared what people would do if they knew and saw the whole puzzle,' says Handy. 'Human assets shouldn't be misused. Brains are becoming the core of organizations – other activities can be contracted out.' He points to Singapore which has largely exported its manufactur-ing activities elsewhere, but retains managerial control. And he calls on schools to become places where students develop a portfolio of compe-tencies which are continually enhanced and added to throughout life.

Such approaches are necessary, he argues, if organizations are to achieve the objectives summed up by one chief executive 'as half as many people being paid twice as much to do three times as much work'.

Handy's world view is humane and liberal, though increasingly bleak. He stands apart from the mainstream of fads and fashions, believing that the organizational world is dominated by paradoxes – like the empty raincoat (inspired by a sculpture in Minneapolis). Perhaps the central paradox is the failure of technology to enhance the quality of our lives and work. Technology leads to greater efficiency which requires a smaller workforce; the company is then taxed to support those out of work through its increased efficiency.

'If economic progress means that we become anonymous cogs in some great machine, then progress is an empty promise. The challenge must be to show how paradox can be managed,' says Handy, who saves his most vehement turns of phrase for 'yellow-page economies of glitz and extras', where mass consumerism and consumption are out of control.

It is a message which, Handy recognizes, is unpalatable to many. Managers putting faith in people, for example, will lose some of their traditional power. 'Managers have been brought up on a diet of power, divide and rule. They have been preoccupied with authority rather than making things happen,' he says, adding a warning: 'Since *The Age of Unreason* I have become more aware that you can't consider the professional class in isolation from the rest of society. Though the world is a good one for professional executives, they are a minority of the human race. If they only look after themselves they will run out of customers.' They have to learn to manage paradoxes, surrender some of their power and take risks with people.

'Work is more than a job,' says Handy. 'In the past, business was the employer of all those who wanted to work. In the future there will be lots of customers, but not lots of jobs.' He does not expect companies to become charitable institutions – 'The job of any business is to be as effective as it can' – but for expectations and working practices to fundamentally alter. 'The principal purpose of a company is not to make a profit, full stop. It is to make a profit in order to continue to do things or make things, and to do so ever better and more abundantly. Profit has to be a means to other ends rather an end in itself.' Handy points to the need for organizations and people to develop senses of 'continuity, connection and direction' – ever more important in a business world beset by disorientation.

His image of the organization of the future has evolved from a shamrock in *The Age of Unreason* ('a form of organization based around a core of essential executives and workers supported by outside contractors and part-time help') to the 'doughnut principle' of *The Empty Raincoat* – 'Organizations have their essential core of jobs and people surrounded by an open and flexible space which they fill with flexible workers and flexible supply contracts'. Handy argues that organizations have neglected and misunderstood the core while expanding and developing the rest of the doughnut. He attaches the same image to people's personal development, suggesting that many need to sit down and return to first principles if they are to achieve a balance in their lives.

The 'federal' organization is something which Handy continues to champion – 'an old idea whose time may have come'. Through federalism Handy believes the modern company can bridge some of the paradoxes it continually faces – such as the need to be simultaneously global and local. 'Every organization can be thought of in federal terms,' he says, adding the challenge: 'Federalism is an exercise in the balancing of power.' Handy accepts that federalism is often neither clear-cut nor easy to implement, instead it is often nebulous and on the verge of being out of control.

Increasingly, Handy seems to offer a dark view of the world of work, organizations and governments. But, he sees himself as articulating the fears of many in business and beyond. 'A lot of people have similar concerns and questions as I have, but they don't know how to pursue them or articulate them so they are suppressed,' says Handy. 'In the end I have only suggestions. There is no formula or perfect solution. This is the tide of events. We can't turn the tide, but we can ride it.'

STUART CRAINER

Further Reading

Charles Handy:
Understanding Organizations, Penguin Books, London, 1976.
The Future of Work, Basil Blackwell, Oxford, 1984.
Gods of Management, Business Books, London, 1986.
The Making of Managers (with John Constable), Longman, London, 1988.
The Age of Unreason, Business Books, London, 1989.
Inside Organizations: 21 Ideas for Managers, BBC Books, London, 1990.
Waiting for the Mountain to Move, Arrow, London, 1991.
The Empty Raincoat, Hutchinson, London, 1994.
Beyond Certainty, Random House, London, 1995.

* Recommended reading

Leadership

'Our prevailing leadership myths are still captured by the image of the captain of the calvary leading the charge to rescue the settlers from the attacking Indians. So long as such myths prevail, they reinforce a focus on short-term events and charismatic heroes rather than on systemic forces and collective learning.'   *Peter Senge, MIT*[1]

'A leader is a man who has the ability to get other people to do what they don't want to do, and like it.'   *Harry Truman*[2]

'Leadership can be felt throughout an organization. It gives pace and energy to the work and empowers the workforce. Empowerment is the collective effect of leadership.'
Warren Bennis[3]

[1] Senge, P, *The Fifth Discipline*, Doubleday, New York, 1990.
[2] Quoted in Prior, P, *Leadership is not a Bowler Hat,* David & Charles, Newton Abbot, 1977.
[3] Bennis, W, *An Invented Life*, Addison Wesley, Reading, Mass, 1993.

OVERVIEW

Stuart Crainer

Leadership is one of the great intangibles of the business world. It is a skill most people would love to possess, but one which defies close definition. Ask people which leaders they admire and you are as likely to be told Gandhi as John Harvey-Jones, Margaret Thatcher as Richard Branson. Yet, most agree that leadership is a vital ingredient in business success and that great leaders make for great organizations.

'Broadly speaking there are two approaches to leadership. You can theorize about it or you can get on and do it. Theorising about it is great fun, hugely indulgent and largely useless. Doing it – or doing it better – is demanding, frequently frustrating and of immense value,' says Francis Macleod, former chief executive of the Leadership Trust. 'Those who want to change an organization must be able to change people and in that process there is only one starting point that makes sense. Learning to lead oneself better is the only way to lead others better.'

When considering leadership in the business context most routes lead to the military world. Management, long used to the concept of divide and rule, has perenially sought its leadership role models from the military. The temptation to view the business world as a battle field is, even now, highly appealing. Indeed, the success of Hsun Tzu's *The Art of War* as a management text points to the continuing popularity of this idea.

Leadership re-emerged on the management agenda in the 1980s after a period of relative neglect. A great many books were produced purporting to offer essential guidance on how to become a leader. These tended to follow military inspirations, with the business leader portrayed as a general, inspiring the corporate troops to one more effort.

Even so, there are some useful inspirations in the military world for today's corporate leaders. One of the most persuasive, and under-estimated, is Field Marshall William Slim. Slim believed that the leadership lessons he had learned in the army could readily be applied to the business world. In his book, *Defeat Into Victory*, Slim described his thoughts on raising morale:

'Morale is a state of mind. It is that intangible force which will move a whole group of men to give their last ounce to achieve something, without counting the cost to themselves; that makes them feel they are part of something greater than themselves. If they are to feel that, their morale must, if it is to endure – and the essence of morale is that it should endure – have certain foundations. These foundations are spiritual, intellectual, and material, and that is the order of their importance. Spiritual first, because only spiritual foundations can stand real strain. Next intellectual, because men are swayed by reason as well as feeling. Material last – important, but last – because the highest kinds of morale are often met when material conditions are lowest.'

The doyen of the military-inspired approach is the UK leadership writer and practitioner, John Adair, who was himself in the army (as well as spending time on an Arctic trawler and various other adventures). Adair has identified a list of the basic functions of leadership: planning, initiating, controlling, supporting, informing and evaluating. Central to Adair's thinking is the belief that leadership is a skill which can be learned like any other. This is one of the fundamentals of the military approach to leadership – leaders are formed in the crucible of action rather than through chance genetics.

In the management world there is a tendency to fluctuate between the two extremes. On the one hand, managers are sent on leadership development courses to nurture, and discover, leadership skills. On the other hand, there is still a substantial belief that leaders have innate skills which cannot be learned.

Modern leadership writers tend to suggest that leadership as a skill or characteristic is distributed generously among the population. 'Successful leadership is not dependent on the possession of a single universal pattern of inborn traits and abilities. It seems likely that leadership potential (considering the tremendous variety of situations for which leadership is required) is broadly rather than narrowly distributed in the population,' wrote Douglas McGregor in *The Human Side of Enterprise*. The American Warren Bennis, inspired by McGregor, has studied leadership throughout his career. Bennis also concludes that each of us contains the capacity for leadership and has leadership experience. He does not suggest that actually translating this into becoming an effective leader is straightforward, but that it can be done, given time and application.

While such arguments are impressively optimistic about human potential, they are disappointed by reality. The dearth of great leaders is increasingly apparent. This suggests that either innate skills are not being effectively developed or that the business world simply does not encourage managers to fulfil their potential as leaders.

The new leader

The increasing emphasis in the 1990s has focused on leaders as real people managing in a concensus-seeking manner. Instead of seeing leadership as being synonymous with dictatorship, this view sees leadership as a more subtle and humane art. It also breaks down the barrier between leadership and management. Traditionally, in theory at least, the two have been separated. 'Men are ripe for intelligent, understanding, personal leadership, they would rather be led than managed,' observed Field Marshal Slim. Increasingly, management and leadership are seen as inextricably linked. It is one thing for a leader to propound a grand vision; but this is redundant unless the vision is managed into real achievement. While traditional views of leadership tend eventually to concentrate on vision and charisma, the message now seems to be that charisma is no longer enough to carry leaders through. Indeed, leaders with strong personalities are just as likely to bite the corporate dust (as Bob Horton found to his cost at BP). The new model leaders include people like Percy Barnevik at ASEA Brown Boveri, Virgin's Richard Branson and Jack Welch at GE in the United States.

The magic which marks such executives has been analyzed by INSEAD leadership expert Manfred Kets de Vries. 'They go beyond narrow definitions. They have an ability to excite people in their organizations,' he says. 'They also work extremely hard – leading by example is not dead – and are highly resistant to stress. Also, leaders like Branson or Barnevik are very aware of what their failings are. They make sure that they find good people who can fill these areas.'

Leonard Sayles, author of *Leadership: Managing in Real Organizations* and *The Working Leader* is representative of a great deal of the new thinking. Sayles suggests that leadership affects managers at all levels, not simply those in the higher echelons of management. 'It is leadership based on work issues, not just people issues, and is very different from the method and style of managing that has evolved from our traditional management principles.'

Sayles argues that the leader's role lies in 'facilitating co-ordination and integration in order to get work done'. Sayles is dismissive of the perennial concept of the great corporate leader. Instead his emphasis is on the leader as the integrator of corporate systems. The leader is a kind of fulcrum 'adapting, modifying, adjusting and rearranging the complex task and function interfaces that keep slipping out of alignment'. Instead of being centred around vision and inspiration, Sayles regards the leader's key role as integrating the outputs of his or her work unit with those of the rest of the organization. To Sayles, 'managers who are not leaders can only be failures'.

Interestingly, and unhelpfully for the practising manager, leadership attracts such aphorisms rather than hard and fast definitions. Indeed, there is a plethora of definitions on what constitutes a leader and the characteristics of leadership. In practice, none have come to be universally, or even widely, accepted.

The very individualism associated with leadership is now a bone of contention. The people we tend to think of as leaders – from Napoleon to Winston Churchill – are not exactly renowned for their team-working skills. But these are exactly the skills management theorists insist are all-important for the 1990s and beyond.

'In some cases, the needs of a situation bring to the fore individuals with unique qualities or values; however, most leaders have to fit their skills, experience and vision to a particular time and place,' says psychologist Robert Sharrock of YSC. 'Today's leaders have to be pragmatic and flexible to survive. Increasingly, this means being people- rather than task-oriented. The "great man" theory about leadership rarely applies – if teams are what make businesses run, then we have to look beyond individual leaders to groups of people with a variety of leadership skills.'

Indeed, the pendulum has swung so far that there is growing interest in the study of followers. Once the humble foot soldier was ignored as commentators sought out the commanding officer, now the foot soldiers are encouraged to voice their opinions and shape how the organization works. 'Followers are becoming more powerful. It is now common for the performance of bosses to be scrutinized and appraised by their corporate followers. This, of course, means that leaders have to actively seek the support of their followers in a way they would have never have previously contemplated,' says Robert Sharrock.

Phil Hodgson of Ashridge Management College has analyzed the behaviour of a number of business leaders. His conclusion is that the old models of leadership are no longer appropriate. 'Generally, the managers interviewed had outgrown the notion of the individualistic leader. Instead, they regarded leadership as a question of drawing people and disparate parts of the organization together in a way that made individuals and the organization more effective.' He concludes that the new leader must add value as a coach, mentor and problem solver; allow people to accept credit for success and responsibility for failure; and must continually evaluate and enhance their own leadership role. 'They don't follow rigid or orthodox role models, but prefer to nurture their own unique leadership style,' he says. 'And, they don't do people's jobs for them or put their faith in developing a personality cult.' The new recipe for leadership, centres on five key areas: learning, energy, simplicity, focus and inner sense.

In the age of empowerment, the ability to delegate effectively is critically important. 'Empowerment and leadership are not mutually exclusive,' says INSEAD's Manfred Kets de Vries. 'The trouble is that many executives feel it is good to have control. They become addicted to power – and that is what kills companies.'

Knowing when to let go has become an integral part of the skills of the modern leader. There are many examples of leaders who stay on in organizations and in governments far beyond their practical usefulness. De Vries contends that leaders, like products, have a life cycle. He identifies three stages in this: entry and experimentation; consolidation; and decline, and estimates that life cycles for leaders are shortening.[1]

The growing interest and belief in the human side of leadership is, in itself, nothing new. Leadership thinker James McGregor Burns coined the phrases 'transactional' and 'transformational' leadership. Transactional leadership involves leaders who are very efficient at giving people something in return for their support or work. Followers are valued, appreciated and rewarded. Transformational leadership is concerned with leaders who create visions and are able to carry people along with them towards the vision.

The ability to create and sustain a credible vision remains critical. Harvard's John Kotter identified three central processes in leadership: establishing direction; aligning people; motivating and inspiring. The way in which these core elements are put into practice is continually being refined. But, at its heart, is an appreciation that the leader cannot act alone. Peter Drucker has observed that leaders habitually talk of 'we' rather than 'I'. The great leaders appear to be natural teamworkers, a fact overlooked by heroic models of leadership. In *The Tao of Leadership*, John Heider produces another aphorism – but one which cuts to the heart of modern leadership: 'Enlightened leadership is service, not selfishness.'[2]

STUART CRAINER

Further Reading

Adair, J, *Understanding Motivation*, Talbot Adair, Guildford, 1990.
De Press, M, *Leadership is an Art*, Doubleday, New York, 1989.
McGregor, D, *The Human Side of Enterprise*, McGraw Hill, New York, 1960.
Oates, D, *Leadership: The Art of Delegation*, Century Business, London, 1993.
Sayles, L, *The Working Leader*, The Free Press, New York, 1993.
Syrett, M, and Hogg, C, (eds) *The Frontiers of Leadership*, Blackwell, Oxford, 1992.

References

[1] de Vries, MK, 'CEOs also have the blues', *European Management Journal*, September 1994.
[2] Heider, J, *The Tao of Leadership*, Wildwood House, Aldershot, 1986.

THINKERS

Warren Bennis

Born 1925: educator

In many ways, Warren Bennis is the epitome of the modern-day management thinker. Now based at the University of Southern California, he has a lengthy academic pedigree – beginning as a protegé of Douglas McGregor, author of *The Human Side of Enterprise*, to become the *eminence grise* of contemporary leadership, advising four US presidents. His work has become steadily more populist and popular.

The most widely-read of Bennis' numerous publications is *Leaders: The Strategies for Taking Charge* (1985), co-written with Burt Nanus. This examined the behaviour and characteristics of 90 leaders and sought to reach general conclusions. The leaders studied were a truly eclectic – and somewhat eccentric – group, including Neil Armstrong and Karl Wallenda, a tight-rope walker. Bennis concluded that the leaders possessed four vital competencies:

- Management of attention – the vision of the leaders commanded the attention and commitment of those who worked for and with them in attempting to achieve it.
- Management of meaning – the leaders were skilled communicators, able to cut through complexity to frame issues in simple images and language. They were expert distillers of information.
- Management of trust – 'Trust is essential to all organizations,' observes Bennis. For the leaders, trust was expressed through consistency of purpose and in their dealings with colleagues and others. Even though people sometimes disagreed with what they said or did, the leaders were admired for their consistency of purpose.
- Management of self – the leaders were adept at identifying and fully utilizing their strengths; and accepting and seeking to develop areas of weakness.

To Bennis, leadership is a skill which can be learned by the manager willing to put in substantial effort. It is, however, fundamentally different from management. 'To survive in the twenty-first century we're going to need a new generation of leaders, not managers.

Education: Antioch College; MIT
Career: Army during World War 2; provost at SUNY, Buffalo, 1967-71; President, University of Cincinnati, 1971-78; University of Southern California since 1979.

The distinction is an important one. Leaders conquer the context – the volatile, turbulent, ambiguous surroundings that sometimes seem to conspire against us and will surely suffocate us if we let them – while managers surrender to it.' He goes on to list the fundamental differences between the two as:

- the manager administers; the leader innovates
- the manager is a copy; the leader is an original
- the manager maintains; the leader develops
- the manager focuses on systems and structure; the leader focuses on people
- the manager relies on control; the leader inspires trust
- the manager has a short-range view; the leader has a long-range perspective
- the manager asks how and when; the leader asks what and why
- the manager has his eye on the bottom line; the leader has his eye on the horizon
- the manager accepts the status quo; the leader challenges it
- the manager is the classic good soldier; the leader is his own person
- the manager does things right; the leader does the right thing.'[1]

The last element has become something of a catch-phrase, another in a long line of neat aphorisms which don't, in the end, bring the practitioner nearer to how to actually develop leadership skills.

Bennis has to some extent become a victim of pigeon-holing. His work actually covers a far wider span of issues than leadership. In the 1950s, for example, he studied group dynamics and was involved in the teamworking experiments at the US's National Training Laboratories. In the 1960s he developed a reputation as a student of the future – in a 1964 *Harvard Business Review* article, Bennis and co-author Philip Slater, accurately predicted the downfall of communism ('Democracy is inevitable,' they wrote).

In the mid-1960s, he was predicting the demise of the modern organization – a prediction which has taken 30 years to begin to be fulfilled. 'Bureaucracy emerged out of the organization's need for order and precision and the workers' demands for impartial treatment. It was an organization ideally suited to the values and demands of the Victorian era. And just as bureaucracy emerged as a creative response to a radically new age, so today new shapes are surfacing before our eyes.'[2]

Curiously, Bennis' career actually follows many of the patterns of Douglas McGregor's. McGregor was president of Antioch College during the time Bennis was an undergraduate and advised Bennis to move on to MIT. In 1959, when Bennis was teaching at Boston University and Harvard, McGregor recruited him to MIT to establish the new organization studies department. McGregor moved from being an academic to an administrator before returning to academic life. Bennis has done similarly – his academic career was interrupted by a spell as provost at the State University of New York at Buffalo and as president of the University of Cincinnati. This proved disappointing. 'The very time I had the most power, I felt the greatest sense of powerlessness,' Bennis observes in the autobiographical *An Invented Life*. In practice, Bennis found that his ambitious intentions were hamstrung by the very organization he purported to lead. Despite the power attributed to him through his job title, in practice he was powerless.

Bennis then returned to academic life, attempting to understand the lessons learned and to convert them into more general lessons about the nature of leadership and the relationship between the individual leader and the organization. His search has not, however, been for the perfectly formed, one-line summation, but rather an enduring study of the humanity behind leadership.

STUART CRAINER

Further Reading

Warren Bennis:
Leaders: The Strategies for Taking Charge (with Burt Nanus), Harper & Row, New York, 1985.
On Becoming a Leader, Addison-Wesley, Reading, 1989.
Why Leaders can't Lead, Jossey-Bass, San Francisco, 1989.
An Invented Life: Reflections on Leadership and Change, Addison-Wesley, Reading, 1993.

References

1 Bennis, W, 'Managing the dream', *Training Magazine*, 1990.
2 Bennis, W, 'The coming death of bureaucracy', *Think Magazine*, 1966.

THE WORK OF THE LEADER

Donald L Laurie

A fundamental shift is underway in the work of a leader creating and sustaining customer responsiveness. It is a shift from a command and control style to one where the leader creates the conditions under which the ambition can be achieved. Leaders are learning, however, that letting go of control and giving people more authority in their area of responsibility is extremely difficult to accomplish.[1]

There is a need for a contemporary theory of leadership to provide a framework for mobilizing people. In my experience, too many managers describe the work of the leader with a series of clichés: 'to provide vision', 'to set direction', 'to motivate people', etc. In practice, senior executives and managers seem to respond pragmatically to problems – calling on their own experience, common sense and selected management principles they have come to believe in over the years. Beyond this, the terms 'leadership', 'authority' and 'power' tend to be used interchangeably and in a sloppy way.

My research has involved interviewing 22 chairmen and chief executives on their work as leaders in creating and sustaining customer-responsive organizations. They include John Nordstrom of Nordstrom, Sir Colin Marshall of British Airways, Jan Timmer of Philips, Bernard Fournier of Rank Xerox, David Sainsbury of J Sainsbury, Gene Fife of Goldman Sachs and others. My conversations with them provided me with insights that confirmed and further developed my thinking.

As a starting point, we need to distinguish between technical problem-solving and adaptive work, and between leadership and authority. I shall then discuss the challenges that emerged from the research in terms of achieving greater customer responsiveness while maintaining profitability. I conclude by suggesting six strategic principles for leadership.

Technical versus adaptive work

Technical problems are routine problems where solutions are known or can be provided by technical experts. Most problems, however, are under-defined and have no ready solutions. The various constituents will frequently have different power bases and competing values or guiding principles, which will give them a vested interest in one solution or another. In such cases, adaptive changes in values and behaviours – the habits of a working lifetime – will be required.

Business process re-engineering serves as an interesting example of both technical and adaptive problems. A technical skill is required to map business processes and there are effective and routine methods to document and communicate changes in these processes. This technical skill is not, however, sufficient to re-engineer an organization effectively. If the adaptive work is not done, the process will not work and the opportunity and investment will be lost. Unfortunately, in practice many executives focus on the technical dimension of problems and give too little attention to adaptive change.

In the concluding chapter of their best selling book *Re-engineering the Corporation*, Michael Hammer and James Champy support this view.

'Sadly, we must report that . . . many companies that begin re-engineering don't succeed at it. They end their efforts precisely where they began, making no significant changes, achieving no major performance improvement, and fuelling employee cynicism with yet another ineffective business improvement programme. Our unscientific estimate is that as many as 50 per cent to 70 per cent of the organizations that undertake a re-engineering effort do not achieve the dramatic results they intended.'[2]

Leadership and authority

Authority serves its functions differently in adaptive and technical situations. Where a problem is clear cut, the executive can authorize a technical expert to provide solutions. The need for leadership arises when the nature of the problem is unclear and the solution yet to be defined. The work of the leader in this situation is to mobilize other people to work on the problem rather than to provide solutions. Authority is the *holding vessel* that allows this difficult work to be done. Leadership is not the preserve of people at the top of large power bases; it is performed every day by many people in different parts of every organization.

Authority is both a resource and a constraint in performing the act of leadership. As a practical matter, authority is conveyed to individuals in exchange for services: 'I'll give you this power as long as you deliver as we agreed.' This applies equally to a chief executive, a sales manager or an auto mechanic – You can keep your job as long as you deliver the budget; you can work on my car, as long as you fix it.

Authority acts as a constraint, however, during a crisis or period of change because people have clear expectations of authority figures. In times of crisis, people want their leader to protect them by restoring order and getting things back to normal. They seek even greater clarity regarding their role, task, job and boundaries. Most of all, they want the leader to maintain the norms that, in all likelihood, got them into the problem. Tinkering with the norms is a perilous activity. The values imbedded in any organization are regarded as sacred.

When these pressures arise, authority figures are vulnerable to being drawn away from the difficult work, which people often want to avoid.

Nor are authority figures and managers necessarily leaders. Too many executives are maintenance engineers, controllers and instruction-driven administrators of their area of the business. Time is spent managing the numbers, 'keeping the lid' on problems, competing with internal adversaries and managing politics upwards.

Exercising leadership from a position of authority in adaptive situations is not easy because it usually means going against the grain. Rather than fulfilling the expectations for answers, one provides questions; rather than quelling conflict, one generates it; instead of maintaining norms, one challenges them; instead of orienting people to their current roles, one disorients them so that new relationships develop; rather than protecting people from external threat, one exposes them to it in order to stimulate the work required to adapt. All this requires leaders to move carefully and to pace the work. This was confirmed in the interviews. If people are challenged too fast, they will bring the leader down for failing their expectations. If people are challenged too slowly, then the leader will be destroyed because of making no progress. A combination of these forces toppled John Akers of IBM and Bob Horton of BP.

The challenges for leaders

Within this concept of leadership, four challenges emerged from the research. First, leaders need to maintain a deep sense of purpose. Second, leaders need to bring conflict out into the open and counteract resistance to adaptive change. Third, leaders need to live and make visible the values that will guide the organization while purging negative behaviours and attitudes. Fourth, leaders need to have customer priorities driving each dimension of the infrastructure so that these can be aligned in order to support adaptive change.

In my discussions with the leaders, I posed the following questions:

- How do you manage a paradox?
- How do you manage resistance to change on your team?
- Do leaders manage values?
- How effective are the key levers of management?

1. How do you manage a paradox?
Asking people to be more customer-responsive while top management downsizes the organization, or asking people for their loyalty while pushing for higher productivity, seems paradoxical.

As Jan Timmer of Philips put it:

'Crisis management is not the best environment in a company. In underperforming divisions fighting for survival, it is difficult to convince people to do more now and reap the benefits later. A certain amount of security is required to embark on leader-driven challenges such as quality or customer responsiveness.'

Credibility of the leader

Managing credibility during tough times emerged as a critical issue. Leaders are finding there is no place to hide. You can't fool the financial analyst or the stock market; you can't fool the employees; and you certainly can't fool the customer. Leaders must simultaneously balance long-term competitive situations while dealing with a real-time ticking clock that forces decisions regarding competition, cost structure, reduced cycle time and the mobilization of people. All of these relate to the customer but in different time-frames. Consistency is central to maintaining integrity.

If the leader is isolated and has different messages for the organization – one day the customer, next day budget reduction – he or she loses credibility. When someone on the front-line asks 'When it comes to the crunch, what do you want me to achieve?' the leader needs a credible and consistent response.

'You must reflect on and question what you initially communicate,' pointed out Jan Timmer. Did you ask too much or promise too much? Did you warn people that setbacks were inevitable? Managing expectations and making sure people understand the magnitude of the task facing them is critical. There is a big difference between achieving $1 million profit and fighting for $1.5 million profit.

Sir Colin Marshall, BA chairman confirmed this:

'At British Airways, we manage the paradox by trying to get people to understand there are better ways. It is our responsibility to get people to believe and accept they can reduce the unit cost of delivery. We can't reduce overall cost; we *can* keep unit costs down.

'When it comes to paradoxes or conflicts in specific situations, everyone knows we take decisions based on the best interest of the customer. It's not unusual for me to hear operations people preparing the daily operations report saying "we did this for the customer and here's what it cost". You can hear some disgruntlement – they know they did the right thing for the customer but they hate not making their budget. The customer must be the discriminating factor in our business.'

According to David Sainsbury, chairman of J Sainsbury:

'It's not a paradox, it's a decision. People are not starry-eyed, they have extremely good radar. They know what the leader really cares about – quality and customer responsiveness, or figures.

'When my cousin John went into one of our shops, he always did the same thing. After checking on the freshness of the produce, he'd go immediately to talk to the people on the floor to identify areas we could improve.

Other leaders in his position within our industry would come into a shop and head right to the back room to review the figures.'

An image came to my mind of a leader standing in front of an organization facing a crunch. The leader's left hand represented 'do the right thing for the customer'; the right hand represented 'short-term financial results'. The leader had a gold ring which could be put on one hand or the other at this crucial time. It became clear to me that organizations know their leaders. They know exactly which finger he or she will put the ring on when it comes to the crunch. In practical terms, this decision was most likely being replicated in thousands of decisions and trade-offs across the organization every day. It is the cumulative effect of these decisions that determines whether an organization is customer responsive or not.

Leaders concerned with paradoxes and conflicts in their organization should ask themselves:

- Is the paradox real?
- Do we have a discriminating factor in our decision-making? If so, is it the customer or something else?
- Am I credible? Do I represent a sense of purpose that people can understand and relate to? Or do I say one thing and do another?

2. How do you manage resistance to change on your team?
People classify problems in relation to their own experience. There seem to be two basic types of people – creative and innovative versus controllers and organization men. Freedom for the creative managers is the opportunity to explore new areas. Freedom for the controller is escape from innovation. These two types of people have a different vocabulary. They each hear what the other says but they have very different interpretations. Finding the right balance can be difficult. When the innovators are loose, costs go out of control; when too much authority is vested in control-oriented people, they kill all innovation. I agreed with Jan Carlzon when he indicated: 'Getting these conflicting styles to work together is one of the most interesting missions in management.'

Weapons of resistance

I have observed senior managers who have highly developed weapons of resistance and work-avoidance techniques. *Maintaining silence* in meetings allows people to remain uncommitted. *Reinterpreting* agreed plans or intentions after a meeting allows any action to be linked to a personal agenda. *Sabotaging* a decision or a colleague can undermine unwanted initiatives. *Escalating* issues that divert attention from the real problems, or launching personal attacks on present or absent colleagues have the same effect. Such behaviour polarizes perspectives and opinions.

112

It is like watching gladiators entering a ring. Each 'gladiator' is well prepared by their staff who wait anxiously to hear how their gladiators defended them and their position. How effectively were they able to gore an adversary with an opposing view? Exciting stuff, but dysfunctional when you pause to realize these people are on the same team.

The attempt to sideline important issues or give the work back to the leader means that the real work remains undone.

Counteracting resistance to change is difficult. It requires the leader to use his or her authority to *hold* the group and dismantle the weapons of resistance. People in the group need to both trust the leader and, to some degree, fear his or her authority. The work of the leader is to identify conflicts central to the success of the business and bring these out into the open, so that real learning can take place. Creating the conditions under which debate can take place is critical to improving the quality of decision-making and central to the development of each individual on the team.

If teams are to understand the sources of conflict and the competing values at stake and clarify the real 'problem' they are trying to solve, the mindset is critical. Executives who respectfully listen, deepen the debate with questions, and consult with each other are likely to reach a better solution to which everyone is committed.

Leaders concerned with resistance to change, might ask themselves:

- Am I making visible the ways in which people on my team resist change?
- Are we investing time to understand the competing perspectives represented by various constituents on our team? Am I helping people learn from each other as part of the conflict resolution process?
- Am I seeking a technical solution to an adaptive problem?
- Do I p*ut the lid on a problem* to avoid conflict?
- Am I asking the rest of the organization to change while my team remains resistant? If so, am I aware how much damage this can do to my credibility and potential to achieve our objectives?

3. Do leaders manage values?

Values, guiding principles or business principles exist in every organization. Either they channel the attitudes and behaviours of people towards the customer or they do not.

Jan Carlzon of SAS, reinforced the point:

'The leader must have a view on the culture required to deliver business results and provide people with an opportunity for meaning in work. You walk the talk and you are credible. If you don't, you're not credible and everyone knows it.'

David Sainsbury echoed the message, with a particular emphasis on living the vision and values:

'When it comes to the crunch, there is no sense having a vision and then letting a shoddy product out the door and saying, we'll fix it next time. That's a very strong message but don't have the illusion you can have it both ways. If you want commitment and trust within the fabric of the organization, you had better live the ideal you represent. You had better underpin that through rewards and commitment to your people. You lead by what you do. Full stop.'

When top teams discuss values, they inevitably focus on the positive values they wish to instil or reinforce within the organization – putting the customer first, respect and trust, openness, integrity, and so forth. Not all leaders and their top teams 'walk the talk'. Paradoxically, those who do not live the values, and who tolerate negative values, are usually very high performers.

Let me give you the example of Matt. Matt is an executive vice-president reporting to the chief executive of a large, multinational company. Year after year, Matt has delivered revenue and profit. He is the most dependable line manager in the business. He is charismatic and a gifted speaker. He is recognized as the most skilful negotiator in the company. He is the number one salesman in a sales-driven organization. He is extremely determined. People who deliver for Matt get promoted. Matt is the best.

At the same time, there are deep-seated concerns regarding Matt's personal integrity. Everyone knows he gives different interpretations of the same event to different people. People within the organization fear retribution if they are not loyal to Matt, who seems to find malice in the motives of those who don't agree with him. His formidable negotiating skills, turned internally, yield ruthless win-lose situations that have destroyed careers. Matt sabotages decisions and colleagues that could inhibit his personal agenda. He is a master of how to drive a command-and-control organization, often using his power in destructive, self-serving ways. Matt is the worst.

Matt's skills often seem to be essential in moving a company out of a near-term crisis. At the same time, he is a major inhibitor of change within the organization.

Matt is a partially fictitious character. Individuals with such characteristics can rise to the top of large organizations, where they have a deep impact on the culture. Individualism takes the place of teamwork, mistrust replaces trust, people cheat instead of behaving with integrity, people become obedient rather than creative, people become afraid and often paralyzed.

Negative values create an image of two equal forces. Think of it as 10,000 lb of thrust pulling in different directions. No matter how much good or positive force there is in the system (and there is usually a lot), the organization will not go forward while there are negative forces pulling in the opposite direction. Remove the negative forces and performance will be turbo-charged because people will feel better about their work.

Everyone is looking for meaning in work. Successful leaders create the conditions under which the human spirit can soar. They recognize the need for clear ground rules in a complex world where the attitudes and behaviour of

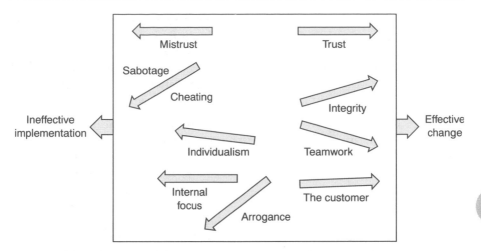

Fig. 1 Negative behaviour destroys organizational energy and momentum

people in their everyday interactions, trade-offs and decision-making are of key importance. They live the values they represent to their organization in a consistent and visible way. Leaders can't delegate living the values; it is central to their credibility and moral authority when they put the organization to work on the tough and constant challenges facing the business. Without credibility, people do not respond. Business is about achievement in terms of industry leadership, differentiated strategy, productivity and financial results. But, in the end, people define achievement in terms of how far the human spirit can reach.

Leaders concerned with the culture, problem-solving or implementation effectiveness might ask themselves:

- What is our adaptive challenge?
- What difficult behavioural issues undermine our capacity to implement strategy or solve business problems?
- What is our belief system? What are our positive values and what are the negative values that need to be purged?
- Do I live the values? Do I provide people with a sense of purpose beyond achieving financial results? Am I helping people discover meaning in work?

4. How effective are the 'key levers' of management?

Every leader I spoke to stressed that the traditional administrative levers need to be aligned if greater customer responsiveness and profitability are to be achieved. The technical factors identified to support adaptive change included: standards, measures and benchmarking; rewards; recruitment; appraisal and promotion; systems; business processes; and organization structure.

I use the term 'technical' factors because each leader was familiar with these instruments and with the theory of how they are, or should be, applied in organizations. That said, the leaders sometimes seemed unsure of how to get these key drivers aligned and supporting their objectives. They also seemed to be searching for more innovative ways to apply these instruments.

Bernard Fournier of Rank Xerox explained the dilemma:

'We have a whole language about measures which has been built up during the last 20 years and everyone is familiar with the jargon. Sometimes, this reinforces our internal orientation, not our customer responsiveness. Too many measures become permanent and that is the last thing we need. What we actually need are the right measures and frequently it is very difficult to determine what they are.'

Denis Tunnicliffe of London Underground added another perspective:

'I am convinced we measure irrelevant things because they are easy to measure, and don't measure many critical things because they are intangible or difficult to measure. For instance, we should measure *unpleasantness* but we can't; we don't know how. It's not the sum of the parts. This doesn't mean its not an important point of every manager's job.'

David Sainsbury told me a story of how productivity measures can go awry:

'Operations set targets for items processed per person hour at the checkout counter. We received a customer complaint letter which described an unfriendly checkout girl with her head down, firing the items one after another over the electronic scanner. She was moving so fast, the customer was worried her arm might come out of the socket. During all this, the customer looked behind her – there were no other customers in line. "Why are you working so fast?" asked the customer. "I have to keep up my items per hour," replied the checkout girl.'

'First, the clock; second, the customer', said David, sighing. 'It is hard to get these things right and then aligned.'

The same themes emerged when we discussed changes in compensation, the implementation of new systems and process re-engineering. The leaders recognized that the origin and real purpose of many measures and standards was control rather than change, and, there was uncertainty regarding how to measure, and indeed what to measure, in a changing environment. Not only is it hard to define the technical factors that affect the change process, but the application of these factors differs significantly depending on whether the objective is control or adaptive change. Furthermore, change in one area can create unforeseen changes in other parts of the organization. It is like a drug that cures one disorder but creates unexpected side effects elsewhere in the body.

Most of the leaders I interviewed had lost confidence in the ability of their experts to align the various strategic and short-term financial objectives, customer responsiveness, business process objectives, programme implementation goals, productivity gains, and so forth. At the same time, they recognized that these factors underpin the business and cannot be ignored.

Even seemingly technical problems require an adaptive change mentality if they are to be resolved.

I have drawn two conclusions about the way to approach the problem. The first conclusion is that the customer must be the discriminating factor in decision making for the whole organization as well as of the leader. Too many organizations start with their strategy and objectives and build their management system, organizational structure, and business processes in relation to internal standards. In addition, multiple initiatives trying to achieve competing objectives add more complexity. Alignment under these conditions is extremely difficult. Once the customer becomes the discriminating factor in decision-making, the opportunity exists to align standards, measures, rewards, processes, and delivery and management systems.

David Sainsbury reinforced the starting point: 'The flow of information to drive decisions should come from the customer. From there, we can think about measures, rewards and processes.'

My second conclusion concerns the definition of problems. Too often, executives seek to address complex problems with administrative or infrastructure solutions. Usually this doesn't work.

Problems need to be described in different dimensions: strategic/intellectual context, behavioural considerations, the learning and competence required to address the issues, as well as the administrative agenda. Think of a problem in your organization and mark from low to high the energy focused on each dimension of the problem on each factor. As a mapping device, use the centre point as low and the outer points as high.

This is a more appropriate approach to relating administrative issues to the strategic and adaptive problems in the world of rapidly changing customer demands for responsiveness.

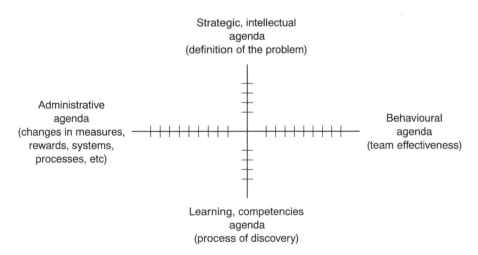

Fig. 2 Administrative solutions in a wider context

Source: Dr. Jim Scholes, Leadership and Strategic Change Ltd, London

117

Strategic principles

Leadership is an experiment. Those who experiment walk the razor edge of challenging people too fast, challenging people too slowly, or allowing operating imperatives to outweigh the importance of people in getting things done. The difficult work of leadership is putting people to work on problems that have no easy answers or ready solutions. To lead the process of adaptive change successfully, consider these six basic principles:

1. *Rise above the playing field.* Recognize the difference between the activities and interactions needed to solve routine, technical problems while maintaining a perspective on the patterns of resistance and adaptive work required to achieve objectives. Find a balcony above the field of play.
2. *Identify the adaptive challenge.* Diagnose the situation in light of the values at stake; differentiate between technical and adaptive problems – unbundle the problem you are trying to solve.
3. *Maintain disequilibrium.* Raise the intensity for change to a level which causes distress. Maintain the intensity at a level which neither overwhelms the people nor restores order. People who are overwhelmed can't do their work; restoring order results in complacency.
4. *Focus attention and close off escapes.* Identify and direct attention to the real issues, counteract work avoidance mechanisms like denial, scapegoating, externalizing the enemy, pretending the problem is technical or personal attacks by one executive on another.
5. *Give the work back to the people.* Identify the relevant teams, develop their capacity to take responsibility, and expect them to become part of a solution that requires collective action. Don't accept polarized perspectives, opinions and personal agendas which put the work back to you.
6. *Find partners and protect mavericks.* You will need confidants to help you keep perspective and allies to collaborate with you in the difficult adaptive work across functions or business. Protect those who raise hard questions and generate distress by pointing to the internal contradictions within the organization. Often these are the people who are able to provoke rethinking of the difficult issues.

The work of the leader – *making it happen*

The leaders who participated in the research clearly distinguished between leadership and authority in the exercise of their roles. In addition, the focus of their work was on adaptive change rather than on providing solutions. They were intent on providing a clear sense of purpose and creating the conditions under which people could find meaning in their work. They emphasized setting the context and articulating the problem to be solved, rather than responding to people's demand for answers. Curiosity and learning were seen as essential in adaptive problem solving. They understood that people need to learn their way to the solutions of problems which are not clearly defined and often cross multiple levels and functions of the business. They saw this as central to the shift from a command-and-control culture to one in which people throughout the organization were 'doing their work' to ensure customer responsiveness was achieved.

Donald L Laurie is managing director of the consulting firm, Laurie International, dividing his time between Boston and London. He teaches leadership at the Senior Executive Programme at London Business School and is the author of *Leadershift*.

Further Reading

Laurie, DL, *Leadershift*, Nicholas Brealey Publishing, London, 1995.
Heifetz, RA, *Leadership Without Easy Answers*, Harvard University Press, Cambridge, MA, 1994.
Gardner, JW, *On Leadership*, The Free Press, New York, 1990.
Pascale, RT, *Managing on the Edge*, Simon & Schuster, New York, 1990.

References

1 Many of the leadership concepts in this article have been derived from Ronald A Heifetz's *Leadership Without Easy Answers* (1994). Heifetz and Laurie have collaborated on consulting, teaching and writing articles on leadership for 10 years. The examples cited are from the author's on-going 'Work of the Leader' research which includes interviews with some of the world's leading executives.

2 Hammer, M, and Champy, J, *Re-engineering the Corporation*, Nicholas Brealey Publishing, London, 1993.

BRITISH PETROLEUM

Peter Phillips

British Petroleum (BP) is recreating itself as a radically different organiza-tion. In 1990 the company began a fundamental change of its culture, strategy and organization to position itself to face future challenges. As a result, the BP group now has three operating businesses and a small corporate centre (less than 200 staff). Decision making is pushed down to the lowest appropriate level. In general the company focuses on its core activities with the non-core being outsourced or bought in. There is a move towards sharing ser-vices between businesses and between regions.

For employees the changes have obviously been dramatic, BP was tradition-ally a cradle-to-grave organization. Downsizing and delayering, together with the constant process of change, have had a major impact on morale. Individuals have had to learn to adjust to new ways of working and develop new understandings of career and development. In effect there is a new employment partnership between BP and its employees.

Even though BP has emerged in good financial shape, more change is seen as inevitable and the pressure to reach new and higher levels of performance is intense.

Clearly the impact on leaders in the company has been dramatic. They are pivotal in the change process but have been no less affected by the changes in BP than other staff. In addition their roles have fundamentally changed. Prior to 1990 BP managers' roles were relatively clearly defined. There were rules and procedures covering most things, a vast guide to personnel policies, and a plethora of committees. Authorities were clearly delineated and controlled.

In an organization where all recruits were highly qualified, managers were selected on technical or professional excellence. Managers tended to solve the difficult problems and direct, check and control the work of their staff. Information was shared with those who needed to know and no further. Upward management – managing your boss – was a key skill, admitting weak-ness was frowned upon, the size of your empire was an indication of success, other groups were a source of competition.

These side effects of its long-established approach were offset by the fact that the company took care of its staff. There was a a sense of being in an enti-tlement culture providing careers and jobs for life. With the onset of the major organizational and structural changes, the role of the company's managers became radically different. In the new cost conscious organization the compet-itive advantage was to come through the people. The leaders had to recognize and learn new skills to operate in the new world and build empowered teams to deliver the new agenda. A new set of 'OPEN' (Open Thinking, Personal Impact, Empowerment and Networking) behaviours was identified as essential for all employees in the new culture.

During 1990 and 1991, although the company as a whole arranged programmes to start and energize the change process, each leader had to help their team come to terms with and operate effectively in the new culture.

The primary focus at this stage in the organization was on achieving the radical new culture. The company's performance began to deteriorate – due principally to the decline in oil price, economic recession and a high level of debt. Financial results were poor and major changes were made (including the then chairman resigning). These changes inevitably were focused on restoring the financial fortunes of the company. Costs needed to be cut, staff numbers were reduced in line with new priorities; a performance culture had to be quickly established to drive forward a leaner organization.

The impact on morale was serious as the company's declining fortunes were debated in the media. Leaders faced the challenge of achieving tough performance targets while rebuilding morale in an atmosphere of downsizing, outsourcing and cost cutting. In the performance culture the principles of the original culture change had been reaffirmed, but how these two cultures would gel had not entirely been explained. This tension needed to be managed by the company and its leaders.

The new balance of leadership

Leaders in the new organization must balance a number of tensions – such as between people and performance; the short and long-term; sustaining current performance and growing for the future. While cost-cutting skills are important, leaders need also to be able to spot and take new business opportunities. While keeping their eyes on the performance indicators, leaders have to encourage creativity, risk taking and challenge; skills for the future must be developed while delivering this year's targets. Performance has to be maintained and morale rebuilt and new understandings of the employment relationship established – living under the constant threat of more change.

To be successful BP has to be globally effective: its leaders have to be able to operate effectively in different cultures, to manage and relish cultural diversity. They have to be able to obtain both the benefits of localization and those from being part of a major corporation. They need to be able to work effectively in non-BP or part-BP cultures, such as alliance and joint ventures.

Leaders have to be flexible and adaptable to translate group strategy into different local environments, build the relationships, sell the message and build and sustain performance. Strong technical and professional skills are no longer sufficient. The ability to understand and influence people inside and outside the company is critical. In such an environment, an ability to develop and maintain strong personal networks becomes essential and in international assignments tends to require longer assignments than has traditionally been the case.

On international assignments there is comparatively little support and relatively few dictates from the business centres. The leaders have considerable independence within light frameworks to deliver the performance target, but have to be aware that they, in their local environment, represent BP. Often the senior leaders in countries are representing more than one business – yet, frequently while carrying this more general responsibility they are directly accountable for one particular business. This requires a knowledge and understanding of the strategy and goals of each business and a range of contacts not easily developed when development tends to be in one of the major businesses rather than through a more general approach.

For the most senior leaders of the group their role has also changed, though clearly the need to set the strategic direction and vision for the business is still key. They need to be able to inspire others and model the desired culture. The ability to lead change becomes critical, and organizational development skills – the ability to create the organization to deliver the agenda – are essential. They have to become coaches to their own staff to provide the appropriate level of support and challenge both to sustain current performance and to grow for the future. They have to ensure that the whole organization is motivated and focused to reach its goals.

How leaders develop ʹ

Now, there is a premium on effective and relevant leadership development to help those who need to do so to learn new skills and prepare for the future. In the old organization there was a miasma of development committees, a paternalistic approach to staff development and an expectation of progress. The principal tool of development was job movement, usually anticipated every one to two years.

BP has long had a fast-track scheme regarded by many as a model to benchmark against. The process identified high-fliers early in their careers – often in their late twenties – and ensured focused development through key assignments towards senior positions. This process was essential, partly to ensure a pool of high calibre successors for the group, also to ensure that, given the hierarchical structure of the group, people progressed fast enough. It also reflected the norm of promoting from within and reinforced the group culture.

The changes in the group since 1990 have dramatically altered this approach to development. The flatter smaller organization clearly had a major impact on opportunities, and business demands now call for longer periods in jobs. Responsibility for development shifted primarily to the individual, albeit in a partnership with the line manager. Personal development plans prepared by the individual and supported by the line are a key part of the performance culture.

A major contribution to the development of senior leaders in BP has been the Leadership Competency Model. This model which describes the key leadership behaviours required by tomorrow's leaders now underpins all group leadership development activities. These competencies were developed with and owned by the businesses. The model provides the linking thread in BP's leadership development framework, which openly lays out the process for developing leaders at all levels. Rather than seeking to identify high-fliers early and predict and accelerate their development to their ultimate potential, the framework breaks the leadership pool into broad bands and outlines the key development processes and experiences in each pool. Attention is focused on development within the band and acquiring the qualities required for the next level – it is accepted that individuals will move through the band at their own pace, some of course will not move into the next. It is generally accepted that for most individuals development will occur primarily within one business. Movement into the group sphere (or fast-track scheme) occurs when individuals have established their technical base, demonstrated strong leadership and commercial skills and have a track record of delivering performance.

Development processes have been opened up to enable individuals to form a clear development plan (and career plan). The ground rules of the general employment relationship and personal development are being clarified so that both sides understand the requirements and expectations.

The competency model is being used to profile the strengths and weaknesses of the senior leaders of the group through 360 degree feedback and assessment processes. These enable the individual and line manager with other appraisal processes, to focus on the short and long-term development needs which are critical for both personal and organizational growth.

The model also informs and interacts with the succession planning process by making individual and job matching a more objective process. It also enables the company to focus on key roles such as associate presidents (the lead individuals in each country) and to identify particular skill requirements, develop succession plans and specific training programmes etc.

Within the leadership development framework the group attempts to align all development processes so that they are part of the same jigsaw and closely associated with company performance. Given that individuals expect to spend longer in jobs, development now has to involve a much broader range of processes. Individuals have to find ways, with line support, to grow in their existing jobs and although training (internally or externally) has a role to play, other activities such as projects, short-term job swaps, external activities, coaching and computer-based and distance learning need also to be considered.

Within the parameters of the leadership development framework and the competency model, individuality, flexibility and scope for mavericks must be retained. The purpose of the development is to identify and develop the leaders who will deliver superior performance today and in the future. The aim is to let talent develop and flourish, not to clone leaders or apply a cultural straitjacket. The models must work globally and apply to all leaders irrespective of nationality, sex, etc. The organization needs to constantly review its models and processes in the light of strategic performance and environmental changes. This is vital for organizational renewal.

It is also accepted that competencies in themselves are not the complete picture. There are other factors involved. Personal attributes, such as moral integrity, sense of mission and will to win, are vital to really outstanding leadership. These must be monitored and developed in leaders. Accepting that these individual characteristics are important, it is essential that all managers demonstrate enthusiasm, commitment and curiosity.

Monitoring, measurement and reward are key parts of the process. They are essential to ensuring that the individual and the organization are developing in tandem. The vital role of the leader in shaping performance and coaching becomes fundamental to the organization's success.

The leader's role has changed and become more complex and, arguably, even more critical to the organization's success. They must:

- ensure that high performance levels are achieved and sustained;
- handle complexity and ambiguity; enjoy leading the change process;
- ensure that the organization, and its processes, are constantly developed to deliver the strategy and performance;
- ensure that the people within the company are motivated, developed and rewarded to produce outstanding results.

These are highly demanding tasks and skills. Developing leaders with the capacity to learn, adapt, coach, support and inspire others is a critical challenge for major companies. Meeting the challenge requires commitment, investment and creativity.

Peter Phillips is manager of Leadership Programmes at BP.

Strategic Management

'The strategist's method is very simply to challenge the prevailing assumptions with a single question: Why? and to put the same question relentlessly to those responsible for the current way of doing things until they are sick of it.'   *Kenichi Ohmae*[1]

'Strategic management is a comprehensive procedure which starts with a strategic diagnosis and guides a firm through a series of additional steps which culminate in new products, markets and technologies, as well as new capabilities.'

Igor Ansoff[2]

'Strategy is not the consequence of planning but the opposite: its starting point.'   *Henry Mintzberg*[3]

---

[1] Ohmae, K, *The Mind of the Strategist*, McGraw Hill, New York, 1982.
[2] Ansoff, HI, 'A contingent paradigm for success of complex organisations', in *Milestones in Management Volume 5*, Schaffer Poeschel, Switzerland, 1994.
[3] Mintzberg, H, *The Rise and Fall of Strategic Planning*, Prentice Hall, Hemel Hempstead, 1994.

OVERVIEW

Costas Markides

Every company needs a strategy – either explicit or implicit. Yet, there is surprisingly little agreement as to what strategy *really* is. Consider, for example, how two of the most famous strategy academics define strategy: Michael Porter defines it as the positioning of the company relative to its industry environment; while Henry Mintzberg defines strategy as the embodiment of a company's visions.

Confusion as to the true nature of strategy is not restricted to academics: senior executives often ask what the differences are between vision, mission, strategic intent, objectives, goals, strategy and tactics. Given this, it is little wonder that a recent editorial in the *Economist* concluded that 'nobody really knows what strategy is'.

This confusion is made worse by the frequent birth (and equally frequent death) of new ideas and concepts about strategy. Concepts such as core competencies, strategic intent, learning organizations, systems thinking, etc, emerge as the popular business fad of the day, only to disappear into anonymity before the year is out. Equally worrying is the following phenomenon observed in numerous companies: formal strategic planning is often taken to be the actual strategy, while the analytical tools developed by academics and consultants to help managers *process information* are frequently also confused as the strategy itself.

Finally, there is general confusion as to the process one goes through to develop strategy. Do you start with an industry analysis and then design the organization to fit its environment? Or do you start with an analysis of the corporation's core competencies and try and leverage those in the environment?

As a result of this confusion, there is a growing disillusionment with strategy. Many managers now regard 'strategizing' as an occupational hazard – a distraction from the real business. In many companies, strategic planning has become just one more annual ritual. Once the cycle is complete and the planning folders safely on the top shelf, managers get on with managing.

Strategy processes are supposed to help managers look into the future. But the 'forecasts' that today's strategic plans contain are often little more than straight-line extrapolations of the past. Even when a rigorous market analysis underpins the plan, the result can disappoint: a plan that is indistinguishable from one produced by competitors using the same tool kit on similar market data. From this common starting point, profitless 'me-too' strategies can easily emerge.

The confusion surrounding strategy manifests itself in a variety of ways. But, in reality, the confusion is unfortunate – and unjustified. Strategy is a very simple thing – at is simplest it is five or six creative ideas that tell us how our

126

company is to fight the competitive battle in its industry. It is not a plan; it is not a hundred-page report; it is not a budget; and it is not a goal. It is just five or six creative ideas. If your company cannot put down its strategy on one sheet of paper then it does not have a strategy.

The question then becomes: how can you develop these five or six creative ideas? Nearly all companies go through the normal 'strategy cycle'. They collect information, analyze it, develop ideas, evaluate them, select a few and implement them. The real added value in this exercise lies in the development of ideas. Yet, only a few companies are truly creative in their thinking and innovative in their implementation to actually come up with ideas that make a difference – ideas that actively break the rules of the game in the industry.

Developing a strategy: two fundamental principles

Consider the following *real* experience of a *real* company. Let's call it company X. Back in 1976, company X started producing a brand new product in a new industry. It cost about £200 pounds to produce this product. The following year, through learning and aggressive elimination of costs it was able to produce the same product for £150. Aggressive cost cutting continued for the next few years so that by 1985 this company was able to produce the same product for about £16.

This seems an impressive feat. Such cost-cutting achievements appear the stuff of commercial dreams. Yet, in 1984 this company nearly went bankrupt. It did so for a very simple reason: while it was cutting costs from £200 to £16 per product, its competitor was cutting costs from £200 to £10 per product. As a result, the competitor was able to underprice company X and nearly drove it out of the market.

This simple example highlights two fundamental principles that should guide the thinking of any manager:

1. the goal of good management is *not* to make the company a good company. The world is full of good companies which go bankrupt every day. Rather, the goal of good management is to make the company a *better* company; and when we say better, we mean *better relative to the competition.*

This is a simple principle, but one consistently misunderstood. Open any annual report of any company. The first two pages are usually devoted to a letter by the chairman to the shareholders. Almost always, the letter starts out like this: 'Dear shareholder: I am happy to tell you that 199x has been another good year for our company. Revenues went up by 15 per cent and profits increased by 10 per cent...' This begs a simple question: sales and profits may have increased, but relative to what? The answer is that the increase is relative to past performance rather than to the performance of the company's competitors.

A company will make profits only if it enjoys a competitive advantage relative to competitors. But a competitive advantage is nothing more than doing something better than the competitors. The moment the competitors start doing the same thing, a company loses its competitive advantage. Hence, for example, suppose you are the only company in your industry to have adopted Total Quality Management (TQM). That ought to give you competitive advantage that would allow you to make profits. However, the moment your competitors also adopt TQM you have lost your advantage. This does not mean that you have to throw away TQM: you need it just to stay on par with the competition. But to stay ahead of the game you need to develop another competitive advantage – you have to find another area where you are better than the competition.

2. the second guiding principle of good management is that there is no such thing as a sustainable competitive advantage. No advantage lasts for ever. The moment you 'discover' something new that gives you competitive advantage, thousands of other companies will try to imitate it or improve on it.

This has a crucial implication: the *only* way to stay ahead of the game is to *continuously* come up with new ideas. The essence of management is continuous strategic innovation. A company that wants to survive in the future needs to become a moving target.

The only source of competitive advantage is *strategic innovation*: finding new ways of competing in an industry; of breaking the rules of the game in that industry. This does not mean that a company should aim for grand ideas. As the chief executive of SAS, Jan Carlzon once said: 'We did not seek to be 100 per cent better at anything. We seek to be one per cent better at 100 things.' Remember: '100 one per cent improvements are better than a single 100 per cent improvement.'

Once these fundamental principles are internalized by the management of a company, the task remains of how to move the organization forward.

Developing a strategy: first things first

It is impossible for anybody to develop a meaningful strategy unless it is perfectly clear what the strategy is trying to achieve. In other words, a company cannot develop its strategy before it formulates its objective. As shown in Fig. 1, the objective tells you the *what* or the *where*. That is, it answers the questions: 'What does this company aspire to become?' or 'Where does this company want to be in 10-15 years' time?' It is only after these questions are explicitly answered that a company can ask the *how*, that is: 'How am I going to achieve this objective?' The *how* is the strategy.

The *what* or the *where* is the company's goal. This goal has come to be called a variety of names – such as vision, mission, strategic intent, objective, long-term goal, etc. Although there are slight differences between these terms, none of the variations in definition are significant enough to justify the tremendous confusion which they often create in people's minds. For all practical purposes they all mean the same thing: a company's objective.

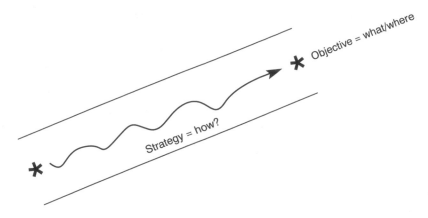

Fig. 1 The 'what' or 'where' of company strategy

Every company needs an objective – it gives its people direction and focus. A recent letter in *Business Week* highlights the importance of the objective:

'President Clinton's effectiveness is waning simply because he has failed to articulate a vision for the country. A flurry of initiatives (health-care reform, Bosnia, trade, Haiti, North Korea, welfare reform, and so on) is no substitute for a compelling conception of where this country should be going.'

Consider also the following lament from a senior NATO planner (Field Marshal Sir Richard Vincent) regarding Western policy in Bosnia:

'The first principle of war is: "For God's sake decide what you are trying to achieve before you go out." Would you please tell us what you want us to achieve? What *is* the objective?'

The importance of having an objective for the organization has been widely recognized. Most companies have taken the trouble to develop and communicate to their people a mission statement or a long-term goal. In fact, companies display amazing creativity in how they choose to communicate their goal: some companies put the goal on plastic cards which they then distribute to all their employees; other companies frame their mission statement and put it on every office wall; a few have actually written their goals on watches which they then present as gifts to their employees.

Most companies do have a mission statement. About 99.9 per cent are useless.

Why are practically all mission statements not even worth the paper – or the watches – they are written on? Some people have argued that what makes mission statements useless is the fact that most of them tend to state the obvious; or are too generic and thus fail to give guidance in making decisions and trade-offs; or are too unrealistic; or not shared by the employees.

Others argue that developing a 'good' mission is a very difficult thing because a good mission has to find the right balance on many parameters. Thus, for a mission to be 'good' it needs to be specific enough but not too restricting; it needs to be flexible and adaptable but should not be changed every year; it needs to be inspirational but not unrealistic; it needs to be measurable but not constraining; it must be easy to understand but not simplistic; it needs to be based on real customer needs but mindful of the other stakeholders' needs as well; and it needs to set a time target but not compromise quality as a result. Needless to say, achieving the right balance on all these parameters is extremely difficult.

Experience suggests that the most powerful missions are the ones that have an emotional content – that is, the ones that have captured the imagination of the people. The question then becomes: 'How can I make my mission inspirational to my people?' Undoubtedly, there are a variety of ways to make the mission inspirational; but for your people to actually buy your mission, what you need to do above anything else is to sell it to them. In other words, nobody will buy anything from you unless you first try to sell it to them.

This leads to the next key question: 'How do I sell the mission to my people?' In thinking about this question, you should also consider how you actually sell a product or service to your customer. The actual content of the product is obviously important, but so is the marketing and selling effort. Thus, mission statements that set ambitious or stretching goals for your people; or that clearly identify the enemy; or are altruistic and/or strong on values and morals; or are developed by involving people, will be easier to sell. However, this does not mean that you should not actively try to sell them. No mission statement, no matter how many grand words it contains, will inspire people at face value. The value-added lies in the effort and energy you spend selling it to your people.

The major reason most mission statements are useless is that companies do not spend the time and energy selling these missions to their people. Most companies spend all their efforts and creativity on developing regal statements and then communicating them to their employees through a variety of unique ways. But communication is not enough. Employees need to not only know the mission, they also need to understand *why* their company is pursuing a particular mission, and also what they themselves are going to get out of it. No one in business would ever dream of selling a product to a customer without first persuading the customer that he or she stands to benefit by buying the product. The same principle applies to mission statements.

Developing a strategy: breaking the rules

Once an ambitious objective has been formulated and 'sold' to the rest of the organization, you can then get down to developing the *how* element – how to achieve this objective, your strategy. As argued above, this should ideally be five or six creative ideas on how to compete in your business by breaking the rules.

There is no one best way to do this but, at the very least, strategy formulation needs to take into account the industry in which your company is competing. No company operates in a vacuum; it operates within a certain industry environment. And what a company needs to do strategically depends on the industry it is operating in. Hence, understanding your industry is the first task of strategy formulation.

You can proceed to understand your industry in any way you feel comfortable. One of the tools that has proved useful in helping people understand their industry is the five-forces framework developed by Professor Michael Porter of Harvard Business School. This framework basically suggests that there are five competitive forces in any industry (customers, suppliers, substitutes, rivals and potential new entrants) that affect the profitability of any company in that industry. The logic behind this is the following:

- If your *customers* have bargaining power over you (for whatever reason), they will exercise that power and squeeze your profit margins; hence your profitability will suffer.
- If your *suppliers* have bargaining power over you (for whatever reason), they will exercise that power and sell you their products expensively; hence your profitability will suffer.
- If there are *substitutes* to your product or service, they will place a limit to the price you can charge and will therefore limit your profits.
- If there is intense *rivalry* (ie competition) in your industry, it will force you to engage in price, R&D and advertising wars, all of which have an adverse effect on profits.
- Finally, if *new entrants* move into your industry, they bring with them resources and the desire to steal market share from you. As a result, rivalry increases and profits go down.

Given the logic of these five forces, a strategist needs to decide what to do about them. Traditionally, most people assumed that the way to proceed was to assume these five industry forces as given and then try and position their firm towards these forces. This is fundamentally wrong and this is probably the most serious misconception about strategy that has developed in the 15 years since the five forces framework was developed.

Instead, what the strategist ought to do is to creatively break the established rules of the game by actively changing these five forces in the company's favour. In other words, the essence of strategy formulation is coming up with creative ideas in response to the following five questions:

- How can I reduce the bargaining power of my customers?
- How can I reduce the bargaining power of my suppliers?
- How can I reduce substitutes to my product or service?
- How can I limit rivalry in my industry?
- How can I prevent new entrants from coming into my industry?

Needless to say, there are no right answers to these questions. It all boils down to creativity and open-mindedness. This is also the area where outsiders to the company or external benchmarking could help in the generation of new ideas.

The next step: company analysis

Once a list of ideas has been generated, each one of these ideas will have to be evaluated – just because you thought of idea X, it does not mean that you should implement it as well. For example, you need to consider whether you have the resources, skills, technology, culture, people, time, etc, to implement an idea. To do a proper evaluation of the ideas generated you need also to carry out an analysis of your company. Developing a list of your company's strengths and weaknesses will allow you to evaluate ideas in a timely and rational manner. This, in turn, will allow you to decide which ideas to keep and which ideas to throw out. It will also enable you to think of what kind of resources and capabilities you will have to create or build up over the next few years so as to implement your ideas. In deciding which resources and capabilities to build, you have to be guided by the thought that the resources which are most valuable (ie give you long-term competitive advantage) are the ones that are rare and cannot easily be imitated or substituted by competitors.

Analysing your company's weaknesses and strengths (or core competencies) has another benefit – it allows you to think proactively about how to leverage your core competencies. By asking the question: 'What are my core competencies and how can I leverage them?' you will (hopefully) think of even more ideas of what you can do in your industry to gain competitive advantage.

As argued so far, a company needs to start out its strategy formulation process by doing an industry analysis which is then followed by the company analysis. One of the biggest academic debates of the day is whether this is the best way actually to formulate strategy. Many academics, and especially those who belong to the 'resource-based' view of the firm, would argue that it is better to start with the company analysis, identify your core competencies and then decide how to leverage these capabilities in your industry. This debate could easily be resolved by arguing that the actual order of doing things is not that important – as long as both the industry and company analyzes are actually carried out (preferably with an open mind). Personally, I prefer to start with the industry analysis because starting with the company analysis runs the danger of focusing the mind internally and thus constraining creativity.

Implementing strategy

The collection of ideas that has survived the evaluation process is nothing more than your strategy. All that remains to be done is actually implementing these ideas.

Implementation is where most strategies fail. At a theoretical level, a strategist needs to ask two questions in thinking about implementation:

● First, given the broad strategy formulated above, what kind of functional policies does the company need to reinforce this strategy? By *functional* policies we mean marketing, R&D, manufacturing, HR, accounting, etc.

- Second, given the strategy formulated above, what kind of culture, structure, people and incentives, do we now need to implement this strategy successfully?

The essence of asking these questions is to first of all identify the *fits* that we have to create internally to support our chosen strategy; and second, to compare what we think we will need with what we actually have now, so as to determine what needs changing and how.

The final step in implementation is actually to develop a detailed action plan of how we will proceed. Hence, it is not enough to say that to implement our strategy we need to change our culture from X to Y. *How* specifically are you going to achieve that? Over what time frame? Who is going to resist you? How are you going to overcome resistance? These are only a few of the questions that need to be asked in preparing a detailed action plan.

Again, a sizeable academic controversy has arisen over implementation. We argued above that first you develop a strategy and then think what new culture, structure, people and incentives you will need to implement it. Many people argue that this is not practical – many companies have a given culture or a given structure which are very difficult to change to accommodate a new strategy. Hence, they suggest that a company take its culture and structure as given (ie as constraints) and proceed to formulate a strategy in the face of these constant constraints.

Such arguments are reactive. The constraining effects of culture, people, etc, should already have been integrated during the evaluation of ideas. Remember that one of the questions asked at that stage was: 'Do I have the right resources, culture, people, etc, to carry out this idea?' If that was done in an honest way then the implementation phase should proceed to change – what needs to be changed for the chosen strategy to have any chance of success?

Changing the strategy: a next to impossible task

One of the most difficult issues in strategic management is knowing when to change a company's strategic direction. Assume, for example, that your company goes through the experience depicted in Fig. 2: for about 10 years your profits are on the rise but then suddenly they take a plunge and before you know it, the company is facing a financial crisis. Given this scenario, *when* in this time period are you most likely to undertake serious restructuring (ie strategic change)?

Typically, the majority of managers would probably begin *thinking* about restructuring sometime around point B in Fig. 2 and then start *doing* something about it after things get even worse – right in the middle of the crisis. This is only natural: why change when everything seems to be going so well and the company is enjoying record profits? 'The moment the rate of change inside the organization is lower than the rate of change outside, the organization is in deep trouble,' observes GE's Jack Welch. But surely that does not mean restructuring a perfectly healthy company?

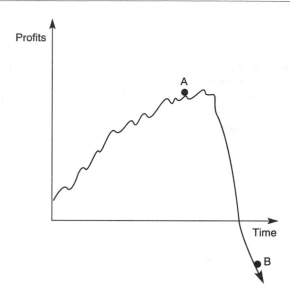

Fig. 2 A steep profit plunge. When to restructure?

Most strategic changes are indeed undertaken when a company is facing financial difficulties – and that is the worst possible time to change. When a company is facing problems, the last thing on management's mind is long-term strategy; instead, they are pre-occupied with putting out the day-to-day fires and staying alive. However, if restructuring is not part of a company's long-term strategy, it is bound to fail. Predictably enough, the majority of restructurings that are undertaken when a company is facing a crisis, fail.

In the example given above, the best time for the company to restructure is at point A, right when it is enjoying record profits. The crucial question, then, becomes: 'How could I possibly know three or four years *before* a crisis occurs that I need to change, and that unless I change now, I will face a crisis in four years' time?' Surely no one can predict the future that well.

To be in a position to 'predict' the future and discover that you need to change three or four years before the crisis, today's managers need to switch their attention away from the financial health of their companies and start measuring the *strategic health* of their organizations. Measuring the financial health of a company is easy: all you need to examine is your profitability, market share and other financial indicators. Unfortunately, these financial numbers tend to be misleading indicators of a company's future health; and they are misleading because they all measure the *past*. There are countless examples of companies which seemed to be in good financial health, only to discover three or four years later they are bankrupt.

A company needs to go beyond the financial figures to examine its strategic health. The strategic health of a company tells you whether your company has a bright future ahead of it even if it is currently making losses. But how can you measure the strategic health of your company? Several readily-available indicators can be used to do this. Examples include: customer satisfaction; employee morale; your financial health *relative* to your competitors'; your strategy relative to industry trends; feedback from distributors, etc. For example, even if you are currently making profits, if these profits are consistently low relative to your competitors', that should give you a hint that something may be wrong. Similarly, if you discover that your customers are not totally satisfied with your product or services, you may have them as customers today (hence you are making profits) but in a few years' time, the chances are you will lose them as customers (hence the crisis).

The best time to change the strategic direction of the organization is well before the crisis arrives; and the best way to know if a crisis is bound to arrive in three to four years is to continuously monitor your strategic health, not your financial health.

A final reminder

Every organization tries to become more competitive so as to outperform its competitors. Very few succeed. What usually differentiates the 'winners' from the 'losers' is nothing more than attitude. The winning companies have internalized the fact that the search for competitiveness is a never-ending search for new ideas and new capabilities. *Sustainable* competitive advantage does *not* exist; rather, competitiveness appears to require a continuous process of innovation, improvement and resolution (or balancing) of dilemmas and trade-offs. Hence, in the race for competitiveness it is not correct to talk about winners – it is better to talk about 'leaders' rather than 'winners' because today's front runner may stumble at the next hurdle. Only companies that internalize this fact and continuously strive for innovation will survive in the long term.

Costas Markides is Associate Professor of Strategic and International Management and Director of the Accelerated Development Programme (ADP) at London Business School. A native of Cyprus, he studied economics at Boston University and has an MBA and DBA from Harvard Business School. He is the author of many articles which have appeared in journals such as the *Harvard Business Review, Strategic Management Journal*, and *Long Range Planning*. He is also the author of *Diversification, Refocusing and Economic Performance* (1995).

Further Reading

Ansoff, HI, *Corporate Strategy*, McGraw Hill, New York, 1965.
Ansoff, HI, *Implanting Strategic Management*, Prentice Hall, New Jersey, 1984 (2nd edn, 1990).
Markides, C, *Diversification, Refocusing and Economic Performance*, MIT Press, Cambridge, Mass, 1995.
Mintzberg, H, *The Rise and Fall of Strategic Planning*, Prentice Hall, Hemel Hempstead, 1994.
Moore, JI, *Writers on Strategy and Strategic Management*, Penguin, London, 1992.
Ohmae, K, *The Mind of the Strategist*, McGraw Hill, New York, 1982.

Igor Ansoff

Born 1918; educator

In 1965 Igor Ansoff's *Corporate Strategy* was published. 'This book represented a kind of crescendo in the development of strategic planning theory, offering a degree of elaboration seldom attempted since,' Henry Mintzberg later observed.[1]

Unstintingly serious, analytical and complex, *Corporate Strategy*, had a highly significant impact on the business world. It propelled consideration of strategy into a new dimension.

'The end-product of strategic decisions is deceptively simple; a combination of products and markets is selected for the firm. This combination is arrived at by addition of new product-markets, divestment from some old ones, and expansion of the present position,' writes Ansoff. While the end-product was simple, the processes and decisions beforehand produced a labyrinth followed only by the most dedicated of managers. Ansoff's sub-title was 'An Analytical Approach to Business Policy for Growth and Expansion'. The book provided a highly complex 'cascade of decisions'. Analysis – and in particular 'gap analysis' (the gap between where you are now and where you want to be) – was the key to unlocking strategy.

The book also brought the concept of 'synergy' to a wide audience for the first time. Today, the word is over-used and much abused. In Ansoff's original creation it was simply summed up as 'the 2+2=5' effect. In his later books, Ansoff refined his definition of synergy to any 'effect which can produce a combined return on the firm's resources greater than the sum of its parts.'[2]

While *Corporate Strategy* was a notable book for its time, it produced what Ansoff himself labelled 'paralysis by analysis': repeatedly making strategic plans which remained unimplemented. He recently wrote:

'Strategic planning was a plausible invention, and received an enthusiastic reception from the business community. But subsequent experience with strategic planning led to mixed results. In a minority of firms, strategic planning restored their profitability and became an established part of the management process. However a substantial majority encountered a phenonemon, which was named "paralysis by analysis": strategic plans were made but remained unimplemented, and profits/growth continued to stagnate.'[3]

Undaunted, Ansoff looked again at his entire theory. His logic was impressively simple – either strategic planning was a bad idea, or it was a part of a broader concept which was not fully developed and needed to be enhanced in order to make strategic planning effective. Characteristically, he sought the answer in extensive research. He examined acquisitions by American companies between 1948 and 1968 and concluded that acquisitions which were based on an articulated strategy fared considerably better than those which were opportunistic decisions.

Reinforced by his conviction that strategy was a valid, if incomplete, concept, Ansoff followed up *Corporate Strategy* with *Strategic Management* (1979) and *Implanting Strategic Management* (1984). In each of which he sought a broader concept which would include strategic planning and would assure effective implementation of strategic plans. In 1972 he published the concept under the name of 'strategic management'. The concept embraces a combination of strategy planning, planning of organizational capability and effective management of resistance to change, typically caused by strategic planning.

Using the concept of strategic management, Ansoff formulated a Strategic Success Paradigm which specifies conditions which optimize a firm's profitability. This paradigm (the result of 'fifteen years of sweat, tears and smiles and occasional flashes of creativity') has five key elements:

'1. There is no universal success formula for all firms.
2. The driving variable which dictates the strategy required for success of a firm is the level of turbulence in its environment.
3. A firm's success cannot be optimized unless the aggressiveness of its strategy is aligned with the turbulence in its environment.
4. A firm's success cannot be optimized unless management capability is also aligned with the environment.
5. The key internal capability variables which jointly determine a firm's success, are: cognitive, psychological, sociological, political and anthropological.'[4]

Being aware of the spotty record of strategic planning, Ansoff (with the assistance of his graduate students) devoted the next 11 years to empirical validation of the Success Paradigm. The paradigm was tested in over 500 firms in the US, Japan, Indonesia, Algeria, Abu Dhabi, Australia and Ethiopia. The statistical results gave strong support to the paradigm. Ansoff translated the paradigm into a diagnostic instrument, called 'Strategic Readiness Diagnosis' and used it in his consulting pratice.

Education: Stevens Institute of Technology, degree in engineering and MS in maths and physics; PhD Brown University in applied mathematics; UCLA senior executive programme. *Career*: Rand Corporation; Lockheed; Carnegie-Mellon University; founding Dean School of Management, Vanderbilt University; Professor European Institute for Advanced Studies in Management, Brussels; now Distinguished Professor of Strategic Management, US International University, San Diego.

Having identified behaviours by firms which optimize their profitability, Ansoff has re-focused his research on management behaviours which cause firms to behave optimally.

STUART CRAINER

Further Reading

Corporate Strategy, McGraw Hill, New York, 1965.
Strategic Management, Macmillan, London, 1979.
Implanting Strategic Management, (2nd edn), Prentice Hall, London, 1990.

References

[1] Mintzberg, H, *The Rise and Fall of Strategic Planning*, Prentice Hall, Hemel Hempstead, 1994.
[2] Ansoff, HI, *Strategic Management*, Macmillan, London, 1979
[3] Ansoff, HI, *Milestones in Management Volume 5*, Schaffer Poeschel, Switzerland, 1994
[4] *Ibid.*

MISSION, VISION AND STRATEGY DEVELOPMENT

Andrew Campbell

MOST (Mission, Objectives, Strategy and Tactics) is an acronym used in many strategy courses. Yet, it gives managers a completely wrong impression of the task of creating strategic direction. It suggests there is a structure and order which managers can follow. First the organization should choose a mission. Then it should define medium and short-term objectives. This makes it possible to develop a strategy for achieving those objectives. Finally, tactics are short-term decisions for implementing the strategy.

In practice, the real process of strategy development and direction setting is much more messy, experimental, uncertain, iterative and driven from the bottom upwards. There are five reasons for rejecting the MOST framework. First, the competitive economic system in which companies act provides constraints that are often interpreted as objectives. Second, strategy and objectives are intertwined, not linear. Third, it is useless to develop a separation between strategy, tactics and operations – insights about creating value come as often from operating details as from broad strategic concepts. Fourth, academics and consultants differ in their views about how insights can best be developed and captured. Fifth, there are also differences in view about how best to implement strategy in an uncertain world.

Competitive economics

Many companies consider the creation of shareholder value as an important organizational objective. Others may balance this or supercede it with an objective of maximizing value to the customers. These objectives are commonly found in mission statements. Yet, they are little more than a reiteration of the rules of the economic game companies are playing. They are constraints on the freedom of action of managers rather than worthy objectives for an organization. The reason managers make so much noise about them is to signal to shareholders and customers that they intend to play by the rules and to communicate these rules to employees.

The stakeholder model (Fig. 1) is helpful in understanding the nature of the constraints imposed by a competitive economic system. The company must win and retain some loyalty from each of the active stakeholders – shareholders, customers, employees and suppliers. Without support from all four of these groups, the company cannot function – it cannot finance itself, sell its products, recruit suitable employees or purchase suitable supplies. These are active stake-holders not only because they have a commercial relationship with the company but because they are infinitely greedy: they want to get as much as possible out of the relationship. Their greed is fuelled by the existence of com-petitors. Suppliers, normally viewed as being the most passive stakeholder, are comparing the benefits of dealing with company A versus company B. If the relationship with company B is viewed as being more valuable, company B will receive more attention, better deliveries, fewer poor quality components, faster response on rush orders and so on. Employees compare their current job with alternative work near where they want to live. Customers, often viewed as the most active stakeholder, regularly compare competitors and often buy from competitors just to see what the product or service is like. Finally, shareholders compare the performance of an investment in company A with alternative opportunities in similar sectors with similar risk profiles. In other words, in our economic system competitors are always trying to woo active stakeholders away from their rivals. Company A must deliver either in monetary terms or in terms of products and services. It has to provide a stream of value to each stakeholder that is viewed to be at least as good as the stream of value offered by competitors, taking into account switching costs. The objective of creating shareholder value is no more than an economic constraint on action. If a com-pany takes actions that fail to deliver sufficient shareholder value, it will lose the loyalty of its shareholders and, as a result, will go out of business. The same is true of its relationships with the other active stakeholders.

There are other less active stakeholders – the government, the community, special interest groups, etc. These other stakeholders are distinguished from

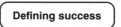

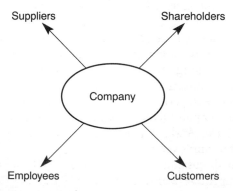

Fig. 1 The stakeholder model

the active stakeholders because they are not infinitely greedy. They have specified requirements, constraints which it is often fairly easy for companies to live with. The requirements of the other stakeholders are demanding but achievable. Consequently, it is not normal for managers to define their company's prime objective as being to pay taxes or obey the law.

The reason why managers often state company objectives in shareholder or customer terms is that it can be very difficult to provide these stakeholders with sufficient value. This is because sufficient value is defined in competitive terms. If one competitor increases the value it delivers, this raises the hurdle for all other competitors. A company can only be confident of delivering sufficient value to its stakeholders if it has competitive advantage. As a result, our competitive economic system demands that companies have as one of their driving objectives, or constraints, the search for and creation of competitive advantage. This is the link between the stakeholder model and the strategists' model. When strategists talk about competitive advantage they are saying no more than 'superior delivery to stakeholders'. To describe competitive advantage or stakeholder value as an objective that drives thinking about strategy is to misunderstand these universal constraints.

There is another and more valid reason why companies choose shareholder value or customer value as a major objective. This is an implementation reason. In certain kinds of businesses managers are better able to create a competitive advantage if they are driven by a focus on shareholder value. Instead of being an objective that guides strategy development, shareholder value in these companies is an objective that guides implementation.

Objectives, strategy, objectives

The use of shareholder value as an implementation objective rather than a direction-setting objective illustrates the second reason why the MOST framework is flawed. Some people distinguish between objectives (things that come before strategy) and targets (things that are used to motivate implementation). This can be a useful distinction once a clear strategy has been formulated. Before this point, the principle of *objectives first, followed by strategy* is misleading.

Take, for example, a typical management team using the objectives first principle. Let us assume that they understand the stakeholder model and recognize that competitive advantage is not so much an objective as a minimum requirement for long-term survival. They hold a planning meeting to develop some agreed objectives before formulating a strategy. One manager says that he would like the company to be in the FT-SE 100. Another says that she would like the company to be a dominant market leader with at least 30 per cent market share. A third says that he would like a more empowered company with better employee relationships.

Immediately the discussion turns to realism. Which of these objectives is achievable in a competitive world? Achievability depends, of course, on whether the management team can generate a strategy for reaching the objective, given the stakeholder constraints. If the group cannot think of a realistic strategy, they are likely to reject the objective as unrealistic. Which, therefore, comes first – objectives or strategy? The reality is that they are intertwined until the moment when a combination of objectives and strategy is chosen.

After lengthy debate the management team agree to go for dominant market share as the driving objective and to implement a strategy based on their proven ability to develop new products faster and more effectively than competitors. At this point, market share becomes an objective towards which the strategy is aimed, and a target, such as three new products this year, becomes an objective whose purpose is to aid the implementation of the strategy. Unless the term objective is used only for the former, and the term target only for the latter, strategy and objectives are intertwined not only in the development of strategy but also in its implementation. Rather than risk confusing managers with the concept of a linear relationship between objectives, strategy, tactics and targets, it is better to explain the interaction between them.

Strategy, tactics and operations

It is common in many texts to distinguish between strategy and operations – between policy and implementation. In fact, most of the leading authorities argue that managers at the apex should formulate policy, and managers lower down in the hierarchy should implement these policies. This distinction is one of the justifications for hierarchies.

The reality of strategy development is much different from this. The key to a good strategy is a good insight about how to create more value than competitors. What is a value creation insight? A value creation insight is an understanding about the production and delivery process or the needs of stakeholders that allows the possessor of the insight to see ways of creating value that are superior to those of competitors. So an insight is an understanding, normally about some pretty detailed issues, which is sufficiently practical to point to a new way of doing things – a superior way. The insight can be about the relationship with suppliers, about the details of the recruitment process or the needs of a particular group of employees, about a segment of customers, and about the value equation being used by shareholders. Sometimes the insight is a grand idea to completely reconfigure the company or the industry. More normally it is a discovery that some process can be operated with fewer people or that some customers require a particular additional service. The very nature of insight means that it is usually possessed by a certain line or operating manager who may not be fully aware of its significance.

This reality leads to two important conclusions about strategy, tactics and operations. First, separating strategy formulation from operations is unlikely to be a good idea. Most of the insights important to strategy formulation are likely to be in the heads of the operating managers. It is true that operating managers are often not the best strategists; but excluding them from strategy development results in the exclusion of many important insights.

142

Second, tactics and operations are not only about implementing today's strategy, they are also about discovering tomorrow's strategy. Tomorrow's insights arise out of tomorrow's operating experiences. Unless implementation is also viewed as being part of strategy development, tomorrow's strategy is likely to be short of insights.

One way to achieve this is to design experiments as part of the implementation of today's strategy that are likely to generate insights for tomorrow's strategy. The degree to which tactics and operations are confused with strategy development can then be minimized or, at least, controlled. But in an uncertain, even chaotic, world the danger is that the insights for tomorrow's strategy do not lie in the areas of experimentation defined by today's strategy. Only by viewing all implementation as an experiment from which new, more powerful insights may emerge can the strategist be comfortable that he or she is not systematically screening out the important information.

A final nail in the coffin of maintaining a distinction between strategy and tactics is the example of McDonalds versus Wimpy in the UK. At one stage the Wimpy managers spotted that McDonalds' restaurants were usually cleaner than Wimpy restaurants. It is common knowledge that cleanliness is a critical factor for success in fast food operations and, as a result, Wimpy managers were eager to raise their standards. Despite a number of experiments, management could not find a way of achieving the same day-to-day cleanliness without spending an excessive amount on cleaning. They concluded that McDonalds' advantage lay in the attitude of its staff – their willingness to use any gap in the flow of customers to mop up, tidy up and polish.

Is this strategy, tactics or operations? Clearly the McDonalds operating procedures and culture were giving it a strategic advantage; but where should the analyst draw the line between objectives, strategy and tactics, and what was the order of events? Did McDonalds' managers decide on an objective of cleanliness, develop a cleanliness strategy and then implement some cultural tactics? Did the longstanding policy of having staff clean up around them result in staff with more concern about cleanliness, who in turn created an environment cleaner than that of competitors? Either way, the objective, strategy, tactics distinction is not a useful one. What Wimpy (now Burger King) needs are some insights either in this area or in some other area that will enable it to offer the customer as good a value proposition as McDonalds.

Developing insights

The McDonalds/Wimpy story leads to the crux of the problem that faces managers seeking to develop strategies, objectives and missions. How do they develop the insights that underpin the whole edifice? Without the insights, objectives are unachievable, missions are dreams, and tactics fail. The problem is that managers, academics and consultants are all equally uncertain as to how these insights can be generated. In these circumstances there are inevitably rival camps selling different solutions. What is important to remember is that we do not know the answer. There is no proof one way or the other that any particular method is better than another. Don't be seduced by the sales pitch. If we knew the answer to this problem, we would not have so many uncompetitive companies.

Before describing some of the solutions on the market, it may be worth pondering whether the problem is solvable. The definition of an insight is that it should enable the possessor *to see ways of creating value that are superior to those of competitors*. If one of these solutions really works, all competitors will immediately start using it, and we will be back to square one, searching for a way of gaining advantage over competitors. Hence, there is no long-term solution to the problem. There are only temporary solutions: periods where a few companies have a process for generating superior insights. As the process is more widely used it is less of an advantage. Failing to use it will be a disadvantage, but using it will not solve the problem.

It is for this reason that management fads are so faddish. Companies scramble to cover the processes used by competitors. Whether it is total quality management, benchmarking, process re-engineering, strategic planning, empowerment, core competence analysis or some other concept, managers are right to experiment with any new solution, even if it only has a low probability of being more than snake oil. The penalty of being late onto a new way of generating insights is severe. At the same time, however, managers must remember that there is no long-term solution. They will always have to cover any proposed solution that appears to offer benefits. The question is only how best to do this with minimum disruption and loss of momentum. Keeping the organization fresh and ready to try the next solution may be the real challenge. The danger is that the leadership has cried wolf once too often, and the organization has no appetite left for new processes when a solution that offers real improvements comes on the market.

The current solutions to the problem of how to develop insights fall into three camps: those that focus on operating issues, those that focus on future-gazing, and those that focus on behaviour and culture.

The operating camp includes process re-engineering, time-based competition, benchmarking, quality, empowerment, and many other tools for examining the effectiveness of today's operations and searching for better ways of doing things. Undoubtedly these tools and processes produce improvements. It has to be said, however, that there are few examples of great strategies being developed out of such processes. There are plenty of examples of strategies being developed out of insights gained from solving operating problems – such as Toyota's development of the *Kanban* process, which resulted from trying to solve a space problem in its warehouses – but these examples seem more normally to come from unexpected places, rather than energetic re-engineering efforts. Nevertheless, the operating camp points to operating details as a major source of value creation insights. Strategic plans are then built on the back of operating competencies and insights.

In the future-gazing camp are processes that involve attempts to define the factors that will be critical to future success. Having defined these factors, the strategic plan involves choosing where to compete (which critical success factors to try to match), and then designing an organization with the appropriate capabilities. Competitive strategy analysis in the Michael Porter mould, developed from the work of management consultants such as McKinsey and Boston Consulting Group in the 1970s, is one way of defining the critical factors for success. Scenario analysis, a Shell tool, is another way of getting at the same outcome. More recently, Gary Hamel and CK Prahalad[1] have developed a way of thinking and a process involving many managers in many thousands of hours of analysis and debate that they believe helps generate industry 'foresight'. At a more mundane level, tools such as the technology S-curve of Richard Foster, and technology maps developed by Motorola, are ways of understanding the future. Finally, chaos theorists are beginning to have an influence. Using the discovery that chaotic systems have stable patterns to which they periodically return, the chaos theorists are arguing that companies should define critical success factors in terms of these stable patterns, and ignore the truly chaotic periods in between which defy analysis.

The behaviour and culture camp brings together two groups of proponents. The first group are the data-free planning enthusiasts. Building on theories about the creative subconscious, they believe that a clear vision is the key to successfully discovering insights. Individuals who are able to convince themselves that they will achieve something, and can imprint this achievement on their egos, engage something called the creative subconscious. This starts to work overtime to eliminate 'cognitive dissonance', a concern that is created by the present being different from the vision. At one extreme, failure to eliminate cognitive dissonance results in madness. The individual creates the vision as a reality in his mind, even though it does not exist, and lives in that reality. At the other extreme, the individual makes things happen such that the vision does come about. Ideas like Hamel and Prahalad's 'strategic intent' fall into this group, as do many of the purveyors of mission and vision thinking. These theorists are trying to operate at the level of the organization as a whole: trying to create an organizational cognitive dissonance that harnesses the organization's creative juices.

The second group focuses on organizational learning. Chris Argyris is famous for his double loop learning principles and his exposure of defensive strategies and defensive routines that are anti-learning. By exposing these defensive routines, he argues we can open ourselves to learning and, as a result, see the insights that are there to see. Many others are also working on the idea of a learning organization – a culture in which insight development is more likely. Peter Senge, for example, argues that system thinking is one of the keys to increasing learning and developing more insights.

The existence of so many different camps and groups with different theories about how insights are developed demonstrates that we do not know the answer and suggests that all theories have something to offer. Managers should beware of becoming over-attached to any one theory.

Implementing strategy

The final reason why the MOST concept should be rejected is that there are differences of opinion about how strategy should best be implemented and these differences get confused with the issue of strategy development.

Managers and academics alike agree that effective implementation is about defining what needs to be achieved, and motivating capable people to want to achieve it. But there are disagreements about both how best to define what needs to be achieved and how best to motivate people.

A simple way of capturing these disagreements is to compare the supporters of the concept of mission with the supporters of the concept of vision. These two often confused words have very different meanings. Stephen Cummings and John Davies in an article entitled 'Mission, Vision and Fusion'[2] provide a revealing description of their derivatives:

'Our word mission is a derivative of the Indo-European *(s)meit*, meaning throw or send. Interestingly, the first sense of *meit* seems to have been to throw, as cow dung at a wall, to dray for fuel, hence the word s*mite* from the meaning "spot on the wall, where the dung strikes".[3] Stemming from this is the Latin *mittere* or *missus*, meaning to let go, to cause to go, to send, throw, hurl, or cast. Hence the emergence of *mis*sion (the duty on which one is sent), and related words such as *mis*sile (a weapon thrown forward), dis-*miss* (a sending away), de*mise* (death, a sending away), e*mit* (send forth), inter*mit* (cease at times, interrupt, send apart), per*mit* (allow, send through), and pre*mise* (a foundation, proposition sent forth).[4] Extrapolating into a modern organizational context, one can see mission as the intent, spirit, or rallying cry which constitutes the organization's and its members', primary duty or way of behaving, the foundation and force which throws, sends, or casts itself into the future towards its goals and targets.

Vision has quite a different basis – the Latin *vide* meaning "to see!", the exclamation mark implying something seen other than by ordinary sight. *Vide*, is a derivative of the Indo-European *weid*, *woid* or *wid*, meaning "to see and to know", where "I have seen" is synonymous with "I know".[5] This origin connects also to wit and is the basis of ad*vise*, de*vise*, re*vise*, super*vise*, pro*vision*, and to provident, words which imply knowledge and foresight. Etymologically, vision can be seen to conceptualize something seen which is not actually present or historical, something which may be a notion of the future which can provide something to anticipate and aim towards or away from.

Mission and vision viewed historically mean quite different things. Both can inspire, both can provide one, or a group, with motivation, inspiration and a purpose. A mission empowers through a force which casts or steers the individual or group into the future in a particular direction. A vision empowers through the provision of knowledge or expectation about the future which can be aimed for, a future state which becomes more known, and more real in the present, and hence more likely to be achieved in the future, because it has been envisaged.'

They go on to explain that these two words refer to different theories of motivation:

'If it can be assumed that the value of a mission or a vision is in aiding an organization's members to work with a commonality of purpose in a unified or co-ordinated manner, then it follows that a preference for mission or vision, or vice versa, will be related to our beliefs concerning what motivates people to work in such a way. Given the basic definitions sketched in the etymological survey above, vision and mission operate with very different theories of motivation. These underlying theories can be equated to goal-setting and reinforcement theory.

In the late 1960s, Edwin Lock proposed that intentions to work towards a goal are a major source of work motivation.[6] This view has become known as *goal-setting theory*. Indeed research has shown that specific goals, particularly those that are both perceived as difficult and accepted by those to whom they apply, do increase performance. There seems little doubt that the articulation of future intentions are a potent motivating force for many, and it is in this way that a statement of corporate vision adds value.

Whereas goal-setting theory is a cognitive approach (albeit a collective one when applied to a whole organization), proposing that articulated intentions direct an individual's or an organization's action, *reinforcement theory*, is a behaviourist approach which argues that existing structures and systems condition and guide action, reinforcing behaviour seen as appropriate within a corporation's context. Reinforcement theorists, clearly at odds with goal-setting theory, see behaviour as being environmentally caused. A mission should provide just such a reinforcing structure by articulating the types of behaviour an organization sees as guiding its progress into the future. Mission should be an everyday reference point for behaviour.

Both goal-setting and reinforcement theory are ideologically opposed, but neither can be proved *better* than the other. Their co-existence simply illustrates the fact that different people can be predisposed to different approaches.

Further, Cummings and Davies suggest that vision and mission have even deeper differences:

'Mission and vision also operate on different world views. One could characterize this difference by categorising a belief in the primacy of vision over mission as parallel to a belief in existentialism (*à la* Jean-Paul Sartre) over structuralism.

Sartre's brand of existentialism, outlined in *Being and Nothingness* and *Existentialism and Humanism*,[7] is under-pinned and driven by the belief that we are at all times free to create and recreate the meaning of our world in terms of a project of future possibilities. Humans can choose to transcend what is given in the past and present by defining and aiming towards new horizons of possibility. We are, according to Sartre, what we make of ourselves. It follows that organizations, as collective human agents, are at liberty to create visions and achieve them.

Structuralists would beg to differ, maintaining that we become what we are because of the structures, social frameworks, and behaviourial patterns already about us. Most structuralists would argue that these structures are beyond the conscious control of individuals, but if a mission is an articulation of accepted behaviourial patterns emerging over time, then this will be seen by structuralists as a far more viable and powerful reference point for developing a common sense of purpose than a vision.

A structuralist ontology cannot be proved better or worse than an existentialist one, but they should not be considered in such terms. Again, their co-habitation reflects the plurality of human thinking.'

To suggest to managers, as the MOST concept does, that these differences do not exist or can be reconciled is to mislead and obfuscate. Not only are mission and vision different ways of thinking about implementation, they are also different ways of thinking about strategy development.

So, what practical advice can be drawn from this analysis? It is easy to take down the ideas of others and set one theory against another. It is much harder to synthesize, create fusion and resolve dilemma.

Managers need first to understand the constraints of the competitive economic system in which companies operate, and make sure they do not confuse objective setting with constraint definition.

Second, managers need to understand the primacy of insights about value creation, the diversity of the sources of insights and the large number of methods companies use to search for them.

Third, managers need to develop a personal philosophy driven mainly by their character and skills, but also driven by the nature of the industry they are in, about how to fuse the process of developing insights and implementing strategy. The academic's role in this personal philosophy building should be one of coach and counsellor, not guru or salesman.

Andrew Campbell is founder director of the Ashridge Strategic Management Centre. He is the author and co-author of a number of books including *A Sense of Mission* (1993). Most recently, he has co-authored *Corporate-Level Strategy* (1994) with Michael Goold and Marcus Alexander.

Further Reading

Campbell, A, and Tawadey, K, *Mission and Business Philosophy*, Heinemann, Oxford, 1990.

Campbell, A, Young, D, and Devine, M, *A Sense of Mission*, FT/Pitman, London, 1993.

Collins, JC, and Porras, JI, *Built to Last – Successful Habits of Visionary Companies*, Century, London, 1995.

Goold, M, Campbell, A, and Alexander, M, *Corporate-Level Strategy*, John Wiley, Chichester, 1994.

Hofstede, G, *Cultures and Organizations*, McGraw Hill, Maidenhead, 1991.

Kotter, JP, and Heskett, JL, *Corporate Culture and Performance*, Free Press, New York, 1992.

References

1 Hamel, G, and Prahalad, CK, *Competing for the Future*, HBS Press, Cambridge, 1994.

2 Cummings, S, and Davies, J, 'Mission, Vision and Fusion', *Long Range Planning*, December 27:6.

3 Shipley, JT, *The Origins of English Words – A Discourse Dictionary of Indo-European Roots*, John Hopkins Press, Baltimore, 1984.

4 Kennedy, EL, *A Stem Dictionary of the English Language*, Book Tower, Detroit, 1971.

5 Klein, E, *A Comprehensive Etymological Dictionary of the English Language*, Elsevier, London, 1967.

6 Locke, EA, 'Towards a theory of task motivation and incentives', *Organizational Behaviour and Human Performance*, May 1968.

7 Sartre, J-P, *Existentialism and Humanism*, Methuen, London, 1948; *Being and Nothingness – an Essay in Phenomenological Ontology*, Citadel Press, New York, 1964.

CORPORATE VALUE CREATION: IMPLEMENTING VALUE-BASED MANAGEMENT

Neil Monnery, Thomas Lewis and Eric Olsen

Corporate value creation should be the primary objective of all senior managers. This is not to play down the importance of developing strategies that deliver customer value and build competitive advantage, but these must be crafted in such a way as to create value for shareholders. Strategy provides the plan by which businesses are able to deliver the profits, growth and/or cash flow that drive value creation.

A focus on value creation implies that decisions and actions are judged in the context of how much value they will create, and that value-creating behaviour is encouraged throughout the organization.

Establishing a culture driven by value creation demands a wide-reaching organizational transformation and, in many cases, the most radical change is required at the top of the organization.

Motivations to manage value

An increasing number of companies are adopting value creation as a key corporate goal. Behind this growing recognition of its importance are a number of external pressures on executives. In the 1980s, the chief threat was from corporate raiders, poised to bid for companies with under-performing shares. Latterly, challenges have come more from institutional investors – the activist shareholders who demand long-term value creation from the companies whose shares they own. This activism has been most dramatic in the US where it is supported by SEC regulations which mandate the reporting of value creation in the proxy statement.

In the UK, too, pressure has shifted from the threat of take-overs to shareholder activism, often centred on the subject of top managers' pay and its weak relationship to corporate performance. The NAPF/ABI guidelines on remuneration, for example, propose a clearer link between performance and pay, and some companies now explicitly target value creation, neatly aligning managerial interests with those of shareholders. Of course, improved compensation is not the only incentive motivating management behaviour. There is also the simple desire to improve your company and to enhance your professional reputation. Management success, prestige and visibility are increasingly driven by value achievements, which in parallel drive the success of companies over the longer term. In both the UK and the US, the lists of most admired companies are dominated by those that have created significant corporate value.

The benefits are not limited to a select group of individuals: value-creating companies will have opportunities for professional growth at all levels. Furthermore, such companies will have greater access to funds for growth and investment; they will also usually comprise businesses that both deliver customer value and enjoy competitive advantage. A value focus is frequently a way to establish a virtuous circle of value creation, long-term competitive advantage and staff fulfilment.

But, in practice, creating value is demanding. First, managers need to know exactly what they are targeting: how specifically do you measure value creation? Second, they need to understand how to work towards that goal: what are the drivers of value creation? And third, they need to discover how to encourage people to do things differently: how do you align behaviour throughout your organization?

Total shareholder return

To harness the energies of the organization to the goal of value creation, it is essential to be able to measure value creation in a consistent and robust way. It is often said that 'what gets measured gets done': managers involved with quality or re-engineering efforts, for example, are well aware of the importance of measures in influencing behaviour and promoting organizational effectiveness and change. The same is true in the arena of value management. A focus on value requires a clear understanding of how to measure its creation, so that progress can be assessed, potential alternative courses compared, and appropriate behaviour encouraged.

Numerous measures have been suggested as yardsticks of corporate performance. Many are accounting-based: some static measures, such as company size or profits at a given moment; others dynamic, showing movements of these indicators over time. These measures are often calculated as ratios: earnings per share (EPS), return on capital employed (ROCE), and return on sales (ROS). Other measures, like market capitalization, derive from market valuations, while a handful are economic, taking account of such factors as inflation. But all of these measures represent only part of value creation.

Effective measures of value creation should be aligned with shareholders' definition of value creation, and must therefore include both the dividend stream and capital appreciation of a share. A measure that is rapidly becoming a standard is total shareholder return or TSR. This measure represents the internal rate of return (IRR) of three cash flows associated with a share: its original purchase (cash out); the dividend stream received by the investor (cash in); and its sale at the end of the holding period (cash in).

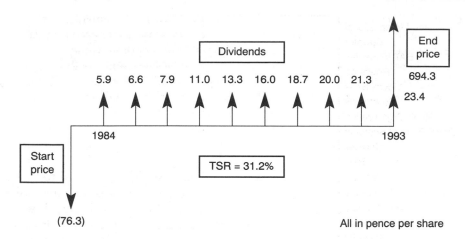

Fig. 1 Total shareholder returns for Reed International 1984–93

The TSR measure shows the absolute performance of a share in terms of the IRR of the shareholder's cash flows. But, for both shareholders and managers, it is usually more helpful to compare company performances: of one share versus another, or against the market index or some other peer group. For example, we have calculated the cumulative TSRs of the original *Financial Times*-Stock Exchange (FT-SE) 100 companies over the ten-year period since the index was launched, and then ranked them by value-creating performance. The accompanying chart shows the top quartile of that group, the 25 companies that created most value for their shareholders between 1984 and 1993.

TSR comparisons for the whole FT-SE 100 reveal very significant differences in corporate value performance over the past decade. For example, investing £1 in the top ten performers at the start of the period would have produced £12.30 at its close; a similar investment in the bottom ten, only £0.85.

Also, the top quartile contains a diversity of companies in terms of their industry, starting profitability and competitive strength. Similarly, no particular method of achieving such outstanding performance appears to be the norm, nor does anything uniquely notable about them in 1984 predict their future success.

We have also looked at comparative TSR performances across different markets, examining companies in 14 countries over the years 1991–93. Using a TSR measure that excludes differences in local market movements, and takes account of currency fluctuations and contrasting costs of capital, we can compare and benchmark internationally. The outstanding value creation of such companies as Home Depot, Intel, Hoffman-La Roche, Murata Manufacturing and Ericsson (the top five) offer useful lessons in value management.

The TSR measure of corporate performance corresponds directly to the performance measures used by investors and fund managers. And, just as active fund managers aim to outperform the market, so corporate managers should aim to achieve returns superior to the average. Otherwise, investors will be better off buying the index.

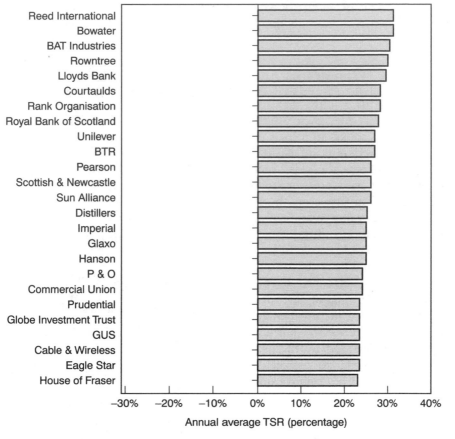

Fig. 2 Top quartile FT–SE 100 TSR performance 1984–93

This focus on relative performance has two implications. First, it insulates managers from macroeconomic factors which are beyond their control, but which move the whole market significantly. (These include tax and regulatory regimes which affect the real cost of capital, as well as expectations of inflation.) Second, it creates a high hurdle since, by definition, half the companies in a given market will under-perform the average. Beating the market consistently is difficult: industry factors, competitive pressures and investor expectations typically limit companies' ability to outdo the market repeatedly, and even those in attractive industries with strong competitive advantages are challenged.

Nevertheless, the overall goal must be value creation. But, what does that mean in terms of corporate target-setting? Outperforming the market more frequently than you under-perform it might be one objective. An even more ambitious goal might be to appear consistently in the top quartile of your chosen peer group. Historical data provides some benchmarks: over the long term, to be an average performer in the FT-SE 100 over a three-year period required a TSR of about six to eight per cent (plus the inflation rate), while top quartile performance required an additional five to eight per cent.

Drivers of corporate value creation

It is possible to describe the factors that have led to various companies performing well for their shareholders. Typically, these include good management, sound strategies, effective implementation and operating skills, and an appropriate skill base in the management and workforce. But how do companies pursue the value creation objective going forward? Is it simply being good at everything, or are there some useful guides to help set priorities?

A first step in answering these questions is to build a model or mental map of what drives value creation. Since TSR itself can be measured only for traded companies and only after the fact, a forward-looking model is needed to help managers make decisions today. This should encompass beliefs about what drives value, and be usable throughout the organization.

In reality, all managers have such a model, either implicitly or explicitly, which they use to guide their decisions. The appropriate tests of such models are whether they fit (do they accurately predict how value is created?) and whether they are usable (normally a question of are they sufficiently simple and well understood by the users?). The right trade-off between these two somewhat contradictory objectives will vary from company to company. A good model will be sophisticated enough so as not to miss important value drivers within your business, but no more complicated than is really necessary to ensure appropriate decisions and actions.

One practical approach is to use an 'internal' TSR throughout the company to look at the potential value creation of individual businesses or even of individual products. Many managers are familiar with the discounting of future cash flows when considering incremental investments in the capital expenditure process. But this discipline also needs to be applied to the larger amount of assets tied up in the base businesses. An internal TSR does this by capturing both the changes in the value of a business (the difference between today's 'market' value and the 'terminal' value at the end of the planning period), and the associated cash flows or 'internal dividend' during that period.

Behind the capital gains and 'internal dividends' are the financial drivers of corporate value performance that are under management's control. These can be further peeled back layer-by-layer to the operating drivers in the business, but at the financial level there are three: improving the returns on existing assets (raising profitability), investing in incremental projects that earn above the company's cost of capital (profitable growth), and delivering cash for investment (free cash flow). The first two actions primarily drive capital gains; the third creates value through funding dividends and growth elsewhere.

Capital gains result in part from the simple action of growing a business. All other things being equal, the market ascribes a higher value to bigger companies

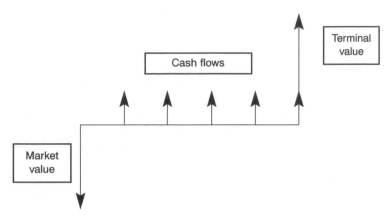

Fig. 3 Internal total shareholder returns

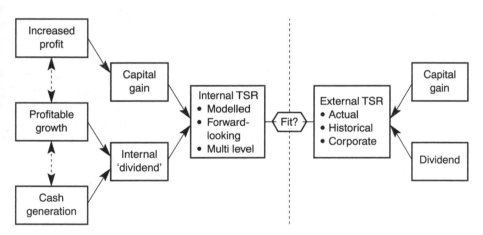

Fig. 4 Value drivers

than smaller companies in terms of assets employed. This is reasonably obvious, but other things are often not equal. In particular, some businesses earn higher returns than others, the corollary of which is that, for the same size, a more profitable company will be worth more than a less profitable one.

These observations are behind the first two value drivers, and have a number of implications: first, the need to balance profit improvement and growth, estimating an appropriate trade-off; second, the value of a good measure of profitability that encourages managers to focus on real profit enhancement rather than accounting adjustments; and third, the importance of an understanding of the cost of capital to indicate what growth is profitable.

The third constituent of value creation is the generation of net cash flow, and here too there is a balance or trade-off to be considered. Growth usually, and profit enhancement sometimes, require investment, thus reducing the available cash flow. Balancing the value of profit improvement, growth and cash generation is essential, and value managers try to include all of these drivers in their assessment of a business. They also understand that different businesses will place different levels of emphasis on the different drivers.

In general, poor return businesses should focus more on profit improvement and cash. High return businesses should tend to grow or throw off cash if their growth is constrained. Successful value creation demands balancing the contribution of each driver, and managing the trade-offs between them. This requires good strategies founded on accurate measures of your profitability, growth, cost of capital and net cash flow. The measures should be tailored specifically to your businesses.

Understanding how to craft strategies that will optimize these levers or value drivers, and then delivering the strategy are at the heart of value management. This is illustrated by the performances of some of the most value-creating companies of the past few years. These are companies that have achieved comparable success despite starting from very different positions. They confirm that any company has an equal chance to achieve value success if they make the most of the value drivers at their disposal, and manage the trade-offs in the appropriate way.

Reed International, for example, the best performing company of our FT-SE survey, demonstrates how dramatic capital gains can be generated through improved profitability. Its exceptional value creation was concentrated in two periods: 1984–87, when it transformed from a conglomerate into a publisher; and 1992–93 when it refocused on high quality international publishing, supported by a merger. Beginning with businesses earning returns below the cost of capital, Reed's corporate strategy has led to high returns businesses across the organization. Initially, there was little focus on growth and, in fact, overall, sales have declined. At the same time, cash returns on investment have risen from 3 to 18 per cent, and EPS have tripled.

Home Depot, the top performer of our international survey, demonstrates the benefits of growth. The American retail DIY chain's value creation is the result of a very simple model: growing very high return businesses at incredible speed. The company has grown at an annual average rate of 50 per cent over the past decade. At the same time, its ROS and ROCE have remained fairly constant at 20 per cent. Underlying this success is a strategy that combines high volume, excellent customer service, and low prices stemming from a sophisticated logistics system. And not only has the profitable asset base grown rapidly, but the cash cost of the growth has been relatively inexpensive because of ever-increasing experience in opening new stores.

BAT Industries is a company that derives much of its value achievements of the past decade from the third driver, cash generation. Its story falls into two: first, the company pursued diversified growth prior to 1989, notably with a move into financial services in 1984; second, after a hostile take-over bid in 1988, it was forced into a huge restructuring in which tobacco and financial services became the core focus. Aiming to maintain a high level of profitability in an environment of low growth has led BAT to continue to put pressure on its cash-rich tobacco operations, offering a very high dividend yield while leaving scope to finance investments. The combination of being highly cash generative, and growing at above the cost of capital has been very productive of value.

Lloyds Bank, another good performer in our FT-SE survey, is a company that had reasonable profitability at the start of the past decade, and has based its success on a judicious mix of the value drivers. By avoiding some of the mistakes of other banks, growing carefully and organically rather than by acquisition, and increasing returns, it beat the market nine years out of ten. Lloyds has worked hard to focus its organization on value creation – for example, its 1989 annual report states that 'Lloyds Bank's primary objective is to create value for its shareholders – by increase in the dividend and appreciation in the share price. This is the driving force behind our decisions and actions.'

Value drivers are evidently not the same for all businesses, and their management requires careful evaluation of the trade-offs. For example, if, like BAT, you begin with high rates of return but little opportunity to grow, it will be value-creating to focus chiefly on cash generation. In contrast, with businesses earning below the cost of capital, as Reed began the past decade, the focus should be more on improving returns. These companies pursued strategies that were appropriate to their starting positions and which drew on an appropriate mix of value drivers. Such strategies are entirely situational: not only do they vary across companies; but since they depend on your starting position at any given moment, they also vary over time.

In addition, appropriate strategies require consideration of the market's expectations of your future performance that are already priced into the current share price. Future strategy must be designed so that these expectations are continually beaten in order to outperform the market. This is both a challenging and encouraging prospect: managers face a clean slate on which constantly to improve to maintain TSR performance above the market average. But, at the same time, whatever your past value performance, you have an equal opportunity to create value in the future. It is not where you start that matters; it is what you do from there in selecting and executing appropriate value-creating strategies.

Implementing value-based management

Companies are complex systems, with skills, people, processes, histories and heritage, and differing opportunities. How does a company marshal those resources to look for value-creating strategies and then to deliver them? In small companies, an individual may drive this. For corporate restructuring decisions, a small group at the centre may decide. But for most large companies, the key is to encourage operating units to understand clearly how their actions and decisions contribute to value creation.

The greatest long-term potential for value-based management is generally found at the operating level. This is often where the decisions with the greatest effect on external TSR are made; it is also where the focus on internal TSR is typically least developed and least exploited. Operating managers need to focus explicitly on value, both in making strategic choices about which products, which markets, how to compete, and when to expand, and in managing day-to-day operations.

The method by which such value-based management is implemented will be different in each company, but, in general, it should be based on adapting existing management processes and measures. These processes – strategic planning, annual budgeting, capital expenditure evaluation, and incentive compensation – and the measures used within them can be used to direct behaviour in your organization. In seeking to change that behaviour, the challenge is to translate the goal of value creation into practical tools that refocus and motivate behaviour within different business situations and company cultures.

How is this to be done? First, you must examine your processes to assess which are the important ones in your organization, who is involved in them, whether they are effective in addressing real business needs, what effect they have on behaviour, and whether their focus is on value creation. Effective processes are a prerequisite for getting the organization to focus on the second step, the measures within those processes.

Fundamental to aligning your processes and decision tools with value creation is the development of an appropriate set of internal measures that quantify, track and reward value-creating performance. Understanding existing measures will help determine whether the measures on which people make decisions are a good guide to future TSR performance. Often this will not be the case as managers pursue EPS, ROCE or ROS goals that are generally only loosely or circumstantially connected to real value creation.

One way of assessing the starting position of your processes and measures is to draw a performance measurement map. This should consist of the key management processes, the various measures used in them, and the strength or weakness of their effects on behaviour. This map can help explain what is driving behaviour in the company, allowing candid discussion of the strengths and weaknesses of the system as a whole.

A performance measurement map may indicate, for example, that your planning process is too weak to generate alternative strategies, that some measures are poorly aligned with value creation, that different measures are used in different processes with different behavioural effects, or that behaviour is driven by an old model of value creation. Whatever the outcome, there are likely to be valuable lessons about the appropriate means of implementing value management, and its different application in different processes.

Value management in the strategic planning process should typically be conducted in the context of an internal TSR target set by the centre or by the business. Business managers can then develop a set of strategies that are realistic in terms of the company's starting position. These alternative plans, once valued, are compared on their potential value creation. Care should be taken not to focus on a single value driver, such as pushing up profits by 15 per cent

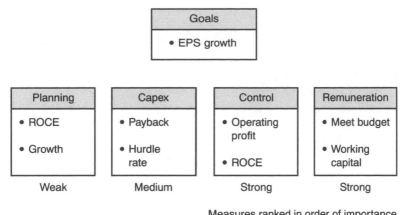

Fig. 5 Sample performance measurement map

regardless of the consequences for cash flow and growth. The planning process must be loose enough to encourage debate around different drivers and to allow room for management creativity, but tight enough to ensure that all discussions tie back to value creation.

Valuing strategic plans needs an appropriate value creation model, such as internal TSR. The model should incorporate accurate measures of financial performance and cash flows, and a means of calculating and comparing the current value of the business – its market value – with its expected value at the end of the planning period – its terminal value. The market value of a business provides a benchmark from which to assess its future value creation.

In tailoring your company's value model, you should balance the needs of accuracy and simplicity: in order to generate strategic alternatives, the value model must be simple enough that line managers can engage in the debate, but accurate enough that the decisions made connect with TSR. One common mistake is to use a complex black box model which only a couple of people understand – this excludes many from the debate, potentially including those who know the most about the real alternatives for the business.

This is not the place to describe these models in detail, but it is worth noting that accurate models of market values include a recognition of the impact of market expectations on TSR performance, and the tendency of high and low performing companies to 'fade' to market norms over time. This reflects investors' views that neither high nor low performance will be sustained in perpetuity. External forces will push returns and growth towards sustainable averages, with out-performers experiencing competitive pressures in the product markets, while under-performers face investor pressures in the equity markets. These expectations have an important impact on the appropriate performance required.

Once a value-creating business strategy is agreed, it must be implemented and delivered. In many companies the most important delivery contract is the annual budget, which should be a short-term reflection of the strategy set out in the plan: if the budget is delivered, then the strategy should be delivered too. The problem is that budget accounting numbers can often be delivered in ways that fail to deliver value. It is therefore vital to have a set of measures that align budgets with strategy and ultimately with TSR performance, again using the principle of 'what gets measured gets done'. Similarly, the measures used in strategy formulation, like internal TSR, need to be cascaded into simpler financial and operating measures that can be used throughout the organization.

Many measures of profitability, for example, are notorious for encouraging people to behave in ways that will not deliver value. The most commonly used ones are accounting-based, and suffer from numerous distortions, notably failing to reflect the underlying cash performance of a business. Hence a complex economic measure such as cash flow return on investment (CFROI), which avoids the shortcomings of traditional measures, will reduce or eliminate bias in behaviour and decisions. CFROI is analogous to the IRR for a new project, comparing the cumulative cash invested in a business with the cash the business is currently producing, while recognizing the importance of asset ages, asset lives and inflation.

CFROI is highly accurate, and avoids most accounting distortions, but it is more complex than traditional measures. We use it as a benchmark measure, to assess the distortions in a company's existing measures, and to tailor a set of new measures from a spectrum of simplified alternatives. The intention should be that the chosen measures reduce complexity while eliminating the biases that cause most distortions in your business. Again, there is a trade-off between simplicity and accuracy: the challenge is to ensure that the measures and targets you use on a daily basis are both aligned with value creation and simple enough to drive behaviour.

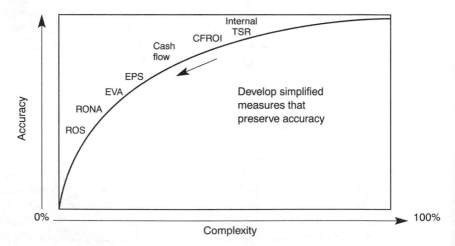

Fig. 6 Spectrum of measures

The primary objectives of a value measurement system should be accurately to reflect actual TSR performance and transparently to encourage actions and decisions that will improve TSR. The ideal trade-off between accuracy and simplicity will vary by company and business. In general, simpler businesses will be able to use simpler measures. But in all businesses it is essential that the measures used in different processes are aligned with one another. Managers and employees are frequently influenced by conflicting signals from the strategic planning and annual budgeting processes. While achieving alignment need not mean that the same measures are used everywhere, it is vital that the measures are consistent with one another and with value creation.

This means that planning and budgeting must also be aligned with the other key processes of incentive compensation and capital expenditure evaluation. The latter is often the process where value is currently most explicitly considered through the use of discounted cash flow techniques. Strangely, new projects are frequently evaluated with value tools, before becoming core businesses and being assessed using traditional measures. In seeking to align internal processes to take full advantage of a company's value creation potential, the measures that signal success for planning, budgeting and compensation might well be borrowed from the capex process.

Finally, the measurement system must be cascaded down through your organization. That need not mean pushing TSR all the way down the line: it is unlikely and undesirable that every single employee will be motivated by corporate value creation. But measures at lower levels in the company must be aligned with the value drivers of your business. A properly designed and implemented value management programme will create a common language between senior management and staff, providing appropriate tools for making complex choices throughout your organization, and allowing greater latitude for informed decision-making.

The value of value creation

Launching a value-based management programme generally requires a transformation of the organization at all levels. The most fundamental change will come at the top: the corporate centre must operate a variety of direct and indirect levers to encourage the whole company to deliver value. Paradoxically, at a time when the pressures to do this are growing, companies are increasingly decentralising and downsizing their headquarters. This gap between resources and responsibilities means that the centre must become even more effective, particularly concentrating on the use of indirect levers. Tools such as the design and implementation of a value-based measurement system allow carefully focused yet powerful intervention in all operations by the centre.

That is not to say that the centre no longer uses direct levers on value. There remain many important corporate decisions which must be addressed from a value perspective, including issues of corporate shape, portfolio planning and resource allocation; mergers, demergers and acquisitions; and financial policies, such as leverage, rights issues and dividends. For example, value creation and erosion are conspicuous in the area of M&A; equally, demergers offer value opportunities for some companies.

One of the central messages of value-based management is that while the TSR goal should be similar for all companies, the means by which you achieve it can vary considerably. The same applies to where you choose to begin the implementation process. Some companies may start at the planning process, involving a fairly small group of senior managers; others may introduce value-oriented measures on a broader scale, perhaps through the budgeting process; while still others may reorganize the remuneration system to encourage value-driven behaviour. From each of these starting positions, it is essential to push for wider awareness of the goal and the actions needed to achieve it, spreading the value message down and across the company.

Value-based management is much like implementing any programme of change. Indeed, it is a management approach founded on change and the need for continuous improvement. For this reason, it is important to convey its analytical and behavioural objectives clearly. People's basic beliefs about what drives their businesses are challenged, suggesting that participation, buy-in and ultimate ownership are crucial to successful implementation. Training and induction processes will not always be easy, but are central to implementing a value creation culture throughout the management structure.

It is important to be aware both of these organizational issues and of traditional strategic management in relation to value creation. In reality, there should be little conflict in most companies: superior TSR benefits not just shareholders, but also employees and customers. The former gain security, greater opportunities and improved compensation; while the latter benefit from the company's ability to attract more and less costly capital which it can invest in better meeting their product and price needs. Such valuable benefits are why a growing number of companies are successfully exploiting the power of explicit value-based management programmes to rejuvenate their organizations, to improve their TSR performance and to build long-term competitive advantage.

Neil Monnery is a Vice President at the Boston Consulting Group's London office. He was educated at Exeter College, Oxford, and Harvard Business School. He leads BCG's Corporate Development practice area in the UK and Europe, and has worked with a number of UK and European companies to implement value-based management.

Thomas Lewis is a Senior Vice President at the Boston Consulting Group's Munich office. He leads BCG's worldwide Corporate Development practice and has worked with German, Austrian and Scandinavian companies on issues of value management. He is author of a German language book on value management, *Steigerung des Unternehmenswertes: total-value management* (1994).

Eric Olsen is a Vice President at The Boston Consulting Group's Chicago office. He was a founding partner of HOLT Value Associates, which later merged with BCG. He has worked extensively in the field of value management for a number of US corporations.

Further Reading

Monnery, N, *Corporate Value Creation: Implementing Value-Based Management*, FT/Pitman, London, 1995.

CREATIVITY IN THE SEARCH FOR STRATEGY

Simon Majaro

The corporate winners of the rest of this decade and the beginning of the next century, will be those enterprises that learn how to harness the creative talent within their organizations in a systematic way. Traditionally it is something managers have ignored and often stifled.

Though there are isolated and spectacular examples of truly creative organizations, creativity remains an ill-defined area of management, often regarded as a useful bonus, rather than a practical necessity. Utilized and developed, creativity can enrich the process of innovation and, during strategic planning, can do a great deal more than simply help to identify creative strategies.

'**D**o you want your company to be creative?' It is very unlikely that any manager would respond negatively to this question. Yet when asked a second simple question: 'Is your company creative?' most managers find it extremely difficult to answer. Some are likely to respond in the affirmative; others in the negative and many would say that they simply do not know. While the majority of managers feel that creativity is vital for success, most are unclear what the word means in practice; how to measure it or how to enhance creativity among members of the organization. Most managers want their organizations to be creative, but very few know how to go about implementing such a task.

Confusion is usually evident elsewhere in the organization. Organization development personnel are not sure where to slot creativity-enhancement in the firm's hierarchy of development needs. Some say that creativity cannot be taught. Others suggest that too much creativity can be disruptive to business. Yet others say that the firm is trying to recruit creative people and, as a result, there is no need to undertake development activities in this area. 'Once creative, always creative', they argue.

Senior managers are also uncomfortable when asked to think when they last used creative thinking and creative techniques in seeking to develop a strategy for the firm's future. They usually respond with silent embarrassment.

What is creativity?

It is important to emphasize at the outset that creativity, in a corporate context, is an input for a greater purpose. Creativity does not live alone. Its main role is the enrichment of the innovation process. The two words creativity and innovation are often used in tandem, without people stopping to reflect what exactly what they mean and the relationship between them:

- Creativity is the thinking process which helps us to generate ideas
- Innovation is the application of such ideas towards doing things better and/or cheaper and/or more effectively and/or more aesthetically

Creative ideas can be wild, outlandish and impractical. On the other hand innovations must be practical, realistic and results-orientated. Why bother with crazy ideas? The answer is simple. Many of the most successful innovations in the annals of business history started life as 'intermediate impossibles'. These are ideas which at first glance do not deserve a second look. Yet through a generous and imaginative analysis managed to be converted into implementable solutions.

Moreover research suggests that, on average, 60 ideas are needed before a single innovation is put into practice. A plethora of ideas is necessary before one can be identified as deserving of implementation. While creativity represents the *quantity* of input; innovation is the *quality* of output. One without the other is like a child without a parent.

Figure 1 describes the relationship between creativity and innovation in a diagrammatic form. It highlights their inter-dependence.

A company which wants to innovate must organize itself to be able to harness the creativity which lies dormant among its personnel.

Even so, it should also be remembered that companies can innovate without having any creative input from inside the firm. If an organization goes out of its way to scout for competitive products and practices, possibly on a global

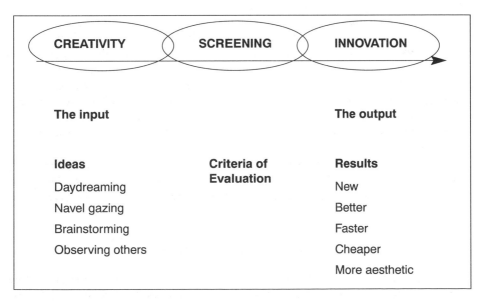

Fig. 1 The relationship between creativity and innovation

scale, it should be able to pick up creative successes from the outside environment. By emulating and even improving upon them companies can promulgate innovations. However, this does call for a conscious strategic decision to behave as a follower rather than a leader.

In some respects such a strategy entails a modicum of creativity. The danger is that one can easily run out of ideas to plagiarize. Japanese companies, for example, are renowned for their ability to innovate on the back of creative concepts developed in the rest of the world. Some such companies have found to their cost that a point is reached when there is little left for them to copy or plagiarize. At that point the lack of creativity can be a painful reminder that innovation based on your own creativity is safer than innovation resulting from simply improving other people's good ideas.

Figure 2 provides a simple matrix that helps to position enterprises on the combined effectiveness of both creativity and innovation.

Creativity and innovation at the top

For some mysterious reason it is often assumed that creativity is simply an important ingredient on the operational side of a firm. Sales forces are expected to be creative. Advertising campaigns are considered effective when the audience regards them as creative. An innovative distribution system is always applauded and almost expected.

Yet, the notion that the people at the top, senior managers driving corporate strategy, can derive considerable benefit from the use of creativity in the

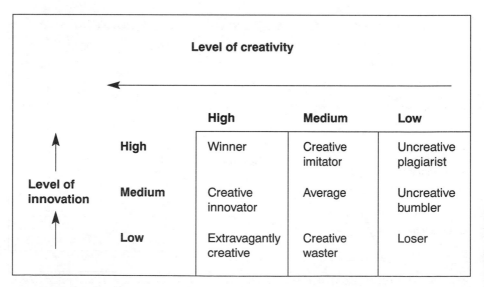

Fig. 2 A combined audit of the firm's creativity and innovation

search for a quantum leap in the firm's strategic direction is less often recognized. Instead, senior managers often expect their subordinates to behave in a creative manner, but shun the process themselves. If a simple technique like brainstorming can help to solve a packaging problem why could it not be used in the search for a new strategy? It is difficult to think of a convincing response to such a challenge.

Creative input can be of enormous value at all levels of management. Figure 3 represents a simple conceptual model of the firm with its three levels. Against each level a list of items that can be enriched by the injection of creative ideas is provided on the side of each level shown. Our main concern here is to explore how creativity can enrich the main tasks which fall within the orbit of the strategic level of the firm.

Creativity during the search for strategy

It is often overlooked that members of a company at strategic level are the cerebral part of the organization. Essentially they are the thinkers responsible for charting the future course of the enterprise. They need to devote a good portion of their time to thinking rather than doing activities. Clearly if thinking is a significant part of their job, creativity must be an integral part of the whole process. Creative thinking is better than uncreative thinking. Moreover, creative strategists at the top can provide the cue for the rest of the organization. It is not enough to exhort people to become more creative without providing the leadership through role-behaviour and example.

Planners are essentially concerned with the future of the firm. As shown in Fig. 3 a number of inter-related, macro-thinking activities must be undertaken

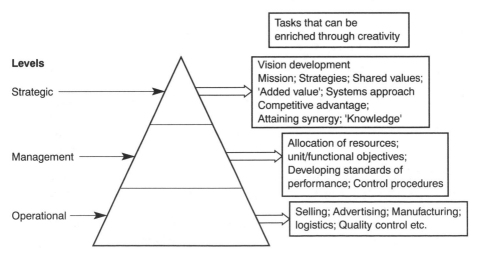

Fig. 3 A conceptual model of the three levels of the firm and their tasks which can be enriched through creativity

during the strategic planning cycle. A few of these macro-activities can be summarized in the following list:

- vision development
- mission and strategies
- identification of core products and/or core competencies
- sustainable competitive advantage
- need for added value
- product differentiation
- a systems approach to corporate strategy
- development of 'shared values'
- knowledge as a competitive advantage.

All these items represent important issues during the search for a strategic direction for the firm. They do not all descend upon top management simultaneously but, sooner or later, create a major challenge to thinking strategists. Unfortunately the process of responding to any of these challenges is hampered by the fact that people at the top are often too close to the business to have a truly objective perspective.

In addition, when company strategists find themselves involved in day-to-day activities and fire-fighting tasks, the absence of a cohesive strategy soon becomes apparent and the organization simply drifts along the route that was charted for it in the past. In responding to the needs of the future environment in which the firm is likely to be operating, time and creative thinking must be devoted to the various key items listed above.

Vision development

When one talks about the future the word 'vision' immediately springs to mind. To many it is not much more than an intellectual cliché that represents a vague attempt at imagining the way in which the world around us is likely to develop. To others, a vision is a continuous and iterative process of providing the firm with a long-term platform upon which to build its plans, direction, aspirations and values, in a manner which is fully empathetic with the needs of the society and marketplace of the future. When vision and the company's plans are in harmony a meaningful basis for action is generated. If the vision points to a more environmentally conscious world, the basis for a greener approach to the firm's strategy becomes more compelling and can provide a practical basis for implementation.

Now, how can managers and organizations inject creative thinking into the process of formulating a vision?

A modified version of the well-trodden brainstorming method can be used with great effect. This modified technique is known as *scenario daydreaming*. Unlike scenario writing it takes place verbally while a scribe records the salient features that emerge during the deliberations. A group of senior people is invited to create a scenario of the world at a given future point of time, say year 2004. Each member of the team is allocated a factor for in-depth exploration, such as economic and demographic trends, the physical and social environments, politics and geo-politics, finance and cost of commodities, technology, etc. Topics for exploration are selected in accordance with an agreed list of factors which are deemed to be of major relevance to the firm's future direction. The topics chosen for daydreaming are allocated in advance to members of the team in accordance with people's specific knowledge and/or personal expertise. Obviously there is little point in asking an actuary to envision the future of channels of distribution or media development of year 2004.

The important point to remember is that all the discussions during the plenary session must be centred around the notion that '*today is year 2004 (or some other future point of time chosen) and this is what is happening in the world around us...*' The use of the future tense must be avoided at all costs. A scribe records the main issues that emerge and through an open and iterative process of distillation a vision is produced. If necessary the exercise can span a number of sessions until the group emerges with a logical and meaningful scenario highlighting the strategic implications for the company.

There is little doubt that the summation of the collective knowledge and wisdom of the team can provide a much more credible vision than the one imposed by a single chief executive. Moreover the fact that the whole team becomes the 'owner' of such a vision helps to create a deeper commitment to its implications.

It is worth remembering that the most important point about planning generally is the process itself rather than the document that emerges. Similarly the vision development exercise is particularly important because of the opportunity it provides for reflection and analysis rather than the written output which may be published at the end of the exercise. The process itself provides the basis for cerebral reflection and creativity and, to that extent, it can enrich the company's strategic planning cycle.

Mission and strategies

Now that the firm's strategists are in possession of a creative vision they can commence the process of injecting a creative input into the next step: the development of a mission and strategies. Once again, for some the whole concept of defining their corporate purpose is objectionable and irrelevant. For others it is a popular pastime. They feel that without an elegant mission statement, encompassing a number of fundamental principles, the firm is incapable of attaining success.

In reality both schools of thought are wrong. The mission statement is neither an intellectual irrelevancy nor a hollow string of slogans. When done properly it represents a well thought out banner under which the firm intends to operate in the future. It should encapsulate a carefully defined analysis of the organization's perceived unique strengths and core competencies, as well as an assessment of the opportunities implied by the vision developed. It is a logical and practical assessment of what business the company ought to be in if it is to exploit its unique strengths to the full. It is not so much the elegance of the output which matters; it is much more the clarity of purpose and single-minded focus that underlies the statement which can be helpful.

When a pharmaceutical company declares that it is seeking to become the best and largest supplier of central-nervous-system drugs to the hospital sector it represents a well-focused mission. One can assume that the firm's strategists have recognized the unique strength that the company enjoys in marketing to hospitals rather than the medical profession as a whole. The firm has accepted the fact that its other products, the non-CNS drugs, are simply blurring the firm's clarity of purpose and, therefore, ought to be divested. At the same time, the company's vision has convinced its managers that the type of market niche they intend to concentrate upon is increasing rather than decreasing. This has the elements of a well-focused mission. It also requires that everyone in the organization is clear as to where the firm is heading. Such pithy and far-reaching mission statements call for enormous managerial courage but provided the homework is carried out calmly through analytical debate, the outcome can be very potent in imparting to the firm a unique sense of direction.

A good mission statement must fulfil a number of basic criteria:

1. It must be specific enough to have an impact upon the behaviour of individuals throughout the business.
2. Be focused more on customer need-satisfaction than products and/or technology.
3. Be based on a realistic assessment of the company's true strengths and weaknesses.
4. Recognize the opportunities implied by the vision.
5. Be realistic and attainable.
6. Be flexible enough to allow for changes that a dynamic marketplace may entail.

Ideally the mission should also incorporate imagination and innovation. By definition this means that a creative input can turn the mission into an instrument of excitement and uniqueness. The various techniques that enrich creative thinking can be used here in a most valuable way. In particular one can use brainstorming, round robin and trigger sessions. The whole idea is to break away from the straitjacket of a corporate mindset. By adopting a unique mission, organizations can find themselves operating in a unique way. To that extent a life assurance company that adopted the bizarre mission that it 'seeks to provide its clients with the process of alleviating their posthumous guilt' has opened the door for most interesting added-value products which would not normally be considered by an insurance company. They may, for example, add a 'will-drafting service' for clients who represent too high a risk on medical grounds.

A particularly useful technique in this connection is *metaphorical analogy*. The method is based on an attempt at drawing an analogy between a problem identified in one type of business and a proven solution in another business. At a higher level of sophistication one can compare a problem in industry or commerce with a well-known solution in remote spheres, such as nature.

By casting one's attention to the way very successful organizations have dealt with the process of defining their route to success, one can derive relevant inspiration for analogous strategic change. SMH, the company marketing the 'SWATCH' range of products, has achieved remarkable success by applying creative marketing principles, derived from non-watch industries, towards turning its cheaply produced, but very fashionable, time pieces into collectable items. If SMH simply tried to emulate other watch manufacturers it would have probably vanished into the corporate graveyard, like many other Swiss watchmakers.

Creative management requires that managers learn to cast their attention and observing skills beyond the myopic perimeter of their own industry. Simply emulating each other in the same sector is a formula for incestuous stagnation. It often amounts to no more than doing the wrong things better and better. Looking over the fence can enrich one's approach to the whole process of designing a meaningful mission, and creativity can be the element that resolves the debate as to whether the whole notion of mission is valuable or not. Indeed, a mission can impart a most powerful cutting edge. However, like everything else that managers have to do in a competitive marketplace, it must incorporate an innovative element and that in turn calls for creativity.

Sustainable competitive advantage

There is no need here to emphasize the importance of competitive advantage in the search for a strategic route to success. The company that has created for itself a unique and sustainable competitive advantage is more likely to succeed than one which simply trails behind somebody else's practices.

This is an area which can benefit enormously from the incorporation of creative ideas and innovation. We all know that innovation often entails differentiation and differentiation needs creative leaps. Therefore, in addition to brainstorming one can use two useful techniques: *attribute listing* and the *strategic creative leap*.

Attribute listing is especially helpful when the main strategic task is based on the need to find ways to improve an existing product or service. It entails listing the current features or attributes of the firm's existing product and exploring ways in which each one could be improved. A bank can, for example, list all the attributes its current services contain and then explore how each one of these attributes can be modified, improved and enriched. Provided such steps are taken in conjunction with a clear understanding of what customers are looking for, the outcome can provide a creative platform for the development of customer-focused competitive advantage.

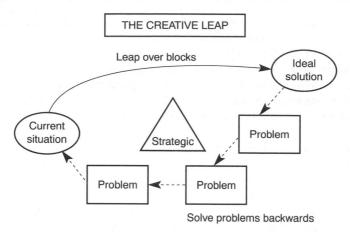

Fig. 4 The strategic creative leap

The strategic creative leap is described in Fig. 4. The aim here is to fantasize about a world in which the company has achieved a quantum leap towards providing a leading-edge and highly innovative product or service. To that extent the exercise is not dissimilar to a scenario daydreaming session. The only major difference is that the exercise converges upon the firm's own standing in this ideal world we hope to live in. Once the perfect product and service are defined it is necessary to start the backward process of identifying the problems and constraints which will stand in the way of attaining such perfection. The quantification and removal of the constraints is easier when one has an image of the end-product in mind.

Added value

Added value is a popular phrase among strategists. The theory avers that the more value that can added to a product and/or service the more differentiation can be communicated to potential clients.

A personal computer that provides a built-in printing facility offers more value to the customer than a normal PC. Add the whole gamut of multi-media facilities, as well as a shredder and franking machine facility, and considerable value is added to the package. Value can consist of intangibles such as status, social acceptability, convenience of use, etc. The more value that is added, and provided such value is appreciated by the marketplace, the fewer competitors are likely to be encountered.

In a fast-moving technology the added-value must be capable of protection, either through the various intellectual property protection systems or through the complexity of the manufacturing process itself, or both. Strong branding of an innovative product with high added-value can lengthen the period of quasi-monopoly.

Microsoft provides an admirable example of a company which enjoys a strong position in the marketplace through technological added value coupled with branding and intellectual property protection.

Adding value is an activity which can derive enormous benefit from the injection of creative ideas. Attribute listing is a particularly valuable technique in this area. Once again other useful methods include metaphorical analogy, brainstorming and morphological analysis.

Brainstorming is a useful technique if managed effectively and conducted by an experienced facilitator. Most people have had experience of brainstorming in the context of solving operational problems or exploring opportunities in day-to-day activities. But, brainstorming can also be very helpful at the strategic level during the search for strategy development in general and the enhancement of added value in particular.

Pictorial brainstorming – a fun variation on the theme. This is especially useful when the design of a new product concept is involved. For instance, if invited to add value to a Walkman one can do it in a pictorial way and produce great ideas during the exercise. Participants are given a card and are asked to brainstorm pictorial images of a novel product or packaging. Every five minutes or so the card is passed on to the neighbour on the right who is invited to add some extra features or benefits to the drawing. After about six or seven such moves the results are explored in a plenary session and the various novel ideas explored.

Morphological analysis is an impressive name for a fairly simple method. Essentially it is a multi-dimensional matrix. Up to three dimensions can be shown graphically. If the number of dimensions exceeds three it can only be shown in columns of items where all the various permutations can then be listed – if necessary, with the aid of a computer.

The idea underlying this technique is to identify a number of dimensions that may have a significant relevance to the ultimate nature of the product or service that one is hoping to develop, while breaking away from the prevailing mindset. A camera manufacturer, for example, can select three inter-related dimensions for exploration: the shape of the unit; the purpose for which it can be used and the type of users who may benefit from such a development.

Creative thinking about each of these three dimensions may yield a list of items, such as:

Shape	*Purpose*	*Users*
Telescopic	Souvenirs	Police
Pencil shape	Home security	Army
Snake	Bank security	Doctors
Brick	Military	Surgeons
Picture	Medical	Foresters

Shape	*Purpose*	*Users*
Statue	Politics	Surveyors
Chair	Structural	Engineers
Lamp-post	Environmental control	Teachers
Light switch	Energy control	Insurance Adjusters
Telephone	Navigation	Lawyers

While this is a fairly contrived example it is evident that by combining 10 × 10 × 10 a total of 1,000 ideas have been generated. As stated earlier, it can be illustrated in a diagrammatic form as shown in Fig. 5.

This now entails a gigantic screening and evaluation task. However, a thorough analysis of all this input may lead the company to new and unexploited sectors for development. For instance a camera that can wind its way like a snake in industrial structures and can be used by engineers and/or surveyors may be discovered as a unique and high added-value concept. Assuming that

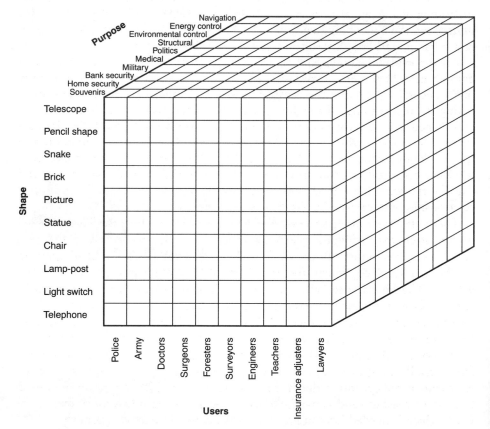

Fig. 5 The search for ideas in the camera business through morphological analysis (example only)

174

the detailed analysis shows that a vast new opportunity is revealed for the company's technology a fresh look at the firm's mission may be required. Instead of declaring that: '*We are in the camera business*' the firm's strategy may need to be adjusted to: '*We want to be prime suppliers of systems that can monitor structural faults which are normally invisible to the naked eye ...*' The technology will not need to be changed dramatically as a result of this exercise, but a radical change in the firm's marketing focus will be required. Moreover, if the planning homework is carried out in an effective manner, the firm may find itself in a high added-value sector and with limited competition. Clearly this is not a strategic route that the faint-hearted organization can pursue.

A systems approach

This is an area in which creativity can play an important role. Imaginative strategists have come to recognize that the development of a *systems* approach to the company's products and services can provide an effective combination of adding value as well as a sustainable competitive advantage. The idea underlying the concept is that when a system offering is provided, a long-term relationship marketing can be established with one's customers.

All the evidence shows that retaining customers is a less costly affair than gaining new customers. A systems approach is an effective way for retaining one's clientele. Probably the most impressive example of a relationship-marketing strategy attained through a 'systems' approach is the way Tetra Pak has established a long-term and continuous liquid packaging service for its customers. In practice when a firm adopts the Tetra Pak system it is committed to that packaging concept for a long time and is unlikely to wish to depart from it. Other organizations can draw a metaphor with the Tetra Pak approach and explore the way they can develop a similar high added value and continuous relationship with customers based on a similar concept.

There are many other successful examples of how companies have attained unique strengths through a systems approach. If properly conceived and executed a systems model can provide its originators with the kind of uniqueness in the marketplace which the suppliers of discrete products seldom can achieve. The financial services industry would benefit from such an approach. Customers would welcome having all their financial services needs catered for by one service provider. However, this does not happen because of the way such companies are structured and the overly traditional way of marketing their services. A group of dentists in the United States offer a dental service from 'cradle to grave'. Clients pay a small fee every year, almost like an endowment policy, into a dental fund. In early years little attention is needed but the increasing fund is available to take care of the much more expensive work which is needed later in life. This is definitely a systems approach.

Brainstorming, the creative leap and metaphorical analogy, are the important techniques which one can apply with great success in this area.

175

Developing shared values

Top management often forget that people in any organization are searching for a role model to follow and emulate. An inspiring leader can provide a cutting edge to the organization through personal practice and behaviour. An honest leader can, through example, stimulate a high level of integrity. On the other hand, a top manager who indulges in devious and irresponsible behaviour patterns should not be surprised if the lower levels imitate such behaviour. It is difficult to expect others in the organization to behave in a manner which is more honourable and desirable than the one demonstrated from above.

An excellent company seeks to articulate a set of values which represents the organization's desire to distinguish itself from the rest. If seeking to become customer-orientated is a desirable path to attaining the firm's aims the people at the top must demonstrate their active participation in such an ethos. If creativity is considered the secret ingredient for excellence, the strategic level must partake in creative sessions and show, through active example, that they believe in its value.

The process of identifying the cluster of shared values which top-management wishes to adopt is an important task. It cannot be delegated to others and deserves considerable thought and wide communication once a decision has been taken. Creativity can provide a valuable aid to the whole process.

A useful technique in this area is the metaphorical analogy method. The ability to draw inspiration from analogous successes from other areas of human endeavour and from history can be of powerful help. Exploration as to how various religions have managed to propagate their underlying values, or the way the Scout movement has sought to develop more caring youngsters can provide case studies for analysis.

The important point to remember is that shared values which are compatible with the expectations of customers, and which pervade the whole organization can impart to the firm a powerful competitive advantage.

Knowledge as competitive advantage

Knowledge is one of the most powerful areas for developing a competitive advantage. There is little doubt that the excellent companies of the future will be those that know more about their customers' needs that those customers know themselves.

An organization that manages to assemble an accurate and up-to-date information flow which is, at the same time, valued by its customers, is more likely to be a winning player in the marketplace. Customers gravitate towards firms that are able to offer comprehensive and anticipatory knowledge relating to the various areas of concern which they are trying to grapple with. Suppliers who can tell their customer how to provide more satisfaction to his or her own customer is better placed than those who cannot. Moreover, a supplier who possesses data about trends in the marketing environment, as well as in technology, is even better placed. The whole gamut of Information Technology tools is now available to those who truly want to build a knowledge data bank that can enrich their strategic standing in the competitive environment.

Knowledge can also enrich the firm's own vision, mission and strategy-development processes. It is much more meaningful to develop such elements in the firm's planning cycle when the supportive inventory of knowledge is accurate and dynamic.

Can one enrich the process of knowledge-acquisition through creativity? The answer is obviously in the affirmative. The first step is to identify 'What one needs to know' and the cost-benefit that can be gained through the acquisition of such knowledge. Through iterative brainstorming sessions top-management can conjure a list of data which ought to be collected in order to enrich the firm's strategic standing among its customers and, possibly even, among its customers' customers. Regrettably this kind of process is often delegated to lower levels of management. To work successfully, the formulation as to what the firm needs to know ought to be undertaken by the strategic level itself, although implementation can be delegated to lower levels.

Senior management must involve itself more intimately in the creativity and innovation processes and there is no better time and place to start than during the search for strategies within the planning cycle. Though often unrecognized and frequently dismissed, the benefits which emerge from utilization of creativity are almost self-evident. However, it is important to highlight the fact that one of the most important pay-offs is gained through the sheer process of resorting to creative exercises at top-management's level. By using creative methods the people at the top can provide the rest of the organization with a powerful management development role model, one which will be emulated and hopefully perpetuated.

Professor Simon Majaro is co-director of the Centre for Creativity and visiting professor of marketing strategy at Cranfield University's School of Management. He is an international consultant; a barrister; and author of numerous books including *Managing Ideas for Profit: The Creative Gap*; *International Marketing: A Strategic Approach to World Markets*; *Marketing in Perspective: The Creative Marketer* **and** *The Essence of Marketing.*

Further Reading

Majaro, S, *Managing Ideas for Profit: The Creative Gap*, McGraw Hill, Maidenhead, 1988.

THE ROLE OF PROJECT MANAGEMENT IN IMPLEMENTING STRATEGY

Eddie Obeng

Project management was once the sole preserve of the building and construction industries. Building a bridge was regarded as a project – a series of activities and plans involving a small number of people neatly isolated from the remainder of the organization's business.

Today, projects are regarded as a key management tool in all areas of the business world. In particular, project management is having an important impact on the implementation of change programmes and quality initiatives. But, while projects have become highly complex and sophisticated, managers' attitudes and behaviour can remain rooted in the traditional bridge-building mentality.

If projects are to be utilized to successfully implement strategy, then they need to be thoroughly understood from the outset. And, to be effective, organizations need to understand how both the nature of strategy and the nature of projects has changed.

Recent years have been filled with talk of a paradigm shift. This is supposed to have fundamentally altered the relationships between business variables. Intellectually, managers have been able to convince themselves of the possibility that all the rules and formulae surrounding effective business and organizational management have changed. Emotionally, many hope that things are still the same and little effort is put into trying to fully understand and act on the implications of this shift.

As the variables and parameters of the business world changed, business schools and academics continued in much the same way. They published and taught models of strategic implementation which were mostly variants of the one represented in Fig. 1 (a modified version of the one produced by Thomson and Strickland in their 1990 book *Strategic Management: Concepts and Cases*[1]).

While theorists saw a logical progression from vision to mission, and then to strategy, and finally implementation, real life organizations were experiencing a number of effects which simply didn't fit the models. Such neatness is no longer translated into reality (if it ever was with any degree of regularity).

The historical reasons for this are many and varied. First, it was unlikely that the corporate vision or mission was clear and unwavering. 'Many managers

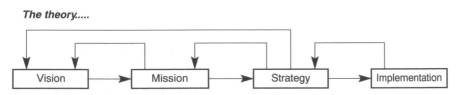

Fig. 1 Traditional model of strategic implementation

misunderstand the nature and importance of mission, while others fail to comprehend it at all,' concluded Andrew Campbell and his co-authors in *A Sense of Mission*.[2] Many reasons are cited for this – most memorably by US President Bush who admitted his difficulties in getting to grips with 'the vision thing'.

From a corporate point of view, difficulty with the *vision thing* meant that the strategies emerging from organizations were far from being the complete picture. Either new initiatives would be introduced during the period between strategic reviews, or some of the areas of strategic policy, which started off as central to the activity, would be conveniently lost during the period between reviews.

Direct implementation tended to be obscured by task force activities and initiatives. Not content with single initiatives, organizations launched a plethora of them in the hope that one would move the organization forward or that their collective force would do so. Companies would start several major initiatives on quality, re-engineering, benchmarking, activity-based costing, cost reduction, competencies and so on, *simultaneously*. Often the initiatives had conflicting goals and, though it was common to hear about them starting, it was unusual to hear about them reaching an end. Implementation of the overall predetermined strategy tended to get lost under this mountain of activity.

This breakdown of the implentation process was, and continues to be, further complicated by the growth in managements fads. The number of instant

Fig. 2 The simultaneous launching of conflicting initiatives

solutions and panaceas available to managers has increased exponentially over the past two decades.

The initial paradigm which converts vision into implementation cannot be instantly dismissed. In less turbulent times, obtaining *fit* between the organization and its environment and future needs was possible. Many models, often borrowed from the military strategist, assumed that through intelligence one could determine the lie of the land and the location of enemy threats. This was achieved by developing a strategy.

Leading texts of a decade or more ago (such as those by Igor Ansoff) viewed the role of strategy as a way of obtaining *fit* in the long term. Strategy was a matter of analysis in which, for example, the activities of the organization were matched to the environment in which it operated. A strategy or strategic plan was created. The plan was usually developed by senior managers or a specialist unit. It made full use of all the history and learning which the organization had previously captured. The strategy was developed by intelligent extrapolation of the past. This gave several advantages in implementation. Most of the managers who would be expected to help to deliver the implementation were largely doing things which they had done before. The other major advantage was that there was a continuous thread between past and future. Working procedures were already in place and could be used as the mechanism for implementation. Implementation was largely through policy and, occasionally, task forces or working groups.

If resources needed to be aligned in a significant way to allow the implementation of the policy this would be accompanied by a re-organization. New departments or divisions would be developed or old ones reassigned.

But, as the world has accelerated and become more complex and unpredictable, this approach to strategy has become increasingly ineffective. Using the military analogy, it is as if the enemy is in fact many enemies and instead of having their strategic targets in fixed positions they are constantly moving them round and changing both the number and type of weapons deployed. In such a battlefield the old way of looking at strategy becomes increasingly ineffective. As IMD's Peter Lorange puts it: 'In today's situation it should be acknowledged that there is no one best design, rather the design of such strategic management systems will probably have to be based on the particular strategic context of a firm.'[3]

New and numerous paradoxes

The paradigm also creates a series of perplexing paradoxes. For example, new competitors are hard to identify. They may arise from entrants which are not traditional competitors. A company producing aircraft for routes primarily patronized by business people going back and forth to meetings will find itself in competition with other opportunities for carrying out meetings, such as video conferencing. So, for any organization which intends to make money both now and in the future, a pre-requisite to guaranteeing current revenues is that the organization must concentrate on improving its performance at what it does today. This means that all the organization's key resources and best people should be given responsibility for improving what is currently in place. Furthermore, controls, rewards, measurements, policies and power structures must also be arranged to ensure that there is focus on today's needs.

However, if the future is going to be very different from the present and will include several discontinuities then it makes sense to concentrate on doing something different to meet tomorrow's needs and challenges. This implies that all the organization's key resources and its best people should be given responsibility for creating what will need to be in place tomorrow to generate future revenues. And they should be as unconstrained by controls, measures and policies as possible.

This resource and control paradox is at the bottom of many organization's efforts in continually organizing and re-organizing.

Another paradox which emerges as organizations attempt to gain some influence over the chaotic business environment is that they will not be able easily to predict where the next challenges will arise. This, in turn, implies that organizations should concentrate on being able to respond to change with what the telecommunications company Mercury in its values statement labels 'awesome velocity'. Alternatively, if the environment is really going to be so unpredictable, then the best way to manage it is to get in first, to push and precipitate change yourself. The best way to predict the future may be to create it yourself.

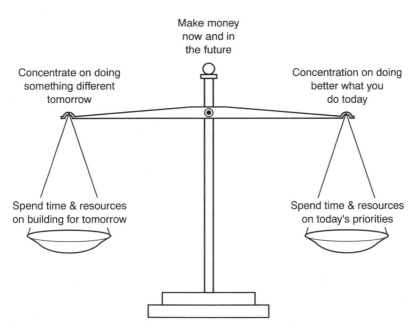

Fig. 3   Balancing the action: preparing to meet tomorrow's needs and challenges

The first response implies rapid analysis followed by rapid implementation, while the second implies high levels of innovation followed by creative implementation. This time the organization is torn between the needs to forecast accurately and to be able to move proactively and reactively at lightning speed.

By far the most perplexing paradox relating to implementation is the fact that, however good the strategic analysis, it is of no use unless it can be brought to life, unless it can be implemented. This itself raises another paradox. Both analysis and implementation are more complex than ever before. They probably cover global issues and yet need to be carried out quickly. The organization then has to decide whether specific groups should be given responsibility for ensuring that focus is maintained. Or, alternatively, should the people responsible for the analysis also be responsible for implementation, in order to make sure that there is co-ordination and continuous iteration back and forth.

In his book *The Icarus Paradox*,[4] Danny Miller describes how successful organizations become stuck in paradigms of their own making. He labels these as *recipes*. Recipes arise when the past strategic or functional domination becomes completely intertwined with the organization's culture. Organizations begin to believe subconsciously that they know the rules for success and they stick to them. They also build control and measurement and reward systems to enforce and encourage the existing recipe.

Recipes can be tremendously useful in focusing an organization's attention and learning on a limited range of activities which give it the best chances of success. So, on the one hand, having and developing an appropriate recipe is highly desirable. However, as global turbulence leads to an increasing segmentation and shift in customer needs it becomes more and more likely that any recipe is going to become unfocused on real market needs. This implies that recipes must be avoided at all costs.

There is a real and natural tendency for recipes to become fixed and invariate. This is partly due to the logical drive described in the resource and control paradox above. Analysis and creative learning outside the recipe, a prerequisite for successful strategy development and implementation, is severely curtailed. Also, because of the strong controls and limitations of the recipe, the recipe comes into immediate and serious conflict with strategy which requires actions which are deemed as outside the recipe.

A new definition of strategy

As the world speeds up, processes of change become condensed into shorter periods of time. A year, once the budgeting and reporting cycle (a short time), has become a long time as more and more and different events are packed in. It is now more likely that the budgets will show variances before they are complete and signed off. To think about strategy in terms of long-term or short-term has lost its meaning. It is far more useful to think of it in terms first described by

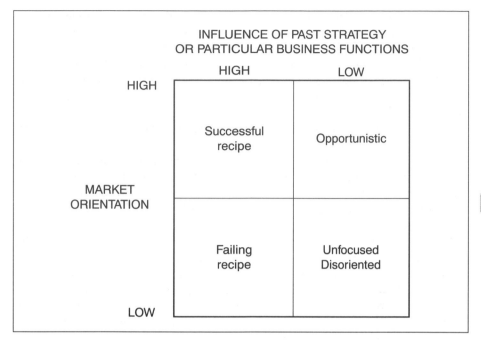

Fig. 4 Occurence and effectiveness of organizational recipes

Peter Drucker: 'Long-range planning does not deal with future decisions. It deals with the futurity of present decisions.'[5] Strategy has to be redefined to become the *conscious manipulation of the future*. That is, it concerns both actions taken now, which we expect to have a long-term effect, and actions which will take a period of time, possibly into the long term, to carry out.

This definition is the last nail in the coffin of elegantly constructed *complete* strategies. Instead, it recognizes that the only way to succeed and sustain strategy is to manipulate many key strings in parallel. The organization must address the strategic problems that it faces each on its own merit and in isolation. Some of these problems will be understood and acceptable while others will neither be understood nor acceptable to the organization. Indeed the strategy must succeed *in spite* of the organization and its recipe for success. It must succeed, one *battle* at a time, managing change in bite-size 'chunks' or projects. With some understanding of the business's goals (making money now and in the future) then the strategic problems or opportunities faced can be identified and dealt with on an individual basis.

It is for this reason that organizations are starting to use projects as the basic unit for implementing strategy. Because of the degree of control gained by redefining major change as projects, they provide a powerful means of implementing a complex and continuously changing strategy.

The final drive behind the move to projects as a way of implementing strategy is that many modern strategies demand global actions. They must transcend national or regional cultures. Any effective project will build its own project culture, and by harnessing the unifying aspects of a common project culture it is possible to address and overcome many of the transnational blockages and resistances to change. Furthermore the project culture can be extended and used to form the basis of the post-implementation culture.

Are all strategic problems the same?

One way of categorizing types of strategic problems faced by organizations is by the likelihood that they are within an existing recipe. Four categories have been used. The category that the organization's problems fall into depends on a dynamic ratio. The ratio between how fast external events (the business environment) are changing (BEC) compared to how fast the organization can learn and build its experience in any particular area (OLE).

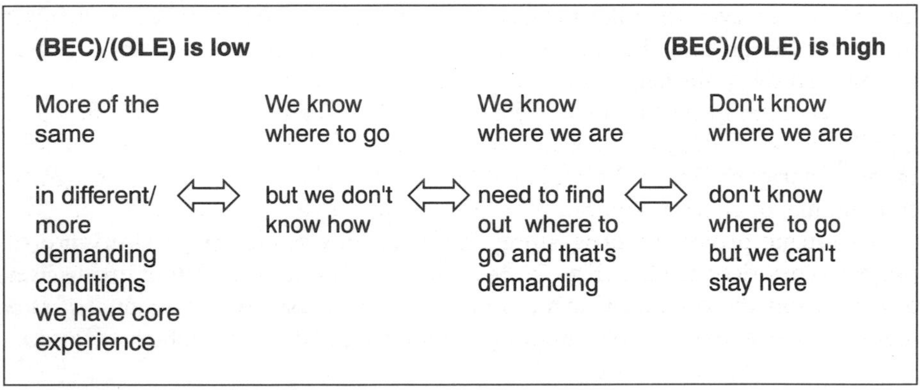

(BEC)/(OLE) is low			(BEC)/(OLE) is high
More of the same	We know where to go	We know where we are	Don't know where we are
in different/ more demanding conditions we have core experience	but we don't know how	need to find out where to go and that's demanding	don't know where to go but we can't stay here

Fig. 5 Types of strategic problem

At one end of the scale, the organization is facing a strategic problem where it has previously captured most of the learning and experience it needs to tackle the problem. At the other end of the spectrum, the world and events have changed much faster than the organization's ability to learn. As a result the organization finds itself wrong-footed, but unsure of exactly how to get out of that position.

Organizations often find that most of the problems they face are skewed towards the right-hand side of the spectrum. This is not surprising given the increasing pace of change. Historically, strategic processes have been focused on the type of problem in the first category.

Achieving strategy through projects

Henry Mintzberg has described strategies as deliberate or emergent, depending on the level of cognition and cohesion of ideas preceding implementation.[6]

The types of processes likely to be associated with the problems on the right hand side of the spectrum are emergent processes or/and emergent strategy. In general, organizational problems get translated into actions, changes that must be carried out, projects, initiatives or policies. If the impetus for the projects comes from the left-hand side of the spectrum, the organization has a good understanding of what it is embarking on, it understands how it is to be done. In short the options for the project leader are closed.

If, however, the impetus for the project arises from any of the other three categories to the right, then the organization tends to be either unsure of what it is attempting to achieve through the project, or how it is be carried out, or both. This is the sort of project where the organization says that it is embarking on business process re-engineering or benchmarking and yet no senior executive can really explain what is to be achieved or how and, as a group, senior management doesn't have a shared view of the purpose of the project. This time the options seem open. This can be very frustrating for the project manager. It feels like an opportunity for a feasibility study or pilot project. However, even the pilot project suffers the same ambiguity and is difficult to get off the ground. Furthermore, events keep changing at such a rate that the pilot study is obsolete almost before it is complete.

Projects used to be simplistically described as something with a beginning, a middle and an end. Now we know that modern projects must come in a wider range of varieties. This is helpful as it allows managers to deal with the significant chunks of change required to implement strategy.

A strategic project or programme is likely to be made up of a mixture of project types described in Fig. 7. A project becomes strategic when it arises directly from the organization's attempt to manipulate its future, or if it is a major change activity whose failure would be catastrophic to the organization.

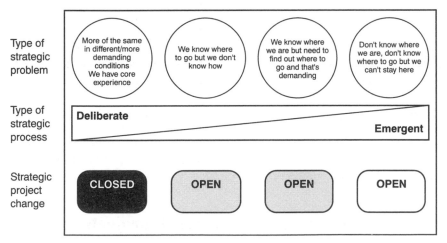

Fig. 6   Relationship between the type of problem, the type of project, and the appropriate process for managing implementation

Unlike an operational project whose failure tends to have localized impact, it is common to find a series of projects, which together influence the organization's future, described as a programme.

Understanding how modern projects work

Figure 7 illustrates the four main types of project change relevant to implementing deliberate and emergent strategies.

P – The **Painting-by-numbers** type of project is formally known as a *closed* project. Traditional projects tend to be of this kind. In fact many organizations still only recognize this type as a project. In *closed* projects you and most of your stakeholders are sure of both *what to do* and *how* it is to be done. These projects arise when the organization is repeating a change of which it has significant experience. Generally the strategic development is from within the organizational recipe and is directional in nature.

At the outset exactly which skills are going to be required is known. The organization will usually have written methods, procedures and systems describing what and how things were done in the past. Such projects might

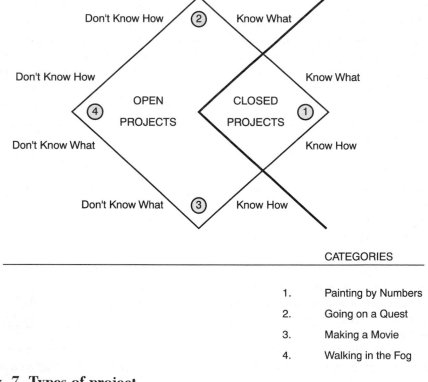

CATEGORIES

1.	Painting by Numbers
2.	Going on a Quest
3.	Making a Movie
4.	Walking in the Fog

Fig. 7 Types of project

186

include a pharmaceutical company carrying out drug trials on a new substance or an established construction company putting up yet another building.

In these cases the project's success is determined by it being managed effectively through four stages:

- **Definition** The specific objectives of the project are set, along with estimates of time and cost.
- **Planning and resourcing** The project deliverables are broken down into subtasks. The resources required are determined and obtained. It is common here to use planning and scheduling software extensively to establish critical paths and resource requirements.
- **Implementation** The tasks are carried out as scheduled against a programme of milestones.
- **Handover** The project deliverables are established as day-to-day working practices in the organization.

Paradoxically, closed projects are difficult because the organization knows both what and how the project is to be carried out. The projects tend to be large, involved and very complex. The challenge is to do it better, faster, bigger or with less resources than last time. Metaphorically, the secret with these types of projects is to spend care and effort in drawing out the outline and numbering each shape and then painting in the right order, light colours first, and checking that everyone paints right up to the line perfectly.

M – the Making a **Movie** type of project is formally known as a *semi-open project*. In *semi-open* projects you and most of your stakeholders are very sure of *how* the project should be conducted but not of *what* is to be done. Typically, the organization has built up significant expertise and investment in the methods it intends to apply and has several people very committed to the method. An example of this is a project to develop new products or market uses for a new invention or technology. It is also the typical experience an inventor goes through looking for applications for a new technology.

Because you know how the project is to be run, it is tempting to spend your time on defining and planning the *how* part of the project. You must, instead, put tremendous effort into finding yourself a good script and the movie will write itself.

Q – the Going on a **Quest** type of project is formally known as a *semi-closed project*. In *semi-closed* projects you and most of your stakeholders are very sure of *what* should be done. It is usually a very seductive idea, such as having a paperless office or a new management information system. However, you are unsure of *how* to achieve this.

The secret of a successful quest is to get your knights fired up and then send them off to 'seek' in parallel, different places at the same time, returning on a fixed date to report progress and share it with others.

F – the Walking or Lost in the **Fog** type of project is formally known as an *open project*. Strategy implementation is occurring well outside the recipe. If you are running such a project you really feel as if you are caught in the fog.

You can't stay where you are, so you've got to move. You are walking in a thick, but uneven fog. In *open* projects you, and most of your stakeholders, are unsure of *what* is to be done and unsure of *how* it is to be carried out. Typically the organization is attempting to do something it has never attempted before. This is usually because the external business, political, legislative or sociological environment has changed or because the organization is implementing a new strategy.

An example would be running a quality-improvement programme for the first time, or developing a brand new product for a market, or segment, which you have not sold to in the past.

In such a project the process followed is:

- **Identifying stakeholders and gaining consensus.** Because the strategic implementation is outside the recipe it becomes important to ensure that all appropriate contributors are involved and are learning the solution. Handover happens during the project.
- **Establishing a communication strategy.** With global projects in particular, outside the recipe projects need high levels of effective communication.
- **Back-from-the future.** Planning in reverse, using structured brainstorms which work backwards from what you would like to achieve.
- **Implementation.** First action taken.
- **Review.** Progress of first actions is widely reviewed.
- **Learning.** Decision making on the next most appropriate actions is carried out.
- **Planning.** Use of back-from-the future techniques (repeat from implementation step).

The secret of success in this type of project is to proceed one step at a time – very carefully but quickly.

Implementing strategy through projects

Much of the success in using projects to implement strategy relies on selecting a full range of projects which address all the issues influencing our ability to actively manipulate the future. It is important for the strategy developers to recognize that, to borrow and modify a concept from Stephen Hawking, they will 'find themselves living in the most probable future of their organizations'. The full range of projects selected will, therefore, arise from a number of strategic considerations and current constraints which will need to be removed – gaps in skills, capabilities, customers, products, etc – between the current state and any future state, and establishing the source and management of future constraints.

In turbulent business environments a large proportion of the projects identified will be outside the current recipe. As a result the projects are likely to be open. At all costs, open projects must be included in the portfolio as they provide the main route to future successful recipes. Furthermore the project culture which develops around a successfully managed project provides an opportunity for the organization to experiment with new ways of working to form the basis of the future recipe.

Bringing implementation to life

Successful implementation revolves around two parallel, but counter-current, processes:

The first involves a number of steps – the interpretation of the strategic problems; developing an understanding of the strategic imperatives; translation of the strategic issues into a strategic project portfolio or programme; selection of appropriate people to manage the individual projects of the programme or portfolio. The process converts complexity and ambiguity into the certainty required for action.

This process flow is from strategic development to implementation and evolves at a slow rate.

The second process involves developing an understanding of the practical day-to-day barriers and constraints to the projects; gaining an understanding of the reactions to project implementation, such as the reaction of competitors or staff to implementation; co-ordinating and reviewing the overall programme or strategic project; translating the key issues into a form to be communicated into the overall strategic analysis process; and informing and influencing the overall strategic analysis process. The process converts the detail of day-to-day activity into a broad vision and context.

This second process flows from day-to-day implementation upwards to strategic development. It usually evolves at a very rapid rate.

Between these two processes, managing both simultaneously, is the programme manager or strategic project leader. This is among the most demanding roles of the modern business.

Getting the right person

As distinct from project leaders who run operational projects, the strategic project leader or programme manager requires a broader and rarer range of skills, ones not normally required in conventional line or project management careers.

Most project management careers are built on delivering operational projects. For these, success equates with completion of the project. In contrast, strategic project leaders are capable of bringing their own projects to an abrupt end, before completion, if they are no longer relevant to the overall needs of the organization.

Success in line management careers is also not usually based on skills to deliver complex and dynamic change. The skills of across-the-line leadership and co-ordination of a network of tasks are unlikely to be finely honed skills.

The preference for the type of change with which the person feels comfortable is also a consideration. For example, open change, arising from the strategic projects on the right-hand side of Fig. 5 requires a personality more at home with ambiguity, creativity and vision; while closed change is best led by an adapter, focused on standards and delivery.

Skills of the strategic project leader

The three sets of skills required by strategic project leaders are:

Strategic management interpretation

- The skills of being able to understand the organization's strategy and being capable of contributing to its development in an economic, financial and marketing context.
- An ability to understand the organization's strategy and its development and to contribute to the future strategic debate, through what is learnt from implementation.
- The strategic project leader or programme manager needs the ability to develop their own vision of the change and understand where the organization's current operations and recipe are in conflict with the future strategic needs. This set of skills ensures that the output of the programme is in line with the needs of the organization and that the paradox of solving tactical versus strategic needs is overcome.

Invisible leadership

- An ability to lead colleagues, directors, senior managers and external stakeholders without becoming ensnared in the political system of the organization.
- The ability to problem solve and transfer ownership through effective process consultation and diagnostic skills.
- The ability to empathize and so work across different cultures, as well as departmental, organizational and often national barriers.

Managing a project portfolio

- An ability to further break down the strategic project into a portfolio of projects and to select appropriate project leaders to manage the different elements. Throughout, maintaining a clear view of the purpose of each element of the project in order to allow them to co-ordinate and monitor progress.
- The ability to effectively mentor and coach a number of project leaders.

There are few things worse than implementing a project which does not improve business performance. Figures 9 and 10 show ways of representing

190

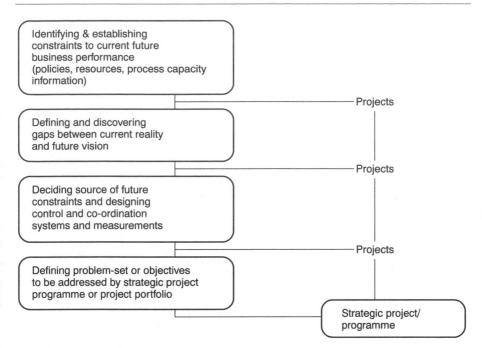

Fig. 8 Process for selection

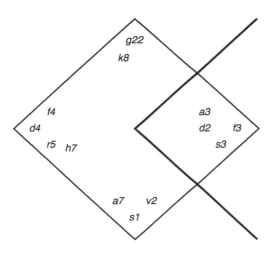

Code	Name	Description	Leader	Sponsor	Links with:
a3		Decentralization	CM	FES	a7, v2
a7	Pits	Market research	PT	IF	a3, k8
d4	EUJV	Design joint venture	EAD	JH	
h7		Network development	KT	CS	s1, s3

Fig. 9 Project portfolio: by project type

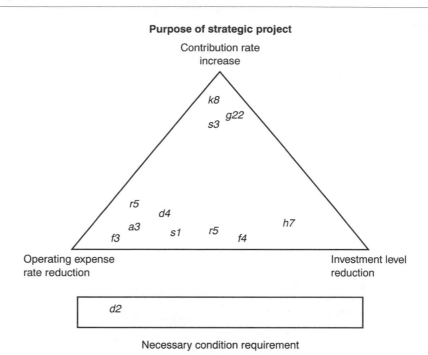

Purpose of strategic project

Fig. 10 Project portfolio: projects by business objective

the programme of projects. Figure 9, by project type, provides an ongoing overview of the degree and frequency of intervention required to successfully manage each project within the portfolio. Figure 10 provides an overview of the purpose of each project. Figure 8 is typical of the range of projects which would be expected of an organization pursuing a cost leadership strategy.

Project profile maps for each quarter show the evolution of projects with time.

Strategy implementation has become more difficult and at the same time absolutely essential. Continuing and chaotic change means that the only chance of success lies in treating implementation as a series of discrete and parallel project activities. By selecting the right person, and by monitoring the implementation as a portfolio or programme of linked changes, successful implementation can be achieved. However, the skills required by the programme manager or strategic project leader are not likely to have been developed during a conventional functional career. Skills development in this area is of vital importance.

One thing is certain, eventually organizations will learn how to manage strategy in a chaotic business environment. Those which do not will cease to exist as the focused competitive pressures on them grow. Those that succeed will do so on the basis of a different mindset, one of managing all change, and especially strategic change, in discrete but manageable projects. They will use closed-project approaches to reinforce and upgrade today's recipe in as fast and effective a way as possible. They will use open projects as a way to break away from today's recipe and prepare for tomorrow.

Dr Eddie Obeng is founder director of Pentacle, the Virtual Business School, and a director of the NWLM Health Trust. He has lengthy experience of making projects happen and of managing change in real situations. As a project leader with Shell he ran development projects; he also instituted a re-engineering programme at Ashridge. He is co-author of *Making Re-engineering Happen* (1994) and author of *All Change! The Project Leader's Secret Handbook* (1994).

Further Reading

Geddes, M, Hastings, C, and Briner, W, *Project Leadership*, Gower, Aldershot, 1990.
Lock, D, (ed.) *Project Management*, Gower, Aldershot, 1992 (5th edn).
Obeng, E, *All Change! The Project Leader's Secret Handbook*, FT/Pitman, London, 1994.

References

1 Thompson, AA, and Strickland, AJ, *Strategic Management: Concepts and Cases*, Richard D Irwin, 1990.
2 Campbell, A, Devine, M and Young, D, *A Sense of Mission*, Hutchinson Business Books, London, 1990.
3 Lorange, P, (ed.) *Implementing Strategic Processes*, Blackwell, Oxford, 1993.
4 Miller, D, *The Icarus Paradox*, Harper Business Books, London, 1991.
5 Drucker, P, *Managing in Turbulent Times*, Butterworth Heinemann, London, 1980.
6 Mintzberg, H, *The Strategy Process – Contexts, Concepts and Cases*, Prentice Hall, New York, 1988.

Quality and Beyond

'Quality is free.'   *Philip Crosby*[1]

'Total Quality is a world movement. Regardless of country or industry, the laggards are at risk; conversely, the leaders acquire insulation against failure.'   *Richard Schonberger*[2]

'Quality is a way of life.'
                    Jan Timmer, president of Philips Electronics[3]

[1] Crosby, P, *Quality is Free*, McGraw Hill, New York, 1979.
[2] Schonberger, R, *Building a Chain of Customers*, The Free Press, New York, 1990.
[3] Quoted in Houlder, V, 'Two steps forward one step back', *Financial Times*, 31 October 1994.

OVERVIEW

Tim Dickson

Total quality management, or TQM, has had a mixed reception in the West. Hailed by some as the most powerful management tool of the last 40 years, it was first used to ruthless effect by Japanese manufacturers as they entered foreign markets after the Second World War. Enthusiasts say it remains *the* crucial corporate challenge of the 1990s (even of the twenty-first century), that properly applied TQM demonstrably feeds through into better business results, and that European companies which turn their backs on it can never aspire to world class status.

Other commentators are more sceptical. They point to the large number of businesses which have felt disappointed and let down by TQM over the last 10 to 15 years. They suspect there may be cultural barriers in Europe which even the most experienced quality practitioners find difficult to overcome. And they fear that the original quality message has been corrupted – at least devalued – by acronym-spinning consultants unable to resist peddling new potions.

The acronyms – TQC (Total Quality Control), SPC (Statistical Process Control), and SQC (Statistical Quality Control) to name a few – certainly sow confusion. But the central idea of TQM is not difficult to grasp even if attempts at definition sometimes start by spelling out what it is not. TQM, for example, goes well beyond the traditional notion of product or service quality measured by a fixed, predetermined standard – complaints per thousand or whatever – at the end of a production run. It emcompasses the whole organization. It puts the spotlight on costs, delivery times, product development cycles, business processes, and changes in the marketplace. Above all, it makes total customer satisfaction the over-riding goal of the company.

TQM can only succeed, its exponents often say, if every member of an organization sees himself or herself as having two jobs: the one which they actually perform day in, day out, and represents their formal job description, the other which requires them to stand back and consider how they can improve what they are doing, the process by which they are doing it, and the way they relate to other people. Such energy and imagination can only be unleashed through the 'empowering' of workers by management, another 'big' idea which has developed a life of its own.

TQM is so all-embracing that its disciples tend to claim parentage of most modern management panaceas. Business process re-engineerng – the hot consultancy 'sell' which has captured corporate imaginations on both sides of the Atlantic in the early 1990s, falls into this category.

Pursuing standards and systems is also an inescapable part of TQM, but too strong an emphasis on this can be unhealthy. Achieving certification under

ISO 9000 or its equivalents, for instance, may be a demonstration that a company is able to define its key processes and keep to them. It is merely a rung on the ladder to Total Quality – nothing more. In itself it conveys neither top level commitment nor a mission to serve the customer, both essential features of genuine TQM.

For true TQM adherents – the Japanese especially but also a growing number of US and European companies – the journey never ends, which is why *Kaizen* (or continuous improvement) is one word from the quality lexicon much touted in the West.

TQM's history – not least the way its star first rose in the East – is crucial to a proper understanding today. The leadership which Japan established is sometimes traced to a series of lectures in product quality delivered four decades ago by the American duo widely credited with inventing TQM, Dr W Edwards Deming and Joseph M Juran. Some commentators have suggested that these two somehow gave away secrets to 'the enemy', but such a conclusion is pure rationalization after the event. American audiences heard the same message from these emerging gurus but, whereas Japanese corporate soil was fertile to receive the seed of a new idea, North American soil was not.

Hard as it is to believe today, consumer goods made in Japan were synonymous with shoddy workmanship after the Second World War. As Deming and Juran were soon to find, though, their eager hosts were not without a tradition of quality. It could be found, for example, in Japan's long history of craftsmanship in handmade goods – superior over the centuries to much of what could be found in Europe – and in the military hardware to which the imperial power's best engineers and managers had for years devoted themselves. The shock of losing the war opened Japanese minds to the need for change, galvanized the country into tackling world export markets, and fuelled their determination to address their quality weaknesses.

American corporations, by contrast, saw no reason to change. Given that their products were generally every bit as good as European ones – and of course better than those of the Japanese – their main concern at the time was with lower prices. US manufacturers thus responded in a wholly logical way by lowering their labour costs – moving offshore in many cases – appealing to Washington for tariff protection or to the American public to buy American.

There were certainly sound cultural reasons why the Deming and Juran approach to 'total' quality – ultimately adding up to a management philosophy for the whole organization – found a particularly receptive audience in Japan. The superiority of group action over individual behaviour which lies at the heart of TQM, for example, had become established in the country's rice-growing regions over thousands of years. Deliberately isolated by their feudal Shogunates, the best means of survival for generations of Japanese had been to work together to harvest the rice crop between typhoons. Even today the challenge of growing large amounts of food on tiny or difficult plots of ground encourages co-operation and group consciousness.

The Japanese do not therefore lose kudos when they share ideas or try to find solutions together – an important contrast to the West where the rewards system encourages individuals to take as much credit as possible. It sometimes sets individuals against their peers, even against the corporation.

In an important article which appeared in the *Harvard Business Review* in 1993, Juran also made much of the fact that his Japanese audiences in the early 1950s were the chief executives of major corporations, whereas his North American listeners were primarily engineers and quality inspectors. Part of what he told them – the then state of the art of quality management – was not revolutionary. Manufacturing products to design specifications and then inspecting them for defects to protect the buyer, he pointed out, was something the Egyptians had mastered 5,000 years previously when building the pyramids. Similarly, the ancient Chinese had set up a separate department of the central government to establish quality standards and maintain them.

The other bit of Juran's message, however – that radical quality improvement could be effected by going further than manufacturing to specification and testing for defects – was highly original at the time and eagerly absorbed by his Japanese audiences. The idea was initially inspired by Juran's own analysis in the mid-1920s of the large number of tiny circuit-breakers routinely scrapped by his then employer Western Electric. By scrutinizing the manufacturing process rather than simply waiting at the end of a production line to count the defective products, Juran put his finger on the circuit-breaker problem and worked out how the company could substantially reduce the level of waste. (Ironically, he was told by his boss that this wasn't his job. 'We're the inspection department and our job is to look at these things after they are made and find the bad ones. Making them right in the first place is the job of the production department.')

Armed with Juran's and Deming's insights into organizational barriers of this kind, the Japanese started to pursue a wider, strategic role for quality which laid the foundations for later Western thinking and involved the following:

- Senior executives taking personal charge of quality.
- A 'cascade' approach to training starting at the top and descending through the management hierarchy.
- The use of statistical methods of quality control (this was Deming's early source of expertise).
- The enlargement of business plans to include clear quality goals.

The Japanese also pioneered ways of measuring customer satisfaction and the performance of key processes (such as cycle time for product development and order to delivery). The involvement of senior executives which is now consistently cited as a key factor in TQM success was underlined by the fact that in some leading Japanese companies the quality audit was called the president's audit since the company president personally supervised the presentation meeting.

That a quality revolution did not take place in the United States in the 1960s and 1970s does not mean that the quality of US goods was declining; most studies show that it was slowly improving. The point was, however, that the rate of progress made by the Japanese was much faster, with the result that Japanese companies caught up with and overtook their Western competitors.

Juran believes US businesses were ambushed for two reasons: they assumed their Asian adversaries were copycats rather than innovators, and their chief executives were too obsessed with financial indicators to notice any danger signs on the quality dashboard.

Xerox Corporation is probably the best example of a financially powerful company that was taken by surprise. In the 1950s and 1960s Xerox processes outperformed every other method of copying and the company made a fortune leasing its machines (it had such a stranglehold on the market it wouldn't sell them). In the absence of effective competition it didn't seem to matter that its products broke down frequently – in fact it was even seen as good business, given that the service department made profits. When the Japanese arrived on the scene with more reliable alternatives, however, the effect on Xerox sales was devastating.

The same thing happened with motors. In the 1950s Japanese cars were of such poor quality they were virtually unsaleable in the United States, yet by the mid-1970s their manufacturers were surging into the lead.

If the Western response was slow getting into gear, the TQM bandwaggon started to roll once the corporate sector's mind had become more firmly engaged in the early 1980s. By the end of the decade, quality was widely recognized as one of the most important factors of success in global markets. The President of the United States and the US Secretary of Commerce had personally weighed in with their support, and the message was spreading to Europe. In October 1991 *Business Week* published a bonus issue devoted exclusively to quality which sold out in a matter of days and ran to two spec- ial printings of tens of thousands of copies.

The high profile which TQM has now achieved in the West owes much to the example of companies which have conspicuously used quality as part of their recovery strategies (most spectacularly Xerox itself, for instance) or to establish market leadership (eg, Motorola, Unisys and Hewlett Packard). The creation of role models was encouraged by the Malcolm Baldridge Awards in the United States (derived from so-called Deming Awards in Japan) and the annual competition staged by the European Foundation for Quality Management. In November 1994 Rover Group – a company once almost pounded into submission by Japanese rivals – was awarded the first UK Quality Award with the transport group TNT Express. 'The awards give other companies – not least small but growing businesses – clear examples to emulate,' UK Prime Minister John Major said at the prize-giving ceremony.

For all the rhetoric and for all the companies which have enthusiastically embraced TQM, though, the burgeoning army of quality evangelists has not seen off the doubters. One reason is the lack of evidence in Europe and North America conclusively linking TQM to tangible bottom-line benefits. Two early American prizewinners – Florida Light and Power and Wallace – subsequently appeared to fall well short of their quality reputations and attracted adverse publicity for the TQM approach. A clutch of surveys in the UK suggests that the majority of companies implementing TQM programmes had found the results disappointing. Such surveys – often conducted by self-interested consultants – usually conclude that the implementation is at fault. But there is no panacea.

Most managers in Europe and North America probably appreciate that quality does not follow automatically from beefing up an inspection team, that improved results do not flow painlessly from a group of 'involved' employees like tonic from a bottle. Finding the magic ingredient, though, remains elusive and requires a combination of resourcefulness, experimentation and perseverance. Learning the concept of TQM is not difficult in theory, nor is it necessarily hard to explain the benefits. But while the lists of instructions and modes of action which TQM spawns are hard to dispute – in meetings stick to the agenda, add value when you speak, criticize ideas not individuals, for example – actually doing these things effectively is another matter.

Therein lies one explanation for the acronyms often seen as confusing the TQM message these days. For even progressive companies periodically need to 'reinvent' quality from time to time, to find a new and more inspiring altar on which managers and employees can focus their worship.

The main 'text' in Europe, however, is likely to remain the quality criteria developed by EFQM, not only as the basis for its award, but as the basis for self-assessment and individual quality benchmarking by interested companies.

Essentially the model says that customer satisfaction, employee satisfaction, a beneficial impact on society and thereby good business results are achieved by leadership driving policy and strategy, people management, resources and sound processes. For the purposes of the award, customer satisfaction (with 20 per cent of the available marks) is the most important category.

This model is as an effective means as any of determining whether a company is, or is not, a truly quality-oriented organization:

- Leadership is a critical issue and 'quality' companies will therefore show that their executives are visibly involved in TQM programmes, that there is a consistent TQM culture across the organization, that successes of teams and individuals are recognized, that adequate resources are provided, that customers and suppliers are involved and that the message is promoted outside the company.
- Policy and strategy should reflect the TQM concept. They should be the basis for business plans, should be communicated, and should be regularly reviewed and improved.
- People management is how a 'quality' company unleases its full potential and achieves continuous improvement. It will be reflected in recruitment, training and career progression which retains and develops human skills and capabilities, empowerment of individuals to take appropriate actions, and effective top-down and bottom-up communication.
- Resources are effectively managed and deployed by companies which are practising TQM. These include finance, information and material resources and takes in the way technology is applied.

- Processes are value-adding activities and TQM forces companies to identify the critical ones, use performance measures to review and improve them, encourage innovation, and successfully implement and evaluate changes to them.
- Customer satisfaction is achieved when the company can demonstrate it has satisfied the needs and expectations of its customers.
- People, or employee, satisfaction is achieved when the needs and expectations of the people who work for the company are demonstrably being met.
- Business results are not so much the financial numbers in themselves so much as the achievement of its financial and non-financial targets, and the ability to satisfy everyone with a financial interest in the company.

Tim Dickson is management editor of the *Financial Times*.

Further Reading

Crosby, P, *Quality is Free*, McGraw Hill, New York, 1979.
Juran, J, *Juran on Planning for Quality*, Free Press, New York, 1988.
Schonberger, R, *Building a Chain of Customers*, The Free Press, New York, 1990.

THINKERS

W Edwards Deming

1900–1993; statistician and consultant

The philosophy of quality and productivity developed by Dr William Edwards Deming has exerted profound influence on global managerial thinking. Its argot now peppers the lanuage of management – 'continuous improvement', 'control the process', 'customer first', and many more of today's concepts have their origins in Deming's ideas.

Having earned a doctorate in mathematical physics in 1928 Deming, in the depressed America of the thirties, became interested in the pioneering work of Walter A Shewhart who was seeking to apply statistical methods to the control of variation in industrial production. With the impetus of World War Two, Deming and Shewhart's innovative systems were introduced to American manufacturing in 1942. They resulted in marked improvements to performance in the organizations where they were instituted. However, following the Allied victory in 1945, American industry, which was suddenly enjoying booming markets, reverted to procedures based around product inspection.

It was in Japan that Deming's approach to quality improvement gained a receptive audience. In 1950 he told Japanese business people: 'Don't just make it and try to sell it, but redesign it, and then again bring the process under control...with ever-increasing quality...The consumer is the most important part of the production line.' In 1951, the first award ceremony for the now prestigious Deming Prize was held.

Deming appreciated that no matter how powerful the tool of mathematical statistics might be it would be ineffective unless used in the correct cultural context. So, based upon this foundation of numeracy he built a humanistic philosophy, the two disciplines forming the twin pillars of his theory. This combination of two mutually-dependent and supportive themes, each essential to the other, was eventually labelled Total Quality Management.

Commenting on Deming's work, management writer Robert Heller observed:

'His work bridges the gap betwen science-based application and humanistic philosophy. Statistical quality control is as arid as it sounds. But results so spectacular as to be almost romantic flow from using these tools to improve processes in ways that minimize defects and eliminate the deadly trio of rejects, rework and recalls.'[1]

The 'arid' world of statistics is the coping stone of Deming's approach. Every business generates overwhelming masses of numbers. But, data is not information. The task of turning data into information falls squarely into the realm of statistics. There is no other way, all else is wild guesswork. The questions 'What do these numbers mean?' and 'Do they mean anything at all?' can be answered only by the exercise of number-theory. This is a core element of quality. The statistical process control systems of Shewhart and Deming aim to provide continuous answers to questions such as these. They seek to use the predictive power of probability and significance testing, to tell managers when and when not to take action. This method, teaching how to 'listen to the voice of the process', is a critical element of total quality.

Deming's philosophy was distilled into fourteen points.

Deming's Fourteen Points

1. Create constancy of purpose towards improvement of product and service, with the aim to become competitive and to stay in business, and to provide jobs.
2. Adopt the new philosophy. We are in a new economic age, created by Japan. Transformation of Western management style is necessary to halt the continued decline of industry.
3. Cease dependence on inspection to achieve quality. Eliminate the need for inspection on a mass basis by building quality into the product in the first place.
4. End the practice of awarding business on the basis of price tag. Purchasing must be combined with design of product, manufacturing, and sales to work with the chosen suppliers: the aim is to minimize total cost, not merely initial cost.
5. Improve constantly and forever every activity in the company, to improve quality and productivity and thus constantly decrease costs.
6. Institute training and education on the job, including management.
7. Institute supervision. The aim of supervision should be to help people and machines to do a better job.
8. Drive out fear, so that everyone may work effectively for the company.
9. Break down barriers between departments. People in research, design, sales and production must work as a team to tackle usage and production problems that may be encountered with the product or service.
10. Eliminate slogans, exhortations, and targets for the workforce asking for zero defects and new levels of productivity. Such exhortations only create adversarial relationships; the bulk of the causes of low quality and low productivity belong to the system and thus lie beyond the power of the workforce.

11. Eliminate work standards that prescribe numerical quotas for the day. Substitute aids and helpful supervision, using the methods to be described.

12a. Remove the barriers that rob the hourly worker of the right to pride of workmanship. The responsibility of supervisors must be changed from sheer numbers to quality.

12b. Remove the barriers that rob people in management and in engineering of their right to pride of workmanship. This means, *inter alia*, abolition of the annual or merit rating and of management by objective.

13. Institute a vigorous programme of education and re-training. *New* skills are required for changes in techniques, materials and service.

14. Put everybody in the company to work in teams to accomplish the transformation.

Deming warned not to take his points as a catalogue of commandments cast in stone, to be ritualistically observed by the managerially devout. Nor as a list of rules to be uncritically obeyed by those unable to function without a supporting scaffolding of strict procedures.

While distilling his ideas down to the 'fourteen points', Deming insisted that effective implementation could only be achieved by a full understanding of the underlying theory. 'Experience, without theory, teaches management nothing about what to do to improve quality and competitive position,' he argued.

In the West his ideas were almost completely ignored until the 1980s when the wave of change in Japanese industry became the subject of Western examination and emulation. Interest in Deming's work was initially brought to a mass American audience through a television documentary, 'If Japan can, why can't we?'

The most commonly observed weakness of Deming's 'fourteen points' is his exhortation to 'Drive out fear, so that everyone may work effectively for the company.' If experience, which Deming believed taught managers little, actually teaches managers anything at all, it is that fear still stalks corporate corridors. On this point many attempts at putting Deming's theories into practice have floundered.

It is probably more realistic and profitable to turn Deming's eighth point on its head to read 'Teach courage'. Until this is done the eighth point cripples the other thirteen. Wise leaders cultivate courage by example, training, education, teamwork, trust, integrity – by moral qualities.

In practice, many organizations have claimed to have taken on Deming's philosophy. Often, however, their attempts at implementation come to an abrupt halt because of basic misinterpretations. Quality is not, according to Deming, a matter of setting a standard of how many defects are acceptable. A manager once told Deming: 'I need to know the minimum level of quality necessary to satisfy a customer.' Deming commented: 'So much misunderstanding was conveyed in a few words.'

Also, Deming's philosophy revolves around fundamental changes in the way businesses deal with figures and statistics. Instead of setting aspirational profit targets, Deming argues the emphasis should be on providing quality products and services for customers. By working at constantly improving all processes within a business, customer satisfaction will increase and, inevitably, so too will profits.

Today, his message has been integrated into conventional thinking, in a way that was scarcely imaginable in the late 1970s. It is now generally accepted that inspection is not the route to improved quality; that functions should work together rather than in competition; and that improved processes and systems are more effective than exhortations.

Deming continued preaching his message until shortly before his death in 1993. Companies such as Ford, Rothmans and Bosch are among those which have adopted his philosophy. A prophet without honour in his own country for so long, Deming's last years were spent travelling the world. 'I'm desperate. There's not enough time left,' he is reported to have told a colleague. 'For companies that haven't fully adopted the ideas and practices that Deming, as much as any man, made universal, those last five words will be their epitaph, not his,' concluded Robert Heller.

FRANK PRICE

Frank Price is the author of *Right First Time* (1984) and *Right Every Time* (1990). He is a Fellow of the Institute of Quality Assurance and a member of the Association of Management Education and Development. He is an independent consultant in the field of quality management and cultural change in the work organization.

Further Reading

Aquayo, R, *Dr Deming: The Man Who Taught the Japanese About Quality*, Mercury, London, 1990.

Deming, WE, *Quality, Productivity and Competitive Position*, MIT Centre for Advanced Engineering Study, MIT, Massachusetts, 1982.

Deming, WE, *Out of the Crisis*, Cambridge University Press, Cambridge, 1988.

Price, F, *Right Every Time*, Gower, Aldershot, 1990.

Reference

[1] Heller, R, 'Fourteen points that the West ignores at its peril', *Management Today*, March 1994.

TOTAL QUALITY

Owen Bull

There is a temptation to begin any discussion of Total Quality with a pithy and neat definition of what it aims to achieve and how managers and their organizations can go about putting it into practice. In fact, Total Quality covers too large an area to be contained within a single definition. Indeed, there is much more to be gained from being able to describe it rather than narrowing it down to a definition.

At one level, Total Quality (TQ) is a label. It embraces a number of philosophies, ideas, principles, methods, concepts, tools, techniques and approaches to making improvements in the total performance of an organization. When any of these are examined in isolation they can appear quite simple and, indeed, few of them can be called new.

But, TQ is not just about using a few well-established ideas and methods. Its potential, and indeed its most enduring successes, come from the way its components are blended appropriately and uniquely for the needs of each organization in which it is adopted.

One of the criticisms levelled at TQ is that it is merely a veneer covering what everyone recognizes as good management and commonsense. Although this criticism has some foundation, it is overly simplistic. A brief spell of managerial experience quickly reveals that not everyone – if anyone – agrees about what actually constitutes good management or commonsense.

So, TQ can be seen as a complex blend of many different components and techniques. But, it can also be viewed as the way you would run an organization if you started from scratch on a new site and used your own money. This description seems to appeal to people because it brings a real challenge home very sharply – given the right conditions and with all to play for and everything to lose, isn't TQ the way you would run your own business?

And if at this point your response is 'Well, it's not my money, so that doesn't count', consider how responsible and professional a reaction that is – especially when corporate stewardship is becoming more and more important. Perhaps a more sustainable complaint would be that few of us ever really face a greenfield situation. If that's true, we may need to look for a slightly different description.

In *Winnie the Pooh* – one of the most unlikely sources of inspiration on management theory – there is an apt paragraph: 'Here comes Edward Bear now down the stairs, bump, bump, bump, on the back of his head. He is sure there must be a better way; if only the bumping would stop long enough for him to think of it.' For managers, the bumping goes on. They are frustrated by the fact that they feel they know *what* to do, but are unable to find the answer to *how* to do it.

Organizations become involved in Total Quality for many reasons. In the manufacturing sector, the success of Japanese enterprises triggered much attention in the 1970s. While most organizations merely looked on with interest, others, such as Harley Davidson and Xerox, were forced to take on TQ to survive. Some, of course, ignored all the warnings and perished. While Harley Davidson came out the other side, for example, many other motorcycle manufacturers bit the corporate dust.

Gradually the uptake spread to the service sector. Companies such as British Airways and The Body Shop (to name two diverse examples) have not only survived, but also thrived using TQ-type approaches. But the reasons for getting into this way of working remain broadly similar to those which attracted manufacturers: to survive, beat the competition and to be more profitable.

The same motivation is now spreading to the public sector. Exposure to competition – whether it be in hospitals or refuse collection – has led, in many cases, to a threat of extinction in a way that was unimaginable only a few years ago. A small, but growing, number of public sector organizations are now enthusiastic proponents of TQ, using it to help ensure that they successfully rise to these challenges. And this seems likely to continue, since the principle that society has a right to demand and expect good value from its public bodies is a fundamental one.

Implementing the blend

If implementation of TQ requires that its component parts are blended together, the importance of finding the right blend cannot be over-emphasized. Many failed TQ initiatives foundered because those trying to introduce it did not recognize that the blend was wrong. This is hardly surprising when much of the literature available on the subject serves to confuse more than to clarify. To read one text on TQ is to learn one author's particular dogma. To apply it might be dangerous because it does not fit the needs of the organization closely enough. To read more is to find that recognized authorities on the subject disagree about what TQ is and how it should be adopted. Confusion is the inevitable result. It is far more profitable to read accounts of how different organizations are run or have been transformed, and to understand the values and approaches which underpin their success. These are the real world success stories, where the blend was right.

What of the ingredients of the blend? One way of starting to get the answer to this is to consider this list of questions:

- Does everyone in your organization clearly understand what it exists for?
- Does the organization have clear, measurable, long-term goals, and plans to achieve them, and are people committed to them?

- Is everyone continuously trying to improve things (processes, activities, results) and measuring the results of their efforts in a carefully co-ordinated manner?
- Do people like coming to work in your organization and are they *really* its most important asset?
- Do people regard managers as sources of help and support?
- Does everyone work to meet the needs of those whom your organization serves; its customers?
- Do *all* those who have some stake in your organization feel that it meets their needs?
- Could your organization make major changes in direction without catastrophic disruption?

A positive response to all these questions could only truthfully be given by a small number of organizations worldwide. But this is only a start. To get to the rest of the answer we need to get a much clearer picture of some of the mechanics of the process.

The modern Babel

The Old Testament tells the story of the Tower of Babel. The plan was to build an enormous tower to reach heaven. But, God intervened by confusing the language of the builders so they could not understand each other. The project, in today's parlance, was sub-optimal. It failed.

The tools and techniques of TQ are often the modern equivalent of the Tower of Babel. There is so much confusion and conflict surrounding the subject that the hopes and aspirations of implementors are routinely and regularly dashed – even without divine intervention.

The very existence of tools and techniques suggests there is a tool or technique for every season – all we have to do is to plug into the seven QC tools or QFD, or Policy Deployment, and best practice, continuous improvement and TQ will flow from every pore of the new empowered, enabled organization. The truth is not that simple. Indeed, some of the tools and techniques are fundamentally flawed or limited in their usefulness. So, why are we burdened with them and where do they come from? Some sources are:

- *Study tours* – many study tours whisk eager executives around companies that have been implementing TQ for an impressively lengthy period. They look at Toyota's policy deployment process, Minolta's management and planning tools or Sony's employee suggestion scheme, and return to base with enthusiastic ideas about implementing these things in their own organizations immediately. This approach does not work, because they are trying to run before they can walk.
- *Training organizations* – in the search for the tools and techniques of TQ implementation, many organizations fall into the trap of buying totally

inappropriate training packages which offer tantalizing glimpses of a utopian future. But, start to use the training and you soon realize that very little of it is actually going to have a real impact.

- *Fashions* – organizations are notoriously fashion-conscious. The slavish adoption of new ways of doing things, simply because others are doing them, is unhelpful. Companies often seek to emulate competitors, sister companies, suppliers or companies in the same group. They are more concerned with superficial impressions than practical implementation and are tempted to copy all the things that have worked elsewhere because it's easier than thinking it through for themselves.

Overcoming such pitfalls, in the first place, requires a great deal of thought. The clear lesson from the myriad failed quality programmes is that all the tools and techniques in the world will not help to create large-scale changes unless an organization knows what it is trying to do. Unless some discipline is instilled into a process it will die out, as the initial wave of enthusiasm becomes a ripple on a distant shore.

One approach is to use a quality cycle, linked to the annual business planning cycle of an organization. This is designed to stop TQ going away, to make sure that it is always there, and that it drives the business. Figure 1 shows one such cycle:

The *question* phase begins the change process and is concerned with asking tough, challenging questions of the organization. Importantly, it does not end until appropriate answers have been found.

Areas for questioning include:

- what do we really do?
- what do our customers think of what we do?

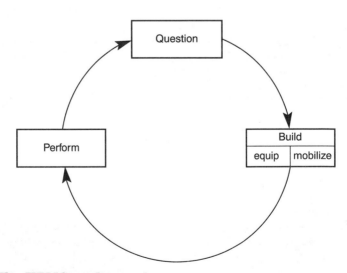

Fig. 1 The KPMG quality cycle
Source: KPMG Management Consulting, 1993

- what do we want to be like in the future?
- what is Total Quality and is it appropriate to the organization?
- what do we need to do during this cycle?

This immediately exposes a critical flaw – it is all too easy to ignore the key issues of what it is an organization really does and whether or not that is correct, and to move immediately on to implementation. TQ requires that the status quo is challenged.

Figure 2 illustrates a technique to challenge organizational assumptions.

The idea is to think about your organization, division by division, factory by factory, product by product, or by whatever level of analysis makes sense, and find out how well you are doing at the things which are really important to customers (ie, do you have your basic strategy right and can you deliver it?). This requires honesty and the ability to be self-critical but, if it is not done, organizations run the risk of improving performance in the wrong areas. If an organization finds anything it does, makes, sells or delivers slipping into the bottom half of the matrix, it could well be heading for trouble.

Inevitably, this does not answer all the questions you need to ask. What it does do is at least make sure that you are moving off from firm ground.

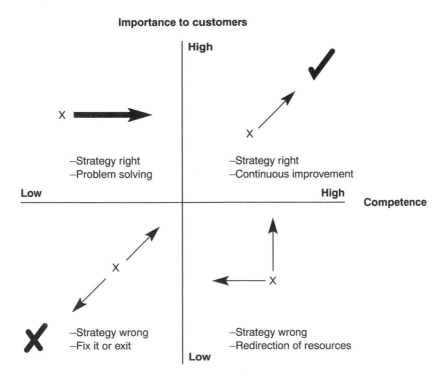

Fig. 2 What is important to customers?
Source: KPMG Management Consulting, 1993

Moving to the *build* phase, we immediately encounter a serious problem. For example, the cycle suggested by the statistician Shewhart follows the pattern: plan, do, check, act. The move directly from *plan* to *do* is liable to create problems. If the organization really is ready, willing and able, this may work. It is, however, extremely unlikely.

So, this phase identifies the critical success factors of the change process and makes sure that vital elements are built into the organization *before* implementation begins. And this introduces a further point which is misunderstood by many: Total Quality is not all about training. Training enables people to do things, but does not empower them to use their skills and the tools and techniques they have been trained in.

The build phase should, therefore, be split into two distinct categories: 'equip' and 'mobilize'. Think of a firework display. You equip yourself with rockets and stakes in the ground ready to launch. But, unless you light the touch paper, you will have failed to produce the outcome you want. You will not have mobilized your resources. Organizations going through change are just the same. They often fail to mobilize their resources.

As an example, in 1902, a 22-year-old was appointed 'technical expert third class' at the Swiss patent office. Three years later, he completed a paper which would later win him the Nobel prize, a doctoral thesis and a special theory of relativity. The following year, Albert Einstein was promoted to 'technical expert second class'.

Resources need to be mobilized. Simply equipping people with skills, tools and techniques is not enough. Their skills could lie dormant – as Einstein's did in his day job.

The split between equipping and mobilizing is critical. This helps organizations to decide what they should be doing in each successive phase. They may then avoid commonly encountered pitfalls. For example, organizations which regard achieving a quality standard (such as BS5750) as a balanced way of improving performance, often find that they have equipped but not mobilized their resources.

Typical issues addressed under the two categories are:

Equip
- quality organization
- quality measurement and systems
- customer orientation training
- tools and techniques training
- personal accountability
- communication systems

Mobilize
- generating and demonstrating commitment
- recognition and reward
- leadership
- communicating

These are not concerned with improving the performance of the organization – that comes next. Instead, they are about creating an environment in which planned implementation will be successful. The key lesson at this stage is the need to build both elements in balance. Move ahead significantly in one area and the process is in danger. Figure 3 can be used to plan the process.

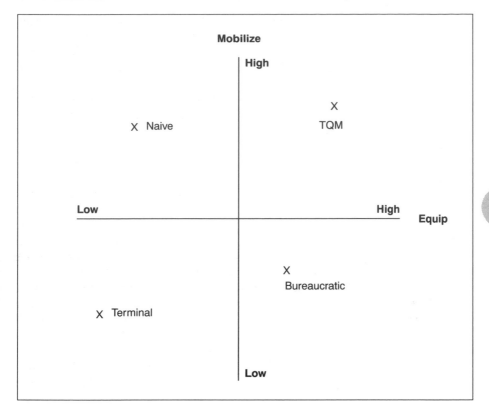

Fig. 3 Equip and mobilize: keeping the balance

Source: KPMG Management Consulting, 1993

The final phase is *perform*. This is where quality improvement activity is highlighted. In this case, however, rather than being a series of isolated incidents, such activity is more akin to the output of a process, one begun by the question phase. And yet, problem-solving and continuous improvement remain prone to disaster – especially if a disciplined, stepped process is not followed.

A typical disciplined improvement process will involve classic problem-solving methods. Figure 4 illustrates one.

An important added ingredient here is to 'check necessary competencies and commitments'. Placed between plan implementation and implementing solution, this in a microcosm is the build phase of the disciplined improvement process. It ensures, in this case, that sufficient resources are put aside (such as training, new software and appropriate communications) to make sure that implementation works and that people are committed to the solution. Again, it is a simple technique, but it makes you stop and think about how you are going to be successful.

To return to the Tower of Babel, the message is clear: tools and techniques are not a universal panacea, a clear path to where you want to go or, even, a

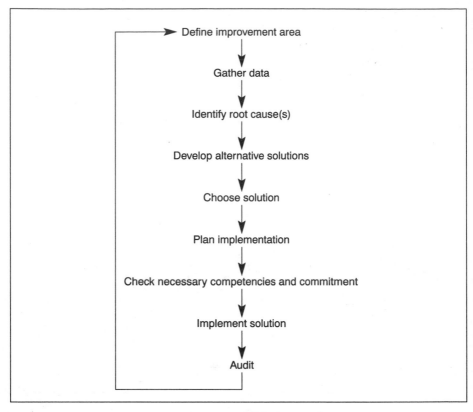

Define improvement area

Gather data

Identify root cause(s)

Develop alternative solutions

Choose solution

Plan implementation

Check necessary competencies and commitment

Implement solution

Audit

Fig. 4 A typical disciplined improvement campaign
Source: KPMG Management Consulting, 1993

stairway to heaven. Your Babel can't be allowed to run into mayhem. You have to really think about what your organization is trying to do and what it needs to do it.

Achieving balance

And yet, there is still something missing. Ingredient X. The final touch. 'Patience be damned, I'm going to kill something!' runs the caption to a cartoon featuring two vultures – one impassively awaiting the demise of his next meal, the other increasingly irritated by the rules of engagement.

To translate this example into corporate reality, take two examples:

1. A manufacturing company needed to change one of its basic fabrication processes. The new method was tried, trusted and virtually risk free. The team which was assembled to sort the change was confident and competent. However, for no reason anyone could really explain, it decided to run a three-

week trial of the new process to ensure that it really did work. Predictably, the trial worked perfectly, but afterwards, the change team was discontented. 'We can't sanction such a major change on the basis of a single trial,' they argued. They estimated that three or four more trials were necessary.

2. A public sector organization was trying to restructure some of its regional operations. A great deal of preparation and planning was undertaken. Objectives were defined and methods assessed. The team leader then wrote to everyone stressing the need for urgency. He required first recommendations in 18 months. 'If two or three of us sat down now, we could solve this in a couple of days and the solution would be at least as good, probably better,' reflected one of the managers.

Companies which allow themselves to be driven by procedure, protocol and detail will lose sight of their goal. The danger exposed in both these examples is of driving intuition out of the TQ process. Rigidity, excessive caution, obsession with data and time-consuming decision-making processes, drain the life from any TQ initiative. As we have seen there is a real need to find an appropriate pace and give careful consideration to what it is the organization is doing and how it should do it. But, when it comes to knowing how and when to apply tools, techniques and ideas there can be no substitute for sound judgement – not, after all, a magic ingredient, but something we all think we possess already. TQ does require team processes and much more – but it also demands intuitive, imaginative, courageous and risk-taking managers if it is to bring sustainable, long-term benefits to your business. Which shouldn't be a problem, because that's what we pay them for, isn't it?

Owen Bull is director of Quality Consulting with KPMG. He has 15 years' experience in international commerce and has, since 1992, been leading KPMG's quality practice. He is author of *Jumping the Q: A Total Quality Perspective* (1994), numerous articles, and is a member of the editorial board of *TQM Magazine*. Before his consultancy career, he spent time with Shell, Wellman plc and Cincinnati Milacron, and has worked and studied in Europe, United States, Japan and South Africa.

Further Reading

Chang, YS, Labovitz, G, and Rosansky, V, *Making Quality Work*, HarperCollins, New York, 1993.
Feigenbaum, AV, *Total Quality Control*, McGraw Hill, New York, 1983.
Juran, JM, *Managerial Breakthrough*, McGraw Hill, New York, 1964.

CUSTOMER SERVICE

Brian Moores

Customer service is a long-established concept – as readily associated with traditional businesses as modern service industry. Yet, it was only in the 1980s that customer service was re-discovered by managers after decades of relative neglect.

Key to this re-discovery was the new belief that customer service is not an indulgence, but a vital competitive weapon. This sparked a huge amount of interest and, as a result, there is an increasing body of work which links customer service to enhanced performance, financial and otherwise, and which provides a blueprint for successful customer service strategies.

In their seminal work, *In Search of Excellence*,[1] Tom Peters and Robert Waterman revealed that some of America's most successful companies placed their customers at the centre of attention to an almost obsessive extent. Apparently unaware that they were doing anything other than applying sound common sense, companies such as Federal Express, Disneyworld, Milliken and Stew Leonard's dairy store, pursued policies which resulted in satisfied customers returning time after time.

The success of *In Search of Excellence* sparked a wave of international interest and, elsewhere, similar success stories were found. Highly customer-focused organizations were identified and examined. Often they had pursued a variety of customer service initiatives for many years without the benefit of any guidebook on best or recommended practice.

Though the topic of customer service has now become a mini-industry in its own right, it is clearly not a newly discovered concept. Unlike some other management approaches with short shelf lives, customer service has evolved over the years in a way which suggests that it will not disappear from management's agenda. And, the research of recent years means we now have a much better understanding of the component parts of an optimum customer service strategy.

Customer-focused organizations appear to:

- Appreciate that it makes financial sense to pursue a customer imperative.
- Devote a good deal of time to determining customers' wants; and realize that these wants need to be prioritized.
- Appreciate the value of contrasting performance on all aspects of their service operations against the best being achieved elsewhere.
- See the good sense of installing monitoring systems to ascertain whether customer expectations about the service provided are being met.
- Recognize that, in a service industry, while things can and do go wrong, this should not preclude a striving for zero defects. However, an awareness

of the theoretical impossibility of constantly providing a perfect service runs in parallel with an appreciation that systems need to be in place to cope effectively when things do go wrong.

- Realize that the delivery of excellent customer service demands the recruitment, training and motivation of suitable staff.
- Know that impressive service standards can constitute an integral part of the marketing mix.
- Are able to capitalize on the fact that many service improvements can be brought about through encouraging the involvement of their own staff in this process.

Why do it ?

The PIMS data base,[2] to which several thousand companies contribute, provides the major economic rationale for policies aimed at improving quality or customer service. It was created to explore the consequence of alternative marketing strategies – PIMS being an acronym for Profit Impact of Marketing Strategy. Opinions relating to the perceived quality of the goods or services provided by participants were also solicited. These perceived quality assessments were then cross-tabulated with the financial returns posted by the contributors. Those organizations rated above average with respect to perceived quality achieved a six per cent year-on-year growth in market share and were able to command a nine per cent price premium. Those rated below average experienced a two per cent annual decline in market share. Figure 1 illustrates the correlation which exists between perceived quality and the two financial performance indicators.

In more recent years, other confirmatory data have emerged to support this link between customer service and overall performance. Many of these stem from analyzes undertaken by multi-branched organizations where the opportunity exists to contrast the performance of different units. The various criteria developed for the Baldrige quality awards in the United States or the equivalent European and British quality awards also provides a template against which a company's service quality performance can be gauged. Many companies have used these criteria for self-assessment purposes, perhaps in anticipation of a subsequent submission. For example, after its Rochester plant won the coveted Baldrige award, other divisions of IBM were obliged to subject themselves to the same assessment process. This reconfirmed a high correlation between quality and financial performance.

Slightly more revealing evidence can be gleaned from a study undertaken by Ryder Rentals, best known for the van rental part of its business. The company undertakes a routine annual evaluation of all its franchisees. This incorporates, among other things, customer ratings of the service they received, visits to the sites to test a variety of characteristics of the operation and *dummy* telephone calls made to the outlet. These and other service attributes are scored and

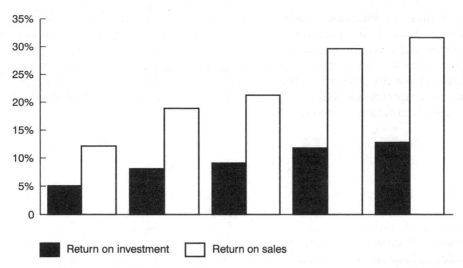

Fig. 1 Effect of relative quality on returns on investment and sales
Source: PIMS database

weighted. The company can determine the sales potential for every site based on local demographics and the size of the catchment population. Actual sales are contrasted with this potential. A cross tabulation of the resulting ratio with the customer service scores is depicted in Fig. 2. A differential of 22 per cent between the best and worst performers is not easily dismissed and the results obviously influence franchising decisions.

These two figures serve merely to illustrate the linkage. Why, though, should companies, whose service performance is highly regarded, produce

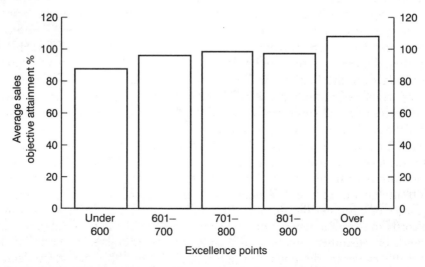

Fig. 2 Commitment to excellence at Ryder Rentals

more attractive financial returns? Because it is likely that excellent quality/service is backed by superior service delivery systems. Another possible consequence might be that companies incur significantly lower costs in putting things right as a result of getting things right in the first place. These kinds of measurement are covered in quality costing. What is not included in the typical cost of quality analysis is the impact of service quality on the disposition of customers to return or recommend others.

Customer retention

Although long recognized as a key characteristic of successful service organizations, the full economic impact of customer retention was not fully appreciated until Sasser and Reicheld produced a definitive 1990 *Harvard Business Review* article.[3] Prompted by an analysis of the reasons for the outstanding financial performance of one particular credit card company, their work has added a valuable new perspective to the concept of the lifetime value of a customer.

Prior to this, the received wisdom was that a supermarket customer, for example, should not be thought of in terms of the £30 of goods contained in his or her basket, but rather in terms of a £15,000 customer who appears every week for the next ten years. Powerful though this basic image is, Sasser and Reicheld's work provides a more substantive framework. They discovered that the key determinant of the success of the MBNA credit card was the amazingly high proportion of customers who were retained by the company. This single statistic differentiated it from myriad other credit card providers.

The reason why customer retention is important in the credit card business might seem to be fairly self-evident. A substantial upfront cost is associated with securing a new customer and it takes several years before that initial investment is recouped. What was not so obvious was that the profit from retained customers increases the longer is their association with the supplier. When these figures are converted to the Net Present Value (NPV) of the profits accruing over the lifetime of the average customer, the results reveal the vital importance of providing a quality of service which ensures that customers do not defect to other suppliers. This relationship between NPV and retention rate for the credit card industry is shown in Fig. 3.

Personal experience suggests that many organizations have little real feel for what is the level of customer defections they experience, or that which prevails in their industry. A determination of just what the current figure is invariably triggers off attempts to reduce defections which, in turn, necessitate uncovering the root causes of customer disaffection. The origin of the cliché that it is five times more costly to recruit a new customer than to keep an old one is lost in time. But, this work on customer retention adds considerable substance to the belief. In view of this evidence, the pursuit of policies which are *not* aimed at producing satisfied, or even delighted, customers would appear to be particularly foolhardy.

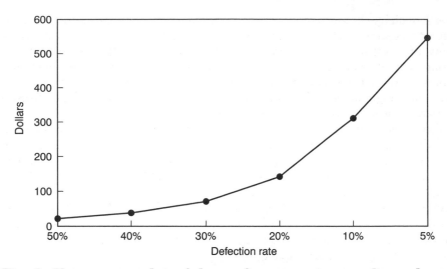

Fig. 3 Net present value of the profit streams in a credit card company, produced over an average customer's life.

What to do

First and foremost is the identification of what it is that customers want from a service encounter. One might be forgiven for assuming that all organizations continually strive to ascertain the needs of their customers. How else do they manage to stay in business? In fact, the evidence is that, all too often, companies appear to operate on the basis that they do not need to ask and are frequently surprised when a competitor's revised service offering strikes a chord with the public. British Telecom, for example, has been forced to recognize that those who make trans-Atlantic calls object to paying for a minimum of three minutes, particularly when the respondent happens to be an answering machine. Airlines appear to be waking up to the fact that even medium-height prospective customers adjudge leg room to be more important than in-flight catering; and the very successful Southwest Airlines has long responded to customers' desire for punctuality, even if it means dispensing with assigned seat numbers and in-flight catering. Financial services companies Direct Line and First Direct clearly tapped into a latent customer demand when they introduced their telephone-based style of operation into the traditional insurance and banking businesses. In a quite different sector, when professionals were presented with the results of a study of what women wanted in a labour suite, they were surprised to discover that top of the list of wants was a TV. The surprise was, in part, occasioned by the fact that nobody had ever seen fit to ask the customers what they wanted.

There are many further examples of this mismatch between what customers want and what service providers think those wants are. An enlightened organization devotes an inordinate amount of time to discovering what these needs are. A willingness and ability to listen is fundamental. Organizations need to put in place multifarious listening antennae to establish the current expectations of customers. These can take the form of formally convened focus groups where small groups of customers are brought together with company representatives for group discussions of around two hours' duration. The overwhelming majority of customers are only too delighted to be asked to participate in such events

Front line staff are confronted with customers with expressed needs day in and day out. Systems have to be put in place for tapping into this form of feedback. Some companies, such as Disneyworld, now routinely organize executives to spend short periods working at the coal face to help tap in to this priceless seam of information. Another hugely successful approach is that adopted by a small restaurant in Boston where each table boasts a card bearing the inscription: *'If I owned this restaurant, the one change I would make would be . . .'* The owners are swamped with good ideas. There is no limit to the ways in which one can listen to customers.

One caveat is in order. In some situations, customers really do have to be provoked into thinking outrageously. This is particularly true when they have become accustomed to indifferent service. Customers have sometimes to be provoked to think outrageously when they are used to being fed on a diet of mediocrity.

Lessons can also be learned from the ways in which other organizations serve their customers. The notion of ascertaining who else is considered an expert at performing some facet of a company's operation is now widely practised in both the manufacturing and service sectors. Benchmarking requires the decomposition of the work of an organization into its component elements and the identification of companies with a reputation for accomplishing those tasks most effectively. Frequently, this results in studying activities in companies whose line of business may be fundamentally different. The literature on benchmarking is replete with examples of such cross-industry fertilization of ideas. Xerox, for example, famously acquired valuable insights on warehousing from L L Bean, the highly regarded mail order company, and on invoicing from American Express. Likewise, staff from a major hospital's accident and emergency department found that they secured valuable insights from a visit to a windscreen replacement company. Similarly, an organization which employs any significant number of staff in a telephone answering capacity can't help but pick up lessons from visiting companies operating similar systems in quite different lines of business. It is comparisons such as these which can provoke an awareness that the standards currently being targeted can be improved, often by a considerable amount.

Which customer needs are most important?

It is self-evident that not all customer needs are equally important. Customers at a Manhattan bank might appreciate the piano music played while they are queuing at lunchtime, but the prospect of shorter queues would doubtless be more attractive. It is important to observe that companies need not necessarily react constructively to all customer suggestions. At Stew Leonard's, for example, customers at its fortnightly focus groups invariably suggest products which might be added to its range. The fact that the store limits its stock items to around 900 in contrast to the more usual 30,000+ carried by the typical supermarket means that all these proposals cannot be acted upon.

Generating a list of customer wants can be an exciting process and can take on some of the characteristics of brainstorming. Attaching priorities is somewhat more problematic. The secret has to lie in some form of forced choice. Some academics propose comparatively sophisticated scaling techniques based on judgemental modelling. In fact, value can be obtained from the use of far simpler approaches.

At Jaeger Tailoring, for example, customer focus groups generated around one hundred possible ways in which customer service could be improved. A small card was produced for each of these service attributes and another panel of customers was asked to rank them in order of desirability. Likewise, in a study of banking service a set of 45 possible service attributes was offered to customers. They were asked to select the ten that they would most prefer and to then allocate 100 points between those ten. The results were highly useful – the top three scores were for faster crediting of cheques, longer opening hours and access to all cash machines.

A visually appealing way of capturing this form of data is via a performance/importance matrix. Having ascertained from customers and company employees which service attributes need investigating, a questionnaire has to be developed which solicits customer evaluations with regard to both the perceived importance of each of these attributes and just how well the company is seen to be performing on that attribute in comparison with competitors.

A less than adequate performance on those issues adjudged by customers as being important is clearly a recipe for almost certain extinction. That said, the service attribute lying in the middle is worthy of some discussion. It would be all too easy to conclude that, because customers do not rate lead time for delivery as important, the company's mediocre performance on that front could be overlooked. In some circumstances, the potential for the real differentiation of the service offering may lie in the lead time. In this particular case, meetings with the company's warehouse staff revealed that it would actually be relatively easy to offer customers a much reduced lead time.

It could be argued that something which is not high on the list of customer priorities does not deserve attention or investment. The challenge then is to place this lead time issue on the customer's agenda. In other words, if economically sensible, it is worth improving performance and then cultivating its importance.

Harvard Business School's Ted Levitt developed the idea of the *generic*, the *expected*, the *augmented* and the *potential* characteristics of a product or service. He depicted these pictorially as a series of concentric circles – this leads to the notion of moving to the outer circles. At the heart of this concept is the idea of exploring how one can construct a service offering which extends beyond normal expectations and might actually engender surprise. This is the stuff of differentiation. Equally importantly, it helps create what is now labelled, *customer delight,* an essential in customer retention.

All the evidence points to the fact that customer satisfaction is a necessary but not a sufficient condition leading to customer retention. Customers who are *very* satisfied are far more inclined to re-purchase, return or recommend than are those who are merely satisfied. When reflecting on those service encounters which have engendered a desire to definitely sample the offering again, it is the level of customer delight which assumes significance. It certainly contributes to the success of Disneyworld which boasts an extraordinarily high level of return business; and Domino's Pizzas which offers delivery in 30 minutes or a free offer. Before Federal Express, the idea of overnight delivery of parcels across the United States must have appeared far-fetched. Confident that it could be achieved, Federal Express's Fred Smith rewrote the rule book and 99.72 per cent of parcels now arrive at their destination the following morning. Some of these service breakthroughs require the use of business process re-engineering concepts but, in others, the key to the success lies in the progressive, ambitious style of thinking the unthinkable.

How are we doing?

Customers are confronted with an ever-expanding set of efforts aimed at ascertaining their level of satisfaction with the service being provided. Sadly, the tools adopted in this quest frequently leave a good deal to be desired. Almost every hotel bedroom now features a guest questionnaire but most can't possibly be of much value given the rather amateurish nature of the contents and presentation. Response rates are typically abysmally low which, in turn, leads one to question the possible bias of those responding. Perhaps, disaffected guests are more likely to fill out such questionnaires. However, another likely reason why response rates are low is that potential respondents have some difficulty in appreciating quite how their completion of the survey will help bring about improved service. All too often, such documents appear to have been dreamed up by a management which is quite patently unconvinced of the value of determining just which issues are of concern to customers. Some even feature answering scales which are incompatible with the questions. It is, for example, not uncommon to encounter questions which demand yes or no answers being coupled with five-point scales.

An effective customer-satisfaction questionnaire ought to cover issues with which customers can readily identify. Surprisingly, the length of the questionnaire does not appear to be a factor which deters respondents, provided the document is sufficiently customer-friendly in other ways. A less than satisfactory visit to a hospital accident and emergency department back in 1974 led to the production of a 46-page 'What the Patient Thinks' questionnaire which features over 500 questions. This survey instrument produces response rates in excess of 70 per cent.

This is probably exceptional and must, to some extent, reflect people's disposition towards commenting on their hospital experiences. It probably also reflects the professionalism of the document and the fact that respondents have reason to believe that action will flow from the feedback secured.

In addition to the fact that the questions relate to issues that respondents perceive to be relevant, in what other ways are they designed to be attractive? Many customer satisfaction questionnaires require respondents to place a cross somewhere on a five- or seven-point scale or a tick in one of five boxes ranging from Very Satisfied to Very Dissatisfied. Respondents appear to be more comfortable with questions which are associated with verbal descriptions corresponding to different levels of satisfaction. The example from the 'What the Patient Thinks' survey instrument shown in Fig. 6 serves to illustrate this approach and also the highly significant differences which emerged from its use in two hospital settings.

Clearly, in Hospital F, there is considerable scope for improvement on just this one aspect of food service. In fact, this issue of preparation is only one of the 12 issues relating to food addressed in the questionnaire. Contrast that with a more traditional approach which would feature a question along the lines of *How would you rate the quality of the food served in the hospital*? Exactly what is implied by the word quality is not readily apparent and will doubtless be interpreted differently by different patients. This form of approach has been adopted by most leading banks which collectively spend tens of millions of pounds securing customer feedback. The following question is extracted from one such survey instrument.

	Hospital		
	C	F	Overall
The meals were usually made to look tempting and appetizing	37%	4%	17%
On the whole the meals were reasonably well presented	56%	47%	56%
From time to time the meals were not as well presented as they might have been	7%	49%	27%

Fig. 4 Example from survey at two hospitals showing different levels of patient-satisfaction

What is your overall opinion of the financial advice you received on this occasion? Tick one box

The advice was tailor-made to fit my needs and was sound and objective.

☐

They gave me quite detailed advice, but didn't seem to take account of my particular needs.

☐

They didn't give me proper advice – they just gave a leaflet.

☐

Don't know/can't remember.

☐

Fig. 5 Extract from survey instrument of a bank

This form of approach differs quite fundamentally from that recommended by Len Berry and his team[4] who have attempted to concentrate on measuring the gap between what customers were expecting from a service encounter and what they perceived of the service they actually received. Their approach requires a respondent to provide answers to a pair of questions on each service attribute. For example, one question might read: '*When an excellent bank promises to do something by a certain time it will do it*'. There is a corresponding question relating to how a specified bank performs on this attribute and in both cases the response scale offered runs from Strongly Agree to Strongly Disagree. It is difficult to see why anyone should score an excellent facility anywhere other than at the top of the scale, so the concept of a gap being measured is probably illusory. This team has also produced a categorization of service attributes bearing the acronym RATER, standing for Reliability, Assurance, Tangibles, Empathy and Responsiveness. They have found that reliability is judged by customers to be the dominant service characteristic. Others argue that reliability should be a part of the core business. The jury is still out on just what are the real dimensions of customer service. It is suggested that continued efforts to identify real customer concerns will reap better dividends than attempting to force these into the five RATER dimensions.

Another way of securing feedback on service delivery is via the use of *Mystery Shoppers*. This approach, which is gaining greater acceptability, involves the recruitment of individuals whose brief is to undertake specified service encounters. They might, for example, be required to partake of a meal at a fast food restaurant or purchase garments from a retail establishment. They are then obliged to subsequently report on the details of the encounter using a proforma reporting instrument. The results can, and often are, converted into scores but they are probably just as effective in revealing where shortfalls in training find their eventual way through to deficiencies in performance.

When things go wrong?

It is clearly not possible to guarantee the perfection of a distributed service delivery system. A checkout operator might give a customer a hard time as a consequence of a set of bad experiences prior to arriving at work. When things do go wrong, systems need to be in place to produce recoveries that become the stuff of legend. Consider the results of the definitive study of customer behaviour by the Washington-based research and consulting agency, TARP. Their research showed that only one respondent out of 26 on the receiving end of a bad service experience would trouble to register a complaint. However, 91 per cent said that they would not return for a repeat experience and that they would tell around ten acquaintances of the episode. Obviously, figures of this magnitude indicate the vital necessity of trying to ensure that system failures do not occur. Less obviously, they also reveal just how important it is to encourage dissatisfied customers to register their complaints. Only then does one have any hope of correcting a bad situation and converting dissatisfaction into delight with the recovery. Equally importantly is the need to prevent the adverse word-of-mouth publicity which would almost certainly flow from unhappy episodes.

It is precisely for this reason that many American companies now make it very easy for customers to register their complaints via freephone numbers. General Electric's Louisville Answer Center receives in excess of four million calls annually. In common with similar operations elsewhere, the calls, not all of which are complaints, are categorized as to reason. This categorization provides valuable insights into where systems are breaking down, thereby enabling corrective action to be taken.

The need to handle complaints in a highly effective manner is, perhaps, best illustrated by another TARP finding which shows that, in some situations, the propensity to repurchase, recommend or return, is greater when a complaint has been handled well than if no problem had arisen in the first place. There is also a second order effect to consider with respect to complaints. If a customer is sufficiently dissatisfied to register a complaint and that complaint is badly handled, then the organization has committed two cardinal errors. In one study for a major bank, while it was disturbing to find that around one in three customers had reason to complain each year, more disconcerting was the fact that 54 per cent were not satisfied with the way in which their complaint was handled.

The people dimension

Customer service is an intrinsically human art. It is not robotic or scripted. This raises important staffing considerations. Can individuals with a predisposition towards customer service be selected? How are they trained to deliver the standards expected? How are they to be rewarded?

Psychologists have been able to devise tests which identify individuals who are more likely to be comfortable delivering excellent customer service. They have also found it valuable to utilize situational tests. If, for example, staff will be contacting customers by telephone, then a part of the selection process ought sensibly to be conducted over the telephone. If they are going to have to work in a closely knit team, then that process ought to incorporate some form of team activity. The restaurant chain Thank God It's Friday (TGIF) places so much emphasis on the outgoing personalities of its staff that, in Europe, each applicant is required to perform on stage for one minute. The so called *buddy* system is widely adopted in the States. This involves high performing staff being encouraged to recommend their friends for employment on the basis that those friends might well possess similar attributes to the recommender.

Training for customer service varies enormously. At Nordstrom, so much emphasis is placed on the original selection that subsequent training is considered to be superfluous. In sharp contrast, the training at TGIF is remarkably detailed. Not only do the staff need to have an intimate knowledge of the vast array of food and beverage menu items on offer, but they also undergo role playing to equip them to deal with difficult situations. Cadet Uniforms in Toronto provides a laundry service to a variety of business users. So concerned is it to preserve its customer retention rate of over 98 per cent that a newly recruited van driver is only allowed out on his own after he or she has been with the company for nine months. In truth, Nordstrom is very much the exception. Even now the investment in people made by outstanding service providers always comes as a surprise.

With regard to rewarding performance, there is a growing move towards incorporating some financial recompense for effective performance in customer service. A number of companies including IBM, the British Airports

Authority and Xerox incorporate a substantial bonus into executive remuneration packages. This is at risk on the basis of customer satisfaction indices. Often the reward takes the form of recognition. In Britain accepted wisdom would have us believe that American and European traditions are fundamentally very different. In the States, hero recognition programmes and ABCD (Above and Beyond the Call of Duty) awards are popular. In fact, European companies which have experimented with such procedures have found that workers find such initiatives satisfying. What is certainly true is that employees have no difficulty in seeing the incongruity of demanding quality but paying for quantity.

Unconditional service guarantees

Assuming that a company has discovered what its customers want, has put in place systems for delivering those wants, recruited staff to support those systems and installed monitoring procedures to ensure that standards are being met, what else might it do to capitalize on the ensuing level of customer service? One expanding approach is the provision of an unconditional service guarantee such as offered by Domino's Pizza if it fails to meet its half-hour delivery time. The most celebrated one is perhaps that of Bugs Burger Bugs Killers which is depicted in Fig. 6.

Both these guarantees feature key characteristics of successful schemes. They are simple and straightforward; there is no small print; the company

---

Bugs Burger Bug Killers

1. Initial charges aren't due until every roach, rat or mouse nesting on the premises is totally eliminated. If at any time dissastisfaction with results leads to cancellation of service, the company will refund up to one year's charges and pay the new exterminator for a year.
2. If a roach or rodent is seen by guests of a Burger client, Bugs Burger Bug Killers will pay the bill, send the guests a letter of apology and invite them back with their compliments.
3. Any fines, due to the presence of roaches or rodents levied by health authorities will be paid, as well as lost profits, plus $5,000 if the facility is closed down.

Fig. 6 An unconditional service guarantee

willingly pays up on failure to achieve the target and the guarantee addresses an issue which is of particular concern to the customer. Before such a scheme can be launched, it is vital that the service delivery systems are sound. The service guarantee will identify weaknesses. Indeed, this might well be the main rationale behind its introduction. But these weaknesses should be in the form of fine tunings to the system which are exposed via the guarantee. Fundamental weaknesses in the systems should not have been there in the first place.

Crucial to the success of any such guarantee is the involvement of staff in its design. They have an intimate knowledge of potential failure points and have to confront irate customers demanding recompense.

In the UK, Magnet Joinery guarantees trades people that if a catalogue item is not available from stock it will be secured within 24 hours and be charged at half the normal price. Hampton Inns, a medium-priced chain of motels, offers a straightforward promise: '*If you're not completely satisfied, we don't expect you to pay.*' Contrary to what sceptics might suspect, only 0.43 per cent of guests action the guarantee which is now the cornerstone of all the company's advertising.

It has to be a particularly short-sighted group of directors or managers who would feel that they command all the knowledge relating to customer service. After all, most rarely come into direct contact with customers. It is front-line personnel who meet customers day in and day out. It is they who have to incur the wrath of customers when service failures occur; who possess the insights into why systems fail and, in truth, who have the capability of putting things to rights. Increasingly, companies are beginning to appreciate this obvious logic. More and more front-line staff are being encouraged to identify and resolve problems, typically in the form of teams.

Staff can become highly motivated to make things change. The reason is very simple. We are all customers and in that role we dislike being on the receiving end of bad service. Even more disconcerting is to be on the delivery end.

Brian Moores is a consultant and lecturer. Originally trained as an aeronautical engineer, he has worked at John Hopkins University, Baltimore; UMIST; Stirling University, where he established the Scottish Quality Management Centre; and Manchester Business School where he created and directed the Institute of Services Management. He has published many articles and is co-author of *Management Structures and Techniques* and editor of *Are They Being Served?* He is now Professor Emeritus of the University of Manchester.

Further Reading

Peters, T, *Liberation Management*, Knopf, New York, 1992
Whitely, RC, *The Customer-Driven Company*, Addison-Wesley, New York, 1991

References

1 Peters, T, and Waterman, RH, *In Search of Excellence: Lessons from America's Best Run Companies*, Harper & Row, New York, 1982.
2 Buzzell, RD and Gale, BT, *The PIMS Principles: Linking Strategy to Performance*, The Free Press, New York, 1987.
3 Reicheld, FF and Sasser, WE, 'Zero Defections: Quality Comes to Services', *Harvard Business Review*, 5, 105–111, 1990.
4 Berry, LL; Parasuraman, A and Zeithami, VA, *Delivering Quality Service: Balancing Customer Perceptions and Expectations*, Free Press, New York, 1990.

Re-engineering

'We cannot be satisfied to lay out a plan that will move us towards the existing world standard over some protracted period of time... because if we accept such a plan, we will never be the world leader. We need rapid, quantum leap improvement.'   *Paul O'Neil, chairman of Alcoa*[1]

'It is not products, but the processes that create products that bring companies long-term success. Good products don't make winners; winners make good products'.

James Champy and Michael Hammer.[2]

'Most people think of the future as the ends and the present as the means, whereas, in fact, the present is the ends and the future the means.'   *Fritz Roethlisberger.*[3]

[1] Devine, M, 'Radical re-engineering', *Directions*, September 1993
[2] Champy, J, and Hammer, M, *Re-engineering the Corporation*, Nicholas Brealey, London, 1993
[3] Roethlisberger, F, *Training for Human Relations*, Harvard University Press, Boston, 1954

OVERVIEW

Stuart Crainer and Eddie Obeng

Twenty years ago, corporate crystal ball gazers predicted an age of leisure. The days of working nine-to-five would, at some time in the not so distant future, be consigned to history. Our lives would be miraculously transformed by technology. At the time, the imagined machines appeared to belong to the world of science fiction. We knew computers existed, but their impact on our lives was minimal, often non-existent. Computers filled rooms rather than laps.

In fact, the leisure age has not yet dawned. People continue to organize their working lives in much the same way as twenty years ago. But the technological miracle has taken place – and continues at breakneck speed.

The paradox is an apparently simple one. Technology has revolutionized our lives and opened up huge new vistas of untapped human potential. At the same time, the way we work and, more vitally, the way modern corporations are organized has failed to keep pace.

This is not a unique phenomenon. A close parallel can be seen in the way product innovation always precedes process innovation. In the case of the organization of the 1990s, high-tech products are there in abundance. Processes, however, are only gradually being evolved as the business world makes tentative steps forward to end the debilitating paradox.

Appearances are deceptive. On the surface companies often appear to be highly proactive. Since the leisure age dream, there have been many changes in the way companies organize their activities and personnel. They are continually refining themselves, introducing subtle variations and adaptations. But, in virtually every case, they are tinkering with an accepted and well-established formula. Change is closed – incremental and evolutionary rather than dramatic and revolutionary. Change, conventional wisdom dictates, comes in steps rather than quantum leaps.

Organizations cannot really be criticized for their relentless urge to subtly re-structure the way they operate. They are creatures of consensus and, anyway, would quickly point to their financial results as the ultimate arbiter of whether constant re-organization has been successful or not.

An alternative insight can be gleaned from an unlikely source. Writing at a time of rapid change in the Roman Empire, Gaius Petronius succinctly captured the frustration that re-organization brings in its wake:

'We trained hard to meet our challenges but it seemed as if every time we were beginning to form into teams we would be re-organized. I was to learn later in life that we tend to meet any new situation by re-organizing; and a wonderful method it can be for creating the illusion of progress while producing confusion, ineffectiveness and demoralization.'

While companies have wrestled with various organizational models, they have also recognized the fundamental need to take part and drive forward the techno-logical revolution. Companies don't shirk from making massive investments in IT and other new technologies. They realize that future success depends on tech-nological competence and excellence and recognize that corporate failure can often be attributed to two factors: failure to learn and adapt as rapidly as com-petitors and/or failure to come to terms with technological innovation.

The key question is straightforward. What effect have such massive invest-ments and innovations had on productivity? One would assume and hope that investment in the latest technology has led to increased effectiveness and improved productivity. Managers benefit from more receptive and accurate information and communication systems. They can become closer to con-sumers, markets and each other. On the factory floor technology leads to faster, less labour-intensive and more reliable production. However, statistics and extensive research from throughout the world suggests that this is simply not the case.

An important aspect of this phenomenon has been pointed out by Peter Drucker who believes that Western industry remains fascinated by innovation rather than productivity, the obsession of the Japanese and others. Drucker has identified increasing the productivity of 'knowledge and service workers' as the great management and business challenge of our times. To achieve this requires that the full potential of technology is utilized.

But it is not only technology which has provided disappointing returns on investment for the business world. Other initiatives have also singularly failed to transform organizations into leaner, fitter and more efficient bodies. In many companies, the most obvious by-product of increased use of technology has been a strident management commitment to quality. As with investment in IT, the intention cannot be criticized. The equation that more efficient and accurate technology enables companies to achieve higher and more consistent quality levels is clear. Many organizations across the world have brought in external experts to launch their own version of quality management. But, as with the continual process of organizational tinkering, too often quality initiatives have bitten the corporate dust or reaped isolated or negligible rewards. Quality guru JM Juran now estimates that less than 50 of the top 500 US companies have 'attained world class quality', a meagre reward for so much investment.[1]

Commonly, quality initiatives lead to a single division or function recording a significant quality improvement. Rarely is this experienced throughout an organization. Similarly, the ideal of continuous improvement has proved to be fatally flawed. Indeed, the service economy and those service elements of industry which now dominate product costs have failed to respond to continu-ous improvement initiatives, evidenced by a reduction in pre-tax profits of 50 per cent over the last ten years.

Fundamental problems clearly remain. Organizations appear unable to trans-late technology into coherent strategy and best practice or to convert quality from an attractive theory into consistent implementation across all their activities. Attempting to buy simple products and services quickly reveals the inadequacies which have survived the quality revolution and various management fads and fashions. A high-tech factory can produce cars more efficiently and more quickly than ever before – yet you can wait a few months for the specific model you require to be delivered. Make a claim to your insurance company and you may well spend three months waiting for the cheque; try to take out a mortgage and the building society can take 28 days to process the paperwork.

The deficiencies in service quality and speed are self-evident in many businesses we come across. It is not only external customers who suffer. Internally, organizations remain prone to functional fiefdoms and silos. Divisions, functions and departments often fail to communicate or blithely continue to exist in their own self-created worlds. Here, too, we would have expected technology to have worked to create more effective organizations. Technology should – and can – bring people closer together. Different departments can share information and communicate it more effectively. Too often, however, technology has merely succeeded in concentrating power in the hands of fewer and fewer people – IT departments, for example, can work as centres and manipulators of power rather than as a means of enhancing communication and bridging functional divides.

The re-engineering solution

In the 1990s, re-engineering has emerged as the latest in the long line of organizational saviours. The interest in re-engineering reflects a growing realization that although the continuous improvements of total quality programmes are critical, they are not enough to deliver productivity gains from massive investment in IT. To do so calls for periodic and radical changes in key business processes and the way business is organized. This fundamentally perturbs any quality system and runs counter to the philosophy of quality management which seeks, and is centred on, continuous improvement.

A common image associated with re-engineering is that it takes a blank piece of paper and starts again. 'Business re-engineering isn't about fixing anything. Business re-engineering means starting all over, starting from scratch,' argue James Champy and Michael Hammer in their book *Re-engineering the Corporation*.[2] In reality, the process of re-engineering has to be a great deal more pragmatic and flexible. There are no blank pieces of paper but, even so, re-engineering involves revolution. It finds out what is getting in the way of the whole organization and attempts to remove the blockage. Re-engineering asks basic questions and seeks to re-create organizations designed around the needs of customers, owners, employees, suppliers and regulators. These are the core constituencies of any business. None can be overlooked if re-engineering is to be achieved or even contemplated.

Re-engineering treats nothing as sacred and any process, resource or idea that stands in the way of satisfying the customer is eliminated. Old job titles are dispensed with; organizational arrangements and structures are not merely tinkered with, but radically re-aligned; the methods of mass production, revered and habitual procedures, are rigorously scrutinized and abandoned.

At this point the manager in the real world of pragmatism and compromise is likely to shake his or her head. How can modern, highly complex organizations start again as if the past never happened?

The managers are right to be sceptical. Instead of accepting certain tasks as inevitable, re-engineering requires managers to ask why they are doing a particular task so they can dispense with work that does not contribute to goals, or simply does not need to be done.

The fuel behind re-engineering is not simply the need to fulfil technology's potential. It is also driven by international competition and the relentless quest for increased quality at lower cost. The demand for re-engineering or, indeed, any solution to the problem at the foundations of business, is substantial. The trouble is that though many corporations have embraced the concept of re-engineering few have succeeded in making it work, and a large number appear not to have fully understood its meaning or intent. Re-engineering guru, James Champy, estimates that 50 per cent of large US companies now claim to be re-engineering, but only five to ten per cent are doing it properly or with sufficient vigour to reap long-term benefits across their organization.[3] Managers and organizations are not natural revolutionaries.

As the re-engineering bandwagon has gained momentum, some companies are already claiming substantial benefits from their re-engineering initiatives. IBM estimates that it has saved £1.8 million a year through re-engineering – this has been achieved mainly through automation. Gateway Foodmarkets in the US piloted a more efficient and focused merchandizing process in six of its stores and increased sales by 50 per cent and the margin on sales by 30 per cent.[4] One insurance company claimed impressive results within two years of implementing a re-engineering programme – administration costs went down by 40 per cent; staff turnover was reduced by 58 per cent; productivity increased by 100 per cent; claims-handling time went down from 28 to four days; and customer call-backs fell by 80 per cent.[5]

GTE, the US's largest local telecommunications company, claims that its re-engineering programme will cut its customer service centres from 171 to 11; revenue collection centres from five to one; and regional centres from 19 to one. These changes will involve the loss of 17,000 jobs over three years and an investment of $680 million to upgrade customer service, administrative systems and software; $410 million for 'employee separation' costs and $160 million to consolidate facilities. GTE estimates the potential annual cost savings to be $1 billion.[6]

The activities of Xerox, one of the world leaders in re-engineering, illustrate its broad ranging nature and the size of the investment – and the risks – involved. 'My objective is to change fundamentally the way we run the company. We need to create discontinuous change; incremental changes will not get us to our vision,' Paul Allaire, chairman and chief executive of Xerox Corporation, has stated.[7]

At Xerox, Allaire has been a prime mover in an attempt to achieve truly revolutionary change. His aims are to increase productivity, lower the company's cost base, be more responsive to customers and improve financial results. This is the managerial equivalent of squaring the circle. To do so requires a sizeable investment: in late 1993 Xerox announced a plan to shed ten per cent of its workforce, 10,000 people, over the following two to three years and set aside $700 million to cover the restructuring. Explaining the restructuring in the company's document-processing division, Allaire said it was 'not a function of any change in the current business environment, but rather it accelerates numerous productivity initiatives that have been under careful consideration for some time'.[8] The change is proactive and attempts to integrate a large number of performance improvement initiatives.

Re-engineering takes on the sacred cows of an organization *en masse*. Xerox's change programme covers four main areas:

- the group's organizational structure
- people and skills
- informal networks, behaviour and culture
- re-design of work processes.

In the UK, Rank Xerox, which has been the champion of re-engineering within Xerox worldwide, is aiming to cut around $200 million from its annual overheads. 'We need dramatic improvements in performance which will be achieved through re-engineering of our business processes,' says Rank Xerox managing director Bernard Fournier. Two teams have been appointed to calculate the value added by every activity in the company and place it within seven 'basic processes'.[9]

While re-engineering first came to prominence in the United States, European companies like Rank Xerox are fast coming to terms with the concept. The Swedish food co-operative, ICA Handlarnas, linked all of its 3,359 retail stores to a single mainframe database. As a result, it has been able to close a third of its warehouses and distribution centres and has halved its overall costs. Its wholesaling workforce has been cut by 30 per cent over three years even though revenue grew by more than 15 per cent during the same period.[10]

As James Champy has observed, only a handful of companies seem to have fully understood the full potential of re-engineering. All too often re-engineering is equated with and inextricably linked to cost reduction. In contrast, full understanding of re-engineering goes far beyond financial parameters – it allows the organization to assess its ability to meet its primary business goals.

In practice, though awareness of the need to change apparently remains high, practical implementation of re-engineering concepts has been held back by two central pitfalls:

1. The human implications are often ignored, overlooked or under-estimated.
2. The revolution does not affect the attitudes and behaviour of managers. This, in turn, exacerbates problems caused by underestimating the human implications of the re-engineering process.

The most obvious pitfall is the fact that much of the extensive theorizing and practice in the field of re-engineering pays scant attention to the concerns and fears of the people involved in making it happen. Talk of turbulence and the relentless progress of change through global business is easy. Talk of the effects of upheaval and change on individual managers and employees is less straightforward, fraught as it is with fears and disappointment.

Re-engineering involves more than analysing processes and re-structuring organizations. Many re-engineering programmes find the changing of culture and people too demanding a challenge. Instead, only processes and systems are changed. It is, after all, easier to re-design procedures and invest in technology which breaks down functional barriers, than to begin to change people's attitudes, beliefs and values. Re-engineering, like any programme of change, must involve and alter the perceptions and behaviour of people. To be effective, change has to carry people along with it. Re-engineering is no different. Indeed, the changes it intends to bring about are far beyond those usually contemplated in total quality programmes or the like.

The key difference between re-engineering and other change programmes is that in re-engineering change often appears to be illogical. By its very nature, proactive change is harder to rationalize and communicate than reactive change where you can point to specific events which have already occurred and are having a clear effect on the business. Indeed, initial responses to re-engineering are emotional – anger, fear, insecurity – though, over time, they may become accepted as logical.

The initial concentration of re-engineering programmes has been on tackling the 'hard' issues – such as processes and systems. The 'soft' issues – people, skills, behaviour, culture and values – are at least as critical, often more so, but have tended to be relegated in importance. Indeed, re-engineering is often preceded by the words 'business process' to suggest that processes are the beginning and end of the programme. They are, it is increasingly apparent, only part of the battle.

There is an on-going debate over whether behavioural and cultural change – through empowerment and team working for example – is an inherent result of re-engineering, or whether it needs to be launched before re-engineering begins. In the US, for example, Bell Atlantic set up its culture change programme two years before beginning the re-engineering process.

At the centre of this discussion is the common belief that a changed organizational structure or more radical re-organization naturally leads to a change in corporate culture. Though this may be the case, changing organizational cultures is a lengthy, time-consuming and delicate process. Re-engineering does, by its very nature, involve cultural change. It emphasizes how organizations *are* as well as what they *do*.

It is unlikely that successful cultural change can be made in a wholesale way. The past is not easily dismissed, nor should organizations want to totally dispense with some of the more positive and established ways of thinking and working. Marrying the old and new cultures is a formidable balancing act.

Having analyzed processes and removed repetitious or needless activities, organizations have a clear view of the processes necessary to satisfy their core stakeholders. But, by its very definition, this requires flexible and variable inputs from people. Employees lose the security of job specialisms and set procedures, while managers suddenly find their performance under closer scrutiny. Managers can no longer fall back on functional hierarchies or traditional ways of doing things to protect themselves. What they do and how they work is stripped bare for all to see.

It is here that the second basic flaw in the practice of re-engineering has emerged. Managers driving through the process tend to underestimate the human side of re-engineering. Cultural and personal issues are relegated below processes and technology. Also, managers are loath to re-engineer their own activities. Too often they espouse revolution and practise conservatism. 'The practice of management has largely escaped demolition. If their jobs and styles are left largely intact, managers will eventually undermine the very structure of their rebuilt enterprises,' James Champy observed in an article entitled 'Time to re-engineer the manager'. He went on to observe that 'the work of managers in a re-engineered organization must change as much as the work of workers'.[11]

Managers, however, are unused to ambiguity and uncertainty. The ambiguity produced by re-engineering covers a number of areas:

- *job definitions* – changes in the scope and nature of job definitions are, for many, deeply unsettling and remove a prime reference point;
- *responsibilities* – people are unsure what they are responsible for and to whom;
- *expectations* – people are uncertain about what colleagues and the organization expects from them.

An obvious adjunct to the process of ambiguity is the disappearance of career ladders. Organizations shorn of their vertical hierarchy can appear to offer little opportunity for progression.

The re-engineered organization is, for many managers, nightmarish. Instead of being tangible it is elusively intangible. Functions are broken apart, some disappear from the organization, sub-contracted to external suppliers. For the manager reared on the old functional certainties the process-based organization is very difficult to manage. The vast majority of managers are not trained or equipped to manage in such an environment. Nor can they attend a short course to be converted from a functional to a process manager. Changing the way you work and think about your work is a process which is more likely to take months, and possibly years, than weeks and months.

It is not surprising that re-engineered companies often report that it is managers rather than grass roots employees who find the transition to process-based work most difficult. As part of its change to more flexible working, the car manufacturer Rover encountered resistance from white-collar workers reluctant to switch jobs to the assembly line. In November 1993, Rover called for 1,000 volunteers to make the change so it could avoid compulsory redundancies among its 33,000 workforce. Only 60 clerical staff volunteered. The end-result is that the company is planning to recruit more workers to make up the short-fall.

Managers often feel threatened by the change, a reaction that is reasonable given the fact that many re-engineering initiatives involve management de-layering. Research suggests that while companies have developed a wide range of supportive packages to help people who have been made redundant they – perhaps not surprisingly – often forget the worries and concerns of those who remain with the organization. In a survey of 50 top UK companies in 1993, recruitment company Cedar International found that a massive 86 per cent had implemented redundancies in the previous year and, in addition, 36 per cent were operating rolling programmes spanning a number of years involving a significant proportion of the workforce.

The second cause of uncertainty is the disruption and destruction of fief-doms and power bases, which causes managers to fear loss of control and authority. Becoming process owners, rather than function heads, can also be difficult for managers. One of Europe's leading re-engineering practitioners, Rank Xerox UK has found that managers struggle to overcome their functional mentalities.

Ambiguity and insecurity are often indistinguishable. Indeed, some organizations have identified insecurity as one of the most valuable aspects of process-based working. There is, however, a disturbing Big Brother element in such an approach. Insecurity is not a great motivator. In the short-term it might yield some performance benefits, but pure fear is hardly a long-term solution.

A more positive motivational approach is to link rewards and remuneration more closely to customer satisfaction or team performance. As we have seen, the disappearance of career ladders can disturb set notions of how a person's career is likely to develop. The association between success and promotion and higher rewards needs to be replaced.

Another important aspect of the human side of the re-engineering is the management of conflict and contention. Managers are often uncomfortable with the rigorous and ceaseless questioning which re-engineering brings with it. Often they are extremely unenthusiastic about the idea of their work being analyzed in anything other than a superficial way. The potential for dissension and conflict is high. If, for example, a team is made up of an engineer, a customer development manager and a company accountant, some sort of conflict is inevitable – and often healthy. There are and will be basic misunderstandings. The manager might ask the engineer why he is doing something in a certain way. Reared on a diet of functional division, the engineer may well say that he has always done it that way and he knows more about engineering than the manager. To make teams work, however, mutual respect must exist or be developed. Managers have to learn to accept objective input from people they regard as outsiders.

In reality, making re-engineering happen involves a complex pot-pourri of skills. Fully understanding how your organization works, approaches problems, and sets about tackling them, is never easy. Measuring every aspect of personal performance is often neither possible or useful.

For managers faced with such challenges, developing new skills is imperative. These include:

- **Interpersonal skills** – managers change from supervisors to coaches. They are there to provide resources, answer questions and look out for the long-term career development of the individual. How they deal with people is key to their day-to-day success and to the progression of their career within the organization.
- **Project management skills** – implementing re-designed processes involves highly developed project-management skills. Experience suggests that today's project manager (more accurately referred to as a project leader) needs training in four key areas.
  - **planning and controlling** – project leaders need to be able to use a variety of methods to ensure they are keeping on schedule and within budget. Even more important, they need to be able to decide priorities for their objectives.
  - **learning skills** – as most project leaders are working in an unfamiliar context it is crucial that they assimilate knowledge as rapidly as possible. This will enable them to adjust their plans and objectives and save valuable time and money. To do this, project leaders need to keep learning, planning, reviewing and changing.
  - **people skills** – project leaders need to be able to negotiate for vital resources; be able to influence people to gain their commitment; be able to listen to, co-ordinate, and control the project; and be able to manage stakeholders from throughout the business.
  - **organizational skills** – project leaders need to be politically astute and aware of the potential impact of wider organizational issues. They should be adept at networking with senior employees, should understand how the organization works, and should have a larger picture of the organization's goals and necessary conditions.
- **Leadership and flexibility** – like any manager who works in a horizontal cross functional and team-based environment, process owners need to coach employees and empower them to feel ownership of the process. This demands a flexible style of managing, with the manager sometimes giving firm directions in order to ensure that the process output conforms to customer expectations, while at other times stepping back and allowing team members to take decisions.
- **Managing processes** – those charged with making processes work require a great range of different skills. Process owners, to use the language of re-engineering, have to be able to manage the boundaries between different processes (which are deeply rooted in vagueness); understand who are the stakeholders in the process; and help establish and monitor appropriate process performance measurements. They also need to be able to operate confidently up, down and across the organization's structure. This ability,

to manage chameleon-like across the organization, is especially important during the early stages of re-engineering when many of the functional vestiges of old processes remain in place.

- **Improving processes** – in the majority of process-based companies, managers are required to refine and improve their business processes on an on-going basis. They need to be able to use the tools of process simplification and re-design, which include benchmarking, process mapping tools (such as systems dynamics, flowcharting and activity diagrams), and require understanding of the potential business benefits of IT applications.

- **Managing strategy** – process ownership is not solely concerned with the nitty gritty of direct implementation. Managers need also to understand how their process aligns with strategic goals and performance measures. They have, for example, to have an understanding of the company's mission, competitive capabilities and core constituencies, as well as some of the basic principles of activity-based costing. This enables the process owner to fully understand and communicate the full benefits of re-engineering – the elimination of non-value adding activities, the enhancement of value adding activities, substantial gains in productivity and far greater market responsiveness.

- **Managing their own development** – to meet the new challenge requires managers to think beyond position and develop comprehensive general skills which will allow them to respond flexibly to organizational needs. They need to be aware of their limitations and skills deficiencies and develop appropriate responses.

- **Teamworking** – managers need to understand the dynamics of team working and be able to operate and manage a wide variety of teams within the organization.

Managers who fail to develop such skills – and organizations which fail to develop their managers – are likely to be stepping from the unknown into nowhere when they begin re-engineering. Those that understand and recognize their current recipe, and develop appropriate skills, are liable to make a leap forward.

Dr Eddie Obeng is founder director of Pentacle, the Virtual Business School. Previously director of project management and strategy implementation programmes at Ashridge Management College, he has lengthy experience of making projects happen and of managing change in real situations. As a project leader with Shell he ran development projects; and instituted a re-engineering programme at Ashridge. He is co-author of *Making Re-engineering Happen* **(1994) and author of** *All Change! The Project Leader's Secret Handbook* **(1994).**

Stuart Crainer is co-author of *Making Re-engineering Happen* **(1994).**

Further Reading

Hardaker, M, *Total Competitiveness*, McGraw Hill, Maidenhead, 1995.

McHugh, P, Merli, G, and Wheeler, WA, *Beyond Business Process Reengineering*, John Wiley, New York, 1995.

Obeng, E, and Crainer, S, *Making Re-engineering Happen*, FT/Pitman, London, 1994.

Regan, J, *Crunch Time: How to Re-engineer Your Organization*, Century, London, 1995.

References

1 Juran, JM, 'Why quality initiatives fail', *Journal of Business Strategy*, July–August 1993 vol. 14 no. 4.

2 Champy, J and Hammer, M, *Re-engineering the Corporation*, Nicholas Brealey, London, 1993.

3 Lorenz, C, 'Uphill struggle to become horizontal', *Financial Times*, 5 November 1993.

4 Devine, M, 'Radical re-engineering', *Directions*, September 1993.

5 Skinner, C, 'Business process re-engineering', *Internal Communication Focus*, December 1993/January 1994.

6 Dickson, M, 'GTE to reduce staff by 17,000', *Financial Times*, 14 January 1994.

7 Devine, M, 'Radical re-engineering', *Directions*, September 1993.

8 Dickson, M, 'Xerox to cut workforce by 10% over next three years', *Financial Times*, 9 December 1993.

9 Lorenz, C, 'Time to get serious', *Financial Times*, 24 June 1993.

10 'The technology pay-off', *BusinessWeek*, 14 June 1993.

11 Champy, J, 'Time to re-engineer the manager', *Financial Times*, 14 January 1994.

THINKERS

Frederick Winslow Taylor

1856–1917; engineer and inventor

The name Frederick Winslow Taylor is now known by few practising managers. And yet, his work forms the cornerstone of much of the management practice of the century. The man may be forgotten, but his legacy lives determinedly on and, once described, would instantly be recognized by most managers.

Taylor was the originator of what became known as 'scientific management'. To the eyes of the late twentieth century observer, scientific management would be considered anything but scientific. Taylor's science was built around minute observation of the best way a task could be undertaken and completed. Having found the best way, people could then be made to follow it, to the second, in the prescribed manner.

Taylorism was built around the notion that there was a single 'best way' to fulfil a particular job; and that then it was a matter of matching people to the task and supervising, rewarding and punishing them according to their performance. The job of management was to plan and control the work.

'Hardly a competent workman can be found who does not devote a considerable amount of time to studying first how slowly he can work and still convince his employer that he is going at a good pace. Under our system a worker is just told what he is to do and how he is to do it. Any improvement he makes upon the orders given to him is fatal to his success,' observed Taylor.

In effect, Taylor sought to de-humanize work. In doing so, he laid the ground for the mass-production techniques which speedily emerged after his death. 'His unforgivable sin was his assertion that there is no such thing as "skill" in making and moving things. All such work was the same, Taylor asserted. And all could be analyzed step-by-step, as a series of unskilled operations that could then be combined into any kind of job. Anyone willing to learn these operations would be a "first-class man", deserving "first class pay". He could do the most advanced work and do it to perfection,' Peter Drucker has accurately observed.[1]

Taylor's theories were first published in 1911 when he detailed how to improve work in a factory in five basic stages:

1. Find, say 10 or 15 different men (preferably in as many separate establishments and different parts of the country) who are especially skilful in doing the particular work to be analyzed.

2. Study the exact series of elementary operations or motions which each of these men use in doing the work being investigated, as well as the implements each man uses.
3. Study with a stop-watch the time required to make each of these elementary movements, and then select the quickest way of doing each element of the work
4. Eliminate all false movements, slow movements and useless movements.
5. After doing away with all unnecessary movements, collect into one series the quickest and best movements as well as the best implements.

Since the rise and fall of labour-intensive, highly functionalist, mass-production, Taylor's ideas have been routinely derided – treating workers as unthinking robots able to carry out carefully prescribed tasks *ad infinitum*. Similarly, the role of managers and supervisors appears to go little beyond holding the stop watch and admonishing – or speedily sacking – malingerers or poor performers. Taylor also emphasized quantity rather than quality.

While there is a great deal of truth in these interpretations, they underestimate the era in which Taylor lived and worked, and the significance (and continuing impact) of his ideas in many businesses. They tend to gloss over some of his insights which do genuinely translate into the modern environment. In *Scientific Management*, for example, Taylor writes: 'It becomes the duty of those on the management's side to deliberately study the character, the nature and the performance of each workman with a view to finding out his limitations on the one hand, but even more important, his possibilities for development on the other hand.' This idea is continually echoed in much of today's management literature.

Similarly, comparisons can be made between the 1990s' fascination with re-engineering – which breaks down organizational processes into their constituent parts – and Taylor's attempts at analysing each and every aspect of the production process.

As Peter Drucker has observed, Taylor's concepts may appear to be inhumane and limited to the modern manager, but he was the first person to really begin to think about the actual act of work rather than taking it for granted. For all his addiction to the stop-watch, Taylor was a truly remarkable man. He patented numerous inventions, excelled at tennis and (perhaps his most significant legacy) persuaded baseball pitchers to throw overarm rather than underarm because, typically enough, it was more efficient.

STUART CRAINER

Further Reading

Taylor, FW, *The Principles of Scientific Management* Harper & Row, New York, 1913.

Reference

[1] Drucker, P, 'The New Productivity Challenge', *Harvard Business Review*, November–December 1991.

RE-ENGINEERING IN PRACTICE

Colin J Coulson-Thomas

A demanding and turbulent business environment, formidable competitors, technological innovation and low barriers to entry put a premium on learning, flexibility and responsiveness. In such an environment, more than incremental adaptation may be required to avoid a negative spiral of cutbacks and layoffs that can result from the scaling down of internal resources to match declining external competitiveness.

In the early 1990s re-engineering has been rapidly embraced as a means of achieving corporate transformation so that organizations become more flexible, responsive, horizontal and team-based. Networks of relationships are sought which can rapidly access and tap relevant resources and empowered people, irrespective of function, distance and time, in order to quickly meet the requirements of individual customers.

Re-engineering returns organizations to their first principles and may focus on one or more business processes, the total organization, or how business is done within their particular marketplace.

Increasingly, re-engineering has come to mean all things to all people. Some consider re-engineering to be but one of a number of change elements that can be employed to transform organizations, while others use it as an umbrella term to embrace those change elements (such as empowerment and increased focus on processes and customers) which they feel are particularly important.

To appreciate what re-engineering is we need to understand what processes are. Processes are at the heart of the concept – which is sometimes labelled Business Process Re-engineering. Business processes are sequences and combinations of activities that deliver value to a customer; while management processes control and co-ordinate these business processes and ensure that business objectives are delivered.

Processes frequently cut horizontally across the vertical functional boundaries of departments such as marketing, production and accounts found in traditional organizations. Various obstacles, barriers and sources of delay are encountered *en route*. In the past, these cross-functional paths have rarely been documented, and no one may have been responsible for them.

Historic investments in training and IT are likely to have been departmental, rather than applied to the processes that actually deliver the outputs sought. Much past effort has been devoted to entrenching vertical channels of command and control and setting self-contained departmental procedures in concrete.

Processes can be improved in various ways, depending upon the degree of change required:

- Process simplification can yield significant but incremental improvements to what exists, typically by cutting out non-value added activities in order to improve throughput times and save on resource requirements. It is not unusual to find 90 per cent or more of elapsed time occurring at hot spots or hand-over points between functional departments.
- In contrast, re-engineering involves radical change. This can involve the re-design or re-building of individual processes, a total organization, or of the relationships between suppliers and customers in a marketplace. Such activities emerge as a result of a vision-led examination of how the basic elements of people, processes, information and technology might be brought together in new ways to achieve a fundamental transformation.

Various lists of *principles* of re-engineering (such as organize around outcomes rather than tasks) have been produced, as major consultancies strive to differentiate their offerings. Certain approaches to re-engineering are little more than process improvement or productivity tools re-named in order to capitalize upon the growth of interest in BPR.

Many of the individual elements of re-engineering are not new. Self-managed workgroups operated in Scandinavia long before they were discovered by re-engineering enthusiasts. However, the combination of change elements under the umbrella of re-engineering does concentrate attention on processes and their outputs. As most organizations are organized by vertical function rather than horizontal process, the potential benefits of such a focus are considerable.

Re-engineering also encourages fundamental, step or frame-breaking change. Dramatic increases in productivity have been chalked up by well publicised re-engineering exercises in such US companies as Ford, GTE, Hallmark, Pacific Bell and Xerox. Response times have plunged from months to days, and from days to hours.

Relationship with other initiatives

The benefits of re-engineering largely derive from thinking, organizing and acting horizontally, in terms of cross-functional processes, rather than vertically in terms of specialist functions and departments. Radical improvements result from challenging assumptions, breaking down barriers, innovative uses of technology, introducing new ways of working, changing relationships and re-drawing traditional boundaries.

TQM is more concerned with continuous improvement, and can complement re-engineering, as when subsequent learning and refinement is built into a re-engineered 'solution'. The tools and techniques of quality can also be, and are, used in the course of re-engineering exercises. However, in comparison with re-engineering, TQM can be a blunt instrument. Thus quality improvement groups could be set up to examine all sorts of activities, whether or not these are part of a critical process.

TQM should result in a focus upon both internal and external customers. It could be a useful precursor to re-engineering, which in turn has been spoken of as a successor to TQM. However, the primary focus of re-engineering is upon end-customers. Ultimately, the external customer is the source of all value and of the rationale of an organization. On occasion, satisfying internal customers can be a distraction.

Initial questions and issues

Re-engineering can be risky and should not be undertaken lightly. Before taking the plunge, an organization needs to clarify its motives, decide how much change is required and establish the scope of what it is trying to do. For example, is it engaged in re-engineering or wholescale corporate transformation?

The motivations, or drivers, for considering or embracing re-engineering can be extremely varied. They could include survival, differentiation, competitive advantage, or a desire for 'early wins' and 'quick fixes'. Some of the drivers may be negative, while others are positive.

Another issue is whether one should begin by tackling management or business processes. Start with management processes and, while they are being reviewed, today's business may die. However, ignoring them can result in an unfocused, unco-ordinated company without direction. As a consequence, re-engineering may be applied to what is not strategically important. Most boards have little if any experience of corporate transformation, and their individual members may need to be equipped with new skills and supported by new management processes that begin and end in the boardroom.

Establishing goals

A re-engineering exercise may be crucial or irrelevant, depending upon the goals set. Objectives range from the modest to the ambitious. Re-engineering initiatives can be relatively self-contained or part of an overall transformation strategy.

The goal of an enterprise-wide corporate transformation could be a world class capability that: delivers value and benchmark levels of satisfaction to customers, employees and business partners; differentiates in the marketplace; and can support ambitious business development and commercial objectives. The re-engineering review process, and subsequent implementation and operation, should also invigorate the people and teams concerned, and provide them with enhanced development opportunities and work satisfaction.

Attacking individual processes will not, by itself, transform an organization. A holistic approach is required. Re-engineering should not become an alternative to creative thinking about different ways of achieving corporate goals and objectives.

Methodologies

A wide range of re-engineering techniques, approaches, methodologies and tools are available from a diversity of suppliers. Various combinations of previously existing approaches and methodologies have been brought together, renamed and repositioned under the re-engineering umbrella.

Most major firms of consultants have their own particular approach to re-engineering, as do some companies and other organizations Which, if any, of these are relevant, or even desirable, will depend upon the situation and circumstances.

Methodologies can be arranged along a spectrum according to the degree of change that is sought. Reference has already been made to the distinction between simplification and re-engineering (Fig. 1).[1]

Simplification usually results in incremental rather than a major 'step change'. Simplification exercises tend to take an existing framework, the limits of installed technology, and current attitudes and behaviour for granted.

In contrast, re-engineering aims at *fundamental* or *frame-breaking* change. A re-engineering exercise would challenge the existing framework, question attitudes and behaviours, and might suggest the introduction of new technology.

A re-engineering exercise could use techniques such as environmental scanning, modelling and visioning that might not be considered by a simplification team. On the other hand, benchmarking, problem-solving techniques, and a range of statistical and process analysis tools could be used in both re-engineering and simplification contexts.

While different methodologies can appear very similar, the uses to which they are put can vary greatly, depending upon the motivations for initiating re-engineering and how the task is approached. Much of what is termed re-engineering operates within an existing framework of attitudes and assumptions, rather than radically challenging them. To the purist, re-engineering is about revolution rather than evolution; fundamental change not incremental improvement.

Process simplification	Process re-engineering
Incremental change	Radical transformation
Process-led	Vision-led
Within existing framework	Review framework
Improve application of technology	Introduce new technology
Assume attitudes and behaviour	Change attitudes and behaviour
Management led	Director led
Various simultaneous projects	Limited number of corporate initiatives

Fig. 1 Simplification or re-engineering?

Maintaining a sense of balance

Techniques, approaches, methodologies and tools are a means to an end, and should not be allowed to become an end in themselves. The purpose of re-engineering is to achieve a radical improvement in performance, not to provide experts with an excuse to plough methodically through endless checklists.

While some resist methodologies and view them as inhibitors of original thought about a particular context, others argue that it is difficult for people to work together without a shared understanding of the steps involved. Much will depend upon the calibre of the re-engineering team. Are they open-minded and courageous? Do they have a tolerance for uncertainty and diversity, an overview perspective, and a desire to learn?

People should not feel compelled to use particular tools and techniques. They should dip selectively into a tool kit and use whatever is thought to be of value. Those who go to the essence of what needs to be done to generate value and build relevant capability, and who keep it simple, tend to be the most successful. No amount of technique can save people from a lack of purpose, direction, shared vision and focus.

What is important is approach and attitude rather than methodology *per se*. One group might plod through the various stages of a methodology with little imagination or enthusiasm, while another could use the same framework to harness and channel creativity and commitment.

The re-engineering process

A review process might pass through modelling, analysis, design and implementation planning phases, and should be tailored to the situation and context. It could involve the assessment of internal and external requirements; the use of benchmarking, environmental scanning, modelling, visioning, design and planning tools; and the analysis of the interaction of people, work processes, information and technology.

Among re-engineering practitioners, there are differences of opinion over the order in which the various steps should be undertaken. Some believe one should not contemplate alternative options until the existing processes have been documented and understood. In the light of this grounding, an alternative model can then be developed and implemented.

Others argue passionately that examining the current reality can condition people and limit their thinking. They advocate ignoring the present state until imaginative thinking has led to a new model. Only then is the time right to examine what is required to develop a programme to migrate from a current situation to a desired future state of affairs.

To ensure that re-engineering supports strategic business development objectives it should be 'front ended' by a strategic review process which includes issue monitoring and management, SWOT and competitor analysis, etc. For organizations new to re-engineering, it is often a sense of crisis which gives rise to the requirement for more than incremental adaptation. Radical action is, too often, only contemplated when the organization is on the brink of collapse.

Once the need for radical action is agreed, what should happen next? There is no right or wrong sequence of steps, so the following example of an approach developed and eventually put into practice, is given for the purposes of illustration only:[2]

- Useful first moves are to assemble a core team and, from the perspective of the total organization, set re-engineering goals, objectives and specific targets. The team should be given both demanding goals and the authority to proceed. Challenging goals are essential as groups tend to stop searching when they feel they have done enough.

- If a particular problem or bottleneck process does not suggest itself as a candidate for re-engineering, the next step is to select a process to re-engineer. Attention should be focused where the potential is the greatest for achieving a significant impact upon business objectives and performance – within an acceptable timescale.

- Rather than be pre-occupied with what is, the team should be encouraged to systematically seek out alternative ways of undertaking whatever is to be the subject of the review. The enquiry should be free and wide-ranging.

- A team in a customer-led organization might at this point spend some time questioning who the customer really is, and the extent to which customer requirements are actually understood. What represents value to the customer from the customer's perspective? What other forms of relationship with the customer could be developed? The answer to questions such as these might be something which does not, but could, exist.

- In a policy-led organization, a team should go back to basics and re-examine the reasons for policies and the nature of policy objectives. Are existing activities dealing with symptoms or underlying causes?

- At this stage, insight and clear thinking are required. If activities being re-engineered do not represent the heart of a problem, improving a peripheral issue or process may distract people from taking necessary action where it is most needed.

- Environmental scanning can lead to unfamiliar and novel options being encountered, perhaps in unrelated fields. The aim should be to obtain a feel for the limits of what is possible.

- Once the team's thinking has become bold and challenging, it may be time to establish a vision for the area that is being examined. This could take the form of a model of operation quite different from that which currently exists.

- In order to design a new model or approach, it may be advizable to agree some design principles. These should not be drawn so tightly as to prematurely close off promising lines of enquiry.

- Once the broad scoping of what is desirable has occurred, the next step is to examine the extent to which it can be achieved. This involves looking at such factors as different ways of learning or performing the work, available technologies, a range of 'people issues', and alternative ways in which people, processes, information and technology can be brought together. Particular attention should be paid to innovations and 'levers' that could unlock breakthrough levels of performance.

- The first principles stage of a re-engineering review should not be rushed, even though others may encourage the team to curtail vague thinking in order to get on with implementation. However, once the major building blocks of a new approach appear to have been identified, the project can move on to a more detailed design phase.
- At this stage, if not earlier, thought should be given to how learning and refinement might be incorporated into the new approach. If some means is not built in to ensure it remains appropriate and current, the sponsoring organization could find itself adopting solutions with a limited life expectancy.
- Up to this point, re-engineering activity has been largely cerebral, namely modelling and analysis, with just enough design work to establish the technical feasibility of an emerging solution. Most organizations will now require some form of proposal with an economic case for moving ahead with detailed design work or implementation planning. Should the team be commissioned to proceed, the cost and impact of a re-engineering exercise can increase quite significantly.
- In the case of a complex process, the project plan could provide for implementation in phases. Interim milestones could be established to focus effort upon one part of a process, or one sub-process, at a time.
- Where the risk of failure is high, and there are existing and ongoing services to deliver, it is usually advizable to test a new approach on a pilot basis.
- Assuming a successful pilot, the full programme can then be rolled out, and its subsequent operation monitored to enable refinements to be introduced, or changes made, as appropriate.

Whether or not the re-engineering team should move on from one stage to the next will depend upon whether further time and additional analysis would result in a materially better 'solution'.

The length of a project

While the length of a re-engineering project will, of course, depend upon the nature of the process being re-designed and its context, 18 months to complete an implementation is not unusual.

More radical changes need not take longer to achieve. A first principles review could involve a relatively short burst of creative thought, while achieving more modest results might require the comparatively time-consuming analysis and documentation of current practice so that improvements can be made.

Some re-engineering exercises are prolonged by a desire to take every relevant factor into account. It is generally possible to speed up the process, for example, by concentrating upon those areas which appear to have the greatest impact upon customers and which consume the greatest amount of resources.

The re-engineering team

Sufficient diversity should be included within a team to encourage active questioning and debate. Team members should be secure personalities, able to think outside the square, while always attentive to impacts upon end customers. A *process owner* should share the vision, goals, values and objectives of the organization, understand the significance of a process, be committed to radical change, and have both the available time and the authority to act.

Consultants should be chosen with care. Their professional backgrounds may prevent them from adopting a holistic overview. Standard and packaged methodologies which do not reflect the unique features of a particular context, and approaches which are over-elaborate and yet incomplete, should be avoided.

Thinking application

To understand what is distinct about re-engineering, compare the above broad phases with the more precise steps of a typical improvement or simplification methodology. When identifying process owners, defining and documenting a process, defining and agreeing customer requirements, and so on, some creative thinking is, of course, required, but many exercises tend to become a matter of filling in the boxes as managers plough through the methodology manual.

With a detailed process improvement, or simplification methodology, the steady plodder can emerge with acceptable levels of performance improvement. However, effective re-engineering can require a very different type of person. One of the challenges of re-engineering is to find people who can push innovation and creativity to the limit without stepping over the boundary of what is practical.

Pragmatic decisions still have to be made. For example, should a complex process be created to handle all the various forms of a transaction that are likely to arise, or should the transactions be screened into different categories, each of which might be handled by a distinct and simpler process or a separate sub-process?

Building learning into processes

Once a particular exercise has reached what appears to be an end point, it should be remembered that situations, circumstances, people, requirements and priorities are ever changing. Hence the importance of building continuous learning, renewal and further periodic reviews of first principles into the re-engineered process.

Particular attention should be devoted to learning, and learning processes (Fig. 2) that enable an organization to continually match its capability and corporate vision to the changing requirements of customers and other stakeholders.

A restless community of seeking, challenging people, for whom aspiring to match or beat the best becomes a way of life, would not need to consider re-engineering as a separate exercise. Its approaches and attitudes would represent aspects of normal business.

Pitfalls of re-engineering

Re-engineering may have been over-sold. While enthusiastic converts talk of nirvana, its early champions warn of nemesis for the naive in view of the risks involved. The more aware practitioners also warn of 'processism' – while a focus upon process can be healthy, an obsession with it and a belief that all one has to do is establish the right processes and nothing but good will follow, can be unhealthy. Judgement and quality of decisions are still needed. Rubbish flowing along world class processes will just produce disappointment more quickly than before.

In spite of the opportunity and potential for radical change, few transformation, re-engineering or quality programmes bring about the changes of attitudes or behaviour that are both desired and required. Quite simply, many re-engineering exercises fail to deliver the hoped-for benefits.

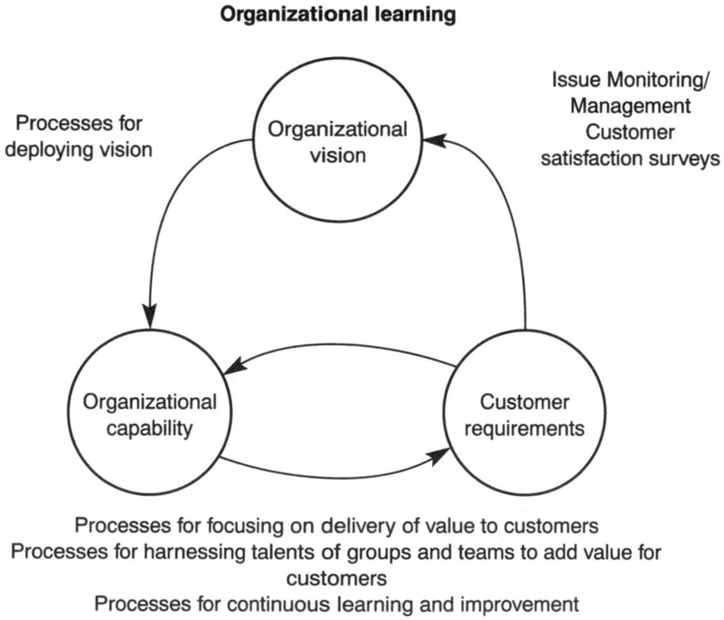

Organizational learning

Processes for focusing on delivery of value to customers
Processes for harnessing talents of groups and teams to add value for customers
Processes for continuous learning and improvement

Fig. 2 The processes of organizational learning

Source: C. Coulson-Thomas, *Transforming the Company*, Kogan Page, London, 1992

People become bogged down with incremental improvements to what is, rather than thinking creatively about what ought to be. The focus of too many exercises is internal, concentrating on the organization and its processes, rather than on what represents value for the external customer.

Approaches to re-engineering are also insufficiently tailored to the situation, circumstances and context. Standard approaches to re-engineering and quality can provide a common language, but they travel better in some parts of the world than in others and they can also destroy diversity.

Many approaches to re-engineering are mechanical and crude rather than creative and sensitive:

- too often, managers are driven simply by reducing staff numbers or the cost base rather than delivering value to customers;
- greater openness and honesty is also required. Many attempts at involvement and participation are crude in the extreme. Speeches and videos are made about how middle managers need to put their backs into eliminating their jobs.

There is excessive focus upon the hard and quantifiable, such as document flows and supporting technology. Insufficient attention is devoted to the softer people issues because these are perceived as difficult or intangible. Re-engineering is being 'done' to too many people who are themselves not sufficiently involved, motivated or empowered.

Some applications of re-engineering can be positively dangerous. Repeatable processes may not exist in creative, dynamic environments. Each 'path through the organization' in response to an individual problem or opportunity may be unique. Establishing, documenting and supporting particular paths may create a new set of inflexibilities, and can be the organizational equivalent of turning the flexible responses of the human brain into the programmed approach of the robot.

Very often what is referred to as re-engineering, turns out only to be process improvement or simplification. Such initiatives may result in worthwhile increases in performance, but they are unlikely to produce the radical transformation promised by advocates of re-engineering.

Success factors

Successful re-engineering requires a number of complementary factors, including a desire to change, the courage to search for ambitious outcomes, the active participation at each phase of the people of the process, and top-management commitment. The latter is sometimes lacking because many of those wishing to undertake 'fundamental transformations' are insecure. They doubt the ability of their people to deliver and are uncertain about whom to trust externally.

While the creative use of IT can transform a marketplace, and IT has become inextricably linked with re-engineering, a radical improvement in performance could result from simplifying IT. One operation was transformed by the introduction of a card index system. Instead of relating only to VDU screens and sending electronic mail messages to each other, people started sitting around a table, talking, and resolving customer problems spontaneously as a cross-functional group.

The critical implementation issues and barriers tend to concern attitudes, beliefs and behaviour. Inter-personal communication and involvement are usually the limiting factor rather than the capability of technology.

Many re-engineering projects are doomed to fail from the moment they are initiated because vital pieces of the jig-saw puzzle are missing. Where success occurs, it is often because other change elements are employed alongside re-engineering. To make a significant impact upon an end-to-end process, let alone a total organization, a holistic approach is likely to be required, comprising of a wide range of elements.

Perhaps the most important success requirement is to assemble the combination of 'change elements' to make it happen in the particular situation and circumstances. No two contexts are likely to be the same, and the key elements needed can vary greatly.

Re-engineering strategy

To develop an effective re-engineering strategy, and before agreeing transformation vision, goals, values and objectives, it is necessary to assess and understand the challenge and the risks; stakeholder expectations; and the various obstacles and barriers. If dramatic breakthroughs in managerial performance are to occur, obstacles and barriers must be both identified and overcome.

Clear roles and responsibilities, and 'vital few' priorities, can ensure that resources are applied where they are likely to have the greatest impact. The review process should address any gaps and deficiencies, while an action programme should detail the next steps to be taken, any missing elements, and the tools and techniques that could be used to overcome implementation barriers.

Successful transformation depends critically upon the selection, combination and application of relevant change elements at each stage of the change process. It is generally easier to get the strategy right than to manage the consequences of getting it wrong.

Imaginative, innovative and enlightened implementation of re-engineering can regenerate the capability of enterprises and communities to compete, deliver value and satisfaction and, if adopted more widely, could offer people a richer variety of work and lifestyle opportunities.

Re-engineering need not be a big company phenomenon. There are market sectors in which small rather than large firms have been the innovators. They have simply out-thought the competition.

It is not easy for flexible and caring forms of organizations to thrive in a social context of restrictive attitudes, unthinking and short-term action, and a reluctance to challenge and change long-established practices. If organizations and societies are to reap the full benefits of BPR, attitudes and behaviours will need to change. Organizations are not machines to be re-engineered by taking pieces out, changing them and putting them back, but communities of people with feelings. Organizations which fail to make this basic recognition are unlikely to succeed in re-engineering.

Dr Colin J Coulson-Thomas, chairman of Adaptation Ltd and Attitudes, Skills and Knowledge Ltd, leads and co-ordinates the European Commission's COBRA project to examine re-engineering experience and practice across Europe. He holds a portfolio of private and public sector directorships, and is regularly called upon to review change programmes and approaches to re-engineering. He is Professor of Corporate Transformation and Dean of the Faculty of Management, University of Luton, and holds visiting appointments at the UK's Aston Business School, Cambridge University, City University Business School, and the IT Instituite of Salford University. Dr Coulson-Thomas is author of a large number of books including *Transforming the Company* (1992) and *Creating the Global Company* (1992); and is the editor of *Business Process Re-engineering: Myth and Reality* (1994)

Further Reading

Bartram, P, *Business Re-engineering: The use of process redesign and IT to transform corporate performance*, Business Intelligence, Wimbledon, 1992.

Carr, DK, Dougherty, KS, Johansson, HJ, King, RA, and Moran, DE, *Breakpoint: Business Process Redesign*, Coopers & Lybrand, Arlington, VA, 1992.

Coulson-Thomas, C, (ed.) *Business Process Re-engineering: Myth and Reality*, Kogan Page, London, 1994.

Davenport, TH, *Process innovation: Re-engineering Work Through Information Technology*, Harvard Business School Press, 1993.

Hammer, M, and Champy, J, *Re-engineering the Corporation, A Manifesto for Business Revolution*, Nicholas Brealey Publishing, London, 1993.

Johansson, H, *et al*, *Business Process Re-engineering: Breakpoint Strategies for Market Dominance*, John Wiley, Chichester, 1993.

References

[1] Coulson-Thomas, C, *Transforming the Company*, Kogan Page, London, 1992.

[2] Coulson-Thomas, C, *Business Process Re-engineering: Myth and Reality*, Kogan Page, London, 1994.

[3] Coulson-Thomas, C, *Transforming the Company, op. cit.*

Human Resource Management

'Man has two sets of needs. His need as an animal to avoid pain and his need as a human to grow psychologically.'

Frederick Herzberg[1]

'What is talent and who is a talented person? Everybody. Everyone has talent. The only problem is to be sure that everyone can give you this talent so that you can use it.'

Jean Francois Cottin, GSI[2]

'Ultimately, whatever the form of economic activity, it is people that count most.'

Lord Sieff[3]

[1] Herzberg, F, *Work and the Nature of Man*, World Publishing, London, 1966.
[2] Quoted in Sadler, P, *The Talent Intensive Organisation*, Pitman, London, 1993.
[3] Sieff, Lord, *On Management: Marks and Spencer Way*, Weidenfeld & Nicolson, London, 1990.

OVERVIEW

Shaun Tyson

There is now a common acceptance that competitive advantage may be achieved by firms from the way their employees are managed. This prescription has gained ground over the last fifteen years to the stage where it may now be said to be conventional wisdom. While one may wish that this is because working people are now treated in a considerate, developmental and respectful manner, one might equally say it is because employees have come to be regarded in the same category as business assets, that is, to be acquired with care, to be developed and utilized effectively. The term *human resource management* (HRM) signifies to managers and to employees a new emphasis on the management of people in order to achieve strategic organizational objectives. Whether the rhetoric which has come to surround the term is intended to disguise and to make attractive the utilitarian purpose, or whether HRM represents a normative management philosophy is a debate which has occupied academics and practitioners during the transition phase.

The debate on how we should manage people has arisen as a consequence of macro economic, social, and political change. Changes to the industrial structure in Western countries, to occupations and to labour markets, and the growing internationalization of business have come at a time when institutions and policies have been under review nationally and internationally. Social, political, demographic and technological change have forced all societies to shift the ideological ground on which values are formed and to question the very foundations of what constitutes good management practice. This has been the backdrop to restructuring at the corporate level.

The 'new' human resource management

It is not surprising that with this degree of social and personal upheaval, there are different interpretations of the changes. Three distinct approaches to the 'new' HRM can be discerned:

1. The first suggests the move from personnel administration to HRM represents a paradigm shift in the way people are managed. The notion here is that because the changes have been so fundamental to organizational life, a new model of the personnel function has emerged with a strategic orientation and a business focus, which is qualitatively different from personnel management.

2. An opposite interpretation is also possible, where HRM is described as virtually the same as personnel management. The new label merely indicates a repackaging of some elements, such as management and organization development, these aspects having become noticeable due to the recent concerns with managing change. According to this view, changes in employee relations, such as reduced trade union militancy, are a response to temporary influences, labour market changes and economic recession.

3. The third interpretation combines both of the other two explanations. HRM is seen as a set of policies with a strong normative content, especially noticeable on greenfield sites, and partly influenced by American and Japanese corporate personnel policies. Ideologically-grounded with a unitary frame of reference, it is argued that the patchy take-up of this approach is due to its reliance on a strong supportive corporate culture.

Situational factors

Situational factors are significant influences on the way HRM operates. There is, of course, a dynamism in the way organizations react to different stakeholders. The policy choices available will, therefore, vary according to the context, and will change as the strategies change.

Ample evidence exists to support the contention that there was a managerial revolution in the 1980s. Just-in-time sourcing; new technology designed to produce flexible specialization; total quality management techniques; and autonomous work groups, all revolutionized manufacturing. New technology also helped to stimulate the service sector, as did institutional changes such as deregulation in financial services. All of these changes occurred at a moment when governments in the UK and the USA had shifted to the right, espousing a new ideology which sought to emphasize the individual employment contract, in place of collective agreements. In the UK, laws to restrict trade union activity and the government victory in the Miners' Strike in 1984, gave the impression that industrial relations were changing.

Trade union membership in the UK has been falling steadily – from 12.3 million members to 8.9 million members between 1981 and 1992 – and, faced with falling revenue and increased costs, there have been a spate of amalgamations between unions. It would be a mistake to assume that the unions are a spent force. They still represent around 40 per cent of the UK workforce, are especially strong in certain industries and in the public sector, and are trying to modernize their image. Unions also have influence beyond their numbers – settlements at Ford Motor Company, for example, or in the public sector, are taken as 'the going rate' for other non-union workers to achieve.

Trade union membership has reduced in Europe over the last decade but recent data shows that in spite of large membership differences (in 1988, the OECD estimated that density ranged from 73 per cent in Denmark to 12 per cent in France) recognition by employers is holding up with little recent change to their influence.

Perhaps the most influential factors to affect industrial relations have been in the labour market. At the time of labour shortage in the mid-to-late 1980s, companies sought a variety of contractual relationships, and cost reduction/utilization strategies have now taken over as the drivers for new contracts. Atkinson's well known model of the flexible firm describes a stable core of permanent employees in each firm, augmented by an array of other contractual arrangements including temporary, casual, part-time, and sub-contractors as well as franchise and outsourcing arrangements.

This provides the company with a pool of labour into which it may expand to satisfy surges in demand without committing itself to permanent employees. Such a strategy also permits withdrawal without heavy costs and, therefore, increases flexibility. Increasingly, the issue becomes one of what should be retained in the core and what should be put in the periphery. Changes of this kind also allow companies to better balance labour demand with supply. For example, the Burton Group changed all its employment contracts within its shops, using the 'key worker' concept. This put people on contracts which ensured the shops were staffed to reflect shopping patterns. Working time changes such as annual hours, flexible shifts, zero hours (call out) contracts and similar arrangements have also sought to create flexibility. There are, of course, training implications for those firms which have opted for a small core. In-house expertise and capability is reduced by a strategy which relies on the external labour market to educate, train and develop people. There are now more people working on non-standard than on standard contracts in the working population, and many people now entirely work evenings and/or at weekends.

A feature of the current labour markets is the increased number of women participating: many of the new jobs created have been filled by women, who now comprise over 50 per cent of the workforce. New employment has come in high-tech manufacturing, distribution, retail and services rather than in the typically male-dominated areas. Industries such as steel, mining, heavy engineering, ship building and vehicle manufacture have, in employment terms, shrunk to a fraction of their former size.

Changes in employment have not been solely confined to non-managerial employees. Career ladders for executives have also disappeared. We now have the mosaic career, sometimes called the portfolio career, made up of a variety of roles performed either simultaneously by working part-time, or being both employed and self-employed, or sequentially, or working on temporary assignments. Although graduate recruitment continues, and blue chip corporations still express a strong desire to find the best possible candidates to enter fast track schemes, the days when most managers could expect to spend a whole working life with one company are long since gone. Even if they are not forced to leave and find work elsewhere, the company itself may be taken over, bought out by management, merged, or go into some other type of collaborative venture, as can be seen from the cases of ICI, now split into two with the creation of Zeneca; National Freight, bought out by its employees; or the Rover Group, now purchased by BMW after a long successful collaboration with Honda, and a previous existence tied in with British Leyland. There is now more variety, challenge and insecurity for executives.

One reason for new approaches to career planning is the move away from large bureaucracies with a central headquarters where hundreds of corporate aparatchiks processed mountains of information, remote from risk-bearing action. The trend towards devolving accountability to strategic business units has gathered pace, and with modern IT systems there is no need for departments to gather or disseminate data. The move towards devolved structures has coincided with a desire to rationalize, and to strip out costs in order to be competitive, resulting in flatter structures, hence reduced promotion prospects, smaller sub-units which allow some form of empowerment, and more flexible approaches to organization design. There is also a less clear divide between a contract of service, and a contract for services.

The emphasis on outputs, on tasks and costs has made organizations more diffuse bodies. The present era has been described as 'post-Fordist' or 'post-modernist' – that is, organization managers have moved away from thinking of their operational activity as replicating a bureaucratic machine, a rational, non-human monolith which delivers standardized products or services with scant regard for customer choice or competitive rivalry. Instead, work is organized in a more organic way, susceptible to rapid change, and to adjustment albeit within a limited range of options. Banking services, for example, are designed as personal financial advisory services, with most routine withdrawals and regular payments handled by machines; car manufacturers have various specification mixes on offer; and airlines try to leverage sales through special packages, air miles schemes and the like.

New, flatter organization shapes have come about as a consequence of delayering. In addition there are diamond shapes, where the top management is supported by technical experts, for example in mechanized production, but there are then only a few employees at the lowest level, as maintenance staff. Mushroom shapes reflect the organization structure in partnerships, for example in medical practice, consultancy, legal services and other professional activity. The smaller, partnership shapes may well be the organization structure most commonly found in the future.

Devolved structures are intended to be more responsive to customers than large centralized organizations. The trend towards divisional structures also reflects conglomerate development. There are numbers of important issues for human resource management which arise from the trend towards divisionalization. Chief among these is the question of where should responsibility for the strategic management of human resources lie? Equally, what aspects of human resource management ought to be controlled from the centre on a day-to-day basis? It has been convincingly argued that HR strategies are typically third-order strategies, downstream from the main decisions taken by the marketing and finance functions.[1] In practice, recent research has shown how influential divisional decision making can be.[2]

Strategies in highly diversified businesses are of necessity formulated at divisional level and go, with the whole weight of the divisional board, up to the main board. While some adjustment seems to be typical, only in the most unusual cases would one expect to see the entire divisional strategic plan rejected. Decisions at divisional level are just as strategic as those at corporate level.

This argument must be tempered with the knowledge that major changes in direction (for example decisions to quit a business area) are likely to require more than just mere approval from the main board. Joint ventures, mergers, acquisitions, divestments and collaboration are fundamental corporate issues and it is here that one normally only sees a major HR contribution during the period of 'due diligence' while the management capacity and the quality of the company to be acquired, is investigated, to check what is being acquired or merged. International businesses can only be conducted through collaboration, and the global market-place made accessible by information technology is stimulating all kinds of partnership, merger, joint venture and franchise deals.

Strategic trends in human resource management

The idea of 'human resource management' is predicated on an assumption that there is a contribution by those with specialist knowledge of HRM to the overall strategic aims of their organizations. Evidence from a study of 30 well-known British companies shows that human resource strategies do contribute to business performance.[3] This study discovered four strategic levers which companies pull in order to adjust HR strategy to business strategy: these were management and employee development, organization development (particularly the management of change, organization design), and employee relations, which includes reward and communication policies.

The new organization development

Creating companies which are capable of continuous change is now a regular management task. Change programmes are designed to question the organizational culture. The new organization development (OD) combines work on culture change with high levels of employee participation. Employees are frequently organized into semi-autonomous work groups, which make decisions about work allocation, training and sometimes even minor disciplinary matters. Such groups permit larger spans of control, and use group pressures positively. Corporate values may also be developed from the bottom upwards, and this approach is consistent with quality circles, learning organization approaches, and the concept of empowerment. Change from the top down cannot work, it is argued, without strong commitment from employees. Participation in decision-making about one's own work does not imply decision-taking on the big strategic issues, but it does involve a sense of pride and commitment to the service, or the output objectives.

The new OD therefore seeks to use organization design, empowerment and TQM techniques to change organizations. Very often a change programme which heightens awareness of the reasons for the change is instituted. The idea is to show top management's vision and leadership alongside employee involvement. Although change may be forced upon the organization – through privatization as in the case of BT or British Airways, and the public utilities or through mergers and acquisitions, the difficulties arise when the first flush of change has passed. Successive changes can breed familiarity and the problem is how to keep people on the edge of performance. This is one argument for the 'learning organization' approach.

Employee development

A corporate vision of continuous change, managed through a learning organization philosophy, requires total commitment throughout the company to employee and management development: institutional pressure for such an emphasis can be found within the 'Investors in People' initiative – a government-sponsored drive to encourage companies to set training standards, and to agree to deliver against these targets. Company training investment can be considerable – for example, the supermarket chain Sainsbury invests £30 million per year this way and that is without recording all the informal learning which is so significant for most employees (the everyday on-the-job help, coaching and advice which is part of both managerial jobs and of colleague/team relationships).[4]

Developing company capability is now seen by many organizations as synonymous with developing employee ability. Performance management is the term given to day-by-day management aimed at developing competencies, for example through appraisal (including customers, peer group and subordinate opinions) and the increasing trend towards openness about weaknesses which are seen as training opportunities. Techniques for enhancing capability are now frequently by distance learning. Through the Credit Accumulation and Transfer scheme, and the National Vocational Qualification schemes, credits towards diplomas and degrees can be built up, encouraging employees to take a long-term view of their development, an injunction entirely consistent with the changing career concept.

Women's development is also now understood to be of particular importance, given the fact that there are still few women in senior positions within industry, commerce, politics, the law or in public life generally, although women have an equal share of the labour market. Some organizations, such as BT and some of the large clearing banks, have encouraged women to develop through specialized training schemes. The argument is as much founded on strategic needs as on any sense of equity: without developing half of their labour force adequately, companies lose out to their competitors.

Reward and recognition

Change has forced companies to simplify their reward structures in an attempt to move away from the bureaucracy inherent with complex job evaluation schemes and salary structures. Keeping such systems up-to-date has proved too expensive a burden. At the same time, organizations have sought flexibility, represented by broad salary bands, and flexible benefits policies, which give the employee some choice. Cafeteria schemes may be slow to be taken up, but the total compensation approach, which accords each job with a total monetary value is gaining ground, as a means of controlling costs. Flexibility with grades encourages mobility within the company's labour market, avoids demarcation issues, and provides learning opportunities for employees.

Corporate recognition for ideas and creativity is now essential. We are in an era of knowledge workers, and this requires policies which motivate employees to think out their own solutions to the problems they face at work.

It is now some years since Scandinavian Air Services (SAS) under Jan Carlson analyzed its business by means of 'Transaction Points' – occasions when customer and employee conducted some form of transaction. SAS discovered ten such points, ranging from the time passengers checked the timetable, made reservations, checked in, were served on board, etc. To improve performance a certain technical standard was established at every transaction point, which was to be seen by staff as an opportunity for creativity, and problem solving – from which a functional quality was expected. Such learning opportunities have to be matched by corporate recognition. Companies such as Westland Helicopters have a formal recognition policy, covering suggestion schemes, group problem solving and individual competitions for new ideas which generate revenue or save costs. The approach to problem solving is, therefore, centred again on individual responsibility, and on-the-spot solutions rather than on passing problems up to management to solve.

The move towards performance-based pay has received a mixed press. All the problems of incentive schemes still remain, including the principal difficulty that payment systems are blunt instruments in the delicate balance of individual motivation. The thesis of Frederick Herzberg remains: people are motivated by exciting work, by challenge, by being given opportunities for personal development, rather than by money, which at best only stands as a symbol for recognition. This has become even more apparent as performance-based pay has been extended to medical practitioners to teachers and to civil servants. While efficiency (ie, savings on non-essentials) may be marginally improved by such schemes, there is no evidence to suggest that surgeons are more careful when on a performance bonus, or that teachers take more care of the children at school if they are promised more money. Disillusionment with performance-based pay is spreading. However, at a time of low inflation, when there is no automatic annual pay rise, only improvements in productivity are likely to generate pay increases. This form of 'performance-based pay', awarded to the group of employees who have all contributed, seems to meet the 'felt fair' criterion, and to be a more potent symbol.

Reward policy is also central to the broad question of what is the nature of the employment contract? In recent years there has been a move in the public sector towards the 'hard contract'. This is based on transaction costs. A deal is struck for that particular piece of work, there is no assumption of promotion, or development. By contrast, the soft contract implies a 'clan' culture, where there is transferability between jobs, a long-term career and a strong development policy.[5] These two extremes pose two different philosophies of people management. The hard contract concentrates on job performance, and gives the individual freedom to negotiate, but no long-term security. It is the ultimate in *laissez faire* capitalism. The soft contract suggests a long-term debt of duty to the corporation, in return for which there is a reciprocal commitment, as used to be the case with large Japanese companies. These different philosophies of management will be apparent in various forms in different business. The two extremes represent the two poles of reward policy options, and balancing between these two raises questions about what the corporation's responsibilities towards its employees really are.

Corporate responsibility, individual responsibility and the role of the State

The demographic trends, together with the problems of long-term unemployment, raise the issue for the next decade, of how will society cope with the economic and social problems it faces? HRM is the functional area which must face the corporate response to the problems of one-parent families, care for the elderly, and changing values, as well as health problems. There is increased incidence of employee drug testing, there are more and more smoke-free workplaces, policies on HIV-affected employees, and corporate recognition of the effects of stress. In addition, many companies now take seriously the problems of sexual harassment and of bullying at work.

As governments are asked to fund ever more expenditure on health and on social security payments, it seems inevitable that whichever political party is in power, employees and individuals will be asked to shoulder a larger share of the burden. Occupational pension schemes are already the only way retired employees can be funded to live at a reasonable standard, and similar approaches to health care can be anticipated. With the state providing the minimum necessary, individuals and their employees will be required to cope with any general improvement. There is a paradox here. Just as employers are seeking to shift the burden of responsibility for career and development back to the individual, with a softer version of the contract for the core of employees, and a harder contract for all those working on various temporary, self-employed and casual contacts, the state is seeking to reduce its own responsibilities by reshaping the Welfare State. At the heart of many of the disagreements over the Social Chapter is the lack of certainty about how to resolve this dilemma.

What is happening to the HR function?

Changing societal values and economic circumstances have been taken as the determining variables which are influencing the human resource function. Clearly there is no one 'correct' model of the function, and any generalization must of necessity simplify. Perhaps it is inevitable that as we approach the end of the century and the new millennium, we reflect on what has gone before, and speculate about what is to come. The changes described here are producing new models of HRM, which set HRM in a strategic direction. This is not to deny that the old models also continue – with their accent on administration, industrial relations, and the provision of a professional service.

The characteristics of the new models are:

- A strong emphasis on HRM as a consultancy service (either internally or externally provided) to senior line management.
- HRM as an activity majoring on the business needs or strategic plans of the organization.
- HRM as a key aspect to the organization's change strategy, playing a process role: enabling and assisting change.
- HRM as a coherent philosophy of management, integrated with other functional areas, but giving line management the authority to manage.
- HRM as a philosophy welded into TQM and the customer focus of the organization.
- HRM working on employee expectations and needs, and using different contractual arrangements to balance these needs with organizational requirements.

At a time of new values, and shifting economic and social circumstances, HRM is unquestionably changing. To give support to the strategic purpose of an organization, the HR specialist must integrate HR policies with the other functional policies, in marketing, sales, production or service management, and finance. But there remains the HR philosophy to which the HR function must contribute chiefly. The philosophy espoused by the organization is as likely to have come about slowly, based on organizational values, just as most strategic plans are emergent and subject to rapid revision and change. The value and efficacy of such philosophies resides in the extent to which the philosophy is capable of changing behaviour and of influencing employees. To know people, how they react, change, develop and what motivates them, angers them, stimulates and challenges them should be the core of HR work. The technical detail of policies and employment laws and contracts are only one side of the HR coin. To be able to use these instruments of policy effectively, knowledge and understanding of people at work stands as the cardinal virtue.

Shaun Tyson is Professor of Human Resource Management, Director of the Human Resource Research Centre and Dean of the Faculty of Management at Cranfield School of Management, Cranfield University, Bedfordshire, England.

Further Reading

Beer, M, Spector, B, Lawrence, PR, Mills, DQ, and Walton, R, *Managing Human Assets*, Free Press, New York, 1984.

Blyton, P and Turnbull, P, *Reassessing Human Resource Management*, Sage, London, 1992.

Storey, J (ed.), *New Perspectives on Human Resource Management*, Routledge, London, 1989.

Storey, J, *Developments in the Management of Human Resources*, Blackwell, Oxford, 1992.

Tyson, S and Fell, A, *Evaluating the Personnel Function*, Hutchinson, London, 1986.

Tyson, S, *Human Resource and Business Strategy: Towards a General Theory of Human Resource Management*, Pitman, London, 1995.

References

1 Purcell, J, 'The impact of corporate strategy on human resource management', in Storey, J (ed.), *New Perspectives on Human Resource Management*, Routledge, London, 1989.

2 Tyson, S and Witcher, M, 'Getting in gear: post recession HR management', *Personnel Management*, August 1994.

3 Tyson, S, *Human Resource and Business Strategy: Towards a General Theory of Human Resource Management*, Pitman, London, 1995.

4 Evans, J, 'Investing in people at Sainsbury's', *Management Development Review*, vol. 6, no. 1, pp. 33-38, 1993.

5 Tyson, S, *Human Resource and Business Strategy, op. cit.*

THINKERS

Richard Pascale

Born 1938; consultant and educator

Richard Pascale urges management to invest the intellectual energy necessary to make an informed choice between *change* (incremental improvement) or *transformation* (discontinuous shifts in capability). He believes a mental muddle surrounds these choices with many change efforts masquerading as 'transformation'. An impassioned critic of management fads, Pascale advocates that organizations commit themselves to relentless self-questioning and re-invention.

Richard Pascale has been described as the 'scourge of the complacent and prodder of the timid'.[1] Undoubtedly, his views and advice have made increasingly uncomfortable reading and listening for managers. He believes that gurus, writers, speakers and the ultimate consumers – managers – are caught up in a game of sound bites and simplistic remedies.

'It's like the practice of medicine in the Middle Ages,' he states. 'A leech under the armpit and one to the groin. With no understanding of bacteria, virus or how the body worked, there were lots of prescriptions by the physicians of the Middle Ages – but cures were largely the product of random chance. A parallel holds today. Lots of remedies but very few successful examples of authentic transformation. Organizations churn through one technique after another and at best get incremental improvement on top of business-as-usual. At worst, these efforts waste resources and evoke cynicism and resignation.

'What is needed is a much deeper inquiry into first, a business's unfolding competitive situation, and second, an understanding of the largely invisible patterns of thinking and behaviour which define the "box" inside which a company operates. Once revealed, it becomes clear whether the organization (improving at a predictable pace given past performance) can successfully meet the demands of competition. If not, there is a need for transformation. This is a difficult but manageable journey.'

On a personal level he is a somewhat reluctant revolutionary. 'I would describe my life as backing away from what didn't work toward a better fit with my gifts and capabilities,' he says. But, Pascale – like other leading management thinkers – has pursued a single-minded path once the course became clear. 'As I was finishing my MBA at Harvard, my colleagues were frantically searching for the "perfect" job. I found myself troubled by the process and unable to engage in it with enthusiasm,' he recalls. 'Then, one day I had an epiphany – what I really wanted to do was spend a quarter of my life teaching; a quarter consulting (to test the relevance of theory in practice); a quarter writing (something I enjoy – and when you put your ideas on paper you discover the holes in the logic); and, finally, a quarter of my life on holiday (to re-create). I have endeavoured to achieve that balance ever since.'[2]

With the first 25 per cent of his time, Pascale, as a teacher, Pascale spent 20 years at Stanford's Graduate School of Business – his course on organizational survival was the most popular on the MBA programme. As a consultant, he has clients that include many of the world's largest corporations.

'Over time, I have focused increasingly on the challenge of renewing large organizations,' he observes. 'I regard my clients as learning partners. Clearly, I am expected to add value and I endeavour to do so. But I am consistently learning from those I work with and always confronted with how much further we have to go to enable corporations to revitalize themselves with a higher likelihood of success.'

As a writer, Pascale's ideas first reached a mass audience through his 1981 book, *The Art of Japanese Management* (co-authored with Anthony Athos). The inspiration for the book was derived from Pascale's work with the National Commission on Productivity (a White House task force of *Fortune 50* chief executives and national union leaders). 'I had spent a year in Japan in the late 1960s,' he states. 'While deeply impressed, I doubted we could learn much from the Japanese as their culture is so different from ours. One night on a flight back from Washington DC, it hit me: why not study Japanese companies in the United States? How would they adapt their ideas to American managers and an American workforce? This became the cornerstone of the study.'

The Art of Japanese Management was a bestseller, eventually published in 20 languages. It drew lessons from archetypal Japanese success stories – such as Honda in the US. Japanese successes, like their best managed American counterparts, derived from a relentless commitment to learning and meticulous attention to the factors that motivate people, reinforce core values and fine-tune the interconnected elements of an organization. Pascale and Athos were the first to coin the term 'Managing by Walking About' (MBWA) and to call attention to the singular importance of *shared values*.

Another contribution of *The Art of Japanese Management* derives from the

Education: Harvard Business School
Career: Member of the faculty, Stanford's Graduate School of Business; White House Fellow, Special Assistant to the Secretary of Labor, and Senior Staff of a White House Task Force re-organizing the President's executive office; consultant to many *Fortune 500* companies including AT&T, General Electric, Intel, Shell, 3M, British Petroleum and Coca Cola.

1970s when Pascale worked with Tom Peters and Robert Waterman (then at the McKinsey consulting firm) and Anthony Athos (a professor at Harvard Business School). Pascale had a hand in developing the 'Seven S' framework. 'It's nothing more than seven important categories that managers use to make an organization work,' he states. The seven Ss are *strategy, structure, systems, style* and *shared values, skills* (an organization's distinctive competence) and people, but to maintain the alliteration we called the people category *staff*.

Despite the book's success Pascale was anxious not to become typecast as a Japan expert. 'I don't define myself as a Japan scholar – what I am interested in is making Western organizations more productive.' Under pressure to come up with a sequel, Pascale wrote a three-page outline on what he believed was the next horizon for improving competitiveness: the importance of constructive contention as the fuel of self-renewal in organizations. 'I thought I could write the book in six months,' he says. 'But all the data and interviews I had in my files only skimmed the surface. People conceal their conflicts; organizations suppress it. The most important contention is often an undiscussable. Yet it is precisely these hidden tensions within an organization that can be a source of vitality if they are channelled effectively.'

Managing on the Edge: How the Smartest Companies use Conflict to Stay Ahead further cemented Pascale's reputation. The book is densely packed with anecdotes and ideas. At their root is Pascale's observation that many of the 'excellent' companies which Peters and Waterman had celebrated in *In Search of Excellence* had fallen from grace within the short span of a few years. At the heart of their vulnerability were the very qualities that historically had enabled them to excel. Paradoxically, internal coherence (an asset during stable times) rendered them ill-equipped to deal with radical shifts in the environment. 'They couldn't get out of their own way,' says Pascale. 'like weight-lifters with tremendous upper body strength suddenly asked to compete in the high hurdles.'

Coincidentally Pascale had also 'stumbled' upon a law of cybernetics known as the Law of Requisite Variety. The law states that for any organism to adapt to its external environment, it must incorporate 'variety'. If you reduce 'variety' internally you are less able to deal with it when it comes at you externally. Then he asked:

> But how does variety show up in a social system? It shows up as deviance from the norm – in other words, as conflict. The problem is that most companies are conflict-averse. For many it is associated with wounded egos, harmed relationships and turf wars. Contention is often mistaken as an indicator of mismanagement. The trick is to learn to disagree without being disagreeable and channel this contention as a means of self-questioning and keeping an organization on its toes.

In practice, Pascale believes 50 per cent of the time when contention arises it is smoothed over and avoided. Another 30 per cent of the time it leads to non-productive fighting and no resolution. Only in 20 per cent of the cases is contention truly confronted and resolved. 'It's ironic,' observes Pascale. 'A threat that everyone perceives but no one talks about is far more debilitating than a threat that is clearly revealed and resources mobilized to address it. Companies, like people, tend to be as sick as their secrets,' says Pascale – who prescribes revealing the 'undiscussables' and that 'breakdowns' be regarded as a source of learning.

His increasingly broad-ranging and holistic world view remains influenced by Japanese thinking. In particular, Pascale argues that Western managers need to become more attuned to the difference between *doing* and *being*.

My exposure to the Japanese language made me aware of two words, *Ki* and *Kokoro*, which refer to the core essence of a person (in other words, who they are being). These terms are as commonplace to the Japanese language as 'me', 'self', 'I' and 'my' are to most Western languages. What this means is that a Japanese, regardless of educational attainment, is constantly cued by his language to pay attention to who they are being while in the process of doing something. (We see in this their seemingly ritualistic approach to the tea ceremony, flower arranging or sumo wrestling.) The way in which this comes to root in business is that it would not occur to the Japanese just to 'do' a management technique – such as Total Quality Management. Of course, they would also 'be' quality. By contrast, they view their Western counterparts as precocious children – always chasing after the latest management technique and striving to distil it down to a recipe for doing. Organizations that churn through a succession of 'doings' (such as TQM and re-engineering) without altering their underlying being often end up older, maybe slimmer, but rarely wiser. Transformation entails a shift in being – at the personal and organizational level.

To transform itself an organization needs to tackle its very core – its context – the underlying assumptions and invisible premises on which its decisions and actions are based. This sounds arcane but is no more complicated than assembling a critical mass of key stakeholders (perhaps the 100 to 200 people who really make things happen in a company) and conducting an organizational audit that reveals the invisible box inside which the company operates. Once revealed, it is easy to have a straightforward discussion about whether the organization, operating at its current level (ie, doing what is predictable), can respond to the unfolding competitive threats. If not, a dramatic shift in organizational capability (ie, transformation) is required.

Pascale points to a number of leading US companies such as Motorola, General Electric and even the department store chain, Nordstrum, as examples of successful ongoing transformation (or reinvention). *Transformation* and *reinvention* are Pascale's coda for the future. 'Many companies need to reinvent themselves,' he says. 'And reinvention is not changing what is, but creating what isn't. A butterfly is not more caterpillar or a better or improved caterpillar; a butterfly is a different creature. Reinvention entails a series of continuous metamorphoses of this magnitude over time.'[3] Pascale plays down his reputation.

I don't think of myself as a guru or as a repository of ultimate knowledge. That's the kiss of death as far as your own continuous learning is concerned. You can witness the undesirable impact of celebrity that accompanies guru-hood. When you become a persona rather than a person, it consumes your energy at the expense of the underlying inquiry upon which your reputation was built in the first place.

STUART CRAINER

Further Reading

* Pascale, R, and Athos, A, *The Art of Japanese Management*, Penguin Books, London, 1981.
* Pascale, R, *Managing on the Edge: How the Smartest Companies use Conflict to Stay Ahead*, Viking, London, 1990.

* Essential reading

References

[1] Lorenz, C, 'Change is not enough', *Financial Times*, 12 January 1994.
[2] Interview with Stuart Crainer, 22 April 1994.
[3] Pascale, R, Athos, A and Goss, T, 'The reinvention roller coaster', *Harvard Business Review*, November/December 1993.

RECRUITMENT AND SELECTION

Elizabeth Hartley and Patricia Marshall

Recruitment and selection lie at the heart of many of the organizational and managerial challenges of the 1990s and beyond. From being sometimes peripheral and often short-term decisions, recruitment and selection have become long-term, strategic, important and highly complex. It is increasingly more demanding to marry the human resource needs of the organization to the developmental and career development aspirations of the individual.

For organizations this situation demands that they develop a better understanding of the variety of options and methods open to them in finding the right person for the job.

Despite relatively high unemployment in many countries, the costs of recruitment are significant – and will remain so. Even in 1988, Michelin, when asked about its annual recruitment costs, estimated these at 12 million French francs and Hewlett Packard in France estimated its at between15 and 22 million French francs. Similarly at a management conference in the UK in 1986 the personnel director of a large publicly-quoted company estimated that the total cost of employing a manager from age 35 to 65 at a salary of £20,000 is a staggering £2.25 million. These figures will certainly have increased in recent years.

Effective selection systems need to identify the superior performer, the person in the applicant pool who is best suited to the job and who will provide the sort of performance the organization needs to meet its objectives. In addition, this goal needs to be achieved without bias towards irrelevant characteristics such as gender or ethnic background. Finally, the operation of the selection system must be cost-effective so that the time and money spent on its design and administration is justified by the quality of the candidates selected.

There are three components of an effective selection system. The first component outlines the process of defining what qualities to look for in an applicant. The second component provides an overview of current selection techniques and outlines recent international trends. The final section describes a means by which the quality of the process can be assessed.

Identifying the selection criteria

Before selecting a person for a job, the first step must be to decide what qualities to look for in the applicant. This is usually done by a process called *job analysis* where the content of the job is studied in detail to provide a description of the skills, knowledge and personal qualities needed to fill that role. The job analysis covers not only the scope of the job itself but also the context in which it is done. It is also important that it is up-to-date: an old job description may be inaccurate and no longer reflect the job as it is today. This is particularly important now as the content of many jobs is changing more frequently than in the past, even though job titles may remain the same.

There are some pitfalls to be avoided in doing a job analysis. It is all too easy to look at what the current jobholder does rather than looking at what the job itself is and what should be done. This is a source of both inaccuracy and potential bias. It can also reinforce another potential pitfall, that of stereotyping. Where the job is currently being done by one gender or ethnic group the job analysis needs to recognize different ways of doing the job rather than focus exclusively on the way it has been done to date.

One approach to this is to start by looking at what the job has to deliver – its *outputs*. This takes as its starting point job *performance* rather than job *content*, an alternative competency-based approach to job analysis and selection which is becoming increasingly popular. A competency is an underlying characteristic of an individual that has been shown to cause or predict outstanding job performance. The competency-based approach to job analysis has become very broadly used in the US and the UK and various automated software packages are available to assist the process. In Asia leading organizations have recently introduced job competencies as the basis for person specifications in some key jobs.

The first step in establishing the outputs of a particular job is to identify the performance criteria required. This may need some discussion by people in the organization who hold jobs senior to the position in question or who depend, for their own effectiveness, on the outputs from the job concerned. However, discussion about what is really wanted from people is valuable in itself because it forces people to think in more radical terms about the characteristics required to deliver performance, and it also prevents the type of assumptions mentioned earlier.

The next step is to identify the personal qualities necessary in job applicants to enable them to deliver the levels of performance defined by the organization. The best way to do this is to identify a group of current job holders whose performance already meets some of these criteria and compare them with a group whose performance is adequate but not superior. Working with these two groups of superior and average performers, the job analyst can identify the personal characteristics, traits, skills and abilities (collectively known as *competencies*) that give rise to superior job performance, and which should therefore be sought in the selection of new jobholders.

If the position is new or current jobholders are not available, then the results of an accumulated knowledge base of 24 'generic' competencies can be used. One such set of competencies researched by David McClelland of Harvard University and management consultants Hay McBer, helps predict superior job performance across a range of professional and managerial roles. These 24 competencies can be grouped in six clusters:

- achievement
- helping/service
- influence
- managerial
- cognitive
- personal effectiveness

However, in any one particular job only a subset of this generic list is important and the list is unlikely to include all the competencies important for superior performance in any specific job. In most organizations there may be competencies unique to the job or to the organization's culture.

Typically, six or seven competencies support the key components of job performance and account for most of the differences between average and superior performers. These competencies should form the prime focus of the selection system. The number in the selection template can also be kept to manageable proportions by deciding which competencies can be trained and which should be selected.

Competencies differ in the extent to which they can be taught. Content knowledge and behavioural skills are easiest to teach. Altering attitudes and values is harder. Underlying motives and traits such as 'achievement motivation' start to develop in the very earliest years and change only slowly in adulthood. From a cost effectiveness standpoint the rule is to hire for core motivation and trait characteristics and then develop appropriate knowledge and skills. Research has shown that most organizations still do the reverse: they hire on the basis of educational credentials and assume that candidates come with, or can be indoctrinated with, the appropriate motives and traits. It is more cost effective to hire people with relevant motives and traits and train them in the knowledge and skills needed to do specific jobs.

Choosing the right selection techniques

The design of the overall recruitment process and the use of different selection techniques within that process is strongly dependent on national norms. Even within Europe current practices differ (see Table 1). For example graphology, which uses analysis of handwriting to predict personality traits, is used in 57 per cent of French firms, yet hardly ever used in other countries; and assessment centres, which are considered to be among the better of the more recent techniques, are not widely used for recruitment anywhere except in the Netherlands.

This 1994 research project found the classic trio of application form, interviews and professional references is the most widely used recruitment tool in all European countries.

Table 1 European recruitment methods (per cent)

	DK	E	F	FIN	IRL	N	NL	P	S	T	UK
Application form	48	87	95	82	91	59	94	83	na	95	97
Interview panel	99	85	92	99	87	78	69	97	69	64	71
Bio data	92a	12	26	48	7	56	20	62	69	39	8
Psychometric testing	38	60	22	74	28	11	31	58	24	8	46
Graphology	2	8	57	2	1	0	2	2	0	1	
References	79	54	73	63	91	92	47	55	96	69	92
Aptitude test	17	72	28	42	41	19	53	17	14	33	45
Assessment centre	4	18	9	16	7	5	27	2	5	4	18
Group selection methods	8	22	10	8	8	1	2	18	3	23	13
Other	2	4	3	2	6	5	6	0	5	6	4

Note: aCV

DK	=	Denmark	N	=	Norway
E	=	Spain	NL	=	Netherlands
F	=	France	P	=	Portugal
FIN	=	Finland	S	=	Sweden
IRL	=	Ireland	T	=	Turkey
			UK	=	United Kingdom

Source: Policy and Practice of European Human Resource Management, Chris Brewster and A Hegewisch (eds), Routledge, London, 1988.

It is, therefore, useful to review the selection methods in widespread use, and consider ways of improving those methods which have been shown to be poor predictors of performance and highlighting others which have been shown to be more reliable or have greater validity. In this context *reliability* means that the selection method will yield similar results if given to the same individual on different occasions or if given to two individuals of the same ability. *Validity* means that the method actually measures what it purports to measure and that the measure is predictive of job performance.

Advertising

The first step in any selection process is to encourage the right sort of applicants to apply for the job. This means that whether advertising is done inside or outside the organization the advertisement should contain accurate information about the job, the rewards and the competencies required. All the evidence shows that using the advertisement for corporate PR, attracting candidates for other jobs or in negative mode, hiding the salary from existing staff, confuses the message and invariably damages the response to the advertisement. Under current international market conditions of high unemployment, combined with shortages of skilled labour, this is particularly important. Using the advertisement to sell the job may put off suitable candidates and is likely to attract too many unsuitable applicants, who will have to be weeded out at substantial cost in the selection process.

Labour market shortages have led to the use of other methods of attracting applicants. As well as a growing use of search and selection consultants and recruitment fairs, new methods such as direct marketing and co-opting are being used in France. Co-opting includes expanding the recruitment function by promoting employees to recruitment positions and rewarding them with benefits. The Compagnie Bancaire, which pioneered the direct marketing technique, writing directly to potential candidates, has been using it for three years. The rate of return, between 5 and 15 per cent is attractive enough to make investment under 100,000 francs worthwhile. However, the French market shows some sign of slackening as too many other companies have adopted this method. Co-opting on the other hand appears to be growing, particularly in the construction and computer industries where Bouygues and Hewlett Packard have officially launched co-opting schemes.

Application forms and biodata

Application forms have been widely used in the recruitment process for some time. However, the information they are being used to elicit has been subject to some significant changes. For example the use of application forms for gathering biodata is increasingly common, particularly in large organizations and in some Northern European countries (see Table 1).

Biodata consists of objectively scored answers concerning a candidate's life history. The questions seek information about two categories – things that were done to a person and the kind of experiences a person has had. The careful choice of questions can produce a profile of likely candidates.

In a competency-based selection process, biodata can be used to measure specific competencies. For example, in a study of executives sent to foreign countries, demanding an 'overseas adjustment' competency, it was found that the most successful executives were more likely to have travelled when young and to have learned to speak a foreign language.

Analysis of the results of biodata studies have shown that validity is good. However, the predictive questions are unique to each job so that large numbers of job incumbents are needed to identify the correct items. The advantage of this method is that once these have been identified the process can easily be computerized and is a cost effective method for screening large numbers of candidates.

Interviews

The interview is widely used throughout Europe, the US and Asia for selection purposes. This is despite a growing body of research which shows that the selection interview is a poor selection instrument. Validity of the method is lower than most other selection methods.

Table 2 Selection methods validities

Method	Validity
Interviews	0.14 – 0.23
References	0.17 – 0.26
Personality tests	0.15
Assessment centre	0.41 – 0.43
Structured interviews	0.54

Source: I Robertson and M Smith, *Advances in Selection and Assessment*

The continued use of the interview ought to be seen in the context of satisfying other objectives. The organization may need to sell itself and certainly needs to evaluate the candidate's ability to be integrated in the organization, to see if he/she is compatible with its value system. The use of interviews can then be justified by the opportunity it creates to discuss with the candidate the job, career perspectives and so on.

In Asia the interview is still the most common selection method. Selection is personalized around the boss–subordinate relationship. However, the limitations of interviews are becoming more widely accepted and the search for alternative approaches and sometimes third party assessments is on the rise.

Behavioural event interviews

The reasons for poor performance at the interview are numerous and the majority can be improved by interviewer training and by setting a clear structure for the interview. Alternatively, use of a special structured interview is becoming more common in Europe and the US. In Asia its use is growing but is is mainly confined to a number of multinationals.

One form of structured interview is the behavioural event interview during which the interviewer asks candidates to describe in detail relevant experiences in their past. The interviewer then probes for evidence that during the experience described, the candidate exhibited the behaviours associated with any of the required competencies identified for selection.

This technique has greatest validity of any of the commonly used selection techniques (see Table 2). it is also highly cost-effective. In one study reported by L'Oreal in New York, 33 salespeople were hired in 1991 using focused interviewing based on a competency template. A further 41 were selected using traditional methods. A careful follow-up study showed that, on an annual basis, competency-selected salespeople each sold, on average, Ecu 71,000 more per year than the other group.

References

References continue to be used routinely in Europe, the US and in Asia where, for cultural reasons, references and associations are a key differentiatior. Who you know and what they will say on your behalf demonstrates your worth. With high staff turnover reference requirements are decreasing and, in Europe and the US, they are often improved through using the behavioural event methodology to generate real behavioural data about candidates. Used in this manner they can generate substantial corroboration of a competency picture for outside candidates.

Psychometric tests

The use of psychological tests has increased dramatically in the past eight to ten years, particularly in the UK. This can partly be attributed to their effectiveness in screening large numbers of applicants, common during periods of extensive unemployment.

There are different kinds of tests available but the types generally used are ability and personality tests. Cognitive ability tests can be used to measure particular aspects of cognitive competencies such as analytical thinking as well as general cognitive ability.

In the US they are used routinely as part of many managerial and executive assessments and are used extensively for selecting sales personnel. Their value is in improving results with minimal cost increase (especially for sales populations). For selecting executives the information gained may have predictive value regarding long-term performance. In Asia, psychometric tests are in widespread use as a back-up to other selection methods in large institutions and the civil service.

Although such tests are cost effective and easy to use they do not automatically produce better selection. In fact they may give a spurious and misplaced sense of professionalism in recruitment.

There are also concerns regarding the fairness of tests. Their use in the US was once widespread but dramatically reduced following legal cases on fairness, particularly in the testing of ethnic minorities.

The following guidelines should be used in deciding whether or not a test will be helpful or will, in fact, adversely impact selection.

1. Is the test going to give information which will help in selection; does it measure the skills, knowledge or attributes required by the job?
2. Has the test been developed professionally with good measures of reliability and validity?
3. The test should have norm groups which are representative of the people to be tested – there should be different norms for men, women, ethnic groups, levels of education.
4. Look for information about what steps have been taken to reduce or eliminate gender and ethnic bias in the test.

Tests that closely simulate actual job demands are likely to be the most effective. For example a test requiring applicants to *identify* effective arguments may not necessarily predict a candidate's ability to *make* effective arguments in writing or in presentations on the job. This may be best tested by a work simulation.

Assessment centres

Assessment centres use multiple assessment techniques including structured interviews, psychometric tests, peer assessment and simulations such as in-tray exercises, written and group exercises.

Practical simulations and exercises add great value to virtually any selection process. They can be designed to mirror as closely as possible the demands of the job. For example, if the job requires teamwork and co-operation, then a group discussion or practical exercise can be designed that requires several candidates to work together to reach an agreement or to achieve some other team-related goal. If the job requires customer service orientation, then a role play exercise can be designed where each candidate deals with a complaining customer played by an actor. If the job requires paperwork then an in-tray exercise can be constructed that simulates appropriate job demands. If behavioural event interviews have been conducted with existing job-holders then critical job-related situations derived from these can provide powerful data to aid in the design of such exercises.

Assessment is by trained observers who watch the behaviours shown during each exercise and assess the levels of competency demonstrated. If managers in the organization are used this can be a useful development exercise in itself.

Assessment centres are becoming increasingly popular in Europe as a selection method. Validity is high although their cost may ensure that their primary use continues to be for internal development purposes rather than selection.

In the US, assessment centres that use realistic simulations are on the rise again after a 10-year decline. Competency-based job analysis and tailored behavioural tests have increased both their face validity with candidates and their predictive value. This has reduced the risk of litigation, the cause of their initial decline. They are now more specialized with the focus on assessment and selection, for example, targeted specifically at production managers. They are still labour-intensive but can generate very thorough, reliable results that improve the quality of selection immeasurably.

In Asia the use of assessment centres is very limited but increasing, particularly for use in career development.

Reviewing the process

To ensure that a new recruitment and selection system is operating properly, follow-up and monitoring are essential. The process should be evaluated against three criteria: Is it delivering superior job performers? Is it fair? Is it cost effective?

Predictive value

Once the selection system has been operating for a few months, the job performance of those hired through the system should be carefully examined to ensure that the new recruits are delivering the results needed. One way to do this is to compare the performance of those identified by the selection system as truly outstanding candidates with the performance of those who were predicted by the system to be capable of delivering good but not superior performance. Recent studies of competency-based assessment methods have shown performance improvements ranging from 19 to 78 per cent with reductions in employee turnover ranging from 50 to 90 per cent.

Fairness

The best way to ensure that the selection system is operating fairly is to collect information systematically on items such as candidates' gender, ethnic background and disabilities and then to monitor whether success at selection is correlated with individual characteristics that should not affect the selection decision. If any correlations are found, the source of the bias should be isolated and remedial action taken.

Competency-based selection systems tend to be fairer than traditional selection systems. For example, in one US study, salespeople were selected on the basis of traditional biodata criteria. One requirement was 'ten years' sales experience' which meant mostly middle-aged white males were hired. Introduction of a competency-based selection system resulted in the recruitment of more female and minority salespeople (without prior sales experience) and increased sales revenues.

Cost-effectiveness

It is possible to assess in quantitative terms the benefits of introducing a new selection technique. This cost-benefit analysis involves quantifying the increased ability of the new technique to deliver superior performers, and multiplying this by the benefit gained from each superior performer. The monetary value associated with superior job performance can be calculated for most jobs and hence the benefit to the organization of the new technique. For example in a recent survey in the south eastern United States the practical economic value of recruiting just one additional superior performer was $3.7 million – which far outweighed the cost of installing the new system.

Cost benefit analyzes of this type should be conducted wherever possible to demonstrate unambiguously that the selection system is worth the time and energy that the organization devotes to it.

Direct recruitment costs are generally three times salary. This includes not only the direct costs but also the indirect costs associated with a new employee taking time to get up to speed. It takes time for them to develop necessary relationships and become fully performing.

Is it also worth weighing up the relative learning lead times. Organizations are likely to increasingly realize that it is easier to add a skill than change an attitude. They will also have to accept that no recruit is a perfect match, but that any selection decision should be backed with awareness of how quickly the missing skill can be developed or acquired.

Elizabeth Hartley and Patricia Marshall are consultants at Hay Management Consultants. Patricia Marshall is also technical director of Hay/McBer Europe.

Further Reading

Oates, D, and Shackleton, V, *Perfect Recruitment*, Arrow, London, 1994.

APPRAISAL

Brian Watling

Automatically and instinctively managers will always claim that they, in management idiom, add value to the company they work for by the work they do. Most will also say that the work they do is of high quality. At the same time they commonly express either dislike or fear of appraisals. The root of this dichotomy frequently lies in the way appraisals are conducted and the fault for this often lies with senior management.

The foundation of appraisal must be the desire to improve performance. This should apply to everyone in an organization – from the chief executive to the newest and most junior employee. The logic is straightforward: if performance is not improving, it is deteriorating – nothing and no one can stand still. To improve, managers must have a clear picture of where they are expected to be in terms of performance; the level of their current performance and how they need to go about bridging the gap between the two.

Appraisal of an individual's performance cannot be contemplated or carried out in isolation from the overall activities, values and direction of an organization. Conclusions on personal performance cannot be reached in a narrow context. Indeed, the context of individual aspirations and performance can be set in the company mission statement. This short and succinct statement identifies values, lays down overall strategy, gives a sense of purpose and direction and encourages the setting of clear precise objectives. Once the whole organization knows the destination, all areas can pull together in the same direction and can ensure that everyone measures progress and performance against a precise target. The first step in the appraisal process, therefore, must be to create a mission statement outlining values, strategy and objectives.

This needs to be explained where necessary and communicated throughout the workforce so that everyone can identify with the corporate strategy. The desired result must be that everyone can see that they are making a contribution. No matter how small or large each task may be, by identifying with the corporate strategy individual performance takes on a new dimension. As a consequence, when individual performance is measured, it should be in the context of adding value and quality to the *whole* organization, not just be a question of completing tasks or doing them a little quicker. Greater understanding produces self-motivation.

Helping individuals improve their performance must start with a clear picture of what acceptable performance looks like. To do so, it must first be established what the jobholder must do to satisfy the reason the job exists must first be established. This is done by writing a *job purpose statement*. This should:

- be short – one or two sentences are sufficient
- say why the job exists
- be specific to the job described
- tie in with the company mission statement.

The job purpose statement identifies key responsibilities and tasks. These, in turn, identify some specific skills or competencies which will be used to measure performance, and during the process of appraisal. Breaking down the job purpose statement into precise areas of responsibility and key tasks will make the identification of competencies relatively simple.

Usually, some competencies will apply generically across a number of jobs, while others will be specific to an individual job. With this information it is possible to write down the key performance indicators and determine how they can be measured. It is worth remembering when appraising performance that both outputs and inputs need to be measured. Outputs are the results of individual performance, and inputs the skills that went into getting the result. Measuring performance is more than simply identifying a result and matching it against a goal or target.

While many of the competencies will apply across a large range of jobs, the levels at which they are performed will vary. It is important, therefore, that a benchmark or anchor point is set and agreed for each competence in every job. This benchmark describes the level at which the competence should be performed and usually ranges over a seven-point scale – one being the lowest level and seven the highest. Once these benchmarks have been set for each job, it becomes straightforward to identify when someone is performing not just to their own job level, but also to a higher job level. This aids in succession planning and looking for personnel within the company workforce and, if a database can be set up and updated regularly, a powerful management resource becomes instantly available.

Appraising the inputs is critical. Achieving high-level performance of the competencies ensures that the outputs take care of themselves. Unfortunately, appraisals frequently concentrate on the outputs. Appraising results which are poor quickly becomes a negative, demotivating experience. Most people are aware of areas where they are performing poorly without being dragged through an interview.

Addressing the skills needed to produce the result is as important as accountability for poor performance. Appraising the inputs allows the appraiser to discover why the results were poor, acceptable or exceptional. Since a lot of appraisals are income-related, there is a tendency to focus exclusively on results. This is an understandable temptation, but there is a strong case for not having appraisals tied to pay increases. Instead, they may be more beneficially linked to career development and performance improvement. If this does happen in an organization the fear, suspicion, dislike and the consequent lack of co-operation associated with appraisals disappears and high morale and productivity are more readily achieved.

Determining key objectives

Creating job purpose statements completes the second step in the process. The third stage looks at setting key objectives for the job, then identifying individual ones.

The key objectives for any job will have their roots in the job purpose statement. With a clear picture of why the job exists it becomes much easier to identify what has to be done to justify the job continuing. Unless the job changes these key objectives remain the same year-on-year. A simple example would be the job of a salesperson – the objective of the job, possibly the main one, is to sell. That is unlikely to change. The job purpose statement of a branch manager in a direct sales company could read: 'To develop the *sales* of the company's products and services by *recruiting* and *developing* quality support management and salespeople within agreed objectives.'

The three main objectives are clearly identified – sales, recruitment and development. A successful manager could be measured against these three objectives. It is unlikely that they will change unless the job changes – for example, a company may decide that all future recruitment of sales people will be handled by head office. If this were to happen one of the objectives would disappear.

The job purpose statement does not quantify the objectives. As a result, five different managers might all have the same job, but with different agreed objectives. The statement also does not stipulate how these objectives are to be carried out. This means that individual objectives could be agreed. In fact it is from establishing the *how* and some means of quantification that we can start to set key objectives for the individual. These may be different for a particular quarter or every year. Some individual key objectives may take a year or two years to achieve. These would roll over from one appraisal to the next until they were accomplished.

Looking at the three main objectives of our manager's job, it is easy to see how key objectives within these three main objectives can be developed. For instance, objective number one is sales of the company's products and services. The individual key objective from this would be to start to put precise production figures forward.

Key objectives should fall into two camps, the outputs – the sales made and the number of people recruited – and the inputs – the competencies needed and desired to produce the results. Once the key objectives are identified and set, both for the job and the individual, then agreement must be reached on how their accomplishment will be measured. While measuring quantifiable results is relatively easy, measuring competencies is much harder and invariably will involve the time of the appraiser. Skills such as decision making, communication and negotiating have to be observed in order to make a useful judgement as to the performance level being exhibited. Feedback of such judgements must be supported by evidence.

Step four in the appraisal process is concerned with measuring performance. In order to keep on track there are some basic rules to follow:

- clearly identify the performance to be improved
- get agreement from the individual as to the performance to be improved
- agree what acceptable performance looks like
- agree the methods for measuring the improvement
- give regular feedback on performance
- separate feelings from facts

By clearly identifying the performance which needs to be improved, and getting the individual to agree that this is the performance to improve, the appraiser ensures that they are not appraising the wrong competence.

Appraising is all about improving performance and to be able to do this you must have a clear conception of what effective performance looks like. Once acceptable performance is identified it is easy to pinpoint what needs to be done by an individual in order for that person to perform at the desired level. Next you must agree how you will measure the performance which is to be improved. Will it be through observation, feedback from clients, feedback from colleagues or a training report once a course has been completed? By getting agreement at the start, the risk of the individual not accepting the results of the measurement is minimized. Regular feedback to an individual trying to improve will ensure that they remain motivated and that they stay on track. It also allows the manager carrying out the appraisal to be seen to be interested and to give encouragement.

Of all the rules, the separating of feelings from facts is critical. This becomes that much easier when the manager is personally involved in the improvement process. Observation which is recorded will ensure that the evidence given to support the judgement is not a matter of feelings but is, instead, a record of facts.

Step five in the process involves the conducting of the appraisal interview. It is important to remember that appraising has as much to do with how the appraisal is carried out as what is actually appraised. Also of importance is where the interview takes place and at what time. This requires preparation and planning. An individual who has spent weeks, probably months, working at improving performance deserves more than a hurried interview. Using an appraisal booklet will ensure that the process covers all relevant points. It will also make sure that the appraiser is prepared with all the reports and notes to be used as evidence to support the rating of performance. The appraisal should be a discussion, a sharing of information that has already been obtained, feeding back positive and negative points on the behaviour and performance of the individual being appraised. Because so much of the appraisal is given to feedback, it is recommended that the following suggestions are observed:

- feedback on what was observed, not on what should have been
- speak plainly, do not use jargon
- avoid feedback based on opinion
- keep the feedback relevant to agreed objectives
- limit the feedback to areas which can lead to action by the person being appraised

- avoid criticism
- be specific
- avoid over-kill

Feedback must be based on what was actually seen and heard and not on what the appraiser would have liked to have seen and heard. It also means that plain speaking, both in terms of easy to understand and non-ambiguous language, is vital. Opinions are of importance only when the appraiser is respected or liked, so giving feedback based on opinion leaves managers open to their opinion being ignored.

There is a limit to how much any individual can take on in terms of improvement. It is preferable to agree, and work on, one or two specific objectives. Once this has been accomplished, the feedback should concern those objectives and should avoid being distracted by anything else the appraiser may have seen. Any other deficiencies can become the objective for the next appraisal period. Inevitably on some occasions the improvement may be beyond the capability of the individual. It is important that the appraiser is sensitive and does not set objectives to improve in areas beyond the capability of the individual. Criticism also tends to be taken personally, no matter how hard the appraiser may try to ensure differently. Statements such as 'you should not have done that' need to be avoided. While avoiding such pitfalls, the appraiser must give specific feedback. General statements attempting to cover the whole performance are unhelpful. Similarly, feedback needs to be limited to the agreed objectives. Spreading the dialogue wider may dissipate the overall effectiveness of the appraisal.

There are eight steps to follow while carrying out an appraisal. Adherence to them will ensure, at the very least, that the appraiser is organized and prepared:

Step one

Make sure that the date and time for the appraisal is set and agreed and that you have all the relevant paperwork and evidence of performance. If you have a pre-printed appraisal booklet, make sure that you have it and that the relevant sections are completed from the last appraisal. The place of the appraisal should be private, somewhere where open discussion and possible disagreement can be aired without fear of interruption or of being overheard. Prepare yourself by being prepared. What you have to hand will be the tools that you can use during the appraisal. If you have forgotten something it can result in an appraisal which is unhelpful and unconstructive.

Step two

Start the appraisal by putting the jobholder at ease. This is a not a grilling or a reprimand. You actually want the jobholder to feel positive about the appraisal and to feel that it is in everyone's interests. Show some genuine interest in the jobholder.

One of the ways to do this is to explain the process, the booklet, and how you will be taking notes that will form part of the next appraisal. Then introduce the objectives set at the previous appraisal and get the appraisee to agree that these are in reality what were agreed. Identify the areas of improvement that were agreed and how these improvements were to be measured. Then move into evaluating the performance, producing all the evidence to support your evaluation. Once you have evaluated the objectives set at the last appraisal you can move on to the next step.

Step three

Now the process moves on to reviewing all the competencies which are associated with the job. This is an opportunity for you and the jobholder to agree an overall evaluation of these skills and whether they constitute a need for further development. This will also give you an opportunity to agree the objectives (the precise competencies you want to improve) for the next appraisal period with the jobholder. By using a rating scale, identifying the competencies which have the greatest need to be developed will be quite easy. However, obtaining agreement may take longer if you have no evidence to support your rating. Do remember to have the anchor points for the job with you when you review the competencies.

Step four

Evaluation of numerical or quantifiable targets that have been set over the appraisal period require some time during the appraisal. These may be sales or manpower targets, the number of items to be produced or service levels to be increased. Again the agreed target will be measured against actual performance so it is important to have all the relevant data close at hand. There is always a danger of over-emphasizing results, particularly financial ones.

Step five

During the appraisal time must be given to covering technical knowledge and skills, including systems and processes. This is more of a conversation, inviting the jobholder to identify any real problems or for the appraiser to feedback on examination results, etc. In the ever changing workplace where technology is playing a bigger and more important role, this section offers the opportunity to discover what, if any, problems are being experienced by the appraisee in relation to technology and technical knowledge.

Step six

Once the evaluation of performance is completed, allow the jobholder to comment on factors that have influenced his or her performance which have been outside their control. Remember, this is not an excuse-making exercise, but an opportunity for honesty and feedback, and for the manager to understand what the jobholder feels are real obstacles to improving performance.

Step seven

Once you have agreed the performance that is to be improved, you move on to agreeing the development needs and the plan of action to bring that development about. It is also a good idea to explore career aspirations and agree competencies that will have to be acquired or honed in order for the aspiration to become a reality. Then you agree the specific methods you will use to ensure that the competencies are acquired or honed.

Step eight

The last page in the appraisal booklet allows the jobholder to make comments – how the appraisal was carried out and how fair he or she believes it to be. Do insist that the jobholder makes a comment or two, not because you are looking for praise, but because honest feedback on your performance will help you to improve also.

Throughout the appraisal the appraiser is giving and receiving feedback. This is because the appraisal is a discussion offering an opportunity for a free exchange of thought and opinion. Instead of being a negative experience, appraisal should be a positive one, for both sides.

Brian Watling is a consultant specializing in management development. He has spent 14 years training managers, most recently as director of management development at Laurentian Financial Advisers.

Further Reading

Bennett, R, *Managing People*, Kogan Page, London, 1994.

MANAGING HIGH-FLIERS

Philip Sadler

Organizations, if they are to survive, need a continuing supply of competent managers, particularly at the most senior levels where decisions of a strategic kind are taken. There are two basic ways of ensuring such a supply. One is to recruit directly into senior positions from outside the organization. The other is to develop managers internally to ensure an adequate flow into senior jobs of people originally recruited as graduates or school leavers. Most organizations pursue both approaches, usually with a bias one way or the other.

Internally identifying and nurturing managers most likely to get to the top – labelled 'high-fliers' – poses a number of central challenges. Organizations must make a judgement about future business conditions and their implications for the nature of managerial work at senior level; they must determine the qualities and attributes needed from those who will fill such roles; identify which young people have the greatest potential; and, finally, having identified the high-fliers there is the question of how best to develop them.

The rapid pace of change makes it continually clear that radically different managerial skills will be needed in the future. Though trying to forecast the key changes which will have taken place in 10 or 15 years' time cannot be avoided, its extreme difficulty should not be overestimated. As Peter Drucker pointed out in *The Age of Discontinuity* – his brilliant study of the business environment in the late 1960s – we cannot predict the future simply by extrapolation from the past. The natural tendency when forecasting is to be acutely aware of current issues of critical importance and to see them as trends stretching ever onwards into the future. Yet, as Drucker noted, the most significant changes in terms of their consequences for business organizations are more likely to arise from discontinuities than from well-established trends. Events of global importance such as the sudden disintegration of the Soviet bloc are inherently unpredictable. Given this, any scenarios of the future must be provisional and tentative and will need constant revision.

There have been many books and research studies focusing on the future business environment. As a result there is a conventional or 'surprise free' view of the future in the early years of the twenty-first century, which, as far as the business organization is concerned includes the following elements:

- continuation of rapid change generally;
- intensification of competition;
- increasing globalization of business;
- continuation of rising customer expectations in respect of product and service quality;

- continuation of rising expectations on the part of employees in respect of the quality of working life;
- increasing public concern about the impact of economic activity on such things as personal health and safety and the environment.

There will undoubtedly be 'surprises' but, taking the conventional view, the implications for the organizational context of management in the future are held to be the following:

- Organizations will need to become more fast-moving, less bureaucratic, more responsive to external forces, more proactive in seeking change.
- Organizations will, on the one hand, become more decentralized or fragmented but will, on the other hand, be integrated through a common culture and information-technology-based networks.
- Organizations will need to improve their capacity to innovate.
- Managerial activity will take place increasingly *across* organizations in line with processes rather than vertically in the context of traditional functional hierarchies.
- Organizations will become increasingly dependent on the quality of their human resource management for the achievement of competitive advantage.
- Organizations will increasingly include members from many different cultural backgrounds.

The future role of management

These changes point to some key features of the managerial role in the future – particularly at senior level:

- greater concern with the planning and implementation of strategic change;
- greater sensitivity to and understanding of the business environment;
- more emphasis on leadership, less on administration;
- greater involvement in lateral, non-hierarchical relationships and transactions including collaborative relationships with customers, suppliers and joint venture partners.

What kinds of managers will be required to fill such roles? Organizations tend to look for the answers to questions of this kind in two different ways. One approach is to try to specify the personal qualities that will be required – things such as intelligence, personality traits, particular aptitudes, etc. The other is to focus more on the skills and knowledge that need to be acquired. Somewhat confusingly the term *competencies* is sometimes used to cover both aspects.

As an example of the personal qualities approach one of the companies studied in the research project *Management for the Future*[1] listed the qualities required as:

independence
openness to change
assertiveness
being respected
being a good motivator
having drive
loyalty
having tact

In another study carried out by the author[2] a French company specified 'people who are creative, adaptable, ambitious for themselves, who are courageous and assertive; open-minded people who think in an international way'.

Such lists indicate that a very wide range of qualities have been identified as linked to success as a senior manager. Even allowing for valid distinctions between one organizational culture and another, the lack of consensus among such lists is disconcerting.

If, however, it is accepted that such lists of qualities have more than face validity, the issue remains of how these qualities are to be accurately measured or assessed. A considerable armoury of weapons is in use for this purpose including the following (which can be mixed in almost any combination):

- Appraisals of potential by assessment of listed personal qualities
  - by superiors
  - by peers (rarely)
  - by subordinates (even more rarely).
- Psychometric tests of various kinds.
- Assessment centres involving various group exercises and individual tasks as well as psychometrics and interviews.

All of these have a degree of face validity but given the inherent difficulty of validation research and the period of time likely to elapse between the assessment of an individual's personal qualities and his or her appointment to the board of directors (assuming the individual stays with the organization that long) there is little serious validation research by companies.

The skills and knowledge approach

This approach, too, is exemplified from the research quoted previously and offers the following profile of the skills tomorrow's senior manager will need:

- awareness of and ability to relate to the economic social and political environment;
- ability to manage in a turbulent environment;
- ability to manage within complex organization structures;
- capacity to be innovative and to initiate change;
- ability to manage and utilize increasingly sophisticated information systems;

- ability to manage people with widely differing and changing values and expectations.

Two questions are raised by such lists. First, are these skills *really* different from those needed by today's senior managers? (Given that they result from 'surprise free' forecasts it is not perhaps surprising if they are not that different.)

Second, as with the personal qualities, how are we to assess the extent to which young managers have the potential to develop such skills?

Characteristics of those who make it to the top

A study of 45 UK chief executives – people who had made it to the top – by Cox and Cooper[3] (using the Cattell 16 PF personality test) found that the scores of the sample were widely distributed over most scales. This points to the conclusion that no one personality profile can be said to be typical of the successful chief executive.

However, 26 of the executives took the KAI (Kirton Adaptor/Innovator) test. All scored in the top half of the distribution, indicating they were innovators rather than adaptors, and 54 per cent came into the top 20 per cent for the population as a whole, indicating that they were strong innovators.

In addition, 30 took a Type A/Type B test, developed by RW Borne. The concept of A and B types was originally developed during a study of patients with coronary heart disease. Type A people are competitive, high-achieving, aggressive, hasty, impatient and restless. They have explosive speech patterns, tenseness of facial muscles and appear to be under pressure. They are so deeply involved in their work as to neglect other aspects of their lives. The results of the 30 chief executives were highly significant. Fifty-seven per cent were type A1 of which there are only 10 per cent in the population at large.

Cox and Cooper also reviewed several other similar studies from both sides of the Atlantic. The overall conclusions to be drawn from these various pieces of research indicated that high-fliers tended to share the following characteristics:

- determination;
- ability to learn from adversity;
- capable of grasping chances when presented;
- strong achievement drive;
- strong self-control;
- a well integrated set of values among which integrity, independence, initiative, people and relationships feature strongly;
- moderate risk taking;
- clear personal and organizational objectives;
- high dedication to the job;
- motivated by the work itself rather than by external rewards;
- a well organized life;

- a pragmatic, as distinct from intellectual, approach to problem solving;
- a high level of 'people skills';
- a high level of innovative ability.

Given the very real difficulties associated with the process of validly identifying high fliers, it is not surprising that there are serious doubts about the whole process. Two potential pitfalls are commonly stressed. The first is the natural tendency for senior managers, when assessing potential and selecting high-fliers, to choose people in their own image and people who seem to fit in well, thus perpetuating the existing managerial culture rather than preparing it for radical change.

The second pitfall is the self-fulfilling prophecy. If the young managers who are initially chosen to be part of the accelerated development programme for high-fliers are then given early responsibility and other development opportunities, they will more or less automatically rise up through the hierarchy providing they don't actually commit any disastrous errors. Their erstwhile colleagues meanwhile, deprived of such opportunities, never get the chance to show what, given similar developmental treatment, they might have achieved.

The reality of the self-fulfilling prophecy is sometimes revealed when an individual, singled out early in his or her career as having high potential, moves rapidly through the ranks and emerges as chief executive. Not all high-fliers who get to the top succeed once they have arrived. Some are conspicuous failures. Career success is not an unambiguous criterion for validation purposes.

The development process

How can high potential be developed? Research findings on this subject have been summarized by Cynthia McCauley of the US Center for Creative Leadership.[4] She has grouped the material under the headings of job assignments; other people and relationships; hardships; and training.

Job assignments

On-the-job experience, particularly when it involves the early assumption of real responsibility is seen as providing the most useful learning opportunities. McCauley quotes AT&T's Management Progress Study which tracked a group of managers over a 20-year period. Initially the sample consisted of 422 who went through a three-and-a-half-day assessment centre. At the end of the assessment process the assessors made predictions as to who would progress to at least middle management level.

Overall there was a significant correlation between the predictions and the level achieved. However, among the college graduates who were predicted to fail but who subsequently experienced challenging job assignments, 61 per cent actually reached top management. Of those who were predicted to succeed but who subsequently did not have challenging jobs, only 30 per cent made it as far as middle management.

Other people and relationships

The research evidence here did not point to such clear conclusions. Nevertheless mentoring and coaching are being increasingly used as developmental processes. Obviously the effectiveness of mentoring depends critically upon the suitability of the mentor as a role model for a future senior manager and on his or her competence in the mentoring role.

There is evidence that those who get to the top have wider networks of relationships than others. McCauley reports a study in which managers in one corporation were asked to identify those aspects of their relationships with their peers which they had found to be most developmental. The things most often mentioned were:

- sharing information – both technical knowledge and organizational matters;
- comparing career strategies and helping each other learn about career options;
- feedback – helping each other gain insight into strengths and weaknesses.

Hardships

The experience of such problems as business failures, expensive mistakes, loss of one's job and other setbacks at work, appear in many cases to have had a positive result – stiffening the individual's resolve and releasing hitherto untapped sources of energy.

McCall and his colleagues, also of the Center for Creative Leadership[5] point out, however, that the lessons learned from hardships are mixed and that some people are scarred by them, retreating into denial and cynicism.

Training programmes

Over the years there has been a rapid growth in executive development programmes – both those offered by external agencies such as business schools and ones offered in-house by large companies. Many of these programmes are specifically designed for 'fast track' managers or high-fliers. For most managers, to be sent on one of the longer executive development programmes at a leading business school is a clear sign that they are among the chosen elite. Such programmes do offer valuable opportunities for individuals to calibrate themselves against other high-fliers from different cultures as well as from different organizations, and there are rich learning opportunities to be garnered by exchanging ideas and experiences with their delegates in addition to any formal learning which takes place in the classroom. The danger, however, is that attendance on such a programme is seen primarily as a *rite de passage* rather than as a real learning opportunity.

In-house programmes vary greatly. At one extreme lies the traditional type of company staff college which is a powerful instrument for perpetuating the existing conventional wisdom and managerial culture. At the other extreme there are in-house programmes which act as major forces for change and organization renewal. One UK financial services company runs an in-house high-fliers programme which involves the participants in developing an alternative strategy for the business. Following the course they are given the opportunity to debate strategic direction with the company's board of directors, the debate being chaired by a neutral management expert from outside the business.

Self-development

Increasingly high-fliers are taking charge of their own careers and assuming responsibility for their own development. This can involve, at the extreme, taking a career break to study for an MBA degree. For many it means part-time study for a degree or diploma. Now that few organizations can offer a 'cradle to the grave' career, high-fliers expect their journey to the top to involve working for several organizations rather than one. Given this prospect they can clearly not just sit around waiting to be developed. Access to open-learning systems has greatly increased the opportunities for self-development.

Another factor encouraging young managers to concern themselves with their own development is the increasing tendency for organizations to become flatter and reduce the number of hierarchical levels, thus reducing the number of career steps and giving rise to the paradox of 'high-fliers and low ceilings'.

Derailment

The research team at the Center for Creative Leadership has also made a particular study of the process of 'executive derailment'[6] which happens when someone who was assessed as having the potential to go right to the top fails to do so.

In one early study 19 top executives who had taken action to derail a high-flier gave their reasons. These included issues to do with personal qualities – such as insensitivity to others, arrogance or betrayal of trust – as well as managerial, or inability to think strategically. Later studies identified six specific clusters of flaws associated with derailment:

- problems with personal relationships;
- difficulty in moulding staff;
- difficulty in making the transition to a strategic level;
- lack of follow-through;
- over-dependence on a particular boss;
- inability to handle differences with higher management.

The researchers suggest the following as ways and means of reducing the incidence of derailment:

- improve the level of understanding of the requirements for real success in high level jobs;
- improve the ability of the organization to assess and develop the competencies, skills or other attributes that match these requirements;
- create an environment in which learning is taken seriously;
- provide more support and counselling when managers reach critical points in their careers;
- plan career development to avoid late surprises.

Issues and problems in the management of high-fliers

In addition to such problems as the self-fulfilling prophecy referred to previously, the research in this field has identified a number of other commonly encountered problems or issues:

- Those who are missed by the system of assessment and not included in the high-fliers group – particularly those who fail only marginally to win inclusion – may become resentful and lose motivation or leave the organization altogether.
- If the high-fliers are promoted too rapidly they may not stay in one job long enough for any real learning to take place, or for valid feedback to become available. It will also be difficult to make a valid assessment of their performance.
- There is a very real danger that although high-fliers are deemed to be a corporate resource, local, national or divisional managers may try to hold on to their best young managers rather than offer them up to the overall company pool of talent.
- The increasing need for future top managers in international businesses to have had international experience is sometimes difficult to meet in this day and age when managers, whether male or female, have spouses or partners with their own careers with different locational requirements.
- Expectations are created which become impossible to fulfil. The international recesssion of the early 1990s, for example, meant that it was often impossible for companies to honour promises of exceptional career progress given in the buoyant years of the 1980s.
- Young people on the high-fliers programme are often under considerable pressure. This can lead to burn-out or some other reaction to stress. It is important that supportive mechanisms, such as access to external sources of counselling, are available.
- Companies often fail to provide adequate routes for young professional, scientific or technical specialists to join high-fliers' programmes alongside those who have been recruited specifically as management trainees. Dr Richard Sykes, Glaxo's group chief executive, began his working career as a laboratory assistant in Halifax Royal Infirmary. A young laboratory worker

today would not easily gain access to a high-fliers programme in any major chemical or pharmaceutical company, irrespective or his or her potential.

There is no universal formula. In the process of identifying those most likely to get to the top, a common point of departure is to take a view about the future context in which senior managers will operate, and from this draw some conclusions about the attributes, skills and knowledge they will need. Studies of yesterday's high-fliers – those who have made it to the top – show that successful achievers share some common characteristics which can be used as a basis for assessment of current populations.

Assessment practices vary. Not all companies attempt to identify high-fliers early on in their careers. Those that do rely mainly on nominations by line managers. Only a minority of companies use full-blown assessment centres. Rigorous validation research is quite rare.

The most effective processes for developing high-fliers appear to be a mix of challenging job assignments and supportive relationships with mentors and co-workers.

Philip Sadler CBE is author of many books and articles, including *Managing Talent* (1993). He was principal of Ashridge Management College, Hertfordshire from 1969 to 1988, and its chief executive from 1988 to 1990. He is now a vice-president of the Ashridge Trust and of the Strategic Planning Society, as well as a director of the Williams Lea Group.

Further Reading

Connor, H; Strebler, M; and Hirsh, W, *You and Your Graduates: The First Few Years*, Institute of Manpower Studies, Brighton, 1990.

Drucker, P, *The Age of Discontinuity*, Heinemann, London, 1969.

Gardner, H, *Frames of Mind: The Theory of Multiple Intelligences* Heinemann, London, 1983.

Howe, MJA, *The Origins of Exceptional Abilities*, Basil Blackwell, Oxford, 1990.

Sadler, P, *Managing Talent*, FT/Pitman, London, 1993.

Smith, M, Gregg, M and Andrews, M, *Selection and Assessment: A New Appraisal*, Pitman, London, 1989.

References

1 Ashridge Management Research Group, *Management for the Future*, Ashridge Management College, 1988.

2 Sadler, P, *Managing Talent*, FT/Pitman, London, 1993.

3 Cox, CJ and Cooper, CL, *High Flyers*, Basil Blackwell, Oxford,1988.

4 McCauley, C, *Developmental Experiences in Managerial Work A Literature Review*, Center for Creative Leadership, Greensboro, NC, 1988.

5 McCall Jr, M, Lombardo, MM and Morrison, AM, *The Lessons of Experience*, Lexington Books, Lexington, Mass, 1988.

6 Lombardo, MM and McCauley, C, *The Dynamics of Executive Derailment*, Center for Creative Leadership, Greensboro, NC, 1988.

WOMEN IN MANAGEMENT

Valerie Hammond

Women's development into management builds on and mirrors their emergence into a wider role throughout the twentieth century. This has been largely in generational bursts with the achievements of one generation being absorbed and built upon by the voice of the next. However, the pace is hotting up. Generational spans, in comparative and in real terms, are getting shorter.

As a result, the role and importance of women in management is recognized as being highly important and, perhaps equally significantly, as a potential source of competitive advantage.

A voice for governance

In the early part of the century, up to and through the 1930s, women directed their attention to securing a voice in the governance of society. Yet even as this was being achieved, Mary Parker Follett, who has been described as the 'mother of modern management', was studying and writing about business management, describing it as 'by far the most interesting human activity at present'. Her focus on leadership and group relations and the integrated nature of organizations can now be seen as far in advance of her contemporaries, including FW Taylor whose thinking about the scientific principles of management so influenced the building of an industrialized society.

A voice for personal choice

In the next period through to the 1960s, and despite the second world war when women did many different kinds of work, they directed their attention towards taking charge of their physical well-being, gaining access to quality education and removing many of the elements of 'chattelship' – cutting free from restrictive property and matrimonial laws. Yet, this was a time of huge advances in the study of management when major thinkers like Abraham Maslow, Elton Mayo, Frederick Herzberg, Douglas McGregor and Peter Drucker were working and writing. That women had a different focus during this period is understandable but unfortunate. Not only did this leave the study of management largely to men, but often women did not even feature among those who were studied. The legacy of much management thought based solely on the experience of men, continues to create problems to this day.

A voice for economic freedom

Earlier experience was played out in the late sixties and early seventies when large numbers of young women streamed into the workforce, filled with aspirations to work and earn and, increasingly, with the education to match. The focus for women was, once again, on legislative change but now it was also on ensuring equal pay and removing discrimination in the workplace. In this period the study of management continued largely to be followed by men. However, far-sighted employers began to ensure that their women staff received the training and development that would enable them to make their full contribution. Most employers did not.

A voice for equality

In the late 1970s and through the 1980s, spurred on by legislative changes, a surge of studies investigated women's development into management roles. This was also the age of new thinking about management, with Abraham Zaleznick, Warren Bennis and Burt Nanus challenging old notions in favour of 'transformational leadership'. Women also appeared among the thinkers writing about management. Seminal texts included *The Managerial Woman* by Margaret Hennig and Ann Jardim,[1] Rosabeth Moss Kanter's *Men and Women of the Corporation*[2] and the poignantly titled *Women Managers – Travellers in a Male World* by Judi Marshall.[3]

Trail-blazing women appeared, especially in service industries. Lone appointments were often presented as evidence that women had 'broken through'. They were the role models who demonstrated career success. Employers invariably believed that it was only a matter of time before other women followed, but this proved not to be the case. Women could get into management roles but, although on the 'right path', they seldom progressed at the same rate as men. Understanding *why* became a dominant focus. Early on there was an assumption that training, specific training for women, would solve the problem. Later it became clear that there was a complex interplay between several elements – the organization, the dominant male group, and even society itself – which needed to be addressed before change could occur.

A voice for leadership and power

Women were now fully engaged in researching and thinking about women's roles in management. Attention was on knowing more about 'difference' – difference in women's experience, in circumstances, in management style. Carol Gilligan's work, *In a Different Voice*, 1982,[4] provided a strong basis for understanding the motivations and development of women. A decade later Judy Rosener's article in the *Harvard Business Review*[5] setting out women's strengths as transformational leaders, stirred a strong debate over whether women should use or hide their different strengths, or even whether they really existed. The need to understand more about the challenges facing women in management was related to a quest for a more detailed awareness of the factors that influenced the functioning of organizations.

This has become even more significant in the recession of the early 1990s when large-scale economic changes have challenged traditional ways of organizing and working, and forced attention onto the business case for women's development. The abilities and behaviours commonly associated with women are suddenly the very skills and work practices most in demand. As asserted by Patricia Aburdene and John Naisbitt in *Megatrends for Women*, 'Today women are transforming the world we live in'.[6] They back this assertion with evidence that five million women run the small and medium-sized businesses in America that will become the business leaders of the future. Similar growth in women-owned businesses is noted by banks in the UK and in some continental European countries.

Growing a management role

It is only over the last 25 years that women in significant numbers have entered management. Previously women were held in check in many different ways. They were less encouraged to aim for high educational achievement, directed into different types of employment and, if they did enter commerce or industry, they were invariably required to resign on marriage. Many of these practices sound so arcane, it is difficult to realize that anyone employed in banking, for example, in the early 1960s would have experienced them. Apart from the effect this had on women's career potential, it also influenced the attitudes of men about the role for women in the workforce. Those few women who achieved prominence were usually unmarried or childless and they followed similar work practices and career routes to men. Rather than being role models for the broad sweep of women, they inadvertently confirmed the view that it was impossible to combine the usual functions of a woman as wife and mother with a career.

The 1990s signify the coming of age for women in management. Not only are the actual numbers increasing but, and perhaps because of this, women are helping to reshape organizations and the way they are managed. When Charles Handy writes in *The Empty Raincoat* of the 'doughnut principle' and describes organizations where many of the prime functions are carried out beyond the core of full-time employees, he described a situation which is familiar to many women.[7] Employment on a project-by-project basis, outsourcing and the necessity to create one's own employment are all situations which many women have experienced. This results in a situation where women are less unsettled by the changes taking place in our organizations and are now frequently more able to capitalize on the opportunities within them. It is often disconcerting to employers to find that the women they have encouraged and groomed for senior management posts are the very ones who choose to leave. These women are attractive to predatory employers but often they leave because the organization is not meeting their career aspirations quickly enough.

The response of employers

With the increasing recognition of the significance of women in the economy, as consumers as well as a skill resource, employers have started to lobby for women's development rather than leaving this to women themselves. The campaign 'Opportunity 2000' was created in the UK by 25 major employers and launched in 1991. Opportunity 2000 has a mission to increase the quality and quantity of women's participation in the workforce. Members are required to set and make public their goals and action plans and to monitor and report on progress. By 1994 membership had risen to 275 separate organizations which, between them, employ more than a quarter of the whole UK workforce. Although the Campaign works to increase women's participation at all levels and occupations, the majority of members use the proportion of management positions held by women as a key statistic to monitor, and to measure against, success.

A distinguishing feature of Opportunity 2000, and of similar initiatives that now exist in several European countries, is the emphasis on the identification of the business case for women's development. It represents a clear sign that employers are looking for a return on their investment in recruiting and training women – in other words women are being treated as a business asset. This is a very different approach from equal opportunities where the aim is to be fair and 'morally correct'. The change is significant and yet, paradoxically, the fact that economic criteria are used results in women being accorded equal treatment.

Each employer's business case is unique, although there are common themes. Examples include: the inclusion of quality human resource practices as part of total quality management programmes; a requirement for increased flexibility; a need to generate greater productivity and competitiveness; and, especially where women form the majority of the customers or are the key decision makers, a desire for a better match with the market.

Does it work? Three years into the Campaign, results suggest that it is a successful strategy but not necessarily an easy or swift one. The UK's Opportunity 2000 employers are able to show that they have higher proportions of women in management overall and at senior levels than is the norm for UK companies. For example, among Opportunity 2000 members, in 1994, women, on average, held 22 per cent of the management posts in private sector firms and 29 per cent of similar jobs with public sector organizations. This is against a figure of 9.5 per cent quoted by the UK Institute of Management for UK organizations in general for the same year. At senior levels the situation is more marked: women form eight per cent of directors in Opportunity 2000 organizations against the national figure of 2.8 per cent quoted by the Institute.

Women are perceived by employers as adaptable, willing to train and re-train, flexible over hours and therefore in tune with the employment needs of the time. They are also described as 'realistic'. This is double-edged as it usu-ally refers to the fact that women will apply for and accept jobs at rates of pay considered too low by men. In the UK, women managers' earnings are 86 per cent of those paid to men for similar work. At director level the situation is worse with women earning only 74 per cent. However, the 1994 Institute of Management survey shows that salaries paid to women are increasing at a faster rate than those paid to men, indicating a growing awareness on the part of employers of the need to improve this situation.

In the frame, but not in the job

After nearly 30 years of attention and action, women are in the pipelines for senior management. Now, in view of the dramatic changes to the scale and shape of corporations, even to government administrations, being in the pipeline is not enough. The type of development that fits an individual to climb a career ladder may be too limited to ensure survival in the flatter more networked structures of the 1990s. This appears to be the experience of many of the men who have lost their jobs in the recession.

Women's adaptability is standing them in good stead especially as the desired skill-sets for the 1990s emphasize many of the attributes that are asso-ciated with women but which were not valued previously. Strong interpersonal skills, good team-work, high-calibre communicators, ability to tolerate ambiguity, multi-channel capacity are all more positively sought after. Of course, many men have similar skills. The important difference is the recognition that they exist in women too, and some would say they are more frequently found in women.

Of course, women face similar challenges to those experienced by men in coming to terms with the changes. However, there is now a history and tradi-tion for women to 'surround their goals' as they seek a 'new voice'. They are prepared to experiment with unconventional strategies. Often these are of ben-efit to the organization as a whole, the men as well as the women who, nevertheless, are the catalyst for the novel approach. One such example exists in the UK's National Health Service (NHS) where a 'Career Development Register' has been established for senior women.

Career development strategies

Among the NHS's one million employees some 80 per cent are women but, despite this huge potential for being in the career pipeline, they accounted for only 18 per cent of management posts in 1991. Faced with a need for several hundred directors and chief executives as part of the health reforms, there was both the opportunity and the need to encourage women to compete strongly for promotion. The Register (in fact a small specialist unit) is the centrepiece of an activity designed to ensure the NHS maximizes its investment in its development of women with capability. The cost-saving potential is huge since the cost of losing and replacing an experienced middle manager can easily equate to £200,000 or more, taking account of the investment over the years in salary alone.

The Career Development Register is located outside the Service but staffed with 'insider' knowledge. It is open to women in the NHS who are well-qualified and already in the resource pool for higher level appointments but who, in the past, seldom put themselves forward for the most senior roles. For some women this was due to lack of self-esteem; for others it was a response to the subtle pressures to limit their aspirations. Through the Register these women are able to take part in development centres and career counselling, which give confidential assessments of their potential and of their development needs. Counselling may open up new directions and opportunities. Development needs can be met through self-development work, projects and assignments, and by participating in training programmes, all without cost to their local management. The Register also supports women through recruitment or promotion so that, while the outcome is dependent solely on the performance of the individual, the whole process is used positively. Experienced managers have thus been retained for the NHS – women who say they would otherwise have left, taking with them the investment, financial as well as knowledge-based, that had gone into their development.

So successful has the Register been in providing career counselling and in encouraging women to bid for and to win senior roles in NHS Trusts, that individual Trusts are to take part in pilots to extend the facility to men as well as women, an activity which they will not fund directly. Women have, therefore, demonstrated a new way of managing career development in the complex and flatter structures of the 1990s.

Upcoming issues

Although there is a greater representation of women in management roles, and some increase in those holding senior management positions overall, it would be a mistake to believe that a self-sustaining critical mass has yet been achieved. In spite of attempts at structural change, organizations generally are still deeply traditional in form and in custom. The corporate climate is one which has many inherent barriers to women despite the fact that women frequently exhibit the key skill-sets for the future. These barriers are often rooted in deep-seated attitudes and behaviours and there is no universal panacea.

Hidden women

There is still only very limited awareness of the wide variety of skills and background among 'successful women'. A bold attempt to challenge this is a travelling exhibition of huge portraits of women from all walks of life. Using a special technique mixing water-colour and film, the artist, Homage, has captured the essence of the personalities behind the achievement. This exhibition is supported by the telecommunications giant, BT, which produces information packs to help teachers run career sessions in schools. It conveys strongly the diversity of women's circumstances as well as their success. It shows women of different ages, different backgrounds, different ethnic groups, women who have children and those who do not. It is a valuable means of challenging the stereotypes of young people, boys as well as girls, while also making an impact on adults.

Relationships for learning

Women already in a management career often need to make contact with those with whom they can network or develop mentor relationships. Ideally this should include other women but, because most firms have relatively few senior women today, this invariably demands creativity. It can be achieved by cross-links with employment sectors where more progress has been made, in finance, retail, public sector for example. Other approaches include learning or self-development sets where groups of five or six women of similar level share their learning, usually working with an external facilitator. At senior levels a valuable approach is the external 'executive coach' who works intensively, one to one, offering mentoring or counselling support.

This is important. Work carried out by the Center for Creative Leadership in the US – examining how managers learn – showed that women place a much higher emphasis than men on the value of relationships as a vehicle for learning.[8]

On the board

Some companies have been dismayed when their senior, role model women have volunteered to take early retirement or redundancy packages. A careful review reveals that these women are rejecting the slow climb through a hierarchy which is, in any case, rapidly becoming outdated. Instead they are electing for portfolio careers, often combining a public role with consultancy. There are issues of power here as well as the desire for control over personal destiny.

Many ambitious and talented career women want to contribute at board level. As yet, very few have broken through this, the new glass ceiling. Competition is undoubtedly fierce and is made more difficult by the way women's careers have been managed in the past. Frequently they have been channelled into staff functions or otherwise discouraged from exposure to general management. Then again, criteria for appointment to the board, especially as a non-executive, often includes the requirement to have held a similar appointment as an executive of a public company. These two factors combine to prevent the appointment even though many women may be able to demonstrate their suitability based on other, equally relevant, experiences.

A creative way of bridging this gap is offered by Prowess and similar agencies which develop and place non-executive directors. Offering a head-hunting type of service, the aim is to identify experienced people with still more potential and to 'place' them on subsidiary or main boards in non-executive roles. Thus, while bringing the benefits of fresh perspectives to the hosting board, individuals acquire a new level of skill to enhance their development within their own company. Conceived as a means of breaking the barriers to women's development at the highest levels, this has already been seized upon as a means of coping with the challenges of providing experience and development for the succession in the flatter structures that are now becoming common. Once again, an initiative introduced for women is being adopted as good general practice.

Flexibility in every aspect

Another area where women are helping to develop the new reality is in relation to the shape of work itself. In Britain, as in many other industrialized nations, a large proportion of women work part-time. Where, in the past, this was portrayed as a barrier to a management career, it is now gaining acceptance that there are very few roles that cannot be handled in a flexible way. Examples exist of senior and even chief executive roles being shared. In the UK the public sector are leading the way so that within the Civil Service, the Home Office for example, has directed that all jobs, including management ones, can be regarded as open to part-timers unless the manager can make a case for refusing. This changes the presumption from a view that career jobs require long hours to a presumption that career jobs can be handled in a variety of ways. Not only is this a change that will make more career possibilities available to women, but it is in tune with the times where there is a growing requirement and predisposition to flexibility in the workforce as a whole. Among Opportunity 2000 members, for example, flexible work policies and practices which were restricted to specific groups of women have been extended, over a three-year period, to all – women and men – at all levels.

Working flexibly creates new challenges. Communication, a frequent cause of problems, needs to be even more effective in flexible or dispersed organizations where people may work from home or be in the workplace for relatively short periods. This is not a problem which is solved solely through technology, though this can help. Rather it places significantly more demands on the manager to create the relationships that ensure good information flow. The Burton Group, for example, emphasizes the critical role of its 'key-timers' – staff who cover the most critical periods. Their contracts are built up from four-hour modules. Deploying this workforce effectively, ensuring it is well-trained and well-informed, are major challenges for managers. Women's communication and relationship skills may be particularly useful here.

A key issue for organizations is that women managers, as well as men, are much more likely now than in the past to be in a family relationship with children. Even where this is not the case, there is likely to be a carer role, perhaps for elderly parents. Although it is becoming more common to provide some form of assistance with child care, this may be of less significance for women managers since they generally earn enough to organize the help they need. However, leading employers recognize the additional burden which arises when the usual care arrangements are disturbed, when residential training is required, for example. These employers demonstrate their own flexibility by offering funds or other additional assistance to make it possible for women to have the training they need without the pressure of worrying about the home situation.

Similarly, the family situation of managers now plays an even greater role in relocation decisions. Women, as well as men, have to consider the effect of any move on their partner, on children and other dependants. The final decisions take place within the family unit but employers are increasingly active in securing work options for the partner.

Flexibility over reward and benefit systems is also helpful to women. This can allow the employee to handle the way that personal needs change over time as well as recognizing that individuals can be motivated in different ways. Women often prefer to trade some of the traditional benefits of a management role, such as a large car, for other facilities or a parental time allowance. Men also are indicating their need for some of these 'alternative' benefits previously associated with women. A cafeteria system agreed at intervals often offers an improved package for the individual while being cost-effective for the employer.

The millennium and beyond

A recent headline reads: 'Today's male managers face extinction – the manager as we know him will be extinct by the year 2001'. While reports of such a demise may be premature, it is clear that the requirements of industry and commerce in the next century will demand more of what have become known as 'female ways of working'. Women managers now have the education, the stamina and the experience. The question is whether in the 1990s they can achieve their 'voice' of leadership and power. Employers' recognition of the role of women as decision makers, consumers, and opinion formers, as well as workers, is a critical factor.

Valerie Hammond is chief executive of Roffey Park Management Institute, Sussex, England. She is an international expert on women's management and professional development. She is the author of a number of books and numerous articles and reports, and was formerly director of the Management Research Group at Ashridge Management College.

Further Reading

Adler, DJ, and Izraeli, DN, (editors) *Competitive Frontiers – Women Managers in a Global Economy*, Basil Blackwell, Cambridge, 1993.

Davidson, MJ, and Burke, RJ, *Women in Management: Current Research Issues*, Paul Chapman, London, 1994.

Hammond, V, Holton, V, with Crainer, S, *A Balanced Workforce: Achieving Cultural Change for Women – A Comparative Study*, Ashridge Management Research Group, Berkhamsted, 1991.

Tannen, D, *You Just Don't Understand: Women and Men in Conversation*, QPD with Virago Press, London, 1991.

References

1 Hennig, M and Jardim, A, *The Managerial Woman*, Marion Boyars, London, 1978.
2 Kanter, RM, *Men and Women of the Corporation*, Basic Books, New York, 1977.
3 Marshall, J, *Women Managers: Travellers in a Male World*, John Wiley, Chichester, 1984.
4 Gilligan, C, *In a Different Voice*, Harvard University Press, Cambridge, Mass, 1982.
5 Rosener, JB, 'Ways women lead', *Harvard Business Review*, November-December, 1990.
6 Aburdene, P and Naisbitt, J, *Megatrends for Women*, Random House, London, 1993.
7 Handy, C, *The Empty Raincoat*, Hutchinson, London, 1994.
8 Van Velsor, F and Hughes, MW, *Gender Differences in the Development of Women Managers: How Women learn from Experience*, Center for Creative Leadership, Greensboro, NC, 1990.

REWARD AND REMUNERATION

Doug Crawford and Vicky Wright

Remuneration is one of the more difficult aspects of human resources to get right – and the degree to which employees use pay as the focus of complaint, dissatisfaction and conflict, bears testimony to its importance in creating a successful business.

According to classical theory, reward management has the objective of attracting, retaining and motivating the employees necessary to deliver a business plan. It is concerned with the design, implementation, maintenance, communication and evolution of reward policies and processes. It is a key management tool. Designed and used properly, it can be a powerful element in harnessing the skills and competencies of an organization's people.

In companies with only two or three employees, pay can be a relatively uncomplicated matter. Pay rates may be set by the proprietor in a fairly informal process perhaps involving some direct negotiation with the employee. The legal requirements too are comparatively straightforward. However, in larger organizations setting pay rates requires more formal policies and processes to be established. The reasons for this are obvious – as more employees work in the company, and the jobs they do become more diverse, it is necessary to provide frameworks for deciding the appropriate rewards relative to the contribution made; and some formal controls are normally required to ensure that costs are adequately managed. As an organization's structure

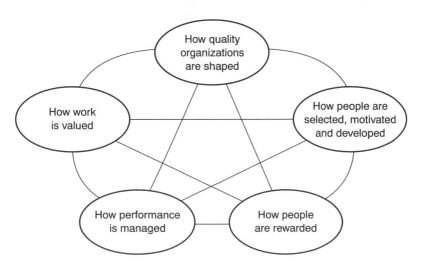

Fig 1 A holistic view of reward management

becomes more formalized, for example through hierarchical arrangements or the formation of teams, pay arrangements need to take account of promotion and career management processes. Similarly, organizations may want to provide arrangements which ensure that high performers are paid for the extra value they add, both as a means of motivating staff to improve performance, and to ensure that rewards are equitably distributed.

Reward management is therefore inextricably linked with all human resource management processes throughout an organization. This holistic view of reward management is an important concept, and is illustrated in Fig. 1.

In taking this broad view of the positioning of reward management it is also useful to consider the non-financial aspects of reward management – the intrinsic and non-tangible rewards that employees can acquire through their work. For the majority of employees, money is an important factor in going to work. But, there are other rewards which can also be highly valued. These might include such elements as: a sense of achievement, status, a sense of being appreciated, recognition of contribution by a superior, or the opportunity to work in a pleasant social atmosphere. In many organizations effective management of these aspects of reward are as important to success as managing pay.

The aims of reward management

Effective reward management processes can have a profound influence on the way in which an organization operates. The following are important aims to consider:

- *compete effectively in the labour market* to attract and retain the right quality people to deliver the business strategy;
- *provide value for money* by ensuring reward is provided in the most cost-effective manner;
- *improve individual and organizational performance* by encouraging employee behaviour that furthers the organization's mission and strategic objectives;
- *support appropriate organization culture* by reinforcing the desired values, attitudes and behaviours in rewards;
- *motivate employees* to achieve high quality performance linked to the attainment of organizational objectives;
- *encourage flexibility* by assisting human resources to be deployed in a manner which meets the organization's needs;
- *increase commitment* by rewarding the contribution that individuals make;
- *achieve an environment of perceived equity and fairness* across the organization by rewarding people according to their contribution;
- *enhance quality* by reinforcing ways of working that produce high-quality results;
- *encourage continuous improvement* by rewarding acquisition and use of new skills and competencies.

310

Motivation and reward

Not everyone is, or admits to being, motivated at work by money. However, those who treat pay merely as an administrative system miss opportunities to use reward and recognition as a means of positively influencing employee behaviour.

There have been many theories developed and research studies conducted into the causal links between pay and performance. Frederick Herzberg's work, for example, in the late 1950s produced his Motivation/Hygienic model. Herzberg found that a group of people he interviewed were satisfied at work through motivational factors (such as responsibility and personal development) and tended to be disatisfied by what he labelled 'hygiene' factors such as job security, salary and working conditions.[1]

Although there is much academic debate on the extent to which pay is a direct motivator there is no doubt that pay plays an important part in the motivational equation and can be used to reinforce other motivational levers such as achievement, recognition, responsibility, influence and personal development.

Despite the ever-present debate there is no right answer to provide a universal panacea in reward management. The effective balance between financial and non-financial motivation will vary between organizations and often between different groups of people within an organization. It is, therefore, of paramount importance that organizations develop reward management processes which meet their particular needs and recognize the requirements of their people, rather than attempt to force the organization into a remuneration straitjacket that constrains their ability to operate effectively.

The components of reward management

The various components which are generally important in developing effective rewards are:

- reward management strategy
- job evaluation
- base pay structures
- total cash package
- benefits
- total remuneration package
- market positioning

Reward management strategy

Because reward practices provide a powerful signal to employees about the nature of the organization and expected behaviour, values and performance, it is important that these reward signals are carefully planned. This is reinforced by the need for most employees to have a reward system that allows them to plan with a degree of certainty about their income. Changing the reward rules is not only difficult for the employer but can be stressful to the employee too. Some of the key questions that should be asked when developing a reward management strategy are discussed below:

- *Business situation* – remuneration is often a major cost element of a business and a key regular cash outflow. How much the remuneration expense varies with revenue and cash inflows can be a major determinant of reward strategy in terms of variable rewards (bonuses, profit share, etc). The business strategy may also have a significant influence on the way jobs are structured, and on hence pay. For example, many manufacturers moving to flexible production need to encourage multi-skilling and better team working. Such changes can be reinforced through skills-based pay and team bonuses.
- *Organization culture* – is the organization primarily technology or customer driven? What is the balance between flexibility/innovation and stability/reliability in organization and work design? Do different sub-cultures exist within the organization? If so, how important is it to recognize and accommodate their particular requirements in reward practices? For example, in investment banking, organizations need to differentiate their pay arrangements between employees who are traders (making a profit 'on the turn') and advisers who earn profits through fees. Different pay arrangements normally apply. Whereas in a more integrated and homogeneous business that seeks to develop a sense of team commitment a common set of policies may be better fitted.
- *Individual motivation* – how important is pay as a motivator to employees and how does its potential impact vary for different employee groups? What other factors are important to employees and how best should they be provided? For example, in healthcare, employees such as nurses are less likely to be motivated by pay than some other groups who may respond well to incentives. But there may be important rewards for nurses that will reinforce motivation – for example, the opportunity to undertake further specialist training.
- *Market competitiveness* – what sort of people does the organization wish to attract and retain? What sort of labour market is it competing in – local, national, or international? How competitive does it need to be in terms of its remuneration package? To what extent should reward be dictated by market forces? There are likely to be very active labour markets in some sectors and in certain professions, which may require a company to keep its pay closely in line with its competitors for some or all employees. In other cases a company may be able to run a less competitive pay policy because, for example, it develops its own employees and they do not participate in the labour market.
- *Control processes* – how should the reward management process be controlled and what degree of flexibility/discretion should be permitted? How much autonomy should be granted to line management? What is the role of the human resources function in managing the reward process? In some organizations the personnel department may control individual pay, in others line managers may have flexibility constrained only by broad guidelines.

Once an organization has addressed these questions it should have a clear picture of the type of reward management scheme that it needs to develop and accordingly will have an appropriate contextual background against which to assess detailed design considerations.

Job evaluation

Job evaluation is the process by which the relative contribution or importance of jobs within an organization can be assessed to establish a systematic order of job size. It often provides the underpinning for developing pay and grading structures.

Most large companies have a form of job evaluation – even if it is a relatively low-key process. It is an important starting point because:

- In organizations with many different types of job it can provide a system for resolving questions of internal relativities. In most, but not all companies, internal fairness in pay is important to employee satisfaction with pay.
- It can provide a means of ensuring line managers set pay in line with the actual and expected contribution of an individual – it can prevent pay costs running out of control.
- It can assist in making outside comparisons.
- Under equal pay legislation, the use of a non-biased, analytical job-evaluation system can be used to defend an equal-pay claim.

Job evaluation is open to much criticism – it is a bureaucratic operation in many companies; the definition of jobs for the purposes of evaluation can be too limiting and disempowering; the flexible nature of some jobs can make it difficult to evaluate them; job evaluation can conceal the need to concentrate on developing skills and competency to improve performance; evaluation systems can encourage 'empire building', etc. Much of this criticism is relevant to the more flexible organizations of the 1990s which need to focus more on individual and team performance in their reward systems. Nonetheless, even in these organizations, some rational underpinning of pay structures is required and job evaluation (or role evaluation) is likely to remain a significant and valuable process.

There are a number of different proprietary job-evaluation schemes and systems in existence. These are supported by management consultancies and have been validated by extensive use in many companies. Other schemes can be developed internally for use in a particular company. All schemes share the same basic principals:

- *Comparative* – job evaluation is concerned with the comparative worth of jobs within an organization, not the absolute size of particular jobs.
- *Judgemental* – although many job evaluation schemes are extremely sophisticated and provide a structured means of analysing jobs into component factors, and rating those factors on a measurement scale, the final determination of the size of a job is based on a judgemental interpretation of the facts.

- *Analytical* – strictly speaking, not all job evaluation schemes are analytical (whole job ranking for example is a non-analytical approach) but the majority of those used by medium/large organizations utilize a systematic and analytical basis for assessing relative job size.
- *Structured* – in addition to being analytical, job evaluation schemes utilize a structured approach to assessing jobs in order that consistent and rational judgements can be made which can be replicated over time.
- *Job or role centred* – job evaluation should focus on the content and context of a job or role, rather than considering how well a job holder carries out the job (this is the role of performance management). Although individuals can 'make a job' the focus on job evaluation is always about the contribution required. A few organizations place a heavier emphasis in their system on skill and competencies of individuals, but this is normally in environments where multi-skilling and flexibility are key determinants of value. Job evaluation schemes can be categorized along two dimensions:

Means of comparison
- *non-analytical* schemes in which whole jobs are examined and compared without any analysis of their constituent parts being carried out;
- *analytical schemes* in which jobs are analyzed in terms of one or more criteria, factors or elements.

Basis of comparison
- *job-job* comparisons where judgements are based on direct comparison between one job and another;
- *job-scale* schemes where judgements are made by comparing each job against a pre-determined scale.

This categorization is summarized in Fig. 2 below.

		Means of comparison	
		Whole job (non-analytical)	By function (analytical)
Basis of comparison	Job–Job	Simple ranking	Factor comparison
	Job–Scale	Paired comparisons Classification	Points factor rating

Fig. 2 Categorization of job evaluation schemes

314

Essentially non-analytical schemes are the simplest but provide little in the way of a robust and defensible rationale for arriving at the final ranking. As such they are unacceptable as a defence against equal-value claims. Analytical schemes on the other hand are more complex to design and administer but do have the advantage of providing a basis for consistency and apparent objectivity over a wide range of disparate jobs. They also provide a rationale which can assist in the development of pay and grading structures and are (subject to the particular design of the scheme) acceptable from an equal value perspective. In addition, proprietary approaches permit comparisons to be drawn with other organizations which use the same method.

The choice of system and the process employed to undertake evaluation depends principally on an organization's particular needs. In the UK most large and medium-sized companies use proprietary methods of job evaluation because they are generally less costly to develop, are validated by experienced outsiders, and can give access to external remuneration data.

Base pay structures

Pay structures are designed to provide a consistent and fair basis for rewarding employees. Internally, they should recognize the relativities between jobs and enable individuals to be rewarded according to job/role size, performance, contribution, skill and competence. Externally, they need to reflect the market for the skills and competencies of individuals and enable their recruitment and retention as required. Pay structures also need to be designed to facilitate the management and control of pay policies and budgets.

There are several different approaches to designing and implementing pay structures in organizations. In determining the most appropriate approach to adopt, organizations should consider the following and their relative importance:

- the characteristics, culture and needs of the organization in terms of size, complexity and the extent to which it is subject to change;
- the type and level of people employed in the organization;
- the need for external flexibility to respond to changes in market rates and possible skill shortages;
- the need for internal flexibility to move people to different jobs or redefine existing roles, without the need to continually reassess individual pay levels;
- the requirement to recognize and reward outstanding performers;
- the need to ensure that consistent decisions covering pay and performance are made throughout the organization and the extent to which local flexibility is necessary;
- the requirement to provide career ladders and development opportunities for individuals;
- the need to exercise control over pay budgets and pay levels and the degree of decision making autonomy that can be granted to line management;
- the extent to which there is a need to reward people for the acquisition and effective discharge of defined skills and competencies;

- the number of pay structures that should be adopted by the organization and the messages that are communicated to employees as a result of adopting multiple pay structures for different functions and/or levels within the organization.

The various approaches to developing pay structures are discussed briefly below.

Graded pay structures

A common approach taken by many large organizations is to adopt a graded pay structure, consisting of a number of job grades into which all jobs are slotted by evaluated size. Attached to each job grade is a pay range, as illustrated in Fig. 3.

In designing graded pay structures the following questions need to be addressed:

How many grades should there be and where should grade boundaries be drawn?

Grades are, to an extent, an administrative convenience for fixing pay for similar sized jobs, but they are normally important in defining promotion and career structures as well. In many organizations they are also synonymous with status. Fewer grades are needed in simpler or flatter organizations, than in organizations which have deep hierarchies or want to distinguish small differences in job size or grade.

How big should each pay range be?

The purpose of a pay range is to allow individuals in the same grade to be paid at different rates. The difference in level may be needed to reflect market rates, performance differences, service differences, etc. Typically, pay range width is expressed in terms of the percentage increase between the minimum and maximum points in the range. It is not uncommon for organizations to

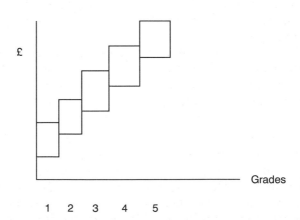

Fig. 3 A graded pay structure

adopt different range lengths for different levels of employees – such as 25 per cent for junior/clerical staff, 40 per cent for middle managers/supervisors and 50 per cent for senior management. Some organizations do not have ranges at all and pay a single spot rate for a grade. This is particularly common where bonuses are payable (for example, productivity bonuses on the shop floor, sales commissions and executive annual bonuses).

How should individuals be positioned in a pay range?

Most organizations have specific policies about how an individual should be placed in the salary range. Positioning an individual in a salary range can be achieved through application of a number of different frameworks:

- The most common approach in large companies is to position pay for managerial grades in relation to assessed performance and experience so that over time an employee's pay rises to a level appropriate to a sustained performance level. For the 'fully satisfactory' performer this may be a position somewhere in the middle of the pay range, such that only sustained high performers reach the top of the range.
- For many clerical workers, and in a number of public sector organizations, position in the range is mainly defined by length of service in the grade – the so-called incremental pay system. These systems are based on the assumption that individuals become more valuable to the organization year by year. The rate of change in organizations makes this a dangerous assumption and many organizations have moved to performance-related increments. While these are similar arrangements to the one above, they differ in that, in time, all employees can reach the top pay rate.
- Performance zoning is another approach to setting pay in which the range is sub-divided into different performance zones. For example, the bottom quarter of the range is reserved for incomplete performers, the next quarter for competent performers, etc.
- Some organizations position individuals within a range solely on their perceived outside market value. This may take account of individual performance, but is primarily driven by considerations of the 'going rate' for their specialist skills.
- Budget approaches to positioning are becoming more common. With this approach a line manager is given a sum of money which can be used to increase individual salaries for his/her subordinates. In these arrangements no firm progression rules apply, but normally performance, and current position, are critical factors in determining individual positioning.

Graded pay structures offer a number of advantages: they are easy to explain and communicate to employees, they provide a sound mechanism for managing reward and they ensure that a consistent approach is taken throughout the organization. However, their operation needs to be actively managed, particularly as organizations become more flexible and less hierarchical, and market pressures and performance differences increase the need to look at pay on a more individual basis.

317

Alternative base pay structures

Although grades/pay range structures are by far the most common approach to base salary management in large organizations, a number of different approaches are suitable for specific organizations:

- *Broad banding.* This is increasingly popular in large organizations which have delayered and have very flexible project working environments. Conventional grades are normally put together and, as a result, five or six bands include everyone from the chief executive to the lowest level employee. The salary ranges are correspondingly large and individual pay is thus determined within a much broader framework. In organizations using this approach pay is closely linked to performance.
- *Individual job ranges.* It is possible to avoid grading by introducing individual job ranges, whereby each job has a pay range associated with it, linked to external market rates. They are typically adopted for senior jobs where it is possible to manage pay on an individual basis.
- *Job family structures.* Simple graded pay structures offer a high degree of consistency and control throughout the organization. However, some functions may have distinctive career structures, and be exposed to particular market pay practices; such situations apply normally to professional and specialist groups (eg, IT professionals, lawyers, accountants, doctors, nurses). In these cases it is often appropriate to adopt separate graded pay structures for defined job 'families'. Each structure can be related to the appropriate market rate and structured according to the requirements of the particular job family. The difficulties in this approach are principally the possibility of equal pay claims, the potential encouragement of narrow specialism and the creation of different values and behaviour in parts of the organization.
- *Competency-based pay.* Competency-based pay structures are normally related to job families with each level in the job family being associated with a defined level of competence. Competence can be defined in a number of different ways but for any competency based pay structure to be meaningful it should be based on the skills, knowledge and behaviours that are necessary to perform the job successfully. The different levels of competency within a job family should therefore represent the requirements necessary to undertake increasingly demanding and challenging jobs within the job family. Progression through a competency-based pay structure should be based on the demonstrable discharge of the required competencies at each level.
- *Pay spines.* Pay spines comprise a series of incremental points extending from the lowest to the highest paid job in the structure. Pay ranges for different grades may be imposed on the spine and progression is normally based on automatic entitlement, although additional increments, or half increments, may be awarded on the basis of performance. Pay spines were common in public sector and voluntary organizations but are gradually being replaced by structures which permit greater scope to pay for performance and allow greater organizational flexibility.

The total cash package

While many employees are used to most or all of their cash pay in base salary, an increasing proportion of earnings is now being paid in the form of bonus or incentive payments. With the move from a 'service' to a 'performance' orientation in many organizations, there has been a growing tendency to link a greater proportion of pay to results, particularly for non-manual workers. However, earlier comments on pay and motivation should be noted – the carrot approach to pay does not always serve to motivate. In changing the reward mix and increasing variable pay the following aspects need to be considered:

What proportion of pay should be variable?

This will depend to a large extent on market practice, the nature of the job, the extent to which defined outputs can be measured, the timescale of their delivery and the work culture of the organization. Generally, it is easier to introduce significant bonuses (say 10 per cent of base salary or more) for individuals with hard measurable outputs (eg, in sales and production) in their jobs.

What should the variable element of pay be based on?

There are two key considerations here: the definition of performance and the extent to which outcomes can be influenced by individuals or teams. Many bonus schemes fail because performance is poorly or badly defined.

Why introduce variable pay?

It is vital to consider the aim of introducing variable pay. Is it with the intention of providing an incentive to individuals (and if so are employees predisposed to be motivated through cash)? Is it the intention to share success with employees? Is it to decrease the element of fixed costs in the organization? Purpose crucially drives design.

How should variable pay schemes be constructed?

Key issues surrounding the structure of bonus or incentive schemes concern:

- who should be eligible;
- the frequency of pay-out;
- whether it should be an individual or team scheme;
- what level of performance triggers payments;
- the planned level of payment;
- whether or not schemes should be capped to prevent individuals earning excessive payments in a particular year;
- the level of discretion that is allowed in awarding payments;
- the interplay between base salary and bonuses.

The commonest types of bonus schemes are decribed in Fig. 4.

319

Performance focus	Time focus		
	Short-term **(a year or less)**	**Longer-term**	**Mixed**
Individual	Individual bonus Incentive gifts	Individual long-term cash incentives	Deferred individual bonuses
Team	Team bonus Gainsharing	Team long-term cash incentive Performance unit plans	Deferred team bonuses
Corporate	Profit-sharing (or corporate success) bonus	Corporate long-term cash incentive 'Automatic' share options Phantom options Co-investment plans Restricted stock	Deferred corporate bonuses
Mixed	Bonus based on multi- level performance criteria Individual bonus from bonus pool	Long-term cash incentive using multi-level perfor-mance criteria	Share options individually performance related on grant Individually geared performance unit plans

Fig. 4 The main types of bonus schemes

Individual bonuses

Individual bonuses have shown the largest growth in recent years – led from the top by significant individual performance payments to executives. At top levels there is no doubt that the boom in bonuses has led to substantial increases in total earnings. These have normally been linked to achievement of corporate financial performance for which executives are held individually accountable.

However, individual bonuses lower down the organization are usually different in nature depending on job role. The commonest types are:

- *Individual output and revenue bonuses* – these apply in roles where measurable outputs are possible eg sales, fee income earned, etc.
- *Individual bonuses based on performance assessment* – these apply in roles where output may not be directly measurable, or where other factors may need to be taken into account. For example, managers are commonly covered by schemes of this type. They can seldom be classified as true *incentives* (which require certainty of a given payment for a given level of performance) and are better described as *rewards*.
- *Bonuses in lieu of salary increases* – an increasing number of individuals are receiving bonuses linked to appraised performance which previously may have been recognized in a base salary increase. For the employer this has two advantages – there is no increase in fixed costs and the reward has to be re-earned by the individual.
- *Spot awards* – these are one-off payments made in recognition of a particular achievement. Often they are paid as a non-cash award (eg, gifts and prizes). Their value is normally in the public recognition afforded to the individual as much as the award itself. Although such awards are frequently regarded as rather 'American' they have a proven record of success in Europe and other parts of the world.

Team bonus

Team bonuses are becoming more common as greater emphasis is given to working in teams. Their commonest forms are:

- *Gain sharing* – particularly common in production environments. These share efficiency savings made between employee groups and the employer.
- *Team bonuses* – these can be found almost anywhere in environments where team working is essential for success. Examples include branch banking, customer service teams and development teams.

Company 'success sharing'

An increasing number of organizations have arrangements by which employees can share in the profits or increase in shareholder value created by them. In part this has been encouraged by legislation favourable to certain schemes from a tax viewpoint – for example, profit-related pay, profit-sharing share schemes and share option schemes.

Such arrangements are normally only available to private sector employees, and certainly (in particular executive share options and restricted share arrangements) are usually the exclusive preserve of the top management.

Benefits

Benefits are elements of reward granted to an employee in addition to his or her cash pay. They are usually designed to increase commitment to the organization and satisfy basic security and other personal needs. They also can provide a tax-efficient method of rewarding employees.

The range of benefits made available to employees generally varies according to status within the organization, market practice and the organization's perception as to how important a particular benefit is from the point of view of attraction and retention of suitable staff. The most common benefits provided are pensions, private health insurance, sick pay, holidays and company cars.

Over the past few years there has been a growing recognition by many organizations that they are not getting the best value from the benefits elements of their reward packages and may be incurring substantial future costs as yet unrecognized. This has led to two fundamental changes. First, the introduction of flexible (or cafeteria) style benefit packages whereby employees can select various elements from a benefit 'menu' to meet their specific circumstances, including the conversion of certain benefits into cash alternatives. In Europe the growth of such schemes has been slow, though they are now relatively common in the US and Canada.

Second, several organizations have begun to review pension arrangements. The enquiry launched following various pension fund controversies did not recommend major changes but long-run funding issues, increased use of early retirement, increased employee mobility and changing employment patterns are encouraging reviews of the established UK pattern of defined benefit pension plans.

The total remuneration package

Figure 5 shows a breakdown of the typical employee remuneration package at clerical, managerial and executive levels in the UK.

Market positioning

Reward policies and practices should be driven largely by the internal needs of most businesses, however they cannot be determined without some reference to the market. In cases where labour is very mobile and scarce (for example, in parts of financial centres such as London and Frankfurt) external considerations may predominate.

Organizations need to be able to gain intelligence as to what competitors are paying for their human resources. Often informal contacts will give a reasonable picture, though individuals are often economical with the truth about their own pay. To gain a sound market view more methodical examination is required:

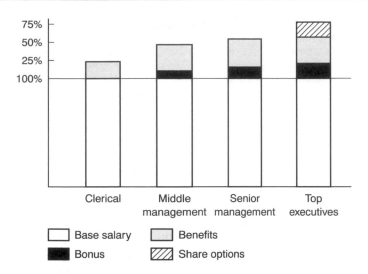

Fig. 5 Typical employee remuneration package at three levels

- *What market?* To start a study it is important to define the appropriate market to survey. Labour markets can be local, regional, national or, exceptionally, international. They also may be specific by sector (eg, oil, pharmaceutical, etc), or function (eg, lawyer, accountant), or both (eg, pharmaceutical research scientist).
- *Degree of accuracy required?* If a general indication is required it may be possible to buy an off-the-shelf survey or ask a recruitment company. More specific, and comprehensive, data may need greater investment.
- *Proprietary surveys.* A number of firms have data on specific employee groups, sectors, etc, and the best normally limit access to their data to the companies which help to provide it. To get the best data it pays to ask providers about who is in the survey, how much data there is, and, of course, its cost.
- *Running your own survey.* A number of firms run their own 'club' surveys in which individual companies share their data on a confidential basis.

After collecting the data, using market surveys to establish internal pay policies has to be managed carefully. Very few organizations have to make pay decisions solely based on the market; indeed there may be dangers in doing so. Can the organization afford to pay the full market rate? Does it need to? In lifting one company's pay, will it encourage others to follow suit thus creating a pay spiral? How accurate is the information anyway? The answer to adjusting pay in line with the market is necessarily one of balanced judgement.

Future trends

Changes in legislation, taxation and attitude occur continuously. All have a significant effect on human resource and reward practices in organizations. In addition, the internal focus on reward has changed with new human resources management needs:

- There is a greater emphasis on performance in pay with consequentially less emphasis on service and internal equity based on jobs.
- Organizations are delayering, resulting in less hierarchy. Pay structures have to reflect the decline in promotion opportunities, even for high fliers.
- Team work and empowerment are two trends in a work organization that need to be reflected in the way individuals are rewarded.
- Jobs are being less rigidly defined and there needs to be greater recognition that in more cases 'the person makes the job'. This will lead to less use of high-profile job evaluation and more flexibility in grading.
- As competition in business increases there will be a need for better alignment of pay to business needs both in terms of cost and reward for those who are delivering the goods. Devolution of pay decisions to line managers and decentralization to business units are common emerging themes.

Doug Crawford and Vicky Wright are reward and remuneration consultants with Hay Management Consultants in London.

Further Reading

Armstrong, M and Murlis, H, *Reward Management* (3rd edn), Kogan Page, London, 1994.
Armstrong, M, *Managing Reward Systems*, Open University Press, 1993.
Bowey, A, *Managing Salary and Wage Systems*, Gower Press, Aldershot, 1989.
Schuster, J, and Zingheim, P, *The New Pay*, Lexington Books, Lexington, Mass, 1992.
Pritchard, D, and Murlis, H, *Jobs, Roles and People*, Nicholas Brealey, London, 1992.
Greenhill, R, *Performance Related Pay for the 1990's*, Director Books, London, 1990.

Reference

[1] Herzberg, F, Mausner, B and Snyderman, B, *The Motivation to Work*, John Wiley, New York, 1959.

CAREER MANAGEMENT

Peter Herriot and Carole Pemberton

Profound structural changes within organizations throughout the Western industrial world have changed the fundamental context of managerial careers. Organizations are increasingly obsessed with how to attract, develop, motivate and retain the highly skilled and knowledgeable workforce they need to take them into the next century. Yet, paradoxically, they must remain lean and cost-competitive while at the same time encouraging innovation and quality.

Organizational turmoil has created an unpredictable employment jungle. Managers can no longer plan their career in the traditional way. Plateaux are reached earlier; career ladders have disappeared to the extent that the entire notion of having a career can be questioned. Alternatively, this uncertainty can be seen as nothing new – individual careers have always been ad hoc rationalizations of chance events and opportunities.

Making sense of this climate of change demands that managers take responsibility for their careers rather than following a prescribed organizational path. Instead of career paths being set in tablets of stone, careers are now flexible and constantly changing, demanding a new psychological contract between employer and employee.

The way managers manage their careers is intrinsically linked to the way organizations behave, shape themselves and regard their managers. To ignore this basic truism is to risk misunderstanding the complex nature of career management in the 1990s.

Organizations have, and are, changing in dramatic ways. At the beginning of the decade a large sample of UK-based organizations was asked what they were doing to respond to new challenges and opportunities within their business environment.[1] The most frequent response (88 per cent) was: 'Creating slimmer and flatter organizations'. Next, with 79 per cent, came: 'More teamworking'. These corporate responses to ever more competitive business pressures are the key influencing factors in any examination of careers in organizations.

The radical change in the career context can be seen in the way that specific roles and careers within organizations have been transformed. Twenty years ago, professionals happily beavered away in like-minded groups. R&D boffins pushed back the frontiers of knowledge regardless of applicability; development engineers produced only the best, when all that was needed was to meet specifications; lawyers and accountants were more concerned to maintain professional standards than to promote the business.

These are historical stereotypes but, often, the stereotype was close to reality. Now, increased competition has eliminated such insular practices. R&D

people, for example, have to work in mixed teams, with design, production and marketing people. They have to communicate with customers or clients. The need for decreased time to market makes successful collaboration with others in project teams a necessity for corporate survival.

IT has also had profound effects upon professionals. Many of the skills of which they claimed sole ownership have been automated. The ring fence of exclusivity has been broken down – access to professionals' routine skills is now available to all via the computer. Consequently, professionals have had to buy in to the corporate strategy. If this strategy is one of cost competitiveness, then they have, first, to surrender their skills to control systems; and second, be prepared to act as bought-in contract workers rather than permanent employees. If the strategy is one of beating the competition in terms of quality of new products or services, then professionals have to be innovative to earn their keep.

Finally, throughout Europe the non-managerial, non-professional work-force has, at the beginning of the 1990s, faced a profound change in the nature of the employment relationship. The deregulation of the labour market, allied to free market political ideology, has resulted in an increased variety of employment contracts. The contracting-out of services, the use of part-time labour and the introduction of fixed-term contracts, have all increased. While these developments may be construed as increasing organizational flexibility, they are perceived by employees as fostering career uncertainty and insecurity.

The career consequences

Much of our thinking about careers has been based on the assumption that the normal model in organizations is the *internal labour market*. In an internal labour market, vacant positions are filled primarily from inside the organization, except at entry level at the bottom of the hierarchy. There are well-defined job ladders leading up the hierarchy with multiple rungs offering regular promotions. Increased skills and knowledge, especially managerial skills which require a considerable amount of organization-specific knowledge, are required for promotion. Organizations such as IBM and leading banks have been typical examples of the internal labour market model.

This idealized picture has always had many exceptions. Knowledge-based professional firms, such as accountancy practices or media companies, have had fewer levels and typically have brought in high performers from outside at all levels of the hierarchy. Organizations with a prospector business strategy, such as Hanson, BAT and other conglomerates, have always been less hierarchical, and recruited externally. However, recently – under the competitive pressures of a deregulated global economy – the vast majority of organizations have followed suit in delayering and downsizing.

The consequences for our traditional notions of career have been profound:

- because there are less rungs on the career ladder, there are less promotions available;
- with downsizing and the increased use of casual labour, the probability of working for one organization throughout one's working life has decreased to near zero;
- cyclical recessions, however, temporarily put a stop to all job movement, both within and between organizations;[2]
- mergers and takeovers result in new career contexts, especially for those in the smaller partner;
- the ever-increasing rate of business, and hence of organizational, change renders it ever more difficult to predict the future. Attempts to match the aspirations and expectations of employees to employers' promises and assurances are extremely hazardous.

As a result, organizations and managers have to replace old concepts of career with new ones. Instead of secure positions in an occupation and an organization for life, with regular and predictable promotions ensured by the organization's management of the career systems, we have an entirely different career scenario. Employment is insecure, and an individual's main asset is his or her employability. They will move between organizations and occupations unpredictably as opportunities arise. And the responsibility for managing their careers will be their own.

Career management by organizations: past practice

Historically, organizations have managed careers in such a way as to support their business strategy.[3] Those organizations which defended their share of a particular market, and had no intention of moving into new markets, tended to grow their own managers. Progression up a well-defined ladder occurred predictably, and was closely related to age. So much company-specific knowledge and commitment was required that it was assumed that individuals could only acquire it gradually. Utilities and services such as gas and electricity, rail and air travel, are prominent examples; so are single-commodity manufacturers. These companies had retention as their primary career management objective.

As we have mentioned, other organizations, with alternative business strategies, managed careers differently. Prospector organizations have recruited high performers, but expect to lose them again before long. Analyzer organizations, which move carefully into new markets while retaining their stake in their main market, have concentrated on development. To acquire a share of a new market, analyzers such as IBM need to develop their people in the necessary new expertise and knowledge required to ensure success.

The consequences of these business strategies, and the alignment of career management strategy to support them, was a sophisticated set of career systems. Those systems used by prestigious analyzers, in particular, became regarded as best practice. Many organizations, regardless of their business strategy, felt they ought to emulate the likes of IBM, Shell, ICI and others. To take one example, succession planning at senior level was considered a career management imperative. Complex matrices matching people and jobs were drawn up (although frequently individuals not on the plan were mysteriously promoted).[4] In order to ensure that these heirs apparent had been broadly enough developed, fast-track schemes were instituted. Individuals were selected at a relatively early stage in their career, usually by means of assessment or development centres. They were then progressed through a planned sequence of jobs and training experiences designed to broaden their knowledge of the business. So brief was their stay in each job that they seldom had the opportunity to learn from their mistakes; this was because the consequences of their mistakes became apparent only after they had moved on. Other organizations, particularly those which could be classified as 'defenders', allowed the education system to do their selection for them. Those who had achieved a degree were automatically put onto a management development scheme from the start.

Career management by organizations: current issues

Today, organizations are beginning to manage careers in totally different ways. These changes have been forced upon them by the contextual changes described earlier. The issues now are much more immediate and pressing, and include:

- People are now reaching the highest level they will reach in the organization by their mid-thirties. Announcing plans to cut back to a mere four managerial layers, Sir Anthony Cleaver, chairman of IBM UK, said it meant 'a maximum of one promotion every ten years, and even this is for the one man [sic] who makes it to the top'.[5] How are organizations to retain and motivate managers who have previously experienced regular promotions?
- The difference between each hierarchical level in the organization is now a major one – in many organizations, for example, there are three or four managerial grades. How are organizations to ensure they have people capable of making substantial jumps from one level to another?
- In the interests of cost savings, corporate personnel functions have been stripped to the bone. As a consequence, responsibility for developing people has been vested in line managers. How are organizations to help line managers in the execution of this vital responsibility?
- The workforce as a whole has been reduced to levels which can appear incompatible with quality of product or service. How do organizations ensure they fully utilize all of the potential of all the workforce? How, in other words, do they identify talent, and break down the barriers to its expression?
- Organizations are expecting more and more from their people. Can they engineer greater commitment, or do they need to think more carefully about what it is they are offering in return?

Career management by organizations: current responses

In response to the uncertainty of anything except change, many organizations have sought to identify the competencies which will be needed to cope with change. Table 1 presents the competencies for the future identified at the UK's National Westminster Bank.

Table 1 Competencies for the future identified by National Westminster Bank

- information search: environmental scanning
- conceptual flexibility: considers alternatives simultaneously
- interpersonal search: explores and understands others' viewpoints
- managing interaction: involves others, builds teams
- developmental orientation: helps others develop.

Source: A P Cockerill, 'The kind of competence for rapid change', *Personal Management* 21 (9) 52–58, 1989

Research from the London Business School[6] indicates that many of these competencies will be intellectual in nature: the capacity to search out and make sense of information about the business environment. Of course, the identification of these competencies requires imagination and vision; they cannot be based on an analysis of jobs as they are. And, once identified, how may they be developed in individuals, teams and organizations?

Which raises a second issue – *development.* While self-development is the popular catch-phrase, organizations are realizing that unless they provide the context in which self-development can occur, the slogan will simply be regarded as an abdication of their responsibilities to employees. Self-development requires support by a variety of systems made available to the employee. These can include: learning resource centres; career workshops; development centres; job vacancy information; study leave; career discussions separate from performance appraisal; managers' rewards dependent upon subordinates' development; and personal development plans.

A third current concern is with *plateaued employees,* in response to which a variety of approaches are being developed. It is now realized that being plateaued is a function of organizational structure, rather than of individual incapacity. It has taken the recent flattening of the organizational pyramid to make it abundantly clear that by definition *everyone* reaches a plateau above which they will not be promoted. The decreased age at which the plateau is reached, plus the added workload resulting from downsizing, present a major problem. A first approach is to recognize that while they may be structurally plateaued, people are not necessarily psychologically plateaued too. They may well actively welcome more variety in their present job or the acquisition of new skills in a sideways move across functions or across businesses.

Alternatively, if they wish to continue in their primary area of expertise, they may move from a particular role in one project team to a different role in another larger project. Their career then becomes one of development through project work rather than transfer to a managerial ladder to which they are neither attracted nor suited.

However, faced with the shock of plateauing, many mid-career employees benefit from the opportunity to reflect upon what they really do want from the rest of their career (and, indeed, from the rest of their life). Table 7.7.2 presents an account of a career workshop run by Wellcome (UK) which has these objectives.

Table 2 Career and personal development workshop: Wellcome

Stage 1: Exploring
- Who am I?
- What is my world like today?
- How do I adapt to change?
- What are my skills, values and interests?

Stage 2: Understanding
- Making sense of what I've learned.
- What changes do I want, if any?
- Developing a vision of the future.

Stage 3: Action Planning
- How do I make it happen?
- Setting objectives.
- Writing action plans.
- Developing a personal support group.
- What if it doesn't work out?
- Coping with disappointment.

Issues:
- Volunteers not conscripts.
- Those facing career blocks.
- Confidentiality, and therefore impression of subversion.
- Personal as well as work careers.
- Integration with other human resource processes.
- Demonstrating value for money.

Source: C Jackson and J Barltrop, 'Career development in organisations', CBI Conference, London, 17 February 1994

As for the subsequent, more specific systems which are appropriate to this problem, these largely depend on which career motivations individuals have expressed and the human resource needs of the organization. The possibilities include:

- *Job redesign* In an era of unremitting change, jobs are constantly changing. In research on managerial jobs it was found that half of the jobs to which managers moved were newly created ones.[7] Job enlargement and enrichment is certainly possible.

- *Sideways moves* Research by the UK's Institute of Management tracked the career development of over 800 managers from 1980 to 1992. It found that sideways or downwards moves among managers had more than doubled in the past decade, rising from seven per 100 managers in 1980–1982 to nearly 15 per 100 in 1992. 'Managers need to look at their careers differently. They have to see sideways moves as an opportunity to develop the broad portfolio of skills they now need,' says the IM's Trudy Coe.[8] One of the reasons middle managers and professionals stay so long in one job is that they know it so well that they are indispensable. Line managers are unwilling to lose them because they know that they will fail to meet budget targets without their aid. 'Swap shops' have already been developed whereby business heads are 'encouraged' to exchange high-fliers. There is no reason this should not be extended to other employees as well.

- Varied employment contracts and rewards. Some people at mid-career welcome the opportunity of part-time contracts. Others would like to become self-employed consultants with some guaranteed work back in the organization. Many are dissatisfied with the assumption that money is all that motivates them; technical professionals, for example, often value conferences and study leave. Yet the problem they sometimes face is that no one has ever asked them. One-to-one career discussions can provide an answer.

A final form of human resource intervention now popular is really more of a general managerial programme than specifically oriented towards careers. However, it is important to careers because it assumes that the interests and values of individuals and organizations are, or should be, identical.

These interventions are called *culture change programmes*. Their aim is to ensure that employees buy into a vision and a mission defined by top management. In order for vision and mission to be achieved, it is thought that employees have to share the same value systems and assumptions about business, and engage in behaviour which accords with these value priorities. Commitment to the corporate values results in continued rewards and approval; failure to express commitment and buy in to the vision can result in encouragement to leave and blocks to further promotion. The evidence that imposed culture change programmes achieve their desired effect is highly unfavourable. Effective change usually occurs at grass roots level.[9] Further, the assumption that all employees should share the same value priorities is both impossible to achieve and hostile to creativity and innovation. Research scientists will always have different values from salespersons, whatever organizations do to them. The real task is not to try to make them conform; it is to facilitate teamworking so that their different perspectives combine creatively.

Individuals' careers: the context

Contextual changes have transformed our view of individual careers just as they have forced us to redefine organizational careers. Until recently, the two were little different. Once the individual had reached career maturity, he or she was supposed to settle down to spend the rest of his or her life in one occupation, probably in one organization. Individual careers were, therefore, typically the different trajectories which individuals followed within their employing organization.

Furthermore, different career stages were proposed which fitted into the patterns of people's lives very neatly. One such theoretical framework follows the course of exploration, establishment, maintenance and decline. Different career motivations were attached to each of these stages, so that, for example, promotion is supposed to be a particularly strong motivator at the establishment stage.

These career stages were assumed to be related to particular life stages, in particular the varying role requirements we face at different periods of our lives. Thus, not only were organizational and individual work careers closely related, but also individual work and life careers.

Inter-occupational and inter-organizational mobility render the first of these equations outdated; changes in social attitudes and behaviour and in the composition of the labour market, the second. Women compose an ever-increasing proportion of the workforce, and their career pattern certainly seems not to follow the traditionally male timetable. Nor, indeed, is the difference simply one of women following the male pattern until maternity, and then later returning, only to be eternally handicapped in the tournament because they missed out on some of its rounds. Rather, both men's and women's careers follow different patterns from the traditional one. Instead of a single male breadwinner, with a wife at home, the dual-career couple is the norm; and, more and more, so is the single-parent breadwinner, male or female. Such careers go in cycles, with periods of concentration on career alternating with periods of concentration on family.

There is no clear age-stage relationship any more. Often, middle-aged women are developing fast towards the pinnacle of their career while their male partner is collapsing, exhausted, into semi-retirement.

Individuals' careers: the motivation

Career stages, then, fail to reflect the fluidity of the modern social context. Traditional accounts of career motivation also fail to do full justice to current reality. There have been two highly influential models of career motivation. The first, by American academic and consultant, John Holland, is represented in Table 3.

Holland supposes that people initially choose or subsequently move to occupations and organizations which are congruent with their interests.

The second model, by Ed Schein, proposes that, once mature, we have a single 'career anchor', which is the underlying career value which we could not surrender. Schein's career anchors are displayed in Table 4.

Table 3 Holland's occupational interests

Realistic:	a preference for activities that entail the explicit ordered or systematic manipulation of objects, tools, machines, animals; and an aversion to educational or therapeutic activities.
Investigative:	a preference for activities that entail the observational symbolic, systematic and creative investigation of physical, biological and cultural phenomena in order to understand and control such phenomena; and an aversion to persuasive, social and repetitive activities.
Artistic:	a preference for ambiguous, free, unsystematized activities that entail the manipulation of physical, verbal or human materials to create art forms or products; and an aversion to explicit, systematic and ordered activities.
Social:	a preference for activities that entail the manipulation of others to inform, train, develop, cure or enlighten; and an aversion to explicit, ordered, systematic activities involving materials, tools or machines.
Enterprising:	a preference for activities that entail the manipulation of others to attain organizational goals or economic gain; and an aversion to observational, symbolic and systematic activities.
Conventional:	a preference for activities that entail the explicit ordered systematic manipulation of data, such as keeping records and an aversion to ambiguous, free, exploratory or unsystematized activities.

Source: J L Holland, *Making Vocational Choices* (2nd edn), Prentice Hall, Englewood Cliffs, NJ, 1985

These well-researched theories have the advantage of emphasizing the point that people have different career motivations. People at the top of organizations who determine career policy often assume that everyone's career motives are the same; all, they believe, are attached to Schein's 'managerial' anchor, the need to take more responsibility for bigger budgets and more people, and to be visibly recognized by rewards and status for so doing. In this assumption, they are probably projecting their own motivation onto others. As a consequence, they fail to recognize diversity and to institute career management policies which recognize and utilize such diversity.

A more modern view of individual career development and motivation would probably use the idea of *identity*. As societies become less homogeneous, identities become more diverse. Instead of identities derived from traditional roles – husband, breadwinner, organization man – people are seeking to express and also to derive their identities in and from their careers. Identities with the component 'woman' as the focus are becoming more frequent. Professional identities as knowledge workers with allegiance to their peers and their discipline rather than to their organization will become more common as professional work is contracted out more and more frequently.

Table 4 Schein's career anchors

Technical/Functional
- exercising particular skills
- reluctant to give up expertise
- managment *per se* of little interest

Managerial
- being accountable for total results
- willing to abandon technical for generalist role
- integrating the efforts of others

Autonomy/Independence
- freedom from organizational restrictions
- control of how, when and what to work on

Security/Stability
- geographic, financial, organizational security
- performs well in certain types of organization only
- sees career management as the organization's responsibility

Service/Dedication
- achieving something of personal value/concern
- would change organization to be able to do so
- would leave organization whose values were
- incompatible

Pure challenge
- the process of winning is central
- problems or opponents are there to be overcome
- search for novelty and variety

Life-style integration
- identity is tied to total life rather than to organization or occupation
- balance sought between home and work

Entrepreneurship
- building something new
- accepting risk.

Source: E H Schein, *Career Anchors: Discovering your Real Values*, Pfeiffer, San Diego, CA, 1990

Careers are, therefore, becoming women's careers, accountancy careers or life careers, rather than organizational careers.

The implications for individuals are profound. Simply by reconstruing their careers in different terms, individuals open up options which they might not previously have even considered. The corollary is, however, that individuals now have to work at a variety of career tasks which they never used to have to face. They need to ask themselves fundamental questions and come to some sort of answers:

- Who am I, and what are my value priorities?
- What roles would I like to play in my life, and how does a work role fit in?
- Who would I like to become, and what roles would help me get there?

- Do I need to work in an organization to play these roles?
- If so, what sort of organization do I need to look for, and how do I recognize it?
- How do I reach a satisfactory contract, such that I'm satisfied with the balance between what I give and what I get?
- How do I keep myself employable so that I'm not dependent on one organization?

These questions lead to the final section, which addresses the most crucial issue of all: how may the career interests and aspirations of organizations and individuals be reconciled?

The psychological contract

In a buyer's labour market, few organizations recognize the above issue as an issue at all, let alone as the most crucial human resources issue they will face in the future. In a buyer's labour market, the power is with the organization to the extent that they can impose and prescribe conditions of work. In times of recession, there is less overall demand for labour. Of course, there are still a few areas of skill shortage where a seller's rather than a buyer's market is operative. There was, for example, still a seller's market for senior managers with international experience during the recession of the early 1990s.

However, all the signs are that there will be ever-increasing skill shortages up to the millennium as jobs increase in skill and knowledge requirements, faster than skill and knowledge acquisition occurs.

In knowledge-based companies, seller's rather than buyer's labour markets will become the norm. Organizations will, therefore, be unable to manage employees' careers without taking account of their aspirations and motivations. Instead of human resource policies imposed on individuals to support the business strategy, careers will have to be negotiated between organizations and individuals. Psychological contracts will have to be agreed, explicitly rather than implicitly.

Historically, psychological contracts have always existed, but have tended to be implicit. In many organizations, for example, the contract used to be: 'you give us loyalty and service and we'll give you security and promotion'. However, circumstances have forced organizations to break these implicit contracts. The anger of long-serving middle managers made redundant is evidence of the strong feelings which such breaking of contracts arouses.

Some organizations have now recognized that there are two perspectives from which careers are viewed – the individual and the organizational.[10] For example, ICL (UK) categorizes its career management processes in terms of individual, joint and organizational career planning processes (Table 5).

Table 5 Career management processes at ICL (UK)

Individual career planning processes	Joint career planning processes	Organizational processes
Occupational choice assessment and counselling	Appraisal and development reviews	Appointment processes
Career planning workshops	Potential assessment centres	Career structures
Self-development plans	Career guidance/ development centres	High-flyer schemes
Pre-retirement courses	Mentoring	Grade structures
Career seminars	Outplacement	Experience opportunities
Computerized career planning	Career breaks and alternative contracts	Manpower planning
CV writing		Expatriate policies
		Person specs for jobs

However, for a true psychological contract to be agreed, more is needed than systems. If a contract is to be explicitly agreed, then each party needs to know, first, what both parties can offer and, second, what they want or need. So, for example, an organization might be able to say that it could offer an above-average salary, the opportunity to work on a project at the cutting edge of technological change but no job security, apart from the assurance of three months' notice of redundancy.

In return, the organization expects up-to-date technical expertise, and the willingness to work long hours in a team to tight project-completion deadlines. The individual might offer the requisite expertise, plus experience of having worked on a similar project for a major competitor. The individual's need is to keep his or her expertise up-to-date and to be free enough and rich enough to take a six-months break.

Clearly, labour market power will largely determine the outcome of the negotiation. The individual will be unlikely to demand a well above-average salary if there are other appropriate experts available for recruitment. However, the satisfactory execution of the contract may well depend on whether parties feel the contract is equitable. Does the contract reflect distributive justice ('Is this deal really fair?') or procedural justice ('He held a pistol to our heads')?

A final point to note is that wants and offers will change for both parties over time. In our example, the organization might lose the leader of the project to which the individual was recruited, and wish to put him or her into that vacated role. The individual's personal situation may also alter.

What emerges is a new definition of career. A career is the repeated negotiation of the psychological contract between organization and individual over time, as the needs and resources of each change.[11] Only such a definition can do justice to the career needs of both individuals and organizations in an era of continuous change.

Professor Peter Herriot is associate director at the Institute of Employment Studies and formerly was director of research at Sundridge Park Management Centre. He is author of *The Career Management Challenge* (1992) and co-author of *Competitive Advantage from Diversity* (1994) and *New Deals* (1995).

Carole Pemberton is research consultant at Sundridge Park Management Centre, and co-author of *Competitive Advantage from Diversity* (1994) and *New Deals* (1995).

Further Reading

Clark, F, *Total Career Management*, McGraw Hill, London, 1991.

Golzen, G and Garner, A, *Smart Moves: Successful Strategies and Tactics for Career Management*, Penguin, London, 1992.

Gutteridge, TG Leibowitiz, ZB and Shore, JE, *Organizational Career Development*, Jossey-Bass, San Francisco, CA, 1993.

Herriot, P, *The Career Management Challenge*, Sage, London, 1992.

Mayo, A, *Managing Careers: Strategies for Organizations*, IPM Press, London, 1991.

References

1 Coulson-Thomas, C and Coe, T, *The Flat Organization: Philosophy and Practice*, British Institute of Management, Corby, 1991.

2 Inkson, K and Coe, T, *Are Career Ladders Disappearing?*, Institute of Management, London, 1993.

3 Sonnenfeld, J and Peiperl, M, 'Staffing policy as strategic response: a typology of career systems', *Academy of Management Review*, 13, 588–600, 1988.

4 Hirsh, W, *Succession Planning: Correct Practice and Future Issues*, Institute of Manpower Studies, Brighton, 1990.

5 Quoted in Dixon, M, 'The benefits of a switchable personality', *Financial Times*, 26 January 1994.

6 Cockerill, AP, *Validation Study into the High Performance Managerial Competencies*, London Business School, London, 1993.

7 Nicholson, N and West, MA, *Managerial Job Change: Men and Women in Transition*, Cambridge University Press, Cambridge, 1988.

8 Inkson, K and Coe, T, *Are Career Ladders Disappearing?*, Institute of Management, London, 1993.

9 Beer, M, Eisenstat, RA and Spector, B, 'Why change programs don't produce change', *Harvard Business Review*, 68, 158–166, 1990.

10 Mayo, A, *Managing Careers: Strategies for Organizations*, IPM Press, London, 1991.

11 Herriot, P, *The Career Management Challenge*, Sage, London, 1992.

CREATING HIGH PERFORMANCE WORK ORGANIZATIONS

Edward E Lawler

In the traditional command and control organization, managers do not concern themselves with employee involvement and participation. Now, as organizations move to less hierarchical structures, the onus is on maximizing human talent and performance – in all areas of the company.

Various approaches, from empowerment to suggestion schemes, actively involve people in the overall performance of their organization. And with the growing use of teams and flatter structures, it is likely that creating high performing organizations will become a more pressing managerial challenge.

Involvement or commitment-oriented approaches to the design and management of work organizations are an increasingly popular solution to the motivation and performance challenges that face today's companies. The advantages of the involvement approach are said to include higher quality products and services; increased job satisfaction and motivation; less absenteeism and staff turnover; better decision making; improved problem solving and decreased management overheads. In short, these approaches can yield greater organizational effectiveness.

Examination of the suggested approaches to involvement reveals that there is not a single approach, but at least three different approaches. All of them are designed to encourage employee participation and decision making. But, research, shows that they result in very different kinds of involvement and are likely to result in a variety of organizational performance gains because they affect employees in different ways.

The three approaches are:

- suggestion involvement
- job involvement
- high involvement

They differ in the degree to which they move four key features of an organization to the lowest organizational level. The features can be summarized as:

- *information* about the performance of the organization;
- *rewards* that are based on the performance of the organization and the contributions of individuals;
- *knowledge* that enables employees to understand and contribute to organizational performance;

- *power* to make decisions that influence organizational practices, policies and directions.

When information, rewards, knowledge and power are concentrated at the top, traditional control-oriented management exists. When they are moved down the organization, employee involvement is being practised. Because suggestion, job and high involvement have different strategies for positioning power, information, knowledge and rewards, these approaches tend to fit different situations and to produce different results. Consider how each of these three approaches operates, and the results they produce.

Suggestion involvement

In suggestion-involvement programmes employees are asked to solve problems and produce ideas that will influence how the organization operates. The programmes are a parallel structure to ongoing organizational activities. They take people out of their regular organizations and put them in a separate new structure or situation that operates differently from the traditional organization.

Quality circles are an extremely popular approach to suggestion involvement. They are often installed as one part of a total quality programme. Like written suggestion programmes, they ask employees to recommend ways by which the operations of the organization can be improved. Suggestions are developed through a group or quality circle. The group process may lead to better suggestions and better developed suggestions than a suggestion-making process run on an individual basis. In quality circles, considerable training is carried out to enable the group to function effectively and to help individuals become efficient problem solvers. The groups do not have the power to implement and decide on the installation of their suggestions, instead they depend on management to accept and to implement their ideas.

Suggestion involvement programmes do not represent a major shift in the way control-oriented organizations deal with most issues. Instead they rely on a special parallel structure to change the relationship between individuals and their organization. This structure gives people the chance to influence things that they would not normally influence and, in some cases, to share in the financial results of this new activity. It also often leads to some additional information being communicated, and to individuals acquiring greater knowledge. However, the change in knowledge, information, and rewards is often limited to a small percentage of the workforce. In addition, it is encapsulated because individuals are asked to use it only when they are operating in special suggestions-type activities. During their regular work activities, it is work as usual.

Research suggests that the suggestion involvement approach can lead to improvements in organizational performance, particularly when it is part of a total quality management programme.[1] Case after case shows that individuals and groups often come up with suggestions that save a considerable amount of money. There also seems to be no question that employees do enjoy the opportunity to participate in problem-solving and that they learn new skills and obtain new information. As a result, they are often more satisfied with their work situation, are absent less, and are less likely to leave the company.

Quality circles and other parallel structures are often easy to install and start quickly. The problem-solving groups can be small and do not need to disrupt the organization. They can be easily installed in a single plant or even in a department of a larger organization. However, because they do not change the existing organizational structure, they are more supportive of strategies of continuous improvement than of major transformational change.

European and American management literature contains a number of well-documented studies revealing the limitations of the parallel suggestion involvement approach. They tend to be thought of as simply programmes, temporary initiatives with limited significance and life expectancy. Parallel structures are also expensive to establish and operate. In some situations, they run out of suggestions because individuals do not have enough expertise to solve the more complex problems. They are also often resisted by the middle levels of management because parallel structures threaten their power and put them in the position of having to do extra work. Conflict can develop between those who are in parallel structures and those who are not. Non-participants can come to resent being left out. Finally, suggestion involvement approaches that are not supported by changes in reward and other systems in an organization may lose their momentum and disappear. This comes about because they do not systematically change an organization's way of operating or the way the total workforce relates to the organization and its performance.

Job involvement

Job involvement approaches focus on designing work in ways that will motivate and enhance job performance. One strategy, job enrichment, focuses on creating individual tasks that give people feedback; increases their influence over how the work is done; requires them to use a variety of skills; and gives them a whole piece of work. This approach has an extensive research history in the United States that goes back to the 1950s, when job enrichment programmes were tried in IBM, AT&T, and a host of other large organizations.

A second job-involvement strategy calls for the creation of self-managing work groups or teams. This approach also has an extensive research history, going back to the 1940s. It differs from individual job enrichment in that it takes the work group as the primary unit of involvement. It tries to create group tasks and group performance measures and to make all the members of a group feel responsible for its performance. Groups designed according to this approach are often called autonomous work groups, self-managing groups, semi-autonomous work groups, or work teams.

The job-involvement approach has significant implications for how an organization is structured and managed. In essence, individuals are given new skills and knowledge, new feedback, an additional set of decisions to make, and may be rewarded differently. Both the individual and the team approach have these effects, although the team approach carried to its fullest has it to a greater degree. With the team approach, interpersonal skills and group decision-making skills need to be developed. The reward system is also changed to a greater degree with groups or teams, since skill-based pay is often used.

Finally, teams can make certain decisions that individuals usually cannot. Both individuals and teams can control the way the work is done. They can practice quality management, inventory, and other task-related activities, but teams can also make personnel management decisions about hiring and firing, and may select their own supervisors. Recently, many corporate re-engineering programmes have created work teams that are responsible for entire work processes as part of their efforts to remove layers of management.

Overall, job involvement represents a significant change in the fundamental operations of an organization. Individuals at the lowest levels receive new information, power, skills, and may be measured and rewarded differently. The changes relate to a particular work task; typically they are not concerned with the structuring and operating of the whole organization or the development of its strategic direction. Unlike parallel suggestion approaches, the day-to-day work activities of all individuals are affected. Involvement is not a special activity, it is the way in which business is done.

Studies of the job involvement approaches show improvements in productivity, quality, job satisfaction, motivation, absenteeism, and turnover among individuals working in enriched jobs and in teams. They also can lead to a reduction in management layers and overhead costs because less supervision is needed. The net result for the organization is usually significant performance improvement. Unlike suggestion programmes, job involvement structures seem to have reasonably good stability, particularly in the case of teams, since they represent cohesive organizational units that are difficult to dissolve.

The limitations of the job-involvement approach are primarily those of lost opportunities. Because they limit employee involvement to immediate work decisions, they do not capture the contributions that individuals can make to strategic decisions, and to higher level management work. This can lead to a tendency for individuals in work teams to optimize their own performance without paying a great deal of attention to overall organization performance. Job involvement approaches may be subject to cancellation if they do not influence higher level strategic decisions. Unless major restructuring is done to support it, supervisors are often in the position of being able to unilaterally change jobs in ways that take away the critical decision-making power. Job involvement efforts are particularly likely to be cancelled when they affect small parts of an organization. Like parallel structures, they can be installed on a limited basis and, as a result, create friction between participants and non-participants.

Work involvement efforts do have significant start-up costs. They always require training and frequently require new layouts of equipment and new information systems. Often overlooked is the need for training the supervisor and for dramatically changing the supervisor's job. Work involvement efforts can be resisted by middle managers because they feel threatened by the new power which others have and they often are not able to learn the skills which it takes to manage successfully.

High involvement

The high-involvement approach has also been called the *commitment approach*, *high performance, empowerment, total employee involvement,* or perhaps more descriptively, *business involvement.* It builds upon what has been learned from the suggestion involvement and job-involvement approaches in an effort to produce high performance organizations. It structures an organization so that people at the lowest level will have a sense of involvement, not just in how they do their jobs or how effectively their group performs, but in the performance of the total organization. It goes considerably further than either of the other two approaches towards moving power, information, knowledge, and rewards to the lowest level. It creates an organization in which individuals care about the performance of the organization, because they know about it, are able to influence it, are rewarded for it, and have the knowledge and skills to contribute to it. In order to have high involvement management, virtually every major feature of the organization needs to be designed differently than when the control approach is used.

In the case of decision power, employees need to be involved in decisions about their work activities, and to play a role in organization-level decisions concerned with strategy, organization design and other major areas. In order to make this happen, organizations need to be designed around business or customer-based units, rather than divided into functional areas. Staff groups need to be kept small and placed in a service role. Perhaps most important of all, a flat structure with relatively wide spans of management is needed. Task forces need to be used to get cross-sections of employees involved in making important organization design and strategy decisions.

High-involvement management

Job design:	Work teams and job enrichment.
Organization structure:	Business or customer focused.
Parallel structures:	Task forces for major business issues.
Performance information:	Focus on business performance.
Knowledge:	Team skills; business economics; problem solving.
Decision power:	Employees make work method and work unit management decisions; have input to strategic decisions.

Rewards:	Egalitarian; skill-based pay; gain sharing and/or profit sharing, employee ownership.
Personnel policies:	Employment stability, equality of treatment, participatively developed and administered policies.

In a high involvement organization everyone's rewards need to be based upon the performance of the organization. Profit sharing, gain sharing and some type of employee ownership are appropriate. In addition it is important that individuals be rewarded for their contributions. In most cases this is best handled by using skill-based pay for all employees. Pay information also needs to be open so that employees can understand how the pay system operates and participate in decision-making concerning the pay of other employees. Finally, where practical, a policy of employment stability for all employees can help reinforce the organization's commitment to its members.

As with the other forms of involvement, employees need to have expertise in problem analysis, decision-making, group process, and self-management. They also need to be cross-trained so that they understand the entire work process in their work area. In order to understand their organization's pay-for-performance system and to participate in business decision making they need to be trained in business economics and the basic elements of business strategy.

Getting relevant business information to all employees is a key to success in a high involvement organization. Modern information technology represents a valuable tool because it has the potential to give operating data to employees throughout an organization. This data needs to be the kind that will both inform them of how the business is performing and allow them to make business decisions even though they are not at a senior management level. The information systems also need to be designed to provide a good upward flow of information about how the organization is operating from a process point of view. Attitude survey data, sensing sessions and grievance information channels can be used to do this. Finally, lateral communications need to be supported by using cross-functional task forces, encouraging horizontal career moves, and where possible, creating channels in the information technology system.

Creating a high involvement organization is clearly a much different and more complex task than implementing job involvement or parallel-suggestion involvement. Many of the methodologies and approaches for such practices as pay, selection, and training are readily available and well developed for control-oriented management. Installing them is simply a matter of taking established systems and making them operational. Virtually every feature of a control-oriented organization has to be redesigned and, in some cases, innovation in design is necessary because the right approaches simply are not developed and available.

There is relatively little data on the effectiveness of high involvement organizations. Indeed, there are few examples to study. The closest organizations to this approach would appear to be the many team-based new plants which have been started around the world. The performance data on these plants is favourable, but limited. In addition, there are some very successful organizations which have started with this approach such as Nucor Steel, W L Gore, and Herman Miller. Finally, there are some large corporations, such as Xerox and Motorola, moving towards it.

Though the evidence on high involvement organizations is sketchy, it generally shows superior operating results. They tend to be relatively flexible, adaptive organizations which are very quality and customer-oriented with low costs and low overheads. It also suggests that this approach helps solve many of the human problems associated with traditional organizations. Motivation and satisfaction, for example, tend to be higher because individuals can make a difference and can continue to learn.

My research suggests that high involvement management is particularly effective when the work of an organization is complex knowledge work and is highly interdependent. Thus, it fits particularly well in high-technology businesses, complex service businesses such as consulting, and in process industries such as chemicals and food. One implication of this is that high involvement management is likely to be most popular in developed countries because it fits the type of work which is likely to be done there.

Edward E Lawler III is director of the Center for Effective Organizations, based at the University of Southern California Business School. The Center has studied a variety of approaches to organizing complex organizations for the past fourteen years and is internationally known for its research on employee motivation, organizational effectiveness and large-scale organizational change.

Professor Lawler is the author of many books and articles. His books include *High Involvement Management* (1986), *Strategic Pay* (1990) and *The Ultimate Advantage* (1992).

Further Reading

Galbraith, JR, Lawler, EE, *et al.*, *Organizing for the Future: The New Logic for Organizing Complex Organizations* Jossey-Bass, San Francisco, 1993.

Lawler, EE, *High Involvement Management*, Jossey-Bass, San Francisco, 1986.

Lawler, EE, *The Ultimate Advantage*, Jossey-Bass, San Francisco,1992.

Lawler, EE, Mohrman and Ledford, *Employee Involvement and Total Quality Management*, Jossey-Bass, San Francisco,1992.

Reference

[1] Lawler, EE, *High Involvement Management*, Jossey-Bass, San Francisco, 1986.

EMPOWERMENT

D Quinn Mills and G Bruce Friesen

Increasingly popular, though perennially misunderstood or poorly applied, empowerment has become an all-embracing term. Complex interpretations and approaches should not, however, distract from what is, at heart, a simple concept. Empowerment can be succinctly defined as the authority of subordinates to decide and act.

To work successfully, empowerment cannot be practised half-heartedly, occasionally or in isolated pockets of the organization. Commitment to empowerment has implications for virtually every area of managerial and organizational work and, therefore, has to be implemented across all an organization's activities.

Empowerment describes a management style. The term is very close in meaning to delegation, but if it is strictly defined, empowerment means the authority of subordinates to decide and act. It implies a large degree of discretion and independence for those who are empowered. Generally, empowerment takes place within a context of limitations upon the discretion of those empowered.

This careful definition allows clear distinctions to be made. For example, a committee is not an empowered team. A committee studies and recommends; an empowered team decides and acts. A traditional employee carries out the instructions of his or her supervisor; an empowered individual acts on his or her own initiative to achieve the company's goals. In extreme cases, neither empowered teams nor individuals have supervisors. Instead, the traditional structure of a business organization is radically changed to facilitate empowerment.

Colloquially, the term is not so precise. Many people speak of 'empowerment' when they mean not delegated freedom of action but merely the opportunity to be consulted by a superior about decisions the superior will make. In reality this is employee participation or consultation. Other persons use the term with a meaning that is at the opposite end of the spectrum from participation. They regard empowerment as autonomy, that is, empowerment without constraint. They object to the term empowerment – though they use it – because it implies that employees have to receive power from superiors in the firm's hierarchy. They regard genuine empowerment as implying full independence of action for the employee.

Organizations are engaged in efforts to empower employees because evidence suggests that empowered persons are more productive and effective employees. Empowerment permits a firm to do more work with less people, and often is accompanied by better customer satisfaction. This is largely because empowerment permits decisions to be made more quickly and with a greater understanding of the nature of the customer's need. The empowered worker is likely to have more direct contact with the customer than his or her supervisors or higher level executives of the organization.

Though it has become increasingly popular, empowerment as a management style is not a new idea. In their research in the 1960s Burns and Stalker observed it being used in laboratories where complex experiments were performed by multi-disciplinary teams of scientists. Rather than rely on managers to co-ordinate activity, the scientists collaborated on work-related decisions for themselves; their managers concentrated on administration and budgeting.

In their research Robert Eccles and Dwight Crane observed similar behaviour in investment banks. Rather than rely on managing directors to co-ordinate work on specific deals, associates 'networked' among themselves to get the work done; directors tended to handle client relations or administrative matters. Harvard Business School's Shoshana Zuboff (1988) reports similar experiences from the factory floor in certain highly technology-intensive industries; under such conditions employees are being given a much greater say in the management of the workplace than in the past.

Traditional management uses hierarchy as an organizing device to reduce administrative costs. However, hierarchy generates efficiency in management at a hidden price – that of inefficient communication. Companies in research or investment banking – which demand continuous innovation as a priority – require a more rapid response to new ideas and faster internal communications than hierarchy can deliver. It is as organizations seek greater responsiveness that empowerment emerges.

From hierarchy to de-layered structure

Three modifications of traditional hierarchy are required to create a de-layered structure. These are described below:

- The rules of decision-making are changed. The benefit of perspective – which pushes decisions upward from the point of action in traditional hierarchy – is traded for responsiveness. In de-layered structures this pulls decisions downward to the point of action.
- Employee specialization is reduced. Rather than split work from management, employees from customers, or staff from line, these functional distinctions are submerged in employee teams. To cope with much broader job descriptions, employees augment their technical training with problem solving and other management skills so that they can make decisions when working with customers or team-mates.
- Long formal lines of communication are curtailed. In a de-layered structure it is accepted that anyone – regardless of position – may ask anyone else for data without going through formal channels. These flexible communication patterns are backed with powerful E-mail and other networking systems based on computer technology.

These changes turn a traditional hierarchy into a de-layered organization structure.

	Traditional	Empowered
(a) Decision making	Issues pass to the closest manager with sufficent perspective to make the decision	Issues pass down to workers closest to the customer with data to make the decision
	priority = completeness	priority = timeliness
(b) Employees are...	Specialized Arrayed by function Given narrow jobs Only given orders	'Generalized' Arrayed by team Given broad jobs Make decisions too
(c) Management...	Holds all authority Arrayed in many levels (narrow span of control)	Authority is shared Arrayed in few levels (wide span of control)
(d) Communications	Data shared only on a 'Need to Know' basis	Data widely shared, few secrets allowed
	Peers and subordinates communicate only through supervisors and managers	Everyone talks to others regardless of level or position
	Vertical channels used by management to issue commands and control activities	Data flows from point to point as command and control are not tied to communication

Fig. 1 Features of organization

Changing management roles

Increased uncertainty in the environment changes management's role in the firm as well as the organization structure. These changes are outlined in Fig. 2.

Time constraints and competitive pressures require that managers must be sensitive and quick to respond to subtle changes. Missing a trend can destroy a firm. Managers can no longer take the time to review results, make operating decisions, and exercise control over activities; this is a *backward* orientation that may cause a company to crash. Empowerment asks executives to shed decisions so that their attention can be directed *forward* to planning and vision.

	Traditional 'control'	Empowered 'support'
(a) Executives....	Make decisions	Delegate decisions
	Review results	Plan for the future
	Control firm's responses	Develop vision
(b) Managers...	Supervise people	Support team building
	Monitor activity	Manage systems
	Make work assignments	Coach teams
	Report to the top	Report to the top

Fig. 2 Management roles

Delegation can be very difficult for executives because they are held responsible for corporate performance and so face the temptation to assert as much control over firm activities as possible.

They may also find that computer networking technology is a double-edged sword. On the one hand, it can support delegation; employees in a company can use E-mail to begin exchanging data without involving managers. On the other, it can lead to centralization; computers can be programmed to copy E-mail for review. How the technology is used depends on how executives feel about authority – empowerment requires them to release it.

The role of the middle manager also changes. An empowered organization places employees in work teams instead of functions. These teams are driven by goals, not by orders; their performance is measured by results, not behaviour; and managers do not supervise, they find people to do the work and let them use their own judgement while doing it. A manager's role becomes one of facilitating work, keeping communication channels open and managing resources for teams; most reporting is done through management information systems rather than personal contact.

Facilitate work

Management's role as intermediary between executives, who set strategy, and employees, who carry it out, does not disappear under empowerment. Managers must continue to help translate strategy into team goals and relay team concerns back to the top. They become facilitators. This change in roles also requires new ways of thinking.

Traditional management asks managers to extract obedience, maintain conformity and reprimand failure. Empowerment requires supportive behaviour from managers. They must lead by example, counsel those who ask for help without judgement, and maintain tolerance for new ways of getting work done.

Maintain communication channels

Under empowerment, managers assume responsibility for supporting communications. As communication channels are composed of people as well as technology, the responsibility becomes one of managing the quality of relationships so that communication proceeds smoothly.

There are two types of communication channel: intra-team and inter-team. Managers have limited dealings with intra-team communications; members are expected to interact directly. However managers must be prepared to help new members blend into a team through introductions and orientation. People will not be expected to naturally assimilate.

Managers will have greater dealings with inter-team communications. While employee freedom to communicate extends to other teams and to top management if necessary, limits will appear. If an employee does not know anyone in another team, for example, he or she must have point of reference – someone who knows who to call and *how* to make that call. Someone must also serve as the external contact point for a team. That person must have credibility with outsiders – customers, suppliers, and executives – and influence enough in the team to get its attention. These are natural roles for a manager with years of experience in both industry and company.

It is important to remember that being a contact point does not mean supervising the group or acting as an *exclusive* source of data. The role is one of information distribution – ensuring that those who need to know something find out in an accurate and timely manner.

Managing resources

Managers still select and hire employees, arrange training, keep a hand in administering the performance appraisal system, and may also administer rewards. Although they do not supervise, managers maintain a vital outside perspective on team functions and should be the first person a team turns to for help when it encounters difficulties it cannot solve for itself.

While team members will have multiple skills, they may not have the management skills needed to analyze more complex business situations. These situations will be picked up by the manager who will be in a position to tap outside expertise or solve the problem for the team.

Elements of an empowered management style

A study conducted at the Harvard Business School found four basic elements of managerial style: administrative ability – organizing work; the ability to 'control' others – holding people to procedures; empathy – the ability to relate to others; and generating vision – the ability to see (and plan for) the future.[1]

Managers in traditional firms would tend to score highly on administrative and control elements, which are key to traditional management, and less highly on empathy and vision, which are not. An empowered firm is ill-served by a managerial style that is heavy on administration and control. Managers whose self-image requires them to dominate others will not survive in an empowered environment which requires empathy and vision to operate smoothly.

Incentives and controls in an empowered firm

While empowerment and traditional management rely on *similar* incentives (intrinsic and extrinsic rewards) to elicit performance, each deploys these rewards in a different fashion to achieve its ends. These differences are summarized as Fig. 3.

Frederick Herzberg (1965), among others, has shown that increasing intrinsic motivation (autonomy, involvement) causes increased work performance while increasing extrinsic motivation through pay increases has little positive effect on performance. This is why empowered firms tend to emphasize intrinsic rewards; empowerment was *designed* with autonomy, variety and involvement of employees in mind.

Traditional management can make only limited use of intrinsic rewards as a by-product of its basic design; employee involvement is not a hall-mark of hierarchy. Traditional management must rely on less effective extrinsic incentives such as increased pay tied to promotions in rank. However, managers using empowerment do not have it all their way. As the scope of hierarchy is reduced, people cannot expect personal advances in rank; they can only gain pay when their team does well. This can limit individual extrinsic incentives (and as Herzberg *also* showed – limiting pay can reduce performance). Further, empowered work places tend to rely more heavily on results than specified job behaviour, so pay for performance becomes the norm. Good employees can be hurt by poor team performance, reducing their motivation.

Empowerment also uses different control mechanisms from traditional management to guide the firm. Vision, goal setting, and performance indica-

	Traditional	Empowered
(a) Rewards are...	Primary extrinsic (money and benefits) Little intrinsic possible	Lean to intrinsic (but extrinsic often equal to traditional)
(b) Basis for pay	Job duties performed People supervised	Business results Team output
(c) People receive	Fixed salary Small bonuses (pay for behaviour)	Variable salary Large bonuses (pay for performance)

Fig. 3 Rewards

tors like unit profitability or cost gain importance. The close supervision of specific behaviours found in a hierarchy become much less important.

Empowerment uses a 'control' cycle that begins with vision, moves to mission statements and goals, and concludes with measurement. As teams achieve goals they are rewarded *and left alone*; should a team fail to achieve its goal, management steps in to review resources (skills, people, equipment), redefine the goal, or both.

Vision provides the frame or reference in which mission statements are written and goals selected. If vision is ill-formed, mission statements will be vague and goal achievement will be hard to measure.

How does one know when one has a good vision? First, it must be consistently and easily comprehended by *all* who hear it – length dilutes clarity. Second, it must be articulated as inclusively as possible. Involvement in the process counts nearly as much as the end product. If few people write the vision, the process is not inclusive even if the result is outstanding.

Third, it must be *action-oriented*; not a forecast or a prediction. Fourth, it must 'stretch' the firm; if a vision is too easy to realize it will not challenge those who hear it. The National Aeronautics and Space Administration's vision of the 1960s – 'to put a man on the moon' – is an example of a good vision. It is short, action-oriented, created a similar image in the minds of everyone who heard it, and stretched the existing organization.

	Traditional	Empowered
(a) Vision setting	Limited activity	Critical activity
(b) Goal setting	Top-down activity	Bottom-up process
(c) Performance appraisal	Supervisor/Mgr only Closely-guarded process	Customers have input Team mates may share
	One-on-one assessment	May have team element
	Relies on managerial judgement	Uses 'result-based' performance data
(d) Choosing leaders	Boss/bosses appointed to lead work groups	Leadership rotates inside a work team
	Critical management activity	Personal control is much less important

Fig. 4 Control Systems

> *Who are our customers?*
> *What do our customers want from us?*
> *Who are our competitors?*
> *How do they compete with us?*
> *Who are our suppliers?*
> *Why are our suppliers important to us?*
> *What are the principle drivers of cost in the firm?*
> *How does our 'business system' create value?*

Fig. 5 Articulating a vision

The raw material for vision flows from strategic industry analysis. The company uses this data to answer the questions of Fig. 5.

A good mission statement addresses the company's vital constituencies – customers, employees, investors, and the community in which the firm operates. A mission statement should not be confused with goals; it provides a context for goals; it tells teams how to shape their goals to suit the firm's purpose. Goals themselves must exhibit several characteristics to be effective.

- First, goals must be *understandable*; otherwise those who are given them must seek further input before acting. Since they cannot act on their own, it follows that they have not been empowered.
- Second, goals must *contain a time dimension* so that those being empowered will know when their progress will be measured. This helps them to accept empowerment and stop looking for direction.
- Third, goals must be *achievable*. Goals that are too ambitious will de-motivate as people realize they cannot reach them. Goals that are too easy will de-motivate as they insult those assigned to them.
- Fourth, goals must be *carefully drawn*. They must be broad enough to support independent action but not so broad that confounding factors prevent their achievement. For example, monthly sales goals for a product requiring a two-month sales cycle are too narrow – measurement occurs before the team can close a single sale. On the other hand, asking a team to keep the company's stock price above a set level is too broad – the price of a company's equity is influenced by factors beyond the control of any one team.

Fifth and finally, a good goal is one that can be aligned with other goals across the organization to facilitate co-ordination among work teams. Goals are aligned when the same goal is not assigned to different teams and all goals are assigned to at least one team.

Measurement completes the loop of vision, goals, and measurement which lets management exercise control without the close supervision of traditional management. There are four types of measurement available under empowerment – financial, market-driven, operational and organizational measures – each has its advantages and drawbacks.

Financial measures range from the simple – spending against a budget – to the complex – revenues, cost of sales, profits, or rates of return on assets. Such measures are useful in an empowered environment because they are based on objective data that are usually already quantified by the team in its normal functioning, which makes them easier to track than if they had to be charted separately.

It is important to remember that financial measures may not be practical in some situations. Even empowered teams may not be able to control all cost inputs and so reported profits may not be entirely under their control. Also, it makes no sense to track rates of return on assets for teams if assets among them must be shared. Pushing such measures on teams will only cause inter-team rivalry to see who can saddle whom with 'joint' costs that should be shared.

Market-driven measures include market share, which may be segmented by product, demographics, or geographic region, as well as customer-retention and loss rates or service satisfaction indicators. These measures may be derived from industry sources, third-party surveys, or surveys done by the team or an internal audit group.

Market measures are useful in the context of an empowered team because they force teams to target customers. Although the data on which they are based may be easy to quantify, an analyst must remember that they are less objective than financial data. Further, some types of market measure – like market-share data – will be more objective than 'after-the-fact' satisfaction data, which must not only rely on recall but also on application of fixed rating scales to a subjective experience. Finally, it is important to note that market measures may not be appropriate where a team has no real customer. Some firms try to solve this by assigning an artificial internal customer to such teams; this may not necessarily produce the same results as real customers would.

Operational measures include productivity or quality indicators. Such measures are useful in the context of empowered teams because they force teams to focus on efficiency. Although operating data may be the equivalent of financial data in its objectivity and ease of tracking, there are still caveats to its use. For example, a team located at a station in the middle of the production process may not be able to fully control either the timing or the quality of the materials it receives.

Appropriate allowances must be made if operational measures are to provide effective feedback in such cases. Some teams may also operate in businesses where data on efficiency is elusive; for example, in the service sector. The fact that data is harder to obtain does not mean operational measurements should be abandoned – it only means they need to be weighed for a relative loss of objectivity.

Organizational measures are the least easily quantified and most subjective. They include such ideas as flexibility, innovation, harmony, and co-operation observed in team settings. Data for such measurements must be obtained by team surveys and external observation by customers and managers. Much work has been done to build survey instruments which can track organizational measures to determine how well the team is functioning. Critical incident techniques are available to help observers filter organizational data.

Practicing empowerment

Traditional management uses managers as a focal point. It presumes that managers identify strongly with company objectives and so can be trusted to administer rewards and punishments on behalf of the company. In contrast it is assumed that the majority of employees are unable to think for themselves (or the company) and so should be asked only to obey orders. Neither assumption is consistent with modern experience; many organizations have found their chief executives getting paid more for worse results, while society heaps ridicule on order-takers regardless of their status as managers *or* employees.

Empowerment does not use managers as a focal point. It presumes employees have brains and ambitions too and so it asks them to internalize vision and goals so as to develop commitment as managers do. When used properly, empowerment can transform motivation; allowing a company to motivate without supervision.

The reduction in the use of formal authority under empowerment does not leave a vacuum. Results-oriented rewards can be used. Both team work and peer pressure – either of which can be more effective than an ineffective supervisor – remain available to an organization designer.

Traditional management uses the asymmetric distribution of power found in hierarchy for purposes of co-ordination. Specialized workers have limited perspective; they *must* turn to managers to make decisions in ambiguous situations because only managers can see the context in which decisions are made.

Empowerment deliberately reduces employee specialization and broadens employee perspective. It achieves this through building teams, writing broad job descriptions, providing administrative skills training, and allowing point-to-point communications – and does not rely on asymmetry to co-ordinate and control work. Yet, the psychology that puts managers in charge is hard to break. Empowerment continues to assign managers the roles of rewarding and punishing behaviour; of setting performance criteria and goals; and of hiring and firing workers. And so it can still seem risky to take initiative.

Practising empowerment requires a company to makes changes in employee psychology. While empowerment broadens perspective among employee level to *encourage* initiative, getting employees to *take* initiative is another matter.

Managers may find employees setting self-imposed limits on their perception of authority unless steps are taken to introduce fault tolerance to the workplace. It is fault tolerance that changes the psychology of the workplace by explicitly setting conditions under which mistakes are not punished.

In setting fault tolerance, managers must consider carefully their still large powers of influence in the firm. If they say one thing, but do another – the action dominates. Managers must also consider what behaviours they really want. To encourage action, action must be rewarded and inaction punished. The first time an action inside the zone of fault tolerance is punished the wrong signal will be sent.

There are six conditions commonly used to set fault tolerance:

1. when a mistake allows something new to be learned
2. when a mistake is not part of a pattern
3. when a mistake is made in pursuit of assigned goals
4. when a mistake falls within assigned authority
5. when a mistake is consistent with law and principles
6. when proper procedures are used

The first and second conditions arise because there is often more value in the failure of a specific action rather than its success. Success does not teach very well; people replicate successful behaviour *until it fails*. If an error can teach the company something new it should be tolerated. By the same token, managers must come down hard on *repeated* (patterned) mistakes to encourage teams to share their experience and to stop the same mistakes from recurring.

The third and fourth conditions arise from the broad delegation of authority that occurs under empowerment. It is easy to have teams wander off-purpose when close supervision is withdrawn and internal dynamics begin to play a role in getting work done; to encourage teams to stick to assigned goals, mistakes made in reaching *beyond* these goals should be punished. However, as long as the team stays *inside* the lines defined by assigned authority, mistakes should not be punished, subject to the other conditions on the list above.

The fifth condition arises because companies do find themselves running into legal trouble as a result of the actions of employees. This criterion tells employees they are not protected in illegal behaviour.

The sixth and last condition is controversial. Teams can cast off ties to a manager only to become tied to a procedures manual instead. But procedure can also be important; documentation is often key to learning. The firm must know what the team did and a procedures guide can help ensure that value is extracted from errors – in the form of modified procedures.

Fault tolerance sets the stage for the development of trust. Trust is actually a complex psychological contract that gives employees comfort in taking actions. The higher the level of trust that management can generate, the greater the level of empowerment achieved.

Predictability is the weakest form of trust; when it is present employees can assume that the employer will act in its own interests, although these interests may or may not be shared with the employee. Predictability makes it possible for employees to anticipate what is likely to happen if they undertake certain actions.

There are two methods of building predictability – personal contact and consistency. Personal contact is important because written orders and telephone calls provide little context for action. Employees cannot glean context from the content of orders alone, they also need body language and facial cues which come only with personal contact. Consistency in management is also important to predictability; it is as managers handle similar situations in a similar fashion that employees come to predict behaviour as a guide for future action.

Reliability is a somewhat stronger form of trust. When it is present employees can assume the employer will follow through on promises, even if they are not always in the employer's interest. Reliability raises the relationship between employee and employer to a longer-term status and permits more of a two-way exchange of views; sometimes the employer contributes, sometimes the employee.

There are three methods of building reliability – keeping promises, using candour, offering support. Keeping promises means more than consistent behaviour. For example, a manager may reward employees who come in early by letting them go home early – behaviour that builds predictability; or the manager may start flextime – a promise that those who come in early may *always* go home early. It is keeping the promise that builds reliability. Using candour is also important in building reliability. Candour ensures that the 'promises' to be kept are clearly understood, even at the cost of personal discomfort. Finally, offering support builds reliability as managers talk to subordinates – even if the news is bad.

Mutuality is the strongest form of trust; when it is present employee and employer share expectations of each other and so feel comfortable to take action with limited communication.

There are two methods for building mutuality – taking time to care, and providing as much security as possible given the conditions in which the company must operate. In taking time to care, a manager remembers critical aims/objectives of employees or personal aspects of work relationships. Employment security may be hard to provide, but it generates the maximum degree of mutuality. Consider the position of the partner in a professional service firm – the partner is, to a significant degree, the partnership to which he or she belongs.

Those who establish teams must also understand their own role in the context of empowerment. Managers must help team members cope with stress. Empowerment is designed for ambiguous environments, but many employees are not; previously they held assigned tasks. Managers must learn how to give and receive constructive criticism and to listen carefully without asserting their remaining authority too strongly.

A company should always aim for the highest level of trust possible to ensure maximum scope for independent action and should never presume to have more trust than it has earned. Without securing at least predictability, employees are unlikely to take any actions that have not been directly approved. If mutuality is secured, full empowerment can be almost automatic.

G Bruce Friesen is a management consultant in D.Q.Mills Inc, a private consulting practice based in Boston, Massachusetts. He is a 1985 MBA graduate of the Harvard University Graduate School of Business Administration.

D Quinn Mills is the Albert J Weatherhead Professor of Business Administration at the Harvard University Graduate School of Business Administration. He is the author of numerous books including *Rebirth of the Corporation* (1991) and *The New Competitors* (1985).

Further Reading

Mills, D Quinn, *The Rebirth of the Corporation*, Wiley and Sons, New York. 1991.
Zuboff, S, *In the Age of the Smart Machine*, Basic Books, New York 1988.

Reference

1 Friesen, GB and Mills, DQ, *Elements of Managerial Style*, unpublished survey research. Further information is available from the authors.

INTERNATIONAL PRACTICE

Semco

Ricardo Semler

Every week groups of executives from leading multinationals visit a once unheard of company based in the outskirts of São Paulo, Brazil. The location is not the attraction – a nondescript industrial complex. Nor is the company's technology exciting or its products – pumps and cooling units – the most thrilling in the world. The difference lies in the revolutionary way the company is run. Its innovations in the way it and its people work has been covered in the *Harvard Business Review* and featured in Tom Peters' *Liberation Management*.

I took over as chief executive of the company, Semco, at the beginning of the 1980s. Previously it had been run by my father. On taking over I set about reconstructing the company along three basic values: employee participation, profit sharing and open information systems.

Now, as they walk through the door, visiting executives immediately notice that there is no receptionist. Everyone at Semco is expected to meet their own visitors. There are no secretaries, nor are there any personal assistants. Managers do their own photocopying, send their own faxes and make their own coffee. Semco has no dress code so some people wear jackets and ties, others jeans.

But, Semco's approach goes far beyond these superficial elements. A few years ago, when we wanted to relocate a factory, we closed down for a day and everyone boarded buses to inspect three possible sites. Their choice hardly thrilled the managers, since it was next to a company that was frequently on strike. But we moved in anyway.

The first step towards this was the elimination of needless layers of hierarchy. Originally there were 11 layers – now a front-line lathe operator is one layer away from the general manager of the division.

One plant, for example, had 300 people using a complex, but slow, computer system. Quality was poor, inventory excessive and deliveries often late. In response, we split the plant into three. Initially, this produced duplications and a loss of economies of scale. We had separate entrances, computer systems and telephones for each of the newly-formed units. It seemed excessive, but it worked.

This approach continues whenever units become too large – between 100 and 200 people. We simply separate them. In the first case, the split had an immediate effect and it continues to work. Not only are people brought closer together, but sales increase substantially as people seek out new ideas and opportunities.

In 1990 the company was experiencing a collapse in the market – inspired by the government's seizure of 80 per cent of the country's cash. After talking to our employees and putting in place their suggestions to cut costs we turned to them once again. The shop-floor committee agreed to a 30 per cent pay cut on three conditions – increased profit sharing from 24 per cent to 39 per cent; a 40 per cent pay cut for managers; and a member of the committee would co-sign every cheque written by the company. With these conditions in place the company revived and survived.

Openness and mutual sacrifice has spawned more innovative approaches to workplace democracy. Everyone at the company has access to the books; managers set their own salaries; shopfloor workers set their own productivity targets and schedules; workers make decisions once the preserve of managers; even the distribution of the profit sharing scheme is determined by employees.

Semco has also championed a borderless system of short-term, non-contractual task assignments. This goes far beyond outsourcing. Instead, it involves unsupervised, in-house, company-supported satellite production of goods and services sold to Semco and other manufacturers by employees, part-time employees, ex-employees and people who simply work on the company's premises using its equipment.

This appears a recipe for anarchy and, to a large extent, it is uncontrollable. As there is no one at the centre (only 14 people at the company's head office) managers in the field cannot turn to someone else to ask for their assistance. They have to make an immediate decision alone – knowing that they will be supported. It means that people often don't have a great deal of security and it requires a huge reservoir of trust on both sides. But, it unleashes people's imagination and entrepreneurial instincts in ways which would simply not be possible in a conventional organization.

As these arrangements evolved, we eased the transition as much as possible – people were instructed in cost control, pricing, maintenance and other aspects of running their own business. Now, around 50 per cent of the company's manufacturing is handled by what we call satellites and we estimate that a further 10 to 20 per cent will follow in the near future. As a result, Semco now employs 200 employees rather than the 500 in 1990.

Our realization has been that there are very few activities which have to be done in-house. We have narrowed these down to senior management, applications engineering, some R&D and some high-tech, capital intensive skills.

For managers such changes clearly represent a formidable challenge. Managers are constantly appraised by Semco workers rather than a coterie of fellow executives, and they have to become used to the idea of accepting that their decisions are not sacrosanct. There are people at Semco whose styles I don't actually like. I wouldn't have recruited them but quite clearly they do their jobs effectively – otherwise people wouldn't support them.

The chief executive's job rotates between six people who take six-month stints at acting as chief executive. As a result, despite owning the capital of the company, I haven't hired or fired anyone for eight years or signed a company cheque. From an operational side I am no longer necessary, though I still draw a salary because there are many other ways of contributing to the company's success. Indeed, what many consider the core activity of management – decision making – should not be their function at all. Only when bosses give up decision making and let their employees govern themselves does the possibility exist for a business jointly managed by workers and executives. That is true participative management.

The plea for businesses to become more democratic and humane is a familiar one. The trouble is that listening to people, accepting their decisions and inculcating people with the need for democracy is far from easy. But, the era of using people as production tools is coming to an end. Participation is not a case of management opting out of making difficult decisions or delegating power to the extent that they are redundant. In fact, it is infinitely more complex to practise than conventional unilateralism, but it is something which companies can no longer ignore or pay lip-service to.

Today, Semco is a unique success story. It has managed to buck Brazilian commercial chaos, hyper-inflation and recession to increase productivity nearly seven-fold and profits five-fold. Though people in the media and other business people tend to call what we have done 'revolutionary', it is in fact nothing of the kind. We have refused to squander our greatest resource, our people.

There is still a substantial amount of scepticism about Semco's approach. The mistake people make is assuming that Semco is some kind of role model. This is just one more version of how companies can organize themselves and succeed. Democracy alone will not solve all business problems. In fact, as we constantly see, nothing prevents autocratic companies from making money.

Ricardo Semler is president of Semco, Brazil's largest marine and food processing machinery manufacturer. He is author of *Maverick!* (1993) and of a number of articles in the *Harvard Business Review*. He has been voted Brazil's Business Leader of the Year and Latin American Businessman of the Year. He has served as vice president of the Federation of Industries of Brazil.

Further Reading

Semler, Ricardo, *Maverick!* Century, London, 1993.

Making the Organization Work

'The hierarchy is under siege because it's increasingly inefficient and many of the most effective workers in our companies
are sick of it. They're tired of the rituals, the lack of real communication, the delays in making decisions and taking actions.
With new technology diffusing information widely, many feel
that the issue isn't who you are in the structure but what you
get accomplished.'   *D Quinn Mills*[1]

[1] Mills, DQ, *Rebirth of the Corporation*, John Wiley, Chichester, 1991.

OVERVIEW

Stuart Crainer

Organizations have traditionally been seen as vertical structures. This has been the critical ingredient of the conventional recipe. Though organizations have tried many different ways of representing their structure most, if not all, end up with some sort of vertical axis from top to bottom. It is a striking truth that today's organizations remain modelled on the principles described by Adam Smith in 1776.

Smith's fundamentals were later developed by the American FW Taylor into what became known as 'scientific management', a doctrine built around specialization and the division of labour. Practical use of Taylor's ideas reached a high point with the advent of the mass-production line with workers performing repetitive tasks on a mammoth scale. Management followed similar structures with different functions – such as marketing, sales, R&D and production – being ruthlessly separated.

Mass-production techniques reaped impressive early dividends. Henry Ford, the arch exponent of the art, generated a huge fortune built on the increased productivity brought by mass production. 'It is not necessary for any one department to know what any other department is doing,' he propounded. 'It is the business of those who plan the entire work to see that all of the departments are working . . . towards the same end.'[1] Ford believed that managers should work in isolation, unencumbered by the problems of their colleagues, simply concentrating on what they are employed to do.

Ironically, it was Adam Smith who identified the potential problem. 'A man who spends his life carrying out a small number of very simple operations with perhaps the same effects has no room to develop his intelligence or to stretch his imagination so as to look for ways of overcoming difficulties which never occur. He thereby loses quite naturally the habit of using these faculties and, in general, he becomes as stupid and ignorant as it is possible for a human being to become.'[2]

The downside of such 'scientific' management is now well known and accepted. Ruthlessly satirised by Charlie Chaplin in the film 'Modern Times', such 'science' brought with it worker alienation, a lack of co-ordination between different functions and a complete absence of flexibility. Any sense of individual responsibility was sucked away by the system. Imaginations were never stretched; intelligence was not developed.

Though the production line model of Henry Ford is disappearing, and arguments over demarcation no longer fill the headlines, Taylorism persists. In the organization of the 1990s, Taylorism has spawned a vast number of controllers, overseers and supervisors. Middle managers, planners and accountants have established themselves as middle men between technology and implementation. Technology, brought in to reduce complexity, has more often than not brought with it teams of managers each intent on finding or creating their own place in the corporate order.

Hierarchies have expanded and new layers have been added with each technological step forward – note the growth of IT departments, strategy departments and so on. Companies have preoccupied themselves with bridging the gap between management and workers or organizing the workforce to perform more efficiently. Little attention has been paid to the role of customers; the layers of management or the core processes which enable the business to attract and retain customers.

Over the last twenty years great strides have been made in eradicating Taylorism from the factory-floor. Management demarcations have, however, usually emerged unscathed. The current fascination for re-engineering may emerge, perhaps, as a means of tackling white collar business processes in a way that has never before been convincingly attempted. It seeks to bridge the gap between management and employees to create a seamless organization geared around the needs of core constituencies rather than functions.

Sceptics of re-engineering may argue that the functional organization works. Undoubtedly, it does. Companies have been organized along functional lines throughout the twentieth century. They have not failed, but they have worked inefficiently. The functional system isn't broken, but it needs fixing.

The central problems of functional organizations are:

1. Goal setting

Functional organizations set goals that are functional rather than business oriented. This means that groups of people in different functions have their own alternative targets and *raison d'être*. There may be overall corporate strategies and objectives, but they are effectively relegated in importance. A manager working in a functional organization first and foremost requires that his or her function succeeds. Performance bonuses are usually related to divisional performance and managers are well aware that functions which succeed attract resources and the most talented people.

The end-result of this is that the performance of different functions within the same organization is often desperately uneven. This can be seen in companies which have developed excellence in one particular area of their business. They may well be financially brilliant, but overall their organization is not achieving its full potential. A company with an excellent R&D department may well be unable to transform ideas into practice thanks to a poorly performing production function.

2. Senior to junior process steps

A business process frequently passes from one hierarchical level to another as it moves from one function to another. It is common that a junior person needs an input from a senior manager, a signature or some other task. In most of these cases the senior manager fails to take the work seriously. They may delay the work in preference to other work, even if the customer needs it urgently, or may make errors which the junior person has to correct.

3. Job definitions

Harnessed by the restraints of their particular function, staff are overly specialized. The language used in one function may be unfamiliar or obscure to another. Usually the concepts they hold dear are at odds with the pragmatic demands of customers. Because of this they are unable to react to increasingly diverse customer needs. Instead of maximizing the potential of people, functional organization denies it. As a result, people become bored and frustrated, leading to higher staff turnover. Job definitions strongly reflect the functional nature of the organization. There are few jobs – apart from chief executive – which bridge the gap between different functions (and the chief executive may well have a specialized functional background). Job titles are unlikely to include the word 'customer' in them. Those that do are vested with little in the way of power or seniority.

4. Responsibility

In functional organizations customer service is not usually the responsibility of any one person. Any problems or customer queries spanning more than one department are passed on and on. Alternatively, problems are identified in purely functional terms – there is a problem with sales or an accounting problem. Identified in functional isolation they are solved in a similar style. At one organization – pre-re-engineering – some salesmen looked after several hundred customers and an engineer typically handled around 100. Responsibility was effectively diluted until very little existed.

5. Communication

The functional organization is often characterized by Byzantine communication chains. Paper passes back and forth between departments. Delays are inevitable as in-trays become more full and customers more irate. The entire process is time consuming and inflexible.

At Bell Atlantic a 15- to 30-day order-to-delivery cycle contained a mere 10 to 15 hours of actual work. The rest of the time was spent in waiting, or was simply wasted as one department passed paperwork on to another. Similarly, at AT&T a design cycle included 80 'hand-offs' from one department to another and 24 meetings. (This was later reduced to 17 and one respectively.)

6. Corporate Bermuda Triangles

In the Pacific Ocean there may well be no such thing as the Bermuda Triangle. In corporate *terra firma* its existence is more easily established.

Functional organizations often have stages of the process where no one has been assigned responsibility. Because processes tend to move to and fro between functions they remain unmanaged.

One chief executive said that an important part of his job was identifying who has responsibility for what in his organization. He found that managers were in the habit of passing things on to him when they were unsure of to whose domain they belonged. By abdicating responsibility, the managers believed they had solved the problem. The chief executive then had to decide who should take responsibility for the particular issue. In effect he found himself in charge of the Bermuda Triangle.

The irony is that the functional organization appears to offer clarity of responsibility. In practice it often overlooks the grey areas between different functions where no one takes responsibility.

7. Self-perpetuation

As new functions and divisions are added to the basic functional structure, the old ones are never replaced. A company may have functional divisions as well as product divisions and, quite possibly, geographic, national, strategic and market-driven splits between different activities.

There is nothing new in revealing the inadequacies and limitations of vertical and functional structures. They have been recognized for a number of years, but attempts at breaking them down have tended to be isolated and short-term. Companies have turned to temporary project teams, task forces and various alternative matrices at times of crisis or to tackle specific localized problems. Once the problem was solved, they resorted to their old ways, continuing to gloss over the fundamental problem.

Functional organizations inevitably produce functional solutions to their problems. Functional organizations produce functional managers. Managers become hidebound by managing things rather than getting them done.

If a company is patently struggling, different functional heads will advocate different functional-based solutions to the problem. The marketing director will argue that the company needs to increase its investment in marketing. If only they had more sales people making direct contact with customers they would be better able to give customers what they want. They might also suggest that the sales team would feel more confident if they had a new glossy brochure to hand to prospective customers.

The finance director is liable to shake his or her head at this point. From their point of view, the company's troubles are cost-related. If the company reduced costs it would be leaner and fitter. The production director will, in turn, argue the case for investment in better quality, more modern machinery. The chief executive, beset by arguing factions who are unlikely to ever agree, is likely to strike a balance – giving a little bit more money to each function or coming up with a company-wide initiative which each function will interpret as they wish and then ignore.

In his book *Administrative Behaviour*, Herbert Simon, summed up this process and coined a phrase for it: 'satisficing' – settling for adequate instead of optimal solutions.[3] This is an in-built characteristic of the conventional functional organization. Past strategy is fused with current organizational culture, so that people begin to believe that they know how things are done and stop questioning the assumptions behind their thoughts and actions. The recipe for success takes over and doubts about the company's ability to actually deliver success are automatically repressed.

Making the modern organization work

Making the new organization work involves a plethora of new skills and demands on organizational structures and managers. This involves radical perspectives on traditional practices.

Instead of having narrowly defined functionally-based goals, the emphasis is now on having broader corporate goals which are clearly articulated and communicated. These are supported and supplemented by team-related goals and targets, often based around an individual project. While once wider matters of strategy were under the control of a small coterie of senior managers, responsibility for developing and implementing strategy is now spread throughout the organization. Managers are all strategists now; and teams are the means by which the strategies are translated into action.

No longer are processes based around comfortable hierarchies. The emphasis is on networks of communication and information, so that the best decisions can be reached – no matter where they are made in the organization. The routine and often needless exchange of paperwork is replaced with speedy flows of information; automatic delegation by coaching and empowerment.

Instead of functionally-based job descriptions and definitions, the growing emphasis is on healthily (or dangerously) ambiguous job descriptions, if any.

For function, now read resource. Increasingly, making the organization work involves providing resources in a timely and supportive way. As an example look at the changing fortunes and perception of the marketing resource.

Clearly, marketing is a core activity of any organization. Its role is often critical to success. Marketing identifies customer needs, suggests products to satisfy the demand and then operates a follow-up support system to ensure consumer satisfaction. The marketing department is the customer's mouthpiece in the organization.

At the beginning of the 1990s there was a shift in attitudes and practice. Some organizations have realized that, despite their talk of being market-driven and market-focused, they have instead become *marketing-driven* and *marketing-focused*. Marketing is not any less important but, instead of dispensing blank cheques to marketing departments, companies are beginning to question and examine the role and achievement of marketing managers in attaining their objectives. No resource is an island and organizations want to establish how marketing best fits and relates to the rest of the organization and, most importantly, how effective it is in meeting the needs of customers. There is no point in having a corporate lubricant if all it does is support cyclical motion in a narrowly-defined area.

Financial services company Allied Dunbar is an archetypal example of an organization which flourished in the 1980s, thanks to effective marketing, and lost its way in the early 1990s. In 1991, a new chief executive began a radical process of assessment. It was discovered that the company had a distorted view of its marketplace relying on a 'market segmentation' model which had little connection with the changing demographics of reality. Allied Dunbar set about finding out what clients thought of the company and what they expected from it. As a result, it hopes to be able to measure the relationship between client satisfaction and profitability – this will enable marketing to be properly directed and be more responsive to customer needs.

Some companies are already re-organizing their marketing resources so that they become more truly aligned to the needs of customers; interact more effectively with the rest of the organization and are treated as a process rather than as an unwieldy and often isolated department. In *Tomorrow's Competition*, Mack Hanan, sums up this challenge. The modern marketing challenge, writes Hanan, is to 'make your business competitive by making the businesses of your customers more competitive'.[4]

One company tackling the issue is Elida Gibbs, the UK personal products subsidiary of Unilever. Its brands include Fabèrgé Brut, Pears, Signal and Timotei. In a revolutionary move, Elida Gibbs abolished the post of brand manager and re-invented the sales team as the 'customer development process'. Brands are now the responsibility of brand development managers.

The changes at Elida Gibbs stem from criticisms of its performance in the late 1980s. Poor delivery standards and an old-fashioned ordering system were a source of irritation to customers. As a result, Elida Gibbs introduced teamworking at one of its factories in 1988. Responsibility for each production line was transferred to those working on it. As well as these changes, Elida Gibbs reduced the number of its suppliers and gave suppliers more responsibility for quality control, testing and development. The roles of the company's managers were also re-defined on the basis of processes. Functional divisions were replaced by 'seamless teams'. Many of the day-to-day contacts with retailers which used up brand managers' time have been passed on to customer development managers.

On one production line change-over time over the last three years has been reduced to less than four hours, when it previously took an entire day. In addition, 90 per cent of orders are now correctly completed – against 72 per cent in the past. Between 1989 and 1991 the company's pre-tax profits rose by 73 per cent and margins widened from 6.5 per cent to 10 per cent. In April 1993 Elida Gibbs launched its first major product since its internal changes. It involved a development process of less than six months – half as much time as development had previously taken.

Similarly, SmithKline Beecham has spent much of 1993 overhauling its marketing activities. It believed it had been hampered by the company's division into geographic units. SmithKline Beecham studied other companies, including Procter & Gamble and Unilever, and then set up six teams – each responsible for a product category. The teams were given free rein to co-opt managers from national subsidiaries. Sales in consumer brands rose by 11 per cent in 1993 and product development cycles have been accelerated – a new toothbrush was developed in 40 per cent of the previous time.[5]

Harvard Business School's Benson Shapiro argues that truly market-driven companies have three characteristics:

- information on all important buying influences permeates every corporate function;
- strategic and tactical decisions are made inter-functionally and inter-divisionally;
- divisions and functions make well-co-ordinated decisions and execute them with a sense of commitment.[6]

The emphasis is on being cross-functional, utilizing co-ordination. Use of cross-functional teams and the dismantling of functional divides allows crucial market information to circulate more easily and more widely throughout the organization. Teamworking leads to more decisions being made by people working through the issues and available information together. Finally, clear understanding of the organizational goals and the company stakeholders leads to marketing decisions being made within an overall process of measurable performance rather than as isolated one-offs. The lessons increasingly being learned in corporate marketing departments are applicable elsewhere. Within all traditional functions, instead of being internalized, isolated and thought of in functional terms, resources need to be unlocked.

Further Reading

Obeng, E, *Organizational Magic*, FT/Pitman, London, 1995.
Thompson, JD, *Organizations in Action*, McGraw Hill, Maidenhead, 1967.

References

1 Crainer, S and Clutterbuck, D, *Makers of Management*, Macmillan, London, 1990.
2 *Ibid.*
3 Simon, H, *Administrative Behaviour*, Macmillan, New York 1947.
4 Hanan, M, *Tomorrow's Competition*, AMACOM, New York, 1991.
5 Jonquieres, G de, 'Buying the Bactroban with the bath oil', *Financial Times*, 10 January 1994.
6 Shapiro, B, 'What the hell is market oriented?', *Harvard Business Review*, November–December 1988.

MANUFACTURING STRATEGY

Jay S Kim

It has been more than two decades since the American academic Wickham Skinner called manufacturing the missing link in corporate strategy. Since then, many companies have developed and implemented a manufacturing strategy as a bridge to unite the 'missing link' with the rest of the organization. In parallel, many researchers have worked to define the concept and to make it operational. As a result, the operations function now receives increasingly significant attention from the top management of manufacturing companies throughout the world.

Yet, integrating manufacturing into broader corporate strategies is now ever more complex. Globalization and the need to accelerate and re-align product development and processes have increased the demands on operations and their role in the organization – and other people's understanding of that role.

Acceptance that manufacturing is a critical function is growing among many organizations. As such it must be integrated with business strategies. The development of a manufacturing strategy is central to establishing this linkage.

World events, however, have changed the context in which this integration must occur, and, in turn, the role of manufacturing in the organization. The nature of markets and the scope of competition have changed significantly as manufacturers rapidly expand their global operations. The Total Quality Management (TQM) revolution, which preoccupied industry during the last decade, forces manufacturing executives to pay much closer attention to who their customers are and what they expect. Fast changes in product and process technologies require manufacturers to adapt rapidly to the changing technical environment. As a consequence, new product development has become a crucial agenda for many firms, and the fundamental re-alignment (or re-engineering) of value-added business processes faces most producers of goods, as well as services.

Do these changes provide an opportunity for the manufacturing function? Or, do they represent another hurdle? How can manufacturing strategy help executives address the challenges arising from the new business context? During a recent forum of senior manufacturing executives, a vice-president of operations of a large telecommunications equipment manufacturer made an apt comment: 'Manufacturing strategy got us here, but it may not get us where we need to be in the next decade.'[1]

What can we learn from the experience of manufacturing executives who worked so diligently with manufacturing strategy, and how can we take advantage of this learning for future changes? There is a gap between the emerging issues that currently occupy the minds of senior manufacturing executives and the perspectives underlying the traditional manufacturing strategy concept. To bridge this there is a need for a fundamental shift in the framework of manufacturing strategy so that it matches the emerging needs of manufacturing managers.

Manufacturing strategy: has it worked?

When manufacturing strategy was first conceived by Skinner and other leading scholars, it was described as plans and policies for structuring the manufacturing function over a long-term period so as to develop the function to become a company's competitive weapon. The focus on a *single manufacturing task* was one key component of manufacturing strategy, and internal consistency among plans and policies in supporting that single manufacturing task was the other.[2]

Manufacturing strategy was expected to fundamentally change how the manufacturing function was managed and evaluated. Management emphasis was to move from a pre-occupation with productivity and cost to a broader view of competitive contributing to the business strategy. Short-term requirements (such as, did we meet the shipping target last month?) were to be replaced by long-range strategic planning (such as, what is the competitive advantage that the manufacturing function brings to our market strategy?). Structural issues (such as, investing in flexible process technologies) were to receive more attention than daily operational issues (such as, order scheduling decisions). Systems design (such as, organizing plant layouts and establishing workforce responsibilities) was to be directed by the general manager rather than by technical specialists.

All in all, manufacturing strategy existed to make the manufacturing function more proactive (as opposed to reactive), and to integrate structural decisions of the manufacturing function with the goals and objectives of the business strategy. If all was done correctly, it was expected that manufacturing would become a competitive weapon, not a corporate millstone inhibiting strategic initiatives.

Did manufacturing strategy work? What did it bring to manufacturers? Figure 1 sums up what Skinner believes manufacturing strategy has done for the operations function. Without manufacturing strategy, the operations function had to work hard on its generic task – to improve productivity and reduce costs. Reality to the manufacturing managers, however, was that costs always went back upward (or, foreign competitors with low wage rates negated any gain in cost advantage), making operations' job harder and harder. What manufacturing strategy did was help managers recognize that there existed many other ways to compete, and define different targets for different performance criteria. With priorities and focus, manufacturing was able to perform well on the strategically mandated variables, and the corporation began to recognize manufacturing as supportive of business strategy.[3] Manufacturing strategy certainly made the manufacturing job easier, with better results.

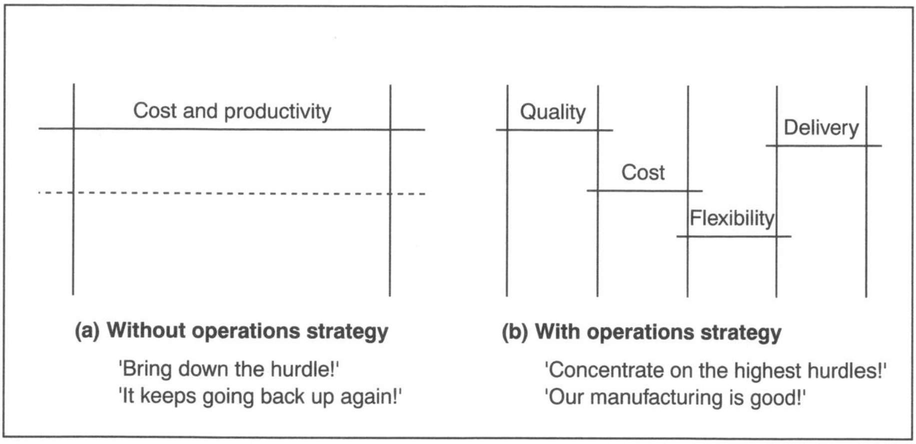

Fig. 1 How did manufacturing strategy change the manufacturing task?
Source: Ideas for this were presented by Professor Wickham Skinner at the Manufacturing Executives' Forum, Boston, 1993.

Consequently, in many organizations, manufacturing strategy has been an important factor in changing the role of manufacturing from one of caretaker to business partner. More than ever, senior management considers manufacturing a critical element in the successful realization of corporate strategy, and operations' position carries more weight in the organization. According to the 1992 Manufacturing Futures Survey, a study conducted by Boston University's Manufacturing Roundtable every two years, the operations function has gained significant ground in business strategy development lately.[6] Results from the 1987 survey indicated that the marketing function then had a dominant role in formulating business unit strategy. In 1992, however, manufacturing managers perceive that there is more balance in strategic influence among marketing, manufacturing, and engineering functions. The manufacturing and human resource functions have gained the most ground in the strategic planning process, and the large gap in influence between marketing and manufacturing is considerably reduced. Furthermore, the respondents to the 1992 survey indicated their belief that manufacturing and R&D will influence strategy development more significantly in the future.

Manufacturing strategy: will it continue to work in the future?

Despite these achievements, there are managers and researchers who have different views on whether manufacturing strategy has worked successfully. A few, including Skinner, believe that its implementation in industry is modest at best. Others argue that its practical achievements to date have been limited.[5] Furthermore, many believe that operationalizing a manufacturing strategy is even harder than developing one. 'Now that we know where to focus, what do we do?' asked one manufacturing director. The implementation process still remains a black box, an art. Some manufacturing managers have gone even further in criticizing manufacturing strategy. 'It's a trap! It forces the manufacturing function to become a mere implementer of what marketing says we have to deliver. Maybe we should start with customers.'

These concerns appear to have affected the perceived value of manufacturing strategy. The 1992 Manufacturing Futures Survey reports that the effectiveness of manufacturing strategy in enhancing a firm's competitiveness has slipped lately. As shown in Table 1, manufacturing strategy was identified in 1990 as the fourth in payoff among 27 improvement action programmes by senior manufacturing executives in the United States. In just two years, however, its ranking had dropped to tenth. Manufacturing strategy, having served its initial goal, is losing its momentum. Unless its core value is re-vitalized, this downward trend may continue, and manufacturing may eventually retreat back to its 'reactive' nature.[6]

Table 1 Declining payoff from manufacturing strategy

Ten action programmes with greatest payoffs:
Results from Manufacturing Futures Survey

1990 Survey	1992 Survey
1. Manufacturing reorganization	1. Closing/relocating plants
2. Interfunctional work team	2. Interfunctional work team
3. Statistical Quality Control (SQC)	3. Statistical Quality Control (SQC)
4. **Manufacturing strategy**	4. Manufacturing reorganization
5. Just-in-time (JIT)	5. Worker training
6. Computer-aided design (CAD)	6. Computer-aided design (CAD)
7. Reconditioning physical plants	7. Supervisor training
8. Supervisor training	8. New process development for new products
9. New process development for new products	9. Quality function deployment (QFD)
10. Worker training	10. **Manufacturing strategy**

For what reasons might manufacturing strategy stop serving the organization's goals and objectives? Why is it losing ground to other programmes in contributing to competitive improvement? What makes it hard to manufacturing executives to move further with this functional strategy concept? There are some fundamental changes occurring in manufacturing practice which require changes in our conceptualization of manufacturing strategy.

The new context for manufacturing strategy

World events over the last two decades have changed the context within which manufacturing strategy has to work. During the 1970s, when Skinner proposed the focused factory concept as a basic principle of manufacturing strategy, manufacturing executives were fighting to stay competitive against the inflows of inexpensive foreign products. Some of the foreign competitors appeared to have competitive advantages in product quality as well. Under those circumstances, the role of manufacturing strategy was to provide a fresh perspective on the competencies required of the operations function. The notion of priorities was a powerful tool which managers could use to identify and focus their 'competitive requirements'.

What are the competitive requirements for manufacturing in the 1990s? In order to explore the emerging context for manufacturing strategy, 40 senior manufacturing executives who participated in a recent executive forum were asked: 'What are the most critical tasks that must be accomplished by your manufacturing function now?' Through a round of brainstorming and group discussion, these managers agreed on the nine key manufacturing tasks listed in Table 2.

Table 2 Nine key tasks for the manufacturing function

- *Customer focus*: finding out and truly understanding what external customers want.
- *Broader responsibilities*: operation of the supply chain (as opposed to production) including order fulfilment and distribution.
- *Global scope*: establishing a global network; simultaneous roll-out of products around the world.
- *Extremely flexible and quick*: absorbing rapid changes in product and processes; reducing cycle time to develop and deliver new, as well as existing, products.
- *Have to do all well*: lower cost, higher quality, AND better delivery; no sacrifice on one for another; value as opposed to cost.
- *Change in culture*: exploiter or creator rather than caretaker.
- *Member of business team*: requiring broader knowledge about business (not function).
- *Reach out:* actively seeking external partners (including customers and suppliers).
- *Product development role*: earlier and more significant involvement.

These executives also rated the importance of these new tasks for their business unit on a 5-point scale (1 = non issue and 5 = critical). Average scores from the respondents are summarized in Fig. 3. All nine tasks received average scores above or close to 4, which was defined in the survey as *very important*.

The most important new task identified was making manufacturing more customer-focused. Twenty-one executives rated customer-focus as *critical* (scale = 5), and the other four as *very important* (scale = 4). Manufacturing executives believe that it is imperative for the operations function itself to find out what customers want, rather than waiting for marketing research. They also believe that important customer needs have to be translated into specific decisions in the value delivery chain.

The second most important task was becoming extremely *flexible and responsive*. Manufacturing executives perceive that the capability to absorb rapid changes in products and processes will be critical for the future. The notion of flexibility is not limited to the factory floor. Rather, the business process as a whole has to be flexible. The participating managers emphasized that the entire supplier-transformation-distribution chain has to respond quickly to the changing needs of customers.

For many companies, manufacturing's role in the *product development process* is becoming increasingly important. Many manufacturing executives are already involved in new product development projects, often in considerably earlier stages and with stronger influence than before. Several respondents highlighted this item as the most important, saying 'the role we play during new product development defines the complexity and uncertainty of the manufacturing tasks down the road.'

The expectation of *continuous improvement* is another element of the context that surrounds today's manufacturing. Changes are everywhere – in products, processes, customers, and competitive scope – and today's good performance does not guarantee future success. Similarly, organizations are less willing to accept the trade-off notion: improvement in one dimension should occur without sacrificing performance in other dimensions.

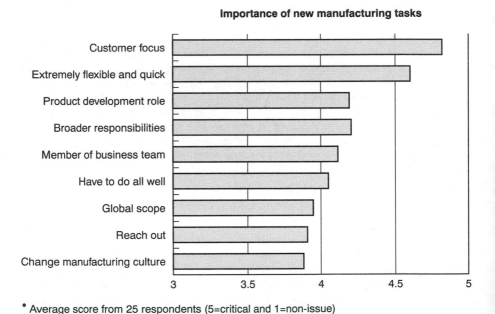

* Average score from 25 respondents (5=critical and 1=non-issue)

Fig. 2 Importance-rating of nine key manufacturing tasks

These trends indicate that the future role of manufacturing managers will be quite different from their traditional tasks. Customer focus, a strong need for a flexible value-delivery chain, emphasis on product development, and the task calling for broader responsibilities, highlight the importance of extending the role of manufacturing beyond the factory walls. In consequence, manufacturing executives perceive the need to reach out to other functional managers in the value chain, and co-operate with them as a cross-functional business team. They will spend more time working with managers from other functional areas, and even with managers from other business organizations like suppliers and customers. The scope of their actions is stretching far beyond the four walls of conventional factories. Their roles are clearly shifting from housekeepers to leaders of cross-functional teams, and further to business partners.

The old manufacturing strategy cannot serve the emerging manufacturing challenges

These observations provide us with some understanding of the emerging context within which manufacturing strategy has to function in the future. Besides the traditional tasks (like being functional experts in cost improvement, quality, and flexibility), manufacturing managers are now requested to have broader business knowledge. Customer expectations, market values of products, and external business partnerships are more frequently on the manufacturing executive's homework list. The entire supply chain, not just the factory, is now manufacturing's task. Product development now requires a significant input from manufacturing.

Can 'old' manufacturing strategy support manufacturing managers in coping with these emerging roles? The answer proposed here is 'no', for two important reasons. First, the process with which manufacturing's role is defined in the old manufacturing strategy concept is too restrictive. Second, the scope of decisions to be governed by manufacturing strategy is too narrow. Figure 3 represents the traditional framework of manufacturing strategy, which highlights the notion of competitive priorities (the *process*) and their links with structural and infrastructural decisions in manufacturing (the *scope*).

The first reason deals with the *process* of developing and implementing manufacturing strategy. Some manufacturing executives confess: 'Even if we know what business strategy is and what manufacturing strategy should be, it is very hard to operationalize. To make things worse, rapidly changing competitive environment does not allow a business strategy to remain stable for a long period, and as a consequence, the operations function is constantly requested to develop a new set of manufacturing capabilities to support the "new" business strategy. However, manufacturing capabilities cannot be built overnight. It takes a long time to establish a quality foundation, for example.'

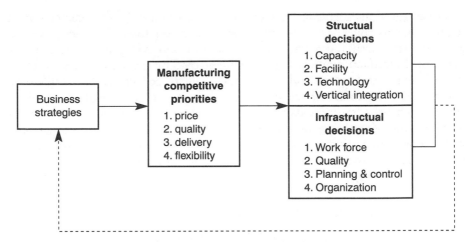

Fig. 3 Traditional framework of manufacturing strategy

Source: S. Wheelwright, 'Manufacturing strategy: defining the missing link', *Strategic Management Journal*, vol. 5, 1984

Can we build a manufacturing strategy without a clearly defined business strategy? What should we do if the current business strategy is becoming obsolete? The traditional way of formulating manufacturing strategy is guided by the top-down perspective, where business strategy defines the priorities of the manufacturing function and these competitive priorities guide key manufacturing decisions. If the business strategy changes, manufacturing's priorities have to be adjusted promptly. Because it takes a long time to develop a different set of capabilities, however, manufacturing strategy cannot effectively support the new business strategy. In today's rapidly changing business environment, this top-down process of formulating manufacturing strategy cannot work.

Does the process always have to be top-down? What needs to be changed in the manufacturing strategy concept in order to reverse this direction?[8] These questions directly challenge the old framework of manufacturing strategy, and today's business environment makes them even more alarming.

The second issue addresses the *scope* of decisions which manufacturing strategy governs. TQM efforts over the last decade have pushed operations managers to look outside their factories and to pay much closer attention to who their customers are and what they want. In many companies, operations managers now have much better understanding of the complex nature of customer requirements than before. One manufacturing vice-president of an office equipment manufacturer recently claimed: 'We now know what customers really want and what they just say they want. What we see from a consumer report is not always what they really need. In that sense, we know about our customers much better than our sales people do.' How does the manufacturing function incorporate these insights into the manufacturing strategy? Where does the customer come into the picture? Which function is responsible for customer satisfaction?

These questions challenge the scope of the decisions that manufacturing strategy has to cover. Traditionally, manufacturing strategy was supposed to guide the structural and infrastructural decisions in managing a plant or plant network. Manufacturing decision categories typically mentioned include facility, capacity, technology, planning and control, quality, and workforce management. In contrast, the questions being raised more recently tend to cover much broader areas like order fulfilment, value delivery, and product development. Manufacturing managers' concerns go much beyond the factory walls. The scope of manufacturing strategy must be expanded into areas which have been regarded in the past as the responsibilities of other functions.

A 'new' manufacturing strategy: focus on customer values and broader scope

Senior manufacturing executives need a new conceptual framework that can guide them through the emerging challenges. Manufacturing strategy has to play that role, but, as noted above, its traditional framework is becoming obsolete. As the role of manufacturing managers expands, the manufacturing strategy concept has to be modified. This paper proposes two changes for establishing a new framework: one on the process of defining manufacturing's task, and the other on the scope of decisions to be addressed by manufacturing strategy.

Cumulated capabilities in delivering customer values

Traditionally, manufacturing strategy practices and literature have recognized that manufacturing's competitive capabilities include cost, quality, delivery, and flexibility. It has been argued that there exist trade-offs among these capabilities, and that the first role of manufacturing strategy is to determine the relative importance among them in such a way that they are consistent with the goals and objectives of the business strategy. Consequently, the concept of focus has long been the central issue of manufacturing strategy. Recent developments in manufacturing, however, challenge this top-down process of determining manufacturing's critical capabilities in two ways.

First, trade-offs among capabilities are no longer acceptable in many instances. Many manufacturing executives now believe that, with intensifying global competition, they cannot afford to allow any slippage in one particular capability to gain more in the others. Nor are these trade-offs always necessary, as noted earlier. Researchers are presenting cases where this trade-off notion does not have to be applied.[9] As manufacturers build higher levels of capabilities in multiple dimensions (without sacrificing others), there are growing arguments that these competitive capabilities need to be approached with a framework of cumulative process rather than one of trade-off. If trade-offs are neither acceptable nor necessary, the notion of priorities becomes less critical as a component of manufacturing strategy. Rather, the more relevant question becomes 'How can an organization accumulate multi-dimensional capabilities and use them as a strategic weapon?'

Second, manufacturing's capabilities should, and could in many cases, influence the formulation of business strategy. As we observed earlier, rapidly changing competitive environments make it harder for organizations to maintain a stable business strategy long enough to develop necessary operations capabilities. In addition, as manufacturing managers are requested to become proactive business leaders rather than reactive caretakers of business strategy, the notion of core competencies is increasingly recognized as a critical source of competitive advantage.[10] Capabilities that are accumulated within the operations function are one such core competency. These trends imply that the top-down process of determining manufacturing's priorities from the market-oriented business strategy needs to be refined.

How can manufacturing accumulate competitive capabilities so as to make them a lasting competency? How can manufacturing's capabilities influence the goals and objectives of business strategy? In order for manufacturing managers to play a more significant role in the strategic planning process, they need concepts that transform manufacturing's unique capabilities into the business strategy. The notion of *customer value* should play this role. The primary results from manufacturing improvement have to be tied to the creation of better values for customers. The requirements and expectations of customers have to be directly tied to manufacturing strategy, and efforts to improve current manufacturing have to start with specifically identifying what customers really want.

Some researchers now propose that the strategic planning process must start by defining which customer value a business unit wants to deliver and how that value should be created. For example, Treacy and Wiersema recently presented three distinctive forms of customer values: operational excellence, customer intimacy, and product leadership.[11] Each of these value disciplines certainly requires a unique combination of capabilities, and an organization must make a prudent choice among them as their strategic focus. Capabilities accumulated in the operations function should guide an organization in determining which form of customer value it can best create and deliver. Table 3[12] shows how capabilities accumulated in manufacturing can help create some unique value to a customer.

For example, if a manufacturing organization progressively accumulates capabilities in conformance quality, dependable delivery, broad distribution, and cost efficiency, it is properly positioned to provide 'operational excellence' as a primary customer value. In contrast, if it builds capabilities around conformance quality, performance design, new design flexibility, and new product introduction flexibility, then a primary customer value it can offer better than its competitors would be 'product leadership'. Manufacturing executives should be able to recognize the strategic consequence of building various operations capabilities, and a new manufacturing strategy should provide them with that roadmap.

Table 3 Possible linkages between manufacturing capabilities and customer value

Accumulated manufacturing capabilities		Possible choice of customer value discipline
Conformance quality Dependable delivery Broad distribution Cost efficiency	⟶	Operational Excellence (delivering reliable products at competitive price with minimal difficulty)
Conformance quality Product flexibility Design flexibility Customization After-sales service	⟶	Customer Intimacy (tailoring products to exactly match the requirements of the selected market)
Conformance quality Performance quality Design flexibility New product flexibility	⟶	Product Leadership (offering leading-edge products that consistently exceed customer's and competitor's expectations)

In the new manufacturing strategy, therefore, manufacturing capabilities should be recognized such that:

- certain capabilities are accumulated on others, rather than traded off;
- the primary contribution of manufacturing's competitive capabilities is to enable the organization to excel in delivering a particular customer value.

Fig. 4[13] thus presents an alternative view on the relationship between the operations function's competitive capabilities, choice of the target customer value, and business strategy.

From structural/infrastructural decisions towards core processes

As the scope of the manufacturing executive's role expands to the other business functions, the context within which these capabilities are addressed has to be broadened. Manufacturing executives are increasingly involved in activities that are beyond the factory walls. Their responsibilities are expanding to cover the entire value chain, and the production activities are tightly linked with the design engineering and marketing functions. As increasing value to customers becomes the primary role of operations, manufacturing strategy should incorporate issues that are beyond the traditional structural and infrastructural decisions in a plant or plant network. Unless manufacturing managers have a proper framework to organize and prioritize them, these broader responsibilities could simply mean that they have to do more than their traditional tasks.

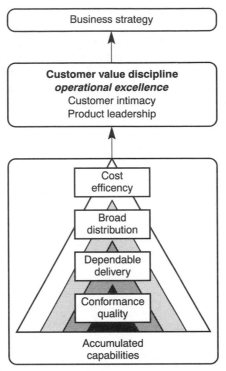

Fig. 4 Cumulative competitive capabilities toward customer valve

Manufacturing strategy needs to provide these senior manufacturing executives with a framework which can guide them in prioritizing their time and efforts.

In defining what decisions a new manufacturing strategy has to address, we can apply the lessons from industry's experiences with TQM. With a broader and deeper awareness of customer expectations, senior management now understand that the cross-functional business processes should be the focus of strategic initiatives. In other words, the notion of customer focus should be the focal point of manufacturing strategy, and it should be approached with a process perspective rather than with the traditional functional orientation. The story of Corning-Vitro's recent experience in establishing its global manufacturing strategy highlights how this process orientation helped a large manufacturer develop a cohesive plan for improving operations capabilities.

'By understanding customers and their requirements, and by defining key processes around them, the Corning-Vitro's manufacturing strategy team was able to identify the required information, generate strategic alternatives, and establish critical initiatives. Rather than trying various improvement programs and attempting endless restructuring, this rigorous process thinking helped us identify crucial opportunities for long-term profit improvement'[14]

New manufacturing strategy should be directed towards cross-functional value-added processes rather than functional decisions. It does not mean that the traditional decisions in the structure and infrastructure of plant network no longer need be addressed by manufacturing strategy. They are still important factors in developing operations' competitive capabilities. What needs to be changed is the perspective with which these decisions are approached. A decision on facilities, for example, should not be guided by the goal of minimizing transportation costs. Rather, it should be regarded as a component of designing the value-delivery process. Pepsi's operating strategy is an example:

'In 1988, Pepsi established its operating strategy, which defined a fundamentally different way of doing business. By looking at our business processes from the customer's point of view, we recognized that there were too many unnecessary steps in our delivery chain. Our process-driven analysis revealed that every can or bottle is picked up and put down as many as 21 times before it gets to the final customer's hand! Pepsi's operating strategy recognized the need to synchronize the value-delivery chain so that it contains only the processes that add value to the customers. A large-scale redesign of the delivery chain was implemented, and our decisions on bottling operations and distribution centers were guided by this new chain design'[15]

What are the core processes that should be included in the new manufacturing strategy framework? Companies have various definitions on what key business processes should be. For example, Davenport reports that IBM identified 17 business processes as a part of its re-engineering effort, ranging from order creation process to customer service processes. Xerox has 14 core processes, and British Telecom has 15.[16] Certainly, different business natures require that manufacturers organize their activities around different processes. As a framework for new manufacturing strategy, I propose to focus on three generic flows of entity that have to go through the manufacturing function: flows of material, information, and technology. Materials have to move from suppliers through manufacturing facilities to reach customers. Information on customer orders and delivery schedules has to be co-ordinated with production planning systems. New product technologies have to go through the manufacturing process in order to reach the marketplace. Manufacturing managers need to understand how these flows of material, information, and technology interact in their daily operations.

Furthermore, they should understand which process needs additional improvement in order to increase 'the right values' to the customers. If 'operational excellence' is the key customer value on which the business unit chooses to compete, for example, the flows of materials and information have to be managed better than competitors'. If a business unit aspires to excel in 'product leadership', the flow of technologies in the new product development process becomes more crucial. Manufacturing strategy should direct the operations function's capability building efforts in these processes. In other words, manufacturing strategy should include within its framework core processes such as:

- supply process (procuring raw materials and components through the supply chain)
- order fulfilment process (receiving and fulfilling customer orders through the delivery chain)
- product development process (developing, designing, and manufacturing new products through the product development cycle).

Manufacturing has long been held accountable for lagging competitiveness in global markets. It has also been by-passed by corporate strategists. In recent years, however, manufacturing has worked diligently to establish itself as a critical source of competitive advantage.

Manufacturing is no longer just a place where things are made. Rather, it is where technologies are translated into customer requirements. Manufacturing managers are not simply caretakers of the business. They are responsible for customer satisfaction. Manufacturing is not just a place where the details of the business are taken care of. Manufacturing is now at the front edge of the business, and manufacturing managers are being challenged to become cross-functional leaders who will translate the customer-driven business strategy into operational excellence.

An increasing number of manufacturing executives are now faced with new challenges as well as new opportunities. If they cannot manage these new challenges, they may be forced to retreat to the earlier status of caretakers and housekeepers. If they can capture this moment of opportunity, their past

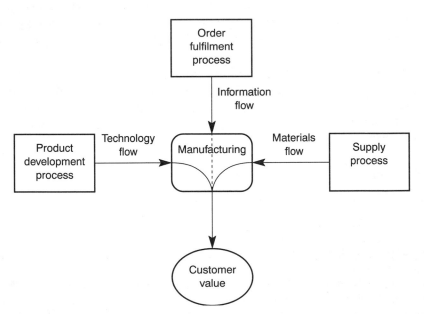

Fig. 5 A new manufacturing strategy: core processes

efforts and subsequent improvements in manufacturing will be translated into business success, giving them a greater leadership role in the future. Although manufacturing strategy has contributed to the enhanced status of the operations function, its traditional framework is not broad enough to help manufacturing executives cope with the new challenges. They need a new and broader framework for managing the operations function, and the entire business process, under these challenges.

Two critical changes need to be reflected in the new framework of manufacturing strategy. First, manufacturing's competitive capabilities have to be understood as a cumulative concept. These strategic capabilities must be directly linked with increasing value for customers. Second, manufacturing decisions have to be approached with a process orientation. Core business processes – such as the supply process, order fufilment and product development – must be the centre of strategic decision making, rather than the conventional structural and infrastructural decisions regarding the 'factory'.

These perspectives are not completely new, and some leading manufacturers are beginning to deploy their manufacturing strategy with a focus on customer value and process orientation. Skinner's 'focused factory' has served manufacturing executives well for over two decades. It is time to contemplate a new manufacturing strategy that can help manufacturing managers exploit emerging opportunities and meet the new leadership challenges.

Jay S Kim is a member of the operations management department at Boston University's School of Management.

Some of the ideas presented in this chapter were motivated by discussions at the Manufacturing Executives' Forum in April 1993. The author acknowledges Professors Miller and Skinner and all the participants for their contributions.

Further Reading

Davenport, T, *Process Innovation: Re-engineering Work through Information Technology*, Harvard Business School Press, Boston, 1993.
Hayes, R and Wheelwright, S, *Restoring our Competitive Edge*, John Wiley, New York, 1984.

References

[1] Kim, JS, 'Operations Strategy: Changing Roles for Manufacturing', Boston University Manufacturing Roundtable Research Report, 1993.
[2] For more information on the traditional role of manufacturing see Skinner, W, 'The focused factory', *Harvard Business Review*, May–June, 1974, and Wheelwright, S, 'Manufacturing Strategy: Defining the Missing Link', *Strategic Management Journal*, vol. 5, 1984.
[3] See Wheelwright, S and Hayes, R, 'Competing through Manufacturing', *Harvard Business Review*, January–February, 1985.
[4] For more information about this survey see Kim, JS and Miller, JG, 'Challenges for

building the value factory: key findings from the 1992 US Manufacturing Futures Survey', *Operations Management Review*, vol 9. no. 3, 1993.

[5] See Corbett, C and Van Wassenhove, L, 'Trade-offs? What trade-offs? Competence and Competitiveness in Manufacturing Strategy', *California Management Review*, Summer 1993; and Hayes, RH and Pisano, GP, 'Beyond world class: the new manufacturing strategy', *Harvard Business Review*, January–February, 1994.

[6] See Corbett, C and Van Wassenhove, L, *op cit*.

[7] Kim, JS and Miller, JG, 'Challenges for building the value factory: key findings from the 1992 US Manufacturing Futures Survey', *Operations Management Review*, vol. 9, no. 3, 1993.

[8] See Hayes, R, 'Strategic Planning – Forward in Reverse?', *Harvard Business Review*, November-December, 1985.

[9] See Ferdows, K and De Meyer, A, 'Lasting Improvements in Manufacturing Performance. In Search of a New Theory', *Journal of Operations Management*, vol. 9, no. 2, 1990.

[10] For an example see Hamel, G and Prahalad, CK, 'The Core Competence of the Corporation', *Harvard Business Review*, May–June, 1990.

[11] Treacy, M and Wiersema, F, 'Customer Intimacy and Other Value Disciplines', *Harvard Business Review*, January–February, 1993.

[12] For the items in value discipline see Treacy, M and Wiersema, F, 'Customer Intimacy and other Value Disciplines', *Harvard Business Review*, January-February, 1993; and for the items in manufacturing capabilities, see Kim and Miller.

[13] The idea for accumulated capabilities was first presented by Ferdows, K and De Meyer, A, in 'Lasting improvements in manufacturing performance: in search of a new theory', *Journal of Operations Management*, vol. 9, no. 2, 1990.

[14] Presented at the 1993 Manufacturing Executives' Forum, Boston, USA.

[15] Kim, JS, 'Operations Strategy: Changing Roles for Manufacturing', *Boston University Manufacturing Roundtable Research Report*, 1993.

[16] Davenport, T, *Process Innovation: Re-engineering Work through Information Technology*, Harvard Business School Press, Boston, 1993.

LOGISTICS MANAGEMENT

Douglas Macbeth

Logistics or supply chain management once centred on the distribution of products to customers. Now, a broader perspective is commonly taken which encompasses the full flow of logistics and its strategic and financial importance within organizations.

Instead of being regarded simply as a cost, the growing emphasis is on harnessing the power of the logistics process as a whole.

The Greek root of the word logistics emphasizes computation, but contemporary interpretations of logistics have been founded on the military approach to the issue. The military has long recognized the importance of soundly managed logistics. Armies cannot fight unless supplied with the means of battle – human provisions, ammunition, equipment, fuel, maintenance capability, intelligence information and decision support. These elements require planning and integrated support so that the appropriate quantities are delivered to the right place when they are needed.

Translate the military images and words into a business and organizational context and the importance of the role of logistics to all human activity can be seen. We see, for example, with all too frequent regularity that the relief of major human disasters is to a high degree dependent on the logistical support able to be provided. Globally it has been said that there is no shortage of food to feed all the world's population, but it is in the wrong location at any given time, and the means of getting it to the point of need are either not in place are or demonstrably unable to operate effectively.

In the business world logistics has been, until recently, associated with the physical distribution of finished goods to customers. A more systemic view is now coming to the fore and, with it, a number of different terms for the activity. We can create different images to describe the staged progression of goods, from raw material through different value-adding, intermediate stages, until acceptance and use by a final consumer whose use of the item extends over a period of time before its disposal in some form (wholly or partly). One preferred image is of a chain of customers and suppliers in interaction, passing material along towards the final consumer, with information and payment passing in the opposite direction. Thus, the term *supply chain management* is often used. The importance of adding value (and not waste) at each stage is integral to the concept of the *value chain*. Other images are used to recognize the dynamics involved. For example, *value stream* or *supply pipeline* capture the very important images of flow.

The analogy of a chain allows other flights of imaginative co-existence of words. Forces of tension and compression are distributed along the chain; failure of the chain (and resultant customer dissatisfaction or calamity) can be the result of failure of any one link, far removed from any particular site of current focus. Each member in the chain (and the consumer at the end of it) is, therefore, dependent on all the others performing, and increased friction on any one of the links increases the likelihood of inefficient operation and potential failure.

With this background in mind, logistics (or supply chain) management can be defined as: 'The management of the two-way flows of materials and equipment, information, finance and people along the chain of customers and suppliers, from raw materials to final consumer.' The activity involves selecting appropriate partners in the chain, co-ordinating effective interaction and relationships to the best economic advantage, and to the advantage of customers, within an environmental and socio-political framework which emphasizes waste reduction.

Before looking at aspects of this definition in more detail, there has to be a recognition that different industrial, commercial and organizational activities create the need for variations of emphasis. Even within these broad categories different sectors or segments will require different aspects of the total product/service package mix to be varied. This often creates a dynamic and variable set of challenges for the supply chain system.

Also of importance is a recognition of the essential differences between manufacturing and service-based systems. The presence of a physical item for sale provides opportunities for production in advance of actual demand, and the storage of the item until a customer appears. Of course, this incurs costs (typically 25 per cent of the cost of the item), but allows the production stage to be separated from the customer contact stage – if this is desired.

In service-based systems the service is time-dependent. If a customer is not available, but the capacity is, then the capability to provide is lost for ever. In pure services, customers are in contact with the supplying system throughout the creation of the service. The customer also defines what the service is: for example, at the hairdressers or in a legal consultation.

The transportation service is one where the logistics element is very high and visible. Other systems require similarly effective logistics, but these are not so visible. A further differentiating factor between manufacturing and services is in the degree to which customer satisfaction in the services is very largely dependent on the person from the service-provider with whom the customer is in contact. The skills, personality profile and training of these customer-contact people then becomes very important.

Within the industrial sector, product differentiation is a key means of separating competitive offerings in the marketplace. At one extreme, pure commodities may well be indistinguishable except in terms of the price being asked. In such situations a supplier would be advised to examine the other parts of the product/service package to look for differentiating factors. If unit price is the sole basis for competition a 'pure' adversarial marketplace is likely to be the most economically efficient. As the service and interaction aspects increase then differentiation becomes more feasible and defensible.

Fast-moving consumer goods markets have long recognized the importance of logistics, especially in the distribution of goods through retail channels. Often, however, it is not recognized that the supply side to the manufacturer offers similar opportunities. Durables are rapidly following the same path with some products increasingly resembling fashion items and others behaving as if they were commodities. In capital equipment markets the switch to customer-order-driven processes is more complete and the timescale may be extended. However, the cost of failure can be enormous.

In each of these slightly different marketplaces, and often in sub-sections or segments within them, the critical factors for success will be slightly different. Some aspects will act as qualifiers to play the game – without a satisfactory level of performance an organization will simply not be considered. These qualifiers do not positively distinguish one organization from another. What is needed is the extra ingredient which wins the customer's order. Order-winners and qualifiers vary with time, competitors' actions and customer expectations, and it is these changes which provide the dynamic challenge for the supply chain.

As organizations evaluate how their markets are moving, they are constantly juggling with features of product innovation, customer supply and service, product manufacture, distribution and delivery, and perhaps after-sales service or financial packaging of the customer's purchase. Logistics has its role to play in supporting these qualifiers and order-winners, but the supply chain exerts its major leverage through certain of the processing elements of quality, very extensively through the performance against delivery requirements, and makes a significant contribution to cost control and reduction.

The financial figures behind this array of images and commercial imperatives are impressive. The Chartered Institute of Purchasing and Supply (CIPS) reports that supply chain expenditure in the UK in 1993 was of the order of £750 billion and reports some of its senior members having a responsibility for spending £6 million per day.

While the quantity of the sums managed is vast, quality is paramount. By thinking, designing and operating systems to prevent any possibility of poor quality occurring, it becomes possible both to satisfy current customer requirements and, by a process of continuous improvement, to exceed these to delight customers by providing either or both of enhanced value and reduced real cost. The Total Quality message must be heard, understood and comprehensively applied throughout the extended supply chain, for quality failures expose weak links very quickly.

Once quality is in control and performance is increasing, the next big target is to manage delivery.

Rather than extended supply chains, an interconnected network of chains might be a more realistic image. Each of the various actors involved in this complex web is interdependent. Each unit acting as a customer is totally dependent on input from its suppliers to allow it to process that input, add value and transmit (as a supplier) onwards downstream to the next customer. An alternative analogy is of a complex relay race where physical batons pass in one direction, information resources pass back and forth, while financial resources pass in one direction in one chain, but switch round to drive other chains from all of the intermediate points on the chain. The importance of the delivery promise is simply that the next stage of the relay requires the timely arrival from the previous stage.

Delivery reliability is the heartbeat which sends the commercial pulse round the network. Without delivery reliability the waste of inventory is built in, to buffer the stages. This is rather as if the baton was delivered, not from speeding hand-to-hand but had arrived in some variable-length queue to wait in turn until the next runner decided it was time to pick up a baton and move on. World records are not created in this way. The waste of inventory allows each stage to operate at its own speed. Looked at in this way, it could almost be regarded as efficient, but the overall race cannot be won. Logistics should be about focusing on the ultimate purpose of speeding the overall flow while minimizing such wastes.

Talking in this way might suggest that speed is always important – it is not, but reliability is. Speed can be important. For example, perishable goods, innovative products, life-saving drugs, all require fast responses. In these cases the speed order-winner might be the most important, but it is wrong to assume that all customers need to have the same response time. If the delivery performance is reliable then customers can confidently plan their activities to meet the requirements of their own customers. In capital projects, for example, the response or order lead time may be measured in months. In other cases (such as convenience food retail) a failure to hold stock means a lost sale – no response time is allowed. Inventory must be carried, but then the attention switches to how much inventory and how it should be managed and replenished.

New interpretations of costs

The common denominator in business is money. The logistics or supply chain activities provide mainly place and time utility which certainly support revenue generation but, perhaps more visibly, contribute massively to cost generation. If all one sees are the financial numbers, the tendency to control these costs and seek to reduce them is a strong one. There is, however, a fundamental principle that costs are not real of themselves. They are an expression of resource usage in performing other activities. It is these other activities and their balance of contribution to revenue or cost which should be controlled or improved.

Costs are only labels, surrogates for more difficult concepts or imprecise substitutes for proper data. Costs, therefore, cannot be controlled or reduced – activities must be modified. Costs are outcomes of doing other things. This sequence of cause and effect is not sufficiently understood and frequently not used in managerial controls and decision processes.

The whole nature of cost accounting is under examination as attempts are made to create an activity-based approach. In the meantime, existing and extremely dated approaches continue to send spurious signals to cause inappropriate action.

Knowledge of the true cost of activities is important to support decisions across all areas of business life. Decisions in the supply chain as to which activities to retain as core to one organization and which to buy from another are very much influenced by relative cost arguments. If these are constructed on dubious assumptions from the costing system, can we be sure the decision is valid?

One of the difficult costs to establish is the real cost of doing business with a supply partner and also the true costs of providing a given level of customer service.

From a logistics perspective, customer service can be broken into three stages: pre-transaction, transaction and post-transaction.

At the *pre-transaction* stage are the preparatory actions which can make the organization easy for the customer to deal with. This covers aspects of organization, policies and flexibility of response.

The *transaction* relates to the personal attention elements while the customer is in contact with the system, as well as aspects of item availability (for storable product). Some traditional service measures relate to the non-reliability of the delivery promises or the failure to carry sufficient stock to cover for all unpredictable demands. Such measures may be regarded as poor quality, but may be acceptable to customers if the recovery through special action response is swift.

Post-transaction can relate to spare-part provision, repair/service response time, product warranty and complaints procedure. Some of these approaches suggest the rather impersonal treatment of customers as aggregated numbers rather than valued partners and might, therefore, only be appropriate in situations where customers, and perhaps suppliers, have little to differentiate them one from the other. In similar vein, the transaction is a useful unit of analysis, but suggests a discrete, non-repeating process. Certainly that can be the case, but many situations are actually repeating transactions where the service history is as important as the single transaction. In fact, existing customers are often surprisingly tolerant of a supplier's repeated failings in certain areas and therefore recognize (often implicitly) that other aspects of the transaction are acceptable. Regular customers are extremely valuable since the effort and expense of finding, as opposed to retaining, customers is quoted as ten times greater.

A concept somewhat similar is customer profitability. This calculates the relative revenue benefit versus service cost of each customer and is followed by a reallocation of resources. This makes sense *if* trust can be placed in the cost information available and in the estimated values of future business volumes and frequency.

Often, customers and suppliers are not impersonal ciphers, and a strategy of selecting customers and suppliers to form a specific supply chain to mutual benefit removes the need for second guessing and wasteful buffering.

Some of this buffering takes the form of inventory stored or in transit between processing stages. In this sense inventory can substitute for either or both imperfect information or slow response. Conversely, faster information transmission avoids the need for the inventory buffer. It is in this area that EDI (Electronic Data Interchange) promises much. The ideal of speed of light communication of orders, response information, invoices, etc, has the potential to remove time, duplication and error-creating wastes from the chain and creates an image of extended networks of companies working in unison.

That ideal has not yet been reached. A number of organizations have established EDI links from customer to supplier but the spread and integration depends on finance, relative importance, multiple and conflicting demands and standards. Here again a coherent vision of the chain and a design appropriate for all in the chain would pay dividends. It is important, however, that EDI is not seen simply or solely as a technical solution. The organizational and people linkages are even more important and need just as careful design and management.

One area where communications and computer information systems come together is in the area of order processing and allocation of capacity. In manufacturing, forecast orders and/or firm customer orders can be used to create production plans based around Material Requirements Planning (MRP) logic. This expands the order information out into its constituent parts, accounts for any existing stocked or in-transit inventory and the time needed to respond, and produces lists for the production system to work to. MRP systems push orders into the system and if the forecasts are wrong (as they often are) the wrong things will be produced, creating the waste of extra inventory while failing to satisfy the real customer demand. Within the goods distribution part of the chain, Distribution Requirements Planning (DRP) works to the same logical plan to action the transportation of goods. Just-in-Time (JIT) systems work from the opposite end of the chain by not producing or supplying until a customer actually pulls items out of the end of the system. JIT works with much lower levels of inventory and while very simple in concept is more easily applied in managed demand situations.

The prime example of a logistical information system in a service industry is airline booking. Here we are approaching a true network where travel agents can interrogate, book and confirm travel arrangements across different airlines' systems, routes and pricing structures. Without such a system the difficulty of matching variable, and often short notice, demands with fixed capacity scheduled flights could only be done with massive fluctuations between poorly utilized aircraft and overbooked flights with exasperated would-be travellers.

In road transport, radio communications, satellite tracking, computerized route planning and real time modification makes it possible to react to new opportunities and problems with greater ease. Retail distribution is an area where the scheduling of deliveries to retail store unloading areas is timed and scheduled with great precision. In a similar vein, manufacturing plants working in JIT mode often need transportation companies to operate sophisticated 'bus routes' moving around their suppliers and delivering the parts to the assembly plant just as in the retail sector.

Another function performed by the inbound or outbound transportation logistics system is to add value through the aggregation or kitting of parts for the next stage or, alternatively, by breaking a shipping quantity down into smaller units for onwards transmission.

There is a whole related area of expertise around the relative cost benefit of unit load sizes for sea, land, rail, road and air transport. Each has associated time, speed, dimension, information and material handling issues. When the transportation extends across state or national boundaries, considerations of customs and excise, security and crime prevention, insurance, liability and safety all come into play.

These are all issues which need to be captured in the total acquisition cost of buying from a supplier, as should the quantification of the costs of any failure. With this perspective the unit price of the item becomes but one of a number of considerations in selecting sources of supply. Physical goods also need to be moved, stored and controlled. Here again the design of the physical logistics systems can extend over many technologies and more, or less, computer assistance. The complex logistical selection, transportation, packing and despatch of goods from a mail order operation requires sophisticated computer supported decision processes to handle the variety of demands on the system.

In the distribution part of the chain, issues of intermediate warehousing location need to be considered, and hub and spoke patterns emerge with bulk goods trunked between the hubs and smaller loads transported along the spokes in smaller vehicles. Variations on this theme can be seen in air freight, as well as road, and, of course, mixed mode operation is possible. These physical and systems concepts have to be integrated with decisions about customer service so that an optimal balance is reached.

A factor of increasing importance is environmental protection and the associated legislation. Many of the processes employed along the supply chain are energy intensive, destructive of resources and create waste by-products. In packaging, for example, two trends are notable. One is the increasingly unique presentation packs and the other is the back-to-basics functionality with no frills attached. In both cases the need to consider recyclable materials is growing. Some material handling items are capable of re-use but this raises the other logistical problem of returning the once-used item for re-use. In some cases customers can be enlisted to help – for example, the Body Shop has refillable cosmetic bottles. In some cases whole or high percentages of products are designed for recycling even if some progressive degradation has to happen. The logistics of the return trip and the recycling transformation adds to the overall complexity.

Transportation systems consume finite energy resources while expelling chemicals into the atmosphere; and power generation systems create environmental impacts over extended geographical and time dimensions. Vehicle emissions are but one problem of transportation systems but the vibration, noise and environmental displacement associated with air, road and rail transport systems generate more public concern in the developed world each year. The safe treatment and disposal of chemical effluent must also be carefully managed.

The management of logistics or supply chain management has, as we have seen, very many aspects and covers a wide area of activity. At the detailed, operational level there are major challenges to both enhance revenue generation through increased levels of customer satisfaction in potentially larger numbers, and to reduce real cost by removing the wastes of inefficiency and ineffectiveness from the supply chain.

There is a major strategic aspect to these issues. Elsewhere, partnership sourcing is discussed and examples given of the potential and actual benefits achievable through working in collaboration with partner organizations in the supply chain. This is not an easy process to establish, particularly if an organization's history, systems and people all have habitually reinforced adversarial behaviour. Making the change to collaborative, partnering approaches is, however, a change process which is also amenable to careful management. Choosing the right partner does become a highly strategic decision. Once established in a partnership sourcing approach it should take a major dislocation to break that link. This means that the chances for new organizations to break into the chain will be few. At the same time, the partners in the supply chain will need to be alert to extreme threats and opportunities (particularly associated with new technologies) so that what is currently a highly tuned, competitive chain does not atrophy to a cosy, unchallenging old pals act. Choosing a partner has much to do with deciding what is going to be the core of your organization – which you will develop continuously while non-core, peripheral activities can be obtained from partners.

Anticipating the demands of the future is difficult. There is a real danger that unless plans are made (perhaps in collaboration with the partner organizations) to monitor and perhaps exercise some of the out-sourced activities on an ongoing basis, organizations could be making good decisions today which might cost them dearly in the future. Such sensitivity to the learning potential in the supply chain (or elsewhere across the network) may well be the key capability of the successful organization of the future. In this, the role of logistics or supply chain managers to support or drive the building of strong, two-way inter-organizational links or partnering approaches may be very significant. The relative importance of this area of management may be greatly enhanced. This will not be brought about from a narrow functional perspective,; it demands a wider systemic and business viewpoint.

Douglas Macbeth is Professor of Supply Chain Management at the University of Glasgow and is sponsored by the Chartered Institute of Purchasing and Supply and the Supply Chain Management Group. He is the co-author of *Partnership Sourcing: An Integrated Supply Chain Approach* (1994).

Further Reading

Macbeth, DK, and Ferguson, N, *Partnership Sourcing: an Integrated Supply Chain Approach*, FT/Pitman, London, 1994.

Lamming, RD, *Beyond Partnership: Strategies for Innovation and Lean Supply*, Prentice-Hall, 1993.

Hines, P, *Creating World Class Suppliers: Unlocking Mutual Competitive Advantage*, FT/Pitman, London, 1994.

Contractor, F and Lorange, P, *Co-operative Strategies in International Business*, Lexington Books, Massachusetts, 1988.

Farmer, D and Van Amstel, P, *Effective Pipeline Management*, Gower, Aldershot, 1993.

Christopher, M, *Logistics and Supply Chain Management*, FT/Pitman, London, 1992.

Schonberger, RJ, *Building a Chain of Customers*, The Free Press, New York, 1990.

OUTSOURCING

Hilary Cropper

Businesses need to respond to increased competition, margin erosion and market turbulence. This requires every part of an organization to dramatically improve its contribution in terms of a higher value, more flexible service, at lower cost. This is particularly true for information systems services. Chief executives want services which react competitively to business needs rather than reflect the staffing costs and skills of the existing IT department.

Directors responsible for IT are responding proactively to this challenge, differentiating between activities which must remain in-house, those where outsourcing can offer long-term best value, and those ruled by lowest cost options. The second type of activity requires a strategic approach in selecting and building a long-term relationship if today's solution is to keep pace with future needs. Selecting today's best-of-class supplier is not enough. The intrinsic culture and behaviour of the parties must form a good fit to provide the openness, trust and flexibility for mutual benefit.

One of the most significant lessons for businesses in all sectors during the 1980s was how easy it is to become distracted and for an organization's activities to become unfocused. Many continue to pay the price for not focusing attention on the critical factors of their business and allowing peripheral activities to become a distraction. Companies in a wide range of industries dissipated the time and energy of top managers on activities of relatively minor importance. While appearing to have a clear business focus, many companies allowed themselves to acquire service operations ranging from their own local taxi firm to captive printing plants. The initial rationale for these acquisitions or developments of internal service departments was often perfectly sound in isolation. But the potential savings all too often remained potential and the expansion of employee numbers meant that the proportion of the workforce adding real value to the business was declining.

Outsourcing was an inevitable backlash against these excesses. Companies began to look at their service departments critically, attempting to establish just how necessary they were to the efficient functioning of the business. They analyzed the true costs of buying-in services against maintaining in-house functions. Government, spurred initially by the difficulty of privatizing businesses that came with a built-in burden of support functions, followed suit. Catering, security, publishing, office cleaning and other specialized activities were among the first to go. In recent years, however, organizations have begun to outsource major activities, such as information technology or human resources, which have a much greater impact on the viability and long-term performance of the business.

Evidence of the rapid growth in outsourcing is shown by the 1994 *Holway Report* into the financial performance of UK computing services companies. It calculated that the outsourcing revenues of the main computing services companies grew by 25 per cent in 1992 and by 33 per cent in 1993 to £665 million. The report estimates that by 1997 the annual outsourcing market in the UK in this area alone is likely to be worth more than £2 billion.[1]

In many cases, the drive to outsource has been the inability of the internal function to meet top management's expectations. In-house IT departments, in particular, have suffered from a lack of confidence in their capacity to deliver business solutions to meet rapid change, within the time frame and cost constraints required.

Because the functions being outsourced are so important to these businesses, managers need to have a clear understanding of the full implications of outsourcing. They also need effective processes with which to manage a very different type of relationship, both with in-house functions and with traditional suppliers.

A business' activities can be divided into four main categories:

Category	Reasons for outsourcing
Peripheral Providing no source of competitive advantage; not essential to the core purpose of the business.	Relatively easily sourced from suppliers; minimal risk.
Supportive An essential but not core activity – but failure in this area would cause serious damage to the business.	Managers' time and resources better spent on fundamental activities; expertise in maintaining the necessary level of excellence more readily available externally.
Strategic An actual or potential source of competitive advantage.	Enhanced or better value resources for strategic thinking and capability.
Core The primary activity(ies) of the business.	None.

The increasing intention of companies to become lean and highly focused has meant that the initial emphasis on outsourcing peripheral activities is gradually being matched by outsourcing at the supportive level. This is particularly true for IT. In addition, a number of leading companies are evaluating the potential for enhancing their strategic positioning by well-managed outsourcing.

The nature of the outsourcing that takes place with peripheral, supportive and strategic activities is necessarily different. In particular, they match relatively closely the three major types of business relationships: transactional, alliance and partnership.

Transactional relationships are simply a series of one-off deals between customer and supplier. Customer loyalty is based to a large extent on the performance of the last job. The benefits one partner derives may be much greater than those for the other. Price rather than value plays the major role in the contract decision.

Transactional relationships work best when the activity is insufficiently important to the business purpose to warrant the management time and effort to establish a close understanding and appreciation of each other's goals and culture. Put simply, it isn't worth the customer's time to develop a close relationship.

For most companies, transactional relationships are still significant in that they provide the bread and butter business of multiple one-off jobs. Good personal relationships between the customer and the supplier's sales and operations staff are essential to maintain the flow of orders.

Problems arise when companies apply the transactional approach to activities which are really supportive or strategic. Decisions to outsource to reduce costs may be sound in principle, but the savings made usually occur once only. The real benefit to an organization comes from continuous improvement. In a support area, for example, the transactional relationship is generally inadequate. From the customer's point of view, there is a danger of being trapped into an inflexible contract, which becomes increasingly irrelevant as requirements evolve, or too expensive to change, even though the business really needs a new arrangement.

Typical of the grey areas, where it is easy to underestimate the amount of relationship building required, is a contract to develop and install a major computer system over a period of years. At one level, this is just another transaction. However, the more important the system is to the customer organization, the greater the need for the supplier to understand and commit to the customer's business goals – and the more the relationship needs to assume aspects of an alliance.

Alliance relationships emphasize mutual but different benefits and tend to be longer term. At their most effective, they depend upon a level of collaboration that extends beyond the contractual to the spirit of the agreement.

The benefits of alliances are that they make it possible to explore the future together, to develop competitive advantage alongside a customer or supplier. They do, however, require a great deal of goodwill to make them work and the benefits must be fairly spread between the partners. Gary Hamel of London Business School has suggested that anyone entering into an alliance should start by designing how they are going to get out of it. As Hamel's comment suggests, alliances frequently have a limited and specific timespan, based on the achievement of mutual objectives. Experience suggests that a 'divorce clause' ensures a clean break between the two sides, either at the end of the project or if circumstances change drastically.

Alliances provide a useful and effective approach for managing the outsourcing of support services. But, success only comes if both parties are sufficiently open and honest about their ambitions for the relationship and are committed to making it work. In the IT industry, a common form of alliance is facilities management, where companies will subcontract responsibility for all their equipment and processing, to an external supplier. The supplier assumes responsibility both for delivery of the service and provision of hardware.

The benefits of this kind of arrangement are that the company avoids tying up capital in obsolete equipment and, therefore, has greater flexibility to respond to changes in technology and market opportunities. The company also gains access to a much wider range of expertise than it would normally be able to justify maintaining in-house.

This 'box-minding' type of facilities management has driven much of the outsourcing market growth to date. However, it is now becoming a commodity service as the benefits it offers decrease and the market matures into outsourcing higher value activities, such as application management and maintenance. These tend to require greater technical knowledge and skills.

In our experience this kind of outsourcing relationship can be highly rewarding if both parties use efficient alliance management as the starting point for a broader relationship, in which the supplier focuses on adding value to the activity. Two cases illustrate the way in which leading companies are now demanding higher quality relationships from potential suppliers.

BT made a strategic decision to sub-contract the enhancement, support and maintenance of several of its business systems off-site. It wanted to concentrate its IT resources on new developments, which would enhance the company's competitive edge. To define the relationship, BT negotiated stringent service level agreements that included seven-day round-the-clock support for some of the systems. In selecting a partner, the key factors were the ability to develop a close working relationship and a high degree of mutual trust. Once the relationship had become established, BT was sufficiently confident to extend the agreement to cover the development of new systems as well.

When Barclays Bank decided to outsource the support and maintenance of its Barclaycard IT systems, its selection process went significantly beyond price considerations. Barclays based its decision on an assessment of the long-term value potential partners would bring to the business and the quality of the business relationship it could expect. These were the issues it focused on when visiting existing customers of potential suppliers. Cost-effectiveness was regarded as an important, but less significant, factor.

Successful alliances frequently have the potential to evolve a valuable step further, into fully-fledged partnerships. Partnership relationships involve an integration of objectives between the two organizations; strong sharing of benefits; and a strong mutual respect for each other's culture and values. They are long-term, symbiotic relationships that depend upon a very high level of trust and commitment. They usually arise because the customer can identify clear strategic advantages from close collaboration with a specialist supplier. The dividing lines between customer and supplier become blurred and, to a large extent, irrelevant. There are significant benefits for both customer and supplier in achieving partnership collaboration.

With the offerings of the IT services business now becoming a commodity, increasing emphasis must now be placed on competing on quality rather than price alone. Inevitably, that means focusing on how to help customers achieve strategic objectives or add significant value to their activities. That, in turn, means that providers of IT services must move closer to customers, to understand what they need and to differentiate the solutions offered.

For some, including my own organization, this is a natural progression. We have worked over the years to develop partnerships with our own preferred suppliers (our associates), with our employees and with our providers of capital. It was inevitable that we would seek partnerships with customers, too.

Partnerships provide additional value to the supplier because they focus on long-term revenue and lasting customer relationships. They also allow the customer to concentrate resources on core skills for their business, while knowing that the important advances in the outsourced area will still be covered.

Two cases illustrate how partnership relationships can be built. In these examples, between FI GROUP and Whitbread and The Co-operative Bank, there has been a significant transfer of staff to FI and a clear understanding of how both parties will gain long-term added-value from the arrangement.

Whitbread was insistent from the start that choosing a partner was very different from choosing a commodity supplier. Having developed several of its successful retail businesses through strategic alliances, Whitbread realized the importance of partnerships as a core competence for both parties. It spent several months assessing the potential for developing a lasting, effective relationship with FI, taking time to understand our culture, and visiting customers. In particular, it was concerned to establish excellent working relationships with FI managers. Only after Whitbread was satisfied on these points did it negotiate a comprehensive and demanding contract that included detailed service levels, key performance indicators and penalties for non-compliance, termination clauses and procedures for revising services and prices. An important part of the agreement is a profit-sharing arrangement, which allows both parties to share the benefits of major cost or productivity gains.

At The Co-operative Bank, an important consideration in outsourcing systems development, enhancement and maintenance of IT systems was the well-being of the 128 staff currently employed. Both the Bank and FI consulted the staff about transfer into FI's employ, with the result that a union ballot was four to one in favour of the arrangement. The similarity of values towards people in the two companies was an important factor in the decision by both the Bank and the staff affected.

To ensure that the seven-year agreement delivered the benefits promised, FI and the Bank spent considerable time and effort devising an effective framework for the relationship and key performance indicators to measure success.

How to develop effective partnership relationships

Partnerships, by definition, require at least two parties, and a clear understanding of what each must bring to the relationship. From the customer's perspective, the process involves the following steps:

1. Be very clear about the kind of supplier partner you are seeking. After all, this is intended to be a long-term relationship with major impact on the business. To what extent must they reflect your organization's values? Do they have to be at the leading edge of technology or should they be very efficient followers? Most importantly, is this a supplier which already has a track record of effective and lasting alliances and partnerships?
2. Understand the implications of trusting a supplier with a critical activity for the business. Are you genuinely prepared to let go? Are you willing to share sensitive information and plans? What are you going to have to put into the relationship to develop trust and deep collaboration? How are you going to ensure that you still manage the strategic issues surrounding that activity?

   'Failure to think through the real implications of outsourcing can mean a loss of control of critical IT resources ... disrupting the organization and costing the business far more than retaining the IT function in-house,' warned one report on outsourcing IT.[2]
3. Consider carefully the impact upon employees. Outsourcing does not have to mean getting rid of people in the internal function. On the contrary, partnerships are greatly strengthened by retaining and developing wider opportunities for the original staff. Among the benefits is that these people already have extensive networks of relationships within the company. A supplier's willingness to take on existing staff is an indication of how seriously they will approach partnership development.
4. Negotiate a contract that allows a strong win-win outcome not just at the start but as the businesses evolve. Ensure that both parties share the benefits of cost or productivity improvements. Build in the flexibility to allow for continuous changes in requirement – indeed, make this the core of the agreement.
5. Develop structures for continuous review of the relationship – this ensures that continuous improvement applies at the relationship level as well as in the quality of service and in the technology provided.

How should a customer evaluate a potential partner? The answers provide a good starting point for defining the objectives a supplier should set for developing its own organization, to make it more attractive to potential partners. In particular, the partnership supplier must:

- Have a good track record, preferably in managing partnerships, but at the minimum in delivering consistently a high quality of service. A high proportion of long-term customers is a useful indicator and it is a wise precaution to talk to some of these about what it is like to work with the potential partner.

- Have a broad and constantly maintained expertise at or near the leading edge of the service provided. The customer partner has to have confidence the supplier will remain best in class over the long term. For an IT supplier, this means constantly upgrading the technical skills of staff, and deliberately seeking challenging assignments that will break new ground and stretch their capabilities.

  Useful clues here are the kind of assignments the supplier is currently tackling, the extent to which it invests in developing its people, the volume of best practice methodologies it can demonstrate, and whether its investment in new technology is planned and continuous or spasmodic and *ad hoc*.

- Be flexible enough to react swiftly and positively to the customer's changing business requirements. Is the partnership likely to enhance or get in the way of significant shifts in priority?

- Be able to develop a deep understanding of the goals of the customer (and often of the customer's customers). To what extent does the supplier already seek to understand its key customers?

- Identify and drive best practice. In delegating responsibility for a key activity, the customer is relying upon the supplier to identify opportunities to save money, to create or to reinforce strategic advantage. They must, in effect, be a source for constant innovation.

- Have a compatible culture and values. Being compatible does not mean being exactly the same, but there must be sufficient common ground to allow people from both organizations to work closely and comfortably together and to trust each other's motives.

  Maximizing the potential of employees is a key ingredient in this. They are the people who provide the IT solutions that are at the heart of our offering, and commitment to them can be essential in being able to deliver on the partnership promise.

Experience with genuine partnerships is still relatively narrow for most companies, so it is difficult to be definitive about the generic requirements for making sure the relationship lasts and fulfils its potential. Experience suggests that the cultural affinities must be more than skin deep; they must be real drivers of the way people think and behave. Similarly, mutual respect, a recognition of mutual dependence and an ethical approach to business are essential building blocks. If these are absent, the chances of achieving lasting partnerships are small.

Outsourcing – at both the alliance and the partnership levels – will continue as business pressures maintain the trend towards more focused, performance-oriented organizations. Partnership sourcing will gradually evolve from an arrangement initiated in most cases by suppliers into one initiated mainly by customers. The search for genuine, long-term value will increasingly define business relationships into the twenty-first century.

Hilary Cropper is chief executive of the FI GROUP PLC, a position she has held since 1987. Under her leadership the company's profits have improved sevenfold. In 1991

she led a successful workforce buy-out which has resulted in 40 per cent of the equity being held by the workforce. She has a BSc in mathematics and prior to joining FI spent 15 years with ICL where she became its most senior woman in management. She is currently a non-executive member of the Post Office Board and a member of the British Overseas Trade Board. She was a founder member of the City livery company, The Worshipful Company of Information Technologists, is a companion of the Institute of Management, a fellow of the British Computer Society and a fellow of the Royal Society of Arts.

References

[1] *1994 Holway Report*, Richard Holway, Farnham, 1994.
[2] *A Business Guide to Outsourcing IT*, Business Intelligence, 1994.

BUILDING CUSTOMER–SUPPLIER RELATIONSHIPS

Kenneth Cherrett

The traditional relationship between purchasers and suppliers has been adversarial, often built around a basic lack of trust and fuelled by insecurity. Increasingly, this conventional and limited relationship is being replaced by 'partnership sourcing' the process of building strong, long-lasting and mutually beneficial relationships between customers and suppliers.

Initially developed by large multinationals as a means of improving quality and lowering the total cost of purchases from smaller suppliers, partnership sourcing is now gaining wider use and growing in importance as a weapon in improving organizational competitiveness. To work, it clearly demands fundamental and far reaching changes in the way customer-supplier relationships are managed. For managers, partnership sourcing is a significant challenge in that it questions ingrained and habitual behaviour and overturns many long held attitudes.

Partnership sourcing, like so many other strikingly simple and effective ideas, is well-established in Japanese organizations where close relationships between customers and suppliers are unexceptional. Co-operation is standard practice. In the West there is growing awareness of the potential of partnership sourcing, though a degree of scepticism remains, suggesting that the traditional adversarial approach is too enshrined in Western business culture for it to be easily changed.

Partnership sourcing seeks to transform the relationship between customer and supplier to one of collaboration and co-operation. Partnership sourcing means rejecting the master/servant syndrome where the supplier is merely instructed what to supply and the customer told the price. The traditional lack of trust and insecurity is supplanted by commitment to a long-term relationship based on clear, mutually agreed objectives, so that the two parties work together as partners to strive for world class standards of quality, delivery and service.

This is not as great a cultural or practical leap as is sometimes imagined. Relationships between organizations and their customers have evolved considerably over recent decades. Companies are now more likely to target particular groups and appoint managers to manage their relationship with identified key customers. Account management is widespread and undoubtedly offers a more sensitive customer-oriented approach. Despite its benefits, account management does not create a relationship based on mutual collaboration and partnership.

Identifiable benefits of partnership sourcing

Growing Western interest in partnership sourcing is stimulated by a number of factors. At a macro level, the increased globalization of business is clearly a spur. By their very nature, global organizations are reliant on an array of local and global networks. They require flexible and supportive partners both inside and outside the organization if they are to work to their full effectiveness.

Another factor is growing realization that the purchasing power of organizations is often unrecognized or left unmanaged. Yet, it has been calculated that for most companies a one per cent cut in the money spent on purchasing has about the same effect on the bottom line as at least a 10 per cent increase in sales volume.

Partnership sourcing is not idealism or philanthropy. The aim is to secure the best possible commercial advantage, based on the principle that teamwork is better than combat. If the end-customer is to be best served, then the parties to a deal must work together – and both must win. Partnership sourcing works because both parties have an interest in each other's success.

Partnership sourcing can help organizations:

- achieve world-class quality standards;
- cut lead times and increase flexibility in response to market fluctuations;
- slash stock and administration costs and bolster cash flow;
- improve planning through long-term, information-rich relationships with customers and suppliers;
- reduce production down-time and boost capacity;
- cut time to market – the time-lag between identifying a market and introducing a new service or product to that market;
- innovate through better information from customers and suppliers, and gain access to the technical resources of both.

Range of partnership

One of the main attractions of partnership sourcing is that collaboration can cover a wide range of different activities – distribution, manufacturing, marketing, R&D, and so on. In practice, partnership sourcing tends to focus on five main areas:

1. **Finance:** Partnership sourcing can markedly reduce the factors that determine total cost. By working with suppliers, organizations can reduce stockholding and lead times. Just-in-time delivery (JIT) has become an integral part of everyday working life for much of industry. But to work effectively, JIT requires a partnership sourcing arrangement to be in place and operational before it is introduced. Partnership sourcing should also ensure that suppliers are paid on time; within a partnership sourcing agreement should be a clearly stated intention to pay on time, every time.

2. **Research and Development:** Partnership sourcing can provide both sides with better knowledge of their mutual R&D capabilities. This can allow them to draw on relevant expert knowledge from their partner organization where appropriate and to develop closer working relationships in areas of potential mutual benefit. From the perspective of the supplier, the longer term nature of partnership sourcing can provide the confidence to go ahead with projects which would otherwise be regarded as commercially risky for a small firm.

As an important adjunct to R&D collaboration the learning benefits of partnership sourcing are also increasingly being recognized. Working with other organizations can offer valuable insights into how a particular company works, how it approaches problems and issues, and deals with external organizations.

3. **Design:** Many partnership sourcing relationships have encouraged suppliers to come up with design proposals which are innovative or which represent cost advantages over in-house design. Manufacturers, particularly in the automotive industry, have liaised with component manufacturers at an early stage to ensure that design is taken into consideration in good time. Some European-based Japanese car plants have demonstrated how quickly they can develop a new model, using these techniques, compared with their traditional competitors.

4. **Production:** Partnership sourcing allows companies to redraw the boundaries between their responsibilities for production, allowing improvements in efficiency and supply chain management. Medium- or long-term agreements give suppliers the confidence to make long term plans for capital expenditure on factory premises, in the knowledge that a major contract is secure provided they can meet their part of the bargain.

5. **Quality:** Greater trust in a limited number of suppliers makes quality assurance essential. Within the relationships provided by partnership sourcing, suppliers are provided with feed-back about quality problems and assisted to trace and cure the causes. Quality assurance standards, such as the European standard ISO 9000, have become almost a pre-requisite in manufacturing industry and are also gaining ground within the best service-based companies. In fact many purchasers now insist that their suppliers are at least working towards attaining a quality standard. For partnerships to develop satisfactorily with benefits accruing to purchaser and supplier, a quality ethos within both partner companies is absolutely vital.

Partnership sourcing in practice

Partnership sourcing at the computer company ICL brings all of the above elements into play. The company began to develop its relationships with suppliers in 1990. ICL found that out of 6,500 suppliers, it did 70 per cent of its business with a mere 200. As a result, early in 1991, it launched a 'vendor accreditation programme' to cement long-term relationships with key suppliers.

The programme's main elements are straightforward. Accredited suppliers must conform to high standards of quality and submit to frequent performance evaluations. Suppliers are also expected to hook into ICL's electronic trading system which speeds up ordering and, increasingly, delivers components directly to production lines. From being anonymous suppliers, companies are now labelled 'strategic partners' and ICL's relationship with them is managed by newly created vendor managers. It is anticipated that, in the future, the partners will play a greater part in product development and, as less qualified suppliers disappear, they are likely to receive more of ICL's business.

ICL executives say quantifying the benefits of partnership sourcing has been difficult. Overall quality improvements have cut spending by £160 million during the past five years, in part because better quality from suppliers has enabled the company to eliminate costly inspection. As excess suppliers are dropped, ICL aims to reduce the management time taken up with overseeing those that remain.

One of ICL's suppliers, Texas Instruments (TI) was an early convert to the concept of partnership sourcing. In 1988 TI identified a need to establish strategic partnerships with its principle customers and developed a programme called 'Total Cost of Ownership'. It recognizes that only by working together in all aspects of business can the breakthrough needed for true differentiation be achieved.

Before approaching customers, TI made sure that everyone within its own organization understood what it was doing and the commercial rationale behind it. Managers and staff were given training on how it would affect them as well as what was expected from them. Next, TI ensured it had a process for working with customers: it developed tools to help identify priority cost areas and measure the effect of the partnership.

It began with a few strategic customers of which ICL was one. These customers were chosen against the following criteria:

- strategic value/size of opportunity
- adoption and awareness of total quality principles
- willingness to change
- ability to determine improvement priorities

The TI/ICL partnership now extends to purchasing, design, testing and marketing. Among its cost saving improvements are:

- the elimination of incoming inspection for TI parts
- lower inventory levels
- potential for automated handling of supplier receipts using bar-code labelling
- qualification to ICL requirements handled by TI
- automated order entry through Electronic Data Interchange

In the late 1980s British Airways (BA) identified 300 small companies whose products were strategically important but of relatively low value. As a result it helped two distributors – one specializing in aircraft bearings, the other in aircraft fastenings – to set up local distribution centres to provide parts for the airline. The idea was to let each party concentrate on its strengths, thereby becoming increasingly able to compete effectively. The fastener supplier with its expertise in low-cost high-volume business was able to offer an attractive package whereby it would act as a purchasing agent for this material. This released BA's purchasing and other personnel from the administrative function to more beneficial value-adding tasks.

In practice, BA's agreement with suppliers involved 'open book' contracts. These required suppliers to stock a comprehensive range of material which BA could call off via an electronic data interchange process without its buyer being involved. The supplier would perform part of the receipting process directly onto the BA computer and prepare goods for daily collection. A number of specific and significant benefits accrued for BA:

- lower costs
- reduced lead times and inventory holdings
- a daily 'just in time' service with guaranteed quality
- reduced administration costs by contracting for a service rather than buying individual items

Confidence gained in the relationship has led to more business and closer relationships. One example of this related to BA's continuing programme of supplier rationalization.

For the suppliers these partnership arrangements deliver specific benefits:

- a longer term deal
- lowered risk (certainty of long term business)
- expanded level of business

One BA supplier says:

> The typical bid-buy approach does not provide a way for customers to evaluate performance and reduce problem areas and will often result in an adversarial relationship between the customer and supplier. The idea of partnership is to set up a system between a customer and supplier which improves the flow of goods to the customer for the mutual benefit of both.

Partnership sourcing can also involve major organizations working closer together to develop a strategically beneficial relationship. In the late 1980s Midland Bank began a programme to move document processing away from branches to a number of purpose-built centres. This in turn encouraged the bank, which used a number of carriers, to extend its strategic supplier programme by introducing the concept to security carrier, Securicor.

The strategic supplier programme had been operating successfully at Midland for a number of years, but chiefly in the Information Technology supplier arena. Suppliers were selected for that programme on the basis of:

- their strategic importance to the bank
- Midland's high dependency on that supplier's product or services
- the value of the business placed with those organizations

Securicor fulfilled these criteria and managers from both organizations now meet every month to discuss operational issues. These meetings led to the joint development of Service Level Agreements (SLAs) covering a range of activities. Both partners had to adopt a more structured approach to management information to enable the SLAs to be effectively monitored. Executive management reviews were set up twice a year and a strategic review at director level was arranged annually. These reviews go beyond day-to-day operational and contractual issues and give both organizations the opportunity, not only to discuss current business, but also to outline future plans. Each partner can adapt and co-ordinate to allow advantage to be gained by the other's development. As a result of this proactive approach by both parties, Securicor's business with Midland has grown – in areas such as office cleaning, delivery of stationery, vehicle maintenance and archival storage, not normally associated with Securicor.

A strategic co-ordinator was appointed by Securicor to co-ordinate the whole span of its involvement with Midland, in effect giving a single point of contact to Midland. Brainstorming sessions were set up, an initiative not new to either organization, but novel in that it involved people from both companies. It worked. For instance, routes were rationalized, giving benefits to both companies. New invoicing procedures cut Midland's administration and made sure Securicor was paid on time – a good example of continuous improvement working outside manufacturing.

The partnership has successfully developed beyond the immediate business relationship. Midland has introduced Securicor to a number of its other suppliers of goods and services, some of which now use Securicor's services.

The challenge of change

Research conducted in March 1993 by Bath University shows that the concept of partnership sourcing is gaining ground. Virtually all of the 350 companies polled had heard of partnership sourcing compared with 90 per cent in 1992 and 71 per cent in 1991. Not surprisingly there was a significant gap between awareness and implementation and 56 per cent of purchasers and 38 per cent of suppliers were implementing either in part or in full. However, it is recognized that full implementation is not always a desired objective for either purchasers or suppliers. Most are keen to protect their key or core customers/suppliers and strategic partnerships are formed within this group. Therefore partial implementation tends to be common.

In practice, partnership sourcing tackles some fundamental conceptions and provides a number of significant challenges:

- **Sensitivity of information** – managers and organizations are unused to sharing information and have to remain carefully selective about which figures, if any, they share with partners.
- **No excuses for poor performance** – by its very nature partnership sourcing means that the buck can no longer be blithely passed on to suppliers. Both sides are fully accountable.
- **Organizational culture** – if an organization does not have an internal partnership culture it is difficult to create one externally
- **Communication** – constant communication is vital and, again, not usually something widely practised.
- **Power differences** – both sides of a particular partnership are unlikely to be equal. This has to be accepted and worked upon through regular mutual evaluation.
- **Risk awareness** – companies that commit themselves to a single source of supply run the risk that the supplier could be hit by a strike or go bust or attempt to push up prices. Similarly suppliers that become over-dependent on one large customer, or who reveal too much about the details of their business, might also be making themselves vulnerable.
- **Multi-cultural issues** – increasingly partnerships are being made which are international in nature and practice. Cultural obstacles tend to slow down the rate at which a close relationship can be built. In one Japanese-American partnership the first five years were negated by cultural obstacles – it has now been established for 20 years.

There is an increasing number of similar international examples of companies overcoming cultural barriers to working more closely together. With continuing globalization, the body of evidence supporting the practice of partnership sourcing is likely to grow.

Kenneth Cherrett is director general of Partnership Sourcing, a non-profit-making organization established by the Confederation of British Industry and Department of Trade and Industry in 1990. Prior to taking this position, he held a number of senior appointments with TSB Group plc, the most recent as director of corporate relations.

RESEARCH AND DEVELOPMENT AS A BUSINESS RESOURCE

Michael Kenward

Ten years ago, few companies showed much detailed interest in the fate of their investment in research and development. Now, when research managers get together from different companies, as much as anything talk concentrates on *how* they approach R&D rather than *what* they do.

The historic view of the R&D function was that it indulged in strange activities that no one else in the company could comprehend. The notion was that R&D would, by some mystical process, deliver the products and technologies that the company needed to progress. It was almost as if the concepts of *management* and *R&D* were alien. You couldn't manage R&D. It was a random process.

Just as companies have looked long and hard at the productivity of their sales and marketing activities, for example, they now want to know that their R&D laboratories are delivering the goods. They increasingly see R&D as an activity that can succumb to the same managerial scrutiny as more mainstream activities.

R&D was once thought to be an arcane domain inhabited by people in white coats. But, in the harsh commercial light of the 1990s, it has to justify its existence. Researchers have to listen to what marketing people say before embarking on new projects. Inspiration alone is no longer sufficient. Alternatively, companies increasingly expect their marketing experts to know what is going on in R&D so that they can contribute to the development process, bringing back to R&D news from customers.

The rise of R&D management as an issue in the UK coincided with the rebirth of the notion that manufacturing continues to have a role to play. R&D management has also been under the microscope in the US, where there was never any suggestion that the service sector would come to dominate the economy. There other factors have played a role. For example, it has become increasingly obvious that a large R&D budget does not guarantee a company the ability to dictate the technological agenda in industry. As Gary Hamel and CK Pralahad ask in their book *Competing for the Future*: 'Where is the evidence that Philips's research budget, which in many years has been substantially larger than that of Sony, has produced a proportionately higher number of new product winners?'

IBM is another example of the lack of linkage between R&D and business success. The company's laboratories might win Nobel prizes – two years in succession – but can they help to win customers? IBM spent nearly $4.5 billion on

R&D in 1993, 13 per cent less than in the previous year, and significantly lower than the $620 million it reached in 1990. Between 1992 and 1993 the company fell from fourth to sixth position in the international league table of corporate R&D spending. The year was also a financial disaster for IBM as a whole, with losses around $10 billion. The company subjected research to the same 're-engineering' as other business activities.

Many companies shut down central R&D facilities during the 1970s and 1980s. In the same way that many companies deliberately reduced the size of the corporate centre in favour of local management, within operating divisions, a significant number of companies devolved R&D to their divisions. At one time it looked as if IBM might go the down the same road. IBM is now a rare animal, with not just one corporate R&D centre, but three. The company has two large establishments in the US, at Yorktown Heights in New York State, and Almaden in California, and a third near Zurich in Switzerland. It was the Zurich laboratory that collected two successive Nobel prizes for scientific achievements.

IBM's response to its predicament was to pull out of research areas that had little or nothing to do with its role as a supplier of computers and computer services. For example, it withdrew from the frontiers of science and threw its resources into the development of software.

The changes went beyond IBM's R&D portfolio. This had not, in any case, been the main problem. IBM was an organizational nightmare. The R&D teams might come up with world shattering ideas – Yorktown Heights was an early player in ink-jet printing, a technology that, in the hands of the Japanese company Canon, has revolutionized the market for cheap printers for the computer market – only to have them rejected by the manufacturing divisions. Even when projects went ahead, they often did so at a snail-like pace.

IBM not only pushed its R&D staff into closer proximity to others in the company, it lowered the barriers between its own researchers and people from other companies. The R&D operation even won the right to launch its own products, should ideas land on deaf ears elsewhere in the company.

Rethinking the R&D function has not been limited to companies facing extinction. Even the pharmaceuticals sector went through a bout of navel gazing, as the pressure on prices, and the threat of health-care reform in the US, slowed the apparently ceaseless rise of the profits spiral.

Before companies could begin to manage their R&D, they had to know what was going on within their laboratories. A major problem facing R&D managers is the difficulty of measuring the productivity of R&D. How does company A compare its innovativeness with that of company B?

The first tool for comparison is to measure R&D spending and to compare it with that of the competition. It is only in the past five years that the UK has had access to the simple numbers of corporate R&D spending. Since 1991, the Department of Trade and Industry has sponsored the Scottish research company, Company Reporting, to produce a league table of company spending, the UK R&D Scoreboard. This now lists all publicly quoted companies that itemise R&D in their company accounts.

The *UK R&D Scoreboard* also details R&D spending by the top 200 companies worldwide. This showed that during 1993 British companies increased their R&D spending at a faster rate than their competitors in the US and Japan. But that came after years of slower growth. In any case, growth rates are only one yardstick. The R&D scoreboard also looks at research spending alongside company profits, sales and dividends.

By many measures, British companies fare badly against foreign competition. For example, 13 British companies featured in the international top 200. Their investment of nearly £4.8 billion on R&D represented just 2.3 per cent of their sales, 29 per cent of profits, and 74 per cent of dividends. By contrast, there were 11 German companies in the top 200. Their R&D spend, £12 billion in all, was 6.8 per cent of sales. R&D was 4.8 times the companies' profits and more than 9 times dividends.

While these indicators tell us something about the relative importance of R&D to companies in the two countries, these crude numbers should necessarily carry a health warning. Germany and the UK are different countries, with different institutions. Financing differs in Germany and the UK, for example. To try to unravel the true value of R&D, there have been attempts to devise more useful comparisons for R&D spending and its effectiveness. One such attempt compared a company's R&D spending with its 'value added', the value of a company's sales minus the cost of its purchases of materials and services.

If there are arguments about the meaning of figures that appear in corporate accounts, it is far more controversial to talk of such indicators as value added. It is even harder to compare companies on an international basis. To bring some semblance of order to this subject, the OECD has, for the past 30 years, promulgated what has come to be called the Frascati Manual, more correctly known as 'Proposed standard practice for surveys of research and experimental development'.

The OECD published the latest revision of this document in the middle of 1994. In the decade since the previous edition, there had been significant changes in the way in which companies conducted their R&D. For example, the 'globalization' of R&D continues apace. Companies are now more happy to conduct R&D where expertise, and costs, make it attractive to do so. A number of companies have been attracted to the former Soviet Union, where there is considerable expertise in software development.

The new Frascati manual set out to deal with the globalization of R&D. It also recommends the use of more detailed categories and provides more precise instructions for identifying government support for R&D. The manual also offers guidelines on the treatment of expenditure on software development, an increasingly important issue as software becomes a more important ingredient of many products.

The OECD is also working on a manual on 'the use of patents as science and technology indicators'. These manuals do not in themselves tell us anything about R&D spending, and certainly not its effectiveness. However, they do help to ensure the comparability of data collected by different organizations. For example, if companies work to the same definitions, it is much easier for them to benchmark their R&D productivity.

The pharmaceuticals industry has done more than many to scrutinize its R&D spending. Given the extent of that spending, this is not surprising. The UK R&D Scoreboard showed that the pharmaceuticals sector spent just over £2.2 billion in 1993, approaching a third of the country's total industrial R&D spend of £7 billion. Glaxo was the UK's biggest investor in R&D, at £739 million, more than a tenth the total for corporate Britain as a whole. (Of course, not all of this money was spent in the UK.) Four of the ten biggest R&D spenders were pharmaceuticals companies. The companies in this sector also spend far more than those in other industries on R&D as a percentage of sales and profits.

Facing the chill wind of price restraint, and the threat of a complete overhaul of the US health care system, many of the larger drugs companies took a long and hard look at their R&D spending, and at the results that it delivered. One objective of this analysis was to assess projects at an early stage to see if it made commercial sense to continue them, or to terminate the activity. R&D projects all too easily develop a life of their own, and continue long beyond the stage when they can hope to repay costs, let alone deliver profits.

Costs escalate rapidly as projects leave research and enter development. It clearly makes sense to apply hard business criteria as early as possible. Zeneca, the pharmaceuticals 'spinout' from ICI, takes a rigorous approach to its analysis of R&D. Zeneca's analysis of its R&D portfolio hinges on calculating the net present value of products under development, tempered with an analysis of the likelihood of success. It is relatively easy to look at the whole portfolio at an executive level. 'You can plot risk and reward very simply,' says Peter Doyle, an executive director of Zeneca Group and the company's R&D director. 'The process that Zeneca goes through brings together many different functions within the company. It is a good way of having a dialogue between R&D people and marketing people on an on-going basis,' says Doyle.

The Wellcome Foundation is another drugs giant that has closely scrutinized its R&D performance. Until recently wholly owned by a research charity, the Wellcome Trust, business issues had long taken a back seat to scientific excellence at the Wellcome Foundation. This couldn't continue in the commercial world, let alone one where a blockbuster drug is seen as an automatic licence to make money. So Wellcome put its R&D portfolio under the microscope.

Wellcome first arrived at a target list of therapeutic areas, diseases that it wanted to treat, after a detailed assessment of its current business and its R&D portfolio. This showed that the company had a lot of projects at both early and late stages of development. This is not the ideal pattern. There should be more 'early stage' projects, with a gradual winnowing out of those that are less likely to contribute significantly to the company's business. It made it difficult for the company to fund everything in the development pipeline. Glaxo, by contrast, had been much more hard nosed about getting rid of projects.

Rather than hacking away at its R&D portfolio with a chainsaw, Wellcome developed a strategy to assess projects, new and existing. Weeding out projects would allow the company to dedicate sufficient resources to projects at a later stage. It also allows Wellcome to target products with potential.

Corporate strategy must come before R&D policy. Underlying everything is Wellcome's desire to refine its product portfolio. The aim is to build a critical mass of products in priority customer segments and disease areas. Wellcome's strategy was to look at the diseases treated by its 'prescriber customers', the people in the medical profession who provide most of its business, and to find more products that it could offer to these specialists. For example, a major moneyspinner for Wellcome is the AIDS drug Retrovir. The very nature of AIDS, which attacks the body's immune system and hence its ability to fight off other infections, leads to a complex mixture of medical conditions. The doctors who prescribe Retrovir also have to treat fungal infections, for example. Wellcome wants its sales force to be able to go into AIDS specialists with a raft of appropriate products.

The company's parallel review of its product portfolio and R&D strategy started as a way of assessing opportunities to establish 'strategic alliances'. Like many other companies in the pharmaceuticals sector, Wellcome sees collaboration with other companies as a way of gaining access to new technology, particularly in the growing field of biotechnology. This more biological approach to drug discovery and development has posed something of a problem for the drugs majors, with their emphasis on chemical approaches to therapy. Biotechnology is characterized by a host of small, R&D-oriented companies pioneering novel treatments. If an opportunity comes along to develop a new product, Wellcome looks at how the product would fit into its strategy to create a coherent product portfolio.

Wellcome and other drugs companies also take an increasingly hard look at the potential size of markets that might arise from R&D projects. No matter how startling the science, if it will not deliver a big enough turnover, the R&D effort will go no further.

Thus Wellcome now has a detailed template against which it can test an R&D project. Will it add to its product portfolio in the company's target areas? Will it deliver a high enough turnover?

The fact that a potential product does not offer a big enough market does not necessarily spell its demise. A number of larger pharmaceuticals companies have shown themselves to be increasingly open to offers from smaller companies that can turn a profit from lesser markets. One such company, Medeva, has quickly established itself on the basis of acquired technology. The company has no plans to emulate the R&D intensity of the drugs majors. Formed in 1990, Medeva has rapidly built up its turnover to more than £200 million a year on the back of compounds licensed from a number of the major drugs companies.

Focusing R&D on a company's business objectives is just one way in which companies are seeking to manage their R&D operations and to improve their productivity. Corporate alliances are also among the tools they are using to leverage their R&D spending. The complexity of technology is one factor pushing companies in this direction. As Dr Michael Elves of Glaxo has put it: 'The range of expertise and technical resources required for success in drug discovery is now so wide that no one organization, be it pharmaceutical, biotechnology company or academic institution, can expect to be self-sufficient.'

The growth of contract research is another outcome of the realization that companies cannot hope to breed all of their own technology. For example, the Association of Independent Research & Technology Organizations (AIRTO) represents around 30 contract research bodies. AIRTO's members employ 7,000 people and have an annual turnover in excess of £320 million.

Some of AIRTO's members are finding increasing demand for helping companies to manage their R&D portfolios. Paul Auton, the current chairman of AIRTO and managing director of Cambridge Consultants Limited, a subsidiary of Arthur D Little, estimates that consultancy work now accounts for around 20 per cent of his company's business.

Thus there are several tools and techniques that companies are using to enhance the productivity of their R&D operations. In the final analysis, the key decision is to treat research just like any other business process. As Hamel and Prahalad say in *Competing for the Future*, an important factor is 'the ability to successfully integrate diverse functional skills – R&D, production, marketing, and sales – to produce a successful product'. The first step is to remove the mystery behind R&D. This may be easier said than done, for it means not just that researchers have to understand the rest of the business process, but also that others in a company have to begin to understand the processes of technical innovation, perhaps even the technologies themselves.

Michael Kenward OBE, science writer and editorial consultant, has written on R&D management for various publications, including *Director* magazine, and *Professional Engineering*.

Further Reading

Hamel, Gary and Pralahad, CK, *Competing for the Future,* HBS Press, Boston, 1994.

MANAGING MARKETING

Robert Smith

The 1980s saw the apotheosis of marketing. Its standing – and its budgets – rose. But, the 1990s have seen a more realistic assessment of the role of marketing in the organization. The emphasis is now on measuring the effectiveness of marketing activities and integrating marketing into the organization as a whole, rather than allowing it to act in isolation.

It was Peter Drucker, the American management guru, who said: 'Business has only two basic functions – marketing and innovation.' As the function that traditionally identifies and meets the needs of customers, marketing has typically had budgets as high as its profile.

Marketing has changed its emphasis and priorities with the times, but certain constants have remained:

- in many organizations marketing is the quickest route to the top;
- marketers can and should be the innovators and free thinkers in organizations, and, as such, beyond normal controls and measures;
- marketers really do lead organizations.

Yet all this is changing. Recent research by Coopers & Lybrand shows that the prestige of marketing is now on the wane. In the extreme, it is believed that the skills required of the contemporary marketing manager involve cutting costs, general administration, progress-chasing and the provision of information to decision makers. The personal qualities required include lack of ambition, subservience and a liking for routine.

Ill-defined in its remit, over-indulged in its spending and lacking in relevant performance measures, marketing is failing to fulfil its original role, or is a function failing to live up to its pretentions. So what has happened?

The sea change started early in the 1980s when retail, leisure and financial services companies – indeed, even government agencies – built marketing departments as big as those in the Fast Moving Consumer Goods (FMCG) sector, just as the balance of power in FMCG swung decisively to the retailers. Having established their marketing departments, they did what they did best: pursued non-existent segments which became fragments, talked ambitiously about lifestyle marketing and increased 'brand support activity' finding ever more imaginative ways of concealing discounts.

The recession of the late 1980s and early 1990s provided further impetus to these trends. In the tough economic climate, 'lifestyle' marketing failed to sustain profitability and companies focused on harder, more accountable disciplines, such as key account management.

Marketing departments responded almost universally, with increased promotional discounts and, in some cases, greater advertising, in an effort to raise sales. But many such short-term measures have proved to have been misguided – products were discounted too often or too heavily, invariably causing irreparable damage to the brand. Without appropriate performance measures, marketing departments often acted in ways that were counter-productive to the business as a whole.

Other conditions were compounding their difficulties. Global competition was on the rise and customer requirements were rapidly changing. As product life cycles continued to shorten, the competitive advantage went to those companies which strove to be at the forefront of new product and service development through a profound understanding of their customers' needs. The traditional role of marketing, as the interface between the company and its customers, became even more crucial. Unfortunately, this coincided precisely with the point when many marketing departments were forced to capitulate to deep cost reductions – largely, though not totally, a situation brought about through their own making.

As the marketing function failed to respond to, and to shape, a changing and infinitely more complex environment, there was a further turning of the screw. Businesses were increasingly focusing on cross-functional disciplines and approaches to improve performance – such as Total Quality Management, business process re-engineering and Just-In-Time. Cross-functional working became the way in which businesses were managed. Marketing, aloof and elitist, was on the outside looking in.

A recent survey of 100 blue-chip organizations, by Coopers & Lybrand, provides a snapshot of the status and role of the marketing function in the mid-1990s. For all those involved in marketing, it makes depressing reading.

The picture emerged of a function which is:

- anachronistic, living on past glories and the hype of the 1980s;
- marginalized from other departments and from the key cost and performance drivers of the business;
- vulnerable in that it lack roles which create value and profit;
- poorly positioned for the future, stuck with a narrow and increasingly irrelevant skill base.

One of the study's main findings, and a prime cause of the malaise marketing finds itself in, stems from uncertainty about the scope of the marketing department's activities. A total of 22 per cent of respondents said that marketing had complete or primary responsibility for negotiating with suppliers, while 30 per cent said it had none. Similarly, 29 per cent gave marketing complete or main responsibility for setting and monitoring customer service standards although 24 per cent gave it none. There was a general consensus that marketing departments are responsible for certain traditional functions such as advertising, but substantial disagreement over the extent of their involvement with customers.

Ominously, the study also showed a significant gap between the perceptions of marketing directors and their managing directors. Marketing directors consistently overestimated the importance of their contribution to strategic planning, while managing directors consistently overestimated the degree of responsibility which marketing departments really bear for customer service and sales.

The evidence suggests that in expanding their role, marketing departments have moved away from their traditional focus and have assumed responsibility for activities that would be better delegated to other functions or even dispensed with altogether. They are responsible for the development of advertising, but not for the strategy on which it is based. They are not responsible for the generation of sales revenues, although they are supposed to support this process. In short, marketing is not responsible for any outputs. Distanced from the key cost and performance drivers for the business and rose-tinted in its view of the strategic contribution it makes, marketing is at risk from being marginalized.

The situation has been exacerbated by the extent to which marketing functions fail to reflect marketing as a process. Although the marketing department is usually responsible for identifying the market and creating customer profiles, it is the sales department which handles the process of generating new and repeat orders; the accounts department controls invoicing and payment; while the engineering and maintenance department deals with complaints, returned products, repairs and so forth.

Clearly, the situation as described above cannot and will not be allowed to continue. A function which traditionally has been a pivot to the success of many companies is simply failing to function. A function, which in many companies is the single largest budget holder has few means of justifying what it spends, or how much. The marketing function is fragile and vulnerable. Change, however laudable its intentions, risks destroying it, if it is not guided by three overriding principles.

First, marketing's 'problems' are not related to the discipline *per se*. Its classical role – as the interface between a company and its customers – is as relevant today as it has ever been. Indeed, in increasingly complex and fragmented marketplaces, its relevance is potentially greater than it has ever been. The challenge is to make sure its functions fulfil its classical role; the challenge is not to become overly intellectual or esoteric over what that role should be.

Second, for good and bad reasons, marketing is different from other disciplines. It relies heavily on intuition rather than fact, to achieve its ends. Many of its 'responsibilities' are discretionary. Many of the tasks it undertakes on behalf of the organization are managed through influences, not authority. There is little data on marketing effectiveness. These are merely random examples of how marketing is different – the multiplicity of differences mean that any standard application of business process re-engineering to the marketing function will not begin to do justice to the subtleties of how marketing 'works'.

Third, marketing departments cannot be changed prescriptively by applying a best-practice template. A striking feature of marketing has been the extent to which it has been influenced and then dominated by ideal models. These were then fitted through force, usually inappropriately, to diverse marketplaces. So, change needs to be organization-specific, and driven by customer perceptions, not existing organizational norms, and certainly not by a mythical concept of best practice.

Such changes in the way marketing is organized and managed can be achieved. Though the nature of these changes is broad-ranging, all should aim exclusively at three simple objectives:

First, marketing must be made more efficient. Given the current typical lack of true control, there is usually scope to minimize the internal and external costs attributed to marketing. There is scope to cut costs substantially through eliminating duplicated processes and examining flows of activity. There is also room for more closely defined transaction times, so that it is clear who has responsibility for which tasks.

Second, the quality of marketing must increase. The consequential costs of ineffective marketing, such as opportunities lost through a misconceived product launch, should be minimized.

Third, the adaptability of marketing must increase. The function must become more responsive to customer, competitor and market change. It must become quicker at introducing new products and more adept at recognizing when old products should be phased out.

So, what must the marketing department become if it is to survive the current crisis? The answer is not prescriptive, but there will be a number of tell-tale indicators.

First and foremost, it will be clear who manages the customer. The process of influencing the customer often becomes fragmented, with many of the activities that impinge on customers outside the control of the marketing department. But, if companies are to make the most of their marketing, these activities must be harmonized. They must either be re-engineered so that every point of contact with customers falls within the scope of the marketing department or, where a task is better completed by another function, responsibility must be transferred.

The new marketing function must be able to show a massive increase in productivity, and reduction in cost base compared with current levels. To demonstrate this, there will also need to be a classification of both group and personal objectives and performance measures.

It will be organized to meet marketplace requirements, rather than fitting in with organizational charts. In some markets, this might be best achieved through the creation of project-centred marketing departments. In others, it might be best achieved through the creation of a planning secretariat reporting at board level, and subcontracting resources as appropriate to business units. Whatever kind of option developed, it is likely to be more flat, and less hierarchial than at present.

It will be an intelligent user and interpreter of open information systems. Marketing has been one of the last functions to recognize the benefits of information technology to streamline its own processes and to increase the quality and speed of its work. Much of the workload for young marketers has been the interpretation of data on an *ad hoc* basis. The successful marketing department of the mid-1990s will not dissipate its efforts and discourage young talent through negligent ignorance of information systems.

Crucially, it will also nurture a different kind of individual. The archetypal marketer is all-too-often recruited as a generalist and never truly loses that tag. In the future, marketing is likely to nurture two types of individuals. On the one hand, these will include people who are comfortable as functional managers in a number of areas, only some of which are formally in the marketing function. They will move cross-functionally throughout their career. On the other hand, there will be technical specialists, in areas such as database marketing, who update their skills in a particular discipline and whose career moves are within that specialist discipline.

Organizations which accept that the imperative is for action and radical change, and a fundamental realignment of day-to-day marketing practices in line with the classic concept of marketing, will have genuine competitive advantage.

They will achieve this through:

- Developing new products more quickly and in line with customer requirements. Marketing, as described above, will be more integrated into the organization and better able to marshal disparate resources to meet customer requirements.
- Becoming increasingly responsive to customers and to competitive change. Since marketing will be measured rigorously, and increasingly focused on value adding activities, there will be every incentive and opportunity to innovate and stimulate change in the organization.
- Providing more consistent customer service. With one function responsible for the customer interface, it is clear where the buck stops. This can involve apparently mundane activities which, to the customer, are critical.
- Becoming better able both to achieve sales opportunities and build long-term customer relationships. Winning companies will not have ivory tower marketers. The only way to meet objectives will be through contact with the customer and a thorough understanding of the profitability of initiatives and actions. Irrespective of specific responsibilities, every marketer will have a direct and continuing role in achieving sales growth and margin improvement.

The last remaining question is, can this fundamental change happen, given the parlous state of marketing? The Coopers & Lybrand survey provides a clue. Managing directors are optimistic about the future of marketing, 60 per cent predicting more influence for marketing over the success/failure of companies, with only three per cent expecting less. A total of 47 per cent anticipated increased staffing levels for their marketing departments with only six per cent expecting less.

There is the will to reorganize marketing. Only if this is translated into action will marketing fulfil its traditional role – which remains its core objective even in the 1990s – of identifying, meeting and nurturing customers.

419

Robert Smith is a consultant with the Coopers and Lybrand Marketing Group, based in Birmingham, UK. He is one of the co-authors of the report, *Marketing at the Crossroads* (1993).

Further Reading

Levitt, T, *Thinking About Management*, The Free Press, New York, 1991.

MANAGING A SALESFORCE

Ken Langdon

Managing a salesforce has all the normal characteristics of managing people in any environment. However, its direct links and relationships with customers make a salesforce a crucial part of any company's armoury. Managing a salesforce and its activities effectively involves managing information, motivation and, most fundamentally, people. In any successful organization the end result must be that the salesforce adds value to the business of the customer or the individual buyer's quality of life.

There is a cyclical, and some would say cynical, view of the lot of a salesperson. Every year salespeople climb slowly, and hopefully, up the gradient represented by their target or quota. The target is management's aspiration for the protection and growth of market share, measured by the total of profitable orders and sales which salespeople generate in their area. Management calculates the salespeople's remuneration based on this performance against target. Reaching target means achieving 'on-target earnings' which probably means that the salespeople can continue the standard of living they maintained when they made target last year. Achieving target also means holding your head up in the office and looking like a winner.

But, it is not simply a question of money. The salesforce is rewarded by vouchers and trips and badges and a variety of other methods of recognition. While the successful wallow in the reflective glory, the unsuccessful watch as their colleagues pack for the annual sales conference taking place at a suitably exotic location.

The journey's main milestone is the end of the company year when the results are posted on the noticeboard to make sure that everyone can see them.

At the beginning of each year management resets the achievement clock to zero and sets a new target. This is almost certainly higher than the previous year's because the salesforce is the front line mechanism by which the company generates its sales and revenue's growth or productivity improvement.

To re-motivate the salesforce is a major management task. Meetings bring together the entire group in an effort to explain the differences in the product which will make the selling job easier. Speakers point to the unique qualities of the product or service and compare these favourably with competitive offerings. The company hands out sales aids and new tools to assist with the task, and the salespeople (possibly with their partners) are told of the exciting new rewards and competitions available for performing the long climb one more time. And so it goes on.

This rather cynical view of the salesperson's life is typical of the feelings of the experienced salesperson. Yet, how management pick, organize, train and motivate the salesforce is a crucial gauge to the success of almost all companies.

The overall aim

It is management's job to make sure that the salesforce is adding value to the customer's business or the individual buyer's quality of life.

This statement remains true, no matter what the product. Customers do not buy a tie because it has bright colours, is made of silk or is washable at 40 degrees. They do so because they imagine how people will think of them when they are wearing it. They do not buy a computer because it has a fast processor, a colour screen or an adjustable keyboard. They buy a computer because it is going to reduce the amount of finished goods stock they are holding and thereby improve their profitability. Neither can it be forgotten that customers have a choice. They can always buy someone else's product.

Getting the sales strategy right

Understanding the customer's real needs

The long-term prosperity of any business depends on satisfying customers and their real needs, as well as their aspirations. Only for a limited period can you sell a shovel to people who do not need to dig a hole.

This simple, but vital, lesson was demonstrated by the 1994 revelations that salespeople in the financial services were selling inappropriate products to their customers. Up to 25 per cent of long-term insurance/savings products were being cashed in within two years, a financial disaster for the customer. Salespeople, also, encouraged their prospects to leave employer pension schemes and take out personal pensions, knowing that by so doing the customer was almost certainly going to have a worse pension to retire on.

Clearly, the financial services industry and its salespeople will pay heavily for this. If prospects and customers do not trust the salesperson they will prove much harder to sell to. They are much more likely to consult their friends or other independent advisers. This, at best, delays the sale and, at worst, adds to the distrust by producing another set of questions and objections.

The key for a sales manager is to understand why the customer needs the product and to ensure that the salesforce is armed with the right set of open and closed questions which will in turn ensure that the right product is recommended.

The next problem is to make sure that the salespeople are talking to the right people. If you want to sell double glazing to a household, you do not direct your selling at the 18 year-old son because he is easier to talk to. You talk to the person (or persons) who will take the decision and whose money is going to fund the project. Yet, this simple point is frequently missed by sales-forces – particularly if the product is complex and they have to have some specialist knowledge.

Ken Wallace, now the chairman of Technology plc, insists that creating a truly customer-facing salesforce requires a 'layered' level of contact. This means that when selling to a large organization you need contacts at all levels, possibly met by their counterpart level in the selling organization. The threat of failing to do this can be very severe. Wallace was involved in managing a difficult sale of new technology to a large company. His salesperson was unaware that his product was priced so uncompetitively in the particular application that the chance of success was nil. The technologists in the buying company, however, were happy to accept the continued efforts and ideas of the salesperson's team. Only a high level of contact could have prevented this waste of resource by discovering the price problem.

Another example can be found in the telecommunications industry. It is a complex business and most of the salespeople charged with selling networks have, at some point, been trained in the technicalities of the product and ser-vices. Then, having become salespeople, they continue talking to the company telecommunications managers. This is the managerial level they are comfort-able with. But, above and around the technical managers are business managers who are responsible for making the company's profits. It is they who will see the innovative possibilities of using telecommunications differ-ently in the normal day-to-day activities. And it is they in the end who will set the telecommunications budget and strategy. So the salesperson who is con-fined to the technical department will once again run the risk of wasting time. 'I'm told it does not meet our return on investment criteria, whatever that might be,' the telecommunications manager is likely to confide. Alternatively, the risk may be competitive. 'Your competitor has spoken to the board and they are impressed, so there's not much we in the telecommunications depart-ment can do,' the manager might say.

In achieving the right level of contact, the sales manager needs a deep knowledge of the marketplace and of customers, and the ability to get the salespeople to talk at the right level – whether it is easy or not. The salesforce has to understand the customer's real need. The easiest way to sell a shovel is to agree with prospects that they really need a hole in the ground.

Clashes of strategy

John Davison, a director of computer company ICL, warns of clashes of strat-egy when the salesforce want to sell the easier route to a customer, instead of the route which causes difficulty in the short-term, but represents a better long-term solution for both supplier and customer.

There are times when a complete change of technology is preferable to the simpler plan of patching and delaying the radical decision. Sales management could find themselves at odds with, not only their salespeople looking for the soft option, but also with the customer's people trying to maintain an easier life. However, the long-term partnership with a client can only improve where sales management and salespeople have held a line and in the end been proved to have been right.

Squeeze profits out of the assets (even the salesforce)

As managers with all types of product and all types of customer consider their selling strategy, productivity is an important driver. A department store manager is likely to ponder: 'Suppose we could get half the shop assistants to try to cross-sell a tie to anyone who bought a shirt, and a tenth of the people asked did buy a tie. That would add more to my bottom line than increasing floor space.'

The simple shop illustration demonstrates 'gearing' in selling. This gearing effect works on two grounds: selling more at the margin and avoiding discounting.

In the first case, the coverage of fixed costs by current sales means that the bottom line impact of selling one more is very pronounced. For example, the average profit on a packaged holiday was less than £3.50. That was if you sold 1 million. If you sold 1 million and 1 the addition to the bottom line was £64.

In the second case, the job of sales management is to make sure that the salesforce understands the real impact of discounting. A purchaser's request for a 10 per cent discount may sound reasonable until you bear in mind that if the margin on the product is 30 per cent, agreement to the discount removes a third of the profit.

The salesforce is an asset. Management has a role in making sure that it is making its contribution to profits and that the selling strategy squeezes as much as possible out of the skills available.

Picking the right people

Hunters or farmers

It is useful to divide the selling job into 'hunting' or 'farming'. Hunting is about bringing in new customers; farming about increasing the amount and type of business you do with your existing customers. The skills sets are different and a major thought in people selection is to consider how much of each activity is involved in the job.

For hunters the main requirement is for persistence and the ability to take knocks. They have the often thankless task of trying to obtain interviews with strangers who may not only be unaware of their need, but antagonistic to an unsolicited approach whether by telephone or personal call. Hunters generally work quickly, have short attention spans and feel very dissatisfied if complications of product or decision-making processes intrude on their getting to the point of closing a sale. They are opportunists and, in most cases, need careful watching to make sure that the product being sold is suitable and will work to the promises made by the salesperson.

Some would say that it is the hunters who give salespeople a bad name, and there is some truth in that, but they are also the people who make innovation possible and *en masse* are important drivers of any economy.

Every salesperson has to have some of the hunter attributes. A good farmer who hates or claims to be bad at new business selling may be too slow to go for the order or not sufficiently assertive to win against the competition.

It is always interesting to listen to the war stories of salespeople – with the hunters the key words are 'got out as quickly as possible', 'I thought I would do one more door'. The hunters also tend to be young. It becomes progressively more difficult as salespeople grow older, to plan and carry out the blitz canvass, where every month he or she knocks on every door in one postal code area.

In contrast, farmers develop skills in long-term relationship building and very deep knowledge of a customer's business A professional sales team selling machine tools, for example, will over the years build a database of customer knowledge which the customer itself may envy. The benefits to management of professional farmers comes in terms of predictable orders, competitive intelligence, market changes and much more. A joint planning session with the sales team working with the customer to build a plan for the next year in detail, and three years in outline, is a sign that your company has truly created the working partnership and added value, which a lot of salespeople talk about while misunderstanding the difficulties and timescales involved in setting one up.

Don't keep hiring yourself

Selling is a very personal job. The old adage that people buy from people, not from companies is true. There is, therefore, a problem in hiring someone from whom you personally would not buy. And yet they could be just right for many of your customers and prospects. Be very suspicious if a sales manager who has a high turnover of salespeople is building a team which looks more like clones rather than the patchwork of different individuals who make up a standard distribution. The danger is that these like-minded people will all find it difficult to do business with some customers, and it can become too comfortable.

Professional sales managers must be objective in hiring, looking for a set of attributes, not for someone they like.

Using role play

In general, salespeople start from a dislike of role play where a manager or another salesperson plays the customer while a salesperson makes a sales call, either in a meeting or on the telephone.

At the end of a real sales call, it is very unlikely that customers will explain to the salesperson how they felt during the call. Thus the salesperson can go away thinking that everything went well. In role play the customer and observers are invited to critique the call, talking about the strengths and weaknesses of technique and strategy. This is why salespeople generally do not like role play.

John Davison's view is that role play in training and development is a very powerful technique. 'Make sure that it is done well by credible people who can avoid charges of artificiality or irrelevance to the salesperson's job.'

The fact is that there is a close correlation between what we do in role play and what we do in real life. Always make role play part of your selection process.

Grow your own

It is remarkable how many salespeople are successful in one company for a protracted length of time, but find it difficult to reproduce their performance with a new organization and set of products.

Of course, hiring experienced and successful salespeople does sometimes succeed, but for value for money, people who you have brought through your organization as trainees or support people often make the most productive salespeople fastest.

Who needs training let's get on with the selling

How much do they need to know about the product?

A key frustration of many buyers occurs when they feel that the salesperson who is talking to them does not know much about the product. In theory it is impossible to know too much about the product you are selling. The danger is to make sure that product training reflects the *application* of the product rather than its manufacture. Lengthy descriptions of the revolutionary new grease which is unique to the product and developed at your specially built laboratories is unlikely to gain a positive response. Emphasizing that the product is guaranteed against rust, however, is significant to the customer.

It is probably useful for the salesperson to be able to explain about the revolutionary grease if the customer asks, but this approach meets the customer's requirement of a salesperson rather than the company's requirement that the salesperson is able to describe the brilliant features of its products.

The clue is role play. In product training as well as technique training, role play is how you train the salespeople to say what the customer needs to hear and get over the competitive edge of your products without a lecture. There is also an important connection between product training and level of contact. If you train your salespeople to be able to handle very detailed questions about the product, you run the risk that they will only talk to the customer staff who appreciate such detail rather than the senior buyers or the people who hold the purse strings.

Combine training in the basics with understanding the customer

There are basic skills in selling, from questioning technique to active listening, from checking that the prospect is genuine to handling objections and closing. Your people need to be thoroughly versed in these and refreshed from time to time.

The most productive way to do this is to combine it with increasing their understanding of the customer. Introduce them to customers. Get managers who have implemented the products you sell to discuss the practicalities of implementation. Persuade users of the products to explain why they are going to buy again, or why they are not. Let them feel like customers do, their joy in the product and their pain when there are problems. The more the salesforce identifies and understands what the customers are going through, the more competitive it will become.

Use role play to illustrate every angle of buying and selling your products and services. Sales managers are vital in the training process. They need to know what the training department is saying so that they can continue the training in the field. They also bring a credibility to the exercises which can be difficult for the trainers.

Targeting and motivating

A director of a smart card company, Norman Strangemore says: 'There are three things you have to do to a salesforce to get it to meet its targets: the first is to motivate it, the second to re-motivate it and the third to motivate it again.'

If buying is an emotional process then we should not be surprised to find that selling has an important emotional side to it as well. The motivation of salespeople concerns confidence and pride in the company which they work for, knowledge of and interest in the market they sell to and a clear reward system which reflects accurately their success in the field. Motivating a salespeople requires:

- Targets which are stretching but achievable. If it is too easy they will sell less than they might; if it is too ambitious they will spend more time proving the task is impossible than trying to achieve it. If it is really too stretching they will find someone else to sell for.
- Added value through effective teamwork. It is a very good idea to have some mutual responsibilities around the team. The pressure of the peer group who have something riding on the performance of a colleague is quite intense and leads to the sort of co-operation which is normally found in teams outside the salesforce.
- Incentive schemes which are straightforward. It is true that salesforces are highly accomplished at finding ways of achieving bonuses or commissions without actually achieving the results management were looking for. Think the scheme through and avoid subtleties.

- Not confusing sales revenue with profits. If you give incentives to salespeople at all levels to take orders they will do so, but if they are in a very competitive environment they may very well do so at the expense of the bottom line. It is easier to sell the cheapest product on the market, so make sure that the salesperson suffers from reducing the profitability of a deal.
- Not rewarding non-performance. Salespeople accept and indeed welcome the fact that their salaries will differ with their results. If they are lucky and get a deal no one was anticipating, they will still expect to be paid. If they are unlucky, it is a mistake to recognize that ill-luck by making up the bonus anyway. It is not good for that salesperson and it is not good for the people who did achieve their objectives.

Promotion and the salesperson

You do not have to promote them to management

It is very tempting to promote your best salespeople to sales managers. They will probably have an expectation that this will happen and be disappointed if it does not. But the logic is different. Your best salesperson may very well be your worst sales manager.

There are two main problems. The first problem is that the highly successful salesperson may find it difficult to allow less experienced or less skilful people who work for him or her get on with doing the selling in their own way. It may prove easier to go out and do the selling on their behalf. This leads to a failure to develop his or her people and a failure to carry out all the other elements of management which need to be done.

The second problem is change. As markets and products change so the way that the salesperson works has to change. It can be difficult for the promoted salesperson to understand. 'This is how I did it and I was very successful' is an attitude which can prevent staff reacting to a required change of behaviour. This syndrome is often seen in the training department when they have been asked to develop courses which help the salesforce to change its methods, only to discover that on returning to the field its managers re-enforce the old ways. This is another reason for making sure that sales management is involved in training.

So, what can you do with an experienced salesperson who wants to make progress in the company and to be seen to be making progress? The answer is to increase their sales responsibilities and place them into a promoted role without putting them in charge of people. The most successful sales companies have all found ways of establishing a professional sales stream which gives a career structure for people who are best used in the field in direct contact with customers.

Don't keep promoting yourself

Exactly the same considerations for the appointment of managers occur as for the appointment of sales people. The best sales managers know that a management team completely comprised of managers of the same style is likely to be limited in its scope.

Management processes and aids to selling

If they see it as a form they'll fill in anything

It is necessary to manage the sales process as you would manage any other business process. The difficulty here is to ensure that the control processes put in place are useful in managing sales, and also useful in *making* sales. If you implement a control process in such a subjective environment as selling which is seen to have no benefit to the salespeople, they will treat it as a series of forms to be filled in. As when providing sales forecasts, they may fall to the temptation of writing what they think management want to read.

Here are two examples of simple processes which monitor the sales process and which, if properly presented to sales people, will generally be accepted as giving management what they want and at the same time assisting salespeople to win business.

Process 1: Managing a complex sale

This process assumes that the sale is complex. It is complex because the customer problem is complex, the products which make up the solution are complex, and there are a number of people involved in the buying process. The salespeople are invited to discuss and agree with their team, or with management, the answers to the following questions:

Customer need
Is it a real need?
Is it strategic to the customer?
Is the campaign worth the necessary selling effort?

Finance
Is the money available in a budget?
Is there a rough cost expectation?
Has the necessary return on investment or value for money judgement been made?

Key people
Do you know all the key people?
Do you have as good access to them as your competitors do?
Are they all informed of the pending buying decision?

Timescale

Have the key people agreed on a decision date?
Is there an agreed implementation timescale?

Solution

Is your solution valid?
Is the risk of your being able to deliver your promises acceptable?

Basis of decision

Have you agreed with the key people their criteria for deciding to go ahead?
Have you influenced this?
Do your unique selling propositions form part of their criteria?

Practical

Are their and your sales and implementation resources defined and available?
Can you support the implemented solution?

Competition

Do you have an advantage?
Is there an acceptably small number of competitors bidding?

If you can answer yes to everything on this checklist, you are probably going to get the order. Where there are negatives you can identify the problems and issues which require attention. This simple, but effective, process is used to ensure that the sales campaign is well-thought through and that there is some control, rather than it being totally driven by the customer.

It is useful to represent the answers to the checklist questions as a radar diagram (Fig. 1).

Process 2: Managing an account for repeat business

Assuming fairly complex selling, the second process examines the quality of the long-term relationship with a client. Once again it starts with discussion of a checklist.

Level of contact

Do you have regular business meetings at all levels:
Senior management?
High level within the product users?
High and wide at technical level?
Where necessary in Central Purchasing?

Customer satisfaction

Do you have an agreed measure of customer satisfaction with the customer?
Do you deliver what you promised on time and within budget?
Does the product give the expected up-time?
Where there are problems are they fixed quickly?
Are you supporting the customer properly where appropriate?

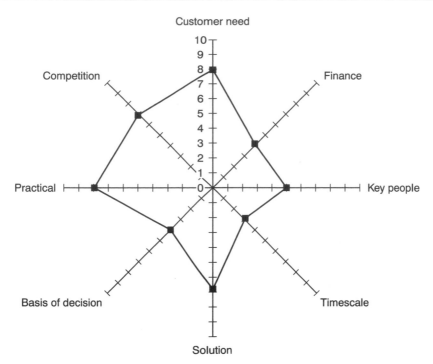

Fig. 1 Campaign checklist

Strategic fit

This area reflects how well the activities and campaign in place, in each part of the customer's business, reflect the selling and buying company strategies.

Are you thoroughly aware of your company's product strategy and can you articulate it to your customer?

Does your plan fit in with your company's strategy?

Is there a connection between your plan and your customer's overall strategy?

Can you see the connection between your plan and some customer critical success factor(s)?

Can you see the connection between your plan and a change in a crucial customer performance indicator(s)?

Competitive position

Are you aware of the strengths and weaknesses of the main competitors you are facing?

Are you aware of your company's strengths and weaknesses in relation to the main competitors?

How vulnerable is your installed base to competitive attack?

Are you seen as price/competitive and value for money?

431

Pipeline

Do you know early enough in the customers' buying process when bids are being invited?

Do you have enough prospects in the pipeline to ensure that you will make target even if your biggest project fails to close?

Have you got a plan for regular prospecting?

Campaign plans

Have you agreed an action plan and timetable within the buying and selling companies to close the business?

Have all your necessary resources agreed to take their part in the campaign?

Is your campaign plan checklist up-to-date and useful as a communication tool?

Market share

Do you have an acceptable measure of what your current market share is?

Do your campaigns deliver marketshare in line with your company's goals?

Inter-campaign leverage

Are you aware of other sales campaigns which are connected to yours, and do you have an agreed plan of action ?

Have you made sure that the appropriate people are involved in your campaigns?

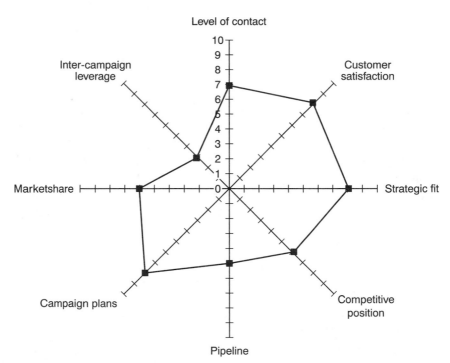

Fig. 2 Account management checklist

Once again it is useful to represent the answers to the checklist questions as a radar diagram.

The salesforce in any organization is a group of people who can be difficult, can get your company into trouble, can be arrogant, can use all sorts of tactics within your company and in your customers' businesses to achieve their ends, but is undoubtedly the bell-wether of a company's ability to grow and prosper.

Ken Langdon is a management consultant and gives courses in business planning and the preparation of sales and marketing plans.

Further Reading

Hopkins, T, *How to Master the Art of Selling Anything*, HarperCollins, London, 1983.
LeBoeuf, M, *How to Win Customers and Keep them for Life*, Piatkus, London, 1991.

DESIGN MANAGEMENT

Raymond Turner

Consciously or unconsciously, every company invests in design. Often, however, this is a casual or bolted-on activity without coherence or conviction which, therefore, misses fundamental opportunities of wealth creation.

Design can play a primary role in translating companies' missions and visions into practical reality. At most points of contact during the customer relationship, design can make a difference to how people are treated and their perceptions of that treatment. Given a broader, more strategic role, managing design effectively creates new competitive opportunities.

The vision thing

Many companies now have mission statements. BAA has as a mission to be the most successful airport company in the world. Unlike many other businesses, BAA also has a vision which defines more clearly what it must do to be the best. The two are distinctly different, often separated, and not necessarily mutually independent.

It is perfectly possible for a company to have a mission, achieve that mission, and be a successful company while having little or no vision. Equally, it is possible for a company to have a mission and for it to make no impact whatsoever on its performance because it has become vague and valueless with no real means of influencing day-to-day actions.

Many missions become compromise statements, ending up as far too general to differentiate the company and create a focus for a management strategy. A mission statement cannot simply be bolted onto an unimaginative, ill-directed company and expected to have a measurable effect.

A vision, however, can become the principal means through which a strategy can be achieved. As an organization, BAA places a high value first on the vision – where it wants to be as a business, and how it can differentiate itself from other companies. With that clearly in place, it can then fulfil its mission.

The BAA vision is driven at the top by chief executive, Sir John Egan, and communicated clearly throughout the rest of the management. It helps determine what makes the company different. It is not a series of vacuous statements, an outline of a process with no clear idea of the end-product. Take the analogy of motor cars. Heavily promoted, they are marketed to customers on the basis of what the driving experience will be like – the vision. Merely describing the manufacturing process to make the car is not enough – that would be a mission, without the content.

At BAA the vision is to provide the best world class experience for customers and to provide quality experiences for everyone the company deals with – passengers, airlines, concessionaires, suppliers, and its own staff. Having defined that, the company can begin to develop the link between the vision, the design inputs necessary to manifest that vision, and so realize the mission.

Combining vision and mission creates a corporate difference which can be very specific to a company, its goals, and the means of delivering that difference which customers will find tangible.

It also provides a clear platform and link between practical daily actions and the end result, allowing individuals to see and measure their own contributions. Design, conveniently, is one process which has a direct practical connection to daily management activity, allowing it to make a point of difference and also to provide the company with a differentiator against any rival company.

It is quite feasible for every design decision to help achieve an overall business objective. This is more than can be said for some other management disciplines. If managers and their companies describe clearly what their objective is, they can then relate design activity in a practical way to achieve that objective. It can even be measured.

At BAA, for example, design managers can manage the experience of the travelling public, airline customers and the company's own people using pragmatic means. Every point in the quality experience process can be looked at, markers can be established for achieving them and design can help to define or characterize that experience.

What does that mean? At BAA it means trying to achieve greater commonality between what the customer expects, and what the company provides at every point where the two meet or come close.

It is also worth defining what is meant by quality. Today, every company putting out a corporate message talks about quality. So much so, that the meaning and the intention can be lost. At BAA quality does not necessarily mean dripping with suspect jewels, but shaping a passenger experience to every venue it controls. While different locations require different levels of investment, it is a question of delivering a quality experience appropriate to every venue, and the traffic it handles, while creating an individual identity for the whole facility. Quality experiences are achieved differently by an imaginative and pragmatic use of design throughout the project management and planning processes.

If the equation is right, the company has used design effectively to achieve its vision. It knows where it wants to be and how to get there. And it knows how to use design as a practical tool to manifest corporate objectives, including the vision.

It is a vision which will not be appropriate to every company. BAA wants to lead the world in the provision and running of airports. Other businesses can be successful by *not* leading. And that may be their vision. For many years, Japanese industries did extremely well by not innovating and leading. Instead, their vision was to look for world innovation and implement it better than anyone else. Arguably their vision has now altered somewhat.

Some companies do not have the courage to lead. Or are pragmatic enough to recognize where they are weak. They may be too small to have the R&D resource needed to turn ideas into reality. On the other hand they may have the vision to take a good idea and maximize its potential through good product development into, perhaps, well-researched niche markets.

Using design effectively

The effective use of design in a business is a bit like a journey of understanding and discovery, recognizing the influence that design can have and then putting in place processes to use it effectively.

There are four important milestones on this journey:

- design in crisis
- design in context
- design in place
- design in management.

Design in crisis

This may sound dramatic but the recognition by a company that its design process is out of control – non-existent even – is more important than the actual state of affairs. It may sound perverse for a design manager to be saying that companies can be quite successful when every visible manifestation of their company is in a chaotic state.

The crisis may only show when there are other business pressures. When this happens, the company needs to use all its management resources – including strategically-focused design – to defend or rebuild its position.

What can design do for a company where its whole design management policy is in crisis? Every company is investing in design to some degree, perhaps unconsciously. Most companies have buildings – shops, factories, workshops, social facilities; communications and information systems – logos, a corporate range of stationery, a corporate brochure, an annual report and accounts, marketing material; perhaps products which they make or buy to sell-on, and product identities or, in the case of some service industries, grander expressions of who they are and what they do, such as 'planes, boats and trains.

They are already investing in design, even if by default, but it is liable to be superficially used, unco-ordinated with any marketing, production or corporate positioning strategy, and with no one responsible for a coherent design plan or strategy. Using design effectively to communicate a common message or set of values through these existing events is, therefore, hardly an 'extra'. It is more a question of recognising the need to use it differently, and more effectively. Look at some simple examples.

Service industries tend to comprise a series of events and experiences which together make up the whole. Whether it is insurance or transport, the net effect can have either a beneficial or detrimental impact on the whole experience people have of their business. At most points of contact during the customer relationship, design can make a difference to how people perceive they have been treated. In BAA's case it is how they feel about their surroundings, their physical and mental comfort while they are using the company's premises, the sense of reassurance they get from properly focused information, the quality and appropriateness of retail and catering activities – in fact the management of the 'journey' through the total experience from departure to arrival.

During this process, design is a logical planning activity as well as an aesthetic one – a means of ensuring value for money and customer satisfaction. But if all design inputs are unco-ordinated and unmanaged, people receive different and uncontrolled messages about the company. When that happens design is in a state of crisis.

It is the same in other types of industry. If you are in the business of making glass bottles, good design can improve the look of the product but, at the same time, it can reduce the amount of raw material needed, cut wastage and use manpower more efficiently through optimising the machinery and the skills of the workforce.

But to return to the premise of design in crisis – companies can carry on their day-to-day business without realizing that design can influence any of these perceptual or practical issues. Once this realization dawns, they can begin the process of moving from design crisis to *design in context*.

Design in context

Once companies recognize that design is out of control, they can then begin to assess the extent to which design touches every part of their business and how effective that contribution is. It is putting design into its correct context, quantifying how it might make a difference to production, sales, the customers, the work environment, shareholder value, corporate and public perception – in fact the essence of a company's wealth-creating capability, the manifestation of its strategic objectives. How can the company use design to do all these activities better?

The first task is to assess exactly where design is or can be used by the business. This does raise the question, who is equipped to carry out this audit? Companies could employ a design consultant or even hire a design manager, but with what brief? Experience suggests that designers and architects can become restricted by their design training. An effective team requires that their skills are coupled with those of a finance manager, who may well be a highly creative person in pragmatic terms and able to make the leap from function to line and quantify design's contribution in terms of the business process. On an international basis, businesses can also draw on the experience of the Boston-based Design Management Institute to point them in the right direction.

The audit should open the eyes of management to all the different parts of the business which do or can use design. It could be print, product design, production engineering, architecture, interior design, information systems and all interfaces with the public, customers and staff. If a company does not have anyone confident of handling such a review, it should consider asking someone from outside, perhaps a counterpart in another industry who does have experience of managing the strategic use of design and can take a dispassionate view.

Design in place

With a clear idea of what design can – or should – influence in the business, it is time to put the appropriate management systems in place to make it effective. It may be appropriate to appoint someone to a design management role. But, sitting in a corporate chair is not always the most effective way forward. Inputting design management to the area of the business most critical to success – marketing perhaps – and achieving some quick 'hits' by the focused use of design may be more meaningful.

There is a great temptation for design managers to elbow their way to the high table, appointed by and reporting to the chief executive or managing director. They do so because it makes design more credible and states unequivocally that it is important. They hope to overcome suspicion and reluctance by being supported from the top.

There is a downside to this – if design managers do not report to an effective business group in the company, their role is much less clear. If what they do and say is not supported at all levels of management, their job is virtually non-existent, albeit supported at a high level.

The appointment of a design manager must carry weight, but it must be seen to be making a direct difference – somewhere, if not initially everywhere – otherwise the role is vulnerable.

Design must be seen to have a value in both strategy and tactics, having a recognizable contribution while those responsible for design must have the authority to review and oversee its use across all aspects of the company.

It is not always easy to achieve this balance – the last thing a design manager needs is a stream of material to merely rubber stamp or to take over responsibility for, because departments can effectively pass the buck. Part of the activity of good design management is also about putting into place processes by which things happen, backed by clear design standards for all parts of the company, training and general communication about how design can contribute to business success.

Design in management

Having said that there are four milestones in the design journey, the road between each stage is not necessarily simple. Logically, companies move up between stages, depending on their starting point, but the final stage, between design in place and design in management, is by far the hardest, achieved by only a few companies and then not always consistently.

The design manager at this level has to do much more than dictate and implement design decisions. The job becomes an entire process of design awareness, opening everyone's eyes in the company to the use and value of design and ensuring that all design decisions taken through the total management process support a clear, strategically-focused, design objective.

In a large geographically spread, project-oriented company like BAA, no design department can merely police and project-manage every design activity. Instead it has to harness the willing support of managers at all levels who are effectively taking design decisions every day in the course of their normal work. Design decisions have to be devolved to the workplace, not taken in an ivory tower. Often the job of a design manager is to advise and guide, providing firm direction with a light management touch.

Design must contribute to the normal work process. It must become implicit in those actions. If it has to be stuck on afterwards, it has failed.

How BAA uses design

To achieve this intuitive level of understanding in an organization like BAA, which is spending more than £1.5 million a day on developing its facilities, a total culture change is demanded, actively supported by the highest levels of company management and by clear communications and training showing design in its correct business context.

Even companies which have a design management department do not always understand this difference – they have to change from giving advice to effecting the change in belief. They have to show that effective design is everyone's responsibility as much as financial awareness or total quality management.

It is a long-term process. Despite having been known for years as a design-conscious organization, BAA has not yet fully integrated design into its management process. However, this is an active part of the programme of developing world class processses. It has spent many years with design in place, creating an organization to manage design with established committees and reviews, without having made that leap to total understanding in the group. People have gone along with organizational demands without having fully realized the value of what is being promoted. However, that is now changing, and design is being recognized as a critical factor in satisfying customer needs, improving profitability, and maximizing efficient operations.

No matter how big a design management department may be, it is practically impossible in a large organization for it to handle all daily design decisions.

For design in management to work we need something quite different to the traditional design management structure of a manager plus experts in various design disciplines. But what?

Creating ownership

The aim at BAA is to create 'ownership' of design decisions at line management and project management levels. The design management role will become one of responsibility for groups of processes through which everyone can see a benefit in their daily work lives. These processes will ensure design consultancies keep design activity in line with corporate standards and objectives, the design direction and degree of standardization already having been decided by BAA.

BAA is a very project- and process-oriented company which makes it easier to apply design activity as part of the total activity. It happens that it has a lot of major activities going on at any one time from refurbishment of facilities to total new termini. Equally, there is no reason why less project-driven companies could not take the same attitude and define activities in terms of projects with fixed aims, life, budget, and likely achievement in which design can be shown to have a measurable role.

Of course, it is very easy to say this and also to be critical of how other businesses are not managing their affairs. BAA has defined its need to put design in management. At present implementation of design management in the group is a multi-speed activity. Different parts of the organization are more ahead that others, but that is not untypical of any large company.

Even when design thinking is totally integrated into the DNA of the business, the job does not rest there. As the business changes, so does the need for design to either support that change, or in some instances, to drive it. BAA is now putting into place the perceptual elements which will add design to the mainstream of line and project management thinking and planning. First it is targeting the project board management – perhaps 300 people in all – as part of a programme called 'Building our Future'. This programme shows how design has an influence on that future and also relates it to the customer experience to show how design decisions directly affect passengers' attitude to the quality experience the company wants to provide.

A second attack is on wider management training where a half- or one-day module will be added to a longer course aimed at project managers, demonstrating how design impacts on wealth creation potential and how the management of design can add value to their project, and to the whole customer experience.

New processes will formally review design in the life of individual projects to ensure it is having an influence on the quality and function of any finished project. And BAA is now looking to get design decisions closer to projects, in the same way as finance, where it will become part of the management review of any investment.

It will not all be achieved overnight, since different parts of the organization are running at different speeds in their acceptance of design and only some sectors have a good idea of how design can actually help.

It is perhaps also salutary to mention what design *cannot* do. It is not magic. It is not a panacea for a badly directed and managed organization. It is there to help managers who want to be helped. It cannot become the direction for the company, only support it.

Design has least impact with companies who have no strategic focus. Here, by comparison to its full potential, it could only tinker. Design supports quality thinking in an organization – it can never substitute for it.

It is fundamental that organizations have a clear view of their overall strategic direction and how they will get there. That is vision, and design helps achieve that vision through pragmatic means.

And if you cannot make that visionary leap of understanding, design in your business will fall short of its wealth-creating potential and the jobs of design managers will be wasted.

Raymond Turner is design director of BAA plc. His remit covers all aspects of environmental design, architecture and interior design, product design and development, information system design, and the development and management of the company's corporate identity. Before joining BAA, he was a board member and principal of Wolff Olins, design director for London Regional Transport and ran Kilkenny Design Consultancy, a multidisciplinary design practice, for the Irish government.

Further Reading

Lorenz, C, *The Design Dimension*, Basil Blackwell, Oxford, 1987.

MANAGING CORPORATE IDENTITY

Terry Tyrrell

One of the first targets for attack on ancient battlefields was the standard bearer. Topple the flag and you demoralize the enemy. The power of identity to unite, motivate and communicate has always been recognized in the military area, but like many battle strategies it can be equally potent in corporate competition.

As business becomes more aggressively competitive, identity and its communication is assuming corresponding significance: internally in galvanizing the workforce, and externally, in differentiating and adding value to the organization. More and more companies are actively seeking new ways of better defining, communicating and applying their identities on a continuous basis. A strong identity can be both the glue that holds an organization together and a vital competitive edge.

Any successful company, by dint of its success, is likely to have managed its hard assets well. It will have got the more tangible things – such as factories, locations, machinery and vehicles – right. But these, while still important, are now the basics. The convergence of technology, management systems, pricing structures and other hard competitive tools, means that companies now have to compete over and above these – with human values. So the projection of what could be described as the company's soul – its personality, spirit, values and even sense of humour (one of British Airways' stated values) becomes the key differentiating factor. Communicating these intangibles through the medium of the company's identity – and in particular its visual identity – has become an imperative.

By the same token, organizations with extensive brand portfolios are now beginning to examine closely the cost of running and promoting large numbers of brands. If one brand costs £X to promote and ten brands costs £10X, then surely it makes sense to put all ten under a single corporate umbrella brand and concentrate the marketing spend there. For example, Owners Abroad condensed its many disparate brands under the First Choice identity and Cadbury's products are Cadbury first, product name second. This has catalyzed a new focus on developing the corporate brand, viewing its communication from the consumer's point of view. Balancing levels of endorsement and branding structures have become the new marketing issues and companies are looking to build consumer-friendly values into hitherto reticent corporate brands. These are all activities directly relevant to, if not led by, identity strategy and management.

Identity: the corporate backbone

The shape and structure of the average organization has changed over the past decade, and it continues to change. The truly monolithic company run by dictates from the top is becoming less common. In its place are flatter more decentralized companies which perform delicate balancing acts between disseminated responsibility and essential central control. Mergers, demergers, acquisitions and partnerings are on the increase as organizations fight to keep pace with market forces; and those with a global spread experience special complications as different cultures and markets are expected to assimilate a single company identity and ethos. Predictably, identity management techniques have evolved to meet these organizational changes, moving away from the traditional top-down approach in favour of a consensus-based method designed to suit both the structure and culture of the company in question. Such a system can, in tandem with an effective internal communication programme, make the path of change smoother and internal acceptance far more speedy. The workforce will naturally weather change and pull together more effectively if they perceive themselves as positioned, supported and visually represented by a clear, articulate identity in which they have an active part to play.

What is identity and how can it benefit an organization?

There are two simple levels of identity. The first – basic identification, or badging – ensures that the consumer will recognize a certain company's products or services anywhere in the world. So IBM or Sony stamped on a product in Tokyo will be as recognizable to a visitor from Helsinki as to one from Nairobi.

The second and more complex level is the setting of a style in which the identity is designed. This is where the more subtle identifiers enter the picture to project the values and personality of the organization, as well as simple ownership. And it is this style which should then set the tone for the entire spectrum of the company's visual communication. We all recognize the Coke swirl; Castrol's red, green and white colour palette and British Airways' colours, typeface and underline flash. If the system is strong enough – as these are – and all of the company's visual communications are sending the same message – as they do – then that message is communicated far more clearly and the company becomes correspondingly more competitive.

The logo is the tip of the iceberg: understanding the process

Before even beginning to explore visual solutions for a particular organization an identity consultancy should embark on a vital period of research. This means getting under the skin of the organization, gathering together a comprehensive

443

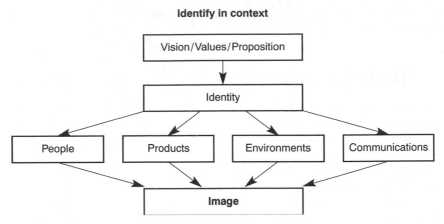

Identify in context

Fig. 1 **If the organization's proposition and its identity are in synchrony, and if the identity is then clearly communicated to and by the organisation's people, its products, its environments and its communications, then all of these elements move closer together. The closer they become, the clearer and sharper the overall company image and the easier it is to sell its products.**

visual audit of the way it currently presents itself against its competitors and conducting interviews throughout all of its various audiences from consumers to staff, suppliers, journalists and City analysts. It is during this first stage that the consultants, together with a management team, should discuss and distil down the core elements of the organization to define its true competitive differential – the proposition ultimately to be expressed through the identity. Far more important than the aesthetics of the identity is whether or not it accurately represents the organization and its intents; whether the workforce will muster behind it and, finally, how well and consistently it is applied. How will the mark look sent through a fax? Blown up on the side of a lorry? Back illuminated on acrylic at 300 metres or on a sports shirt on television?

Some of the most expensive and comprehensive identity programmes make no visible change to the mark at all. The value of an established, well-recognized mark outweighs even tired-looking original graphics. The Ford logo, for example, is not particularly visually pleasing but it has enormously high recall with consumers. It is far easier to bring an old mark up-to-date with incremental change that it is to imbue a new mark with established values. Kodak and Shell have both managed quite major visual change but, because this has been implemented gradually over several years, consumers have been affected only by what they perceive as a sharper, more contemporary overall image. Nevertheless, it is still important to recognize the limits beyond which a brand and its mark cannot be moved. To reach the top end of the car market, Toyota felt the need to create a stand alone brand, Lexus; and Ford bought Jaguar because the Ford mark, though strong, could not be credibly attached

444

to a high performance luxury car. Similarly, Kodak has experienced some difficulty in successfully marketing its business to business products.

The logistics: protecting your identity investment

Developing a new identity almost always represents a substantial investment for the organization – both in time and money. The aim of an identity is to prompt recognition of the company it represents and evoke awareness of a particular set of values attached to that company. If it is copied by competitors – or indeed by anyone – the communication of those values becomes confused and diluted and the company no longer owns them exclusively. In September 1993, the Philip Morris Marlboro brand was valued by *Financial World* at US$39.5 billion. It is easy to see why it is worth registering and protecting a name which in the future can be perceived as having so much accumulated good will with the consumer.

So it makes sense first to develop an identity that is distinctive and memorable, and second, to protect it legally from being copied. Until October 1994, the Act that governed UK trade marks had been on the statute books since 1938, drafted for the very different industrial and commercial conditions of the day. It was overdue for change. The new improved Act, driven by EC pressure to harmonize European trade mark law, extends legal protection into areas where such protection previously did not exist. It also opens new routes for the UK to obtain protection for a trade mark throughout the whole of the EC. And an appendix to the GATT agreement, for the first time, now sets minimum standards for the protection of intellectual property.

This whole area of intellectual property – the protection of patents, trade marks, designs, brand identities and copyright is becoming a central strategic issue for identity managers, who will have to work hard to keep abreast of legal developments and legislation – or risk costly and embarrassing mistakes.

Developing a registerable mark is an art in itself – particularly for an organization with an international presence. 'Registerability' has to be a key element of the design brief. The proper trade mark searches in all of the relevant markets must be assiduously carried out and, finally, the new mark registered by the company as soon as possible to obtain maximum legal protection. Moreover, since the criteria for ownership has now shifted from proven usage to first-past-the-post, it is vital to check and ensure that all of the brands and identities already in the organization's portfolios are legally registered and, therefore, owned.

Making it work

The testing point for a new identity is when the consultancy leaves the client to fly solo. This is when the effectiveness of the system, its documentation and accompanying communications programme becomes evident. Happily the dine-and-dash days of the eighties are long over. At that time some consultancies were known to swoop in, design a logo and basic system, launch it with a media fanfare and leave – presenting the company with a sterile manual on its way out of the door. Today, any consultancy worth its fee will develop a documentation system that is more than just a cold manual filled with guidelines (usually the most infrequently perused piece of literature in the company).

Designed to be as adaptable and fit for change as the organization they describe, today's identity guidelines are educational and motivational tools, allowing the maximum possible scope for interpretation from market to market, situation to situation. The flow of information, advice and updates to all those charged with implementation is, ideally, maintained as an ongoing problem-solving dialogue. Often the consultancy can be involved at a low level of activity for years after the launch, helping to maximize the benefits of what can be a substantial investment.

Building consensus: turning the triangle upside down

Traditionally, identity decisions have been made by one individual at the top of an organization then passed down the line through a straitjacket of rules and 'shalt nots'. But, today's more decentralized companies demand a correspondingly flexible approach to making an identity system work. In parallel with the development of any identity programme it is now crucial to work equally hard at building consensus with those who will be expected to implement it –

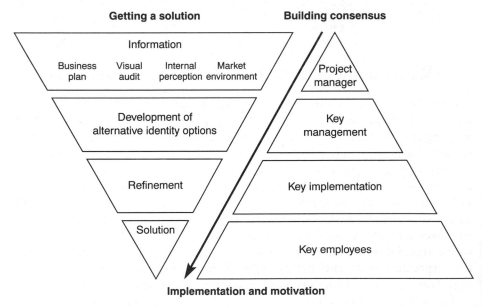

Fig. 2 Building a stong identity system

especially if the identity change is the result of a structural or cultural change. Without it, managers resentful at the prospect of a perceived increase in workload can throw expensive banana skins. A more effective approach is to begin an identity programme by creating working parties of representatives from each of the organization's outposts or divisions. Involved in the decision-making process from the outset these individuals will then assume ownership of, and responsibility for, the ultimate success of the new regime.

In tandem with the ambassadorial efforts of these key people, the organization should instigate a motivational internal communications programme which introduces the new identity, communicates its benefits and addresses particular issues. If employees fully understand the positive commercial impact to be gained by building a cohesive identity they will be more likely to commit to their part in it.

One of the biggest mistakes that companies make when investing in a new identity is to fail to keep the momentum going once the initial excitement is over. Maintaining a high level of interest in and commitment to making identity work throughout the company is the only way of getting a real return on that investment. Another common mistake is to believe that the job is done once the change is safely under way. As developments in the maketplace drive developments in the organization it is important to review and reassess the identity at regular intervals. This way incremental changes can be made to keep the company competitive and avoid wholesale change as a purely defensive measure.

Finally, while most companies are familiar with tracking the effectiveness of their advertising spend, very few bother to set up similar tracing systems for a new identity. It is wise to work with the identity consultancy to set up a system at the outset of an identity programme. Many consultancies, anxious to prove the worth of their efforts, will be willing to share the cost of such a system.

Who should manage it inside the organization?

During the eighties, the average manager in charge of overseeing a company's identity lasted approximately nine months – little more than that of a logocop wielding a hefty rule book. The role was unsatisfying, unpopular and unsuccessful. Now, as image and service increasingly become key differentiators, identity managers are gradually taking on a new strategic role. MBA-level business expertise; experience of brand marketing and strong human resources skills are basic requirements for the job. Working hand in hand with the chief executive at board level, the new breed of communications director is fully empowered to act as guardian of the company's vision and its consistent innovative articulation on all levels. He or she keeps the issue of identity high on the corporate agenda, stimulating and maintaining momentum throughout the organization and ensuring regular re-evaluation against competitors.

The role also effectively bridges the gap between internal communications – usually the province of the personnel department – and the external communications relayed by the marketing department. So the people inside the company are receiving – and in turn communicating – the same messages as those outside.

Doubtless, as this level of communications manager becomes more prevalent; putting in place image tracking and identity management evaluation systems will also become more matter of course. By studying shifts in familiarity and favourability in different audiences, these can help managers to detect warning signs early and act on them before they become problems – as well as evaluating the success or failure of individual strategies.

Working with consultancies

A good corporate identity consultancy should be able to get right under the skin of the client organization, define all of the characteristics by which that organization is recognized and create a workable identity system which identifies and enhances all of its communication. Finding the consultancy which can do all that – and has the right mix of personalities to gel with the client's culture – is not always easy. Most design companies, for example, will claim corporate identity development as a service – yet very few can field the business knowledge, expertise and experience to mount a full scale programme. Management consultancies on the other hand, do have the business acuity, but lack the skills to manifest the change through a visual system.

When choosing a consultancy it is essential to look for one which demonstrates the right mix of strategic, creative and implementation abilities. Bear in mind too that the consultants should be able to demonstrate the intellectual gravitas to argue the case for a solution at board level. Look for a proven track record of projects on a similar scale to the one at hand and an understanding of the prevailing cultures of relevant organizations and industries. Above all, make sure that the chemistry is right – that the consultancy/client culture is compatible and that you personally feel comfortable with the individuals with whom you will be working.

Having selected the right consultancy according to these criteria it will be far easier to develop an atmosphere of mutual trust in which to work together.

Reaping what you sow

The key to harnessing the power of identity is just that – harness it. Left to itself an organization's identity will certainly develop, but towards visual anarchy rather than clarity. The messages it communicates will gradually become diluted, unclear and even conflicting as individuals – aided and abetted by tools such as desktop publishing – change, adapt or otherwise misuse it at will.

Management is crucial. Begin by defining the messages to be communicated through your identity then move heaven and earth to ensure that these are consistently communicated to and by the entire organization at every point of contact. Make someone at director level responsible for managing it on an ongoing basis. Protect it legally and document its use in such a way as to inspire rather than hobble. Appoint outside help when necessary – and always, always put your head above water at regular intervals to be sure that the identity is still fit for both company and marketplace. If you manage all of this you should have developed an identity which can act as a powerful competitive differentiator, a valuable internal motivator and a persuasive corporate ambassador.

Terry Tyrrell is chairman of Sampson Tyrrell a company he founded with Martin Sampson in 1976. Sampson Tyrrell is one of Europe's foremost consultancies in corporate identity and design. In 1986, Sampson Tyrrell joined the WPP Group, the world's largest marketing services group.

Further Reading

Olins, W, *Corporate Identity*, Thames & Hudson, London, 1989.
Identity Issues, Sampson Tyrrell, London, 1993.

Education, Development and Training

'Many organizations now recognize – often for the first time – that the latest management techniques and thinking is important for them if they are to survive and succeed. Management development is no longer seen as a blind act of faith, but a necessary investment for the present and the longer term.'

Peter Beddowes, dean of Ashridge Management College

'Education and training are decisive. [The] single greatest long-term leverage point available to all levels of governement.'

Michael Porter[1]

---

[1] Porter, M, *The Competitive Advantage of Nations*, Macmillan, London, 1990.

OVERVIEW

Theresa Barnett

Ascending in a metaphorical helicopter above the terrain known as management education, development and training, an observer might identify at ground level a few familiar landmarks, and some new features, slightly obscured by mist. Even as the helicopter hovers, it may be buffeted by the aftershocks of minor earth tremors, which are causing rifts and new compacted land masses on the map below.

The animal life moving about the terrain, grazes, preys and socializes. Some animals form herds and seem to be migrating towards a common destination. Here and there individual animals prowl alone, few in number and endangered by the environment.

On this map, the familiar landmarks seen by the observer are the traditional suppliers of education, development and training for managers. These suppliers fall into four main groups which can be broadly described as academic, professional, commercial and organizational. The new features evident in the landscape are the result of restructuring, of new technology, of new ways of learning which seem to be forcing changes in the traditional environment.

Among the animals engaged in this Darwinian survival of the fittest scenario in the landscape, it can be seen that both the herds that are moving together towards a common destination, and the individuals who anticipate and move to solve life-threatening problems, are best placed for survival in the new environment.

As it is with these animals, so it is both in the corporate life of managers and in the twin pressures on their education, development and training. The challenge is to provide both the generic needs of the herd, and the precise just-in-time needs of the individual.

The new realities

The flatter organization structures which Charles Handy described in the late 1980s and which have redefined the geography of major corporations in the 1990s have led to a greatly decreased number of hierarchical levels of specialist or manager. Specialists have already been outsourced in many companies, and it seems likely that this trend will continue so that the management core of a workforce will be small in comparison with the people-heavy organization of the 1980s. Upward career progress with the same employer will not always be an option and career progression is likely to include in-company, cross functional, sideways, job changes. Many managers, therefore, will need to migrate to new companies and new environments if they are ambitious for upward progress.

The new pressure on the manager is to take ownership of his or her own career, to ensure that success in business and in learning is documented in a way which has transferable value to a new employment situation, and to invest time and money in personal development. In effect, managers must ensure that their personal profile of achievement holds value in the alien territory of a different corporation.

A steadily increasing number of women are also joining the managerial workforce. This group will face all the pressures experienced by their male colleagues and in addition may need a more family-friendly approach to learning – more flexibility of learning events and a balance between face-to-face, residential, and distance learning. The new style of management, which is being sought by major corporations, shifts the emphasis away from traditional aggressive individual competition to the softer more difficult to develop skills, of collaboration, teamworking and life-time customer alliances built on skilled negotiation and high-level interpersonal interactions. At the same time, performance-based pay systems, generally based on individual achievement will need to change to include the team performance element, or managers will regard the new cultural requirements as unrealistic.

Looking ahead, with salaries currently being a very major cost to most organizations, it seems likely that the employed manager will become a slightly rarer species, and that all but the core group will be employed on a contracted basis, with a complex package of benefits which may include access to accredited learning events. There is no doubt that the contracted manager will be motivated to keep skills up-to-date, and to obtain proof in the form of an accredited updateable qualification of their potential worth in a future contract. The present trend towards accreditation of standards, competencies and harmonized EU qualifications should converge to support the contracted individual in developing a meaningful portfolio of achievement.

With flatter corporate structures, the manager may acquire a much greater span of control, in addition may be a member of a project team, and yet be the leader of a particular business unit. Many more managers will be working with foreign partners or customers. Some managers working in a matrix structure will have to relate to direction from multiple sources of authority. In the new business structure the manager will require objectivity coupled with smarter, harder, business-like approaches which take into account international cultural diversity. This 'hard' business behaviour will need to be backed with a 'softer', more sensitive and intuitive interpersonal approach to building long-term profitable relationships.

Faced with these paradoxical challenges, how is the manager served by the suppliers of management education, development and training? Clearly, if the suppliers are to prosper they will have examined the changing requirements of the corporate market with great care.

Established suppliers: academics

Across the world, universities and the business schools associated with them, offer a range of academically taught and examined business qualifications, the most sought after of which is an MBA. These qualifications have traditionally been offered as a high-level education either for practising managers, with those attending programmes aged generally in their late twenties or early thirties, or for postgraduate students. The twin strength of these institutions lies in the high level of theoretical knowledge and the real life business consultancy experience of the academic staff who teach on the programmes.

There is, however, a tendency for each subject to be taught in its own environment – as a result, often there are academic silos, each of which rarely mixes or crosses into the terrain of another discipline. This requires the student to be capable of making conceptual and applied connections across multi-academic disciplines and being able to transpose these into usefully applied techniques back at the workplace. Many exceptional students will certainly be able to do this – others may struggle to achieve a real return on the investment of time, money and energy which they have made.

Universities and their business schools are moving to address this problem. At the University of Pennsylvania's Wharton School, for instance, courses are no longer taught as isolated disciplines. Students study 'integrative' case studies and also do practical work in companies. Professors at the school work as a team or 'flying squad'.

A common problem in the current economic environment is that potential students, if they are already employed, will certainly be loath to spend as much time away from the workplace as the traditional minimum one-year or two-year full time commitment required to obtain an MBA.

Perceiving this threat to traditional markets, universities and business schools have offered flexible alternatives both for part-time and distance learning equivalent qualifications. It is no easy option to study for an MBA and also to hold down a management position in the time and task culture of corporate life. However, these new methods of study have opened up opportunities for many managers who would have found full-time attendance at business school impractical because of family or work commitments. In 1993, these new channels opened access to MBA programmes to an additional five managers for every one who attended a traditional full time course. Students working on distance learning MBA programmes can work from home wherever that may be and because of this flexibility many of the students are from locations worldwide, and far distant from the university. Universities have responded proactively to this distant market, by running tutorial and examination segments of programmes in major cities across the globe, and by redesigning their programmes.

The MBA qualification with its international currency, could provide a useful platform for managers from many diverse cultures. A key skill for a manager working in an international market will be to understand business customs and ethics in countries with markedly different approaches to their own. Unless, however, the students analyze and discuss a very wide internationally based curriculum with a focus on case studies in which diversity, ethics and national cultures are a critical business element, the opportunity for this may not be fulfilled.

The current challenge to business schools and universities is how to increase flexibility in redesigning their own programmes to attract even busier, more pressured managers. At the same time, they must maintain standards and adapt to growing interest in company-specific programmes – which may be accredited by the university as an academic programme and have points towards a qualification associated with their completion.

Customized programmes are increasing significantly. At Wharton and Duke University in the United States, 65 per cent of their executive education is tailored; at London Business School and Ashridge Management College, 45 per cent of revenue comes from such programmes.

Faced with these diversions, many providers have turned away from a complex third challenge. This is emerging from the novel technological infrastructure of the information superhighway which brings opportunities to link together universities, businesses and students in a flexible and innovative approach to learning. The seeds of this new approach, however, may be gleaned from networks currently used by universities to communicate with both students and academic staff. A concern is that a global divide already seems to be established with major continents such as Africa, lagging behind in the development of a technology infrastructure.

In Japan, where the future value of information has been identified as a weapon in terms of competitiveness, the Ministry of International Trade and Industry is proposing to create 19 'information' cities called 'Technopolis'. These cities will be ringed by optic fibre which will deliver services such as databases, information services and telemarketing. [1]

This will give Japan a unique technological opportunity to distribute learning services direct to the desk of a busy executive. The Japanese multimedia university with its satellite learning centres already reaches many thousands of students, most of whom would not have had the opportunity of gaining qualifications by other means.

The insecurity experienced by individual managers maintaining employment status in a fast moving business environment has led to an increased value being put on qualifications, both by the manager who may need to move from one company to another, and by the employing organization which requires more precise information on the individual potential of managers. In some countries, France for instance, only the most highly qualified become managers, and management is an intellectually based occupation. In the UK there is a clear trend towards qualification of managers which is being driven by both the desire for qualification by the individual and by corporate hunger for more confident and smarter performance from its human resources. But if performance is the goal, then the essential paradox is that an MBA education doesn't teach the manager how to manage people, but mainly how to analyze facts, figures and other information.

Established suppliers: professional institutions

Professional institutions have traditionally offered qualifications in particular specialism. Unlike universities and business schools, there is no equivalent to the internationally recognized MBA among these qualifications. As a consequence of this anomaly, professional qualifications are not generally transferable internationally except within old colonial boundaries. For example, a teacher qualified and experienced in the UK will certainly have to take a new and different qualification if working in the USA. Naturally it is not only desirable, but in many cases essential that professional specialists have the relevant qualification, and legislation currently under consideration in Europe looks at the harmonization of such qualifications. A future in which transferable qualifications were established – in marketing, management, personnel, accountancy, banking, engineering, law and the whole range of business specialist activities across a spectrum of types of business – would encourage cross-border transfers of staff and a more international approach to recruitment and career development.

In each country, professional institutions offer nationally recognized qualifications. A recently increasing trend has been for these institutions to insist on continuous professional development for those who wish to maintain member status. This is particularly so in the business-related professional institutions. This gives an opportunity for the institution to offer update programmes to those already qualified and for them to be flexible in offering new ways of achieving the continuous development requirement. One flexible method is for the professional institution to work with other providers such as universities, commercial bodies and the in-house departments of companies, to accredit short courses and programmes run by these other providers as part of the continuous professional update process.

In the UK, for example, the Institute of Personnel and Development has worked with three organizations to accredit the in-house teaching of stages one and two of professional membership of the Institute: the Post Office, Ford and TSB, who have pioneered this work at their training centres.

Looking across the professions, it seems certain that there could be a generic management element to professional qualifications which, like the possible generic element in management education, could apply to all comers. This generic element which might be a mix between a diploma in business administration and a diploma in management studies would be internationally recognized and instantly used in professional or managerial work worldwide.

Professional institutions have long been engaged in a range of distribution channels for their qualifications. Correspondence courses, evening classes, distance learning, have now been joined by in-house professional qualifications gained through attendance on an accredited programme run by the large corporate training department. This move will surely support an increase in professional qualifications within large corporations and the professionalization of the workforce.

The challenge to the professional institutions is to get closer to the universities, large corporations and to media and publishing houses who work with the institutions to bring out published materials. They could, as a result, offer newer and more relevant routes to qualification to a workforce of managers whose working environment has become more precise, more time pressured, and more eager to employ those with an appropriate qualification.

Generic solutions: commercial providers

At the top end of the scale, the greatest of the commercial providers span a range of institutions from universities and business schools, to management colleges, specialist training companies and consultancy groups. These great providers run commercial businesses based on their curriculum of short, generally modular programmes, and events. Few of the programmes offered last for longer than ten days, but may well be designed to span six months with four or five short residential modules spaced out over the desired time schedule. Many are both innovative and excellent.

These include large and small providers. There are thousands of individual consultants working at a local level to offer training at a more economic price to a diversity of small and medium-sized businesses. One of the effects of right sizing in large companies is the outsourcing of some functions. One of the functions outsourced may well be the company management training department. If it is fortunate it will be able to offer its services back to the organization on a contract basis.

Among residential training colleges, the recession has had an effect and lower academic head count with a higher number of associate staff has been the result. The effect of this has been to release consultants into the market. The best of the providers have had to become global suppliers in order to maintain their market share, and in many cases the proportion of international business has increased.

One feature of the large commercial provider is the diversity of programmes on offer, covering cognitive subjects such as finance, small group issues such as team roles and team leadership, work techniques such as project management, personal efficiency – for instance rapid reading – time management, lateral thinking, and organizational development issues such as managing change. Many of the established group of colleges and specialists have adapted to the new time-pressured world of their clients, the managers in larger corporations, by introducing shorter more intense, more carefully spaced, more action-learning-based programmes. It is surprising that only a few of these providers have linked their short programmes to any accredited qualification.

This is particularly surprising where the same college actually offers an MBA or other academic award.

Ideally, the manager who is the target market for these programmes, would take away a recognizable credit towards a qualification from attendance on a relatively expensive, albeit short, residential module. This credit would need to have international currency to allow a greater marketplace of delegates, and to have relevance whatever the national or multinational base of the sponsoring organization. The managers and the sponsoring organizations are both currently showing clear signs that every expenditure on education, training and development must give a measurable return on the money invested. One such measure would be the increased qualification level of the managerial workforce and the overall value to the company of its managers as an intellectual asset. The challenge to management centres is to provide precision in their offerings while still maintaining an acceptable level of utilization and take-up on courses. This challenge can be faced by getting closer to the corporate customer and by designing more precisely what that organization needs.

In the United States, for example, Johnson & Johnson worked with Duke University to produce its own custom-based training and development programme for its managers. The objective was to make managers more aware of customer needs and to increase awareness of competitors. The cost to Johnson & Johnson was $2,700 per student, but the returns were high as one part of the company reduced inventory levels by 43 per cent and another cut the production cycle by half.[2]

Specialist training providers may major in one particular type or style of training. In this group, there are many types including outdoor training providers working on individual challenge and, team and leadership issues, specific skills training providers – Time Manager International for instance, offers a well presented, entertaining and strictly copyrighted programme on time management. There is a large number of companies in this supply group and it seems likely that only the excellent will survive in the years to come.

The challenge to these specialist training providers is to anticipate how their particular specialism can be applied by a corporation in order to gain competitive advantage and then sell this concept to the organization. A further challenge is how to lock already established programmes into the competence or academically accredited points system so that such individual offering can be seen as part of an overall approach to learning by the buyer.

Clearly, individual consultants and small training providers are not in a good position to advertise accreditation and academic modules. These providers however, are often particularly well placed to offer a more interpersonal range of activities such as work team facilitation, influencing skills, interpersonal role play and action learning based on real life business problems. A large amount of company training is carried out by such individual consultants offering open courses on a wide variety of topics. The worrying aspects to this are that standards and value may vary, that there is no particular recognized qualification for a training consultant and that the consultant is quite likely not to have been able to be selective in the type, level, age or previous knowledge of the delegate attending the programme. Value to individuals could, therefore, be affected through the imprecision of the material offered in relation to the diverse and precise needs of the individual attending. This is slightly less likely to be the case where the consultant acts with the company training department and tailors material, level and method to those attending the programme.

The challenge to consultants working in the corporate environment will be how to keep up with the customer, as organizational change and re-structuring affect the established relationships the consultant may have formed with the corporate buyer. Alternative forms of supply are appearing in the market. One such alternative is the Open Learning Centre. This may stock a range of commercial published materials in a variety of media which can be used by managers visiting the centre. In Poland, Solidarity has sponsored Open Learning Centres in Gdansk and Warsaw. These centres give the opportunity to learn languages, accounting, finance, operations and a range of management skills.

As a consequence of market pressures, consultants have been eager to gain Government sponsored tenders to work on multinational projects in alliances with large corporations, universities and specialist training providers. Substantial projects sponsored by the EU in support of training and development in Eastern Europe, for instance, have provided seed corn for both specialists, consultants, technology-based training companies and universities in equal measure.

Generic solutions: organizational providers

The role of the manager within an organization has taken on an increased strategic importance as a factor in creating competitive edge, particularly in terms of increased efficiency of production, within the company, and in terms of excellence of service in relation to its customers and the community.

A new ethical concern with stakeholders such as staff, shareholders, customers and the community is shaping organizational approaches to learning and development. The effects of the recession caused many companies to take a microscopic look at the value obtained from expenditure of every type, and the identifiable budgets of in-company training and development departments were no exception. As a consequence, various trends emerged.

The first was that large identifiable amounts of expenditure – company residential colleges, for instance – were rationalized, outsourced, floated as independent businesses or integrated with other training and development resources within the business. Out of this change came a new message to company managers: old style structured learning was on the way out, and new-style structuring of a learning environment which would support the manager engaged in self-managed learning was put in place.

The second trend was the widespread introduction of non-residential, distance learning and technology-based methods for knowledge-based learning.

Across the countries of the world, learning centres filled with machines and software, able to be supervised by a single low-cost administrator, have offered managers and staff alike, the opportunity to undertake individual self-paced learning on a variety of topics.

Typically, the US General Accounting Office has developed software packages to teach management skills through computer simulations of real-life situations. The skills taught include 'motivating to achieve results; assessing personal management skills; leading effectively; performance appraisal and conducting successful meetings'.[3] The challenge of this new methodology is both how to measure its effectiveness and how to lock such modules into accredited qualification.

Both these trends in learning methods foster a just-in-time approach to training provision. The busy manager needs precise training or support for learning at just the right time, and there is some evidence that organizational training departments are making every effort to provide delivery methods which satisfy that requirement.

In this environment, it is important that the supplier understands the likely learning style of the student and designs programmes which will prove easy for the student to undertake, which will fit with their learning profile, and satisfy precisely the need identified.

The new focus on human resources as a strategic issue has also shifted company attention on to moral and ethical contracts with its employees. As part of this contract, the company may provide learning opportunities for managers and will, in return, expect the individual's commitment to personal development and life-long continuous learning. The individual manager will almost certainly perceive an advantage in gaining some tangible evidence of the learning that has taken place and, as a result, will press for the opportunity to gain qualifications which are transferable.

A few companies recognizing the need of staff to be valued and educated in order to perform well, have set up internal provisions for management development. NEC has its own Institute of Management which trains its managers throughout the world. In the UK, GEC has its own management college. General Electric, in the United States, trains 6,000 managers every year while Banque Indosuez trained 1,200 managers during 1991.[4]

Some have even established their own in-house 'universities'. Motorola University, for instance, contains an educational curriculum which is relevant to the corporation, to the job and to the individual. It works to design programmes that accrediting boards will certify and which traditional universities will accept. The Motorola University works in partnership with established universities in giving feedback on the programmes attended by Motorola sponsored employees.[5]

A further effect of the focus on human resources as a strategic issue has been to expose the very real need for every level of manager, from the most senior to the newly appointed management trainee, to make a visible commitment to increasing their own learning. While this is quite usual at management trainee level, it has been more exceptional at director and board level. The message given to the company by this form of top-level commitment to learning can have a very positive and measurable payback.

Recent concerns on corporate governance, and the legal responsibilities of directors are live issues, and company directors have become increasingly motivated to gain a professional qualification in, what could be called, 'company direction'. In the UK the Institute of Directors director development centre offers an accredited diploma, director business updates and a range of services to support this new market. The type of curriculum developed by an in-house education and training department will have both generic and precise offerings aimed at every level, every job and every functional type of manager. This creates a learning environment in which some aspects are job specific, some function/profession specific, and some generic to education, some generic to interpersonal issues or to relationships.

The in-house department has had to examine every cost. It is no longer likely to consist of large numbers of well paid 'lecturers'. A much wider range of skills now needs to be called into play. Organizational training departments have been leaders in setting up part-time contracted resourcing for their programmes, in selecting top level business school and consultant contribution and input to senior programmes, and in developing strategic action-learning projects with real business outcomes for senior managers to own and shape on behalf of the organization.

The strategic business focus of the organizational training department is now an acknowledged factor in the best companies, and ownership and sponsorship of projects and action learning has moved to board level in some cases.

Clearly in organizations, qualification is a growing requirement. There are many companies currently gaining accreditation for internal competence-based training programmes, which will add to points gathered from external or internal educational modules. Ideally every effort of the individual would have some tangible outcome. Without international agreement on transferability of qualification, however, this may be of limited value to those managers who see their career developing on an international front.

The current environment in which companies operate clearly puts certain pressures on their training and development departments to work proactively to create change and to implement strategy among the key influencers in an organization, its managers. It may be that where this process is working well, the organization perceives other stakeholders, who may benefit from involvement in company sponsored training.

Some companies now undertake team action-learning projects, jointly with the customers, or business partners with whom they may need to develop a good working partnership. Digital's AIMS programme for senior managers, designed by INSEAD, uses action-learning projects and team building not only cross-functionally within the company, but across boundaries to include business partners and customers. GE in the US at its Crontonville Institute has developed an emphasis on customer education, and has moved from a focus on knowledge, to a focus on fundamental change within the GE businesses including the concept of boundaryless working between functions, divisions, business partners and customers.

Other companies support the community by providing places on in-company programmes for charity aid workers whose own organization's budget does not allow for more than very basic training. Managers from large corporations can now be involved in working on community projects, in order to apply new skills and gain confidence while at the same time contributing to a major charitable effort. TSB offers non-paying places on its short management programmes through recommendation from the TSB Foundation which manages an annual programme of charitable donations. The TSB also runs an innovative development programme for young managers as part of which each manager works for 100 hours on a community project. A final workshop on this programme brought together the 24 delegates, 24 charities, company trainers, HR director and the group chairman to share the learning outcome of this experience.

The challenge to the organizational training department is to be viewed by the organization as a strategic asset, without which company business and human resource initiatives would face major disadvantages in implementation. Where a company does see training as a strategic contribution this will undoubtedly form one feature of the annual report to shareholders – Dresdner Bank, for instance, reports on yearly growth in training effort and expenditure.

A clear challenge to the company today is to produce meaningful measurement of what has been achieved through education, training and development. The topic of measurement has to be of strategic importance in its own right, and where companies have applied new measures there have been some notable payoffs achieved.

There is little doubt that the landscape of management education, development and training will continue to change, with a larger number of diverse suppliers chasing a falling number of managers in the target market. Managers will increasingly be looking for a life-long learning process which provides just-in-time training, distributed through on-the-desk, multimedia, open learning centres and distance learning. By using these new techniques, the manager will attempt to balance the pressure of work and home life while gaining qualifications. The infrastructure for education and training is changing rapidly with the old ivory towers between education, training and development starting to fall as they integrate into *learning*.

New alliances are emerging between universities and publishers, universities and large corporate training departments. Training and development is becoming an inclusive event at which companies, customers and the community work together on strategic issues using project-based action-learning techniques. Tomorrow's company will certainly provide access to learning as part of an ethical contract with managers in order to support the individual's development of a life-long portfolio of achievement in learning. The challenge for the experts employed in the education and training environment is how to retain the leading edge of expertise and add to it a credible understanding of the business environment in which learning can be put into action.

Theresa Barnett is deputy principal, learning and development, at the TSB Group Management College. The College activities include management and director development, professional development, management skills programmes, team facilitation and consultancy. She has worked for a number of years on the integration of technology into management learning and was responsible for a number of award-winning innovative interactive programmes. *A Case of Disappearing Pills* has been included in the US Smithsonian Institution interactive teaching laboratory as an example of best design.

References

1 *Journal of Management Development*, 11.7, Florida Atlantic University.
2 Wiley, C, 'Training for the '90s', *Employment Relations Today*, Spring 1993.
3 Abbott, J and Dahuus, S, *Journal of Management Development 11.1*, Florida Atlantic University.
4 Devine, M, 'Dismantling the ivory towers of management education', *Directions*, December 1992.
5 Wiggenhorn, W, 'Motorola University, When training becomes an education', *Harvard Business Review*, July/Aug 1990.

THE ROLE OF BUSINESS SCHOOLS

Arnoud de Meyer

Faced with increasing competition from other providers of management train-ing and development, business schools are undergoing a rigorous process of re-examination.

Bridging the gap between research and best practice is central to the debate. The measure of the future success of business schools is likely to lie in the quality of their research and the productiveness of partnerships the schools forge with the business world.

Being an effective manager is not a black and white issue. Managers are nei-ther good nor bad. In reality, being a good manager is a matter of being marginally better than and different from your competitors. It is a question of being a little bit faster; able to spot an opportunity somewhat earlier; or react-ing quicker to a new threat. These are the elements which make the difference between a successful and a less successful manager. This marginal advantage may be based on talent, flair or natural leadership. But, knowledge of manage-ment can provide this decisive advantage. A sophisticated manager must, as a result, constantly update his or her knowledge of the latest concepts, insights and experiences in management thinking.

The education of managers encompasses a wide, and well known, array of possibilities. These include on-the-job training, special assignments, work-shops, conferences, support through consulting, and short and long training courses. Business schools have a special role to fulfil in this portfolio. Traditionally they have three major differentiating characteristics. They have the ability to offer a complete package which ranges from basic to very sophis-ticated training. They offer an opportunity for managers to get in touch with the latest thinking based on the research carried out by their faculty. And they are able to preserve an independent outlook towards the world of business.

In contrast to most other providers of management education, business schools often offer a complete portfolio of educational programmes. The thor-ough training of an MBA programme exists alongside general management programmes for experienced managers and specialized or topical programmes. For the business school this has the advantage of different programmes being able to cross-fertilize with each other – the insights that a faculty member may learn from top executives will have a positive impact on the teaching in a graduate programme. But, more importantly for organizations which want to use management education as a key element of their management development programmes, this offers substantial advantages. It means that managers and executives at different levels of the organization can be confronted with the same concepts, expressed in the same language and put into practice by similar approaches. Though the teaching methods will differ for different levels in the organization, and though the conceptual approach must be adapted to the particular challenges confronting different levels in the organization, a close partnership with a business school enables a company to create some coherence between the education and development of its different management levels. People will communicate more effectively because they use the same idiom, they will be able to discuss issues on the basis of the same underlying concepts and, in general, it will be easier to apply some of the insights gained in management education, because the company environment will be more familiar with the concepts taught at a business school.

The coherence that a business school may provide between the education of different organizational levels is only valuable when the commonly acquired insights and concepts are state of the art. This leads to the second vital differentiating characteristic for a business school: its research and development activities. Research at business schools is often denigrated. Practitioners are quick to talk of ivory towers, academic playgrounds, and categorize research as esoteric and overly theoretical. Yet, good management research is absolutely essential to the competitive performance of companies. A good management concept – one that can provide a competitive advantage to your organization – has a limited time during which it can provide such an advantage. Only in the first months or years after the discovery of such a concept can one build an advantage on it. Afterwards it becomes a common good, available to all, and organizations simply have to apply it in order not to fall behind their competitors. At that stage, the advantage has evaporated. This process can be seen in recently developed concepts such as activity-based cost accounting, strategic quality management or the concept of core competencies. The first companies to apply these concepts, clearly extracted an advantage from them. But for the bulk of organizations, the latecomers, it is simply something you *have* to apply, even if it does not provide you with a real competitive advantage.

In order to serve its partners, the business community, a business school must carry out research, and further the understanding of management practice. Management research is essential to the business community. Collaborating with a business school is for many companies a privileged method of gaining access to the latest management thinking, before it gets published in trade journals or popular books. And working with the scholars who developed these concepts may be one of the fastest ways to discover not only the *what* of the concept, but also *how* to implement it effectively.

Essential to good research is the critical and independent mind of the researcher – the third differentiating characteristic of a good business school as a source of management education. As a consequence of its financial and organizational structure, and the type of faculty it attracts, a business school may develop a spirit of independence that is difficult to achieve in other educational environments. It is the duty of a business school to challenge company executives on commonly held beliefs, to shake confidence in their current practices, to help them think about wider socio-economic and political responsibilities. Business schools should not train administrators, but managers and entrepreneurs who contribute to the growth of the economy and the improvement of society. A debate on ethics in an international economic environment or an analysis of preconceived ideas on culture is often easier in the free academic environment of a business school than in the business itself. Business schools must provide a non-threatening environment in which executives and managers can simulate the impact of alternative ideas, and see how they can create a beneficial effect in the long term.

The mistake of some business schools is not to recognize that their major competitive advantage is in being at the forefront of management education. Business schools should not be the best or the most effective in mass training of basic management concepts but, instead, their uniqueness must be based on high quality and rigorous research. Offering education based on leading-edge research will become ever more important in the future. It will become the competitive arena in which business schools can and should compete. This obviously does not imply that research should be totally disconnected from current business needs.

Rigour in research is important but business schools do not have to be ponderous. Instead, they should be able to shorten the design cycle time of research efforts, in order to be faster in responding to business needs. Serving the business community *faster* is the first challenge for business schools. The traditional approach to management research takes too long.

At the risk of being too simplistic, one could describe the research system as follows. Some excellent companies are having interesting experiences using a particular approach. Through case studies or other forms of empirical research, scholars try to gain an understanding of these experiences. After having gathered enough data, the scholars begin conceptualizing and modelling in order to make that experience available and actionable for other companies. And those models are consequently taught in management education programmes. This, in itself, is not a bad model. But, it has the disadvantage that the cycle time from first observation to practical application can easily take five or more years. In the current business environment this is too long.

Business schools have to find a way of speeding up the process of concept development and testing. Like companies they have to go from sequential problem solving in research to simultaneous approaches. Action-oriented management education can play a very positive role in achieving this. Programmes tailored to particular organizations can fuse analysis of experiences and practices with the concept development. Executives can then be stimulated to critically analyze their own experiences. The resulting insights can be used by the executives in projects carried out in their own organization. The projects can then be used as case studies of how particular concepts can be applied in a particular organization. Such close collaboration between the company and the business school enables both sides to develop some of the building bricks of new management concepts. At the same time, the business school evolves from a teaching institution towards a learning institution. In these circumstances, the business school is no longer a place where students are taught, but becomes an institution where everybody – participants as well as faculty, researchers or doctoral students – learns from each other.

A second challenge for business schools is to increase the impact they may have on participants and companies. INSEAD's Yves Doz has developed a simple model to explain this (Fig. 1). The first dimension in this model concerns who receives the impact of education: one individual, a few key individuals, a larger group of managers, or the entire organization? The second dimension reflects the content: are business schools teaching technical tools and skills, or are they more strategy-oriented, or do they try to change values, culture and attitudes? The third dimension indicates to what extent the company environment is integrated in the management education: do business schools simply neglect cultural implications, is it acknowledged, is it integrated or do they try to change the company environment?

Traditional management education usually stays close to the centre of this three-dimensional model. A few individuals are taught skills and tools, or perhaps strategy, and the specific company environment of that individual is neglected or ignored. Yet, in order to have a real impact on the management capabilities of individuals and organizations, business schools need to explore

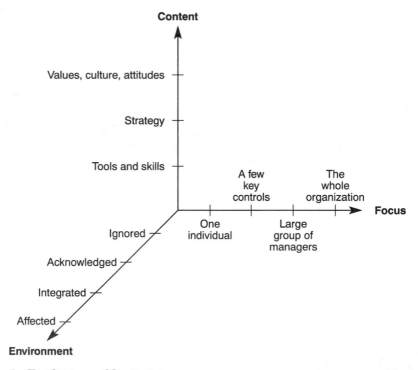

Fig. 1 Evolution of learning process

how they can offer education that is away from this centre. How can they offer activities that will impact on the whole organization, that help the company to transform its environment, and that will enable the company to adapt its culture? The answer is not necessarily to organize more tailormade programmes. That is only one answer to the need to increase the impact of business schools. Cleverly designed combinations of on-the-job training, international assignments, combined with well chosen open enrolment programmes in business schools, may do an equally effective job.

What is needed to meet these two challenges? A partial answer to both of them lies in the creation of partnerships between business schools and outstanding business organizations. Such partnerships go beyond the organization of educational programmes and encompass the full range of activities, such as support for and collaboration in research and development, training at different levels of the organization, contributing to the graduate programmes and hiring of MBA graduates.

Describing the need to develop such partnerships is straightforward; but implementation requires a large amount of adaptation from both sides. Experience at INSEAD suggests that three conditions have to be fulfilled to give any partnership a chance.

First, the company and the business school must know each other at different hierarchical levels. Too often the partnership is managed by one gatekeeper or account manager on both sides. The impact of such a gatekeeper is often insufficient inside the respective organizations. As a result, a partnership that was initiated with good intentions dies quietly away because the power structures in both organizations do not adhere to it. In order to make the partnership work, both sides must be prepared to invest in multiple and repeated contacts at different hierarchical levels in the organization. Deans must talk to top managers, faculty must interact with executives, and research assistants and students must interact with the company's rank and file management.

Second, a partnership between a business school and a company can only survive if the two parties respect the difference between each other's long-term objectives. For example, the company's objectives in terms of competitive position and return on investment often require secrecy and the protection of new ideas. The business school's academic objectives require broad diffusion of ideas through publication, conference presentations and teaching. The conflicts that may arise as a consequence have to be brought to the table early on in the discussions, and a *modus vivendi* has to be found.

Third, business schools and companies have very different organizational structures and value systems. Business schools are very flat structures built around a group of professionals whose loyalty is divided between the school and their profession. Companies often have a stronger common sense of direction, and authority has a clear meaning. These differences reflect the difference in goals and are appropriate for the two types of organizations. But, as misunderstandings are inevitable, any short-term partnership has a high risk of failure. Organizations often do not understand that the concept of academic freedom gives a very different meaning to authority. One could argue that faculty cannot be told to collaborate with a company, but that they have to be seduced into working with a company. In such an environment partnerships must be given time to develop. Partnerships can only work when they are designed with a long-term perspective. The two organizations have to get to know each other, have to understand each other's weaknesses and strengths, and have to gradually build the partnership through a succession of small concrete achievements.

Successful partnerships are often initiated through a fairly straightforward management development programme. Having built a climate of confidence, faculty develops several case studies and begins to understand the organization. This gives the company confidence in the capacity of the business school to come up with relevant concepts and ideas, and leads the company to invest in a major research programme. This may, in turn, evolve into a highly sophisticated management development activity for the executives of the company, based on the joint research. The end result can be that the company and the business school engage in myriad activities stretching from specialist training, consortium programmes with other companies, as well as research and support for the school's most senior programme.

One consequence of the partnership idea is that business schools cannot limit their activity to the delivery of an educational programme. More and more they need to take responsibility for the application of concepts in the partnering organizations. This does not imply that they have to go into the consulting business. But, it does imply that business schools have to take more responsibility for what happens before and after the programme. Participants who come well prepared to the management education programme get a lot more out of the faculty than other participants. Understanding the specific goals of the programme, or coming to the programme prepared with a set of concrete problems that the participant wants solved during it, may help tremendously in increasing the return on the investment in training. It also makes it easier for a business school to react to the specific needs of the participant and to indicate what the potential tools for the implementation of certain ideas and concepts are.

Finally as we know, no learning is more effective than learning by doing. Sitting on a school bench for several hours and listening to a dry lecture is a very artificial exercise for a modern manager. A real partnership requires that business schools should take a share of the responsibility for the diffusion and application of what the participant learned. Thus the implementation side must feature prominently in business school programmes. Action learning through project work, structured debate and exchange of experience between participants will have to gain importance in programme portfolios. Again, to make this work, business schools require the active support of their partner companies.

Partnering is not easy and cannot be done on a large scale. Experience suggests that, at any one school, the number of partnerships will have to be limited. Both business schools and companies must carefully select the organizations they want to partner. Companies need to look for partner schools that offer the best in research relevant to the company's challenges. A business school's strength starts and ends with the rigour, the quality and the relevance of its research. This is the force that will enable and nurture such partnerships.

Arnoud de Meyer is associate dean for executive education and professor of technology management at INSEAD. A graduate of the State University of Ghent, Belgium, he is the author of numerous books and articles. His areas of specialism include manufacturing strategy, international R&D management, implementation of process technology and information systems in manufacturing.

Further Reading

Bickerstaffe, G, *Which MBA? A Critical Guide to the World's Best Programmes*, The Economist Intelligence Unit, London, 1994.

TOP MANAGEMENT DEVELOPMENT

Robert Sharrock

Much that is written about management development has a formulaic quality. It concerns what can be done to managers to enhance their effectiveness, and the processes which can be put in place in organizations to deliver *management development*. Yet, if there is one factor which underpins the success of top managers, it is the ability to benefit from developmental opportunities created by themselves – this has been called *manager development* rather than the more procedural and less active *management development*.

Manager development resists formulae. It is intuitive, less formal than conventional approaches, and is rooted in the actions of managers. There is growing awareness that throughout their careers managers can enhance and enable their own development. The skill of managing personal and career development is set to become vital to personal and organizational success.

Organizations are in a state of flux and the pace of future change is likely to accelerate. The trend of corporate down-sizing is set to continue as organizations become more focused, flatter and more closely aligned to their customers. In the US, for example, it has been forecast that by 2000, 85 per cent of the workforce will be employed by companies employing 200 people or less.[1]

These are truths almost universally acknowledged. But, while the changing nature of organizations is well documented and understood, the changing nature of organizational responsibilities is less well accepted. In such a turbulent environment notions of organizational responsibilities will become more complex. They will involve balancing the interests of the entire range of stakeholders – going beyond shareholders to encompass customers, employees and society at large. Public interest in commercial issues, environmental and consumer power and an ever-more vigilant media have all, as Sir Adrian Cadbury has observed, forced the *social agenda* into the boardroom. These factors, though now sometimes seen as thorns in the side of senior executives, will constitute a commercial force which agile and aware organizations will harness to secure competitive advantage.

The effect of these organizational trends will be that developmental experiences obtained within one organization are likely to be insufficient, both in terms of quantity and quality, to achieve senior management positions in the future. The reality of this is already apparent. In 1993, for example, Barclays Bank appointed a chief executive, Martin Taylor, a former financial journalist and chief executive within the textiles industry who lacked direct banking experience. Ironically this was felt necessary in spite of the bank's own

470

management development programme, designed to identify high fliers. These trainees are given a range of relevant experiences through job placements to equip them with, what Barclays feels, are the required management skills for the future.

The reduction in opportunities for vertical promotion and the loss of the traditional lure of promotion as a means of development and motivation means that managers will need to re-construe the nature of the psychological contract between them and their organization.

This, in extremis, is captured in Table 1.

Table 1 The changing psychological contract between managers and the organization

	Traditional	*Future*
Duration of tenure	long-standing	time-limited
Certainty of tenure	safer	less certain
Management development	planned by the company via promotion	opportunistic, self-determined via company changes
Motivational drivers	loyalty	enhancing future employability
Salaries	lower, incremental, predictable	higher, offset by risk, less predictable

The key to the new psychological contract will be an increased need for managers to take responsibility for their own development and sets of skills. To do so requires a high and consistent degree of motivation. A key element of executive success is the drive to achieve results and make an impact, and personal motivation is, in some individuals, permanently high. This may be due to psychological factors, such as a craving for recognition and status.

For others, however, motivation varies in relation to personal circumstances and stages of life development. A rapid promotion following a job change, increased monetary needs coinciding with family life or the self-confidence that follows from a close, mentoring-type relationship with a charismatic boss, can each provide a fillip to an executive's aspiration and drive.

One manager noted that his career overseas, running a large plant, had become static. 'It was comfortable for me and my family, but eventually I decided I had to act, to get noticed and to create more opportunities.' Having secured a head office role, he achieved rapid promotion to become chief operating officer. He is now chief executive of a governmental organization seeking to become more commercial, where his skills and background are seen as adding particular value.

People must create and seize the opportunity. As Rosabeth Moss Kanter argues in *When Giants Learn to Dance*, if security of tenure no longer follows from being employed, then it must come from having a sufficiently broad and marketable skills base to ensure employability. A precursor will be a capacity to tolerate risk and ambiguity. In short, a new skill will be required for managerial success in the late 1990s and beyond – that of career management.

Top management skills of the 1990s and beyond

What, then, are the skills which top managers of the future should be acquiring and developing? Since the seminal work of Richard Boyatzis, in *The Competent Manager: A Model for Effective Performance* (1982), there has been a great deal of research on management competencies, defined as skills and characteristics which result in effective or superior performance. Though Boyatzis' work was well researched and of high quality, it was conducted overwhelmingly on sizeable numbers of middle managers in large, American corporations, with clearly defined roles. There is a risk, inherent in the static and mechanistic approach to how competencies are defined, that what emerges are lists of skills which underpin how things are done. Such an approach can produce limitations and deficiencies which are self-perpetuated rather than give emphasis to how things should or could be done, either now or in the future. It emphasizes probabilities rather than possibilities.

Examples of research into the skills which underpin executive success are summarized in Table 2. For the purposes of classification, skill areas identified by the researchers have been condensed into four broad headings: problem solving, drive, interpersonal and business experience.

The differences in emphasis in the various studies reflect the range of groups under investigation. In his book, *Peak Performers* (1986), Charles Garfield's interest, for example, is skewed towards the entrepreneurial American chief executive; his list of skills is closer to Andrew Kakabadse's in *The Wealth Creators* (1991). Alan Mumford's study, *Developing Top Managers* (1988), on the other hand, concentrated on UK directors. His key skills tend therefore to be more closely related with corporate and boardroom issues.

The important implication is that there is no one way of being a top manager. The ideal set of skills for an executive role will undoubtedly depend on the following factors:

- Size, stage of development and nature of the business. A charismatic, risk-taking and visionary individual may be responsible for the rapid growth of a company but with size, divestment of ownership and the need to manage through others rather than directly, a new set of management skills may be required.
- Rate of change of the business environment. Slower changing areas of business (such as bulk chemicals) where new entrants are deterred by high entry

Table 2 Research into top management competencies

Author	Problem solving	Drive	Inter-personal	Business knowledge
Kakabadse (1991)	Flexibility	Create their own opportunities		
		Drive and ambition to succeed	Highly interactive	Broad knowledge
		Resilience		
Garfield (1986)	Course correction[2]	Self-mastery[3]	Team-building and team-playing	
		Missions that motivate		
			Change management	
		Results in real time		
Mumford (1988)	Identifying direction	Working to high standards	Operating effectively in different cultures	Managing external relationships
	Taking a corporate perspective			Profit centre responsibility
			Influencing key executives	
	Grasp of data and broader principles		Getting others to act on your behalf	International exposure
	Planning the future			

costs, are likely to demand different management skills and styles from more rapidly changing businesses, such as the IT industry.

- The requirement of skills of strategic value at a point in an organization's development. For example, an organization seeking to become more customer-driven may appoint a chief executive with particular strengths and skills in marketing or customer service. The appointment of Sir John Egan, who had successfully turned around Jaguar Cars based on quality and customer focus, to chief executive at BAA (British Airports Authority) is a notable example.

● Culture. The attitudes, skills and behaviours valued within an American multinational company will be different from, for example, those within a Swedish multinational.

● Relationships with stakeholders and business partners. Some organizations can function fairly autonomously of external investors – others are crucially dependent on their relationships with bankers and shareholders. Again, the implication is that different skill sets have a premium depending on prevailing circumstances and needs.

Given the variety of business environments, a key need for executives is to identify their own strengths and style. They can then seek out situations where these skills will add most value and to recognize when these skills are no longer required. The value of insight, written about by American business psychologist Paul Brouwer as early as 1964, will increase as top managers need to be yet more active in managing their careers.

The relevance of insight

In *Peak Performers*, Charles Garfield refers to the key skill of self-mastery – orchestrating and developing capabilities and seeking opportunities within organizations which further personal growth.[4] Manager development must begin with the individual. The truism that 'He that would govern others, first should be the master of himself,' has never been more true.

The starting point, therefore, is a level of self-knowledge. At its simplest, this includes an accurate appreciation of strengths, limitations and goals. Several levels to insight can be discerned. At the most basic, individuals may lack any understanding of how they impact upon others and of their key strengths. Psychological factors behind such limited insight may be the lack of capacity to take perspective and see oneself as others might, or a defensiveness to the views of others based on a fragile self-esteem. With greater insight comes an appreciation of personal goals and strengths, normally somewhat over-valued, but with it often comes a lack of awareness about how to act as a result. The highest level of insight is accompanied by a sense of taking responsibility, learning to address limitations and in creating and seeking situations which harness strengths.

Interestingly, contemporary accounts of intelligence are beginning to encompass notions of how these insights can be levered by individuals to their practical advantage. Robert Sternberg, in *Intelligence Applied* (1986), for example, draws distinction between academic intelligence, usually measured by an ability test, and more practical intelligence which relates to the capacity to achieve goals in practical settings. He argues that tacit knowledge, knowledge that is not openly stated or learned, is key to practical intelligence, and includes knowledge about the self (motivations) and the ability to assign priorities to tasks, in addition to career management skills (including a knowledge of the value of reputation, and convincing others of the worth of one's ideas).[5]

Table 3 Levels of insight

Level	Characterized by
1. Lack of insight	Little appreciation of impact on others; little knowledge of key strengths and weaknesses
2. Developing insight	Growing appreciation of personal goals and strengths; little or no awareness of how to take advantage of strengths or correct weaknesses
3. Insight	Sense of responsibility for managing own development; addressing limitations; seeking and creating situations to utilize and maximize strengths.

Top managers can lose insight, or never acquire it, quite easily. One reason is that increasing distance from peers and a boss, combined with growing power, may lead to the views of others – once a source of constructive feedback and criticism – drying up. Another reason is that repeated success experiences may cause an individual to lose sight of external factors (for example, market growth or the role of the immediate team) behind the success, and the implications of these for career management. Under these circumstances, top managers can benefit from confidential counselling to consider their personal goals, skills and the needs of the business situation.

Creating and harnessing career opportunities

Faced with the new psychological contract, potential top executives will need to be more energetic and creative in identifying career opportunities within and beyond their immediate organizations. In her evocatively titled book, *How to be Head-Hunted* (1991), Yvonne Sarch constructs a case for career management round the theme of reputation – building it, proving it, earning it and holding on to it. She speaks of the need to create opportunities through projecting one's strengths to best effect.[6]

With the emergence of consultancies and a premium of specific technical skills, for example, some managers may find themselves with insufficient exposure to general management to progress to the top. One manager, now IT director with a £500 million turnover business, determined to obtain broader management exposure having worked for an international management consultancy. 'I knew I needed good management experience if I was to progress in a commercial organization.' Having regularly received phone calls from search consultants, he arranged to meet several and was shortly in the running for two jobs. 'I had to decide between organizations – a major UK financial institution, and my current employer. Talking about the decision with a business psychologist, I decided a smaller organization where I would be closer to the top decision-makers, and have free reign in my actions, would suit my style, play to my strengths and provide better learning opportunities.'

This degree of proactivity requires a certain psychological safety to enable one to take measured risks, such as pushing one's case to those in authority and changing job. Top executives of the future will need to manage their lives such that the taking of measured risks can be readily entertained. Important implications include:

- Having work and other spheres of one's life in balance. Ideally, work should not obliterate other areas of life and no one should be too dependent upon it for their sense of psychological worth.
- Smoothing financial ups and downs through the use of debt, savings and pension planning. Managers of tomorrow are more likely to have to take financial risks – for example, raising capital prior to a management buy-out or accepting lower paid work.
- The need to construe mistakes as learning opportunities rather than disasters. Decisions of the future are more likely than ever to involve ambiguity and uncertainty. Mistakes are, therefore, unavoidable. The ability to learn from them will be key.

There is a powerful analogy between the marketing of top manager's own skills and the marketing of a company's products. As John Viney and Stephanie Jones have pointed out, in *Career Turnaround* (1991), both start with an appraisal of goals and objectives, and what amounts to a SWOT analysis – the identification of strengths, weaknesses, opportunities and threats.[7]

Such analysis can stimulate thought and lead to careers taking new directions. A manager in an international fast-moving consumer goods company had joined as a marketing trainee. He achieved good rather than spectacular promotions but, after a few years, began to think more creatively about his career. 'Analogously to a marketing plan, I asked myself where my skills might best be used. When an opportunity arose to apply my skills to an environment needy of marketing skills and the approach of an outsider – a traditional high street clearing bank – I seized it with enthusiasm.' He is now senior executive responsible for a major product line within the bank.

The following series of questions serves both as a checklist of some of the key aspects of executive career planning and means of enhancing opportunities.

Identifying, strengths and limitations

1. Are you aware of your strengths?
2. Do you have a clear goal of what is your next ideal job?
3. Do you have a good idea about what you are trying to achieve through your work?

4. Are you aware of your limitations?
5. Do you have levels of drive and ambition ahead of your peers?
6. Do you have the opportunity to talk about your career planning with an insightful friend, mentor or professional?
7. Do you have a good idea of how you are perceived by your colleagues?
8. Do you know what your boss thinks of your work?
9. Do you appreciate your financial needs?
10. Do you understand what kind of organizations you feel most comfortable in (large or small; entrepreneurial or conservative; people or task oriented)?
11. Are your work and other aspects of your life in reasonable balance?

Creating and enhancing opportunities
1. Are your skills increasing in demand, and if so, in which industries or settings?
2. Do you regularly scan the jobs pages of a quality newspaper?
3. Do you have an up-to-date CV which emphasizes your achievements rather than your responsibilities?
4. Do you seek to enhance your reputation for achieving results and producing high-quality work?
5. Do you have personal contacts in organizations which value your skills (eg, competitors)?
6. Do you make an effort to meet people who may present you with future opportunities?
7. Are you sufficiently financially secure to take work-related risks?
8. Do you have effective means of dealing with stress?
9. Have you met an executive search consultant ('head-hunter') in the last three years?
10. Have you applied for another job in the last three years?
11. Do you have enough personal security and self-confidence to take measured risks at work?
12. Do you seek out opportunities for your own development at work?
13. Do you work in an organization where personal development and achievement are valued?

Learning processes

'Experience is inevitable; learning is not,' say Russo and Schoemaker in their 1989 book *Confident Decision Making*.[8]

In the light of the research and the trends already noted, how are top managers to gain the appropriate skills to equip them for the careers of tomorrow? A good starting point here is to consider how, in general, top managers learn and consider how these processes can be harnessed to best effect. Perhaps the most extensive research in this respect has been done by Alan Mumford. Mumford's investigation into the processes of top management learning revealed that development processes tend to be informal, intuitive and, in the case of talented managers, followed from their own management actions. Mumford distinguished between three types of actual learning. Only a very few of the managers he questioned mentioned formal, planned learning as having had material impact – and then it was having participated in teaching rather than learning experiences.

Even formal learning opportunities often contain a large amount of informal learning. Completing an MBA is perhaps the most formal and usual means of enhancing problem-solving capabilities. For one manager, it provided a means of honing down problems to his key parameters – 'I learned to question and to sort out ideas which are fad and fashion from those which will stick. I learned to get along with people from different cultures and see problems from a more global perspective.' The credibility and awareness that arises from such international experience is now well harnessed – as a country managing director for an international consumer goods company.

Identifying which means of learning is most effective is an impossible task. There are wide variations in managers' approaches to learning as well as in the quality of experiences encountered. Furthermore, this is a notoriously difficult area to research, since most learning of skilled behaviour occurs at an unconscious level and is therefore difficult to identify and discuss during interview.

Nevertheless, Alan Mumford has made a number of interesting observations:

- The development value of learning through the job seems to increase in line with novelty content. Changing organization has more learning value than promotion, for example, where managers carry with then significant knowledge of job content.
- Learning through others seemed to be less important than the literature suggests, with its focus on the boss-subordinate relationship. For example, in only a few cases did mentoring, defined as a confidential, supportive, informal or formal relationship with someone other than a boss, appear to have a beneficial influence. It is possible that Mumford's sample of directors may have been unable (or unwilling) to articulate which influential managers in their experience had had a beneficial effect. Certainly, many talented managers build up a collage of behaviours, probably a small part of their total repertoire, which are either acquired or reinforced by charismatic role models.

Executives differ in their temperamental capacity to learn and can be expected to respond differentially to the learning processes outlined above. David Kolb has identified four key parts of a general learning cycle, represented in Fig. 1. Furthermore, individuals differ in their preferred style of learning. Cautious and introverted individuals may push themselves gingerly into novel experiences which present learning opportunities, although they may review more thoroughly the experiences they do have. Kolb has described such individuals as *assimilators*, with a bias towards concepts and ideas. Less cautious and more extroverted managers, on the other hand, will tend to have a preference for learning from others and by doing. Kolb has described such managers as *accommodators* due their flexibility in the light of changing circumstances.

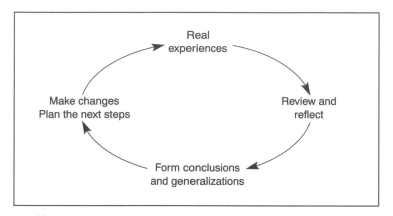

Fig. 1 Kolb's learning cycle

Source: D. Kolb, *The Learning Style Inventory*, McBer & Co, Boston, Mass, 1976

One of Mumford's observations was that only rarely did executives seem to exploit the maximum value from the learning opportunities. On this analysis, management learning can be greatly enhanced by increasing the emphasis on reviewing and forming conclusions, rather than simply doing – the preferred style of most action-oriented executives.

Seemingly off-beat experiences can have a direct and powerful affect on the way managers manage – but only if the lessons are learned and their potential application recognized. Managing internationally, for example, requires an understanding not so much of particular cultures in which the manager is working but of the fact that differences exist and need to be taken account of. One manager, having graduated in physics, began his career with a year's spell of teaching with Voluntary Service Overseas. 'I learned how to put my message across so that it was understood, and developed a self-confidence in my ability to work away from my home.' Now working for a UK-German electrical company, he observes: 'There is nothing unique about management in Germany or anywhere else. Things have got to get done and problems solved. What is helpful is a need to consider the different perspectives of other cultures and take account of them. The confidence, though, to approach problems head-on is key'

Other factors which affect top managers' capacity to benefit from developmental opportunities include:

- *Intelligence*. A key finding from occupational psychology is that aptitude tests seem to be most effective in predicting the success of training. In general, strategic capabilities can be seen as an amalgam of intelligence, experience and an orientation towards results.
- *Psychological blocks to learning*. One, referred to by psychologists as a 'positive attributional bias', relates to claiming credit for outcomes over which, in reality, little control of influence was achieved. The corollary block is rationalizing to avoid the pain of mistakes, including blaming

others or altering preferences to reduce the impact of failure (such as, 'I never wanted the job anyway').

- *Lack of feedback*, caused by inadequate business information, too distant a relationship with a boss (such as, running an autonomous business unit) or 'jobhopping' before the effect of decisions are fully apparent.

How best to learn management skills

Current knowledge is not yet in a state to allow us to say precisely what kind of learning is most effective for whom, for which set of skills. However, the following pointers will enable us to specify some broad factors which will promote development.

- Recognize the novel, learning experiences which occur in the natural course of work, and make the most of them.
- Harness the developmental impact of changing job and organizational requirements.
- Maximize learning from doing by focusing on the conclusions and learning points, as well as the business results, which follow.
- Gain information about the effect of management actions, particularly in those circumstances where feedback may be insufficient.
- Be proactive in seeking learning opportunities where new skills can be acquired.
- Be aware of learning blind-spots, such as *post hoc* rationalizations, and guard against them.
- Seek learning opportunities, such as management training, which are relevant to work and help solve business problems.
- Seek to work with others who can act as role-models.

The examples quoted are based on real consulting experiences. They have been altered to preserve the anonymity of the individuals and their organizations.

Robert Sharrock is a professional psychologist with YSC in London, a consultancy specialising in organization and management development.

Further Reading

Garfield, C, *Peak Performers: The New Heroes in Business*, Hutchinson Business, London, 1986.
Sternberg, RJ, *Intelligence Applied*, Harcourt, Brace & Jovanovitch, Orlando, 1986.
Viney, J and Jones, S, *Career Turnaround*, Thorsons, London, 1991.
Mumford, A, *Developing Top Managers*, Gower, Aldershot, 1988.
Kolb, D, *The Learning Style Inventory*, McBer & Co, Boston, 1976.

References

1 'Futurists gaze into business's crystal ball', *Washington Post*, 20 July 1989.

2 Refers to the recognition of an individual's capabilities and deploying them proactively to the best effect, either within the current environment or by seeking a fresh business environment.

3 This captures the mental agility to see rapid ways of achieving goals and to adapt behaviours in the light of experience.

4 Garfield, C, *Peak Performers: The New Heroes in Business*, Hutchinson Business, London, 1986.

5 Sternberg, RJ, *Intelligence Applied*, Harcourt, Brace & Jovanovitch, Orlando, 1986.

6 Sarch, Y, *How to be Headhunted*, Business Books, London, 1991.

7 Viney, J and Jones, S, *Career Turnaround*, Thorsons, London, 1991.

8 Russo, EJ and Schoemaker, PJH, *Confident Decision Making – How to Make the Right Decision Every Time*, Guild Publishing, 1989.

9 Mumford, A, *Developing Top Managers*, Gower, Aldershot, 1988.

10 Kolb, D, *The Learning Style Inventory*, McBer & Co, Boston, 1976.

EVALUATING TRAINING EFFECTIVENESS: THE STAKEHOLDER MODEL

Mark Easterby-Smith

Evaluating the effectiveness of management training, education and development has, in times of cost-cutting and recession, taken on an entirely new significance. With organizations assessing and often reducing their training budgets the increasing onus is on providing effective means of measuring the bottom-line impact of training.

Such issues strike at the very heart of managerial attitudes to development – is it to be seen as intrinsically good no matter what or can its commercial and personal impact be efficiently gauged?

There is an old debate about whether management should best be seen as a science or an art. Supporters of the former view suggest that optimal procedures can be defined for managing processes, for making strategic decisions for allocating resources, and so on. Those supporting the alternative view argue that once a procedure can be fully prescribed and codified it may be automated or delegated. It then can be said to fall outside what is conventionally understood to be a managerial role. They also point out that the most difficult and intractable problems within contemporary organizations are to do with enabling people *to deal with highly ambiguous and uncertain futures*.

The same issue surrounds the evaluation of training effectiveness. The most common advice within training literature is that systematic procedures should be applied to the evaluation of all training activities. These involve some kind of cycle, such as: determine objectives, carry out training, measure reactions, measure job-related behaviour, measure impact on work unit, relate back to objectives, modify training design, etc. There are many problems with this so-called systematic model.[1] To mention three problems briefly: first, it tends, because of its emphasis on measurement, to pick up mainly trivial data; second, because it is so long-winded and cumbersome it is hardly ever applied in practice; and third, any data collected are rarely used because they do not have much relevance to the highly political environment that inevitably surrounds training.

It is the political nature of the evaluation which has made me conclude, from experiences over two decades, that it must be essentially an art, rather than a science. This does not mean that appropriate procedures and techniques are not important. It is just that their entire value depends on determining clearly what the purpose of any particular evaluation is, and how the results will be used.

The purpose depends on who are considered to be the primary stakeholders for a particular evaluation, and on the kind of questions that these stakeholders want to have answered.

Purposes and stakeholders for evaluation

If one follows the advice of training textbooks, evaluation is simply a matter of good training practice; it demonstrates a professional approach to training, and incidentally signals the end of a particular course to participants. And by far the most common purpose for evaluation is *ritual*. There are, however, at least four other general purposes which might be served by evaluation which I shall describe in the following sections, and these are then summarized in the model in Fig. 1.

It is often said that as soon as corporate budgets come under pressure the first thing to go is the training department. Therefore, it is a matter of personal and departmental survival that one is able to show and convince decision makers that training and development activities are not only making a significant contribution to overall organizational aims, but also a *necessary* contribution. In a sense, what is being required is some kind of proof that training is valuable and should not be cut, so *proving* is the second general purpose.

Unfortunately, in most cases, if nothing is done about evaluation until the training department comes under political threat, the chances are that evaluation data will simply be too late to avert disaster. In a slightly different context, this form of evaluation is useful when organizational structures and costing systems are being changed. As a result, many training departments are now being required to charge a major portion of course costs to client departments within the wider organization. They, therefore, need some reasonably tangible and immediate evidence to convince senior managers and other budget-holders that it is worth investing time and money in these programmes. This becomes even more important when internal market arrangements are established so that potential clients can take their business to any competing providers whether they be inside or outside their own organization.

A third reason for establishing evaluation procedures is to use them to ensure that standards and quality are maintained throughout a training operation. It is most common to find this form of *controlling* evaluation within larger organizations, particularly where there is decentralized training activity which nevertheless needs to conform to some general pattern. This is often the case with safety training and technical courses in large private organizations, and with general training programmes in public sector organizations. In these latter cases there are legislative reasons why particular standards and procedures of training must be adhered to. In this way evaluation procedures may be used not only to control the overall delivery of courses, but also the performance of individual tutors and lecturers. As competition intensifies among consultancy providers, colleges, and business schools it becomes increasingly important for their managers to know how individual tutors are being rated by trainees. It is then possible for them to take remedial action either through changing workload allocations or offering remedial training to ensure that customers remain satisfied.

Feedback systems which are geared to monitoring the overall quality of provision will enable identification of the stronger and weaker courses, or of individual trainers, but are unlikely to indicate precisely *how* to make any of them work more effectively. This, therefore, introduces the fourth possible role of evaluation: to focus on how training and development activities might be *improved*, either immediately or at some time in the future. Such attempts at improvement might involve minor modifications to existing activities, or fairly radical changes. They might also be conceived at the level of overall training and development policy or at the detailed level of how to run a particular session in a better way. What is important about this kind of evaluation is that it not only focuses on potential problem areas but also can allow for some creative leaps from past activities to future potential.

The mention of creativity leads to the fifth potential purpose for evaluation, where it is designed specifically to become an integral part of the *learning* process itself. It is well known that the classic forms of evaluation conducted in education establishments (ie, examinations) are extremely valuable in

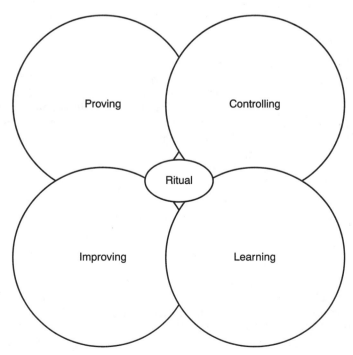

Fig. 1 Purposes of evaluation

motivating students and focusing their attention, at least over the period immediately preceding the examination. Similar principles can be applied through evaluation to training programmes and – not necessarily in such a draconian and judgemental way – but through providing review and reflection procedures as a way of focusing individuals' attention. Such procedures can include getting trainees to clarify, and specify, their own learning objectives in advance of attending courses, or through the establishment of review processes where they discuss with their bosses, and record in writing, the extent to which their learning is being put into practice on the job.

These five main purposes of evaluation are illustrated in Fig. 1. The reason for differentiating between them is that each one leads logically to rather different evaluation procedures and methods; in general it is not cost-effective to attempt to satisfy a multiplicity of such purposes. One way of deciding which purposes are likely to be most significant for the training activity it is to consider the potential needs and interests of different stakeholders, assessing which stakeholders are likely to be most significant from the point of view of the training activity. Thus, when the training activity is coming under financial pressure or potential criticism from senior managers, an emphasis needs to be given to the *proving* forms of evaluation. If there is no immediate political threat from the upper hierarchy then internal reference points may be more relevant. In this case, training managers, as stakeholders, are more likely to be interested in maintaining quality and overall control of the activity. Meanwhile the trainers are more likely to be interested in ways of improving their programmes and interventions, while the trainees themselves will be more interested in forms of evaluation which maximize their learning opportunities and the benefits to be gained from their efforts.

Over time it is probable that the relative significance of different stakeholder groups will vary. This is very easily noted within UK business schools where the long-standing tussle for supremacy between industrial and academic stakeholders has recently been disrupted by the intervention both of government and of individual students as stakeholders.[2] Since the mid-1980s government pressure has led to a succession of increasingly stringent audits

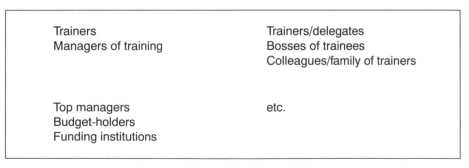

Fig. 2 Potential stakeholders

and quality assessments within universities and management schools which have led to marked changes in evaluation procedures. Individual students are also becoming much more powerful because the supply of courses, particularly at the post-graduate level, now exceeds demand, and institutions are anxious to solicit more business. Government pressure to increase the depth of academic audits adds to the power of the individual student because, for once, his or her voice actually has a direct impact on institutional status and funding. Meanwhile, the academics and industrial organizations with their respective interests in improving and demonstrating the applicability of training and education are becoming less dominant.

The design and conduct of evaluations

Essentially, evaluation involves gathering a certain amount of data from around training or development interventions, and feeding that information back to whichever people are in a position to make use of it. Consequently, the ideal design of the evaluations will vary according to the way the data is to be used (ie, the purpose), and the nature of training intervention that is being studied. In addition it is important to be aware that common practices for training and its evaluation vary considerably in different national or cultural contacts. This section, therefore, describes typical evaluation procedures which may be linked to three distinct types of training intervention, and then builds a general model for looking at the design of evaluations.

Example 1: A short skill-based course

This is a two-day course intended as an introduction to situational leadership' for junior managers. In this case the most commonly used form of evaluation is the end-of-course 'happiness' sheet which asks participants to rate the event and teaching quality on a range of multiple point scales. End-of-course questionnaires do no particular harm, provided it is understood that their primary use is diagnostic, in the sense of providing immediate feedback to course organizers on which elements were perceived to be more or less useful. Thus the main stakeholders for this kind of evaluation are the trainers themselves, and possibly their managers. Since the questionnaire is mainly diagnostic, there is little point in going into great detail and sophistication; normally fifteen questions on one side of paper should be sufficient.

The wording of such questionnaires will normally reflect key features of the course objectives and content. For example, if it is based on a number of short spots for visiting lecturers then it is normal to ask for ratings of each lecturer. If it is a more integrated course, provided by one or two tutors who work alongside the group the whole time, then it might be better to focus on distinct sections and activities within that course. The beauty of 'happiness' sheets, if one can call it that, is that they are quick to administer and collate, and can be used to provide a common database over a very wide range of courses or events. In extreme cases it is sometimes possible to use this kind of information for 'proving' by showing data of trends, or of single courses, against average results. But it is essentially flawed because it is based on immediate reactions from participants without any independent observations.

A more important criterion with a skills-based course is to assess to what extent participants have actually acquired skills and been able to use them successfully in their work. This requires some kind of follow-up study, either by questionnaire or interview, which includes gathering data from the participants themselves, and possibly from colleagues or others at work. The ideal time period before gathering this data would perhaps be three months. This allows space for the individual both to try out the new techniques, and to decide whether or not they are actually useful. These follow-up studies are quite expensive to conduct because, even when simply based on postal questionnaires, they require considerable administration and effort to track down ex-participants. Therefore, it is particularly important to be clear about the purpose of such an exercise. In this case the most obvious purposes are providing *proof* of the value of the intervention, and as a *control* mechanism which might encourage those responsible for providing the training to focus more on the thorny issues of application. However, it is often very difficult to find

Please indicate your reactions to the following questions about the course and return the sheet to the tutor before your departure.						
	Poor				**Excellent**	
Joining instructions	1	2	3	4	5	
Accommodation	1	2	3	4	5	
Meals	1	2	3	4	5	
General organization	1	2	3	4	5	
Lecturer A	1	2	3	4	5	
Lecturer B	1	2	3	4	5	
Lecturer C	1	2	3	4	5	
Lecturer D	1	2	3	4	5	
Length	Too short	1	About right	2	Too long	3
Level	Too low	1	About right	2	Too high	3
Pace	Too slow	1	About right	2	Too fast	3
	Little				**Very much**	
Knowledge gained	1	2	3	4	5	
Skills gained	1	2	3	4	5	
New approach gained	1	2	3	4	5	
Relevance to work	1	2	3	4	5	

Fig. 3 Typical 'happiness' sheet

conclusive evidence of behavioural changes in the work setting, even when everyone is personally convinced that they have taken place.

Example 2: An action-learning programme

Action learning, or project-based management development programmes, are based around real problems occurring in the workplace, which may be provided either by individual trainees or by other clients. Formal educational or theoretical inputs are usually only justified in relation to dealing with the specific problem that has been encountered. Such programmes are also quite long, between 6 and 18 months, and rely on small groups which meet together on a regular basis (perhaps for one day each month). Action-learning programmes are often personally and emotionally challenging since individuals are dealing with very complex and intractable problems and it is normal for participants to go through periods of frustration and elation – these are seen as natural elements of the learning process.

From an evaluation point of view, there is little point in focusing on ratings of the inputs of formal lectures, nor in using 'happiness' sheets at any single point. The wide variety of experiences of different participants also suggests that standardized questionnaires will be of little value. If the main aim of the evaluation is about *proving* then it is most useful to focus on outcomes and changes in beliefs and behaviour. These can potentially be picked up either from participants themselves or from peers/bosses, and it is possible to use both questionnaires and interviews. Questionnaires can possibly be used two or three times over the period of a lengthy action-learning programme, but they do require much co-operation and goodwill from the people who are completing them. With interviews the response rate will be much higher since it is harder to evade a persistent interviewer who has institutional backing than simply not completing a questionnaire. But interviewer time is also very expensive, and it is hard to justify carrying out interviews more than once or twice, on financial grounds, therefore in most cases it is necessary to take a sample of the trainees rather than the whole population.

One way of increasing the level of co-operation from participants is to emphasize the potential *learning* objectives of this kind of evaluation. Participants themselves may be extremely interested in the views of an external commentator on how they appear to have changed over the period, and responsibility for these observations may well be integrated with the tutor role, or may even be based on participants carrying out evaluations of each other. This, in a sense, introduces a form of collaborative evaluation which is neatly aligned with the underlying philosophy of action learning.

If, on the other hand, the evaluation is being carried out primarily for the trainers, then an emphasis on the process of the programme and the experiences of participants while they are on it will be of greatest value. This is likely to surface naturally through regular reviews and discussions in the course of the programme. The question is, how much of it should be recorded in mechanical or written form, and how is this best analyzed and used? One possibility, which also starts to invoke the object of *improving*, is for diaries to be kept by both tutors and participants. The diaries might then form the basis for periodic review and evaluation discussions. It is important here that the tutors are able to generalize from their experiences so that they not only know how to change the design and interventions within the current programme, but also in subsequent programmes. Finally, the objective of controlling is not unduly relevant in the case of an action-learning programme. Such programmes are essentially unique and attempts to standardize are likely to be at best irrelevant, and at worst downright harmful.

Example 3: A collaborative degree programme

This is where a company contracts with an educational provider to send a specified number of employees on a tailor-made programme which is also award-bearing. Such programmes are becoming increasingly common in the UK as a result of the growing importance of certification for managers and the much tighter competition in the educational market, which has required institutions to adapt their products as much as possible to corporate needs. These programmes are likely to contain elements of both the examples given above, with the relative emphasis on specific skills and project activities depending on the aims of the programme designers. The additional element is that there is likely to be some formal academic content and curriculum which is prescribed by the educational institution as a necessary part of certification.

From an evaluation point of view it may, therefore, be important to look at the way different elements of the formal content are received (probably through using 'happiness' sheets), and at how much is learnt and applied by the participants. The normal assessment system of the institution is likely to focus primarily on the levels of knowledge and understanding achieved by participants, which leaves the evaluators from the corporate side free to focus more upon areas of application. One of the difficulties in studies of this kind is, of course, that with the partnership between a company and an educational institution there are even more stakeholders with interests in the nature and outcomes of the programme.

Because so much of the design and delivery is controlled by the educational institution it is likely that the people from the corporate side will be most interested in checking up on the overall training activity (*proving*) since they will find it hard to have any direct influence on *improving*. This means that the stakeholders within the company, as the key funders of the programme, will primarily be interested in whether or not to continue sponsoring the particular programme. There is, however, one additional feature that is important here. This is that the success of collaborative educational programmes is often measured in terms of the degree of immediate or intermediate application into participants' jobs, and this depends to a large extent on the degree of support that an individual participant gets from his or her immediate manager. By introducing *learning* as an explicit objective of the evaluation, and therefore recognizing the participants themselves as implicit stakeholders, it becomes possible to involve both participants and their bosses in periodic reviews which can be recorded on paper and collated centrally. This also has an element of *control* as far as the behaviour of the boss is concerned. One system recently established on this basis is used by the Ford Motor Company in relation to advanced technical training and requires both boss and participant to have an annual discussion in which they answer four or five brief questions about their expectations, degree of support, main areas of learning, specific areas of application, and elements that appear to be problematic.

Choosing the focus for evaluation

In the course of the three defined examples I have occasionally mentioned different elements of the training activity upon which one might focus. These can be differentiated in general terms as follows:

- context
- administration
- inputs
- process
- outcomes

A focus on 'outcomes' is important when the emphasis of the evaluation is on *proving* and where the training programme contains expectations that knowledge will be applied. The focus on 'process' is most relevant when the purpose of the evaluation involves *improving*, because it is most likely to help the trainers understand how they can do things better. The process focus is also particularly relevant with training programmes that are highly interactive, whereas in more formal and didactic programmes a focus on the quality of 'inputs' and lectures is more likely to be of relevance. The fourth focus, 'administration', has not been mentioned explicitly above, but it is often useful to include the odd question about accommodation, the quality of joining instructions, and general organization, in any questionnaires. This is not only to pick up problem areas, but it also provides a useful benchmark against which to compare the more specific educational elements of the programme. If the accomodation hotel is rated higher than the trainers have rated it then you definitely have a problem. If the hotel is rated somewhat lower than the trainers' rating then the accommodation needs to be changed in future. But there is also a possibility that some of the criticism that people would aim at the course is actually being directed at the wider setting of the programme. This may need to be watched carefully. Finally, the 'context' of a programme concerns both the way participants came to be chosen to go on it, and the broader setting within the organization which led to some kind of training or educational need being identified. It may not immediately be evident that this should become a focus for evaluation after a course has started, but issues of selection and nomination are often very significant for how a course runs; a course which is mandatory is likely to have a very different atmosphere from one that is highly selective and perceived to be elitist. Any trainers or educational institutions wishing to maintain and improve the quality of their product will be prudent to include some form of contextual monitoring within the evaluation procedure that they establish.

Issues and problems with evaluation

I have so far resisted providing any single prescription as to how evaluations should be defined and conducted. Instead, I have tried to show that different evaluation problems and stakeholder groupings can lead to a wide range of evaluation techniques and methodologies. The key point here is that evaluations should be useful, and this means being clear about the purposes they are intended to serve, so that they do not become purely *ritual* exercises.

Five different issues frequently arise from evaluation studies irrespective of the particular design or context involved.

1. Timing. As noted, the collection of data is costly, both in terms of evaluator time and goodwill from informants. It is rare to get more than one or two shots at it, and this means choosing the target well. If the bulk of data is collected during or immediately after the training event, that data will naturally emphasize the importance of the event. If, on the other hand, evaluation focuses primarily on the workplace some time after the formal training activity has been completed, the results are likely to put a different set of pressures upon those responsible for designing and running the training course. The former is likely to lead to an improved quality of performance of the trainers and their institution within existing main parameters; the latter is more likely to provoke uncomfortable and difficult questions which force trainers to think

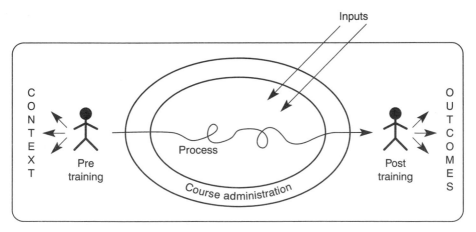

Fig. 4 Different focuses for evaluation

and act outside the framework of their existing knowledge. It will, therefore, come as no surprise to realize that the former approach is more likely to be in the interests of training providers, and the latter more in the interests of training purchasers and consumers.

2. Culture. The second issue is discussed under this general banner and it includes both organizational and national culture. At the organizational level the main cultural issues are concerned with decision-making procedures and the acceptability of different forms of data. In a strongly hierarchical organization the interests of senior managers, as stakeholders, are likely to be a predominant concern of the evaluation, and the general standing of training and development as an activity is likely to effect the degree to which proving becomes a necessary part of the evaluation process. It is also noticeable that some companies set great reliance on scientifically gathered and quantifiable data, whereas others base their judgements more on anecdotes and opinions gathered from trusted informants within personal networks. The astute evaluator is advised to ensure that outputs of any evaluation activity conform reasonably well to the data processing behaviours of key stakeholders.

The cultural issue becomes more complex when one looks at national differences. Here, there are not only the problems of different organizational conventions for handling and using data, there is also the further problem that contexts will be very different and educational processes may be both experienced and judged on different bases. When gathering data to evaluate a programme involving people from different countries, one should recognize that individuals are likely to have substantively different problems (for example, language, communication, and problems of application to different work contexts). They are also likely to form very different judgements about exactly the same educational events. The evaluator should therefore be sensitive to the possibility of such problems when working with an international context or group.

3. Who should carry out the evaluation? Should it be the trainers themselves, professionally trained (external) evaluators, or, as in the example on action learning, the participants? Here there may be some link to the apparent purpose of the evaluation. If the aim is *improving* then it may be best for the trainers to be closely involved; for *proving* it may be best to use external professional evaluators; for *controlling* an internal specialist unit may be advizable, and if the aim is *learning*, one could expect a greater involvement of participants themselves in the process.

4. Who owns the data collected? Given the range of people who might be involved in the evaluation this question might well be asked, similarly who owns the conclusions from the evaluation? To start with, the normal conventions about the confidentiality of informants should normally be maintained, unless there are good reasons to do otherwise. This means that anyone involved in gathering data should not communicate the identities of informants either directly or indirectly to anyone outside the study. Beyond this is the question of how widely the overall results of the evaluation are likely to be disseminated; the wider this is, the more likely that those responsible for training will try to reduce the impact of any possible negative information because this may be directly harmful to their interests. The stakeholder model would suggest that this problem is best handled by circulating draft conclusions to all of the principal stakeholders well before any final report is produced. It is important then that such people's views are obtained about both the accuracy of data gathered about the past, and the possible courses of action which should follow on from this. In some respects this phase of consulting with stakeholders can be seen as an integral part of the evaluation process with the emphasis upon making the best use of the data that is generated.

5. Costs. This is an issue which has already been touched upon at various points. As implied above, the cost includes both financial expenditure and personal time/goodwill. My advice is: try to be minimalist with the design of evaluations, and remember that there is usually a diminishing rate of return on data that has been gathered. It is all too easy for evaluation studies (like many management research projects) to become overwhelmed with data that never gets used to any clear purpose. And this returns us to the starting point: one should attempt to clarify the primary purpose(s) of the evaluation before starting to gather data. Without some clarity of purpose the whole exercise is likely to be a waste of time and resources. But remember that this purpose may still evolve and change over time.

Mark Easterby-Smith is head of the department of Management Learning at Lancaster University Management School. Since the 1970s he has been involved in evaluating management development programmes and systems for many companies and educational institutions. He is author of numerous articles on management learning and of the book *Evaluating Management Development, Training and Education* (1994).

Further Reading

Bramley, P, *Evaluating Training Effectiveness: Translating Theory into Practice*, McGraw Hill, Maidenhead, 1991.
Easterby-Smith, M, *Evaluating Management Development, Training and Education*, Gower, Aldershot, 1986 and 1994.
Newby, AC, *Training Evaluation Handbook*, Gower, Aldershot, 1992.
Patton, MQ, *Creative Evaluation*, Sage, Beverley Hills, 1981.
Revans, RW, *Developing Effective Managers*, Praeger, New York, 1971.

References

[1] Easterby-Smith, M, *Evaluating Management Development Training and Education*, Gower, Aldershot, 1994.
[2] Easterby-Smith, M and Lee, M, 'United Kingdom Management Education in the 90s: Policies and Priorities', discussion paper, Department of Management Learning, Lancaster University, 1992.

OUTDOOR MANAGEMENT DEVELOPMENT

Nicola Phillips

Management development in the outdoors is a technique that is increasing in popularity, so much so that it is in danger of being seen as a panacea for a whole range of management development and teambuilding issues.

The central idea behind outdoor development is that by taking managers away from their familiar environments, it is possible to enhance their awareness of their own behaviour and interaction with other people. By removing the familiar paraphernalia of job titles, hierarchy, company politics and national cultures, this kind of development can lay bare the fundamental principles involved in the management of individuals, groups, and resources.

Outdoor management development is now used extensively in the UK, is reasonably widespread in the United States, but less so in Europe and the Far East. Some European countries even find it insulting that they should be asked to 'play games' as they perceive it.

While numbers are growing, all too often neither the participants nor those who send them have any idea of what management development is really about, or what it is designed to achieve. Outdoor management development is certainly being used in international development as a way of bringing individuals together with a common bond, in that they are doing activities that they have probably never tried before. This helps to eliminate the tendency to indulge in national stereotyping.

'Managers apply their skills to a range of tasks which are quite different from those they face at work, but which are challenging and real. The results of their actions are immediately apparent, providing clear evidence of their performance,' say Chris Creswick and Roy Williams of the Food, Drink and Tobacco Industry Training Board. 'Although the outdoor tasks are not *normal* they are inescapably real. Managing an outdoor situation is like managing life ... the underlying management processes are laid bare.'

The onus, therefore, is on trainers and consultants to balance the risk of alienating the participants with a remote concept, and giving them an experience which will allow them to develop their interpersonal skills. There is no stock answer to this; as with all management development, it will depend on the skill of the trainer, the culture of the company and the outcomes the company is looking for.

The heart of management development in the outdoors is the idea that, in order to become more effective as an individual or as a team member, people need to develop an awareness of themselves and the way they operate. But in any training and development programme, there is only a very limited period of time in which to increase this self-awareness. One of the major advantages of outdoor development is its *immediate* impact. The mental and physical stimulation involved in outdoor activities provoke thought, while the fact that the development takes place in a different environment helps to heighten awareness.

The objectives for an outdoor development programme can be diverse, and can operate at one or more of the following levels:

- **At the individual level,** management development in the outdoors involves understanding one's own behaviour, improving self-awareness and gaining insights into personal styles of management.
- **At the team level,** the development activity aims to develop effective team-work, and to provide a greater understanding of how teams work and the roles individuals take in teams.
- **At the inter-team level,** outdoor development looks at issues concerning how to manage effectively between groups, and aims to improve understanding of competitive and collaborative behaviour. This is particularly useful with international teams.
- **At the organizational level,** outdoor development examines how to create effective strategies and to manage change.

The most common issues this management development technique is used to examine are:

- communication and interpersonal relationships
- assessing individual strengths and weaknesses
- personal development
- confidence building
- self-awareness
- teambuilding
- maximizing team potential
- leadership
- decision making
- problem solving
- resource and information management.

Management development in the outdoors is also sometimes used as a kind of incentive event, an enjoyable group experience which is provided as a reward for employees. This should not be confused with the more serious approach of development training, and participants need to be adequately briefed about the purpose of the event.

In practice

Many myths and misconceptions have sprung up regarding the activities used in outdoor training programmes. Most of these are based on second-hand knowledge or hearsay about dawn swims in icy mountain lakes, and other masochistic exercises.

Many of these myths date back to the early days of outdoor training, when it was chiefly used by the army. Development in the outdoors was, and is, used by the military to develop 'character' and leadership skills, and to build teams. The first outdoor training centres and organizations were set up and staffed by ex-army personnel. Their tendency to emphasize physical exertion highlights one of the major problems with management development in the outdoors. Because the environment is so different from the average workplace, the experience can cloud the very issues that participants are there to investigate.

The kind of outdoor development offered by today's specialist training providers is rather different. Perhaps the main difference lies in the increased emphasis on teamwork. While the more military-style organizations believe in an authoritarian, leader-centred approach, the new training providers favour a greater emphasis on teams.

The actual activities offered by outdoor training providers are now wide-ranging. They include mountaineering, abseiling, canoeing, orienteering, construction of bridges and other large structures, and caving.

They are usually, but not always, put into the context of a major task, usually a quest of some kind. There are probably well over a hundred providers of outdoor programmes now operating in the UK alone. Many of these providers also work in Continental Europe, as there seem to be fewer native outdoor development trainers. In the United States, there are numerous organizations which provide outdoor development with activities ranging from 'rope courses' (where participants undertake a variety of activities involving ropes), to very dramatic desert survival programmes. Wherever the providers are based, their backgrounds are similar. Some are specialist outdoor organizations, diversifying into management development in search of a wider customer base. Others are experienced management trainers who choose to use the outdoors as their medium.

Exercises can range from twenty-minute, simple problem-solving exercises, to more complex exercises and to projects lasting several days. The exercises may involve both indoor and outdoor components. Normally, planning will take place indoors, while the activities take place out of doors.

Some rules of good practice

Any outdoor training should aim to offer a programme which provides a whole range of new situations and experiences for the participants. And obviously, the activities should be carefully tailored to the participants' own levels of fitness.

The standard approach to learning in the outdoors, adapted from Kolb's learning cycle[1] is shown in Fig. 1.

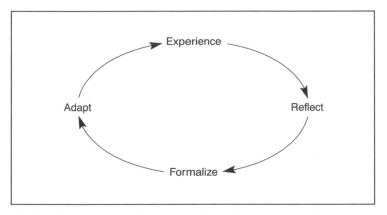

Fig. 1 Kolb's learning cycle adapted for learning in the outdoors

Source: D. Kolb, *Organisational Psychology: An Experimental Approach*, Prentice Hall, New Jersey, 1971

Participants on outdoor programmes are typically given a task to complete. Once they have completed the task, they are asked to reflect on what happened and how it happened. The tutor's role is to facilitate this process, to provide formal theoretical input, and to help the participant to understand why things happened in a certain way, and what implications that has for their way of working.

This demands a broad range of skills from outdoor management tutors but, above all, it demands the ability to achieve a balance. Those who offer training in the outdoors need to possess both the technical skills needed for the outdoor exercises, and the facilitation and management development skills needed to make sense of them in a development context. If training organizations cannot provide an individual with both kinds of skill, then they need to ensure that they can provide two or more trainers who have both between them. The international dimension also demands both cross-cultural experience and sensitivity to international management issues.

The tutors have to make sure, on the one hand, that they are not allowing the group to flounder in unfamiliar situations, but on the other hand ensure that they are not taking over the decision-making process.

This process of reflection can take place at the end of an activity, or it can be done in the middle of an exercise. At the end of this review process, the group should be ready to move on, and start to adapt their behaviour, either in readiness for the next exercise, or back at the workplace.

In the outdoors, no amount of rationalizing can alter the fact that a group of people are standing amid the ruins of a task that has failed because of their own behaviour. It is the reflection upon the failures and successes of the outdoor exercises that provides the core of any good outdoor programme.

The tasks and activities that people are asked to perform, while essential to the learning experience, are only a means to an end.

It is very difficult to have a 'mediocre' experience on an outdoor course. Generally, participants welcome their very difference from other forms of training. In some cases, this assessment is due to the participants' pleasure in what they have achieved, or to their sheer relief. This in itself is not a bad thing, but it is not the primary aim of a good management development programme, particularly if it has been achieved at the cost of the main objectives.

What is crucial is the participants' ability to transfer their experience on the programme, back to the workplace. One of the first questions that anyone investigating this kind of training should ask is: how does the provider intend to relate the activities to what goes on in the participants' real place of work?

If the facilitators of management development in the outdoors are doing their job properly, they will constantly be asking participants to evaluate their experience, and to assess its relevance to their working lives. In international teams, the learning payoff is sometimes greater in terms of understanding and breaking down barriers to communication.

Client organizations, too, have an important role to play in ensuring the transfer of learning. Arrival back at the workplace after an outdoor programme is a crucial time for further evaluation and assessment. Individuals should, at the least, be debriefed by their line managers, preferably against objectives set before their departure for the course.

Some training providers will send their tutors back to the client organization after about three months to talk further to the participants. The transition back to work is often a lot easier, if a whole work team has been involved in the programme. The shared memory of such an event can lead to remarkably strong teams.

Outdoor programmes cannot guarantee improved performance in the workplace. Outdoor training should never be perceived as a replacement for other types of management development carried out indoors. Rather, the two types of development should be seen as complementary.

Perhaps the most distinctive feature that the outdoors can add to a management development programme is the fact that it is a great leveller. It can be an invaluable means of getting away from the hindrance of job titles, company hierarchy, national stereotypes and corporate politics. It is very difficult to pull rank on your fellow managers when you are all dressed in the same rainclothes, soaking wet and a long way from achieving your target.

Handled well, it can lay bare the more fundamental principles involved in the management of individuals, groups and resources. At a time when an organization wants to introduce major change, management development in the outdoors can be a valuable medium for dealing with the unknown.

Valuing the difference

This becomes especially true when dealing with multinational groups. After a recent merger, one multinational restructured its sales and purchasing teams cross-functionally. The idea was for creative, technical and finance people to work together worldwide to increase productivity and development. In reality, however, people from each discipline and country rarely listened to each other. Indeed, there was a great deal of hostility between them, to the point where they would not share new product ideas. One of the main problems for these teams was that they were composed of people who were all at a similar level of seniority, working in a very competitive environment, chasing a small number of promotions worldwide. This was hardly calculated to foster trusting, co-operative relationships.

The organization's human resources director was familiar with these issues, but felt they would be better managed by an outsider. With a consultant, he designed a one-and-a-half-day development workshop called 'Valuing the difference'. The workshop looked at practical ways of building and developing multinational and multifunctional teams in a changing environment. The aim was to create more versatile and cohesive teams, which were able to break down national and functional barriers and use their differences to recognize opportunities and create quick, workable and appropriate solutions The aim was to harness the enormous range of talent within the teams, and encourage them to collaborate rather than compete.

The outdoors was chosen as a medium for several reasons: the short time scale demanded something quick and intensive, and an experience that was out of the ordinary for all participants was perceived to be one way of starting with cultural and functional equality. The workshop began with a large, group outdoor exercise to identify some of the problems being faced by the teams. The exercise involved them planning together, prioritizing work and allocating resources, in order to locate various pieces of equipment necessary to complete their task. One-third of the team set off immediately to look for the items, without consultation. When they eventually found them, they had no idea what to do with them, and had alienated the rest of the group, although they felt self-satisfied about having located the equipment, and therefore completing what they perceived to be their task. This exercise vividly illustrated the group members' lack of respect for each other's skills, and the lack of communication within the teams, which in the workplace resulted in duplication of effort, and unproductive use of resources. In the next exercise, the participants were grouped into their usual work teams to discuss how the issues that had arisen as part of the exercise were reflected in their work reality. The process was painful for some, but most saw it as an opportunity to say things they had wanted to say for some time.

The final stage of the process was to get together as a group and discuss how they could work together in instigating and managing the changes within the organization.

As a result of the workshop, the teams were able to:

- recognize cross-cultural issues in their teams and identify ways of dealing with them;

- identify ways to value their differences rather than see them as an obstacle, or use them as an excuse;
- examine ways of maximizing their negotiating power as a team, rather than individuals.

In this instance, the outdoor exercise was used to release the tensions and highlight the real dynamic issues for the group. By acknowledging its diversity, the team could maximize the resources it had to draw on.

The key elements in considering management development in the outdoors are:

- the skills of the provider;
- the organization's expectations;
- the participant's expectation.

The skills of the provider

Some organizations conduct a great deal of research into the different providers of outdoor training before they select one. For many, the fundamental criteria are the provider's standards of safety and hygiene. Quite sensibly, they take the view that any organization that could not conform to these rudimentary requirements would be unlikely to provide them with a good programme of management development in the outdoors.

However, it is also crucial, as we have seen, to find an organization that will concentrate on the developmental process, and on the transfer of learning to the workplace, rather than on the outdoor activities alone. It is also important, of course, for the provider to establish a rapport with the client, and to develop a good understanding of its needs.

The skills of individual tutors are one of the decisive factors in the success of any programme. The most creative, exciting and well-planned exercises can fall apart if the tutor lacks the appropriate skills to relate the tasks that have been achieved to the processes and problems of management.

Tutors need the skills to help the group to deal with conflict, and to face up to the implications of their actions, when all they want to do is to complete the task in hand. They need to be able to spot when the group has reached the limits of its ability, and adjust the exercise accordingly, without intervening too soon or too often.

The organization's expectations

Organizations need to take a realistic view of what can be achieved through a management development programme in the outdoors. In order to run a successful outdoor training programme, the client organization must be very clear about what it wants to achieve, and have discussed this thoroughly with both the training provider and the participants. Without clarity of objectives it is impossible to know what has been achieved when the programme is over. These objectives should be discussed and agreed with the provider prior to the programme, and constantly reviewed during the course of the programme also on return to work.

When choosing a provider, organizations need to ensure that:

- all the tutors have sufficient knowledge of the organization in order to understand both the focus of the programme and the culture of the participants;
- The tutors have adequate facilitation skills to manage the group dynamics.

The participant's expectations

Many reluctant participants in outdoor development often feel a great deal of apprehension about what will be expected of them before the course. They may assume that there will be over-demanding physical challenges, and worry about being fit enough, or being the wrong size or shape. Many participants fear that they will not be able to complete the tasks required of them. The often unfamiliar environment of outdoor programmes can further add to their fears.

In order to calm these fears, participants need to be thoroughly briefed on the activities involved and, most importantly, on the purpose of the whole programme. They need to understand the connection between outdoor activities and everyday work issues.

However, it will never be possible to quieten all the apprehension aroused by an outdoor development programme. Indeed, a certain degree of apprehension is a desirable part of an outdoor programme. Learning to deal with individual and group apprehension can be one of the most positive results of an outdoor event. It has clear parallels with change management, for apprehension is often a large part of the resistance to change.

An effective multinational, multicultural team is one where all the members have tasks that are recognized as important, and are respected as part of the team. No matter how disparate the team members are in terms of nationality, professional function or skill, each member needs to be able to accept the fact that the others have something to contribute. Homogenized teams, made up of people with similar characteristics, rarely produce innovation, and difference should be welcomed. The outdoor medium is very effective in bringing people face to face with team issues very quickly, but very intensely. Managing and focusing the intensity of the group dynamics, and having the ability to relate the group's experience to the workplace, is the art, essence and advantage of outdoor development.

A checklist for running international management development in the outdoors

Observance of the following criteria are crucial to the success of any programme of development in the outdoors:

- the programme should have very clear objectives;
- it must be designed as part of an overall training programme;
- careful checks need to be made on the training providers' safety standards;
- the provider should be familiar with the client organization;
- the programme must be tailored to individual client needs and objectives;
- the course should have a high tutor to participant ratio;
- the programme and the tutors must relate each activity back to the workplace;
- the emphasis should be on reviewing the process, not on the outdoor activity itself, from day one;
- the tutors must be capable of conducting continuous reviews;
- the course should be followed up with evaluation sessions in the workplace.

Nicola Phillips is a management development consultant. She has worked in various organizations as human resource manager and is the author of *Managing International Teams* and *One to One Management*.

Further Reading

Phillips, N, *Managing International Teams*, Pitman, London, 1993.

PART

2

MANAGEMENT TOOLS AND TECHNIQUES

Managing the Management Tools

'Behaving like a manager means having command of the whole range of management skills and applying them as they become appropriate.'   *Herbert Simon*[1]

2

[1] Simon, HA, 'Making management decisions: the role of intuition and emotion', *Academy of Management Executive*, February 1987

OVERVIEW

Darrell K Rigby and Crawford S Gillies

Industrious managers, barraged by the onslaughts of global competitors and anxious to demonstrate that they can cope with a new world of discontinuous change, are turning to management tools and techniques in unprecedented numbers. The term *management tools and techniques* now encompasses a broad spectrum of managerial aids – from simple planning software, to complex organizational designs, to entirely new outlooks on the business world. The choices are myriad – re-engineering, horizontal organizations, service guarantees, benchmarking, core competencies, empowerment, and TQM – to name just a few. But they all have one thing in common: they promise to make managers more efficient and effective.

Unfortunately, until very recently there has been no objective evidence on whether increased usage of such tools was good or bad for companies, let alone which tools have produced what results over what period of time. And using the tools haphazardly does have its pitfalls. As one middle manager at a large insurance company said: 'Our people are so confused by the conflicting message of these training seminars that they're starting to think it's all just a big joke, an expensive snipe hunt devised to amuse top management.'

An in-depth survey of 500 senior managers conducted by Bain & Company in conjunction with the Planning Forum (a non-profit management organization) demonstrates conclusively that management tools, despite their potential for performance improvement and their dramatic growth over the past decade, are often not properly understood or applied.

We interviewed senior executives and conducted extensive literature searches to identify 25 of the most popular and topical management tools. Most, if not all, will be familiar to executives. Among the companies surveyed, the two most popular tools were mission statements (a 94 per cent usage rate), followed by customer surveys (90 per cent). Total Quality Management (TQM) came third with 76 per cent. Benchmarking and re-engineering were placed sixth and seventh respectively and are clearly attracting increasing interest. The least utilized tools included value chain analysis (27 per cent), five forces analysis (24 per cent), and mass customization (21 per cent). In 1993 the average company responding to the survey used 12 of these tools. In 1994, they planned to use 16 of the tools – an increase of more than 30 per cent. Clearly, tool usage is high and growing. Sadly, we found no correlation between the number of tools used and satisfaction with the financial results of a business.

On the other hand, there was a strong correlation between satisfaction with financial results and a company's ability to build distinctive capabilities that serve customer needs better than the competition. Further, we found that management tools vary significantly in their ability to improve a company's results along the four key dimensions that drive improved performance:

Customer equity Helping to increase market share, generate greater customer loyalty, and produce higher customer value.

Long-term performance capabilities Expanding growth capacity, improving product development, and contributing to higher employee skills and morale.

Competitive positioning Building stronger barriers to competitive entry and expansion. Helping to create more advantageous bases for competition, improved relative economics, and a better position for achieving market leadership.

Organizational integration Increasing teamwork, leading to greater sharing, learning, and faster and more innovative decision making.

Some tools were better at discovering customer opportunities, others at exploiting competitor vulnerabilities. Some were effective at building distinctive capabilities, and others at bringing organizational activities together by strengthening integrative skills. It was confirmation – if confirmation were needed – that the secret to success is not in discovering one magic tool or in trying to use all of them. The secret is applying the right tool to the right job – learning which tools to use, how, when, and where.

Senior managers need a rational system for selecting, implementing, measuring, and integrating management tools and techniques to improve the results of their business units. On the basis of our research, we can offer four suggestions on how to effectively manage the management tools for improved results:

1. Put the strategic agenda firmly in the hands of managers, not tool gurus.
2. Diagnose which elements of the strategy are most seriously constraining performance.
3. Lead the organization to properly sequence and address constraints.
4. Choose the right tools for the job.

Put the strategic agenda firmly in the hands of managers

Line managers and tool gurus do not always have perfectly aligned agendas. Gurus can derive satisfaction from provoking stimulating debate, but managers must manage. Managers cannot afford to be seduced by novelty; they have to stay focused on results. However, they often do need innovative ways to sustain the delivery of superior returns. Producing such results requires managers to strengthen the essential elements of strategy and bring them together in creative collaboration. While tool usage may help line managers in this process, it should never drive them.

Our research shows that tool users fall into four segments. The first two, which we call *leaders* and *faddists*, share some common elements. They are both early adopters of management tools and techniques; they feel that it is important to stay on the cutting edge with the right tools; and they believe that strategic planning is important to the success of their business.

The segment called *leaders*, however, places heavy emphasis on managing cultural change in the organization. They are highly sensitive to the impact that tools will have on their culture, and they use tools as an important ingredient in the change management process. *Leaders* also like to focus the organization on complementary tools. When they find something that works, they stick with it, and then add additional tools that fit well. For example, they may take a programme that includes customer satisfaction surveys and roll it into a customer retention effort. They prefer to get the whole organization focused on unifying concepts and techniques. This segment of users creates the best financial results.

In the second segment, the one called *faddists*, tools are typically given higher priority, while organizational structures and information systems are given lower priority than they receive from the *leaders* segment. Historically, *faddists* have pursued more major tool programmes than the other segments. *Faddists* believe that tools can solve their major problems and that people will just have to learn to adapt to the new techniques. As a result, their people are often highly cynical. They know that the latest tool the chief executive has just introduced with a great fanfare will probably be forgotten in 12 months – when the next major (and often contradictory) initiative is launched. The *faddists* deliver (by far) the worst financial results.

Managers in the third segment, the *followers*, wait for a tool's track record to become public before implementing it. Unfortunately, given the biases and paucity of information on tools, this approach does not always lead to good or timely decisions. *Followers* adopt tools after the *leaders* have already gained first-mover advantages – sometimes after a turn in industry or economic cycles make the tool less useful than it had been. In addition, this segment does not tend to stick with the same tools over time. This is partly because they do not have much success with the tools, but partly because they are more interested in watching and copying what others are doing. Their results are down where we would expect them to be: second from the bottom.

The fourth segment, *sceptics*, are people who do not believe tools are helpful. They feel that strategic planning is a waste of time. Surprisingly, *sceptics* use just as many tools as the other segments do, but they hate doing it. They probably expect less of a tool and introduce it with less enthusiasm. It could be that companies in this segment are reacting to someone powerful in the organization pushing a new tool through the system. The middle managers know it won't work, so they don't put much effort behind it. Sure enough, it doesn't work. Surprisingly, the results are not as horrific as one might expect. In fact, the results of *sceptics* are a little better than those of *followers*, though not as good as those of *leaders*.

These findings suggest that a manager should probably choose to be either a *leader* or a *sceptic*, and avoid getting stuck in the middle. In other words, discover how best to apply the cutting edge of management tools and use them as an essential ingredient in a sophisticated change management process, or don't waste too much of the organization's time and effort on a fad.

Diagnose which elements of the strategy are most seriously constraining performance

A business's performance level is determined by its weakest strategic component. If customer needs are inadequate to drive demand, revenues shrink. Without distinctive capabilities to create supply, a firm will produce sub-par quality at above-par costs. Unless competitors' vulnerabilities are constantly pressured, they will be free to make assaults of their own. Their counter initiatives will derail your firm's strategies and whittle attractive returns down to mediocre margins. And unless all of these issues – customer needs, distinctive capabilities, and competitor vulnerabilities – can be creatively integrated by a motivated team focused on achieving breakthrough results, all the efforts will be unavailing.

Clearly, the first logical step is to learn which elements of the company's strategy are most seriously constraining performance, then consider what might be done to strengthen them. Measuring strategic performance and identifying the areas that require the greatest management attention is never easy. A practical diagnostic test is worth serious consideration. This diagnosis leads managers through a rating of 25 critical performance areas in the most important strategic arenas: [1]

- Are we delivering superior results?
- Are we discovering unmet customer opportunities?
- Are we building distinctive capabilities?
- Are we exploiting competitor vulnerabilities?
- Are we developing superior integrative skills?

The objective of the diagnosis is to provoke a thoughtful discussion of the business's true condition and performance constraints. Higher scores are clearly correlated to better financial results. Further, the scoring patterns can be interpreted to identify logical action implications. For example:

- When the scores along most performance dimensions are high, but one area is low, the best results are achieved by focusing on ways to strengthen the lowest performing strategic component.
- When the scores in all strategic components are uniformly low, companies tend to do best by focusing first on customers and capabilities. These components push low-performing companies to master the basics: first, defining what customers want, then using customers' needs to identify new products and to drive major improvements in current business processes.

509

- When the scores are uniformly high, heavy emphasis on the development of integrative skills yields the strongest results. Moreover, some high performers can successfully drive all strategic components simultaneously to higher levels.

Armed with the insights from this diagnosis, a manager is prepared to rank the critical performance dimensions and address the elements constraining success.

Lead the organization to address constraints

Again, some of the lessons learned from *leaders* can be very helpful in this process. *Leaders* believe even more strongly than other segments that management tools require top-down support to succeed. Once they discover a tool that works, they tend to use it over and over again. They work hard to find the right tools for their particular situation, staying well educated on cutting-edge techniques. They also care more than other segments about having the whole organization focused on the same tools at the same time. They work hard at increasing teamwork, managing cultural changes, improving employee satisfaction, designing organizational structures and improving strategic planning. They avoid contradictions that reduce organizational focus and commitment. And they do not tie their personal credibility to a glib guru's high-powered sales pitch.

Gurus who preach that the only way for a company to improve its performance is to put a trendy tool at the top of every meeting's agenda show no appreciation of the chief executive officer's job, and even less understanding of how things really get done within an organization.

The case history of the head of a national chain is instructive. Under serious pressure to improve performance, he was persuaded that re-engineering was the answer. So he raised the re-engineering banner, hired an expensive consulting firm to manage the process, and tied his future to its success. When the project ran into trouble, and the management team lost confidence in his sense of direction, he decided that his personal credibility was now inextricably tied to re-engineering. He pushed even harder to make re-engineering work, became distracted from more critical growth issues, watched sales continue to decline, and engineered himself out of a job.

Championing failed fads is a sure-fire way to undermine the confidence of employees in their leader. Employees begin to doubt the leader's ability to create needed change, and new programmes are greeted with increasing scepticism.

Executives would be wiser to champion compelling strategic directions, while regarding the specific techniques for getting there as expendable tools. For example, leaders should espouse the principle that real job security comes from understanding and winning profitable customers. They should not be championing the latest customer satisfaction measurement technique. They should articulate the benefits of building cohesive teams of world-class experts and not become cheerleaders for the latest guru's much publicized organization design.

Choose the right tools for the job

The final step, of course, is choosing the right tools for the job. The survey proves that different tools offer very different strengths. Mission statements, for example, received the second highest scores in overall satisfaction. But they rated below average in boosting customer equity, performance capabilities, and competitive positioning. The only thing they are really good at is organizational integration – getting everyone focused on common objectives and working together to pull in the same direction.

If a business needs to improve customer equity (increasing market share, generating greater customer loyalty, or producing higher customer value) tools such as customer surveys, mass customization, customer retention, and service guarantees deliver high satisfaction ratings.

Businesses that want to increase performance capabilities (expanding growth capacity, improving product development, or contributing to higher employee skills and morale) might consider cycle time reduction, re-engineering, strategic alliances, or Total Quality Management.

Those needing to improve their competitive positioning (building stronger barriers to competitive entry, helping to create more advantageous bases for competition, improving relative economics, and a better position for achieving market leadership) may benefit from competitor profiling or micro marketing.

And businesses that need to improve their organizational integration (increasing teamwork, leading to greater sharing, learning, and faster and more innovative decision making) will want to explore the benefits of groupware, horizontal organizations, mission statements, or self-directed teams.

In implementing any of these tools, however, a manager should keep in mind three vital lessons from the research:

- Every tool carries a set of strengths and weaknesses. Success requires understanding the full effects (and side effects) of each tool, then creatively combining the right ones in the right ways at the right times.

  The survey shows that a tool's performance ratings differ widely between high-performing and low-performing users. Pay-for-performance works well when a company is doing well, but is very dangerous in cyclical industries or in companies that are doing poorly. Weak performers tend to give much higher satisfaction scores to activity-based costing than high performers do. Core competencies produce passable results when highlighting existing competencies in strong performers – essentially reminding them to preserve current strengths. But companies starting from weak positions experience very little success using core competencies to identify and build new strengths that are not already present.

- Major efforts produce significantly higher satisfaction levels than limited or trial usage does. Often it is better to pursue five related tools as major efforts than it is to adopt 15 different tools in more limited trials.

- Tools exist for the benefit of people, not *vice versa*. Properly applied, tools can help to inspire fresh thinking, stretch the personal and professional development of individuals, and reinvigorate enthusiasm for the business. But tools should always be positioned as the means to an end. The 'end' is results, which will only be achieved when people build capabilities that serve customer needs better than their competition. Tools are expendable instruments that come and go as their usefulness to people evolves.

Management tools are credited by their advocates with saving corporations – almost as loudly as they are blamed by their critics for destroying them. The truth is, tools do neither. People make companies succeed or fail. If they are wise, people can use tools to improve their performance and job satisfaction. If they are unwise, they will adopt expensive tools without seeing any performance improvements.

Now, while many of the world's most powerful companies are struggling to establish new directions, and while organizations are searching for new leaders who can establish clear and compelling visions for the future, is not the time for theoretical tools to dictate management actions. It is time for results-minded managers to take control of their businesses, and to actively and creatively manage their management tools.

Darrell K Rigby is a director in the Boston (USA) office of Bain & Company, the international strategy consulting firm. He joined the firm in 1978 after receiving an MBA from Harvard Business School and has led several practice areas for Bain, most of which have centred on corporate strategy. His current research on management tools and techniques, co-sponsored by the Planning Forum, has been widely cited in leading business publications.

Crawford S Gillies is a partner in Bain & Company's London office. He has extensive experience of helping clients in a variety of industries throughout Europe to develop and implement corporate strategy and organizational change.

Reference

1 Rigby, DK, 'How to manage the management tools', *Planning Review*, November/December 1993.

Henry Mintzberg

Born 1939; educator

The work of Canadian Henry Mintzberg counters much of the detailed rationalism of other major thinkers of recent decades. From his first publication, *The Nature of Managerial Work*, Mintzberg has challenged orthodoxy, arguing the case for a more intuitive and humane approach to strategy formulation and practice, as well as to the structure of organizations. *The Nature of Managerial Work* exposed many of the myths surrounding senior managers, revealing them to be creatures of the moment rather than far-sighted strategists carefully planning their next move.

Mintzberg has generated a unique reputation, as someone apart from the mainstream able to analyze basic assumptions about managerial behaviour.

His most recent work tackles head-on the role and process of strategic planning. Mintzberg argues that intuition is 'the soft underbelly of management', and that strategy has set out to provide uniformity and formality when none can be created.

Despite a series of highly important and influential books and appointments at two of the world's leading business schools (McGill in Canada and INSEAD in France) Henry Mintzberg remains something of an outsider in the world of management thinking.

While his books are scholarly rather than populist, he emphasizes the creative and spontaneous, the right-side of the brain rather than the left-side with its prediliction for analysis and rationality. He is a wry humanist who carries out his work with academic rigour. 'A well published waif' is how he jokingly describes himself. 'Perhaps the world's premier management thinker,' says Tom Peters.[1]

There is a sizeable dose of cynicism in Mintzberg's world view. Though, when asked, he is quick to add the explanatory coda: 'I am sceptical about everything except reality.' To keep hold of reality, he eschews the management guru merry go-round. 'There is a lot of obnoxious hype about being a "guru" to the extent that the medium can destroy the message,' he says, 'I'm in one of the most competitive fields around, but I've never felt competition for a moment. You can compete by competing head-on or by not competing at all. I care about doing things well, not doing them better – that is a low standard.'

Mintzberg's name was initially brought to a wider audience with his first book, *The Nature of Managerial Work* (1973). An article in the *Harvard Business Review* ('The Manager's Job: Folklore and Fact')[2] brought Mintzberg's research further into the public eye. Its origins (and those of subsequent books) lie in Mintzberg's grand plan. 'In 1968, I set out to write a text called *The Theory of Management Policy*, to draw together the research-based literature that helps to describe the processes of general management.' Mintzberg's plan has expanded – each of the three central chapters became books, and an early section of the fourth chapter also developed into a book.

At the time of its publication, *The Nature of Managerial Work* was radically alternative and rapidly dispensed with much conventional wisdom. 'I had a lot of difficulty getting my first book published,' Mintzberg recalls. 'One publisher said they were publishing a book just like it – 20 years later, I have yet to see the book.' In his research, Mintzberg got close to managers actually managing rather than pontificating from afar. His research involved spending time with five organizations and analysing how their chief executives spent their time. While this tracking approach is now commonplace, in the early 1970s it was ambitious – previous research had concentrated on the people managed by managers and the structure of organizations rather than the day-to-day reality of managerial behaviour and performance.

The Nature of Managerial Work revealed managers to be hostages to interruptions, flitting from subject-to-subject rarely giving undivided attention to anything. 'The pressure of the managerial environment does not encourage the development of reflective planners, the classical literature not withstanding,' Mintzberg observed. 'The job breeds adaptive information-manipulators who prefer the live, concrete situation. The manager works in an environment of stimulus-response, and he develops in his work a clear preference for live action.' Instead of being isolated figureheads analysing and generating carefully thought-out strategy, managers were suddenly exposed as fallible and human.

Mintzberg's research led him to identify ten key managerial roles split into three categories:

1. Interpersonal:
- the figurehead role where the manager performs symbolic duties as head of the organization;
- the leader role where he/she establishes the work atmosphere and motivates subordinates to act;
- the liaison role where the manager develops and maintains webs of contacts outside the organization.

2. Informational:
- the monitor role where the manager collects all types of information relevant and useful to the organization;

- the disseminator role where the manager gives other people the information they need to make decisions;
- the spokesman role where the manager transmits information to the outside world.

3. Decisional:
- the entrepreneur role where the manager initiates controlled change in the organization to adapt to the changing environment;
- the disturbance handler where the manager deals with the unexpected changes;
- the resource allocator role where the manager makes decisions on the use of organizational resources;
- the negotiator role where the manager deals with other organizations and individuals.

These neat categories should not disguise the challenge put out in *The Nature of Managerial Work*. The corrolary of Mintzberg's conclusions was that if we don't understand how managers spend their time and what they do, how can management be improved and the skills of managers appropriately developed?

Twenty years on, Mintzberg's style and approach has remained determinedly iconoclastic. 'My books succeeded because they were different,' he says. 'If you think differently and execute it poorly you are dead.'

His background in mechanical engineeering might explain the root of Mintzberg's techniques and thinking. 'Mechanical engineering is not concerned with image or status. It is about reality and requires a certain kind of thinking,' he says, recalling a college assignment to design a pump. While all the other students went away and looked at the latest catalogues to copy a design, Mintzberg didn't look at anything and came up with a pump virtually identical to pumps when they were first invented. In his later research, Mintzberg also seeks to re-invent or establish first principles for himself.

'I am not an intellectual. I am a writer and researcher,' he says. 'I write primarily for myself, to find things out. I never write anything to boost my reputation or image – sometimes it is *appropriate* to publish something in the *Harvard Business Review*. When I am writing, the painful stage is getting an outline and then there is joy when things click and integrate.'

After his initial success, Mintzberg's focus shifted to organizational structure. In *The Structure of Organizations* he identified five types of 'ideal' organizational structure:

- simple structure
- machine bureaucracy
- professional bureaucracy
- divisionalized form
- adhocracy

Even so, at the core of Mintzberg's work is a belief in the excitement and spontaneity of management and faith in people rather than organizations – 'I don't like to be organized – I am a voyeur'. He has little time for the formal dictates of the organization. 'We have become prisoners of cerebral management. I'm sympathetic to the management process which is intuitive, based on immediate responses,' he says. Instead of seeing strategy as the apotheosis of rationalism Mintzberg has famously coined the term 'crafting strategy', whereby strategy is created as deliberately, delicately and dangerously as a potter making a pot. To Mintzberg strategy is more likely to 'emerge', through a kind of organizational osmosis, than be produced by a group of strategists sitting round a table believing they can predict the future.

Mintzberg regards full-time MBA programmes as perpetuating the obsession with 'cerebral management'. He no longer teaches on MBA programmes and contentiously advises: 'Regular MBA programmes should be closed down. It's the wrong way to train people who weren't managers to become managers. MBA programmes are confused between training leaders and specialists. At the moment, we train financial analysts and then expect them to become leaders. If accountants were forbidden to be chief executives it would probably be an enormous benefit.'

Mintzberg argues there is more to business success (and life) than MBAs. 'To be superbly successful you have to be a visionary – someone with a very novel vision of the world and a real sense of where they are going. If you have that you can get away with murder. Alternatively, success can come if you are a true empowerer of people, are empathetic and sensitive. Often, visionaries create companies and success is continued by empowerers.' These, he makes clear, are not qualities which conventional MBA programmes are likely to nurture. 'Conventional MBA programmes mostly attract neither very creative nor very generous people and the end result is trivial strategists who sit in their offices and look for case studies.'

Education: McGill University; MIT.
Career: Worked for Canadian National Railways 1961–1963; later he was visiting professor at a number of universities and business schools; President of Strategic Management Society 1988-91; consultant to a large number of organizations; visiting professor at INSEAD; director of the Center for Strategy Studies in Organizations at McGill University; professor at McGill since 1968.

His most recent work takes on the full might of conventional orthodoxy, countering the carefully wrought arguments of strategists, from Igor Ansoff in the 1960s to the Boston Consulting Group in the 1970s and Michael Porter in the 1980s. 'Too much analysis gets in our way. The failure of strategic planning is the failure of formalization. We are mesmerized by our ability to programme things,' says Mintzberg, identifying formalization as the fatal flaw of modern management.

The Rise and Fall of Strategic Planning is a masterly and painstaking de-construction of central pillars of management theory. Arguing that 'strategy is not the consequence of planning but the opposite: its starting point', Mintzberg exposes the fallacies and failings at the root of planning. These include:

- *Processes* A fascination with elaborate processes creates bureaucracy and strangles innovation.
- *Data* Mintzberg argues that 'hard' data, the lifeblood of the traditional strategist, is a source of information; 'soft' data, however, provides the wisdom. 'Hard information can be no better and is often at times far worse than soft information,' he writes. In *The Nature of Managerial Work*, Mintzberg similarly observed that managers relied on 'soft information' rather than exhaustive written reports.
- *Detachment* Mintzberg refutes the notion of managers creating strategic plans from ivory towers. 'Effective strategists are not people who abstract themselves from the daily detail but quite the opposite: they are the ones who *immerse* themselves in it, while being able to abstract the *strategic messages* from it.'

Looking at the development of his work, Mintzberg observes: 'My perception of what constitutes effective management is not so different as it was. But now there is a lot more ineffective management.' In *The Rise and Fall of Strategic Planning*, he produces a typical paragraph (on the role of the effective strategist) which has the air of someone thinking aloud, but perhaps sums up Mintzberg's own approach: 'Perceiving the forest from the trees is not the right metaphor at all ... because opportunities tend to be hidden under the leaves. A better one may be to detect a diamond in the rough in a seam of ore. Or to mix the metaphors, no one ever found a diamond by flying over a forest. From the air, a forest looks like a simple carpet of green, not the complex living system it really is.'

STUART CRAINER

Further Reading

Henry Mintzberg:
** *The Nature of Managerial Work*, Harper & Row, New York, 1973.
The Structuring of Organizations, Prentice-Hall, New Jersey, 1979.
Structures In Fives: Designing Effective Organizations, Prentice-Hall, New Jersey, 1983 (this is an expurgated version of the above).
Power In and Around Organizations, Prentice Hall, New Jersey, 1983.
** *Mintzberg on Management: Inside Our Strange World of Organizations*, The Free Press, New York, 1989 (Collier Macmillan, London).
The Strategy Process: Concepts, Contexts, Cases (with JB Quinn), 2nd edn, Prentice Hall, New Jersey, 1991.
** *The Rise and Fall of Strategic Planning*, Prentice Hall International, Hemel Hempstead, 1994.

**Essential reading

References

[1] Peters, T, 'Plans down the drain', *Independent on Sunday*, 24 April 1994.
[2] Mintzberg, H, 'The Manager's Job: Folklore and Fact', *Harvard Business Review*, July/August 1975.

Financial Management

'Business is other people's money.'   *Mme de Girardin*

'Profit is a concept, cash is a fact.'   *proverb*

'The only member of the board who must always be consulted on every single strategic decision is the financial director.'
                                        Sir John Harvey-Jones

OVERVIEW

Steve Robinson

In the highly functionalized organization, now increasingly consigned to history, managers could often proceed through their entire careers with only a limited knowledge of finance. Now, however, few managers can afford to claim a knowledge of finance is unnecessary. The breaking down of functional barriers in many companies has led to a demand for a broader range of expertise and awareness among managers. Most strategic business decisions are qualified in financial terms and a failure to understand how businesses manage their finances can create day-to-day difficulties for managers – and, ultimately, reduce the potential of their businesses. In the hyper-competitive 1990s everything has to be driven by the business. Cash is no longer king; it has become the dictator.

Measuring performance

The growth in importance of financial management is not simply an internal issue. The assessment of business performance in financial terms is demanded by ever more attentive investors, lenders, supplier creditors, employees, tax authorities and Government agencies – not to mention the host of media commentators and analysts eager for every morsel of data.

For managers, extracting the information they require – and have to provide – can be a daunting and intimidating experience. Financial reports can appear nightmarishly complex and deliberately obtuse to the untutored eye. Breaking through some of their mysteries is an important first step to enhancing awareness and knowledge of how an organization is performing.

The information in a financial report is basically divided into three parts:

1. The profit statement or income statement
This provides the profitability picture for the whole business. More detailed breakdowns are provided in the reviews of the chief executive and operating company executives. Information disclosure requirements are becoming more exacting.

2. Cash flow statement
This provides an analysis of cash movements which can be divided into:

Inputs:
- generated by the business
- supplied by owners

- supplied by lenders
- realized from asset disposals and divestments

Outputs:
- paid in dividends
- paid in interest
- invested in assets and acquisitions

3. Position statement or balance sheet

This provides an overview of the state of the business. It covers long-term issues of funding, such as retained profits; loans and share capital, as well as long-term investment (fixed tangible assets; intangible assets and strategic investments).

It also covers matters of short-term funding (including bank overdraft, supplier creditors) and short-term investing (stock, debtors and cash).

Financial reports are clearly important documents and a vital starting point in understanding the financial situation and outlook for a particular organization. There are, however, many useful sources of data, such as market forecasts and pay agreements, which exist outside of financial reports.

The successful interpretation of the interaction between environmental factors and the specific situation of the company is the key to predicting future performance. Four aspects of the business are likely to have major financial implications for the future:

- **People:** the more people there are in the business, the greater their impact on cash now and in the future.
- **Borrowing facilities:** the balance sheet gives details of actual current borrowings, but an important additional component is the availability of further borrowings, both committed and uncommitted. Large numbers here are a measure of confidence by lenders and an indication of the attitude to risk adopted by the board.
- **Fixed asset investment:** often the largest part of fixed asset investment is property. This is, of course, subject to market fluctuations. (In a controversial case at the Queen's Moat Houses hotel group, its properties were valued at £2 billion in 1991; and £861 million a year later.)
- **Environmental impact:** it is increasingly certain that companies damaging the environment will pay the financial price – and that their shareholders will suffer.

Accurately assessing the financial performance of a business involves bringing together a wide variety of information and data:

Component: Cash Flow

Approach: Identify major inflows and outflows; isolate non-recurrent items.

Calculate: 'Operating' cash flow (cash generated after day-to-day expenses); 'post-financing' cash flow (taking out the cash costs of funding the company interest and dividend); 'post capital expenditure' cash flow (taking out the necessary investment for the future to protect and maintain current earnings potential); 'free' cash flow (the cash available for investment in the long-term growth of the business after all the above payments).

Component: Profitability

Approach: Identify major profit contributors (by geographic area, product group and market sector); relate investment and return in as many as possible of the analyzes above; isolate non-recurrent profits and losses and establish repeatable earnings (profit after tax, interest and minorities).

Component: Gearing

Approach: Identify the relationship between 'owner investment' and long-term borrowing; refine the analysis to show the effect of intangible assets, the impact of including off-balance sheet finance; redefining the boundaries of debt and equity and of the length of the 'long' term.

Component: Growth

Approach: Volume and margin growth will be found in the profit statement. It is important to look at both, as the key is often the interaction of the two as seen in the operating profit figure. A more general overview can be obtained from the balance sheet. Strength does not come simply from the acquisition of assets, but also from employing them in order to generate cash return in excess of their financing cost.

Component: Capital Expenditure

Approach: Compare the expenditure by category with the amount of depreciation in the fixed assets schedule in the balance sheet notes. This will give an indication of whether it can be maintained. A study of the relevant accounting policies will be necessary to reach a judgement. The proportion of capital expenditure being generated by the 'post financing' cash flow is a good indication of the ability of the business to fund growth without borrowing or shareholder investment.

Getting it wrong

Of course, there are no guarantees. For all the complex financial mechanizms now available and widely practised, the most common reason for going out of business is quite simply that the company runs out of cash at a critical time. There are many reasons why a company may find itself in a crisis or even facing imminent death. These include:

- inability to collect cash owed from debtors
- withdrawal of borrowing facilities
- speculation using financial derivatives
- investment in fixed assets – using short-term finance and failing to produce short-term returns
- stock building
- enforced payment of creditors
- failure to restrict non-productive costs to a level appropriate for the volume of business
- uninsured assets loss
- uneconomic pricing policies

Every aspect of running a business has a cash flow implication. The importance of cash flow – no matter what the size and scope of the business – can never be under-estimated. Effective business management monitors the causes and effects of events and decisions on a continuous basis. It is now key that companies and their managers remain close to customers and suppliers – partnership sourcing, for example, can lead to innovative solutions to perennial cash flow problems. Cash flow must also be monitored continuously at all levels.

In practice

The perennial and increasing drive to reduce costs has forced industries and individual businesses to develop new and more exacting ways of examining their cost structures – all of which aim to reduce the chances of crises arriving.

The emphasis, therefore, is not on spells of enthusiastic cost cutting – usually followed by periods of corporate munificence – but of developing cost control and consciousness into a continuous activity. The search for cost reductions has led to an analysis of every aspect of cost and the questioning of the value delivered. The nature of costs is continually undergoing change. Increased automation, for example, has reduced direct labour costs – typically they are now around five per cent of total costs (compared with a likely figure of around 60 per cent 30 years ago). The proportion of direct material costs to total costs has fallen equally sharply. Traditional methods of overheads appointment and absorption have often relied on labour hours or material cost as the basis. In many cases neither of these are now appropriate as they are no longer key influences or drivers of cost.

A technique used increasingly to identify cost drivers is Activity Based Costing (ABC). It aims to align organizational (indirect overhead) costs with operational activity to enable costs to be accumulated around a product or service. The approach focuses on what is actually generating the cost rather than simply allocating it to a particular activity or function.

The use of the technique ensures a clear understanding of costs and how they relate to particular activities – in a more general sense, ABC clearly has close parallels with re-engineering which seeks to examine processes more intensely than ever before.

The use of ABC can be taken more widely to encompass other techniques such as zero-based budgeting, where each budget cost-head starts with zero and has to be justified. The total concept has become known as Activity Based Management (ABM) or Value Based Management (VBM).

The new challenges

In the state of flux many businesses find themselves in during the late 1990s, financial management has taken on a new importance and, as well as emerging techniques such as ABC, fresh dilemmas and challenges are constantly being produced:

Adjusting to high borrowing and falling asset values

The legacy of the late 1980s has been the high level of corporate debt incurred by fast-expanding acquisitive companies. The impact of changing – usually declining – asset values has questioned their financial stability in many cases. Refinancing has been necessary and two groups of losers are left nursing their wounds. The banks have had to write off trillions of dollars lent to highly leveraged management buy-outs which failed to generate sufficient cash in the harsh recessionary conditions necessary to survive. Stakeholders, keen to join the heady atmosphere of enormous potential gains, have seen the value of their investment fall dramatically.

A high profile case illustrating both high borrowings and fall in asset values was Saatchi and Saatchi, the global advertising and business services conglomerate. Saatchi and Saatchi was one of the fastest growing companies in the UK during the 1980s. At its peak, in 1987, it confidently proposed a merger with the Midland Bank – then twice Saatchi's size.

The Saatchi and Saatchi share price reached the heady heights of 700 pence in 1986; by the end of 1990 it was 37 pence and cash flow was negative.

Even before the dramatic departure of Maurice Saatchi and other senior executives at the beginning of 1995, Saatchi stakeholders saw their holdings dilute from 100 per cent to 16 per cent as the banks and other lenders exchanged their virtually worthless debt for potentially valuable shares. Saatchi expanded mainly by acquisition financed by almost every possible option – right issues, convertibles and debt. It was not affected by falling tangible asset values – such as real estate – largely because its acquisitions had brought few of such assets. Instead, Saatchi bought the even riskier class of asset; intangibles – brands, creative human resources and client bases. The intrinsic value of such assets lies only in their ability to generate cash. If the assets have gone the potential is zero.

The changing role of the centre

Cost pressures have forced many companies to reconsider the role of the centre and how it adds value to the business. There will be continuing need for consolidated financial reporting and specialist corporate finance and taxation expertise in companies. But, the majority of the operational financial management and business-driven development initiatives will originate out in the divisions. Development of higher levels of expertise has been a feature of recent years. In the past the centre forced financial discipline on its subsidiaries. Now, subsidiaries increasingly have the specialist knowledge and the systems to make their own decisions within the strategic framework of the group.

Coping with internationalization

Business has become increasingly international and companies cannot ignore the effect of currency changes on cash flow, profitability and the overall position of the company. No company is wholly immune. Exports are affected by the value of the home currency in relation to other trading partners. Raw material imports affect production costs; finished product imports are often competitors in the domestic market. The risks extend beyond the trading sphere. Finance is a global industry and companies borrow and invest in many currencies. It is not sufficient that only financial people understand how currency risks are created and managed.

The 1990s have brought regular corporate casualties involving major losses from foreign currency dealings and the use of financial derivatives or instruments. Derivatives are financial arrangements between two parties derived from the future performance of underlying assets such as currencies, debt bond shares and commodities. The market is huge – the Chicago Mercantile Exchange handles $200 trillion worth.

But, the alarm bells are already ringing about derivatives. In 1991 Allied Lyons suffered the biggest ever loss in foreign exchange dealings incurred by a UK company. The £150 million it lost resulted from 'dealings in foreign currency instruments which were inappropriate, and in which it lacked the requisite trading skills', its chairman later reported.

Such massive errors are now increasingly prevalent. No one and no organization is immune. The mining, metals and industrial group Metallgesellschaft was in Germany's top 20 companies in 1993. On 6 January 1994 the company stunned the market when it announced revised losses for 1993 of Dm 2 billion. By March 1994 the company had total debts of Dm 9 billion.

Already in the 1990s companies which appeared financially strong have fallen. In the future only the truly expert will be able to survive.

Steve Robinson is author of *The Financial Times Handbook of Financial Management* (1995). He is a client director and is finance subject leader for the MBA programmes at Ashridge Management College. A qualified management accountant and certified accountant, he worked in industry for a number of years before becoming

principal lecturer in financial management at the Metropolitan University of Manchester. He has an MBA from Bradford University Management Centre and is an active consultant for a range of companies.

Further Reading

Mills, R and Stiles, J, *Finance for the General Manager*, McGraw Hill, Maidenhead, 1994.
Robinson, S, *The Financial Times Handbook of Management*, FT/Pitman, London, 1995.
Smith, T, *Accounting for Growth: Stripping the Camouflage from Company Accounts*, Century Business, London, 1992.

MANAGEMENT ACCOUNTING

Sydney Howell

Management accounting is increasingly regarded as an integral part of the strategy process. Providing crucial and continuous information, it is taking on a number of more dynamic and flexible forms – including Activity Based Costing and Time Based Analysis. Such new interpretations and techniques bring management accounting into the mainstream of information provision and strategy formulation while distancing it from financial accounting.

It is vital to understand what management accounting can do, but also vital to understand its limitations. Essential features of management accounts are:

- They break the total business down into smaller complete businesses, or business units.
- Inside each business unit, the management accounts identify the key ways that the unit can earn revenue (products, services, customers, salespeople, etc) and all the key resources that it uses (staff time, machine time, raw material, asset delay time, customers' delay time, etc).
- Important resources don't usually carry a price tag at the moment when a junior person in the business uses them. By putting a money value on a physical resource like time, compressed air, machine hours, etc, management accounts are a bridge between managing the physical resource, and managing the money outcome of the business.
- Management accounts are for managing people, as well as resources. It's vital to report outcomes to anyone who directly or indirectly controls a resource or a revenue. Problems are inevitable if the management accounting reports do not clearly line up with a sensible allocation of power and financial responsibility in the organization.

Unfortunately trade-offs are often unavoidable in the way we design or use a management accounting system. Sometimes we need to 'multiplex' the system, so that it provides different data to support different decisions (eg, variable costs for short-term output decisions, and average full costs for longer-term investment decisions).

What kinds of decision can management accounting support?

Economic information includes:

- **Pricing:** what price would cover our variable cost or our average total cost? What price would meet our target return on sales, or on assets or on capital employed? Whatever price we finally set, we need to know what effect it will have.

- **Procurement:** we need to decide where to buy inputs, and what mix of inputs to choose.

- **Product mix:** which products should we emphasize, and which de-emphasize?

- **Forward and backward integration:** should we sell our product as it is, or add further value to it before selling it, or drop some existing stages of processing. (For example, should a computer company make its own printed circuit boards or buy in? Should an airport run its own catering, or subcontract?) Likewise should we make or buy inputs? Sometimes these decisions should be driven by strategy, and not by short-term cost at all (for example, a computer company may want to build economies of scale, or an airport may wish to suppress abuses by its staff).

- **Process improvement:** we need to know what is the cost of poor quality or poor yield, so that we can allocate effort to the most profitable improvements.

- **Investment and disinvestment:** it is clearly vital to identify areas of high return on investment, so that we can reinforce success. Low return may not be a signal for retreat. A careful analysis of competitors may show where we are wasting resources, so we can correct the problem.

All of the above decisions exist in a world without uncertainty, but business is full of uncertainty, and management accounts are an important tool for managing it. If we are off-course, is this merely a nuisance, or life-threatening? Where has the problem arisen? What size of correction do we need to bring us back on course? Can we make this correction inside the affected area? If not, how much do we need to make up elsewhere? Tools like Cost Volume Profit Analysis and Variance Analysis can help.

Extra problems arise in motivating managers. We need to be able to allocate praise or blame, and to develop each manager's career, economic skills and sense of responsibility. Other aspects of the human side of management accounting will be discussed later in this article.

Is there a difference between management accounting and financial accounting?

The gap between management accounting and financial accounting is probably growing. In its early days, management accounting was simply a more frequent form of the annual financial accounts, with extra supporting detail, and its job was to predict and control the year-end financial result (or even to support it, by valuing the inventory). The management accounts at the end of the year 'added back' to the same profit as the financial accounts. This is less and less true. We must of course be able to explain, and if needed remove, any difference between the management accounting profit and the financial accounting profit, but there seems less and less wish to make the two identical.

One reason is behavioural. In a major multinational group, a factory in a high tax area like, say, Denmark, may need three different price levels: a low selling price in the financial accounts (to minimize tax), a higher selling price in the management accounts (to motivate Danish managers and to guide their investment decisions), and a special 'variable cost only' price to ensure that the group overall makes efficient use of any spare capacity.

Strategy is another factor. Management accounts need more and more to report information that does not arithmetically form part of the financial accounting profit (eg, quality, customer satisfaction, market position). It is also vital to take decisions on a longer-term basis than one year's profit – a skill the Japanese are very strong in.

What are the basic techniques of management accounting?

The central technique is to share out assets, revenues and costs to different activities and managers. Managers' 'own' budgets for each of these, and the system reports actuals against budget. Comparisons against the same period last year, or year to date last year, or the size of overspend or underspend at this stage last year, are always useful. It is also helpful to compute the rate of spend required for the rest of the year, if the original budget is to be met (rather like the required run rate in a cricket match).

Cost Volume Profit Analysis is another powerful tool. Suppose our business has fixed overhead costs of £20,000, and variable costs of £8,000 for every load of product it sells. If the selling price per load is £12,000, each load makes a 'contribution' (to overhead and profit) of £12,000 – £8,000 = £4,000. After five loads, the business has broken even, since the contribution of £20,000 from five loads equals the fixed costs of £20,000, and there is neither profit or loss.

If we sell 10 loads, we'll make a profit of £20,000, as total contribution will be 10 × £4,000, and fixed costs will take half of this.

Sales: 10 × £12,000	£120,000
– Variable Cost 10 × £8,000	£80,000
= Contribution	£40,000
– Fixed Costs	£20,000
= Operating Profit	£20,000

It is a fact of arithmetic that our 'average cost per load' for these 10 loads is £10,000. But it is a fact of economics that no single load actually cost us

£10,000. If the business were to sell one load more or less, its costs would change by £4,000, not £10,000. It can be seriously misleading to base pricing and output decisions on yesterday's average full cost. Products or customers that appear to make a loss on full accounting cost may be increasing the total profit of the business.

Variance Analysis is a powerful way to explore deviations from plan. In accounting language, a 'variance' is simply an underspend or overspend, compared to a plan, budget or standard.

Suppose, for example, we planned to spend £855 on raw material, in order to make a piece of equipment, and we actually spent £1,000, partly because we used extra material (100 units instead of 95), and partly because we paid a higher price than planned per unit of the material (£10 per unit instead of £9). We have overspent by £145 in total, but how much of the overspend (the 'variance') was due to inefficiency, and how much to the unexpected price rise?

Management accounting has several ways to tackle this question, to which there is no exact answer. We can write out the planned spend (say 95 units at £9 per unit)

A

Planned units used	×	Planned price/unit	=	Planned spend
95 units	×	£9/unit	=	£855

Now change the 'units used' from 'planned' to 'actual'. This gives a spend we might have made if it was only our efficiency that had been worse than plan:

B

Actual units used	×	Planned price/unit	=	Potential spend
100 units	×	£9/unit	=	£900

The difference of £45 between the A spend of £855 and the B spend of £900 was caused by changing only the efficiency of material usage, so we call B – A an 'efficiency variance'. By subtraction, the remaining part of the total overspend must be due to price variation, so we call it a 'price variance' of £100.

C.

Actual units used	×	Actual price/unit	=	Actual spend
100 units	×	£10/unit	=	£1,000

The difference between A and B is the efficiency variance of £45 and the difference between B and C is the price variance of £100. These two variances add up to the total variance (overspend) of £145. In algebra, of course, the difference B – A reduces to:

$$(\text{Planned units} - \text{Actual units}) \times \text{Planned price}$$

This is how many accounting textbooks define the efficiency variance. Under this rule, a positive variance is an overspend, and a negative variance is an underspend. Of course, price and effiency variances can be of opposite sign, eg, we may save £80 by using material more efficiently than planned, but lose £110 from paying a higher-than-expected price for the material, leading to an overall overspend of £110 – £80, or £30.

Many complex variances can be calculated, both for sales items and revenue items. They can reflect the effects of selling more or fewer units than expected, of input or output prices higher or lower than expected, of gaining or losing market share, of movements in currencies, etc.

The strength of variance analysis is that it gives a quantified diagnosis, a target and an action plan: 'We've lost £45 due to inefficiency inside the factory, and £100 from adverse market movements; if we get the efficiency right again we'll save £45; try to squeeze £100 from the buying and/or selling price.'

A slight disadvantage of variance analysis is that it isn't exact. Different methods give different answers. For example, some accountants find it natural to measure the effect of price before they measure the effect of efficiency. They start, as before, from the planned spend:

A

Planned units used	×	Planned price/unit	=	Planned spend
95 units	×	£9/unit	=	£855

but they next change change price from 'planned' to 'actual'. This predicts the spend we might have made if only our price were worse than plan:

D.

Planned units used	×	Actual price/unit	=	Potential spend
95 units	×	£10/unit	=	£950

In the present example D – A gives an efficiency variance of £95, which is different from the C – B efficiency variance of £100 (and the algebraic formula is different, too). In more complex systems there are more than two choices for what is called the 'order of variance extraction', and all of them usually give different answers. Not every accounting textbook mentions this discrepancy.

It turns out that nothing can make the price variance and the efficiency variance independent of each other, and no method is logically perfect. Luckily the differences between various methods are small, provided all the individual variances are small (say 10 per cent of total plan). The moral is that variance analysis is not an exact science, and its strongest signals (ie, the largest variances) are likely to be the least accurate. Here, as in some other ways, management accounting is safer as a guide for fine-tuning than for major policy change.

Of course the management accountant has to make many arbitrary policy choices in addition to the order of variance, such as depreciation rules, stock valuation rules, currency translation rules, etc. Management accounts are at best a 'model' of the business, and any model, in some circumstances, can give misleading advice.

Similar problems arise in estimating how costs will change if we vary the mix of output, or vary the level of any other activity which supports output (eg, redesigns, order line administration, batch setups, etc). In extreme cases, such as oil and chemical companies, where all products interact very strongly, and compete for resources, it is vital to take decisions for all the products simultaneously, using optimizing methods, such as linear programming. For them, today's average cost should guide neither today's decision nor tomorrow's.

Even if linear programming isn't needed, a safe rule of thumb is that whenever the management accounts seem to favour a large change in product mix, or price or volume, it's always wise to make a special study to predict the new total effect on costs, revenues, customers and competitors. Bring in the interaction effects which conventional accounting often assumes away, such as the effects on customers, and what parts of the costs of both outputs and activities are fixed and variable.

What are the other behavioural pitfalls of management accounting?

We've mentioned the effects of setting too high or low a transfer price. Splitting cost and profit across too many different managers can make departments squabble over resources, and managers are unable to spend a pound in one department in order to save ten pounds elsewhere.

Is it fair to hold managers to account for things they do not control? If we believe in empowerment, perhaps we should only judge a manager by those financial outcomes which he or she can actually influence (ie, leave out overhead spending by other departments, or the effects of currency fluctuations, and economic cycles which the manager can do nothing to control). But if no one is responsible for environmental setbacks, and no department ever suffers from the overspending of other departments, who will ever be motivated to take corrective action? Some degree of unfairness is in fact vital.

However, if you use the management accounts over-aggressively in setting and enforcing targets, this can can cause managers to game play. They may spend more time and effort managing the accounting numbers than in running the business. They may deliberately or accidentally take decisions that damage the business, solely to improve their own short-term accounting performance.

What are the critical things to remember in designing and using a management accounting system?

The key design decisions should reflect the way your business uses resources and generates revenue, and the way you *want* to use resources and generate revenue (ie, there should be a match between your corporate strategy and goals, the way you divide economic power and responsibility between managers (especially profit responsibility), and the design of the management accounting system. What should be the profit centres, cost centres and revenue centres?

Common design mistakes are to split responsibility and/or reporting for resources that should interact, and to ignore the effect of fixed and variable and shared costs. Many Western accounting systems also omit or under-emphasize asset management and cash flow.

In practice a common mistake is to misforecast or misinterpret the timing of expenses. A seemingly large under-, or over-, spend can arise simply because a big spend moved a week or so earlier or later, or because the budget is spread evenly over the months, without allowing for their different numbers of working days. Other common errors are to over-interpret short-term results, or to use the wrong level of cost in a decision. For short-term decisions, avoidable variable costs may be most useful, but for long-term decisions total average costs can be useful.

What are the important recent developments in management accounting?

Important recent trends include Activity Based Costing, Strategic Management Accounting, Time-Based and Asset-Based Analysis, and Multiplexed Analysis.

Activity Based Costing uses the idea that activities such as order entry or batch setup may have very different impacts on different products, and/or different customers. You should cost one-offs or small orders, and you may find them very expensive indeed. What you can do about this is a complex matter.

Strategic Management Accounting uses the idea that longer-term and non-accounting goals may be as important as short-term profit. Strategic goals may require the reporting of 'non-accounting' numbers, and of some variables which have little impact on short-term profit (perhaps including environmental information).

Time-Based Analysis and Asset-Based Analysis are a break from the traditional Western obsession with the profit and loss account, and with direct labour cost. The logic is that:

$$\text{Return on assets} = \text{Margin on sales} \times \text{Asset turnover}$$

If we boost the asset turnover sufficiently high, the size of the profit margin can be as low as we like, and the business will then earn a high return on assets at a very competitive price, and will need little cash to fund its growth. Key goals include flexibility, and speed of asset movement, rather than cost *per se*.

Multiplexing drops the fiction that nothing affects anything else. Multiplexing uses database technology to look directly at interactions, and to simulate major policy changes. For example, suppose Activity Based Costing suggests we should double the price of small lots of product X. How will this affect each of our major customers? How will it affect our average minor customer? How will it affect our costs for product X, and our costs in total? Do we have to charge the same price increase for every customer, or should we discount for a few sensitive majors?

These are sensitive and controversial issues yet they lie at the heart of accounting and, indeed, of managing in complex environments. With managers deluged with a welter of information, management accounting offers a dynamic means of understanding, communicating and using information to the benfit of the organization as a whole.

Sydney Howell is a lecturer in management accounting and control at Manchester Business School. He is author of *Analysing Your Competitor's Financial Strengths* (1993).

Further Reading

Howell, S, *Analysing Your Competitor's Financial Strengths*, *Financial Times*/Pitman, London, 1993.

Johnson, HT and Kaplan, RS, 'The rise and fall of Management Accounting', *Management Accounting* (USA), January 1987, pp.22–30.

Smith, M, *New Tools for Management Accounting*, FT/Pitman, London, 1995.

MANAGING THE FINANCE FUNCTION

Charles Colman

Often isolated, misunderstood and under-utilized, the finance function remains mysteriously aloof in many organizations. Yet, few executives or companies would deny its critical role in supporting and forming strategy, and in allowing companies to improve their financial and overall performance.

The major objective for a finance function is to help define and then value the best business opportunities for the company. This requires members of the function to be highly trained and motivated in order to achieve this objective. Increasingly, achieving such objectives demands teamwork and the breaking down of functional barriers.

Evolution of the finance function at Procter & Gamble (P&G)

The early development of financial management at Procter & Gamble followed a traditional 'command and control' orientation. As Keating and Jablonsky discussed in their book *Changing Roles of Financial Management: Cutting Close to the Business*,[1] this traditional functional organization, with a chain of command style of management, stressed corporate oversight, operating efficiency, and conservation of corporate resources. In this type of organization, the finance function provides independent financial assessments of product initiatives and profit plans, but is not heavily involved in strategic business analysis.

P&G still maintains a command and control orientation in areas such as treasury (centralized), global financial systems, internal audit, and the profit forecast process. In other areas of finance P&G is now evolving a 'competitive team orientation', driven by strong competition in the global market and a renewed focus on building shareholder value.

The competitive team orientation, as described by Keating and Jablonsky, occurs in firms where financial work is focused on the market and integrated into the business organization via a matrix style of management. It requires the finance organization to have an intimate knowledge of the business issues facing a firm. The end result from this design is an increase in shareholder value because the firm makes improved business decisions based on relevant financial analysis.

The challenge faced by a finance organization is to balance the two approaches – 'command and control' with the 'competitive team orientation'. Each approach is appropriate for different circumstances and finance personnel must learn to switch between modes. For instance, a strong internal audit group can look for both control weaknesses and business building opportunities. A prime example of this is the work that must be undertaken to 'standardize' procedures in an acquired business unit with the parent company's procedures. The internal audit group, if responsible for this, can ensure that normal control requirements are met but also identify synergies which can reduce the dilution effect of the acquisition's purchase price.

In a centralized, information-hungry organization, there will be tension between finance's control orientation and the competitive team orientation. Other functions in a firm might regard the control orientation as 'finance carrying a stick' because of data exclusively available to finance. Finance members must make a transition beyond this in order to become full partners on business teams and not be perceived as 'spies' by other team members. Leaders of the finance function must reinforce this partnership approach with the leaders of other functions in the presence of the finance members of business teams. A finance functional leader can quickly destroy the trust of other functions unless he or she is very sensitive to the requirements of finance's team orientation.

For example, it is unwise to release sensitive financial data on upstream research projects in response to a rush request from a centralized control group. This communication must be jointly managed with research to ensure the trust relationship between finance and research is maintained.

Establishing a functional vision

A firm needs a clear idea of what it wants to do if it is to successfully build competitive advantage. No finance function will be successful unless a Corporate Purpose is established and is fully understood. At Procter & Gamble the 'Statement of Purpose' reads as follows:

'We will provide products of superior quality and value that best fill the needs of the world's consumers.

We will achieve that purpose through an organization and a working environment which attract the finest people; fully develop and challenge our individual talents; encourage our free and spirited collaboration to drive the business ahead; and maintain the Company's historic principles of integrity, and doing the right thing.

Through the successful pursuit of our commitment, we expect our brands to achieve leadership share and profit positions and that, as a result, our business, our people, our shareholders, and the communities in which we live and work, will prosper.'

With P&G committed to implementing this Corporate Purpose, the finance function's mission statement was created as follows:

'To provide leadership to business decision making, and sound, innovative planning and managing of the Company's financial affairs to maximize long-term profits, cash flow, and return on investment.'

The finance function's mission statement can be related to the fact that the corporation will produce products of superior quality and value in order to maximize long-term profits, cash, and Return on Investment.

Strategy deployment

Now, vision and mission statements will provide little guidance to a finance function (or a total firm) unless the question 'What can I do?' is answered. All members of the finance department need to share the same understanding of the 'Statement of Purpose' and of the function's 'Mission Statement'. This does not result from one-time deployment. It requires continual reinforcement and tracking, formally and informally, by all leaders of the function.

With a guiding vision in place, the firm's business strategies can be deployed straight to the business units. The finance function should have joint ownership of these strategies and specific ownership of certain sub-elements. The right strategy deployment process can focus the organization quickly and powerfully on the right things. This business focus is essential for a financial department dealing with the increasing globalization of markets, rapid world-wide deployment of technologies and products, and continuing change in consumer needs and requirements. The strategy deployment process creates business and functional alignment, appropriate workload distribution, and meets the internal need for clarity of direction. It answers the question 'I know what needs to be done, but how do I make it happen across thousands of people?' It also prevents the situation where the finance department finds itself working on a lot of things that don't fit together.

Having said all these positive things about strategy deployment, what technique can be used to ensure it is efficiently applied?

A powerful deployment tool that can be used is called 'OGSM' (Objectives, Goals, Strategies, and Measures). It has worked extremely well for me in both the US and Europe, in established and acquired businesses. This tool can cascade a company's strategies to the individual business units. Just as importantly, the OGSM process can be incorporated down to individual work and development plans, allowing an individual's contribution to be clearly defined.

The intent of strategy deployment via an OGSM process is to focus on the critically few choices that will win in the marketplace. In keeping with the essence of strategy, it focuses as narrowly as possible for as long as possible. It is *not* intended to comprise the complete work and development plan of a member of the financial department, but rather to focus on those choices that will achieve breakthrough results. OGSM allows the entire organization to understand what is required, why it is required, and how to get there. Other methods can be chosen to gain alignment, but they must achieve the objective of guiding finance to an involvement in the business which permits the function to consistently value the project opportunities of the company.

In addition the OGSM process clearly defines the groups responsible for delivering strategies and links these strategies throughout the organization in terms of what 'I/we can do'. The emphasis is clearly on what it will take to achieve a strategy, not negotiation to a lower need. Regular reviews are at the heart of this system. This is schematically represented in Fig. 1.

Figure 2 provides an example of how an OGSM is used to transfer business strategies from the chief executive officer to the individual business unit. In this example, the chief executive sets a specific company profit objective, with year-by-year goals and strategies to support this objective.

The company strategy shown in Fig. 2 is of increasing the return from new product introductions. This strategy recognizes the importance of innovation to the business. New product introductions can either exploit opportunities

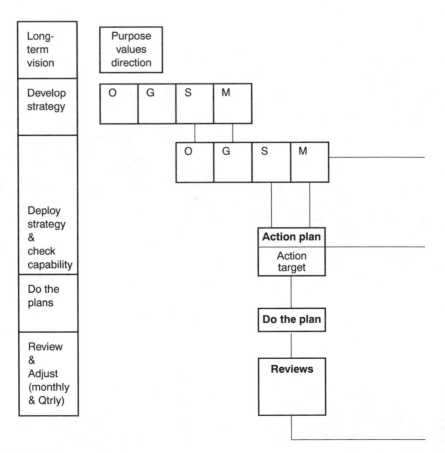

Fig. 1 Strategy deployment

Company

OBJECTIVE	GOAL	STRATEGY	MEASURES
Grow profit to X by year X by increasing volume and profit margins		1. Increase the return from new product introductions 2. ... 3. ... 4. ... 5. ...	Initiative Success Rate from 30% to 60% by Year 5. Total Profit from New Products + 200% by Year 5.

GOAL:

	Year 1	Year 5	Year 10
Volume	BASE	+50%	+100%
Margin	BASE	+25%	+50%

Business Unit (Finance Function)

OBJECTIVE	GOAL	STRATEGY	MEASURES
Increase the return from new product introductions	Initiative Success Rate from 30% to 60% by Year 5. Total Profit from New Products + 200% by Year 5.	1. Introduce Risk Analysis to new product team. Weed weak projects. 2. ... 3. ... 4. ... 5. ...	Complete Year 1. 25% portfolio profit improvement Year 1.

Fig. 2 OGSM example

(on a global basis) or deal with competitive threats. The company's measure, in this case, requires an increase in both the new product success rate and the total profit expected from new products. This strategy is then cascaded down to a business unit where finance translates the strategy into an objective. The objective of increasing the return from new product introductions in turn requires a strategy of introducing risk analysis with a specific Year 1 measure for the profit centre. The point here is that the finance function takes ownership for a specific element of a business unit's OGSM as derived from the company's OGSM. Other functions can also take ownership for specific elements of OGSMs at either the company or business unit level. This process requires a significant amount of dialogue to create alignment, but leads to clear management of a finance function.

An individual in a business unit's finance department can learn to use a 'Competitive Team' or a 'Command and Control' orientation for each OGSM strategy being deployed. An OGSM strategy of cost control will require that the 'command and control' hat be worn, yet the same strategy can also require innovation and will play to the 'competitive team' orientation. Finance department members have to be sensitive to when a strategy requires a control orientation, and when it requires a team orientation. Failure to do this will create barriers to finance's ability to function as full team players.

An OGSM is better deployed if there is a wide span of control under a single manager. Unnecessary layers in an organization prevent the spread of good ideas. A wide span of control allows for both the detail penetration necessary to properly coach people, yet provides the motivation that comes from delegation of responsibility.

Portfolio analysis

Portfolio analysis is the central role which the finance function must play. This is how finance can value the best business opportunities of a company.

In *The Competitive Advantage of Nations*, Michael Porter describes firms that create competitive advantage by receiving or discovering new and better ways of competing in an industry and bringing them to market.[2] Porter describes innovation as including both improvements in technology and better methods or approaches to marketing, and/or new forms of distribution. These innovations can shift competitive advantage when rivals don't see the new way of competing or are unable or unwilling to respond.

In order to facilitate innovation, the financial function must be fully integrated with all aspects of the business, including project teams, the scientists developing the upstream projects, the manufacturing groups developing new processes and cost savings ideas, and those departments, such as sales and marketing, which interact with the customers and consumers. The financial group can then value the myriad ideas which can be generated in a firm and help develop the optimal strategic direction or resource deployment.

In *Managing Across Borders: The Trans-National Solution,* Christopher Bartlett and Sumantra Ghoshal point out that in order to achieve global competitive advantage, costs and revenues have to be managed simultaneously. Efficiency and innovation are both important and require the 'trans-national' corporation to make selective decisions. Therefore, a finance member of a global team will, at times, wear either a 'Command and Control' hat (efficiency) or a 'Competitive Team' hat (innovation).

Global companies often find that innovation opportunities and the resources necessary to realize these opportunities are in different locations (eg, manufacturing and research centralized in one location). Linkages are required between the business unit identifying the opportunity and these resources. Regional/global business teams can create this integration. Financial partnership on the teams becomes key to identifying an innovation's economic potential. The financial team member can also bring economic perspective to bear as different profit centres negotiate a co-ordinated approach. A firm will only achieve a growth rate equal to its potential if it can allocate its scarce resources to the most attractive opportunities.

For this to happen, the finance function must be capable of representing the best business judgements within the firm, with associated risks. Such an approach is necessary both for the utilization of current assets of the firm and, importantly, for new business ideas. Members of the finance function must be able to communicate evaluation techniques and analysis in an easy-to-understand manner to the owners of the business building projects. Supposing these owners to be a 'project team', then members of the team need to be as conversant in the economic implications of their choice as the finance department.

The first step is to choose a financial measure that permits consistent value comparisons across projects. Few firms can staff all 'good' projects and, therefore, require a screening mechanizm. Net present value (NPV) is best for this purpose. NPV values the increase in a firm's wealth by discounting a project's cashflow by the firm's cost of capital. The alternative concept of an 'acceptable rate of return' can be limiting. It's possible to achieve an acceptable rate of return yet generate a low NPV on projects where, for example, there is a low capital investment but a formulation's cost upcharge is barely offset by an increase in the amount of product sold. A rate of return is generated which is above the company's cost of capital, but the NPV is unacceptably low when compared to other projects. A project team that focuses on NPV will have the correct perspective on how best to increase shareholder value and will attempt to raise NPV in order to gain resources. It will focus on reducing costs and/or increasing consumer appeal and in the process spend more time evaluating the key levers driving the NPV results.

The second step is to benchmark a project against previous results. Project teams will be unable to design their initiatives for maximum NPV unless they have a database of similar initiatives to measure themselves against. Benchmarking of previously implemented projects is key if proponents of new ideas are to understand what amount of economic contribution to the firm's value is necessary to receive resources. Benchmarking permits project teams to understand what has contributed to the success of other company initiatives. Teams can penetrate the differences between their ideas, and other, formerly implemented, projects (both successful and unsuccessful ones) to improve the project's value and probability of success.

Finally, it is all very well to use the NPV tool to analyze a business prospect, but when projects are competing for resources, then it is important that the finance function present the relative net present values using comparably weighted assumptions. This requires risk analysis so that one project does not make an optimistic assumption (eg, the ability to take a price increase) while another (better) project has been conservative (eg, avoided the reliance on pricing to deliver a high NPV). Easily available risk analysis software packages make this type of dialogue with a project team an easy one. Risk scenarios are quickly calculated and easily understood by all. The financial department can then present a portfolio of projects to be prioritized in the knowledge that relative risks have been equally considered.

I want to emphasize the importance of the training which project teams should receive from the finance function on financial concepts and risk analysis. The walls between functions are those of 'functional lore'. Yet, winning firms need business teams whose members all fully understand and *own* the financial evaluation techniques in use and the results which are being measured.

Character of the financial department

It is worthwhile to develop a characterization of a finance department that functions as perfectly as we would like. Perhaps it would look as follows.

The finance function understands what it takes to improve the stock price of the company. It consistently delivers high-quality results. It is integrated in an ongoing development of its own capabilities with its members engaged throughout the business so that key issues are fully understood and anticipated. It is always focused on improving business processes. It makes a difference in business decision making.

Members of the finance function are technical masters who can convert skills and new ideas into practical applications. They are creative and innovative. Each member is data oriented and recognizes that only through very thorough analysis can the best solution be identified. Members seek first to understand, then to be understood. They recognize cultural differences. They can build commitment to ideas, and work effectively with others. They function equally well as leaders or as team members. Initiative and follow-through are superb so that multiple priorities can be handled, obstacles overcome, and risks taken where appropriate.

Such a profile can be circulated as a 'Gold Standard' to motivate employees and measure their performance. It can also be developed into a series of 'Key Performance' factors that can be shared with all members of the function and extended to the profile used to recruit new members to the firm.

Expectancy and competitive advantage

Expectancy theory states that the motivation to do something is a function of the outcomes which a person expects to result from a certain behaviour and whether these outcomes are attractive or not. The theory applies to behaviours under the voluntary control of the individual which in turn relates to the amount of effort put into an activity and the desire to innovate. I find this theory to be relevant in ensuring that a function has a 'will to win' for the firm. If an OGSM is used for strategy deployment, then individual members of the finance function can be motivated to perform via clarity of expectations, a reward structure linked to results, and the chance for individual participation and ownership in moving the firm forward towards its Statement of Purpose.

It is important to foster a spirit of 'creative interpretation' of the company's goals so that new strategies can be continually developed. The finance department's responsibility for portfolio analysis is an area where creativity is important. By linking a firm's vision to strategy deployment and portfolio analysis, the finance function can provide competitive advantage.

Charles Colman is finance director of P&G's US Laundry Category and has worked extensively in Europe.

Further Reading

Sprent, P, *Management Mathematics – A User-Friendly Approach*, Penguin, London, 1991.
Lynch, RL and Cross, KF *Measure Up – The Essential Guide to Measuring Business Performance*, Mandarin, London, 1992.

References

[1] Keating and Jablonsky, *Financial Executives Research Foundation* series on Innovative Management.
[2] Porter, M, *The Competitive Advantage of Nations*, Macmillan, London, 1990.

MANAGING LONG-TERM INVESTMENT DECISIONS

Eddie McLaney

In essence, certainly from a financial point of view, a business can be seen as an organization which raises finance from various sources (shareholders, long-term lenders, etc) and uses this finance to make investments. These investments might be of a wide variety of types, including shares in other companies. More typically, however, for most businesses, the investments will be made in land and buildings, plant and machinery, stock-in-trade, etc, which will help the investing business to produce a product or to provide a service which can be sold at a profit. Businesses will employ labour to manage their investments, ie, to cause the product or service to emerge and to be marketed.

Given that the business of a business is to raise finance and deploy that finance in profitable investment, two crucial activities of a business are financing it and making investment decisions.

It would be difficult to overstate the importance of making long-term investment decisions. They are important because:

- They often involve amounts of finance which are significant relative to the size of the business concerned.
- They tend to commit the business for fairly long periods of time or, at least, are so intended when the investment is made.
- The costs of abandoning unprofitable investments are often very significant.

These factors combine to mean that a series of bad investment decisions, or perhaps just one significant error, could cause the business to fail.

The objective of investment

A central issue in the management of business investment is the objective in whose furtherance the investment is made. It is not possible to make effective investment decisions unless the decision maker is clear on which objective or objectives the business is pursuing.

Finance and management literature is awash with discussion about what is, and what should be, the central objective or objectives of private sector businesses. Various suggestions have been put forward, including maximization of turnover, long-term stability and seeking to strike a balance between the requirements of the various 'stakeholders' in the business. Ultimately the one financial objective which encapsulates what most businesses are seeking to achieve is *to increase the value of the business*. Put another way, the objective is for the business to generate wealth. This means that, all other things being equal, businesses would seek to take on investment opportunities which are expected to generate wealth. Where there are mutually exclusive opportunities, those which enhance wealth the most will be selected.

The wealth-enhancing objective has been objected to by some commentators on the grounds that it concentrates too much on the welfare of the shareholders and not sufficiently on that of other participants in the business, such as employees and customers. However, there is nothing about a wealth-generation objective which, of itself, is contrary to the interests of these other participants. In a free, competitive market employees, customers and all other stakeholders are likely to benefit from a relationship with a business which is generating wealth, since this implies the ability of the business to continue in operation and to raise finance for expansion. This ability to prosper should provide the employees with good and expanding employment opportunities and customers with continued supplies. The disciplines of the market should ensure that none of the stakeholders can be exploited, not at least for any great period of time.

Ultimately, exploitation of any of the stakeholders would lead to diminutions of business wealth. For example, a business which acquired a reputation as a bad employer would probably experience a high labour turnover and its accompanying costs. Similarly, a business which tried to sell substandard merchandize would not normally be able to establish or to maintain a profitable market. Other stakeholders provide similar examples. Clearly, the objective of wealth enhancement seems entirely consistent with enhancing the benefits to all stakeholders.

Even if it is true that wealth enhancement is too limited an objective against which to assess investment opportunities, it certainly would be true that any business which consistently made decisions which led to diminutions in its wealth would have a very limited future, to the detriment of all stakeholders. So, it appears to be the case that, even if we accept that wealth enhancement may not be the only credible objective for a private sector business, the effect of any investment decision on wealth must be a key consideration.

There is a great deal of research evidence, much of it gathered by surveying the opinions of managers, on the subject of the financial goals pursued. This points fairly clearly to wealth generation as the primary objective of investment decisions.

The search for investment opportunities

Given that businesses are in the business of making investments with wealth enhancement as the objective, it is important that those businesses are constantly seeking new investment opportunities, both to replace expiring ones and to expand activities. These opportunities may be concerned with new products, new markets, new production methods, etc, or simply maintaining the existing nature and scale of operations. What this involves in practice will obviously vary very widely from one industrial sector to another and from one business to another, so it is not possible to do more than generalize.

Businesses need to consider carefully their commitment to the search for investment opportunities. This search may involve highly sophisticated research and development, conducted 'in-house'. On the other hand, it may involve the rather more mundane activity of scanning the trade press in a search for a new machine which will enable the business to make its product or to provide its service more cheaply. It is likely that the business's competitors will exploit opportunities to invest, so to remain competitive and to survive the business needs constantly to search out profitable investments. Rarely will such opportunities present themselves without a systematic search.

The search for profitable investments is at the centre of the management of long-term investment decisions. Other activities are essentially subordinate to it. However, little of the literature on investment management seems to be concerned with this search.

Forecasting the outcomes from an investment

Having identified a possible investment opportunity, it then becomes necessary to try to assess its ability to make a positive contribution to the wealth of the business. The first step in this process is to identify the relevant financial effects of making the investment. As with the search for investment opportunities, the means of identifying the financial effects will vary depending on the nature of the investment under consideration. If the investment is in the production and marketing facilities for a new product or service it may be appropriate to use market research to try to assess its acceptability, including forecasts of sales volume at various price levels. Estimates would need to be made of the production costs which would be engendered. Tax payments and receipts caused by the investment must also be estimated.

In many cases there may be less obvious financial consequences of a particular course of action. For example, the successful launch of a new product or service may have an adverse effect on the sales of some other output of the business. If this is the case the financial consequences must be estimated.

For all of these estimates we are interested in the cash flow effects, in terms of both amount and timing, of making the investment. The reason for this is that it is not until cash flows out of the business to meet the costs that it needs to be taken away from some other beneficial use – for example, generating interest in a bank deposit account. Similarly, it is not until the cash actually flows in from the investment that it can be used for some other profitable purpose. One important cost which must be estimated is the cost of the finance which will be used to make the investment.

With the estimations of the various revenues and costs should be some assessment of how confident the decision makers can be of the reliability of these estimations. The estimations relate to the future and cannot, therefore be seen as completely reliable. The confidence of the decision makers in the reliability of the estimations will have a significant effect on how the estimates are used in the analysis of the investment.

Appraising the investment opportunity

It is then necessary to take the various financial estimates and to ask the question, if these are the estimated effects of making the investment, would the investment be expected to generate a net increase in wealth? Here we can generalize – for all businesses seeking to enhance their wealth, the assessment process will follow the same pattern.

At this point we have estimates of the cash flow effects of making the investment under consideration, including the cost of finance. We also have some idea of the reliability of these estimates, usually referred to as their riskiness. The question of risk and how we might deal with it we shall leave until the next section. Probably the best way to proceed is through an example:

A business wishes to assess an investment in a new production facility. Establishing the facility will cost £10 million, payable immediately. It is estimated that sales of the new product will generate net cash benefits, taking all revenues and costs into account, except financing cost, as follows:

	£m
Year 1	3
2	4
3	5
4	3
5	2
6 & thereafter	zero

For the sake of simplicity we shall assume that the cash flows occur at the ends of the relevant years.

The cost of finance to support this project is 10 per cent per annum. Will this investment enhance the wealth of the business?

Were the net cash inflows all to occur at the same time as the £10 million outflow, we could simply say that, since the sum of the net inflows (£17 million) exceeds £10 million, undertaking the project would enhance the wealth of the business by £7 million and should, therefore, be undertaken. Since the cash flows do not all occur at the same time (a standard feature of investments) the assessment is not quite so straightforward. This is because £s at different times have a different effect on wealth; it is invalid to make the direct comparison between the £10 million and the £17 million. No rational person would see receiving £1 in a year's time as acceptable compensation for giving up £1 now.

We know the effect on the business's wealth of spending £10 million to make the investment, but what is the present *effect* on the wealth of the business of receiving £3 million in a year's time, £4 million in two years' time etc? If we were able to assess the present value of future receipts, we could make a valid comparison of the net effect on wealth of undertaking the investment. By present value is meant the value that the business would presently place on those future receipts.

Let us simply consider the £3 million that is estimated would be received after one year should the investment be made. On the face of things, the amount cannot affect the business's wealth until it is received. Due to the existence of financial markets, however, it is possible to turn a receipt scheduled for next year into an immediate receipt and enhancement in wealth. The business could immediately borrow such an amount, that with one year's interest on it would equal the £3m. With an interest rate of 10 per cent, this would be:

$$\frac{£3m}{1 + 10/100} = £2.73m \text{ [Note that £2.73m + (£2.73m} \times 10\%) = £3m]}$$

Thus, with a finance cost of 10 per cent pa a receipt of £3 million expected to be received in one year's time enhances present wealth by £2.73 million. The effect of other years' expected receipts on present wealth can also be assessed. The effect of any receipt (R) on present wealth is:

$$\frac{R}{(1 + i) n}$$ where i is the annual interest rate and n is the number of years into the future that the receipt will occur.

(Note that this general point is equally true of the present detrimental effect on the business's wealth of future payments.)

Thus the total net effect on the business's wealth of the future receipts in our example is:

			£m
Year 1	$\dfrac{£3m}{(1 + {}^{10}/_{100})^1}$	=	2.73
Year 2	$\dfrac{£4m}{(1 + {}^{10}/_{100})^2}$	=	3.64
Year 3	$\dfrac{£5m}{(1 + {}^{10}/_{100})^3}$	=	3.76
Year 4	$\dfrac{£3m}{(1 + {}^{10}/_{100})^4}$	=	2.05
Year 5	$\dfrac{£2m}{(1 + {}^{10}/_{100})^5}$	=	1.24
Total enhancement of present wealth			£13.42m

Fig. 1 Calculation of investment returns over 5 years

This can now be compared with the cost of making the investment (£10 million) to conclude that the investment would make the business more wealthy by £3.42 million and should, therefore, be undertaken.

In effect the business has the opportunity to 'buy' for £10 million the opportunity to receive future cash flows which have a combined advantageous effect on wealth of £13.42 million. Buying investments for less than they are worth will help a business, whose objective is to generate wealth, to achieve that aim.

As is probably obvious from this analysis, calculating the net effect on wealth in this way implicitly takes account of the financing cost of undertaking the investment. This is because future cash flows are 'discounted', by the cost of financing them, from the time of making the initial investment to their receipt.

This approach to investment decision making is known as the net present value (NPV) method. Though it is not the only one which is used in practice, it is certainly the most logical approach for the business pursuing a wealth-enhancement objective.

Appraisal methods used in practice

Research evidence shows there to be three other approaches used in practice to appraise investment opportunities as well as the NPV method.

One of these, the internal rate of return (IRR) method, is very closely related to NPV. In effect IRR asks what is the financing cost which will cause a business to be indifferent to a particular investment opportunity? Thus it is the interest rate (i) which will give the opportunity a zero NPV. If we look back at our example, we can see that, if the financing cost were to be increased above 10 per cent pa, each of the future cash inflows would be discounted by a higher figure and the total enhancement of wealth (or present value) would fall below £13.42 million. There is a finance cost at which the present value would be exactly £10 million. At this hypothetical finance cost, the investment would have a zero effect on the wealth of the business. This finance cost is the IRR of the investment.

If the IRR is greater than the actual cost of finance for the investment, the project is worth undertaking. If there are two or more competing projects, the one with the higher or highest IRR would be selected. Strictly, for the business seeking wealth enhancement, IRR is not the most appropriate method because IRR is concerned with a percentage rate of return, not with the direct effect of an investment on wealth. In most practical cases, however, IRR provides identical advice to that given by NPV.

The payback period (PP) method looks at the length of time it takes for the initial investment to be repaid from the cash flows generated. In the above example, this would be three years because it would not be before the end of the third year that sufficient cash would have flowed in to cover the initial £10 million investment. Users of the PP method would seek investments which would pay for themselves fairly quickly. Users would probably have a 'hurdle' period which would serve as a maximum acceptable to them. Investments with a longer payback period would automatically be rejected. With competing investments, the one with shorter or shortest payback period would be selected, provided that it fell within the hurdle period. To the business seeking to enhance its wealth, PP is badly flawed. It is not concerned with wealth, but with liquidity. It takes little account of the timing of the individual cash flows within the payback period and totally ignores those which occur outside it. There is no obvious logic for the choice of hurdle period and this makes using the PP method somewhat unscientific. Its advocates claim, however, that it gives a perspective on an investment which is different from that which is provided by NPV and IRR.

The other method found in practice is the accounting rate of return (ARR). This takes the average accounting profit and expresses it as a percentage of the average investment. Users would normally have a 'hurdle' rate which investments would have to satisfy, with the higher or highest ARR being selected from competing investments. As with PP, selection of the hurdle rate is rather arbitrary. ARR generally lacks logic. This is mainly a result of using a means of reporting economic performance for a short period in the life of a range of investments (accounting profit) to assess a particular investment over its life-time. Although accounting profit should be concerned with the amount of wealth generated, financial accounting PP based on some rules, whose use can, and usually will, lead to distortions when applied to assessing an investment opportunity. Since, ultimately, accounting flows and cash flows should be the same in total it seems better to use NPV or IRR which more correctly handles the data in the context of a wealth-enhancement objective.

There is a large body of research on the use of the four appraisal methods by UK businesses. Most of this research relates to larger businesses. The most notable findings of the various studies include:

- Most businesses typically use more than one method to appraise invest-ments. For larger businesses this has averaged three (of the four discussed above). Smaller businesses tend to use about two methods, on average. The research does not establish whether businesses use different methods for dif-ferent types of investment, whether individual divisions have their own favourite method which varies from one division to the next or whether all investment opportunities are appraised using more than one method. The truth probably lies with all of these to some extent. If, as seems likely, busi-nesses use more than one method to appraise all investment opportunities, or at least the more significant opportunities, this does not imply a lot of extra effort. The raw data for all four methods are estimates of potential cash flows. Once these estimates have been made, it is relatively simple to apply each of the four methods to them.

- It can be argued that the use of more than one method implies some uncer-tainty by decision makers on the objectives being pursued through the investment process. Businesses which seek to enhance their wealth should be using NPV, since this is the only one which relates directly to that objec-tive. On the other hand, decision makers may prefer to have a number of perspectives. It seems quite likely that where multiple methods are used for particular decisions, one of the methods will be the major determinant with the others giving additional views.

- Nearly all larger businesses use NPV or IRR. As pointed out, IRR is con-ceptually less correct for businesses whose goal is wealth enhancement. IRR does, however, normally give identical advice to that proffered by NPV. Smaller businesses seem less enamoured of these 'discounting' methods. Whether this implies that smaller businesses tend not to be so clearly focused on wealth enhancement or whether their managers are more com-fortable with the less sophisticated PP method is a matter of conjecture.

- PP remains a very popular approach with businesses of all sizes and seems to be increasing in popularity over time, even among larger businesses. For smaller businesses it is overwhelmingly the most popular of the four methods.

- ARR is the least popular of the methods and is becoming less popular over time. This is not so surprising since it seems to offer no insights which are not better provided by the other methods.

UK experience in the use of investment appraisal methods is broadly shared by the United States.

Risk in investment appraisal

An ever present feature of all decision making is the extent to which what we expect to happen will not actually occur. What particularly tends to concern us is that things will turn out worse than was projected. This is an obvious concern with investment decisions since their time scale and size combine to mean that outcomes are difficult to estimate and errors in estimation could have profound effects.

Assessing and allowing for the risk associated with investment opportunities is not an exact science, any more than any other aspect of an investment decision. In practice, various approaches are used. Some decision makers attempt to ascribe statistical probabilities to various outcomes. Another approach is to look at various 'scenarios', that is, possible outcomes for the investment as a whole when different assumptions are made about the inputs. From the effect on the overall outcome of alterations to various inputs, decision makers are able to make some assessment of how sensitive is the success of the investment to particular input factors. In this way the 'key' variables may be able to be identified.

There are sound theoretical reasons to believe that the most appropriate way to deal with risk, in the context of NPV, is to increase the required rate of return, ie, to discount future cash flows more heavily. Certainly, in practice, we see plenty of examples that investors seek higher returns from risky investments than they do from safe ones. Typical yields from Government stocks fall well short of those provided, on average, from the equities of commercial and industrial businesses.

Though there is a body of theory which relates risk to required return, investment decision makers are ultimately likely to be left to use their own 'gut' feeling in setting the required rate of return for a particular investment opportunity.

Post audit and monitoring

It is generally seen to be good management practice to review decisions and to monitor their outcomes, a process often known as 'post audit'. The nature and scale of many investment decisions makes review and monitoring particularly important. Post audits are conducted in an attempt to assess and, where necessary, take steps to improve the investment decision making process. This would normally involve questioning all of the assumptions and predictions on which the original decision was based and, where possible, comparing them with the actual outcomes. Valuable conclusions may then be able to be drawn on the extent to which the decision-making process was effective and where it was deficient. In the latter case, it may be possible for the post audit process to lead to improvements in the decision-making routines which could be implemented to the benefit of future investment decisions.

Another valuable purpose of post audits is to assess the investment for its own sake. Monitoring an existing investment may reveal that it is not operating as envisaged when the original decision was made. In that case it may be possible to take action to correct for any shortfall in performance. The conclusion from such analysis may be that the investment has gone irretrievably wrong and abandoning the investment needs to be considered. Logically any abandonment decision should be based on a full assessment of all future cash flows from continuing to operate the investment, on the one hand, and the cash flows which will result from abandonment, on the other. It is logical to address constantly the question of abandonment. When, at any point, it becomes more wealth enhancing to abandon than to continue, the abandonment decision should be taken.

Eddie McLaney is a chartered accountant who has considerable experience of teaching, writing and consultancy in the fields of accounting and finance. He is a Principal Lecturer in Accounting and Finance at Plymouth Business School, University of Plymouth and author of *Business Finance for Decision Making* (1994).

Further Reading

Brealey, RA and Myers, SC, *Principles of Corporate Finance* (fourth edn), McGraw-Hill, Maidenhead, 1991.

Lumby, S, *Investment Appraisal and Financing Decisions* (fifth edn), Chapman and Hall , London, 1994.

McLaney, EJ, *Business Finance for Decision Making* (second edn), Pitman Publishing, London, 1994.

MANAGING FINANCIAL RISK

John Heptonstall

Prior to the 1970s, financial risk was associated largely with credit. From the viewpoint of the lending institution, the key consideration was counterparty risk. Risk management was primarily a matter of funding the loans with deposits of corresponding maturity, assessing the credit-worthiness of the individual borrower and negotiating an appropriate risk premium to be incorporated in the lending rate. For the borrower, the key considerations were the determination of the amount of debt that might safely be carried, and the impact of the resulting capital structure upon overall cost of capital.

These issues remain important, but now make up a small part of financial risk management which is a vastly more complex subject than it was two decades ago.

The growing complexity of financial risk management can be attributed to a number of factors. The dramatic increase in risks associated with market rates – and this includes currency market prices, interest rates, equity prices and commodities – now command far more attention than the traditional risk areas. The upsurge in market rate risks has given rise to the development of a wide range of new hedging instruments and techniques; and these in turn have triggered new and less obvious forms of risk.

The upsurge of volatility in financial market rates stems from a number of macro-economic developments. First and foremost of these is the breakdown, during 1972–1973, of the post-Bretton Woods system of 'fixed' currency exchange rates. During the life of this system the combination of a fixed value for the US dollar in terms of gold – and of semi-fixed parities for other participating currencies in terms of the dollar – provided long periods of stability. The relative spot market values of the dollar and of the pound, for instance, were held within a band of two per cent for eighteen years. In such a system, hedging – the management of currency risk – is not a high priority (and speculation is not rewarding). The collapse of the system led to a massive increase in volatility. Now, that same dollar/pound spot rate could easily move by one per cent in a single day. The attempt by the original members of the EEC to set up a localized fixed rate system, the 'snake in the tunnel', was no more successful than the fixed rate system itself. After 1973 the Western world had entered a period of 'dirty floating'. Currency price movements were now largely unpredictable, and currency rate risk became a major preoccupation of treasury staff.

A second major development in the financial infrastructure has been the proliferation of floating interest rates. During the late 1960s and throughout the 1970s the Eurocurrency market expanded vigorously and syndicated lending, which rapidly became the dominant form of transaction, and is virtually all done at floating rates: loans may be for ten years or more, but the interest rate typically has a six-month reset period. London Interbank Offered Rate (LIBOR) became the world's most important interest rate.[1] After the LDC debt crisis came to a head in 1982/83 the syndicated loan market fell in importance, but was replaced by a rapid growth in a new floating rate instrument in the Eurobond markets – the Floating Rate Note. By 1986 the FRN market was itself declining in importance, to be overtaken by newer and 'disintermediated' instruments such as the Issuance Facility and the Medium Term Note. All of these are essentially floating rate instruments.

This increase in the use of floating rate financing techniques coincided with an increase in volatility in the interest rates themselves. A significant milestone here was the change in Federal Reserve policy during 1979/80, when the then newly-elected chairman, Paul Volcker, attempted to manage the US economy via the monetary aggregates rather than through the previous close control of interest rates: during the following twelve months both US Prime and LIBOR rose by more than ten per cent. The shock waves arising from this period have long subsided, but other factors now contribute to interest rate volatility. The escalation in the size of the currency markets has seriously eroded the effectiveness of conventional intervention operations, so that the attempts of governments to influence the values of currencies are increasingly made through interest rate policies. Above all, the governments of the mature industrial economies now consider that their primary obligation is to control inflation, and look to interest rate policy as their primary weapon in doing so. The imposition of such policies – and their subsequent relaxation – can cause massive swings in interest rates: as in the UK during 1992/93, when bank rate fell from 12 per cent to 5.25 per cent after the attempt to hold sterling's ERM parity was abandoned. In the light of such volatility, interest rate exposure has joined currency rate exposure as a major concern for financial institutions and for a wide range of businesses.

During the period of relative stability in financial market rates there was little incentive to develop new ways of managing financial risk. After the mid-1970s, however, the nature of the market was transformed. Increasing risk called forth increasingly ingenious risk management techniques. The subsequent decade gave birth to more new financial instruments than had the previous fifty years, and innovation continues to the present time.

Categories of financial risk

The preceding section explained how increasing volatility has produced levels of market rate risk that have stimulated the development of new hedging instruments. The instruments themselves and the ways in which they are employed have, however, produced new categories of risk. It is now necessary to recognize four separate types of risk in the financial markets.

Market rate risk is conceptually simple: the danger is that changes in financial market rates, whether in currency markets, in interest rates or in equity markets, will have an adverse effect upon the organization's earnings and/or cash flows. A risk of this type is generated whenever a business invoices its export sales in the buyer's currency, accepts an invoice for its own imports in the supplier's currency, engages in cross-currency borrowing, or contracts to make any payments – of royalties or licence fees, for example – in a currency other than that in which it incurs the majority of its own operating costs and measures its financial results.

Basis risk is less widely recognized and arises largely from the techniques used to hedge the primary market rate risks. It is the risk that the subsequent price/yield performance of the instrument used in setting up the hedge is not the same as that of the 'cash' position being hedged. A bond portfolio may be hedged with a position in Treasury Bond futures, but a change in the slope of the yield curve changes the premium or discount of the futures market price relative to that of the bonds themselves. An extreme form of basis risk – which should be given a different name, such as 'proxy risk' – arises when a cash market position is hedged with a different instrument. A treasurer with an existing floating rate loan at US Prime rate, for example, might seek to hedge against the danger of rising interest rates by hedging in Treasury Bill futures. Any subsequent rise in short-term rates will certainly affect both Prime and the T-Bill rate, but they will not necessarily rise by exactly the same amount and the hedge will be imperfect.

Liquidity risk is the danger that a hedge cannot be properly constructed – or unwound – because of a lack of liquidity or depth in the appropriate market. Such a situation may arise in the currency markets when the currency of a smaller country has to be hedged, or when the desired maturity in a forward market transaction is unusually long. Even in the most active of the futures markets, which are generally assumed to be very liquid, the depth of the market (as shown by the 'open interest' figures) declines sharply beyond the two nearest value dates. Liquidity problems can also arise when a financial market is significantly 'one-sided'. In the currency options markets, for instance, the financial institutions which are the market-makers experience a distinctly one-sided market in that their natural counterparts, the corporate treasurers, are much more willing to be option buyers than to engage in option writing, even where they could in fact write on a fully covered basis.

Counterparty risk is simply credit risk: the risk that the other party to a transaction will be unable to honour his obligations. In conventional money market and capital market transactions, the risk assessment undertaken by lenders and investors is concerned with establishing the credit quality of borrowers and issuers, and is greatly assisted by the existence of professional 'rating' agencies. The development of new financial instruments, however, has given rise to a sharp distinction between those that are exchange-traded (and therefore settled via a clearing-house) and those that are transacted 'over-the-counter' or OTC. Those markets that use a clearing system are generally considered to be free from counterparty risk, save in the unlikely circumstance of a general financial market 'meltdown'. There is a growing concern, however, that in the OTC markets many participants are exposed to very high levels of counterparty risk.

Traditional hedging methods

Traditional approaches to managing financial risk are largely confined to the foreign exchange markets. Foreign currency transaction exposures can be hedged by the construction of a 'natural hedge', through the forward foreign exchange market, or by replicating a forward contract via the money markets. Prior to the development of the new generation of financial instruments there were virtually no readily available facilities for hedging interest rate risks.

The concept underlying the natural hedge is to look for transactions that can be undertaken *as a part of the company's ongoing operations* that will produce an offset to existing exposures. Thus, a UK company which regularly exports to France and, for competitive reasons, invoices in French francs may seek to hedge the resulting transaction exposure by locating a French supplier for some of its own requirements for materials, components or bought-out sub-assemblies. The resulting French franc debtors balance will offset the French franc creditors arising from the exports, and will create a hedge which is virtually cost-less. Such a hedge is difficult to achieve in practice, however, and should be pursued only if the UK company is making regular export sales to the French market.

By far the most widely used conventional hedge mechanism is the forward market in currencies. The UK company in the above example would in this case simply make an agreement with its bank to sell the expected French franc proceeds of the export sale, for delivery at an appropriate future date. If the franc receivable is due in 90 days, the francs are sold three months forward. No cash flow takes place at the time of agreement, but the forward rate is immediately 'locked in' and the British treasurer now knows exactly how much sterling funds the franc export transaction will produce. The rate of exchange that can be achieved, however, may be significantly different from that currently available in the spot market. Forward market rates are driven by the relative levels of 90-day interest rates in the two currencies, the currency with the higher interest rate being set at a forward discount. If French interest rates for the appropriate maturity are higher than those in sterling the franc will be at such a discount, and the sterling cash flow produced by the forward sale will be correspondingly reduced. The forward hedge does nevertheless achieve the primary objective of eliminating uncertainty by replacing an uncertain future cash flow with a known amount, and is the favoured hedge instrument of most treasurers.

The forward hedge may also be replicated in the money markets, where local regulations permit. The required action of the British treasurer in this case would be to borrow 90-day francs in an amount which, with the addition of interest costs, will amount to the value of the franc receivable. The francs received are immediately sold for sterling in the spot market, the sterling funds are deposited, and the franc borrowing produces a liability which offsets the existing franc asset. The resulting hedge works as efficiently as a forward market sale. The transaction is not cost-less, however. If franc 90-day interest rates exceed those in sterling the borrowing cost will exceed the return on the sterling deposit, giving a net interest cost. In theory, the interest differential is the same as the differential that determines the forward market rates. In practice, because the UK company probably does not have access to inter-bank money market rates, the cost of this 'do it yourself' method will usually exceed the implied cost of a conventional forward.

There is, however, one circumstance in which the money market hedge may produce significant savings. The British company borrows 90-day francs and sells them for spot sterling as before, but rather than placing the sterling funds, is able to use them to draw down or eliminate an existing high-cost overdraft line, or to avoid or delay new local borrowing that would otherwise be necessary. Instead of making a sterling deposit at, say, five per cent, the funds are used to reduce a borrowing line on which the company is paying six per cent, and the one per cent gain makes the hedge more cost-effective than a forward.

Such opportunities to reduce hedging costs are frequently overlooked. Finance has become a highly specialized function. The team within treasury who are responsible for exchange exposure management may not liaise effectively with the team concerned with local currency funding, and the opportunity is lost.

The development of financial futures

The fundamental operations of futures trading are long established. Futures markets for agricultural commodities date back at least to the previous century, and possibly further: it has been suggested that something very like futures contracts existed in the Osaka rice market as early as the mid-eighteenth century. Only during the last two decades, however, has there been a rapid development in futures contracts based upon financial instruments, and this is now the biggest of the 'derivatives' markets.

The futures contract is essentially similar to the forward contracts long established in the foreign exchange markets. There are many superficial differences. The futures market uses a brokerage structure for all transactions, while in the currency markets only a minority of deals are brokered. A clearing house plays a key role in all futures markets and is a counterparty to every buyer or seller, but in the currency markets buyer and seller have direct counterparty risk in respect of each other. The existence of the clearing house means that each party to a transaction can be given the choice whether or not to make or take physical delivery (and the great majority of futures market participants have no intention of doing so, intending rather to discharge their obligations via a second, offsetting contract), while in the forward currency market the parties to the transaction bind themselves to exchange currencies on value date. Nevertheless, the basic contract agreement – to make or take delivery of a specified package of assets at an agreed price and on an agreed value date – is essentially the same as in any forward contract.

The fact that the future and the forward contract are essentially similar has had an important consequence. It has meant that in the currency markets, where the forward contract was already well established, there was little need for a largely duplicate instrument, and the market in currency futures has remained relatively small. In the interest rate area, however, no such forward market had established itself. The interest rate futures contract consequently filled an important need, and its growth has been enormous. Virtually all major futures exchanges trade contracts on their respective government bonds and treasury bills. The IMM[2] Three Month Eurodollar time deposit contract is one of the most heavily used instruments, with open interest of more than one million contracts (with a face value of $1,000,000 each) at the time of writing. The LIFFE Three Month Sterling and Three Month Euromark contracts and the Matif (Paris Futures Exchange) Three Month Pibor contracts are also very heavily used, and there is active trading in the LIFFE Three Month Eurolira. Euro Swiss Franc and Three Month Ecu contracts. The interest-rate based futures contracts, in short, offer highly liquid instruments for hedging short-term interest rate exposures in all major currencies.

Nevertheless, financial futures are far from being perfect hedge instruments. They are essentially short term in nature, the liquidity declining very rapidly beyond the two or three nearest delivery dates. They are also relatively inflexible. For any contract to be exchange-traded it must obviously be exactly specified. The contract amount of, say, a Three Month ECU contract is set at one million ECU, and is not negotiable. It is therefore impossible to hedge an exposure of ECU 5.5 million efficiently: it must be either under-hedged with four contracts or over-hedged with five contracts.

A rather bigger problem is the fact that most contracts have only four delivery months per year – which means that closing out a position usually means buying or selling contracts that are still some way from delivery (maturity). This produces considerable price uncertainty. At delivery the market value of a futures contract will be the same as the spot market price of the underlying commodity or financial instrument: because any difference will rapidly be arbitraged away. The price of a contract that is still some time away from maturity, however, is determined through a very different mechanism: the carrying cost of the underlying commodity or instrument. In the case of a financial futures contract, this *carrying cost* is the cost of the funds that would be used to finance a position in the actual instrument, less any income produced by the position. In the case of a holding of treasury bonds, the carrying cost is the cost of the short-term funds that the bond dealer uses to finance the position minus the coupon interest received: with an upward-sloping yield curve the carrying cost will be negative (and bond futures will trade at a discount to actual bond prices), but with a reversed yield curve there will be a true carrying cost (and bond futures will trade at a premium).

It is this mechanism that gives rise to the *basis risk* referred to earlier. In the treasury bond example used above, the futures contract will provide a bondholder against changes in the overall level of interest rates: that is, any parallel shift in the yield curve. But any change in the slope of the yield curve will change the market price of the futures relative to actual bond prices, and thus reduce the efficiency of the hedge. As a result, it can be said that interest rate futures eliminate market rate risk but, in many cases, replace it with basis risk, replacing a larger uncertainty with a smaller one.

Forward rate agreements

The rapid growth of financial futures – and their shortcomings – motivated the banking world to develop a futures-type instrument of its own. This is the Forward Rate Agreement or FRA. Intended as an instrument that banks could offer to their non-bank customers as an alternative to market-traded interest rate futures, it has in fact become a widely used instrument in inter-bank trading. Being a tailored or over the counter instrument it does not suffer from the inflexibility of exchange-traded products, and can be written to fit the counterparty's exact needs in both maturity and amount.

The FRA's flexibility is matched by its inherent simplicity. The two parties agree upon a future target level of a specified interest rate, the 'settlement indicator': for example, a rate of six per cent for three month LIBOR one month from now, and a face amount, say $50 million. If, in one month's time, LIBOR is at seven per cent, the seller of the FRA will pay to the buyer an amount equal to the present value of one per cent interest on $50 million for three months. But had the LIBOR rate fallen to five per cent, a similar payment would have been made from buyer to seller.

The FRA provides the same form of protection that could be achieved by hedging the above exposure in the Three Month Eurodollar market, but with far greater flexibility. Its popularity is easy to understand. The FRA is less widely used in the North American markets, where interest rate futures were already well established before its appearance. In the UK and European markets it has become a major instrument.

Even the FRA has some imperfections. Being an OTC instrument, it does not offer the facilities of a clearing house interposed between the two parties, and counterparty risk does exist in this case, although clearly only in respect of the incremental interest cost and not the capital amount. Its pricing does not enjoy the transparency of the futures markets with their 'open outcry' trading, and futures market prices may have to be used to provide a price reference. Lastly, like the futures markets themselves, it is essentially a short-term instrument and provides no protection against long-run interest rate exposure.

Hedging longer-term interest rate risk: the swap market.

The maturity limitations of the forwards, futures and FRA markets provided a niche for the development of yet another instrument, the fixed/floating interest rate swap. Far from remaining a niche player, however, the swap market is now one of the biggest of the derivatives markets, rivalling the financial futures markets in magnitude.

Interest rate swaps grew out of a simple arbitrage operation. In all parts of the money and capital markets the market rates include a risk premium. The borrower or issuer with a strong credit rating can access funds at a lower price than can a lesser credit. These risk premiums are not uniform, however, and tend to be lowest in short-term, floating-rate, bank dominated markets, and highest in long-term, fixed-rate, investor-driven markets. The swap vehicle has developed as a means of arbitraging the excessive difference between the two. In the process, it gives the strong credit an opportunity to use its privileged position in the fixed-rate markets to obtain floating rate funds at particularly advantageous terms, and the weaker credit to have access to fixed-rate funding that would otherwise be unobtainable. This is, in fact, the one part of the financial markets in which a free lunch might be said to exist.

In early swap transactions the parties were typically both corporate entities, with a bank playing the role of match-maker and facilitator. One party, a larger company with ready access to the fixed-rate markets, would raise fixed rate funds at, say, ten per cent per annum. The other party, a smaller company, wanted fixed-rate funds but did not have access to them. The smaller company had ready access to the floating rate markets, however, and borrowed the funds it needed at perhaps a one per cent margin above LIBOR. The parties then negotiated an agreement by which the larger company undertook to service the smaller company's debt. In return, the smaller company agreed to make regular payments to the larger at a fixed interest rate of, say, 11 per cent.

The result was that the smaller company obtained the kind of funding that it required, while the larger company had in effect obtained floating rate funding at a very attractive rate: the one per cent gain on the fixed rate side offset the floating rate payments to produce floating rate funding at LIBOR flat rate, normally available only in the interbank market. Note, however, that it is only the obligation to make regular debt service payments that have been 'swapped': not the obligation to repay the principal amount. Counterparty risk is unchanged. In the event that the smaller company goes into liquidation, it is the lending banks who are the losers, not the larger company.

The swap market rapidly became an attractive one for banks, providing a ready opportunity to generate fee income. And as the market grew, banks wishing to be major players quickly found that they could not wait until they had found two suitable counterparties and could arrange a marriage. They must now be willing to act whenever one potential swap counterparty is located, and play the opposite role to that which the counterparty wishes to take. Thus, if the counterparty wishes to pay out fixed rates and receive floating rates the bank must be willing to do the exact opposite. Banks which are active in the swap markets in this way are said to be 'swap warehousing': accumulating a collection of 'half swaps' in the hope that they will have an overall balanced position. They publish the rates at which they are willing to pay or receive fixed rate funds, with the floating rate payments all being at the market (LIBOR) and the 'spread' between the fixed rates representing the bank's profit margin.

The swap can of course be used purely as a funding instrument, by large companies and other entities issuing fixed-rate paper simply to generate below-market floating rate funding, and is used in this way to such an extent that at times the volume in the Eurobond market is determined almost entirely by swap market activity. It can just as easily be used to change the nature of existing borrowings, however, and used in this way becomes a major instrument for managing interest rate risk. Thus a treasurer who has taken out a large, ten-year floating-rate loan on the assumption that the general trend of interest rates will be downward, and who now after one year reverses his expectations, will seek to eliminate his exposure to rising interest rates by swapping into fixed rates. A short position in interest rate futures would allow him to hedge his risk over the coming year, but a fixed/floating swap allows him to lock in the hedge for the entire remaining nine-year life of the loan.

As the swap market has grown it has also become diversified. In addition to the basic fixed/floating swap with a fixed amount and with both liabilities in the same currency (now frequently called a 'plain vanilla' swap) there are sinking fund swaps, 'sawtooth' swaps with seasonal fluctuations in the swap exposure, fixed/fixed cross currency swaps, fixed/floating cross currency, floating/floating or 'basis' swaps and even swaps based upon the market price of a commodity, usually oil, as the floating rate side. The cross currency forms are different in one very important respect, in that in these transactions it is quite common to exchange responsibility for the repayment of principal as well as the debt servicing, so that counterparty risk is clearly very much greater in these forms of swap. The fact that swaps are all OTC instruments has given rise to widespread concern recently, and there has been discussion about the need for better regulatory control and/or the development of a swap clearing house. By far the largest sector, however, remains the original fixed/floating type of transaction in which counterparty risk is limited to the future service payments.

A new dimension: options on financial instruments

All of the instruments described so far – natural hedges and forwards, futures and FRAs and the swap in all its many forms – have one important common characteristic. All of them, properly used, can provide effective protection against the impact of an adverse movement in financial market rates. All of them, however, are just as effective in eliminating the windfall additional profit and cash flow that would otherwise have arisen from a favourable rate change. A treasurer who hedges against rising interest costs through any of these methods gives up – for the life of the hedge – the opportunity of a reduction in interest cost that would have come from a decline in market rates.

The treasurer who has a large floating rate borrowing and is concerned that interest rates will rise during the next three months will be interested in buying protection against that risk – but will not necessarily want to give up any possible gain from falling rates during the remaining ten-year life of the loan. One possibility is to hedge the current three-month period, using a future or FRA. An interesting alternative, however, is to purchase an instrument that will give protection from interest rising above an agreed level at any time during the life of the loan, while still leaving the treasurer free to enjoy any fall in rates. A bank will be willing to sell him such protection, in return for an up-front cash premium payment. The instrument is called a 'Cap', and if the protection is set at, say, eight per cent then the loan is said to have been capped at that level. In any period in which rates are 10 per cent, the bank will refund the marginal two per cent interest cost to the treasurer. If rates fall to four per cent, however, the treasurer enjoys the full benefit.

The Cap is in fact just one example of a very important family of financial instruments: *options*. Options are unique in that they are only binding upon one party, the seller or 'writer'. The option buyer has the right to exercise the contract if it is in his favour, or to throw it away (allow it to expire unused) if it is not. There are only two basic forms of option, the *Call* which gives the right to buy at an agreed 'strike price', and the *Put*, which gives the right to sell, and all option strategies are combinations of one or more Calls and one or more Puts. The Cap described above is thus a Call option, giving the buyer the right to take up a fixed rate loan at eight per cent – or, more accurately, it is a strip of Call options covering successive three-month periods for the remaining life of the loan.

The option itself is not by any means a new idea: options on shares have existed since the nineteenth century. They remained relatively little known, however, until the late 1960s when option trading was permitted on a number of major stock exchanges. Since this development, the 'listed option' or 'traded option', trading in equity options has grown to the point at which option trading in the New York market sometimes exceeds the volume of trading in the shares themselves. During the 1970s the same principle started to be applied to other financial instruments, with one of the key breakthroughs being the introduction of options on currencies at the Philadelphia Stock Exchange. Progress during the 1980s was rapid, and options now exist on a range of currencies, interest rates and equity index instruments. A variety of hybrid forms exist, including the 'Swaption', giving the right to enter into a predetermined fixed/floating swap on defined terms at any time during a set period.

The pricing of option instruments is complex. In calculating the premium to be charged for an option the writer would have to take into account five variables: the time to expiry, the strike price, the current market price of the underlying cash instrument (ie, share or interest-bearing instrument), the current level of interest rates, and the volatility of the instrument's market price, measured in standard deviation terms in relation to market volatility. This last item adds mathematical complexities, and the formulae used in option pricing are beyond the scope of this article. The potential option buyer, however, need not delve into the mechanics of option pricing to recognize that this is potentially a very powerful risk management tool.

The most rapid growth in this area in recent years has been in OTC options rather than in exchange-traded instruments. The over-the-counter markets are clearly a more appropriate environment for innovation and experimentation, and most new option-type products have appeared in this sector. Much of the development has been focused on managing currency market risk, with some innovations (the 'Boston Option', the Citibank 'Cylinder' and the various types of 'participating forward') seeking to reduce the up-front cost of option hedging and others (the 'average rate' option, the 'lookback') offering greater flexibility. Other innovative forms have appeared in the area of index-linked equity hedging instruments ('knockout' or 'exploding' options). And one of the most innovative of all of these developments is the 'compound option': in effect, an *option on an option*. This instrument offers companies, for the first time, a way of hedging *contingent* market rate exposures – which arise, for example, when it is necessary to submit a foreign-currency bid in a competitive tender situation. There is little doubt that market-makers will continue to look for innovative opportunities in the option area.

The selection of risk management instruments

This article has illustrated the manner in which increasing uncertainty and volatility in financial markets has prompted the development of new and innovative risk management instruments and techniques, particularly the 'derivatives'. The range is now so wide, however, that few people outside the specialist treasury area have a real understanding of their possibilities – or of their limitations. Indeed, the large and widely-publicized losses made by some major companies in recent months suggest that even some corporate treasurers do not fully understand these instruments.

The first point that needs to be recognized is that any instrument that can be used to reduce the risk arising from an exposed position becomes a *risk-generating* instrument if it is used where no such prior exposure exists. A short position in stock index futures contracts is a hedge if the futures buyer already owns or manages a broad equity portfolio – but is a highly speculative position if he or she does not. Similarly, writing options against a portfolio of assets is a highly conservative, revenue-enhancing technique, but writing the same options 'naked' involves unlimited risk. The first requirement in a risk management strategy, therefore, must be fully to understand the risk that is to be hedged, and only to set up hedge positions that correspond to that risk.

Once the risk is understood, the next task is to select the type of instrument to be used. All risk management involves decision-making under uncertainty: it is the *degree* of uncertainty that is the prime consideration here. Take, for example, a UK company treasurer who will have to make a large payment in Swiss Francs in three months' time. Clearly, he or she has a real transaction exposure, and equally clearly he does not know what the spot sterling/franc rate will be at the end of the three months. He may consult his bankers and/or other foreign exchange advisers, but ultimately has to make a decision based upon his own judgement and risk tolerance. Where that risk tolerance is low, his policy may simply be to hedge all such exposures in the forward market. Given such a low-risk tolerance, he would probably undertake all funding operations at fixed interest rates, or swap any floating rate positions into fixed. Such an approach is not uncommon, but can hardly be considered optimal.

If the treasurer is willing to use some judgement and to make decisions on a case-by-case basis, he must now ask himself in which direction he expects the rate to move, and how much confidence he has in his judgement. If he believes that sterling will strengthen during the coming three months – and attaches a 90 per cent probability to that outcome, then his best course of action is obvious: he should leave the exposure uncovered. (Note, though, that in this situation there is no course of action that can be called 'do nothing': if no action is taken to hedge the exposure this amounts to a conscious decision to leave the position open and to finance the transaction in the spot market at whatever the spot price is at that time.) If he believes with equal certainty that sterling will go down against the franc, then his course of action must be to hedge, and the only question is the method to be used: look for a natural hedge, use the forward market or currency futures, or replicate a forward in the money markets. In neither of these situations should the purchase of an option even be considered.

Where the decision-maker does not have such a high degree of certainty, however, the use of an option becomes a serious consideration. A treasurer who believes that there is a 60 per cent possibility of sterling falling against the franc, may not readily want to give up the 40 per cent possibility of a windfall profit if the rate moves in the other direction. He must now look at the cost that would be involved in setting up an option hedge, and decide whether the profit opportunity justifies that cost. And if not, one of the more recent hybrid option instruments will allow him to buy protection at a lower cost if he is willing to give up a part of his profit potential.

Full details of all of these techniques and the ways in which they are used require further reading and research. Only having mastered the basic principles of risk management will a manager be in a position to talk to his or her banker about the determination of an optimal strategy.

John Heptonstall is managing partner of Heptonstall & Associates based in Geneva, Switzerland. He is an associate and programme director at Ashridge Management College and a visiting Professor at IMD in Lausanne. He has also been a visiting faculty member at other institutions, including Instituto de Empresa in Madrid, Groupe

ESC, Lyon, and the University of Melbourne. His primary professional interests lie in the management of financial risk and the incorporation of risk considerations in corporate strategy.

Further Reading

Wunnicke, DB, *et al*, *Corporate Financial Risk Management*, John Wiley & Sons, New York, 1992.

Grumball, C, *Managing Interest Rate Risk*, Woodhead-Faulkner, New York, 1987.

Hull, JC, *Options, Futures and Other Derivative Securities*, Prentice Hall, New Jersey, 1993.

Manson, B, *Practitioner's Guide to Interest Rate Risk Management*, Graham & Trotman, London, 1992.

Marshall, JF, and Kapner, KR, *Understanding Swaps*, John Wiley & Sons, New York, 1993.

References

[1] LIBOR – the cost of wholesale money in transactions between major banks in the international money and capital market. If not otherwise qualified, it is assumed to be the US dollar lending rate.

[2] IMM – the International Money Market (sometimes called the International Monetary Exchange), part of the complex of derivatives trading markets in Chicago.

Marketing

'There is only one valid definition of business purpose: to create a customer.'

Peter Drucker[1]

'A truly marketing-minded firm tries to create value-satisfying goods and services that consumers will want to buy.'

Theodore Levitt[2]

[1] Drucker, PF, *The Practice of Management*, Heinemann, London, 1954.
[2] Levitt, T, 'Marketing myopia', *Harvard Business Review*, 1960.

OVERVIEW

Patrick Barwise

These are 'interesting' times for marketers – partly in the sense of the Chinese curse. The challenges they now face include intense competition. Most product markets in developed economies have excess supply; blurring industry boundaries; constant change; the threats and opportunities of emerging technology; new power relationships; globalization; increasingly sophisticated and demanding customers; and new regulations. The need for marketing has never been greater.

Yet, at the same time this has not led to larger, more powerful or prestigious marketing departments. On the contrary, *many firms have reduced their marketing departments*. Management consultants talk of 'marketing's mid-life crisis' and of marketing being at a 'crossroads'. In the dramatic words of Coopers & Lybrand's Robert Smith: 'Ill-defined in its remit, over-indulged in its spending, and lacking in relevant performance measures, marketing is failing to fulfil its original role or is a function failing to live up to its pretensions.'

This apparent paradox – marketing being more important than ever before but the contribution of marketing departments being critically questioned – ironically reflects the belated triumph of the original marketing concept. As long as 40 years ago, Peter Drucker argued that since the role of business was to create customers, its only two essential functions were marketing and innovation. In 1954 he wrote: 'Marketing is not a function, it is the whole business seen from the customer's point of view.' As markets have matured and become more competitive, especially during the 1990s, this 40-year-old concept has become increasingly widely accepted.

Most people now regard it as self-evident that corporate survival and performance depend on the firm's ability to meet customer needs better (or at a lower price) than the competition. In the UK, much of the success of the early privatizations – especially in competitive product-markets, as at British Airways – has been based on the acceptance of this simple, powerful idea, and its influence on the day-to-day behaviour of managers and other employees. In manufacturing, many firms adopted the marketing concept too little and too late, but it is firmly entrenched in those that survive. Often, an over-emphasis on cost-cutting may reduce the ability to create long-term customer value, but the commitment to fighting it out in the product-market is clear. The marketing concept is emerging intact and, in some quarters, triumphant.

Marketing as a process, not a function

Inherent in the marketing concept is the idea that *market orientation and the creation of customer value are the concern of everyone in the firm, not just of those in the marketing function.* The dramatic improvements in productivity, 'total quality', and customer service since the late 1970s, have cut across all business functions – operations, logistics, R&D, sales, IT, and so on. Until recently, marketing people have, if anything, been less involved in these developments than people in other functions: the impetus has tended to come from the quality movement in operations management.

These developments have had two effects on the marketing function. First, when the marketing concept is successfully implemented across the whole firm, the specific role of a separate marketing department has to be reassessed. Second, in many firms the marketing people have been seen as arrogant and aloof, neither close to their colleagues nor even especially close to the customer.

A further factor has been the *increasing pressure for accountability.* Arguably, marketing people could and should have done more to demonstrate the effectiveness of their decisions and expenditures, although it is in the nature of marketing that much of its value is inherently non-quantifiable – especially for those activities aimed at building long-term value and market position. Either way, marketing's failure to prove its value to the accountants has weakened its influence and encouraged the shift of resources towards activities with demonstrable short-term gains, such as price promotions. A similar worrying trend in many firms is the continuing under-investment in R&D.

We are now seeing the long-heralded arrival of *marketing as a process, a way of running the whole business.* Successful marketing today involves *all* functions within the firm – including the marketing department, which still has a distinct role in such areas as customer communications and market research and analysis, and a shared role in such areas as new product development, pricing, and competitive strategy. In the rest of this overview I discuss six major trends or issues in marketing. All of these are having a major impact on people in marketing, but also affect other functions too. Finally, I return to the specific question of the future of marketing as a function.

The six key trends or issues are:

- relationship marketing
- the use of new technology
- customer value and the blurring of product and service
- measurement and accountability
- innovation and learning
- globalization

1. Relationship marketing

An important trend, especially in mature markets, is the growing emphasis on customer retention and 'relationship marketing'. In many markets, the increasing cost and difficulty of attracting new customers mean that it is more profitable to concentrate on retaining a long-term relationship with existing ones. Increasingly, firms are identifying customer relationships as among their most valuable assets. Of course this depends on the level of customer loyalty, which varies greatly between different industries. But, even in industries characterized by low brand loyalty, there is now a recognition that while products may come and go, successful brands can have an indefinite life and even a marginal increase in customer loyalty can have very high long-term value. (This is related to the concept of 'brand equity' discussed later.)

The issue is complicated by two opposite trends:

- *Most markets are becoming more competitive* with increasingly sophisticated customers and an increasing number of 'lookalike' products in markets ranging from generic drugs, memory chips, and PC clones, to corporate banking, mortgages, premium private label soft drinks, and home-delivered pizzas. Especially during recession, there is a limit to the price premium that can be carried even by strong brands such as Marlboro, Coca-Cola, or IBM. In this sense, customer-switching costs and brand loyalty have never been lower. The result is that as product differentiation becomes harder, the focus tends to shift towards price, distribution, sales, and service.

- At the same time in many markets – especially business-to-business markets – we are seeing the growth of *closer, longer-term partnerships between firms within the same value chain*. This would apply both to, say, DuPont or Bosch and their major automotive customers, and also to consumer goods manufacturers like Procter & Gamble and its top retail customers such as Wal-Mart. These partnerships involve close collaboration on product development and also increasing interdependence of information systems and other processes. A major trend in supply chain management has been to reduce the number of suppliers. All of this involves increased customer-switching costs, justified by the increased competitiveness of the coalition. One effect of these and other strategic alliances has been the increasing blurring of industry boundaries (as in IT and financial services).

These two opposite trends have led to a shift in power from the marketing function towards the sales function, especially key account management. Increasingly, the prime activity in sales is the nurturing of long-term relationships with customers, as opposed to individual transactions. Meanwhile, within marketing departments we have seen organizational changes with brand or product managers tending to be replaced by more market-oriented category or market managers. For instance, in consumer packaged goods, today's category manager is part of a multifunctional team working closely over time with the firm's main retail trade customers. In this sense, consumer goods marketing has become more like industrial marketing, especially in areas such as groceries with high retail concentration.

At the same time, many consumer marketing companies are also seeking to build direct long-term relationships with individual consumers via database marketing, one of the main uses of new technology. This, too, is somewhat reducing the gap between consumer and industrial marketing.

2. The use of new technology

Many of the trends, challenges, and opportunities in marketing relate to new developments in information and communication technology (ICT).

Some of the organizational changes taking place in marketing – as in other functions – are closely related to the use of ICT. The routine use of telephone, fax, voice mail, electronic mail and, increasingly, video conferencing, are essential for the success of innovative organizations, especially those with global reach. In addition, marketing has some unique new opportunities in the use of ICT. These can be grouped under two headings: database marketing and new media opportunities:

Database marketing

Closely related to the trend toward relationship marketing is the increasing use of long-term marketing programmes using large databases with data on individual customers. Database marketing has three key characteristics:

- Increased *targeting* in terms of either market segments or individual customers and prospects: the database enables the marketer to customize marketing communications.
- Increased emphasis on marketing as an *interactive process through time:* the database records not only which communications have been directed at each customer or segment, but also what the response was, which may in turn influence the choice of subsequent communications – we might call this 'mass relationship marketing'.
- Although traditionally associated with direct mail, database marketing today involves a *range of media* combining direct personalized media – mail, telephone, personal selling – with direct-response advertising (eg, with coupons or free-phone numbers).

Marketing has in the past been comparatively slow in the adoption of ICT (typically slower than sales management, which has used ICT extensively for order taking and territory allocation). However, this is now changing with the growth of database marketing.

New media opportunities

Marketing also has some emerging opportunities from new media, like interactive cable TV, and from the further development of traditional media – print, direct mail, and notably (in the UK) radio – all of which are able to deliver audiences which are far more segmented than for television. Opportunities in new media include 'electronic brochures' using CD-Rom at the point-of-purchase, home-shopping via interactive cable TV, video on demand, and so on. These new technologies are likely to develop more slowly than some of the hype about the 'Information Superhighway' suggests: the financial and practical barriers should not be underestimated. Nevertheless, the trend towards more interactive and targeted media will continue. This will pose a threat to commercial TV channels and also to traditional advertising agencies who are already having to adapt to a more fragmented media regime. It will also impact logistics and distribution, as products are increasingly mailed, home-delivered, or collected by consumers from a convenient pick-up point. The long-term effects of these changes will be substantial and marketers need to start exploring them – as both threats and opportunities – now.

3. Customer value and the blurring of product and service

Also linked to relationship marketing is the increasing focus on providing customer value throughout the organization. The clearest symbol of this trend has been the high profile programmes of total quality, *Kaizen* (or continuous improvement), and more recently business process re-engineering, that have been such a major feature of firms in the last ten years. Built into all these developments is the belief that *customer satisfaction is the key determinant of long-term market success.*

This includes the idea that the ultimate judges of product quality are customers not design engineers. But, even more important than customer-oriented product quality, has been the emphasis on *customer service.* This partly reflects the continuing shift towards a service economy but also the recognition that even manufacturers are also service businesses whose customers partly judge them on delivery performance, responsiveness, friendliness, accurate invoicing, and so on.

Within firms, the idea has gained credence that all departments – even those which have no direct contact with external customers – have their own internal customers. Some firms have formalized this through written service contracts between departments. As a result, the concept of customer service is starting to run through entire businesses. Innovations in customer service include the growing provision of unconditional service guarantees and increasing focus on 'service recovery' – the handling of complaints and service failures: the evidence is that customers whose complaints are well handled can end up more loyal than before the service failure.

4. Measurement and accountability

Another related trend is the increasing emphasis on measurement and accountability in marketing as in other functions. This has reinforced the growth of database marketing with its emphasis on measuring the response – or at least the measurable response – to each marketing activity and using the acquired knowledge to adapt further communications to the same customer or segment. Measures of market response and customer loyalty can also be used to allocate priorities between different types of activity. For instance, the database can help marketers assess the long-term value of different types of customer or even customers gained through different media or promotions.

Another effect has been to encourage firms to allocate marketing resources towards those activities with quantifiable results, such as short-term price promotions. It may have become harder to justify investments in long-term brand building.

Brand equity

As a counter to these pressures for financial accountability, there has been much interest in the idea of *brand equity*, ie, that strong, established brands are valuable assets. Further, there have been numerous attempts to place a financial value on these assets, especially in the UK where the accounting rules allow such brand valuations to be included in the balance sheet. However, progress has been limited for two reasons.

First, as with any asset which is not actively traded (eg, shares in large public companies) valuing a brand inherently involves having to make subjective judgements about future cash flows or profits. The valuation also depends on its purpose, eg, acquisition, balance sheet, or internal management. Moreover, in the case of brands one has to make arbitrary judgements about separating the value of the brand from the value of the rest of the business. This is especially problematic for corporate brands, as in most industrial and service businesses.

Second, there has been little if any attempt to standardize brand equity measurement or valuation. This perhaps reflects marketers' traditional obsession with being different and original, resulting in a proliferation of sometimes conflicting definitions, methods, and labels. The resulting confusion has, arguably, reduced the credibility and influence of the marketing discipline. In contrast, the accountants – despite also facing conceptual problems, for instance over the nature and purpose of balance sheets – have been far more consistent in their use of language and methods. Marketing people could learn a useful lesson from the accountants' ability to sing from the same hymn book.

While it may be a mistake to believe that we will ever devise a valid method for estimating the value of brand equity, this does not justify today's total lack of standardization. Marketers should start by developing some standard measures and definitions, as an aid to clear analysis and discussion. This especially applies to firms managing the same brands across many countries.

New data sources

There has been more progress in other areas of marketing measurement. In particular, our ability to measure short-term market response has been greatly helped by the increasing availability of *new data sources*, notably retail checkout scanner data in packaged goods. This approach is now being extended to other industries, eg, the SoundScan system in the United States which measures music (tape, CD) sales. The US has also seen the development of 'single-source' data, consumer panels which measure both purchases and media exposure (especially cable TV) for the same consumers. In many firms, the marketers now have more data than they can assimilate and are looking towards expert systems and other techniques to extract useful information.

Measuring long-term advertising effects

One of the hardest activities to justify within a regime of quantitative measurement and accountability is *long-term media advertising*. In the UK there has been extensive work over the years trying to estimate advertising effectiveness, second only to the United States in terms of sheer research volume. Since 1980, the Institute of Practitioners in Advertising (the advertising agencies' trade association) has run a competition giving awards to documented case histories demonstrating advertising effectiveness. Other countries have followed suit, although there is still no such scheme in the US. Since 1990, the IPA awards have included a category called 'longer and broader advertising effects'. The winning IPA case histories are published in a book under the series title *Advertising Works*, recommended reading for anyone interested in best practice in estimating advertising effectiveness as the basis for future resource allocation. Despite such well-publicized initiatives, it is inherently impossible to quantify the full long-term effects of advertising. This will always remain an area for informed business judgement rather than mere technical optimization.

5. Innovation and learning

Today's emphasis on innovation and learning has several implications for marketing. In *new product development*, speed is now seen as crucial, especially in technology-intensive businesses. If anything, the importance of being first to market may even have been overstated: the evidence is that the long-term winners in emerging markets are not necessarily the pioneers, but rather the players that develop and dominate the market during its crucial second phase of 'early growth'. Recent research shows that the player who ends up dominating the market typically enters several years after the initial pioneer. This again relates to organizational learning. The pioneer has the opportunity to pre-empt all later entrants, but is also more likely to make mistakes in the design or marketing of the new product or service. Later entrants have almost as much ability to learn from the pioneer's mistakes as the pioneer itself, and at much lower cost.

The emphasis on speed to market will rightly continue but we may, perhaps, see a trend towards more frequent, incremental product improvements (as in Japan) and, in some cases, a little more caution by testing the product and its marketing prior to the full launch. For instance, most marketers believe that Unilever was over-hasty in launching Persil/Omo Power. However, once the new product and its marketing mix are ready for launch, the international roll-out is likely to be very fast if not concurrent. In other words, the emphasis will still be on speed as well as on 'getting it right', but focusing as much on shortening the 'time to peak sales' (via fast market penetration) as on further shortening the pre-launch 'time to market'.

Learning about market response

Innovation, learning, and speed are not just passing fads, they are likely to be a dominant feature of management in most businesses for the foreseeable future. We will, therefore, see a continuing trend away from slow, large-scale, step-by-step *market research* towards a range of more responsive approaches. These will still include techniques such as focus groups, conjoint analysis, market response modelling, and the extensive analysis of customer behaviour that is part of successful database marketing. In addition, however, the approach today increasingly involves *working directly with customers*, especially with those customers who tend to lead their industries or – in the case of consumer markets – those who tend to be 'early adopters' or 'opinion formers'. Companies which work closely with such customers may be in a stronger position to sense new trends, and to distinguish these from fads. A related trend is the growing use of free-phone advice numbers, prize-draw questionnaires, and the like, to encourage direct communication from consumers.

There is also an increasing willingness to do experimental or even 'expeditionary' marketing. The former refers to controlled incremental experiments in the real market, with line extensions, trial price packages, and so on. Major retailers have greatly benefited from an ability to conduct low-cost marketing experiments giving detailed confidential data on market response.

Expeditionary marketing refers to a willingness to try more radical product (or marketing) innovations. Paradoxically perhaps, this approach has been a feature of Japanese industries like consumer electronics, mainly noted for their success at continuous incremental product innovation. In fact, this is less of a paradox than it might seem, for two reasons. First, incremental product improvements in Japan are not random, but are sequenced to take the firm along a planned trajectory of performance and cost. Each project is judged as much by the learning and capabilities it will generate as on its direct profitability. It is these capabilities which allow the occasional bolder step. Second, both approaches – incremental and expeditionary – are based on the idea that the way to learn about market response is to keep launching new products in the real market.

A classic case of expeditionary marketing was the Sony Walkman, which was developed in response to a bold hunch, not because of any perceived gap identifiable from market research. This more entrepreneurial perspective reflects the view that, while market research is good at describing what customers think, feel, and do today, and is therefore essential for suggesting and testing possible fine-tuning improvements, research cannot reliably predict how the market will respond to a radical new product like a personal stereo, or even a new service like telephone banking which uses technology with which consumers are already very familiar. In this situation, the crucial marketing skills still include the use of diagnostic research, but also those of *communicating the benefits* of conceptually new products or services and *learning from the market response* better and faster than the competition.

6. Globalization

Finally, all of these trends are occurring in an increasingly global context. There has been genuine progress at reducing trade barriers between countries, especially within Europe. Many of the issues were discussed in Ted Levitt's classic *Harvard Business Review* article 'The Globalization of Markets' in 1983.

In high-technology industries, the main drivers behind globalization are cost efficiency and knowledge sharing. The economics favour players with high expenditure on R&D and product innovation, and with production economies of scale, so that fixed costs are spread over a global market including North America, Europe and Asia Pacific. To achieve this combination, firms need to invest heavily in global distribution, sales, and service. Industries showing this pattern include consumer electronics, cars, pharmaceuticals, IT, aerospace, defence, and engineering. Much of the strength of the mighty German and Japanese manufacturing sectors has been based on the combination of high domestic R&D with global distribution and marketing.

For somewhat different reasons, *many luxury brands and an increasing number of service businesses are also becoming global*, and this trend seems likely to continue. The reasons vary, typically including some cost efficiency and shared learning (as in high-technology industries), eg, the development of a new perfume, a new quick-service restaurant format, or an airline reservation system. In addition, there may be some direct benefit from the use of a global brand, because of its luxury connotations (Chanel, Rolls-Royce), associations with international youth (Levis, Pepsi, Swatch, Benetton) or just because of familiarity and reliability (Holiday Inn).

Managing marketing across borders

There is no clear separation between international marketing (as opposed to a few export sales) and the rest of international management. Among the multinationals, the trend is towards organizations structured into businesses aimed at global or – especially for packaged goods – regional product markets (eg, ICL's business selling IT systems for retailers worldwide; Mars's European pet food business) rather than the traditional collection of national businesses reporting to country general managers. Nevertheless, organizing for transnational operations remains problematic and most chief executives see it as an area for further improvement.

Within marketing, a particular issue is the *balance between global or regional and local branding and marketing* (discussed in a later section by Jean-Noël Kapferer). Another less widely discussed issue is pricing: as national barriers and shipping costs decrease, we are likely to see a reduction in the price differences for the same product in different countries. The management of such price differences is an increasingly thorny problem in international marketing and a source of some conflict and tension within transnational businesses.

The future of marketing as a function

I have highlighted six current trends or issues in marketing: *relationship marketing; the use of new technology; customer value and the blurring of product and service; measurement and accountability; innovation and learning*; and *globalization*. These are all impacting upon the marketing function and other functions as well. In addition, at the start I raised the broader issue that – partly because the marketing concept is now so widely accepted and is increasingly being implemented across all the functions within the firm – the specific role of marketing as a separate function has come under question.

What does all this mean for people in marketing, and for the future of marketing as a function?

Perhaps the main implication is that we are likely to see a continuing *increase in the importance of marketing as a philosophy and a way of running the business, perhaps combined with a decrease in its importance as a separate function.* The competitive pressure for firms to be market-oriented and responsive will, if anything, increase even further. This may mean that the most successful management careers will need to include some experience of both sales and marketing. It is also likely to mean organizational changes that increase the amount of direct customer contact within all functions and at the top of the organization. A notable feature of Germany's extremely successful mid-sized engineering companies is that they are run by people with a solid knowledge of technology who also spend a high proportion of their time working directly with customers. Another aspect of market orientation will be the increasing dissemination of headline information about customer satisfaction and market performance throughout the organization.

The need for marketing as a function will continue. However, we are unlikely to see a return to large corporate marketing departments and even within individual businesses and business units, the number of career marketing people on the payroll may be small. I believe the trend will be towards *sub-contracting much of the detailed research, analysis, and in some cases even the execution of marketing to specialist agencies*, perhaps including ex-employees working from home. Firms will from time to time use such agencies on a one-off basis for *ad-hoc* projects, but the trend will be towards longer-term relationships. This set-up will provide a good blend of mutual understanding, specialist expertise, knowledge of the particular market context, and low fixed costs for the firm. Many marketing tasks are well suited to the move towards 'shamrock organizations' discussed by Charles Handy.

For those marketing people who continue operating within the firm's marketing department, the challenge now is to come down from their ivory tower, to become more efficient and accountable, to spend more time in *direct contact with customers* – both direct trade or industrial purchasing customers and also final consumers or end-users – and to work more closely with their colleagues from other functions (especially sales, operations, and product development) and increasingly from other countries as well. There is also a challenging and crucial task for marketing people to manage the *customer database*, the various *specialists* involved in extracting usable information from the database, market research, modelling, and the development of an *integrated mix of communications*. To succeed, they will need a mixture of human, analytical and time management skills.

Thinking strategically

The need for time management skills relates to what I believe to be the single biggest challenge – and opportunity – for the marketing function: to rise above the day-to-day and start thinking more strategically.

This is much harder to achieve today than even only five or ten years ago. The trends I have described mean that the marketing task has become more complex. The rate of change in products, markets, and technology has increased. Relationships with customers, outside agencies, other functions, and colleagues from other countries are time-consuming, as are some of the planning and control systems resulting from the emphasis on measurement and accountability. At the same time, the number of people in marketing departments has decreased as part of the general downsizing in firms.

The net effect – a more complex task done by fewer people – is that marketing managers are often working very long hours merely to keep on top of their day-to-day tasks. It is extremely hard for them to find the time and energy to stand back and think about broader strategic issues.

This problem is certainly not unique to marketing people, but I believe that in their case it raises a particular threat to the long-term success of the firm because of marketing's role as the main interface with the market environment. Good marketing people have a close and detailed knowledge of the market; a holistic understanding of the firm's competitive strengths and weaknesses; a thought-through view of the external threats and, especially, opportunities it faces; and a perspective on an appropriate longer-term marketing strategy. If the day-to-day pressures prevent the development of this knowledge and vision, the whole firm can become purely tactical and reactive.

One effect of the time and performance pressures is that, although the need to be outward-looking is universally recognized, it is hard to find the time to put this into practice. This includes time with today's customers and time analysing today's competitors – their structures, strategies, capabilities, priorities, and internal financial performance. But, perhaps even more important is the need to spend time developing a better shared understanding of the way the firm's markets may develop in the future, and who its competitors will be tomorrow. What almost destroyed IBM was not Honeywell and Univac but DEC, Apple, and Microsoft. What is threatening Coca-Cola is not only Pepsi-Cola but now also Cott, which makes the concentrate for premium private label colas such as President's Choice in North America and Sainsbury's Classic Cola in the UK. Coke's UK market share has just fallen below 50 per cent for the first time.

Four key tasks for marketing people

Marketing people must find a way to rise above the day-to-day pressures and do four things:

1. Develop a detailed and deep understanding of their *current customers and prospects*. Much of this should come from direct contact, especially with leading-edge customers. Some should also come from ad hoc background research on new issues, values, and trends. (Such research may be harder to justify in today's environment as it neither exploits the main data sources nor is it immediately actionable).

2. Similarly, develop a deep and shared understanding of *today's competitors*. A good mechanism for achieving such understanding, shared within the management team, is to conduct a structured role-play of the competitor. Another, especially in consumer markets, is to 'reverse-engineer' the competitor's advertising and promotional material: what are its strategic communication objectives?

3. Third, and more difficult: develop a similarly deep and shared perspective on *how the market may change and develop in the future*. What are likely to be the new threats and opportunities? What new issues are just over the horizon? Who will be tomorrow's customers, competitors, and channels? What will be the new applications, the new product technologies? As London Business School's Gary Hamel has argued, the way to develop such a perspective is simply for the whole management team to take the time to explore and debate the issues in sufficient depth. But I believe it is the marketing people, perhaps with some of the R&D people, who should play the leading role.

4. Finally, develop a *strategic marketing perspective* on what the firm should do to achieve its objectives, based on an understanding of its current and future markets and capabilities. The issue here is to become more proactive, what London Business School's Tom Robertson calls '*market-driving as well as market-driven*'.

Given the unprecedented time and performance pressures, none of this will be easy, but it is very important and should be pretty interesting too – and not just in the sense of the Chinese curse.

Patrick Barwise is Professor of Management and Marketing and Director of the Centre for Marketing at London Business School. He previously held positions in sales and marketing with IBM, the Austin-Hall Group and Graphic Systems International. He is the author of numerous books and articles, including *Accounting for Brands*, *Must Finance and Strategy Clash?*, *Television and its Audience*, *Unique Value* and *Managing Strategic Investment Decisions*.

Further Reading

Baker, C, (ed.) *Advertising Works 7*, NTC Publications, Henley, 1993.

Hamel, G, and Prahalad, CK, 'Corporate imagination and expeditionary marketing', *Harvard Business Review*, July-August 1991; and 'Competing for the future', July-August 1994.

Golder, PN, and Tellis, GJ, 'Pioneer advantage: marketing logic or marketing legend?', *Journal of Marketing Research*, May 1993.

Robertson, TJ, 'How to reduce market penetration cycle times', *Sloan Management Review*, Fall, 1993.

Levitt, T, 'The globalization of markets', *Harvard Business Review*, May-June 1983.

Webster, FE, *Market-Driven Management*, John Wiley, New York, 1994.

BRAND MANAGEMENT

Chris Styles and Tim Ambler

A brand is any proprietary good or service a firm sells, and as such is the primary revenue and profit generator of the firm. Some firms manage many brands, such as Procter & Gamble, Unilever and Grand Metropolitan, while others manage a single corporate brand, such as IBM, BP or any number of small industrial suppliers. Whatever the case, the assets created by these brands, *brand equity*, are among a firm's most important and valuable assets. The management of these assets should, therefore, be a focal point of the organization.

Management's essential role of refreshing brand equity requires a new perspective. The world of the brand manager has changed dramatically over the last decade. The brand manager now must deal with: consumers who are far more sophisticated and demanding than they used to be; more powerful distribution channels; and threats to national brands from stores' 'own label' brands.

The evolution of brand management

The evolution of brand management is linked to the evolution of brands themselves. Scholars have recently identified four phases in this evolution, which took place primarily in the United States.[1]

Phase 1 – the development of national manufacturer brands

The end of the last century saw the emergence of national brands. Until this time branded consumer goods were limited to a few industries, such as patent medicines and tobacco products, which only tended to be distributed on a regional basis. However, a number of changes occurred at this time to provide the right environment for high quality mass-marketed brands. These included improvements in transportation, production processes and packaging, as well as the greater respectability of advertising, changes in trademark law, and increasing industrialization and urbanization. The management of the new national brands tended to be the responsibility of firm owners and top-level managers, with only low-level tasks delegated to others. Sales promotions (premiums, free samples, etc), mass advertising and other elements of promotion emerged as major marketing tools during this period.

Phase 2 – functional management

The years between 1915 and 1929 saw national brands become an important part of consumer and corporate life. Consumers benefited from an improvement in quality, were increasingly influenced by advertising and made the purchase of brands an important goal. On the corporate side, developing and distributing national brands became the key to success in many industries. During this time, the management of brands started to become increasingly complex, especially in those cases where a company owned many brands. The result was that brands could no longer be managed by the original entrepreneurs. Instead, brand management became 'functional' with the key tasks of sales, product development, advertising and planning being handled by specialists in top and middle management. Decisions were made by groups of managers across the specialized functions. In addition, advertising agencies took over some of the marketing functions such as market research, product testing and sales promotions, in addition to copy development and media placement.

Phase 3 – the birth of the brand management system

During phase two the problems of co-ordination and co-operation between different functions emerged, as did the absence of a focal point of responsibility for each individual brand. The solution of brand management was devised by Procter & Gamble (P&G) in 1931. The idea was that each brand should have its own manager and assistants who would take responsibility for advertising and other marketing activities. This 'brand management system' gave bottom line responsibility for the performance of a particular brand to a single manager. It also allowed large manufacturers to compete more effectively with more than one brand in the same category, as P&G had started to do in the 1920s with Ivory and Camay bath soaps. Interestingly, the brand management system did not spread quickly throughout industry. Many were unaware of P&G's new system, while others believed that functional management was still the superior organizational form.

Phase 4 – the brand management system becomes institutionalized

The 1950s were dominated by the post-war economic boom. The era of shopping centres and television advertising saw the proliferation of new products and new brands. By 1967, 84 per cent of large consumer packaged goods manufacturers in the United States had brand managers. Though titles have changed, this system largely prevails today.

Branding and the brand management process

Defining a brand

There are two approaches to defining a brand. First, there is the traditional *product plus* definition which views branding as an addition to the product. The definition given in Philip Kotler's classic textbook, *Marketing Management*, typifies this aproach: '(A brand name is) a name, term, sign, symbol or design, or a combination of these, which is intended to identify the goods or services of one group of sellers and differentiate them from those of competitors.'[2]

From this perspective a brand is applied once the product issues are resolved. It is an afterthought. Its primary objective is to signal to the consumer the source of the product, thereby protecting both the consumer and the manufacturer from competitors who would attempt to provide similar products.

The alternative is the *holistic* view. This regards the product as just one element of the brand – a single component of the marketing mix alongside price, promotion and distribution. The product is only part of what the consumer experiences of the total brand. A brand from this perspective is the promise of a bundle of attributes that someone buys and that provides satisfaction. The attributes that make up a brand may be real or illusory, rational or emotional, tangible or invisible. These attributes can emanate from one, all, or a combination of marketing mix elements.

This holistic approach to branding is being increasingly adopted to achieve meaningful differentiation. For example, as differentiation in the automobile market becomes harder to achieve on the product front (with the alliances between the major firms, most of the products are very similar), features such as service warranties are becoming more important. For retail brands such as Sainsbury and Marks & Spencer in the UK, the total brand is made up of not only the distribution system (location, product range, etc.), but also the quality of own-label products, price competitiveness and even trading hours. In addition, features such as high-technology ordering systems are now defining and differentiating national FMCG (fast-moving consumer goods) brands from the perspective of the 'trade'.

This approach has allowed brands to be used as umbrellas for numerous products in often quite unrelated categories – for example, Virgin (airlines and cola) and Sony (video tapes and mobile phones). As a brand relies less on a particular product to define it, it is able to leverage the other elements of the marketing mix to launch new product ideas cost-efficiently and effectively. These new products take the form of line extensions (same brand, same product category) or brand extensions (same brand, new product category). Strong, enduring 'mega-brands' are being created as a result.

The brand management process

Brand management can be viewed as a system, with inputs, transformation processes and outputs. This is represented by the 'bucket' diagram in Fig. 1. This diagram shows the inputs as marketing expenditure, brand equity and the ideas, teamwork and energy of the brand management team; the transformation processes of measurement, analysis, planning and implementation; and the outputs of profit, brand equity, and inevitably, some waste.

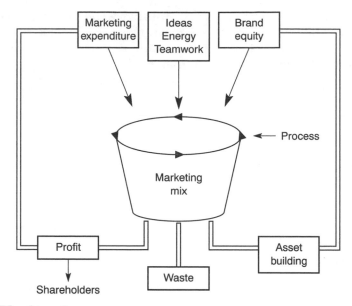

Fig. 1 The brand management process

Source: Tim Ambler, 'Are branding and marketing synonymous?, *The Journal of Brand Management*, vol. 1, no. 1, Summer 1993, pp. 41–48

Most parts of this process would be very familiar to the majority of managers, particularly those involved in the marketing process. Brand equity, however, needs further explanation.

Brand equity

In the brand management process outlined above, brand equity is both an input and output. Brand equity produced today goes back into the system to help build the brand in the future. The actual term 'brand equity' began to be used widely by US advertising practitioners in the early 1980s and was then taken up by academics. The literature which has emerged, confirmed by a recent study conducted by London Business School,[3] suggests two distinct approaches to the definition and measurement of brand equity: bottom-line or financial-evaluation approaches on the one hand, which focus more on the value of the brand asset; and consumer-based approaches on the other, which focus more on the asset itself. This is a primary source of confusion surrounding the concept – the asset and its valuation are not always clearly separated. It is like the difference between a house as an asset and the financial worth of that asset. The house may have many different valuations depending on the circumstances and assumptions used for valuation, eg, for sale, purchase, insurance, probate. The variations of valuation neither change the asset itself nor deny its existence.

To some extent managers choose between taking profits today or storing them for the future. Brand equity is essentially that store. It is the store of later profits and is therefore an asset and a long-term concept. Our definition of brand equity is as follows:

Brand equity is the aggregation of all accumulated attitudes in the extended minds of consumers, distribution channels and influence agents, which will enhance future profits and long-term cash flow.

The key elements of this definition are as follows:

- it follows the holistic approach to branding;
- it is made up of the beliefs, likes/dislikes and behaviours (all three of which make up 'attitudes') of interested parties which come about as a result of all elements of the marketing mix;
- 'extended minds' such as automatic ordering programmes and other systems are included;
- this definition separates the asset and its valuation.

The job of the brand manager is to maximize the *total* of profits plus brand equity, not just sales, market share and short-term profits alone.

Current brand management theory

The current theory dominating management is that of profit or shareholder value maximization, derived from economics. The analytical techniques that have been in development since the era of functional management are concerned with demand, costs and profitability. The key task, in theory, is to find the point of profit maximization where marginal cost is equal to marginal revenue. Within this framework, even the use of the behavioural sciences, consumer behaviour in particular, is directed at solving the optimization problem.

For the brand manager, this has been translated into maximizing sales and market share, with the assumption that this will in turn lead to profit maximization. Brand economics are expressed in per-unit terms – generally, the higher the number of units sold, the lower the per-unit costs and the higher the per-unit, and thus the absolute, profits. The central focus for the brand manager has therefore been the discrete transaction, ie, making a sale. The sum of all these transactions represents total volume (sales revenue), with market share being an indicator of the proportion of total category volume the brand was able to command.

By examining each element of the brand management process, we can see how this paradigm has influenced what brand managers actually do:

Measurement: Brand managers collect a wide range of econometric, objective data. Objective data includes market data from secondary sources (government statistics, etc) as well as the large amounts of consumer research and retail audits regularly provided by market research agencies. This data includes measures of brand awareness, brand usage, attribute ratings, future purchase intentions, and 'movement' (sales) from retailers, expressed in both volume and monetary terms.

Analysis: The objective data collected in step one is used for microeconomic analysis to estimate share, relative positioning (eg, perceptual maps), market potential and volume forecasts. It is also used to measure marketing mix effects through the use of 'sales response' functions and other econometric modelling techniques.

Planning: Most large multinationals have an annual planning and budgeting process. On the basis of the events and outcomes of the previous year, and aided by measurement and analysis, the future environment is predicted, and plans to exploit that environment are made by the brand management team. The individual brand plans are aggregated to form category and corporate plans. Each brand plan usually includes an assessment of past performance, objectives for the future (sales, market share, profit), as well as an outline of the strategies and implementation plans for each element of the marketing mix. Such plans are submitted to top management for approval and serve as the key instruments of control in both a strategic and budgetary sense. Plans are usually revised many times in the course of achieving consensus and a number of alternative 'what if' scenarios are usually generated and evaluated.

Implementation: Once the brand plan has been approved, the brand manager co-ordinates the team, including the advertising agency, sales force, etc, which carries it out.

This approach to brand management has been designed as a, perhaps, mechanical model of economic efficiency. We refer to this brand management paradigm as the 'neo-classical' paradigm. Its core elements can be summarized as follows:

Objective	• satisfy consumer needs; make a sale; maximize profitability.
Consumer understanding	• anonymous consumers who are aggregated into a homogeneous segment; understanding through representative market research; independent buyer and seller.
Competition	• challenge head on.
Key task	• manipulation of marketing mix elements to achieve sales.
Core elements of exchange	• focus on products; sales as a conquest; discrete event; monologue to aggregated segment.

Shortcomings of the neo-classical paradigm

Unfortunately, the single-minded pursuit of sales and profit maximization has led to a number of problems. The principal ones are listed below:

Short-termism: A typical brand manager in a multinational is unlikely to stay in his/her position for a period longer than two years, and often less than a year. During that short period the brand manager's key priority is the manipulation of the marketing mix to achieve improvements in short-term sales, share and profit. These are measured using the vast amounts of economic indicators available, eg, Nielson share data, internal accounting data, consumer research. Bringing about improvements in each of these indicators is the manager's key task, and not building the brand equity asset for the long term.

The bureaucracy of rationality: One of the key benefits of the brand management system was that it had the potential to recapture the entrepreneurial spirit of the original, smaller organizations of the early 1900s. Brand managers were little general managers, all in theory running their own small businesses. Organizations, however, become large in scale with a tendency to move slowly. Risk-averse organizations tend to spend more time on model building and number crunching and less on developing new, breakthrough ideas. A conflict therefore develops between analysis paralysis and the brand manager's self-perception of entrepreneurship.

Inward focus: Analysis, planning and measurement keep the brand manager in the office pouring over reports and working on spreadsheets, instead of keeping 'close to the customer'. The frequency with which a brand manager meets with buyers from major multiples, store managers or consumers, is disturbingly small. Paper displaces people, who are left to agencies and the salesforce to deal with. Yet it is the direct understanding of people's needs which should be the main driver of what the brand manager does.

Inexperienced personnel: The typical brand manager is a young graduate with perhaps two to three years in the company (though such experience is not essential). The selection criteria for most brand management positions is heavily weighted towards problem solving and analytical skills. Such skills are taught well by universities in general, and business schools in particular. However, given that managing brands and brand equity is one of the most important tasks of a firm, is this the right profile for a brand manager? Or is brand management too important to leave to someone relatively inexperienced and new to the company? A firm that would not allow such a person to manage a manufacturing plant, worth £20 million, does allow him/her to manage a brand asset worth many times that amount.

The relational paradigm: a new approach

Brand management requires an update – its own equity needs refreshing. The Relational Paradigm (RP) may provide an answer. The RP essentially shifts the focus of managers away from discrete transactions and towards the formation and maintenance of long-term relationships with key actors relevant to the brand. These key actors include: the brand itself, championed by the brand manager; consumers; retailers; advertising agencies; and even competitors. The focus is on co-operation between actors, to create value, rather than on conflict, which may destroy value. Instead of looking at the market from an industry structure perspective as the economists do, it views the market as a network of 'value-laden relationships'. Brand equity – the store of future profits generated by the 'attitudes' of all the actors – is stored within a brand's network.

The task of the brand manager is still to generate profits in the short term and to build brand equity to ensure profits in the long term. However, the process by which this is done differs significantly from that of the neo-classical paradigm. The focus of managerial activity is the improvement of relationships within the network from the perspective of the brand. The brand manager essentially becomes a network or relationship manager (see Fig. 2).

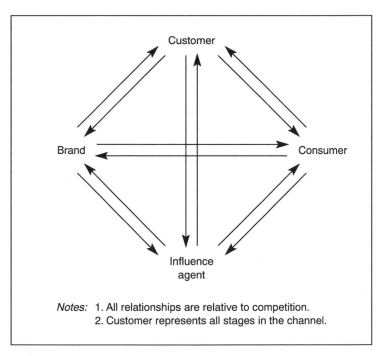

Notes: 1. All relationships are relative to competition.
2. Customer represents all stages in the channel.

Fig. 2 The market as a network

Source: Tim Ambler, 'Are branding and marketing synonymous?, *The Journal of Brand Management*, Vol. 1, no. 1, Summer 1993, pp. 41–48

In practice this means a fundamental shift in the way managers spend their time and other resources. This can be demonstrated by looking at each element of the brand management process in turn:

Measurement: As brand managers are addressing relational issues rather than pure economic issues, the data will be biased towards experiential data. Experiential data is data gained through interactions with, and observations of, network members. For example, visiting stores and talking with store managers, brainstorming with advertising agencies and conducting qualitative market research. Such data gives the brand manager rich insights into the dynamics of the brand's network. This does not imply that economic (objective) data is not needed. In practice, one would expect objective and experiential knowledge to accumulate simultaneously and reinforce one another. Under an RP approach to brand management, however, experiential data is primary and supplemented by economic data analysis, rather than the reverse.

Analysis: Given the emphasis on experiential data, analysis is dominated by individual perception, judgement, and further interaction with actors possessing relevant expertise, eg, advertising agencies. Econometric analysis serves to support this process. The key difference is the recognition that customers and consumers are not wholly rational, something which rational economic analysis does not always allow for.

Planning: Planning under the neo-classical paradigm focuses on economic analysis and the classic 4 Ps of marketing. A relational marketing plan, however, would start with the laying out of the network of channels, contacts and key influence agents and then analyze the relationships from the consumer and customer perspectives. The aim is to establish the relative importance of each relationship for the business and determine the strengths, weaknesses, opportunities and threats that exist. The plan will seek to enhance the relationships within the brand's network relative to competition, ie, seek to develop stronger relationships with key actors than the competitors are able to develop. Because of these strong relationships, there will be less need to meet competitors head on. A relational plan would not only focus on money allocation but also on the time and energy of the brand team, which is often in even shorter supply.

The RP also calls for greater interaction with network partners in the planning process, for example, with re-sellers and agencies. Volume and profit targets are jointly agreed between brand managers and their key customers, eg, agreeing margins with retailers. Key elements of the marketing mix are also jointly planned with key actors. For example, rather than products being developed unilaterally by the manufacturer, products are developed jointly by buyer and seller. Indeed, research has found that the key source of innovation in some sectors tends to be customers and not the manufacturers themselves. For example, a study by Von Hippel[4] in scientific instruments found 77 per cent of all innovations came from users. The RP formally integrates this into the planning process.

Implementation: In the implementation phase, the brand manager becomes the network co-ordinator on behalf of the brand. His task is to direct and influence the dynamics of the network to the brand's advantage. It is during this phase that value created through developing close relationships is drawn upon to make the system work and create further value to be stored within the network for later use. For example, automatic ordering by a supermarket chain using pre-programmed systems that link it with the manufacturer is a result of a high value relationship between the two actors. The relationship is drawn upon to help the network operate effectively in the present which, in turn, will strengthen other relationships, such as that between retailer and consumer as well as manufacturer and consumer. This increases the overall value of the network as a whole – value which can be drawn on by actors in the short and long term.

Marketing is essentially a series of exchanges between parties such that each benefits. Under the RP, what is initially unsure develops into co-operative relationships and ultimately symbiosis. Each business grows with the success of the others.

The RP is summarized in the following way:

Objective	• increase the value within the brand's network; value is realized through short-term profits and future profits stored as brand equity.
Consumer understanding	• well-known customers, treated as individual members of the network; understanding through interaction; dependent buyer and seller.
Competition	• avoid where possible.
Key task	• manage network relationships .
Performance criteria	• increased value within the network-brand equity.
Core elements of exchange	• focus on service; sales as an agreement; on-going process; individual, two-way dialogue and negotiation.

Benefits of the relational approach

The relational perspective is being adopted by practitioners in various ways. Banks, for example, have recognized that it is generally more profitable to extend business with an existing customer than to seek out a new one. The value of a long-term relationship with a customer is much more important than the costs of an individual transaction. Industrial marketers, perhaps the leaders in this area, have long valued the importance of establishing and maintaining long-term supply contracts. Business consultants now look to form on-going partnerships with their clients rather than looking to win individual projects. The specific benefits of the RP's long-term relationship orientation can be summarized as follows:

Long-term perspective: The shift of focus from transactions in the short-term to forming on-going relationships forces the brand manager to take a long-term perspective. Under these circumstances the manager is less likely to take opportunistic action to achieve a sale if it may jeopardize a certain relationship in the long run, even though a short-term indicator may temporarily show improvement. Building brand equity becomes the primary focus and not short-term sales and profit. Firms would also tend to encourage longer tenure by brand managers to ensure strong relationships can be formed and maintained.

Greater market orientation: A brand manager's time and energy will be more devoted to network members, including customers and consumers, than to the internal organization. This will lead to the managers being more market-oriented and customer aware.

Increased economic efficiency: The economic benefits of the RP include lower marketing or 'transaction' costs per customer, and higher sales volume per customer via cross-selling within the relationship. There are also efficiencies to be gained from less support staff needed to maintain data processing and analysis.

More relevant to today's challenges: The challenges outlined at the beginning of this chapter – consumers demanding more; retailers exerting more power; and the emergence of private label brands – are all relational challenges. The emergence of retailers' brands, for example, shows a strengthening of the relationship between large retail chains (eg, Sainsbury and Tesco in the UK) and consumers. Conversely, the relationships between some of the national brands and consumers has weakened, partly perhaps because of the proliferation of short-term discounts and other deals that eroded brand loyalty. Such sales promotions have in fact taught consumers to be disloyal. These challenges require a re-orientation from the one-off sale to on-going relationships in which a series of purchases occurs. Customers and consumers should respond positively to the development of enduring and stable relationships which result in their specific needs being better understood and acted upon.

The way forward for brands

Managing brands should be a focal point of any firm, but there needs to be a paradigm shift in the way this is done. The historical development of brands and their management has led to the widespread adoption of the brand management system. The processes involved in this system are currently being driven by the neo-classical paradigm, which focuses on the goal of economic optimization. Preoccupation with gathering and analysing economic data has led to problems such as short-termism, bureaucratic organizations that are slow to respond to market conditions, managers who spend more time looking inwards than outwards, and the reliance on young, inexperienced managers to manage valuable brand assets.

Part of the answer is to adopt the long-term approach of the relational paradigm with its emphasis on the formation of long-term relationships and the creation of value within networks. This discourages short-term action that may be harmful to the long-term benefit of brand equity that is stored in the network. Economic analysis is valuable but secondary to experiential data-gathering and analysis by managers.

It is our conclusion that, from an organizational perspective, current brand management systems are strong and should continue to be used. They focus the firm's attention on where it should be: on revenue-generating brands. However, we see the future success of the system linked to the degree to which its processes are re-oriented towards the principles of the relational paradigm.

In practice, moving towards the RP means doing the following:

- Balancing the brand manager's short-term orientation with building long-term relationships and brand equity.
- Restructuring reward systems for both brand managers and advertising agencies to reflect the relational emphasis.
- Making it more acceptable to collect and use experiential data for strategic decision making. Managers should become more selective about the amount of economic data they collect. Such data should be regarded as support for data gathered through interactions. Research suppliers should restructure the products they supply to reflect this.
- Organizing budgeting and planning along relational grounds. First, budget allocations should be driven by the brand's relationship priorities. Second, the allocation of a manager's energy and time need to be considered, as well as budget allocations – managing relationships takes all three. Third, managers need to take an interactive approach to planning. This means joint decision making with key network members, both internal and external.
- Making a brand's market network the dominant structural form as opposed to the firm's internal decision-making orientation. Brand managers should look outward rather inward.

Chris Styles is a doctoral student at London Business School. His research and teaching interests include brand management, export marketing and advertising. Previously he was a marketing manager with Procter & Gamble's export division in Geneva.

Tim Ambler is Grand Metropolitan senior research fellow at London Business School. He is the author of *Need-to-Know Marketing* and was previously joint managing director of International Distillers and Vintners, responsible for strategy, acquisitions and marketing. He is a director of Wolverhampton and Dudley Breweries, holds an SM in marketing from MIT and is a qualified chartered accountant.

Further Reading

Aaker, DA *Managing Brand Equity*, The Free Press, New York, 1991.

Haigh, D *Strategic Control of Marketing Finance*, FT/Pitman, London, 1994.

Hague, P and Jackson, P *The Power of Industrial Brands*, McGraw Hill, Maidenhead, 1994.

Hankinson, G and Cowking, P *Branding in Action*, McGraw Hill, 1993.

References

1 This section draws heavily on an article in the *Journal of Marketing Research*, vol. XXXI, pp. 173–190, May 1994, entitled 'Brands, brand management and the brand manager system: a critical-historical evaluation', by George S Low and Ronald A Fullerton.

2 Kotler, P, *Marketing Management: Analysis, Planning and Control* (8th edn), Prentice Hall, New Jersey, 1993.

3 Ambler, T and Styles, C, 'Brand equity: towards the measures that matter', Pan'agra Working Paper, London Business School, 1994.

4 Eric Von Hippel, *The Sources of Innovation*, Oxford University Press, Oxford, 1988.

INTERNATIONAL PRACTICE

Anheuser-Busch

Christopher Stainow

It is estimated that the Budweiser brand is the sixth most valuable global brand ($8.2 billion), and far ahead of any other beer brand. The single beer, Budweiser, commands five per cent of the world beer market. Budweiser, together with other beers made by Anheuser-Busch, accounts for almost 10 per cent of the total volume of beer consumed worldwide.

Like many of the other top global brands, Budweiser has its origins in the US. Importantly, despite expansion worldwide, it has retained the brand's American roots. Perhaps its most signficant achievement is to have developed into a global brand while adapting to the needs of local markets and retaining the integrity of the brand's core values.

Anheuser-Busch is by far the largest brewer in the world, with control of 44.4 per cent of the US market. It began the journey of international expansion using Budweiser as its flagship brand at the beginning of the 1980s. In 1981 Anheuser-Busch (A-B) formed an international division and began the process of selling Budweiser beer in the international marketplace. Thirteen years on, A-B products are to be found throughout the world – including 22 European countries.

In expanding to such a degree, Anheuser-Busch International (A-BII) has relied on two fundamental business objectives:

- to build Budweiser into a leading international brand;
- to build its international business portfolio by investing in leading breweries and local brands in foreign countries through the formation of joint-ventures, equity investments and other partnerships which enables the expansion of the core business: beer.

Strategically, the approach to building the Budweiser brand internationally has three aspects:

- *Budweiser positioning*: making Budweiser a global *icon* brand.
- *Country priorities*: utilizing different marketing campaigns which take into account the landscape of the local market – current size, competitive analysis, potential long-term growth, consumer trends.

    As John Murphy says in his book, *Brand Strategy*: 'The trend towards international branding of goods and services is likely to continue and indeed strengthen. This, however, by no means precludes the need for sensitive brand positioning to suit local conditions.' Such local sensitivity has remained a prime objective throughout the development of the Budweiser brand worldwide.

- *Exchange of best practices*: learning the local market practices and sharing experiences in order to develop strong and innovative marketing efforts.

Anheuser-Busch defines an icon in two ways: as a visual representation of an ideology or symbolic world, and as a trademark that represents more than simply a brand name. All around us, there are good examples of global icon brands including Marlboro, Coca-Cola, and McDonalds. Each of these brands:

- are perceived to be of high quality;
- are seen as leaders;
- possess qualities which extend beyond the specific product virtues;
- retain some sense of a relationship with customers.

For example, Marlboro as a brand name is more than just an American cigarette. Marlboro has come to symbolize the spirit of American independence and wide open spaces. It also evokes the historical narrative of the American West with a host of associated connotations. Above all, Marlboro is seen as a *quality* proposition.

Similarly, Coca-Cola is more than a brand of soft drink; it symbolizes harmony, friendship and happiness. McDonalds is more than just a hamburger; its name symbolizes the all-American spirit of family and values. Each of these brands is a global icon as a result of careful planning and implementation, real local marketplace awareness, and proper brand investment.

In the UK, Budweiser is seen as the pre-eminent US beer, embodying US indigenous craft and tradition, while offering consumers the possibility of partaking in a genuine, attractive and uniquely American proposition.

Around this lifestyle-offering there are a number of other elements, such as the enjoyment of American sports, like American football and drag racing, and music. When approaching the UK, A-B had to consider two fundamental issues:

1. The brand image of Budweiser – the type of person who drinks the beer. This had to be considered in the context of the local perceptions of America, its people, places and culture.
2. The product image of Budweiser – what the likely reaction of UK consumers would be to the beer in terms of its taste, appearance and quality.

Vital to this was the realization that consumers would form an opinion of Budweiser in conjunction with their personal and ideological views of America. Potentially this could work for or against A-B.

Sometimes these perceptions are good. America is vast, free and independent – has a certain 'cool' appeal particularly to younger adults. Americans are honest, adventurous, relaxed and straightforward.

But, rightly or wrongly, perceptions of the US can be negative. America can be seen as the proponent and the origin of the 'junk' fast-food and faddish culture. Americans are sometimes seen as aggressive, arrogant and with little regard for the cultural nuances and mores of countries and cultures outside of the US.

These countering viewpoints have an impact on how Budweiser is positioned in a particular market and how A-B's brand equity is protected in this marketplace. Anheuser-Busch is seen as a big company with strong values based around family ownership. On the other hand, American beer is seen as weaker tasting than a standard European-style beer. The American brewing industry is also seen (in some quarters) as having few brewing credentials. In some areas as well, there is opposition to the prospect of a large American corporation establishing itself in Europe and using its considerable marketing skills and spending power to sell its products to local consumers.

In either case, whether it is its brand or product image, the fact that A-B comes from America has an impact on the image which local beer drinkers have of its brands. In the absence of knowledge, it would have been entirely possible for drinkers to develop only a negative view of Budweiser. The same is probably true for Marlboro and McDonalds when they first embarked on international expansion.

Anheuser-Busch sought to achieve the same level of success. Bridging the gap between international strength and local awareness there are five critical components which underpin the company's brand positioning:

1. A positioning statement – These are words which define what A-B wants the brand to represent and which become the basis for all its marketing activity and could be summed up as follows:

- Budweiser is a premium quality beer with a distinctively refreshing taste.
- Budweiser represents and lets beer drinkers in other countries be a part of the American image they like.
- Budweiser is a popular beer worldwide.

2. Visuals and slogans – a library of visual icons which represents Budweiser's symbolic world:

- the label, widely recognized and very American with its red, white and blue colours;
- the Budweiser bow-tie;
- the long-neck bottle, distinctively American in its shape;
- the slogans *King of Beers* (used for over 100 years) and *The Genuine Article* which denotes the beer's sense of authenticity.

3. Brand personality – a series of images which provide a basis for local beer drinkers to relate to the brand. The Budweiser brand personality could be defined as all-American, masculine, active, social and genuine – consistent with a premium quality image.

4. Scale – marketing that addresses consumer expectations of a *big brand*. A-B's scale relies on aggressive distribution and point-of-sale merchandizing and association with large-scale events such as the World Cup.

5. **A strapline** which embodies the brand essence such as :

- *The Genuine Article*
- *World's largest selling beer*
- *King of Beers*
- *This Bud's for you*
- *The best reason in the world to drink beer*

Aside from building a strong and growing relationship with its consumers, A-B puts an enormous value on building and maintaining meaningful business relationships with its trade partners and customers.

Successful international expansion depends on more than advertising and marketing. Commitment to the local marketplace entails strong ties with the local trade in order to move the product to the consumer through wholesaler and retailer channels.

Anheuser-Busch in the UK operates in a distinctive business environment – distinctive in the priority that trade partnerships play in its success. It works closely with Courage which brews Budweiser on its behalf and with a whole network of national and regional brewers, wholesalers and retailers. In marketing the brand, Budweiser frequently looks to having co-promotional platforms with a range of partners – such as the 1994 World Cup.

A-B's worldwide positioning, as well as Budweiser's brand equity, acts as a considerable incentive for the UK drinks industry to do business with it – and continues to do so regardless of shifts in the industry.

It is apparent that in the UK, as elsewhere, productive trade relations command high priority in A-B's list of business imperatives. 'Making friends is our business,' says the A-B chief executive.

A-B's approach to business in the local marketplace is an expression of the brand equity and momentum delivered by the US and international marketing activity. This can manifest itself both in relations with Budweiser consumers as well as trade partners of Anheuser-Busch. As David Aaker says in his book, *Managing Brand Equity*: 'Brand equity can provide leverage in the distribution channel. Like customers, the trade has less uncertainty dealing with a proven brand name that has already achieved recognition and associations.' A strong brand will have an edge in gaining both shelf facings and co-operation in implementing marketing programmes.

Without these valued trade partnerships, the goal of building Budweiser into a global icon brand would be far more difficult. Budweiser is now the number two premium packaged lager in the UK.

Christopher Stainow is managing director of Anhesuer-Busch European Trade Limited. Previously he was director of sales operations, deputy managing director and export manager. During the 1980s, he helped lay the foundations of Anheuser-Busch's presence in Europe with the introduction of Budweiser and Michelob beers. He was responsible for establishing many of A-B's operations when the company first moved into Europe and is now responsible for charting the company's growth through the 1990s.

THE EUROPEANIZATION OF BRANDS: BEYOND THE GLOBAL/LOCAL DICHOTOMY

Jean-Noël Kapferer

The rise of globalization is taken by some to suggest that brands will auto-matically become global in nature. Others contend that local flexibility needs to be enhanced.

In reality, European brands are becoming more standardized. This is not necessarily caused by the forces of globalization. Such trends have to be seen in a broader light. By its very nature, brand management has to be flexible and pragmatic. Individual elements within the marketing mix may pursue dif-ferent courses while still enhancing brand strength. It is this flexibility and pragmatism which is changing the nature of European brands.

The process of economic, legal, monetary and political unification in which the members of the European Community are engaged has become a symbol in the hot debate between advocates of global brands and defenders of a customized-localized approach. The theoretical arguments of each side are well known and have often been expressed.[1] The increasing homogeneity of the European market is considered as meaning that global branding is an appropriate concept and will soon be implemented in Europe.

While crude dichotomies are useful to launch a debate, brand management is necessarily pragmatic and it has already been suggested that globalization is a myth.[2] This article presents the results of a survey of 210 European brands; it reveals the main tendencies in terms of marketing, advertising and branding behaviour. These facts go beyond the rhetorical controversy about the merits or disadvantages of local or global brands.

In Europe, brands do certainly move towards a standardization of their marketing mix, but this can be expected from brands which were first man-aged locally, with local headquarters being given full independence. The inverse process has been noticed among American brands[3] with little expres-sion of surprise – starting their international expansion on the basis of the same marketing mix used in the US, companies blundered through their lack of adaptation to the local market.[4] To counter this, localized marketing and advertising increased in popularity – for example, the management of Playtex in Europe is now separate from the US.

Instead of questioning the global–local dichotomy, it is more beneficial to focus on each facet of brand management. Some facets may be in the process of standardization while others remain customized and adapted to each market. It should also be possible to identify more types of Europeanization than simply two (local versus global): some brands may globalize particular facets of their marketing mix while different brands standardize others.

As a result, the main goals of our pan-European research were to assess the present state of the art in terms of global branding. Although it is useful to have a clear view of present branding practices in Europe, descriptive statistics fail to indicate which approach is best. Descriptions are not recommendations. Ideally companies would like a normative model to what should or should not be done. To do so requires a criterion. The lack of accessibility to confidential data (such as profits and margins) poses problems, though the market share of each brand may be taken as a good proxy of its success. As a result, the pan-European survey compared the behaviour of strong, moderately strong and weak brands. Although correlation is no cause, it is a first approach towards normative conclusions based on facts rather than armchair theorizing or ideological credos.

The pan-European survey aimed at answering the following questions:[5]

1. How advanced is the process of brand standardization in Europe? How does it vary by product categories or brand country of origin? Is this process linked to the media profile of the brand (TV versus non-TV brands)?
2. What facets of brand management are homogenized throughout Europe and what facets are adapted to local markets?
3. What is meant by local market? Regions, countries?
4. What types of pan-European brands exist at the present time? What is the typical behaviour of each type? Are some products more prone to belong to a type?
5. Is there a relationship between the 'strength of a brand' (its relative market share in Europe) and the identified types of pan-European brands?

A trend towards greater homogenization

Since most brands operating in Europe started as local brands, it is not surprising that the only direction in which they could develop was towards some degree of homogenization. Actually, 81 per cent of the respondents declared they have moved towards a more standardized brand marketing mix, while 12.9 per cent retain localized brand management. As shown in Table 1, there is a clear link between European brand strategy and the brand's country of origin.

There seems to be a segmentation between Latin countries and Anglo-Saxon originated brands. Certainly, the consensus exists in favour of more homogeneity, though the localized approach is much more present among brands originating in France or Italy. Are some countries more prone to the practice of managerial despotism so they can move speedily and forcefully towards homogeneity? This may be caused by managerial culture – such moves require that companies overcome organizational and psychological resistance to a process that suppresses local involvement. However, the results are also

Table 1 Brand standardization tendency and country of origin

	We leave each country free to decide	We push towards homogenization and standardization	NA	(N)
Germany	4.5%	95.5%++++	---	(44)
England	5.3%	94.7%	---	(19)
Japan	---	85.7%	14.3%	(7)
Switzerland	20.0%	80.0%	---	(10)
USA	5.7%	77.1%	17.1%	(35)
France	23.9%++++	69.0%----	7.0%	(71)
Italy	30.0%+	60.0%-	10.0%	(10)
Mean	12.9%	81.0%	6.2%	(210)

Chi Square statistical significance:

+ or −	$p < 0.10$
++ or−−	$p < 0.05$
+++ or −−−	$p < 0.01$
++++ or −−−−	$p < 0.001$

probably due to a number of product categories being over-represented in certain countries. For instance, when one speaks of a brand of French origin it is likely to be a food brand, any of which is more sensitive to cultural differences than high-tech products.

Table 2 presents the relationship between the product categories and the type of pan-European approach. A total of 41 per cent of the sample declared that they had, on the whole, the same marketing mix across all Europe; while 25.8 per cent said they adapted the mix to each country. Finally, 35 per cent segmented Europe into a number of geographical zones.

There are, however, significant differences by product category. The food brands are least prone to globalizing their marketing mix in Europe: they divide Europe into zones. A typical division would create three groups: Latin countries, a group comprising Germany, Austria, Netherlands and a part of Switzerland, and finally the Scandinavian countries. These groups have a common culture and rather similar food habits.

In contrast, cosmetics brands are the most prone to globalizing their marketing mix. Harvard's Ted Levitt has argued that technology would be the most potent force towards homogenization. Cosmetic brands are now based on permanent innovations emerging from biological research. Also they try to solve eternal and universal needs: skin preservation, anti-ageing, looking young and beautiful. Although the results do not reach statistical significance, this technology argument would fit the high percentage of globalization among drugs companies (detergent makers are permanently using chemical research to bring out innovations), as well as the manufacturers of home appliances, hi-fis, videos and cameras. Business to business brands – also generally based on technology – still seem to customize their marketing mix by country, as do the service brands (banks, insurance, employment agencies). Both business-to-business and service brands share the importance of personal contact and direct selling to the customer in the marketing mix. This human facet of the mix naturally produces increased customization. Also, local habits may require some adaptation: for instance, German standards of what is a normal size and comfort for a hotel room led chains such as Novotel, Ibis and Holiday Inn to adapt to allow for some variance in their architecture.

It is luxury brands which are the most enthusiastic practitioners of globalization. This is no surprise. They are also technology-based (Dior Cosmetics, Lancôme Cosmetics) and their core identity is linked to a person, a creator: Yves Saint Laurent for instance, or Ralph Lauren. Such a person is the same throughout the world: Saint Laurent's personality does not change when he travels to Japan or to the US. This creates a strong force against unnecessary changes. If the brand has a real core identity, it should remain identical through time and space.[6] Furthermore, being sold to well-off customers who travel extensively, international homogeneity acts as a reassurance to target customers.

Table 2 European marketing policy by different product categories

	The same marketing mix across Europe	The same mix within zones in Europe	Marketing mix adapted to each country	(N)
Luxury products	64% 0 +++	28% 0	8% −−	(25)
Cosmetics	60% 9 ++	30% 4	8% 7 −−	(23)
Hifi/video/photo	54% 2	20% 8	25% 0	(24)
Home appliances	54% 2	37% 5	12% 5	(24)
Drugs/detergents	53% 8	30% 8	15% 4	(13)
Beverages	40% 0	30% 0	30% 0	(25)
Textile	39% 1	39% 1	21% 8	(23)
Automobile	35% 0	35% 0	30% 0	(20)
Services	30% 8	23% 1	53% 8 ++	(13)
Business-to business	25% 0	16% 7	58% 3 ++++	(12)
Food	23% 5 −−	50% 0 ++	26% 5	(34)
Mean	41% 1	34% 9	25% 8	(210)

Chi Square statistical significance:

+ or −	p<0.10
++ or −−	p<0.05
+++ or −−−	p<0.01
++++ or −−−−	p< 0.001

Media influence on globalization

A third source of the trend towards homogenization – beyond the country of origin (and its style of management) and the product category – is the media factor.

One of the main advantages of global branding is savings in advertising productivity. It is far less costly to do a single TV spot than 12. In fact Table 3 shows that there is a relationship between the typical media used (TV or non-TV) and the willingness to embrace globalization.

Although the vast majority of advertisers aim at more homogeneity (81 per cent) TV advertisers are more likely to do so than non-TV advertisers. There is indeed a high level of overlap of TV across borders, not to mention pan-European TV channels or sports events which receive worldwide or European coverage. As can be seen from Table 4, this homogenizing process is implemented through new ways of organizing the marketing structure and decision process at the European level.

TV advertisers set up international teams who decide on the advertising strategy and copy platform, or even the overall marketing strategy, while non-TV advertisers still leave local subsidiaries with a great deal of autonomy. For instance, BMW has created a 'Brand Circle', made of ten participants from its main foreign subsidiaries and BMW headquarters. The lead country approach is only practised by a minority (6.2 per cent). It introduces authoritative management and stirs up local resistances, such as the 'not invented here' syndrome. It is currently practised by Milka, with the lead country being Germany.

Compelling factors against global brand management

It is well known from international marketing research that the way you look at the data often tells you different stories. In his work, Alfred Boote analyzed

Table 3 European globalization tendency and media factors

	We leave each country free to decide	We push towards homogenization and standardization
TV advertisers	9% 4 −−	85% 2 +++
Non TV advertisers	21% 3 ++	70% 5 −−−
Mean	12% 9	81% 0

Chi Square statistical significance:

+ or −	$p<0.10$
++ or −−	$p<0.05$
+++ or −−−	$p<0.01$
++++ or −−−−	$p< 0.001$

Table 4 Organizing for international branding

International organizational mode	TV advertisers	Non-TV advertisers	(M)
Decentralized: each country is autonomous	2% 0 ––––	9% 9 ++++	(4% 3)
Local autonomy with some co-ordination by headquarters	43% 6	50% 8	(45% 7)
Strategic decisions made by a European team	37% 6 ++++	14% 8 ––––	(31% 0)
Strategic decisions made by a lead country	4% 7	9% 8	(6% 2)
Centralized organization:	12% 8	14% 8	(13% 3)
	100%	100%	

Chi Square statistical significance:

+ or –	$p < 0.10$
++ or ––	$p < 0.05$
+++ or –––	$p < 0.01$
++++ or ––––	$p < 0.001$

a psychographic segmentation in Europe and came to the conclusion that there were striking differences between countries on many attitudinal items, but that the underlying value structures in each country appeared to bear sufficient similarity.[7] There are differences between countries, but it remains up to the European managers to take them into account or to ignore them. To paraphrase a famous sentence, the earth is round, but for the practical purposes of everyday life, it is as well to take it as flat.

It was, therefore, interesting to ask European brand co-ordinators whether specific differences between countries would be sufficient to prevent global brand management and lead to a locally adapted marketing mix.

Legislative differences are ranked first. For example, if one wanted to use a commercial featuring children advertising a cereal, conformity to the British, German, Dutch and French laws would only allow the cereal bowl on screen. Another striking result is that – legislation differences apart – it is a minority of European managers (47.1 per cent) who consider that an inter-country difference should necessarily lead to the marketing mix being adapted. While these are only the views of people whose task precisely consists in thinking internationally, it is interesting to see that even differences in consumption habits are not enough to force adaptation of the mix. Bearing in mind that differences in legislation will soon disappear in the EC, this means that globalising tendencies largely overcome inter-countries differences.

Table 5 Which, between countries' differences, should lead to local adaptation of the marketing mix? (Base N = 210)

Type of differences	Yes, necessarily adapt	Desirable	Adaption unnecessary	NA
Legal differences	55% 2	17% 6	24% 8	2% 4
Strength of competition	47% 1	34% 3	16% 2	2% 4
Consumption habits	41% 0	38% 6	18% 1	2% 4
Distribution structure	39% 0	24% 8	31% 9	4% 3
Brand awareness	38% 1	34% 8	24% 3	2% 9
Level of distribution reached	37% 1	31% 0	26% 2	5% 7
Media audience	37% 1	33% 8	24% 8	4% 3
Success of marketing plans	34% 3	34% 8	22% 4	8% 6
Consumer needs and expectations	32% 9	39% 0	25% 2	2% 9
Media availability	32% 4	39% 5	23% 3	4% 8
Brand images	30% 5	36% 7	29% 0	3% 8
Manufacturing standards and norms	27% 6	18% 6	49% 5	4% 3
Nature of representation locally	27% 1	28% 1	39% 0	5% 7
Brand histories	25% 2	33% 8	37% 6	3% 3
Cultural differences	24% 8	47% 1	25% 2	2% 9
Life style differences	24% 8	39% 5	32% 4	3% 3
Affiliates, turnover	22% 9	31% 0	41% 0	5% 2
Buying power	21% 9	33% 3	41% 4	3% 3
Consumers' age	12% 4	22% 9	61%	3% 8

The second strong result from Table 5 is that the most compelling factors are tied to competition (number and strength of competitors, brand awareness, level of distribution, product life cycle, etc). This is why new concepts with no competition are more easily globalized (such as Mars, Gillette, McDonalds, Coke, Malibu, Bailey's, Jameson). In contrast, the positioning and pricing policy of Orangina is not the same in France, where it is the second soft drink after Coke, as it is in the UK where it competes as a premium brand in the orange carbonated soft drink market against local brands such as Tango or Sunkist. In general, when a subsidiary is strong – for instance, France is Apple's third best-selling country – it is allowed to be autonomous by headquarters. Its specific marketing mix has proven to be locally successful.

Interestingly, cultural and life-style differences emerging from psycho-graphic European studies convince only a fourth of the interviewees. They do not seem to be potent enough to lead to significant local adaptations of the marketing mix. This also holds true for two other consumers' differences: the target's age and buying power.

The facets of brand adaptation

The proponents and adversaries of global branding use a basic dichotomy: to be or not to be global? The reality has more nuances. Even so-called 'global brands' such as Marlboro, Coca-Cola, McDonalds do not fully globalize all the facets of their marketing mix.[8] Certainly, a Mars bar is the same all over the world, but there are more than 100 varieties of Nescafé as the product and advertising is adapted.

Interviewees were asked which facet they adapted from one European country to another, or one zone to another (Table 6).

Interestingly, it is the physical identity (the logo and name) of the brand which is most globalized. In the process of mergers, or of geographical extension, companies have become muddled with similar products having different names. There is, as a result, a desire for simplification – Shell now calls all its motor oil in Europe, Helix.

Table 6 Which parts of the brand marketing mix are globalized in Europe or adapted?

	Fully globalized	Adapted	NA
Brand logo	93% 3	5% 2	1% 4
Brand name	81% 0	11% 4	7% 6
Physical characteristics of the product	67% 1	27% 6	5% 2
Packaging	53% 3	36% 2	10% 5
After-sales service	48% 6	16% 7	34% 8
Distribution channels	46% 7	33% 3	20% 0
Culture & arts sponsorship	32% 4	26% 7	41% 0
Sport sponsoring	29% 5	38% 6	31% 9
Advertising strategy	29% 0	65% 7	5% 2
Advertising execution	29% 0	57% 1	13% 8
Relative price	24% 3	67% 1	8% 6
Direct marketing	18% 1	60% 0	10% 0
Promotion	10% 0	80% 0	10% 0

Ranked next, but far behind, are the characteristics of the product and its associated service and packaging or format. Because sports events are international, sponsorship should be global. This is true for the few brands having access to such events though it seems that most other brands adapt their sponsorship from one area to another. Advertising strategy is fully globalized by only 29 per cent of the sample. Finally, sales promotion tools and direct marketing are always adapted. These are quick-response tools used as tactical devices to match local objectives. The lack of homogeneity of pricing is explained by the objective of maximizing profits locally. The concentration of distribution will cause an obligation to suppress these price differences, which in turn will act as a potent force towards homogenization of the brand positioning.

How does one reconcile the seemingly low figures of Table 6 concerning the globalization of European brands' facets, and the 41 per cent of respondents (Table 2) declaring they have the same marketing mix throughout Europe? The latter figure seems inflated. From results of questioning on the concrete facets of the mix, most prove to have been adapted, perhaps not from country to country, but at least in certain countries. Actually, a cross-tabulation indicates that 50 per cent of those declaring to have the same marketing mix in Europe also declare they have to adapt the advertising strategy here and there locally. For instance, Apple's marketing mix is European but, in line with the humanistic values of the brand, some room for adaptation to each country's culture is left in the advertisements. Each citizen should feel that Apple is speaking to him or her personally.

A typology of Europeanization of brands

Looking at the sample of 210 brands operating in Europe there are types of brands, each one characterized by a typical profile of facets some of which are globalized while others are not. A cluster analysis procedure was undertaken and the hierarchical clustering process was stopped when four types remained, maximizing variance between types and minimizing intra- type variance. Table 7 depicts these four types of European brands.

Type 1 is a typical adapter. Brands of this type are flexible and quickest to adapt promotion, direct marketing and sponsorship to conquer local market shares. They also do not hesitate to adapt the media mix, the below/above-the-line ratio. Finally, although they do not change the advertising strategy more than the sample average, they do adapt creative ideas and copy executions when necessary. One finds in this type such brands as Apple, Ray-Ban, Evian Mineral Water and Estée Lauder. The automobile sector is significantly over-represented in this type (12 car brands among 20 belong to this type). They practise 'global' marketing. Renault is a typical example as shown below.

Type 2 are the beginners. This type inherits a situation where heterogeneity dominates. Cross-tabulations showed that it comprised many brands whose European co-ordinators declared them to be at the first stage of

Table 7 A typology of international brands

	Type 1 (n$_1$ = 58)	Type 2 (n$_2$ = 34)	Type 3 (n$_3$ = 73)	Type 4 (n$_4$ = 45)
% Modifying the				
Brand logo	1% 7 [1]	26% 5	---	2% 2
Brand name	1% 7	55% 9	5% 5	---
Brand packaging	37% 9	91% 2	17% 8	22% 2
Product characteristics	34% 5	67% 6	12% 3	13% 3
After-sales service	22% 4	17% 6	21% 9	---
Advertising strategy				
• Target	27% 6	29% 4	24% 7	8% 9
• Positioning	34% 5	44% 1	28% 8	4% 4
• Promise	29% 3	47% 1	30% 1	6% 7
• Media mix	69% 0	55% 9	68% 5	24% 4
Advertising execution				
• Creative idea	48% 3	58% 8	23% 3	15% 6
• Brand baseline	34% 5	61% 8	27% 4	11% 1
• Brand symbol or spokesman	13% 8	23% 5	4% 1	2% 2
• Copy execution (TV)	46% 6	52% 9	19% 2	6% 7
Promotion	98% 3	94% 1	89% 0	31% 1
Below/above-the-line ratio	58% 6	70% 6	49% 3	22% 2
Direct marketing	96% 6	47% 1	60% 3	22% 2
Sport sponsorship	93% 1	35% 3	17% 8	4% 4
Cultural sponsorship	79% 3	14% 7	5% 5	2% 2
Distribution channels	31% 0	41% 2	42% 5	15% 6
Relative pricing	63% 8	91% 2	95% 9	6% 7

[1] Percentage of the brands of this type which change or adapt the logo.

Europeanization. They include Yoplait, Damart thermo-wear, Heinz Ketchup in Europe, and Nesquick. Cross-tabulations also showed that food product and drugs (detergents, etc) were over-represented in this type (at a statistically significant level). In fact, Procter & Gamble's Ariel in the UK, France or Germany is called Dash in Italy. Johnson's Pledge is Pliz in France and Pronto in Switzerland. As to food brands, one finds again that marketers hesitate to enforce a global approach if food consumption habits are not the same from north to south of Europe. For instance, the first yoghourts to be launched in the UK contained fruits: this positioned the whole product category as a

Table 8 Branding behaviour of a typical adapter: Renault

	Global strategy	Multi-local strategy
Brand	Yes	
Positioning	Yes	
Marketing objectives		Yes
Marketing mix		
Product		
• Name	unique by model	different for limited series
• Packaging	unique on the whiole	options vary
Price		Yes
Distribution		Yes
Communication		
• Benefit		Adapted by country
• Style	Brand unity	
• Signature	when possible	
• Creation		Adapted to local culture
• Media		Adapted to the local environment

pleasurable desert. Later, plain, natural yoghourt seemed dull in comparison. In France, Danone's success and core values were historically based on plain natural yoghourt and its built-in health values. These two visions are radically opposite. From one country to another, Danone cannot use a monolithic marketing-mix to sell the same product.

Type 3 is the tactician. They stick to a global core identity and strategy, but locally adapt such execution facets as the media mix or distribution channels and relative pricing *vis-à-vis* the competition. Typical brands within this type are Club Med, Polaroid, Kodak Color film, Vizir liquid detergent, Rank Xerox and Levi's.

Type 4 could be called the global brands: they standardize all facets of the marketing mix as much as possible. However, even in this group, one finds significant adaptations of below-the-line actions, such as promotion and direct marketing. Luxury brands are over-represented in this type: 14 among the 25 of the whole sample. For instance, one finds Chanel, Moet & Chandon and Nina Ricci, but also Playtex. Interestingly, Playtex Europe uses a different marketing mix from that of the US to adapt to the more sophisticated European woman. Table 9 captures the behavioural and organizational differences between these four types, as to TV advertising.

As expected from a typically global brand, type four imposes the same advertising everywhere. Type 3 accepts only minor adaptations of its single commercial. Type two is just starting to Europeanize: its dominant organization

Table 9 Organizing for international TV advertising

	(M)	Type 1: Adapters	Type 2: Beginners	Type 3: Tacticians	Type 4: Globalists
Each country develops its own creative idea and realizes its own commercial.	(27%)	28% 3	41% 9 ++	20% 4	18% 2
Many commercials are created by central headquarters and local affiliates may choose.	(8.1%)	8% 7	12% 9	6% 1	4% 5
The creative idea is imposed but the execution is left to each country.	(12% 2)	21% 7 ++	16% 1	4% 1 ––	4% 5
The central headquarters impose a single European commercial authorizing minor local adaptions.	(37.8%)	34% 8	22% 6 ––	57% 1 ++++	22% 7
A single European commercial is imposed and translated.	(22% 3)	21% 7	5% 7 –	16% 3	54.5% ++++
		100%	100%	100%	100%

Chi Square statistical significance:

+ or –	p<0.10
++ or ––	p<0.05
+++ or –––	p<0.01
++++ or ––––	p< 0.001

is that of independent agencies acting independently at the local level. Its first move is generally to select an agency with a European network to accompany the process of homogenization. Type 1, the adapters, leave the choice of organization most open.

Brand strength and type of Europeanization process

So far the above tables have been descriptive. They present a picture of the state of the art in Europe. Is it possible to evaluate these Europeanization strategies on a normative basis? Lacking profit figures, one good proxy is the relative market share of the brand in each of the countries where it is sold in Europe. Since the PIMS analyzes have shown that profitability is linked to relative market share, we made two types of analysis:

1. A cross-tabulation of the competitive status of the brand with each of the four types of European brand. The competitive status of a brand is defined as the number of countries where the brand is market leader. Some brands are

leaders in all 18 countries. Some are leaders in none. Finally, some are leaders in specific countries and not elsewhere. Table 10 shows that 51.8 per cent of the adapters are dominating in most of the 18 markets covered by the study. It is the most successful type. Then comes the globalists (35.6 per cent), the tacticians (27.4 per cent) and the beginners (20.5 per cent).

2. A second type of analysis consisted in computing a weighted brand strength score for each brand. Two formulas were used; the first was:

$$BS1 : \text{Brand Strength Score} = \sum_{i=1}^{18} \text{Brand Competitive Status in Country } i$$

In this formula, the brand strength score is obtained by adding the value of the brand's competitive status in each of the countries where it is present. Five levels of competitive status were weighted as follows.

- Launch phase 1
- Follower 2
- Challenger 3
- Relative leader 4
- Absolute leader 5

Thus the maximum brand strength score a brand could receive was 90 (5 × 18).

The second brand strength formula was computed introducing a different competitive weighting to give greater emphasis to market leadership (0.5, 1, 3, 6, and 9 for the position of absolute leader). In addition, each country was weighted according to its economic power. The weight of each country was:

- UK/France/Germany   5
- Italy/Spain   4

Table 10 Market leadership and type of European brand management

Status of the brand and level of presence	Type 1: Adaptors	Type 2: Beginners	Type 3: Tacticians	Type 4: Globalists
• Leader in all 18 countries	19% 0 ++++	2% 9	2% 7 ————	15% 6
• Leader and non-leader, present in all 18 countries	32% 8 +	17% 6	24% 7	20% 0
• Leader and non-leader, present in 11 to 17 countries	32% 8	23% 5	41% 1 +	26% 7
• Leader and non-leader, present in 10 countries and less	1% 7 ————	35% 3 ++++	9% 6	8% 9
• Leader nowhere	13% 8	20% 6	21% 9	28% 9
	100%	100%	100%	100%

- Austria, Belgium, Netherlands,
  Switzerland, Norway,
  Denmark, Sweden   3
- Portugal, Greece, Turkey,
  Luxembourg, Ireland, Finland   1

Thus the second brand strength index reads as follows:

$$BS2 = \text{Brand Strength Score} = \sum_{i=1}^{18} \text{Brand Competitive Status} \times \text{Country Weight}$$

It is possible to compute the average brand score of each of the four types of brands which were identified in the typology (Table 11).

All three analyzes converge: whatever the brand strength formula used, the first type (adapters) regroups brands whose brand strength score is significantly above the average sample mean score. Not surprisingly the beginners have significantly lower brand strengths. The pure globalists come second. Certainly correlation is no cause, but it is a hint at the winning route for international brand management.

A pragmatic approach to globalization

The former results were cross-sectional: they presented a snapshot of European brands. Now, in practical terms how does one move from Type 2 (the beginners) to Type 1 (the adapters) or Type 4 (the globalists)? What step-by-step procedure should one follow? The answer will be very different for new brands or products and for existing ones. In the first case, organizational resistance factors are likely to be low. All countries and subsidiaries have the same status. Headquarters will easily set up teams in charge of defining the optimum European marketing mix and brand positioning. The same team will brief a small number of advertising agencies, select the best European creative concept

Table 11 Brand strength and type of international brand

	Sample mean	Type 1: Adapters	Type 2: Beginners	Type 3: Tacticians	Type 4: Globalists
Brand strength score 1	(41,62)	48.52 +++	31.76 ----	40.51	42.00
Brand strength score 2	(157,23)	183.25 ++	126.21 -	148.72	161.40

Chi Square statistical significance:

+ or −	p<0.10
++ or −−	p<0.05
+++ or −−−	p<0.01
++++ or −−−−	p< 0.001

and message. This is how Procter & Gamble launched Always, a new feminine protection, or Ariel Micro at the European level. Whirlpool's entry in Europe and substitution to Philips was planned from the outset at a global level. The brand switch itself did not take place at the same time in all countries to account for large differences in Philips' local brand equities. However, the brand positioning, and advertising were fully global. Orangina tries to use the same marketing mix in all new countries in Europe where it will be marketed, once a local bottler is found.

Now, for most European brands with strong local equities, the former approach is not practical and, indeed, would be suicidal. Global branding is not an exercise of style: it should not aim at saving money, but making money. The homogenization process will necessarily be pragmatic and modular.

It should be realized that a lot of will and perseverance from headquarters will be needed to overcome local resistance from autonomous subsidiaries. While one does not need international Neros, definite objectives should be set up which will make clear for all where the organization wishes to go. This requires a step-by-step process. The first step is to agree on a common brand platform, some kind of invisible kernel or identity prism.[9] This can be done by answering the questions of the following platform, concerning the spirit, sources and goals of the brand. The second step is to agree on the visible facets of this identity (trademarks, packaging, advertising style, codes and tone or manner).

The Volkswagen Golf, for instance, does not have the same advertising (nor even name) across countries. However, there is a definite style that conveys a common brand core. The following steps can be compared to a ladder corresponding to a progressive homogeneity. For instance, in terms of packaging one may choose between three options:

- A common trademark only, on the products (Danone).
- A common style (Findus).
- A common packaging with information written in multiple languages (Pampers).

Table 12 Brand identity platform

Spirit of the brand (invisible)

1. Why does this brand need to exist?
2. What are the brand's core values?
3. Mission: what benefits does the brand want to bring in people's lives?
4. Positioning.
5. Brand's imaginary client.
6. Brand's personality.

Signs of recognition (visible)

1. Trademarks.
2. Graphic identity.
3. Tone, manner, codes of advertising.

As to advertising, various degrees of increasing convergence can be decided on. Such as:

- Strong trademark visibility and common brand spirit.
- International corporate or umbrella campaign, allowing localized product campaigns.
- Rather rigid executional guidelines, thus reducing the degrees of freedom.
- Common pool of commercials among which countries may choose (Coca-Cola, McDonald's).
- Identical commercials with only some minimal local adaptations (Always, Gillette, Ariel).

To accompany this modular process of brand Europeanization it is essential to create common tools for controlling its progress. Countries and subsidiaries must agree upon common brand equity measures and image surveys.

As a conclusion, it can be said that the key elements for bringing existing strong local brands towards more homogeneity across borders and, if desired, a global approach are:

1. To establish a vision for the brand, its *raison-d'être*, its core identity.
2. To focus on similarities, not the differences. This is mostly a question of frame of mind: it is also a matter of will.
3. To develop as much as possible team skills and work in networks not hierarchies. Only by creating common tasks where all European managers play a role will globalization be internalized.

Jean-Noël Kapferer is Professor of Marketing at Groupe HEC School of Management, Jouy-en-Josas, France. He has a degree from the Sorbonne and a PhD from Northwestern University, where he later lectured. He is the author of numerous books including *Rumors: Image, Uses and Functions* (1990), *Les Marques: Capital de l'entreprise* (1991) and *Strategic Brand Management* (1992).

Further Reading

Kapferer, J-N, *Strategic Brand Management*, Kogan Page, London, 1992.

References

1 Hite, R and Fraser, C, 'International advertising strategies of multinational corporations', *Journal of Advertising Research*, 28(4), August-September 1988; James, W and Hill, J, 'International advertising: to adapt or not to adapt?', *Journal of Advertising Research*, 31 (3), June-July 1991; Kanso, A, 'International advertising strategies', *Journal of Advertising Research*, 32 (1), January-February 1992.
2 Wind, Y, 'The myth of globalization', *Journal of Consumer Marketing*, vol. 3 (2), Spring 1986.
3 Hite, R and Fraser, C, 'International advertising strategies of multinational corporations', *Journal of Advertising Research*, 28(4), August-September 1988.
4 Ricks, D, Arpan, J and Fu, M, 'Pitfalls in advertising overseas', *Journal of Advertising Research*, 14 (6), 1974.

5 To obtain this information 685 European advertising or marketing co-ordinators of the major brands operating in Europe were nominally identified, thanks to the collaboration of the Eurocom advertising network. They represented all product categories from food products to luxury goods, durable to fast-moving consumer goods, and also comprised services and business-to-business products. They all received a mailed questionnaire, in English, German or French. Each questionnaire focused on a single brand. For umbrella brands, source brands or endorsing brands, it concerned one of its product (for instance the Volkswagen Golf or Ford's Fiesta). In all, 210 questionnaires were analyzed, which represents a high rate of return (30 per cent), indicative of the timeliness of the topic. Among the respondents, 71 per cent were TV advertisers, 10 per cent were market leader everywhere, 21 per cent leader nowhere. In this survey, we took an enlarged vision of Europe, not limited to the EEC Members, but comprising 18 countries.

6 Kapferer, J-N, *Strategic Brand Management*, Kogan Page, London, 1992.

7 Boote, AS, 'Psychographic segmentation in Europe', *Journal of Advertising Research*, vol. 22(6), December 1983.

8 Riesenbeck, H and Freeling, A, 'How global are global brands?', *McKinsey Quarterly*, no. 4, 1991.

9 Kapferer, J-N, *Strategic Brand Management*, Kogan Page, London, 1992.

RELATIONSHIP MARKETING STRATEGY

Adrian Payne

In mature markets, strategies aimed at building sales volume through obtaining new customers have proved to be an expensive approach for many firms – often not producing the anticipated profits. Attention is now being directed at building enduring relationships with existing customers.

This change in direction represents a shift from transaction marketing to relationship marketing. Transactional marketing's emphasis is on the individual sale; in contrast relationship marketing focuses on building strong, long-term relationships with individual customers.

2

Relationship marketing is a relatively recent phenomenon. Its emergence in the 1980s, however, was not so much a discovery, but a rediscovery of something which has long formed the cornerstone of many businesses. The contemporary concept of relationship marketing is founded on three complimentary perspectives.

The first is the nature of the way companies view their relationships with customers. This is fundamentally changing from an emphasis on the transaction to a focus on the relationship with the aim of long-term customer retention.

Second, a broader view of the markets with which a company interacts is emerging. In addition to customer markets, organizations are also now becoming concerned with the development and enhancement of more enduring relationships with other external markets, such as those with suppliers, as well as internal markets.

Third, a recognition that quality, customer service and marketing activities need to be brought together. Relationship marketing focuses on bringing these three elements into closer alignment and ensuring that the synergy of their combination is fully realized.

All of these three elements are inextricably linked to customer retention.

Marketing has always been focused on customers. Too often, however, this focus has concentrated on the capturing of new customers rather than nurturing and building relationships with existing customers. Relationship marketing, therefore, is built around seven elements:

- focus on customer retention rather than on a single sale;
- emphasis on customer value rather than product features;
- long timescale rather than a short-term perspective;
- high customer service emphasis;
- high customer commitment;
- high customer contact;
- quality as the concern of all rather than a matter for operations.

While there is increasing awareness and appreciation of relationship marketing, the transaction bias remains strong in many organizations. The investment made in winning a new customer, once successful, is immediately transferred to the next prospect – typically little effort goes into keeping that customer happy.

Organizations often acknowledge that existing customers are easier to sell to and are frequently more profitable than new customers. However, while managers intellectually agree with this view, greater emphasis and resources are often placed on attracting new customers, and existing customers are frequently taken for granted. It is only when some breakdown in service quality occurs, and the customer is on the point of defection, or leaves, that the spotlight focuses on the existing customer.

Of course, new customers are highly important, indeed they are essential to the success of most service businesses. But, a balance is needed between the effort directed towards existing and new customers. Without such a balance any organization is failing to fulfil the potential of its interaction and relationships with customers.

The ladder of loyalty

Relationship marketing can be explained by reference to a ladder of customer loyalty. The traditional approach concentrates on the first two rungs, on converting a prospect into a customer. Relationship marketing emphasizes developing and enhancing relationships so that customers become clients, supporters and, ultimately, advocates.

The relationship marketing concept is increasingly being championed. 'It has always been incredible to me how insensitive companies can be to their customers. Most of them don't seem to understand that their future business depends on having the same customer come back again and again,' laments William Davidow in *Marketing High Technology*.[1] Indeed, it is only in recent years that significant research has been carried out into the commercial advantages of transforming customers into advocates. 'The economic benefits

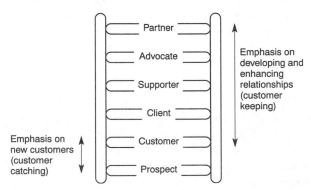

Fig. 1 The relationship marketing ladder of customer loyalty

of high customer loyalty are considerable and, in many industries, explain the differences in profitability among competitors,' concluded Frederick Reichheld of Bain & Company in a 1993 *Harvard Business Review* article.[2] He pointed to the example of credit card company MBNA which calculates that a five per cent increase in retention grows the company's profits by 60 per cent by the fifth year. 'Building a highly loyal customer base cannot be done as an add-on. It must be integral to a company's basic business strategy,' argues Reichheld. 'Creating a loyalty-based system in any company requires a radical departure from traditional business thinking. It puts creating customer value – not maximizing profits and shareholder value – at the center of business strategy, and it demands significant changes in business practice – redefining target customers, revising employment policies and re-designing incentives.'

One study of the American car market found that a satisfied customer is likely to stay with the same supplier for a further 12 years after the first satisfactory purchase. During that time, the customer will buy four more cars of the same make. To a car manufacturer, it is estimated that this level of customer retention is worth $400 million a year in new car sales.[3]

Clearly, building such a relationship also expands the traditional concept of the key components of marketing activities. While once these were centred on product, price, promotion and place (the 4 Ps), relationship marketing adds three crucial new elements – people, processes and proactive customer service. Customer service is no longer an added extra, but at the very heart of all of these activities.

The relationship chain

Growing disenchantment with functional approaches to organizational work has focused attention on processes. The trend now is to organize the flow of a company's work around company-wide processes, rather than narrowly defined functions. An integral part of this is the realization that processes revolve around customers and customer service.

The limitation of conventional views of processes is that they are regarded as linear. The focus is on stages and steps which may add value to a business. In contrast, the relationship chain focuses on how value can be created and sustained through improved relationships.

The relationship chain has five core components:

• **Defining the value proposition**
It is important that organizations create value which goes beyond the tangible benefits or uses of their product or service. They have to offer enhanced value. Central to this are:

– identifying key service issues
– measuring service preferences
– competitive benchmarking.

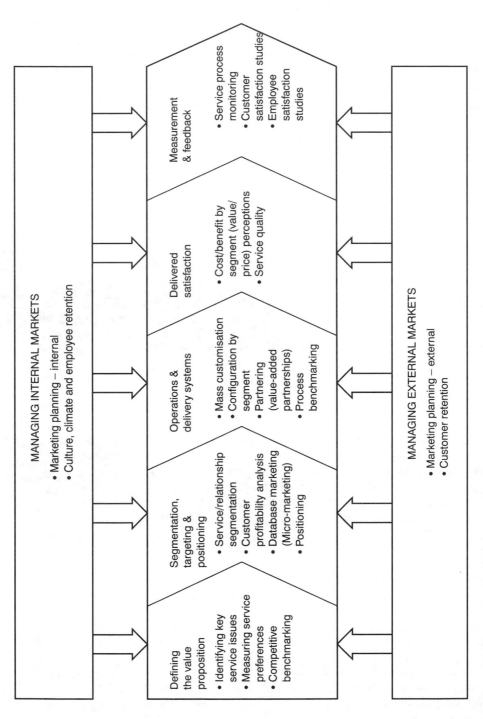

Fig. 2 The relationship management chain

• Segmentation, targeting and positioning

Awareness of the importance attached to various service attributes enables organization to identify patterns which emerge among customers. If one group of customers has, for example, a distinct set of priorities from another group then it would be reasonable to think of them both as different service segments. The company then has to decide which of these segments to target and how it should position the service offered to these segments in relation to the competition.

Among the techniques which can be used at this stage are customer profitability analysis, cluster analysis, and database marketing.

• Operations and delivery systems

The way in which an organization configures and manages processes is a critical element in achieving success. The ability to meet ever-increasing demands for variety, flexibility and quality provides sizeable challenges. There are a number of critical aspects of the design, management and planning of operations and delivery systems:

- mass customization
- configuration by segment
- partnering
- process benchmarking.

• Delivered satisfaction

Organizations can differentiate themselves from the competition not just by the quality of their core product. Customer satisfaction and the maintenance of the customer relationship is dependent on how well a product or service measures up to the customers' original expectations of quality. Each segment and delivery of service quality needs to be reviewed.

Total value must be regarded as something more than price. Customers do not buy products, they seek benefits. Delivered value can be thought of as the total value offered to a customer less the total cost.

Defining service quality remains contentious. But, one analysis breaks it down into three useful dimensions: the technical quality of the service; functional quality; and corporate image.[4]

• Measurement and feedback

In order that the process of relationship management becomes a continuous cycle of improvement, systems of measurement and feedback must be installed. The aim should be for constant feedback rather than occasional research. It is not sufficient to inspect the final output of a process as a means of controlling quality. If the process is under control the end-result is guaranteed. It is vital, therefore, that critical points where malfunctions or failures could lead to loss of quality are identified and performance continually monitored.

Feedback needs to be obtained from both customers and employees. In 1969, researchers identified five factors which constitute the overall concept of job satisfaction (satisfaction with the work itself; satisfaction with pay; satisfaction with promotion prospects; satisfaction with supervision; and satisfaction with co-workers).[5] These remain the core of employee satisfaction studies – though others, such as satisfaction with the working environment, corporate communication, senior management performance and company image, can be included.

Customer satisfaction must also be measured regularly, While a product or service may not change, the expectations of customers invariably do so, Surveys need to be objective (whether they are questionnaires, interviews or focus groups) and must use criteria which reflect the needs and preferences of customers. Ideally results should be compared with customer satisfaction data relating to the products and services of competitors.

Each of these elements has critical activities, processes and linkages which need to be managed to implement relationship-focused strategies. The chain helps identify those value-adding activities that can be carried out in different elements of the chain. Once identified, external and internal marketing plans need to be developed to ensure communication and delivery of the value proposition.

The management of internal and external markets has an impact on every part of the relationship chain. An understanding of the significance of each is a prerequisite to the successful implementation of any relationship marketing strategy. The external marketing issues are mostly directional in nature. In contrast, the internal marketing elements are facilitators, which, if managed correctly, create an environment conducive to cross-functional working and the effective delivery of customer satisfaction.

Managing external markets

The marketing planning process: This process aims to determine where the company is, where it wants to be and how it can get there. Traditionally marketing plans have taken narrow definitions of markets and opportunities. Relationship marketing takes a broader perspective and, therefore, in addition to marketing plans for existing and potential customers, a company needs also to consider developing plans for supplier markets, referral markets, influence markets, recruitment markets and internal markets.

Customer retention: Companies must invest in retaining customers. Established customers tend to buy more, are predictable and usually cost less to service than new customers. Also, they tend to be less price-sensitive and may provide free word-of-mouth advertising and referrals. Retaining customers also makes it difficult for competitors to enter a market or increase their share in that market.

Managing internal markets

Internal marketing planning: Planning for external markets is well-established and understood. Internal markets are not normally subject to the same sort of planning and scrutiny. The principles of planning remain the same. Critical to planning for internal markets is that everyone in the organization can seen the linkage between what they do and its impact on the eventual customer. The internal marketing plan is a means of bringing these issues to the fore and on focusing attention on improving performance of the internal customer chain.

Culture, climate and employee retention: Relationship marketing can only be successful if it is backed and driven by a truly customer-oriented corporate culture. In turn, the culture dictates the climate – the policies and practices characteristic of the organization.

Internal marketing remains complicated – and compromized – by the fact that it rarely exists as a formal activity. A Cranfield School of Management study found that internal marketing is:[6]

- generally not a discrete activity, but is implicit in quality initiatives, customer service programmes and broader business strategies;
- comprizes formal structured activities accompanied by a range of less formal ad hoc activities;
- a critical part of competitive differentiation;
- a key weapon in reducing conflict between different functions;
- evolutionary, involving the slow erosion of barriers;
- reliant on effective communication;
- an experimental process, leading employees to arrive at conclusions themselves;
- used to facilitate an innovative spirit;
- more successful when there is commitment at the highest organizational level;
- more likely to be successful as part of an approach that permeates an entire organization to become part of the overall philosophy rather than if it is overtly packaged.

The people factor

While the link between culture and high quality service is increasingly accepted, the connection between customer retention and employee retention is less obvious. The limitations of accounting systems mean that the costs of high employee turnover (such as increased costs of recruitment and training) are rarely monitored. Their effect on customer service is also often overlooked or simply not realized. Relationship marketing stands or falls on the quality and willingness of the people who implement it – this requires that organizations have a truly integrated approach to marketing and human resource management.

Traditional marketing thinking conspicuously fails to integrate employees into an organization's marketing strategy. An important aspect of seeing people as part of the marketing mix is to recognize the different roles which employees have in various marketing tasks and in direct contact with customers.

One academic has developed a scheme which provides categories based on involvement in marketing activities and customer contact. The categories are: *contactors* (who are heavily involved in conventional marketing activities and have frequent or periodic contact with customers); *modifiers* (such as receptionists who need to have a clear view of the company's marketing strategy if they are to convert into meeting customer needs); *influencers* (such as market researchers, who are key to implementing marketing strategies but often have little or no customer contact); and *isolateds* (people from support functions).[7]

While such categories are useful, the key realization must be that relationship marketing revolves around highly trained and motivated employees continuously providing high levels of customer satisfaction and retention.

Adrian Payne is Professor of Services Marketing and Director of the Centre for Services Management at Cranfield School of Management. He holds Masters degrees in Business Administration and Education and a Doctorate in Business Administration. He is author and co-author of a number of books including *The Essence of Services Marketing* (1993), and, with Martin Christopher and David Ballantyne, *Relationship Marketing* (1991).

Further Reading

Albrecht, K, and Bradford, LJ, *The Service Advantage*, Dow Jones-Irwin, Homewood, Illinois, 1990.

Christopher, M, *The Customer Service Planner*, Butterworth-Heinemann, Oxford, 1992.

Christopher, M, Payne, AFT, and Ballantyne, D, *Relationship Marketing*, Butterworth-Heinemann, Oxford, 1991.

Cowell, D, *The Marketing of Services*, Heinemann, London, 1984.

Payne, AFT, *The Essence of Services Marketing*, Prentice Hall, New Jersey 1993.

References

1 Davidow, W, *Marketing High Technology*, The Free Press, New York, 1986.
2 Reichheld, FF, 'Loyalty-based management', *Harvard Business Review*, March-April 1993.
3 *Business Week*, 4 April 1983.
4 Grönroos, C, 'Innovative marketing strategies and organizational structures for service firms' in *Emerging Perspectives on Services Marketing* (eds Berry, Shostack and Upah), Rand McNally, Chicago, 1983.
5 Smith, PC, Kendall, LM and Hulin, CL, *The Measurement of Satisfaction in Work and Retirement*, Rand McNally, Chicago, 1983.
6 Payne, AFT and Walters, D, 'Internal marketing: myth or magic', draft paper, Cranfield School of Management, 1990.
7 Judd, VC, 'Differentiate with the fifth P: people', *Industrial Marketing Management*, 16, 1987.

DATABASE MARKETING

Patrick Forsyth

The burgeoning development of information technology and the computer has propelled database marketing to the forefront of the marketing activities of many organizations. Yet, despite growing sophistication, database marketing is still sometimes regarded merely as enabling easier use of direct mail. If database marketing is to achieve its full potential within an organization, perception of its role must go far beyond this.

Database marketing is driven by the need to establish and develop strong long-term relationships with customers. Overlooking this fundamental objective provides a recipe for marketing disaster.

2

Database marketing refers to any interactive and individual marketing – specifically promotion and communication activity – based on the use of information from a central database direct to its focus. It is often characterized by a cycle of information – using information to direct an approach designed to prompt a response, which in turn provides new information which can be returned to update the original database. The approaches used can include any of the many communications methods within the promotion mix.

Simplistically, database marketing can be regarded as sending out mailshots to customers and prospects. Although direct mail is often involved, best practice in database marketing is highly, and increasingly, sophisticated. Database marketing stimululates on-going and persuasive contact with existing and potential customers. It aims to build, maintain and develop customer relationships; and in so doing it may use a full range of communications methods from telephone to newsletters, as well perhaps as direct mail. In addition, it may link to other personal contacts, such as internal sales support offices or field salesforces.

No marketing activity can work effectively in isolation. Database marketing is no exception and most often works in tandem with other marketing methods. Figure 1 shows, in graphic form, an example of the kind of communications flow it can be, and the cycle of activity and events involved.

In looking at Figure 1 one should imagine a range of mixes. Some organizations use a predominantly database-orientated approach; others use database marketing as part of a wider mix of methods. In order to produce the best results the mix must be tailored to the particular product or service and the market in which it is sold.

Another key ingredient, illustrated by Fig. 2, is the relationship between different methods of customer contact and the blend of control (in terms of the message) and personalization to which they lend themselves. One of the

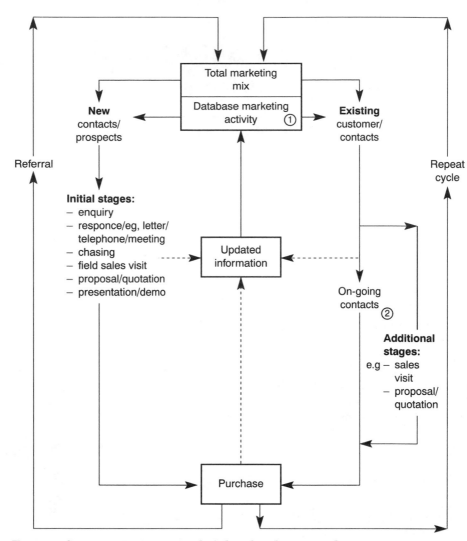

Fig. 1 Communications cycle: the database marketing activity (1) as part of initial process and (2) acting as 'flywheel' to maintain awareness and prompt ongoing response

central strengths of database marketing is that it allows a considerable degree of both control and personalization.

Perhaps the key to database marketing is in the development of relationships. Communication from banks, car makers, book clubs and many others share a common objective – all are attempting, with varying degrees of effectiveness, to create and maintain customer relationships and to make them profitable. There is nothing new in this. However, technological development has made the management of the database itself easier, less costly, and much

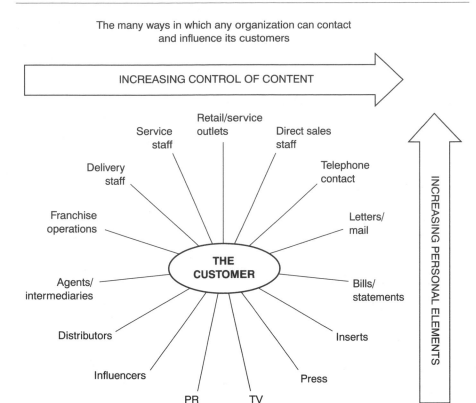

The many ways in which any organization can contact
and influence its customers

INCREASING CONTROL OF CONTENT

Service staff
Retail/service outlets
Direct sales staff
Delivery staff
Telephone contact
Franchise operations
Letters/ mail

THE CUSTOMER

Agents/ intermediaries
Bills/ statements
Distributors
Inserts
Influencers
Press
PR
TV

INCREASING PERSONAL ELEMENTS

Fig. 2 The customer contact spectrum

better able to prompt accurate, tailored approaches to different groups of customers rather than a mass approach. Database marketing combines some of the benefits of both the shotgun and the rifle. It makes possible approaches that are more likely to find favour in the marketplace, because it enables action to be taken which more customers feel is tailored to them as individuals.

The advantages of database marketing methods

The objectives of database marketing can be the same as any other method of promoting goods and services. They might include recruiting new customers; stimulating demand; increasing the frequency of purchase; or expanding the take-up of the product range.

While its objectives are commonplace, its measurable advantages are that it is:

Selective: perhaps this is the greatest advantage, it can focus communication on specific groups. Car distributers may send customers material directed at them as individuals not only as a purchaser of a car, but of a particular model now so many years old; they may even have variants of that approach for others who have the same type of car but have a different personal profile in terms of, say, age or home area.

Personal: this goes closely with the above – it allows individual approaches to be addressed by name rather than by generic terms.

Measurable: because responses are, for the most part, linked specifically to individual action, it becomes possible to measure the responses and, as a result, the financial return that comes from them.

Adaptable: both the format and scale of approach can be tested and adapted to maximize returns. A communication can, for example, be sent to customers in one area of the country (or purchasers of just one product or any other limited category) and results assessed before the approach is extended. Fine-tuning of exactly what is done is also made possible along the way, with the nature and form of what is done evolving in the light of experience. The approach is adaptable, too, in terms of timing, and can be controlled so as to allow communications to go at exactly the right moment to coincide with the likelihood of a positive response (using knowledge of when that moment is).

Such an individual approach coincides with what is happening in the market. In both industrial and consumer areas of marketing the costs of mass marketing approaches are rising, and niche marketing is focusing effort on smaller and smaller segments of groups of consumers, groups who value the individual approach, and are more likely to respond when treated as individuals. This aspect of database marketing makes it valuable in terms of competitiveness. There is a strong overlap with customer service. Dealing with customers in a way they find acceptable, better still in a way they like, and find more attractive than the way in which they are approached by others, builds loyalty and can increase sales at the expense of competitors. Database marketing offers an important means of differentiation.

All these factors make database marketing less a specialist technique than one available (and in many cases used) across a wide range of fields – commonly these include utilities, such as gas; telecommunications companies; banks, insurance companies and other financial services; charities; travel companies, such as airlines and hotels; retailers and mail order companies. Nor is database marketing the monopoly of larger organizations. For smaller organizations, database marketing can offer a cost-effective means of approaching and communicating with prospects and contacts. They do so by systematically communicating effectively with a smaller number of carefully selected people, rather than using a shotgun approach, possibly at greater cost and lesser return.

Dividing the market

Effective database marketing must clearly begin with the database. There is a dichotomy here. Groups which it is intended to approach need to be large, to produce economies of scale; and small, so that tailored approaches will appeal to individuals, and that communications to them are not seen as a standard approach. If database marketing is to work well in the market then the smaller groups should predominate, and the computer system should enable this to be dealt with on a manageable and cost-effective basis. The groups defined are only a form of market segmentation. This is a basic tenet of marketing, simplistically it states that there are rarely mass markets for anything. Markets are made up of segments. Groupings must be established that are right for the individual business. This can involve demographics, the age, sex and other characteristics of those involved, or the size and type of companies. But it can also relate to many other possibilities of categorization, for example:

- customers and non-customers;
- large and small customers;
- recent, less recent or dormant customers;
- those relating to particular sources (responders to advertising or direct mail, or those with whom the sales team have had direct contact, for instance);
- purchasers of specific products;
- those in particular geographic areas, nationally or internationally;
- buyer types (in industry ranging across directors, technical people or any particular level or job function or specialization that may be pertinent).

Groupings are not mutually exclusive; what may, in fact, be of most use are categories with quite complex definitions. For instance, a bookshop might keep a list of those who had purchased a business book in the last year and lived near enough to revisit the shop. Categories may have still greater complexity. Again with a computer system, summoning up the names of those meeting a number of specific criteria may take only a moment; though it is worth noting that the more cross referencing is involved the longer, and more costly, it is to keep records up-to-date.

Any database marketing system must include the ability to update accurately and promptly. Any failure in this area quickly means that the process becomes less cost-effective, as communications go to those who are in fact off-target, and can soon dilute customer goodwill. Spelling a customer's name incorrectly may be forgiven as an isolated error, provided it happens only once; contacting a retired octogenarian about hang gliding holidays three times in a week and addressing him 'Dear Madam', destroys credibility and makes it very unlikely that he will plan booking his next holiday with the perpetrator.

Developing contact strategies

Having established a database – something that may mean locating the names as well as entering them into the system or evolving less sophisticated customer and prospect records into a more usable form – then a strategy needs to be adopted for its use. The possibilities are considerable. For example:

- are all target groups equally good prospects?
- what frequency of contact is appropriate for each group?
- what needs to be said to them?
- what method of communication (it may well be a mix) is to be used?
- what co-ordination, for example with the salesforce, is necessary?

The use of the record must be actively planned. The longer term sequence of contacts and the mix of methods is very important, as is the continuity. Consider again the example of the car distributor. The distributor has a number of opportunities. They want customers to have their cars serviced and, if necessary, repaired there. They want customers to replace the car there, and maybe to buy others (as someone might for a spouse or within a company). They may also seek the sale of extras and hope to prompt recommendations to others who may become new customers.

This requires information which categorizes each buyer, entered at first contact. The distributor knows something about each customer, their organization and motoring needs. They can then plan the on-going communication accordingly. This should aim to create and build a relationship, and instil trust and loyalty. This is a typical part of a sequence of contact, valid in many businesses, and planned to move people 'up the ladder' and through the stages necessary to create sales and revenue: suspects to prospects, to first-time buyers, to repeat customers, to regular customers, to major customers (buying across the range); or to influence advocates – those who recommend or influence others to buy. It is said that the first prerequisite to repeat business is to be remembered. While this is clearly sensible, communications will quickly become repetitive if they only say: 'We're still here'. If the car distributor creates a sequence of helpful messages: reminders of the next necessary service, an invitation to the launch of a new model, a note about some topical issue such as new legislation about tyre wear; does the whole thing well, personalizes the approach, adds an occasional incentive and rings the changes in terms of contact method (eg, alternating telephone and post), then it becomes very difficult for the customer to take their car elsewhere.

None of this, however, happens in a vacuum. People receive communications about other cars, and though loyalty may well be as good as the quality of the last supplier contact, that quality is judged in the light of the impression created by others. Clearly this thread of communications also runs parallel with the actual process of doing business. If a car is not serviced well or the personal courtesies that are involved are neglected, then the overall effect is destroyed; or, at the very least, diluted.

It is the systematic and creative use of the database that makes it an effective and differentiating process. Information about the contacts is used to decide the precise nature of the activity that is then deployed to communicate with them. If the information is right – if it is helpful to customers and prospects in making decisions about what to do – if it is up-to-date and accurate and if the approaches are seen as personal, individual and pertinent, then they are likely to produce good results. That is not to say this is a panacea to sell anything.

The image, the product, the service – all the other factors inherent in marketing retain their importance. Any technique is only as effective as the quality of the way it is implemented. Here the efficiency of the way in which contact is initiated, and the subsequent way in which customer relationships are nurtured, have a direct relationship with the level of business produced.

In addition, other factors need attention, for instance:

- Outgoing activity should be suitably coded, and steps taken to encourage feedback and ensure information is sought to verify marketing method and update records.
- Such feedback can be summarized to produce overall information about trends, and provide assistance on a predictive basis as future activity is planned and, most important, the whole process can be linked back to such areas as marketing planning and product/service review and act as a catalyst for change.

This integration of database activity with overall marketing and its direction extends its significance. Database activity can be regarded only as a marketing method, something which is instrumental in prompting sales of whatever is coming through at the moment. But by enhancing customer relationships, promoting feedback and acting to put the organization closer to the customer, it has broader implications. The information base can in various ways act as a corporate resource – for example, contributing to the quality of business planning or product development. None of this is possible, however, without careful consideration of the systems aspects.

System considerations

Computers are something with which many in management have a love-hate relationship. It is now impossible to imagine life, business life in particular, without them.

Even so, anyone struggling to maintain effective customer contact using old style record cards may well find them inadequate to the demands of marketing in the nineties. A database in the sense in which it is dealt with here must aid *future* opportunities, not simply be a record of the past. It must match market needs and customer expectations, enabling a form of communication to be established which makes sense to the customer, and achieves the strike rate and returns demanded by marketing plans. This means it must be based on sound analysis of the market, the competition and customers; it must be accurate and up-to-date and the way it is stored must facilitate the way it needs to be used.

This may demand some internal reorganization, or at least some thinking that is not locked into old style departmental thinking. For example, in a hotel the front office and the meetings side of the business were traditionally separate entities, one seeking to fill bedrooms, the other meetings, conference and banqueting space. In seeking new prospects for the meetings business, accessing records of who stayed in the hotel (all of whom filled in a registration form which included such details as their organization and job title) helped locate new contacts – who of course already knew the hotel. Originally this could not be done – the two departments hardly spoke to each other – but one central database made the totality of the information available to the whole overall marketing effort; new prospects and business quickly resulted.

Of prime importance is the system on which the database is housed. Computer power is such that the hardware is less of a problem than it used to be (though sensible choices and possibly outside advice is necessary), but software certainly is. In this crucial area specialist advice needs to be sought.

Though the systems available change rapidly, there are three principle ways of progressing in this area:

- bolt a marketing module onto an existing accounting package;
- purchase a package, and fine-tune it to meet the specific needs involved;
- build a database from scratch.

The first approach is likely to have drawbacks in that the original system was designed for rather different purposes. It may well make it difficult to include contacts and/or prospects in the required way, in addition to the customers it is designed to deal with. The third is time-consuming, and often needs the kind of budget that makes even the more adventurous weak to think about it. The package route makes good sense for most. Here the trick is to locate a basic package which is close to your requirements so as to minimize any fine-tuning. Though some fine-tuning is likely to be necessary, the whole purpose of the database is that it relates to specific marketing objectives; it is no place for too much compromize.

Now, it is common for *standard* packages to be intended not as all things to all men, but to have a reasonably specific focus – for example, Pro-ACTION *professional* is designed for professional service firms, such as accountants. Such a choice is likely to have some of the fine-tuning that might be necessary with something more generic already built in.

It needs to be a selection you are sure of, and flexibility in dynamic times is a major consideration. Who can truly know everything they will demand of their system in the future?

The information necessity

Marketing is, of course, a process that must – above all – be customer-focused. The premise of database marketing is very simple. It recognizes that marketing must utilize information to do a proper job, and that the best results come not from seeing what information is available and using it in the best way possible, but from analysing what information is *necessary* to maximize the effectiveness of customer communication, assembling it and creating a system to make it conveniently usable. The right information, the right system, integrated into the total marketing process, and thus involving all the key members of the marketing team (all this has tentacles in many areas and cannot be organized as a backroom department), can create genuine differentiation in the market and repay the cost and effort of its inception.

Knowing your customers and staying in contact with them are basic tenets of marketing. Approaches based on database marketing, and those which initiate creative communications – providing real reasons to do business – can form a powerful element of many organizations' marketing activity. Like everything else, it needs careful application, and must be set up in such a way to allow cost-effective as well as persuasive contact to take place.

Marketing is a complex process. It is as much art as science, and its success is dependent as much on the orchestration of its many elements, so that they work well together, as it is on the quality of individual actions and methods. Database marketing is no different in this respect. It is not a magic formula, and success with it does not just happen. But with care it can be an important part of the mix, one that can pay dividends in what for most is an increasingly competitive market, and may cast at least a small spell that can improve sales and profitability for many organizations.

Patrick Forsyth is a consultant. He runs Touchstone Training and Consultancy which specializes in training in marketing, sales and communications skills, and works across a wide range of industries. He is the author of a number of books including *Marketing Professional Services*, *The Selling Edge*, *Agreed! – Making Management Communication Persuasive* and *First Things First*.

Further Reading

Forsyth, P, *Marketing for Non-Marketing Managers*, Pitman/Institute of Management, London, 1992.

COMPETITOR ANALYSIS AND BENCHMARKING

Tony Bendell and Roger Penson

Dismantling machines to discover how they work has been part of business practice for time immemorial. But it is only recently that organizations have attempted to correlate and measure other aspects of their performance in comparison with competitors or other organizations. Benchmarking, as the process has been labelled, involves seeking out, identifying and attempting to emulate and improve on best practice wherever it may be found.

In the late 1950s, Japanese industrialists visited many thousands of companies around the world, mainly in America and Western Europe, specifically to absorb ideas that they could adopt, adapt and improve upon throughout manufacturing processes. They investigated Western products and processes to understand their good and bad features, and then built superior alternatives at a lower cost. They also transferred good practices and technology used in one business area to a completely different one, driven by a commitment to company-wide continuous improvement.

The use of benchmarking by the Japanese was not a revolutionary step into the dark – though it may have appeared so at the time. Various commentators have pointed out that benchmarking is a natural evolution of concepts of competitor and market analysis, quality improvement programmes, performance measurements and, perhaps most of all, Japanese management practices. The origins of benchmarking go much further back to the primitive taking apart of competing products to see how they could be copied or made more efficiently.

The modern Western conception and practice of benchmarking can be traced to 1979 when the Xerox Corporation in America, motivated by a rapidly diminishing market share, instigated an approach to benchmarking every bit as vigorous as that of the Japanese. Xerox felt it had no choice. Its competitors were able to sell products more cheaply than Xerox could make them. To understand why this was, the product features and performance capabilities of competitive machines were rigorously evaluated and Xerox was able to investigate the practices of Fuji Xerox in Japan. The improvement opportunities that were identified and put into place resulted in a swift turnaround for Xerox's fortunes and led to best practice benchmarking becoming a central part of its business strategy. Today, Xerox and Rank Xerox in Europe are generally recognized as the leaders in the benchmarking field in the Western hemisphere.

The lead given by Xerox established the technique in America and it has become a qualifying condition for companies aiming for the prestigious

Malcolm Baldrige Award for Quality. More recently, it has become a criterion in the European and UK Quality Awards.

Such awards attract attention to a growing fact of corporate life: the pressures of global competition mean companies are realizing that they must match, or exceed, best practices from competitors anywhere in the world in order to survive. Further, with the increasing realization that small continuous improvements are insufficient to narrow the major gap behind global competitors, companies are increasingly looking for major breakthroughs – which typically can only be achieved by studying the approaches of others.

To a large degree benchmarking is a natural development from Total Quality Management (TQM). Despite their mixed results, TQM programmes have helped managers to focus on what they are doing badly and how they can do it better. They set themselves targets for continuous incremental improvement. However, unless they raise their eyes from the job in hand to look at what others are achieving and how they are achieving it, they may never realize that it is their business processes themselves, and not just their marginal inefficiencies, which are holding them back. The only way that managers can drive their organizations to excellence is to ensure that they keep their eyes on their competitors and world's best practice in all aspects of the business. They must benchmark performance and internal processes by external comparisons against those better than them in order to improve.

Recent research suggests that the practice of benchmarking is now spreading and is entrenched in many organizations. A survey conducted in late 1991 among small, medium and very large US firms revealed that, compared with one year previously, more than 75 per cent of the survey sampled believed that the amount of benchmarking in their firms had increased. During the next five years, 96 per cent of these organizations expect still more benchmarking. It is interesting that the same survey revealed that 79 per cent of respondents felt that companies will have to practise benchmarking to survive, but that 95 per cent felt that most companies still do not know how to benchmark. Only 28 per cent thought it was a management fad.

Further results indicated that leading companies from most industries are benchmarking and that benchmarking is not limited to any one type of industry. The majority of firms also considered themselves to be novice users of the benchmarking process. Perhaps most interestingly, nearly half of the companies had been conducting benchmarking studies for less than two years, while only 20 per cent had been benchmarking for more than five.

Growing interest in benchmarking has led to an ever-increasing level of requests from companies for co-operation and benchmarking partnerships with others. Interestingly, the survey revealed that, despite this, 82 per cent of the companies sampled still did not have a formal process for responding to such requests.

But, a survey of the top UK 1,000 companies by the Confederation of British Industry (CBI) and Coopers & Lybrand revealed that more than two-thirds of the 105 respondents from the manufacturing, service and other sectors claimed to be benchmarking, with 82 per cent regarding it as successful. Sixty-eight per cent intended to increase investment in benchmarking in the next five years.

Such research is also backed by a number of impressive cases of benchmarking in practice. Car maker, Rover, for example, halved its test times after benchmarking against Honda. Lucas Industries cut the number of shopfloor grades four-fold after benchmarking against a German plant. British Rail reduced the time to clean a train to eight minutes after benchmarking against British Airways.

The meaning of benchmarking

Though increasing in popularity and usage, the term benchmarking remains ambiguous, woolly and mysterious. It appears to require great subtlety of understanding and clearly means different things to different people. Company practices vary dramatically in terms of their implementation, or tentative enquiries, in relation to benchmarking. Some companies look for consortia of partners to, in some sense, get together and exchange information. Others look for rather broad, perhaps superficial, visits to world-leading or comparable companies to get a *feel* for the way of doing things. Others employ consultants, who interpret benchmarking as the collection and comparison of global, primarily financial, measures of company performance. This is often with similar companies in the same industry worldwide, or perhaps, those in comparable circumstances.

Not surprisingly, the lack of clarity about the meaning of benchmarking has provided an opportunity for consultants. However, a consultant's report which shows poor financial performance, customer satisfaction or other high-level attributes, in comparison to the performance of competitors, does not in itself assist the organization to improve fundamentally. At this global, somewhat nebulous level, many of the problems of organizations are well known to the people managing them. These measures are fundamentally of *output performance*. They show how much or how little is being achieved by the organization in comparison to competitors and to world's best practice. They do *not* show the weaknesses in the internal business processes or the strengths. They do *not* show how the competitors and world leaders are achieving their levels of performance. They do *not* show what, if anything, is transferable to the organization's particular circumstance and how to make the transfer. They do *not* in isolation, provide the degree of certainty that management needs in order to make the change necessary in its behaviour or style. They do *not* provide the understanding of the *why* – this can only be achieved through a process of personal discovery.

Benchmarking on global measures by external consultants does not, and cannot, provide the fundamental insight and change of practice that is necessary to transform the organization from a potential world loser to a world winner. Nor can naïve, unstructured, unplanned, uninformed and often iso-lated attempts at benchmarking by individuals within an organization which is not committed to and has not planned what it wants to do with benchmark-ing. The attractive visit to another company, particularly somewhere exotic, may be a perk of the job, but such visits are more likely to lead to a petering out of the interest in benchmarking, or even bring it into disrepute, when they fail to deliver anything substantial.

The real role of benchmarking has to be seen in the context of the organiza-tion that is continuously looking at itself, analysing its performance and internal processes, and continuously implementing improvement.

Modern management jargon might call this a proactive organization, or a Total Quality Management one; the jargon is not important. Such an organi-zation is looking continuously to improve and is planning improvement. In doing this, it will set itself targets and, for most organizations early in the improvement process, it is most likely that these targets will be improvements relative to its current performance. Often, a crucial first step is to identify both what are the key measures of current performance and actually how good they currently are. Once this is done, targets are established for improvement against time and an action plan put in place to achieve this.

There is still, however, one thing missing. If the improvement targets are established in isolation of any knowledge of what others are doing and of what others are achieving, the targets may not be taxing enough to help a company or other organization stay in business.

This view of benchmarking, then, is not just about the comparison of mea-sures, as it has often been mistaken to be. It is, instead, a natural development of the desire to improve and the process of improvement. As well as looking internally, one looks for ideas to borrow, adapt or adopt from those that are doing better, even perhaps in one very specific aspect. In this sense, it is very much an integral part of the improvement process. Nor does benchmarking stop when comparisons have been made and you have been found to be doing well or have been found wanting. This is the first step; *how* and *why* need to be established, and methods of achievement evaluated for potential transfer, improvement upon and implementation. *Implementation is part of the process.*

This concept of benchmarking, like modern approaches to TQM, has as one of its central ingredients, the concept of the *internal business process.* The crucial internal processes of the business need to be identified, and measures and mea-surement points established. Comparisons in processes, and process performance have to be made externally, as well as internally, and process improvement or redesign need to be put in place. Instead of global benchmarking measures, loved by some consultants, *process benchmarking* becomes the key to improvement.

The need for change

Commitment from the top is absolutely essential if the approach is to be suc-cessful and improvements are to follow from the comparative measurement exercise of benchmarking. Times vary greatly, but generally the initial reach activity may take between six and eighteen months to complete. This can require a large amount of resources. Then comes the hard part – making the improvements. Benchmarking is no quick fix with instant payback. Unless senior management show patience and take leadership for the change process, the whole activity is likely to become another short-lived initiative – resulting in frustration and apathy.

There must be a belief in the need for change. This belief is likely to be reinforced when comparisons with market leaders are made, but it is management's responsibility to generate enthusiasm for improvements and to overcome resistance to change throughout the organization. Benchmarking is a tool to help the change process and not the preserve of a few elite specialists. The people who will be asked to make changes following the benchmarking exercise must be involved with the process from the beginning. Their input will help to prevent needless mistakes being made during the study and they will recognize the need for improvement when the comparisons are made.

If their first introduction to the benchmarking exercise comes from analysis and consists of 'Company X can produce twice as much as you can in half the time', without any reference to how, then the reaction is likely to be somewhat different. Not everyone can be part of the investigation team, but it is important to keep people informed of the progress being made by communicating as much information as possible to those who will be involved at the implementation stage.

Benchmarking is a tool for people who are serious about making improvements. Training is necessary, both at the awareness level and for practical application. The benchmarking process needs to be planned, steered, monitored and reviewed if maximum benefits are to accrue. If these activities are absent the exercise is likely to produce statistics rather than action. In addition, trying to do too much too quickly will result in information overload and confused priorities; to allow people to become familiar with the methodology, two or three key areas for investigation are quite sufficient initially. Senior management support and recognition will then act as a spur for further activity.

What is to be benchmarked?

Benchmarking is not about making visits to other companies to vaguely attempt to 'pick up one or two ideas that may be useful somewhere'. It is not industrial tourism. Instead, it is centred around planned research which has been focused by an organization's recognition that it needs to make improvements in critical business areas.

Improvement, generally, is initiated by asking the following questions:

- *Where do we want to be?*
- *Where are we now?*
- *What do we need to do to get from here to there?*

Any activity that can be measured can be benchmarked, but most companies will start with those areas where they know they need to be competitive to remain in business. The company should have a clear mission statement or list of business goals which is used to focus improvement activity. Customer satisfaction is high on most company priority lists, as is the need for a low-cost operation. Deciding these broad areas partly answers the question 'Where do we want to be?' However, these need to be broken down into more specific activities that can be measured. What are the processes that deliver customer satisfaction or processes that eat up the costs? The more precisely you define what you need to measure, the more useful will be the information that you gather to compare it with.

What things are important to customers? What will help them to be successful? How good is the service currently given? What factors cause customer dissatisfaction? An analysis of customer complaints and warranty claims can give some guidance here and, of course, the customer can be asked directly. Questionnaires can be sent out and review workshops can be organized. 'Reliability' is a major requirement of most customers, but what does it mean and how is it measured? The answer may be on-time delivery, performance or levels of defect-free product. What key measures are already in place to monitor both current performance and the hoped-for improvement? What is your current performance in these areas and what is your current practice for achieving these performances?

Common areas for benchmarking are stock levels, work-in-progress, waste and reject levels. Again, the cost for each of these areas must be known, but also it is essential to understand the processes and practices that lead to these costs being incurred. A thorough analysis of what actually happens is necessary, rather than blind acceptance of a theoretical process model.

The benchmarking organization needs to understand how and why the organizations it has benchmarked have achieved their superiority. This goes beyond the levels of attainment that they have achieved. Comparing numbers will not help organizations compete – it is necessary to compare the practices that have given rise to the numbers.

Emphasis has been placed on this initial step because in the experience of leading benchmarking organizations like Xerox, it is here that most companies get it wrong. Until organizations understand their processes fully, and how these processes deliver the current performance in key areas, it is meaningless to make comparisons with other organizations.

When the process is understood, and the critical activities are known and measured, the 'Where are we now?' question has been answered. It should be clear where improvements could be made by investigating best practice elsewhere. It is essential to make sure that the subjects chosen for benchmarking are based on current market demands and not just on areas that the company considers to be important. In the production of electronic components, for example, a defect-free supply is almost taken for granted; the primary requirements may now be for service differentiation and time to market.

Who to benchmark against?

Deciding on who to benchmark against depends on the subject chosen for benchmarking, the resources that can be made available and the challenge that an organization is prepared to undertake. In general, there are often seen to be four different types of benchmarking. Each approach has its own advantages and disadvantages.

Internal benchmarking involves making comparisons with other parts of the same organization. It can be with other departments, other sites, other companies within the same group, either in the same country or abroad. This type of benchmarking is usually straightforward to arrange and fairly common. It is relatively easy to obtain all of the information necessary for a good comparison to be made. If the operations are similar across the different sites, the data will instantly be relevant and usable, but it is unlikely to yield improvements which meet world best practice.

Competitor benchmarking is much more difficult. Any information obtained is likely to be very relevant but, for reasons of confidentiality, it will be almost impossible to get a full picture of how a direct competitor operates. Looking at outputs and available figures can give some information, but they can also mislead if the processes that deliver the outputs cannot be determined. Some larger organizations, however, do exchange information in selected areas in the interest of jointly coming to terms with best practice.

Functional benchmarking typically involves making comparisons with non-competitive organizations which carry out the same functional activity that you are interested in. Examples are warehousing, procurement, catering, etc, that apply to most businesses and other organizations. BA benchmarked with the Oriental Hotel, Bangkok, in an effort to improve the service on its frequent flier programme. The hotel, BA recognized, was expert at looking after its guests and BA hoped to learn how it recorded and utilized details of customers' preferences. This type of benchmarking has several advantages: functional leaders are easy to identify in many areas; confidentiality is not usually an issue; approaches which may be novel for your industry can be discovered; and two-way partnerships can be developed. Weighing against these are likely to be problems in adopting and adapting their practices for your operation.

Generic benchmarking goes a step further and may compare business processes which cut across various functions and in quite different industries. Opportunities discovered by this process are likely to be the most innovative and to create breakthroughs for unprecedented improvement. However, the integration of novel concepts into a different industry is also likely to be the most challenging.

638

The type of benchmarking and organizations chosen to benchmark against depends on many factors. If an organization is large and generally looked on as being a market leader, then the requirement is obviously different from that demanded by a smaller company with perhaps less experience of making quality improvements. The former will have a real need to search out best practices, whereas the latter will probably find it easy to identify improvement opportunities by observing the practices of many successful companies.

Similarly, the level of resource that can be, and needs to be, committed in each case will be different. It makes sense to limit initial visits to local companies if possible; not only will the time and cost be less, but also problems associated with language and cultural differences will be avoided. Obviously, where the opportunity presents itself, internal benchmarking is the ideal place to start. Kodak does this between its various sites, as does Philips. The whole process is relatively easy to manage and helps to build experience in the benchmarking technique.

For other types of benchmarking, there are various sources of information which can aid in the identification of organizations to compare against. A simple starting point is the knowledge already within the company; in the marketing function, for example. Customers, suppliers and other contacts within the same industry can usually contribute good ideas. Consultants, academics and other industry observers can be asked who they think are the leaders in any particular area. Trade journals, magazines, books and other library material are useful, and ideas can also be picked up at conferences, workshops and seminars.

Of course, no research can guarantee that the company selected for benchmarking really represents best practice. (Though organizations have to remember that benchmarking against average performers simply produces more mediocrity.) If research indicates that a particular organization is the best you have yet come across, and their performance is better than yours, then proceed to the next step. Perhaps somewhere there is someone a little better; you may discover them at a later date. It is important to halt the research, temporarily at least, and to start making improvements.

Some companies have side-stepped the issue of who to benchmark against by opting to use as a benchmark the idealized requirements of the Malcolm Baldrige Quality Award. In Japan, companies have prepared themselves for the Deming Award in a similar way, even though the requirements are less clearly defined and structured. The new European Quality Award and UK Quality Award go beyond Malcolm Baldrige in some areas and obviously, too, present an opportunity for making comparisons.

Collecting the benchmarking data

Although the most valuable information will be obtained by the direct exchange of data with other companies, much useful material can be gleaned from indirect sources. The sources mentioned in the previous section can be utilized, supplemented by information from annual reports, public databases, research institutes, government agencies, etc. However, one must beware, since some of the data obtained by these means will be out of date or may be erroneous for other reasons.

Before descending upon other organizations, it is vital to carry out as much desk research as possible in order to optimize the value of any visits. To supplement other sources, questionnaires can be prepared and sent to potential benchmark organizations, for completion and return before the visit. Also, internal discussions should be held before the visits to establish the extent of current knowledge and to focus the requirements of the investigation so that a comprehensive checklist can be prepared.

Many companies which are not direct competitors are willing to allow access and to share information, especially if it will be kept confidential. There will often be a need to sign a non-disclosure agreement. Personal contacts and a professional approach play a major part in opening doors, though there is usually a need to convince target organizations that mutual benefit will accrue. Potential benchmarkers should be well briefed and be given sufficient authority to trade sensitive information. Often, a partnership for the exchange of data develops, with reciprocal visits and regular meetings to compare notes.

Independent bodies can be used to gather data from competitive companies, but here it is often only the numbers that can be obtained and not the processes that deliver the numbers.

Analysing data and implementing improvement

The data from benchmarking exercises will obviously differ depending on the activity that has been investigated. However, it should be made up of two elements: what is achieved in terms of numbers (the performance metrics) and how and why it is achieved (the practice). Neither of these is of much use without the other. These two sets of data need to be considered and compared to your current performance in the same area. A further consideration may well be the difficulty of transferring a process that works well in one endeavour into a completely different industry.

The questions are:

- *How big is the gap between your performance and theirs?*
- *How much of their experience is applicable to your situation?*

If the data collected during the study is directly comparable, the performance gap is instantly meaningful. Even if your performance is superior there may be things to learn from what others do. The main lessons, though, come from studies which show that your performance is inferior. The question 'Where do we want to be?' can now be answered in detail, with quantified goals based on a knowledge of what the leaders are achieving and how. If the processes, products, company size or business areas are not very similar, then the interpretation of the data will be more difficult and the performance gap may not be as meaningful.

It may also be more difficult to answer 'How do we get from here to there?' What can be done to close the gap? How can the positions be reversed, bearing in mind that your competitors are also making improvements and trying to widen the gap? How far will you go to adopt and adapt new practices? What is involved, how much will it cost and how long will it take? What are the broader implications for the organization? These are issues that need to be tackled on a team basis, involving those who can really understand the current practices, those with responsibility for steering the future of the company and those with the authority to make the changes.

Once the decision is made to proceed, implementation of the changes must be planned and steered. New targets for the critical activity can be set based on the benchmark data, and good leadership will be essential to maintain focus and prevent backsliding. Progress towards the new objectives will need to be reviewed regularly and senior management have a key role to play in overseeing and providing support for the whole implementation process.

Managed in this way benchmarking is worthwhile. It can transform a traditionally managed company into a proactive one, constantly looking at the competition and world's best practice for new ideas. Consultants can help, but benchmarking should be done by an organization for the organization. The responsibility to achieve this rests with management.

Tony Bendell is East Midlands Electricity Professor of Quality Management and director of the Quality Unit at the Nottingham Trent University. He is also principal author of *Benchmarking for Competitive Advantage* (1993) and *Implementing Quality in the Public Sector* (1994).

Roger Penson is senior consultant with Services Limited.

Further Reading

Bendell, T, Boulter, L, and Kelly, J, *Benchmarking for Competitive Advantage*, FT/Pitman, London, 1993.

Utilizing Technology

'You must accept the fact that if the computer is a tool, it is the job of the tool-user to know what to use it for. So the first thing practically everyone must learn is to take information responsibly.

This means asking what information do I need to do my job, from whom, in what form, and when. And you're going to have to ask what information do I owe, to whom, in what form and when – not only so that others can do their jobs, but so that they can enable me to do my job. Unfortunately, most of us still expect the chief information officer or some other technologist to do that. It won't do.' *Peter Drucker[1]*

---

[1] Drucker, PF, 'Introduction' to *Techno Vision*, Wang, CB, McGraw Hill, New York, 1994.

OVERVIEW

Chris Yapp

In the first fifty years of the computer industry's existence, the worldwide market has grown from zero to around US$900 billion per annum. It has created some giant corporations, such as IBM, and new kinds of organizations, such as Microsoft. Since the emergence of the personal computer, from Apple and IBM in the late 1970s and early 1980s, there has been widespread adoption of computing within the workplace and, increasingly, in the home and in education. Tens of millions of people are employed by the industry worldwide with hundreds of millions of users.

Investment in information technology (IT) has reached huge proportions. In the US during the 1980s, $1 trillion was invested in IT. Capital expenditure in IT has been compounding at around 20 per cent annually over the last ten years and now accounts for some 70 per cent of all capital investment.

The logic behind such investments is clear. From a business perspective, it appears obvious that IT is a resource with which to achieve business results.

Yet, the numerous studies into the deployment of IT show that it often conspicuously fails to add value to organizational performance. At a macro level, productivity growth in the leading Western economies falls far below the average of three per cent sustained over the last 100 years. And, in addition, research at MIT and other institutions supports the fact that companies investing in IT in the 1980s show little in the way of productivity gains. General Electric vice president Gary Reiner has observed: 'We have found that in many cases technology impedes productivity.'[1] This is a startling observation. Technology is *supposed* to make our lives easier and organizations more productive. If it is failing to do so we must begin to question either the nature of the technology or the way in which we put it to use.

Senior managers now commonly complain that the cost of IT continues to rise without significantly contributing to the bottom-line. Academic surveys confirm this, and various studies suggest that the contribution of IT to organizational productivity is nil or negative.

Even studies of professional IT managers show similar concerns. A recent study of IT managers in the finance sector indicated that they believed that 50 per cent of their projects failed. Spectacular failures, such as that with TAURUS, the ill-fated UK stock exchange system, where the total write-offs may be as large as £300 million, only serve to suggest that IT is a resource that is not well managed, or maybe even understood.

A second area of concern lies with the speed of change in the technologies. Since 1960 the IT industry has delivered a 25-30 per cent improvement in price-performance year-on-year, with many forecasters seeing nothing to stop this for the foreseeable future. Each fresh wave of technology has spawned new companies and competitors. Very frequently, the established suppliers in the market have been wrong footed by smaller, more dynamic organizations which apparently appear from nowhere. Seemingly invincible competitors over many years, such as IBM and Digital, drop from enviable profits and reputation into drastic losses with remarkable speed. Similarly, Wang grew explosively through the 1970s and early 1980s only to collapse in the late eighties. It is now a fraction of its former size and glory. The speed of change of the technologies is matched by rapid change in the fortunes of suppliers.

However, for the user community, while the technologies may change rapidly, the business systems that they support often have much longer lives, frequently running into decades. Managing the risk associated with technology change lies at the heart of many of the problems reported by organizations.

A third area of concern lies with the *IT culture*. While many business men and women are quite happy to argue with specialists in such areas as finance, marketing or human resources even from a limited knowledge of these disciplines, the complex jargon and impenetrable concepts of the technologists leave many cold. Managers remain unsure of the meaning and implications of ideas such as ROCE, pay for performance and object orientation.

Turn to the technology specialists and the culture divide becomes clear. 'We ask the users what they want but they never seem to know,' the specialists lament. Since the advent of the personal computer another complaint is widespread: 'Just because they know how to use a spreadsheet they think they understand IT'. A number of surveys have highlighted the social characteristics of the successful IT professional. They are logical, pay attention to detail and tend to be introverted. This is a stereotypical, but often accurate, perception.

In summary, the IT industry has grown rapidly over fifty years but stands accused on three broad fronts. First, the returns from the trillions of dollars of investment world-wide are hard to find. Second, it changes so fast that it is difficult to make sensible choices and, finally, the culture gap between the IT professional and the professional manager is unbridgeable.

What is a computer?

As the basic technology of the IT industry, it may seem overly simplistic to question what constitutes a computer. In the days when there were only mainframe computers, they were easily identifiable by their size and the environments in which they were housed. Indeed the personal computer is readily identifiable. However, in the late 1960s a study of future computing trends made a pretty good effort at identifying the principle trends of the industry. One area that it overlooked, however, was that of *embedded* systems.

Today, there are many devices that contain embedded within them microprocessors, the core technology of computers to provide various control and computing functions. Cars, cameras, lifts, vacuum cleaners and washing machines are all available which contain 'computer' elements.

In practice, it is less useful to ask what a computer *is* than to ask what a computer *does*. Essentially, a computer takes input and produces output, the conversion being achieved by programs which access stored information or data. Data can both be retrieved or stored by programs. Computers can also communicate to other computers over telephone and data networks. This is all very basic. But, when you look at the operation of a modern petrol pump, the problem becomes a little more obvious. First, when the pump handle is lifted from its housing, a message is sent to a device at the garage paying point. Also, a program is triggered which determines the price of the petrol grade selected. As the petrol is poured, dials show the quantity and cost of the fuel delivered. When complete, the handle is returned and a message is sent to the paying point. The driver may choose to present a credit card which is 'swiped' by a card reader. The card details, along with the cost of the fuel, are transmitted to a computer programmed to check the availability of credit on the particular card. This is the use of data, processed into output using stored data and communicated to another computer. So, is a petrol pump a computer? This difficulty in defining the boundaries of the computer industry is one that will become increasingly blurred over the coming decade.

The critical feature of modern computing is *digitization*. That is to say that information is represented by digits, strings of binary 0's and 1's. Over the years of the computer industry, the types of data that could be represented in this format has been increasingly extending. Today, text, graphics, images, video, sound and animation can all be digitized. Once digitized the information can be manipulated by digital processing. We are all familiar with compact disc technology, the digital representation of sound. Over the next few years we will see the development of digital television for the home. Once digitized the various data types can be stored and processed together, creating the multimedia technologies which now receive so much press coverage. With this generation of technology emerging rapidly in the marketplace it is likely that the majority of computer power will not be in devices that we would generally consider to be called computers.

Another important feature of computing is *architecture*. Computer architecture is a term used at a number of levels within the industry. Hardware, software and systems are all described in terms of architectures. Phrases like 'IBM architecture' or 'open-systems architecture' all reflect the importance of this term to computers and computing. Architecture is, in essence, the imposition of design constraints on system specification. The constraints on computer design in the past are slowly being lifted by new technology developments. Consider the hardware. The processors of modern computers can execute millions of instructions. Millions of characters can be stored on disks. Until the early 1980s however, computers could only speak to other computers at limited speeds, in the low thousands of characters per second. The advent of Local Area Networks (LANS) made it possible for computers to interact at speeds of millions of characters per second for the first time. However, for long distances the speed rapidly fell back to the low thousands. A series of new technologies, called the Integrated Services Digital Network (ISDN), is emerging. Broadband ISDN offers potential for multimillion characters per second networking.

Until now the limit on communication speed has meant that the disks, the processors and other parts of a computer had to be located slowly if overall performance was to be acceptable. Freed from this constraint new computer architectures are emerging where different functions can be distributed over different components networked together. We are moving from an era of computers to an era of networked computing infrastructures. This all-pervasive IT infrastructure is the vision behind the widely publicised information superhighways. The IT industry favours an architecture known as client-server for the provision of this computing infrastructure.

This leads to an issue of *integration*. With rapid changes of technology and comparative longevity of business systems, protection of investment is a major issue. 'Legacy' systems is a significant topic for most major users of technology. Increasing flexibility of software development is opening up better and cheaper means for integrating new and old systems at the hardware and software levels. However, there remain some significant hurdles.

So far, we have concentrated on the technology part of information technology. It is true to say that much of the computer industry has been similarly preoccupied. For the users however, technology is the cost; the value comes from information. Increasingly as the technology grows in power and becomes all-pervasive it will diminish in importance for most users.

The value of information and software

While the hardware aspects of computing can be seen and touched, moving to the information and software aspects presents some different challenges.

In the early days of computing, many computer systems were created for a single purpose such as payroll, accounts or stock-keeping. The processes and the information which were being handled were reasonably well understood and discrete.

However, this situation has changed dramatically. The early applications of computers required large suites of software, which have proven to be expensive to maintain. It is not unusual for 80 per cent or more of an organization's IT budget to be taken up with the maintenance of legacy systems. The software industry is addressing this through new techniques for developing software known as Object Orientated (OO) analysis and design. Put simply, the idea behind OO is to break up software into small chunks or objects which can be reused and modified more easily than previous software. There are some significant issues already identified in reskilling the workforce to the new methods, but these should ease in time. The potential for rapid prototyping and cheaper and higher quality maintenance of software is demonstrable in some early pioneers but is at the time of writing far from widespread.

So, if we can largely ignore hardware, and software is better and cheaper, what is the problem?

Asked to write down three keys words about his or her organization a manager is likely to use words such as customers, markets or products and services. In the public sector a manager might identify the number of patients, scholars or recipients of service as vital factors.

The trouble comes when you walk round the organization and ask staff how many customers, products and markets the organization works in and with. The variation in answers can be amazing. One manufacturing company board gave a range of 1 to 570 for the number of products. One local authority gave a range of 50,000 to 250,000 customers. A finance company gave a range of 4 to 70 for the number of markets. Does this matter? In the days of single application machines it tended not to matter in that for a particular application the definition of a product or customer could be controlled.

Now, however, computers are frequently integrated across internal organizational boundaries and functions. As a result, the problem can easily get out of hand. When computing extends beyond the boundaries of firms to electronic trading, for instance, the problem can be both complex and expensive.

Consider a branch of a bank. The approach adopted in early automation was to computerize by type of account, so that each branch knew how many deposit accounts and savings accounts there were. The emphasis on accounts meant that banks frequently lost sight of the customer. At a recent conference one UK bank director claimed that there was more information in a branch prior to computerization than there is now. How has this come about?

Increasingly businesses are attempting to bring information together in a 'customer centred' way. But what is a 'customer'? Is it someone who has ever bought your product? Or, is it restricted to customers during the last year? Or, does it include all potential customers? The meaning of each term may vary in context.

The design of databases to cope with multiple uses is often seen as a technical exercise, but there are human issues to be dealt with as much as technical issues. Organizations have to establish whose definition or definitions need to be captured and what data is needed on a 'customer' for all the reasonable interpretations it may wish to handle.

This is not an academic exercise. When a manufacturing company attempted to integrate the computers which supported the order fulfilment cycle, the different meaning of data on the various systems made the integration prohibitively expensive.

Turning back to the hardware there is the basis of a solution. One factor that has driven the IT industry, probably more so than any other industry, is standardization. In the early days of computing, each manufacturer built its own computers and these were incompatible with those from other suppliers. This proprietary era meant that each computer acquisition by a company was a strategic decision. It meant more than buying a product, the decision was about buying in to the product direction of the supplier.

In the late 1950s the emergence of COBOL then FORTRAN led to the first standardized languages. This created the benefit of programmer portability. Programmers could move between different manufacturers' equipment taking their skills with them. Since those early days, nearly every part of the IT jigsaw has seen major efforts at standardization. In operating systems, the software that drives the computer itself, UNIX has emerged as a standard. Similarly SQL has emerged as a standard language for information update and retrieval. In networking, X25, ISDN and CSMA/CD are examples of industry standards. In addition to the standardization work of the various international standards bodies, there are numerous examples of *de facto* standards. The most prominent is Microsoft Windows which has emerged as the most popular user interface on today's PCs.

Standardization is important for the computer industry because it has enabled the rapid development of technologies and created open markets without the problems of proprietary lock-in. This is not without its negative repercussions. In the early days a user company could expect support for all its computing from a single supplier. With the increasingly complex usage of computers in organizations and with multiple suppliers, many organizations have found that price reductions brought about by competition can be largely lost in increased support costs. This has led to many organizations seeking 'prime contractors' or 'systems integrators' to manage this complexity. Others have opted to outsource IT expertise from facilities management companies.

While the IT industry has learned the processes for standardization of hardware and software, standardization of information is less well developed. There are good examples of standards for information exchange. These have helped the car and retail industries move to electronic trading. Standardization of technology has largely been supply-side dominated, where there is a greater need for user involvement in data standards. Whether users understand or value this role is open to debate.

When the IT industry is not busy inventing new hardware and software there is a third leg which receives less coverage than it deserves, that is *methodologies*. Methodologies vary in their aims and scopes. There are design methodologies, project management methodologies and business-IT linking methodologies, for instance. Many of the IT disaster stories reported in the press are more likely to be failures to apply methods, inappropriate methods or unskilled management than IT-based failures.

Business-driven IT

As the scale of spending on IT grew, notably in the 1980s, there was an increasing search for competitive advantage from IT and the emergence of methodologies aimed at improving the linkage of business and IT. A wide variety of industry gurus have offered suggestions and highlighted issues in this area. There are a number of key principles that seem to be widely-held beliefs.

First, there is no link between IT expenditure and business results. Some organizations spend little on IT and get good returns. Others spend a lot and have little to show. Broadly, the implementation of technology falls into two camps. On the one hand there is a reactive strategy. In this the business strategy is predetermined and IT is deployed where justified on efficiency grounds. Organizations that see IT in these terms try to use IT to do things better. IT is seen as an enabler.

On the other hand there is a more proactive strategy. In this, IT capability is considered as an input to business strategy. The organization seeks to find out how it could achieve its results given the potential of technology. IT is seen as a creator of opportunities and is about doing things differently. There is much to support the notion that the latter approach is a higher-risk higher-reward strategy. Many of the successful examples of *business re-engineering* reflect the latter approach rather than the former.

Second, the benefits of IT investment come from organizational improvement. Throwing IT at an ill-defined business problem creates more problems than it solves. It is important to improve the organization first before applying technology. The difficulty arises where existing practice is automated. It may be that both bad and good practices are automated, producing solutions that may be faster but also flawed. Organizational improvement includes such issues as streamlining processes, reducing overheads and reskilling staff for the new technologies. Re-engineering has increased management attention on process thinking and understanding. This is not new, but rather an extension of trends seen in initiatives such as Total Quality Management and Activity-based Management. New software technologies known as groupware and workflow are enabling the design of organization-wide process management rather than the task-by-task automation of past practice.

Third, IT is about *change management*. If IT doesn't change something, why use it? IT has some profound impacts on organizations and people – though the latter are often ignored. It is here that the real difference exists between organizations which harness technology for business performance and those which feel mastered by the technology.

IT, organizations and people

Why is it that IT has such an impact on organizational performance for good or ill? Basically, organizational design is about two things. First, you divide up the organization into the tasks that need to be accomplished. Second, the tasks are integrated with co-ordination mechanisms provided. Historically most technologies have been either about the production side of organization or about co-ordination. For instance, the typewriter enabled the production of letters and memos. The telegraph enabled co-ordination within and between organizations to be extended geographically. The richness of modern IT provides both production and co-ordination possibilities.

For example, computer-aided design and manufacturing technologies enable a designer sitting at a workstation to create three-dimensional models of an artefact to be created and transmitted to manufacturing, both faster and to higher quality, in the hands of skilled individuals, than traditionally feasible. Those organizations that have reaped the benefits of this class of technology are those that have moved to newer working patterns. Frequent reports indicate teamworking, flatter hierarchies and pay reflecting multi-skilling for instance. Organizations that have tried to implement CAD/CAM in traditional organizational settings have often struggled or reported limited benefits.

The rapid changes in technologies can have significant impact on skills, competence and esteem. The emergence of the spreadsheet in the early 1980s, for example, enabled the finance departments of many organizations to use IT without relying on their IT departments. There has been a cycle of skills transfer in the IT industry which is rarely recognized. Each IT step change creates a need for new skills – 'Expert Systems' or 'Artificial Intelligence' created the need for people who could facilitate the extraction of knowledge from experts. There is then a tendency for the technology to move from expertise towards the domain of the IT 'general practitioner' as the early experience is captured in improved development tools. Technology then may move into the hands of the general user.

A good example of this can be seen with desktop publishing where software packages exist for every need from a basic system for small leaflets and documents capable of being produced by a layman, to rich systems which require expertise in layout and design to be used successfully.

Traditionally, one set of skills would see an adult through a lifetime of work. With IT, the change in capability of systems and software is such that the working life of useful IT skills in many areas may well be five years or less. The culture divide referred to earlier between IT professionals and business professionals is particularly to be regretted in this area. Organizations following a high-technology route increasingly need to consider the human resource factors in their business cases.

The issue of esteem is potentially troublesome. The CAD/CAM designer may well see the technology as 'liberating', offering improved quality and higher productivity (provided that training is appropriate). In contrast, a system aimed at managers, such as executive information systems, may be seen as 'controlling' or 'remote'. The introverted nature of many IT professionals leads them to assume that solutions will sell themselves rather than becoming involved in the 'selling' process. The development of more 'intuitive' user interfaces to computer systems such as Microsoft Windows alleviates only part of the problem. There is more to a good user interface than colour screens and icons. The need for 'ownership' of systems by users is essential. Feeling in control, through consultation in design and delivery along with training, is important.

Having considered some of the issues involved in the impact of IT on skills, let us consider the impact on organizations in more detail. We have already observed that IT can impact both the production and the co-ordination aspects of organizational implementation and design. It is an important aspect of IT that when a process is automated, information is often created as a by-product of the automation. Many organizations see the benefits of computers only in terms of the benefits of organizations. There is a sense that these organizations are 'information paupers'. The winners with IT tend to reap the benefits of IT investment by creating value from the information. Important potential can arise to eliminate routine reporting and control, functions carried out in the past by middle managers. Rather than automated, these organizations are 'informated' – a term first coined by Harvard's Shoshana Zuboff.

Charles Handy has written extensively on the future shape of organizations, most notably on the 'shamrock' and federal organizations. The new information technologies are making economically possible much richer organizational forms, and Handy's writing fits well with the capabilities that IT is now delivering. There is another model which fits Charles Handy's federal model; the PC Model.

A modern PC consists of a 'bus'. This is a high-speed piece of hardware into which 'boards' are slotted to build a PC. To interface with the bus there are very tight specifications for the bus. Other than that, the design of each board is quite independent. Boards are available from a wide variety of suppliers, so that each PC shipped in the world could be unique. Some boards act as processors, some handle disks or communications, for instance, and others handle devices such as faxes.

Moving from hardware to software we see similar design principles in practice. There is a linking piece of software, a software bus that pulls together 'objects' of software. There is a tight design specification for the software bus, but again the individual objects can be organized according to the tasks they perform.

Increasingly as we move to a faster, leaner flatter organizational structures we see the emergence of an organizational 'bus' with tight specifications linking federal empowered business units into an organic whole. ABB is the most widely described organization which fits this type of organizational metaphor. There are a few tight rules, such as financial reporting rules and inter-company trading, but each company 'board' can organize its own affairs according to its own rules.

Perhaps the real significance of IT for managers is the impact on organizations and skills. For the technophile the constant change and increasing power of technology will continue to excite and offer new opportunities and challenges for many years.

Yet, the lessons of the past would suggest that being seduced by technology can be dangerous. While a knowledge of the potential and indeed the limitations of any generation of technology will become an increasingly important part of every manager's required knowledge, it is how technology is deployed that will separate the winners from the rest.

For the technophobe or the sceptic, it is important to grasp the fundamental management issues associated with technological change. Knowledge of management of change, a rich picture of organization and an understanding of the impacts of IT on skills are more valuable in achieving business value than a deep grasp of the technology.

Indeed, a little knowledge may be a dangerous thing. With rapid change in information technology continuing for many years to come, occasional dabbling may leave a manager with a false picture of IT potential.

The real challenge for management teams is to bring IT closer to the business and to ensure that IT delivers. Management of technical expertise is probably a more important and realistic goal to set than to attempt to turn the general management community into IT gurus and enthusiasts.

Chris Yapp is a consultant with ICL specializing in the managerial and organizational impact of technology. He was one of the ICL group responsible for exploiting the material derived from the Sloan School research programme 'Management in the 1990s' which created many of the key concepts of re-engineering. He has worked in the IT industry for 15 years in a variety of roles, both technical and business. His technical background has mainly been in networking. He was the project manager at Honeywell for the implementation of the world's first multivendor open systems, OSI, network.

Further Reading

Floyd, C *Making Technology Pay*, FT/Pitman, London, 1994

Reference

[1] 'The technology pay-off', *BusinessWeek*, 14 June 1993.

IT MANAGEMENT

Veronica Janas

Information technology and information systems play a pivotal role in managing and achieving change. They are both agents and sources of change. Yet, it is a role which is often not easily understood or assimilated into existing organizational practices and culture.

Enabling IT management to play a full part in managing change involves IT managers developing a broad range of skills and the IT function as a whole being integrated into the mainstream of organizational culture, structure and strategy.

O n a daily basis, the key accountability of an information systems function is to deliver, to agreed cost and service levels, the established operational services on which the enterprise depends.

The story does not stop here as any enterprise is subject, through time, to change in its markets, suppliers, potential products, competitors, the socio-economic environment and so on. Its on-going success is in large measure governed by the ability of its managers to foresee change and take advantage of it.

The companion accountability of the information systems function is thus to keep the facilities in line with the needs of the enterprise, delivering agreed new capability within preset functional, cost, time and quality parameters.

Achieving the two accountabilities together is complicated by the following two factors.

- First, the extraordinarily rapid pace of change in IT has meant in recent years that the unit costs of solutions have fallen and the range of applications which are feasible and cost-justifiable have been dramatically extended. Information systems as a function are thus both an agent and a source of change in the enterprise's on-going efforts to perform better. However, changing the information technology base, or even extending it, is frequently time-consuming, expensive and risky. Also, judging which new facility or supplier to use is fraught with difficulty.
- Second, though an enterprise will formulate an array of policies, objectives and strategies to provide a framework for future action, in practice its top management will expect to be able to exercise considerable freedom in their reaction to specific circumstances.

The implications of this for IT management are profound. On the one hand, the IT manager is often constrained by past investments in *legacy* systems. These may still be performing essential tasks efficiently, but impose a brake on further development and change. On the other hand, the enterprise may be seeking to undertake new initiatives quickly and cheaply – without the cost and delay of systems replacement.

Consequently, the IT manager has the challenge of constantly responding to new requirements while continuing to provide stable operational services. At the same time, he or she must maintain adequate flexibility to respond to future change. The IT manager is not necessarily assisted in this by technology itself. The design of IT products and tools often assumes a conformity and symmetry which does not exist in the real world. This puts a straitjacket on the solution and is further complicated by the legendary incompatibility between many IT products.

These complex challenges mean that the IT manager must understand the current activities of the enterprise and be privy to any of its future plans which have implications for information systems. Equally, to assess, recommend and manage solutions, he or she needs to understand the capability of the available technology and tools and their future capacity.

Comprehensive management skills

The role of the IT manager also calls for comprehensive management skills. The IT manager has to be a planner with a good business and technical under-standing. This is vital and a prerequisite of the principal, traditional role of the management, design and delivery of information systems solutions and their on-going production and support. These also call for the management of rela-tions with top management and customers at all levels in the business. It is also important to manage relations with an array of actual and potential suppliers. The teams running the development projects and supplying operational services also require management and, for salaried staff, personal development.

These activities, of course, have to be performed within the financial con-straints of a budget set in competition with all the other activities in which the enterprise could invest. The IT manager is thus also a financial manager.

This broad portfolio of skills applies to the traditional form of the IT department. Typically, this encompasses systems development, production and technical services. However, this traditional role is changing. The IT function is an agent of change and is itself subject to on-going change in its organiza-tion as well as its tools.

There are three key processes involved in IT management: the identification, planning and provision of the *direction* of the investment; the delivery of pro-duction services or *service management*; and the *management of change* or development and delivery of new facilities.

1. Direction This is the first generic process; it identifies the business issues at which the information systems investment will be directed, and sets the level of investment. It determines the technical direction and the infrastruc-ture through which the services will be delivered. It establishes the overall mechanisms and organization of the IT function through which it will be managed and controlled. The activities which comprise this process typically form part of the planning cycle of the enterprise. All aspects of information systems activities should be covered.

An investment review will confirm or revise the level of the on-going, operational costs. It will also establish the scope for new investments. This may expand what already exists or target new areas. It may include new infrastructure investment, new applications developments, software and hardware acquisition, and system or tool replacement. All these investments are in some degree in competition with each other, depending on what the enterprise can afford and justify. The costs and time to reskill staff should not be overlooked.

A useful technique for the IT manager to apply as part of such a review can be the 'IT Investment Grid'. This enables the comparison of the IT investment profile to be compared with that of the business as a whole.

Here, investments are classified according to two factors: whether their unit costs tend to be low or high, and whether their business benefits tend to be low or high. This establishes categories of investment which can be characterized by their attributes. For convenience these categories are shown as four quadrants of a grid. It is not intended that the grid is used to plot values of cost and benefit; investments are simply placed in the quadrant which is thought most appropriate.

In summary, the steps in the use of this grid are:

- The board determines its desired investment profile by assigning a percentage value to each quadrant of the grid according to its business parameters.

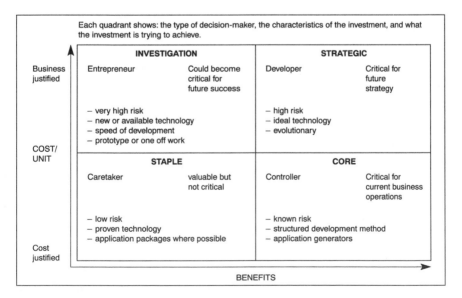

Fig. 1 IT investment grid: category characteristics © OTR

- The elements of actual and projected IT expenditure for the year are similarly categorized and accumulated to assess the current investment profile.
- The actual and desired investment profiles are compared, taking into account any revision to the budget.
- Mismatches and conflicts are resolved and global and detailed investment plans are formulated.

Figure 2 shows an example of investments from different institutions, and how the classification might change with the passage of time.

Having established the broad investment profile, the level of expenditure on current services can be confirmed. This establishes the budget and form of the activities covered by the second process, service management. The budget for new investments and the targets at which it should be directed need also to be clarified and the technical direction or options agreed. These may, of course, be revised as individual projects progress. These are the subject of the third process, the management of change.

It may also be appropriate to review organizational and control options while agreeing the future goals, investment profile and budget for the IT function. Control structures should be established for the IT function, including not only its line reporting but also functional review groups, investment sign-off and project monitoring. Any general policies and standards set by the enterprise should also be made explicit, together with security and audit requirements.

Research across Western Europe suggests that the information systems activities of any enterprise now tend to be managed using one of four organizational models. These are:

- centralized
- devolved
- separate company
- federal

Four different infrastructure investments made by the UK financial sector. Through time, the nature of the investment will change, as indicated by the arrows.

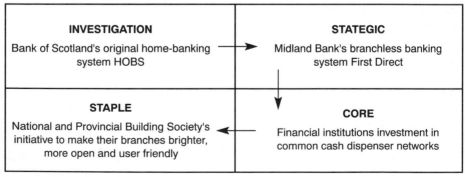

Fig. 2 How technology migrates: different investment types

Furthermore, with the passage of time, there tends to be a migration through these models in a patterned way. Major corporations, such as conglomerates, will also exhibit several of these models at different levels of the organization, for example at corporate level versus subsidiary. It is extremely important for the effective deployment of the enterprise's investment in information systems that the appropriate organizational type is selected. This should be reviewed regularly as part of the planning process. It should be noted that facilities management and outsourcing may be employed within any of the models though they are not themselves deemed separate organizational types. The reason for this is that responsibility for running the IT service of the enterprise cannot take place externally, although the services can be delivered externally.

The combination of all these activities comprises the first process: direction. While much of the process may be performed as part of an annual planning cycle, it is desirable to establish monitoring- and check-points throughout the year.

2. Service management This is the second key process in IT management. It comprises the on-going delivery, support and routine enhancement of the operational systems.

The services may be provided using a central computer installation, or through distributed systems or both. These may be linked or may stand alone. All or part of the services may be contracted out. Whatever the approach, these services are by definition part of the operating fabric of the enterprise. The associated costs have become part of the fixed operating costs of the enterprise and, in the short term, are non-discretionary.

Many management systems are possible. However the roles are structured, there are certain common service management activities which make up this process. The first of these is to understand clearly what the customers' requirements are and to be sure that the services satisfy them. These requirements might include performance, timeliness, integrity and many other attributes. Reasonable service levels should be negotiated and agreed with all the customers in respect of the critical service attributes. Performance against these should be monitored, measured and published regularly to customers. It is also helpful to hold regular review meetings with customers to discuss performance, forthcoming changes, enhancements and so on. As the requirements will change, the service levels should also be reviewed formally at intervals.

The services themselves clearly need to be resourced. This will require a number of technical components and specialist support services, potentially from internal and external suppliers. The capacity of the technical infrastructure to deliver the current services and accommodate planned growth needs to be monitored. If extra capacity is required, this has to be justified, planned and managed ahead of the need. The skills and availability of the support resources need to be managed to achieve the agreed service levels. Where these are being provided from an external source, the contract must be negotiated and managed. In drawing up such contracts, it is vital to identify clearly the services to be provided, the terms, flexibility required, service measures and exit terms. The provision of customer help desks, support engineers or similar services are also part of service management.

Integrating changes is an on-going issue. Change will arise from the suppliers of the equipment or systems software issuing corrections and enhancements. Similarly, package suppliers and applications support staff will be issuing changes – to correct problems or in response to customer requests. New applications will need to be implemented. Changes will be coming from all sides – and may well be incompatible or in conflict in some way. Managing the flow of change to meet customer needs while continuing to satisfy service criteria is a key function of service management.

Overall there is also the paramount need to manage costs within budget. The pressure will always be on the service management function to control or reduce costs while maintaining and improving the agreed services to customers.

As indicated earlier, different parts of the above responsibilities may be carried by several managers in different parts of the enterprise. However, overall, these activities comprise the service management process of IT management.

3. Management of change. This is the third process and concerns, in essence, the management of the project life cycle of all the projects which the enterprise initiates. These are one-off activities to seek to achieve specified benefits for a given investment. A budget for investment in new information systems, infrastructure investments and expansion or replacement, should have been established in the plans by the direction process. The overall level will have been set according to the enterprise's needs and what it can afford. This budget only establishes a framework which, if necessary, the top management could reset at any time.

Expenditure will be sanctioned from the budget on the basis of the specific investment cases and the established authority levels. An outline of at least some of the envisaged investments will have been agreed in the planning cycle. These will be the subject of initial investigation or feasibility studies. The original subjects may equally be overtaken by more pressing matters. Whether or not a particular project was in the plan, a complete project proposal should be prepared for all investments above a standard level, once the need and approach have been confirmed.

Such a proposal should state why the investment is required, what it will achieve and the business case, elaborating all the costs and benefits – and risks. It is helpful to state the objectives of the project in three or four brief statements. These provide a useful focus for the project in its later stages. A preliminary project plan should be included, showing the phasing, deliverables, monitoring points and outline of resources required. Any organizational implications and how these will be supported should be considered. It is desirable to describe the alternatives, with the arguments for and against, including the implications of doing nothing. The assumptions, dependencies and risks should be made clear. How the project will be managed and resourced, monitored, reviewed and controlled should also be stated.

It is important, in a project proposal, to identify the sponsor and customers of the investment. While the IT function will have a significant involvement in preparing such proposals, it would only rarely actually fulfil these roles. Indeed, the proposal may well be compiled and issued by the sponsor.

It is valuable at the point of sanction to assess the 'typology' of the project against a checklist of qualities clarifying its scale and the organizational and technical environments within which it will be conducted.

This assessment can be used to identify the nature of the project, establish the scope of sanction, the appropriate review mechanisms, verify the risks – and determine the competencies required in the project manager.

A sample overview of the project qualities and relevant approaches which may be so demonstrated is shown in Fig. 3.

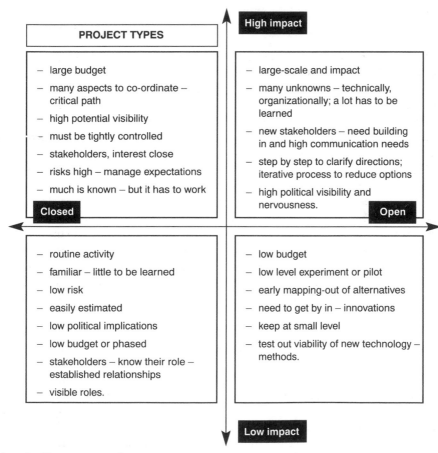

Fig. 3 Project qualities and relevant approaches
Source: Organisation and Technology Research © OTR

Achieving a proper understanding of the nature of the project through this process is a key ingredient in the formulation of an effective project quality plan or 'contract'.

Our research indicates that this is the key point at which the seed of project success or failure is sown.

Managing an on-going project

Once projects are under way, the sponsors, steering committees and principal customers have a vital role to play. They must dedicate the time to fulfil their roles properly and resolve any issues which may arise. They should also give due support and encouragement and release resources to the projects as necessary.

Many projects will be cross-functional and involve changes in jobs and skill requirements. The methods and time to manage such changes, and reskill those involved, should be an explicit part of the project from the outset. Without this, it is impossible to reap the full benefits of the investment.

Similarly, the methods and criteria for managing the testing and acceptance of deliverables should be established at the beginning. Test management should be an active component of the project. There are a number of techniques for this which, if properly applied, will reduce both elapsed time and project cost. Equally, risk management should be an explicit task from the inception of the project. There are again a number of techniques for this.

Project management is a particular skill, and it is important that an appropriately skilled project manager is appointed with a brief, authority and support appropriate to the purpose.

The review of projects also requires particular skills in the senior management concerned. The board could consider establishing one of its number as a 'project controller' to monitor the quality of project and change management across the enterprise and ensure the availability of properly skilled project managers.

All these processes and activities are relevant, no matter how the IT function is organized. Historically, the shape of the IT organization tended to be dictated by the available technology – the mainframe – but, with the increasing range of technical solutions, the enterprise now has the opportunity to structure its information systems function according to its own needs and culture.

Model one A *centralized* structure was the standard model into the 1980s, but has now been replaced in many organizations. This model is typified by a central IT department of significant size with central computers probably performing a dominant role in the information processing. There may or may not also be distributed processing. If there is, it will also be controlled by the central department. The reporting line is likely to be to a main board director, probably with a service role. Policies and standards are likely to be clearly stated and strongly enforced. This organizational model is most applicable today to medium-sized and large enterprises which are characterized by:

- strong product or service branding;
- tightly replicated activities across their sites and outlets;
- large customer or product databases.

It may also be employed by smaller, single-site, tight-knit enterprises.

The supporting IT organization will probably be on the well-established lines of production, support, and development sections or departments, as discussed earlier.

Model two In this model, *devolved*, no overall control or co-ordination of the IT function is practised. There may indeed be no recognized IT function at all. Each component of the enterprise is free to pursue an independent path in all aspects of its information processing. While co-operation is not precluded, it is entirely voluntary. No common policies or standards exist. The devolved model may be observed in the corporate level of a major conglomerate which controls its disparate member companies essentially through financial parameters and requires limited information from the subsidiaries, which it keeps as independent as possible to facilitate divestment. It is also typical of a small company which can satisfy its information system's requirements from commercially available products, such as PC packages.

Model three This is where the central IT department becomes a *separate company* within the enterprise. The new IT company is charged with trading externally as well as internally, and with providing competitively priced services internally. Its internal customers will become free to obtain competitive tenders externally.

This model is intrinsically unstable. In the majority of cases the following occur:

- The IT company has to take on sales skills and costs.
- Unless it has unique and highly desirable products or skills which the parent permits it to sell externally, it does not achieve its sales targets.
- It also becomes an arms-length trader with its internal customers, which have to bear the extra cost, and with which it loses any close or special relationship and, ultimately, their custom.
- The internal customers, in responding to the need to negotiate with internal and external suppliers, establish their own centre of IT competence which become embryo IT departments.
- Any cohesion in the information systems across the enterprise starts to be undermined.
- With non-achievement of targeted revenue and recognition by senior management that IT is not their business, the internal IT company starts to become an anomaly in the corporate portfolio.

Model four The final model is a *federal* structure, where a central IT function fulfils a co-ordinating role between what are otherwise devolved IT activities in, say, member companies of a corporation. Here, the extent of the powers of the central and devolved IT functions should match the control lines of the enterprise. That is, powers which are retained at corporate level should be reflected in the scope of central IT responsibilities and accountabilities. Equally, those which are delegated to subsidiaries should be reflected in local IT responsibilities and accountabilities.

A federal organization will typically be employed where there is a need or desire by the main board and/or powerful central functions:

- to maintain a level of direct co-ordination or control;
- to include within their domain a source of IT planning and advice;
- there is a clear rationale for co-operation across the enterprise.

There are three corporate examples where the federal approach is likely to be appropriate. The first is where the component parts of the enterprise operate in a common supply chain, or common markets, offer common or related products and services or otherwise have a business need to share a significant volume of data and/or services. In the second example, the corporate structure includes central functions which need to access significant volumes of information to common data standards from the subsidiaries and/or impose on them common methods and controls. The third example is where members of the main board wish to have an IT reference point to assist in foreseeing new business initiatives, to check and guide future investment and to monitor the effectiveness of current spend and of information systems activities.

The specific role and scope of the central function should be determined from a study of the enterprise's policies, practices, culture and various requirements.

It should be noted that the central role could be delegated to, for example, the largest or most appropriate IT function in one of the subsidiary companies or divisions. It is not essential for a discrete central IT department to exist for the organization to conform to the federal model. Similarly, the IT function could be deployed between the underlying processes and managed on a matrix basis.

In many enterprises, the IT organization will have experienced a series of changes as depicted in Fig. 4:

Organizational changes – management skills required

Overall, research indicates that there is a permanent dynamic organizational pressure which will maintain some form of central information systems function in most companies.

The requirements from IT managers, in terms of the scope of their activities, their accountabilities, style and competencies will continue to change. In the federal structure, the role of the corporate IT manager may well be focused primarily in the area of the first process, direction, with no direct line responsibility for production and development. In line roles in the federal structure, and in the other organizational models, the management characteristics which

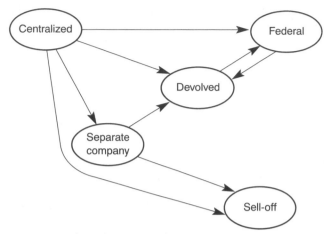

Fig. 4 Changes in the IT organization

are important for a particular enterprise depend on the nature of the dominant activities, as depicted in the IT Investment Grid. Figure 1 indicated the types of management and approaches most applicable in the different quadrants. It can be seen that the service management process will be of particular importance to activities in the 'staple' and 'core' quadrants, while project or change management is very important in the 'investigation' and 'strategic' quadrants. Taking these two views together can be of assistance in recognizing the particular style and range of management skills required.

Veronica Janas is general manager of the project management division of Organization and Technology Research.

Further Reading

Knights, D and Murray, F, *Managers Divided*, John Wiley, Chichester, 1994.
Strassman, PA *Information Payoff*, Collier Macmillan, London, 1985.

MULTIMEDIA

Peter Chatterton

The integration and acceptance of new technologies into the workplace invariably lags behind the pace of technical innovation. Multimedia has proved no exception. Yet, its impact is likely to be considerable over the next decade.

Multimedia brings a range of different technologies together – consumer electronics, computing and telecommunications – in ways which are interactive and immediate. Harnessing its potential is not solely the responsibility of specialists, but needs to be part of overall corporate strategy.

Ask a range of people to explain their understanding of the term multimedia and you are sure to receive many different interpretations. Some will focus on new consumer services such as video-on-demand, virtual reality games and interactive cable TV. Others will be more interested in business applications ranging from desktop video-conferencing to interactive computer-based training. All will have heard of the new information super-highways but may be unsure what this actually means.

These recent innovations are best explained as an evolution of a range of different technologies, broadly classified as consumer electronics, computing and telecommunications. For instance, audiovisual consumer electronics devices make increasing use of microprocessors to provide users with greater interactivity. Compact Disc-Interactive (CD-I) is just such an example of a multimedia device that has evolved from the compact audio disc. When connected to a TV and hi-fi, it will display pictures, video and animation as well as music and speech. Interactivity is provided via a control device that allows the user to pick and choose what they see and hear. Another technology, the microprocessor-based personal computer (PC), has evolved purely from being able to process text and graphics to incorporate pictures, sound and video. Telecommunications technologies, traditionally associated with voice and data transmission, have evolved with new applications, such as video-conferencing, and cable TV is beginning to bring a wide range of interactive services into the home, for example tele-shopping.

The evolution of these three traditionally separate technology areas – consumer electronics, computing and telecommunications – is also characterized by a growing convergence between them. The compact disc for instance, widely known as a consumer electronics product, has now become an essential component of a multimedia PC in the form of a CD-ROM drive. The PC has also become increasingly integrated with telecommunications, giving rise to significantly greater use of worldwide electronic mail and information networks.

While the opportunities presented by these technologies are probably limited only by the imagination, there are a number of drawbacks. First, many are not mature, despite the protestations of the technology companies. For instance, the processing of digital audio and video on PCs and via telecommunications networks needs considerable power/speed requirements. Such infrastructure technologies are not generally in place with agreed standards and at mass-market prices.

Of greater significance is how the technologies are used. Historically, effective applications of technology nearly always lag behind the technology itself – and this is particularly true of multimedia, where rapid and continuing change and development presents continually moving goalposts. To date, the most effective applications of multimedia have been developed by corporations for training their staff, where cost-savings through economies of scale have been the driving factor. Video-conferencing has also been successful and will no doubt increase in popularity as it becomes available at low cost on desktop PCs.

Alongside these relatively simple applications of the technology, many corporations have experimented with sales and marketing applications, such as the creation of multimedia electronic product brochures, located in retail outlets. In nearly all cases, these experiments have failed to spur consumers into buying sprees. They have succeeded in highlighting the complex human and social issues surrounding technology-based retailing.

Applications of multimedia may be divided into two broad areas. First, and the most straightforward, are applications that help to improve internal efficiency and productivity. Video-conferencing and training applications fall under this category. Second, and of greater significance, are the applications in sales and marketing – reaching out and communicating with customers. This is applicable to both business-to-business and consumer retailing. This second area is crucial to nearly all companies as, in time, it will influence marketing techniques, sales and distribution channels and customer buying patterns. As a result, a gradual change in the balance of power in market supply chains will emerge. Companies will need to be aware of these changes and to react positively to the opportunities (and threats) they offer.

The effects will be most noticeable in the media industry where media products can be delivered to office and home multimedia technology, providing new on-demand and interactive service options. This will affect the very heart of how people find and use information, news and education and entertainment services. New concepts will become available such as personalized newspapers, entertainment-on-demand, electronic universities and instantaneous access to worldwide electronic libraries of books, music, film and multimedia publications.

Improving internal efficiency and productivity

The opening up of global markets in the 1980s and 1990s set many challenges for companies, not least the need to be able to respond to the markets with increasing rapidity and effectiveness. The trend for take-overs and acquisitions to exploit these global markets brought a major problem for large conglomerates – the need to respond to rapid market changes with the same speed and flexibility of smaller companies. Most large organizations are now trying to emulate the flexibility found in the smaller business and to minimize bureaucracy, such as by forming federations of autonomous business units and eliminating hierarchal management structures. Whatever organizational structures are chosen, there is a general trend towards collaborative working between multi-disciplinary work-group teams that are created on an ad hoc basis and drawn from both within and outside the organization. These teams may frequently be geographically dispersed, and flexible working arrangements such as tele-working may be favoured.

These organizational trends present many problems, both in maintaining effective internal communications and in sharing and managing documentation, particularly for geographically dispersed work-group teams. Despite the widespread adoption of word-processors, spreadsheets and graphics presentation software, and the emergence of electronic mail, the methods for managing and controlling the creation, distribution, storage and archiving of documents are still largely paper-based. Not only does this limit the efficiency and productivity of such work-group teams, but it also presents problems in maintaining the organization's knowledge base.

Aiding collaborative working

Multimedia aids collaborative working in that it allows all forms of information media to be electronically processed using PCs and PC networks. This has a range of benefits. First, it gives staff the opportunity to express themselves with multimedia – incorporating speech, music, animations, pictures and even video – as well as textual and graphical information. Multimedia documents can be prepared in a number of ways. The most common is to use graphics presentation software that has multimedia capabilities. For instance, music or speech can be added to slide shows. Colour pictures can be incorporated by using a scanner, and videos may even be recorded direct from a VHS player or camcorder. The more sophisticated packages provide interactive capabilities that allow the presentation to be pre-programmed with options for the viewer to choose what they see and hear. Such presentations can be run live off a PC and, for large audiences, displayed via an overhead projector. Many other methods for distributing and showing such presentations are possible including the use of electronic mail, recording on to VHS tape or copying onto CD-ROM using 'writable' CD-ROM drives.

The second benefit is that it gives staff the opportunity to use their desktop PCs to communicate with each other using video-telephony and video-conferencing technology. This allows them to see and talk to each other via their desktop PCs. These may be connected either via a local or wide area network or via a broadband public telecommunications network such as ISDN (Integrated Services Digital Network). Employees can simultaneously use their ordinary PC software, such as a word-processor and each party will see the same document on their remote screens, allowing them to change and develop the document as if they had a single PC between them.

The last, and most important benefit, is the ability for companies to manage and control all their documents electronically. New software, such as groupware, provides an environment for managing and controlling any type of document, be it a word-processed file, a spreadsheet, a multimedia document or a series of scanned images of paper documents. The latter is of significance, as it means that companies can process their incoming post via their PC networks simply by scanning all post on receipt. Similarly, they can process their fax information, by using PCs to send and receive faxes.

Groupware environments provide a range of features that aid collaborative working. Typically, any piece of information is represented by a screen icon or object. This can be a word-processed file, a spreadsheet, a voice message, a series of scanned images or a multimedia combination of all these. The icon is filed and categorized in the same way, irrespective of the format of the information. It is stored electronically in one place and any authorized user can access this information – wherever they are located – including access via public telecommunications networks. This provides flexibility for home-working or for staff who are frequently away from the office.

Document management techniques, such as revision and version control, and security access restrictions are included and the software ensures that the most up-to-date version of any document is available to any authorized person. This gives rise to the concept of just-in-time information, where the PC is used as the first point of call for any information and the need for hard-copy archives is minimized.

Combined with the desktop video telephony and conferencing capability, the PC can serve both as a communications tool and the gateway to all of a company's document processing and management. This underpins flexible and changing organizational structures and working techniques and will ensure that the organization's knowledge base is maintained in a format that may be readily available to authorized personnel, both currently and in the future.

These technologies may be regarded as company 'infrastructure' technologies. Responsibility in this area typically rests with specialist information systems and information technology managers. Increasingly, managers in all areas will be required to better understand the technological possibilities – what technology can do for them and the benefits and pitfalls involved. They will need to closely define their document management and communication requirements and work together to implement the systems. Defining the business requirements of internal customers is an area that is too frequently left to IT personnel. Managers, with their staff, need to take full responsibility for providing a detailed business requirements definition of their needs. It is then the responsibility of the IT manager to co-ordinate the different management needs and develop and implement the appropriate systems.

Once installed, the systems need to be supplemented by staff training. Groupware systems engender a working environment in which everyone uses their PC to prepare, disseminate, store, file, categorize, manage and find information. Managers need to ensure that their staff work towards such a culture change. This is not always easy to implement – even today, the use of word-processors, spreadsheets and electronic mail is resisted, often with spurious and irrational justification. Training should include helping staff to develop their skills in communicating and exchanging information in this new arena. While technology, to a certain extent, can help manage information, it cannot stop people generating poor quality information, or too much of it. In fact, it is probable that word-processing and electronic mail have contributed towards an overload of information – by making it too easy to generate and distribute it. Poor management techniques can also exacerbate this problem. For instance, in some organizations staff attempt to protect themselves by copying everything to everyone.

Managers should, therefore, seek to engender a culture which emphasizes the quality of communications and information exchange. This includes helping staff to understand how best to communicate with specific individuals, to reduce unnecessary information and to ensure the organization records the correct type of information for its knowledge base.

Education and training

The increasing adoption of IT systems as an integral part of a company's way of working, is one of a number of driving forces for better and more cost-effective training techniques. Formal company training is moving more towards self-motivated education in a broad range of skills. In practice, it will be unrealistic and uneconomic for companies to provide such education and training using conventional classroom teaching techniques. More progressive companies are responding to the challenge by providing libraries of interactive multimedia materials as a resource for managers and staff. These interactive materials allow trainees to undertake training at their own pace and convenience, providing greater flexibility in fitting it around busy work schedules. Such techniques also allow students to be monitored and tested, using the technology, and can make large-scale distance learning a practical and economic proposition.

Interactive multimedia training can be employed in one of two ways. First, published materials may be purchased or rented. These types of materials train in generic subject areas. They typically include general business skills, such as in the areas of management, communication, sales and marketing, finance and business. Training in 'soft' skills, such as customer care or safety awareness, is particularly suited to multimedia technology where the use of video information can help staff in interactive role-playing and games scenarios to visualize both good and bad practices.

The second method by which the technology may be employed is applicable to companies which have highly specific training needs; where it is not possible to buy materials of a generic nature. This will include, for instance, training in product knowledge for complex technical products or training in work and safety procedures that are unique to the company, such as in the banking and insurance industries. If this is the case, the company will need to develop its own customized training materials. This method has the advantage that, once developed, the company owns the copyright and can therefore replicate the material in any quantity. If carefully designed, the material can also easily be updated to take account of any required changes and modifications.

The major benefit of technology-based training is through the economies of scale for training large numbers of staff in a flexible and convenient format. Companies which use the technology have different perceptions of the financial benefits, though nearly all agree that there are positive benefits. A major UK telecommunications company, which has extensive experience of technology-based training, reports that traditional classroom teaching techniques costing £150 per trainee per day, can be reduced to £15.

Multimedia in sales and marketing

Sales and marketing managers are now facing up to the fact that customers are better informed and more sophisticated in their purchasing. Furthermore, deregulation has broken down trade barriers. This gives rise to a convergence of consumer tastes across national borders and greater choice in product ranges. This is all raising demands and expectations for quality and personalized service.

In the light of these changes, many companies are rethinking their sales and marketing strategies. Some are questioning the value for money of television advertising and, with the advent of new technology-based direct marketing tools and databases, are moving more towards direct marketing and selling techniques, where they can target highly specific customer groupings.

Multimedia presents opportunities to enhance these direct sales and marketing channels and to help customize and personalize product information towards individual customers. An electronic brochure can present information in ways not possible with other media. For instance, customers choosing home furnishings can use a high-street multimedia point-of-sale kiosk to furnish and design a room with any combination or permutation of curtains, carpets, furniture, coverings and so on. Detailed product information can be provided and a personalized brochure printed. A customer could even take away a personally designed video for viewing in the comfort of their home.

Similar applications can be developed in other sectors. The holiday industry, for instance, could help its customers to better visualize what holiday they are buying and minimize the risk of expectations not being met. Multimedia brochures in the white and brown goods area can provide detailed product and technical information, often not available from poorly trained shop assistants. In the fashion industry, customers could be helped to visualize how different combinations and permutations of clothes will look on them – even when the products are not stocked locally. Such point-of-sale applications can also include transactional capabilities enabling chosen products to be ordered (if not stocked locally) and paid for.

One of the most important benefits of such systems is that companies can talk direct to customers via their computers, although to the customer, the computer appears as a less hostile television. For instance, the way that the customer uses the electronic brochure can be monitored, providing valuable market data as to customer preferences and buying motivations and habits. It can even allow products to be pre-launched to gauge customer reaction – without necessarily having to undergo the total cost of a fully-stocked launch. Transactions can, of course, be recorded and customer details collated to aid future direct sales and marketing campaigns.

Although experiments with multimedia point-of-sale kiosks have not met with significant success, this has mostly been due to a lack of understanding of the human and social issues involved in consumer purchasing and, in many cases, the service has been overly complex. In the United States, the organization Quality, Value, Convenience (QVC) has introduced a simpler type of technology-based retailing application. Viewers watch product presentations on broadcast TV and can make purchases by dialling a free-phone number, paying by credit card. Such simple services may well be the forerunner of more complex interactive brochure shopping which will evolve in the home via technologies such as cable TV and on-line information networks (accessible via PCs).

In certain sectors, the direct sales channel to consumers via home or public-access multimedia terminals will have profound influence on the power balance in supply chains. The food industry, for instance, has already seen a change in the balance of power over the last ten years, moving away from manufacturers' brands to supermarket own brands. It is possible this evolution could change direction and non-traditional companies could instigate home-shopping for groceries. The supermarket retailers may well wish to stall progress in this area – after all, they are experts in maximizing sales revenue via supermarket shopping and could be nervous about developing unfamiliar sales channels. This, of course, opens up opportunities for existing supply chain parties or even new entrants, operating via cable TV channels. They could be successful if they are able to master the not inconsiderable distribution problems that are almost unique to the food industry.

Certain companies may need to change their product and brand strategies. For instance, those involved in textile manufacturing and retailing often brand their different materials and styles under co-ordinated ranges. These help consumers make up their minds in choosing items, by making 'recommendations' for co-ordinated patterns and items – displayed in high quality printed brochures. However, with the aid of an interactive multimedia brochure, customers can be helped to visualize product combinations and permutations in the settings of their own homes. The need for pre-defined, co-ordinated groupings may not be of such importance in helping the consumer to make a purchase and this may result in companies having to re-think their product range and brandings.

In all sectors, the ability to deal direct with consumers using home-based tele-shopping will open up opportunities for manufacturers, distributors, suppliers and new entrants to sell direct to consumers. In particular, the technology will significantly reduce the entry barriers and costs for direct selling, enabling both new entrants and other supply chain parties to consider entering the direct sales market. The advent of QVC illustrates the potential for new entrants to become significant market players. Similarly, on-line information networks that currently offer a range of retailing possibilities from books and computer software to airline and theatre tickets also illustrate how non-traditional parties could influence the supply chains.

Traditional retailers will need to respond to such threats with new services which provide added-value and which are outside the scope of purely technology-based retailing. This may vary from the provision of highly personalized services through to combining out-of-town shopping with theme park entertainment.

Multimedia will, by definition, have the greatest impact in the media industry. To date, technology has had a major impact on production processes. The advent of desk-top-publishing has not only reduced cost bases but has played a major role in reducing the power of the printing unions. But it is in the area of delivery or distribution that multimedia will play an even greater role. Interactive multimedia terminals in the home will provide consumers with a whole range of new services. Video-on-demand trials are already under way in various parts of the world. These provide consumers with a service for choosing any video they want and then immediately watching it on their TV – the video is delivered 'live' via their ordinary telephone cable. Such services will change the whole concept of broadcast TV and will rapidly develop to provide an entire range of other on-demand and interactive entertainment, educational, news and retailing services. The technology will be used to help profile a wide range of these services to individual consumer needs. The media industry will, therefore, need to give a great deal of consideration to its future products and services.

The media industry is particularly vulnerable to new entrant players where the low barriers to entry make it feasible for spin-offs from existing players or new company start-ups. More importantly, existing players frequently find it difficult to adapt to new low-cost production processes and new sales and distribution channels. It is often the middle-management staff in such companies who fail to respond to the challenges, feeling threatened by the changes that need to be implemented and the confusions surrounding the technology.

Developing sales and marketing applications

The rapidity of multimedia technology innovation is matched by the hype that surrounds it. It is created not only by the technology companies, keen to maintain a competitive edge, but also by the press, seduced by electrifying new concepts such as tele-working, tele-shopping, tele-education, virtual worlds and so on. Such hype is dangerous and can lead to false and confusing promises – a story only too familiar to businesses which have past experiences of poor information technology investments.

In the late 1980s and early 1990s this hype gave rose to a spate of early multimedia experiments by large corporations. These were mostly driven by the organization's mavericks and were frequently met with resistance by a large section of staff, prompted by the insecurities, uncertainties and unpredictability of the impact of the technologies, not least on their own careers. These experiments, while not always providing the anticipated degree of business benefit, did provide some key lessons in highlighting the importance of the technology and how to implement it.

One of the key lessons is that, unlike most historical uses of IT, multimedia will have far more strategic importance than simply helping to improve company efficiency and productivity. It will go right to the heart of how companies market and sell their products. It will affect sales and distribution channels, marketing strategies and the provision of customer services. In many cases it may provide the foil against which new products and services are developed and how they are branded. The technology will affect every single aspect of the media industry, from production and operations through to marketing, sales and distribution – direct to the end-user.

In organizational terms multimedia is too important to leave to the IS or IT manager. All management functions will be impacted by the technology, and management decisions on its use will need to be set within the framework of overall business strategy.

How companies choose to devise strategies and programmes to successfully exploit multimedia will vary, depending upon their own choice of management styles and techniques. However, there are two important elements that will help the process:

Learning

Multimedia technology, while having the power to excite, can also cause considerable confusion. Before any trials or developments the company should undertake a company learning process that will help the entire organization to develop a common understanding of what the technology is and will become; its impact on the company and the market it is in; how it can be used; the benefits and pitfalls involved and what should be done next. It is essential that this exercise is undertaken internally through the use of work-shops with contributions from all management and relevant staff. Outside facilitation could aid this process although it is preferable to appoint an internal facilitator who has hybrid-type skills. In many cases, it is helpful to set up demonstrations of current applications to help staff to visualize the possibilities and see how others are using it.

This learning process should help to develop the company vision of where it will be in its market in the longer term and also help develop consensus on how to get there.

Gain experience

Most companies will be treading new waters with the technology. First-hand experience is vital and an early part of the development process should be to trial the technology. This may simply involve its internal use, such as with interactive multimedia training or desktop video telephony. These internal applications help staff to familiarize themselves with the technology and to understand its potential and limitations.

Alternatively, some companies may wish to jump in at the deep end and choose a customer-facing trial. This could, for instance, involve a public-access kiosk application or a home-shopping application, possibly carried out in conjunction with a cable TV company.

Whatever development route is chosen, expectations must not be raised too high and the objectives and perceived benefits (both tangible and intangible) should be clearly agreed before implementation. It is important that the mistakes experienced in the implementation of IT are learned from and not repeated.

Peter Chatterton has worked with many organizations in helping them to implement multimedia strategies and programmes. These have been applied to new business development, creation of new sales and marketing techniques, improving customer services, implementation of cost-effective educational and training programmes and in the development of information sharing and communication support systems to aid collaborative working. He is the author of *Does Your Company Need Multimedia?* (1993) and *Technology Tools for Your Home Office* (1993).

Further Reading

Anderson, C, and Veljkov, M, *et al*, *Creating Interactive Multimedia: A Practical Guide*, Computer Books, 1990.

Burger, J, *The Multimedia Bible*, Addison-Wesley, Reading, 1992.

The CD-I Design Handbook, Philips Interactive Media Systems, Addison-Wesley, 1992.

Chatterton, P, *Does Your Company Need Multimedia? – How to Maximize the Commercial Benefits*, The Financial Times/Pitman Publishing, London 1993.

Chatterton, P, *Technology Tools for Your Home Office*, Kogan Page, London,1993.

Feeney, M and Day, S, *Multimedia Information*, Butterworth, London, 1991.

Feldman, A, *Multimedia in the 1990's*, British National Bibliography Research Fund, 1991.

Introducing CD-I, Philips Interactive Media Systems; Addison-Wesley 1992.

The Oxford Reference Dictionary of Computing, Oxford University Press, Oxford, 1991.

Tucker, RN, *Interactive Media: The Human Issues*, Kogan Page, London, 1989.

Wodke von, M, *Mind Over Media: Creative Thinking Skills for Multimedia Computing*, McGraw-Hill, New York, 1993.

Further Information

British Interactive Multimedia Association (BIMA); 6 Washingley Road, Folksworth, Peterborough, PE7 3SY, UK

European CD-I Association, 188 Tottenham Court Road, London, W1P 9LE, UK

European DVI Developers Group, Digital Vision International Ltd, 202 The Foundry, 156 Blackfriars Road, London, SE1 8EN, UK

European Information Industry Association (EIIA), Boite Postale 262, Luxembourg L-2012

Interactive Multimedia Association, 800 K Street NW, Suite 240, Washington DC 20001, USA

Learning

'The organizations that will truly excel in the future will be the organizations that discover how to tap people's commitment and capacity to learn at all levels in an organization.'

Peter Senge[1]

'Learning is the new form of labour. [It is] no longer a separate activity that occurs either before one enters the workplace or in remote classroom settings ... Learning is the heart of productive activity.'

Shoshana Zuboff[2]

---

[1] Senge, P, *The Fifth Discipline*, Doubleday, New York, 1990.
[2] Zuboff, S, *In the Age of the Smart Machine*, Heinemann, Oxford, 1988.

OVERVIEW

Jane Cranwell-Ward

The classic psychological definition of learning is any relatively permanent change in behaviour which has been brought about as a result of experience or practice. Traditionally attention was focused on individual learning and then learning within a team. In organizational terms there is now a growing emphasis placed on the *learning organization*. This recognizes the need to go beyond individual and team learning to embrace the capability of the organization to transform itself to achieve continuing business success.

How people learn

As long as 25 years ago Harvard Business School's Chris Argyris was emphasizing the importance of managers being helped to learn from experience. In the UK, the academics, Peter Honey and Alan Mumford, developed a questionnaire to enable managers to identify their preferred way of learning.[1] The way to maximize learning from experience is to structure the learning using a variety of methods which encourages activity, reflection, drawing some learning points, then applying the lessons learned. While individuals have a preferred way of learning, it is possible for them to develop less preferred styles.

Managers need to maximize opportunities for learning. Ian Cunningham in *The Wisdom of Strategic Learning*[2] refers to learning from success – for example, Ian MacLaurin turned round the fortunes of the supermarket chain, Tesco, after studying successful practice in the US. Managers must also learn from failures and the mistakes they make, and those made by others. Richard Branson of Virgin Airways studied why small airlines failed and observed that their mistake was to try to compete on price. He has succeeded with Virgin by focusing on service and customer care rather than price.

In one of the most well-known concepts in the field of learning, Chris Argyris differentiates between single-loop and double-loop learning. Single loop learning occurs where errors or mismatches are detected, but the underlying assumptions and values are not questioned. By contrast, double-loop learning requires individuals to re-examine the fundamentals. According to Argyris, many organizations continue to repeat errors and fail to derive the benefits of double-loop learning, because the staff have suppressed feelings and develop defensive routines for fear of a sense of failure and the feelings associated with failure.

Managers need to develop a more open approach to learning, by being prepared to take more risks, allow feelings to surface, and challenge ways of working on the grounds that 'it has always been done this way'. Double-loop learning, therefore, requires a shift away from defensive rational reasoning towards a search for continuous improvement and being open to novelty.[3]

Leading-edge organizations are establishing systems which encourage feedback from a number of sources and ensure the information is acted upon. Most companies use 360-degree feedback as a means of developing both the individual and the organization. The customer forms a crucial link in this feedback process. Environmental and internal turbulence has resulted in the growing need for continuous learning and development to enable managers to respond to the changes. In a recent report by Price Waterhouse, reference was made to a survey by the British Institute of Management in which 100 per cent of respondents identified the human resources of an organization as a critical success factor.[4]

Why continual learning and development?

In the last ten years the pace of change has increased dramatically. In particular, organizations have been facing much greater competition. As a result, to keep at the leading-edge, managers have needed to learn new skills, increase their knowledge and find new ways of working. The ability of organizations to learn faster than their competitors may be the only sustainable competitive advantage.

Darwin was the first to stress the importance of adapting to the environment and the notion of survival of the fittest. However, the business market provides a different sort of competitive pressure for organizations, and the time scales are much shorter. Many of the important changes now under way have important repercussions for the skills a manager must possess. Many demand continuous learning:

- Downsizing and delayering have been the outcome of organizations striving to cut costs and remain competitive. For many managers, particularly middle managers, this has resulted in redundancy and the need to learn and develop new career paths. Some have made dramatic changes moving to self-employed status often helped by their previous employers as part of the redundancy package.
- In striving to remain competitive many organizations have focused on the importance of quality. Sustaining high levels of quality often requires process improvements which, in turn, has development implications for managers. From being highly bureaucratic, many organizations are – through re-engineering – bringing functions together to co-operate far more closely.
- International organizations require their managers to cope with the complexity of global markets and operations. They need to retain flexibility to employ different solutions for varied situations around the world. BP has responded to these challenges by managing information more effectively, simplifying and flattening the organization structure. It has developed a structure based around the business unit which has a geographic product

market. Managers are required to network across functional boundaries working in multifunctional project teams often brought together on an ad hoc basis. Much less emphasis is placed on the formal organizational hierarchy with its associated grades and status. This form of network organization has been adopted by other multinationals including General Motors, Ford and Digital. Individual commitment and motivation to succeed and a changed managerial style are critical success factors for this type of organizational change.

- Technological change is another important driver of continuous development. Organizations increasingly need to change their structures to maximize the benefits of new technology. Ten years ago few managers used PCs on a daily basis. Managers who survive into the next century will be those who develop themselves to gain maximum benefit from the technological resources available.

What skills are needed? The competency approach

Having recognized that continuous learning is essential, what skills do managers need to meet the challenges of the 1990s? In 1988, the UK's Management Charter Initiative was formed to address growing concerns about the lack of adequate training for managers. This led to growing interest in competence or dimensions of behaviour which relate to levels or standards of performance and can be defined in output terms.

Henley Management College and Northern Regional Management Centre have conducted research on behalf of MCI to develop senior management standards.[5]

The research findings recognized the importance of key behaviours which constitute good practice and satisfactory outcomes. The model of senior competence also acknowledged the importance of knowledge and understanding which underpin performance. The third component was personal competencies, the underlying abilities which help contribute to highly effective performance.

The research highlights several areas of activity to enable senior managers to develop and implement strategy and provide leadership. The areas were summarized as:

- **Reading the environment** – identifying and evaluating opportunities and threats for the organization in the internal and external environments.
- **Charting the way ahead** – contributing to the development and communication of the mission, goals values and policies of the organization and its units.
- **Planning the action and making the pace** – developing and implementing programmes, projects and operating plans for the organization.
- **Evaluating and finding ways of doing things better** – reviewing and evaluating objectives and policies and their implementation.

In terms of personal competencies, a number of skill areas were identified to enable senior managers to contribute to the organization and its achievement of objectives. They include influencing skills, team building, communication skills, strategic and information-gathering skills.

As a result of MCI many organizations now map the particular competencies needed by their managers to help the organization to compete successfully. Organizations identify competencies in relation to the environment in which they operate, and the steps that are to be taken to sustain competitive advantage while being cost-effective.

Internationalization

Increasingly the international dimension is driving the learning of many managers. Deutsche Aerospace AG (DASA) generates 75 per cent of its turnover through its co-operation with international partners. The only way in which the high-tech aerospace industry can support the necessary R&D and remain profitable is to seek global markets. DASA's strategic goal of competing through co-operation with international partners, produces a constant need for key skills from DASA managers. The need goes beyond training in intercultural communication to bicultural team development. DASA sees itself as a transnational corporation centred on Europe, and managers work to the maxim 'think global act local' as they conduct business in France, the USA, UK, Italy, Spain, Japan and elsewhere.[6]

Similarly, Hitachi-Europe has a programme to enable its managers to manage effectively across different cultures. The programme is run in the UK and has nominations across mainland Europe including Germany, Holland, Sweden, France and Norway. Sessions help managers to develop a greater understanding of managing and working in cross-cultural teams.

The US places great emphasis on managers valuing diversity of race, gender, sexual orientation, age and disability. The New York-based company, Colgate Palmolive is addressing the issue of understanding cultural diversity in global terms. It operates in 170 countries and receives 70 per cent of its revenue from overseas markets. Apart from recognizing the importance of shared values across the organization, it also recognizes the importance of understanding and valuing individual cultures. Different styles of managing, communicating and negotiating must all be learned.[7]

Empowerment

Many organizations seeking to achieve excellence and sustain their competitive position have recognized the importance of empowering staff to achieve a performance culture. Northern Telecom, a telecommunications company based predominantly in the US and Canada but operating worldwide, initiated a quality change programme from HQ. It had been benchmarked on best practice from companies such as IBM, Motorola and Xerox. The UK division had some concerns as to the likely success of this initiative and therefore sought to change the culture of the division by empowering staff. For managers this meant the adoption of a shift in management style from an authoritarian to a liberating style. Self-awareness development helped managers to understand self-limiting and self-blocking behaviour. Managers were thus enabled to achieve self-directed change.[8]

The manager as a developer

The manager of the future is likely to need the skills to support, coach and develop the experts doing the work. Most organizations are now recognizing the importance of a supportive rather than an authoritarian style of management. The Hearsey and Blanchard model of leadership helps managers appreciate the need for a flexible approach when managing others. Managers need to develop delegation skills to encourage their subordinates to become less dependent and to take responsibility for their own learning. Developing staff is an important element of this process and requires managers to make far more use of coaching to maximize work-based learning.

The manager as a leader

Organizations which are striving to become more commercial are recognizing the need to help managers to develop as leaders as well as managers. The manager as a leader requires a different set of skills – he or she needs to motivate and inspire, create a shared vision, as well as having communication, influencing and networking skills. These skills contrast with the more traditional skills of planning, organizing and appraisals skills. Many of the companies recently privatized in the UK are concentrating on developing leaders rather than managers and organizations in general report a greater need for leadership capabilities.

The manager as a generalist

Managers are increasingly required to develop generalist skills and to work cross-functionally as they are faced with more complex problems which need to be addressed in a more integrated way. This places demands on the manager to develop functional skills, in particular finance and marketing expertise. Until the 1980s, managers were able to leave financial matters to accountants. Today, the pressure for cost-effectiveness requires managers to have a far greater financial understanding. In addition, managers need a way of working cross-functionally which emphasizes problem solving and project management skills.

The manager as an innovator

Organizations are increasingly recognizing the need to develop their managers as innovators to enable them to find new and better ways of operating. Tom Peters has emphasized the importance of innovation in all his books and quotes 3M, Apple, Hewlett Packard and Boeing as excellent companies in this respect. To be innovative managers need not only the tools and techniques which help reach creative solutions, but also the capability to withstand change, ambiguity and uncertainty. Managers also need to create an environment where people feel confident to take risks and take personal responsibility for making a positive and effective contribution to the overall result.

Current trends in management development

HR and management development specialists are meeting the challenges of the 1990s in a number of highly significant ways. In particular, development is much more focused and tailored to meet clearly specified needs. Organizations are also seeking to form partnerships with providers of development to ensure that managers are given the techniques and frameworks to apply to live issues and receive appropriate support at work to gain maximum benefit. As part of the partnership approach the HR function is enabled to help the business both formulate and implement the business strategy creating and changing the culture where necessary.

Managing in a turbulent and changing environment has highlighted the need for far greater flexibility in terms of learning experiences provided, methods employed to encourage learning, and the way learning is delivered. Apart from encouraging continuous development, organizations are also looking to providers of development to make their offerings far more flexible.

In a survey of 500 companies, conducted by the Institute of Personnel Management and Lloyd Masters Consulting, 58 per cent had a board director responsible for training. Another trend highlighted by the survey was the tendency for organizations to delegate responsibility for training to line managers. This has led to line managers becoming enablers, facilitators and coaches. The training function takes on a supporting role to the line in helping them fulfil responsibilities.[9]

The concept of the learning organization has developed from a growing recognition of the need for continuous development and the importance of learning for both the individual and the organization. Many organizations now operate a formalized mentoring scheme to help ensure maximum learning from experience.

As organizations have become clearer about the training needs of managers they have formed partnerships with training providers to develop more focused development for managers. The programmes are highly tailored to meet specific learning objectives and usually complement in-house development activities. Many organizations follow a competence route which identifies key competencies at specific levels which are demonstrated by highly successful managers. Some organizations run development centres prior to training programmes and then help managers to follow a personal development plan to address specific needs.

Organizations frequently provide managers with the opportunity to obtain a management qualification. This has been the trend for many years, but more recently steps have been taken to help managers obtain a qualification by giving recognition and accrediting prior learning. This encourages a move away from teaching and emphasizes the importance of what a manager has learnt in day-to-day work.

In response to the need for managers to become more outwardly focused, for organizations to become more competitive and develop networks across company boundaries, progressive organizations have started to join a consortium of companies to help develop managers. One such consortium was formed by Digital in conjunction with key customers and a business school, to help senior managers understand the issues relating to globalization of key customers and of Digital. The programme was developed to enable managers to meet the challenges of managing in a particularly turbulent environment. It provided a solid foundation of managerial skills and knowledge which would serve as base throughout the managers' careers. The programme also allowed managers to take effective action in complex situations and changing environments, drawing on their skill-base and knowledge. The programme had an action research component with managers addressing live issues.[10]

Companies sponsoring managers to undertake MBA programmes have also recognized the benefits derived from the consortium approach. Managers from Ford learn alongside managers from British Aerospace, Unilever, Brent Council and Nationwide. The companies host workshops which supplement a distance-learning programme. Practising managers demonstrate best practice in key areas of the business. Recently a European consortium has been developed to enable managers to benefit not only from learning across organizational boundaries but also across cultural boundaries. The programme gives managers the opportunity to attend modules in several countries including Germany, France and the US in Houston, Texas. Partners in the consortium are Deutche Aerospace, Mercedes, AEG, Intercontinentale and Henley Management College.

Measuring the benefits of development is a growing concern of HR specialists, When using an external provider, many companies have opted for tailor made programmes for managers in preference to open programmes which were extremely popular in the 1980s when the economy was more buoyant.

Several organizations including McDonalds, Unipart and Motorola have set up their own universities. This step helps to ensure that all levels of staff are appropriately trained and can contribute to a process of continuous improvement and deliver a high quality service to customers. Motorola established its university approximately 11 years ago and aims to have the best world class training function.

There is much that other organizations can learn from Motorola, particularly those who want to demonstrate how training adds value to the bottom line. About eight years ago it established a special evaluation unit tasked with the collection and evaluation of data for quality assurance purposes and as a process for continuous improvement. Motorola has developed a thorough evaluation process involving both the training function and line management to help assess how training adds value to the bottom line. It is a four-level process of evaluation:

Level one – assesses the level of customer satisfaction with a programme and is a form, filled out anonymously. This level is completely automated.

Level two – involves a test to assess whether the training has achieved its stated objectives.

Level three – requires the learners to create action plans with staged objectives and success measures. They are then assessed on the extent to which they have implemented their objectives. Apart from the action plans, learners are observed undertaking their jobs and their behaviour is assessed to ensure that learning is transferred to the workplace.

Level four – assesses organizational impact, traditionally the most difficult level of evaluation. It compares work performance against clearly defined criteria of those who have completed a training programme with a control group who have not received the training.

At Motorola, its energies are being channelled into getting levels two and three right, before progressing to level-four evaluation.

Different forms of learning

The manager has a range of different forms of learning which are suitable at different stages of the learning process, and will vary in terms of effectiveness, depending on the preferred style of learning of the manager. Most development professionals would agree that managers learn best when they approach their development in a range of different ways.

Distance learning – is for those who want flexibility in timing and location. It is a good method for developing the basic knowledge, skills and attitudes needed by managers. Material is usually very carefully developed and defines the target audience and learning objectives. In this way learners will be quite clear of what they can expect to achieve when they have completed the package.

Distance learning can appeal to different styles of learning. It can be designed to make good use of the multimedia approach with the development of interactive video, the CD Rom and training videos. CD Rom stores computer programs, sound, video and graphics on a CD and allows learners to use a mixture of learning media, and to plan their own learning path.

Recently, many providers of distance-learning programmes, particularly those leading to a management qualification, have worked with organizations to provide a range of features to maximize the learning experience. These include the development of a programme schedule which provides the learner with milestones to achieve and monitors progress by a programme co-ordinator. Other features include line-manager support, the use of mentors, the use of subject experts via telephone hot lines, the use of IT for computer conferencing and access to tutors and peers, and written assignments to check understanding and help assimilation of learning. Finally, workshops can very successfully complement distance learning.

Coaching and mentoring – coaching involves a process of helping a person solve a problem or complete a task better through discussion and guided activity. It is a highly developmental process and is a useful way for learning through experience and continuous development. Coaching is vital for ensuring that work-based learning takes place.

Coaching can sometimes be confused with mentoring. Mentoring involves a one-to-one relationship with another person, the mentor, who not only coaches but uses other techniques such as counselling, facilitating, and networking. It is therefore a much broader development technique. It is particularly useful for senior managers who may have a mentor from another organization to add breadth and more outwardly focused development.

Projects – these are often linked to more formal development programmes and enable managers to apply lessons learnt to the work situation. They may be undertaken individually or on a team basis. If projects are to be motivational, a company sponsor, who has a definite need for the project to be undertaken, must be nominated. When undertaken individually it provides a good opportunity to apply problem solving techniques. The most successful projects are those which allow the manager to complete a project which helps him or her to achieve personal business objectives. When undertaken in a team, individuals can practise team skills as well as networking and working cross-functionally, or cross-culturally.

Networking – a flexible arrangement, aimed at encouraging people to learn from one another. Networking can take place internally, socially or via informal contacts. It may be encouraged by setting up a process of mentoring or by actively seeking opportunities to interact cross-functionally. Managers are now also encouraged to network with people from other organizations. Benchmarking is one way of learning about best practice in other organizations and now regularly takes place whereby competitors meet on a regular basis to discuss key issues.

Self-managed learning – a form of learning in which managers take responsibility for their own learning. They set their own learning objectives, decide how to achieve them, how to measure them and how to integrate them with the needs of the organization. Managers participate in learning sets which provide scope for effective learning. The rest of the learning takes place within the organization where managers learn from one another.

Hiram Walker has successfully used self-managed learning. Managers were given a comprehensive handbook of materials on a wide range of topics, rather like a mini resource centre. They could also obtain help from external resources organized by the company. At the end of the programme, managers presented evidence of achievement to their peers; they also met with a director for a de-briefing on the programme. The results were logged on personnel files, thus acknowledging the programme as part of the career development process. A range of benefits can be attributed to the programme. It increased self-awareness, self-motivation and self-initiative. It helped to break down departmental barriers, created a greater understanding of roles, as well as enhancing strategic skills and a broader business perspective. Finally managers appeared more open and receptive to change and had a more positive attitude to learning and development. The company has assessed its cost-effectiveness and believes that it is one of the most cost-effective methods it has used.[11]

Self-development – this form of learning requires managers to take responsibility for their own learning. This approach encourages continuous development as individuals strive to become competent. The manager identifies the development need and then takes responsibility for addressing the need. The organization can facilitate the process. Within the Civil Aviation Authority an in-house framework of management competencies was developed initially for the appraisal system. These competencies are now included in a Development Options Guide. Ways of developing capability in each of the competencies are listed in the guide, including books to read and steps to be taken to develop skills. Within the career development project, information and opportunities are also provided for all employees to analyze their skills, attend courses, development centres, career development workshops and take part in career guidance discussions.

Team development – the purpose of this form of development is to help teams understand patterns of interaction, process and task issues. If it involves team building it is conducted with actual teams. Team skills may also be learned in a group, away from the real-life team.

Team development usually involves an external facilitator. At the preparation stage, the facilitator conducts preliminary interviews with team members to get to know the team and its key issues. A team development event is then run which addresses the strengths and blockages to team effectiveness. Sometimes teams will undertake outdoor training to emphasize key issues and help develop team spirit.

Eurocopter SA employed team development after the French-German merger to help foster the overall success of the enterprise by enhancing its transnational identity and develop synergy between the two cultures. An inter-cultural communication workshop was run separately for the French and Germans followed by a joint problem-solving workshop. This helped both cultures to work more effectively in an integrated team and formed the basis of a common business culture.

Secondments – this is a very practical way of learning and appeals to managers who are pragmatists. It is a cost-effective form of learning and, where second-ments are undertaken in another organization, enables the manager to gain a broader business perspective. Learning is maximized when the manager on secondment is coached effectively and the process is linked to the company appraisal scheme.

Jane Cranwell-Ward is director of company programmes at Henley Management College.

Further Reading

Cunningham, I, *The Wisdom of Strategic Learning*, McGraw Hill, Maidenhead, 1994.
Mumford, A, *How Managers can Develop Managers*, Gower, Aldershot, 1993.
Wilson, G, *Self-Managing Work Teams*, FT/Pitman, London, 1994.

References

[1] Honey, P and Mumford, A, *A Learner's Guide to Using Learning Opportunities*, 1990.
[2] Cunningham, I, *The Wisdom of Strategic Learning*, McGraw Hill, Maidenhead, 1994.
[3] Argyris, C, 'Teaching smart people to learn', *Harvard Business Review*, May-June 1991.
[4] 'Organizational trends – who is doing what?', Price Waterhouse, London, 1992.
[5] Lane, G and Robinson, A, *The Development of Standards of Competence for Senior Management*, AMED Research and Development Conference, 1994.
[6] Boem, T and Wichmann, D, *Internationalization and intercultural competence: a report on DASA and Eurocopter experience*, Forum 94/1, EFMD, 1994.
[7] Solomon, CM, 'Global operations demand that HR re-thinks diversity', *Personnel Journal*, July 1994.
[8] Rooke, D and Jones, M, 'Empowerment – lessons from Northern Telecom organiza-tions and people', AMED, 1:3, 1994.
[9] Saggers, R, 'Training climbs the corporate agenda', *Personnel Management*, July 1994.
[10] Bouchami, H, 'Developing managers in turbulent times', AMED Research and Development Conference, 1994.
[11] Cunningham, I, 'Imbibing a new way of learning', *Personnel Management*, March 1993.

THINKERS

Chris Argyris

Born 1923; educator

A superficial look at Chris Argyris' work and career gives an impression of the classic academic. Argyris has spent his entire working life at some of the leading centres of American academic excellence – at Yale in the 1950s and 1960s, at Harvard Business Schoool since 1968. But, the scope of his thinking defies conventional academic strictures. 'Working in academia is both exhilerating and infuriating,' he admits. His work is driven by high-quality academic research, rather than unsubstantiated opinion. It is also, he admits, not highly accessible. 'My books are not easy to read. It is the way I think,' he says. 'I write articles based on anecdotes and books based on research. I don't want to research, raise basic questions and then stop.' [1]

Underpinning Argyris' career has been a humane desire to develop and nurture individuals within organizations. 'I am interested in social sciences in organizations of any kind,' he says. 'Discipline-oriented people can feel I'm a traitor.' Argyris' intellectual armoury includes a Baccalaureate in psychology; a Master's degree in economics and a Doctorate in organizational behaviour.

Tracing his *raison d'etre* back through his career, Argyris observes: 'What drives me now has motivated me for the last 40 years. It sounds corny but I love learning for its own sake and, after serving in World War Two, I wanted to do something when I got back. I am optimistic, believing there can be a better, more just world. Though I am an unabashed romantic, I have always been connected with reality. A true romantic has a vision without it being operational. Being a soft-hearted romantic is deadly. In my case, research and theory provide the quality control. Success has always to be compared with one's values.'

For Argyris research has gone hand in hand with teaching and consultancy. He does not compartmentalize his interests in the way of some other management thinkers. Instead, the three

> *Education*: Baccalaureate in pyschology; Master's in economics; Doctorate in organization behaviour.
> *Career*: Taught at Yale in 1950s becoming Beach Professor of Administrative Finance in 1965; joined Harvard Business School, and became James Bryant Conant Professor of Education and Organizational Behaviour in 1971.

strands support and interrelate with each other. His work is based around the fundamental belief that if organizations allow and encourage individuals to develop to their full potential will be mutually beneficial. Argyris' research constantly challenges his natural optimism. Executives are often poor communicators, unwilling to challenge the status quo or to learn from their experiences. 'Some executives can't cope with changing anything. When new ideas are implemented the old theory of control is left intact. This is a source of continual disappointment, but my disappointment is tempered with a sense of understanding,' says Argyris. 'I am not angry, but I just think let's face reality. Disappointment is an opportunity for leverage for change.'

What Argyris has constantly observed is a mismatch between people and organizations. To fit people into organizational structures, they have been limited rather than developed, constrained and contained. People have, in turn, failed to develop themselves or accept responsibility for their actions. 'Responsibility is not a one-way process,' he says. 'We are personally responsible for our behaviour but, unfortunately, many companies change their parking space and not people's sense of responsibility.'

The origins of the development of the now popular concept of the learning organization can be traced to Argyris. In a 1991 *Harvard Business Review* article he wrote:

'Any company that aspires to succeed in the tougher business environment of the 1990s must first resolve a basic dilemma: success in the marketplace increasingly depends on learning, yet most people don't know how to learn. What's more, those members of the organization who many assume to be the best at learning are, in fact, not very good at it. Because many professionals are almost always successful at what they do, they rarely experience failure. And because they have rarely failed, they have never learned how to learn from failure.'[2]

His pleasure in the growing interest in the role of learning is combined with fears that it might be short-lived. 'I am pleased that organizational learning is in vogue but I worry that if we are not careful it will become another fad,' he says. 'I have little difficulty in talking about organizational learning to chief executives but, as you go down the hierarchy, it is regarded as being a bit dreamy.'

Argyris' contribution to the debate was the seminal work, *Organizational Learning* (1978), which he co-wrote with MIT's Donald Schon. Together with Schon, Argyris developed the concept of single-loop and double-loop learning. Argyris later explained the idea:

'Learning may be defined as occurring under two conditions. First, learning occurs when an organization achieves what it intended; that is, there is a match *between its design for action and the actual outcome. Second, learning occurs when a* mismatch *between intention and outcome is identified and corrected; that is, a mismatch is turned into a*

match ... Single loop learning occurs when matches are created, or when mismatches are corrected by changing actions. Double-loop learning occurs when mismatches are corrected by first examining and altering the governing variables and then the actions.'[3]

In short, single-loop learning does not question underlying assumptions while double-loop learning tackles basic assumptions and beliefs. The vast majority of learning falls into the category of single-loop learning, though Argyris believes that double-loop learning is now more widely recognized – 'Double-loop learning is gaining credence as a practical thing'. Indeed, the preoccupations of the early 1990s suggest that managers are more willing to tackle (or at least to contemplate) the big issues and to question and re-establish first principles.

Argyris believes that IT has a crucial role to play in furthering the acceptance and practice of learning within organizations. 'In the past the one-way, top-down approach gained strength from the fact that a lot of behaviour is not transparent. IT makes transactions transparent so that behaviour is no longer hidden. It creates fundamental truths where none previously existed.'

Argyris' ability to dedicate time and energy to getting under the skin of organizations is forcefully demonstrated in *Knowledge for Action* (1993). In this book Argyris examines the behaviour of one of his consultancy clients, itself a consultancy group. The consultancy arose when seven successful consultants decided to establish their own company. They hoped that it would be free from the Machiavellian political wrangles they had encountered in other organizations. In practice, their dreams were disappointed. Indeed, by the time Argyris was called in, internal wrangling consumed too many of its productive energies.

The company preferred to remain anonymous. 'I have always advocated not naming the companies I carry out research in,' says Argyris, recalling, 'When I worked with IBM Thomas Watson Junior said name the company – at a stockholder meeting someone asked why the company employed Communist consultants!'

The consultants featured in *Knowledge for Action* were, in fact, falling prey to what Argyris calls 'defensive routines'. Faced with a personally threatening problem, the executives were adept at covering it up or bypassing it entirely. Board meetings, therefore, concentrated on trivial topics – there was always one person keen to avoid discussion of an important issue. Outside the boardroom the big issues were discussed and blame apportioned, so that divisions built up relentlessly between the original founders. This approach affected the behaviour of the rest of the organization – others consciously kept information to a minimum so that executives weren't forced to face up to something new.

The fact that Argyris' client is a group of management consultants helps convey the importance of his message. If highly trained, intelligent executives fall into such traps, what chance have ordinary mortals?

Argyris' work forms a bridge between theory and practice in a way few other academics have managed. He says:

'*In education it is important that students connect what they learn to what they actually do. Executive education goes on every day, not simply by sending executives to a classroom. Too much formal executive education reinforces the status quo of the organization and too many academics are romantic in the pejorative sense. They run away from developing new approaches so you read 600 pages on leadership and it adds up to what? There are academic standards, but theories need to be tested. Academics and executives have a love-hate relationship. Academics say that executives are too shallow; while executives are interested in the pay-off. What executives now complain about is not the newness of the concepts but that the new concepts don't keep implementation in mind. You get unconnected fads and ideas so that managers can't use them.*'

While critical of formal processes of executive development, he points out that practising managers have a negligible record when it comes to developing important ideas. 'Practitioners don't come up with the ideas, the great theories which influence and create best practice. There have been people like Sloan and Barnard, but they were exceptional.'

Even so, Argyris identifies strongly with managers. 'I feel sorry for managers to some extent. There tends to be a fundamental assumption that if anything needs correcting it is management. And they are now being asked to deal with a lot of information. But I don't think they will ever be asked to deal with an amount beyond their competence. The amount is not the issue. The human mind is finite though managers sometimes act as if it wasn't.'

STUART CRAINER

Further Reading

Personality and Organization, Harper & Row, New York, 1957.
Overcoming Organizational Defences, Allyn & Bacon, Boston, 1990.
Organizational Learning: A Theory of Action Perspective* (with Donald Schon), Addison-Wesley, Wokingham, 1978.
On Organizational Learning,* Blackwell, Cambridge, 1993.
Knowledge for Action,* Jossey-Bass, San Francisco, 1993.

* Recommended reading

References

[1] Interview with Stuart Crainer 29 May 1994.
[2] Argyris, C, 'Teaching smart people how to learn', *Harvard Business Review*, May-June 1991.
[3] Argyris, C, 'Problems in producing usable knowledge for implementing liberating alternatives', Address to the International Congress of Applied Psychology, July 1982.

THE LEARNING ORGANIZATION

Phil Hodgson

'Learning has replaced control as the fundamental job of management,' wrote Shoshana Zuboff of Harvard Business School in her 1982 book, *In the Age of the Smart Machine*. Despite a great deal of research, the exact nature of the learning organization remains elusive in theory and even rarer in practice. Yet, the importance of creating organizations geared towards, and built around, learning is recognized by a growing number of managers and management thinkers.

With the emphasis on fully utilizing the talents of people to gain and retain competitive advantage, the concept of the learning organization has proved increasingly attractive. Interest has further been fuelled by the destruction of hierarchies so that organizations demand more from less people; and, from the perspective of the individual, by the growing demand for self-managed development and career management.

The learning organization has assumed mythological status in the later part of the 1990s. Its exact meaning and examples of best practice remain steadfastly elusive, but few managers would want to stand publicly against it. Managers might observe that it sounds attractive, is probably harmless and relatively inexpensive. In fact, the learning organization encapsulates a whole series of complex and untidy processes into a single easy-sounding phrase. This gives the impression that you can install a learning organization as easily as you can install a new piece of equipment. As a latest fad, the learning organization disappoints because it doesn't come in turnkey form. The biggest disservice the term does is to suggest that it is an end state – a product. In reality the learning organization is not a product; it is a process.

There are many kinds of processes that can dominate the culture of an organization. Imagine three roughly equal-sized companies competing in the same market. One prides itself on its creativity; the second emphasizes action; and the third learning. They are similar in terms of market share and financial details, and they all employ good people. The one difference between them is that they have each concentrated their recruitment and development activities towards encouraging a different component of human skill and ability, in order to create a different culture. The creative company continually searches for the new and different; even if its staff are not clear what they will do with it once they've invented it. In the action-oriented company people are always going somewhere, doing something, even if they are not clear why. The people in the company which emphasizes learning are not as strong in sheer creativity or decisive action as those in the other two organizations, but they do find the time to review what has happened, and to discuss how they could improve it. In short they are prepared to learn, from each other, from the market, and from their competitors.

It is increasingly evident that the company with a culture geared to and driven by learning may have a headstart in the hyper-competitive future. Managers, and the people who study managers, are involved in a frantic search for ways to understand what learning is, what and who it involves, and when it is applied to organizations. They want to turn the concept of the learning organization from a great theoretical idea into something that can be directly usable. The importance of learning more about *how*, *why* and *when* in organizations can no longer be understated or put to one side. 'The rate at which organizations learn may become the only sustainable source of competitive advantage,' says Ray Stata of Analogue Devices.[1]

What is a learning organization?

Definitive definitions of the learning organization are elusive. The phrase was coined during the 1980s, and referred to the aims – even visions – of a growing number of companies trying to bring about rapid and, in most cases, dramatic transformation of their organizations. Companies such as British Airways, Rover Group, Rank Xerox, 3M, and most of the oil companies, recognized that the route to a successful future in a less and less predictable world depended on the ability of everyone in their organization. They needed to mobilize their full skills and aptitudes continually, to recreate and rediscover from the existing organization a new organization best suited to that future.

Continual experimentation and adaptation to a changing set of circumstances is not a new idea. It looks very like the mechanism that governs the survival of every organism on the planet under the rules of engagement sketched out by Charles Darwin more than 130 years ago. When evolution involves deliberate experimentation and adaptation it is only a short step to describe it as learning.

Definitions of what constitutes a learning organization are in abundant supply. In *The Learning Company*, Mike Pedler and his colleagues say it is: 'An organization that facilitates the learning of all its members and continuously transforms itself.'[2]

The various definitions struggle to reconcile the learning of individuals and the concept of organizational learning. 'Although organizational learning occurs through individuals, it would be a mistake to conclude that organizational learning is nothing but the cumulative result of their members' learning. Organizations do not have brains, but they have cognitive systems and memories...organizations' memories preserve certain behaviours, mental maps, norms and values over time,' says Hedberg.[3]

The best known champion of the concept and practice of the learning organization is Peter Senge from the Massachusetts Institute of Technology (MIT). 'In the simplest sense, a learning organization is a group of people who are continually enhancing their capability to create their future,' says Senge. 'The traditional meaning of the word *learning* is much deeper than just *taking information in*. It is about changing individuals so that they produce results they care about, accomplish things that are important to them.'[4]

In his book *The Fifth Discipline* (and the subsequent *Fifth Discipline Fieldbook*[5]), Senge suggests that there are five components to a learning organization:

- **Systems thinking** – Senge introduces the idea of systems archetypes. In practical terms this can help managers spot repetitive patterns, such as the way certain kinds of problems persist, or the way systems have their own in-built limits to growth.
- **Personal mastery** – Senge grounds this idea in the familiar competencies and skills associated with management, but also includes spiritual growth – opening oneself up to a progressively deeper reality – and living life from a creative rather than a reactive viewpoint. This discipline involves two underlying movements – continually learning how to see current reality more clearly, and understanding how the ensuing gap between vision and reality produces the creative tension from which learning arises.
- **Mental models** – this essentially deals with the organization's driving and fundamental values and principles. Senge alerts managers to the power of patterns of thinking at the organizational level and the importance of non-defensive enquiry into the nature of these patterns.
- **Shared vision** – here Senge stresses the importance of co-creation and argues that shared vision can only be built on personal vision. He claims that shared vision is present when the task that follows from the vision is no longer seen by the team members as separate from the self.
- **Team learning** – the discipline of team learning involves two practices: dialogue and discussion. The former is characterized by its exploratory nature, the latter by the opposite process of narrowing down the field to the best alternative for the decisions that need to be made. The two are mutually complimentary, but the benefits of combining them only come from having previously separated them. Most teams lack the ability to distinguish between the two and to move consciously between them.[6]

There is a perennial danger of allowing the concept to overtake the reality. Academic definitions cannot be instantly applied in the real world. Managers need to promote learning so that it gradually emerges as a key part of an organization's culture. Being convinced of the merits of the learning organization is not usually a matter of dramatic conversion. Former chairman of Rover, Sir Graham Day, describes the evolution of his realization: 'During the mid-1980s a number of us, particularly in manufacturing business, somewhat belatedly became aware that our international competitiveness was being negatively impacted by the static knowledge and skills of our people at all levels. It was a small but critical step to translate this understanding into programmes to lift knowledge and skills on a continuing basis...Rover's need to establish what we now term a learning organization came from the imperative to secure the company's survival. Now it contributes to Rover's increasing competitiveness and value as a business.'[7]

Potential benefits

In a 1988 article, Arie de Geus, a former planning director at Shell, showed that one-third of *Fortune 500* industrial companies listed in 1970 had disappeared by 1983. A few organizations were identified, however, which had survived for 75 years or more. De Geus suggested that the key to their longevity was their ability to conduct 'experiments in the margin'. They were always looking for new business opportunities which continually challenged the organization to grow and learn.[8] This ability to grow (although not necessarily in size) and learn has become the backbone of any organization wishing to survive and prosper in changing and turbulent markets.

But this increased adaptability is not the only benefit that emerges from an organization that concentrates on learning. Learning to adapt, to cope with the market and the environment is important, but that is learning about what is already there. The other kind of learning that accrues to this kind of organization is an increased curiosity about what isn't yet there. Senge identifies this as *generative learning* and contrasts it with the coping kind which he calls *adaptive learning*. Generative learning occurs when people start looking at the world in new ways.

Acknowledging truths that contradict previously held views may lead to major business opportunities, but may be painful. In *Managing on the Edge*, Richard Pascale tells the story of how Honda decided to launch its bikes into Los Angeles as part of a grand strategy to sell into the USA.[9] Honda sent some people to California expecting to promote its larger bikes. In order to get around town, the sales people used some of the newly-developed small 50cc bikes. These attracted a lot of attention wherever they went. Eventually the sales team got enquiries, not from motorcycle dealers, but from sports shops and other retailers. It seemed that fewer people were interested in the large machines, and against Mr Honda's and the American teams' expectations the 50cc bikes were to become the biggest seller. They opened up the USA market to Honda, and within four years Honda was marketing almost 50 per cent of all motorcycles sold in the USA.

In this case it is interesting to look at the readiness of Honda's managers to learn rather than criticize. For instance, the team in America did not call back to Tokyo to say that (as Toyota had found previously) the strategy for launching the larger machines into the USA was failing. Instead they offered the alternative idea that everyone wanted the small machines. Yet, here was an organization that had spent a lot of effort in putting together a strategy to sell a product into a major market. A variety of alternative actions might have been taken – the sales people could have been fired for incompetency because they failed to sell the big bikes; a different sales strategy involving more or different advertising could have been adopted; and so on. Many organizations would have been loath to let go of their hard-fought-for strategy, especially on account of a few comparatively junior people several thousand miles away, in a market that had not yet proved itself.

This ability to be generative really shows its advantage when things start to speed up. A spokesman for 3M has said that the majority of its computer products are obsolete within 12 months. The old design and production cycle of 24 months just wasn't good enough to compete successfully in that kind of environment. A 3M motto is 'change is the driving force for success'. To this end it has given a major overhaul to all of the jobs on its Texas site. Referring to their need for thinking and ideas and learning to be brought into every kind of work, from the most senior manager to the most junior cleaner, 3M says that there is no such thing as a mundane job any more – even in the cafeteria. Tom Peters summed it up after a visit to a 3M site. He said that 3M's view is, 'if you ain't getting better, you're getting worse'.

Creating the learning organization

How do you create, or at least enhance, the learning capabilities of an organization? First take heed of the warning of William O'Brien, chief executive of Hanover Insurance companies: 'Why don't people create such organizations? I think the answer is leadership. People have no real comprehension of the type of commitment it requires to build such an organization.'[10]

O'Brien goes on to say that the classic leadership roles of making key decisions and setting direction are inappropriate, as they reinforce attention onto short-term events and, when there is a crisis, place their faith in the leader's charisma. The learning organization needs leaders who will act as teachers, designers and stewards. There are different skills to be deployed too: challenging mental models, building shared visions, and encouraging more people to think about the entire system rather than just their part of it.

In *The Learning Company* Pedler and his co-authors identify a series of characteristics which they argue are significant in creating the learning environment. They include:

- encouraging a much wider debate on strategy and policy formation;
- creating an environment where tensions are welcomed as they can precede creative solutions to problems that were previously seen as 'win-lose' resolutions of difficulties;
- 'informating', that is using information technology to inform and empower for the many rather than for the few;
- exchanging information – getting closer to internal and external customers and suppliers;
- using the people who meet external customers to bring back useful information about needs and opportunities;
- collaborating rather than competing and making internal and external best-practice comparisons;
- encouraging self-development opportunities for everyone in the organization. Individuals are encouraged to take responsibility for their own learning and development.

Pedler also observes that managers need to see their major responsibility as encouraging a learning climate by facilitating learning from experience, and experimentation. There also needs to be the recognition that some learning has to come as the result of making mistakes. So although managers don't encourage people to get it wrong, they do encourage everyone to try it out. In this way generative learning will have occurred.

It is hard for managers to learn to let go, but it is possible. Mike Walsh, chief executive of Union Pacific, made enormous changes to the effectiveness and morale of his huge and widely dispersed organization. He said: 'My biggest challenge is to be worthy of the staff, and the staff in this and most other companies are capable of a great deal more responsibility than most managers have a clue.'

What are the first steps?

The initial steps towards becoming a learning organization are usually taken for a reason. It may be a change of chief executive, an obvious challenge in the marketplace, or a new opportunity posed by technology. But it also comes from recognizing a need that has usually been there for some time. The need is not confined to the top of the organization, or even to its management. The need is simply that most people feel under-used or wrongly used at work, and would love to do it differently. Recognizing that need, publicly and privately, is often one of the key steps to moving the organization along the road to becoming a learning organization.

Angela O'Connell and Mike Mulholland of Barclays Property Holdings say:

'When we started, we did not have a specific plan, there was nothing to refer to and it has been a learning process in itself. With hindsight, much has seemed painfully obvious, a lot of what we have done is about unlocking what is natural in people anyway. However the process is painful, since people are not encouraged to view work as an environment in which they learn and develop.'

Rover Group realized after the turbulence of the 1970s and early 1980s that the organization had unwittingly become dependent, petulant, and almost an anti-learning organization. Understanding that the predominant view of training was of something that was *done* to you, led to a series of actions. Rover wanted staff to be keen on learning as something you could do *for yourself*. It led to the creation of The Rover Learning Business as a separate organization, a business within a business. Its primary aim is to provide a top-quality learning and development service to all employees as customers, regardless of geography and with equal opportunity. It is committed to providing assistance to everyone wishing to develop themselves. One of its first products was the REAL programme (Rover Employees Assisted Learning).

The REAL programme allows each employee to receive an amount of money per year for pursuing some kind of learning programme. The programmes very definitely do not have to be linked to work – in fact the only limitations that are put on choice of subjects are those where tax regulations need to be complied with. Learning to swim, learning in-shore navigation, learning Japanese, have allowed staff whose previous experience of 'education' was generally to be a failure at school, to now appreciate that they too can participate in learning, and what's more it can be fun. Rover reports that in parallel with the REAL programme, suggestions from employees have burgeoned. Quality circle groups operate widely across the organization, and in 1992 alone, suggestions saved the company over £10 million which, coupled with suggestions from previous years, meant that nearly £20 million had been saved.[11]

But tackling the entire organization as one unit, may seem very daunting. Theresa Barnett, deputy principal of the TSB Staff College says: 'You don't have to convert the whole company in one go, you can develop smaller cells of learning activity and then link those cells together.'

Of course, just because you have split up the organization into a series of smaller learning units does not mean that the work load is any less, or that the challenge to adapt to a new way of thinking is reduced. 'To ask department A and department B to learn from each other is a big leap, but once they have developed their learning abilities in cells, then it is easier to link these interactively together. But it takes a lot of work to connect across a complexity of learning departments – especially in a large organization. That is often one vital role of a management college,' says Theresa Barnett.

Problems, costs and risks

The interest in improving learning is quite similar to the interest in improving quality which was very attractive five years earlier. Sadly, there is mounting evidence that more than half of all quality initiatives fail within two years. Will the learning organization prove similarly disappointing?

There are probably three main problems to be overcome in setting up and sustaining a learning organization. The first is the loss, or more precisely the handing over of control from the managers to the people who are doing the learning. If they are to learn, then they have to be able to experiment. If they are going to experiment, they need to have the flexibility and authority to 'try it a different way'. Many managers find this shift in their own jobs disconcerting. The manager has to change from certainty to uncertainty. They are suddenly inhabiting a place where the right thing to say is, 'I don't know but try it anyway, I'll support you if it goes wrong.' Apportioning blame remains endemic and automatic in most organizations.

In addition, the skills of listening and asking good questions, not always apparent in top management, are the ways to steer a project. Simply dictating adds no learning value. For a person who wants power, the facilitating stance seems a poor substitute. But where the transition has worked, direct but static power has been traded for dynamic influence. And time and time again, managers have found that you can achieve more with less if you go by the second route.

A telling comparison can be made between CNN and CBS. CNN has very little bureaucracy, makes most of its big decisions on the run, and spends less in 24 hours than CBS spends in one hour for apparently equivalent news coverage. The people at CNN are powerful because they keep moving, they don't use fixed authority, they appear to invent it each time afresh. It is very tiring, and people do get burned out, but it is also tremendously competitive.

A key challenge is that of trust and having the confidence to trust people. In most organizations in which learning has been successfully introduced, people have had to learn to trust each other. It is a sad fact, but in the past, the Western world seems to have been especially good at creating organizations that ran without the need for trust. The price of that omission was a belief that learning had to be institutionalized to be taken seriously. The learning organization is fuelled by trust, but how many managers are good at creating and extending trust at all levels (not just their own) in the organization? And it doesn't stop there. The really effective organizations bring suppliers and buyers into their workplace in order to involve them in the total process of design and delivery. Managers who learned their management skills in a non-trust environment usually have some difficulty in changing their ways to suit and promote the new culture.

'We have transformed from a service division within an institution into a market-oriented business. We are encouraging curiosity, trust and the belief in others' abilities, helping people to feel good about themselves, feeling valued and important. Sadly the culture of an institution often tends to emphasize the negative, avoiding risk – the 'yes, but' syndrome,' say O'Connell and Mulholland of Barclays Property Holdings.

The final problem area is coping with risk. The inescapable fact is that as experimentation increases, so mistakes will increase, and in the short term performance is likely to suffer. It can require strong nerves to weather that initial dip in performance, if the pressure to perform is on. How do you cope with risk? The obvious answer is to start slowly, and in a limited way, create the learning. That is certainly feasible, but another feature comes into play, which is that once people have started down this route, they find their view of what is and what isn't a risk changes. Things that used to take weeks – waiting for approvals, can now be done in hours or minutes. If you can suddenly learn to move at that sort of speed, you can afford to make some mistakes, because you are now achieving much that was previously beyond you.

How to sustain the learning organization

The business imperatives are strong, and any organization that improves its performance in the way that Rover Group has done could be forgiven if they instructed their staff to keep on learning. But of course they don't, because something even more powerful is at work. The simple fact is that most people appear to like learning. It makes them feel better, and it encourages them to come to work, and to work better at work. The difficulty in sustaining this style of organization is found when it has been imposed from above rather as a passing fad or fashion. In this case then, like fashion, the learning organization will last until the next fashion comes along, and the organization will probably not last many of those.

Airlines SAS and BA found that after they had radically reorganized their operations and considerably improved market share and profitability, in a few years customers had got used to the improved levels of service, and wanted more. The dramatic learning curve that all their staff had gone though during the first revolution had tailed off, and it was time to stand at the foot of another apparently vertical learning rock face.

While learning can now be shown to be a significant component of getting ahead, continuous learning appears to be an even more significant part of staying ahead. But that is often a complex process. As Paul Turner, TSB's director of personnel for credit and operations, says:

'Models of a learning organization are worthless, unless you are prepared to understand the intricacies and complexity of that organization. Changing our culture from that of a traditional bank has meant an acceptance that we can all change. It has been a challenge to simplify the processes and also recognize that implementation requires more sophistication than was needed in the past.'

Every event can have a learning payoff. Even a humble meeting can play its part. 'They should be seen as a learning process, as an opportunity for systematizing learning for the organization,' say O'Connell and Mulholland.

Becoming a learning organization requires new ways of thinking and a lot of work. But for organizations determined to keep at the leading edge, is there any choice? 'Learning is the key to *sustaining competitive advantage*,' says TSB's Paul Turner – and this must be the most compelling reason for every employee to take the learning organization seriously.

Phil Hodgson is a psychologist turned strategist. He is director of action learning at Ashridge Management College. He has been a volunteer worker in the West Pacific, a software engineer, human resource manager and business development manager. As a consultant and trainer, he has worked extensively in the areas of leadership development and the management of strategic change. He is the author of a number of books and many articles.

Further Reading

Pedler, M, Burgoyne, J and Boydell, T, *The Learning Company, A Strategy for Sustainable Development*, McGraw-Hill, Maidenhead, 1991.

Senge, P, Roberts, C, Ross, RB, Smith, BJ and Kleiner, A, *The Fifth Discipline Fieldbook*, Nicholas Brealey, London, 1994.

Senge, P, *The Fifth Discipline: The Art and Practice of the Learning Organization*, Doubleday, New York, 1990.

References

1 *Sloan Management Review*, pp. 63-74, Spring 1989.
2 Pedler, M, Burgoyne, J and Boydell, T, *The Learning Company, A Strategy for Sustainable Development*, McGraw-Hill, Maidenhead,1991.
3 Hedberg, BO, 'How organizations learn and unlearn' in *The Handbook of Organization Design*, (eds Nystrom, P and Starbuck, W), vol. 1, Oxford University Press, 1981.
4 Quoted in Napuk, K, 'Live and learn', *Scottish Business Insider*, January 1994.
5 Senge, P, Roberts, C, Ross, RB, Smith, BJ and Kleiner, A, *The Fifth Discipline Fieldbook*, Nicholas Brealey, London, 1994.
6 Senge, P, *The Fifth Discipline: The Art and Practice of the Learning Organization*, Doubleday, New York, 1990.
7 Day, G, Preface to *Implementing the Learning Organization*, Thurbin, PJ, Financial Times/Pitman, London, 1994.
8 Geus, de, AP, 'Planning as learning', *Harvard Business Review*, March-April 1988, pp. 48–62.
9 Pascale, R, *Managing on the Edge*, Viking, London, 1990.
10 Senge, P, *The Fifth Discipline: The Art and Practice of the Learning Organization*, Doubleday, New York, 1990.
11 Bower, DG, 'The Learning Organization: A Rover Perspective', *Executive Development*, vol. 6 no. 2, 1993, pp. 3–6, MCB University Press.

SELF-MANAGED LEARNING

Andrew Constable

When it came to management development, managers were once pawns in the hands of the organization. If the company thought a manager needed a particular skill they were speedily despatched on a suitable course. In some companies development is still regarded in these terms. The trouble is that the skills needed by managers in the 1990s are so broad ranging that picking off skills is no longer enough. Managers and their organizations have to be more selective and focused.

As part of this growing trend, there is growing realization among managers – and their companies – that developing managerial skills and techniques is not simply a corporate responsibility. Managers, too, have a role to play in being proactive and identifying areas in which they need to develop. Today, instead of being pawns moved around by corporate might, managers are increasingly encouraged to examine their own strengths and weaknesses to develop the skills necessary for the future.

Self-managed learning (SML) can be defined as a process whereby individuals determine *what* they learn and *how* they learn *with others* in the context of their unique situation.

Understanding self-managed learning can be helped by drawing comparisons with other forms of development activities. In the vast majority of these, centre stage is occupied by the teacher, lecturer or expert who imparts knowledge more or less effectively to expectant students. The learner has a passive role and often fails to engage with the process. This is not to deny the value of the knowledgeable and wise, but to suggest that learners frequently fall short of deriving maximum benefit from such approaches.

In contrast, with SML it is the learner who is the central figure in the process. All activities which the programme encompasses are designed primarily to assist the learner. It is they who set learning goals and objectives for the programme and then choose the methods by which they will achieve them. These might include attending a lecture or conference, but could also feature listening to audio-tapes in a car, researching a topic of a particular interest to the individual or spending time tapping the knowledge of someone inside the organization. These are only a few examples of the infinite variety of ways in which we can learn. The important point is that it is the *learner* who chooses.

This can give the impression of encouraging individualism to an extreme extent. But, to work successfully, SML should act as a framework which enables individuals to learn and study different areas at the same time while participating in a common process. This is a feature which is particularly attractive both to participating individuals and to sponsoring organizations. Experience clearly suggests that individuals rarely, if ever, have identical development needs. This raises serious questions about the generic approach to developing people whereby large numbers go through the same programme (in which they have often had little or no say) and are expected to emerge with certain pre-determined changes in their knowledge, skills or behaviour. Inherent in the SML process is a respect for the worth of the individual and the valuing of differences between individuals.

Origins of self-managed learning

SML can be viewed as a synthesis of the best features of a range of approaches to developing people. The key influences come from action learning, independent study, open learning, distance learning and, what might be called, the self-development movement. The advantages and drawbacks of each approach are described below:

Action learning

Advantages	*Drawbacks*
● Learning is focused on real issues.	● Emphasis on action, *not* on learning.
● Some risks involved.	
● Group context for learning.	● Learning is unplanned, too haphazard.

Independent study

Advantages	*Drawbacks*
● Learner chooses what/how to learn.	● Too isolated.
● Can include use of learning contracts.	● Too academic.
● Responsive to individual needs.	● Does not recognize the importance of social contact in the learning process.

Open learning

Advantages	*Drawbacks*
● Flexible on time and place.	● Pre-packaged materials – rigid, disconnected from our experience.
● Choice of learning materials.	
● Accessible to a wide range of people.	● No choice of goals, learning methods and assessment processes.

Distance learning

Advantages	*Drawbacks*
● Learner chooses when and where to study.	● Can seem very remote and detached.

- Range of learning materials.
- Can cater for large numbers of students.

- Impersonal.
- Solitary activity.

Self-development movement

Advantages

- Responsibility rests with the learner.
- Encourages independence.
- Equips individuals with life-skills.

Drawbacks

- Can appear vague.
- Not structured.
- Often no clearly defined goals.

SML seeks to combine the advantages of each of these approaches and to augment them with other features in an innovative and powerful way.

The growing interest in using SML can be attributed in part to changes in organizations, such as the increasing importance of networks, and organizations becoming leaner, flatter and more flexible. The disappearance of career ladders means that managers have to make the right career moves which bring them into contact with important and useful new skills.

In turn these changes have influenced the ways in which organizations seek to develop their workforce. The increasing interest in empowerment has highlighted deficiencies in training and development. There has been a noticeable shift towards more on-the-job learning and greater importance being attached to individual relationships, through approaches such as coaching, mentoring and networking. SML contains both these elements: much of what individuals learn takes place as part of their normal work activities and the process encourages participants to form close relationships with their colleagues and with their line manager. As a result, learning is not separated from work in the way which characterizes many development approaches. As has already been implied, participants on an SML programme have much greater power than is usual in development processes.

There can, of course, be myriad reasons why an organization decides to adopt the SML approach. They might want to use an approach which would be congruent with, and support, broader organizational and cultural changes, such as encouraging individuals to take greater responsibility for what they do. Alternative attractions may include offering both individual and organizational development and benefits; the strong emphasis on the development of internal resources; an approach which can cascade throughout the organization; and cost-effectiveness.

From the individual's perspective SML can be a powerful and profound process. By its very nature SML avoids the problem of learning transfer which often diminishes the value of other development activities. It deals with the whole person and recognizes that emotions, physical health, spiritual well-being as well as intellectual, can be legitimate areas for development. (There is, however, no pressure applied to individuals to focus on any area they do not want to.)

This approach recognizes that many managers have neatly compartmentalized their lives and refuse to acknowledge links between their home and working lives. SML can remove the barriers which prevent managers learning lessons in their private lives which might be useful in their business roles. It regards development as a continuous process, taking all aspects of a person's behaviour and outlook rather than one small aspect of it.

As a result, the changes which take place in individuals are likely to be of a more permanent nature than is usually the case. Instead of a quick fix, SML seeks to be developmental over time.

Key elements of SML

Mapping the field

This metaphor is used to describe the process of providing an overview of the context in which individuals will pursue their learning goals. This will vary in accordance with the type and nature of the programme.

For example, an in-company programme may have as its field a number of management competencies which have been identified as critical to the future success of the organization. Individuals develop their learning objectives based on these competencies.

The mapping process provides an anchor for the programme, without which much of the potential value would be lost. Organizations sometimes fail to recognize the importance of this process – it is not then surprising that individuals choose areas to work on which appear to bear little relation to broader organizational needs and objectives.

Learning contract

This is essentially a statement of what an individual is going to work on in the programme. It comprises a series of learning goals and objectives which also include the method of learning to be used and the evidence of learning which will be produced at the end of the programme. The number of goals and the amount of time spent developing them will be dependent on the overall length of the programme. A rule of thumb is that one-third of the total programme should be devoted to developing the learning contract, and two-thirds to fulfilling the goals.

The term *learning contract* originates from the United States and is now becoming more widely used in Europe. The *contract* refers to the agreement that the individual makes with him or her self, and with the other members of the learning set, as to what they are going to work on. Alternatives such as *development agreement* and *personal development plan* can also be used where the language is felt to be more appropriate.

A simple but powerful framework of five questions can be used to help individuals develop their learning contracts. This is set out in Fig. 1.

The process of defining and clarifying learning goals is in itself very valuable, especially when assisted, challenged and supported by others. It helps individuals to focus their minds and to choose areas which will have the greatest impact on them and their effectiveness at work. Questions which participants on an SML programme would typically ask themselves when defining their learning goals include the following:

- How do I wish to develop my role? How do I wish to develop my career?
- How does that role or direction fit with the overall strategy of the organization?
- What area of knowledge, skills and qualities do I need to be effective in that role, in this organization?
- What are my present areas of knowledge, skills and qualities?
- What do I need to learn?

Support for the use of learning contracts is provided by research which suggests that individuals who engage in the process of setting goals are likely to outperform those who do not. They provide a discipline to the learning process and enable progress to be measured.

Learning sets

A set is a group of five or six individuals working together with an adviser to provide challenges, support, and the benefit of their experience to each set member in relation to their learning.

A *set*, or *learning set*, is different from other groups such as discussion or brainstorming groups, project teams and committees. The primary purpose of a set is to assist the learning of each individual within the set. In order to achieve this, set meetings have a particular structure which is again different from the structure of other meetings managers may attend. A typical pattern is set out below:

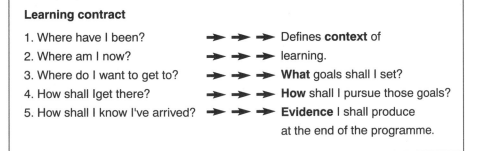

Learning contract

1. Where have I been?   ➤ ➤ ➤ Defines **context** of
2. Where am I now?   ➤ ➤ ➤ learning.
3. Where do I want to get to?   ➤ ➤ ➤ **What** goals shall I set?
4. How shall I get there?   ➤ ➤ ➤ **How** shall I pursue those goals?
5. How shall I know I've arrived? ➤ ➤ ➤ **Evidence** I shall produce at the end of the programme.

Fig. 1 The learning contract

1. 'Check in'

At the start of a set meeting, each individual briefly talks through the key things that have happened to him/her since the last set meeting which are not directly related to their learning contract.

2. Setting the agenda for the set meeting

This involves:

- negotiating time;
- ordering time slots (names);
- identifying if there are any set issues for which time needs to be scheduled.

3. Individual time slots

This is the principal element of a set meeting. Each individual has a slot of time in which to use the set for helping their learning. Each set member does not need to take the same amount of time and indeed, the way in which the total time is allocated will invariably be different from one set meeting to the next. (On a long-term programme, sets will meet typically once a month).

4. Set issues

Time may be given over at the end of a set meeting to discuss set issues.

5. 'Check-out'

The metaphor here is taken from leaving a hotel. In a set meeting it consists of a series of brief individual comments about how each set member experienced the set meeting.

A useful comparison is to see a set as a group of wise, experienced consultants whom you have at your disposal for a limited period of time and it is up to you to make best use of them. Sets tend to generate their own ways of working and their own ground rules, which is very much in keeping with the philosophy of the approach. (General guidelines can be provided as a stimulus for this.) How set members choose to use their 'air-time' is their individual responsibility.

The process of learning in a set can also yield other organizational benefits. These include cross-functional working, the development of a team ethos and cross-cultural co-operation. It is worth considering these additional advantages when sets are being formed at the start of a programme.

Set adviser

The set adviser has a vital role to play in the effective functioning of the set. It is *not* a role that someone can step into without preparation or training, and not an area in which to cut corners.

1. Qualities of a set adviser

- individual *and* group focus;
- good interpersonal skills: questioning and listening;

- able to identify significant patterns in people's behaviour and ways of thinking;
- inner assurance;
  - *not* to take the lead in the set;
  - to raise difficult issues;
  - to assist individuals to work through confusion;
  - to feel comfortable with not having an expert role in the set;
- patience;
- persistence;
- resilience.

2. Key activities

- demonstrating effective behaviour in the set;
- ensuring a balance is maintained between challenge and support;
- helping to make the learning of set members explicit;
- ensuring the set is working effectively;
- maintaining the focus on learning;
- adhering to the structure of the set meeting.

Examples of the kind of interventions a set adviser might make, include the following:

- Is this a useful line of questioning?
- What have you learned from this?
- What will your next steps be?
- What will you do differently next time?
- Is this a set issue which we should put some time aside for later?

It is also worth pointing out that the set adviser is not there to prop up the set or to take decisions for it or to be the sole timekeeper. It is not an easy role to perform and certainly not one for the faint-hearted. In fact, some of the most effective set advisers have themselves had recent experience of being a set member. It has been this experience which has encouraged them to take on the role of set adviser. The transition is an attractive means of cascading SML down through an organization and equipping some employees with additional skills through taking on the role of set adviser. This does not obviate the need for specific training in these skills but it accelerates the process of becoming proficient in this role.

Assessment

This is an important part of an SML programme and takes two forms: continuous assessment and final assessment. Continuous assessment is provided through regular set meetings during which individuals present the work they have completed since the previous set meeting. They will be asked questions by the other set members and receive comments and feedback. This usually proves highly beneficial to each individual and contributes substantially to the learning process. In the light of observations made by others, individuals may then modify their way of working, consider a new perspective on a subject or choose to focus their efforts in a different area.

Final assessment starts with the individual making a judgement as to how well individuals have done in relation to the learning goals agreed and negotiated in the set. Each individual makes a case for him/herself. For example, if someone had five learning goals they might argue that three of them had been met as specified, one of them had been only partially completed and the other had exceeded the target. The other set members would then offer their assessment of what had been achieved. As a result, responsibility for this process is thus shared between the individual and his or her fellow set members. In other terms this could be described as self and peer assessment. The set adviser also contributes to this process.

If the programme leads to a recognized qualification there will be a further level of assessment provided through external moderators. There is no doubt that assessment on an SML programme demands much more of the participants than on a more traditional course where they are typically not involved in the process. Part of the rationale for this approach is based on the belief that competent individuals should be able to judge and assess their own work accurately and effectively.

Individuals will know much more about the process of learning they have experienced than anyone seeing only the work produced at the end of the programme.

Questions sometimes arise about the rigour of the assessment process. They tend to come from people who have not experienced SML and who are more accustomed to the rigour being provided through the powerful position of teachers and examiners on more traditional programmes. SML programmes are at least as rigorous as more traditional courses and sometimes more so. If there is a difference, it is often that individuals are tougher on themselves than others would be, and they set very high expectations of what they should achieve. The set process acts as a useful check and balance in helping individuals identify appropriate target levels of achievement for themselves. Rigour is therefore certainly present but, as with many aspects of SML, is created in a different way.

What does a self-managed learning programme look like?

Figure 2, provides a blueprint for an SML programme. It is important to mention that this is not a rigid structure and that some of the elements shown are not present in all programmes. A good example of this is the use of mentors on this type of programme. Mentors can enhance the value of the learning undertaken by participants in an SML programme and also provide a further link back to the organization. However, some organizational cultures are not conducive to having mentors so alternative ways of providing the same bene-fits would have to be examined.

Key points to note from the blueprint are the following:

- The programme is divided into two phases. Phase 1 is concerned with develop-ing and agreeing with other set members a learning contract. Phase 2 is about delivering on the learning goals/objectives contained in the learning contract.
- Phase 1 typically lasts one-third of the length of the programme; Phase 2 takes up the other two-thirds.
- The actual length of the programme can vary between a few months and two years. (In theory it could go beyond two years, although there are likely to be practical difficulties with this.)
- Parallel processes of *Information Gathering* and *Information Processing* take place in Phase 1 of the programme. There are a variety of ways in which these process can be managed and delivered.
- Dialogue between participants and their line managers around the learning contract is an important feature. It helps to secure line managers' commit-ment to the process and ensures that what individuals are learning is relevant to the needs of the organization.

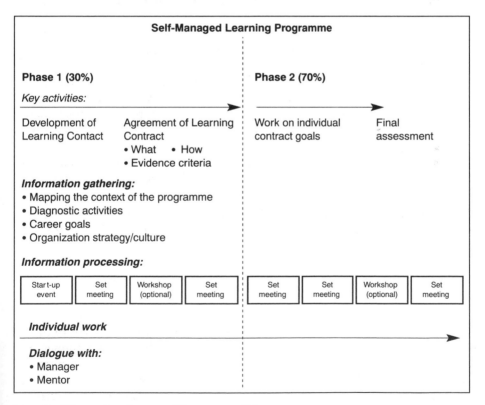

Fig. 2 Blueprint for a self-managed learning programme

Potential pitfalls

● **Failure to provide a clear context for the programme** What are the boundaries within which individuals can develop their learning contracts? SML is at its most powerful when individual and organizational objectives are linked.

● **Participants do not attend set meetings regularly** Clearly the set process is a vital thread running through this type of programme. If set meetings are frequently missed by individuals, they themselves will fail to derive the benefits of this process and, equally important, this will have an adverse effect on the other set members.

● **Insufficient time and effort is spent developing learning contracts** This runs the risk of individuals working on areas that may not be the most important either to them or their organization. The process of negotiating and challenging learning goals/objectives in the set is critical to the success of the programme.

● **The temptation for set advisers and others associated with the management of an SML programme to try to provide all the answers to participants' issues/problems** This can be particularly appealing at the start of a programme when the participants are struggling with uncertainty and trying to determine what it is they are going to be learning. The role of the set adviser and any other people supporting the programme is to assist the participants to work through these challenges for themselves.

● **Unrealistic expectations of immediate changes in participants** SML is essentially a long-term developmental process. The type of changes that do take place are often of an altogether different order to those on a more traditional programme.

Even though many companies are now expressing an interest in SML, the trouble is that the habits of a generation are hard to break. Managers fed on a diet of conscripted training are uneasy about having the burden of their own development thrust upon them. Being *sent* on a course is something you can complain about – sometimes with justification. It is completely different when you have to identify your own needs and the best methods of satisfying them.

There are other reasons why SML is a difficult concept for many managers to come to terms with. Some point to a lack of motivation. Why, they say, should they develop themselves when their company offers little or nothing in the way of support or rewards? There is also a strong fear of failure. In some areas, training has traditionally been regarded as a last resort, an admission of inadequacy. Other managers are simply unsure of what to do. They don't know where or how to start the process and, even if they begin, don't know how to maintain momentum. Another disincentive to following self-managed development is simple lack of knowledge. Managers may be unable – or perhaps unwilling – to identify areas in which they need to develop and have little or no knowledge of the myriad techniques, approaches and activities at their disposal.

● **Failure to provide sufficient training for set advisers** It is unreasonable to expect people to take on the set adviser role without adequate preparation and training. This applies both to managers and trainers/developers who wish to become set advisers. It is a different type of facilitation to that which most trainers/developers are accustomed and indeed many do not find it easy to make the transition from their more traditional role. Thorough training can go a long way to overcoming this potential problem.

Potential benefits

Individual

- New knowledge, skills and abilities defined in the learning contract.
- Improved management skills.
- Strategic thinking.
- Ability to cope with and manage change.
- Enhanced interpersonal skills.
- Greater self-awareness.
- Better understanding of how they learn.
- Greater confidence.
- Self-reliance.
- Belief that they can, to a large extent, determine their own future.

Organization

- Matches individual and organizational needs and objectives.
- More versatile and flexible workforce.
- Can support broader organization and cultural changes.
- Can link with other development initiatives (see next section).
- Congruence with project/enterprise/change environment.
- SML is an approach which is 'owned' by the organization – with a strong emphasis on the development of internal resources.
- Can cascade throughout an organization.
- Facilitates cross-functional working and networking.

Links with other initiatives

SML can link with and support a whole range of other organizational initiatives and, indeed, in our experience, is often at its most effective when this is the case. A *map* showing some of the other activities with which SML has been or could be linked is shown in Fig. 3:

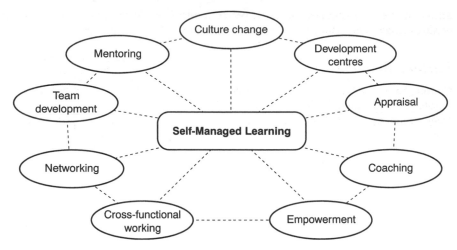

Fig. 3 Other initiatives with which SML can be linked

An important feature of this map is the interconnection of the different initiatives. This has been, and will no doubt continue to be, attractive to organizations which are considering SML because they can start anywhere on the map, ie, with any of the processes shown. SML can not only facilitate any of these processes but can also provide a link between a number of different activities as shown. It does not matter where you start because they are all connected. This enables organizations to adopt a more strategic, long-term approach to developing their people and provides a framework for such an approach.

SML has moved from the fringes of development activity to the mainstream and is now seen as the way forward for many organizations. It is closely linked with the notion of the learning organization which is gaining popularity across the globe. Interest and popularity seem likely to continue to grow.

The sceptical might suggest that SML is an abdication of a company's responsibility, a means of shifting management development onto the already loaded shoulders of their managers. But if it is to work, SML involves and relies on the participation of the manager's organization. The company has a vital role to play, providing opportunities, support and resources.

Fundamentally, however, it is the individual manager who has to take final responsibility and control. And he or she can't do this in isolation. Companies can't abandon their managers to plough their own furrow. Also, people need and want to share and test ideas with others. Self-managed learning revolves around relationships with a wide range of people – from colleagues on courses to mentors and coaches; from the manager's boss to family and friends. The key relationship, however, must be with the organization.

Andrew Constable is assistant director of Roffey Park Management Institute. Prior to joining Roffey Park in 1992, he worked for the Manpower Services Commission and Abbey National. He is account manager for a number of Roffey's major clients and tutors on open programmes, including personal effectiveness, and power and the enterprising manager, for which he is programme director.

Further Reading

Cunningham, I, *The Wisdom of Strategic Learning: The Self-managed Learning Solution*, McGraw-Hill, Maidenhead, 1994.
Dent, F, Macgregor, R and Wills, S, *Signposts for Success*, FT/Pitman, London, 1994.

COACHING AND MENTORING

Joanna Howard

The traditional homogeneity of organizations is increasingly being replaced by encouragement of individuality, variety, innovation and difference. This, however, runs the risk of losing some of the key attractions of the traditional organization – stability and security.

Coaching and mentoring seek to bridge the gap between traditional expectations of the organization and more contemporary approaches. Several key features of coaching and mentoring, for individuals and organizations alike, make them increasingly attractive. They can encourage a culture of learning and mutual help, and combine both individual and organizational development.

Both coaching and mentoring are natural human activities, often intuitively practised by managers. Although many managers practise them without thinking, many others have not developed these natural skills or have allowed them to stagnate or disappear.

Mentoring and coaching are distinguished from each other generally by the work-distance and time-frame of what is being discussed. Typically, managers coach those who report to them, about fairly immediate work developments. A mentor is often organizationally more distant from the person they are mentoring (by seniority or by being outside the organization or department); and can work with the mentee on longer term issues of personal development and career planning.

Coaching and mentoring in the organization

The significance of coaching and mentoring for the modern organization lies in four key aspects:

- **The attention to the individual** provided by these activities. This in itself is a shift from previous attitudes to the management of subordinates. This attention can provide a point of stability that makes people more able to respond effectively to change.
- **The individual becomes a skilful and reflective learner.** This is the underlying aim of both activities. Individuals increasingly use their own experience as the key material for learning, assisted by the knowledge and wisdom of the coach or mentor.
- **The importance of the relationship.** Both activities are examples of what has been described as 'developmental working relationships'. A large part of the success of the mentor or the coach depends on the way they manage

the relationship at a human and personal level. This ability transfers into other working areas, as not only a survival skill in the new style of organization, but as a means of sharing knowledge and expertise.

- **The effect of organizational climate, and the effect on it.** Though the one-to-one relationship is clearly central in coaching and mentoring, to be fully effective it needs to be part of an organization-wide appreciation of the value of learning as a driver for relevant change. Effective coaching and mentoring relationships can help to develop this wider process as well as deriving benefits from it.

Coaching and mentoring frequently run alongside, or are an intrinsic part of, a self-development process set in place by the organization. This process can vary; with personal projects and personal development plans at one end of the continuum, and an organization-wide self-managed learning programme at the other. They are linked by an emphasis on development becoming something for which individuals have to take responsibility themselves.

One of the most important conditions for coaching and mentoring to be successful is the assumption that learning is a respectable activity, and that everyone can and should be engaged in it. The mentor and the coach challenge and support individuals in their learning, and help to provide the organizational framework in which it happens.

Success is also more likely where there is a clear, though evolving, picture of the nature of a person's job or role, and where it fits into the organization and the corporate goals. This requires a degree of clarity about job or role expectations: well-developed and thought-through criteria of success, clear regular feedback, some sense of the resources necessary to achieve the targets set, and an understanding of the work context, both internal to the organization and in the marketplace. This clarity is never easy to achieve, but a move towards it sets the scene for effective coaching and mentoring.

Coaching

Effective coaching depends not only on the skills of the coach and the receptiveness of the person being coached, but also on the conditions outlined above being present (clarity about success criteria, usable feedback, etc) in the work setting. At the same time, when managers start to coach, if they are working effectively there is a better chance of the surrounding conditions being improved. Coaching conversations may lead to increased clarity about job expectations, for instance, and may provide regular feedback and the opportunity to think through standards and criteria for success. There is a close two-way relationship between effective coaching initiatives and a favourable learning climate, each enhancing the other.

The concept of coaching remains most easily associated with sports coaching where the purpose of the coach is to help the person they are coaching to reach their personal best. Interestingly, the nature of sports coaching is undergoing basic changes – ones which are, to some degree, mirrored in organizations. There was a time when the coach was the person who drove the athlete on, forced the pace and continually instructed. Increasingly, coaches are now moving to an approach which involves accurately targeted questioning to help the athlete become increasingly aware of 'what works' – for instance, the environment in which he or she performs best, how this feels, and what the obstacles are to achieving this repeatedly. Despite this changing emphasis, some traditional aspects of coaching remain – for example, the coach also celebrates victories and supports the athletes through bad times.

In the same way, the manager who is coaching subordinates finds a way of getting them to reflect on their performances, become aware of what they are doing and how they are doing it, so that each individual in the end learns to monitor his or her own performance. At the same time, the manager provides essential information and knowledge where there are gaps that need to be filled. While doing this, they are working to develop a climate where learning and innovation – as well as achievement – are expected and rewarded. The coaching approach challenges the manager to think about the nature of the roles of the people they may be coaching, and this is a developmental experience for the managers. Many HR functions are devolving some of their management development responsibilities to the line, and the concept of 'manager as coach' is seen as part of this trend.

Mentoring

Mentoring has something in common with coaching but, at its best, has a different emphasis. The mentor has less of a vested interest in the mentee's performance results – the mentee's results don't directly have an effect on the mentor's business performance. This makes it easier for the mentor to take a long-term view and a broader approach to the mentee in his/her working life. The mentor is free to be objective, challenging or supporting as necessary, and is able to help mentees think through their overall career development, while their immediate manager or coach may quite properly bring in the more immediate or short-term focus.

Mentors are often used to help individuals manage the process of transition: graduates entering a large organization; someone moving to increased responsibility; a person moving to a level in which they may be seen as unusual (such as women promoted to a level where there are very few women).

Many organizations now have a well-established system of mentor selection and training, induction for mentees and monitoring of the process. For example, GKN has a mentoring system for employees of high potential on a self-managed learning programme; at supermarket chain ASDA, a senior store manager from a different area will be a mentor for people who are being prepared to be store managers; at a division of the Prudential Corporation mentoring is used for women returning to work after maternity leave; and the

UK Stock Exchange has a system of external mentors to support senior management through a major change scheme.

Although widespread mentoring is a fairly recent development in Europe, it is more notably acknowledged as an essential developmental experience in Japan. Research carried out by Warwick and Stirling Universities, compared the 'factors in growing as a manager' reported in paired British and Japanese companies. The emphasis on the effect of role models and mentors was cited most frequently by the Japanese, while the British emphasized education and wider experience of life.[1]

The process of mentoring, when mentors come from within an organization, can have an organizational impact. Senior managers come into contact with, for instance, recent recruits, and this can give the mentor a fresh view on the organization and on the new generation of thinking. At the same time, the mentor who is working at a strategic level can be in a position to convey the corporate direction to the mentee in a way that is direct and immediate. In this way, the mentoring relationship can strengthen organizational cohesion.

Challenges for coaches and mentors

The most challenging aspect for coaches and mentors is the change in mind-set that is required. They should no longer give the impression of knowing best or insist on instructing or commanding. Instead, they should work alongside their colleagues – a position that remains rigorous and targeted but in a very different way. For people who are used to a 'telling' style, the ideas and approaches of coaching and mentoring can seem *softer*. In fact they are not; they are more demanding on both parties in that they require thinking, sophisticated attention, sensitivity to nuances, and a commitment to outcomes while abandoning the need to be in control of people or of situations. People surmount these difficulties more easily when they see the positive effect of working in this way, particularly in organizations which are going through changes such as restructuring, downsizing or change in corporate focus. Individuals blossom and develop, become more creative and more aware of the scope of their job and of the critical success factors. They perform better.

Skills and activities of coaching

There are many possible approaches to coaching. They may involve watching what a person does and giving feedback on what you notice; working on problems with someone and learning together; asking stimulating open-ended questions; talking through your own thinking processes aloud, and encouraging the other person to do the same; encouraging analysis of what really works for individuals; finding your own way of seeing the work and the learning from the other person's point of view; and using questioning as a way of helping a person understand their own thought processes.

Coaching can be thought of as two kinds of conversation: mapping-related and performance-related.

Mapping-related conversations may focus on:

- the organizational setting or culture – 'what works around here?', 'where does this project fit into the overall strategic plan?'
- identifying problems and possible causes – 'what exactly is going wrong?', 'has this happened before?'
- establishing overall desired outcomes – 'what are you trying to achieve?', 'what is the general purpose here?'

Performance-related conversations may focus on:

- what the person is doing – 'what exactly did you do?', 'how are you going about this?'
- comparisons – 'is this different from what you did last time?', 'are other people doing the same thing?', 'can you learn from them?'
- questions about thinking – 'how are you thinking this through?', 'what evidence are you looking for?', 'what assumptions are you making?', 'do they need checking?'
- questions about resources – 'would it help to organize your resources differently?'

Managers as coaches face a number of common pitfalls in their conversations, for any of the following reasons:

- having moved into coaching before establishing a certain amount of rapport and trust;
- being unclear in their own minds about what they are trying to achieve by engaging in the conversation;
- not listening properly because they are too busy deciding whether what they are saying is *right* or not;
- only using questions which demonstrate their knowledge;
- avoiding questions to which they don't know the answer;
- answering their own questions;
- not picking up signals as the conversation goes along about how useful it is for the other person.

These pitfalls can be avoided by keeping in mind the purpose and desired outcome of the coaching activity.

Coaching to improve unsatisfactory performance

A further and more skilful area of coaching is in the area of challenging or confronting for performance improvement. When a person is not delivering the performance required, he/she may have a variety of emotional reactions such as despair, resistance, self-justification, or even complete unawareness.

The coaching approach in this situation is to deal with these by focusing on clear expectations. Often these expectations have not been properly mapped out or clearly understood.

Gathering information and agreeing where the problem lies are essential next steps, at the same time as staying aware of the other person's reactions.

In dealing with underperformance, the following pattern, for a coach, can be useful:

- get clear in your own mind what the situation is: what is the current performance, and what it is expected to be;
- lay aside feelings of blame and irritation and gather information about how individuals are reacting, their awareness of the performance shortfall, and what they see as the problems.
- get the persons being coached to share in identifying the problems, adding their own perspectives and ask them for possibilities to resolve them. This is a stage where it is particularly important to maintain a positive and clear relationship, focusing forward on next steps and change.
- establish a process whereby the employee will set up a plan for informing the coach/manager of progress against clearly stated goals.

Learning to coach

The value of coaching is that it establishes an effective and dynamic working relationship in difficult and changing situations.

In many cases, managers are encouraged to coach by 'manager as coach and developer' initiatives. These may take the form of workshops or of elements of management development programmes. As training and development responsibilities are being devolved more and more to line managers, the pressure on them to work in this way increases. Lack of time or other priorities often get in the way, with the widespread feeling that in current working conditions it's quicker just to tell someone how to do things or, alternatively, to let them get on with their job, rather than taking time to coach. Because of this, there is often a certain amount of resistance to adopting a coaching style of management in the first instance; this resistance may also be in reaction to the hype that is in some cases connected with approaches to coaching.

Resistance may be overcome by starting the coaching from the top. The managers who are expected to move to a coaching style may themselves need to be coached. This experience helps them to understand the value of coaching at first hand, and to get an intuitive sense of how to do it themselves.

Skills and activities of mentoring

What is required of a mentor? The most favoured attributes appear to be acting as a sounding board for ideas; being a source of organizational knowledge; and helping people to see themselves more clearly. Interestingly, few potential mentors choose a *role model; someone who exemplifies good practice* although this is frequently the reason a mentor is chosen by a mentee.

Each variant of the mentor role requires different skills, but a core might include some familiar and well developed techniques, to be used during a mentoring meeting:

- listening openly without making judgements;
- asking open-ended questions;
- summarizing;
- clarifying;
- reflecting back;
- being aware of differences between verbal and non-verbal behaviour;
- helping the mentee explore potential options and their outcomes.

Behaviours which may be tempting but that are particularly unhelpful in a mentor include:

- passing judgement;
- filling in a silence too quickly;
- asking questions when the mentee is trying to figure something out;
- being or feeling patronizing or condescending;
- telling the mentee what to do before he or she has started to think it through for themselves.

The main purpose of the mentoring relationship is to help mentees develop their own thinking and planning about their career and development, with someone supportive who has organizational experience and knowledge. Unhelpful behaviours such as those listed above sabotage this process.

It is noticeable, when working with potential mentors, how easy it is for them to fall into the trap of asking leading questions or of disguising statements or opinions as questions. These are habits acquired from an earlier style of management and it is easy not to be aware of them, or their inappropriateness, in the mentoring situation.

For senior managers, mentoring involves a change of behaviour but an even more dramatic change of thinking. Senior managers have mainly got to where they are by being effective and decisive and by (quite appropriately) knowing what people should do and getting them to do it. Working with someone who is junior to them but whom they do not manage can initially be quite challenging. This stretch of style is one of the benefits that mentors identify as a personal gain from being involved in the mentoring process.

Learning to mentor

Many organizations provide orientation or training for mentors, to provide a base-line or a common approach. Attending a mentoring workshop can be a welcome opportunity to engage in some personal development, to revisit the skills of listening, establishing rapport, reflecting on one's own behaviour; skills that may have become rusty in the journey to a senior position. The usefulness of mentors lies partly in their knowledge and experience; but as this becomes less relevant with changing times, mentors' key value is in their ability to help their mentees to gain knowledge and experience of their *own* in their current role, and to develop their ability to make effective judgements in ambiguous or uncertain situations.

Setting up mentoring schemes

Key factors in a successful mentoring scheme are similar to those in any organizational initiative. That is, commitment and modelling from those with most power and influence, clear and user-friendly systems and procedures, clarity about the reasons and desired outcomes of the schemes, and widespread and appropriate communication to all stakeholders. In the case of a mentoring scheme, the stakeholders include not only mentors and mentees, but also the mentees' managers.

In some organizations, only selected people are offered a mentor in a formal scheme. Mentoring may be provided for potential high-flyers, for women, for new recruits. These choices may have an impact on those who are not offered the same provision. Communication and explanation are therefore important. Mentoring may also be seen, usually wrongly, as a 'gateway', a way through to the fast track with a powerful protector; these notions need to be contradicted if they are not the case, and the real reasons for the selection widely disseminated.

An essential element of the communication is clear briefing for all involved (mentor, mentee, mentee's manager), which may also include an element of training for mentors. Bringing mentors together at intervals supports this communication process as well as providing support for the mentors themselves.

Informal mentoring

Many people have experience of an informal mentor; someone who took them under their wing at a crucial stage in their career. In a wide variety of organizations there are traces of this process, being, as it is, a very normal and well-respected human activity. This mentor may have been chosen in some sense by the mentee, or may have themselves chosen the mentee. One approach to promoting mentoring in the organization is to encourage this process by, for instance:

- describing it as a valuable process;
- encouraging new recruits to select a mentor;
- including developmental activities such as mentoring in appraisal criteria for senior managers.

International or cross-cultural implications

Cross-cultural research indicates that managers in different national cultures work from different sets of assumptions and priorities. The individualist assumptions in cultures such as those of the UK or the United States, for example, contrast with the collective assumptions in Japanese or Latin American culture. Assumptions will affect the pattern of mentoring and coaching in these countries, with varying emphasis on the individual's career and personal development or the good of the organization or group. The assumptions about how status is attained (based on one's own achievements, or on the group a person was born into and their personal connections) vary between countries and cultures, and this will affect the choice of mentors, and how they are valued by mentees. Expected behaviours by mentors in different countries or cultures with a history of mentoring may also vary.

There are also implications for mentoring in multinational organizations, particularly where there are managers of different nationalities working in the same company. In the light of known cultural differences, attitudes and understanding of what mentoring is to be in the organization need careful clarification, with shared meanings being developed.

Joanna Howard is programme director for the MBA by self-managed learning at Roffey Park Management Institute. Before joining Roffey Park in 1988, she was senior lecturer at Thames Polytechnic's School of Education and Community Studies.

Further Reading

Boydell, T and Megginson, D, *A Manager's Guide to Coaching*, Bacie, London, 1979.
Parsloe, E, *Coaching, Mentoring and Assessing*, Kogan Page, London, 1992.

Reference

[1] *Personnel Management*, March 1991

PROJECT-BASED LEARNING

Bob Dodds and Bryan Smith

The cost-effectiveness of training and development approaches is always high on corporate agendas. Bottom line payoffs, together with the integration of on and off-the-job learning, enables project-based learning to make a major contribution to the effective development of managers.

Moreover, projects can provide an important context within which bosses and sponsors can coach and mentor managers as a natural and integral part of day-to-day working relationships.

Projects as a method of learning have grown in prominence over many years in management development both inside and outside organizations. In education, projects have been used to provide essential linkages between theory and practice. Projects are, in essence, tasks – though the terminology paradoxically suggests feeling restricted and moving forward in a practical way to the future.

So, for many managers involved in a development process the concept is not new, but the context often is. 'Doing a job', 'completing a task', 'getting things done', is the everyday stuff of managing. In these day-to-day situations some managers will reflect on their learning, many will not.

The project-based approach to management development prompts an integration of learning while carrying out the project. In a modular development programme some elements of learning can be deliberately designed into the first module to facilitate effective learning transfer through the project, such as networking skills, managing change, influencing and persuading, time management.

Tomorrow's business environment

In the present situation, where the future seems to have arrived too soon, there can be perceptions of too much change too quickly, and too much complexity. This can be highly disorienting. Managers undertaking projects, particularly where the project takes the manager outside his or her domain, are frequently at the forefront of change. Where such change can be effectively integrated with learning, then individual learning and the potential stock of organizational learning can be greatly enriched.

Much has been written in recent years about the organization and business environment which we will see emerging as we approach the end of this century. Charles Handy in *The Age of Unreason*[1] describes the impact of the shamrock form of organization, based around a core of essential executives and workers supported by outside contractors and part-time help, highlighting

723

the ramifications of the growth of this way of organizing in the big businesses and in the institutions in the public sector. He also describes the transition towards individuals having a 'portfolio' of work categories directed towards differing activities and sources of income. In this scenario, individuals will typically be contributing differing activities to several organizations, depending on the nature of the organization's shamrock of requirements and the available portfolio of individual offerings.

For project-based learning and development, this scenario has the following significance.

- Achieving business objectives and operational requirements will increasingly be accomplished by employing a mixture of internal and external resources, managed as a set of parallel running projects. Resources will come and go, and be allocated and relinquished, in accordance to the needs of the business. It will become increasingly important that organizations take steps to capture and build on the learning that takes place during a project, as there will be fewer permanent core staff to act as the repository of organization learning. Indeed, older staff may be moving from a core role to a part-time role and developing the portfolio nature of their work.

- Our understanding of the term 'organization' will become less clear as the boundaries within and between organizational activities become fuzzier. The concept of the 'virtual' organization, consisting of internal and external components, will make it more difficult to locate the centre of expertise for a given business activity.

- Existing businesses in the developed world will be under increasing pressure from competitors emerging in the developing world. One route to competing effectively will be a shift towards higher added value, low-volume offerings, offerings which cannot readily be provided by the developing world. For success, the importance of capturing knowledge and developing the know-how base rapidly will be paramount. Information technology, including the electronic super-highways envisaged in the US and the European Union, can make an important contribution to this. However, of more importance will be the encouragement of creativity and innovation within organizations. Project-based learning and development provides the vehicle for releasing and focusing creative energy and for breaking the mould of organizational inertia.

- The continuing advances in the availability and sophistication of IT systems will provide additional means for supporting project-based learning and development activities. A key part of any learning activity is the opportunity of interacting with the sponsor, coach and others involved in the learning process. IT systems can provide the means of extending the interactive learning environment across distance, enabling dialogue to take place at times which are flexibly suitable to the needs of the manager and the project.

Impact of technology

In considering how technology may influence the way we learn in the future, it is useful to reflect on how the ubiquitous television has already caused the major shift in how we obtain our entertainment. The movement from participation by large groups in cinemas to small groups at home has had dramatic impact on the entertainment industry. Currently TV entertainment is still predominantly a 'broadcast' phenomena (ie, the programme is transmitted to all viewers at the same time), although the video recorder has provided the means for varying the time at which we choose to view.

Major developments currently under way in the telecommunications industry make possible, and commercially viable, the provision of teleshopping and of 'video on demand' services. The significance of such developments in the context of learning is the interactive nature of the services – ie, it has become possible for the user to have a dialogue with an 'intelligent television', and at the time of day which suits their individual circumstances.

Such interactive, on demand, facilities are well suited to the support of project-based learning and development. We are already aware of the benefits obtained by small groups of managers meeting at a time and place of their choice with their coach to review progress and exchange ideas concerning their projects, and such face-to-face gatherings will continue to be important. However, the availability of on-demand interactive multi-media facilities will result in significant changes in the learning environment and approach adopted in organizations. Project-based learning, with its inherent flexibility in terms of time scheduling and the direct link to the work context, will be at the forefront of such change.

Many of the anticipated changes in organizations are likely to facilitate the development of learning through projects (individual and group). The harnessing of information technology and the acceleration of technological change will require an effective integration best achieved through project working. Also, the higher priority which will increasingly need to be given to new product development, quality, customer service and their changing needs, can provide scope for projects containing essential learning for individuals, groups and organizations.

Organizational learning

A major difference that these technologies may provide is the ability to capture learning which arises as part of the outcome of project activities and, going further, to allow interactive access to the knowledge base at the stage where new projects are being initiated.

As a result, the learning benefits from projects can be captured, retained and used widely within the organization. This, in turn, will help organizations improve their responsiveness to changing business needs.

'The rate of learning should be equal or greater than the rate of change in an organization,' says action-learning guru Reg Revans. If technology is influencing and increasing the rate of change in an organization, then technology may become an essential component in ensuring that the rate of learning keeps pace in order for the organization to flourish and compete effectively.

On a wider perspective, project-based initiatives, particularly involving groups, can be part of a company's strategy for loosening up its structure, generating structural flexibility and moving towards a situation of greater involvement and participation at all levels. Also, once project-based learning has proved its value then the project group approach can underpin thrusts in key business activities such as product development, productivity improvement and strategic planning. The opportunities are immense at individual, group and organizational levels.

Critical success factors

In the context of modular project-linked programmes, there are several factors which are critical to success:

1. Establishing conditions for successful project completion.
2. Applying criteria to the choice of a project.
3. Establishing an appropriate infrastructure to support project-based learning.
4. Integrating learning with doing.
5. Identifying and valuing learning outcomes.
6. Securing organizational bottom-line benefits.

Establishing conditions for successful project completion

- Before the project is started there should be adequate discussion with the participant's manager (and the project sponsor if different) to ensure there is common understanding of the project objective.
- Regular communication with the manager/project sponsor should be established and maintained throughout the project.
- An appropriate time requirement is agreed and `protected for the project' so that the participant does not suffer extreme frustrations or become demoralized and fail. It is unlikely that the time requirement will be less than 10 days for a programme where modules are separated by six months.
- Ideally the participant should have a strong interest in the major issue or type of problem to be tackled, which is chosen as the subject of the project. Alternatively, the issue, while not of strong interest, may be perceived to have development potential for the participant. There have been occasions where, with a low level of initial commitment, remarkable results have been achieved.

- The participant should be given the freedom to approach the project in the manner in which he or she sees fit. This does not preclude coaching support from the sponsor.
- The project should be as clearly defined as possible. Again, account always needs to be taken of the dynamic nature of organizations.

Applying criteria to the choice of a project

- The project should be concerned with a major problem within the participant's area of operation (or a related area) and which in solving would involve gaining a broader understanding than the confines of the department or business function.
- It must offer a substantial challenge and stretch the participants' managerial skills.
- It should not merely be a gathering and collating of information, yielding little potential for learning.
- It should not be directed at the solution of problems which are exclusively technical.
- The project is likely to contain a 'people' element.
- It should require the gaining of co-operation and commitment of other colleagues.
- It should enable some real impact to be made on the issue/problem, and preferably devise a plan for implementation. It is possible that the participant may be involved in implementation prior to the second module.
- Typically, the project may be linked to some planned or ongoing major change.
- It should include diagnosis, making recommendations and, where appropriate, initiating necessary action.
- The project should not be an issue or problem which is so intractable that it is not capable of solution, nor should it be too complicated for one individual to effectively tackle.
- Though primarily a learning vehicle, the project should yield some worthwhile benefits to the sponsor/organization. Indeed on completion, it should be feasible to highlight both learning and bottom-line benefits.
- It should provide such a testing experience that the participant emerges stronger and more confident to handle and manage major change situations.

Establishing an appropriate infrastructure to support project-based learning

- In embarking on project-based learning the infrastructure may be rather basic as in Fig. 1:

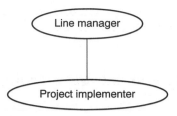

Fig. 1 Basic infrastructure

- It may, through linking off and on-the-job learning, develop to include others (see Fig. 2).

Typically roles will be exercised in relation to the project implementer including mentor, coach, adviser, critic, assessor, learning facilitator, support(s) – 'fellows in opportunity'. Clearly, with the impact of delayering, learning opportunities can be utilized through the expanding and developing of a network of relationships.

Integrating learning with doing

Carrying out a project spread over a period of several months frequently mirrors the reality of managers' work patterns – what they really do. While managers will often embark upon their projects by adopting a classical approach of planning, organizing, co-ordinating and controlling (because it's a project!) the actuality, even at junior levels, often soon reflects John Kotter's 'efficiency of seemingly inefficient behaviour',[2] as the project becomes part of the manager's agenda, interweaved with a network of day-to-day interrelated

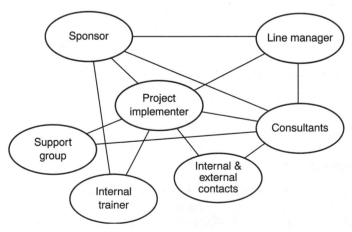

Fig. 2 Linking off- and on-the-job learning

problems and issues. The idealistic intent of securing big chunks of time for working on the project is rarely experienced in practice.

Identifying and valuing learning outcomes

Typically, learning outcomes will be evident to the participant(s) at the stage of preparing for the presentation of the project to sponsors and support group. Some recent learning benefits highlighted in such presentations have included:

- Managing change skills.
- Establishing/improving effectiveness of relationships.
- Practical problem-solving – applying techniques.
- Managing risk in making decisions.
- Influencing styles/skills.
- Improving self-management.
- Managing conflicting objectives.
- Gaining understanding of interdependencies of departments/functions.
- Value of reviewing learning while reviewing project achievement.

Such benefits have often been realized through painful as well as pleasant experiences.

In essence the project, in providing a learning opportunity, also presents a challenge to managers in seeing how effectively they can utilize the opportunity for learning.

Prior to commencing the project, managers have gained an increased awareness of their learning style preferences, using the Honey and Mumford Learning Styles Questionnaire.[3] In learning styles terminology, most projects will tend to relate more to Activist and Pragmatist preferences than Theorist or Reflector. However, development and application of theories, concepts and models is emphasized. Also periodic reflection throughout the project is stressed and high reflector styles are clearly in evidence at the project presentation stage, when learning outputs are highlighted.

Securing organizational bottom-line benefits

Organizational benefits vary widely from the rare sponsor statement of 'Just what I'd expect, but a useful confirmation' to 'I'm sure the board will be delighted with the recommendations. I'll arrange a presentation for you'.

The scale and scope of projects often point to likely subsequent benefits. Project topics might include:

- develop a marketing strategy for new products;
- develop a new product development plan;
- develop a strategy for open learning;
- initiate culture change;

- recommend/implement a downsizing programme;
- carry out a market research survey to develop a new image and improve standards;
- develop proposals for operation and marketing of technical consultancy service;
- review effectiveness of communications with customer network – recommend cost effective improvements;
- produce a strategy to help improve sales performance;
- develop a plan for revamping inadequate service departments;
- establish a PR strategy for the business and implement the initial stage;
- develop/implement new or revised systems, which might cover management information, cost control, information technology, stock control, performance appraisal, or TQM.

In essence many projects provide an intervention wherein major change is implemented more quickly than would be the case without such intervention. Bottom-line benefits have frequently been realized and expressed in five and six figures.

In practice: Volvo[4]

To develop its younger managers, Volvo established a partnership with Sundridge Park Management Centre. It was decided that with 70 plus managers scheduled to attend the programmes within a year-and-a-half, then individual projects might result in an indigestibility of change. Group projects were therefore identified against the criteria for choice. As it transpired 15 group projects were completed, the groups being formed from 70 managers.

While projects were identified and offered to the programme, managers' choices were made, based on a mix of criteria including:

- interest and perceived results;
- functional mix of disciplines;
- balance of team role preferences and styles;
- logistics of project group meetings.

By the end of the first module, project groups were ready to start work on their projects. Occasionally groups made contact with sponsors during this module to seek clarification or possible modification of project aims.

An intermediate workshop (between modules) provided an opportunity to share progress, seek further help, and to look towards project completion. Since the projects were high-profile opportunities for gaining kudos, presentation skills was a main element of the workshop.

On the second module, presentations were attended by sponsors and bosses. As many as 20 guests attended these presentations; a clear indicator of top-management commitment. Many of the project recommendations were implemented. For example:

- greater willingness to begin to regard job mobility (lateral moves) as a development opportunity;
- better co-ordinated approach to head office secretarial utilization and development, resulting in savings of £20,000 pa;
- establishment of a set of criteria to improve the selection of potential Volvo dealers, and hence minimize risks of failure;
- collation of diverse competitor information to support sales and marketing (external consultancy quoted £10,000 for the project);
- reductions in overhead costs amounting to £25,000 pa;
- foster a culture more supportive of innovation.

In practice: ICI

Project work was initiated through the Foundations of Business programme which is a key part of ICI's Core Development Programme in which younger managers participate, normally within the first four years of joining the company. These managers have usually joined ICI directly after completing their university education, typically in a science discipline, and have spent their first few years gaining experience in an operational or technical role. The focus of the programme is to lay the foundations of a thorough understanding of business management in a business-led organization.

Project work has been an integral part of the programme for several years, and over 800 individual projects have been undertaken. In the earlier years of the programme, the project work centred around developing an improved general understanding of the mission, the objectives, and the critical success factors of the particular business unit to which the participant belonged. Gaining experience of differing functional perspectives (eg, marketing, production, research) and the interfaces between functions, also formed an important aspect of project work. In this way, project work helped participants to gain an improved understanding of general business management issues and become less dominated by the technological orientation of their environment.

A further benefit of the project work has been that it provides a common framework for participants to share their know-how and insights concerning a diverse range of businesses within the ICI portfolio, and in so doing recognize common issues and approaches to analysing and solving problems, which might otherwise be obscured by local technical jargon.

More recently, increased priority has been given to selecting projects which focus on current business issues in the changing ICI business environment. The de-merger of the company to form a new ICI and the biosciences company Zeneca, along with other company re-organizations, has provided participants with opportunities to undertake projects which allow them to explore potential new roles and familiarize themselves with new, emerging business environments. This focus of projects on current issues has been undertaken in parallel with a stronger involvement of sponsoring managers in the selection and review of projects and also with an increased contribution by local ICI trainers as facilitators in the support of project activities.

The benefits

Project activities are seen as providing twin track benefits, both in terms of applying and reinforcing the learning for the individual and also in providing tangible benefits for the organization. The tangible benefits can indeed be significant. In the setting of the high cost technological environment with which ICI operates, it is not unusual for project initiatives to result in significant savings, measurable in tens or hundreds of thousands of pounds. The less tangible, individual benefits of projects are of course equally important. The increased understanding and confidence that individuals gain from project work can continue to provide benefit to the organization on many occasions throughout their employment with the company.

The principles and practice: individual projects

- Where the criteria of choice have been rigorously applied, projects with a strong prospect of success have been proposed.
- Again the 'right' project can certainly provide a means of both testing and developing an individual.
- Sometimes actual benefits of the project follow some time after recommendations. It is important to handle an individual's expectations during this stage, so that there is no risk of demotivation.
- It is vital for sponsors and line managers to have realistic expectations of project outputs, also to have a suitable level of involvement with the project and provide appropriate support.
- It is important to establish the right balance in measures of success between the project being a learning vehicle and providing the organization/sponsor with bottom-line benefits. Where there is a clear bias towards the former, then it is important to understand/handle an organization's reaction to what may be seen as an unsuccessful project, ie, lack of bottom-line benefits.
- Moreover, for a project which is perceived to have failed, it is important to be aware of the effect of such failure on the learning process and to reinforce the value in learning from an analysis of what went wrong.
- One of the most profound benefits gained by managers has been a greater understanding of different parts of the business.
- Modular project-linked programmes may be part of a key strategy for a wider establishing and valuing of action learning.

Principles and practice: group projects

- The increasing rate and complexity of change is omnipresent and is predicted to continue. Carrying out too many projects simultaneously in an organization can be hazardous. However, competitive business forces may just be prompting such a scenario.
- Again, as with individual projects, commitment/involvement of sponsors is vital. Group projects are likely to be bigger, which should sharpen sponsors' involvement. Also, in scoping such projects, the likelihood of acceptance of recommendations should be carefully considered. For instance, it could be very important to the sponsor's career development.
- Furthermore, sponsors' needs should be clearly understood by groups, together with what they value and reward. The size of group projects may often have a potential impact upon the organization culture.
- The criteria for choosing project groups are important and should be owned by the members. Though potentially messy the same ownership should apply to the process of applying the criteria.
- When project performance contributes towards the accreditation of a programme for a management qualification, then the handling of any inequalities of contribution among group members becomes critical – there is no room for passengers.
- Organizations are never static. Projects, which are all about change, can impact on the development of the organization.
- The role of the sponsor is critical to the learning/development outputs of projects. Many sponsors would benefit from developing effective coaching skills to help individuals/groups maximize on learning benefits.

The truth remains that, for managers, learning is not something which is measured, evaluated and rewarded; it is at best a secondary activity to performing effectively on-the-job.[5] Project-based approaches represent an attempt to place learning higher on the agenda of managers. It can appear an ambitiously utopian goal, but with a strong thrust through projects and other initiatives the day may not be too far away when managers will value learning as highly as they now value doing and achieving, and the dream of effectively integrating learning with doing will become a reality.

Bob Dodds and Bryan Smith are consultants at the Sundridge Park Management Centre, Kent, part of the PA Consulting Group.

After graduating as a physicist, Bob Dodds worked for some twenty years in the information technology industries, in the UK and Germany, in both technical and business development roles. He joined Sundridge Park in 1988. He is the Client Director responsible for the management development programmes for several major clients, which make particular use of project work to accelerate the transfer of learning to the workplace and to facilitate organizational change.

Bryan Smith spent 15 years in the engineering industry, initially qualifying as a Chartered Engineer. His core skills and experience has been in management development with Cummins Ltd, British Timken, the Food Drink and Tobacco Industry Training Board, the Central Training Council/Manpower Services Commission, The College of Management, Dunchurch (GEC), and as an independent consultant. He joined Sundridge Park Management Centre in November 1984 where he is now Director of Studies. He has written numerous articles and is editor of *Industrial and Commercial Training*.

Further Reading

Honey, J and Mumford, A, *Manual of Learning Styles*, Honey, Maidenhead, 1992

References

1 Handy, C, *The Age of Unreason*, Century Business Books, London, 1989.
2 Kotter, J, *The General Manager*, The Free Press, New York, 1982.
3 Honey, J and Mumford, A, *Manual of Learning Styles*, Honey, Maidenhead, 1992.
4 Branch, J and Smith, B, 'Project-based management development – the Volvo story', *Journal of European Industrial Training*, vol. 16, no. 1, 1992.
5 Mumford, A, 'Making a career through learning', *International Journal of Career Management*, vol. 2, no. 1, 1990.

USING CONSULTANTS

Stuart McAdam and Mark Pinder

Among managers, consultants often have a mixed reputation. In some cases, consultants bring a fresh insight to a key problem, or work effectively with client staff to achieve real, meaningful benefits. In others, consultants are criticized for stating the obvious; addressing peripheral issues; and charging excessively.

For these and other adverse reasons, many business people rapidly become disillusioned with their consultants. What they frequently fail to realize, however, is that the fault is often as much their own as that of the consultants. Many managers are poor at selecting consultants, communicating with them, managing the relationship with them, making use of their skills properly and, above all, ensuring that the benefits of the consultants' work are realized.

There is an ever increasing number of consultants available to business people, no matter what the business or the problem or challenge facing them. While the choice is growing rapidly, there are equally numerous and valid reasons to hire a consultant. Commonly, these include:

- Not having the expertise within the organization to carry out an important project: for example, an organization may know something is wrong, but does not have the specialized personnel or expertise to put it right.
- Not having the resources to address a key problem or issue thoroughly.
- Wishing to gain an insight into current thinking in a particular industry or sector and to benchmark accordingly.
- Wishing to undertake some work which requires complete independence – for example, to gain acceptance to change that is unpalatable or difficult to achieve.

Whatever the precise circumstances, using consultants successfully requires that three critical factors (shown in Fig. 1 as the three points of the triangle) are in synergy from the outset of any project:

- **Perceiving the problem** – the client needs to have a perception of the problem they would like to be resolved. This may be a limited or incomplete perception. The solution to a particular problem may be vague. But, at the very least, the client needs to be able to articulate the nature of the problem and in what way they want things to be different. Expecting a consultant to suddenly understand a business and come up with an instant solution is wishful thinking.
- **Track record** – consultants *offer* independence, professionalism and round-the-clock client care. In many cases it will be the truth, but the client should be looking for more than this. They should look for evidence of previous

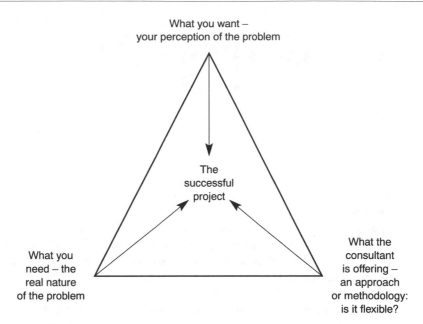

What you want –
your perception of the problem

The
successful
project

What you
need – the
real nature
of the problem

What the
consultant
is offering –
an approach
or methodology:
is it flexible?

Fig. 1 The need for consultancy – three critical factors

success, flexibility in approach and, above all, evidence that the consultant is genuinely capable of understanding particular business issues and developing meaningful solutions that will work. Many consultants have developed standard approaches and methodologies to client issues which, having served them well in the past, form the cornerstone of their work. There is nothing wrong in this, as long as the approach can be adapted to suit the individual needs of an individual business.

- 'Need' or 'want'? – what a client needs may be (though not necessarily) very different from what he or she expresses to want. In one instance, a retail finance company that had recently been through a merger was having problems with its staff. Increasingly, people were expressing dissatisfaction with the grades they were in, and their status relative to other staff they regarded as their equals, but who came from the other merger partner. The company decided a new job evaluation scheme was the answer to the problem. A firm of management consultants was brought in, who designed and implemented a new job evaluation scheme which was fair, rigorous and introduced a common grading structure. The company received even more complaints about pay and grading than it had before.

In fact, the problem was that a new job evaluation scheme was what the company *wanted*, but not what it *needed*. The consultants were technically competent and dedicated to their task, but they made no attempt to question the client as to the real nature of the problem. Had they done so, they would have realized the root of the problem was staff motivation and the lack of progress made at integrating the staff of the two former entities following the merger. Unless these issues were addressed, it was inevitable that disquiet concerning status and grade would continue.

Ensuring that there is synergy between what the client wants, what the client needs, and what the consultant is offering, requires *continuous dialogue* between client and consultant, from the outset and throughout the duration of the project. This dialogue begins even before the project gets under way: in selecting the right consultant for the job.

Selecting a consultant

It is essential that clients follow a consistent, logical process with a number of clearly-defined steps. Cutting corners in the process may result, quite simply, in selecting the wrong consultant, or there may be a deep misunderstanding between the parties about needs and objectives.

Step 1: Prepare a long list of consultancy providers
Once an organization has a more or less clearly-defined idea of what work they want the consultants to do, they have to identify the consultancy providers. There are many potential sources of information, including:

- word-of-mouth (eg, other people in the same professional network who have used consultants to do similar projects to the one contemplated);
- advertisements placed by consultants in newspapers, trade journals, etc;
- direct marketing approaches by consultants;
- consultancy registers (a variety of organizations maintain registers of approved consultants and are happy to give information and advice concerning their selection).

It is important at this stage that clients do not limit the scope of their choice too much, but make use of as many sources of information as possible to compile a comprehensive list. They should not rely solely on consultants' publicity material, or the opinions of colleagues who may have used consultants successfully but for different purposes.

Step 2: Prepare a short list
The next step is to produce a short list of consultants to be invited to tender for the project. The number of consultants included in a short list depends on the size and nature of the project, but between four and six is about right for a typical project.

The most common method of selection is to contact all consultants identified in writing, giving them brief details about the project and a description of the client organization, and asking them to express their interest in bidding. This may automatically reduce the number of potential candidates (some may express no interest or even fail to reply). Of those interested in receiving further details, selection criteria will include:

737

- **the quality of response:** do they appear to understand the particular industry and the nature of the problem? Does their reply attempt to identify the client's needs? Have they taken the trouble to investigate further (for example, by seeking additional information to help them understand key issues?)
- **track record:** have they done similar work in the sector and when was the work performed? (A prestigious client named in a brochure may indicate no more than one individual attending a workshop run by the consultancy on a completely different subject.)
- **the experience of other clients:** if possible a prospective client should contact one or two previous clients to establish the *modus operandi* of the consultants.

This could cover how they behaved; the success of the project; their ability to meet their own objectives; meeting deadlines; their responsiveness to the organizational culture; whether they provided value for money (and the accuracy of their invoices); the competency of individual consultants on the team and whether the organization believes that it still needed consultants in the first place and whether they would use the same consultants again.

Questions such as these provide real insight into what actually happened during a consulting project. While it would be unreasonable to expect perfection in every aspect, information on how difficulties were overcome can be very revealing. As in any other service industry, moments of truth matter. A reliable and professional practice will guard its reputation jealously and should be ready and willing to provide references.

Step 3: Invitation to tender

The shortlisted consultants should be required to prepare formal proposals setting out their approach to the project. This should be done through the medium of an Invitation to Tender.

If the consultants are professional in their approach, it is likely they will try to arrange a meeting with the prospective client, before they prepare a formal written proposal, to discuss the background to the project and the company's needs. Other objectives of the meeting may include: demonstrating their professional credibility; establishing mutual rapport; identifying any key players in the client organization; finding out if there are competitors for the work, and who they are; and gaining a feel for the likely scope of the project, including the timescale and budget. It is as important for the client as for the consultant that this meeting fulfils its objectives. There is no point, for example, in the consultants selling the benefits of their work to a person who cannot influence whether it goes ahead or not, or having an unrealistic view of the scope of the work involved. With the requirement for dialogue between client and consultant if the project is to be a success, the initial meeting is usually the most important means of establishing a real understanding from the outset.

Consultants' proposals come in many different forms and sizes. In some cases, a one or two page letter, covering the gist of a previous conversation with the client, is sufficient. In others, the proposal will be a full-blown report in its own right, running to many pages of text, making use of flow-charts and diagrams to illustrate aspects of the work and perhaps with a separate volume of appendices and CVs. At the very least, any proposal should contain the following details:

- a brief summary of the background to the project;
- a description of the client's requirements;
- a description of the approach the consultant will take in carrying out the work;
- an indication of the amount of consulting time involved and the overall elapsed timescale;
- details of the staff who will carry out the work and what their roles will be;
- the fees that will be charged (including any direct costs such as travel, accommodation and report preparation);
- most importantly, the outcome and deliverables of the project, highlighting the main benefits.

Consultants' proposals are contractual documents which, should the contract be won by the consultant, can be referred to at a later date to ensure that the terms of reference of the project are adhered to. They should, therefore, be studied in detail and *any* areas of misunderstanding clarified before proceeding further.

Step 4: The beauty parade

Most consultants expect to be asked to make a formal presentation of their proposals at a beauty parade – a process in which they are invited to appear in front of the client and demonstrate why their approach is preferable to that of their competitors. From the client's point of view, beauty parades can be invaluable in determining how professional the consultants really are, and in bringing together key decision makers to agree on the final choice. All tenderers may be asked to make a presentation, or just the two or three who have put together the best proposal.

A good presentation will have been rehearsed beforehand, will involve all members of the proposed project team and will give ample opportunity for questions (many of which should have been anticipated in advance). A poor presentation should be regarded with suspicion; this is a strong indication that the consultant hasn't prepared thoroughly and doesn't have a true understanding of the client's business issues and requirements.

Step 5: Making the selection

Key considerations in making the final choice should include:

- **Clarity:** how well have the consultants understood and described the issues that led the work to be commissioned in the first place? Have they helped the client organization to define its real needs and to develop its own understanding?
- **Structure:** have the consultants specified clearly how they would structure the project?

- **Who, when?:** who will be working with the client? Dealing with a large consultancy, companies need to be alert to proposals that are vague about exactly who will be working on the assignment. It is worth having a precise indication of the time input of each consultant and insisting on meeting the people involved and having copies of their CVs. Obviously all consultants aim to maximize their earnings, and many apply the taxi-rank principle of waiting for clients on a 'first come, first served' basis. A lengthy selection process may lead to the preferred consultant being unavailable.
- **Deliverables:** have the consultants specified exactly what will be delivered? The term deliverable may include many things, such as:
  - written reports;
  - fully-developed methods or systems including equipment, materials and training provision;
  - transfer of skills to client managers and staff;
  - fully analyzed research data;
  - a technical specification for a system or process;
  - facilitation in which consultants work closely as advisers with the client's management team.

The client must ensure that they know exactly what will be delivered by the consultants and that it meets their requirements in full.

- **Cost:** the relative cost of different consultants is clearly important in the decision-making process. Unfortunately some consultants are deliberately vague about costs and fees: beware of any that hedge their bets. Thus a proposal suggesting 'we anticipate this work will take us between 30 and 50 days at an average fee rate of £1,000 per day' is of little value. Clients should ask for a detailed breakdown of fees relating to the tasks and staff involved. If this is not forthcoming they should look elsewhere for assistance.

  Something else to be very clear about is the provision of facilities and the costs of support services. Some consultancy teams bring a secretary with them to prepare reports, presentations, etc. Others will ask for access to secretarial assistance.

Beginning the relationship

The value of meetings with the consultant should not be under-estimated. They are a vital component of any engagement in ensuring understanding and the generation of valuable opinions and ideas. A start-up meeting at the beginning of the project is particularly important. From the client's point of view, it is necessary to build rapport and ensure that the consultants are aware of their expectations. From the consultants' point of view there are many practical matters to be agreed if they are to be able to proceed without delay with the project work. These include:

- **Fact-finding:** which staff do they need to see, where are they based, when are they likely to be available? What other sources of information relevant to the project exist?
- **Hopes and expectations:** how are people throughout your organization likely to react to the project? How much do they know, and how much do they need to know? Jointly managing staff expectations may be a delicate task.
- **Administration:** the extent of clerical or secretarial support and office facilities available for the project, and the involvement of client counterparts, need to be agreed.

At the start-up meeting the next steps in the workplan should be agreed in detail, so that both sides know exactly what will happen next and by when it will happen.

Client counterparts

In many circumstances, client counterparts (ie, staff seconded to work with the consultants on the project team) are essential to the success of the project. Critically, they are the conduit by which key skills and knowledge frequently essential to the implementation of project recommendations are transferred to the client. They may also play a vital role in enhancing the consultants' understanding of the client, and in assisting with project monitoring.

Managing counterpart staff can be a nightmare for consultants, as all too frequently staff with entirely the wrong characteristics are selected for the job. A detailed specification of the type of person(s) required, and the skills and abilities they must possess should be agreed. Things to avoid are:

- counterparts with little or no knowledge of the technical content of the work, assigned to the project team to develop their learning;
- staff who will in reality have little time to devote to the project and who therefore may duck out of their involvement, or, equally important, will have little to do with the implementation of the work once the consultants have finished their work;
- staff who it is felt would benefit from working with consultants 'for personal development reasons' (all too frequently, code for staff whose managers are pleased to get rid of them for a period of time).

Clients need to bear in mind that consultants sometimes try to pass the blame for their own failings onto counterparts who, for one reason or another, have not fulfilled their objectives.

Establish mutual respect

Consultants can become quite cynical about their clients, and *vice versa*. Neither party should allow this to happen. Problems can occur because the relationship between client and consultant is, in most cases, a short-term one and there is a temptation to form quick judgements about the abilities of the people you are dealing with. It is important to give a good initial impression.

What do consultants respect in clients? Here is a comprehensive, but by no means exhaustive, list of the main characteristics:

- **Perceptiveness:** consultants respect people whom they consider to be intellectually their equal and with whom they can talk through key issues.
- **Challenging:** clients will gain more respect from your consultants if they challenge their views rather than meekly accepting them.
- **Interest in their work:** not surprisingly, consultants expect their clients to show this. The number of clients who do not, and get a poorer piece of work as a result, is little short of amazing.
- **Commitment:** working long hours is part of the consultancy ethos and people who demonstrate commitment to their work tend to command respect.
- **Decisiveness:** clients who do not make decisions (and who therefore slow down projects or cause unforeseen changes to terms of reference) are the consultant's curse.
- **Business acumen:** consultants are particularly impressed by entrepreneurial prowess in their clients (perhaps because, as advisers rather than businessmen, many of them lack this characteristic themselves).

Displaying some, if not all, of the above characteristics at an early stage during the relationship should lead to a good working relationship between client and consultants.

Managing the relationship

Many clients, having commissioned a project, are content to leave their consultants to get on with things and are totally dependent on what they choose to tell them about the progress they are making. This is a major error. The client should be proactive in seeking information concerning overall progress, problems encountered, key findings and, in particular, any changes to, or deviations from, the original workplan.

All consultants have workplans, usually broken down in detail into the specific tasks required, the amount of time allocated to each, the deadline for completion and the deliverables emerging from different stages in the project. They should *not* simply be for the consultants' own use. Clients should ask to see details of the workplan, at the outset of the project and at regular intervals thereafter. They need also to monitor the progress being made and question any areas where there appears to be divergence between what was supposed to have happened by a particular date and what has actually occurred.

The consultant's workplan is a guideline and in many cases there may be valid reasons why it needs modification as a project gets underway.

Nevertheless, clients should know about any modifications in advance and must have the facility to give them their approval.

Two key aspects of consultant project management, from the client's point of view, are:

- **The project manager.** Particularly for larger projects, it is essential that one of the more senior consultants acts as project manager with responsibility for controlling the work of the consultancy team. This person should also be the key link with the client, with the specific task of reporting on progress, receiving client feedback and ensuring that this is acted upon.
- **Regular progress meetings.** Whether the project is large or small, the work-plan should have written into it a regular series of meetings to report on progress and issues, and ensure that client feedback is conveyed back to the project team. These meetings need not be formal, and should involve only a small group of people including the project manager and the main contact within the client organization.

  If held on a weekly basis one would not expect project meetings to last more than an hour in most cases, but this clearly would depend on the number and complexity of the issues to be explored. The project manager should be expected to start the meeting by giving a clear and concise report of progress made, following which, discussion should take place on any issues encountered.

The client should be looking for three key things from their consultant: *delivery to the terms of reference, delivery on time,* and *delivery within budget.* Any deviation from the original agreement in one or more of these areas should be explored thoroughly to minimize the possibility of unpleasant surprises at the end of the project. There may, of course, be valid reasons for changes to the terms of reference, for example, unforeseen difficulties in obtaining agreement to key recommendations, or changes to the workplan being required as a result of technological change or new legislation. The key point, however, is that the client must know in advance of any proposed changes, and must discuss and agree them in full before giving their commitment.

Most consultants value their clients sufficiently to take the consequences (in terms, for example, of additional time or resources input) when they have mis-judged an issue. However, it is as well to be watchful for the following:

- **Poor project management:** you should not expect to pay extra fees if, for example, the consultants have simply misjudged the amount of work required, or have brought in additional consultants at a higher fee rate to do the work.
- **Agreed deliverables being dropped or modified because they are proving difficult:** clients should insist on the consultants coming up with *all* the agreed deliverables, and to the quality standards required.
- **The 'sell-on':** consultants will always look for opportunities to sell more work to their clients, and one of the easiest ways for them to do this is to build on the back of an existing client relationship. If a client is considering

commissioning more work, they should make sure this is something they need rather than something their consultant wants.

Many consultants declare that they are 'always seeking to give added value'. The dividing line between added value and 'scope creep' (ie, where the client is trying to obtain additional free work from the consultant that is nothing to do with the original terms of reference) can be a fine one, but clients should not be dissuaded from asking consultants for more if they genuinely believe it is needed.

Ensuring implementation

Ultimately, there will come a time when the consultants depart. This can be a difficult time for clients, which perhaps explains why so many of them cling to their departing consultants like jilted lovers. Implementation difficulties can include:

- implementation taking longer than originally anticipated;
- lack of understanding or resistance amongst staff affected;
- problems created by poor co-ordination mechanisms;
- other priorities occurring which distract attention from implementation.

Although clients may have to solve these and other issues alone, they should expect some help from the consultants through their development of the project. Have they, for example:

- provided an implementation plan, setting out key tasks, timescales, resources required and responsibilities for implementation?
- have they anticipated problems and issues and discussed these during the project? Have they suggested solutions?
- have they involved key players in the client organization, so that they understand and support the project and are committed to implementing it?
- have they transferred skills to the client's staff to help them maintain systems and procedures and explain the benefits to other staff?
- have they provided clear recommendations that leave no doubts about what needs to be done and why?

Most consultants are professional enough to care about the impact of their work, and are therefore willing to give ad hoc advice after their formal involvement in a project has come to an end. Effective implementation must be the core objective of both sides.

Stuart McAdam is group human resource director of Mercantile and General Reinsurance. Before joining M&G, he spent seven years in consultancy, principally with KPMG Peat Marwick's human resources team. He was previously head of employee relations at the Confederation of British Industry and has an MBA from Bradford Management Centre.
Mark Pinder is an independent consultant specializing in change management, human resources management, training and organization development. He has worked

extensively throughout Europe and is the author of *Personnel Management for the Single European Market.*

Further Reading

Pinder, M and McAdam, S, *Be Your Own Management Consultant*, FT/Pitman, London, 1993.

Communication

'It is vital for the success of our companies that businessmen and women emerge as real leaders and demonstrate their ability to communicate effectively, internally and externally.'

Sir Colin Marshall, chairman, British Airways

'Communication in stressful change situations requires sustained and extensive interpretation and reinforcement. Competent, high-trust firms are in a position to communicate the same basic messages to all levels, from middle management to shop floor, with nothing left out on the grounds that those below would not understand it.'

Tony Eccles, London Business School[1]

'No manager can be effective in his job unless he is able to communicate. It is the most essential single skill. I hope that managers everywhere will seek to improve their ability, for it is one that can be learned.'   *Sir John Harvey-Jones*

---

[1] Eccles, T, *Succeeding with Change*, McGraw Hill, Maidenhead, 1994.

OVERVIEW

Heinz Goldmann

Communication lies at the very heart of management. We expect that the heads of large organizations should be effective communicators able to use a variety of forms of communication, tools and techniques. Yet, it is something which managers are notoriously poor at doing successfully.

Examples of poor, inadequate or misdirected communication abound. Change programmes and quality initiatives routinely break down simply because managers have poorly communicated the rationale behind them to the rest of the organization. The commercial logic may be flawless, but if it is not communicated successfully people will quickly become de-motivated and unenthusiastic. The surge in poplularity for re-engineering programmes at the beginning of the 1990s provided ample evidence of this seemingly terminal deficiency in managers. Programmes have floundered because of the lack of communication skills in those who are supposed to make them happen. It is one thing identifying all the processes which make up a business' activities, quite another to inform, inspire or communciate with the people who have to bring the processes to fruition.

Take one view of what characterizes a quality-oriented organization: 'Charismatic leadership, contrary to popular belief, is not one of the features of successful companies. Instead, the common factor is leadership which is both forthright and listening. It is very assertive about standards and objectives, making clear that quality is non-negotiable and that customer service is genuinely and consistently the number one priority. At the same time the leadership not only encourages employees to give their views about how to improve quality, it actively listens to those views, acts on them and draws on the knowledge and experience of staff at all levels.' This was one of the conclusions George Binney drew from analysis of the quality programmes of 46 companies across Europe.[1] Only if there are two-way messages can the process be honestly defined as communication.

Such two-way communication is vital to achieving the full potential of any such programme, and in making virtually anything happen in an organization. Participation, empowerment and involvement all revolve around communication.

Part of the reason for the general malaise which affects communication may lie in the general lack of formal training in communication tools and techniques. Courses at some of the world's leading business schools and management institutions miss out communication entirely. They have separate courses on marketing, strategy, finance and so on, but avoid communication as either too simplistic, unimportant or something managers do automatically anyway. Or they dismiss the issue by offering a public speaking course.

Communication is too important to be ignored or treated so lightly. It demands practice, coaching and training. And, like the other skills of management, it is something which can be learned.

Effective communication needs to be built around this simple foundation and realization: communication is a dialogue, not a monologue. In fact, communication is more concerned with a dual listening process. Too often managers spend nine-tenths of their time talking. At the end of a speech they have a cursory look round the room and ask if anyone has a question. They then appear surprised if no one responds to their half-hearted invitation. The reason no one normally replies is that during speeches people become bored. They have no choice but to listen and often applaud just because they are relieved it is finished. If they are not involved and participating actively from the very start, how can they be expected to suddenly take up an invitation to say something (which sometimes even leads to trouble, as such a question is easily interpreted as criticism).

It should always be remembered that:

- Preparation is the key – it starts much earlier than the event. You have to ask questions to find out something about your audience – their expectations, motivations, mentality and attitudes (the famous 'EMMA' formula). Mutual knowledge is to be built up all the time.
- Dialogue is a means of making sure you are not making a mistake. Decisions taken in isolation can be dangerous and, sometimes, plain wrong.
- So-called 'audiences' are more interested in participating in a discussion rather than listening to a speech. Listening is painful, and one person addressing scores of others is an unnatural event. Unless you are an excellent speaker you should forget about making speeches and conduct conversations.
- It is not important what you say, but what people perceive. Managers usually over-rate the receptiveness of people and their willingness to understand.

Though putting them into practice continues to stretch the minds of the most prominent executives, the skills of communication are succinct and simple:

- **Empathy.** Managers must be able to put themselves in someone else's shoes. They must understand the implications of what they are saying or doing for colleagues, employees, customers and anyone else their behaviour affects. The ability to empathize – understand people – diminishes dramatically when they have to act outside their protected hierarchical realm.
- **Common denominator.** If managers are to communicate they have to find, establish and express a common denominator with their target group. There needs to be a bond of solidarity. With growing internationalization, intercultural differences make it even more difficult to build such bonds and communicate effectively. Yet, these relationships are essential.
- **Projection or impact creation.** If the delivery is boring then empathy won't help. The impact created is based on projecting a strong message, portraying

a powerful personality, impressing by determined (yet acceptable) persuasion. Empathy and projection are not necessarily correlated. Similarly, projection and impact are not automatically helped by using the latest in high-technology devices. In fact, there is an ever-present danger that technology will lead to a greater number of monologues as executives become consumed by what technological gimmickry can do rather, than the message they are trying to communicate to their audience. An exhausting parade of charts stifles interest. Also, face-to-face communication is 90 per cent more effective than written or printed messages.

Managers become increasingly aware of their limitations. Even at a very senior level managers are conscious that they are not good communicators. But to make it work effectively demands that executives invest time in learning to communicate. Percy Barnevik of ABB estimates that he spends one-tenth of his time deciding on the strategy, and the rest communicating it. Such a bias says a great deal about the critical importance of communication. It is not an indulgence or a distraction, but a *must* for any manager in any organization.

Heinz Goldmann is chairman of the Heinz Goldmann International Foundation for Executive Communications in Geneva and founder chairman of the Mercuri Group. He and his organization coach, instruct and train executives in communication throughout the world. He has personally instructed over 450,000 people in 38 countries.

Dr Goldmann is the author of *How to Win Customers* and *Communicate to Win.*

Further Reading

Goldmann, H, *Communicate to Win*, FT/Pitman, London, 1995.

Reference

[1] Binney, G, 'Rising above the bureaucracy of quality', *Directions*, May 1993.

COMMUNICATING WITH EMPLOYEES

Brenda McAll

In the last few years, managers throughout industry have seen more changes than many of them could have expected to see in their entire working lives. Having to communicate information which often leads to feelings of insecurity and fear has become a key activity.

From being ill-organized and peripheral in many companies, employee communications has become a constant corporate need. This raises two substantial challenges. Information is often complex and has to be communicated effectively to a dispersed and diffuse workforce. Yet, it must appeal to people as individuals. There is no such thing as a typical employee, and employee communications are bound to fail unless they take account of the individual needs of every employee within an organization.

For BT the 1980s saw liberalization and privatization and in the 1990s the process of change has, if anything, accelerated. Since 1990, BT has been turned inside out and upside down, to ensure that it is a marketing-led customer-responsive business, one that instinctively looks outwards at customers and competitors, rather than inwards at its own processes and the way things were done in the past. Since 1990 BT has reduced its workforce by more than 80,000 people (or 35 per cent) on a voluntary basis, and further downsizing is anticipated.

Internal changes have been matched by increasing pressure from competitors in all market sectors. BT has had to learn to market and to sell and to be driven by customer perception. From being an engineering company, BT is now remaking itself as a service company.

The role of employee communications in such a context is to build people's self-confidence, to persuade them that change is not only inevitable but that it also brings opportunities.

This is not an easy task. People tend to be somewhat sceptical – they feel as if they are losing touch with the company after working for it for many years. Most of the old certainties have been stripped away – employees have had to face up to the fact that they no longer have a job for life; they cannot assume that they will always be doing the same work in the same place; their hours of work and attendance patterns will have to change; the way they work will change; the company they work for may diversify into places and areas of business they are unfamiliar with.

People respond to this predicament in a number of ways. Some of them are already so cowed and dispirited by apparently endless change that there is precious little you can say or do that will make any difference. At the other end of the scale are the zealots, evangelists for change, usually mavericks who need to be carefully managed.

The bulk of the population however is likely to fall into two main categories: the *pragmatists* and the *highly anxious*.

The pragmatists are, to a greater or lesser degree, disengaged from the company ('It's only a job', 'I've got to pay the mortgage'), have low expectations of what they can get from the job, have a relatively short-term perspective, and only experience loyalty, if at all, to the local team rather than to the company as a whole.

The highly anxious are a more volatile group, feel that they are not in control of their destiny, and are angry with the company, believing that it has let them down.

The identification of these groups highlights the importance of providing attraction and interest for every group within the organization. There is little point in admonishing the fearful to seize opportunities with both hands; just as there is not much mileage in relying heavily on the selflessness and loyalty of the pragmatists.

This is precisely why middle and line managers are so key in the employee communications process. They are the people who know the people to whom the company wishes to convey messages.

Why communicate with employees?

It is essential to establish from the start that employee communications is not an act of altruism. It should not be motivated by a vaguely-held belief that we are 'that kind of company'; or out of some sense that it is good to talk to the workforce. Companies must do so because they believe it makes sound business sense.

The purpose of employee communications is quite simply to support senior line managers and help the company deliver its operational (business) objectives as efficiently and cost-effectively as possible. In a service company it is vitally important to have everyone lined up behind a commitment to the highest levels of customer service.

If people are to do the best possible job, they must understand that job and their own responsibilities; how the objectives of that job relate to the objectives of the team, division and company; where the company is going; and how they, as individuals, can make a contribution. Quite simply, informed people make better contributions.

Employee communications policy

BT's company-wide employee communications policy puts responsibility for successful employee communications firmly with line managers:

'Communications with our people must be consistent in approach, tone and design, and messages and channels must be clearly owned and managed in a total quality way. Employee communications are a principal line-management responsibility, and open and effective two-way communication between managers and their people is key.'

All the research carried out by BT on a range of communications issues points to the same conclusion: people prefer to get their information face-to-face, and they prefer to get it from their line managers. That is the key relationship and where arguments (and hearts and minds) are won or lost.

Employee communications in practice

Company-wide employee communications in BT are managed from the Corporate Relations Department, and organized on an account management model. A company-wide account management team provides the links between the 'owners' of messages and the employee communications community in the field at all levels.

The account team produces the annual, company-wide employee communications plan; it monitors employee communications performance, sets targets for improvement, and produces guidelines for local communications planning.

First principles of communication

1. Effective employee communications must be led from the top
Effective communications require the active commitment and endorsement of senior managers. It is not enough simply to develop a 'vision statement' or formulate in general terms the values by which the company lives. Behaviour is what counts. Managers must be seen to behave in a manner that is consistent with the ethos they are promoting.

2. The essence of good communications is consistency
At all costs, avoid following fashion and tinkering. If you try to improve communications and then fail – because your messages are inconsistent or are 'good news only' – things will not quietly settle back into the way they used to be. You will inevitably have created expectations, and may have to live with the consequences of having disappointed those expectations.

3. Successful employee communications owe as much to consistency, careful planning and attention to detail as they do to charisma or natural gifts

4. Communication via the line manager is most effective
It is an opportunity for people to ask questions and check that they have understood the issues correctly. However, the reality is that the volume of business and the need for timeliness may make it necessary, on many occasions, to inform employees directly rather than relying entirely on the cascade process. (Though managers will still need to answer people's questions and listen to their views.)

5. Employee communications are not optional extras, they are part of business as usual and should be planned and budgeted for as such
An employee communications plan – relating key themes, targets, objectives and resources – provides a context in which to deliver initiatives that arise at short notice.

6. There must be integration between internal and external communications
There must be a fit between what you are telling your people and what you are telling your customers, shareholders and public. (By the same token, there must be a fit between what you are telling your people, and what the external media are telling them.)

7. Timing is critical
However clear, eloquently expressed and presented your message may be, if it arrives at the wrong time, you might as well not have bothered. Old news is often worse than no news. Consequently, it is important to ensure that the channels you use can really deliver in the requisite time.

8. Tone is important
Expressing gushing enthusiasm about a technical change of little real significance is scarcely calculated to make people take your message to heart.

9. Never lose sight of the 'what's in it for me?' factor

10. Communication is a two-way process
Employee communications are not reducible to a one-way information dump. Capturing feedback is of critical importance, and if you are not seen to be listening and acting on what you are told, why should people bother telling you?

11. A single key theme or a couple of key themes is a means of giving coherence to a range of diverse employee communications initiatives
In recent years, the overriding theme of BT's employee communications has been the impact on the business of competition, regulation and recession. Many messages and initiatives can therefore be evaluated according to the light they shed on one or more of these key themes.

12. Set your standards and stick to them

Determine which channels should be mandatory and which should be optional; establish quality standards for all channels and review these at least annually.

Channels and channel management

The key to managing communications channels is discipline, commonsense, timeliness and a respect for your audience.

Of all the channels, team meetings remain the most significant, provided managers get into the habit of conducting them in a professional manner, delivering any core briefing, and answering questions (admitting when they don't know the answer and committing themselves to finding out).

As an adjunct to running team meetings, managers at all levels should be seen to walk the job and, if appropriate, offer 'surgeries' for their people. It is also desirable for managers to attend team meetings held by their subordinate managers.

Employee publications are an important element in any employee communications portfolio, but one should resist the temptation to assume that they can solve all your problems – there are certain things that publications can do well and certain things that they can't. BT has a full-colour company newspaper that goes to all employees and pensioners at their home addresses. It has resisted, as far as possible, the growth of local publications which, if unchecked, can become a rampant cottage industry. However, it does publish nine editions of the 24-page newspaper. There is also a bi-monthly, features-based magazine for all managers and another for BT people working overseas.

In publications of this kind, you are unlikely to enthuse your readers by uncritical recycling of the company line. On the other hand, fearless exposés of all the company's problems are unlikely to win much management support for the magazine. It is, therefore, essential that employee publications should have very clear editorial policy, and be monitored consistently, to ensure that they are meeting their objectives.

Corporate briefings – whether directly addressed or cascaded through the organization – are another indispensable part of employee communications. BT has the capacity to brief a range of audiences from the top 100 managers to all employees.

Video is a communications channel that should always be approached with great care. Not only is it an expensive medium but it is rarely very effective. Every year, companies spend large amounts on making videos about the need for culture change, and seem entirely to lose sight of the fact that video is a visual medium, and is not comfortable in dealing with management abstractions. In BT, videos tend to be used only to support or report on events – meetings, conferences, etc – for those who couldn't be there.

Of course, managers need support if they are to communicate effectively. BT has recently published a style guide for managers, which seeks to make people more conscious of what they write and how they give presentations, and has also produced a practical guide to communications, which provides guidance on everything from how to walk the job to communicating bad news.

Because of the inevitability, speed and comprehensiveness of change in modern business, companies are quite frequently in the position of having to communicate developments in advance of having all the detailed information. General statements of intent and reassurance are rarely effective. People want to know as much as possible as soon as possible – in particular they want to know what will be happening to them as individuals.

The general rule is: tell people as much as you can as soon as you can – and if you can't provide details, then at least put the initiative in context and commit yourself to providing the detail when it is available.

In other cases, however, it is not the lack of hard information that is the problem, so much as the lateness of that information. The more conventional employee communications channels – company newspapers, briefing packages, team meetings and so on – are not always flexible enough or fast enough.

BT has devoted considerable resource (and used its own technology) to improving the speed of information flow. The problem hasn't been entirely overcome as more than half of its people are 'on the road', rather than office-based, but significant progress has been made.

As part of this, the company has set up a service called Newsline, a 24-hour-a-day, seven-day-a-week, dial-up news service. It's toll free, so people can call from home if they wish; it can be updated in minutes, several times a week, or even several times a day. It is able to respond very fast to breaking news stories and consists of a mix of news reports and interviews with key managers.

One of the great benefits of this particular channel is that it enables companies to graft facts directly onto the grapevine which, of course, remains one of the speediest and most influential communications channels. Each caller will talk to colleagues and customers – and the service helps bring more consistency and control to such informal contacts.

Electronic mail systems are rapidly being deployed throughout many organizations. This is obviously a very powerful channel, but raises issues of 'etiquette': who should be able to mail the chairman? how easy should it be for people to broadcast company-wide messages?

BT has also invested in a business television network and produces a regular, fortnightly, live news programme aimed specifically at middle and senior managers. More than 50 programmes have been made, including one-off specials dealing with major alliances or year-end financial results. And a number of formats, including phone-ins have been tried. (Other parts of the business are catching on to the advantages. The sales community in particular has been exploiting the team-building potential of the medium in a series of sales-related programmes.)

One of the perennial problems is that much of the financial information a company would like to communicate to its managers is potentially share price-sensitive. Consequently, BT releases its quarterly financial results to the Stock

Exchange before it can release them to its people. This inevitably used to mean that most managers first learnt the company's results from external media. Now, within half an hour or so of the news being released to the Stock Exchange at 7.30 in the morning, BT's managers are able to see the top team talking live, on its own business television network, about the results (and analysts commenting on them), while everyone else in the company can get the essential information from Newsline.

Business TV need not be hugely expensive. The unique thing about BT's business television programme is that it has not been handed over to a facilities house. Instead, it uses a mix of in-house expertise and a number of freelancers, and has invested in a small studio and editing suite.

Nevertheless, however much you keep on top of costs, it is clearly not a cheap medium, particularly if you are only showing one programme a week, or even if you are showing ten, there's still a lot of time when you are not getting anything back from the network. The job is to find other uses for that channel, and BT is currently trialling broadcast teletext. Provided that the TV monitors are always switched on (and someone has to be responsible for ensuring that they are), and people get into the habit of looking at them at least once a day, teletext has the capacity to make a big contribution to timely communications.

All these services – Newsline, Business TV and teletext – can be linked to a Fax Information Retrieval System and those who need it can request hard copy of further information. For example, when BT is communicating financial results, the headline figures are given on Newsline and teletext, and anyone who wants more details can call off hard copy by fax.

The beauty of fax information retrieval is that it is energy-efficient. You only get the paper to the people who need and want it, thereby saving trees and avoiding information overload. Communication of this kind is customer – rather than supplier-driven. And that is a key change.

There are three other notable developments:

- Integrated Services Digital Network or ISDN links also have enormous potential for employee communications as you can send data as well as voice over these lines.
- Compact disc technology is also likely to be very important in this area. Microsoft, for example, has launched a CD called Art Gallery – for less than £50 you can have access to 2,000 of the world's greatest paintings (plus animation, commentary and text on techniques). Increasingly, this is the way images are going to be stored and used.
- Finally, there is the fact that there are something like 70,000 PCs in BT alone. This means that it already has a communications channel that terminates on the desk of a large part of the audience. In a year or two, it will be able to communicate with these terminals over a broadband network. Already, the company has the capacity to store text, images, even full motion video on disk, and all these can become a key part of the employee communications mix.

A two-way process

What is so interesting and challenging about the new technology is not just that it enables companies and managers to do the same things that they have always done, only better, faster and cheaper, but that it provides the opportunity to re-negotiate the contract with the audience. In the past, the unspoken assumption may have been 'anything that you need to know, we will tell you'; now we can say 'anything you want to know about, we can help you to find out about'.

The new technology also enables managers to look again at issues of feedback. In the past, companies had to ask 'what did you think of what we told you?' Increasingly, they are now able to say 'choose what you want from this selection' and they can then monitor, in real time and at little additional cost, the choices that are being made. Companies are becoming better at listening as well as quicker at telling.

Employee research

Measure and monitor what you do. Commit publicly to a research programme that will enable you to measure progress. Since 1989 BT has been running one of the largest employee attitude surveys in Europe – CARE (Communications and Attitude Research for Employees). A questionnaire is sent to everyone in BT every year or so, and managers are asked to encourage their people to complete the questionnaires in their teams – often at team meetings.

The defining characteristic of CARE is that it is action-oriented. All managers with more than ten people working for them receive an individual report – this means producing no fewer than 3,500 individual reports.

BT also test markets and researches the effectiveness of individual employee communications products, from roadshows to business TV, using readership surveys, focus groups, and questionnaires. It has also launched an 'omnibus survey'. Every eight weeks or so it conducts interviews with around 800 BT people to gauge channel performance and reactions to the content of important communications initiatives. From this a picture of how communications might be improved can be built.

It is important to recognize that the very act of asking questions is significant – an acceptance that communication is a two-way process. The act of consultation is a major step towards becoming an 'open company'. It gets everyone thinking about things they might once have taken for granted, and asking questions. Is improving quality part of my normal job? Do I understand where the business is going? How do I rate my manager's performance?

A commitment to survey work entails a parallel commitment to good communications, not just news of the results, but also of what is being done about them. Consequently, the golden rules are that you should only ask people questions to which they have some way of knowing the answer, and you should not ask questions if you are unable to act on the answers.

If you want to know what your people think and feel, what excites them and what doesn't, what they think of their managers and the company that pays their salary – then the easiest way is to ask them. You may not always like what you hear, but nobody can say you didn't ask.

There is now someone with responsibility for employee communications on most of the major project teams in BT. Communications is on the main business agenda and there is an increasing recognition in the company that it needs to be planned and managed professionally.

Not everything has always gone according to plan. Employee communications often feels like a no-win exercise – people complain that they have insufficient information about the company's operations, but when something is done about it, they are still likely to complain that they are too busy to read/watch/listen to the new material.

The messages are often hard. Where people's jobs and lifestyles are at stake, it is scarcely surprising that they can get very emotionally involved – and it would be surprising if they didn't sometimes blame the messenger for the unpalatable message.

However, people have a right to know what is happening to them and their company and they have a right to hear about the things that affect them and their teams from their managers. This may not be very comfortable for managers, it may make them feel vulnerable, they may believe that they lack the necessary skills (a training issue, by and large) or the necessary resilience (delivering bad news is never pleasant), but it is a vital part of leadership.

Brenda McAll is BT's controller of employee communications.

Further Reading

Davenport, J and Lipton, G, (eds) *Communications for Managers: A Practical Handbook*, Industrial Society, London, 1993.

INTERNAL MARKETING

Kevin Thomson

Customers and markets, once considered as existing only outside the organization, are now seen as existing within it as well. What is true of the external market – that best satisfying its needs is what drives the organization – is true also of the internal market. Both need to be served if companies are to continue to meet corporate goals.

Where there are markets, marketing activity follows. As a result, a new discipline, internal marketing, is emerging, not as a pale shadow of external marketing, but as a powerful new force with a strong link to revenue generation.

Internal marketing is a process which recognizes that people within the company have a big influence on customers. How people get on with their employers, managers, and with others inside the company, has a direct bearing on the quality of their own relationship with people outside the company – the customers of the organization.

It is not the faceless company, but its people who create the added value the organization is seeking to provide to its customers. People make a company. What they are capable of delivering in terms of commitment knows no bounds when they buy-in to goals and when they are involved.

Internal marketing creates the environment in which good internal relationships lead to more effective business performance and a drive towards individual and corporate goals. To that extent, internal marketing is concerned with new ways of doing things. What it seeks to bring about is `buy-in' to change, whether that means enhanced levels of customer service, the adoption of new tasks following restructuring and merger, or greater empowerment and accountability, and so on.

For the customer-focused company, and those organizations adopting quality as a competitive strategy, internal marketing is clearly critical. It is directed at effecting a *continuous* improvement in marketing performance that goes beyond the traditional remit of external marketing.

Conventional marketing may be proficient at attracting customers, but it is only through the desire of people within the organization to provide quality service and products – to each other and to the final customer – that marketing promises can be delivered, and customers retained and nurtured.

This reality is already being recognized in job recruitment. The text of a recent advertisement makes the point:

'Customers must trust you and the promises you make. Your team will respect you for your commitment, enthusiasm, support and creativity in achieving new standards of performance, through inspirational leadership and commitment to their personal development.'

These are not matters that have traditionally been the concern of external marketing. Marketing, as we know it, has very largely been a matter of logistics – of winning customers by getting the right product to the right place at the right time and price.

Now the 'tell' and 'sell' approaches with which marketing has at one time or another been associated, are giving way to the much softer concept of persuading would-be customers to '*buy*' into the products, services and objectives of the organization over the long term because of the mutually-advantageous added-value they are seen to offer.

If such added-value is not to be a price advantage or features innovation, in all likelihood it will be realized through the company's own people. This may follow an improvement in their quality and service levels, effected not through command, but through involvement, empowerment and local participation in the attainment of corporate and marketing goals.

Clearly, this requires a holistic response from the organization, one in which external marketing co-exists with human resources, quality, PR and its own people in a pervasive process of satisfying customer needs.

Quite who manages this broadly-based internal marketing role has yet to be resolved in most companies. A few have appointed internal communication specialists, though in practice internal marketing is much more than internal communication, which is only part – albeit a key part – of the process.

In other companies it has yet to be seen whether marketing, HR or PR will pick up the gauntlet, though it is interesting to note that HR managers are becoming aware of the need to market their own function internally. At this stage, many companies are turning to specialist consultants for strategy and implementation.

Whoever holds the reins, the introduction of internal marketing pre-supposes a number of cultural and structural changes. They can be imposed, and sometimes are. But, realistically, a new culture cannot be expected to thrive in unprepared ground. Organization goals which are meaningful to management and worth backing, may not seem so meaningful to others.

It is only through the application of internal marketing skills associated with missions, visions, values, communication channels, matching corporate and individual needs, involvement, feedback and response, that such values can take root and provide the green shoots of new growth.

Internal marketing – key questions to consider

- As an organization, to what extent do you regard internal customers in the same way as your marketing department regards external customers?
- What data do you possess that will allow you to assess accurately your internal customers' needs now and in the future?
- What do your internal customers like about you, both on a business and on a personal level, and what don't they like?

- What differentiates your products and services from those of your external competitors in the eyes of your internal customers?
- How involved are your internal customers with your long-term strategy?
- What are the main 'business' issues facing your internal customers?
- How do your business issues match the personal needs of your internal customers?
- Do you know the 'what's in it for me' for each of your internal markets?

Organizations set on introducing internal marketing practices first need to take a new view of the people within the organization and the way in which they are managed. If people are seen as customers (internal customers) then it follows that each has a supplier (their colleagues).

The organization can then be thought of as comprising a series of internal markets, each of which needs to 'market' to the other in the common cause of best meeting external consumer requirements. The next step is to get the people in the organization to take the same marketing-based view.

As with external marketing, the company should start by understanding its new customers. What do they want? What motivates them? What do they think of the 'service' they currently receive? What will persuade them to buy-in to the proposition that they themselves are customers, and, indeed, suppliers to their colleagues? It is by listening and understanding the needs of its own people that the company can convincingly respond to the big question sure to follow, 'What's in it for me?'. Why, for example, should people within a company respond to exhortations to improve customer satisfaction if there is no recognition of their own needs?

There is more than ample evidence to indicate that unless internal customer needs are matched with the needs of the organization, then people may comply but they will not buy-in or change to any meaningful extent. Only when people willingly involve themselves in the organization's goals is the ground prepared for transferring responsibility for action to those nearest to the customer.

Everything proceeds from this. It involves much more than replacing a top-down command structure with, let us say, team briefing. Indeed, it explains why a new report says that 72 per cent of team briefing users regard the process as having failed to meet their expectations.

What's required is not team briefing but the much more robust approaches of internal marketing, particularly on this point of matching needs. The director-general of the Institute of Personnel and Development, Geoff Armstrong, says:

'You have to know the people, to recognize cultural differences, to analyze their capabilities and to relate all that to the business environment to create sustainable business advantage. Without that, important ideas such as total quality management and business process re-engineering become no more than flavours of the month.'[1]

The phases of an internal marketing process are shown in Fig. 1.

761

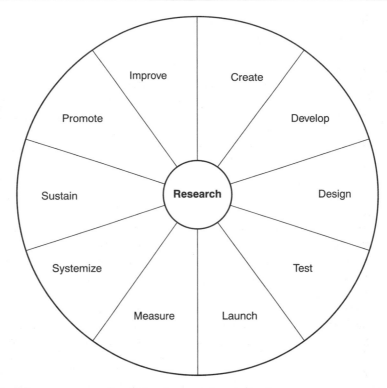

Fig. 1 The process wheel for internal marketing

It is worth paying particular attention to the media adopted to carry the communication. Having got their messages right and their market well-targeted, some companies then choose the wrong media.

The problem is that traditional communication channels of house journals, memos and even electronic communication media, are simply not up to the job of servicing what will ultimately become a three-way communication process – top-down, bottom-up and side-to-side. If internal marketing processes are squeezed down existing channels very little will emerge at the other end.

Again, the needs of the market must dictate the media, not the other way around. If people feel that they need a good *listening* to, *talking at* them through the house journal will be counter-productive.

Internal communication as part of the internal marketing process needs to be co-ordinated. Printed material will certainly be involved, but media should also embrace face-to-face discussion and local activity groups, audio and tape presentations, questionnaires, and a feedback and response mechanism.

It may well involve internal television and the like, so selecting the mix of media is critical. But what really makes the difference is the way in which the media are scheduled to prepare everybody so that all messages and responses are continuously well-received and acted upon positively.

The wheel approach to implementing internal marketing recognizes that matching individual and corporate needs has to be a continuous process in the same way that external marketing tracks and meets customer needs on a continuous basis. It is not a one-off activity.

Where feedback is continuous, high confidence and positive attitudes are generated, whereas a lack of feedback is accompanied by high hostility and low performance. It would not be going too far to say that feedback and local initiative should drive the internal marketing process. We hear a lot about the need for directors to 'own' or 'live' the mission, but they and their managers need to go further than that if the company is truly set on continuous improvement. It is their responsibility not to command but to make it possible for people to realize their own potential and goals, by directing them towards the objectives of the organization.

This may sound difficult, but it can be achieved with great mutual benefit in even the most unpromising, not to say, cynical circumstances.

Winning hearts and minds, then, is a priority objective of internal marketing. But there is more. If everybody is both an internal customer and internal supplier, then individuals or groups should ideally market to each other, for much the same reasons that the organization is marketing to them. Here, internal marketing evolves from top-down, bottom-up to become a side-to-side process as well. In this way a virtuous circle of continuous improvement is formed. The tools to do this are available and the skills can be taught.

The pervasive nature of the internal marketing process was borne out in a Cranfield School of Management survey recorded by Martin Christopher, Adrian Payne and David Ballantyne in their book *Relationship Marketing*. Among its findings, the study identified internal marketing not as a discrete activity, but as implicit in quality initiatives, customer service programmes and broader business strategies. Internal marketing was viewed as performing a critical role in competitive differentiation. It was seen as an experiential process, leading people within a company to arrive at conclusions themselves.

It has a role in reducing conflict between the functional areas of the organization and it leads to the erosion of barriers. And, not surprisingly, communication was considered to be critical to internal marketing's success.

Yet, internal marketing is not solely associated with marketing considerations. Its implementation is equally applicable within organizations where some other condition is bringing about need for change – delayering, restructuring, re-engineering and acquisition. In the case of the latter, generating a 'feel good' factor about an acquisition, both among those people within the acquired company and those within the purchasing company, will clearly be important to morale, motivation and staff retention. Unless both parties buy-in to the benefits of the merger the perceived advantages of the acquisition may never be realized.

In an acquisition in 1994 involving two of the leading names in the computer industry, attitudes to the merger which had been 20-80 per cent against, completely reversed – recorded in the feedback – when internal marketing processes were introduced. And having those processes in place made it much easier for the merged organization to win the support of its people for the restructuring, not to say re-engineering, that followed.

This a key point. Organizations planning to re-engineer their business processes should first re-engineer their internal marketing processes – such as they are – if they are to increase the chances of change-management success and reduced the risk of failure. If, on the other hand, considerations about communicating change are taken on board only at the implementation stage, then the prognosis for BPR is not good.

Internal marketing, then, is appropriate to most types of organization, not just to those who have actually established internal markets – that is to say autonomous profit centres that compete in an internal market. Here, it might be expected that internal marketing would be most visible.

In their book *Internal Markets*, Halal, Geranmayeh and Pourdehnad made the point that where internal markets were established, managers should actively strive to make the idea work by marketing their services to clients, working with them closely to solve problems, and developing methods to evaluate their satisfaction. But internal marketing of this kind is not noticeably prominent in the UK's National Health Service which pioneered the concept of the internal market in the public sector. Perhaps it explains why internal resistance to the new way of doing things remains entrenched.

One of the newest roles for internal marketing is among those companies learning to adapt to the peripheral workforce. Here the main human resources consideration is how to manage people whose relationship with the organization is semi-detached. Again, it is through internal marketing that such companies need to determine what their contractual people value so that these can be matched to corporate objectives.

One thing is certain: what they value will not be the traditional ones of corporate career patterns and rewards. But, whatever they are, they need to be identified and addressed if outsourcing is to be an effective means of conducting the company's business.

And one could go on. There is a key role for internal marketing beyond the internal customer, one extended to get the best out of federations and communities of suppliers and strategic alliances, for example. Others, too, can be brought to buy-in to an organization's objectives, so that what was once a three-way, becomes a four-way marketing process.

Small wonder that companies are coming to see internal marketing as having strategic significance, and it is the view of some commentators that internal marketing is the biggest challenge now facing everybody involved in change of whatever nature.

Kevin Thomson is a consultant with Marlow-based MCA. He is the author of *Managing Your Internal Customers*, **FT/Pitman Publishing, London, 1993.**

Further Reading

Halal, Geranmayeh, Pourdehnad, *Internal Markets*, Wiley, New York, 1993

Thomson, K, *Managing your Internal Customers*, Pitman, London, 1993

Christopher, M, Payne, A and Ballantyne, D, *Relationship Marketing*, Heinemann, Oxford, 1991

Reference

[1] Institute of Personnel and Development Conference, October 1994.

NEGOTIATING

Jane Hodgson

Negotiating is a vital, often unacknowledged, part of management. In one form or another negotiating accounts for large amounts of managerial time. As a skill which can be enhanced and developed negotiating is all but ignored. Yet, by developing skills which allow for full and complete negotiations – rather than overly quick or confrontational ones – managers can achieve results which are mutually beneficial.

If you ask a group of managers to identify the words they associate with negotiations, the pervasive emphasis tends to be on competition, hostility or combat. Similarly, the negotiations which come to public attention also appear to have an aggressive element to them, with both parties locked in seemingly unalterable, opposing positions. This confrontational stereotype can overshadow the fact that most managers need to negotiate as part of their workload. Negotiating with customers, suppliers and contractors is, for many managers, a normal part of their day-to-day activity. Other managers may not regard negotiating as an essential part of their job but they will, nevertheless, find themselves negotiating budgets, workload, accountability, deadlines or timescales.

The skills involved in negotiating are an essential part of any manager's toolkit. Often they are taken for granted or lie dormant and undeveloped. Yet, good negotiators are made, not born – negotiation strategies and skills *can* be learned.

Approaches to negotiating

Many negotiations start with the two or more parties involved preparing their case and stating their position. As each negotiator develops more and more arguments in favour of their own position, they tend to become more convinced of the rightness of it, more entrenched in the stance they have developed, and less willing to move away from it. Each step they take away from this position will be hard fought for and grudgingly conceded.

This entrenched position, and the determination to achieve the most favourable deal regardless of the other party, tends to lead to an outcome which is often labelled win-lose – if one person wins, another loses. One negotiator comes out of the encounter having achieved most of their objectives, but as a consequence, the other comes away feeling that they have given away more than they intended.

Fisher and Ury, in *Getting to Yes*, label this win or lose approach *positional bargaining*. They suggest that a more constructive approach is what they call *principled negotiating*, where the focus shifts from the position of the various parties to the problem which all those involved need to solve. This is much more likely to lead to both parties achieving at least something of what they want so that the situation is resolved to the satisfaction of both.

The essence of this problem-solving approach is that the focus shifts from the people involved to the problem to be solved; from the relative positions of the parties to the interests they have – what they actually want to achieve from the event. A collaborative rather than competitive climate is created, with the aim being to have both parties working together to solve the problem rather than win a battle. In this way, a win-win outcome, where both parties feel satisfied at the end of the negotiation, is achieved.

There are four specific steps which strengthen the problem-solving approach. They are:

Focus on the issue to be resolved, not the person involved

Negotiating often involves personality as well as business problems. The difficulty of negotiating a settlement may feel as if it has more to do with the person doing the bargaining than with the problem itself. It is easy to be drawn in to feeling that you have to get the better of the person sitting opposite, especially if they got the better of you last time. Focusing on the problem to be solved and divorcing that from your feelings about the person with whom you are negotiating, removes some of the tension and increases the likelihood of achieving a solution.

Widen your horizons

Do not assume that there is only one solution to the problem. This can limit the problem-solving capacity of otherwise brilliant negotiators. People get into the habit of thinking of one best solution, or a range of solutions incorporating a fixed number of variables. Thinking creatively about the scope for solutions outside the obvious ones can create new perspectives and solutions which provide greater benefits to both parties. For example, if two people cannot agree on the price one of them should pay for some goods the other one wants to sell, potential solutions can be increased by bringing in considerations such as discount for prompt delivery or penalties for late delivery, credit agreements or cash payment, guaranteed orders, and so on.

Look for a solution, not a battle

The problem-solving approach involves building a bridge to help the person on the other side move towards you. If you see yourself and the other person involved as equally interested parties needing a solution to a common problem, you avoid becoming locked into your corner, having to fight a battle to achieve a compromise which may feel less than satisfactory.

Set up meetings to be constructive

At the beginning of a meeting, summarize its purpose in positive terms. Look at why you are both there. Make it obvious that you are taking a problem-solving approach by asking questions which show that you appreciate that the other party has a right to their wants, needs, opinions, demands. Involve them in the process of reaching a conclusion, making it obvious that it is a joint problem which needs to be solved, using phrases which include the word 'we'.

Preparation

Good preparation is one of the keys to a successful negotiation. As in many other areas, it is easy to react quickly and effectively if you have the facts and figures at your finger tips, if you know what to expect from the other party, and are familiar with the background to the case. It is not so easy to do a good job if you are caught on the hop and asked to provide information which you have a vague idea about but are not too sure.

There are two essential parts to preparing for a negotiation – the first is preparing your own case, and the second, less obviously, is thinking about the other party.

Preparing your own case

1. Focus on end results. Any standard text on negotiating will tell you that you need to have clear objectives and know what you want to achieve from the negotiation. This is undoubtedly true. If you start negotiating without a clear idea of what you want you could end up with a lot of gifts, in that anything you got would be an achievement, or you could be robbed, ending up by giving away valuable concessions while receiving little of any value.

However, it is important to focus on the end result you want to achieve rather than a specific goal. If you need to buy a particular product at a specific price, you may have boxed yourself in to a win-lose position. If you can't get the product at the price you want, you will have lost. If you do get it at that price, your supplier will have lost. By focusing on the end result you want, cost saving perhaps, you and the supplier may be able to come to some arrangement which would enable you to save costs in another way – for example, by making adjustments to delivery schedules or quantity purchased. It is advisable to deliberately generate a wide range of options of possible outcomes, thinking in the long term about what the eventual implications of those outcomes might be.

2. Know your priorities and your limits. It is unusual to have just one issue to bargain about. Once you know your overall objective, break it down into its constituent parts, then prioritize. What is essential? What is important? What is less vital? What would be totally unacceptable, the limit beyond which you are not prepared to go?

3. Plan to package the issues you need to deal with. Rather than having to negotiate one issue at a time, be prepared to treat them as a whole, trading gains in one area for concessions in another.

4. Focus on the potential for common ground. What might you be able to agree about at an early stage in the meeting?

5. Have a range of negotiating positions rather than negotiating around a single fixed point. The most commonly used technique for achieving this is setting out your *ideal*, *realistic* and *fallback* positions. This is a useful way of establishing your parameters for the negotiation, formalizing your thinking about what you want to achieve and the limits beyond which you are not prepared to go.

Your *ideal position* is what you would really like to have. In an ideal world, this would be your outcome. This is the place at which you are likely to start when you state your position at the beginning of the negotiation. One trap which many negotiators fall into is having an unrealistic ideal position. They may ask for a wildly inflated version of what they want, thinking that if they ask for more they may end up with more. This does not always work, as the outrageous may be recognized and countered with the exorbitant, or may provoke a refusal to negotiate at all. Your ideal position should be achievable.

Your *realistic position* is what realistically you might expect to obtain, given that you recognize the need to be flexible in achieving your objective, and that in order to gain some of what you want, you may need to give something to the other side. A problem which can arise with the realistic position is that it is too rigid. Some negotiators are inclined to look at their ideal and fallback positions and put the realistic position firmly in the middle, with little or no flexibility built in.

Your *fallback position* is your bottom limit, the point beyond which you are not prepared to go. Beware of setting your fallback position too high. Be realistic when you work out what your limits really are. Having to go lower than a settled and stated fallback position engenders feelings of defeat and anger and can cause you to lose face with colleagues.

Fisher and Ury suggest the idea of a BATNA – a 'Best Alternative To a Negotiated Agreement'. If the person with whom you are negotiating refuses to settle on a solution to the problem which satisfies your fallback position, you might need to fall back on your BATNA. This is something which needs to be thought through before you begin to negotiate. If you cannot come to an acceptable agreement, what will you do?

Thinking about the other party

Try to predict what issues or solutions might be raised by the other side. Think about what you think their objective, priorities, ideal, realistic and fall-back positions might be. Considering the wants and needs of the other party, and putting yourself in their position, means that you can make educated guesses about the demands they are likely to make and the limits they may have. It means that there may be fewer surprises in the negotiation and that you are better prepared for the eventualities which may emerge. However, let the guesses you make about the other party be hypotheses, be prepared for them to be wrong.

Having a realistic appraisal of the balance of power is an important facet of any negotiation. Negotiating with the chief executive may feel very different from negotiating with someone who reports to you. Power is important in negotiations because it can affect the ability of the negotiators to make decisions, and because the person with more power is likely to achieve more of what he wants – partly because he may have the power to impose his solution. Power depends very much on the environment, the situation in which it is used. A judge has the power to impose a fine on someone for speeding, but elsewhere, depending on their role, the guilty party may have the power to deny the judge planning consent or permission to board a full bus.

Perceived power can be more important than power itself. How much real power does the other person have in that situation? Is it power based on position, expertise, reputation or connections? Do not underestimate your own power. If the other party has power based on position, you may have power based on expertise. If they have power from their connections with the powerful, your reputation may stand you in good stead. People tend to negotiate only if they believe that the other person involved has something which is valuable to them, be it resources, skills, or something more intangible such as influence or good will. So the balance of power in a negotiation may weight the likely outcome, but need not mean it is a foregone conclusion.

Skills

The skills involved in successfully negotiating a satisfactory outcome are those which help to build a bridge between the two parties, so that they can meet somewhere in the middle.

Questioning and listening

Questions are one of the key tools of the effective negotiator. They can be used to collect and clarify information, avoid stalemates, defuse anger, obtain thinking time, stimulate creative thinking and discover visions and motivations. The intelligent and generous use of questions can make it much easier to negotiate. When you are negotiating, it is useful to have as much information as possible about the facts the other side possesses, not to mention their thoughts, opinions, needs, and desired outcomes. Increasing the amount of information you have increases your power.

Asking questions can have the effect of discovering extra facts which might put a completely different light on the subject, and even uncover the route to future agreement. They can be used to provide extra thinking time by deferring reactions to suggestions, proposals, or statements of fact or opinion, made by the other side.

Questions can also be used to move out of stalemate by stimulating thinking about new and different ways of approaching a problem. Questions such as 'what if', 'suppose we', 'how would it be if...' all encourage a wider exploration of the field.

Perhaps the most effective use of questions in negotiations is to avoid disagreeing directly with what the other party has said. If you don't understand or don't agree, don't say so, ask a question. Exactly how do they propose it might be implemented; what precisely would be involved in doing it that way; what specific costs might be involved, what other factors might be implicated?

Many negotiators find it difficult to listen in negotiations because their minds are so full of what they want to say, to hide or find out. Their anxiety to put their own point across, means that they are waiting for the other person to finish speaking rather than listening to what they have to say. Concentrating on what the other person is saying becomes easier if they recognize that asking a question at the end not only gives thinking time, but gives extra valuable material to add to the infrastructure of the negotiation.

Bargaining strategies

There are four essential strategies involved in effective bargaining: giving and receiving signals, creating possibilities, trading and packaging proposals.

Giving and receiving signals

A crucial skill of fast and efficient thinking in negotiating is the ability to both send signals about your willingness to move from your starting position, and pick up the signals which the other person is sending about their willingness to move.

These signals are sent non-verbally and verbally, consciously and unconsciously. Unconscious signals are usually sent through body language and tone of voice, and most people are very good at picking up and interpreting these non-verbal signals.

It is sometimes easy to miss the verbal signals people send unless you are looking out for them. Phrases such as 'At the moment we can't reduce the price'; 'We can't give you a discount under these circumstances'; 'As things stand, we cannot change the size' – all these indicate that given certain movement or change, the price, discount or size might actually be negotiable.

771

Creating possibilities

Giving the other party a picture of what life might be like if certain things were to happen can help to move the negotiation along. There are phrases which do not commit anyone to a specific course of action, but set out some options for routes which could be taken to reach a satisfactory outcome. Phrases such as 'suppose we...', 'suppose you...', and 'how would it be if....', paint a picture of what the future could be like if a certain course of action were followed. They suggest possibilities in a tentative, non-threatening way and can be used to extend the range of the bargaining arena.

Trading

Once willingness to move has been signalled and possibilities created, the next stage is trading one item for another. This is where the bargaining really starts. It should be a process of give and take to ensure a win-win outcome. There are some rules which can help you to decide instantly if you are trading, bullying, or caving in.

1. Give away things which are of little value to you.
2. Try to gain things which you value in exchange for what you give.
3. Only give away things you can afford to give.
4. Make sure that you won't regret it later.
5. Don't give away anything without getting something in return. This may not necessarily be an obvious asset, it may be as intangible as goodwill or a quiet life – but it should be something that you value.

Packaging

If more than one issue is involved in the negotiation, it can be irritating and counter-productive to negotiate them one at a time. Regarding them as a package of issues to be settled means that it is possible to give something away on one issue while gaining something on another, so that a compromise agreement does not need to be reached on every single item. It makes it easier to assess the outcome as a whole, to evaluate the concessions the other party may be making against their demands. If all the issues to be negotiated are brought out into the open at the beginning of the meeting, problem solving is made easier.

Characteristics of skilled negotiators

A major research study into the behaviours used by negotiators during the negotiation meeting was carried out by the Huthwaite Group in the late 1970s. Using behavioural analysis techniques, they looked at the differences in behaviour between average and skilled negotiators. They defined skilled negotiators as those who were rated as effective by both sides, had a track record of significant success which stood the test of time, and a low incidence of implementation failures. They found that skilled negotiators differed considerably from average negotiators in their interactions, using some behaviours significantly more than average negotiators, while avoiding others.

The Huthwaite Group found that skilled negotiators used these behaviours more than average negotiators:

1. Seeking information. Skilled negotiators asked for more than twice as much information as average negotiators, asking questions both to obtain necessary information with which to bargain, and as a deliberated strategy to control the discussion, avoid direct disagreement or reduce the other party's thinking time.

2. Testing, understanding and summarizing. Skilled negotiators checked that a statement or proposal had been understood, and summarized by recapitulating the outline of part or all of the discussion so far, more than twice as much as average negotiators. Both behaviours clarify interpretation and reduce misunderstandings. Whereas average negotiators, anxious to reach agreement, might leave ambiguous points to be cleared up later, the skilled negotiator tended to have a greater concern for successful implementation, so would check out and eliminate any ambiguities when they arose, rather than leave them as a potential problem for implementation.

3. Behaviour labelling. Skilled negotiators tended to give advance warning of the type of behaviour they were about to use. For example, rather than asking: 'What is the deadline for this?' they would say: 'May I ask you a question? What is the deadline for this?' Instead of saying: 'I think we should assimilate x with y', they would say: 'I'd like to make a suggestion – we could assimilate x with y'. The advantages of labelling behaviour are that it leads to clearer communication by drawing the attention of the listener to what is coming next, and ensuring that the whole of the proposal, statement or question is in focus. It slows down the negotiation, giving more time for thought and introduces a little formality, which can keep the negotiation on an even keel.

The only exception to this was disagreeing. Skilled negotiators were less likely to label disagreeing whereas average negotiators were inclined to label disagreeing more often. Labelling disagreement can have the effect of annoying the other party or causing them to lose face. Skilled negotiators were more likely to lead with reasons and explanations before concluding these factors led them to disagree.

4. Feelings commentary. The common perception of a skilled negotiator is someone with a poker face who keeps all their cards close to their chest, revealing very little about their thoughts and feelings. The Huthwaite Group found that, in fact, skilled negotiators were more likely to give information about their thoughts and feelings, but less likely to give information about concrete facts or expressions of opinion. The advantage of giving information about thoughts and feelings is that it appears to reveal what is going on in the mind, which, whether or not it is genuine, gives the other party the sense of motives being open and above board. It is worth being careful about the way these feelings are expressed – 'I'm feeling a bit confused because some of this information seems to be contradictory', is a lot less inflammatory than: 'You're confusing me,' or 'You are making contradictory statements.'

The Huthwaite Group found that skilled negotiators avoided the following behaviours:

1. Irritators. They found that certain types of phrase such as 'reasonable offer', 'generous terms', 'fair', 'honest', 'impartial', etc, which referred in favourable terms to the negotiator's own side, tended to be inflammatory and to lessen good will. This type of phrase had no positive effect used as self-praise, and irritated the other side because of the implicit insinuation that they were *not* generous, reasonable, fair, impartial, or honest. One surprising result of this research was not that skilled negotiators avoided this gratuitous self-congratulation, but that average negotiators used it quite often, nearly five times more than skilled negotiators. Any television coverage of an industrial dispute will give a good example of this.

2. Defend/attack spirals. Some conflict is often involved in negotiations, which involves defend/attack spirals. Defence looks very much like attack to the observer, and human nature means that when a negotiator feels he is under attack, his natural reaction is to defend. This can lead very quickly to an escalation from one unguarded remark to full scale conflict as each side defends itself from attack by the other. Skilled negotiators tended to avoid being drawn into these spirals, instead defusing conflict by asking questions, and when they did attack, doing so hard and without warning.

3. Counter proposals. During negotiations, or in fact any meeting, one proposal is often greeted by another, counter proposal. It is natural that this should happen because one idea of how to achieve an end often triggers other thoughts and suggestions as to how to achieve it. Skilled negotiators tended to avoid making counter proposals as the effect is often counter productive. The disadvantage of counter proposals is that they are made at a time when the other party is least receptive, having their own proposal uppermost in their mind, so the counter proposal is often perceived as blocking or disagreeing. Also, they introduce an additional option which can confuse or cloud the issue making it more difficult to resolve. A better way of altering or moving on from a proposal is to ask questions about it, giving the proposer the satisfaction of having his idea considered, and the opportunity to find the flaws in it for himself. Then make the other proposal.

4. Argument dilution. The research found that contrary to commonly held beliefs about the weight of the argument – which suggests that the more arguments on your side of the equation, the more likely the scales will tip in your favour – quality rather than quantity was key. Skilled negotiators tended to use a few good reasons for their argument, rather than backing it up with many smaller ones. One reason for this is that it is easier for an opponent to find the flaws in the weaker reasons, and so disregard the good reasons. Another reason is that many minor reasons for the argument can have the effect of trivialising rather than substantiating it.

Many people become worried about the prospect of having to conduct a negotiation. It seems from the outside to be a process shrouded in mystery, performed by the expert. In fact it is no such thing. Most people are involved in negotiating on a daily basis, and have been ever since they swapped conkers or lollipops. Looking at it as a problem-solving rather than point-winning exercise, preparing thoroughly and imaginatively, and using some simple skills and strategies, can help to ensure that agreements are made which are not only satisfactory to both parties immediately, but stand the test of time. Settlements which are reached quickly, with a superficial compromize agreed, have a huge potential for breaking down because of misunderstandings, cosmetic consensus, or a failure to explore the issues thoroughly enough.

Negotiators who focus on the long-term outcomes of the agreements they make, perhaps spending a little longer preparing beforehand and using questioning and other strategies more skilfully during the meeting, are not only most successful in achieving successful results, but are those with whom other people have no qualms about negotiating again.

Jane Hodgson worked in the public sector and in financial services before becoming a management development consultant. She specializes in the development of people and communication skills, and the stimulation of organizational development initiatives. She has worked in the UK, Europe and the United States with clients in the public and private sectors. She is author of *Thinking on Your Feet in Negotiations* (1994) and co-author of *Effective Meetings* (1992).

Further Reading

Fisher, R and Ury, W, *Getting to Yes*, Arrow Books, London, 1981.
Hodgson, J, *Thinking on Your Feet in Negotiations*, Pitman, London, 1994.
Kennedy, G, *How to Negotiate and Win*, Arrow Books, London, 1982.
Kozicki, S, *The Creative Negotiator*, Gower, Aldershot, 1994.
Nierenberg, GI, *The Art of Negotiating*, Pocket Books, New York, 1984.
Nierenberg, GI, *The Complete Negotiator*, Nierenberg & Zeif, New York 1986.

NETWORKING

Vivien Whitaker

There are different interpretations of the term networking. It is often linked to information technology and 'hard' networks. In contrast, what is sometimes referred to as 'soft' networking, is concerned with relationships between people. It has been defined as 'all the different ways in which people make, and are helped to make, connections with each other'.[1]

Networking has had a bad press in the past – talk of the exclusiveness of old boy networks, links with political issues. However, as traditional formal hierarchies are changing and professionals are increasingly engaged in home-working, virtual teams and global organizations, networking has become increasingly important.

Some networks exist within organizations; others are external to organizations and may be linked to professions or special interest groups. The potential to network is immense. The question is whether managers capitalize on these opportunities.

Networking is not just about recognizing the connections we have with others, it is also making the most of these connections. It is something we can all do, all the time. We have the opportunity to make connections with each other whenever we talk – through face-to-face conversations, meetings or telephone calls – and whenever we write – through letters, internal memos, E mail, proposals or reports.

Networking can add value for us as individuals and also contribute to the results of our organizations. Take two examples:

Two managers, from different organizations met on a management develop-ment programme. During discussions they became aware that they both had similar problems. They used time outside the formal sessions to share ideas and brainstorm solutions. They kept in touch after the course to discuss how each problem was resolved.

A quality assurance manager in a computer systems integration company noticed that the head of a unit he was visiting was planning to spend 20-person weeks developing some new software. The quality assurance manager knew from visits he had made to other units that someone else was working on something very similar. Although it was not formally part of his job he shared this information and the units were able to exchange ideas and save time in development of a new product.

The connections we make when we are networking are more than an information exchange or cascade, and often do not reflect the formal structure of the organizations we work in; in fact managers often circumvent them when they need to get things done quickly.

Increasing recognition of the importance of networking has prompted managers to discover ways to enhance the usefulness of these informal links. Some managers arrange focus groups or retreats or 'away days' with their staff so they can keep in touch and brainstorm new ways of working. Others work systematically to develop informal networks.

After the reform of the UK's National Health Service in the late 1980s many medical practitioners were required to take on a greater managerial role. Helen Jones, working for the NHS in Yorkshire, recognized that no informal networks existed between the medical and managerial professions. She started with a small core of medical practitioners who were keen to learn about management They then networked with colleagues about the benefits of their management development programme. Several programmes with doctors from different disciplines were set up and regular conferences for participants were held so that learning could be shared. Some doctors then went on a development programme in which managers from industry were brought together with doctors. This enabled the doctors to extend their networks to industrial and service managers and also to other doctors in other regions who were experiencing similar problems.[2]

Network analysis

We can be more aware of our internal networks and the way we use them by undertaking a Network Analysis.[3] This involves drawing maps or diagrams of three types of relationship networks within the organization:

- **Communications network** – this reveals the employees who talk about work-related matters on a regular basis.
- **Advice network** – this indicates the prominent people in the organization on whom others depend to solve problems and provide technical information.
- **Trust network** – this reveals which employees share delicate political information and back one another in a crisis.

Network analysis can help managers to look at where they see themself on these networks – are they a 'hub' in the centre of a network or a 'node' on the edge of other people's networks? Are each of an individual's network diagrams similar to each other or is there a lack of congruence between them?

Drawing your communication network

Draw a diagram of all the people you talk to or write to every day. Then using a different coloured pen include all those people you communicate with at least once a week. Use another colour to identify those people you connect with occasionally but who offer you crucial information. Indicate by arrows whether communication is one-way or two-way.

The American academics Krackhardt and Hanson were asked to undertake a network analysis of 24 branches for a bank whose customers were not satisfied with the information they were receiving about banking services. A study of the communications networks of the branches showed that it was not the *amount* of information flow which distinguished the more profitable branches; it was the *quality* of communication which determined their success. Non-hierarchical branches with two-way communication between people of all levels, were 70 per cent more profitable than one-way communication patterns between 'superiors' and staff.

The communication networks of two branches located in the same city illustrated this point.

Branch 1 had a central figure, a supervisor, with whom many tellers talked on a daily basis about their work. The supervisor confirmed that employees talked to her, but she reported communicating with only half of these tellers about work-related matters by the end of the day. The tellers resented this one-way information flow as they regarded information as central to their success. They complained that the supervisor was cold and remote and failed to keep them informed. As a result, productivity suffered.

Branch 2 had very few one-way communication lines but many mutual, two-way lines. Tellers in this branch said they were well informed and reported greater satisfaction with their jobs.

As a result of the network analysis, management changed from a 'more is better' communication strategy and began exploring ways of fostering mutual communication in all the branches. The bank sponsored mini-seminars in the branches, in which the problems revealed by the maps were openly discussed. These consciousness-raising sessions spurred many supervisors to communicate more substantive information to tellers.

It may be helpful to get colleagues and staff to draw their communication networks to compare maps and identify common issues.

Drawing your advice network

Using a different sheet of paper draw a diagram of those people you go to for help or advice at least once a week. Taking a different coloured pen indicate those people whose advice you seek occasionally.

Drawing your trust network

Using a third sheet of paper draw a diagram of those people whom you would trust to keep in confidence your concerns about a work-related issue.

Company founder and chief executive, David Leers, thought he knew his company well. In fifteen years the company had trained a cadre of loyal professionals who had built a strong regional reputation for delivering customized office information systems.

The company's structure was typical of many businesses. The field design group had been the linchpin of the company for years, but had recently become dissatisfied when resources started flowing to other groups. Leers decided to involve them in planning and set up a strategic taskforce composed of members of all divisions, but led by a member of field design to signal his continuing commitment to the group.

The group started well but after a month had made little progress; within two months the group was completely deadlocked by members championing their own agendas. Leers turned to Krackhardt and Hanson for help.

An analysis of the company's trust and advice networks helped Leers to get a clear picture of the dynamics at work in the taskforce.

Taskforce leader Tom Harris held a central position in this advice network. However, he was in a very weak position on the trust network. This, Leers concluded was the main reason for the taskforce's inability to produce results. Harris was interested in technical issues, not people, and didn't possess the skills to moderate conflicting views, focus the group's thinking and win the commitment of taskforce members to mutually agree on strategies. He decided to re-design the team to reflect the strengths of the trust network.

Referring to the map, Leers looked for someone in the trust network who could share responsibilities with Harris. He chose Bill Benson, a warm amiable person who occupied a central position in the network and with whom Harris had already established a good working relationship. He publicly justified his decision to name two taskforce heads as necessary, given the time pressures and scope of the problem.

Leers (CEO)			
Software Applications	Field Design	Integrated Communications Technologies	Data Control Systems
O'Hara (SVP)	Calder(SVP)	Long (SVP)	Stern (SVP)
Bair	Harris	Muller	Huttle
Stewart	Benson	Jules	Akins
Ruiz	Fleming	Baker	Kibler
	Church	Daven	
	Martin	Thomas	
	Lee	Zanado	
	Wilson		
	Swinney		
	Carlson		
	Hoberman		
	Fiola		

Fig. 1 The Leers company structure

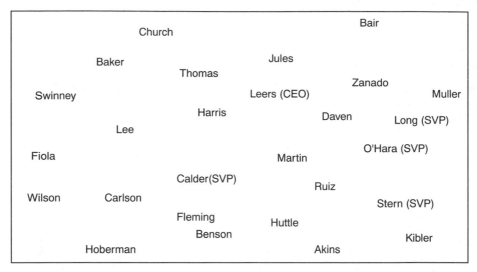

Fig. 2 The advice network

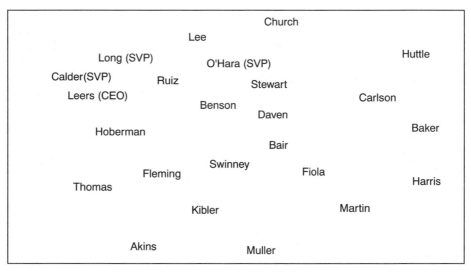

Fig. 3 The trust network

Within three weeks, Leers could see changes in the group's dynamics. Because taskforce members trusted Benson to act in the best interest of the entire group, people talked openly and let go of their fixed positions. During the next two months the taskforce made significant progress in proposing a strategic direction for the company. And in the process of working together, the taskforce helped to integrate the company's divisions.

Comparing networks

Set out your three networks side-by-side and look at them together and answer the following questions:

- Do your networks conform to the formal structure of your organization?
  If they don't, what do the diagrams tell you about the 'informal' structure within your organization?
  How can these help you with your networking in the future?
- Do your networks overlap?
  If they don't, would it be helpful if they did?
  What do you need to do to make this happen?
- Can you identify 'bow-ties' in your networks where a lot of people are dependent on one person?
  What happens when this person is out of the office or away sick?
- Have you spotted 'holes' in your network – people you should be talking to in your organization but who are not on your diagrams?
  How can you plan to close these holes?
- Do you communicate sufficiently with other departments in your organization?
  Are there opportunities for networking which you are not capitalizing on, which may help you in your work?
- Are you using people on your networks effectively?
  Could you get more value from your networks by planning or attending more meetings, informal get-togethers or by lunching in the staff restaurant?
- Are you in the 'hub' at the centre of your department's networks or are you on a 'node' at the edge of other people's networks?
  Do you need to network more actively so that people around you begin to see you as a source of information/advice?

Now draw together an action plan of what you need to do differently in order to maximize the use of your internal networks. Do it under three headings:

What I need to do   Who can help me?   When I will start

External networks

It it useful to look beyond your organization and observe networks you belong to which are not linked to your organization – your professional association, your local chamber of commerce or small business club, links you have established with people from other organizations while on training courses or conferences, or in previous jobs, friends you have known since college or university.

Drawing your external network

Create a diagram or network map of your external networks and the key people involved. It may be helpful to use different colours to highlight different links.

External network of a training manager working for a housing association

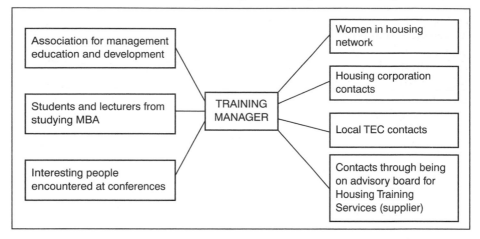

When you have completed your map ask the following questions:

- Are there key people you rely on a lot?
  Could you diversify your contacts? Why not aim to double the number of contacts that you have?
- Can you identify people whom you would like to contact but haven't found the time or courage to yet? Add them to your map.
  Who could help you to make contact with them?
  Do you have a mentor or more experienced manager who could help you to develop your external networks?
  If not, how could you find one?
- Do you find it difficult to recall people's names?
- Are your networking relationships of value to both parties?
  If not, is there a way of making them mutually beneficial?
- Do you use lack of time as an excuse for not talking to your contacts?
  Do you try to 'be strong' and resolve all your problems yourself?
- When planning your next career move are you able to identify people who are currently in a job you would like, and go and talk to them to find out more about the post?
  Add their names to your map and identify contacts who might introduce you to these people, if this is necessary.
- How do you use your external networks to learn about other people's good practice and new ideas?
  How do you publicise your own good practice and develop new ideas and ways of working?
  Can you set up a learning network with colleagues where you share learning and good practice on a regular basis?

Now add to your action plan all those things which you need to do differently in order to capitalize on your external networks.

Techniques which assist networking

1. Event + response leads to outcome

This equation helps us to be aware that any outcome is a result of both an event and our response to that event. For example, attending a conference and not talking to anyone does not increase a participant's network. The participant who takes the trouble to talk to other people will naturally expand his or her network.

The difference between these examples is that *the participant influenced the outcome by taking action*. The people with the most effective networks are the people who take action to create networks and maintain them. Look around your organization and spot the effective networkers. If the organization uses Belbin's team roles[4] these people will probably be the resource investigators who enjoy developing contacts and exploring opportunities.

2. I'm the kind of person who...

We often hold back from taking action because we are not the kind of person who is good at socializing, or the kind of person who asks questions at a conference, or introduces themselves to other professionals whom they don't know.

Yet there is only ourself and the messages we tell ourself that holds us back. We *can* become the kind of person who asks questions and introduces him/herself to others if we *change the messages we give ourselves and take a few risks*.

Behavioural scientists have discovered that it takes just 30 days to create a new habit if you practice your new behaviour each day.

3. Go for it, anyway

Often, the most important step is to recognize that you have nothing to lose and much to gain from taking action.

Barriers to networking

Although many new initiatives in organizations, such as virtual teams and virtual offices, depend on managers' skills in networking to be successful, other new initiatives, like competitive tendering in the public sector, actually discourage networking. Colleagues who previously would ring or meet to chat over ideas are now having to cost and code each activity, or having to negotiate a contract to do so. Many of the new systems do not appear flexible enough to accommodate the sharing of ideas and good practice across departments, or between organizations, at the moment.

Learning networks

What these systems have not yet recognized is the value of sharing learning. If we can learn from other people's experience and so avoid mistakes it can help us not only to keep apace with, but to 'ride the waves of change' successfully.[5] By using networking to learn more quickly we are gaining competitive advantage.

Perhaps most persuasively, research has shown that every professional in the world is connected to every other professional by a chain of no more than five links long. It is worth remembering this when you are daunted about taking risks in networking – it is relatively easy to obtain an introduction to anyone you want to meet.

Vivien Whitaker is a consultant. Her consultancy work has included projects on problem solving, strategic planning, managing change, team development and action-learning based development. She has worked with a wide variety of public and private sector organizations and is author of *Managing People* (1994).

Further Reading

Hastings, C, *The New Organization*, McGraw Hill, Maidenhead, 1993.

References

[1] Hastings, C, *The New Organization*, McGraw Hill, Maidenhead, 1993.
[2] *Ibid.*
[3] Krackhardt, D and Hanson, JR, 'Informal Networks: The Company Behind The Chart', *Harvard Business Review*, July–August 1993.
[4] *Ibid.*
[5] Belbin, M, *Team Roles At Work*, Butterworth-Heinemann, Oxford, 1993.
[6] Morgan, G, *Riding the Waves of Change*, Jossey-Bass, New York, 1989.

MANAGING INTERNATIONAL PUBLIC RELATIONS

John Graham

Public relations has tended to reside in a managerial and corporate grey area, its importance underestimated or unrecognized. Now, the complexities of a changing global business environment make it crucial for companies to understand what role public relations should play in defining and implementing corporate strategy.

Technological advances, such as the advent of worldwide networks, instantly access corporate audiences on a global scale. This is supplemented by a growing demand that companies not only operate responsibly but are seen to be doing so. For any modern organization, satisfying and communicating with a variety of stakeholders is a constant necessity.

Public relations deals with all the communications that a corporation or organization conducts with its key audiences. These audiences can include not only the media and shareholders, but employees, industry analysts, the community, customers, suppliers and governments in every country in which the company operates. Decisions by representatives of each – or all – of these groups can affect company strategy, tactics, growth and profits.

Public relations has traditionally been used as an umbrella term to cover a wide range of areas, including corporate communications, issues management, media relations, product publicity, investor relations, financial communications, lobbying, public and community affairs, crisis management and sponsorship. These various aspects are increasingly being drawn together, as more and more companies become concerned with managing their reputations wherever they do business, into what is now labelled *reputation management.*

A 1993 survey of senior public relations executives in large US and European corporations indicated how much the practice of public relations has changed and developed in recent years, and how it will continue to do so.[1] Just over 45 per cent of respondents believed that public relations will become more:

- strategic
- international in scope
- involved in investor/government/media relations
- involved with other operating groups within the company

Of the top five public issues projected to have a major impact on companies throughout this decade, Americans and Europeans agreed on four: global competition, technological innovation, environmental concerns and regulatory matters. Figure 1 shows the top 10 areas of concern mentioned by survey respondents:

To cope with such a diverse set of issues, public relations has to be an approach rather than simply a technique; a framework that ensures consistency and maintains transparency, not a means to hide uncomfortable facts. If the trends in the US are indicative, this will become an important element for survival. The US already has a thriving watchdog industry, with report cards on company behaviour produced regularly in areas such as disclosure of information, equal opportunity, environmental behaviour, community involvement

Rank	US %	Europe %
1.	Global competition 74	Technological innovation 62
2.	Environmental issues 68	Environmental issues 58
3.	Health care costs 68	Global competition 58
4.	Technological innovation 55	Regulatory issues 49
5.	Regulatory issues 48	Corporate expansion 30
6.	Retirement benefit costs 28	Downsizing/layoffs 23
7.	Labour relations 16	Executive compensation 18
8.	Product liability costs 15	Labour relations 17
9.	Corporate expansion 15	Product liability 16
10.	Women in management 13	Healthcare costs 12

Fig. 1 Ten top areas of major concern revealed by 1993 survey of senior public relations executives in USA and Europe

and political affiliation. This awareness is increasingly having an impact on how people view a company's products and services.

Although there is less of a tradition of corporate openness in Europe, the prospect of a unified market has sharpened the understanding that European-based companies have about the need for good communications and reputation management.

Internationalization of business will call for consistency of performance on a global scale. Some of it will be forced on companies by increasingly stringent legislation spanning areas ranging from treatment of the workforce to advertising and packaging. As a result, working within a closely monitored ethical framework – both internally and with all external relations – will make good business sense. These trends all have important implications for how organizations communicate to stakeholders and key audiences.

Organizing public relations

While each company has to define its public relations strategy in the way best suited to its needs, there are several common issues:

- the position of public relations compared to other corporate functions;
- the role public relations plays in supporting marketing;
- programme management and evaluation;
- choosing and using external consultants.

In comparison to functions such as marketing, production or finance, public relations remains in the early stages of its development. This can make the job of the person in charge less clear cut. He or she can be a unit head, manager or director. Chief public relations executives can enjoy widespread responsibility and be on equal footing with their fellow directors, or they might be used simply as messengers. Some can be in charge of the entire corporate communications network; others may have responsibility for a single function, such as media relations. This inconsistency can be contrasted to the US where heads of communications routinely play a central role in corporate activities, with some reaching the board. They are being elevated to the same level as chief financial or legal officers. This example has yet to be followed widely in Europe.

The qualities these chief communications executives must possess include a demanding combination of functional, managerial, organizational and negotiating abilities. As they become more senior, and associate with other senior executives as equals, there is increasing emphasis on improving the communications skills of all management.

In the final analysis, the senior communications executive can be truly effective only with the backing of the chairman or chief executive. The head of public relations, or chief communications officer, should have a direct line to top management, if not a direct reporting relationship.

It is crucial that the head of communications is able to cut across all the major functions of a corporation. Not only do company heads set the tone for corporate communications, they can spend almost three-quarters of their time on communication/presentation of one sort or another. In public companies, chief executives have to be closely involved in dealings with investors, bankers, analysts and the financial press. Relationships with employees, customers, senior government officials and the local community also have to be nurtured.

Although the structure of the public relations function varies from company to company, a conventional approach might encompass the following:

- At the top sits the head of public relations, the director of corporate communications, for instance, reporting directly to the chairman/chief executive.
- Under him/her can be a department of considerable size which covers a wide range of functional areas, or one which is quite lean and handles only essentials. This latter particularly characterizes companies with a strongly centralized headquarters.
- Product/brand publicity/public relations is pushed down to the operating companies. The public relations people there might report to the marketing director, although there could be a reporting route to the centre.
- There might also be a head of public affairs/relations in a division, depending on the autonomy of the operating companies.

Deciding on the role of the senior communications officer depends on the size of the company, the nature of its products and its business objectives. In many companies, communications managers increasingly have reporting lines to other public relations personnel all over the world. This structure stems from the need for consistency allied to technological advances in communications: if an event occurs in Germany which will have an impact on the corporate reputation around the world, effective and co-ordinated action needs to be taken to deal with the ripple effect as the news travels from country to country.

The corporate public relations department can combine a number of different disciplines. This can encompass specialists in media relations, investor relations, internal communications, public affairs, sponsorship and events as well as other related fields. In consumer goods companies, brand publicity can fall under marketing budgets, with a looser reporting relationship to the centre.

Carrying out public relations

Media relations

Public relations executives increasingly recognize the importance of media relations. Communications are fully allied to an internationally competitive media, which means that it becomes increasingly pointless to practise fortress building and leak prevention. News knows no boundaries. Companies have to deal with a hungry and diverse collection of journalists who themselves have different audiences to satisfy and different constituencies to address. It is essential to foster a professional relationship with the media because of the impact that relationship can have on corporate activity.

Making generalizations about media relationships in different countries is as dangerous as making any stereotypical comments. But, having understood the power of good media relations for some time, US companies have generally been much more open and communicative than their European counterparts. This has changed over the last few years, particularly as the enormous surge in hostile takeovers in Europe forced companies to realize the powerful role the media plays in winning the battle or warding off predators. This process will accelerate across the Continent as more companies are confronted with the growing demand for information from their range of audiences.

In such an environment, companies need to be more open, honest and willing to deal with uncomfortable news. To determine the quality of a company's media relations, most business journalists consider the following criteria to be the most important:

- fast reaction to enquiries
- an open and honest media relations policy
- willingness to deal with unfavourable news
- comprehensible information

Marketing

In the past, the relationship between marketing and public relations/communications has often been confused. One reason has been the lack of understanding about what marketing is. Use of the term has often been synonymous with sales or advertising. In organizations where marketing is viewed strategically rather than functionally, this gulf of misunderstanding is narrowing. This, in turn, shifts the perception of public relations, transforming it into more of a management service, alert to issues, perceptions and changes in the environment and their impact on corporate reputation.

Exploiting important issues as an adjunct to consumer communications is already a common practice in the US. Defined as issues-led marketing, there is growing interest in this practice in Europe because brand differentiation, like brand loyalty, is increasingly difficult to achieve.

As the branding of both products and the company itself is occupying more management time, companies are seeking ways to use public relations in marketing products and capturing changing consumer tastes where the emphasis is increasingly placed on value.

When brand publicity is well thought out and integrated, its payback can be enormous. But there has to be tight co-ordination among different groups for a more integrated marketing approach to be effective and consistent with the communications policy as a whole. This might mean that the marketing director has control over all brand public relations, while serving as regular liaision with the in-house communications manager.

Investor relations

While it is important to maintain a steady flow of consistent information to all target audiences, particularly customers and employees, investor relations demands special skills. Investors read the press, carefully monitor financial strategies and are becoming more vocal and more demanding, a trend underpinned by increasing interest in corporate governance.

Investor relations is coming to the fore as companies engage in cross-border takeovers. This requires persuading shareholders of the benefits and looking for new sources of capital. These activities usually demand a more prominent and better understood profile.

How investor relations is handled is a subject of continuous debate. The chairman should always be involved. But who should direct the activity? The finance director, company secretary? Director of corporate communications? Powerful institutional shareholders will usually want to speak with the chairman or finance director. As a result, some companies put investor relations under the finance director/company secretary, with the head of communications playing a strong role in presentation. While the investor relations manager will often have a depth of expertise in complicated matters, such as taxation, a close relationship means that general matters can be handled in a co-ordinated fashion by his/her communications colleague.

Good investor relations has to be built up over time, not hurriedly cultivated because of the appearance of a predator, for example. The information flow should be frequent. Apart from earnings announcements, other face-to-face elements could include facility visits and small group meetings with investors.

Internal communications

Calling employees 'internal customers' has become a central tenet of corporate thinking. It means that everyone in the company is seen as an essential part of the process, whether they deal with the outside world or not, and as crucial elements of the organization's success. Employee communications programmes can include in-house newsletters, videos and group meetings.

Forward-looking companies are combining all these communication activities, so the senior public relations person handles both external and internal communications in a consistent fashion.

Public affairs

Dealing with governments and other regulatory bodies at a local, regional and transnational level has become a major focus of public relations. The key to participating in the contemporary political process is finding a common vocabulary and a way to construct alliances and relationships with people who share common goals. To create their market, companies must become part of the political process. They must first help shape the dialogue at the national level – and, in Europe, at EU level as well. They must demonstrate how their actions can benefit both country and business interests. And they must enhance their credibility and extend their reach by building strong relationships with allies and activists. Having well-defined connections to the appropriate people, from a local mayor to national politicians, can often make the difference to a company if it is confronted with what it considers an ill thought-out piece of legislation.

In Europe, increasing numbers of companies are hiring experts to serve as envoys to the European Commission, a key organization in an era of growing regulation. That job can involve lobbying and helping company affiliates in the EU to co-ordinate their own lobbying efforts. An important part of the government affairs executive's job is keeping senior management at corporate, as well as regional, headquarters informed of developments in the EU and at a national level that can affect the business.

Crisis management

A crisis concentrates the corporate mind like almost nothing else. Suddenly the need for public relations/communications becomes clear. So many things can go wrong, including: product recall; factory fires, explosions, etc; accidents; strikes; sudden resignations; a takeover threat; or the discovery of fraudulent activities.

Because the sheer number of events which can give a company instant, unwanted headlines can be overwhelming and unpredictable, it is imperative to devise a system which outlines personnel procedures and policies that go into action should such an event take place. The fact that events are unexpected does not preclude planning. It would now be naive for any consumer goods company, for example, to not have a tried and tested policy for product recall, from physically removing defective or tainted products from shelves to having pre-agreed channels for publicity.

One problem is that companies are too reactive. Crisis situations – rather than the underlying issues – are managed, or organizations try to manage parts of an issue, with little knowledge of where it came from or the trends to which it is connected. Companies can also equate issues with problems, and not opportunities. Managing issues after they have become politicized means that management options and the likelihood of success are both limited and expensive.

The head of communications must try and think the unthinkable and then be prepared for it. Sometimes this effort can be as straightforward as making sure there is access to extra telephone lines. Crisis management is not just about having a manual for action, but about having enough forethought to face the unexpected with a fast but effective response. In fact, having a rigid manual could be too restrictive. There should be at least some sort of guidelines on who can talk to the media, what needs central clearance, who will speak for the company depending on what problem it faces, and so on. Often an effective communications system is one based on trust and delegation as much as pre-planning.

Programme management

Management of a public relations programme can be handled on a continuous or project-by-project basis, or both. Public relations objectives should be as carefully thought through as any management task, and budgets should be set accordingly. Clarity of aims will contribute to allocating sufficient resources and deciding on measurements of success. The problem with some public relations practice is that it is assumed that media coverage alone is the way to judge success.

Programme management consists of several stages:

1. A need is identified because of an opportunity, problem or difficulty, or as a result of an organization's overall objectives.
2. Overall objectives are discussed among the relevant managers (including outside consultants where used). At this stage, research can be carried out to provide a more solid foundation for activities.
3. The programme is devised and implemented.
4. Programme evaluation. This should be based on briefing discussions and encompass:
   - programme objectives;
   - results of interim measurements of progress towards reaching objectives;
   - results of measurement of impact on the attitudes and behaviour of key audiences.

Research plays an increasingly important role. It can be used at the outset of a programme to refine objectives and contribute to decision-making about the programme; to provide measures of progress during the programme; and to establish whether results have been achieved at the end. More companies are doing initial research to judge carefully who its target audiences are, and what sort of messages are important to reach them. To some extent this is a result of increased pressure to find more formal ways of measuring effectiveness, which arises out of the quality movement, with its emphasis on research, setting benchmarks and then measuring achievements and results.

There is a long and short-term aspect to evaluating the effectiveness of public relations. Long-term means measuring over time what can be small but significant shifts, while short-term evaluations can be carried out for specific campaigns. Using research to measure public relations success is still a relatively new concept, while millions have been spent creating sophisticated measurement systems for advertising campaigns.

Companies, as they invest more in their communications efforts and become more aware of that investment, are increasingly prepared to put money into measurement of both internal programmes and those run by external consultants. For instance in investor relations, indicators include changes in the share price, share appreciation versus goals, share performance measured against that of peers and analyst opinions. Surveys of advertising awareness, results from targeted marketing campaigns, sales completed or new accounts are signs of success for marketing and sales support programmes. Executives responsible for government relations can point to legislation or regulations passed, dropped or amended. The primary methods used to evaluate public relations results include surveys, focus groups, external comparisons/benchmarks, awards, outside appraisals and mentions.

These approaches can work even in the more elusive area of gauging corporate image. It can be measured by surveying important target audiences, though it can seem hard to put a monetary value on image until something goes wrong. What the public relations practitioner is doing is preparing against something that will, it is hoped, never happen, and in the meantime demonstrating to senior management why this preparation is important.

Management should be made aware of two truths of any professional communications plan: results take time, and there are no guarantees.

Choosing and using consultants

There are three main criteria for selecting an agency: chemistry, creativity and capabilities. And there is a number of reasons why companies call in outside public relations consultants, including:

- **strategic planning:** strategy development, strategy implementation, help with major developments, a second opinion/sounding board.
- **tactical development/implementation:** filling experience/capability gaps, access to contacts/target audience, an extra pair of hands, or as a stalking horse, where the consultancy puts something forward for the in-house executive to present to those above him/her.

Companies that make the best use of consultants bring them in and make them an integral part of their management team. The relationship needs to be grounded in a clear understanding of objectives and of the skills and resources necessary to achieve them. The areas where companies turn to consultancies cover a wide range, from media and investor relations to sector specialities such as healthcare and technology.

The best relationships are based on close co-ordination between the external agency and the internal public relations executives. Expectations need to be defined early and then continue to be redefined as needs change. That includes being realistic about both briefs and budgets. With briefs, companies can make the mistake of not thinking through the exact nature of the issue they want to address. That will obviously affect budget development and can cause problems on both sides as the relationship progresses. Clearly spelling out of objectives in the first instance will help to avoid one of the biggest problems clients and consultancies have: a mismatch of expectations on both sides.

Knowledgeable clients are establishing a structural framework and code of practice within which their suppliers can operate. And this can be as effective internally as externally in making in-house people think through objectives, messages and target audiences.

There is also the cross-border factor to take into account. Sooner or later, the time will come when the implementation of a pan-European and/or international communications strategy will require reinforcement in major markets around the world.

Companies – particularly US companies – must come to terms with the fact that there is a multiplier effect in Europe. They have to recognize that it will cost more to cover the same sort of market area as the US because it is not just a question of doing different translations, but dealing with different markets.

The issue of who controls co-ordination is also one that will become increasingly central to international public relations. Giving responsibility to an international account executive in a big agency is one solution sought by many international clients, but this demands complete confidence in the agency's capability. Alternatively, clients can plug into a large consulting network but co-ordinate themselves and/or add outside consultancies where the local satellite seems weak. Some companies choose to put together their own consulting network based on selecting local firms in each market.

The best solution for any company ultimately depends on the complexity of the proposed programme or project. Even if a company has decided to exploit a consulting network already in place, it is crucial to investigate all the members individually and test capabilities. Once the relationship is established, the agency can apply some of the central co-ordination, including message development, budget management and quality control.

What consultants cannot do – and should not be expected to do – is to act as co-ordinators for cross-border activity in place of the client's own management. Clients need to have already thought through their organizational structure across national borders.

And, in an age of increasing integration, these corporate structures will have to be able to handle communications activities not only across borders but across disciplines as well. This demands a sophisticated matrix of responsibility which effectively oversees and aligns the output of all marketing services firms, including public relations, advertising, direct marketing and sponsorship, in the name of corporate consistency.

John Graham is chairman and chief executive officer of Fleishman-Hillard, the largest independent public relations firm based in the US. He joined Fleishman-Hillard in 1966 and became president in 1974 and chairman in 1988. During his career, John Graham has worked in nearly all aspects of public relations.

Further Reading

Dunn, J, *Successful Public Relations*, Hawksmere, London, 1988.

Reference

[1] *Public Relations 2000*, Fleishman-Hillard, 1993.

GOVERNMENT AND PARLIAMENTARY RELATIONS

Patrick Law

Governments wield considerable power over the business world whether through legislation and regulation, or their purchasing of goods and services. Yet, the relationship between companies and government is often ignored. In doing so, companies miss an opportunity to shape policies which may have a direct effect on how they do business.

An engineer, a management consultant and a politician were arguing about whose profession came first. 'The world was built in six days – clearly a great engineering feat,' argued the engineer. 'Agreed, but it was we who drew up the plans to create order from chaos,' the management consultant responded. Finally, the politician simply asked: 'But who do you think created the chaos in the first place?'

This is hardly a flattering or realistic assessment of the nature of the political process. But it does capture the stark choice that organizations now face: either to seek to influence relevant political and regulatory decisions or spend considerably more effort in managing the adverse impact decisions may have.

The reality is that free markets exist only in economic text books and political rhetoric. In the UK, for example, the government controls over 40 per cent of gross national product with many companies and organizations owing their continued existence to the way in which this money is spent. Direct expenditure, legislation and government-inspired regulation heavily influence all organizations from private and public companies to voluntary groups. Companies are rarely negligent enough not to assess the threat to a product from a rival. Yet, many appear content to ignore potentially larger threats which their regulatory framework may contain. Failure to manage this environment is to neglect a critical factor in the success of any major organization.

The reasons why organizations often fail to manage political and regulatory issues are threefold.

First, some see political and regulatory decisions as peripheral to their business. This may be true, but it is not an assumption that should be made by default. There should always be an assessment of the potential political or regulatory threats that might exist.

Second, the political world is often seen as remote and closed to outsiders, where decisions are difficult to foresee and harder to influence. But, with a comprehensive understanding of the way in which policy is made and implemented, many opportunities can be identified and threats avoided.

Third, some hold the view that trying to influence the formulation of public policy is the 'devil's work'. There are, of course, illegitimate ways of trying to influence decisions. But this should not disguise the fact that organizations have a wholly legitimate role in informing those who make decisions about the consequences of those decisions. And the decision makers have a legitimate remit in asking for representations. Decision making can only be improved if the consequences are properly thought through on the basis of all the available information.

The management function that seeks to understand and influence the formation of public policy is known as government relations, parliamentary liaison or public affairs. The labels are not particularly important, though they do give an impression of what priorities the department might have.

Government relations suggests the machinery of government – the civil service; regulatory authorities; agencies and committees; *parliamentary liaison* suggests relations with members of parliament or elected assemblies; while *public affairs* suggests a wider remit including those who influence public policy (such as pressure groups or think tanks) as well as government and parliament. For convenience, this article refers to public affairs.

Best practice

Irrespective of its title, the department dealing with public policy issues can maximize its value to the organization by having a major input in three areas:

- assessing and advising on the public policy agenda
- preparing the case to be argued
- advocating the organization's interests

As a generalization, organizations tend to concentrate more on the latter element. This is particularly the case where the public relations department is given the remit to manage public policy issues. The focus then becomes telling people about the organization rather than listening to the concerns of the political system and formulating a way to deal with them.

An essential aspect across all three areas is co-ordination. Organizations will often have a range of contacts with government and related bodies outside the public affairs department. Where these are co-ordinated, intelligence can be shared and arguments used to reinforce each other. Where they are not co-ordinated, policy makers will question which aspect of the organization is the authoritative source.

Assessing the public policy agenda

This essentially amounts to contributing to corporate strategy. Organizations do not operate in vacuums. They must make a realistic assessment of the threats and opportunities that the public policy agenda provides. This outside-in management demands the ability to gather detailed intelligence about how key decision makers view an issue and then persuading the organization to act upon the information. Internal advocacy is often as important as external.

Detailed intelligence-gathering depends on a relationship of trust with officials, advisers, politicians and party workers. It is not about breaking confidences or inducing indiscretions, but rather understanding the thinking and decoding public statements. Organizations that claim to perform this role will often go little beyond parliamentary monitoring and reading of government press releases.

These relationships cannot be built up overnight. They depend on a long-term commitment to building the necessary contacts. The ideal position is to reach the point where your organization will be brought into the policy-making process at the earliest point. In this context, there is a movement towards the recruitment of people with a background within the system rather than internal line managers. Former insiders understand the priorities of the system and speak the same language.

In gathering the relevant intelligence there is a series of factors that should be addressed:

- What are the regulations/decisions that affect you?
- Who makes the decisions that affect you and what are the constraints or influences that operate on them?
- How do they see your organization and its objectives in relation to the issue under consideration?
- Are the issues administrative/technical or are there political considerations? If so, what are they?
- What type of solutions would be acceptable to the system?

In general, the further down the list, the more difficult the questions are to answer reliably.

First class intelligence is worthless if it does not become part of the basis of internal decision making. Organizations need to value the advice they receive on public policy issues – however uncomfortable that advice may be. The best reporting arrangements within an organization for the public affairs department is a popular, but uninteresting, debate among practitioners. In the end the reporting lines are less important than the relationship the department has with the organization's chairman or chief executive. It is essential for them to be able to step outside the organization and see it as others see it.

Case preparation

Research and preparation are vital in contributing to the formation of public policy. It is a much neglected area with some practitioners preferring the quick headline or the glossy brochure to the well constructed argument. In essence, arguments must be constructed so that they are difficult to dismiss. It should also be remembered that politicians or policy makers who examine your representations may not have detailed specialist knowledge.

Relatively junior politicians often do not have the resources to examine a case in detail but their approach is still likely to be penetrating. There are numbers of important rules which should be followed in preparing your case:

- Produce arguments that bear in mind the outlook of those you are addressing, based on the intelligence you have already amassed. If you can solve their policy problems so much the better.
- Do not argue exclusively from your own self-interest. Look for the wider beneficial effects of what you are proposing and get third parties to advocate it as well.
- Avoid argument by assertion and emotion.
- Be prepared to justify everything you say.
- Work out in advance the weaknesses of your case and provide answers.
- Anticipate the case that others may argue and understand its strengths and weaknesses.
- Do not over elaborate and smother the main point in irrelevant detail.

Advocacy

Direct advocacy of your case should only start when you are clear what you are trying to achieve and what your strategy for achieving it is. In determining the tactics the intelligence-gathering exercise is again vital. For instance, it will provide a view on whether quiet, low-key advocacy will be sufficient, or whether high-profile campaigning to mobilize public support is required. Far too many organizations waste time and money on ill-thought through programmes of political activity. The Public Policy Unit has estimated that approximately £40 million every year is wasted by business in unnecessary entertainment programmes or literature production.

The three critical aspects to remember in any programme of advocacy are *timing*, *targets* and *techniques*.

Timing – The simple truth is, the earlier in the policy process the better. It is always easier to influence the development of policy than to change it once it is established. The person doing the first draft of any proposal has the hardest task. They start with a blank sheet of paper and often need expert input.

Quality intelligence will once again be important in alerting an organization to when issues are under development. High-profile campaigns are, of course, often required, but this is sometimes because earlier activity has been neglected or has failed to produce the required decision.

Targets – Background preparatory work will have identified the key people in the process you are trying to influence, hence the people who need to be contacted. Within the civil service a great deal of information is available through publications. Details of ministerial responsibilities are also available. This information is raw and an assessment will need to be made of the importance various people have in the web of influence.

Two common mistakes are made. First, organizations tend to aim too high. It is rare for senior politicians to devote time to an issue in detail unless it is of considerable importance or political sensitivity. And then they tend to consider it late in the policy process. Most issues will be dealt with by junior ministers or officials. It is, therefore, important not to neglect special advisers, middle-ranking officials and ministerial personal private secretaries.

The second mistake is to take too scattered an approach. The number of people directly interested in an issue is often small. Those able to influence the decision is smaller still. So, it is a waste of everyone's time casting around for irrelevant junior politicians to entertain. It is rare that pure numbers are important.

Techniques – Good presentation does matter. However, by itself it is never enough. The most important element is tailoring your case to the needs of those you are contacting. A concise letter tailored to a politician's specific interest sent from someone whom he or she has had contact with in the past is likely to get a reply. A recent MORI survey of UK MPs found that 41 per cent spontaneously mentioned written briefs, and 34 per cent cited personal contact, as the most important things a company could do to maintain and develop good relations with MPs. By contrast, 40 per cent mentioned sending too much junk mail as something that organizations did to contribute to poor relations with MPs.

Contact programmes

Many organizations have a contact programme involving lunches, dinners and corporate entertainment. Such programmes have advantages – they establish personal relationships, promote greater understanding of an organization's objectives and can shape opinions in advance of specific lobbying. But they are not a substitute for a well-researched case and too often become the end rather the means. Do not mistake acceptance of your hospitality for acceptance of your arguments. Indeed, there is a growing trend for politicans to want briefing sessions on specific issues rather than lengthy dinners with no specific focus.

Use of consultants

There is a growing army of consultancies offering their services on government and parliamentary relations. They fall into three broad categories:

- parliamentary monitoring services
- specialist lobbying companies
- public relations companies with a lobbying facility

Outsourcing monitoring services is usually non-controversial and cost-effective. The latter two types of company can offer a range of expertise and knowledge, but too many organizations employ consultants because it is the done thing. So, before deciding to employ an agency, an organization needs to understand its own needs. Answering the following questions may help:

- How will the consultancy add value to work of the in-house team?
- What exactly do you want the consultancy to achieve? Do you want them to advise you or directly advocate your views?
- Would a long-term relationship best fit your needs or is the work project-based?
- Do you want a specialist lobbying company or would a company with ability to gain press coverage and mobilize public opinion be preferable?

In deciding between agencies, probe the track record and the relevance of their skills and experience to your position. Always ask them what they cannot do as well as what they can do. Above all, keep asking why they are proposing a certain course of action. There are no easy answers so be suspicious of consultants who claim there are.

The most successful approach to public affairs is invariably careful research and preparation, followed by a well-thought-through programme specifically designed to achieve your objectives. There is a measure of contempt among policy makers for the gin and tonic approach to public affairs which places contact-making first and policy development second. Contacts may, of course, be helpful in establishing a platform to advocate your case. It is human nature to listen more carefully to someone you know. But, in the end, the critical factor in determining the degree of influence you have is the quality of your arguments.

Patrick Law is Parliamentary Affairs Manager at British Gas.

Further Reading

Bright, C, *The EU: Understanding the Brussels Process*, John Wiley, Chichester, 1995.
Miller, C, *Lobbying Government, Understanding and Influencing the Corridors of Power*, Blackwell, Oxford.
Muggeridge, H (ed.), *The Whitehall Companion*, Dod's Publishing and Research.

TEAMWORKING

Graeme Leith

Teamworking is the very antithesis of what traditional models of management preached and practised. Management was concerned with the skills, drive and actions of strong individuals in achieving organizational goals; teamwork was the preserve of the lower echelons of the organization.

Such isolation is no longer recognized as a productive means of motivation or of achieving corporate goals. Instead, the onus is now on managers to create effective teams throughout the organization; teams that interlink and interact continuously at all levels. For managers weaned on a diet of divide and rule, learning these new skills and attitudes, to allow teamworking to operate successfully is a formidable challenge.

In the recent past, the emphasis of industrial management was on de-skilling jobs. This meant that little or no training was given in each job, and managers could exercise greater control. Everything was done to provide stability and predictability – as exemplified by production lines in the car industry.

The knowledge-workers of the late twentieth century are less and less willing to put up with the old style of management, based on rank and power.

Today's workers are better trained and educated than ever before, more experienced and also more expensive. They work in less predictable environments and use their technical abilities, as in computer programming, with larger areas of discretion. Furthermore, businesses need greater creativity and innovation at all levels. Managers using old-style rank and power authority damage the effectiveness of such people. Today's knowledge-workers require *interdependence*. This is formed through sound teamwork and responsibility, by authority and accountability being devolved as far down an organization as possible.

Asea Brown Boveri (ABB), widely recognized as one of the world's best run companies, employs about 250,000 people in countries throughout the world. Percy Barnevik, its chief executive, sees the prime aim as being the devolution of power as far down the line – or put differently, as far away from group headquarters – as possible. How else could he run such an enormous, complicated and technical set of businesses? Barnevik's message, and example, is that modern business is too complex for one person – or even a single group of people to be omniscient managers. It demands teamworking from the very top to the very bottom of the organization.

A team can be defined as *two or more people working for a common goal for which they hold themselves* mutually accountable. Teamwork is *achieving* the more successful completion of a task by working *together,* than the separate individuals would have done by working *alone.*

Most teams can be classified in one of three ways:

- teams that make recommendations
- teams that make or do things
- teams that run things

Teams can be internal – within a department, across departments – or, as they are increasingly, external – with suppliers or customers. Wherever they are found, successful teamwork is based upon three fundamentals for each team member:

- esteem
- trust
- confidence

Esteem provides respect and integrity to both oneself and the other team members. Trust shows that a team member believes in him or herself and also the other team members. Confidence is generated by the knowledge that the task can be done.

Each fundamental is interdependent – if a team-member's esteem is reduced, so, too, is their self-confidence. Damage to any one fundamental will adversely affect the others. All three are absolute requirements for top performance in a team. Each fundamental is reciprocal – to earn trust, each team member needs to show trust in the others. The whole context of teamwork is based on building-up relationships with each team member. Each step or stage in team-building is about developing esteem, trust and confidence in each team member.

Team members must be able to work with and through others, to complete their tasks. While most managers are very well trained in their specialism, such as marketing, many have had little or no training in the other side of the equation within their job – the people side.

It is increasingly apparent that skills and technical expertise are practically worthless, unless associated with the ability to create and work in effective

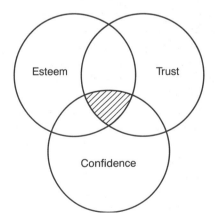

Fig. 1 The three fundamentals of teamworking

teams. The main bottlenecks in achieving a strategy or completing a project are often caused by concentrating on the task, to the detriment of the team.

The benefits of successful teamwork to the team members are:

- co-operation
- expertise
- stimulation
- job satisfaction
- group achievement

The benefits of successful teamwork to the business include:

- motivation, commitment and involvement
- fewer ideas, though more usable with better risk assessment
- distribution of work and bringing skills together
- problem-solving and decision-making
- information and idea-collection and processing
- co-ordination and liaison
- management and work control
- testing and ratifying decisions

The three fundamentals of teamwork underpin every team transaction and form the first of four issues found in all team interactions. These are the need for:

- **Inclusion** – the desire to achieve the three fundamentals of esteem, trust and confidence.
- **Information** – the need to express and receive ideas, perceptions and feelings.
- **Aims** – the need to integrate the different individual motivating factors within the process of the aims-setting, problem-solving and decision making.
- **Control** – the need to regulate, co-ordinate and control the team.

Each issue is interdependent and iterative. All four issues need constant attention, but their priorities will alter depending on such aspects as maturity of the team, or the time available to the team. This will apply to both the team as a whole and each member. The team's ability to resolve each issue will directly affect its performance.

A sustainably successful team will address these issues of relationship-building, while also addressing the task of the team. The different steps that such a team undergoes can be shown graphically as in Fig. 2.

This model oversimplifies the real complexities, but does provide a means by which to focus on the important issues at any one time.

The various steps in developing these elements are:

Step 1 – Direction
Inclusion as a member of the team is the most important question here. Members seek acceptance by showing they are worthy of esteem. Each team member needs to believe he or she can make a worthwhile contribution.

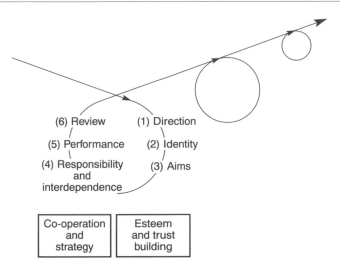

Fig. 2 The cycle of teamworking

At the same time, the question on the other side of the equation is 'Do I want to belong?' For this, each member needs to believe the task of the team is important and useful. Furthermore, that it is a task that will be done better in the team than by the individual alone.

Each member must be convinced that their skills will be useful and used; their opinions will be listened to; and their influence will be felt. If any team member is not able to answer these questions of direction successfully, they will feel disorientated, uncertain and apprehensive, and their performance will suffer.

The focus of the team at this point will be emphasized when they know their results will receive the attention of someone important to them, and that that person will respond to them.

Successful completion of this step will allow the team members to tackle other relationships and task issues with greater confidence. This will be seen to have happened when each team member has satisfactorily answered his/her own questions about the team's purpose, and his/her own membership and fit within the team. In other words, whether all team members think the team is worth joining and they feel that they have been properly *included*.

Step 2 – Identity
This step focuses on building trust focusing on the pivotal question 'Who are you?' Everyone needs to discover what they can about the others, such as their background, approach and experience. Each needs to determine whether the other is competent to do the task and whether they will 'get on' with each other.

The hidden or reverse question in this step is 'What do they want or expect from me?' This hidden question needs a positive response before the team member will feel trusted.

Trust must be both given and received in equal measure for this step to be constructive, and enable the team to move forward to the next. The degree of trust obtained can be gauged by the feelings of mutual esteem team members have for each other, their openness and candour and, more generally, by their spontaneity, or lack of guardedness.

Without trust, information flow is severely hampered, and communication more reticent, even though their outward appearances will be of general friendship and intent.

Just as a management decisions need reliable information, so good team-work needs trust-building at this stage.

Step 3 – Aims

Having obtained the fundamentals of Steps 1 and 2, the team's next fundamental is to be certain of its aims and each member's role in achieving these.

Here, the question underpinning everything is 'What are we doing?' and information is the lubricant for its resolution. The type of information required will be the options available to the team, and its rationale for making its choice coupled with key issues or concerns of the members at this stage.

The most common mistake of managers is the assumption that all the team agrees on its aims. Most teams carry at least one official aim, along with a variety of sub-agendas such as personal aggrandizement, or disinterest, even apathy.

Time must be given to clarify the aims for the team, and to obtain consensus on it purposes, values and operating assumptions. When these are clarified and agreed upon, the roles and functions which are needed, and the people who will undertake them needs to be determined. Each role will require its own, agreed authority and responsibility levels, while the tasks will be differentiated to avoid conflict, yet be sufficient to complete the team's aims.

Signs that this step has not been completed satisfactorily are team members' apathy or unnecessary competition. Focus will be on the trivia coupled with argument, or disinterest generally. Frequently, at this point a great deal of energy and time is lost over conflicting activities and jockeying for position.

Managers must realize that team members are driven by their own personal, as well as, the team's aims. They must recognize that these aims co-exist and work within, and for, both sets of parameters.

Once these are sorted out openly, and their aims and roles are agreed, then the team will be able to change from looking internally and focusing on the team, to looking externally and focusing on the task.

By now, the three key aspects of teamwork – esteem, trust and confidence – will have been addressed, providing a sound platform or foundation for co-operation in reaching their aims.

Step 4 – Responsibility and interdependence

This is the time – when the aims and options have been determined – when the members take up their responsibilities, or duties, to ensure that the team's aims can be attained. It is the first real step towards co-operation. This is one of the most trying times and tests each member's commitment. It is the equivalent of 'action stations'. The process for this step is negotiation and clarification of each role and the expectations that that carries. The team members need to generate their own clear and concensual vision and how each will contribute to its realization. Responsibilities are agreed, before action commences.

To meet their responsibilities properly, other parameters of resources such as time and money have to be agreed. Once these aspects are sorted, the ways of working together must be formalized. How will decision-making be carried out? How will information be shared? When will they meet?

The strength of the team at this step will be seen by the levels of dependence displayed. Little understanding or acceptance will be seen by member's dis-owning their own responsibility for the team's success, while not showing any particular approval or disapproval for suggestions from the others.

Alternatively, this reaction may be displayed with hostility. Rather than accept any proposal, the team member will be negative, complain or use sar-casm. If this occurs then the team needs to reaffirm, through discussion and agreement, its understanding and acceptance of its aims and roles.

Taking a short cut, or forcing or imposing one's own view, will seriously affect the team's chances of high performance. This may seem to some, espe-cially those who have already been through and committed themselves to each step, to be time-wasting. In fact it is essential, and time very well spent for the team. Without the amount and degree of responsibility and interdependence agreed and committed to, the team will be like a house whose foundations are built on sand, rather than rock.

Once responsibilities have been agreed, the sequence of work will be the next prime issue. This is where the team accepts the control of a work sched-ule. It is also the time when the team is free to act. Decisions have been made and agreed and they are now free to get on with it.

Just as a good car driver is one who drives well and smoothly, so the team will need as smooth an operation as possible. This is through proper sequenc-ing and timing of actions. A number of techniques exist for this, such as critical path analysis or PERT charts.

Self- and team-discipline are the key ingredients to success here. Difficulties at this step will be seen through confusion, conflict and missed deadlines, resulting in energy-sapping frustration. The team leader's role here is to enable or empower his or her team, by 'servicing' their needs for integration, and contin-ued commitment. This is best done when everyone is clear of the whole picture and their place within it, and may require frequent review and reinforcement.

Step 5 – Performance

High performance, or true synergy, is neither logical nor predictable, and the degrees of success in performance are also highly variable. However, high per-formance does usually fall into two categories.

Crisis can be the energizer that forces a team to work together. An example of this is a company which was severely affected in a recession. The threat to the company's very survival brought together an otherwise rather disparate team of managers, and made them focus on the job in hand. In this instance, their combined efforts were required for nearly two-and-a-half years, before the company could be said to have weathered the storm. This is longer than most crises. Usually, high performance in crisis is only required for a limited period, and is often thereafter referred to by team members as having been very exciting, even enjoyable, and may well go down as one of the 'legends' of the company or team.

The second and more usually found reason for high performance in a team is when there is mastery, step by step, of the team-building, which can be affected by timing, the team's chemistry or the 'freedom' allowed for the team to act. This performance is more predictable, although not constant, and at a lower rate or pace than that found under crisis, primarily because it is spread over a longer time. *Esprit de corps* is generated, each member of the team makes a contribution, feels needed and works harder for the team, than he or she would probably do so for him or herself.

Characteristics of the performing team are control or discipline within the team, and flexibility, especially of roles and also leadership. As the expertise of one team member is needed, so the team's leadership is likely to pass to that person for that time. The nominal or hierarchical leader's role then is to act as coach or facilitator, and so enable the team to work within and through these changes.

In addition, being confident of the internal machinations of the team, a successful team is able to concentrate upon, and respond quickly to, their external environment, such as clients. This outward focus builds on internal confidence, especially after a success or two, and so generates a strong team spirit and allows individual team members to 'shine', perhaps by portraying particular artistry or creativity.

A fully-developed, performing team will be able to respond seemingly intuitively. Members will be able to work on presumptions of the other members because they will begin to second-guess each other, or anticipate each other's needs and responses. They will play to each other's strengths and bring out the best in each other.

A further characteristic in a highly proficient team is that members' intuition and confidence allows them to take up risks or challenges, that they would not accept individually.

However, not every occasion needs such teamwork. It will be a waste of time seeking such abilities in an activity which does not need high levels of energy or creativity, such as a mundane, maintenance type of task.

Step 6 – Review
Whether this step is taken at the end of a particular project or task, or is carried out as an assessment of continuing work, reviews – of success or failure – are highly rewarding and they can refocus and re-energize the team. It can be by using such questions as 'What went wrong or right? How could

we do it better next time?' or even, 'Are we on the right track or focusing on the real issue?' So, both personal and task-related issues can be addressed. An example is one turn-round consultancy team which is very successful at, and thoroughly enjoys, turning a troubled unviable business into an effective and profitable one in a set time-scale; at which stage they hand the newly-viable business to another management team who will run it indefinitely. Each of the teams work to their best strength, ie the first in the excitement and challenge of revitalizing the business; and the second in their ability to maintain and further grow the business. At the hand-over stage, the consultancy team reviews its success and handles the change, in conjunction with the incoming team.

At whatever time this review is completed, and it usually needs to be carried out more often than it usually is, and not just in the case of failure, the most important question is whether the aims of both the individual and the team still match?

Given such a match the individuals and team as a whole can be re-enthused and re-invigorated. Any doubts about the match need to be openly discussed. An instance of this was in a professional partnership which was losing its impetus after four years of highly successful business. On reviewing how the team was working, two of the partners felt they could no longer support the focus of the business, and left, amicably. The process of the review revitalized the rest of the partnership into a high-performing team again.

Such reviews are needed more frequently than is usually accepted, because teams experience so many continuous changes, such as the external environment, a new boss, team members leaving or joining and other significant alterations. Each of these will effectively put the team back, frequently to Step 1 and 2 again. To a high-performing team who handles its reviews well, such a set-back will be minor and it will soon have adapted to suit the new environment. To a team in difficulties these changes can make life impossible.

These are the six steps which will develop a highly-performing team. However, they are simplified for ease of explanation. All these steps will be occurring all the time, though with different emphasis at different times. No one aspect can be ignored at any time, although the focus of concentration will change, according to the point of development the team has reached.

To further complicate teamwork, different individuals will progress at different speeds. For example, in a recent project team, two individual team members were left behind by the speed of progress achieved by the other five. One had joined the team as a new member seven months into the project, but had not been taken through the developmental steps, and felt hurt and ignored; the other had a fundamental disagreement with the aims of the project. They had become casualties in the team. This team under-performed and lost ground to its schedule until these two individuals were given attention and brought up to speed.

Teamwork can only progress at the speed of the slowest.

Barriers to teamwork

These are the most frequently found reasons why a team is not performing to its potential, and result in low synergy:

- **Time** – too little time is allowed for a team to develop. Frequently, there is no recognition given that time is needed for this. In work, team development tends to take weeks and months to come about, unless the task is the only one each member is responsible for.
- **Hierarchy** – the belief that every one who reports to a manager is a team. No organization chart will ever make a team.
- **Power** – the presumption that the hierarchical leader is the right one to lead the team.
- **Control** – the refusal of a nominal leader to either achieve the credibility needed for the team to work together, or to provide enough 'space' for the team to work together.
- **Task** – the task is not seen to be worthwhile.
- **Feedback** – no, or too little, response feedback is given to the team about its progress. A further, major reason for disenchantment of a team is when no credit is given for its work.
- **Sabotage** – a team, or some of its members, may seem to accept the task or challenge, but in reality feel it is a waste of time. Members tend not to disagree openly, simply do as little as they can get away with.
- **Groupthink** – this is a form of complacency exemplified by ridiculing ideas from other teams, ie, the 'not-invented-here' syndrome, and also disallowing ideas contrary to their accepted norm, especially from within the team itself.

Prime performance enhancers

- **Core beliefs** – concensually-agreed visions, values and goals provide the direction and energy for the team, and need to be frequently and openly 're-negotiated'.
- **Accountability** – the team and the team members being given or obtaining sufficient accountability to carry out their work fully.
- **Date** – a crisis schedule does marvels for team spirit! More often, the team becomes highly motivated and energetic as the date of completion nears – usually because it is way behind!
- **Recognition** – of the work and results it achieves by people important to the team.
- **Feedback** – both internally and externally to the team, feedback can provide helpful insights to the working of the team, and, along with recognition, is the number one motivator for both the team overall, and for its individual members.
- **Time** – time is required for adequate team-building and task completion. Time allowed for the first steps of teamwork will provide real returns on

the investment not only for the task currently undertaken, but also for others later on.

In conclusion, experience has shown that the two aspects of teamwork that are most frequently ignored or missed through ignorance are *time* and *feedback*. Major leaps forward in team performance will be achieved if these two aspects are addressed properly. When in doubt, give more. There is nothing altruistic in the business's endeavour to develop teams. It is an entirely commercial demand.

Graeme Leith is a consultant at the Sundridge Park Management Centre, Kent. He specializes in strategy, leadership and teamworking for senior managers. He previously ran his own consultancy company and works for organizations throughout the world.

Further Reading

Adair, J, *Effective Teambuilding*, Gower, Aldershot, 1986.

Belbin, RM, *Management Teams: Why they Succeed or Fail*, Heinemann, London, 1981.

Hicks, RF and Bone, D, *Self-managing Teams*, Kogan Page, London, 1990.

Katzenbach, JR and Smith, DK, *The Wisdom of Teams*, Harvard Business School Press, Boston, 1993.

Margerison, C, and McCann, D, *Team Management*, Mercury, London, 1990.

Stewart, R, *Choices for the Manager*, McGraw Hill, Maidenhead, 1982.

Belbin, M, *Management Teams – Why they Succeed or Fail*, Heinemann, London, 1981

Bradford, L, Gibb, J and Bennek, T, *Group Theory and Laboratory Method*, John Wiley and Sons, New York, 1964.

Sanborn M, *Team Building*, Career Track Publications, Boulder, 1989.

Shelton L , *Creating Teamwork*, Career Track Publications , Boulder, 1986.

Woodcock, M and Litt, D, *Team Development Manual*, Gower, Aldershot, 1989

Drexler A, Sibbet D, and Forrester R, *Teambuilding: Blueprints for Productivity and Satisfaction*, NTL Institute and University Associates, 1987

CRISIS MANAGEMENT

Lex Van Gunsteren

Crises are commonplace in management. Yet, the same mistakes in handling them are made repeatedly. Indifferent or complacent managers remain in their positions for too long. Owners often appear to be loath to change a once successful management team, and managers with crisis management skills are brought in too late to become saviours. Similarly, the signs of impending crisis are routinely overlooked as commentators, analysts, investors and managers concentrate on hard financial data rather than soft data which points to other conclusions. The crisis has, at some time, to be faced up to and management during a crisis demands sets of skills not usually found in managers who have led the organization prior to the crisis.

The word *crisis* originates from the Greek, *krinein*, to decide. A *company crisis*, therefore, is a decisive moment, a time of great difficulty or danger in a company's history.

It is useful to distinguish two fundamentally different types of company crisis:

- unpleasant-surprise crisis
- management crisis

An *unpleasant-surprise crisis* can happen to any company. A product may unexpectedly have a quality problem causing sales to stagnate; a war may break out in a country where the company generates most of its turnover; or a world crisis – such as the Gulf war – may affect a particular type of business, such as air lines, travel agencies and hotels. It is impossible to avoid such crises. They simply come, like rain or sunshine. But, in the same way as we can prepare for bad weather by taking an umbrella or raincoat, a company can establish some guidelines and policies on how to act once there is a crisis. Such preparation can make a substantial difference because, frequently, the harm done to the company is often severely worsened by managerial blunders during the early stages of a crisis.

A *management crisis*, in contrast, does not come as a complete surprise to insiders. Usually, executive secretaries and directors' chauffeurs foresee a company crisis caused by inadequate management before financial figures start to deteriorate. The saying: 'When you do not make a profit, you are either in the wrong business or have the wrong management' is only true from a short-term perspective. Happening to be in the wrong business is a failure of management – it did not change the scope of business at the right time. So, if a business consistently fails to make a profit, it simply has the wrong management.

Failing management always blame external circumstances, conveniently forgetting that 'a collapse of the market', 'unfair competition from low-wages countries', 'competition from substitute products', etc, do not suddenly emerge, but can be foreseen and anticipated.

Management history and literature is filled with such crises. A number of key messages emerge. In the case of the unpleasant-surprise crisis the main message is: *be open and genuine*. Any attempt to conceal relevant facts and to manipulate the situation ultimately backfires and increases the damage to the company. A management crisis usually originates from arrogance and complacency. The success of a company tends to make its management arrogant; they believe that anything they touch will turn into gold. Employees may also become complacent; they take their salary and fringe benefits for granted. Though it appears simple to avoid these pitfalls, experience suggests that it is not. A management used to success through secretive and manipulative behaviour has great difficulty in displaying openness and honesty as is required in an unpleasant-surprise type of crisis. It is equally difficult for an entrepreneur not to be misled by success and recognize *in time* that his or her success formula no longer works and has to be replaced by a new one. As a result, in spite of the mass of insight as to how managers should cope with both types of crisis, the same mistakes are made repeatedly.

The unpleasant-surprise crisis

During times of trouble you learn who your real friends are. Likewise, in an unpleasant-surprise crisis the real nature of a company's culture surfaces. Usually, management has only limited control over the situation. It cannot prevent all its employees from talking to the press, nor prescribe what finally appears in the newspapers. When faced with unforeseen predicaments employees have to act according to their own judgement rather than to instructions from senior management. The public, being aware of this, tends to base its judgement of a corporation on its conduct during a crisis. If a serious quality problem with its product was initially covered-up, the damage to the company's reputation can be noticeable for years. Conversely, if such a crisis is dealt with in an open and genuine manner by the company's management, the event can considerably strengthen the reputation and goodwill it enjoys.

In his book, *How to build a corporation's identity and project its image*, Thomas Gabett provides some guidelines for handling media interest during an unpleasant-surprise crisis:

- *Public relations can not resolve the crisis*. Words alone cannot make the problem go away. That requires decisive management action.
- *Long-range considerations should outweigh short-term costs*. The long-term goodwill the company enjoys from its customers should be kept in mind when considering the short-term costs of corrective measures.

813

- *Deciding what to say in a crisis is not a passive experience.* The public affairs department must engage operating managers, as well as lawyers, when preparing public statements.
- *The company always has the responsibility to communicate with employees.* Interpreting the crisis and its implications to employees is vital because they are also members of the community and are seen as authoritive sources of information.
- *It is not necessary to respond to every lunatic accusation made.* It may even be counterproductive, as it may dilute the information to the public on the real issue.
- *Media coverage of a crisis occurs on two levels: the event itself and the handling of the event.* As a result, you have to fight a war on two fronts and your performance on both is equally important.
- *Do not speculate.* Be prepared to say: 'We do not know yet.' Speculation can easily shape the perception of the public and be very difficult to correct later.
- *Immediately assume the public's point of view.* The tendency will be to see the event from the point of view of the management, playing down its seriousness. Never underestimate what the press can do with it.
- *Monitor the news.* You have to know what the press is saying.
- *Speed is essential.* Any delay in responding may be interpreted as a cover-up.
- *Designate your 'hitter'.* The most credibility comes from the highest management. The level of response is an indication of the importance management places on the problem. It may be useful to assign your 'hitter' at a high management level, but such a spokesman should be cautioned not to speculate.
- *A crisis will not run its natural course if social activists are involved.* In that case, do not expect the crisis to go away naturally. You may have to fight a lengthy guerrilla war.
- *When faced with a choice between saying nothing at all or expressing the company's position, choose the latter.* When balancing between candour and legal caution, remember that there is as much risk in underestimating what the press can do with undisclosed information as there is in what the court can do with the disclosure.
- *Politicians respond to public fear.* When communicating with them, keep in mind that they want to respond to their constituents.
- *View a crisis as requiring countering urgency tactics.* The interest of management may waver when other issues seem to require priority. Responsibility for follow-up should then be delegated to a competent executive, in particular when activists are involved who are just waiting for negligence on the part of management.

Such advice is helpful, but of little value when the required conduct is not in line with the corporate culture, when it does not fit naturally with the prevailing norms and values.

To the outside observer, for example, it was astonishing to see how long Perrier's management maintained that its mineral water did not contain any

814

toxic element in spite of overwhelming evidence to the contrary. When they finally admitted the failure, apparently persuaded by public affairs experts, the damage to the public image was already done.

A more recent example is the washing powder battle between Procter & Gamble and Unilever. P&G attacked its competitor by advertising that Unilever's product 'Omo Super Power' had shown excessive wear and tear in various tests. Initially, this was dismissed by Unilever's management as unfair advertising, but was later admitted to be true. By that time, sales of the product had dramatically stagnated. To regain the confidence of the public, not only had the defect to be cured, but enormous amounts of money had also to be spent on extra advertising campaigns.

There are, of course, many examples of the right action being taken. The company which, at great cost, withdrew its oranges from the market when it became clear that a lunatic was injecting them with poison, was rewarded with great customer loyalty once the criminal was caught.

In 1993 a fully-erect crane was wrecked during discharge in Long Beach, causing great financial damage to its Japanese builder, Mitsui Paceco Portainer. The chief executive of the shipping company concerned, Dock Express, took the first plane to Japan and explained the accident as candidly as he could. His prompt and genuine action was so much appreciated that the relationship with Mitsui continued.[1]

When, some years ago, Shell was under heavy attack from activists because of its policy to stay in South Africa, its management ordered a discrete investigation to discover what the 'silent majority' thought about the matter. The investigation, let alone its results, was never made public. Its purpose was not to be used in the media, but to check if the management's view had sufficient support in various relevant circles of society.

A company's culture is a decisive factor during times of crisis. This becomes most apparent at times of war. Company loyalty is what induces employees to save valuable assets, like records and drawings, or to make duplicates and store them secretly. An example of this concerns a Rhine inland shipping company, which had a culture typical of so many family-run businesses – 'the company takes care of you and you take care of the company'. After the Second World War, when the allies wanted to know where ships were sunk, it emerged that during the war employees had made notes on the locations of shipwrecks. As a result, the company had its fleet operational much earlier than most of its competitors.

Management crisis

A manager has a *serving function*, one that is aimed at realizing the objectives, the mission, of the organization or the organizational unit. A management function becomes critical when the objectives of the organizational unit seem to be unattainable.

Crisis management is aimed at reversing this trend, and making the objectives attainable. The crisis comes to end when the objectives seems to be within reach once more. Their actual realization, however, can still be in the remote future.

A crisis is a *perception*. At the beginning of the Second World War, when the British people felt Hitler had the winning hand and that the objective of remaining a free nation was virtually unattainable, a crisis was at hand. The actual downturn had begun much earlier, but without awareness, there is no crisis. In times of crisis, the continuity of the entire organization is perceived to be at stake by its members. As a result, the willingness to make personal sacrifices in the interest of the whole is much greater. Alongside this is the acceptance of a leader who takes hard measures which could also affect the individual (it was only after people became aware of the true nature of the crisis that Churchill could take over from Chamberlain). When the crisis is over, the crisis-leader is usually replaced by someone with a softer profile.

Management functions can become critical through changed circumstances or through management itself. Sometimes a crisis comes from a combination of the two: unfortunate circumstances coincide with a manager who is unfit for the task at hand.

Changes in circumstances can occur because of a variety of reasons. General trends which play a role are:

- External factors are now more prominent elements in success or failure. This requires a strong external orientation in addition to attention to internal efficiency.
- The need for participative planning and decision-making has increased, both with respect to the quality of plans and decisions and their acceptance in implementation.
- The complexity of most businesses has increased.

The result of these changes is that old success formulas no longer work. When the manager is the cause of the crisis, two factors prevail:

- *Arrogance* through success, resulting in:
  - Less willingness to learn or adjust;
  - Ego-tripping: a need to be in the limelight which makes him or her more oriented towards him or herself than towards the business;
  - An urge to leave a monument behind as 'a crown on his or her career';
  - Fear of losing face.
- *The effect of the manager's life cycle.* The manager's energy has declined, as has his or her feeling for the market. They have lost contact with the company's environment, primarily because their external contacts are based on old relationships. Former clients and colleagues have no influence on what happens in the market. The manager is no longer aware of modern techniques, nor is he or she prepared to make a serious effort to develop essential new skills.

In this last situation, the attitude of the manager is directed towards preservation of the status quo. He or she does not want to take any risks, especially if there is the risk of being blamed if the efforts fail.

This is illustrated in Fig. 1. Imagine there are two alternative options available, option A and option B. The manager estimates that alternative A provides the company with only a limited chance of survival, and that option B gives a much better chance to survive.

However, if in situation B things do not work out, the manager could be blamed for having made a mistake and his or her reputation could be badly damaged. They could be accused of not being cautious enough. Choosing option A, continuing the present course, never attracts blame – there are no attributable mistakes, but he or she has taken proper care of the business. The administrator type of manager will always go for option A, even when aware that option B would be better for the company. Only a true crisis manager would dare to choose option B. Such individuals are prepared to stick their necks out and risk their reputation.

Cycle of fair-weather and bad-weather managers

When the chief executive function or the functions of other managers become critical, a number of *symptoms* can be observed:

- Horizontal leakages in the second echelon, ie, the second echelon of management knows a lot more than it is supposed to know and the managing director is unaware of this.
- Passing on problems to others and covering oneself through memorandums.
- With respect to running the business, there is a shift of attention from external to internal affairs; a reduced awareness of the relevant external events; the internal order is more important than the client.
- At the same time, there is also a shift from internal to external affairs which actually have little connection with running the business: the symptoms of

	Continue present course	Decide for a breakthrough
Chance of survival for the company	small	great
Personal damage for the manager in case of failure	small (the outside world has done it)	considerable (the manager *himself* has done something)

Fig. 1 Willingness to take personal risk

817

diversionary tactics; managers begin to mingle with famous politicians and in employers' organizations. They want to give the impression that they are more important than their position as managing director of the firm suggests.

- Attention is almost always centred on keeping the wolf at bay and solving short-term problems, and rarely on the realization of opportunities.
- Optimistic planning; the plans are actually wishes: planned sales and returns are repeatedly not realized (Fig. 2).
- Indecisiveness at the top.

The latter is an important signal that the turning point in the cycle of fair-weather and bad-weather managers is forthcoming. This can be seen in Fig. 3, where the cycle is presented schematically.

The different phases are as follows:

- Initially the business does well. There is *decisiveness* and, as a result, *success*.
- Because of the continuous success, *arrogance* appears. The arrogance becomes apparent in various matters: the managing director not only has time to run the business, but is also involved in trade organizations, in symposia and in the media; there is an increasing preference for prestige projects; a new, larger and more luxurious office building is moved into, conveniently forgetting that when a jacket is too tight, there are two possibilities – either the jacket is too small or the person is too fat.

A second characteristic of this phase is *harmony*. People are overbearingly friendly to each other. Failing managers are not fired; the directors systematically avoid such painful tasks.

The result of these two characteristics is that indirect costs, especially the costs of staff and office, increase more than the turnover.

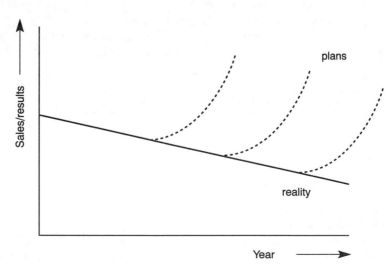

Fig. 2 Tomorrow it will be better

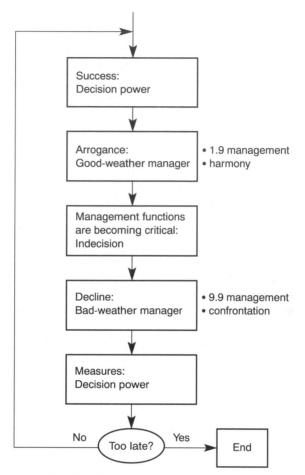

Fig. 3 The fair-weather/bad weather cycle

This fits into the typology of Blake and Mouton's 'managerial grid'.[2] Blake and Mouton identified what they labelled the 'country club' manager. Such a manager has golf clubs in the back of the car and popular talk in the front. He or she has a particular interest in the personal lives of colleagues, and has a desire to be loved by everyone. He or she is, in contrast, uninterested in the finer points of the company's levels of productivity. Often he or she belongs to the second or third generation in a family business. During the rule of such fair-weather managers, bad-weather managers stand on the sideline.

- Another result of high costs is that the firm earns a reputation of being too expensive while margins become ever smaller. A few prestige projects do not work out, and financial results deteriorate. Initially, this is obscured by exploiting financial reserves and realizing book profits, but after a certain period, which can go on for some years, the elasticity is exhausted. Unpleasant measures are unavoidable, but the current management is reluctant to take them. There is *indecisiveness* at the top. The top-management function has become critical.

- After further deterioration, it becomes clear to the fair-weather managers that they can no longer avoid taking action and, indeed, they do something: they take a step sideways to give the *bad-weather managers* some room. They, in turn, go assiduously on their way in a style which can be characterized as *confrontational*. The real bad-weather manager, with an interest in both the people and productivity aspects of the business gets his chance.
- During the ruling period of the bad-weather manager, there is *decisiveness*. Necessary measures are taken, even when these are drastic and painful.
- If the fair-weather managers step aside at too late a stage, it can still go wrong. If the changing of the managerial guard is on time, the company can crawl back to a new period of success. Then the *fair-weather managers* seize power again and the whole cycle repeats itself.

This cycle is an internal wave movement. In fact two wave movements can be identified:

- External, economic climate: fair weather/bad weather.
- Internal, management: fair-weather/bad-weather managers.

The difference in the phases of these two wave movements determines the degree of gradualness at which the changes take place:

- **In phase:** bad weather outside coincides with the reign of the fair-weather managers. The result is that the firm goes into crisis.
- **Out of phase:** bad weather coincides with the interregnum of the bad-weather managers. The fair-weather managers have the wind from behind. The result is that there are no major transition problems.

The changing of the managerial guard, therefore, should take place on time. This is not easy, because that change is a painful, emotional event.

Behaviour at downturn

With an approaching crisis, the top manager often behaves similarly to those involved in the process of a dying partner. For a manager, saying good-bye to the company can be just as difficult as saying good-bye to a dying life partner.[3] The two experiences share some common characteristics:

- Initially, the manager denies that there is anything wrong. 'Everything is fine with us!', 'Declining results? Gossip from jealous competitors!', etc.
- In the next phase, the manager becomes angry and protests. Everyone else is guilty: 'The press has written us into the grave', 'Prophets of doom have spoiled the atmosphere', 'The government does not do anything', 'The unions are undermining us', etc. This phase is equivalent to the complaints from the partner about doctors or nurses administering the wrong treatment.

- This is followed by a sense of desperation, which the manager tries to conceal as much as possible.
- Finally, in the last phase, the manager is able to create enough distance to face reality and make way for constructive bad-weather management.

The crisis manager

The bad-weather manager, or crisis manager, who takes over from the fair-weather director possesses *individual prominence*. He or she has self-confidence, charisma, a power to convince, knows how to motivate, is honest and open, communicates clearly, knows how to get things done, but is certainly not a pusher. The way that a crisis manager works can be characterized by:

- Dividing attention between short and long-term issues.
- Concentrating on what is *relevant*, not on what he or she is good at or likes to do; he or she has an eye for both urgent and important issues (Fig. 5). In the management function which has become critical, only the urgent issues seem to be dealt with, and then only partially.

Phases which a remaining partner goes through	Time frame
1. Denial	Hours/days
2. Protest	Weeks
3. Despair	Months
4. Detachment, taking distance	Gradually

Fig. 4 For a managing director, acknowledging the downturn of the firm can be as difficult as saying good-bye to a dying partner

	Problems	Opportunities
Short term	urgent	important
Long term	important	important

Fig. 5 Identifying urgent and important issues

The crisis manager takes a project-based approach to short-term issues – composing two lists on which is ranked: major problems or opportunities, and strong managers he or she has at their disposal in the company.

The crisis manager assigns the best manager, P, to the most important issue A, and then Q to B, R to C, etc. Winston Churchill is a good example of this approach: the best field marshal goes to the most important battle field. There will always be protests that the executives P,Q,R,S,T cannot be missed in their current functions. Only when it concerns key figures who are from 'spear heads' – promising activities which are essential for the future of the firm – will the crisis manager give in to this.

The long term receives attention not only in order to be able to develop the business after the crisis has been overcome, but also because it is an absolute prerequisite for motivating personnel. They want to see that there is a long-term future. The positive long-term vision of the crisis manager must become evident – for example, by allowing the continuation of research and development on a limited scale. Verbal or written statements to this effect are not sufficiently convincing.

Changing the managerial guard

This section primarily pertains to a management crisis, although some points are also valid for an *unpleasant-surprise* crisis.

The bad-weather or crisis manager can do a lot, but cannot ensure that he or she comes to power in time. Others are responsible for this timing. It cannot be expected that the current good-weather management will take the initiative at the appropriate moment to place themselves on the sideline. Action will have to be taken by the board of directors, the bankers and the employees' council who are all in a position to influence the changing of the guard. Since it is so important that changes occur at the proper time, they have the moral obligation to actually use the power they have. Almost without exception, this happens at a very late stage or sometimes not at all. This is hardly surprising.

Only in public companies, and generally in larger firms, is the supervisory board responsible for appointing the first echelon of management. The character

Major problem/opportunities	Strong managers
A	P
B	Q
C	R
D	S
E	T

Fig. 6 The crisis manager assigns the best managers to the most important issues

of the supervisory board of such large firms is usually such that avoiding damage to their personal reputations plays a dominant role (Fig. 1). In smaller firms this is less apparent. In these non-public companies, however, appointing or firing the managing director is the prerogative of the general meeting of shareholders, at which, more often than not, the managing director holds decisive power. Supervisory board members have in such situations only one sanction at their discretion: resignation, and they are only likely to use this in extreme situations. Most board members see their responsibility as being at their posts, particularly during a time of crisis. A more appropriate influence for supervisory board members in non-public firms is, therefore, desirable.

The banker only feels empowered to act when the financial figures justify intervention, and that is almost always too late. Financial figures can sometimes be kept at acceptable levels for a lengthy period, even though action has been necessary for quite some time.

The employees' council often recognizes the approach of a crisis earlier than the responsible management. But they are trapped in the myth of rationality: if something cannot be made concrete with financial figures, then it is not taken seriously by the sitting management. When the employees' council has a feeling that things are going wrong, they would be wise to seek external professional help, not only to clarify the diagnosis, but also to devise an appropriate intervention strategy before it is too late.

Given these circumstances, it is little wonder that, when asking managers about problems concerning the changing of the guard, the following reactions come to light:

- Changing a failing managing director usually happens too late.
- In general, the initiative to change does not come from within the company (management, employees' council), but from outside and usually not from the supervisory board, but from the actual owner (family or bank).
- Half of the managers consulted feel that the successor usually also fails to fit in.

So, how does the right manager get a chance at the right moment? Obviously, awareness of the symptoms of a coming crisis, as described in the previous section, is not enough.

It is not only important to know where to look, but also to be aware of why people ignore visible signals. In practice, the four most important causes are:

- *Cognitive dissonance*: 'That's what we have decided, so we will stick to it.'
- *Catch 23*: 'It won't go that fast.'
- *Cassandra information*: The signals are too threatening for the people involved (risk to their own reputation).
- *The performance of people is undiscussable (a taboo) without hard information.*

These factors explain why the initiative for changing the managing director(s) should be expected to come from the actual owner (family, bank) rather than the supervisory board or works council.

Cognitive dissonance

Research shows that leaflets and advertisements about cars are not primarily read by people intending to buy a car, but by people who have just bought one. The explanation for this curious phenomenon is given by Festinger's theory of cognitive dissonance.[4]

Cognitive dissonance means that when individuals have to make a choice between two mutually exclusive, but similarly attractive possibilities, they develop a feeling of discomfort. This feeling of discomfort is stronger the more important the issue is and the more the pros and cons are equal to each other in the perception of the person. Cognitive dissonance is stronger when it relates to the decision to change jobs, than when you have to decide whether or not to take a raincoat because of the chance of rain. Cognitive dissonance is stronger the more the attractiveness of the new job weighs up to the present one.

After the person has decided for him or herself (the official decision can be much later) the feeling of discomfort persists. The person then will try to get rid of that unpleasant feeling by filtering information, so that the decision made is confirmed. This explains the interest in leaflets giving information about a car consumers have already bought: after some time there is no doubt about the right choice.

The same principle applies to the appointment of managers. The manager is appointed by the board of supervisors who, directly after the appointment, necessarily go through a process of *cognitive dissonance reduction*. Information that points out that the supervisory board made the right decision is emphasized; positive information about dismissed candidates is trivialized.

Years later, the circumstances facing the manager could have changed, so that the director is no longer qualified for the task. This is rather difficult to understand and accept for people responsbile for the original appointment. Perceptions are limited. This is not dishonesty, but predictable and explainable in the light of 'That's what we decided, so we stick to that' (the effect of cognitive resonance reduction). Many other seemingly illogical phenomena in business practice, such as indecisiveness in stopping loss-generating activities, can be explained in the same way.

Catch 23

Catch 23, which was coined by Edward de Bono, reads: 'It is essential that something gets done, but it never makes sense to do it at any particular moment.'[5] In other words, managers are liable to say 'it doesn't go that fast, so we can postpone the painful matter for some more time'. This can go on until it really is too late.

Cassandra information

Of the information that comes to the attention of directors, only a part is relevant for the fulfilment of their tasks (Fig. 7). That information we may call *used information*, since it is both relevant and paid attention to. The information that is not relevant, but nevertheless receives attention, may be called *confusion information*, because the covering of irrelevant details leads to confusion and losing the essence of the issue at hand. The essence often concerns relevant information which does not get attention: *Cassandra information*. (The god Apollo, being in love with Cassandra, the beautiful daughter of King Priam of Troy, gave her a present: the ability to predict the future. When she rejected him in spite of that gift, he could not take it back because a gift from a god is a gift for ever. Therefore, he provided her with another: no one would ever listen to her. When she warned the Trojans about the wooden horse, her advice was ignored and the town was subsequently destroyed.)

The causes of Cassandra information are:

- the *accessibility* of the information is insufficient;
- the information is *too threatening* – the information that the war with the Greeks was not over was too threatening for the Trojans.

The latter aspect often plays a role when failing executives need to be replaced. The consequences of failing are unpleasant and threatening for the board members concerned, and therefore, the inclination is to ignore the signs of imminent failure. In that process the abundance of confusion information is sometimes used as an excuse to ignore Cassandra information ('I could not pay attention, because I already had so much to read').

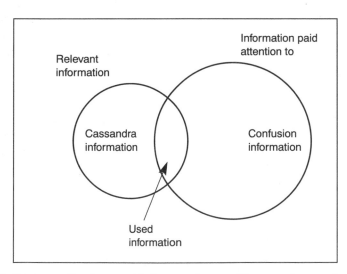

Fig. 7 Only a small piece of information paid attention to is relevant

The performance of people is undiscussable without hard information

Hard warning signals, such as declining financial figures, are usually noticed at a very late stage. By the use of creative accounting, declining results can often be hidden for a long time.

If corrective measures are to be taken in time, then attention must be paid to 'soft signals', which can be noticed much earlier than declining financial results. These soft signals often concern the functioning of people (Fig. 9). If there is a taboo on discussing a person's performance, then this must be resolved first.

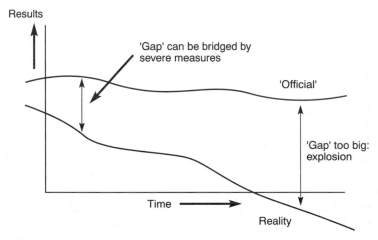

Fig. 8 The danger of creative accounting

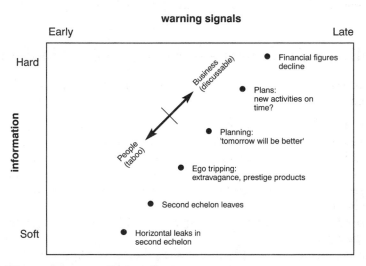

Fig. 9 Discussing people is taboo

Finally, there is the question of why a successor often also appears to fail. Before all, it should be realized that there are no similar cases of succession. Wisdom and courage from the side of those having a say in the matter – supervisory board members, shareholders, employees' council members and the predecessor himself – are the first condition for a successful changing of the guard. The following observations from practice can only provide some supplemental guidance.

Finally, one needs to realize that it can be too late to turn the tide, even if one succeeds in finding the right superman. From the outside, it will seem as if the wrong successor was appointed, while, in fact, bad timing caused the fiasco.

Pitfalls for the internal successor: the succession paradox

With succession from within the company, we often notice disappointments because the shareholders or supervisory board appointed an excellent number two, who was bound to fail in a number one position. Entrepreneurship, the tension of solitude at the top, and the need to take unpleasant decisions, can put him or her under great pressure. This is especially true in the case of an owner/director of strong personality who left a heavy mark on the company. Such personality tends to have a strong preference for his second in command, who for years followed his directions with great loyalty, above a candidate who, in the eyes of the outside world, might perform even better than the predecessor himself. In such cases, more often than not, the problem is what we may call the *succession paradox*: if the departing chief executive accepts the candidate for his succession, you can be sure that he is the wrong one; but when you have found the right one, the leaving chief executive is unlikely to accept him.

Pitfalls for the external successor: cultural mismatch

With succession from outside the company, the following pitfalls can be recognized:

- *It does not click with the second echelon*. Profit or loss is the positive or negative outcome of a multitude of operational decisions at the second hierarchical level. The first echelon can give impossibly intensive attention to a great number of things. Companies are run by the second echelon. A good manager in the second echelon, someone who can choose where and for whom he works, has a need of:
  - *Room for development of his own vision* and of his own initiative.
  - *Respect for the boss*.

  The top manager's ability to establish these two things for his subordinates is far more important than his own professional and technical skills.

827

- An interim manager is appointed or the function is temporarily delegated to a supervisory board member who shows insufficient attention and involvement.
- The new manager cannot cope with some aspects of the corporate culture; for example, dealing with representatives of the owner's family.
- The mentality and background of the new manager does not fit with the *development phase* which the company finds itself in: expansion, consolidation or maturity.
- The new manager falls back on *success formulas from his own past*, which do not fit the new situation. For example: starting up R&D activities to develop own products, while the company is historically of a licence-taker or jobber type.

Lex A Van Gunsteren is a business consultant and teacher. He also is an innovator in ship propulsion a field in which he holds several patents and has written numerous articles. He graduated as a naval architect and received his Ph.D from Delft University. He has served as a managing director to several international corporations. His teaching and consultancy are mainly concerned with managing innovation, crisis management, and strategic management in small and medium-sized enterprises. He is the author of *Management of Industrial R & D: A Viewpoint from Practice* (1992) and co-author of *Bad-weather Management, Myth and Reality* (1991).

Further Reading

Bibeault, DB, *Corporate Turnaround*, McGraw Hill, New York, 1982.

Gunsteren, LA Van, and Kwik, R, *Bad-weather Management: Myth and Reality*, Eburon, Delft, 1991.

Gabett, Thomas F, *How to Build a Corporation's Identity and Project its Image*, Lexington Books, Lexington, Mass, 1988.

Meyers, GC *Managing Crisis: A Positive Approach*, Unwin, London, 1988.

Slatter, S, *Corporate Recovery: A Guide to Turnaround Management*, Penguin, London, 1984.

References

[1] *Cargo System*, May 1993.
[2] Blake, RR and Mouton, JS, *The New Managerial Grid*, Gulf Publishing, Houston, 1978.
[3] Menges, LJ, 'Dying of a partner' in *The Coming End*, Intermediair, 1975.
[4] Festinger, L, *Theory of Cognitive Dissonance*, Stanford University Press, 1957.
[5] de Bono, E, *Future Positive*, Penguin, London, 1983.

PART

3

MANAGING

INTERNATIONALLY

The Transformation of the International Economy

'You want to be able to optimise a business globally – to specialize in the production of components, to drive economies of scale
as far as you can, to rotate managers and technologists around
the world to share expertise and solve problems. But you also
want to have deep local roots everywhere you operate – building
products in the countries where you sell them, recruiting the
best local talent from the universities, working with the local
government to increase exports. If you build such an organization, you create a business advantage that is damn difficult to
copy.'   *Percy Barnevik, chief executive, ABB*[1]

3

---

[1] Taylor, W, 'The logic of global business: an interview with ABB's Percy Barnevik', *Harvard Business Review*, March-April 1991.

OVERVIEW

Bruce McKern

An introduction to the topic of international management can hardly emphasize enough the profound transformation of the international economy that has taken place over the last forty years. This has brought far-reaching implications for the international division of labour, the welfare of populations, the governance of corporations and the autonomy of nation-states. This transformation has occurred with remarkable speed, and the thinking of managers and policy-makers has not yet fully adjusted.

Not only has trade between nations greatly expanded, at a rate faster than the growth of the global economy as a whole, but the primary actors in international trade are no longer mainly corporations of one nation transacting at arm's length with corporations of another. Instead, increasingly they are international corporations whose transactions are largely conducted with their own affiliates or subsidiaries distributed around the globe.

Furthermore, a considerable (and increasing) proportion of the sales of these affiliates is derived from their local operations. In fact, by the UN's estimate, the sales of international corporations[1] accounted for one-quarter of the world's GDP in 1991 (and a higher proportion of *private sector* output).[2]

According to this source, there were some 36,600 international corporations (ICs) active in 1991, whose operations encompassed 170,000 subsidiaries worldwide. The sales of these international corporations in 1991 were estimated at $US 5.5 trillion, of which inter-affiliate exports represented one-third or $1.3 trillion. The world total exports of goods and services in the same year was $4.0 trillion. ICs' operations in host countries are thus already more important than arm's length international trade. For some countries this ratio is much higher – in US companies, for example, the average ratio of total IC sales to exports is 4.1.

The inter-affiliate transfers noted above are an important manifestation of the high degree of economic integration practised by ICs in their search for worldwide efficiency and growth. ICs transfer materials, components and finished products between affiliates, sourcing where most appropriate for each subsidiary and distributing through their operating units in each country. In fact, in manufactured products, arm's length trade now has the minority role in international transactions: transactions internal to ICs (ie, between affiliates) account for 75 per cent of world trade of manufactures.

Measured by share of ownership of foreign direct investments, the US was still the leader in 1991, holding 24 per cent of the worldwide stock of Foreign Direct Investment (FDI). But this ratio is not much greater than would be

Table 1 Foreign investment and international trade

	$ US billions, 1991	%
All countries		
FDI outflows	180	
FDI stock	1,800	
Foreign sales of ICs	5,500	
Gross domestic product	21,500	
Gross domestic investment	4,900	
Total exports of goods & services	4,000	
ICs inter-affiliate exports (est.)	1,320	
For sales of ICs as % of world exports		138
Sales of ICs as % of world GDP		26
FDI flow as % of gross domestic invest		3.7
Developed countries		
FDI outflows	177	(1992 est: 145)
Gross domestic product	17,200	
Gross domestic investment	3,800	
Exports of goods & services	3,000	
Developing countries		
FDI inflows	39	(1992 est: 40)
Gross domestic product	3,400	
Gross domestic investment	800	
Exports of goods & services	930	

Source: UNCTAD, Programme on Transnational Corporations, *TNCs and Integrated International Production*, 1993

implied by the importance of the US in the world economy. Japan, with 12.9 per cent of the stock, has leaped to prominence, just behind the UK (13.3 per cent), while France (7.7 per cent) has also grown rapidly.

Since the investment data are based on the book values of equity held, they understate the leadership of the US in terms of the current value of total assets or sales. But it is clear that the stock of investment by ICs from the five major developed countries has doubled in the last five years and that the greatest growth has come from Japanese and French ICs (this can be seen in Table 2). German and British ICs have held their share, while the US share has slipped, reflecting a slower rate of growth of its outward investment. The strength of Japan's thrust into foreign economies can be seen in the increase in the value of its FDI stock, which grew by $US 173 billion between 1987 and 1992. British investment grew by $124 billion in the same period, while US stock grew by only $135 billion.

The Japanese urgency to become insiders in foreign markets is clearly reflected in these figures. German firms have also increased their production activities in foreign countries. Yet, by comparison with the foreign presence of

Table 2 Outward foreign direct investment, by major source

| | $ US billions | | | |
| | Stock of FDI owned | | Outflow of FDI | |
Source country	1987	1992	1991	1992
France	41	151	24	17
Germany	91	186	21	17
Japan	78	251	31	16
United Kingdom	135	259	18	15
United States	339	474	29	36
World	1000	1949	183	150

Source: UNCTAD, Programme on Transnational Corporations, *TNCs and Integrated International Production*, 1993

US ICs, Japanese and German firms still have a long way to go. In 1989 US ICs registered $4.10 in total sales for every dollar of exports, whereas for Japanese ICs the figure was $2.60. The even lower ratio for German companies ($1.50) reflects the over-dependence of German ICs on Germany as a source (Table 3), with damaging consequences in the climate of weak domestic demand, high costs and a strong Deutschemark experienced early in the 1990s.

The foreign operations of ICs are concentrated in the developed world, particularly in what Kenichi Ohmae has labelled the Triad[3] of rich countries (Western Europe, Japan, the US and Canada). In 1991, for example, developed countries as a whole harboured 80 per cent of the world's total of foreign direct investment. Western Europe was host to 41 per cent, North America 32 per cent and other developed countries 7 per cent (Table 4). For the size of its economy, Japan hosts a considerably smaller fraction of the world's foreign investment than the other countries of the Triad (Fig. 1). However, 1992 saw a major shift in the flows of FDI in favour of the developing world, as Triad firms rushed to invest in Asia. This trend is likely to continue into the next century.

Table 3 Affiliate sales and exports of international corporations, 1989

Country of domicile	Sales	Exports[a]	Ratio of sales to exports
US	1,266	307	4.1
Japan	534	203	2.6
FR Germany	372	251	1.5

[a] Excludes inter-affiliate sales

Source: UNCTAD, Programme on Transnational Corporations, *TNCs and Integrated International Production*, 1993

Table 4 Inward foreign direct investment, by host region

By host region	Inward FDI Stock % of world total		Flows of FDI $ US billions			
			Outflow		Inflow	
	1987	1991	1991	1992	1991	1992
Developed countries	78.7	80.1	177	145	108	86
W Europe	35.7	41.1				
N America	34.2	31.8				
Other	8.8	7.2				
Developing countries	21.2	19.8	5	5	39	40
Africa	2.2	2.0				
Lat Amer & Caribb	8.4	7.5				
Asia	10.6	10.2				

Source: UNCTAD, Programme on Transnational Corporations, *TNCs and Integrated International Production*, 1993

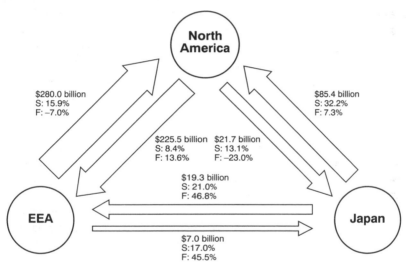

Note: Dollar figures show stock of FDI. Percentages are annual growth rates of stock (S) for 1980 – 90; flows (F) for 1985 – 91.

Fig. 1 Foreign direct investment between Triad countries, 1990

Source: UNCTAD, Programme on Transnational Corporations, *TNCs and Integrated International Production*, 1993

Spheres of influence

ICs have tended to gravitate toward zones of traditional influence. Investment by Japanese ICs in East Asia as a whole is relatively more important than that by European and US ICs in that region. European ICs are better represented in South Asia than are US and Japanese ICs. And Japanese and US ICs have under-invested in Western Europe relative to European firms.

Conversely, however, Japanese firms are relatively more active in North America than European firms, and this has important implications for their future success. Experience in establishing operations in the US strengthened the competencies of Japanese ICs for entry into the UK and other European countries. These competencies include better understanding of customers, establishing supplier networks, dealing with unions and more individualistic employees, and setting up distribution systems. The US has been a useful proving ground for Japanese firms intending ultimately to operate in Europe, as the examples of Honda, Nissan and Toyota confirm.

By contrast, the difficulty experienced by the other Triad countries in establishing insider positions in Japan has reduced their opportunity to reap the benefits of Japan's strong growth. Just as important, they have had fewer opportunities to test and improve their organizational competencies in a difficult environment where adaptation is a requisite for success. They have consequently been less equipped to succeed in other testing markets, such as the fast-growing East Asian economies, which are destined to become the centre of gravity of the world economy in the next century.

The fundamental ideas on which the Japanese management system has been built include certain enduring principles which can be continuing sources of organizational advantage. These include:

- continuous improvement, which in turn depends on a workforce educated and motivated to take responsibility for change;
- production systems that are customer-focused and driven by demand;[4]
- participative decision-making with clear strategic direction from the top.

The Japanese practices of life-long employment, promotion by seniority, and consensual decision-making were valuable in implementing these principles for Japanese companies in a high-growth environment supported by a community-based culture. However, it is not obvious that each of these practices is appropriate for US or European firms, or for all industries, or indeed that they will survive unchanged in a low-growth Japanese environment. Wellford Wilms, for example, shows that the NUMMI joint venture between Toyota and General Motors succeeded in part because it forged a new culture embodying many of the Toyota principles, but adapted to US circumstances.[5]

Japanese ICs will probably have to adapt their management processes to gain greater flexibility to handle severe economic fluctuations. Certainly, they will move to diversify further geographically in order to be less dependent on their domestic market. European companies, likewise, will need to shift more firmly into foreign operations, particularly Asia, as they surmount the recent difficulties. US firms, despite the renewed strength of the domestic market and a favourable exchange rate, will need a much more determined approach to the growth opportunities of East Asia.

Globalization and opportunities for ICs

Firms evaluate a foreign country for investment in terms of its attractiveness (adjusted for risk) as a *market* for the firm's products or services, as a source of *resources* (such as labour), or as a *centre for rationalization* of the firm's worldwide operations in its drive to achieve global efficiency.[6] The overwhelming importance of the developed nations of the Triad in the past as destinations for FDI is clearly attributable to their large, rich markets and stable governments. More recently, the growing integration of the European Union has stimulated firms to gain efficiencies in the Western European market by consolidating their operations. Their recent entries into Eastern Europe are stimulated by mixed motives: to establish an early position in small but growing markets, and to use lower labour costs in the East for sourcing products for the West.

Preoccupation with events close to home may have distracted European firms from the nascent opportunities in North America. The creation of the North American Free Trade Area accelerated a trend already under way. Tariffs against Mexican or Canadian goods entering the US market had been low for some years (averaging some 4 per cent *ad valorem*, although higher on some specific goods) and a number of ICs had positioned investments in Mexico to serve that growing market, with an eye to supplying as well the huge market to the north. With the signing of the NAFTA, Mexico has become an even more attractive source for the whole region, provided ICs are prepared to satisfy requirements for local added value.

While the attention paid to Europe and North America is understandable, it has been at some neglect of the expanding markets of Asia. As noted, US and European firms are relatively not as strongly represented by direct investments in the East Asian region as Japanese ICs. Yet Asia in total represents 31 per cent of the global market, much more than Eastern Europe and the CIS (7.7 per cent) or Latin America (8.2 per cent).[7]

Within Asia, of course, there are big income disparities between and within countries. Japan alone accounts for a third of the Asian market, and 10 per cent of the world total, but China (9.9 per cent) has been growing much faster in the last few years. India (4.9 per cent) has also begun to grow more quickly under the spur of liberalization. South Korea (1.5 per cent), Indonesia (1.3 per cent) and Taiwan (1.0 per cent) are the other major fast-growth Asian markets.[8] The opportunities for ICs differ markedly among these countries. Taiwan and Korea are richer markets, with concentrated *per capita* purchasing power, at roughly half the level of the US or Japan, whereas individual purchasing power in China is no more than 5 per cent of the US, and in India it is perhaps 2 per cent.[9] Indonesia is somewhere in between.

Despite these low average levels of individual purchasing power, each of these three countries is large enough to include a sizeable middle class with higher incomes. For example, 90 per cent of households in the largest three cities of China (Beijing, Guangzhou and Shanghai) are reported to have incomes above $73 per month. A total of 44 per cent of households in Bombay, Delhi and Calcutta have comparable incomes, and the middle-class population of India is estimated to number between 100 and 150 million.[10]

Asian nations have enormous infrastructure developments under way which can be accessible to ICs. The Long-Term Credit Bank of Japan estimates the value of projects planned for the next ten years at $1 trillion. Recognizing and seizing such opportunities demand a strong commitment to Asia from a marketing organization on the ground, backed by local operations. For large infrastructure projects where critical items may be exported from an IC's Triad operations, local representatives are needed to work closely with government, as standards are idiosyncratic and the IC can often influence the requirements. There is usually a demand for local procurement, so fabrication operations, local design and (ultimately) research facilities strengthen an IC's bargaining position against regionally-based competitors. In manufactured goods, a local factory producing for export may be critical for access to the local market, and in the case of consumer products, it permits the corporation to be more responsive to local needs. Frequently, distribution in a developing country is complex, sales outlets and service facilities are hard to establish, so that a direct investment, often with a local partner, may be essential.[11]

Asian markets are not without difficulty and risk. Western-style democratic governments are not the rule, corrupt practices are commonplace, and government influence on business transactions is pervasive.[12] These problems exacerbate the market risk firms have to face in a new environment. But the potential of Asia is so great, that ICs cannot afford to ignore it. By the World Bank's purchasing power parity estimates, China's economy is closer to one-third as big as the US economy, rather than one-fifteenth, as the current exchange rate indicates. Not only in China, but for many countries in the region, economic growth is expected to be strong in the next few years, in contrast to Japan's near-term difficulties. If these countries continue to grow at rates roughly double those of developed countries, there will be a re-ordering of the relative importance of nations within a couple of decades. On a purchasing power parity basis, China will have the largest GDP in the year 2020, some 40 per cent larger (in PPP terms) than the next country (the United States) followed by Japan, India, Indonesia, Germany and Korea.[13]

A transformation of the international economy is well established. It is a transformation into a system of globally integrated networks controlled by international corporations. Asia will be the fastest-growing region of the world well into the next century, and to succeed there, ICs from Europe and North America will need to establish insider positions through active investment.

The uncertainty of foreign environmental data complicates foreign market entry decisions, and the choice of entry mode in a particular case needs a careful balancing of opportunity versus risk. When the market opportunity is highly attractive, and risk low, a wholly-owned subsidiary is usually the optimal entry vehicle. When the market is attractive, but the risk high, it is often safer to enter into a joint venture with a local partner. In less attractive markets, exporting or licensing are preferred modes. In several interesting Asian economies (China, India, Indonesia, for example) joint ventures have until recently been virtually the only means of direct investment. These policies have changed and will continue to evolve but, for the time being, joint ventures may be the best way of serving local markets, and essential for certain sectors or activities such as distribution. In any case, the trend is for greater direct investment, and this strategy will place increased demands on ICs to manage effectively in more complex environments.

The challenge of international competition: environmental complexity

Among the challenges international managers describe when asked about their world, 'increased complexity' is often mentioned. Complexity can be thought of in terms of three dimensions:

- diversity
- rapidity of change
- density of relationships or linkages

What do these dimensions mean, and in what sense have they intensified in recent years?

Diversity

International managers have always faced diversity in dealing across countries – with foreign customers, suppliers and distributors, with governments and legal systems, with competitors and with employees. Today, however, as argued above, ICs must be far more deeply integrated into foreign countries than before. As they seek opportunities to exploit proprietary technology, brand names, capital resources and managerial competencies, particularly in newly opened or emerging markets of Eastern Europe and Asia, the spectrum of national diversity has greatly increased. The presumption that the demand for many of their products or services will be 'global', ie, undifferentiated across countries, and the need to follow (or preferably pre-empt) foreign competitors, are forces which have propelled ICs into a wider variety of markets and national cultures.

Although the essential nature of many products and services may be the same across the globe (jet aircraft, VCRs, Swatch timepieces and retail banking, for example), adaptations to national differences are essential, particularly in those operations which are close to the customer, such as marketing, sales and service. These issues are rendered more complex, not only by the increased diversity of cultures encountered as firms diversify, but also because most of the new markets are in a weaker state of development and under quite diverse systems of government.

839

The problem of increased diversity originates at the local level, but its effects are systemic. International corporations depend on the creation, transfer, and protection of *knowledge* throughout their worldwide network. Increasing diversity threatens the effective communication of this competence. As Carnegie-Mellon's Herbert Simon notes, the IC's multicultural network throws into sharp focus the tensions between the loyalties of individuals toward national versus corporate cultures.[14] This tension is a barrier to effective communication.

ICs have traditionally coped with the problem of diversity in a variety of ways that have as their objective the establishment of the corporate culture as the over-riding value system. Their approaches have been conditioned by their home country cultures. American firms, for example, have tended to rely on comprehensive planning systems, emphasizing achievement of quantitative goals – especially financial targets. Japanese firms have relied largely on expatriate managers imbued with the parent company culture, reporting through a strong formal hierarchy, and interconnected through carefully nurtured and long-standing informal relationships.

European companies have more commonly relied on the socialization of home country and foreign managers to the corporate culture and objectives, achieved through careful selection, training, indoctrination, job rotation and frequent communication.[15] Almost inevitably, the corporate culture is also suffused with the national culture of the parent corporation, and this sometimes works against integration by inhibiting the flow of information from the periphery.

Today, as national cultures are giving way in many parts of the world to a more diverse set of cultures based not on nation, but on ethnicity, race or religion, the international manager's world is not only more diverse, but shifting more rapidly. Greater diversity has appeared, not only in customers, competitors and governments, but also within the IC's workforce. International corporations, irrespective of where the parent is domiciled, will need to tap the creativity and skill of increasingly diverse front-line workers and managers. Benefiting from this increased diversity will depend on changing the attitudes of managers, which will require adopting new organizational processes.

Rapidity of change

The pace of change in a corporation's environment is a critical variable, but one which has been largely neglected, until recently, in theories of strategy. A characteristic of all organizations is *inertia*, the tendency for the organization to resist change. If the task of the corporate strategist is to shape the firm's strategy to the demands of its environment in the quest for 'rents' or sustainable above-average profitability, then inertia is the strategist's enemy. Inertia blinds managers to the need for change and when the need is recognized, resists implementation of the necessary actions.

Environmental change in an industry has been characterized as 'fast cycle', 'standard' and 'slow cycle', according to the rate at which the market prices of the industry's outputs change. Slow cycle environments, according to Jeffrey Williams,[16] are markets in which prices rise slowly over long periods; in standard cycle environments, they remain stable; and in fast cycle environments they fall rapidly. The pace of change is a reflection of the sustainability of the competitive advantages of incumbent firms.

The strategy and actions needed by a firm to fit a fast cycle environment are, needless to say, different from those needed in a slow cycle environment. In a slow cycle environment, the firm's competitive advantage depends on control over local resources, or *isolating mechanisms* which protect it over the long-term (as seen in public utilities, or Microsoft's MS-DOS operating system). Standard cycle industries are traditional oligopolies, where the firm's competitive position depends on efficiency, economies of scale and brand loyalty (automobiles, domestic appliances, paper products). In fast cycle industries (such as consumer electronics, digital PBXs and personal computers),[17] competitive strength depends much more on innovation and speed to market. The competencies a firm develops to fit the pace of fast cycle environment include embedded organizational knowledge, much of which is intangible and difficult for others to imitate.

Business history is replete with examples of companies which failed to recognize a major environmental shift in their industry, and particularly shifts which increased the pace of change. The difficulty lies first in recognizing that an environmental shift is under way, and second in making the organizational transformations needed. Organizational inertia tends to oppose both actions.

It is a common perception that all industries are now fast cycle environments. This is not the case. Where the isolating mechanisms are strong, a slow cycle industry may remain slow paced for some time. International industries have often been standard cycle industries, where competition is often oligopolistic and based on product differentiation.[18]

But even within such industries, entry into a new country can expose a company to a faster pace of change. When Procter & Gamble entered Japan in 1972, it faced not only the increased diversity of a new set of customer requirements, but an environment in which the pace of change was more rapid due to the innovatory capacity of local competitors. The company's difficulty in surmounting these twin challenges required a recognition of the more rapid pace of change in the Japanese market, and hastened the development of an R&D organization in Japan. Painful as the Japanese experience was for P&G, it had long-term value by forcing a shift in the firm's perception of the dynamics of its industry, to the benefit of its competitive strength worldwide.

Many ICs depend largely on technological competencies for their success in foreign markets. In many of these industries ICs deal with rapid technological change, both in product and process technologies. The more rapidly changing environment is partly due to the adoption of the techniques which gave the Japanese electronics and mechanical assembly companies their long run of successes. The spread of these ideas to US and European companies has been a process of necessary catching-up, rather than innovatory change. Adopting these techniques has not given them a competitive advantage, but rather has simply admitted the firms to the international competitive arena.

In fast cycle industries, such as personal computers, consumer electronics and (increasingly) pharmaceuticals, speed of change equates to rapid cost reductions and new product introductions. In such industries the speed at which an organization can capture learning efficiencies to reduce cost and at the same time speed its product development, is a critical determinant of success. Early adopters which have the competence to recognize, assess and quickly implement newer technologies of design and manufacture, such as rapid prototyping, can achieve a temporary edge. However, international corporations which have been preoccupied in the last few years with restructuring and reducing numbers may have lost expertise which will be needed for these two challenges. Those which have concentrated more precisely on re-engineering to improve cross-functional efficiency and cycle time, and on fostering entrepreneurship and integration, will be the stronger competitors in the future.

For many ICs, therefore, a dynamic pace of change will be commonplace in the future. Competitive positions in individual products will be transitory, so firms in fast cycle industries will need the capacity for continuous product renewal. Overcoming organizational inertia in order to succeed in this environment is still a major task for many firms.

Density of relationships

An international corporation can be viewed as a network of interpersonal relationships, both internal and external to the firm. These relationships transmit information, elicit behaviour and conduct transactions. As ICs grow and diversify, the number of possible inter-connections expands exponentially. Individuals face growing complexity in processing information, understanding its meaning, and acting appropriately. The quality of information may also deteriorate as the number of sources and intervening filters grow.

Of course, no individual has to transact with every other individual in a corporation. But consider the IC with multiple product divisions (or Strategic Business Units) and multiple foreign countries of operation. Each geographic operation within a product division is potentially important to every other, whether through material flows or through information flows – about product variations, process improvements, marketing concepts, new technologies, and so on. Likewise, although product divisions are distinct, there may be core competencies which support several divisions. So for most managers, there will be important actual or potential linkages within their division, within their country, across countries, across functions and for some, across divisions. These potential linkages increase as the firm grows.

The traditional response to the density of relationships is a structural one. The corporation develops a structure of formal reporting relationships which are intended to portray the transactional connections. Job descriptions describe and circumscribe the expected behaviour of each individual and the responsibility for action.

International corporations have adopted well-known archetypal organization structures in an attempt to manage the complexity resulting from the twin dimensions of product and geographic diversity. In businesses where the market is homogeneous worldwide and the strategy is 'global', the structure is based on one or more worldwide product divisions. For the 'multidomestic' strategy, where markets differ greatly from country to country, a regional or area structure is more common. For businesses where the pressures to gain the benefits of global concentration are as strong as the need for country-by-country responsiveness, a matrix structure is sometimes used.[19] These structural archetypes are rough frameworks, and in specific cases are modified by factors such as the extent of the firm's international production activities, as well as the importance of its international sales compared to its home country business.

The problem with formal organization structures, as John Hunt has noted,[20] is that the formal structure does not recognize the realities of the informal organizational relationships, and in particular, the power or social influence exerted by each of the participants. The power relationships in the informal network are the means by which the organization performs its tasks, and 'reorganizations' which ignore the real power relationships are destined to fail.

The informal network in an organization can be mapped with individuals as nodes connected by communication links.[21] The density of the linkages to a node or individual is an indicator of his or her importance and power in the network. Such a map is a more accurate depiction of the linkages in an organization than the formal organization chart.

More important than structure, as Christopher Bartlett and Sumantra Ghoshal[22] argue, is the behaviour of managers. Ideally, every manager should behave as if the 'matrix is in the mind'. In other words, every manager makes the compromises between the conflicting pressures of global and local forces mentally and through every action. Every manager should 'think globally, act locally' (and I would add, 'think strategically, act tactically').

Managing diversity, change and density of linkages

How can managerial behaviour be modified to deal with the tensions implicit in the increasing density of linkages – the inherent conflict in an international network between product-line, geography and function? It is not yet clear what approach will be most effective in this new environment. It is clear, however, that an effective approach will depend much less on structure and much more on *process*. I believe the keys to this process can be summarized as:

- simplifying the vision or strategic intent
- rationalizing information
- encouraging entrepreneurship at the front-line level

Vision

The role of vision is to simplify the market environment and make explicit the direction of the corporation. For example, Canon's vision of distributed photocopying, based on small, low-speed, affordable, desk-top copiers, gave a clear direction to its strategy for overtaking Xerox. Emerson Electric's 'best-cost' motto expresses a simple vision of a high-quality, low-cost strategy which drives every one of the company's businesses. This vision is expressed in detailed planning at the level of each business, together with a disciplined regular review process led by top management. Vision reduces complexity by focusing on the key implications of the firm's strategy for front-line and middle managers.

Information

Information is critical to planning and control in all international corporations. It is the necessary tool of top management in measuring performance. But in the 'network' organization, it takes on an ever greater importance if it is used to provide front-line and middle managers with the data they need to cope with complexity.

The purpose of vision is to simplify and guide initiative at all levels of management, so front-line and middle managers need appropriate information to make the vision operational and to clarify the actions they need to undertake. In the re-engineering of business processes, for example, access to a common data base is needed to reduce unnecessary interactions and to speed decision-making. Exchange of information in common data bases is already enhancing co-operation among R&D groups located thousands of miles apart. It routinely enables global treasury managers to pool foreign currency exposures from subsidiaries and reduce hedging costs. For ICs to operate efficiently as networks, however, we can expect that data-sharing will need to become much more commonplace in areas such as benchmarking between affiliates, new product testing, marketing and promotion campaigns, and logistics. ICs with increasingly multinational shareholders may also find value in adopting a 'global currency' for reporting and internal control.[23] Similarly, automated language translation, today a reality only under narrowly constrained conditions, may become commonplace as an aid to communication.

While it is too early to predict precisely the pattern of uses information will take, it seems clear that it will be far more important in providing ICs with a competitive edge. How best to arrange access, who should have access, and what data should be available, are problems to be resolved. Certainly, at the operational level, the rapidly falling cost of communication by voice, electronic mail and video will make it even easier for managers to communicate directly.

Bartlett and Ghoshal[24] have described the managerial processes in ABB, a company many observers consider to be 'transnational'. They observe that top management's role appears to be to set an organizational context

844

encouraging initiative and creativity, collaboration and learning: its role is 'creator of purpose and challenger of the status-quo'. Top management in ABB establishes the strategic mission and performance standards, and nurtures organizational values.

Middle management's role is reviewing and supporting initiatives, linking skills, knowledge and resources across the network, and creating and maintaining trust. Since international networks depend on lateral communication more than on vertical flows, companies such as ABB rely far less on centralized staff than the traditional IC. This means that middle management needs to place more emphasis on facilitating information flows and mediating lateral conflict rather than decision-making in a vertical chain of command. In ABB, as Bartlett and Ghoshal describe it, their efforts are mainly directed towards internal benchmarking, technology transfer and identifying and encouraging best practice, rather than in filtering information or reviewing vertically-flowing decisions. They facilitate information exchange and reinforce cultural norms, playing a supportive, rather than deciding, role.

A broad information base, accessible to all managers, puts important information in the hands of front-line managers. Middle level managers, without large staff groups, and lacking superior information on operational matters, are thus freed to focus on integration. Their information set should be oriented towards data which help to explain differences in market opportunities, performance and resource use across the firm's operating units, which can be used to drive exchange of useful ideas and practices. For network firms to be successful, the information base needs to be designed to suit this different approach to the control of information. Information is power, and the power of a network to operate quickly depends on its information set.

Entrepreneurship

A necessary characteristic of firms in rapidly changing environments is the ability to recognize or anticipate changes in the marketplace and make decisions quickly. The flatter structure of a network is designed to reduce the time delays inherent in bureaucratic vertical information flows, delegating to front-line managers greater responsibility to run their business in an entrepreneurial manner. Changing the behaviour of middle managers, accustomed to being gatekeepers and controllers of access to information and top management support, is a major cultural task in which the role of top management in forcing the shift is critical.

Just as important, front-line managers need to understand the vision, to have appropriate information access, and to be fully involved in setting operational targets. Incentives need to be oriented towards achieving a sensible balance of short-term profit targets and long-term goals of innovation and growth. Front-line management has both an entrepreneurial and an operational role: creating and pursuing opportunities, managing personal networks and operational interdependencies, and reconciling long-term goals with short-term performance. As Bartlett and Ghoshal observe, the front-line managers in ABB are able to operate as entrepreneurs only because the vision is made concrete and explicit for each business through the planning process; because strategic planning and major decisions are transparent and participative; and because upper management creates a climate of confidence and trust through its behaviour and communications. An important additional characteristic, I believe, is that profit responsibility is pushed down to the front-line managers at ABB.

Robert Burgelman's studies of internal corporate innovation,[25] conclude that successful US firms are characterized by an environment that provides funds for experimental innovation outside the mainstream, support for those developments which promise to be viable, and recognition and reward for the successful innovators.

The important difference in such an IC is the different set of assumptions about the role of front-line managers. These are:

- In a dynamic environment, the front-line manager is seen as the source of entrepreneurial action. The firm is, therefore, an aggregation upwards of many small entrepreneurial units, rather than the disaggregation downward of a central entrepreneurial unit. In Emerson Electric, for example, the smallest business group has sales of only $40 million, yet it operates in several countries and has a global mandate.
- Front-line managers have control over most of the firm's resources. They are relatively independent of the corporate center, but are more *interdependent* with horizontally related units. Interdependence is fostered by the strategic intent, by middle management, by the shared information base, and by the firm's cultural values.
- Managers are accountable for the whole activity of their business. The planning process is participative, goals represent a 'stretch' from current performance, and front-line management runs the business. Top management monitors critical operational performance measures, is available for consultation, and is focused on the strategic variables, intervening only when necessary.[26]

Bartlett and Ghoshal claim that, at least in ABB, the culture of the firm encourages learning, initiative and trust. These values, if widespread, are no doubt conducive to the smooth working of a decentralized, flat, entrepreneurial network. However, it is certainly not a trivial matter to shift a firm's culture to these norms. Learning and initiative can be encouraged by incentives appealing to individual benefit, and are more likely to flourish in individualistic societies. Trust is developed over time from the experience of consistent positive behaviour in others and is more likely to be easily developed in communitarian societies such as Japan than in highly individualistic ones such as the United States or Britain.

If trust is in fact a critical determinant of success in a network organization, corporations whose majority culture is individualistic will face more difficulty in adapting to the new form. However, other qualities may be more important, such as acceptance of change, or tolerance for uncertainty. US and West

European managers tend to be relatively flexible on this dimension; Japanese, Taiwanese, and Korean managers less so. Clearly, more needs to be known about the cultural problems of encouraging and developing entrepreneurship in international corporations.

Building the network organization

Over the past forty years, international corporations have wrought a remarkable transformation of the international economy. Commerce between nations has shifted firmly away from traditional arm's length trade, towards manufacture for foreign markets *in situ*. Under the impetus of their search for new markets and driven by the imperatives of efficiency and responsiveness, ICs have created integrated businesses linking multiple activities worldwide. Their operations, already so important in the integration of economies, are also a powerful force for political rapprochement. Their emphasis on the developed Triad has left open major opportunities in emerging markets such as East Asia, in which Japanese ICs have led the way.

The recent great surge of transnational integration, during which the worldwide stock of foreign investment doubled in five years, coupled with recessionary economies in the developed countries, has intensified competitive pressures on ICs. In response, they have focused on their organizations and work methods and found ways to create value for customers by deploying fewer resources more efficiently.

Japanese corporations based their global expansion on innovative processes for managing mass manufacturing and rapid product development, providing tangibly higher quality to their customers. American ICs began catching up ten years ago and many have reached parity with the Japanese ICs in these two areas. European companies have been trailing, but are also now making strong efforts to improve.

From manufacturing and product development, the competitive arena has shifted to other business processes and to the structure and culture of the firm. American firms have been leaders in restructuring activities, which have included layoffs, organizational streamlining and the re-engineering of business processes. Many US companies, aided by a weak dollar, are ahead of their Japanese counterparts in this undertaking, while European companies have further to go.

For many international corporations, all of these changes have been necessary, but not sufficient to deal with the increased complexity of the environment. The network organization is an adaptation which seems to be better suited to this new context. The characteristics outlined above – vision, information and entrepreneurship – are likely to be important to the success of international corporations. Firms that succeed in modifying their organizational processes in this direction could prove to be the most adept at meeting the challenge of international competition in the next millenium.

Bruce McKern is Professor of International Business and President of the Carnegie Bosch Institute for Applied Studies in International Management at Carnegie Mellon University, Pittsburgh. Professor McKern has been a Visiting Professor at Stanford University, INSEAD, IMD and the Chinese Academy of Social Sciences. He was Director of the Stanford Executive Programme and Founding Director of Macquarie University's Graduate School of Management in Australia. His most recent book is *Transnational Corporations in the Exploitation of Natural Resources* (1993).

Further Reading

Bartlett, CA, and Ghoshal, S, *Managing Across Borders: The Transnational Solution,* Harvard Business School, Boston, MA , 1989

Dunning, JH, Multinational Enterprises and the Global Economy, Addison-Wesley, Wokingham, 1993

Robock, SH and Simmonds, K, *International Business and Multinational Enterprises,* Irwin, Homewood, Illinois, 1989.

References

[1] International corporations are variously defined as 'global', 'multinational' or 'transnational', depending on their broad strategy. Here I use the term 'International Corporation' generically, without a specific strategy implication.

[2] UNCTAD, Program on Transnational Corporations, *World Investment Report: Transnational Corporations and Integrated International Production*, New York, 1993.

[3] Ohmae, K, *Triad Power*. Free Press-Macmillan, New York, 1985.

[4] Kampouris, EA and Miller, RA, 'Demand Flow Technology for Transnational Companies', *Carnegie Bosch Institute Working Paper* no. 94–5, January 1994.

[5] Wilms, WW, Hardcastle, AJ and Zell, DM, 'Cultural transformation at NUMMI', *Sloan Management Review*, Fall 1994.

[6] Stopford, JM, 'The Impact of the Global Political Economy on Corporate Strategy', *Carnegie Bosch Institute Working Paper* no. 94–7, January 1994.

[7] Economist Intelligence Unit, *Crossborder Monitor*, vol. II, no. 34, 31 August 1994.

[8] *Ibid.*

[9] *Ibid*

[10] Economist Intelligence Unit, *Crossborder Monitor*, vol II, no. 9, March 9, 1994.

[11] Lucente, EE, 'Managing a Global Enterprise', *Carnegie Bosch Institute Working Paper* no. 94-2, January 1994.

[12] Stopford, JM, *op cit*.

[13] *The Economist*, London, October 1-7 1994.

[14] Simon, HA, 'Is International Management Different from Management?', *Carnegie Bosch Institute Working Paper* no. 94-1, January 1994.

[15] Bartlett, CA and Ghoshal, S, *Managing Across Borders: The Transnational Solution,* Harvard Business School, Boston, MA , 1989.

[16] Williams, J, 'How Sustainable is Your Competitive Advantage?', *California Management Review*, vol. 34, no.3, 1992.

[17] Examples are from Williams, *op. cit.*

[18] Caves, RE, *Multinational Enterprise and Economic Analysis*, Cambridge University Press, Cambridge, UK, 1982.

[19] Doz, Y, *Strategic Management in Multinational Companies*, Pergamon Press, Oxford, 1986.

[20] Hunt, J, 'Structural and Organizational Changes in Global Firms', *Carnegie Bosch Institute Working Paper* no. 94-4, January 1994.

[21] Krackhardt, D and Hanson, J, 'Informal Networks: The Company Behind the Chart', *Harvard Business Review*, July/August 1993.

[22] Bartlett, C and Ghoshal, S, *Managing Across Borders: The Transnational Solution*. Harvard Business School Press, Boston, MA 1989.

[23] Ijiri, Y, 'Global Financial Reporting using a Composite Currency: An Aggregation Theory Perspective', *Journal of Accounting*, forthcoming.

[24] Bartlett, CA, and Ghoshal, S, 'Beyond the M-Form: Toward a Managerial Theory of the Firm', *Strategic Management Journal*, vol. 14, Special Issue, Winter 1993.

[25] Burgelman, R and Sayles, L, *Inside Corporate Innovation: Strategy, Structure and Managerial Skills*, The Free Press, New York, 1986.

[26] Bartlett and Ghoshal, 1993, *op cit.*

3

ACHIEVING GLOBAL COMPETITIVENESS

Hans A Wüthrich

The success or survival of a company operating within a social market economy depends entirely on its competitiveness. Achieving global competitiveness is a sizeable ambition. 'All you need is the best product in the world, the most efficient production in the world and global marketing. The rest takes care of itself,' says former Sony chairman, Akio Morita.

Due to the increasing rate of change in markets, technologies and competitive structures, companies are continuously forced to improve their competitiveness as part of a learning process. To achieve a clear superiority over competitors, managers and their organizations must adopt a consistent policy towards four interdependent strategic components and optimize them in a balanced and sustained way: achieving global competitiveness must be built round global market efficiency, global cost efficiency, global environmental efficiency and management efficiency.

Recent years have witnessed an explosion of opportunities for creating competitive benefits thanks to a phenomenon diagnosed over ten years ago by Harvard's Ted Levitt: *globalization*. This trend and its practical consequences are now of intense interest to many managers.

'National borders have become irrelevant for determining market dimensions. Depending on the feasibility of handling goods and services, market dimensions fluctuate between a city quarter (hairdresser) and the whole world (chemical and car industries). As soon as market dimensions exceed national boundaries, a national territory becomes nothing other than a region within a larger economic space,' says Franz Blankhart.

The growth of foreign directed investment (approximately 34 per cent per annum since 1983) is a useful yardstick of globalization; it was almost four times larger than the increase in world trade in the eighties.[1] The UN's *World Investment Report*, published in 1994, showed that after investment flows peaked in 1990 (DM 232 billion) and after the subsequent recession, a rise of about 9 per cent to DM 195 billion was recorded in 1993 compared with DM 171 billion in 1992.[2] The number of transnational companies behind these figures is constantly growing. At present, some 37,000 parent companies already control over 200,000 subsidiaries abroad. Some 40 per cent of the total assets of the world's 100 largest companies, excluding providers of financial services, are already located outside their home countries. As in the eighties, the globalization of economic activity is being driven strongly by companies originating

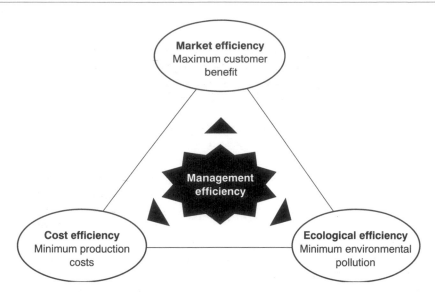

Fig. 1 Components of strategic competitive strength

from the US, the UK and Japan, and also from Germany and France. At the same time, the US and Europe are the most important target countries for investments. Recent estimates show that after a decline in investment flows during the period before 1990, the developing countries now participate much more strongly in the globalization process than they did even a few years ago, namely to the tune of 40 per cent.

The growing intensity of cross-border trade and the foreign activities of companies which once had a purely national focus has led to increasing concern with the phenomenon of globalization in both business and financial literature and in practice. The diversity of the resulting discussions can be explained by the vagueness of terms such as globalization, global competition and the global company. This makes it more difficult to compare various statements or the results of research.

In an economic context, the *concept of globalization* can be viewed from two angles. The *macroeconomic* perspective refers to the efforts of countries, regions or districts to encourage cross-border activity in their economies by adopting suitable policies. Liberalization, the dismantling of barriers to trade and investment, as well as the creation of common economic spaces are visible signs of this development. The *microeconomic* perspective sees this concept as an extension of business activity by companies beyond their domestic market. But globalization does not merely mean corporate activity oriented towards international or multinational markets, it implies that the world market, or at least the most important national markets in the triad, are treated in the same way.[3]

This definition brings out an important feature of globalization, namely the existence of a global market where a product can be sold anywhere in the world without the need to adapt either its properties or its marketing strategy to a particular country. Numerous indicators support the perception of a clear trend towards the convergence of consumer behaviour and thus of a global market for an increasing number of goods and services. This is due not least to the increasing global networking of communications and media services.[4]

Seen in this way, a global company:

- operates with one global strategy in place of diverse strategies oriented to national markets;
- acts within a homogeneous or increasingly homogeneous market;
- markets a standardized product globally, and makes consistent use of the opportunities offered by the international division of labour with the aim of realizing economies of scale and synergy effects.[5]

The automotive industry is the pre-eminent example of a global industry. On the basis of the above criteria, however, it is evident that even this most global of all industries is still far from doing full justice to the label.[6] Despite international networking, in the form of co-operative agreements and alliances for procurement, R&D, and production, most car makers are still clearly focused on their domestic markets. The only exception is Honda, almost equally well represented in all three triad markets.

Even if this example corrects our notion of the current status of globalization, there are unmistakable signals pointing in this direction. Many markets around the world are opening up following the gradual introduction of market principles to almost all former communist countries. This change was triggered by fundamental political upheavals such as the end of the cold war and the dominating East-West conflict, the disappearance of the Warsaw Pact and the dissolution of the Soviet Union. Despite numerous obstacles and sporadic setbacks, the intensive efforts to set up multilateral trade agreements show the current commitment to deregulation and liberalization and the will to create a common arena as a basis for a more free exchange of goods and capital.

The need for global integration

The degree of globalization of business

A critical question for every company is whether it currently forms part of a global industry or whether it can expect to develop in this direction. The following portfolio provides a rough guide for orientation. It distinguishes four types of businesses: purely global, blocked global, multinational and local national businesses, and assigns typical industries to each type.

The criteria listed in Fig. 3 provide a rough classification for companies whose businesses are not explicitly contained in this portfolio:

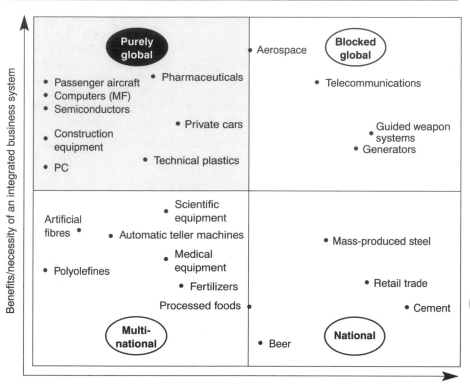

Fig. 2 Typical industries in four types of businesses

Source: W Rall, *Globalisierung von Industrien und ihre Konsequenzen für die Wirtschaftspolitik*, Göttingen, 1986, p.160

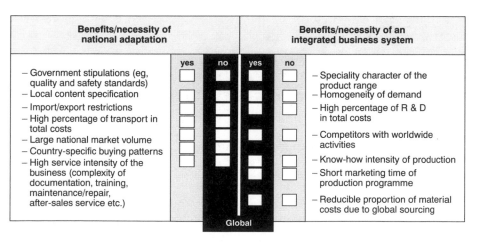

Fig. 3 Indicators of degree of globalisation

Source: G Yip, *Total Global Strategy: Managing for Worldwide Competitive Advantage*, Prentice Hall, New Jersey, 1992, pp. 31–62

Globalization potential of a business

The globalization potential of a business or industry can be determined by looking at specific indicators known as 'globalization drivers'.[7]

If we discern a potential for globalization within an industry, we must ask what are the practical benefits of gearing business activity to the entire planet. What competitive benefits arise from, and only from, a global integration of value-added activities and what are the consequences for customers?

Benefits of global integration

A consistent global integration of all value-added activities yields benefits in the following functions.

Research and development:
- Reducing the complexity of the range of a company's products and services.
- Creating time benefits through improved innovation management aimed at avoiding short product life cycles and eliminating the problems arising from imitation.
- Assuring greater flexibility in dealing with the accelerated rate of technological change and the volatile nature of customer demand.
- Improving efficiency through the worldwide networking of R&D activities.

Procurement:
- Increasing market strength in sourcing (also on financial markets).
- Improving standardization of incoming materials, range of functions and quality.

Market drivers	Cost drivers	Governmental drivers	Competitive drivers
– Common customer needs	– Global scale economies	– Tariffs	– Exports
– National global customers	– Steep experience effects	– Subsidies	– Imports
– Multinational global customers	– Sourcing efficiencies	– Non-tariff barriers	– Competitors from different continents
– Global channels	– Favourable logistics	– Compatible technical standards	– Interdependent countries
– Transferable marketing	– Differences in country costs	– Common marketing regulations	– Competitors globalized
– Lead countries	– High product development costs	– Government owned competitors	
	– Fast changing technology	– Government owned customers	

Fig. 4 Globalization drivers

Source: G Yip, *Total Global Strategy: Managing for Worldwide Competitive Advantage*, Prentice Hall, New Jersey, 1992, pp. 31–62

- Creating time benefits thanks to an improved response to changes in the procurement market.

Production:
- Creating economies of scale, comparative cost benefits and structural cost reductions.
- Reducing the complexity of products and processes.
- Consistent utilization of the international division of labour.
- An improved negotiating position *vis-à-vis* governments and authorities, eg, when seeking approval for manufacturing sites.

Marketing:
- Getting ahead of the pack by harmonizing marketing stance and establishing a global brand.
- Obtaining efficiency benefits by using the global media overspill, reducing insertion costs, improving product overspill as well as standardizing processes in the sectors of information, planning and control.
- Achieving learning benefits thanks to the transfer of know-how across borders.

Distribution/sales:
- Keeping ahead of rivals thanks to the worldwide availability of a company's range of products and services.
- Obtaining learning/time benefits through the worldwide use of information technology.

After-sales service:
- Obtaining efficiency benefits due to the reduced complexity of the product range (reduced logistical problems in the spares procurement sector, fewer complaints by reducing the product to core functions and standardizing quality).
- Obtaining efficiency and learning benefits by standardizing the training requirements of the service team.

Components of global competitiveness

What are the preconditions and procedures required to achieve global competitiveness for a company that already operates globally or will do so in the future? Bearing in mind the comments on strategic competitive strength made at the outset, we can identify the components of global competitiveness in Fig. 5:

1. Global market efficiency

Global market efficiency can be understood to mean maximum customer benefit. It results from a range of products and services that satisfy needs, globally

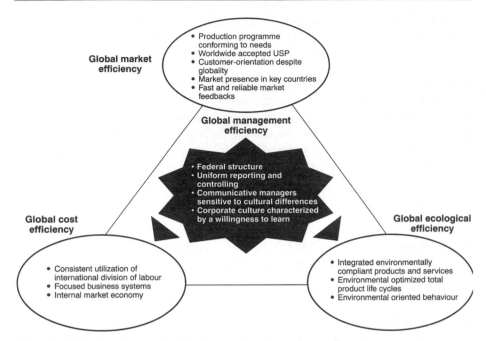

Fig. 5 Components of global competitive strength

accepted unique selling propositions (USPs), customer orientation and market presence in key countries as well as timely feedback from the market.

Production programme conforming to needs

'Success in global competition demands a product that already acquires its global character on the drawing board,' says Herbert Henzler of McKinsey & Co. If a company wishes to be a global player, its products must have a global character. In particular, it must resolve the dilemma of standardization and cost benefits versus local adaptation and enhanced customer benefits. Examples of companies with global operations show that the conformity of their production programme to customer needs must take precedence over a global approach that is motivated purely by cost factors. Thanks to a modular product design, local adaptations can now be made at reasonable cost, according to the principle: 'As global as possible and as local as necessary.'

In the essentially global market for passenger aircraft, sales of Boeing's 737 model stagnated in the early seventies. After trying to target the Third World in the hope of extending the life cycle of this product, the US plane maker had to concede that the 737 was unsuitable for the new environment for three reasons. The runways were shorter and softer and the pilots were not as well qualified as in other markets. These factors led to landings of the 737 that were often too hard, and there were multiple touchdowns, so that the brakes failed. By making minor adaptations to take local conditions into account

856

(thrust of the engines, redesign of the wings as well as the incorporation of tyres with reduced pressure), Boeing made its standard product into one of the best selling passenger aircraft in the history of civil aviation.[8]

Worldwide accepted unique selling propositions

The factor that distinguishes a company's range of products from its competitor's is known as the unique selling proposition (USP). It is important in maintaining competitiveness, particularly in a global context, and in view of the fact that the products and services offered by competitors are becoming increasingly similar. By focusing on a particular sales feature, the company attempts to convince the consumer of its superior level of service. In striving to achieve global competitiveness, a company uses this approach to establish and maintain a global quality or performance standard, as well as to build up credibility and confidence in its products. Thus some companies even accept a guarantee that their standards will be maintained.

An example is Delta Dental, a large American insurance company which guarantees:

- *Fast customer service*: if a client's question cannot be answered at once, a Delta representative calls back with the answer within 24 hours, otherwise the company pays the client $50.
- *Faultless processing of invoices*: 90 per cent of the invoices submitted for payment are correctly processed within two weeks, the rest within a month, otherwise Delta waives the client's administrative charges for a month. These can range between $120 and $12,000 per month.
- A saving of at least 10 per cent: If the Delta client does not save at least 10 per cent of the standard dental fees, Delta will remit the difference.[9]

An increasing level of education and a higher level of skills among consumers leads to more critical buying behaviour. This is forcing companies to present the benefits of their products and services to the customer by means of objectively testable criteria and verifiable comparisons. Thus global advertising can increasingly ill afford to communicate simplistic images. The trend is towards advertising that can verify its claims.

Customer-orientation despite globality

Numerous examples from real-life situations show that customer focus is another important element of global market efficiency and means far more than lip service being paid to the global availability of a company's products and services. The personal contact involved in selling the product and the intensity of the after-sales service also represent key factors for competitiveness in a globally-oriented business.

The Japanese commonly observe: 'For many Europeans and Americans a business transaction is finished when the sale has been made, whereas for us that's when the business relationship really starts.' This points to the special importance the Japanese place on customer focus. In an extreme case this implies the ability to provide a service or deliver a product within 24 hours around the clock. Or to reply to a request, deal with a complaint or prepare a quotation on the same day.

When the Japanese talk of customer focus, they do not limit it to their sales staff alone, but involve the entire company. This includes the close interest paid by the management, in a conceptual sense and, above all, in real physical terms. Top managers of large Japanese consumer goods manufacturers regularly visit their sales offices and personally sell washing machines or stereo systems.

Market presence in key countries

Global orientation does not automatically mean that all regional markets are treated in the same way. What are known as pacemaker, or key, markets play a special role in achieving and maintaining secure competitive positions in global business. These markets are of particular importance to the main competitors within an industry because of their large volume and strong purchasing power. They tend to be characterized by intense competition.

Exceptions to this rule are markets with a monopolistic supply structure. A company's presence in these pacemaker markets alone can give it the necessary sensitivity to the industry and competitive trends and allow it to discern technological changes affecting the market in global competitiveness. Because of their demand structure, these key markets provide the necessary basis for establishing a worldwide image and a global brand. Their greater market volume allows a company to increase the number of its target customers and to enhance its focus on them. In this way, they can achieve levels of performance which would be impossible, for reasons of scale, if they were solely oriented to their domestic market.

Fast and reliable market feedback

If a company is to achieve sustained market efficiency, it cannot dispense with a corporate feedback system. In global corporations where several thousand customer contacts per day are the rule, the level of customer benefit cannot be taken for granted. Strategic monitoring provides real-time information on customer satisfaction. It constitutes the critical element of quality assurance and provides the basis for in-house learning processes. Suitable instruments, such as interactive telephone systems, allow market information to be obtained in the field and then made available to the entire company within a short time.

The Hilti company, based in Liechtenstein, manufactures assembly equipment and markets its products primarily via a direct selling system. More than 3,000 of its service engineers visit construction sites around the world, producing over 40,000 customer contacts per day. These are then systematically evaluated by means of a corporate feedback system. The results form the basis for new or improved products. At Sharp, the creative lifestyle planning group maintains continuous contacts with about 600 customers.

2. Global cost efficiency

Global cost efficiency means optimizing the costs required to attain the targeted corporate performance. To this end, the benefits of an international division of labour must be consistently utilized, business systems must be given a clear focus and market mechanisms must be introduced within the company.

Consistent utilization of the international division of labour

Despite convergence, at least within the major economic blocks (EU, ASEAN, NAFTA, EFTA, etc), and increased efforts towards harmonization and regulation at the political level (GATT), significant differences relevant to costs continue to exist between countries in many sectors. These include the various stages of the value-added process as well as the factors affecting production, such as human resources (work) availability of production sites (land) and sources of funding (capital).

Global sourcing can already yield cost reductions at the beginning of the value-added chain, namely at the *procurement* stage. The example of the Ford Escort car illustrates the degree of global sourcing now practised. The intermediary products for the Escort model are obtained from no less than 15 countries. These include not only raw materials, but components and entire systems which come from a worldwide network of subcontractors and suppliers, from all three regions of the triad. The fact that these regions are at the same time the pacemaker countries of the automobile industry points to the strategic orientation of the procurement and production sectors. For reasons of economies of scale, the final assembly is concentrated in only two plants in Halewood (UK) and Saarlouis (Germany).

But, we cannot ignore the drawbacks that go hand-in-hand with the benefits of global sourcing. In addition to the obvious increase in procurement and logistic costs, a number of intangible factors also increase with greater transportation distances. Together, these make global sourcing consistent to only a limited extent with a supply situation that is well synchronized to the needs of the production process.

A number of redundancies may well be desirable in some sectors of *the research and development process*, as at Philips NV, where this principle has been adopted by decentralizing the company's R&D activities. However, this can lead to the 're-inventing the wheel' syndrome that remains a cost trap for many companies with global interests, but whose principal focus remains domestic. The art of consistently utilizing the international division of labour can no longer be limited to locating and exploiting comparative benefits, but increasingly demands the intelligent networking of a company's R&D activities. Communication barriers must be dismantled and local technical competence increasingly tapped by the entire corporation by using IT systems installed around the world.

The opportunities offered by the international division of labour are also consistently exploited in the *production* sector.

From the perspective of cost efficiency, globalization means that a company must constantly monitor the make-or-buy-ratio. Sustained cost optimization can be achieved only by examining the contribution of every stage of production to the value added, and comparing the results with the worldwide potential for outsourcing.

Focused business systems

A company's complexity and costs structures depend largely on the size of its product range and the diversity of variants. During the period 1980 to 1990 this diversity increased by a factor of 3.5 in growth markets and by a factor of 5.2 in stagnating markets. Experience shows that every time the number of variants doubles, costs increase by between 20 and 30 per cent. The meaning of product focus becomes evident by looking at the examples of Caterpillar and International Harvester. By pursuing a strategy based on Ford's, Caterpillar managed to survive, despite a profound crisis in the industry. Two-thirds of the manufacturing costs in the market for construction equipment are accounted for by the core areas of engines, axle systems, transmission and hydraulics, and these depend greatly on volumes. After retrenching to standardized core components for the product lines serving its regional markets, the company shifted its production to a few large factories. The assembly plants in which the necessary local adaptations were made are located in the main markets of Australia, Brazil, Japan and Europe.[10]

The doggedly national market focus of International Harvester, one of Caterpillar's competitors, indicates what can happen if a company elects to buck the tide of globalization. In the mid-seventies the company was able to service every national market with customized products. At first sight, this sounds like a clear competitive advantage. But the problems that grew from this strategy were soon apparent within the organization. Fifty-seven different types of engine were manufactured in no less than eight factories, and the diversity of models and types proliferated without limit. The company fell into a cost trap from which it was unable to emerge despite rationalization programmes. By the early eighties, Caterpillar had one competitor less in the construction equipment industry.

Focusing business systems means concentrating on those parts of the company's product range that correspond to its core competencies, the consistent reduction of the diversity of variants and a clear orientation towards key customers. The message is that 'Not every customer is king!'

Internal market economy

Linear budget reductions or cost cutting, often designed as one-off economy programmes, rarely have the desired effect. Global cost-effectiveness can be sustained only if a company is oriented to the market-based mechanisms of supply and demand *within* the company. These optimize the costs required to manufacture the company's products on the basis of self-organization. A number of features characterize an internal market economy: the breakdown of production units into profit, service and cost centres, the introduction of an internal customer/supplier relationship with clear transfer prices as well as of performance-oriented remuneration. But also the reduction of purely co-ordinating management tasks and of transverse subsidies as well as the conversion of overheads into value-added.

A large telecommunications company makes extensive use of the principle of an internal market economy for large projects. Each development engineer represents a profit centre. He or she sells his/her services proactively by speci-fying his/her technical qualifications and hourly rates when approaching the leader of a project he or she wishes to join. Very good engineers are wooed by the project leaders and can obtain correspondingly high rates. Research work-ers and developers who are not fully occupied simply leave the company.

Experience shows that the introduction of market principles is blocked largely by mental barriers tied to specific corporate cultures.

3. Global ecological efficiency

'We call those companies "eco-efficient". They are making progress on the path to corporate growth which is sustainable in the long term by improving their operating methods, substituting polluting materials, introducing clean technologies and products and trying to use and re-use resources more effi-ciently,' says Stephan Schmidheiny.

Not only economic efficiency, but ecological efficiency in the sense of mini-mizing the environmental pollution caused by corporate activity is becoming increasingly important. A survey run by the German Federal Working Group for Environmentally-Aware Management (Bundesdeutscher Arbeitskreis für Umweltbewußtes Management, BAUM) showed that consumers feel that com-panies have a greater ecological responsibility than the relevant government departments.[11] It is not altruism, but hard-headed economic and business arguments that urge a consistently ecological stance by corporate manage-ment. The natural environment represents a production and waste-disposal factor that will increasingly become a cost burden for companies in the future. Economic efficiency must be based on an aggressively proactive style of envi-ronmental management.

Integrated environmentally compliant products and services
It makes no sense merely to launch a 'green' product or a 'green' line onto the market by making a few technical innovations and then wrapping it up with a decorative PR exercise. Policies of this kind are counterproductive for the company as fundamentally they lack credibility. An integrated environmen-tally-benign product and service structure must mean gradually bringing the entire range of products into line with ecological principles. This process must be oriented to technological improvements. A programme that focuses the product range to ecological values will then lead to ideas for innovative prod-ucts that are attractive to customers.

Environmentally optimized total product life cycles

Environmentally-benign product design must relate to the entire product life. Starting with the procurement of the raw materials right up to waste disposal, the whole idea must be to design each of these process stages in an environmentally optimal way.

A conflict of goals may well arise between cost and ecological efficiency, especially in companies with global operations that make consistent use of the opportunities offered by the international division of labour. A worldwide production network leads to significant environmental pollution, especially through the transport of goods. Another unsatisfactory situation arises when companies shift parts of their production to other regions with less restrictive environmental laws. Ecological optimization of the product life cycles must be based on product policies that quantify and balance the environmentally polluting effects over its entire life cycle.

To increase the life cycles of their products, an increasing number of companies are starting to replace defective parts and then return the product to the customer (rebuilt products). Thus Canon now offers recycled machines in addition to new photocopiers. A factory in Ireland simply replaces defective parts of the machine with new ones. Canon then sells the recycled copiers at a reduced price.

Environmentally-oriented behaviour

'Corporate commitment to quality means satisfying customers' requirements by using the fewest possible resources of every kind,' says Fritz Fahrni of Sulzer AG.

Ultimately, ecological efficiency can be achieved only when employees at all levels of the company are able to, want to and are allowed to, accept personal responsibility for the environment. Organizations must renounce the 'organized lack of responsibility' once so common. Employees can recognize and avoid environmental hazards at the workplace. Experience shows that moral exhortations have no effect. The required knowledge of ecological interrelationships and an awareness of environmentally benign action, as well as the willingness to pursue it, can be achieved only by the total involvement of all employees.

In conjunction with the D&RSW AG consulting company of Zürich, the Sulzer company has developed an interactive ECO programme called 'the economy and ecology'. More than 10,000 of the company's employees are working on this cascading programme. Four to six employees each create three illustrated posters. The first one deals with general environmental trends, such as air pollution or the greenhouse effect. The second poster analyzes the economic and ecological consequences of specific actions, for example the economic and ecological effects of air travel and video conferences. The resulting impulses for action are illustrated in the third poster. The ECO programme also stimulates the search for new business opportunities in a directed way.

In addition, the practice of environmentally-benign behaviour calls for appropriate corporate structures. Thus incentive systems must be worked out so that ecologically-friendly behaviour also pays off for the individual.

4. Management efficiency

Management efficiency is the central component and integrating factor of any strategy. Because the objectives set in trying to reach global efficiency in marketing, costing and ecological action are to some extent contradictory, high demands are made on a manager's co-ordinating skills. Global management efficiency is characterized by four dimensions: a federal structure, unified reporting and controlling, communicative managers who are sensitive to diverse cultural factors and a corporate culture characterized by a willingness to learn.

Federal structure

'Federalism offers a well-recognized way of dealing with paradoxes of power and control: the need to make things big by keeping them small, to encourage autonomy but within bounds,' says Charles Handy.

The worldwide flows of information, technology and products resulting from the international division of labour means that a global company has a large number of organizational interfaces. The critical question is: what management structure should be implemented to exploit core technologies and economies of scale worldwide without jeopardizing local market presence and responsibility? Many large companies such as General Electric, Johnson & Johnson, and Coca-Cola in America, Grand Metropolitan and British Petroleum in the UK, Accor in France, ABB in Switzerland and Honda in Japan are moving towards a federal structure. Behind this move lies the conviction that the principle of subsidiarity provides the most effective basis for dealing with complexity in a global corporation. Head office needs to intervene, while respecting the principle of subsidiarity, only where the decentralized units are unable to fulfil their business mission. And corporate headquarters must create the conditions that allow decentralized subsidiaries to realize their own objectives (autonomy before synergy). The principle at work here is: the greater the complexity of the corporate structure, the greater the leeway of its parts. The following are important characteristics of federal structures.[12]

- Small, transparent and results-oriented market units embedded within a corporate network (small within big is beautiful). The units are designed as profit centres or centres of excellence. They are responsible for operative business management in each local market.
- Clearly-thought-out matrix structures that realize the benefits of a worldwide presence and the company's group synergies.
- Consistent decentralization of staff and support functions all along the line, or the establishment of service centres that offer their services at market prices.

ABB's Percy Barnevik has stated his company's aspirations: 'We want to be global and local, big and small, radically decentralized with centralized reporting and control... If we resolve those contradictions, we create real organizational advantage.'

ABB operates with about 1,200 legally independent local companies with an average workforce of 200 and about 4,500 profit centres each with about 50 employees. ABB makes a distinction in its matrix dimensions between 'business areas' that bear long-term strategic responsibility for the worldwide success for their specific products and services, and 'regions' whose responsibility lies in the operating business. The headquarters was reduced from 1,600 to 100 employees and looks after the functions of corporate finance, corporate development, corporate control, legal affairs, etc. The overall co-ordinating functions devolve upon the 13-member executive committee.[13]

Global management efficiency means more than merely managing corporate structures *within the company*. In a market in which it is increasingly difficult to obtain the required resources for going it alone, value-added partnerships and strategic alliances are often the only way of surviving. The choice of a suitable partner and the elaboration of the contents of co-operative agreements make particularly high demands on management. Alliances alone do not by any means ensure global competitiveness. In statistical terms they often involve more risks than opportunities.

Unified reporting and controlling

Management efficiency in a decentrally managed global company requires IT-supported reporting and controlling procedures designed on a uniform pattern. They must be based on a company's strategic plans and the objectives and budgets derived from them. Wal-Mart, the world's largest retail chain, has installed a nationwide point-of-sales system which provides the company's managers within hours of closing time with all relevant information on sales figures, goods turnover for all products, sales locations and regions either individually or in aggregate. This is the only way of reducing the time lag between corporate perception and decision-making so that time becomes a global competitive advantage.

Communicative managers sensitive to cultural differences

'A proper federation needs a common law, language and currency – a uniform way of doing business,' says Charles Handy. Specific demands are made on managers in a global company. The following personal qualities are required:

- They must be capable of fostering a climate of consensus and must not be authoritarian. This is the only way of harmonizing global objective with national interests.
- They must nurture a high sensitivity towards cultural differences. In a global environment, management efficiency must be measured against the background of national cultural differences. These comprise different social standards and sets of assumptions, education systems with a different bias, characterized either by traditional or religious mind-sets, or different social structures. The daily clash of collective Asiatic lifestyles and ideas with individualistic Western ones represents a real challenge to managers. The ability to achieve intercultural integration is becoming a key management function.

- They must be multilingual and be able to communicate effectively.
- They must be able to deal with paradoxes. Future management situations will be characterized increasingly by constellations that we may call paradoxical. Generally applicable principles no longer exist. Whatever is of value today may well prove to be useless tomorrow. *Lego* describes these paradoxical requirements on management very well in its mission statement.

Corporate climate characterized by a willingness to learn
'Companies with a high learning efficiency learn from their customers, suppliers, competitors and their employees. They know that the sources of today's success can be the causes of tomorrow's failures,' writes David A Nadler.

We must accept that the survival of a company fundamentally depends on its willingness to learn. The more dynamic the operating environment, the greater the demands on organizational learning based on the principle of self-organization. **TEFCAS** is the acronym given by creativity expert, Tony Buzan to describe the general learning formula that he claims is also applicable to companies. Learning presupposes Trials. Such experimentation leads to an Effect. By means of an ideal/actual comparison (Feedback) the result to be obtained can be Checked, thus allowing corrections to be made (Adjust). Success is the result of the learning process. There are only two blocks to learning for individuals and companies alike: refusing to permit further trials and not obtaining timely feedback. Managers can make a critical contribution to creating a climate of learning in their organization by their personal style of leadership and by establishing in-house systems to encourage learning.

- to be able to build relationships with one's staff... *and to keep a suitable distance*
- to be able to lead... *and to hold oneself in the background*
- to trust one's staff... *and keep an eye on what is happening*
- to be tolerant... *and to know how you want things to function*
- to keep the goals of one's own department in mind... *and at the same time to be loyal to the whole firm*
- to do a good job of planning your own time... *and to be flexible with your schedule*
- to freely express your own views... *and to be diplomatic*
- to be visionary... *and to keep one's feet on the ground*
- try to win consensus... *and to be able to cut through*
- to be dynamic... *and to be reflective*
- to be sure of yourself... *and to be humble*

Fig. 6 The 11 paradoxes of leadership

Source: K Bleicher, *Paradoxien Unternehmerischer Dynamik*, unpublished manuscript, 1994, p. 29

Outlook

'Equipped with simplistic stone-age thinking, we fight for survival in a high-tech environment. The traditional success recipes and power formulas have gone by the board, the ultimate cost and efficiency revolutions remain without effect, caught up in obsessive ideas spawned by conventional management concepts,' says Ian I Mitroff, director of the Center for Crisis Management at the University of Southern California.

In the future too, not all sectors will be affected by the trend towards globalization. Ultimately, the customer or market will decide on the degree of globalization of an industry. The competitiveness of global companies obeys its own laws, and these differ from those applicable to companies that are focused on their home markets. The alignment towards a global strategy is more than just a fashionable trend, it implies a fundamental transformation urged by changing competitive structures. Global competition is not a partial phenomenon, it inevitably affects the entire company. In view of the planetary scale of environmental destruction and in response to the growing pressure of public opinion, quite apart from factors of market and cost efficiency, an integrated ecologically-oriented style of corporate management is urgently needed. The discussions that used to pit ecology against the economy have become obsolete.

However, we cannot lose sight of the fact that highly efficient management is the primary factor in achieving global competitiveness. Decision makers must deal in a meaningful way with objectives that may, as we have seen, involve mutually contradictory elements. How far must, and should, local adaptation go when a company's range of products and services are being designed? In what way can the international division of labour be exploited while ensuring an acceptable degree of environmental pollution? How much autonomy can be granted to decentralized operating units without jeopardizing vital group synergies? How can managers succeed in encouraging learning and innovation in a guided way? To come up with effective answers to these and similar questions, an organization must place a premium on learning capability, must draw on specific management qualities to deal with paradoxes and must ultimately be prepared to throw unreflected management myths overboard.

Hans A Wüthrich is Professor of International Management at Munich's Universität der Bundeswehr. He studied economics at St Gallen University where he later completed a doctorate and joined its faculty of strategic management. He is a partner in D&RSW AG (a management consulting company) and lectures at St Gallen University.

Further Reading

Bennett, S and Wallace, T, *World Class Manufacturing*, Oliver Wight, 1994.

References

1 *International Direct Investment: Politics and Trends in the 1980s*, OECD, Paris 1992, p.11.

2 *World Investment Report 1993*, United Nations, New York, 1994.

3 Levitt, T, 'The globalization of markets', *Harvard Business Review*, no. 4, 1983.

4 Kreutzer, R, *Global Marketing, Konzeption eines länderübergreifenden Marketing*, Wiesbaden, 1989, p.59.

5 See Hamel, G and Prahalad, CK, 'Creating global strategic capability', in Hood, N, *Strategies in Global Competition*, 1988, p.11; and Wortzel, L, 'Global strategies: standardization versus flexibility', in *Global Strategic Management, The Essentials*, New York, 1991, p.137.

6 Solvell, O, 'Is the global automobile industry really global?' in Hood, N, *Strategies in Global Competition*, London, 1988, p.200.

7 Yip, G, *Total Global Strategy: Managing for Worldwide Competitive Advantage*, Prentice Hall, New Jersey, 1992, p.17.

8 Peters, T, *Liberation Management*, Knopf, New York, 1992.

9 Henzler, H and Rall, W, 'Aufbruch in den Weltmarkt', *Manager Magazin*, no. 9, 1985, p.186.

10 Gege, M, 'Motive einer umweltorientierten Unternehmensfübrung', in Hansmann, K-W, *Marktorientiertes Umweltmanagement*, Wiesbaden, 1994, p.90.

11 Handy, C, 'Balancing corporate power: a new federalist paper', *McKinsey Quarterly*, no. 3, 1993, p.159.

12 Müller-Berghoff, BH, 'Asea Brown Boveri AG - Ein multi-domestik Konzern', in Hoffmann, F (ed), *Konzernhandbuch, Recht, Steuern, Rechnungslegung, Führung, Organization, Praxisfälle*, Wiesbaden, 1993, p.503.

THINKERS

Michael Porter

Born 1947; educator

Michael Porter of Harvard Business School is probably the world's most successful academic. While other management thinkers have compromised their approach in search of popular appeal, Porter's work is unashamedly academic in tone and content. Seriousness and rationality is all pervasive. 'His work is academic almost to a fault,' observed *The Economist*. 'Mr Porter is about as likely to produce a blockbuster full of anecdotes and boosterish catch-phrases as he is to deliver a lecture dressed in bra and stockings.'[1]

His approach is based on surgical precision, the dissection of the vital organs of companies and industrial nations. Porter's books, not surprisingly, have been few in number, but high in their ambition and influence.

'Strategic thinking rarely occurs spontaneously. Without guidelines few managers knew what constituted strategic thinking,'[2] he lamented in a 1987 article. His work has set about constructing the guidelines. This has brought him into conflict with a number of other leading thinkers. Henry Mintzberg, the champion of spontaneity and intuition, has been critical of Porter's 'enthusiasm for generic strategies and checklists of all kinds'.[3]

His first book was *Competitive Strategy* (1980) which, instead of tiptoeing round the edges of management theory, went straight to the strategic heart. Porter tackled the apparently imponderable question of how organizations can achieve long-term competitive advantage. He sought a middle ground between the two polarized approaches then accepted – on the one hand, that competitive advantage was achieved by organizations adapting to their particular circumstances; and, on the other, that competitive advantage was based on the simple principle that the more in-tune and aware of a market a company is the more competitive it can be (through lower prices and increased market share).

Porter managed to absorb both these concepts. From analysis of a number of companies, he developed 'generic strategies'. This was not an instant template for competitive advantage – Porter insisted that though the 'generic strategies' existed, it was up to each organization to

Education: degree in aeronautical engineering at Princeton; doctorate in economics, Harvard.
Career: Joined Harvard faculty 1973; also now runs a highly successful consultancy business, Monitor.

carefully select which were most appropriate to them and at which particular time. The four 'generic strategies' are backed by five 'competitive forces' which are then applied to five 'different kinds of industries' (fragmented, emerging, mature, declining and global).

Porter's five forces of competition include one internal to the industry (rivalry among existing firms) and four external forces. The five forces are:

- threat of substitute products
- threat of new entrants
- bargaining power of buyers
- bargaining power of suppliers
- rivalry among existing companies

For managers, Porter's 'generic strategies' framework is seductive. It is clear and the logic irrefutable. The trouble is that, while Porter suggests that the model should only be used to stimulate thinking, organizations often regard it as a direct route to competitive advantage. There is considerable irony in companies using the same model to differentiate themselves from each other.

Porter contends that there are three ways by which companies can gain competitive advantage – by becoming the lowest cost producer in a given market; by being a differentiated producer (offering something extra or special to charge a premium price); or by being a focused producer (achieving dominance in a niche market).

To examine an organization's internal competitiveness, Porter advocates the use of a 'value chain' – analysis of a company's internal processes and the interactions between different elements of the organization to determine how and where value is added. Viewing everything a company does in terms of its overall competitiveness, argues Porter, is a crucial step to becoming more competitive.

'In a volume of over 500-pages it is easy to miss Porter's one reference to human resource management. It occupies only two paragraphs,' observes the UK management writer and thinker, Philip Sadler, of *Competitive Advantage*.[4] The human element is not often to be found in Porter's work.

This is even truer of *The Competitive Advantage of Nations* (1990). Probably Porter's most ambitious project, it is a detailed study of the competitiveness of the world's top eight economies which emerged from Porter's work on the Presidential Commission on Industrial Competitiveness set up by Ronald Reagan. Interestingly, Porter produces a more pragmatic view of the world in this book. He is highly critical of general prescriptions and the worldwide application of management fads such as just-in-time. What works in one country, fails miserably in another, he warns. This runs counter to much of the prevailing wisdom of globalization. Indeed, instead of national differences and characteristics becoming less pronounced, Porter found them to be as important as ever.

'You can boil Porter's magisterial work down to just three words: "vigorous domestic rivalry". That is: firms that engage in the most intensive competition in their home market tend to improve fastest,' commented Tom Peters, saluting Porter as 'an unlikely prince of disorder'.[5]

Again, Porter's research produced a tidy checklist. His 'national diamond' framework identified four factors which influence the competitiveness of nations:

- resources
- related and supporting industries
- demanding home customers
- domestic rivalry

While Porter has attracted some criticism for his willingness to boil his mass of theories and ideas down to all-embracing bullet-points, without them it is unlikely that his complex ideas would either be accessible or understood. That they are so influential is a triumph for Porter's abilities of dissection and logic.

STUART CRAINER

Further Reading

Competitive Strategy, Free Press, New York, 1980.
Competitive Advantage, Free Press, New York, 1985.
The Competitive Advantage of Nations, Macmillan, London, 1990.

References

[1] 'Professor Porter PhD', *The Economist*, London, 8 October 1994.
[2] Porter, M, 'Corporate strategy: the state of strategic thinking', *The Economist*, London, May 23, 1987.
[3] Mintzberg, H, *The Rise and Fall of Strategic Planning*, Prentice Hall, Hemel Hempstead, 1994.
[4] Sadler, P, 'Gold collar workers – making the best of the best', *Directions*, December 1992.
[5] Peters, T, *Liberation Management*, Alfred Knopf, New York, 1992.

CULTURAL FACTORS IN INTERNATIONAL MANAGEMENT

Fons Trompenaars

In a globalizing environment the development of the international manager is a strategic activity. In developing truly international managers, organizations are simultaneously fostering their own process of becoming international in outlook and practice. Central to this process is respect for, and awareness of, cultural diversity.

The successful international manager reconciles a number of key dilemmas which are common to all cultures. Failure to reconcile these dilemmas will lead to the failure of an organization's international aspirations and strategies.

Management in a global environment is increasingly affected by cultural differences. The way management is deployed in a multicultural environment is, and needs to be, dependent on the broader strategy and shape of an organization. The process of developing international managers is a reflection of how truly international an organization is and, in turn, produces the specific level of internationalization of the corporation.

The international manager needs to go beyond awareness of cultural differences. He or she needs to respect these differences and take advantage of diversity through reconciling cross-cultural dilemmas. *The international manager reconciles cultural dilemmas.*

Basic to understanding other cultures is the awareness that culture is a series of rules and methods that a society has evolved to deal with the recurring problems it faces. They have become so basic that, like breathing, we no longer think about how we approach or resolve them. Every country and every organization faces dilemmas in relationships with people; dilemmas in relationship to time; and dilemmas in relations between people and the natural environment. Culture is the way in which people resolve dilemmas emerging from universal problems.

While nations differ markedly in *how* they approach these dilemmas, they do not differ in needing to make some kind of response.[1] The succesful international manager reconciles dilemmas more effectively.

Dilemmas in relationships with people

How does a society deal with rules? The universal truth versus the particular instance

Universalist societies tend to feel that general rules and obligations are a strong source of moral reference. Universalists tend to follow the rules and assume that the standards they hold dear are the *right* ones and attempt to change the attitudes of others to match. Particularist societies are those where *particular* circumstances are much more important than the rules. Bonds of particular relationships (family, friends) are stronger than any abstract rule, and responses change according to circumstances and the people involved.

In order to test these extreme definitions 15,000 managers worldwide were asked to consider the following dilemma:[2]

You are a passenger in a car, driven by a close friend, and your friend's car hits a pedestrian. You know your friend was going at least 35 miles an hour in an area of the city where the maximum speed is 20 miles an hour. There are no witnesses.

The lawyer of your friend says that if you testify under oath that the speed was only 20 miles an hour, it may save him from serious consequences.

This example produces two basic questions:

- What right has your friend to expect you to protect him?
  My friend has a **definite, some** *or* **no** *right.*
- Would you help your friend in view of the obligations you feel for society?
  Yes *or* **no.**

The chart in Fig. 1 shows the result of putting these questions to a variety of nationalities. North Americans and most Northern Europeans emerge as almost totally universalist in their approach to the problem. The proportion falls to under 70 per cent for the French and Japanese while, in Venezuela, two-thirds of respondents would lie to the police to protect their friend.

Time and again universalists respond in a way that as the seriousness of the accident increases, the obligation to help their friend decreases. They seem to be saying to themselves: 'The law was broken and the serious condition of the pedestrian underlines the importance of upholding the law.' This suggests that universalism is rarely used to the exclusion of particularism, rather that it forms the first principle in the process of moral reasoning. Particular consequences remind us of the need for universal laws.

As Fig. 1 shows, universalists are more common in Protestant cultures, where the congregation relates to God by obedience to his written laws. Predominantly Catholic cultures retain more relational and particularist features. A person can break one of the commandments and still find compassion

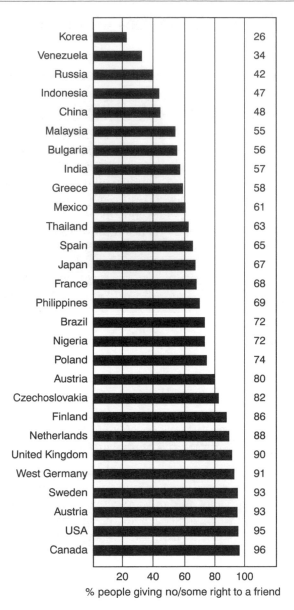

Korea	26
Venezuela	34
Russia	42
Indonesia	47
China	48
Malaysia	55
Bulgaria	56
India	57
Greece	58
Mexico	61
Thailand	63
Spain	65
Japan	67
France	68
Philippines	69
Brazil	72
Nigeria	72
Poland	74
Austria	80
Czechoslovakia	82
Finland	86
Netherlands	88
United Kingdom	90
West Germany	91
Sweden	93
Austria	93
USA	95
Canada	96

20 40 60 80 100
% people giving no/some right to a friend

Fig. 1 The car and the pedestrian – universal versus particular

for their unique circumstances. God, for the Catholics, resembles them. Moreover, he will probably understand that you were lying for your friend, particularly one so unfortunate.

Universalist cultures tend to take contracts very seriously. They regard them as containing the universal truth which transcends all kinds of particular situations. Universalist cultures, therefore, tend to have many lawyers to protect the 'ultimate truth' written down in a document. Particularist cultures tend to go for building trustworthy relationships, which are particular by definition. The time that is 'lost' initially is gained back later when no lawyers have to intervene.

Reconciling universalism and particularism

We have identified seven such cultural dichotomies. Universalism versus particularism is the first. Interestingly, the two extremes can always, in a sense, be found in the same person. The international manager is very often caught in the dilemma of the universal truth and the particular or local circumstance. On the one hand, he or she needs to listen to the universalities of headquarters. Alternatively, the particular needs of the local environment requires responses which do not fit the demands of headquarters. The most effective international manager reconciles this dilemma by acknowledging that the particular instances require universal rules in order not to slip into a local pathology. Intuitively the international manager goes through a cycle in which the middle is held by his or her talents. Fig. 2, devised by Charles Hampden-Turner,[3] illustrates this.

Take the following example. A series of interviews of managers was conducted for managers at Advanced Micro Devices, which has its headquarters in

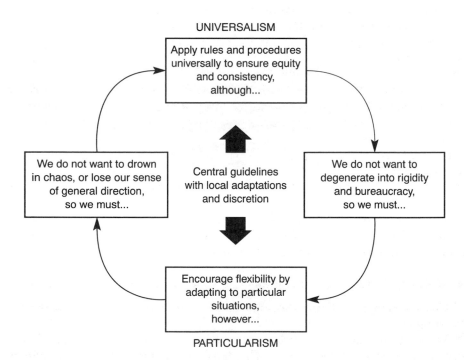

UNIVERSALISM

Apply rules and procedures universally to ensure equity and consistency, although...

We do not want to drown in chaos, or lose our sense of general direction, so we must...

Central guidelines with local adaptations and discretion

We do not want to degenerate into rigidity and bureaucracy, so we must...

Encourage flexibility by adapting to particular situations, however...

PARTICULARISM

Fig. 2 Universalism versus particularism

Sunnyvale, California. Managers working in Europe said: 'We need to become more adaptive to the particular needs of European clients such as Nokia, Thomson, Philips and Ericsson. These customers want slight adaptations to the chip. When we discuss this with our American colleagues they keep complaining about our exceptions. The Americans at headquarters keep on emphasizing that all adaptations to the existing universal chip threaten economies of scale. Furthermore, it increases the pressure on the production capacity. Manufacturing can't cope with demands without all these adaptations.'

We asked the managers from the US *and* Europe if they saw any potential of reconciliation. It was surprising how powerful this methodology worked. The European managers suggested that a regular invitation of their clients to California to co-develop the next universal chip would solve the problem. The quality of the newly-developed universal chip needs to be measured by the number of particular applications it can serve. To universalize particulars and to particularize the universal is essential to internationalization.

The group versus the self: individualism versus collectivism

The conflict between what each of us wants as an individual, and the interests of the group we belong to, is the second of the seven dimensions covering how people relate to each other. Do we relate to others by discovering what each of us individually wants and then try to negotiate the differences? Or, do we place ahead of this some shared concept of the public and collective good?

Individualism has been described as 'a prime orientation to the self', and collectivism as 'a prime orientation to common goals and objectives'.[4] Just as for the first dimension, cultures typically vary in putting one or the other of these approaches first in their thinking processes, though both may be included in their reasoning. The 15,000 managers who answered the following question demonstrate this, although the division here is not quite so sharp as for the universal versus the particular example.

Two people were discussing ways in which one could improve the quality of life.

One said: 'It is obvious that if one has as much freedom as possible and the maximum opportunity to develop oneself, the quality of one's life will improve as a result.'

The other said: 'If the individual is continuously taking care of his fellow human beings the quality of life will improve for everyone, even if it obstructs individual freedom and individual development.'

● Which of the two ways of reasoning do you think is usually best, A or B?

Charles Hampden-Turner sees the issue as essentially circular, with two 'starting points'.

We all go through these cycles, but starting from different points and conceiving of them as means or ends. The individualist culture sees the individual as 'the end' and improvements to collective arrangements as the means to

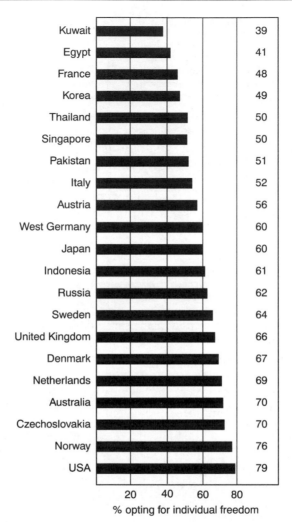

Fig. 3 Individual versus collective

achieve it. The collectivist culture sees the group as its end and improvements to individual capacities as a means to that end. Yet, if the relationship is truly circular; the decision to label one element as an end and another as a means is arbitrary. By definition, circles never end. Every end is also the means to another goal.

The effective international manager is close to the conviction that individualism finds its fulfilment in service to the group. They regard group goals as of demonstrable value to individuals, only if those individuals are consulted and participate in the process of developing them. The reconciliation is not easy, but possible. One particular company has applied this thinking very effectively to its international pay-for-performance system. The highest individual

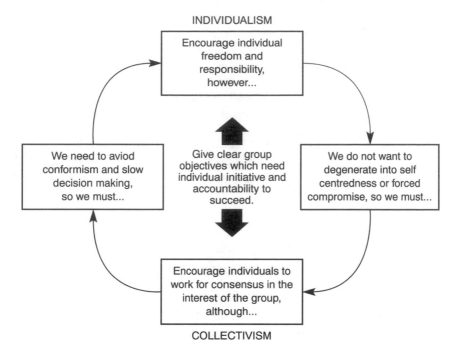

Fig. 4 Individualism versus collectivism

bonuses were given to those who were the best team-players. Teams could get significant rewards if they had nurtured individual development. It is something the Japanese do naturally.

Do we display our emotions?
Affective versus neutral relationships

In relationships between people, reason and emotion both play a role. Which of these dominates will depend upon whether we are *affective*, ie, show our emotions, in which case we probably get an emotional response in return, or whether we are emotionally *neutral* in our approach.

Typically, of course, reason and emotion are combined. In expressing ourselves we try to find confirmation of our thoughts and feelings in the response of our audience. When our own approach is highly emotional we are seeking a *direct* emotional response: 'I have the same feelings as you on this subject.' When our own approach is highly neutral we are seeking an *indirect* response. 'Because I agree with your reasoning or proposition, I give you my support.' On both occasions approval is sought, but different paths are being used to this end. The indirect path gives us emotional support contingent upon the success of an effort of intellect. The direct path allows our feelings about a factual proposition to show through, thereby 'joining' feelings with thoughts in a different way.

To philosophize about their products and approach, the French division of Elf Aquitaine launched the following expression in their advertisements: '*La passion a toujours raison*' (passion is always right). This could only be developed in France. When the British branch of Elf saw the verb they could not resist saying: 'Yes, we know that for the French passion leads to the truth, but that is good for the French and very bad for our business in the UK.'

Overly affective (expressive) or neutral cultures have problems in relating to each other. The neutral person is easily accused of being ice-cold and heartless; the affective person is seen as out of control and inconsistent. When such cultures meet, the first essential for the international manager is to recognize the differences, and to refrain from making any judgements based on emotions, or the lack of them.

How far do we get involved?
Specific versus diffuse cultures

Closely related to whether we show emotions in dealing with other people is the degree to which we engage others in *specific* areas of life and single levels of personality, or *diffusely* in multiple areas of our lives and at several levels of personality at the same time.

In specific-oriented cultures a manager *segregates out* the task relationship she or he has with a subordinate, and insulates this from other dealings. But, in some countries, every life space and every level of personality tends to permeate all others.

National differences are pointedly displayed under the headings of specificity and diffuseness. The range is clearly illustrated by responses to the following situation:

A boss asks a subordinate to help him paint his house. The subordinate, who doesn't feel like doing it, discusses the situation with a colleague.

The colleague argues: 'You don't have to paint if you don't feel like it. He is your boss at work. Outside he has little authority.'

The subordinate argues: 'Despite the fact that I don't feel like it, I will paint it. He is my boss and you can't ignore that outside work either.'

In specific societies, where work and private life are sharply separated, managers are not inclined to assist. As one Dutch respondent observed: 'House painting is not in my collective labour agreement.'

Diffuse cultures tend to have lower turnover and employee mobility because of the importance of loyalty and the multiplicity of human bonds. They tend not to headhunt or lure away employees from other companies with high (specific) salaries. Takeovers are rarer in diffuse cultures because of the disruption caused to relationships and because shareholders (often banks) have longer-term relationships and cross-holdings in each other's companies and are less motivated by the price of shares.

878

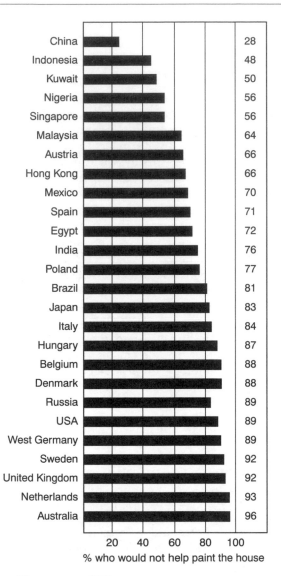

China — 28
Indonesia — 48
Kuwait — 50
Nigeria — 56
Singapore — 56
Malaysia — 64
Austria — 66
Hong Kong — 66
Mexico — 70
Spain — 71
Egypt — 72
India — 76
Poland — 77
Brazil — 81
Japan — 83
Italy — 84
Hungary — 87
Belgium — 88
Denmark — 88
Russia — 89
USA — 89
West Germany — 89
Sweden — 92
United Kingdom — 92
Netherlands — 93
Australia — 96

20 40 60 80 100

% who would not help paint the house

Fig. 5 Specific versus diffuse

Reconciling specific/diffuse cultures

This is perhaps the area in which balance is most crucial, from both a personal and a corporate point of view. The specific extreme can lead to disruption; the diffuse extreme to a lack of perspective; a collision between them results in paralysis. It is the interplay of the two approaches which is most fruitful for the international manager. They must recognize that privacy is necessary, but that complete separation of private life leads to alienation and superficiality; that business is business, but stable and deep relationships mean strong affiliations.

Do we work for our status or is it given? Achievement versus ascription

All societies give certain of their members higher status than others, signalling that unusual attention should be focused upon such persons and their activities. While some societies accord status to people on the basis of their achievements, others ascribe it to them by virtue of age, class, gender, education, etc. The first kind of status is called *achieved status* and the second *ascribed status*. While achieved status refers to *doing*, ascribed status refers to *being*.

Achievement-oriented organizations justify their hierarchies by claiming that senior persons have 'achieved more' for the organization; their authority, justified by skill and knowledge, benefits the organization. Ascription-oriented organizations justify their hierarchies by 'power-to-get-things-done'. This may consist of power *over* people and be coercive, or power *through* people and be participative. There is high variation within ascriptive cultures and participative power has well-known advantages. Whatever form power takes, the ascription of status to persons is intended to be exercised as power, and that power is supposed to enhance the effectiveness of the organization. The sources of ascribed status may be multiple and trying to alter them to promotion on the grounds of achievement can be hazardous.

In ascribing cultures, status is attributed to those who 'naturally' evoke admiration from others, ie, older people, males, highly qualified persons and/or persons skilled in a technology or project deemed to be of national importance. To show respect for status is to assist the distinguished person to fulfil the expectations the society has of him or her. The status is generally independent of task or specific function.

Towards reconciliation

Look at the following global dilemma. You are HR manager of a US firm and are deciding who to send to your subsidiary in China as its new general manager. You feel that Ken Martin, a high-potential Harvard graduate, 36-year-old male is the best candidate. In case you decide to send him to join the management team of five senior Chinese managers, you need to imagine what will happen. Ascribed status in China is particularly based on age and family and regional background. 'But we don't have a senior person with the knowledge they need in China,' might be your argument. Reconciliation could be achieved by making Ken Martin assistant to the more senior Chinese manager. This could be done before retiring the last general manager. But, do send Ken Martin. Reconciling is not identical to compromising by sending older males or no one at all.

How do we organize our time? Past, present or future orientation

If only because managers need to co-ordinate their business activities, they require some kind of shared expectations about time. Just as different cultures have different assumptions about how people relate to one another, so they approach time differently. This orientation is about the relative importance cultures give to the past, present and future. How we think of time has its own consequences. Especially important is whether our view of time is *sequential*, a series of passing events, or whether it is *synchronic*, with past, present and future all interrelated, so that ideas about the future and memories of the past both shape present action.

In his Declarations, Saint Augustine pointed out that time as a subjective phenomenon can vary considerably from time in abstract conception. In its abstract form we cannot know the future because it is not yet here, and the past is also unknowable. We may have memories, partial and selective, but the past has gone. The only thing that exists is the present, which is our sole access to past or future. Augustine wrote: 'The present has, therefore, three dimensions. . .the present of past things, the present of present things and the present of future things.'

The methodology used to measure approaches to time comes from Tom Cottle, who created the Circle Test 5.[5] The question asked was as follows:

Think of the past, present and future as being in the shape of circles. Please draw three circles on the space available, representing past, present and future. Arrange these circles in any way you want that best shows how you feel about the relationship of the past, present and future. You may use different size circles. When you have finished, label each circle to show which one is the past, which one the present and which one the future.

Interestingly, when the Japanese were trying to take over the operations of Yosimite National Park in California, the first thing they submitted was a 250-year business plan. The intitial reaction of the Americans was: 'That involves 1,000 quarterly reports.' Americans tend to think about the improvement of the next quarter, while the Japanese do not ignore the short-term but tend to place it in the context of the long-term future. That is as close as managers can get to reconciling different time frames.

The international manager is often caught in the dilemma of the future demands of the larger organization, needing visions, missions and managing change towards it and past experiences of local populations.

A last example shows that the synchronous approach can accelerate sequences. I was checking out from a hotel in Strasbourg. Like most guests I placed myself at the end of the queue, since there was only one lady available to do the check-out procedures. After a few minutes we saw a French couple going straight to the check-out counter. As they were being dealt with, an Englishman in the queue approached them and informed them of the queue's existence. They were genuinely surprised. This confirms our stereotype of the French, but the rest of the story is also notable. When I got the opportunity to check out, the lady at the counter asked for my electronic key. She pulled it through the electronic reader and asked if I would like to read the invoice first. I had hardly

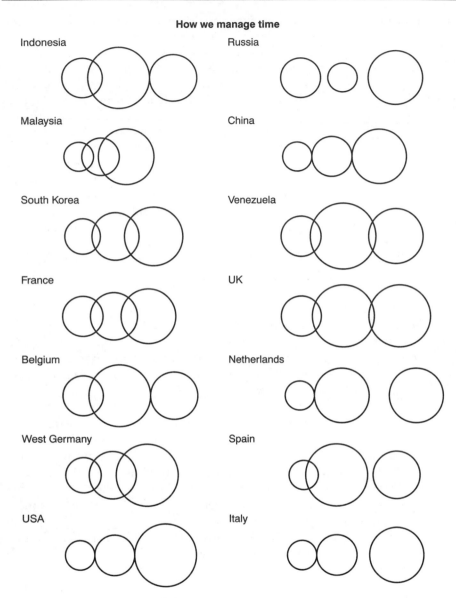

Fig. 6 Past, present and future

answered when she pushed the printout into my hands. She then immediately turned to the people behind me and asked for their key. When she gave the printout to the people to read, she turned back to me and asked: 'OK, sir?' I now understood – the 'dead moment' for reading my invoice was used partly to serve another client. This polychronic approach speeded up the total sequence of people checking out and was an improvement on pure sequentialism.

Do we control or are we subjugated? Nature orientation

The last culturally-determined dimension concerns the meaning an actor assigns to his or her (natural) environment.

In cultures in which an organic view of nature dominates, and in which the assumption is shared that man is subjugated to nature, individuals appear to orient their actions towards others. People become *other directed* in order to survive, their focus is on the environment rather than themselves. The traditional view of nature was dominated by a belief in what the American psychologist, Rotter, calls *external control.*[6]

Conversely, it has been determined that people who have a mechanic view of nature, in addition to the belief that man can dominate nature, usually take themselves as point of departure for determining the right action. This *inner-directedness* is also reflected through the current fashion of customer-orientation.

The mechanistic cosmology triggered in the Renaissance, still dominates much of our thinking today. It is characterized by a separation of natural relationships and social relationships. The latter, we clearly see in Western society, where the champions of internal control are the engineers and the MBAs.

Working in the 1960s, Rotter developed a scale designed to measure whether people had *an internal locus of control,* typical of more successful Americans, or an *external locus of control,* typical of relatively less successful Americans – disadvantaged by their circumstances or shaped by the competitive efforts of their rivals. The questions he devised we also used to assess our 15,000 managers' relationships with natural events. The answers suggest that there are highly significant differences between geographical areas. These questions all take the form of alternatives; managers were asked to select the statement they believed most reflected reality. The first of these pairs is as follows:

A *It is worthwhile trying to control important natural forces, like the weather.*

B *Nature should take its course and we just have to accept it the way it comes and do the best we can.*

Fig. 7 shows the percentage of respondents who chose A, ie, the inner directors.

Again this requires reconciliation by the effective international manager. Looking at the circle we see a process in which the international manager realizes that in a largely controlled world many things can be controlled and that a focus on the environment can increase our internal strength:

This also requires reconciliation by the effective international manager. In industry there has been a lengthy discussion on whether new products are developed through *technology push* or by *market pull*. In an inner-directed culture one prefers to point to technological renewal. We have seen where this can lead to at Mercedes-Benz. At the beginning of the 1990s this car manufacturer became a victim of its own successful technology push of the 1980s. With the S-class, the company found a new, very exclusive 'niche market': a market without clients.

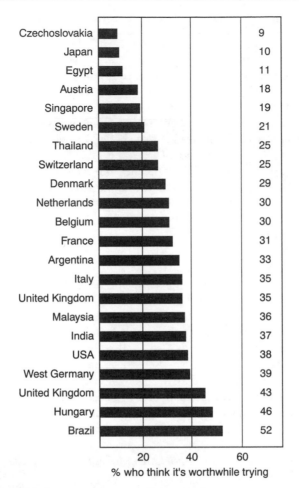

Fig. 7 Internal versus external control

In an external-oriented culture managers concentrate on the market. This approach also has its restrictions. The client often doesn't know what it wants. Or one listens to the customer for such a long time that the product is already dated as soon as it is launched. Also, in this case we see the power of reconciling both cultural orientations. The push of technology can determine the choice of a customer to one who is willing to listen. The pull of the market can give guidance to the choice of which technology to push.

Reconciliation of cultural differences: the major human talent of international management

The international manager strives toward riding the waves of intercultural differences rather than ignoring them or leading to one specific culture. Almost

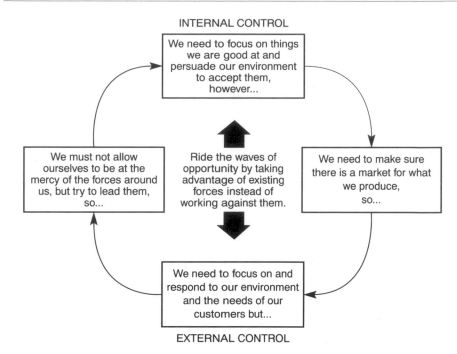

INTERNAL CONTROL

We need to focus on things
we are good at and
persuade our environment
to accept them,
however...

We must not allow
ourselves to be at the
mercy of the forces around
us, but try to lead them,
so...

Ride the waves of
opportunity by taking
advantage of existing
forces instead of
working against them.

We need to make sure
there is a market for what
we produce,
so...

We need to focus on and
respond to our environment
and the needs of our
customers but...

EXTERNAL CONTROL

Fig. 8 Internal versus external

all our problems, and their solutions, are recognizable all over the world. Internationally-operating managers are in the middle of these dilemmas.

There is another important respect in which all the world's managers are the same. Whichever principle they start with, the circumstances of business and of organizing experience requires them to reconcile the dilemmas. You can only prosper if as many particulars as possible are covered by rules, yet exceptions are seen and noted. You can only think effectively, if both the specifics and the diffuse wholes, the segments and the integrations, are covered. Whether you are at heart an individualist or a collectivist, your individuals must be capable of organizing themselves and your collectives are only as good as the health, wealth and wisdom of each member.

It is both true that time is a passing sequence of events and a moment of truth, a now in which past, present and future are given new meanings. We need to accept influences both from the depth of our inner convictions and from the world around us. In the final analysis **culture is the manner in which these dilemmas are reconciled, since every nation seeks a different and winding path to its own ideals of integrity.** Businesses will succeed according to the extent by which this reconciliation occurs, so we have everything to learn from discovering how others have travelled to their own position.

Fons Trompenaars is managing director of the Centre for International Business Studies in the Netherlands, a consultancy and training organization for international

management. He is the author of *Riding the Waves of Culture* (1993) and co-author, with Charles Hampden-Turner, of *The Seven Cultures of Capitalism* (1994).

Further Reading

Trompenaars, F, *Riding the Waves of Culture*, Nicholas Brealey, London,1993

References

1 See Trompenaars, F, *Riding the Waves of Culture*, Nicholas Brealey, London,1993.
2 Developed by Stouffer, SA and Toby, J, 'Role conflict and personality', *American Journal of Sociology*, LVI-5, 1951, pp. 395–406.
3 For a general outline of his methodology of reconciling dilemmas read *Charting the Corporate Mind*, Basil Blackwell, Oxford, 1991. For an application of reconciling dilemmas in various cultures read *Seven Cultures of Capitalism*, Charles Hampden-Turner and Fons Trompenaars, Piatkus, London, 1994.
4 Parsons, Talcott, *The Social System*, Free Press, New York, 1951.
5 Cottle, T, 'The circles test: an investigation of perception of temporal relatedness and dominance', *Journal of Projective Technique and Personality Assessments*, no. 31, 1967.
6 Rotter, J, 'Generalized Expectations for Internal versus External Control of Reinforcement', *Psychological Monograph* 609, 1966, pp. 1–28.

IDENTIFYING AND DEVELOPING INTERNATIONAL MANAGEMENT COMPETENCE

Kevin Barham and Claudia Heimer

From simply being a well-used phrase *managing internationally* is now a constant reality for more managers and organizations than ever before. What skills and characteristics are required of managers in the highly demanding and fast-moving international business environment? How are organizations to assess international management potential? And how are they to help managers develop the necessary international capability?

Some companies use a competence-based approach to address these questions. This has attracted controversy with critics doubting the strategic and developmental advantages of generic competencies for international managers. But, with organizations increasingly forced to operate in a global context, competencies can provide a foundation from which to integrate and develop the skills of managers. When applied in a dynamic and flexible way, a competence-based approach can help human resource practitioners to provide people in their organizations with focus and direction without restraining innovation and change. In an international organization effective use of competencies can allow the company to accommodate *and* to benefit from its local diversity.

Originally, the competence approach was derived from research commissioned in the 1970s by the American Management Association. The research – carried out by the US company McBer and its then chief executive Richard Boyatzis – set out to identify the personal characteristics which result in effective and/or superior performance within a job.

McBer's work sparked a continuing debate about the usefulness of the competence approach. Some of the key points in the current debate concern:[1]

- **The level of competence** (skill level versus underlying characteristics). Some competence approaches primarily value the measurement and definition of skills. Others primarily value the underlying characteristics which lead to demonstration of a particular behaviour. The international management competence framework, presented later, attempts to address both aspects.
- **The degree of competence** (effective versus superior performance). Some definitions of competence emphasize 'threshold' competencies – qualities that a person needs in order to do a job; others focus on underlying characteristics which differentiate superior performance from average and poor

performance. Again, the underlying characteristics described in the international competence framework are important for superior performance internationally.

- **The specificity of competence** (generic versus company-specific competencies). Some competence approaches concentrate on defining competencies for a particular organization; others attempt to define a generic set of competencies. The international competence framework is generic and intended to serve as a starting point for organizations in developing their own tailored approaches.

- **The durability of competence** (emerging versus maturing versus core, stable competencies). Some competencies may not be relevant now but will become more important in future. This competence framework recognizes both competencies that are enduring and those that are more changeable.

What are the strategic benefits and pitfalls of a competence-based approach to developing managers with international responsibilities? Some academics argue that competencies have proved to be a successful tool to create both horizontal and vertical integration of human resource policies and practices. On the vertical axis, it is possible to demonstrate their link to effective performance in line with business strategies. Horizontally, competencies also create consistency in human resource strategy and tools. In the international context, the competence approach can also help tackle the issue of internationalization of a company culture and its managers when combining consistency and integration across international operations with flexibility to accommodate and benefit from different local perspectives.

Some management development practitioners suggest that when aligned with business strategy and mutually strengthened by links to other human resource tools, management development is more effective through a competence approach. It is also argued that this is more easily achieved when a strategic focus exists within the organization, and a tailored, company-specific, rather than a generic competence approach is used.[2] Competence-based approaches can not only create a common language to talk about what effective performance consists of within an organization, but also have the potential to create more focused and accurate feedback. This overall transparency in what an organization expects from individual managers allows them to participate more actively in their own development.

Some of the worries with the competence approach concern a potential over-emphasis on job-person fit, rather than the overall effectiveness of the organization, leading to a myopic and mechanistic application of the model. The search for person-organization fit based on the values of the organization is another potential danger that can produce narrow behavioural engineering and cloning. It has also been suggested that organizations run the risk of concentrating on past or present competence profiles, without paying sufficient attention to the future.

There are also concerns about the transferability of competence frameworks and assessment techniques across different national contexts when competencies are behaviourally-anchored. The competence approach has been developed in the US and has been mostly used in Anglo-Saxon countries so there is a need to know more about its use in other cultural contexts. Certainly, rigid lists of competencies produced by the corporate centre are less likely to be transferable internationally than culturally-sensitive approaches that leave space for local interpretation.

A number of factors need to be taken into account when applying the approach specifically to the development of international managers.

Different types of international manager

An important part of any competence-based approach to international management development is to recognize that there are different types of international manager and competence. These may relate, at the organizational level, to the requirements of different international strategies or, at the individual level, to the needs of different management positions within an organization. Nancy Adler and her colleagues at McGill University in Canada suggest that companies move through different phases of international evolution and that each phase demands a different strategy and structure, different approaches to cultural interaction, and different kinds of international manager:[3]

1. **A domestic stance** in which the company operates primarily in its home market and is structured as a centralized hierarchy. Here, few managers (if any) are sent abroad, although export skills may be needed when the firm starts to go international.
2. **A multi-domestic phase** where the company has expanded internationally and each country in which it operates is managed separately within the decentralized hierarchy. Here, expatriate managers from the home country need country-specific skills for adapting culturally to a single country abroad.
3. **A multinational phase** where the company integrates domestic and foreign operations into worldwide lines of business but headquarters tightly controls major decisions worldwide through a centralized hierarchy. Here, international management roles are focused on top managers who are drawn from all parts of the worldwide organization and whose role is to integrate the company. Managers in the international cadre require a greater understanding of the world business environment and the cross-cultural skills needed to deal with a multiplicity of cultures. Cultural differences will be minimized by assimilating them into the dominant organizational culture.
4. **A transnational stage** where companies, structured as non-hierarchical 'networks of equals', are both globally integrated and locally responsive and depend on worldwide organizational learning. In companies of this kind the old distinctions between local and expatriate managers become obsolete because people from all over the world must constantly communicate and work with each other and consciously manage their cultural diversity. The overwhelming majority of managers have international responsibilities and

require the ability to move between local responsiveness and the global perspective. They need to be able to integrate worldwide diversity and create cultural synergy, collaboration and learning.

Models like this mean that a company should think about its current stance and whether it needs to shift its position. They do not mean that all firms should move as quickly as possible through the different phases; not all firms will aspire to a transnational stage. A company needs to consider the implications of its current and desired approaches to the international arena for the competencies needed by managers now and in the future. One drawback of Adler's model is that it does not highlight the co-existence in any organization operating internationally of different types of international manager to the limited types inherent in the model.

It is worth developing a practical overview of the international tasks and responsibilities that different managers actually fulfil. When, for example, Fiat, the Italian car manufacturer, set internationalization as a strategic business objective, it conducted a review of current roles and responsibilities in the company. It discovered that 40 per cent of the managerial jobs in the company dealt with international matters.[4] Fiat's human resource director said: 'We discovered a simple truth. At the beginning of the research, we thought that our international managers were the people that we sent abroad. But we found that the real problem of the international manager is not linked to the people sent abroad. It is the people who have to manage the international structure. The problem was not how to handle and care for the "foreign legion". The problem was here (in Italy). How international can our managers here be?'[5]

Fiat identified four types of management positions, each of which was exposed to the international business environment to a greater or lesser degree:

1. **Transnational positions:** operating over the whole geographic area covered by the business.
2. **Multinational positions:** operating in the context of several different countries.
3. **Open, local positions:** operating within the context of a single country, with significant links, reference points and dependence on elements outside the country (generally head office).
4. **Local positions:** operating within a single country, influenced by locally-determined variables, without significant interaction with other countries.

With these provisos about different types of international managers in mind, let us turn to an example of a competency framework focusing on the requirements of an increasingly significant type of international manager. The example also illustrates a fruitful methodology to determining relevant competencies.

An international competence model: the multi-country manager

One particular type of international manager is becoming increasingly prominent. With barriers down (witness the European Union, the North American

Free Trade Area, and moves towards free trade in South America), and with organizations trying new forms of international co-ordination and integration, the international manager is likely to be someone who can manage across a number of countries and cultures simultaneously, either globally or regionally.

To find out about the competencies needed by such key multi-country managers, Ashridge Management Research Group interviewed managers in companies as diverse as Asea Brown Boveri (ABB), Airbus Industrie, Barclays Bank, Cathay Pacific, Nokia Maillefer, Rohm & Haas, Skandia International, SKF and Tiphook.[6] All the managers interviewed had substantial experience of managing internationally, including working as expatriate managers. This meant that the study was able, not only to consider their current responsibilities as multi-country managers, but also to explore how they had developed their competence and what they had learned in working internationally that equipped them for their current jobs. It was felt to be important that many of the managers had worked in fast-moving and rapidly changing business environments as these are increasingly the conditions that international managers will encounter. Interviews with the managers focused on their past international experience including, in particular, critical learning experiences in different countries and cultures; on their current responsibilities; and on their aspirations and development needs for the future.

The findings of the study produced a view of international competence which includes both 'skills' and 'underlying characteristics'. Where appropriate, we illustrate the competencies with the words of the managers themselves. The findings offer a generic competence framework that firms can use as a starting point for developing their own tailored approaches.

'Doing' competencies

The interviews revealed three aspects to international management competence. The first involves active 'doing' competencies involving observable skills and knowledge bases and consisting of four main roles:

- championing international strategy;
- operating as cross-border coach and co-ordinator;
- acting as inter-cultural mediator and change agent;
- managing personal effectiveness for international business.

Champion of international strategy

As champions of international strategy, the challenge for international managers is to keep operations moving in the overall direction set by corporate strategy while dealing with the different and often conflicting priorities of local countries. They work with managers from other countries to envision the future and formulate strategies to take the organization forward. They set up forums for crafting strategy to draw upon the knowledge and expertise of local managers and to spread ownership of the international strategy.

International managers are responsible for keeping local units informed about the big picture and what is going on in other parts of the operation. In particular, in an age of accelerating product life cycles, a crucial task is to speed up business development where possible by exploiting and adapting learning between different countries and markets.

The international manager takes care to educate people at the corporate centre about international initiatives and to 'warm up' or secure the support of top management for those initiatives. Said one manager: 'You can spend 50 per cent of your effort convincing people to support you. It means that people in head office must be internationally-minded themselves. My international management starts at home because a lot of the initiative and a lot of the drive can only come from the support and compliance of head office.'

To underpin the role of international strategy champion, the international manager must remain globally aware. This means staying abreast of the world standard of competition and what it takes to match and beat it. It also means finding and learning from best practice in one's technical or professional specialism wherever it resides in the world.

Maintaining global awareness and implementing international strategy depends greatly on the manager's ability to build strong personal networks both internally and externally. Successful international managers are very active networkers and accept that effective networking depends on reciprocity.

Cross-border coach and co-ordinator

As cross-border coach and co-ordinators, international managers are increasingly working with local management teams. They collaborate as equals, encourage local managers to contribute their own ideas and help them to extract the learning from their experiences.

What such international managers want from local management is early warning of problems building up. But they also recognize that controlling local managers rigidly and penalizing failure can undermine strategy.

An open, collegiate coaching style of this sort is essential in managing the transnational matrix or network with which some firms are experimenting. The international manager has to rely on persuasion rather than formal authority and must help local managers to understand that they are complementing each other rather than competing. The task is to turn local managers into internationally-thinking managers who will look outside their own subsidiaries and understand that they are interdependent with the rest of the company.

At the same time as they are coaching local teams, the international manager will often be concerned with building teams within countries and across countries. Some companies, for example, are using international project teams as experiments in changing the organization by encouraging mutual understanding and collaboration between different parts of the organization.

Multicultural, dispersed teams meeting only at intervals often have problems in maintaining commitment and momentum. The international manager is particularly concerned to spend a lot of time at the beginning of the project building the team, surfacing assumptions that arise from cultural differences, and ensuring that every team member feels fully included and valued.

Intercultural mediator and change agent

Creating flexible yet cohesive international organizations involves considerable change and demands new ways of thinking and working. These may sometimes run counter to cultural norms in some countries, as recognized by an Italian manager in ABB's Italian operations: 'We Italians are very individualistic. But this can be a problem in a company like this. We have to learn to listen to other people's opinions.'

As intercultural mediators and change agents, international managers need to switch their frame of reference rapidly between different cultures. They must not only be aware of their own cultural underpinnings and of the need to be sensitive to cultural differences, but also manage change in different cultural contexts and push the boundaries and test the limits of different cultures. They must not assume, however, that approaches to change which work in one culture will work in another.

One manager pointed to the need to build on what already exists rather than trying to impose a totally different approach: 'As an international manager trying to introduce change, you must be aware of current reality in cultural terms and try to add on to it. You can't get them to do somersaults. If you are trying to introduce change, you have to get *them* to do it, and sit back and have faith in them.'

One of the biggest problems for the international manager is to dig below surface explanations to understand what is *really* happening locally. Some managers try to address this problem by cultivating a 'culture guide', perhaps a respected senior manager in the local unit, who can help interpret the situation.

In the past, companies have assumed that managers will acquire international skills merely by giving them international assignments. If change is to be a central component of the international manager's work, this alone may not be sufficient in the future. One UK manager with extensive international experience worried about a missing element in his development: 'My overseas experience has certainly made me more flexible and adaptable, but that has a downside. It means that one is prepared to take things as given rather than perhaps working to change them.'

Managing personal effectiveness for international business

A further critical competence is the individual's ability to manage his or her personal effectiveness for international business. Managing time is a vital issue for the international manager. A central fact of their lives is the large amount of time spent visiting the operations for which they are responsible. Although some firms are supplementing the telephone and the fax with other means of communication, such as videoconferencing, most managers still feel that there is no substitute for face-to-face communication with their local managers and teams.

Determining how much time to allocate to visiting operations abroad and how much time to spend at base is a difficult decision. Said one manager: 'If you travel half the number of days that you are working at home then that is too much because you exceed the point where, although it's good to have contact, you need time in the office afterwards because the follow-up is important.'

The international manager's job involves a great deal of travelling and a lot of stress. The average number of days that the interviewed managers spend away from their home base is about 120 per year. In other words, they spend a third of their lives away from home. This makes it very difficult to achieve a satisfactory balance between home and private life and the costs imposed on the family can be considerable. 'You never travel too much for the company and always too much for the family,' said one manager.

Another tension is that working at a distance from the scene of operations threatens the manager's sense of control over events. According to a British manager working for a Swedish company: 'What causes stress is that you can't spend the time to really go into things the way you would like to. Sometimes you want to get more involved than you can. The inability to influence certain things causes stress because you cannot go in there and do it yourself. You can only work through people. Sometimes you feel that life goes too slowly and that things are not happening in the way you would like them to.'

'Being' competencies

The job of the international manager is challenging and makes heavy demands on both the individual and the family. Nevertheless, many people clearly thrive on the challenges. From our research it became clear that successful international managers have a philosophy of life or 'being' that enables them to do so. This second aspect of international competence relates to the 'underlying characteristics' that facilitate the demonstration of skilled behaviours. It underpins the active side of the job and concerns the way that the manager thinks and reasons, the way they feel, and the beliefs and values that motivate them. It consists of three mutually sustaining parts: cognitive complexity, emotional energy, and psychological maturity.

Cognitive complexity

Cognitive complexity is the ability to see several dimensions in a situation rather than only one and to identify relationships and patterns between different dimensions. This is particularly important in the highly complex and fast-moving world of international management. In the international arena, managers need to be able to put aside their habitual assumptions and to enter into the minds of people who have different perspectives from their own.

This facility critically depends on the capacity for active listening. This is related to the insight provided by another study of international managers carried out by Indrei Ratiu: 'For the "most international", things are assumed to be not what they seem, and need to be constantly checked and re-checked against the new data'.[7] Psychological studies have found that cognitively complex people 'tend to search for diverse (not only confirmatory) information and are more sensitive to and more able to utilize minimal cues'.[8] As Ratiu notes, the emphasis of the 'least international' managers in his study was 'less on data collection and more on early explanations and rapid conclusions'.

Research at Ashridge Management College shows that among successful international managers, cognitive complexity is related to two additional features: a certain sense of humility and a degree of fluency in at least one other language. The first point may seem surprising, for such individuals may be perceived as having little to be humble about. One manager explained how it works in practice: 'Initially, I rely on local people to guide me. I'm not embarrassed about this, quite the contrary. I tell the local people: "Help me so that I don't make a mistake".'

This attitude contrasts strongly with the image of the arrogant international manager who imposes his or her way of doing things on each location.

Language fluency is significant for cognitive complexity because it can contribute to deeper cultural understanding and sensitivity. Furthermore, psycholinguistic studies have shown that individuals who speak more than one language are exposed to a number of alternative ways of seeing things. Ability to speak the local language means also that the international manager, in his or her attempt to understand what is going on locally, is able to engage with a wider range of people than just the local top team.

Learning the language presents an emotional challenge. One manager described his experience of trying to speak the language in Brazil: 'There was a period of months, nearly a year where I felt that I was stripped of my personality because I was not able to convey my personality along with my words. I was so intent upon simply trying to get a thought across, there was no personality to find... Language programmes alone do not prepare people for that feeling: the difficulty of learning to cope with feeling inadequate.'

If working in the local language can be painful, however, it can be that very 'stripping of personality' which facilitates the putting aside of habitual assumptions and the development of cognitive complexity.

Emotional energy

International managers need to bring a great deal of emotional energy to their work. They have often developed an emotional resilience that allows them to take interpersonal risks and deal with personally uncomfortable or stressful situations such as that described by the manager in Brazil. This resilience is often fostered through earlier career experience abroad.

The willingness and ability of international managers to express and reflect upon emotions appears to be an important distinguishing feature. As Indrei Ratiu found in his study, 'the ease and readiness with which they (the most international managers) can recall the stress symptoms indicative of culture shock contrasted with the other managers who claim never to have experienced culture shock or else refer to it only obliquely, and with discomfort.'

Psychological maturity

International managers have also developed a psychological maturity that depends on three core values. First, their strong curiosity to learn stays vibrant throughout their career. Second, they believe in living for the moment. This allows them to apply a great deal of psychological energy into unravelling the current complexity. This contrasts strongly with the 'backward looking' approach to making sense of a situation. This was found to be characteristic of less international managers who tend to perceive and use only data that confirms their previous conclusions.

Third, many successful international managers have also developed a strong personal morality. They believe in respect for all persons, regardless of nationality or race. They also believe in contributing to the wider organization rather than focusing on their own bottom line. This is particularly important in companies that are trying to implement transnational matrix or network structures. One Swedish manager in ABB said: 'I am paid to run my own local operation in ABB in Sweden, but I think I also have a mission to contribute knowledge so that we can improve the overall activity of ABB in my business area. There is not very much payback in my pocket for that; in fact, it probably takes money out of my pocket.'

Becoming international

How are the qualities described here to be fostered and developed in international managers? Exposure to different working contexts and cultures has been and continues to be an important route to internationalizing managers. Understanding how to develop the combination of the active 'doing' with the 'being' competencies in a career-long process of 'becoming international' remains a challenge. This approach concentrates primarily on the learning process of the manager and builds on the crucial moments in any individual's development where there is very high potential for transition in their 'being'. Looking back, individuals identify experiences, at or away from work, that enabled them to see themselves and the world in a different light. Individuals and their managers can design learning opportunities that enable such transitions to occur. These may include a new job (in particular, an international assignment); a secondment; membership of an international project team; or participation in a management programme.

Whether or not such a transition takes place may depend on the way the experience is facilitated. A key element in the learning process is often missing in the work and development experiences of managers: the need for reflection in order to understand and make better sense of an experience, draw out the learning and assimilate it in new behaviour. Successful international managers do not consign what others consider to be everyday episodes or interactions with other people to the wastepaper basket. Instead, they reflect on and glean as many lessons from them as possible.

Many managers, however, do not have or do not take the time or opportunity to extract the learning in an experience because they are constantly moving on from one activity to the next.[9] At worst, they experience 'superstitious' learning because they do not explore the various factors that impinge on a situation, and they draw conclusions without being challenged. A key challenge for management development, therefore, is to build opportunities for reflection into the work of managers, rather than creating additional 'activities' for them to experience. The opportunity to reflect in dialogue in 'learning relationships' is particularly valuable, whether it be through discussions with peers, coaches, or mentors, because they allow the manager to explore different interpretations of events and behaviours. We have already noted the way in which international managers seek out the help of 'culture guides' when working in new countries; they might apply this strategy to help them learn and reflect on a wider plane about their work.

Using a competence-based approach to international management development

Competence models can be useful starting points for thinking about the requirements for international managers, and can help human resource practitioners think about how they can contribute to developing international management competence. They can serve as a point of departure for the elaboration of company-specific profiles. As human resource specialists and line managers increasingly recognize, it is essential to take a business-driven approach that integrates management development with business strategy and other human resource management practices. The development of such a tailored approach involves a number of steps.

A first step is to identify the competencies required of the company's international managers. Some international companies, including Cadbury Schweppes and British Petroleum, have certainly used generic competence frameworks as a starting point. These companies have further developed and validated the frameworks through internal feedback processes such as focus groups in their international subsidiaries or research conducted in the organization by external experts.

If they decide to start a tailored competence approach, companies can initiate either small or large-scale internal research processes to identify the required competencies of their international managers. These consist of interviews using repertory grid techniques and/or 'critical incident' analysis, carried out with individuals or groups of stakeholders. Discussions with senior managers are particularly concerned with their views on future demands on managers. While external partners as objective investigators are certainly valuable, there are also advantages in getting managers themselves to identify the competencies and heighten their understanding of new development approaches that might arise.

Part of the process involves research into the different types of managerial roles with international responsibilities that exist in the organization. This provides a framework for the development needs of the different types of international managers within the organization. As Nancy Adler's work shows, competencies developed for the entire management population of an international organization can be further tailored to expatriates, multi-domestic, multinational or transnational managers, all requiring similar generic competencies as well as skills specific to their situation.

Having identified the required competencies, the next step is to assess individuals to determine their development needs. Typically, this involves career counselling interventions and development workshops which, to give managers ownership of their own assessments, are carried out in the spirit of self-assessment with the help of human resource professionals. They provide vehicles for needs analysis and also constitute a developmental experience for the managers concerned. The outcome of such interventions are action plans to guide the future development of the individuals.

Competencies can inform both the content and the design of management development activities and can help in their evaluation. In the international arena, in particular, experience-based approaches such as planned international assignments and international project teams can play an important developmental role. A survey by IOC-Ashridge shows that managers themselves feel that participation in international project teams is one of the most powerful development opportunities.[10] A competencies 'road map' can provide a useful framework for individuals trying to make sense of their experience and reflect on what they are learning by underpinning their experience and maximizing the support provided by 'culture guides', mentors, cross-cultural facilitators, coaches or peers.

Clearly communicating the competencies required of managers during experience-based, or formal, development activities enables the creation of an environment that favours self-managed learning. The ability to consciously take part in their own development, and to drive it, is an emerging competence of the international manager. In the future, in a constantly-changing international business environment, the ability to drive their own development process – the 'becoming' competence – will be one of the most important criteria for the successful international manager.

Kevin Barham and Claudia Heimer are research and development partners with the Ashridge International Institute for Organizational Change based at Archamps, France.

Kevin Barham is author and co-author of a number of books including *The Quest for the International Manager* (1990) and *Management Across Frontiers* (1992).

Further Reading

Boyatzis, RE, *The Competent Manager*, John Wiley, Chichester, 1982.

Mitrani, A, Dalziel, M and Fitt, D (eds), *Competency-Based Human Resource Management: Value-Driven Strategies for Recruitment, Development and Reward*, Kogan-Page, London, 1992.

References

1 The first three items can be seen in Hogg, B, Beard, D and Lee, G, 'Competences' in *Development Centres: Realizing the Potential of your Employees Through Assessment and Development*, (eds Lee, G, and Beard, D), McGraw Hill, Maidenhead, 1994. The fourth element is analyzed in Sparrow, PR, and Bognanno, M, 'Competency Requirement Forecasting: Issues for International Selection and Assessment', *International Journal of Selection and Assessment*, vol. 1 no. 1, January 1993.

2 Tovey, L, 'Competency assessment: a strategic approach - part one', *Executive development*, vol. 6, no. 5, 1993.

3 Adler, NJ and Bartholomew, S, 'Managing globally competent people', Academy of Management Executive, vol. 6, no. 3, 1992; and Adler, NJ and Ghadar, F, 'Strategic human resource management: a global perspective' in Pieper, R (ed.), *Human Resource Management: an International Comparison*, de Gruyter, Berlin, New York, 1990.

4 Auterio, E and Tesio, V, 'The internationalization of management in Fiat', *Journal of Management Development*, vol. 9. no. 6, 1990.

5 Barham, KA and Devine, M, *The Quest for the International Manager: A Survey of Global Human Resource Strategies*, Special Report no. 2098, Economist Intelligence Unit, London, 1990.

6 Barham, KA and Wills, S, *Management Across Frontiers*, Ashridge Management Research Group and Foundation for Management Education, 1992.

7 Ratiu, I, 'Thinking internationally: a comparison of how international executives learn', *International Studies of Management and Organization*, XIII (1-2), 1983.

8 Streufert, S and Nogami, GY, 'Cognitive style and complexity: implications for I/O psychology', in Cooper, CL and Robertson, I, (eds), *International Review of Industrial and Organizational Psychology*, John Wiley, Chichester, 1989.

9 Berthoin Antal, A and Gonin, D, 'Rethinking management: what the participants think', *EFMD Forum*, no. 2, 1992.

10 Barham, KA, Berthoin Antal, A and Heimer, C, *International Organizational Change in the 1990s*, IOC-Ashridge Discussion Paper, 1994.

TRAINING THE INTERNATIONAL MANAGER

Bruno Dufour

Identifying the attitudes and competencies essential to the international manager has exercised many minds over recent years. The lack of solid conclusions has implications for how and where managers can be trained to become truly international in outlook and practice.

Business schools have made strenuous attempts to bridge the gap between their teaching and best management practice. Yet, there still remains a need for a fundamental shift in emphasis in their approach – the future demands that managers possess a mastery of different cultures, broader industry awareness and entrepreneurial, rather than administrative, skills.

Military academies are supposed not only to train bureaucrats, but also active fighting leaders. In the same way, business schools should be expected to train not only administrators, but also entrepreneurs. Recent years have shown that business schools have become overly focused on technical skills and administration processes rather than on developing business people as entrepreneurs. The leading-edge qualification, Master of Business Administration, succinctly states the objective: administration. Even now, though some schools have been changing their curriculum, there is no such thing as a Master in Entrepreneurial Studies.

Criticism against business schools and MBA programmes is commonplace. Henry Mintzberg, for example, has widely criticized the disciplinary approach within MBA programmes. Parallels have also been drawn between the decline of American industry and the rise of MBA programmes and MBA-trained managers.

In 1992 a survey was carried out among over 50 chairman, chief executives, vice-presidents, directors and human resource managers in 35 international companies based in 14 European countries. Initiated by the European Round Table Working Group on Education and Groupe ESC Lyon, it provided an insight into how senior managers viewed the training and development needs of the future, and the ability of established providers to meet them.[1]

The managers advocated a truly international approach. 'At the moment I see an awful lot of narrow focus and nationalism in the teaching of business schools,' said Brian Goldthorp, director of personnel at Trafalgar House. 'In the future, I would not send any rising development executive to any institution that could not demonstrate to me that it had, first of all, a European focus, a European strategy and a European faculty. Beyond that, I want a world focus as well.'

The managers also called for greater emphasis on the human side of management and business. 'Teaching ...must include more of the social aspects of business and life,' said Justus Mische of Hoechst. 'We are getting very intelligent young people from the universities, but they don't know how to work in an important sector of research, which is incredibly complicated and specialized. They have difficulties in communicating inside the firm on an everyday basis. They are not trained in social techniques, in how to solve a problem with people who have a different point of view. If the universities and business schools do not develop them, then the companies have to.'

This point has recently been forced home by the international recession. In recessionary times managerial innovation was notably more characteristic of companies than of business schools. While business schools can be innovative when the environment is stable, their own 'time to market' is too long to be reactive enough to adapt to such turbulent situations.

In their efforts to become transdisciplinary, business schools are caught in a perpetual struggle with the prevailing academic culture. The entire profession is geared towards the development of tenured academic careers within precise fields, such as marketing or finance.

Today, companies no longer care about such disciplinary approaches. Instead, they are looking for managers with different sets of skills. They require problem-solvers, project managers, people with the 'soft-skills', doers more than thinkers. Importantly, companies demand entrepreneurial skills, rather than administrative ones.

As a result, MBA students are often regarded as overly-analytical and their discipline-based skills as irrelevant. Too often, they fail to master enough foreign languages or to come to terms with a variety of cultures. They are not at ease in multicultural settings and, frequently, they also lack knowledge and know-how about the use of new technologies and the development of productivity in management. Clearly, such a failure to meet the new needs of the marketplace means that the management education model is outmoded and needs to be totally revised and adapted.

Many institutions are attempting to be innovative in the ways by which they train the international managers of tomorrow. Through rigorous selection and high quality faculty, business schools succeed in supplying companies with *qualified* managers. But the cost of this training is high and increasing every year. It resembles *haute couture* prototyping rather than an industrial process.

Companies require that continuing education should not be discontinous. Continuing education should try to bring, at the right moment, at the right place, the right information to the right people. It should be just-in-time executive education; entrepreneurial, multicultural, anticipative and integrative, making full use of new approaches and the latest in information technologies. It should build up knowledge in a constructive way using accessible and navigable groupware.

To achieve this, to become proactive leaders, business schools should go through value analysis. Instead of teaching the same old courses in consumer goods marketing, corporate finance or basic accounting, business schools should try to be more efficient and integrate various disciplines from the beginning of the programme through a global approach. Subjects such as project management, management of technology, environmental management, and industrial goods marketing, demand integration so that students will be forced to get back to basics on their own – rather than sitting in a classroom listening to something they can find in text books and databases. Instead of simplifying issues through a discipline-based approach, managing and coming to terms with complexity has to become a day-to-day business.

In addition, graduate students should be exposed to research processes and methods. These can be supported by multimedia so that all the basic information required can be accessed through networks or with CD-ROMs or CDI. Basic courses could also be delivered in distance learning processes which cut the cost of traditional MBA programmes in saving the time and money of the first residential months of the MBA.

A normal executive education programme divides its cost into three equal parts: housing and accommodation; salaries and wages of the participants (or the equivalent in unpaid salaries for participants) and teaching costs. Using new technologies such as distance learning, multimedia and just-in-time open learning through networks, students and faculty can get together and share information and training. Students need to come to courses only when necessary – if they need interaction or direct contact with other participants, or if they need explanations for implementation or something from a group or an expert.

Behind such innovations must be an awareness that, in the sphere of international management, European management is based on a fundamentally different approach from American or Japanese management. The crucial element in this is diversity. The European Round Table/Groupe ESC Lyon research concluded that best practice in European organizations revolved around six characteristics:

- managing international diversity;
- leading as well as managing;
- fulfilling a broader social role;
- thinking long term;
- recognizing and using the benefits of Europeans' inherent individuality;
- combining a world outlook with global strategies.[2]

It identified the key skills of the Euromanager as:

- the capacity to change;
- an open mindset;
- the ability to learn from others, adapting their ways to your own situation;
- an entrepreneurial spirit;
- communication skills, including other languages.

The European model of management is based around a less formal economic model than those of the United States or Japan, and it is also characterized by the management of diversity. European cultures vary from country to country and Europeans are anxious to keep it that way.

In such an environment, managers have to master multicultural attitudes and different value systems. It is not just a question of knowing how to behave in a specific country. It is also a question of understanding the history, the religious values and specific conditions under which business has developed in each European country.

In Europe, management is increasingly becoming a cultural activity rather than a technical one.

In the same vein, companies are asking managers to know more about industry sectors and less about techniques. Most companies have established their own individual techniques and approaches to areas such as finance and marketing. They usually teach these techniques to new recruits within a matter of days. However, it takes a lot longer to understand the dynamics of each industry sector at a global level.

An approach based on cultural sensitivity, awareness and knowledge is, therefore, highly useful in coming to terms with the culture of a global industry, the specific culture of a national industry in the same sector and the specific culture of the company.

The key questions now faced by managers are no longer easily answered by business schools. These include: What is the competition? What are the technologies? What are the issues? What are the key factors for success? What decisions does the company have to make in order to become more competitive?

In response, business schools must totally re-design how they organize their faculty. Instead of going through marketing, finance, management and so on, faculty should be focused on specific sectors with an emphasis on using project managment to become truly transdisciplinary. Business schools could then be differentiated from each other by addressing specific industry sectors. This emphasis would be complimented by knowledge and awareness of the classical academic fields. Schools, in turn, could gain support from local entrepreneurs and companies to develop this specific approach. In doing so they would become closer to the local business environment (and be able to gain financial backing from the same sources).

The emphasis on the courses of these re-designed schools would be to give participants the opportunity to fully develop projects and to be involved in business start-ups. Entrepreneurial research and transdisciplinary studies would be encouraged. This would prompt faculty members to address issues in a different and non-traditional academic way.

In recent years business schools have dealt mostly with academic issues, constructing new knowledge, methods of research, and technical approaches. New content has been introduced onto courses – such as, environmental issues, ethics and global business. Recession has also forced them to deliver courses, such as starting new businesses, which are more relevant to the business community. But, it is difficult for academic bureaucracies to do what they teach: the implementation of change. Unfortunately, intelligence is frequently correlated to resistance to change and unless their very survival is on the agenda, very few institutions will joyfully re-engineer their academic organizations.

For those who lead business schools, achieving and implementing change requires a shift in emphasis. They have, for a long time, been defending faculty from external threats from university bureaucrats and others. In the near future they may have to do exactly the opposite and encourage faculty members to become more productive, to use new technologies, to dismantle what they have cherished for so long, to totally rethink their programmes. In such an atmosphere of turbulence the international managers of the future will be developed.

Bruno Dufour is director-general of Groupe ESC Lyon, the Lyon Graduate School of Business. He holds Master's degrees in business studies and economic psychology and was a fellow at the Creative Problem Solving Institute at Buffalo, New York. He was head of market research at the Coca-Cola Export Corporation in Paris until becoming a Professor at Groupe ESSEC. Since 1974 he has been managing director and co-founder of a textile group and became dean of Groupe ESC Lyon in 1982. In 1987 Dr Dufour became ESC's director-general.

References

[1] The results of the survey can be found in *Euromanagement*, Bloom, H, Calori, R and de Woot, P, Kogan Page, London, 1994.
[2] *Ibid.*

MANAGING THE GLOBAL COMPANY FROM THE CENTRE

Robin Buchanan and Richard Sands

Successful management of the global company from the centre requires a clear understanding of how the centre adds value to the local operations, and careful selection of the local markets in which the company is to compete. The centre can add value to local operations in many ways: by providing services; developing infrastructure; monitoring, controlling and challenging; realizing synergies; and allocating resources.

The best global companies clearly understand the needs of their local operations, and perform some or all of these roles to meet those needs exceptionally well.

Selecting the best markets is not easy. It requires the centre to evaluate the size of the opportunity each market represents, and the potential the centre has to add value to each market. The next difficult decision is the timing of entry. Too soon means high risks and a long wait for returns, too late means the opportunity will be gone. Finally, each market must have the right allocation of senior management attention. These resource allocation decisions need to be based on facts and informed judgement rather than emotional response.

The chief operating officer of GlobeCo has just landed at the city airport – it could be Budapest, Sao Paulo or Taipei – and is looking for the taxi to take him to his hotel. He's tired after a long flight (probably across several time zones), but knows he's going to have to spend several more hours at the hotel going through the strategic plan for the local market in preparation for the next day's meeting. He can't help wondering if he's wasting his time.

After all, with operations in more than 50 countries, he can't spend more than four days a year on each – not much to spot opportunities the local managers have missed. He can't keep up-to-date with local market conditions. He is overwhelmed by details of local laws and regulations and doesn't understand the language or much of the culture. In the strategic planning meeting he will have difficulty knowing if the answers he receives to his questions are true or false. Of course, the regional manager will be there, but she may feel closer to the locals than to GlobeCo head office. What's more she hasn't got the chief operating officer's detailed understanding of GlobeCo's overall objectives and constraints, so cannot be relied on to help him communicate the corporate viewpoint.

Given all these difficulties, how can the chief operating officer and his colleagues at GlobeCo head office add the most value to GlobeCo's local operations? To add value from the centre, managers based at head office need to make two fundamental decisions, and both must be made well if the centre is to add value.

The first decision is about role: in which ways can head office managers add value to the businesses? The second decision is about focus: upon which geographic markets should head office managers concentrate? The companies where head office managers add the most value are those where they have defined their role and focus in terms of a clearly-thought-out corporate strategy.

Corporate strategy for the global company[1]

Business unit strategy is about making a particular business the best in its industry. That is, producing superior returns to shareholders by outperforming competitors at serving customers, building capabilities and achieving economic performance. Corporate strategy, in contrast, is about being 'the best parent of the best businesses'. Many companies focus either on the role of the parent or on the selection of businesses, giving peripheral attention to the other side of the equation.

Having businesses with potentially strong competitive positions is vital: a group cannot be successful as the ideal owner of businesses with no development potential, any more than an expert surfer can succeed without waves to ride. At the same time, a group can destroy shareholder wealth if it owns high potential businesses, but intervenes inappropriately to make them underperform. In fact, the parent company must actually enable the businesses to achieve performance they could not achieve on their own *or with any other potential parent*.

For a multinational company competing in a single industry, this translates into two prerequisites for a successful corporate strategy. First, the head office managers have to understand the needs of the local businesses, and to ensure that they are in a better position to meet those needs than the head offices of other possible owners (ie, to ensure they are being the best parent).

Second, the head office managers have to understand which *local markets* offer the best potential for the development of *businesses* under their ownership. This second pre-requisite requires explanation. There are different ways for a business to be attractive. For example, a business may be attractive because it has a leading position in a very competitive (low return) market, or because it has a secondary position in a less competitive (high return) market. A company that has demonstrated the capability to operate successful businesses in some markets, and wishes to expand, will have to ask itself which markets to develop. Where are the margins attractive? Where is the growth potential? Where can the company's businesses establish leading positions? Answering these questions requires assessment of the attractiveness of local markets.

For companies operating in multiple industries, as well as multiple countries, the issues are the same but the decisions required are more complex. Consider Pirelli, the manufacturer of tyres and cables operating in markets around the world. Should Pirelli's priority be to develop its tyre businesses, its cables businesses, or both tyres and cables in, for example, Argentina? Are the needs of Pirelli's local operations for central support driven more by the businesses they are in or their locations? For the rest of this article we assume (for clarity) that we are dealing with a single business multi-geographic company, but acknowledge that this is an over-simplification.

Role: how management at the centre can add (or destroy) value

When asked, head office managers will list a number of different roles through which they add value to the businesses. For these roles to operate effectively they must match the businesses' needs. However, the match is often poor. If so, the head office may destroy value in the businesses it controls. It is a problem which local managers invariably recognize: 'Hello, I'm from head office and I'm here to help you,' is a joke that will draw a laugh, or an exasperated sigh, in almost any company.

The five most commonly listed roles for parental value addition are:

- providing services
- developing infrastructure
- monitoring, controlling and challenging
- realizing synergies
- allocating resources

Providing services

There are certain functions linking a global company to the outside world for which the centre must be responsible. Examples include, maintenance of the group shareholders' register and preparation of an annual report. Most corporate centres, however, provide far more services than these essential functions of a public limited company. Frequently, for example, the centre provides training, information technology and purchasing services.

The centre may decide to provide a particular service because it believes it can do so more cost effectively than the local operations themselves or third party suppliers. This may be right if the company's needs are unique and common to each market. However, a third party supplier stands or falls by its ability to provide a responsive and cost-effective service in its chosen field, and usually has far greater experience than an in-house department can provide. A third-party supplier is also less likely to be deflected by corporate politics. Hence, a company which centralizes services in-house will want to question if it really is 'beating the specialists', or if the delivery of the service is a mask for another value addition mechanism.

Whether or not the service is sub-contracted to a third party, someone within the company must be responsible for ensuring that high-quality cost-effective service is delivered. The local operations are the customers. Therefore, a reasonable starting point is that each country should be responsible for its own needs, using in-house departments or third party suppliers as it wishes. Transfer prices can be set to encourage the local operations to purchase in-house if this is in the collective interest.

Central management only needs to get involved if responsibility for managing an important service would be a major and unnecessary distraction for local management. In these circumstances, head office managers add value to the local operations by *providing services so that business managers can focus on business issues.*

Different companies will come to different conclusions about the central provision of services. For example, General Motors recently centralized purchasing to achieve economies of scale and to enable its local managers to concentrate on the critical issues of marketing, sales and distribution. In contrast, the Ladbroke Group recently decentralized purchasing to its businesses. Although purchasing is fundamental for both its hotel and retail businesses, but also the purchasing success factors for hotel and retail businesses are distinctly different.

Developing infrastructure

We are often told that the centre adds value by developing infrastructure (organization structures, policies and communication channels) within which the businesses are to work. On closer examination, it becomes apparent that this infrastructure is of three types:

- **Infrastructure within the businesses.** For example, Procter & Gamble has developed a systematic approach to new product development which must be used by all its businesses, and which helps those businesses outperform their competitors in this key function. Procter & Gamble's accumulated experience in product development has enabled it to identify do's and don'ts it knows will maximize the chances of a successful product launch. Individual businesses would take years to learn these through experience and so can avoid many mistakes by following the rules. When central management does this it adds value by *providing infrastructure so that business managers can learn from the companies' accumulated experience.*
- **Infrastructure linking the businesses to the centre.** This kind of infrastructure is a mechanism for the centre to monitor, control and challenge the businesses, and is discussed further below under monitoring and controlling.
- **Infrastructure linking the businesses to each other.** This kind of infrastructure is a mechanism for achieving synergies among the businesses, and is also discussed later under 'Realizing synergies'.

Monitoring, controlling and challenging

Many head office managers believe that they add considerable value by monitoring the performance of their businesses, intervening to rectify underperformance and pushing strong performers to do even better. However, for monitoring and control procedures to be effective two conditions must be met.

First, the monitoring criteria must be appropriate. The criteria must be few enough so as to be actionable but of sufficient number to be comprehensive. For example, if local managers are measured only on margins, they may raise prices even if the consequence is a large and inadvisable drop in sales. Hanson uses financial monitoring and control effectively because it has a tried and tested set of measures it knows are appropriate for slow-growing manufacturing businesses. If a Hanson business is failing to meet its targets, this is identified quickly and the centre can exert control. Hanson adds value *by providing controls when there is a need for direction.*

Second, the targeted performance levels must be appropriate. If the targeted levels are too low the businesses will underperform, and if they are too high the management of the businesses will give up. One approach which avoids some of the difficulties of setting targets is to maintain a constant push for improvements. Allen Sheppard's aggressive, you-can-do-better approach succeeds in raising the performance of Grand Met's businesses. This is a good example of the centre *providing challenge so that business unit managers are stretched.*

Realizing synergies

Many managers claim that the centre adds value by realizing synergies among the businesses owned. Managers should not, however, simply assume that because particular businesses have some common characteristics there must be synergies to be realized. In many cases, the costs of achieving synergies far outweigh the benefits. The centre thinks only about the direct costs of establishing systems to realize the synergies, and forgets other costs, such as consumption of scarce senior management time, loss of focus by the centre and feelings of disempowerment on the part of local managers.

Where the potential for synergies does exist, the most efficient way to realize them is often to provide the local managers with information and structures which make the synergies apparent to them, so that they realize the potential for themselves. Head office managers who do this are providing *information and structures so that business managers may exploit opportunities.* One of BAT Financial Services' roles is to create a dialogue between the managements of Eagle Star, Allied Dunbar and Farmers in order to realize synergies. On the other hand Harrisons & Crosfield has recently dissolved its divisional structure, recognizing that the opportunities for synergies between its varied agriculture businesses are few.

Allocating resources

Head office managers often assert that they add value by allocating resources among the local operations more effectively than anyone else would. Usually they are thinking of finance, human resources and, sometimes of other central assets, such as brand names and customer lists. If markets were perfect there would not be any such role for head office managers. Local operations would be able to raise finance themselves if their investment proposals merited it. They would headhunt employees from other operations within the Group and externally, so that each manager ended up in the place within the organization where he or she could add the most value.

Of course, most markets for people and finance are far from perfect, and there is a role for the centre in using its detailed understanding of its businesses to allocate resources more effectively. Internal resource allocation can also be much quicker than the external markets. Finding a suitable finance director for a new acquisition would take six months or more in external markets, and so companies like Hanson and BTR have internal cadres of professional managers they can move almost immediately to the areas where they are most needed. These companies add value by *providing privileged and rapid access to scarce resources.*

In practice: ABB and Unilever

Successful global companies will choose from among these five possible central roles those elements that will be most relevant to their own circumstances.

ABB and Unilever are examples of successful global companies whose head offices add substantial value to their local operations. ABB is one of the world's largest electro-technical companies, with 1993 revenues of about $28 billion. It employs more than 200,000 people in approximately 1,500 local companies. Unilever's 1993 revenues were almost $42 billion, spread across four business groups – food, detergents, personal products and speciality chemicals. Unilever has 294,000 employees in more than 60 countries around the world.

Corporate strategy insights
ABB and Unilever both have clear insights into how to add value to the businesses they own. ABB has recognized that through thoughtful structuring of its organization it can help its businesses achieve many of the benefits of centralized scale and decentralized market focus at the same time. ABB has also recognized that managers in engineering-dominated companies can be more motivated by engineering prowess than by profit. Such companies build up overheads and lose focus on profits, an imbalance ABB can help restore.

Unilever has identified the benefits of sharing product, marketing and technological information, ideas and skills across FMCG businesses in different product groups and different countries. In addition, Unilever has realized that independent FMCG businesses tend to under-invest in research and new product development, and that the parent has a role in ensuring that sufficient investment is made.

Implementing the insights

ABB and Unilever have developed skills and mechanisms which enable them to exploit their value creation insights into the businesses they own. ABB has a matrix of business areas and country managers which breaks the ABB businesses up into small, focused profit centres which consequently become closer to their results (these centres employ, on average, just 40 people). This is providing *challenge so that business unit managers are stretched.* The structure is, however, tight enough to retain the advantages of both national scale and global sharing of technical developments. This is *providing information so that business managers can exploit opportunities.* ABB also has particular expertise in integrating businesses into this structure. It knows how to realize the benefits of rationalizing production across countries, cross-selling products, sharing technical developments and transferring best practices. Between 1988 and 1991 it did this for 126 companies employing 100,000 staff. This is *providing services so that business managers can focus on business unit issues.*

Unilever achieves synergies between its businesses through an array of different mechanisms, including the transfer of managers among businesses, and small head office teams of highly experienced staff with a brief to facilitate co-ordination. This is *providing privileged access to resources* and *providing information so that business managers can exploit opportunities.* However, Unilever is careful not to impose co-ordination on the businesses which would reduce its ability to respond to local conditions. The company has developed central expertise in marketing and product development, but these services are also bought by, rather than imposed on, the businesses. This is *providing services so that business managers can focus on business unit issues.*

The mechanisms for interaction used by ABB and Unilever have evolved over many years and strike fine balances between centralization and decentralization, co-ordination and independence. Consequently, they are hard for other companies to duplicate. It is this that makes the competitive advantages of these companies sustainable.

Identifying the value added (or subtracted) by the centre

We have seen how the five head office roles to achieve value addition in businesses are open to misconception and misapplication, and are perhaps more complicated than at first sight. We now describe some analytical approaches which head office managers can use to identify the value added (or subtracted) by their own companies' centres, and arrive at a clear understanding of their options for head office role.

The value added by the centre can usually be identified by careful examination of three areas: The people at the centre; the organization (both formal and informal) linking the centre to the businesses; and the functions, services and resources the centre provides.

The people

Value added by the centre through its people can sometimes be traced to exceptional individuals, such as a brilliant product technologist or a visionary chief executive. Just as often, it stems from the head office team in aggregate, and the way this team approaches business issues, ie, the rules of thumb and models it employs to synthesize information and take decisions. The team's approach develops from the personalities, education and business experience of the head office managers.

Interviews are a vital source for understanding the people. Discussions with senior management should be the starting point, but the views expressed may reflect their desires rather than the actual situation. Others can often give further perspectives on the value added by these people. Middle managers (at the centre and in the businesses) will have different perspectives on what the senior team adds. Competitors' managers can (and often will) articulate what they most admire about their rivals. Customers, suppliers and advisers can give other external perspectives. Head-hunters can give particular insights if asked what types of people they would place in the centre, and why. For example, managers who are successful at Grand Met have to thrive on change, whatever their functional specialization.

The organization

A review of the organization should consider the formal structures and processes, as well as the way the organization operates in practice. The formal structure will highlight official responsibilities and reporting lines. Additionally, a review of budgeting, planning and other processes will identify how, in theory, decisions are made. Actual practice may be effectively identified by selecting important business decisions which the organization has to make, and then mapping out how the decisions are actually made through discussion with those involved. Such a process will also make explicit the boundaries of responsibility between the centre and the local operations, and will often highlight possible efficiencies.

A thorough understanding of such organizational issues may have a dramatic impact on a company's performance. For example, Bain & Company performed this analysis with one branded goods manufacturer to find out where product development responsibility really lay. The review showed 13 different departments participating in the decision, and suggested specific process simplifications. Implementing these simplifications enabled development lead times to be cut from 18 to 6 months.

The functions and services

The functions and services provided by the centre can be listed and analyzed. It is, however, important to get beneath the functional titles to understand what exactly the people in the functions are doing and for whom they are doing it. Auditors devoted to assessing compliance with controls are adding value in a different way from auditors focused on due diligence for acquisitions. Strategic planners who see their prime customer as the chief executive are very different from those dedicated to serving the local operations. The simplest way to get at this information is to ask each function's managers to list their main activities, the 'customers' for those activities, and the time spent on each activity.

The emerging themes from reviewing the people, organization and functions can be confirmed by examining past successes and failures (eg, new operations that worked – and those that failed). Are these 'case studies' consistent with the emerging impression of how the centre adds value? If not, either the roles for value addition have changed, or some part of the analysis is suggesting a misleading conclusion.

The BrandCo case

The BrandCo case study illustrates how the members of the senior management team may have completely different perceptions of their role and head office value addition, even when they have built their careers within the same industry. If an analysis of head office role enables the managers to understand each others' perspectives, debate can move on from questions of role to implementation.

BrandCo is a branded consumer goods company with manufacturing and sales operations worldwide. Bain & Company was engaged by BrandCo to examine the role of the corporate centre and its relationship with the operations in each country.

The senior staff at the corporate centre included long-serving employees formerly from local operations, others who had joined the group through acquisition, and other, mainly functional, specialists who had joined individually. In a series of interviews, we asked each of these members of the senior management team to articulate how the centre added value to the businesses.

The long-serving employees were traditional and somewhat paternalistic, arguing that the centre added value by 'protecting the heritage of long-established brand names' (in other words, that the value of the centre lay in preventing rapid change). Many of the managers who had joined through acquisition focused on corporate development, claiming the centre added most value by deal-making to enhance the global network. The functional specialists stressed processes, and claimed that the centre was adding value to the businesses by giving them effective brand and financial management systems. This analysis showed that there was no consensus among senior managers on the value added by the centre.

The organization reflected these different perspectives on the centre's addition of value. Geographic reporting lines and functional reporting lines were both strong. There were no clear rules for resolving conflicts between the functions and the countries. For example, a proposal to relaunch a product would shuttle backwards and forwards between the marketing director and the country managers for the product's key markets, without agreement ever being reached.

In addition, the centre was providing services which were not wanted by the country managers. For example, the central marketing function saw itself as co-ordinating brand advertising between markets, while the country managers wanted local flexibility.

Attempts to resolve organizational issues were all failing, in part because there was no agreement on the centre's role. Highlighting the different opinions on this issue enabled them to be debated and a new value addition mission for the centre was agreed. This resulted in the beginning of an effective process for organizational change.

Focus: on which local markets should management concentrate?

Having determined fruitful roles, global companies must determine which markets offer the most promising conditions for business development. This brings us to the second fundamental decision, the issue of management's focus.

Decisions about the role of head office need to go hand-in-hand with decisions about the types of businesses upon which the company will focus. Consider ABB and Unilever once more. ABB concentrates on engineering intensive electro-technical businesses where there is potential to create linkages across national borders. These are the businesses it understands well and to which it can apply its value creation insights. These businesses are not all high growth, but they all have the capacity to improve profitability under ABB's control.

Unilever has identified three product groups requiring similar marketing and product development skills, and a thorough understanding of fat technology. A company such as ABB would destroy considerable value in Unilever's businesses – ABB understands industrial and public sector customers rather than retailers and consumers, and would be inclined to reduce rather than increase product development expenditure in the businesses. Of course, Unilever would be an equally dreadful parent for ABB's businesses.

As well as being clear which *businesses* they are going to participate in, ABB and Unilever are clear about which *markets* are attractive to them. In recent years, ABB has made substantial investments in Eastern Europe, identifying many former state-owned enterprises to which its centre can add considerable value. Unilever has different organizational structures for businesses in mature and developing markets. These structures recognize the different success factors in the respective markets. In mature markets, its businesses are based around product groups, acknowledging the primary importance of brand and product development. In developing markets, Unilever has a geographical structure (spanning all product groups) which enables it to take a co-ordinated approach to the critical issues of distribution and relations with local governments.

Selection of local markets

In the single business multi-geographic company, having the best businesses is all about competing successfully in the most attractive markets (where a market is considered attractive if it offers high returns to many competitors *or* the potential to secure a leading position with above-average returns).

An examination of the historic expansion of a multinational business into new markets often reveals one of two patterns of expansion: The first is gradual geographic expansion, conquering a market, then its neighbours, then their neighbours, along the lines of a Roman Legion on the march. The second is not so much a pattern as an apparently random series of market entries dotted around the globe. There is a logic to each of these approaches, but in both cases it is incomplete.

The logic of the 'Roman Legion' approach is that neighbouring markets are likely to share costs and customer characteristics. For example, establishing a manufacturing base in Germany builds German language capability. This can be used to sell into Austria and Switzerland. These markets can then be served with minimal distribution cost, utilizing surplus production from the German factory.

The problem is that geographic proximity is no guarantee of either similarity of market characteristics or size of opportunity. Austria and Switzerland may be easy to serve from Germany, but is the potential market in either of them large enough to justify the increased requirement for senior management time? In other parts of the world, geographic proximity can give minimal indication of market similarity: Japan, China and Korea are neighbouring markets, but fundamentally different in terms of size, opportunity, infrastructure, language and culture. Global strategies based on the triad of geographic markets – America, Europe and Asia – are fundamentally flawed if they overlook these kinds of differences.

The 'random' approach is essentially opportunistic, and is favoured by companies that prefer to grow through acquisition rather than organically. Its logic is that markets should be entered when (and only when) there is an opportunity to secure high short-term returns or a strategically strong position. However, companies that follow opportunistic acquisition strategies may miss the biggest growth opportunities. For example, Foster's Brewing achieved instant market share in the UK by buying Courage, but Anheuser-Busch's decision to establish a joint venture in China may be a much better long-term investment.

Ranking

An approach that we have seen work particularly well is to have a clear list of priority markets to develop, based on factors such as growth potential, cost of entry, opportunity to secure leadership, synergy with the existing network and similarity of management challenge. Centres are good at managing particular types of market as well as particular types of business. For example, Paterson

Zochonis earns attractive returns in the highly competitive soaps and detergents industry by concentrating on developing markets such as Nigeria, Poland and Indonesia.

A company which has a list of priority markets has advantages over companies following either the Roman Legion or opportunistic ('random') approaches. It has a clearer overall plan for expansion, and it can use its list of priorities to evaluate and respond quickly to acquisition opportunities.

Timing

Identifying a particular new market as attractive does not necessarily mean it should be entered now. A decision needs to be made about the timing of market entry. It can be a difficult decision, particularly in emerging markets where there is uncertainty about market development. When managers debate entry into markets, such as Russia and China, they typically fall into three camps:

- The sceptic: *'The political risks and economic instability make it crazy to go in.'*

- The enthusiast: *'The potential returns are enormous: we have to be there first.'*

- The pragmatist: *'We should watch and wait.'*

All three are essentially emotional responses to a question on which the decision should instead be based on fact. In reality, management needs to decide whether there are early mover advantages which justify the additional risks. Will the company lose access to raw materials or distribution channels if it delays? Are entry barriers increasing? Is there a steep learning curve which will give early entrants an unassailable lead? What can be done to minimize the risks of entry and generate early returns? For example, can a strategy be based on a low level of initial investment, progressively ramped up as market uncertainties are resolved? A fact-based assessment is as important in emerging markets as established markets.

The next section sets out one approach that can be used to arrive at such a fact-based assessment of market priorities.

Evaluating market attractiveness

When examining the attractiveness of a business to the company, it is often helpful to split the business's potential contribution into three parts. First, the profits the business is capable of generating on its own and without additional investment. Second, the additional profit that could be generated through acquisition. Third, the additional profit that could be realized through the influence of the corporate centre.

To estimate the first part of the profits, local managers can be asked to prepare growth forecasts for their local markets and development plans for their businesses within those markets. These plans can be subject to constraints on the amount of capital and other resources to be reinvested, and can be based on an assumption of no change in the level of services received or other interaction with the centre. A central review of these forecasts can ensure that they are equally challenging and a reasonable basis for comparison between the businesses.

For the second part, the centre can lift the capital constraints, and allow the businesses to say what else they would do if they were allowed to make major investments or acquisitions. The businesses may well need help to identify acquisition candidates, assess their availability and estimate their price. The centre itself can take responsibility for assessing acquisition and investment opportunities for new markets.

To estimate the third part the centre can think through the value it adds in each of the markets. What more could the centre do to improve the local businesses' performance? What impact would this have? This information, combined with the growth potential including acquisitions, can be used to identify the total value to the centre for each business. The centre can similarly think through the value of each of its businesses to rivals, and identify those markets where it could realize more value through disposal.

By this stage a number of options are likely to be emerging. Some operations will be clear development candidates, others certain for closure or disposal. A decision needs to be made on how to set priorities among the rest, and this can be very difficult because of the number of factors to be taken into account. The following approach is effective in ranking options:

1. Ask head office management to put to one side opinions about the business and markets, and to list its corporate financial objectives and constraints. These objectives and constraints are then used to build a financial model for evaluating options.
2. Ask head office management to forget the financial constraints, and to describe all the options it can visualize for the development of the group.
3. Evaluate each of the options using the financial model with representative acquisitions and investments, and assess the fit with the financial constraints. Critical constraints will be identified and preferred options will emerge.
4. Refine the remaining options, challenging critical constraints (can they be avoided?) and gradually eliminate options until consensus is reached on the strategy to be followed.

The WatchCo case

The following WatchCo case study illustrates how this process can work for a company facing severe management, as opposed to financial, constraints. It shows that selecting the best markets in which to compete can be difficult, even if the value added by the centre is well understood. Care must be taken to ensure assessments of market potential are consistent. Once the best (long-term) markets have been identified, resource constraints may limit the company's options to develop businesses in each of those markets.

WatchCo produces watches, jewellery and other branded accessories which are sold in numerous markets around the world. With the opening up of Eastern Europe and new markets in the Far East, WatchCo could see new opportunities everywhere, but recognized it could not take advantage of all of them. It did not believe it had a sufficiently strong group of country and regional managers to keep all the markets under control, and wanted to know upon which it should focus.

Regional and country managers were asked to prepare five-year forecasts of WatchCo's cash and profit potential in each of 70 markets and potential markets around the world. The forecasts were collated and reviewed centrally to ensure comparability. Many were unrealistic in that they included over-optimistic assumptions of market growth, but were insufficiently challenging in terms of increased sales, market share and margins. Several rounds of reviews were required to bring these forecasts onto a realistic and consistently stretching level.

Next an assessment was made of the difficulty of achieving the full potential in each market. Twenty factors were taken into account, including:

- current competitive position (market share);
- existing degree of control over distribution;
- brand image and awareness;
- complexity of the product portfolio;
- degree and complexity of regulation.

The financial forecast and assessment of management challenge were combined to produce a measure of return on management resources committed for each market. This highlighted the fact that senior management was devoting too much time and attention to large, mature markets. Not only did these markets have low growth potential, but also they were more predictable and their country managers were experienced enough to cope with the problems likely to arise. As a result, WatchCo's senior team directed significantly more of its attention to emerging markets, and is realizing the benefits.

Postscript: The local strategic plan

GlobeCo's long suffering chief operating officer was somewhat taken aback when the local management team concluded the presentation of their annual strategic plan with a chart listing five requests:

- tell us how to plan our advertising campaign;
- help us buy the media we need to launch it;
- tell us where our margins are too low;
- tell us which products are selling best in other markets;
- help us find an engineer who understands our plant.

Was that really all they needed? Perhaps his job wasn't so difficult after all.

Robin Buchanan is the managing partner of the London office of Bain & Company, the international strategy consulting firm. He was previously the head of Bain's Acquisitions and Alliances practice and has had more than 12 years' experience of advising multibusiness and multinational firms on corporate strategy and organization. He is currently writing a book with Lord Sheppard and other Bain colleagues on adding value from the centre.

Richard Sands is a manager in the Warsaw office of Bain & Company and a senior member of the firm's international strategy practice. He has substantial experience in helping clients develop and implement corporate strategy and organizational change, and a special interest in the challenges faced by firms entering the emerging markets of Eastern Europe.

Further Reading

Bartlett, C, and Ghoshal, S, *Managing Across Borders*, Century Business, London, 1989

Goold, M, Campbell, A and Alexander, M, *Corporate-Level Strategy: Creating Value in the Multi-business Company*, John Wiley, Chichester, 1994.

Reference

[1] This section and the following one build on research conducted by the Ashridge Strategic Management Centre, London, and published in the book *Corporate-level strategy; creating value in the multi-business company*. The ABB and Unilever examples are also drawn from that book. We acknowledge our debt to the authors.

MANAGING THE GLOBAL COMPANY

Paul Evans

The process of internationalization has accelerated throughout in the twentieth century. Now, in the mid-1990s, it has reached breakneck speed.

In Britain, Holland and Germany, European firms such as Unilever and Philips, were the first multinational corporations, investing capital outside their limited home markets in the late nineteenth century. Most US firms focused on the immense national market with limited export operations until the opportunity to transfer their expertise pulled them abroad in the 1960s. Japanese firms became multinational in this sense of direct foreign investment only in the 1980s.

The pace of change has been fuelled during the last 30 years with increasing free trade; the decline of national barriers (symbolized by the 1992 European open market and NAFTA); the emergence of newly industrialized countries bringing new market opportunities and competition; and the liberalization of regulated sectors. During the last ten years, the talk has increasingly been of globalization. But from a management perspective, what does globalization imply?

Globalization has led to new competitive pressures, affecting firms that may only be national in the scope of their operations. This adds up to the need to do things better, cheaper and faster. A competitor that can offer goods or services of higher quality, at lower cost, and with the latest technology, can rapidly steal market share.

Conventional management wisdom has been rendered obsolete within a decade. Michael Porter, the strategy guru from Harvard Business School, pioneered the concepts of *Competitive Strategy* in 1980. One of his central ideas was that strategy means a choice on how to compete. Porter's research, grounded in sound historical data, suggested that winning firms made one of two strategic choices.

One choice is market differentiation, competing on the basis of value added to customers (quality, service, differentiation) so that customers will pay a premium to cover higher costs. The other choice is cost-based leadership, offering products or services at the lowest cost. Quality and service are not unimportant, but the strategy of cost reduction provides focus to the organization. Porter's data showed that firms with a clear strategy, either market differentiation or cost leadership, performed better than those which did not have a clear strategy or those which tried to do both.

The trouble was that these observations were already becoming outmoded by events. Some firms were finding ways of organizing themselves so as to offer products or services better *and* cheaper. The Japanese automobile industry, in its competition with American and European firms, is a case in point. With the opening of trade barriers, these firms were free to export and even set up shop abroad, eroding the market shares of established firms. Survival in hyper-competitive industries, such as microcomputers, had become a question of organizing oneself to do things better *and* cheaper *and* faster as well. In this industry, a delay of one month in time-to-market can mean the loss of $100 million of revenues with fixed development costs. Within a decade, what was once regarded as conventional strategic reasoning had become a recipe for corporate suicide.

The evolution during the last decade at Royal Dutch/Shell is an example. Ten years ago, Shell's strategic value was Quality. The corporation did not pretend to be the lowest cost producer of petrochemical products. Instead, it represented reliability, professionalism, safety, value added to customers, and everything that quality implied. But, with low oil prices and increasing competition, those values changed during the mid-late 1980s to Quality at Low Cost. At the same time as Shell initiated a new TQM drive throughout the world, headcount came down from 130,000 to 114,000 people and will continue to decrease, while revenues increase. In the spring of 1994, the strategic values were notched up one step further. Flexibility was announced as the new driver. Better, cheaper, and more responsive to change.

The studies of Christopher Bartlett from Harvard and Sumantra Ghoshal from INSEAD, examined in their book *Managing Across Borders*, showed that multinational corporations from different regions of the world have different management heritages, each with a distinctive source of competitive advantage. The strength of the *multinational* or multidomestic firm is local responsiveness. It is a decentralized federation of local firms linked together by a web of personal controls (expatriates from the mother firm who occupy key positions abroad). Many European firms such as Unilever and Philips embody this model. The *global* firm is typified by US corporations such as Ford earlier this century and Japanese enterprises such as Matsushita, and its strengths are scale efficiencies and cost advantages. Global scale facilities, often centralized in the mother country, produce standardized products, while overseas operations are considered as delivery pipelines to tap into global market opportunities. There is tight control of strategic decisions, resources and information by the global hub. The *international* firm is the third type. Its competitive strength is its ability to transfer knowledge and expertise to overseas environments that are less advanced. It is a co-ordinated federation of local firms, controlled by sophisticated management systems and corporate staffs. The attitude of the parent company tends to be parochial, fostered by the superior know-how at the centre. This is the heritage of many American and some European firms, such as the Swedish telecommunications supplier, Ericsson.

Bartlett and Ghoshal argue that global competition is forcing many of these firms to shift to a fourth model, which they call the *transnational*. This firm has to combine local responsiveness with global efficiency and must have the ability to transfer know-how – better, cheaper, and faster. Thus, Ericsson reorganized in 1990 to provide more power to lead countries, cutting out management levels and reducing staff so as to reduce costs and bureaucracy, regrouping business units, and placing more emphasis on technology development.

The transnational firm is a network of specialized or differentiated units, with attention paid to managing integrative linkages between local firms as well as with the centre. The subsidiary becomes a distinctive asset rather than simply an arm of the parent company. Manufacturing and technology development are located wherever it makes sense, but there is an explicit focus on leveraging local know-how in order to exploit worldwide opportunities.

The matrix management dilemma

How can the transnational firm organize itself so as to compete in this 'better-cheaper-faster' world? Traditional concepts of management – line and staff, the chain of command, vertical hierarchy, conventional management control – have all been questioned. Rather than enabling organizations to rise to the new challenges, they appear to handicap performance.

These challenges come to a head in the matrix management dilemma. When sales outside the mother country are small, an export department or international division can handle these activities. But when international sales reach a certain size, the firm has to set up subsidiaries abroad which gradually build up their own local manufacturing, marketing and development facilities. The firm finds itself with an array of geographic subsidiaries, product divisions, and functions. How can it co-ordinate and control this array when it comes under competitive pressure to be cost-effective and responsive?

The response in the 1970s was that of matrix organization. Its origins lay in the US Space Program of the previous decade where the challenge was to meet President Kennedy's target of putting man on the moon by 1970. This demanded incredibly complex project co-ordination, while meeting Congressional cost constraints. The term *matrix organization* was supposedly coined by mathematically-trained engineers to describe this evolution in project management. Matrix organization, the only new form of organization in the twentieth century, can be seen as a diamond with three roles: the top manager who heads and balances dual chains of command; two or more matrix bosses (eg, product and regional managers) who share subordinates, and the individuals who report to two different matrix bosses on a straight-line or dotted-line basis.

By the early 1980s, many corporations had become disillusioned by matrix. Management observers like Tom Peters commented that matrix structures are so complex that they just do not work. They are afflicted with problems such as power struggles, ambiguity over resource allocation, passing the buck and abdication of responsibility, the cost of support processes and meetings, and frustratingly slow decision making. Many organizations abandoned matrix to revert to business-driven structures with clear accountability, and even once stalwart enthusiasts such as Citibank, Dow Chemicals, and most recently Digital Equipment, have returned to simple structures. Academics were at pains to point out that dual structures must be supported by matrixed processes, such as joint goal-setting, dual evaluation and rewards systems, matrix leadership behaviour and individual skills. Their advice was that one should not touch matrix unless there is no other alternative. However, even though ultimate accountability may clearly lie with product divisions, most multinational corporations retain some matrix features. And a recently created corporation, ABB, is built on matrix responsibilities.

In spite of such insights, matrix-type pressures have increased rather than decreased, especially in hyper-competitive global industries such as telecommunications, computers, and pharmaceuticals. Alongside the need for clear accountability with business units are pressures to be close to local governments and markets, where service levels and distribution channels may be important for product differentiation. Customer segments need to be managed by account managers, whose responsibilities cut across geographic and product boundaries. Cost pressures often argue the need for centralizing functions, such as manufacturing or information technology, on a regional or worldwide level. Cost pressures also argue for spinning off component manufacturing and other services to outside companies, but the necessity to speed up time-to-market argues for close relationships with manufacturers such as those practised for decades by Marks & Spencer (known as 'a manufacturer without factories'). Best practice and the lessons of success or failure need to be rapidly transferred from one subsidiary to another.

Today, the precept is to keep the structure clear and as simple as possible, minimizing the number of straight and dotted line matrix relationships – for example, locating profit and loss responsibility clearly with business division managers – while building the matrix into the minds of key leaders and their relationships. Operationally, this means that no one should be appointed to a major business unit responsibility unless they have proven themselves in a country position beforehand.

This is a lesson that companies such as AT&T and Eastman Kodak learnt when they decentralized their organizations, giving P&L responsibility to divisions and business unit managers. 'There was nothing wrong with our aim of giving clear accountability to business managers,' said a senior Kodak executive. 'Handicapped earlier by a slow-moving, functionally driven organization with regional subsidiaries, we gave the responsibility to talented and ambitious business managers. However, most of them had no geographic experience outside the United States. And in so doing, we neutered the regional side of the matrix. The pendulum swung too far, and now we are trying to get the balance right. This means ensuring that senior business managers have international experience, and that senior regional managers have product line experience.'

The lesson behind this is that structure is only one form of integration. Structure is the formal and hierarchic technology of management. But there is another complementary management technology, that of informal or horizontal integration – the network technology of teams, project groups, informal co-ordination mechanisms, relationships, and influence over attitudes and values. Corporations are paying much more attention to these informal types of co-ordination, which can be thought of as *glue technology*.

Once again, Shell is an example. In terms of profits, Shell in 1994 is the largest corporation in the world, the only remaining member of what used to be an exclusive group of corporations known as 'the five billion dollar club'. But for the last 40 years, its basic organizational principle has been decentralization – in Shell's jargon, local autonomy to the 300 operating companies that constitute the formal structure of the group. This is even incorporated in the name of the corporation, 'the Royal Dutch/Shell Group of Companies'. However, the flip side of autonomy is that Shell pays a great deal of attention to what it calls 'cohesion management'. As Lo Van Wachem, former chairman of the Group, would say, there are three things that hold the companies tightly together. The first is the strategic values symbolized by the pecten logo, as mentioned earlier. The second is rigorous attention to performance evaluation of companies. In earlier times, this meant financial control. Performance was evaluated on the basis of the same financial systems so that there is equity in this process. However, recognizing that financial systems lead to short-term measures of success, Shell has been attempting to broaden its concept of performance evaluation to include broader 'balanced scorecard' measures.

The third source of cohesion, and the deepest, is management development. The soft side of this is training. Decentralization implies paying rigorous attention at the centre to technical standards, and to the creation of a management network via selective central training. The aim is to create a situation where 'you always have a friend in Uruguay'. If some important matter is on your desk concerning that country, you remember a friend from a seminar whom you can call. But the deepest source of cohesion, according to Van Wachem, is the career mobility that creates the matrix in the mind. Prior to assuming any post of significant leadership responsibility, key executives should have job experience on different sides of the matrix.

Shell has a matrix organization at the level of its senior management, 25 group vice-presidents, known as co-ordinators, responsible for business areas such as oil exploration and marketing, geographic areas and country operating companies, and management functions such as finance, IT, and human resources. This is supported by sizeable staff support groups, but it is cohesion technology that makes it work.

Glue technology

There are three elements to this glue technology of global management – building face-to-face relationships, project management, and career/mobility management.

Face-to-face relationships are the basic element, recognizing the common-sense fact that things get done through people who know each other. If people do not know each other, there is no alternative but to forget about co-ordination or to refer matters up the formal hierarchy. The tools to build these line-to-line relations that take over from the staff bureaucracy are company conferences, annual 'jamborees', regional or worldwide functional meetings, exchange seminars, workshops between two companies after a merger, or central training programmes. While there may be some informational or educational input at these meetings, the main objective is to build necessary relationships. Appropriately designed, they can develop the interpersonal networks that are fundamental to the functioning of the transnational enterprise.

For example, a few years ago, INSEAD's Euro-Asia Centre was asked by the chairman of a group of companies headquartered in Southeast Asia to develop a seminar for selected executives, tailored to various strategic and organizational priorities. On the final evening of the two-week programme, the chairman flew in for the traditional closing speech, where he said: 'I look forward to hearing your recommendations and proposals, which I hope this meeting has generated. But I want you to know the main reason why I asked you to attend this special programme – I sent you here to get drunk with each other!'

You can imagine the reaction of the seminar faculty at the back of the room. Afterwards, they discussed this with him, concluding that he was a shrewd businessman. He explained: 'The reason why I commissioned this programme was that I have so many detailed problems on my desk that I can't do my job – I can't see the wood for the trees. And the reason why I have these problems is that Mr Goh in Singapore isn't collaborating with Mr Williams in London, and Dr Muller from business area X isn't working with Mr Ismail in business area Y.' He had personalized these problems in terms of key executives who had to collaborate, and then he had decided to lock them up together for two weeks, both to build personal relations (and there may be some truth that inebriation facilitates the breakdown of barriers) and to develop a common sense of problems and opportunities.

Similarly, the president of a newly formed European corporation, resulting from the merger of a British and French company, invested seriously in building relationships in the new top management team. Its members were flown into the middle of the Arabian desert and given one week to find their way to Riyadh – an extended outward bound exercise! Following this, this team spent a week in the luxury of a Riyadh hotel successfully constructing the strategy for the new company.

The second element in glue technology is *project management*, managing external opportunities or internal problems via teams drawn from across the formal structure. More than 20 per cent of ABB's business comes from projects which cut across the formal structure. While these are managed by a small group at its Zurich headquarters, the resources for such teams lie with the businesses. As in many other companies, development projects that used to be run by central staff departments now draw upon people from the operating business units of the firm.

This has an important implication for the changing role of the manager. The line-staff distinction that has held sway for most of this century becomes obsolete. It has its origins in Frederick Taylor's scientific management, separating the planning of work (staff) from its execution (line). But in a complex global corporation, this leads to a bureaucracy that handicaps responding to pressures to do things better, cheaper, and faster. Staff departments were the first to be cut back in the wave of downsizing and decentralization that started in the 1980s. However, the sheer amount of planning and development work has increased, not decreased. This project work is now built into the line manager's role, which becomes matrixed. The traditional 'managerial' part of the job is operational, the department or unit for which one is accountable. But what used to constitute 98–100 per cent of the job now has to be managed in, say, 60 per cent of one's time. The other part of the job, taking, say, 40 per cent of the time and more associated with leadership, is the project role that once was assumed by staff managers. This involves working on external development projects, internal improvement projects, and project teams that cut across the formal structure. Freeing up the time for this project role requires greater delegation of operational responsibilities or empowerment, a related aspect of this changing role.

Staff roles change rather than disappear. The role of the staff manager changes from that of analyst or problem-solver to that of a network leader, someone with few direct resources but with the credibility to call the shots and command the attention of line managers. The role of country managers must also change. Instead of being kings or queens of their territories, their role becomes a more complex job of making this new project-oriented organization function. Few companies have been successful in converting traditional country managers into these new roles, which typically require changes in staffing.

There is a substantial learning curve in developing project management capacities. Over-ambition is a frequent trap, setting up too many project groups that overstretch the capacity of the organization. If working on project groups becomes synonymous with wasting time, line managers learn to avoid them. Most project groups are highly dependent on the resources of a few technical and managerial leaders, and this means paying close attention to staffing, staffing them for success and not just with the available people (who are rarely the right people). New sets of skills are needed: defining clear goals and breaking a project down into operational sequences, as well as skill in working with cross-functional and cross-cultural teams.

This may go further in terms of matrixing dual or multiple responsibilities into the same job – a product manager within a particular country may also assume the role as country manager. The human resource manager for one country may have regional responsibility for management development. A particular country may be responsible as a centre of competence for information technology in the region, or for a project to enter emerging markets in Asia or Eastern Europe. The organization is less linked to physical location, and key decisions may be made by teams who meet at airport offices or hotels, leading to what is known in some sectors as 'virtual organization'. In hyper-competitive environments the life cycles of business units become so short that it is more appropriate to consider them as projects rather than allowing them to become institutionalized.

Alternatively, the management decision-making structure may be organized around development and marketing stages rather than having one single structure. Thus at the development stage of a new product, decisions are reached by a management committee under the leadership of a divisional manager that consists of senior R&D executives, a manufacturing executive, with occasional attendance by product managers from lead countries, and regional managers. When the product moves to worldwide commercialization, the management team changes. Regional managers assume the leadership, with a team drawn from lead and other countries, with business unit and development managers attending when required.

Project management, especially where the organization is becoming more akin to a series of projects than to a stable structure, raises new management challenges. How do we measure the performance of people with dual project and operational roles, and how do we reward people for both local and global performance? How can the job-evaluation system be changed so that salaries are more linked to competencies than to jobs? How do we persuade strong local business or country managers to release talented people for important projects? What are the leadership competencies that are necessary to function in this way, and how can we best develop them? How can we manage the careers of people who are assigned full time to important transnational projects, including the shock of re-entry when they go back into a traditional operational role?

Career and mobility management is the third element of glue technology. People are products of their own experiences. If their prior experience is narrow, exclusively within a single functional area and a single country, then they are unlikely to be able to function well in this matrixed environment. The careful management of experience builds the matrix into the attitudes and competencies of leaders.

Take, for example, two functions, such as manufacturing operations and marketing. With distinct operating cultures, these require their separate functional identities. Yet, they must collaborate closely and resolve frequent conflicts. Traditionally, this meant substantial hierarchical centralization (reporting structures, central staff, planning and control systems). The cumbersome hierarchic apparatus can, over time, be lightened by introducing an explicit career path rule: no senior executive in either function can hold that office unless he or she has proven him or herself in a previous line job in the other function.

Sticking to this rule leads to a number of desirable outcomes. First, it ensures that senior functional executives not only have the necessary depth of experience within their own function but also that they acquire the needed leadership perspective (they have to prove themselves in a managerial job where they have no expertise, where their only resource is their leadership competence). Second, this fosters the network of relationships accompanied by trust via which difficult problems get resolved. Third, it ensures that senior managers acquire perspective, knowing how their own function is viewed from the outside. And fourth, this affects behaviours lower down in the firm. Ambitious young managers learn that they must take people in the other function seriously, and their interest in interfunctional training and projects is boosted. They realize that if they undermine their counterparts in the other function, this will catch up on them when they are in their rotational job, damaging their career prospects. Over time, this builds the matrix into the culture.

Such career pathing is used by firms, including Dupont and Unilever, to ensure that managers have breadth of perspective. Honda in Japan provides some interesting examples. Research, engineering and manufacturing have until recently been autonomous companies at Honda, with research as the *primus inter parus*. But they are linked by a variety of subtle career norms. For example, the implicit norm is that the president of research will become the president of Honda. This signals the importance of research to the other companies. It also ensures that research collaborates closely with engineering and manufacturing – otherwise the future president will inherit problems of his own making!

Shell, Hewlett Packard and Unilever ideally want to have local managers running local businesses. But none of these companies would entrust a local with a leadership responsibility unless that person has proven him or herself in a headquarter or regional staff role, and ideally also in a management post in a country that has to collaborate closely with their own national subsidiary. The perspectives of the person would otherwise be narrow. Co-ordination with other centres and adopting the higher level corporate perspective would not be a priority for the individual. Mechanisms such as cross-functional training and project work may serve to broaden perspectives, but the necessary *depth* of broad perspective is fostered through such mobility experiences.

Mobility is also useful, indeed vital, to transfer learning and best practice from one part of the firm to another. Exchange on best practice may be helpful, but what gives the confidence to put the innovation into action is often the presence of a champion who has done it before. Mobility also develops the network, the nervous system of a firm that facilitates responsiveness. The soft signals and information on competitive moves, technological shifts and the like are transmitted through the network of relationships, rather like the proverbial grapevine.

There is little in business which confers substantial competitive advantage that comes easily. Relationships, project management know-how, and career development take time before the benefits materialize. Typically, companies require a three- to five-year investment before they begin to see the payoff. Perhaps, not surprisingly, many executives prefer to use the heavy tools of structure and systems to resolve these matrix management dilemmas, swinging the pendulum in one reorganization after another from centralization to decentralization, from simple to complex structures and back, from privileging the country managers to privileging the business managers.

Gaius Petronius, Roman Governor and adviser to Nero in AD 65, put it well: 'We trained hard... every time we began forming up into teams, we would be reorganized. I was to learn later in life that we tend to meet any new situation by reorganizing... and a wonderful method it can be for creating the illusion of progress while producing inefficiency and demoralization.'

Paul Evans is Professor of Organizational Behaviour at INSEAD.

Further Reading

Barham, K and Oates, D, *The International Manager*, Pitman, London, 1992.

THE EVOLUTION OF MERGERS AND ACQUISITIONS IN EUROPE

Didier Pène

The frequency and value of mergers and acquisitions (M&As) suggests that their commercial and strategic justification is unquestionably accepted. In the era of globalization, cross-border M&As appear to offer a direct route to greater internationalization. Even after the M&A boom of the 1980s, activity remains high – in the first half of 1994 over 600 European companies made acquisitions outside their home countries.

However, research and experience continually point to mixed results – financially and organizationally – from M&As. On paper and in theory M&As often appear to offer synergies and opportunities for growth, but the reality is that companies are often sold off, or anticipated returns do not emerge.

Mergers and acquisitions have been a fact of corporate life since the second industrial revolution of the nineteenth century. Since the 1960s, however, the popularity of mergers and acquisitions has grown substantially.

In the United States, the most active country in this field, the valuation of transactions has grown from $43.6 billion in 1968 to $340[1] in 1988. This represents a multiplication of more than 2.5 (in constant 1972 dollars) over this period. In Europe, the number of mergers and acquisitions recorded by the European Community grew from 480 in 1984–1985 to 1,122 in 1988–1989.[2] In France, along with the UK, one of the most active European countries, the value of mergers and acquisitions has increased from 10 billion francs in 1981 to 65.5 billion in 1985[3] and 147 billion francs in 1990. These figures apply only to acquisitions in foreign countries.

Despite their profusion in the 1980s the M&A market is highly cyclical. In the United States, for example, their number fell from 4,462 in 1968 to 2,106 in 1978. The value of the transactions was divided by more than five (in constant 1972 dollars) between 1968 and 1974, dropping from $52.8 billion to $9.4 billion before rising again to around $130 billion in 1988, dropping to less than $30 billion in 1991 and rising, yet again, since.[4]

In Europe too, after a sharp increase in the 1960s and a decrease in the 1970s, a new wave of M&As emerged in the 1980s, before slowing down after 1990 and rising again over recent years in countries which recovered first from recession.

In general, long-term growth in M&As has mirrored the pace of growth of the GNP of individual countries. The second general trend is that mergers and acquisitions activity follows cycles of economic activity and even seems to amplify them.

Despite this clear cyclical pattern, the major question must be whether the financial, economic, and strategic aspects of M&As have changed since the 1960s? Paradoxically, there is evidence of continuity in activity over this period. Even so, the differing corporate environment of the 1990s has had a demonstrable effect on the evolution of M&As.

Although this article concentrates on analysis of mergers and acquisitions in Europe, trends and activities in the US cannot be ignored – the US often provides the impulse for change in this activity as in many others, and it remains a highly active partner in European M&As.

The rationale behind M&As

The reasons used by companies to explain their desire for external rather than organizational growth haven't changed a great deal over time. Most frequently, they cite a desire for synergy or diversification. Synergy includes the search for critical size, increased marketshare and so on.

Diversification doesn't simply include the search for reduced risk through the combination of cyclical and countercyclical activities, but also moving into new promising activities, preparing a progressive move from a mature field to a more dynamic one, testing and learning new jobs, and so on.

There are always aggressive M&As where a company tries to increase sales or/and marketshare and defensive ones, where a company merges or buys in order to face strong competition or to prevent a competitor buying the target company. In addition, there are always mergers and acquisitions aimed at concentrating on core business.

Generally, external growth aimed at increasing market share, reaching a critical size, diversifying into new fields, testing new products or new technologies, and at learning new jobs, takes place more often in periods of economic growth. Concentrating on core business and divesting occurs more often in periods where economic activity slows down.

Another stable characteristic of the M&A market is the doubt often expressed about the financial benefits of external growth for shareholders, especially from the purchasing company.

Modern financial theory teaches that the optimal portfolio strategy with respect to equity is to buy the market index. The reasoning behind is that the market portfolio provides the highest possible return for a given risk and the lowest risk for a given return.

To hold this market portfolio should allow the optimum combination of return and risk. Even a mutual fund invested in many companies is considered an imperfect portfolio and, in the long-term, should perform worse than the reference index.

A company having developed through external growth, and with a limited number of firms, is an even more imperfect portfolio and should, on average, perform even less well than mutual funds invested in shares.

Most studies in this field show that, with respect to return and risk, the market portfolio usually out-performs mutual funds and that mutual funds beat conglomerates.

Academic studies throughout the world repeatedly show that buyers don't generally receive a significant financial return from external growth. The financial benefits of M&A remain open to basic questions.

These studies typically look at the *ex ante* market reaction to the announcement of a merger. These take the expected costs and benefits of the merger or acquisition into account. In this respect, an acquisition is financially interesting if it earns a return higher than the normal one which one could get without external growth.

Usually it is the shareholders of acquired companies who emerge as the big winners. In the United States, on average they receive a 20 per cent premium in a friendly merger and a 35 per cent premium in a hostile takeover.[5] Elsewhere, the results are similar.[6]

While the motives of sellers can be readily understood, studies don't explain why so many buyers devote large amounts of time and effort to M&As when the financial results are often negligible or non-existent.

Ex post studies made by leading consulting firms like McKinsey are generally even more pessimistic. These studies look at the success or failure of merger programmes after their completion. Twenty-one years ago, a study analyzed M&As in Europe during the 'merger wave' of the sixties, between 1965 and 1970.[7] The sample included 407 European companies which had been involved in M&As. The survey asked the chief executives what were the initial objectives of the merger. A few years later, at a time when one would think the merger or acquisition should have reached these objectives, the same executives were asked if the expected results had materialized. Whether the acquirer of a company was American, European in its home country or the acquisition was made by a European company in another European country, the results were disappointing. Around half of acquisitions were considered by acquirers as successes, and half as failures or partial failures. So, the strategies developed by competent managers intended to achieve external growth failed to provide better results than sheer chance.

More recently, McKinsey studied 116 acquisition programmes made between 1972 and 1983 taken either from the *Fortune 200* largest US industrials or the *Financial Times* top 150 UK industrial companies.[8] It judged a programme to be successful if it earned its capital cost. In other words, income after taxes as a percentage of equity invested in the acquisition programme had to exceed the acquirer's equity cost of capital.

The results were even more disappointing than those of the first study: 61 per cent of the acquisitions ended in failure; only 23 per cent in success.

More positively, the probability of success can be improved when the buyer acquires a smaller company in a related business and when its core business is particularly strong.

Most studies are pessimistic, although some are more optimistic about the *ex post* results of M&As. But, generally, the optimistic ones study small samples, cover periods which are too short to provide general lessons on their results or take market values as proxies for accounting ones. Clear, or credible, conclusions are few.[9]

The chances of success appear small and the macroeconomic function of M&A in making the business world more efficient is elusive. But it is also true, that in spite of the failures, many M&As actually succeed. Optimism may be a necessary characteristic of buyers. Their purpose often appears to be negative – they want to avoid performing badly rather than using M&A to perform better.

While these characteristics – and mysteries – of M&A remain consistent, many other aspects of M&A have evolved rapidly since the 1960s. The main one is that the end of the seventies and the eighties brought about what has been labelled the third industrial revolution.[10] The reasons for this revolution are manifold. One can mention the conversion of formerly centrally-planned communist economies to capitalism which brought about the end of the cold war; the end of 'colonial' wars like Vietnam and the ten-fold increase in energy prices from 1973 to 1979.

But, the main reason is probably the fact that the causes of rapid growth in the 'old' industrial countries during and after the second world war progressively ceased to operate. Roads, housing, private and office buildings, railroad, air transportation, hotels, tourism, television, telephone and so on were developed and aspirations fulfilled. Most basic durable goods which were developed after the world war, like cars, television, home equipment, air planes, and so on, reached their maturity. The improvements in the standard of living slowed down the consumption's growth rate. The birth rate also started to decline.

During this period, productivity was volume-based and built around fast increasing demand. But, the third industrial revolution relies less on volume and more on productivity improvement based on cost reduction. Changes in demand caused an excess capacity to occur in many industries like steel, tyres, cars, computers, and so on. The search for cost-reducing productivity put even more emphasis on technology and added to the capacity-expanding technological change an obsolescence-creating one.

This evolution favoured a large movement of liberalization, deregulation and privatization in Europe, as well as in the United States. Companies tried to find other markets around the world, this precipitated the globalization of trade and brought with it new customers and new competitors.

Many companies hit by these changes didn't have many choices other than bankruptcy, or important changes in organizational practices, including downsizing or mergers and acquisitions. Fortunately, capital markets and financial institutions provided a response to the need for M&As. In the US, 35,000

M&A transactions occurred between 1976 and 1990 with a staggering total value of $2.6 trillion in 1992 dollars.

In Europe the number of transactions reached similar levels, with Europe catching up the United States at the end of the period. For instance, in 1989, 1,314 transactions occurred in Europe and 2,599 in the world.[11] Even so, on average the value of transactions remains higher in the US.

The third industrial revolution has brought internationalization, a vital element in the modern M&A field. In the 1960s, acquiring a company in a foreign European country was not straightforward. The Common Market was in its infancy and currency controls were applied in many countries. Economic nationalism was still strong and national administrations protected national companies from undesired foreign takeovers with general efficiency.

The 1980s saw a fundamental change. The decision made in 1985 to create a single European market in January 1993 was taken seriously by the business world and many companies quickly sought to prepare themselves. The number of M&As between companies from different European countries grew from 99 in 1984/1985 to 250 in 1987/1988.[12] And, from 1984 to 1988, the percentage of transactions inside the same European country decreased from 65.2 per cent to 55 per cent, while the percentage between different European countries grew from 20.6 per cent to 24.4 per cent.

But, the increase of international mergers and acquisitions in Europe didn't mean the development of a European fortress. From 1984 to 1988 the percentage of M&As between companies located in the Common Market and outside increased from 14.2 per cent to 20 per cent. The US was by far the most important partner outside the Common Market. Between 1983 and 1987, UK and Dutch companies acquired more companies in the US than in the Common Market, while France and Germany bought slightly more in the Common Market than in the US. In the M&A field, the US is really part of Europe.

During the same period, from 1984 and 1989, the golden age for M&As in Europe, internationalization didn't develop at the same pace in every country. While British, French and Danish companies acquired more than they sold; the reverse was true for companies in Germany, Italy, Spain and Portugal. Even so, large companies have now largely outgrown national boundaries. There are now few large companies which could proclaim themselves to be simply French, German, British or Dutch.

Over the period from 1984 to 1989, most M&A activity occurred in industry, but M&As in the service businesses grew at a faster rate. The need for restructuring occurred first in industry after the oil crisis, while services like banking and insurance were not as severely hit and remained under national regulations. The new Common Market rules related to deregulation in banking and insurance pushed many companies to look for M&As in other European countries at the end of the 1980s. While recession at the beginning of the 1990s slowed down this wave of international M&A, it didn't bring it to a halt.

The second significant development in the European M&A field, also caused by the third industrial revolution, is that external growth is increasingly a continual process of buying and selling companies or parts of companies. Twenty years ago, acquiring a company was an important and rare decision. A company was motivated by a desire to grow its business. Usually a larger company acquired a smaller one without any intention of selling it. M&As were vehicles for external growth. The emphasis was on the purchasing side of the process; selling was not implied. Indeed, acquisitions were supposed to last and to divest was considered a sign of failure.

'Companies will generally not divest... a successful business except in a comparatively few special cases,' observed Michael Porter in 1987.[13] Analysing the histories of a sample of 33 large diversified US companies between 1950 and 1986, he continued, 'companies divested many of the entries in our sample within five years, a reflection of disappointment with performance'. He even added, 'most of them had divested many more acquisitions than they had kept. The corporate strategies of most companies have dissipated instead of created shareholder value'.

This dissipation which Porter identified in the US spread to Europe in the second half of the 1980s. For example, Pinault-Printemps in France completely changed its core business in a relatively short time – from timber to specialized retailing and department stores – through acquisitions, financing its acquisitions with debt and the sale of former acquisitions.

Similarly, Bolloré sold subsidiaries in power distribution, ships and other fields acquired only a few years previously. There are many other companies, such as Crédit Lyonnais, Fiat and Air France, which are now selling large parts of what they proudly acquired in the eighties. There are, in fact, hundreds of European companies engaged in selling businesses considered as sound strategic investments a short time ago.

In many cases, the ceaseless process of buying and selling can be attributed to poor management. Companies appear seldom to be able to resist the opportunity to acquire a company if the conditions appear favourable, even if it doesn't always fit in with its official strategies and objectives.

But, as there are no reasons to think that today's business people are less competent than their predecessors and as exceptional opportunities don't materialize every day, there must be other reasons to explain all this activity.

One cause is probably that the economy has become more cyclical. While the number and the value of transactions seems to decrease with recession, it is likely that companies with aggressively acquisitive strategies during growth periods increase the probability of being obliged to sell when the cycle turns down.

It is also likely that the increasing rhythm of economic change, the opening of more and more countries and increasing deregulation, make business strategies unstable. New competitors emerge, substitutes abound, suppliers change, customers' tastes develop, production technology and so on move faster and oblige many companies to speedily change their strategies if they want to survive. This may motivate them to acquire and sell in order to develop their new strategy. If keeping still is the route to oblivion, then M&As are a means of appearing to be continually on the move.

Increased flexibility and speed is mirrored in M&As. Companies have to move fast to sell subsidiaries or divisions whose outlooks no longer seem so bright and to seize opportunities to make acquisitions in industries which unexpectedly appear more attractive.

Adding fuel to this process has been the evolution of the banking system, particularly in continental Europe. The deregulation of the financial system means that individual banks which get into trouble will not automatically be saved by a national bank. They are, as a result, less willing to take risks. In practice this means that companies often have to find their own sources of finance. This often involves the sale of subsidiaries and divisions. Such sales may also reduce debt and make banks and financial markets readier to provide assistance. This is all very well, but while banks and financial markets provide help when companies are doing well, they are less so inclined when companies experience a crisis and genuinely require assistance.

The new emphasis is on flexibility. Multibusiness companies are dividing themselves into business units, stand-alone businesses, which can be sold off. In order to manage and maximize value – the course recommended by consulting firms – companies have to be completely flexible, ready to sell and buy almost everything at every moment. To make possible divestiture easier, identifying the cash-flow of individual business units is not enough. Instead, one has to determine business-units tax rates, capital structure and even the cost of capital. The consequence is that companies structured on this basis can be considered as the sum of autonomous businesses.

The permanent process of acquisitions and sales of businesses is now much easier because of the financing instruments developed during the 1980s. Junk bonds made many acquisitions possible – the cost of issuing junk bonds was less than that of raising equity. Similarly, the development of mezzanine debt – a high-interest form of financing between debt and equity – provided many opportunities.

The use of equity or quasi-equity without voting rights makes acquisitions possible without, or with only limited, dilution of control. Leveraged buy-outs, including every kind of senior and junior debt and secured by the target company's assets, make acquisitions possible almost without equity. A good example of this kind of financing is the 1988 leveraged management buy-out of UK company Bricom. In this case, equity with voting rights represented scarcely more than one per cent of the acquisition.

This kind of financing enables acquisitions without money and also helps small companies to take over larger ones. Although risky, such financing continues to be used – though with more caution than was evident at the end of the eighties.

It is also notable that investment banks are increasingly active in finding buyers of possible divestments and sellers for possible acquirers. They are now armed with data banks and sophisticated information systems which let them know, for example, that a subsidiary or division belonging at the moment to a group which needs cash or is modifying its strategy would be more efficiently managed by another which can buy it.

Back to the future

Many companies remain set on M&A strategies. There is a trend, however, back to more traditional M&A strategies:

- **concentrating on core businesses:** Sanofi recently sold its businesses in bio-industries and others in perfumes, like Jacques Bogart and Stendahl, to finance the acquisition of Sterling Winthrop so that it could become stronger in drugs and health products.
- **increasing market share:** Companies are intent, for example, on broadening the scope of their operations in Europe or elsewhere – the British hotel group Forte bought Air France's Meridien Hotels in order to increase its market share in Continental Europe.
- **financing investments in new industries:** Increasingly companies are using M&As, alliances and joint ventures to enter new areas, such as multimedia, in order to, if possible, gain some control on prices. TCI, Time Warner, ATT, Mitsushita, IBM, Sony, Motorola, and so on have already done so in the US and Japan. European companies like Philips, Bertelsman, Canal Plus, France Telecom and Deutsche Telekom are among others attempting to do the same.

But, borderlines between traditional M&As and permanent acquisitions and sales are flexible. Sanofi, for example, grew mostly through acquisitions and developed three branches, drugs, bio-industries and beauty products. In 1994 it decided to concentrate on drugs and health products. This represented a fundamental change in strategy – it was only in 1993 that Sanofi acquired the beauty products company Yves Saint-Laurent. Its change in direction was a matter of seizing the opportunity – Eastman Kodak was in a a hurry to sell Sterling Winthrop. Companies were sold to finance the acquisition of Sterling Winthrop, as Sanofi's mother company, Elf-Aquitaine didn't want to help its subsidiary financially.

Decisions are no longer clear cut, nor can they be assumed to be long-term. Many factors now work in favour of a more active acquiring-selling approach than long-term strategic thinking. So, weighing up what to buy and sell occupies executive minds to a far greater degree and far longer time than was previsouly the case.

An interesting aspect of this evolution is that it brings the behaviour of companies closer to that of the financial markets. Theorists of the financial markets who consider a company as a sum of investment projects, tend not to like M&As, whose financial interest for shareholders doesn't seem obvious.

By splitting companies into business units, pushing firms to buy and sell continuously, transferring as many activities as possible to subcontractors, companies are seeking the sort of flexibility found in financial markets where parts of companies, in the form of shares and bonds, can be bought and sold at any moment.

This evolution may have been caused by the strengthening of the relationship between the financial markets and industrial and service companies, which has occurred over the last 15 years. But, the timing of the 'real' economy which has to take into account preparation, decision making, communication, time to convince, transportation, negotiation, working up, and so on, cannot be the same as the instantaneous world of the financial markets. But, the more flexible companies are, the more able they are to apply the recommendations of the market.

The nature of the power in these fundamental relationships is continuously shifting. While financial theory considers groups as imperfect portfolios, financial markets exert pressure on companies in order to make them closer to flexible, better and acceptable portfolios.

Will this trend go further or reach a limit because the changes demanded of companies and managers are excessive? The answer is not obvious.

Didier Pène is Professor of Finance at HEC Group in France. He has written many articles on financial management, companies' evaluation and mergers and acquisitions. He is the author of *Evaluation en regroupements d'entreprises* (1979) and *Evaluation and prise de contrôle d'entreprise* (second edition, 1993). Educated at the Sorbonne, the Institut d'Etudes Politigues de Paris and Stanford Business School, he is also a consultant to a number of major companies.

Further Reading

Jenkinson, T and Mayer, C, *Hostile Takeovers*, McGraw Hill, Maidenhead, 1994

References

1 Copeland, T, Koller, T and Murrin, J, *Valuation: measuring and managing value*, John Wiley, New York, 1990; and Jensen, M, 'The modern industrial revolution, exit and the failure of internal control systems', *The Journal of Finance*, July 1993.
2 Club Finance Internationale, 'Les restructurations en Europe; les operations de Rapprochement Trans-Européennes, actualisation des faits', HEC, 1991.
3 Pène, D, 'Arbitrage entre croissance interne et externe en France', *Revue d'economie Financière*, no. 5/6, 117, June-September 1988.
4 Copeland, T, Koller, T and Murrin, J, *Valuation: measuring and managing value*, John Wiley, New York, 1990; and Jensen, M, 'The modern industrial revolution, exit and the failure of internal control systems', *The Journal of Finance*, July 1993
5 Copeland, T, Koller, T and Murrin, J, *op cit*, p. 315.
6 Husson, Bruno, 1987, La Prise de Contrôle d'Entreprise, PUF, Paris, 53–72.
7 Kitching, J, *Acquisitions in Europe*, Business International SA, Genève, 1973.
8 Copeland, T, Koller, T and Murrin, J, *op cit*, p. 318.
9 Healy, P, Palepu, K and Ruback, RS, 'Does Corporate Performance improve after Merger?', *Journal of Financial Economics*, vol. 31, no. 2, April 1992.
10 Jensen, M, 'The Modern Industrial Revolution', *op cit*.
11 Club Finance Internationale, 'Les operations de Rapprochement Trans-Européennes', HEC, 1990.
12 Pène, D, 'Les Prises de Participation et de Contrôle en Europe', unpublished, 1991.
13 Porter, M, 'From Competitive Advantage to Corporate Strategy', *Harvard Business Review*, May–June 1987.

INTERNATIONAL JOINT VENTURES

Peter Lorange

If mergers and acquisitions were the strategic mantra of the 1980s, international strategic alliances and joint ventures are the strategic call of the 1990s. These forms of co-operative effort have become an integral part of modern business strategy.

Yet, the rationales behind them seem to be shifting. Also, as they become more established, the issue of how they can be developed and evolved is emerging – as is how to exit from an international joint venture. Only by having a realistic exit as a potential option can a company's values be protected and strategic flexibility gained. The final key issue facing such partnerships is how to safeguard sensitive core competencies while still fully co-operating with a partner.

Purposes of international strategic alliances

The traditional purposes for forming international strategic alliances stemmed from various forms of resource constraints among one, or several, of the co-operating entities. For instance, there might be a problem with finding financial resources to pursue a certain strategic direction; a partner would then be called in to help underwrite the effort. Typically, such alliances might occur when a particular company has an interesting technological opportunity, but lacks the funds to take it further. A second type of classical international strategic alliance is concerned with access into certain countries. In many parts of the world, it has been difficult for foreign companies to enter the market. It takes resources, willingness to take political risk and time to develop a meaningful presence in such markets. One solution is to bring in a local partner. Sometimes this partner may not play much of an active role beyond legitimizing the activities of the joint venture in its home country. At other times, however, the true expertise of a local partner might be very helpful. Even though the world is becoming more open to business, with protectionist moves decreasing, this type of international strategic alliance remains prominent.

While the rationale for the above-mentioned type of strategic alliance is clear, it should not be denied that if the initiating actors had free choice, irrespective of resources or other constraints, they would in most cases prefer to go it alone. As such, joint ventures have often been branded as a second best option. This sense of scepticism tends to be further strengthened when operational problems occur in the alliance. Despite this, there has been growing recognition of the role of international joint ventures as a preferred option, irrespective of resource constraints. This has been highlighted by the fact that technological and other forces rapidly make all businesses global. Thus, the *speed* of commercializing a new business concept globally is critical. Few corporations can achieve this fast enough on *all* the frontiers they may be participating in. As a result, it can be an attractive option for today's progressive corporation to share in the rapid global development of many of its activities with other progressive corporations. We are now seeing increased activity among leading multinationals in teaming up within specific business areas to jointly take them global. The driving force is speed and utilization of a unique common position and not resource constraints *per se*.

We are also increasingly seeing strategic alliances as a way of achieving global economies of scale and/or scope, while at the same time, adding flexibility in terms of remaining 'local' in various key markets. The fact that each participant in a joint venture does have a home base and, typically, enjoys certain areas of strength, makes it possible for a modern strategic alliance to create an advantage beyond what the wholly-owned multinational firm might achieve. This approach, which can create a more credible local perception, while also achieving the benefits of global focus, is probably easier to achieve through a network of strategic alliances.

With a shift towards the emergence of positively motivated strategic alliances, where the international joint venture approach *is* the preferred option, it is also more and more common that such alliances take a longer-term, strategic form. Undoubtedly, it requires a great deal of effort to put together and manage an international joint venture. The investment in time and energy can only be justified if the international joint venture option is covering a central strategic concern.

Formation of international joint ventures

In this discussion I shall draw heavily on a conceptual model for how to form joint ventures developed jointly with Dr Johan Roos.[1] Fig.1 shows this model.

Its main features are as follows: a joint venture is not formulated as a typical discrete or finite decision, but is a result of a 'gradual formation', based on an iterative process among the prospective partners, gradually leading to common understanding and trust. This formation process goes through an initial phase and a main phase. Also, while there is a number of rational and analytical issues to be covered in this process, behavioural and psychological issues related to the various decision makers and stakeholders involved, on both sides, are also prominent. The process is partly analytical, partly behavioural.

During the initial phase it is important, from an analytical point of view, to create a clear and easily understood 'win-win *raison d'être*' for the alliance. It is also important that the basic joint venture philosophy and approach is endorsed, explicitly or implicitly, by all key stakeholders in both organizations.

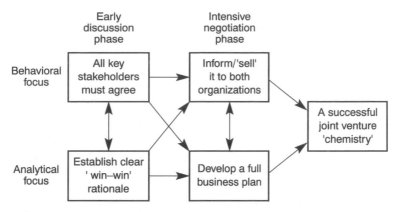

Fig. 1 The joint venture formation process

During the main negotiation phase which follows, it is necessary to develop a clear analytical plan for *who* does *what* and *when*, together with the resource commitments needed. In parallel, however, it is also important to 'sell in' the prospect of a strategic alliance in both participating organizations, so that this new way of working will be welcomed, rather than resisted. A proper formation process is fundamental to making a joint venture work. Even though the joint venture may be based on a brilliant strategy, it is unlikely to yield the expected results unless embedded in an appropriate formation process.

When attempting to create a win-win situation, it is important to keep in mind that realistically this can only be achieved if *all* prospective parties feel reasonably equal. The big multinational corporation must be aware that it may run into nationalistic sentiments when it is dealing with a local entity in developing a strategic alliance. The sensitivity to the perceived dominant attitude of a multinational corporation must be kept in mind. Similarly, in some cultures the preference for full ownership is very strong. These cultures tend to have a propensity to cultivate a win-lose attitude in their societal activities. It may be particularly difficult to create an appropriate win-win attitude if such a preference is culturally prominent, ie, when the ultimate motive may be to dominate.

In achieving support from all of the key stakeholders, it is important to remember that it may be hard to find 'who is who' when dealing with international joint ventures. In many companies in different parts of the world the classical hierarchical organization, prominent in many Western companies, simply does not hold. It is often not obvious who are the key stakeholders. For instance, large corporate groups in the Far East can still be run as if they are family-owned, even though the formal ownership stake in the various companies of the group may not be too high.

Another cultural characteristic in bringing all key stakeholders on board has to do with the fact that a 'yes' does not mean an agreement. Similarly, a 'no' may not mean a no. The way one negotiates is very different from culture to culture. Recent experiences in developing strategic alliances in the former

Soviet Union emphasize the difficulties of identifying who are the key stake-holders and being able to determine whether in fact there is commitment to take the joint venture foward or not.

In developing a strategic plan for an international joint venture, achieving a realistic resource focus is often particularly challenging. How can companies ensure that the quality of resources, particularly when it comes to human resources, is adequate from each side? Does each partner have the technologi-cal competencies, as well as the commercial competencies, that are assumed? Similarly, it may be difficult to judge the overall financial strength of a prospective partner, given the lack of commonly accepted procedures for how accounts are being reported. The fact that many international commercial groupings consist of loosely affiliated legal entities, makes the issue of develop-ing an understanding of the overall resource realities behind a particular strategic plan even more of a challenge.

Finally, when it comes to the 'selling' of the strategic alliance within both partner organizations, it is important to be sensitive to cross-cultural resistance and national sentiments. Many cultures are fearful of a foreign intrusion. This should be kept in mind when it comes to explaining the rationale for the alliance. Most importantly, the self-respect of both parties must be maintained.

Overall, the formation process for an international joint venture is highly demanding. Research suggests that the more experienced the management teams are on both sides, both in terms of having participated in joint ventures before, and, perhaps even more importantly, being truly international in experience and focus, the more realistic international joint venture formations will be.

The evolution of an international joint venture

It has been noted that a joint venture or a strategic alliance never represents a stable situation, but is always evolving from one stage to another. It has also been said by some that a joint venture represents a managerial marathon between the various partners, and that the ultimate winner within such a working relationship is the party which is best able to maintain its drive and commitment to the alliance over time. Why is it that a joint venture typically does not represent a steady state way of working?

This is caused by a number of forces, three of which can be highlighted:

Organizational learning

There is likely to be learning taking place among the parties, which may allow for more effective ways of co-operation. When an international joint venture is put together, it is frequently based on a concept for each party to contribute its part to the business equation, where the specific activities to be carried out typically rest with the parents. The joint venture, as an organizational entity, is more or less 'empty'; it is a contract regulating the co-operation between the parties. As time goes on, and the learning accumulates on both sides, it often becomes apparent that executives involved in the strategic alliance should be dedicated to these tasks on a more permanent basis to not only ensure efficiency, but also so that they can benefit from being together and form an effective team. After all, organizational learning can most effectively take place around a business, rather than around particular, free-coupled functions. One frequently sees activities gradually transferred into a new organizational entity and that more and more organizational learning takes place within the joint venture itself. As an additional benefit, this brings an opportunity to develop a more committed organizational culture for the alliance.

Needless to say, there can be particular challenges in developing a designated organization for an international joint venture. It could, for instance, mean moving key executives across borders. It could also mean that the parent organizations may have to give up certain activities, possibly leading to the closure of plants at home. Nevertheless, the advantage of business-based organizational learning and the commitment effect that can be achieved from this tends to be very powerful. If one or two of the parents resist such an evolution, insisting instead on the status quo, this may lead to a gradual weakening of the joint venture and perhaps even to its ultimate demise.

Responding to competitive threats

A related argument is the growing need to respond more rapidly and forcefully to competitive threats, as well as to be able to take more proactive advantage of related new business opportunities created by the joint venture. When it comes to responding to competitive threats it goes without saying that this can be a slow and, at times, confused process with the responsibility for responding split between the two parents. Internal co-ordination problems and debates regarding how to respond are quite frequent within international joint ventures, and an evolution towards a more co-ordinated way of responding is thus key. While this does not necessarily have to be done through a common organization, at least not as a first step, it typically leads to a designation of responsibilities to a few specific executives, perhaps within one of the parent organizations. This 'asymmetry' may then propel further development towards a fully free-standing organization. The issue of new opportunity seeking is of course also potentially difficult if one or both parents continue to compete actively in other aspects of the business. A parent may be hesitant to see the strengthening of the joint venture organization, fearing that this might lead to the creation of a future competitor. This has to be balanced against the benefits from having a strategic alliance which is able to create positive value from the opportunities as follow-on from the initially established base. Many parent organizations eventually allow the alliance to evolve into a more free-standing organization with the resources and the management capabilities to respond to new business development.

943

Organizational resistance

There may be resistance among the parent organizations to changes and re-configurations in the international joint venture. We have already touched on the fact that this also may lead to diminished activities in one or both parent organizations, and/or lead to change in the relative importance among the parents. It is, therefore, of critical importance that a clear and current concept of the win-win rationale is constantly re-articulated among the partners as the alliance evolves. Both parties will be required to reiterate what the win-win equation is at relatively frequent intervals. There is nothing unnatural about an evolution of the basic rationale behind the joint venture. This can, however, become a problem if the lack of attention to such a reformulation of objectives leads to a creation of a dysfunctionality among the parents. A key factor here is being sensitive to national pride and prestige. It is important that the reformulation of the win-win concept never gets linked to any sense of 'mistake', or lack of 'performance', or the emergence of winners and losers among any of the parties. Evolution in an international joint venture can only take place based on a feeling of mutual success.

The exit issue

It is clear that an international joint venture can have a lot of risks associated with it. The commercial risks that a joint venture runs may in themselves be quite formidable. In addition, there are the potential risks of a lack of working success of the strategic alliance due to organizational difficulties. It follows that realistic exit clauses must be built in to any strategic alliance. However, the problem is that these often tend to undermine the very co-operative spirit which is necessary to make an international joint venture work. If discussion and quarrels regarding how to stop the alliance prevail, then it will naturally have a very limited life. Even when it comes to such seemingly straightforward issues as resolving disputes in terms of a vote among the parties where, for instance, a 51 per cent majority shareholder votes down the 49 per cent minority partner, the joint venture may be rapidly on its way towards becoming ineffective. The important thing is that all parties must act *as if* they are fifty-fifty parties, despite the fact that the legal side of their alliance-agreement may say something different. Only then will the true complementary efforts from the parties emerge and only then will full positive value creation beyond the capabilities of each partner emerge. If this understanding is not brought to bear, then legally-driven actions can handicap the alliance. For executives with their roots in legally-driven environments, this can be a problem. Thus, while exit clauses are important they should not be allowed to hamper the evolution of the alliance.

This leads us to the fundamental issue of how each of the partners might receive their ultimate pay-off from co-operation. In order to address this it is important to keep in mind that the evolution of the alliance typically leads to the development of a more and more free-standing organization, as we have seen, with indigenous capabilities of tackling its own business. An organization will gradually be created with a commercial value on its own. At this stage, each of the parents owns an asset which has a commercial value and can be sold. Each has the option to sell out without destroying the value of the joint venture itself. In contrast, selling out *before* such a free-standing organizational entity has taken hold will, in all likelihood, lead to the destruction of the owners' value. Whether one of the partners buys its previous partner, or whether an outside entity is brought in as a new party to the joint venture, becomes an issue of negotiation, rather than an issue of how the joint venture's value and operation will continue to take place. Typically, however, one of the existing partners will buy out the other. Such a buy-out must be very sensitive to the fact that nationalistic sentiments must not be allowed to create a negative image of what is happening.

The 'black box' issue

As we have seen from the discussion of the evolution of a strategic alliance, as well as from the discussion of how to develop a meaningful exit strategy, it may be desirable for each partner to have some type of safeguard control over its stake in the joint venture. The legal contract does of course play an important role here as a way of protecting the parties. It should be kept in mind, however, that an international joint venture's legal contract can be quite difficult to enforce. An appropriate arbitration mechanism must be specified, with a location chosen for where to arbitrate. Similarly, patent protection and technology agreements can contribute in some ways to creating protection for a partner, a 'black box'. Here too, however, the enforcement issue can be a monumental challenge.

A complementary and perhaps more effective black box protection can be created, based on the *latent* power that each partner may be perceived to have *vis-à-vis* the other partners in case the joint venture is broken off. This latent power can, for instance, stem from a technology base which is constantly being renewed through innovative R&D, or through maintaining a strong market position – values that any partner appreciates and may be reluctant to cut itself off from.

A technology-based latent power position, developed by a partner, through emphasizing its own R&D, can only offer protection, however, if it is *signalling* its progress and overall strategic direction to the other party typically at quite frequent intervals and deliberately. By doing this, the other partner understands that it is part of a flow of new technologies and anticipates future benefits from this. If it breaks off the joint venture, this will of course mean latent future opportunity losses while no longer being part of the partner's technological-based progress.

Similarly, when it comes to market-driven latent power, demonstrated through investing vigorously in local market development, brand name enhancement, active contact with the distribution chains, etc, it is again important that a partner is able to signal its progress to the other party, so that the latter understands that breaking off the strategic joint venture might lead to a difficult situation in the marketplace. Latent threat of losing the market is of course also a strong deterrent against breaking off a joint venture. Thus, it is an advantage if each of the partners in an international joint venture can take an active stand to develop their complementary 'black box' positions. As such, each party will also perceive that they have teamed up with a true winner, making it easier to justify why this international joint venture should continue. Anticipated future benefits, and the latent threat of seeing such benefits being taken away is an effective way of protecting one's interest in an international joint venture, complementing a legal-driven approach and patent position.

The future

International joint ventures are already a prominent part of the strategies of many multinationals and leading national companies. More and more can be expected to emerge. Over time there is likely to be a managerial know-how advantage dimension that can be expected to accrue for firms with practice in being effective participants in such international joint ventures. Success is experience-based. The very fact that one has already previously participated in such co-operative activities will be an asset.

Beyond this, however, it is important to structure a competent way to build up the execution of international joint ventures along the lines suggested. This requires clearer understanding of the analytical and behavioural sides of creating an effective formation process; more realistic focus on the evolutionary side of a joint venture; clear focus on the aim, enabling the creation of an ultimate exit position to recuperate one's value (not, of course, to be confused with premature exit discussions which can only lead to 'working accidents'); and, finally, the creation of a 'black box' position to help glue the joint venture together in a co-operative way – while still being able to protect one's own interest. All of these elements are essential aspects of successful international joint venture management.

Dr Peter Lorange is President of IMD, the International Institute for Management Development, based in Lausanne, Switzerland.

Further Reading

Faulkner, D, *Strategic Alliances*, McGraw Hill, Maidenhead, 1995.
Lorange, P and Roos, J, *Strategic Alliances: Formation, Implementation and Evolution*, Blackwell Publishers, Oxford, 1992.

Reference

1 Lorange, P and Roos, J, *op cit.*

JAPANESE MANAGEMENT

Jacques Gravereau

At the beginning of the 1980s 'Japanese management' appeared in the West like a bolt from the blue. This sudden discovery was part of the rude awakening for American industry – beginning with the automobile industry – which had believed itself to be the best in the world.

In the 1960s the United States was three times as productive as Japanese industry in terms of man-hours. By the 1980s, Japan had risen to the top. With the increase in value of the yen in 1986, the colossal wealth of Japan in dollar terms reinforced the impression of Japan's superlative power. If 150 Japanese companies appeared in the *Fortune 500* at the end of the 1980s, having started from almost zero 20 years earlier, it was because the Japanese must hold a secret. The secret, so the West believed, was Japanese management.

At the end of the 1970s and the beginning of the 1980s, seminars on Japanese management began to appear everywhere, notably after the publication of the first wave of excessively laudatory books, such as *Japan as Number One* (1979) or *Theory Z: the Japanese Challenge* (1981). This was not love at first sight, but the combination of a number of factors. At the beginning of the 1980s, Western managers noticed that the 'universal' principles of the American management model (from which stemmed their arrogance in the subject) were no longer valid, or in any case less efficient. At this time, it was also realized that national cultures could affect management practices to an enormous degree – this marked the birth of intercultural management.

Origins of Japanese management

As with love stories, fact and fiction are interwoven. In reality, most of the features of modern Japanese management date from after the war and were borrowed from America which, as we tend to forget, had a huge and determinant presence in Japan from 1945 to 1952. So-called Japanese methods, such as quality circles, very often have their roots in the West and existed long before Japanese management became fashionable.

Astonished and delighted by being the height of fashion, the Japanese themselves discovered, to their surprise, that there could be a Japanese style of management. This was highly flattering to their sense of national pride.

In reality, 80 per cent of management practices within a Japanese company are the same as in any other company worthy of its name. The functions (identified or not by an organigram) are perceptibly the same.

What makes the difference is the remaining 20 per cent which have their roots in Japanese culture.

Certain 'Japanese' elements have in fact been imported and adapted and improved for local use. Even the theory of management, borrowed from the West, has been re-developed locally, going from scientific management, passing by behavioural sciences to contingency theory. Even today, Japanese companies send whole battalions of their managers to watch Western management closely, in every field possible and in remarkable strength: there are, for example, 12 times more Japanese in professional positions in Europe than Europeans in Japan which, furthermore, enables Japanese management to adapt quickly.

If the West has seen Japanese management as a quick answer to emulate Japan's economic success, the Japanese themselves have never pretended to be the inventors of modern management concepts and techniques, even ones identified as 'Japanese'. Inside Japan, a clear distinction is often made between foreign techniques and native features. There are even terms for this in Japanese. Before the era of the Meiji one spoke of *Rangaku* (Dutch science) for foreign techniques. Later, the 'foreign' Japanese syllabary, *Katakana*, (rather than *Hiragana* or *Kanji*) continued to be applied to products and techniques of foreign origin, in order to discern at a glance if an element suspected of being 'foreign' is really so.

Of course, a technique or information is only worth the use to which it is put, and the same goes for company values. It is here that Japanese management is truly interesting; even if the question of its transferability, which we will examine later, is not necessarily easy nor a magic formula.

The reality behind the myth

Seen from afar, there exists a single stereotypical Japanese company. This is without doubt an optical illusion caused by geographical and cultural distance.

In reality, Japan is a society which works at several speeds. The employees of the major companies only represent a quarter of the Japanese salaried workforce. The others, sub-contractors, second-class companies or small services (which represent half the population of Tokyo for example) constitute a class on their own. For this part of the Japanese workforce, the fight for survival takes precedence.

It is also dubious to talk of the benefits of Japanese management in the case of, say, human resources, when one looks closely at the composition of the wage-earning classes of companies. The main Japanese principles of lifetime employment, or of seniority-based promotion, apply to incumbents. Women, seasonal workers and employees on short-term contracts escape these rules, and often find themselves in a job market which is sometimes difficult (but also extraordinarily active). The concept of lifetime employment, therefore, may attract the attention of Western commentators, sometimes with naïvety, but it is not applicable to all.

Finally, all Japanese companies without distinction are often grouped together under the label 'Japanese management'. But, it is apparent that Japanese companies may have totally different management styles. Some are slow, lumbering and bureaucratic, often the large-sized companies, or part of the old establishment (more than three generations). Others, and sometimes the same ones, at the level of their head offices or functional services, have a deplorable rate of productivity, of which Japanese company-chiefs are aware. Some are built round human relationships, while others venerate the organization. *Mitsui-no-hito* (which equals men) falls into the first category; *Mitsubishi-no-Soshiki* (which equals organization) falls into the second category. Other companies may be very personalized and/or very charismatic, such as Matsushita or Honda, and the process of down-top decision-making, which is a prerogative of Japanese management, often then becomes a formal, even hypocritical, exercise. Similarly, the reactivity of Japanese companies may be very different from one company to another.

Is there such a thing as 'Japanese Management'? What seems certain, is that Japanese society as a whole is determined by a very strong national identity, reinforced by insularity. Furthermore, the Japanese believe that they are unique. There exists a Japanese culture, under-pinned by values which are shared by all, which is very different from Europe or America. The Japanese social structure is very strong. It affects organizational culture, the ideologies of Japanese companies and, to a large extent, management practices.

Japan is a group-oriented and also a vertical society. The values which support and govern society put the accent on the group, the hierarchy, and personal status. Interpersonal communication depends on the status of the interlocutors and the Japanese language even has three levels of courtesy for each verb, according to the level of the interlocutor on the social scale. The big difference with an individualistic society (European values of the Greco-Christian legacy), which is a doing-oriented society, resides in life in the group. Japan is a control-oriented society, which emphasizes harmony, unity, loyalty, reciprocity. The motto of the Japanese state is even *wa* (harmony), which reflects the Confucian vision of a family-like society.

Yet the group does not necessarily submerge the individual. Instead, it is a community ruled by, apparently harmonious, interpersonal co-existence. The group takes priority over the individual. The function of the group is to ensure peace and comfort to its members, as in a family or in a small village or household, which the Japanese call *ie*. Japan is thus a society of duties (as opposed to individual 'rights'). A Japanese has a continual and frantic need to compare himself with his neighbour, not in technical terms (correct or incorrect), but rather in moral terms (good or bad).

The spirit of Japanese management, its content and its practical achievements are largely determined by this strong cultural context. The Japanese company is lived by its members as the *ie* (family household). It dominates to the point of becoming the centre of the world and to the detriment of the family, hobbies and private life. First and foremost its function is to protect its members (at least in the major companies that can afford such protection).

If one characterizes management as the organization and movement of ideas, things and people, the Japanese put an accent primarily on people. Where the Americans process facts, the Japanese gather people. Thus we have the crucibles of Japanese management, which really took shape after the Second World War: the life-time employment system (*Shushin-Koyo*), seniority/merit promotion (*Nenko-Joretsu*) and internal company trade unions (*Kigyobetsu-Kumiai*).

The roots of company structures

Other characteristics of the Japanese company flow from these crucibles. The Japanese company aspires to recruit brilliant (by Japanese standards) young non-specialist employees, to which they give on-the-job training through job rotation (a standard training which ensures only average competence). The emphasis is on co-operation; not individual competition (as in the West). There are no precise job descriptions nor contracts. The rewards (rank, salaries, perks) are seniority-based. Above all, there is a high concern for employees, which may be called 'Total Concern for People'. The company, granting life-long employment, also has comprehensive welfare programmes.

To cement the group, the company has an ideology, clearly expressed in its principles and continually repeated: the seven spirits of Matsushita, the ten rules of Dentsu and so on. Each puts an emphasis on the spirit of the founder, the tenacity of its predecessors, abnegation and tenacity (*Gamman*).

As a family-like organization (at least in spirit), the company appears as a tangible group sharing similar outlook and living in one place (or one 'village'). The vertical relationship between members of the family (father, child number one, number two, etc) is reflected by a very precise ladder of titles, which are of extreme importance, as they provide legitimacy to their holders, whether they are *Kakaricho*, *Bucho*, *Kacho* and so forth.

The aim of the organization is to maintain harmony within the collectivity. It seeks to do so through the peculiar Japanese technique of consensus building: the *Nemawashi* process. *Nemawashi* is a gardening term which quite literally means to free the roots of a tree before transplanting it. In other words, it means including all the potential actors of the group, by seeking their views, either formally (for example, the technique of *Ringi* with an exact document which passes from hand to hand) or informally.

The decision-making processes may not be drastically different from those in the West. What is different is the perceptions of those affected by a particular decision. Workers in Japan often deeply feel they have a part in the process, even if decisions made regarding strategic issues or personal matters are often made by a very tiny group of top people (usually morally accepted and well respected). One may argue, for example, over the kind of dictatorship exerted by the personnel department of a company over job rotation and promotion, where the *Nemawashi* process hardly seems to appear. (In this case there seems to be another kind of TCP, 'total control over people'.)

The first important characteristic of Japanese management is thus the strong emphasis on people, which paves the way to different patterns among the Japanese, Europeans or Americans in response to a given set of similar circumstances. Whereas the system-type of management found in the US and Europe emphasizes the decision-maker, the professional, the individual's creativity and responsibility, the functional relationship, and management by objectives, the organic-type found in Japan makes the boss a facilitator, a social leader and emphasizes group strength, free form command and management by consensus.

It must be understood that 'consensus' is a decision-making process by interpersonal adjustments and consensual understanding, rather than simply good vibrations giving birth to an agreement. Japanese bosses, for example, substantially differ from decision-makers in the West. Their role is to combine people rather than directing them. Their tasks are to activate the group energy with apparent humility, which makes them often seemingly unaware of what is going on in the group. They reward subordinates, instruct them and build a protective wall around them. But again, this is done the Japanese way, that is most often without words (non-verbal communication is essential) and with emotion-sharing (*Kimochi*) rather than formal instructions.

The boss is an expert in dealing with the psychological factors which make a Japanese individual work. The 'natural contract' linking people together is made up of human inclinations mixed with a desire to be protected by a structure. This environment makes personal relationships into a sort of a human balance sheet, where reciprocal moral obligations (*Giri*) make up an endless chain of favours and mutual duties. Much more than a managerial organization, this purely Japanese system of human relationships is the foundation and motor of cohesion and identity of the group. This is upheld by a Japanese vision of nature which considers à *priori* that man is good, and that there is no need to doubt this. As 'sincere' human contact counts more than the formal rules of comportment, one understands why the written law and lawyers play such a small role in Japanese business. For example, there is one Japanese lawyer for every 100 American lawyers. The sphere of reference for human activities is public and not private, where accomplishment of the group counts more than individual achievements. Social or ethical values are of value only if they are valuable to the group.

The individual and the group

The duties given to individuals are not always clearly defined, as opposed to tasks given out to groups, but the Japanese quickly read the circumstances they are placed in and try to respond to the needs arising from the overall situation. In all cases, immense importance is attached to justice in hierarchical relationships.

Japanese companies have developed management practices in accordance with this particular cultural context, which, in a simplified way, may be grouped into four categories: *human resources, mobilization techniques, financial management* and, of course, *production methods*.

The vision of long-term objectives for the company and the Japanese 'communalist' orientation have given birth to the system of employment for life and seniority/merit promotion and pay-systems. The dominant model, it must not be forgotten, is that of the major companies, which in Japan only date back to just after the war, to a baby-boom where the young classes were numerous and available (as a result it was economic to pay more to the less numerous elder classes, although this is no longer the case). The first characteristic is massive annual recruitment (apart from during a recession) of young, preferably well-educated, employees, with a general university degree. Then this new batch of people (which traditionally starts work on 1st April each year) is placed in the company mould, by teaching it rituals, company songs, indispensable loyalty; briefly, creating a group identity. Careers proceed in a predictable fashion during the first 15 years, at least as far as titles and salaries are concerned, as the job-rotation and associate training is intense.

A major city bank, for example, recruits 140 university graduates each year (20 of whom are women, which is a very recent trend). These same 140 will be in the third rank of the hierarchy for three years, then in the second rank, etc, every three years, with corresponding salary increases – and whatever the 'individual' performances (moreover, difficult to judge due to the lack of other than generalized objectives). At the end of 12 years, taking the same example, 140 out of 140 will be promoted to 'deputy manager', then five years later, 130 of them to 'manager'. It is only towards the age of about 40 that the real career race begins, with its stress and frustrations. There are three advantages: retention of key personnel via a predictable career path, teamwork with relative absence of internal conflict, ability to identify with the overall interest of the company.

The large Japanese company is thus 'internalizing' the labour market, as Fukuda says. It recruits, allocates, develops, and utilizes its own human resources. However, as this type of system produces its own blockages, both for the individual (frustrations, doubtful personal achievement) and the company (need for specialists at short notice, for example), there has been a recent tendency for mid-career hiring to develop. Nevertheless, this model remains true in 95 per cent of cases, and is contrary to Western wishful thinking on the so-called revolution in Japanese management.

This model only applies however to corporate first class citizens. The same bank recruits another 140 employees each year to the grade of clerk – all women, who will leave the company upon marrying, on average at the age of 25. In the same way, employment, notably during a period of recession, is regulated by attrition of female workers, part-time jobs, short-term contracts, etc, which make up a reservoir from which it is mainly possible to draw. In fact, Total Concern for People only applies to 25 per cent of Japan's total workforce. It is discussed at length, because it constitutes the dominant ideological model for the Japanese themselves, even those who belong to medium-sized companies.

952

Japan's unemployment rate (which is not calculated according to ILO standards) remains ridiculously low – because women and other seasonal workers do not necessarily sign up at the Employment Agency, and also because the market for small jobs remains extraordinarily active and encouraged by the fiscal structure: company social security costs are between 10 and 15 per cent, as opposed to 50 per cent in France or Scandinavia for example. Hidden unemployment also exists within the company. Managers who are put 'near to the window' (*madogiwa-zoku*) without actually being sacked benefit, as all the others, from the foundation of the Japanese group: security. This is less and less true, as during recession many companies now ask certain managers to leave, in some cases at the age of 50 (the 'normal' retirement age being 55 to 60, depending on the company).

With such homogeneous human groups, Japanese companies are able to develop long-term training schemes. Similarly, with job-rotation, the best managers are able to have quadruple 'training', which later on is very effective at executive level. These privileged few in effect pass from commercial posts to manufacturing posts, and to financial and overseas assignments. They overcome the classical difficulties experienced by European companies of dialogue between technicians, financial and international managers, etc.

Working in groups, solidarity, collective motivation, permanent mobilization, all contribute to the final performance of the company in terms of strategy, productivity, quality, and profits. The strength of the group is used intentionally as a mobilization technique. This gives defensive and offensive advantages to the company. Defensive advantages: the fragility of the company, the permanent menace from the outside and from competition are put forward so as to reinforce the cohesion. In the same way contractors are mobilized (often aggressively) from whom improvement in productivity is continually being asked for, by 'zero-delay', 'zero-defects', reduced prices, etc. Offensive advantages: the group takes precedence over the individual. Similarly facts take precedence over hierarchy. They are treated the same way by everyone: the respect for detailed facts is an essentially Japanese quality.

Information – the Japanese way

In order to respect the facts, they must be understood. In Japan, information (as in the Chinese world) is of major importance. The power of the Japanese technical and financial press is of course well-known (or not known, as 95 per cent is published in Japanese behind a linguistic barrier which is difficult to penetrate). The Japanese economic press is by far the biggest, per capita, in the world, but beyond the figures it is the attention paid to information which is important. In the West, information within a company is often an instrument of manipulation (internal communication in certain cases) or an instrument of power (the legitimacy of the boss is to control more information than deputies). In Japan, on the contrary, according to a local saying 'information is a fresh water spring' to which everybody has access. In the context of confidence and loyalty to the group (and slow advancement) the advantage is obvious. Even if the risk of dissemination exists, the advantages, in the eyes of the Japanese, far outweigh the disadvantages. The value of information, the Japanese way, is only for those who are able to really value it. Information allows one to react rapidly to events, even if they take place on the other side of the world. Furthermore, it is not by chance that the major Japanese trading companies, the *sogo shosha*, play a primordial role: that of gathering technical and commercial information from throughout the world, immediately organizing and spreading it through their own channels. Europe would be right in believing that Mitsui Corporation, for example, has the most powerful computer in the world devoted to technical and commercial information (400,000 messages daily concentrated through four satellites).

The special business environment

Another characteristic of Japanese management rests in the special business environment inside the country, until recently largely protected from the outside world. The business interlocking relationship through cross-share holdings, but above all through interpersonal solidarities developed over a very long period of time, is one feature, whether or not one may argue about the famous *Keiretsu* (financial and industrial groups). The secondary role of shareholders, which allows a certain serenity for company chairmen, is equally well known. Similarly, access to credit is very easy. The 25 years of the Japanese boom have been helped by virtually cost-free credit, arising from extraordinary domestic savings (two times greater than that of Europeans and three times the rate of the Americans), and which is mostly recycled through the group's financial circuits. In the same way, the major groups have the ability to make others bear the costs: the State, builder of roads, which allows for the tight flows of 'just-in-time', or sub-contractors and distributors, which act as 'cost absorbers'. All these features of Japanese financial management are related more to a system of social order than to management techniques, but they are part of the success of Japanese companies.

When one mentions Japanese Management, one obviously thinks of its more visible side: manufacturing techniques. It would seem that the main export item of Japanese management has been a productionist model with attention paid to extreme rationalism for mass production, and adapted to modern times, where the workers are no longer robots but graduates. Frederick Taylor is dead, long live Taichi Ohno! The genial engineer of Toyota has in effect reinvented and adapted concepts which take into account modern industrial data from the sixties up to the present day.

There exists in this preoccupation a combination of three elements: people (who learn, train themselves and interact), customers as 'god', increasingly quality-conscious (and service oriented) and cost cutting (through various techniques). The last element is not new. It was the basis of Taylor and Henry Ford's reflection: how to offer products to a maximum of consumers at reasonable prices. The first two elements are more so: that it is to say, the normal evolution of mature and affluent societies.

As we know from the abundant literature on the question, the three major basic principles of this production management have been '*just-in-time*', *automation with the human touch* (the operator can stop the assembly line) and *TQC* (total quality control). All other management techniques aim at implementing these principles.

The original discovery of Ohno was made on the production site, by inversing the Taylor sequence. 'We take care of what goes before, and not what follows,' says Ohno. Then various techniques were used, beginning with *Kanban*, at each process to withdraw parts from the preceding stage, which in turn uses it to order parts. *Kanban* means a signpost (card, paper...).

As a result, a load-smoothing production scheme was implemented, with the goal to attain zero-inventory. The subsequent slogan of the Five 'Olympic' Zeros has become famous worldwide. This does not only apply to products on the line, but also applies to exchange of tools on the machine, for instance.

Everybody in the company, becomes a 'decision-maker', pays attention to the quality of products, to the immediate work environment, is his own foreman and his own cleaning-lady (which, by the way, allows the latter type of post to be suppressed). For the procedure to become a daily habit, the Japanese company uses simple and easy-to-remember slogans. The three *Mu*, for example (*Muda*=waste, *Muri*=strain, *Mura*=discrepancy). Or the famous 'S' in varying numbers: sometimes the '3S' (*Seiri, Seiton, Seiso*), very often '5S', or even a sixth 'S' – 'Sense' (discern what is important and what is not, appreciate the changes around you).

There is a genuine commitment to quality and customer-reaction. By reverse engineering from American pre-war industry, quality-circles have developed and have become as much the subject of seminars as Japanese management in the 1980s.

Quality-circles do not apply only within the company, but also outside, as quality products are only produced with quality parts. It is in this way that, from 1977, Mazda developed its 'honeybee strategy' for subcontractors. This consists of going from flower to flower to pollinate the quality from company to supplier. More than major innovations, it is a question of daily improvements, little by little, made popular by the *Kaizen* concept (step by step, small improvements).

One finds in the concern for cost-cutting through fine-tuning regard for human resources, as the sequence beginning with waste elimination (meaning eliminating excess time) is followed by the redistribution of work (meaning man-hour savings) and concludes in the elimination of unnecessary posts (meaning people-saving).

As Japanese managerial practices have become an export item, and as Japanese investment overseas has also flourished, notably from the second half of the 1980s, an important question has arisen: that of the transferability of Japanese management.

Japanese management – does the model transfer?

In Japan itself, this management model is not necessarily transferable. The achievements of Toyota, for example, become less and less visible when one descends the chain of medium and small-sized companies. In the same way, this industrial model has little effect on service companies, small or large, which remain over-staffed. What remains (is this an economic feature or a cultural one?) is a widespread quality-consciousness and customer service concern.

Studies on the transfer abroad of Japanese practices in companies having Japanese capital give rise to mixed feelings. The first ones in the seventies asked questions on universal values. Everything happened as if the ideas of Maslow could be applied anywhere to the five human fundamentals (physiological, security, social, esteem, self-actualization). Certain Japanese companies, such as Akai, have even consciously applied this diagram abroad.

In the eighties, Malcolm Trevor, after a careful survey of Japanese companies in the United Kingdom, maintained that the Japanese production system woke up English work ethics, for three reasons:

- the bottom-up approach improves the job routine and workers' participation increases;
- the style of leadership through example-setting is positive;
- the Japanese production system is a rational one, thus teamwork, *Kaizen*, quality concern, etc, are of enormous value.

Over time it has been noticed that a distinction should clearly be made between management values attributable to cultural values, such as group orientation and collective *nemawashi*, and the features attributable to economic incentives, such as life-time employment, seniority-based promotion or job rotation and training.

Some features are only transferable in peculiar cultures. Japanese firms in a Chinese context, for instance, practise seniority-based promotion, and are able to emphasize on group orientation. Japanese firms in a European context cannot do so. Sony, for example, which so far is the only veritable multinational Japanese company, has refined management concepts abroad by making a clear distinction between individual and group values.

What does Sony consider transferable, and what is not? Respect for and confidence in workers, management by communication and information, and fairness are considered as generally transferable values. On the other hand, management methods must often be adapted. The practice of consensus-building and down-top objective-putting, works quite well, but in the West this takes several years to put into place (according to Sony, 10 years). The de-hierarchization of communication or the evaluation of individual performances depend entirely on the local context. It is thus that salaries are individualized and not established by age group, as in Japan.

Does this transfer work? At factory level, early Japanese overseas experiences have, in general, been felt to be successful, and productivity, if not the contentment of the workforce, is often greater than in the same factories in Japan. With pragmatism, Japanese factories have taken care not to transfer all the Japanese gimmicks, such as keep-fit on the workplace. In the US, Japanese car manufacturers have also been astute in setting up in rural zones which have not been 'contaminated' by the all-powerful UAW of Detroit. There are the occasional protests ('We are not Japanese' claimed the workers of Sharp Corporation on strike in eastern France in 1994), but the graft has generally taken well.

In contrast, at managerial level the general ascertation is often more bitter. Each party in effect notices that the rest of the world has a different managerial culture to that of Japan, and *vice-versa*. There are many frustrations expressed by local managers, in the case of the usual methods as well as the decision-making process in Japanese companies. To summarize, Western managers feel that objectives are not clearly presented, that there are time-consuming meetings, and that the methods of performance evaluation and reward are vague. Above all, there is the strong feeling that real decisions are made by Japanese only outside the meeting room and, at the end of the day, there is no promotion for non-Japanese. This gap caused a clash in October 1994 at MCA, when top American managers eagerly rebuffed their bosses from Matsushita for being unable to simply understand their local business and to implement adequate strategies.

Whether 'Japanese management' had been transferred or not, it would seem that the fashion of the 1980s has now calmed. Furthermore, since 1991 Japan has entered into the longest period of recession known since the War, and the Japanese model is being blamed, starting in Japan itself.

Recession and 'restructuration'

The Japanese recession of the early 1990s and the fashionable Japanese word of 'restructuration' reveals, in reality, a three-fold crisis: an economic crisis, which is the most obvious and which obliges companies to adapt, but also a crisis of society and a culture crisis.

One of the strengths of Japanese management has always been to recognize changing environmental factors and to show courage in abandoning old conventions. With the maintaining of a strong 'Japanese' identity in an homogeneous society, changes are not necessarily perceived as a threat, as was seen, for example, during the oil shocks. Moreover, in Japanese the word crisis (*kiki*) is composed of the mix of the characters 'danger' and 'opportunity to rebound'.

However, during the recession, the Japanese are now taking another hard look at, say, life-time employment and the seniority system. The situation of company profit and loss accounts is inciting personnel directors to hire fewer young graduates each year (and sometimes none at all), thus unpriming the fountain of young recruits at low salaries. At the same time, the over-50s are 'incited' to leave the company. Alternative career paths are also offered. Here and there, even on-the-spot dismissals have been reported.

The production model and the life of products has considerably evolved, with or without the recession. The life cycle of products has become shorter and shorter, infected at an extremely rapid rate by the innovations of the whole range of competitors. Mass-production, that is to say the productionist model, finds itself at a dead end: manufacturing industry is in a paradoxal situation where the cost of the chase after large-scale savings is now greater than the advantages.

The talent of Japanese companies to take the right strategic options has also been damaged by the recession. Some companies have emerged well, at the cost of painful financial and human adjustments. Others are not management models, and have done just about everything they should not have done during a recession. This strategic model is thus damaged.

In spite of all this, the costs to the parent company, the rigidity of the human resources system, and in spite of the discussions which are continually being led by company bosses.... the heart of the system, the ideology of lifetime employment and the seniority system, are in reality not seriously brought into question. There may be, it seems, a risk of rupture in the implicit social contract that Japanese company leaders are not (or not yet) ready to take, although it has been talked about for ten years.

The bolt from the blue might perhaps break one day under triple social pressures. First, the general ageing of the population (even more so than in the West) eventually creates problems. There will be less savings, consumers will become less reactive, while this has always been a key element of Japanese economic dynamism. Already middle-aged middle managers are no longer assured of all the rewards and promotion which they could be guaranteed before. In this age-range/rank class, there is often an intense frustration, although not expressed openly in this inward-looking society.

Elements of change – present and future

The drawbacks of Japanese people-management are increasingly apparent. It suppresses individual creativity, by encouraging the employee's dependency. It produces meaningless jobs. On a broader scale, there are the harmful effects of the escalator system and impediments to a formation of a free horizontal labour market. This may be supplemented from time to time by the recourse to firms of executive search (notably for high-level engineers and, more surprisingly, specialists of information systems). Although growing, the head-hunter business remains weak when compared to the West.

The second characteristic of Japanese society is the appearance of a new young class, less submissive (but only relatively) to the company mould. The desire to enjoy life (holidays, travel, hobbies), the wish to have a meaningful job, comparisons with abroad, create many aspirations. Company bosses all deplore the apparent lack of loyalty by young white-collar workers, but when one digs a little deeper, they are concerned only by the difference of attitudes and mode of expression between young and old.

Underneath, nothing has really changed. Young graduates just out of university still rarely turn down job offers from a major company, while being perfectly lucid on what they expect during the first 15 years of their career. Similarly, the 'May disease' (one quits a major company a month after the recruiting ceremony in April) is only a journalistic fashion: in reality, the phenomenon is marginal.

The third element which is changing Japanese society, is women. At present they are still generally second-class corporate citizens, whatever their degrees and qualities, which are often very high. In a few years' time, the major change might well be the growing place given to women (often reluctantly) in management decisions. This is not yet the case, and Japanese management which privileges age, puts the young into a mould, and women aside, is promised some good years ahead.

The greatest challenge, however, for the Japanese company, is without a doubt cultural, and one may wonder about the productionist model, which leads to dead-ends on the subject of innovation, and thereby new markets. For example, Japanese manufacturers of integrated circuits have chosen to concentrate their know-how and financial means on the D-RAM memories – a component used in great quantities – but their over-investment in the production of these memories has resulted in an over-production, causing prices to tumble and the erosion of margins. The veritable 'brains' of the computer, microprocessors, are much more profitable; thus, American companies such as Intel are assured of a dominant position in this field.

Another example of their obstinacy is the refusal to perfect production techniques: the Japanese have neglected the extreme importance of technologies which facilitate the use of products. Recently, the technical perfection of user-friendly products has appeared as a non-negligible value added. However, from the point of view of the company boss, this sector is more difficult to manage; it is easier to carry on with large-scale savings. It is for this reason that managers in areas such as the automobile and electronics industries have made the mistake of over-investing in this field during the years of the economic bubble. On the hierarchy ladder within Japanese companies (in terms of published profits for the last two years), it is furthermore notable to see 'user-friendly' products appear in the lead with Nintendo and Sega in the Japanese Top 10. This upsets traditional hierarchies. To become Number One in the area of mass-production is not necessarily to become Number One in Management.

However, what remains of Japanese management, after the fashion of the eighties and the morosity of the nineties, is positive, because the capacity to constantly learn, the reactivity, lucidity and, above-all, working in the group, remain intact. Are these cultural elements of a peculiar society or Japanese management characteristics? The question is once more asked. If a Japanese management exists, it is because there exists a very strong background of identity and Japanese values. Only foreign techniques penetrate but very few 'values' as such. This crucible is intact. Japanese management lives on.

Jacques Gravereau is director of the Eurasia Institute at Groupe HEC School of Management, Jouy-en-Josas, France. He is a national adviser for French Foreign Trade, a board member of the Japan Management Institute, and of the Foundation for Advanced Information and Research, and the Institute for Fiscal and Monetary Policy. He is an adviser to the European Commission and to the French Ministry of Foreign Affairs. Previously, Dr Gravereau spent 17 years as a corporate executive with positions in Hong Kong, Tokyo and Europe, including being senior vice-president of the Rothschild group of companies.

Further Reading

Pascale, RT and Athos, AG, *The Art of Japanese Management*, Simon & Schuster, New York, 1981.

PART

4

NEW
ELEMENTS IN
MANAGEMENT

The Third Industrial Revolution

'The principal purpose of a company is not to make a profit, full stop. It is to make a profit in order to continue to do things or make things, and to do so ever better and more abundantly. Profit has to be a means to other ends rather an end in itself.'

Charles Handy

'Many of you have long experience in your manufacturing operations of the advantages of substantial, well-contrived and well-executed machinery. If then, due care as to the state of your inanimate machines can produce such beneficial results, what may not be expected if you devote equal attention to your animate machines, which are far more wonderfully constructed.' *Robert Owen addressing the superintendents of his factories in the early nineteenth century*

4

OVERVIEW

Tom Cannon

A new managerial paradigm

In his analysis of the nature of scientific change, Thomas Kuhn[1] challenges the view that science evolves as an 'incremental', 'cumulative', process. He argues, instead, that the development of scientific knowledge is best viewed as a series of 'scientific revolutions'. These revolutions mark major turning points in the way the world is interpreted as the scientific community rejects 'one time-honoured scientific theory in favour of another incompatible with it.' This process has identifiable parallels to the way industries and the prevailing approaches to management change over time.

This type of shift was seen at the time of the first Industrial Revolution. From the middle of the eighteenth century to the beginning of the nineteenth century, there occurred a clear 'break with a tradition of economic life, and a pace of change, which had lasted for centuries.'[2] The impact of these changes on the ways goods were produced, distributed and sold is well documented.[3] There is far less analysis of the impact of these changes on the ways resources and people were managed.

For the first time, large amounts of capital, labour and technical resources needed to be managed on a continuous basis for purely economic ends outside agriculture. This new type of industrial activity shaped the kinds of management systems that emerged. Small scale and relatively local production dominated. The new entrepreneurs and managers combined technical expertise with access to emerging financial markets. The hands-on skills to solve immediate mechanical or technical problems and the ability to adapt to wild fluctuations in economic conditions were more important than continuity and professionalism. Managerial relationships were based on trust, often derived from pre-existing links, eg, family ties, not formal, professional knowledge. This first industrial revolution was founded on the owner-manager as proprietor.

Towards the end of the nineteenth century, a new wave of scientific, technical, economic and industrial changes occurred. This second industrial revolution was linked with a number of factors: a shift from coal to oil-based energy; the emergence of the steel, chemical and engineering industries; and a sharp increase in the scale of production and the size of companies. Alfred Chandler summarizes these changes as 'the managerial revolution'. [4]

The scale of the new enterprise made it hard for entrepreneurial proprietors to maintain their control. Business owners were forced to recruit a new kind of professional manager from outside their immediate, social circles. These professional managers won and held their positions because they had access to a specific portfolio of skills. At the same time, the gap between ownership and control widened as proprietors sought capital from financial institutions and widened the equity base of their businesses.

The fictional character, Gordon Gekko, in the movie 'Wall Street'[5] describes both the zenith of managerial capitalism and the point of change in his speech to shareholders:

'Now, in the days of the free market when our country was a top industrial power there was accountability. The Carnegies, the Mellons, the men that built this great industrial empire made sure it was, because it was their money at stake.

Today management has no stake in the company. All together these men sitting up here own less than three per cent of the company. And where does Mr Cromwell put his $M dollar salary? Not in Teldar stock. He owns less than one per cent.

You own the company, that's right, you, the stockholders and you are being royally screwed by these bureaucrats with their stock lunches, their hunting and fishing trips, their corporate jets and their golden parachutes'

He challenges both the competence and the right of professional, bureaucratic managers to lead the ventures 'owned' by others.

A new, third industrial revolution is taking place. This revolution is altering the economies of the world, just as the first and the second industrial revolutions transformed the world from an agricultural society to an industrial society, then, from a coal and mechanics powered economy to an oil and engineering-based economy. Rapid increases in the rate of technical change shift the locus of economic and industrial power. The organization and structure of companies adapted to new technological and market imperatives. The factory system, for example, grew to accommodate the benefits of concentrating men and machines to maximize production.

New, electronic and computer-based technologies do not require this type of concentration. In many ways, the greatest technological and market gains from the new technologies occur when labour and machines are dispersed. The machines which dominated the first and second industrial revolutions were controlled by hand or arm. This placed a premium on manual and mechanical skills. The machines which dominate the third industrial revolution are controlled by brains. Intellectual and process skills are at a premium today. The new roles, expectations and responsibilities of management reflect this process of change and transformation.

Roles, expectations and responsibilities

The wider society and the nature of the economic order are not immune from these changes. The industrial and technological changes associated with the first and second industrial revolution changed society. The factory system, trades unions, the joint stock company, and business management itself emerged at those times. These innovations were accompanied by debates on the responsibilities of companies which have parallels today. Shifts in the scale and form of business prompted questions about the values and ethics of business leaders and the impact of their enterprises on communities and the environment. The responsibilities of corporations to their communities came under intense scrutiny. In part, this reflected new awareness of the impact of corporate actions on the environment and the disadvantaged.

Elsewhere, the discussions reflected widespread recognition of the changing relationship between companies and communities. New technologies, developments in markets and new ideas highlight the influence of corporate actions and their impact on issues which extend far beyond the conventional remit of firms and their managers. During revolutionary change, these occur at a time when conventional, trusted solutions no longer match contemporary need.

A responsible kind of freedom

Today, the rolling back of the state creates new opportunities and imposes new responsibilities on firms. Corporate leaders are seeking ways to express and define their role in these changing circumstances. The same shifts place increased responsibilities on firms, entrepreneurs and managers. The freedom to act is not the license to abuse. Many of the hostile shifts in political attitudes toward corporate behaviour reflect abuse by specific business leaders. This was true when Rowntree exposed mistreatment by employers. It recurred when the Teapot Dome scandal highlighted abuse of political power. It was highlighted with the Great Crash when the misuse of Stock Market rules emerged. It was seen when Maxwell exploited trustee compliance and executive freedom. Competent corporate leaders recognize the link between rights and responsibilities.

It was the first industrial revolution which brought the issue of corporate responsibility into sharp focus. In part, this was a reflection of the power of the new industrial processes to reshape age-old relationships. Feudal, clan, tribe or family-based systems of authority and responsibility were broken. Simultaneously, the new techniques and technologies gave 'corporations' vast power and wealth. The landscape could be reshaped, cities built. The power of the machine over man raised major issues of responsibility and morality. The wealth of the new industrial classes gave added emphasis to the debate. It enhanced their power while standing in sharp contrast to the difficulties of the new, industrial proletariat.

In *The Condition of the English Working Class (1845)*, Engels wrote:

'One day I walked with one of these middle-class gentlemen into Manchester. I spoke to him about the disgraceful unhealthy slums and drew

his attention to the disgusting condition of that part of the town in which the factory workers lived. I declared that I had never seen so badly built a town in my life. He listened patiently and at the corner of the street at which we parted company, he remarked: "And yet there is a great deal of money made here, Good morning, Sir!"'

During each period of change, responsible business leaders seek ways to define and exercise their responsibilities. Robert Owen represented a generation of business leaders who tried to create a new type of industrial community first at New Lanark, then at New Harmony. His efforts at the start of the nineteenth century reflected both an awareness of the scale of change and a deliberate attempt to respond constructively. Others challenged this point of view. To the Board of Agriculture in 1816; 'the idleness and depravity of the working class' explained their privations. Despite this, a combination of government action through legislation like the Factory Acts in Britain and employer and trades-union-led industrial reform redefined the rights, expectations and responsibilities of employers and workers.

Values and perspectives

Paternalism characterized many of the great business empires of the middle to late nineteenth century. Lord Leverhulme saw Port Sunlight as a personal charge. George Cadbury moved out of Birmingham in 1879. Brewers like the Whitbreads, bankers like the Barclays and others linked their non-conformist religious principles with an acceptance of wider responsibilities to their fellow man. Their religion introduced two important dimensions to their approach to wealth and industry. First, it gave a strong sense of community. In part, this derived from the chapel or communal meeting place. It was, also, a function of a tradition of community support for co-religionists. Second, their religion emphasized the responsibilities associated with wealth and success.

In North America, entrepreneurs like Francis C Lowell shared Owen's vision while other progressives introduced local reform and prompted or supported national action to ameliorate the impact of industrial and economic change. Workers were not passive during these periods of change. New political parties, trades unions and the co-operative movement were among the innovations that sought to redefine economic and social relations in the light of revolutionary change in industry. In Europe, local conditions shaped the ways economic and social responsibilities were defined. In France and Germany much of the impetus for industrialization and change came from government action.

The challenge of the new

This 'partnership' between industry and government developed far more extensively in mainland Europe than Britain. Iron production in the Creusot region of France was partly the result of entrepreneurial action, but equally the consequence of deliberate state action to support this development. *Ingenieurs des mines* played a crucial role in research into mining conditions beside supervising conditions. France had a Ministry of Manufactures almost a century before British governments would consider such a development. The great technical schools of the revolution provided the finest technical education in Europe for most of the nineteenth century. Private finance for the institutions or scholarships for students was provided by the new, industrial corporations and their proprietors.

Development in Germany was largely shaped by the same forces. Industrialization was based on an active and expansionist state and a confident, well-educated middle class. Trades unions were small and weak. The government's control over key sectors like mining and railways seemed to avoid the worst excesses of exploitation while its investment in education reduced the need for private investment. The success of this model was already threatening British hegemony by the 1870s.

In the later years, the nature of the key industries shaped the character of the corporate response to social and economic needs. Two industries dominated: chemicals and electricals. Enterprises operated on a far larger scale than in the cotton or iron industries. They required a better educated, skilled and stable workforce. The mass of artisans which characterized the pool of labour in the first half of the century was inappropriate for the new companies and their leaders.

Corporatism

The companies created by Siemens in Germany, Ford and Edison in the US, Lever in Britain, symbolize the second industrial revolution. Their scale, range of activities and dependence on a technically competent workforce capable of meeting the needs of sophisticated consumer and industrial markets distinguished them from their predecessors. A cadre of new, professional managers emerged in the US and Germany to lead these new ventures. Management education, training and development became increasingly formalized in the US through the business schools and in Germany through the *Fach Hochschule* (engineering colleges). Although these institutions adopted different approaches, both endorsed the view that management involved distinct, specific and 'learnable' skills and competencies. The codification of skills, professionalization and specialization emerged from this process.

The emergence of the new, professionalized management group severed the bond between entrepreneurs and their workforce and often coincided with a process of severing links with a community. This 'local' connection was once a key feature in the character and identity of the enterprise. Lever Bros in the North West of England, RJ Reynolds in Salem, and Hoechst in Frankfurt symbolize the bond between a firm and a locality. Growth, relocation and acquisition have eroded this relationship. If Unilever now has a corporate core it probably lies on Blackfriars Bridge near the City of London. Nestlé took over Rowntree, in spite of efforts to assert a local dimension in the defence.

Investment policies looked more closely at goodwill in the financial community than goodwill in the local community. Unilever's decision in the 1980s to shift production of frozen foods out of the North West of England took little account of 30 years of past production or high local unemployment. This contrasts with Lord Leverhulme's attempts to redevelop the Western Isles of Scotland through an exercise in corporate philanthropy. Mobile, rootless professional managers found little in their professional training, performance criteria or acquired values to justify 'unproductive' investments in communities offering low returns or poor yields.

During the late 1970s and early 1980s, the consensus between 'corporate man' in government, trades unions and industry began to break up. The post-World War Two assumption that the state could solve economic and social problems through planning, direct intervention and high taxes was challenged. Rapid technical change, massive industrial dislocation, increasing unemployment, diminishing competitiveness and environmental degradation were not susceptible to approaches refined over the previous 50 to 100 years. New approaches which reflected the needs of a new industrial era are required. Lessons from the past are useful but successful action is rooted in the present, or in the German saying, 'we must learn from the past – not live in it'.

4

The roots of change

Many of the best examples of corporate social responsibility and good governance from previous eras survive. Examples of paternalism or philanthropy persist. Cadbury has a high proportion of its operations concentrated in Birmingham. Bourneville remains a powerful symbol of affirmative action. Sir Adrian Cadbury's involvement in industry education partnerships and his work on the reform of corporate governance in Britain symbolize a personal commitment to a wider role for corporate leaders. It is a tradition which goes back to the first industrial revolution and people like Robert Owen and Francis Lowell. It was mirrored in the efforts of Henry Kaiser, Andrew Mellon, Werner von Siemens and Alfred Nuffield to tackle the problems created during the second industrial revolution. Today, the mission statements of firms like United Biscuits, The Co-operative Bank, ARCO, Levi Strauss and Whitbread mirror this commitment to their communities.

'Good relations means good business. The equation is as simple as that. Therefore today's most important task is encouraging the good relations that will create good business in the future,' says Whitbread & Co's *The Whitbread Way*.

In specific locations, such as Dresden, Lille, Detroit and Manchester, organizations like the Moss Side and Hulme Business Support Group in

Manchester, seek to: 'Assist in the economic and social regeneration of Moss Side and Hulme and its immediately surrounding areas of Manchester.'

Debate on business ethics provoked by change, dislocation and the power of business has evolved along similar lines.

Managers deciding whether to introduce a new technology face a moral dilemma. They know it might put loyal employees out of work because the new equipment needs fewer people, or their skills are redundant. The trades union officers wanting an 'embargo' against cheap imports from developing countries must decide whether to put the needs of their members before those of third world peasants. The marketing policies of firms raise a host of ethical issues. These range from the kinds of images used in advertising to the types of products offered to the market. The stewardship of private and public assets is at the centre of the policy debate on corporate values. Bribery in Japan, misuse of the funds of Saving and Loans and theft of pensioners' funds at Maxwell Communications are among the issues shaping the agenda.

It is no coincidence that the debate on business ethics is most fierce at a time of change. Established values are challenged, old certainties no longer ring true and the scope for different interpretations and moral ambiguities proliferate. Over time, firms and managers have tried to resolve these questions in a host of ways. The Christian ethic was a powerful and overt influence on managerial behaviour in the last century. Weber linked the rise of industrial capitalism with the protestant work ethic.[6] Shintoism performed a similar role in Japan. The increasingly secular nature of society in the West and the successful industrial development of communities with powerful corporatist or communal traditions has created a more eclectic base for values and morality. The challenges managers face have increased their awareness of the limitations on their ability to predict or control outcomes. This, in turn, has made them increasingly aware of the nature of the ethical challenge facing them in areas like innovation and change, employment, restrictions on trade, marketing, fairness in the workplace and exploitation of the natural environment.

The manager's dilemma

Many social debates centre on the nature and location of employment. The pressure for change prompts companies to invest in new equipment and plant. It is seldom possible to arrive at an exact fit between the skills available to the current workforce and the skills needed by the new technologies. Sometimes, the innovations require changes that those affected are reluctant to accept. Elsewhere, those affected are unable to change. In ports, for example, the changed nature of cargo handling with the advent of containerization eliminated many jobs while changing the character of the rest of the work. Dockers with long service were seldom able to compete with new entrants with more appropriate skills. Communities can be blighted by this process. The change in the mining and steel industries in the US, Europe and Asia demonstrate this.

Production in these sectors was typically concentrated in communities with few alternative sources of employment locally. Closing the mine or steelworks could mean killing the community. The greater the change, the more widespread the effect.

The ethical challenge to managers and firms exists on two levels. These are:

- Should we make the change?
- What responsibility do we have to minimize the impact?

Often, the pressure for change leaves the firm or community with no option. Examples abound of firms and communities that tried to resist technological change. It is hard to identify any which have succeeded. The accumulated evidence is a powerful case against resistance. The threat to the enterprise is often a sufficiently strong argument to end any debate about the necessity of change.

But, the social cost of change is seldom paid by the promoters of innovation and novelty. John Donaldson[7] highlights the problem in his discussion of the newspaper headline dealing with unemployment in the 1980s 'Shock Treatment for the Economy May Have Hurt, But It Has Worked'. He raises the questions: who did it hurt and who did it work for? Commerce is a major source of change and has a clear responsibility to address its social consequences. This is especially true when the changes affect the social values which bind communities. 'In sum, the processes which produce economic and business growth without considering the value implications are inevitably unable to recognize the crises and value consequences because the ideologies attached to the techniques forbid it,' writes Donaldson in *Key Issues in Business Ethics*.

The moral basis for continued change and the social gain to the community and its members requires justification. It is, on one level, akin to the philosophical notion of *prudential obligation*. That is to say, it is in the best interests of corporations to tackle these problems.[8]

A fragile world

The needs of the natural and built environment are especially difficult to accommodate during change and innovation. Goldsmith, Dickens, Kingsley, Hugo and Warner were among the nineteenth century writers who described the impact of early industrialization on the environment. The oil boom in North America at the turn of the century set the model for exploitation of natural resources which has persisted for most of the last hundred years. The sheer visibility of these early forms of exploitation made protest, reform and control attainable. The environmental impact of many new technologies is impossible to predict. This sense of powerlessness is, however, not a basis for denying the ethical and corporate implications of innovation. Constant vigilance and openness are critical features of the attempt by firms to meet their obligations in this area. Effective action is limited by the twin constraints on modern corporate action. These are: the problems of forecasting the long-term technological consequences and the concern about wedding public accountability to competitive advantage.

Contracting into the community

Many corporate leaders acknowledge the bond between their enterprise and the community in which they operate. In even simpler terms 'business has a massive stake in the nation's cities... their balance sheets reflect the cost and value of the assets involved'.[9] This stake was deeply rooted in the links that had evolved between firms, their workers and communities they served. There exists a form of contract between the firm and the community.[10] This includes both an obligation on the state to allow the firm to pursue its activities but, at the same time, an obligation on the firm to meet certain responsibilities. In the UK, Business in The Community was created; initially, to deploy corporate resources to overcome the problems of unemployment.

Affirmative action to help specific groups shifts the agenda for corporate responsibility much further than the immediate interests in minimizing the costs of transition or economic change. It implies that firms have a direct interest in social engineering. The argument of *prudential obligation* was used extensively in North America to justify this type of intervention. The violence in the cities of Detroit, Chicago, Los Angeles, Newark, etc, provoked corporate leaders like Henry Ford II to acknowledge that 'equal opportunity policy means more than the elimination of deliberate racial discrimination'. The latter was required by the law; Friedman's *rules* required it[11]. The new agenda went beyond even *prudential obligation* to an attempt to achieve economic equity. This is often justified in terms of either Locke's[12] *natural rights* or a form of the Utilitarian[13] principle that this will contribute the *greatest good to the greatest number*.

Stewardship

A series of events over the last decade put the issue of stewardship at the centre of the policy agenda. Proper stewardship is a responsibility placed explicitly on all those responsible for the goods or funds of others. It imposes a duty to exercise due diligence, ie, care, rigour and attention, in the management and disposal of all those assets for which the officer is given responsibility. Many of the cases which hit the headlines illustrated the scope for those managing corporate resources to deploy them for their personal benefit. The proliferation of recent cases highlights more widespread collapse of the notion of responsible stewardship. Abuses range from sweetheart deals, which covered every part of the private life of corporate executives from homes to holidays, to remuneration packages which take little note of either competitive conditions or corporate performance. Elsewhere, the notion of abuse of trust recurred. In the US, the Savings and Loan scandals threatened the stability of the Bush administration while Fred Wang's pay-offs, and the wage deals of corporate leaders provoked a host of questions from workers, customers and shareholders. The Anglo-Saxon world is not alone. Lockheed and Nomura in Japan, Michelin and Perrier in France, and Olivetti in Italy have been affected by intense debates about the stewardship of corporate resources. Together they suggest that the ethical codes of managerial capitalism cannot cope with the new environment.

Criticism of the present approach to stewardship has come mainly from; three directions: the reformist left, those within firms and related agencies, and the radical right. The reformers argue for a reform of company law allied to a strengthening of the supervisory agencies such as the Securities and Exchange Commission in the US and the Department of Trade and Industry in Britain. Stakeholders within firms are demanding a clearer say based on better information about policies and rewards. The radical right argue that imperfections in markets allied to external restraints on entry and exit create an environment for abuse. The work of ProNed in the UK illustrates some of the internal reforms of company practice which are deemed necessary by those seeking internal reform. In the US, the United Shareholders Association is an increasingly powerful voice for those who want to 're-assert that directors of companies are fiduciaries representing the interests of the owners.'[14]

The advocates of legislative action and strengthened statutory agencies highlight the failures of the present voluntary systems of supervision and control. These 'mechanisms to constrain behaviour'[15] operate to control the interest groups while asserting the wider public or community interest in responsible stewardship. This is especially true given the increasing distance between the point of ownership and the point of control.

An alternative approach is needed which looks to present capabilities and future needs, not traditional practices. Internal and voluntary reform is the key to sound stewardship in the eyes of many of those who acknowledge the problems. They see government action as likely to impose high costs on all – the responsible and the irresponsible – while addressing the wrong problems in a cumbersome way. They concentrate their attention on establishing internal systems and voluntary codes of practice to ensure that directors – in particular – exercise the duties placed upon them. These duties combine those of an executive with management responsibility and a trustee of assets.

A governance paradox

There is widespread acceptance among shareholders of the proposition that excessive pressure for external control and governance can inhibit effective management. There is, however, less acceptance among top management that shareholders have title and that in a system of private enterprise their rights come before those of the paid executives.

'Excessive corporate governance... can also chill innovation and risk-taking... Corporate governance by referendum, instead of by board of directors, has all the same drawbacks as federal governance by referendum instead of by Congress,' observed the Business Round Table.[16]

A new balance is called for between the needs of managers to *get on with the job* and the rights of shareholders to see *just what job is being done*. The spate of recent frauds, allied to the apparent failure of contemporary arrangements for scrutiny to flag the problems, has provoked a widespread debate on current arrangements. These events question the ability of the external auditor and the professions generally to keep shareholders properly informed about the 'true' state of the company finances and the quality of stewardship exercised by directors.

Fat cats

Self-restraint by business leaders is an important part of the equation. The infamous 'fat cats' visit by President Bush to Japan, the dramatic increases in salaries for directors of newly privatized companies in Britain making headlines in the *Financial Times*, combine to highlight concerns about systems for establishing levels of pay in industry. The debate on compensation is driven by a number of forces. These include:

- the apparent injustices in the process of determining levels of pay;
- the latitude allowed directors and other institutional or corporate leaders;
- the lack of a clear relationship between organizational performance and pay;
- the proliferation of 'packages' or hidden supplements;
- the weakness of the systems of supervision.

These are not issues confined to the private sector although there is a tendency to focus attention on business leaders. There is concern that top management are abusing their positions of trust and using their power to gain private benefit from their role as trustees of corporate resources. This highlights the role remuneration plays in balancing rights and responsibilities[17] while wedding legitimacy to performance.[18] There is an implicit 'ethical contract' by management to establish and maintain systems which link their role as trustees with their needs as executives.

A new paradigm

In *Strategy and Structure* Chandler highlighted the importance of new structures 'to make possible continuing effective mobilization of resources to meet both changing short-term market demands and long-term market needs'.[19] The eras of proprietorial and managerial enterprise were parts of this process but not the final stage. There is every indication that the current stage in the evolution of the market economy will call for the creation of new structures if managers are to work effectively, opportunities are to be developed, community needs satisfied and ownership rights respected.

The new paradigm will need to recognize some traditional responsibilities, respond to current circumstances and recognize the nature of the new environment. At its heart will lie the integration of a sustainable business ethic with an acceptance of personal and corporate responsibilities to all stakeholders in the enterprise. This, in turn, will be linked with a determination to incorporate wider responsibilities to the natural and built environment. Internationalism is a key feature of this new ethic.

Economic development has always been shaped by migration, interaction between different groups and the actions of outgroups. Non-conformists in Britain, Scottish migrants in North America, the Jewish community across Europe, Calvinists in Germany played a disproportionate role in shaping the industrial revolution in the last century. Their debates about the purpose of commerce – from Smith (the Scot) to Hayek (the Austrian migrant) – continue to mould discussion. Their influence on the discussion on corporate responsibility has been, if anything, even greater. The Welshman, Owen, the Non-conformist, Cadbury, and the Scot, Carnegie, symbolize the ability of individuals from outside the establishment to raise new issues and question the values and assumptions of the dominant community. Changes in today's business environment suggest that new players are entering the economic arena. Their aspirations and values are influencing the debate on corporate responsibility and governance.

Some derive their codes of ethics from outside the Judeo-Christian tradition which dominates European and American business. Shinto in Japan, Hinduism from India, and Islam impose different obligations and have different expectations of their believers. Though Japanese products can be seen on every high street, and their factories and offices fill skylines, their ethical codes are seldom incorporated in contemporary discussions of corporate responsibility. It is, however, increasingly important to explore the ways the values of these new players will influence the debate on corporate responsibility. The emphasis in Japan on the group, for example, contrasts sharply with the individualism which dominates Anglo Saxon debate on values and responsibilities. The attention paid to harmony within the group, *Amae*, and with nature, *Shibui*, have few equivalents in European or North American thinking. In Islam, attitudes towards religious observance and social obligation struggle to co-exist with Western materialism. Fate, caste, family and respect play a complex part in shaping the business behaviour of Hindu business.

A more subtle, but, potentially more important change is being wrought by the new generation of female managers and entrepreneurs. There is some evidence that many have a stronger sense of group or community than their male counterparts. The bimodal[20] nature of female employment allied to perceived internal barriers to advancement[21] may create attitudes and values among women managers which differ from those of their male counterparts. The conventional business stereotype of ethics and values based on the Judeo-Christian male values are being reshaped. The modern business community is culturally complex, ethnically diverse, and not gender based. It reflects increasingly the community in which it operates. The nature of the contract between business and its community is being re-negotiated to reflect these changes.

Conclusion

The modern enterprise affects most aspects of modern life – in the home, across the nation and in the international arena. The reluctance of a manager to recruit workers of a different colour, religion or gender can eventually produce riots in the streets or squander talent that the firm needs. Effective industrialists show growing awareness of the challenges they face in addressing issues of change, trade practices, stewardship, employment and investment policies. They acknowledge the impact of their actions and their responsibility to satisfy the economic functions of the firm in an environment of trust. The decision by the community to give industry greater freedom in recent years acknowledges the link between freedom and prosperity. Like all political decisions it is conditional. One of the implicit terms of this contract is that self-regulation delivers the economic benefits while ensuring that the community is maintained and developed effectively at a minimum cost. The values of the executives who are responsible for delivering their side of this 'bargain' are shaped by a tradition of debate which gains added momentum from the new issues and perspectives emerging today.

Today, a new paradigm seems to be emerging. The new paradigm will recognize the unity of a subject which encompasses such issues as business ethics, corporate social action, good governance and sound stewardship, respect for the natural and built environment, and affirmative action by business to play its part in tackling the problems of disadvantage. This view recognizes the economic contract between business and society. This contract shapes the relations between commerce and other groups. Its primary aim is to enable industry to perform its economic function in the most effective manner. This economic function stands alongside but is not separate from the other functions performed in and by society. The defence and maintenance functions performed by society allow business to execute its affairs against a background of security and reassurance. The education and development functions of the state develop the skills and sustain the values which industry requires to build and prosper. The governance function establishes the legitimacy of certain behaviour and defines the rules under which commerce pursues its trade. This contract is explicit in some areas, implicit elsewhere and open to negotiation but underpins all commercial activity.

The *rolling back of the state* is not based on the proposition that tasks of social development and maintenance are unnecessary. The core proposition is that industry, operating within a contract employing a variety of market-based mechanisms, could deliver these more effectively than the state or that the state could deliver them more effectively in collaboration with the private sector. The terms of the contract were redefined to meet contemporary needs and circumstances. Contracts are, however, about deliverables. There is little point in preparing a contract if the parties to it cannot deliver against it, do not wish to deliver against it, or do not believe they should deliver against it. High quality governance and delivery lie at the heart of the effective corporate responsibility management. The onus now lies on the new generation of businesses to deliver.

New responsibilities call for a mixture of new and old skills. The visionary contribution of leaders needs to be matched by improved competence among current specialist managers, ownership by line managers and new awareness of their responsibilities by entrants to management. The long-term impact of education, training and development in business ethics, environmental awareness and corporate governance, needs to be assessed to understand their real contribution to the new paradigm. New generations of specialist staff require the support of top management. This is essential for two key aspects of their work: the internal management of the corporate responsibility function, and transferring this mission to line management. Effective programmes are owned and implemented by and through line managers. They need access to expert staff but the systems of reward and control which shape their wider management behaviour will need to mesh in to determine their response to issues of corporate responsibility.

Many of the changes associated with the new paradigm require industrialists to look beyond their immediate environment. Outside events have forced this. The collapse of totalitarianism in Central and Eastern Europe symbolized the synergy that can exist between corporate responsibility and corporate gain. The newly liberated markets are unlikely to produce short-term gains. They are even less likely to produce long-term gains if businesses in the West fail to play an active role in redeveloping their economies. Part of the wider contract with the international community is ensuring a profitable and successful future. Managing the paradox inherent in wedding pressure to respond to turbulence and rapid change to long-term vision, is as important in building the responsible company for tomorrow as in building the profitable company for the Millennium. The debate about the role and importance of both leadership and empowerment reflects this synthesis of ideas and actions. The rate, pace and nature of economic change is forcing individuals, firms and communities to examine not only the way they manage their operation but the nature of the enterprises they manage and their contribution to the wider good.

Tom Cannon is the chief executive of the Management Charter Initiative, associate rector of Hajioannion University, visiting Professor of Corporate Responsibility at Manchester Business School, and visiting Professor of Business at Kingston University. He is also non-executive director of a number of companies and consultant to leading companies such as Mirror Group Newspapers, Virgin and IBM. He is a prolific author and broadcaster. His books include the bestselling *How to Get Ahead in Business* and *Corporate Responsibility*.

Further Reading

Beaumont, J, Pedersen, LM and Whitaker, BD, *Managing the Environment*, Butterworth-Heinemann, Oxford, 1994.

Burrough, B, and Helyar, J, *Barbarians at the Gate*, Arrow, London, 1990.

Cannon, T, *Corporate Responsibility*, FT/Pitman, London, 1993.

Chandler, A, *Strategies and Structure: Chapters in the History of the American Industrial Enterprise*, MIT Press, Cambridge, Mass, 1962.

Demb, A and Neubauer, FF, *The Corporate Board*, Oxford University Press, Oxford, 1993.

Donaldson, T, *The Ethics of International Business*, Oxford University Press, Oxford, 1989.

Stewart, JB, *Den of Thieves*, Simon & Schuster, London, 1991.

References

[1] Kuhn, TS, *The Structure of Scientific Revolution*, The University of Chicago Press, Chicago, 1972.

[2] Mathias, P, *The First Industrial Nation*, Methuen, London,1983.

[3] Cipola, CC, *The Emergence of Industrial Societies*, Methuen, London, 1975, and many others.

[4] Chandler, AD, jnr, *Strategy and Structure: Chapters in the History of the American Industrial Enterprise*, MIT Press, Boston, 1962.

[5] 'Wall Street', film dir Oliver Stone, 20th Century Fox, 1987.

[6] Weber, M, *The Protestant Ethic and the Spirit of Capitalism*, 1905.

[7] Donaldson, J, *Key Issues in Business Ethics*, Academic Press, London, 1989.

[8] Raphael, DD, *Problems of Political Philosophy*, Macmillan, London, 1982.

[9] Task Force on Urban and Business Regeneration, *Initiatives Beyond Charity*, Confederation of British Industry, London, 1988.

[10] Plamenatz, J, *Man and Society*, Oxford University Press, Oxford, 1963.

[11] Friedman, M, *Capitalism and Freedom*, University of Chicago Press, Chicago, 1962.

[12] Locke, J, *Second Treatise of Government*, 1821.

[13] Mill, JS, *Principles of Political Economy*, Longman, London, 1865.

[14] Dale Hanson quoted in *New Directions in Corporate Governance*, Business International Limited, London, 1991.

[15] Plant, R, 'Responsibility and Accountability', Mimeo, University of Southampton, 1990.

[16] *Corporate Governance and American Competitiveness*, The Business Round Table, Washington, 1990.

[17] Gowler, D, 'Values, Contracts and Job Satisfaction', *Personnel Review*, Autumn, 1974.

[18] Rothe, H, 'Does Higher Pay Bring Higher Productivity?' in Fleishman, EA (ed.) *Studies in Personnel and Industrial Psychology*, Dorsey Press, London, 1961.

[19] Chandler, AD, jr, *Strategy and Structure: Chapters in the History of the American Industrial Enterprise*, MIT Press, Cambridge, Mass, 1962.

[20] Hakim, C, 'Occupational Segregation', Department of Employment Research Paper, London, no. 9, 1979.

[21] Hymounts, C, 'The Corporate Woman – The Glass Ceiling', *Wall Street Journal*, 25 November, 1986.

THINKERS

Peter Drucker

Born 1909; writer

The bare bones of Peter Drucker's career give little insight to the profound effect and influence he has had – and continues to have – on management thinking. Born in Austria, he became an investment banker in London in 1933. In 1937 he emigrated to the United States and worked in newspapers. In 1942 he became a Professor of Philosophy and Politics at Bennington College in Vermont and later a Professor of Management at New York University. During his career he has also been a consultant to many large organizations. Now, Drucker is the Clarke Professor of Social Science and Management at the Claremont Graduate School in Claremont, California (he also lectures on oriental art at the same institution).

Behind these scant details lies a career as a writer and thinker on virtually every aspect of management. Drucker's books are as diverse in content as they are numerous. His first book appeared in 1939, *The End of Economic Man*. A succession of others has followed. In the 1940s Drucker wrote *The Future of Industrial Man* and *The Concept of the Corporation*; in the 1950s, his output included *The Practice of Management*; in the 1960s, came *Managing for Results, The Effective Executive, The Age of Discontinuity*; the 1970s brought the encyclopaedic, *Management: Tasks, Responsibilities, Practices*; the 1980s included, *Managing in Turbulent Times* and *The Frontiers of Management*; and in the 1990s, *Managing the Nonprofit Organization* and *Managing for the Future*. By any stretch of the imagination, this is a phenomenal output.

In addition, Drucker has written novels and the autobiographical *Adventures of a Bystander*. Examining the contents of this book, Henry Mintzberg wryly noted that Drucker was the last of the gurus to be featured. 'It is ironic that the oldest person

Education: Doctorate in international and public law, Frankfurt University 1931.
Career: Journalist in Germany and the UK where he also advised banks; went to the US in 1937 to teach; 1939, *The End of Economic Man* published;1942, Professor of Philosophy and Politics at Bennington College, Vermont; Professor of Management at New York University; since 1971 Clarke Professor of Social Science and Management at the Claremont Graduate School in Claremont, California.

included is listed under new elements of management,' he commented, agreeing that Drucker was in his rightful place.

Drucker has deliberately set himself apart from the mainstream of management education – not for nothing is the greatest management thinker of the century a professor at a relatively obscure institution. He has roundly condemned Harvard Business School and the business school system and, during his lengthy career, has studiously avoided becoming part of any one organization. The theorist has studiously retained an objective distance from organizational practice.

What is notable about Drucker's work is his uncanny ability to spot trends and describe them in an almost downbeat manner, drawing wisdom from an array of sources (though Jane Austen and Trollope remain consistent inspirations to him). Later they are almost always picked up by others and become the height of managerial fashion. Often, their roots can be traced back to Drucker's work a decade previously. His 1969 book, *The Age of Discontinuity*, for example, is now much referred to as writers and managers attempt to come to terms with managing change. In this book he observed that America was 'a knowledge economy' – a theme he later returned to in *Managing for the Future* (1992) in which he observed: 'From now on the key is knowledge.' Twenty-five years on from his original observation, the concept of knowledge-workers and knowledge-intensive organizations is gaining widespread attention (not least from Drucker himself).

Other of his works have ignited interest long after their publication. In the 1973 book, *People and Performance*, he discussed the broader social responsibilities of managers and organizations – once again, this is something organizations are slowly coming to terms with. Drucker called for less hierarchical structures and leaner organizations in the 1960s and again in the 1980s before they became fashionable in the 1990s.

Drucker predicted what is now labelled post-industrialism and examined how this would impact on managerial best practice. Indeed, his recent writings have reaffirmed the radical challenges facing managers: 'The single greatest challenge facing managers in the developed countries of the world is to raise the productivity of knowledge and service works. This challenge, which will dominate the management agenda for the next several decades, will ultimately determine the competitive performance of companies. Even more important, it will determine the very fabric of society and the quality of life in every industrialized nation.'[1]

Perhaps his greatest achievements are *The Practice of Management* (1954) and *Management: Tasks, Responsibilities, Practices* (1973). In the latter, a massive work, he identifies five 'basic operations in the work of the manager'. These are:

- setting objectives
- organizing
- motivating and communicating

- measuring
- developing people (including him or herself)

The length of his career and his level of book production has enabled him to extol a company's virtues and then, later, to point out how and when its virtues became liabilities. Most famously, his book *Concept of the Corporation* analyzed and celebrated GM's divisional structure – in 1991 he recognized that what had once made the company successful, its long-established management practices, were what was now holding it back.

Undoubtedly, Drucker's ideas have evolved – his fascination with corporations, for example, has given way to an interest in small firms and non-profit organizations. His broad brush brings in history, sociology and anthropology and, by its very nature, courts disappointment and failure. *The Economist* observed that Drucker has 'a burning sense of the importance of management. He believes that poor management helped to plunge the Europe of his youth into disaster, and he fears that the scope for poor management is growing larger, as organizations become ever more complicated and interdependent'.[2]

Despite such concerns, Drucker is encouraged that the emphasis is now on changing organizations to become more efficient – rather than on dragging every ounce of energy out of tired managers and employees. He also believes that globalization will produce managers who are more in-tune with the needs of the global environment than politicians. Only then will managers be able to take what Drucker regards as their rightful place as the driving forces behind the great economies.

STUART CRAINER

Further Reading

Peter Drucker:
Concept of the Corporation, John Day, New York, 1946.
The New Society, Heinemann, London, 1951.
The Practice of Management*, Harper & Row, New York, 1954.
Managing for Results, Heinemann, London, 1964.
The Age of Discontinuity*, Heinemann, London, 1969.
Management: Tasks, Responsibilities, Practices*, Heinemann, London, 1974.
Innovation and Entrepreneurship, Heinemann, London, 1985.
The New Realities, Heinemann, London, 1989.
Managing the Nonprofit Organization, HarperCollins, London, 1990.

* Recommended reading

References

[1] Drucker, PF, 'The new productivity challenge', *Harvard Business Review*, November-December 1991.
[2] 'Peter Drucker, salvationist', *The Economist*, London, 1 October 1994.

PUBLIC SERVICE MANAGEMENT

Catherine Fitzmaurice

The last 15 years or so have been fertile for the public sector. They have brought a crop of changes which have altered the structures, dynamics and conceptions of public services. This revolution, like most profound changes, has not been painless nor has it always been welcome, but the process of change continues and its impact remains difficult to assess accurately.

There is another barrier to judgement: where public services are concerned, discussions seldom avoid the pitfall of prejudice. They tend to arouse a very high degree of emotion, involving basic questions about society and politics. However, what can be said is that the process of change has brought with it a new managerial agenda involving new skills and attitudes.

While discussions of public sector management are prey to emotions, the changes in this sector clearly require evaluation. Questions need to be asked about the expectations which now fall on public sector management. The impact of fundamental changes on the senior managers of public services requires examination. We can also assess the needs they now have in terms of both management training and management development.

The portrayal of the public sector at the beginning of the 1980s was simple: it was perceived as large, bureaucratic and belligerent; it was held to be costly and complacent; it was branded as inefficient, insensitive and inward-looking.

The extent to which this portrayal reflected reality remains a moot point. Perceptions are always relative and tend to become polarized when the reference points differ markedly. This was certainly the case as far as public services were concerned. While attachment to the Welfare State conditioned the rhetoric and response of the public sector, attachment to the Market Economy persuaded governments, in the UK and beyond, of the need for radical changes in public sector management.

In many ways, the debate Welfare State versus Market Economy was a non-debate. Indeed, it is equally as difficult to argue that a single system of management (bureaucracy) is necessary to achieve the goals of a philosophy (welfare state) as it is to assert that the endorsement of a political predicate (market economy) is the only and necessary answer to efficiency and effectiveness of the public services (service delivery).

The pursuit of the three Es – Efficiency, Effectiveness and Economy – had, however, started in earnest, and with it came structural changes (privatization, decentralization, etc) and performance measurement (audits, inspections, regulations, etc).

A new world emerged, characterized by the struggle for finite resources in a system where need had to be demonstrated and allocation was dependent on quantifiable performance and defined priorities. A new language also emerged: that of chief executives, governance and business plans; one of targets, market testing, national standards and curriculum, compulsory competitive tendering and charters.

The language, however, fails us in one major way. We have one expression – public sector – and many varied embodiments of what used to fall under this term. But, what now constitutes the public sector? Is it a question of ownership or of accountability? Crucially, the changes have affected the very nature of this sector, yet the language has not moved on. We lack words to define what should legitimately fall under the ambit of scrutiny when 'public' services are concerned.

So, for example, services for water, gas, electricity and telecommunications are no longer owned or managed as they were. They are businesses subject to competition, even if this is somewhat limited and involves, in most instances, the use of an existing infrastructure by the competitors. However, while closer to the image of a private sector company, they are still providing a public service and have to abide by central government regulations and standards of public accountability which do not affect other private sector companies.

Roles, functions and expectations

This attention to linguistics is not a peripheral issue. It crucially affects the way in which we can define the roles, functions and expectations of the senior managers who manage public services. It also helps us to understand their frustrations and the staff demoralization which often stems from the changes they have to manage.

First, they have to face the powerful public perception, implicitly or explicitly stated, that private sector management practices are 'better'. The problem is that the assertion is questionable. The private sector is not immune from inefficiency or waste, inadequate human resource management or poor customer service. Private concerns also struggle with effective strategic planning or leadership, find managing change and communication difficult, have debates about the marketing of their services and face issues of personal effectiveness and corporate culture.

Second, comparing sectors is problematic because there is great diversity in both public and private sector organizations. What is more, while each operate under constraints, the nature of these constraints is not always the same.

So, for example, many public sector organizations still fall within the yearly budget cycle. In some instances, this means that they have to commit their organization to a three-year plan when they ignore the allocation of public funds which will be theirs in subsequent years.

Most are dependent on sudden and sometimes profound changes of policy which emanate from government and over which they have little control. Furthermore, many public sector organizations cannot make a profit or plough back to the organization more than a small percentage of its financial achievements. Nor can they borrow freely for capital projects. For some, dismissal of staff is still difficult, if not impossible, while recruitment and selection can easily be out of the control of the senior management team.

On the other hand, senior managers of public services do not face the vagaries of the stock-market, the threat of takeover bids or competition at an international level. They do not yet face, to the same degree, the possibility of losing senior managerial and professional staff attracted by the higher salaries or benefits offered by competitors.

As a result, it is quite difficult to compare like with like and the dichotomy private versus public offers little comfort, be it intellectual or managerial. The reality is that there is much that private and public service providers can learn from each other. There are also great dangers, as far as public services are concerned, in not assessing and capitalizing on those aspects of public sector management which were, and are, successful.

Managing values or valuing management?

It is worth noting that the public services have always employed a large proportion of professionals: doctors, social workers, lawyers, psychologists, accountants, architects, probation officers, teachers, fire fighters, nurses, researchers. The code of ethics and conduct of these professional groups went a long way to ensure service delivery in conditions which were often far from optimal. Expressions such as 'the goodwill of staff' were often used to describe their commitment despite inadequate working conditions, poor financial remuneration and long working hours.

This is not to say that there was no inefficiency, ineffectiveness or complacency. Nor was this some kind of 'golden period'. However, public service managers – and indeed policy-makers – do need to reflect on what led professionals to work with motivation despite the paucity of external rewards. They also need to think about the reward systems currently contemplated – performance-related pay is a good example – and assess their possible impact on the values which underpin public service provisions. If the values and management of the welfare state are no longer reinforced, there is no reason to expect the same reliance on professional 'goodwill'.

However, there is a pressing need to reconcile, somehow, the values of providing a service to the community to its effective management. Sound management practice may be a quality, a skill or a necessity. It is, however, not a substitute for the value system which underpins service delivery. Put differently, managerialism should not be the paradigm of the organization but a means through which it is to be achieved.

Professional groups also tend to hold very strong views about the assessment of their performance. By and large, it is their peer group and their professional association which are considered relevant and legitimate assessors. Equally, those are deemed to act as guarantors of integrity and ensure adherence to professional norms of conduct. In other words, accountability has been seen by professionals largely as a professional not an organizational matter. These norms, however, are not concerned with costs or resourcing.

Given the proportion of professionals in the public services, the drive to establish efficiency, effectiveness and economy was doomed to a head-on collision with professional values. The health service always offers a varied array of such conflicts, be they in terms of the cost of new and complex procedures, such as multiple organ transplants, or of keeping very premature babies alive or of not treating the teeth of sweet-eating children nor operating on persistent smokers.

The root of these conflicts can only too easily be ascribed to the power of professional groups, their rejection of cost controlling mechanisms and of organizational accountability. It is important too that public service managers examine and analyze how, in the absence of the current sets of performance indicators, audits and inspections (and the bureaucracy they themselves create), professionals assessed, maintained or improved the quality of the service they provided. Those indicators may have been more qualitative and nebulous than the statistics presently generated but the latter are not necessarily more accurate or informative because they are couched in numbers. Indeed, there is now a considerable incentive to ensure a correct profile of results given the financial consequences attached to them.

Professional managers and managing professionals

Reflecting on the values and behaviours which characterized the public services is also important for another reason. As was noted earlier, the public services include many professional groups. At present, many of those professionals are still people who came to their career because they wanted to practise their professional skills. They saw themselves as social workers, surgeons, clinical psychologists, teachers, probation officers, etc. It was someone else's role to ensure the running of the offices, personnel functions or health and safety.

Those were generally administrators and they did not 'manage' as much as 'administer'. They were not 'professionals'. Largely treated as second rate citizens in organizational cultures which were dominated by the 'professionals', their concerns were seen, by and large, as less central and important than the discharge of professional obligations.

The public services revolution has considerably altered that balance of power. Administrators have become managers and as such wield enormous power with which the professionals have had to come to terms. In the process, many have come to realize that the managers are professionals in their own right, highly experienced, often holders of postgraduate qualifications and members of their own professional institutes.

However, more or less concurrently and in many public service organizations, the professionals themselves have either chosen to become managers or have had this function thrust upon them. Devolved budgets have transformed many professionals into middle managers, and most senior professional staff are now part of a senior management team where they are corporately responsible for performance evaluation or for some direct managerial function over staff and budgets.

This change has two effects. The first is that management is often in the hands of people who were never trained for it and, in many instances, are still very uncomfortable, both professionally and managerially, with these new responsibilities.

The second is that, whatever their ability to come to terms with this fundamental shift, they are required to manage other professional staff who themselves have to make this transition from professional to managerial accountability. In many ways, it is very much like helping a bereaved friend when you have been yourself recently bereaved. Helping another may actually help you but it also shifts the focus back onto your own bereavement. Moreover, in many instances, professionals are now accountable directly to a professional manager who can challenge clinical decisions.

It is worth noting too that the fate of chief executives or senior managers drawn from a managerial background is no less difficult. Whether they came from the private sector or another public service organization, they do have to face the inevitable prejudice that generic managers never quite understand the culture, behaviours, history and symbols of the organization they have come to manage. This, of course, is something of a self-fulfilling prophesy as generally, they have been appointed precisely to change the very culture of the organization.

Management training and development

The changes which have affected the public services have a tremendous impact on the needs for management training and development. Three needs are frequently expressed.

First, it is not uncommon for senior managers to experience despondency. It affects them whether they are drawn from a managerial or professional background. This despondency is very much akin to learned helplessness and is clearly related to the pace and unpredictability of changes decided upon by policy-makers at governmental levels. In this respect, private and public sector organizations differ strikingly.

The problem is that the lack of control over policy changes often heavily clouds senior managers' assessment of their potential to fulfill an effective strategic function. This can result in a lack of appreciation of the strategic role they can still fulfill within the boundaries available to them. This is compounded by the fact that senior managers rarely meet colleagues from other public services and often fear revealing their feelings of powerlessness within their own and often competitive organizations.

Formal comparisons of organizational constraints with other senior managers act as an effective means of challenging this despondency over unpredictability. It leads to a realization of the similarity of experiences between services. Importantly, it also reveals different means used by organizations to manage uncertainty. In other words, the acknowledgement of the difficulties is, in itself, part of the process of adaptation. Indeed, it is quite clear that this process is essential for effective learning to take place.

The second need which faces senior managers concerns the strategic function they are to fulfill. Services are at very different developmental points in this respect but, in most instances, strategic change needs to be effective. However, to be effective, these strategic changes require powerful cultural changes which are often totally neglected. Put another way, the need to address change at a strategic level also means making a fairly detailed analysis of what sustains the 'old' organization. It also means that senior managers must decide, on this basis, what is required to operate a successful transition.

The third aspect is very much linked to the second and concerns the role of the senior management team. Corporate cultures and corporate strategies require effective top teams. Because of the powerful professional culture which characterized public services and emphasized independence, the issue is often a difficult and thorny one. In this respect also, management training and development offer a powerful vehicle for change. Indeed, external facilitation is essential as the process presupposes both an ability by each member of the senior management team to scrutinize his or her own strengths and limitations, and an ability to understand differences and build on diversity. This process, of course, is similar to that concerning the leadership function of senior managers. In this context, the appreciation of the effectiveness of different leadership styles is also very much a liberating feature in the development of senior managers.

The challenge of specificity

There are many other areas which are now crucial to public sector management development: the relationship between professionalism and managerialism; motivation of staff in a changing and uncertain climate; quality of service delivery; adherence to both efficiency and effectiveness criteria; and personnel issues, be they related to contracts, performance appraisals, rewards or training, etc.

There are others which also very much affect public service organizations. Competitive tendering, be it compulsory or voluntary, is certainly crucial; the issue of corporate governance is another which, if anything, will increase in consequence and importance; the question of partnerships or contracted services where statutory responsibility remains with the service concerned is another.

However, looking at the three areas identified earlier, the question of the specificity of public sector management can easily be raised. Indeed, adaptation to shifts in policy, strategic thinking or top team effectiveness are not the sole concerns of public sector organizations. In the same vein, other comparisons could be easily established: competitive tendering has a long history in private sector organizations, as has the tradition of serving as a non-executive director or of using subsidiaries to produce goods or services.

Indeed, the management of public services resembles in many ways the management of private sector organizations. The diversity which now characterizes the structure of public services enables even greater comparisons. However, the issue of specificity is still a real issue. It is, incidentally, the same if we look at the private sector: for example, there are areas of communality in management between the banking sector and the engineering sector. Nevertheless, there are many specific features of each type of organization which need to be integrated both in management practice and in management training.

It is clear that effective management entails not the blind acceptance of any management model, but the careful consideration of its applicability to a specific context. It is very much the role of senior managers, helped by management training and development, to ensure that the models either are helpful at a heuristic level or can be appropriately applied given the specific needs of an organization.

The same applies to public services. As we have seen, the public sector is very much in transition. Its history, its past culture, its achievements, its aims and its vision of its future are all part of this transition. Its specificity, of course, is partly due to its obligations in relation to parliamentary accountability.

At a different level, its specificity has to do with its uniqueness as a sector of the economy, directly funded or regulated by central or by local government and charged to deliver the professional services that government policy decided upon and that politicians were elected to ensure they provide. This situation will alter with increasing centralization of performance standards, increased decentralization in terms of managerial autonomy, and increased variety in structures and forms of service delivery.

However, what is currently at issue, and will remain an important challenge for all public service providers be they public or private, is the crucial need to reconcile commercial and community values, to see beyond the storm of change and to identify the most effective means to provide services which are both of quality in their delivery and reflective of care and respect for the communities to which they are offered. This remains an urgent and important challenge for the senior managers and the public services they manage.

Dr Catherine Fitzmaurice is director of the public sector senior manager's programme at Cranfield School of Management, Bedfordshire.

Further Reading

Duncan, C, (ed.) *The Evolution of Public Management: Concepts and Techniques for the 1990s*, Macmillan, London, 1992.

MANAGING THE SMALL BUSINESS

Panikkos Poutziouris

In his 1973 classic, *Small is Beautiful,* EF Schumacher observed: 'Man is small, and, therefore small is beautiful... To go for giantism is to go for self-destruction.' Though small businesses are a key economic driving force, the lure of 'giantism' remains strong.

Managing the small business requires a unique set of skills. Managers must be entrepeneurial, creative, risk-taking and innovative if they are to juggle the complex demands of achieving growth. Yet, they must also retain financial stability and independence. Only if a balance is struck can organizations develop along the path from existence through to survival, comfort and growth.

Small businesses are vital protagonists in economic, industrial and market development. 'Small enterprises are a seed-bed of indigenous entrepreneurship; mobilize so far ungenerated capital; are labour-intensive; enhance indigenous technological learning; contribute to the decentralization of industry; further competition behind protective barriers; use predominantly local resources; cater for the basic needs of the poor; contribute to the more equitable distribution of income and wealth,' accurately observed one academic study.[1]

Small and medium-sized enterprises (SMEs) constitute the backbone of the enterprise system, playing a key role in the regeneration of regional and peripheral economies, the creation of jobs, promotion of innovation and the creation of economic wealth. However, their success in achieving these bold objectives depends on the ability of entrepreneurs to launch new business ventures and to propel young and dynamic firms to growth and development.

The development of a small business is governed by the entrepreneurial aspirations and capabilities of management. The business owner or manager needs to exhibit both entrepreneurial and managerial skills to orchestrate survival and growth strategies, marshalling limited resources in the targeting of market opportunities. Also, the founder of a small family business (it is estimated that over 85 per cent of businesses in Europe are family-controlled)[2] must strategically plan the entreprenerial succession in order to safeguard both the reinforcement of organizational management and leadership.

Small businesses and entrepreneurship

It is easier to describe small businesses than to define them. Because of a lack of concensus as to what constitutes a small business, a three-part definition proposed by the Bolton Report, as early as 1971, is most widely used :

- In economic terms, a small business has a relatively *small share of its market.*
- It is *managed in a personalized way* – with no formal management structure.
- It is *independent* in the sense that it does not form part of a larger enterprise and *the owner/manager is free from outside control.*

The same Bolton Committee, recognizing that a single quantitative definition would not cover a diversity of industries, used eight definitions for varying industry groups. Statistical definitions of small firms continue to vary considerably, from one country to another, and from industry to industry. Criteria used to measure business size include the number of employees, sales volume, and asset size. In Europe, small firms are defined as those with less than 200 employees, medium-sized firms are those with 200 to 500 employees, and micro-firms employ less than ten people.

Qualitative criteria serve as more generally acceptable definitions because they place more emphasis on the motives and characteristics of the founder and/or owners. Clearly, the decision of the entrepreneur to start up a new firm or invest in a business venture is governed by the potential rewards. These generally include:

- **profit:** freedom from the limits of standardized pay;
- **independence:** freedom from supervision and rules of bureaucratic organizations;
- **satisfying way of life:** freedom from routine, boring and unchallenging jobs.

Entrepreneurship lies at the heart of the small business. The start-up of a new firm, or the charismatic management of a growing small business, remain the most idolized forms of entrepreneurship. It is the small business which is routinely celebrated for exhibiting innovative excellence, risk-taking and creativity. And, the survival and success of a small business heavily depends on the managerial charisma of the owner or manager.

Beyond the glamorous entrepreneurial image there are often complications. The small business, characterized by a craft-oriented management and autonomistic business culture, linked to the owner's behaviour and attitudes, can often inhibit the entrepreneurial motivation for business growth. The scenario becomes more complicated when the small business is family-controlled and family politics contradict economic rationality.

Though widely understood, entrepreneurship comes in a variety of subtle variations. *Entrepreneurship* describes the founder or owner as the centre of the company's operations. *Intrapreneurship* describes in-house entrepreneurial activity when dedicated employees assume managerial responsibility and leadership; and the concept of *interpreneurship* refers to inter-generational, entrepreneurial activity following successful management succession in the family business. *Corporate entrepreneurship* refers to the introduction or hiring of external managers.[3]

Managing small business and entrepreneurial ventures

The challenges, problems and issues facing the small business owner or entrepreneur are governed by a great number of factors. They may be personal or family-related, organizational, inter-organizational or, in a wider context, driven by industrial dynamics or prevailing macroeconomic conditions. The success or failure of a small business depends on a number of growth constraints whose nature changes as the business moves along the stages of the organizational life-cycle growth model: existence, survival, comfort and growth.

An important distinction to make is the difference between the owner-manager – mainly found in passive companies – and entrepreneurs. Often the two concepts are mistakingly taken as being synonymous. Some academics make further distinctions – between 'artisans' who seek intrinsic satisfaction from the excellence of their craft, 'managers', who seek recognition from managerial excellence,[4] and 'classic' entrepreneurs characterized by their creativity and innovative charisma. Similarly, others segment entrepreneurs into 'growth-oriented', 'independence-oriented', and 'craft-entrepreneurship-oriented'.[5] Others still, focus on the factors of profit maximization and growth orientation, and offer a more simplistic and vivid distinction between the small business owner and the entrepreneur:[6]

'A *small business owner* is an individual who establishes and manages a business for the principal purpose of furthering personal goals. The business must be the primary source of income and will consume the majority of one's time and resources. The owner perceives the business as an extension of his or her personality, intricately bound with family needs and desires... An *entrepreneur* is an individual who establishes and manages for the principal purpose of profit and growth. The entrepreneur is characterized principally by innovative behaviour and will employ strategic management practice in the business.'[7]

Problems and priorities

The problems – both internal and external – facing small businesses have been the subject of increasing interest. Each stage of development brings with it a set of strategic disadvantages. These can be translated into supply-side gaps (such as finance and technological gaps). Growth constraints (or their sources) govern the structure, behaviour and performance of small firms as they, hopefully, develop.

As the small company launches successful, profitable products and services and establishes a customer base, resources will be built up to pursue potential market opportunities. Small entrepreneurial businesses pursuing growth strategies often experience 'growing pains' and new problems. Small business owners and founders face pressure to adopt more professional management, develop further, or introduce, new managerial functions and tasks (such as design and product development, or recruiting financial and marketing personnel) and even invite outsiders (often corporate entrepreneurs or venture capitalists) to reinforce the business resource base in order to cope with their changing needs.

Although small-business management faces an endless array of potential problems, some of those will never be realized, constitute a threat, nor appreciably affect the owner and the business. Other problems will be persistent and can even be life-threatening if not attended to. Small-firm problems can usually be broken down by functional areas in order to increase strategic awareness of them and to identify priorities.

Small businesses are often centralized and unstructured. This tends to serve the managerial-entrepreneurial motives of the business owner rather than the needs of the organization. The small-business owner often prefers informal communication and control structures which suit his or her management style.[8] Strategic planning is usually limited and the typical 'spider web' organizational form of small business is characterized by lack of delegation and over-dependence on the owner manager.[9]

Despite the external communication disadvantages routinely experienced by small businesses – such as in the monitoring of industrial developments, technological change, and development of infrastructural projects and support mechanisms – there is a number of internal communication advantages. The small business usually has an efficient and informal internal communication network. This is commonly backed by harmonious employment relations, especially in the family business where there is a homogeneous cultural background. These factors enable a speedy response to any internal problems which emerge.

Paradoxically, the attractions and advantages of the small business – informality, family-oriented, personal – can also work against it, as often they may erode the managerial professionalism of those running it.

General management problems

The dominant managerial problems facing small-business management are often rooted in the psychology, technical calibre, and business aspirations of the owner/manager and development of the organizational structure and management style.

● **Time mis-management and lack of management specialization:** The small business owner/manager is often a strong believer in the marriage of ownership and control. This can lead to a failure to seek out or use technical specialists when they are required. Duties are not given priorities and strategic decisions may be overlooked in order to complete routine jobs. The lack of management specialization creates inefficiencies and disadvantages in the innovation process (ie, marketing tactics, design/development of new products/services and technological progress). In family businesses the management function tends to improve with the introduction of a new generation of entrepreneurs.

● **Proliferation of traditional approaches rather than modern management practice:** There is no widespread application of formal systems in the areas of cost-pricing, quality control, inventory and strategic management. Direct experience and informal management practices often prove to be adequate and compatible to the narrow resource base of small firms. But, in some industries, small-business management is characterized by deficiencies which adversely affect other business functions, especially during times of market turbulence, and when business growth demands more managerial expertise and administrative support.

● **Poor management development:** The small business owner overlooks the need for investment in training and management development. As the firm expands in a fast-changing environment, managerial skills become more important than operational-production considerations, thus widening the managerial gap.

● **Negligence of selection, promotion and supervision of personnel impedes managerial professionalism:** Recruitment decisions, especially for managers, need to be governed first by behavioural motives, then by organizational considerations.

● **Poor strategic planning and monitoring of information:** Strategic planning is overlooked in the small business because it requires strategic awareness and a substantial investment of time to collect and analyze information critical to the formulation of profitable business strategies. Information gaps emerge, with respect to monitoring developments in technology, market demand, industrial/trade policy, which adversely affect the design and implementation of business strategies.

Production and operational problems

The central issue in the economics of production is the concept of economies of scale. This constitutes the fundamental rationale for industrial efficiency, associated with specialization, and is the major determinant of business size. The optimum scale of operations is the level at which economies of scale are exhausted, or to be more practical, costs cease to fall rapidly.[10] The optimal point delineates the feasible production zone for small businesses. This is often suitable for niche-strategies not tailored to the economics of a large business with its high overheads.

The size of the minimum efficient scale (MES) is the main determinant of the size distribution and the relative importance of small businesses across industries. An industry with a small MES, is essentially a small-business industry, where there is a proliferation of small firms which do not suffer a unit cost disadvantage relative to larger organizations.

Economies of scale are barriers to entry and undermine the efficient operation of the small business. Cost disadvantages can usually be identified in these areas:

- exploitation of economies from management specialization;
- development of economies by focusing/differentiating competitive products/services;
- adoption of modern/automated technology;
- modernization of management, production, distribution and marketing methods;
- utilization of production capacity;
- research and development to upgrade quality and develop new products/services;
- training programme to upgrade technical and managerial skills;
- purchasing/importing of raw materials;
- distribution, promotion, advertising and selling of products/services.

Small firms are able to compete successfully with large organizations, because they can absorb fluctuations in demand through their inherent flexibility. They employ flexible production strategies and inter-firm co-operation (through subcontracting networks or membership of consortia) to remain viable in an otherwise hostile environment for small businesses.[11]

There are other sources of advantages for the small business apart from the economic benefits of flexibility. Small businesses can pursue innovation-driven strategies in developing customized and quality products or services; flexibly targeting niches in localized markets, or at the higher end of the market; and in providing better service to customers with special contractual relationships and strong feelings of loyalty.

The dedication and leadership of the small-firm entrepreneur may inspire employees to achieve high levels of productivity, enough to offset the cost-disadvantages of being a small business. Family firms often capitalize on high human capital productivity to develop a labour cost advantage. But, their development is hampered by a number of operational problems:

- **Under-utilization of capital and production capacity:** The operations of small businesses are focused – at least in the early stages of development – more towards local markets where often demand is limited geographically and is sometimes volatile or seasonal. As a result of this demand insufficiency, small businesses do not fully utilize their production capacity. The problem is more acute in manufacturing firms equipped with production technology tailored to mass production.

- **Lack of product specialization:** In some small businesses the degree of product specialization or diversification is examined in terms of products and markets: this is determined by the number of product groups and their linkages (common production inputs, technology or distribution system), and the number of distinct markets and their definition in terms of geographical extension, customer groups and customer needs.[12]

Diversifying into producing a greater number of products is one method of reducing market uncertainty and improving the utilization of production capacity. This tactic is more prolific in businesses operating in local markets and among atomistic entrepreneurs who see subcontracting as an erosion of business independence.

- **Cost myopia impedes dynamism:** Conservative and reactive small business owners tend to pursue tactics to minimize costs. In defence of local markets, they copy designs rather than promoting a culture based on their own innovation. Their manufacturing strategy is based on the reproduction of customized products at a more competitive price. Limited financial and technological resources force owners to overlook the competitive advantages yielded by research and development. The cost myopia also impedes the upgrading of labour skills – training is regarded as a waste of valuable working hours.

- **The wrong location:** The small firm may be operating from a location which creates difficulties for both supply and distribution. The concentration of small firms with involvement in inter-firm co-operation or a subcontracting network in industrial districts, creates external economies which can often outweigh the cost disadvantages of small-scale operation.

- **The wrong premises:** The decision about the size and type of premises largely depends on the scale of operations. This is determined by the market, technical considerations and the company's business aspirations. As small firms develop they are liable to experience difficulties with premises.

- **Shortages of highly-skilled technicians:** The intensity of this problem depends on the labour market. Recruitment of multi-skilled technicians remains a serious constraint on the development of the small business for it also hampers investment in technological upgrading. To sustain business growth, limited resources must be marshalled towards the development of technical capabilities and operational flexibility.

- **Technologies are not 'state of the art', either because of poor access and/or under-utilization of capital capacity:** The development of the small business depends on the degree to which the technological base can sustain the competitiveness of the product or service. The success and failure of small manufacturing firms is governed by the technological gap, where the small producer has poor access to modern/flexible technologies.[13] Even if they have access, small businesses are often incapable of fully utilizing particular sets of technologies due to constraints associated with existing physical facilities (premises, market isolation), financing bottlenecks (high capital investment) and 'craft-management'.[14]

Financial barriers

Small businesses face unique financial problems that overshadow the other barriers hindering their performance and development process. Research has shown that the main source of capital in the early stages of development is personal equity.[15] Small firms are initially very dependent on internal capital (private/own, friends and family funds) because their borrowing level is low. As the business develops and grows in size and age, different forms of short and medium-term financing options are available to finance emerging goals and activities.

There are heavy personal and social costs in the start-up, survival and growth phases of a family business, for entrepreneurs, their families, relatives and friends. The over-reliance of small firms on owners' capital injections and funds lent by relatives and friends, is mainly the consequence of finance gaps which occur where external financing requirements (equity and debt) are not fully met. The debate on the nature of the finance gap has evolved, but has always been governed by Binksian Law: 'The smaller the firm, the larger the proportionate increase in the capital required to respond to an increase in demand (depending on the diffusion of demand fluctuation), but the smaller the ability to command loan and equity finance.'[16]

Investigations into the financing of small businesses have found that long-term external finance plays a minor role in their development.[17] This is a result of problems endemic to the economics and dynamics of small firms – such as erratic demand; the conservatism of capital markets which often penalize the small business; and the inadequacies of small-firm management in planning and financial control.

The financial development of small firms is also governed by a number of other unique factors. The autonomistic and idiosyncratic business culture is based on the locus of control and is characterized by an opposition to external financing options because these will erode the control of the business owners. Other shortcomings generally involve poor financial planning and over-dependence on the owner/manager which contributes to problematic financial management and the development of a weak financial base to support business development.

Throughout their lives small companies face a finance gap. During the start-up phase, small business owners finance operations with internally generated funds but, as the company develops, the financial structure varies depending on the financial needs and financing options available. Factors governing financial development will be profitability, the economics of financing small-firm growth (institutional conservatism and asymmetry of information), and the entrepreneurial culture which is often opposed to outside interference and is intent on providing creative solutions to information gaps and financial planning.

The lack of external development finance – mainly in the form of bank loans, including short-term loans and overdraft facilities – evolves depending on the stage of development process. The life cycle of the capital structure suggests that at the early stages of the organizational life cycle, high business risk constrains the supply of short-term bank support (through interest rate penalties, high bank charges and collateral). As the firm develops in terms of size, age and business image, the debt gap improves, but widens as the small firm pursues alternative growth strategies. At the lateral stages of development the small business management will consider other financing options.

Small businesses are also commonly exposed to high gearing and are overdependent on external-debt financing. As a result of the equity gap, small-firm development has to be financed from external sources. The limited capacity of small firms to accumulate internally-generated funds is governed by their business performance and entrepreneurial attitudes of business owners with respect to external equity participation which is reflected in the high level of gearing.

The cash-flow cycle can frequently lead under-capitalized firms into situations of over-trading, poor liquidity, mis-management of credit, inventories and time-period investment. Poor cash-flow often persists through the organizational life cycle of small firms even when they are trading successfully. Often, as result of misallocation of funds (short-term funds financing long-term capital investment) a shortage of working capital emerges. In addition, the limited market power of small firms does not guarantee synchronicity of trade debt and trade credit, a problem exacerbated by discrete changes in demand.

Another obstacle frequently encountered is insufficient asset collateral to secure loan finance. Small businesses are often undercapitalized and can experience a debt gap because of insufficient collateral. The asset-backed collateral is undervalued by financial institutions to ensure the loan is realistically covered in the event of default and mediation. To secure loan finance the small firm owner/manager provides personal collateral in the form of a guarantee or property deed. This erodes limited liability.

The founder/owner of the small business inevitably devotes the majority of managerial effort to the establishment and functioning of the production process and promotion of sales. Lack of management time, as well as poor management development, and limited use of information-accounting systems and health checks can lead to the undermining of financial planning and financing strategies.

Poor credit management – through over-crediting and the slow collection of debt – is also common. The typical lag in the collection of accounts receivable – also due to normal business practices exemplified by 'the cheque is in the post' – creates problematic credit management. There is no widespread use of credit management agencies, like factoring, either because of cost myopia or mostly due to its damaging effect on customer relations. Often small firms offer credit as part of the marketing mix in order to safeguard customer loyalty.

The financing of small business development remains a formidable issue for the small business owner and his or her banker, which needs to be addressed continuously and in conjunction with the overall strategic and marketing orientation of the business.

Problems of marketing and competition

There are two views on the impact of competition on small business strategy and the strategic ability of smaller firms to fend off competition. The small business lacks the human and technological resources necessary to re-orientate strategy to changing market conditions and, as a result, has limited strategic options in coping with competition. A contrasting view is that small businesses largely compete with other small firms, and organizational size does not play a crucial role in the strategic management of competition. Besides, small firms develop competitive advantage in terms of customer relationships and consequently they may successfully and flexibly cope with rivals by pursuing differentiation, innovation and 'nichemanship' strategies.[18]

Niche strategies target, or create, gaps in the market which larger firms find unsuitable for their large investment capacity. The most common identifiable advantage for successful small companies is a narrow scope of operations reflecting market, product and customer specialization. The marketing strategy emphasizes the non-price elements of the marketing mix, such as quality, and satisfying a small, clearly defined market where customers have specialized needs.

Despite the competitive advantage of their marketing operations in terms of flexibility, innovation and personalized service, small businesses often encounter a number of marketing-related problems:

- **Sales performance is insufficient and inwardly oriented:** Despite the ability of small firms to react to changing market trends, their localized customer base, or specialized market niches, are often too small to justify an expansion or technological upgrading programme. To improve the geographical distribution of sales, management has to target new market niches, home and abroad. Small firms face prohibitive cost disadvantages in developing markets.

- **Poor knowledge of market competition and lack of market research:** Small businesses are predominantly owned by artisan-entrepreneurs who lack the managerial time and skills to monitor and utilize market information. Market research to establish the customer profile, source and form of competition, and to identify market trends is often beyond the financial and administrative base of small firms.

- **Lack of a proactive marketing programme:** Small firms often lack the qualified technical specialists and financial resources to support a formal research and development programme to produce innovative products. In response to competitive pressure from mainly larger counterparts, often launching promotional/advertising campaigns, small firms target localized and special markets with high quality, customized products/services.

Small-business marketing is the vehicle of entrepreneurial success where operations put the customer first. Small-business management needs to establish the customer profile in the target market (per segment and niche), analyze the competition, and regularly evaluate capacity to guarantee the consistent delivery of quality products/services more effectively – and then more efficiently – than the competition.

Pillars of small business success

Markets have been shaken by a number of developments that directly and indirectly favour the 'small is beautiful'-driven niche strategies:

- Technological revolution.
- Liberalization, decentralization: privatization, management buy-outs.
- Sophistication of consumers: quality and design culture.
- Ageing population and working women: convenience.
- Vegetarianism, green revolution.

These trends contribute to the intensification of competition, furthering of market fragmentation and shrinking of product life cycles; subsequently creating scope for small-business niche strategies to fill or create gaps in the new markets that large organizations find unsuitable for their investment capacity. The re-emergence of small firms across economies and industries concretely suggests that Michael Porter's dictum that 'national and economic prosperity is created, not inherited' holds and depends on the capacity of business to innovate, upgrade and develop competitive advantage.

In the new business climate the emphasis of competitive strategy has shifted from price and efficiency to quality, design and customer service which entail innovative and flexible customization tactics. Small firms are naturally in a better position than large businesses to meet the rapidly changing customer expectations because they are 'closer to the customer'.

While the most important factor on business growth is the overall market demand for its products/services, management capacity and attitudes towards change do play an equally significant role in determining business success. Not surprisingly, small business owners often eschew growth in favour of other objectives.

Dr Panikkos Poutziouris is a Fellow in Management of Small and Medium-sized Enterprises at Manchester Business School.

Further Reading

Burns, P and Dewhurst, J, *Small Business and Entrepreneurship*, Macmillan, London, 1989.

Longemecker, J, Moore, C, and Petty, W, *Small Business Management: An Entrepreneurial Emphasis*, Thompson, 1994.

Poza, E, *Smart Growth*, Jossey-Bass, London, 1989.

Pinchot, G, *Intrapreneurship*, Harper and Row, New York, 1985.

Pratten, C, *The Competitiveness of Small Firms*, Cambridge University Press, Cambridge, UK, 1991.

Scase, R, and Goffee, R, *The real world of the business owner*, Croom Helm, London, 1980.

Scase, R, and Goffee, R, *Entrepreneurship in Europe*, Croom Helm, London, 1987.

References

1 Schmitz, H, *Flexible Specialization:a new paradigm of small-scale industrialization*, IDS, Essex University, 1987.

2 Golzen, G, 'Pitfalls press on family affairs', *The European*, 15–18 July 1993.

3 Poza, E, *Smart Growth*, Jossey-Bass, London, 1989.

4 Stanworth, and Curran, 'Growth and the small firm', *Journal of Management Studies*, vol. 13, 1976.

5 Dunkleberg, and Cooper, 'Entrepreneurial typologies' in Vesper, K, *Frontiers of Entrepreneurship*, Babson, 1982.

6 Carland, et al, 'Entrepreneurs versus business owners', *Academy of Management Review*, vol. 9 no. 2, 1984.

7 Burns, P and Dewhurst, J, *Small Business and Entrepreneurship*, Macmillan, London, 1989.

8 *Ibid.*

9 Scase, R and Goffee, R, *Entrepreneurship in Europe*, Croom Helm, London, 1987.

10 Pratten, C, *The Competitiveness of Small Firms*, Cambridge University Press, Cambridge, UK, 1991.

11 Carlsson, B, 'Small-scale industry at the crossroads', *Small Business Economics*, vol. 1, no. 4, 1989.

12 Stratos, *Strategic Orientation of Small European Business*, Gower, Aldershot, 1990.

13 Schmitz, H, 'Growth constraints on small-scale industrialization', *World Development*, vol. 10, no. 6, 1982.

14 Ballah, A, (ed.) *SMEs: Technology Policies and Options*, IT Publications, London, 1992.

15 Peterson and Shulman, 'Capital stucture of growing small firms', *International Small Business Journal*, vol. 5, no. 4, 1987.

16 Binks, M, 'Finance for expansion in the small firm', *Lloyd's Bank Review*, 134, London, 1979.

17 Binks, M, et al, 'Finance gaps for small UK firms', *Piccolla Impresa*, vol. 2, 1991.

18 Perry, C, 'Growth strategies for small firms', *International Small Business Journal*, vol. 5 no. 2, 1987.

Corporate Responsibility

'To motivate the worker to peak performance, it is equally important that management set and enforce on itself high standards for its own performance of those functions that determine the worker's ability to perform.'   *Peter Drucker[1]*

'I would not say that social performance is just as important as economic performance, but it is an important factor. We are not something separate – just a body of people founded by some shareholders, operating on their behalf. We are part of the structure of the town we work in and the lives of the people we employ and of the country we live in, and I think it's ridiculous to pretend otherwise.'
Sir Anthony Pilkington, chairman, the Pilkington Group[2]

4

---

[1] Drucker, PF, *The Practice of Management*, Harper & Row, New York, 1954.
[2] Quoted in Bloom, H, Calori, R and de Woot, P, *Euromanagement*, Kogan Page, London, 1994.

OVERVIEW

Peter Spooner

'**M**anagement's total loyalty to the maximization of profit is the principal obstacle to achieving higher standards of ethical practice,' observed Kenneth Andrews, author of *Ethics in Practice* in a 1989 article in the *Harvard Business Review*.[1]

Forty years ago managerial loyalty to the maximization of profit was unquestionable. Asked what is every company's overriding responsibility, anyone in business would have unhesitatingly answered: 'To earn profits'. In *Capitalism and Freedom*, Milton Friedman gave a very simple definition of the social responsibility of business. It is 'to use its resources and engage in activities designed to increase profits so long as it stays within the rules of the game – which is to say, engaged in open and free competition without deception or fraud.'[2]

If today's managers were asked the same question, they would probably respond similarly but justify it by pointing out that unprofitable companies eventually cease to be responsible for anything. That reasoning is unassailable, as far as it goes. But, in the social climate of the 1990s, it hardly goes far enough. Friedman's rules of the game are now constantly changing and the notion of responsibility is expanding across the entire range of the modern organization's activities.

Answers to such questions came more easily in the days when a company was assumed to have a single set of stakeholders: those owning equity shares in it. Today it is generally accepted that there are various groups whose interests are affected, and sometimes even seriously damaged, by the way a company conducts itself. They include employees, customers, suppliers, members of the local community, the general public and (if one fully embraces the environmental cause) virtually all denizens of Planet Earth. Their interests are not identical and conflict at some points. Few of the groups have a direct interest in profit maximization.

The first burst of interest in corporate responsibility came in the 1960s and early 1970s. It was in the spirit of the times: a new generation questioning an old order, the rise of consumerism, growing awareness of the environmental issues that had been so chillingly raised in Rachel Carson's thought-provoking novel, *Silent Spring*. Major companies began to publish ethical codes and expose themselves to a process called 'social auditing'. Unfortunately good intentions often materialized as generalizations rather than specifics.

The movement was probably honoured more in management literature than in boardrooms. 'Social responsibility' tended to take a high moral ground remote from the company's daily activities. Support for charities and community projects seemed worthier than, for example, the development of more equitable employment policies or the raising of safety standards. This approach produced some absurdities. In one well-publicized case, a company supporting environmental projects in other continents was fined for polluting a local stream.

In the mid-1970s much of this emerging interest was blown off executive desks by the cold winds of global recession. It was tacitly accepted that on the corporate agenda ethics came well below survival.

Though the corporate agenda of the 1990s has also been dominated by strategies for survival, there appears to be growing interest in the entire idea of corporate responsibility. The tide seems to be turning again. This time round, will it be seen as part of the mainstream of corporate activity? Will executives accept the argument that in the long run good behaviour is good business, part of the profit-making process? Will a new crop of mission statements really spell out what is expected of a company's personnel, not only at the lower levels but also at the top?

The prospect of subjecting the business community to tighter rules of conduct – thus reducing opportunities to interpret responsibility in the light of specific circumstances – may seem at odds with the current movement towards deregulation. This is not necessarily so. However one looks at it, corporate responsibility is double-sided. On one side there are self-imposed standards; on the other, mandatory standards enforced by law. Neither can achieve much in isolation. But the balance between them needs constant readjustment to meet changes in the economy, in the use of technology, and in social expectations.

The increasing prominence of corporate responsibility can, in part, be accounted for by:

- The radical changes now taking place in the structure of organizations; the flattening of traditional 'pyramid' hierarchies with their fixed lines of responsibility, and the emasculation of middle management. These changes open accountability and responsibility to new analysis and discussion.
- The growth in informal networking (where lines of communication and authority are not charted) coupled with 'employee empowerment' (where shopfloor workers and their immediate supervisors are left to make a wider range of decisions within corporate guidelines).
- The erosion of trade union power which traditionally put a brake on irresponsible conduct affecting employment.
- The growth of outsourcing, with companies losing direct control of many of the people producing their goods or services.
- The emphasis on growth by acquisition and merger, putting corporate policies under the control of directors with no hands-on experience of the activities concerned, and no established loyalty either to the workforce or the external stakeholders.
- Ever-increasing global competition, especially from enterprises with different national cultures.
- Confusion over the interface between government and private enterprise.

- The disenchantment of ordinary people with the examples set by politicians and some high-profile business leaders.

These trends and issues have sparked debate – and some action. This covers: ethics and values; the organization's environmental and social responsibilities; also the financial responsibilities prescribed through corporate governance.

To the individual manager, or company, the range of the debate and the issues can seem daunting. This is prompted by the fact that the activity of companies in a variety of industries is capable of having a greater impact on more people than ever before. Reprehensible conduct by Victorian companies was largely confined to the defrauding of investors, creditors or customers; and the unfair treatment of local workers and their dependants. Much more is now involved as a result of advancing technology, centralized marketing, the greater complexity of products and services, off-shore ownership and other fundamental changes.

Account has also to be taken of the steady shift from manufacturing to service activity. Two decades ago the consumerist movement was primarily concerned with strengthening product liability legislation. Fears were expressed in Western boardrooms that unless its excesses were curbed, the threat of being put out of business by massive compensation claims would not only discourage innovation but lead to the withdrawal of some long-established products. Such fears proved groundless and the interests of all parties were eventually brought into a new and reasonable state of balance. Even so, this may have put a brake on legitimate efforts to protect the purchasers of services, especially in potentially hazardous operations like passenger transport.

After the false dawn of the 1970s, corporate responsibility received relatively little attention in the early 1980s, when the emphasis was on economic growth, entrepreneurial success and material values. Then came a fresh, though unwelcome, stimulus: a succession of disasters that raised serious questions about the 'duty of care' society was entitled to expect, and also about the accountability of companies and their senior officers when those expectations were not met.

The capsize of the Channel car ferry, the *Herald of Free Enterprise*, the Exxon Valdez oil spill, the explosion on the *Piper Alpha* oil rig, the explosion at Union Carbide's plant at Bhopal, India... these and other tragic incidents helped to fire an interest in issues that had not been properly recognized, let alone addressed, when discussion of corporate responsibility had been confined to a narrower band of business activity.

First reactions to such disasters tend to regard them as unfortunate breaches in corporate health and safety performance. Wide ranging moral, social, managerial and environmental issues are often ignored. A refusal to countenance management failure is not unusual in such circumstances. 'It was a shock. A disaster like this was inconceivable. We pride ourselves on being safe. If established procedures had been followed this would not have happened,' said Bill Stevens, president of Exxon, after the Exxon Valdez disaster.[3] The trouble was that by not following safety procedures, the company's employees made such a disaster conceivable and then, appallingly, reality. Senior management's perception of the company clearly differed from what actually happened in practice, and the systems they managed failed to acknowledge human fallibility.

For the hard-headed manager driven by the bottom-line, such disasters pose unwelcome questions. First, they can spell financial ruin. Despite insurance cover, the direct costs of disasters are rising steadily while the hidden costs in image and public relations terms are rising even faster. According to one estimate, over 60 per cent of the industrial sites where there is a serious 'incident' actually cease operating.[4] The scale of financial penalties is demonstrated by the costs incurred by Exxon. The company spent $2 billion clearing up the damage after the Alaskan oil spill, in addition to making payments totalling $1.1 billion to the US and Alaskan authorities.

There is a hard-headed financial solution. BP, an acknowledged leader in safety, now justifies safety expenditure by conducting the same kind of cost-benefit analysis that it applies to all other business decisions. How much would it cost if non-implementation of a particular safety measure were to result in a disaster or major accident? This is increasingly regarded as a realistic approach.

While awareness of the financial implications of corporate irresponsibility provides a salutary warning to some organizations, these disasters prompt examination of more general and vital lessons.

In Europe the Zeebrugge ferry disaster, in particular, provided what many now see as a classic case-history (indeed, it is quite extensively used in management education). This disaster culminated in a landmark legal case in which a company and several senior officers successfully defended themselves against charges of manslaughter. However, its real significance lies in the fact that the tragedy and subsequent events seemed to expose an imperfect understanding, not only in legal circles, of the way companies ought to be run in modern society.

Perhaps most notable among these examples is the woolly thinking that seems to envelop certain areas of corporate governance and management. Consider, in particular, the role of the directors and senior managers who, in a legal action, will be deemed to represent the 'controlling mind' of a company.

- What precisely are their personal responsibilities to the company's stakeholders?
- At which points in the management process can their own acts of negligence be attributed to the company as a legal entity?
- When can they (and therefore the company) be held responsible for offences committed by junior personnel who have broken company rules but have not been properly selected, trained, instructed or supervised?
- How much should people at their level know about the company's day-to-day operations? Is ignorance a credible defence if they have failed to set up and maintain effective reporting systems?
- What level of competence should be expected of them, both as individuals and team members, especially where the company's operations are potentially hazardous?

1005

Satisfactory answers to those questions are rarely found in directors' guidelines or management texts. They are certainly not spelled out in ethical codes or corporate mission statements. Contrast, for example, the reactions of senior managers when disasters occur. When a Japan Airlines Boeing 747 crashed in 1985, killing 250 people, the company's president resigned. Before doing so, he visited the families of every victim with traditional Japanese mourning gifts. He was helped by 17 senior managers, and 420 employees spent time giving assistance to the families of the victims. A government report later showed that the company itself was not directly responsible for the disaster.

Other senior managers conspicuously refuse to make the link between their decisions and the daily performance of the company. After the Zeebrugge disaster, the chairman of the ferry company P&O, Jeffrey Sterling, commented: 'Those on board who were responsible to shut the doors did not carry out those instructions, period. I think it gets a bit far-fetched that somebody sitting on shore should be hauled up in a similar context for that actually specifically not happening.'[5] Sterling could not identify and would not acknowledge any link between management and operational performance.

The Zeebrugge disaster and its aftermath in the courts reveals the uneasy relationship between the legal and non-legal aspects of corporate responsibility. The capsize occurred on the evening of the 6 March 1987, minutes after the *Herald* left the harbour; 192 passengers and crew members perished and there was one subsequent death. Uncertainty over the duties of directors and managers – and how they actually perform their roles – threads its way through the three inquiries and various legal proceedings in the disaster. The inquiry into the technical cause of the capsize made it plain that the ferry owners had not breached shipping regulations. But its final report contained unprecedented criticism of the way the company had been directed and managed:

'A full investigation of the circumstances of the disaster leads inexorably to the conclusion that the underlying or cardinal faults lay higher up in the company. The board of directors did not appreciate their responsibilities for the safe management of their ships... did not have any proper comprehension of what their duties were... From top to bottom the body corporate was infected with the disease of sloppiness.'[6]

The criminal proceedings went still further in uncovering what the inquiry had described as a 'vacuum at the centre'. In fact, this very vacuum became part of the legal defence of the managers and employees directly involved in the disaster. The inquiry criticized the board of directors for not making one of its members responsible for ships' safety. In court the board's failure to do so became its defence: none of the 'controlling mind' defendants could be guilty of failing to perform a specific duty none of them had.

The legal situation regarding incompetent or irresponsible management remains hazy, with interpretations differing from one legal system to the next. The concept of aggregation under which the failings of a number of managers, not necessarily criminal in isolation, can be combined as part of a prosecution case is already accepted in a number of countries, though in the UK it has only recently made a first step towards legislation. Aggregation is one of the issues in a consultation paper on involuntary manslaughter, published by the Law Commission, the UK's official law reform body, in April 1994.[7] This draws heavily on the outcome of the Zeebrugge trial in its section on the liability of corporations.

The criminal justice system, as the Law Commission's paper tacitly accepts, often appears to have an out-of-date conception of how corporations are now directed and managed. But it equally suggests that the business community and their regulatory bodies have not done as much as they should to clarify things.

Guidelines for directors and other senior officers tend to focus on their financial duties, especially to shareholders, and on near-impossible tasks such as defining insider dealing. While increased interest in corporate governance is generally welcome, it runs the risk of continuing this fascination with financial responsibility above all else. Even now, directors are more likely to face legal action for financial irregularity than for subjecting employees or customers to unnecessary pain.

This tunnel vision on accountability is one reason why there is so much uncertainty and division over the way a legal system can most effectively deal with corporate misdemeanours. Should its primary objective be to punish, to deter or to reform?

Further complications in the case of corporate offences are, first, that it is clearly impracticable to imprison a company, and second, that any punishment that puts a company out of action bears heavily on innocent parties such as employees, customers and (with public corporations) taxpayers.

The nature of these abstract issues means that there remains a tendency to focus on the minutiae of safety regulations rather than the core issues of responsibility. The potential consequences of a technical offence are separated from its actual consequences. In *Disasters: Where the Law Fails*,[8] David Bergman argues that the law should make a clear distinction between 'dangerous' companies (which put people at risk by breaking safety regulations) and 'violent' companies (whose misconduct has resulted in death or serious injury).

It is commonly argued that in such cases the criminal justice system is dealing with crimes of negligence or recklessness but not with crimes of intent. No company, however unprincipled or badly run, ever sets out to kill employees or customers. When it happens the company is genuinely shocked. So surely it is reasonable for the law to focus on the technical offence rather than its outcome?

This logic is persuasive but, in the end, it reinforces the argument that the time has come for the 'duty of care' imposed on directors and managers to be defined more clearly, to range more widely than at present, and to be more closely related to the realities of managing a company's operations.

Whatever happens, few businessmen will deny the need for effective deterrents in areas where irresponsible corporate conduct is capable of doing extreme damage. Various measures have been suggested, among them:

- The enactment of new offences more closely related to the potential consequences of corporate misconduct within the present business environment.
- More positive acceptance of the company as a legal entity in cases of serious criminal conduct as well as minor infringements of regulatory law.
- Clearer definition of directors' and managers' 'duty of care' so that penalties (including imprisonment) can be imposed on individuals in appropriate cases.
- Better facilities for investigating possible corporate crimes.
- A more effective range of sentences that take account of a company's financial status and also minimize the adverse effects on innocent parties.

Whatever reforms emerge, it is vital to ensure that in protecting the public and other stakeholders from a small minority of truly irresponsible companies, that managerial drive and legitimate forms of competition are not placed under unnecessary constraints.

It may be thought that by focusing on health and safety, corporate responsibility becomes overly dramatized and the issues with which the average board of directors has to contend are distorted. However, there are several good reasons for using safety as a basis for debate. The drama of incidents resulting in multiple death and injury can illuminate fundamental issues easily overlooked when corporate responsibility debates are centred on more mundane areas.

Not so long ago safety was a major concern for the relatively few companies that used toxic materials, employed potentially hazardous processes, or (as in coalmining) had to expose employees to exceptional risks. Today, the number of companies capable of harming people, both on and off their own premises, has increased enormously. That is shown by the growth of product recalls as well as by 'creeping disasters' involving pharmaceutical and other products once thought to be risk-free. Even the 'user friendly' products of the computer age, PCs, terminals and word processors, are introducing new health hazards such as RSI and sight defects.

No one seriously suggests that an acceptable standard of corporate behaviour can be achieved only through turning the legal screws. Much also depends on the personal quality of the top managers who not only formulate policy but help to shape a company's culture. Their commitment to high standards has to be made very visible.

The more power a manager has, the more responsibility he or she bears (and, of course, the more they expect to be rewarded for that responsibility). But it is unreasonable to expect business leaders, along with politicians and other opinion-formers, to adhere to ethical standards far above those of society in general.

Corporate responsibility is good business. Harvard's Rosabeth Moss Kanter believes that corporate values are a 'genuine competitive advantage... an enduring factor amid so many changes in products and services... a means of changing from a roadblock organization to a flexible organization capable of working across national boundaries.'[9]

Andrew Campbell of the Ashridge Strategic Management Centre puts corporate responsibility in the context of an organization's *raison d'etre*:

'Corporate responsibility is about business purpose. A management team wanting to create a "responsible" corporation is unlikely to have "maximizing shareholder value" as its business purpose. All businesses, whatever purpose they choose, must create value for their active shareholders, customers, employees, suppliers. Long-term profitability is normally a central part of creating this value, but it is not the objective. The need to create value is a constraint not a purpose.'[10]

Of course, there are cases which seem to show that dubious behaviour can be even better business – as long as it does not attract media attention. Nevertheless the arguments supporting the proposition that responsible behaviour can be commercially successful are not unrealistic. There is evidence that good companies attract, motivate and retain good people – the sort they need to assure future profits. In addition, companies sustaining high standards minimize the risk of being faced with excessively high compensation claims, or of finding themselves put on the media rack by 'whistle-blowers' – two relatively new hazards.

Today's business leader often has to make difficult judgements and resist temptations unknown to the old-style industrialist with hands-on experience and a long-standing loyalty to a local workforce. Because of radical changes in the structure of business they may be isolated, both physically and mentally, from the operations for which they are expected to take responsibility.

Given this isolation, there is the temptation for managers and directors to seek to protect themselves by saying to their subordinates: 'Don't tell me what's really going on in case I'm held accountable for it.' It is, however, likely that any businessman or woman following that line will find that the ultimate penalty for lack of responsibility lies in the company's accounts.

Peter Spooner is a former publisher and journalist. He was public relations manager for NCR for ten years before becoming editor of *Chief Executive* magazine. He was co-founder of the Herald Families' Association and is now an active campaigner for higher standards of corporate responsibility.

Further Reading

Crainer, S, *Zeebrugge: Learning from Disaster*, HFA, London, 1993.

References

[1] Andrews, K, *Harvard Business Review*, September–October 1989.
[2] Friedman, M, *Capitalism and Freedom*, University of Chicago Press, Chicago, 1962.
[3] Booth, S, 'Dux at the crux', *Management Today*, May 1990.
[4] *Financial Times*, 28 February 1990.
[5] Interviewed on BBC *World at One*, 9 October 1987.

6 The Merchant Shipping Act 1984. MV Herald of Free Enterprise, Report of Court no. 8074, HMSO, London, 1987.
7 *Criminal Law: Involuntary Manslaughter*, Law Commission Consultation Paper no. 135, HMSO, London, 1994.
8 Bergman, D, *Where the Law Fails*, HFA, London, 1993.
9 Kanter, RM, Speech at the 23rd International HR management Conference, Barcelona, 1991.
10 Letter to *Financial Times*, 14 September 1993.

THE ROLE OF ETHICS IN CONTEMPORARY MANAGEMENT

Thomas M Kerr

Is it right to cut corners on health and safety to increase profits? Would you accept a bribe in a foreign country where it is normal practice? Would you work for a tobacco company? Under what circumstances would you allow sub-standard products to leave your factory?

These are just some of the weighty moral dilemmas which constantly face managers. Until recently, ethical standards within the business world were assumed rather than understood. Now, after the financial and other scandals of the 1980s, ethics is a fixture on management development programmes and an aspect of growing importance for managers of all types.

There are two essential ingredients in achieving ethical performance in business management. One is ethical literacy, which is that managers are as well acquainted with ethical reasoning (moral philosophy) as they are with, for instance, financial accounting. The second is organizational structures and practices which open the way for ethical achievement.

Ethical leadership

Multinational corporations are leading the globalization of trade and finance which is now reshaping business and labour markets around the world. 'Transnational corporations have played a leading role in this process as traders, investors, disseminators of technology and movers of people – thus strengthening the links among national markets,' observed the 1994 *World Investment Report*.[1]

Business managers have become the most influential group of *professionals* in the world. Their decisions have wide effects, outdistancing national boundaries. Certainly, today and tomorrow, their acts are as consequential as the acts of political leaders. No institution more profoundly shapes life, liberty and the pursuit of happiness than business. For these reasons managers should play a statesmanlike role and they must be prepared to do so. Those who can must be those chosen to lead.

Influence brings with it demands and expectations. Consider those who wrote the United States constitution in Philadelphia in 1787:

'Rarely has a generation of activists been so thoroughly schooled in classical political thought... For them the works of the Greeks and Romans constituted neither dead languages or dead learning. Many read Montesquieu in his own language. They liked to cite the great English thinkers – Hobbes and Locke and Hume – against English rule itself.'[2]

One of them, Thomas Jefferson, for instance, had set out to become a learned man. From an early age he aspired to the eighteenth-century ideal of the *philosophe*, the universally informed philosopher, whose knowledge was built on a classical base and whose efforts were committed to reason and the pursuit of useful results.

Similarly, the great British philosopher and economist, John Stuart Mill, was thoroughly acquainted with all the Latin and Greek classics by the age of 12. In the following year he was introduced (by his sole teacher, his father) to political economy and studied the work of the Scottish political economist and philosopher, Adam Smith, and that of the English economist, David Ricardo.

Tomorrow's professional manager should be familiar with, and utilize, an understanding of utilitarian theories and applications, Adam Smith's moral philosophy, Marxian approaches, distributive justice, the rights and responsibilities of individuals, Kant's imperatives of duty to others and respect for persons. Their knowledge and understanding need to be as transnational as their business activities – encompassing Buddhist and Chinese philosophy, Muslim and Jewish philosophical thought and, perhaps, many others. Application of the principles of moral philosophy are – or should be – as usual and familiar to executives as balance sheets and profit and loss statements.

Tomorrow's professional manager will know that the caution attributed to Hippocrates, 'Abstain from whatever is deleterious and mischievous,' is as applicable to many business situations as it has been to the medical profession for which it was intended.

She or he will know that all societies have moral rules that foster certain actions such as truth telling, promise (contract) keeping, and forbidding others like murder and theft. There must be awareness and understanding, also that there are differences between the practices of different peoples, eg, monogamy versus polygamy; the forbidding or permission of abortion; from proffering the normal small change of business entertainment – tickets to sports or theatre, and the odd bottle of spirits – to substantial bribery. She or he may well have considered *Antigone* and Creon as employee and hierarchical manager, and be interested in the societal metamorphosis of usury from sin to perceived virtue, as well as having reasoned on the moral dimensions of managerial decisions in the light of human art and history.

In sum, for professional management we must seek out, hire, promote and encourage, women and men of, and for, all seasons.[3]

Then they must employ the language and considerations of moral philosophy in their day-to-day, indeed, hour-to-hour, leadership. When considering acquisitions they should, for example, be as interested in a target company's ethical practices as in its financial performance. The personal deportment of the manager in the exercise of moral judgement is far more influential than written policy. The manager's constant example is the vital element. She or he will make their position clear and create an atmosphere for others to follow.

Recently, legislatures and courts have established the right of corporate managers to recognize and respond to obligations to the community at large, as well as to employees, suppliers, and customers, in addition to their fiduciary responsibility to shareholders.

But, wrestling with the views and concerns of their various wide-ranging stakeholders is nothing new. This was accepted by IBM's Thomas Watson, Jr, who said:

'Bigness itself is a relatively new phenomenon in our society. Even if nothing else had changed, the vast concentrations of power in our society would demand that businessmen reconsider their responsibilities for the broader public welfare.'[4]

One of the earliest and most noted expressions on the ethical role of management came from Owen D Young, in 1929, when he was head of the General Electric Company:

'It makes a great difference in my attitude toward my job as an executive officer of the General Electric Company whether I am a trustee of the institution or an attorney for the investor. If I am a trustee, who are the beneficiaries of the trust? To whom do I owe my obligations? My conception of it is this: That there are three groups of people who have an interest in that situation. One is the group of fifty-odd thousand people who have put their capital into the company, namely, its stockholders. Another is a group of well toward one hundred thousand people who are putting their labour and their lives into the business of the company. The third group is of customers and the general public. Customers have a right to demand that a concern so large shall not only do its business honestly and properly, but, further, that it shall meet its public obligations and perform its public duties... in a word, vast as it is, that it should be a good citizen.'[5]

The same point of view is often expressed today in the annual reports of major corporations.

In 1981, the *New York Times* reported on a pronouncement on corporate responsibility issued by the Business Roundtable, the prestigious lobby for the largest US corporations: 'More than ever, managers of corporations are expected to serve the public interest as well as private profit.' Employees, according to this report, expect not only 'fair pay, but also such conditions as financial security, personal privacy, freedom of expression, and concern for the quality of life.'[6]

In 1946, Frank Abrams, chairman of Standard Oil Company of New Jersey (now Exxon) described the role of the modern manager as maintaining 'an equitable and working balance among the claims of the various directly interested groups – stockholders, employees, customers, and the public at large.'[7]

The notion of the business leader as steward or trustee has long been accepted, but 'only in recent times have obligations to the community at large been viewed as part of corporate responsibility.'[8]

In *The Modern Corporation and Private Property*, Berle and Means raised the question of how managers, insulated from traditional owner control, might use their power. They noted three possibilities: continuing to serve as trustees devoted to the interests of the powerless stockholders, plundering in the managerial interest, or serving the interest of society at large. They support the third alternative:

'It is conceivable – indeed, it seems almost essential if the corporate system is to survive – that the control of the great corporations should develop into a purely neutral technocracy, balancing a variety of claims by various groups in the community and assigning to each a portion of the income stream on the basis of public policy rather than private cupidity.' [9]

Many business leaders expressed important opinions after the revelations of widespread price-fixing and bid-rigging by US electrical manufacturers in 1960. One of the strongest statements reproving American management generally and, by implication, the management of firms involved in various questions of business ethics, was delivered prior to the next annual meeting of the General Electric Board by a GE director, Henry Ford II, chairman of the Ford Motor Company. Ford assailed American business for permitting a climate that made scandals possible. He called on the nation's top executives to keep their houses in order and, failing to do so, to have the 'plain guts' to admit it, and to pledge that it will not happen again. He observed that the scandals 'could arouse popular distrust and revive old and worn-out hostilities toward American business and industry.'[10]

Corporations are not only useful to society. In turn, society is useful to corporations; it enables them to do business with property rights and civil rights. For example, all the industrial nations provide tax-supported courts and legislatures to vindicate business promises (contracts), and corporations benefit enormously from their distinct legal *persona*.

Today, every corporation is regarded as being responsibly accountable to the society from which it extracts the essentials of its continued existence, as well as to its shareholders.

Long ago Louis D Brandeis suggested that business corporations have positive, creative, obligations to society:

'In the field of modern business, so rich in opportunity for the exercise of man's finest and most varied mental faculties and moral qualities, mere money-making cannot be regarded as the legitimate end. Neither can mere growth in bulk or power be admitted as a worthy ambition. Nor can a man nobly mindful of his serious responsibilities to society view business as a game, since with the conduct of business human happiness or misery is inextricably interwoven.'

'Real success in business is to be found in achievements comparable rather with those of the artist or the scientist, of the inventor or the statesman. And the joys sought in the profession of business must be like their joys and not the vulgar satisfaction which is experienced in the acquisition of money, in the exercise of power, or in the frivolous pleasure of mere winning... As the profession of business develops, the great industrial and social problems, will one by one find solution.'[11]

Brandeis' intellectual aspiration that there is more to business than profit or size is a fundamental principle applicable to business administration today.

Designing organizations to achieve ethical performance

The most important role model to others is the behaviour of those in authority. In the 1968 survey, *An Honest Profit*,[12] it was found that most subordinates accept the values of chief executives. Top management (of the small unit or large, office, depot, department, division, group, or of the entire firm) must project consistent and sincere commitment to ethical practices.

Unless ethical considerations are a part of every manager's thought processes the corporation will fail to exercise the level of responsibility which good business represents and society expects.

Likewise, the perceived motives of those in charge are crucial. Does the management display ambition to produce the very best product or service at the most competitive price? Are they eager to excel? Or, does the management conduct the business merely for their own ends – selling off this business, 'restructuring', 'down-sizing', 'golden parachutes'? Firing employees after mergers or restructuring deeply damages employee loyalty to the firm. Productivity goes down. Many younger people have no compunction about switching from one company to another if it seems to their personal advantage.

Setting the right example requires that there should be a corporate culture of openness and co-operation. There can be a moral 'quality circle'. In his book, *The Manufacture of Evil*, Lionel Tiger observes:

'If an organization's leaders broadcast the implicit message that they are concerned with the organization's ethical as well as economic health, they can mobilize forces of citizenship and commitment, which are also necessary to an organization's general effectiveness. People are energetic for what they believe in, but they may casually inhibit or sabotage what they consider shabby or wrong. Economics and ethics are not mutually exclusive.'[13]

The manager must encourage open decision-making in which differences of opinion are welcomed, abetting discussions in which the relevance of ethical standards to proposals is discussed. They should never say, 'Do not bother me with that,' but instead, 'There is no such thing as a dumb question. We do not shoot the messenger.' The key is communication with the door to the front office always being open.

The 1960 Great Electrical (price-fixing, bid-rigging) Conspiracy was a lesson in practices to avoid and prohibit. The General Electric Company had rigidly enforced a 'one over one' communication policy. This laid down that if you had a business matter to discuss you could contact *only* the person immediately above on the hierarchical ladder. As a result, only a few individuals knew of the continuing anti-trust violations. The US Senate Sub-Committee which later investigated the matter was told: 'You never let the manufacturing people, the engineers, and, especially, the lawyers know anything about it.' In a similar vein, the *New Yorker* commented: 'The clear waters of moral responsibility at GE became hopelessly muddied... by their garbled communications up and/or down the executive ladder.'[14]

Effective leaders encourage and even reward dissent. In his book, *On Becoming a Leader*, the leadership guru Warren Bennis notes of leaders:

'They understand that whatever momentary discomfort they experience as a result of being told from time to time that they are wrong is more than offset by the fact that reflective backtalk increases a leader's ability to make good decisions.'

'Executive compensation should go far toward salving the pricked ego of the leader whose followers speak their mind. But what's in it for the follower? The good follower may indeed have to put his or her job on the line in the course of speaking up. But consider the price he or she pays for silence. What job is worth the enormous psychic cost of following a leader who values loyalty in the narrowest sense?'[15]

The manager thus approaches problems listening to others whom he or she has strongly encouraged to speak up. To hear both sides before giving judgement, is not an astonishing or even a new discovery. Orestes in the *Andromache* of Euripides, says: 'Wise, indeed, was the lesson of him who taught mankind to hear the arguments of both sides.'

In this format every decision situation should be considered only after three preliminary steps:

- Do we have the facts?
- Is there any possible element of harm?
- What principles of moral philosophy are applicable?

What of the people with whom the manager is dealing? 'Treat people as adults. Treat them as partners; treat them with dignity; treat them with respect,' advise Tom Peters and Robert Waterman in *In Search of Excellence*.[16] Give employees the feeling of making a contribution and of being important. Protect their individuality, personal privacy and dignity. Their employment should only be terminated for just cause, and they are entitled to a fair hearing that includes the right to confront witnesses, the right to present evidence, the right to have adequate representation (either an attorney or other type of counsel), and the right to an impartial decision-maker. Job applicants and employees should not be required to answer intrusive questions about their private lives and personal beliefs on 'psychological', 'personality', or 'integrity' tests. There must be positive measures to prohibit sexual harassment. Employees should not be subjected to electronic surveillance through video display terminals, observation by hidden cameras or monitored telephone calls unless there is an express business need to do so *and* the employees are informed of the practices.

There should be no attempts by employers to control private habits or proclivities of their employees: for example, smoking, or those who engage in such risky hobbies as scuba diving, hang gliding, whitewater rafting or motorcycle riding, where there is no relationship between the private activity and job performance. Respecting employees' private rights boosts morale and raises corporate performance.

Xerox Corporation chief executive, Paul Allaire advises:

'Spend a lot of time on the soft part of business, on the people part. Ask yourself: how do I manage in a manner which really unleashes the creativity of my workforce? Paying attention to the people side of management and understanding new ways of organizing, structuring and motivating people are probably going to be the most important lessons.'

Beneficial outcomes?

The German philosopher Immanual Kant would insist that we act as we ought, not for any reward or recognition, but only because that is, indeed, what we ought to do. But the practices and programmes I have discussed are also very much in the self-interest of the firm and it is permissible to recognize benefits to the firm from them.

Robert Reich, the US Secretary of Labour, has observed:

'Watch the workplace. A balance sheet tells investors a great deal about a company's condition – inventories, accounts payable and receivable, debt level. But it misses much else. Hard-to-measure data about the workforce and workplace practices – the quality and loyalty of employees, investment in training and retraining, and health and safety strategies – are especially likely to elude standard accounting. Yet these factors can matter enormously – especially for long-term players like pension funds.'

Indeed, a study by the Gordon Group of financial analysts, found that, from 1990 to 1994, companies with 'high performance' workplace practices outperformed the *S&P 500* by an average 16 per cent each year and beat their industry averages by 7.5 per cent. In contrast, companies with poor workplace practices had substandard financial results.

Clearly, there are collateral returns from an ethical programme:

● It is not too simple to say that all participants at the firm are comfortable. Exceptional employees do not leave, having to be replaced after costly shutdown, search, and indoctrination expenditures. Productivity will be measurably improved.

- Generally, it is not necessary to have so many auditors, lawyers or security personnel.
- Errors are quickly discovered due to open communications.
- Whistleblowers have no need to publish concerns to the wide world, saving on legal and public relations costs (as well as possibly abating regulatory legislation).

These are benefits to the firm that are in addition to, not instead of, competitive rates of return. At the same time an excellent ethical reputation encourages investments that fortify the corporation's fiscal situation, enhancing its ability to produce robust profits. In the United States a recent Roper poll for Cone/Coughlin Communications of Boston, found that, after price and quality, one-third of American consumers consider a company's socially responsible practices next most important in deciding whether to buy a brand. The pithy truth is summed up by Nadine Gordimer: 'The real definition of loneliness [is to] live without social responsibility.'

Thomas Kerr is a former trial lawyer for the antitrust division of the US Department of Justice, former assistant general counsel of Westinghouse Electric Corporation, former commissioner, City of Pittsburgh Commission on Human Relations and former president of the Pennsylvania American Civil Liberties Union. He originated the law and ethics programme at Carnegie Mellon's Graduate School of Industrial Administration where he now teaches.

Further Reading

Andrew, KR, *Ethics in Practice: Managing the Moral Corporation*, HBS Press, Boston, 1989.

References

1 UN Conference on Trade and Development, 1994.
2 Burns, James MacGregor, *The Vineyard of Liberty*, Knopf, 1982.
3 Robert Bolt's dramatization of the life and death of the English humanist priest and Lord Chancellor, Sir Thomas More, *A Man for all Seasons*, Vintage, 1960.
4 Watson, T, Jr, *A Business and Its Beliefs*, McGraw-Hill, 1963, p. 80.
5 Sears, *The New Place of the Stockholder* (1929), p. 209.
6 *New York Times*, 20 December 1981.
7 Frank Abrams, quoted in Edward S Mason, 'The Apologetics of Managerialism', *Journal of Business*, May 1963, p. 11.
8 Herman, ES, *Corporate Control, Corporate Power*, Cambridge University Press, Cambridge, UK, 1981, p. 245.
9 Berle, Adolph A, Jr and Means, G, Macmillan, New York, 1933, (revised edn 1968).
10 Ford, H, II, Speech to the Junior Chamber of Minneapolis, 20 April 1961.
11 From an address at Brown University Commencement Day, 1912. Quoted in *The Social and Economic Views of Mr Justice Brandeis*, ed. Alfred Lief, Vanguard, New York, 1930, pp. 387–388.
12 Baumhard, R, *An Honest Profit*, Holt, Rinehart, 1968.

[13] Tiger, Lionel, *The Manufacture of Evil, Ethics, Evolution and the Industrial System*, Bessel Books/Harper & Row, New York, 1987.

[14] *New Yorker*, May 26 1962.

[15] Bennis, W, *On Becoming a Leader*, Addison-Wesley, Reading, Mass, 1989.

[16] Peters, TJ, and Waterman, RH, *In Search of Excellence*, Macmillan, London, 1982, p. 238.

LEVI STRAUSS & CO

David Logan

Be it T-shirts, jeans or *haute couture*, the sewing business is a tough business. It is not the first place that people would look for a company which exemplifies the best in ethics and good management values. It is highly competitive, regularly featuring in media stories of worker exploitation, price wars and short-term investment practices.

Yet, it is in this environment that Levi Strauss & Co has emerged as the world's largest 'apparel company' with revenues of nearly $6 billion. In addition, it has consistently won awards from public bodies, and praise from business leaders, for its commitment to ethics, values and social responsibility. In a poll of US business leaders, Levi Strauss & Co was voted the country's most ethical private company – an honour shared with the Merck Corporation, which has consistently been recognized as America's most ethical public company.

At Levi Strauss & Co, ethics and values are not an afterthought; concepts bolted on to the business when economic success is guaranteed. They are at the core of its culture and are perceived to be key drivers of business success. The company manages its ethics and values commitments with the same degree of care and attention that it devotes to other critical business issues. As with Marks & Spencer in Britain, Robert Bosch in Germany and Tata Industries in India, the company's commitment to good ethics and values was set by its founding family. But, it has successfully transferred the family's personal commitment to ethics, values and social responsibility into its worldwide business ethos and management practices.

The importance of such historical commitment cannot be underestimated. A culture of ethics, values and social responsibility is built over time rather than overnight. Just as the Watsons influenced the culture of IBM so the Haas and Koshland families influenced the ethics and values of Levi Strauss & Co. The company has been a family-owned business for most of its 140-year history and this connection has been critical in shaping its sense of values.

From its earliest days the company committed itself to the highest quality of product and best possible service for its customers. The owners did everything possible to avoid laying off employees in the depression of the 1930s; they also ensured equal employment opportunity for African Americans in their factories during the 1950s and 1960s when expanding into the southern States. Human rights and a concern for employees remain core values today and Levi's has earned a reputation as being a good employer. In the growing community of San Francisco, where the company still has its headquarters, the Haas and Koshland families were social and cultural leaders in the mode of so many Victorian entrepreneurs and business leaders in Europe and other parts of the world.

As the business expanded the community involvement tradition developed alongside. Levi Strauss & Co now draws over 40 per cent of its revenues from its international businesses and sources product from over 50 countries worldwide. A quarter of its employees are outside the United States and, as it has expanded, the company has taken its approach with it around the world. The same basic business values that are found in San Francisco and Arkansas are now found in Britain, France, the Philippines and Brazil.

This family connection provides the foundation stone on which the superstructure of a modern management system for the company's ethics and values is built. The success of the company in recent years, now led by Robert D Haas, the great-great grand-nephew of the founder, has been to transmute the benevolent paternalism of an earlier era into a more dynamic, modern approach to managing ethics and values, one which engages employees in the process. To do this the company has clarified its ethics and values and created management systems to ensure that they are integrated into the business, monitored and evaluated and that they support the economic success of the company. This strategy has several mutually supportive components.

The creation of an ethical ethos

To create an ethical ethos in a business several factors are necessary, including the role presented by senior managers. There have to be clear written statements of values to which employees can refer and management structures to support them. Levi Strauss & Co has codified and promulgated to all managers and employees the ethics and values which were initially the personal commitments of the company's owners. Like many companies Levi's has a worldwide *Code of Ethics* which is based on four key elements:

- *A commitment to commercial success in terms broader than merely financial measures.*
- *A respect for our employees, suppliers, customers, consumers and stockholders.*
- *A commitment to conduct, which is not only legal but fair and morally correct in a fundamental sense.*
- *Avoidance of not only real but the appearance of conflict of interest.*

This code is further supported by two additional statements which expand on its themes. First, a statement of *Ethical Principles* which sets the tone for the style of behaviour the company wants to see from all its employees. This statement gives a commitment to seek to be honest, fair, show respect for others, compassion and integrity as well as, to keep promises in working relationships. These are values which are hard to live up to, but by setting them down as benchmarks, employees know what, in principle, is expected from them in their business dealings.

The second expansion of Levi's *Code of Ethics* is its *Aspirations Statement*, a document which speaks directly to the human experience of being at work. It challenges all employees, who helped shape the document, to show leadership in 'modelling new behaviours, empowerment, ethical management practices and good communications'. The *Aspirations Statement* also recognizes that people need recognition for their work and positive behaviour, and commits the company to valuing and making good use of human diversity whether by age, race, sex or ethnic group. These statements of principle help to codify basic values, and create a climate within the business about the way in which business and personal relationships should be conducted. They are, in turn, supported by a range of more precise policy statements which make these principles explicit in particular sets of business conditions.

Ethics and values in company policy

As many organizations have discovered, statements of general principle are never enough to ensure that ethics and values are converted into consistent practice. Levi Strauss & Co follows through its general statements of ethics and values in a number of ways at both the levels of policy and personal action. Some issues require specific policy statements. One recent example was the company's relations with its suppliers. Its sewing business sources product from some of the poorest countries in the world, where the treatment of labour and respect for human rights can be very poor compared to Western values and practice. It was a desire to conduct business in a responsible way with suppliers that led Levi's to issue a policy statement on *Business Partner Terms of Engagement*. This set out the company's expectations of its suppliers in regard to matters such as environmental requirements, ethical standards, health and safety, legal requirements and employment practices. The latter are of particular importance and the principles are very explicit with regard to the use of child and prison labour, as well as wages and benefits.

These terms mean that any manager responsible for sourcing Levi products and supplies has clear guidance as to the types of suppliers he or she can do business with. Having developed this statement for application worldwide, Levi Strauss & Co attracted considerable attention when it announced that it would not be sourcing product from China. Levi's judged that many local employment practices, including the use of prison labour, breached the supplier code of practice.

It was suggested that Levi's was following a political agenda, but this is not borne out by the company's previous behaviour in South Africa in the 1980s where it took a similar stand. Then Levi's pointed out that South African apartheid laws required the company to actively discriminate amongst its employees and that would be a breach of its fundamental *Code of Ethics*.

Therefore the company could not, and would not, do business in South Africa under apartheid laws. The company also developed clear policies with regard to the treatment of employees with AIDS, in the early 1980s. These and other such policies are derived from a profound commitment to basic human rights, a commitment which guides the company's activities in many fields not just supplier relations.

Managing ethics and values commitments

General statements of principle and specific policies in respect of any particular stakeholder or issues need to be implemented and evaluated by managers and employees. Levi Strauss & Co has gone a long way towards integrating ethics and values issues into the normal structure of management objectives and annual performance measurements for managers. Managers are not judged by economic performance alone. This is a critical message for the importance of these values to the company. Up to 40 per cent of management bonuses are decided on performance measures relating to ethics, values and personal style in human relations as set out in the *Aspirations Statement* and elsewhere.

In order to help managers and employees meet their required objectives and keep to the ethics and values of the company, they are given training and other forms of support. As part of the management training programme, there is a core curriculum of four days' training around ethics and values. This training is to help professional managers think through and manage these dimensions of their business activities. They are encouraged to raise difficult questions about the way the company does business and to propose solutions to the conflicts that arise between ethical principles and the management of a global business with tight economic performance criteria.

While individual managers throughout the company are expected to take responsibility for ethics and value issues in the day-to-day management of the business, they are backed up by a Social Responsibility and Ethics Committee. This is made up of senior managers and is proactive in developing policy and addressing concerns raised by managers and employees. It is supported by a small in-house research capacity, which identifies issues, analyzes them and, if necessary, proposes solutions or policy changes. Help is also available to individual managers to work through their own solutions to problems in their particular situation.

The company is successful in achieving its goals in relation to ethics and values because it is scientific in its approach to the management of such issues. Levi Strauss & Co long ago realized what many companies have yet to recognize, namely that they cannot rely on an inspired chief executive or a dramatic conversion among individual managers to produce a rounded values-based organization. Many of the most difficult ethics and values questions in business are actually underpinned by careful factual and ethical analysis. This business-led approach allows managers to make decisions about values within a structured framework of options where costs, benefits and policy options are made explicit through the work of employees and in-house research capacity.

Levi's believes that a moral sense is widely shared by its employees, irrespective of status within the organization. What helps employees and managers make good ethical decisions is a commitment to a framework of values and detailed research and discussion of problems. Few major companies have committed long-term management resources and created specialist units devoted to understanding the ethical and social impacts of their activity. They remain reactive, operating on a year-by-year, issue-by-issue basis, rather than having the long-term, strategic capacity, that Levi Strauss & Co has taken the time to develop.

Support for individual employees

A company's ethics and social responsibility programme is not entirely encapsulated within its statements of principle, policy and management objectives. Individuals have to face ethics and values problems on a daily basis. These might range from sexual harassment in the workplace to relations with immediate managers or suppliers and retail customers. Employees and managers within the company can get confidential support to help them work through ethical conflicts in their business lives. The company has counselling and technical support facilities for managers and employees facing difficult business situations with personal, ethical overtones.

Commitment to communities

It is not just the good management of the internal aspects of running the company that marks a business out as a leader in social responsibility; it is also its role in the wider community. Having been leaders in the development of San Francisco, the founding families took the experience of being good 'corporate citizens' and created a policy to ensure that each Levi Strauss & Co plant community everywhere in the world, had a community involvement programme. Few multinationals in the US or elsewhere have made such a commitment. The company spent over $10 million on community activities worldwide in 1993. Most important, true to its basic values and management style, it has teams of sewing machine operators managing its local charitable community programmes. They are supported by line managers and a small professional staff that also run a specialist community programme concerned with economic opportunities for the disadvantaged in the company's plant communities around the world.

Ethics, values and business success

At Levi Strauss and Co good ethics and values have always been supported as being 'good' in themselves. They are also seen to be worth investing in because they are acknowledged to be an asset to the business. They underpin business success and profitability.

For example, in the marketplace Levi's has established a profound sense of trust between itself and its customers. People know they will get quality without question and refunds when necessary. In addition, the company has addressed issues in its advertising, such as its sexual content, and was one of the first companies to use disabled people to promote its product. It has both a human rights view of the power of advertising and an understanding that responsible advertising, which is inclusive of diversity, will bring the company greater acceptance and wider markets around the world.

Another key example of where the company's values help it succeed is in the way in which they create a climate among employees to help management gain their support for radical changes as it repositions itself for a global marketplace. People will accept major changes in the size, structure and working practices of a business much more readily if they believe that those changes will be made with regard to the long-term wellbeing of the business. For example, in an industry renowned for its top-down management style, Levi's has created employee-driven quality circles which empower employees to restructure their approach to work in order to improve efficiency in productivity and significantly reduce poor quality products. These types of changes can only be initiated in a climate of trust based on the shared basic values of the type set out in the company's *Aspirations Statement*.

Chief executive Bob Haas has forcefully argued that an empowered workforce, one sharing the same values and aspirations for the company as managers and owners, will make it a leader in the market. 'You can't energize people or earn their support unless the organization has soul,' says Haas.

The success of Levi's values-driven approach and its 'aspirations' for the future have led to the company being much more productive and competitive. The overall performance of the business shows it. The fact that jobs have been retained and indeed increased by 2,500 in the US in what is seen as a declining industry, shows the benefits to employees of a values-driven approach to management. Not only are jobs secured but the day-to-day experience of being at work is greatly improved.

All this is not to say that Levis is perfect, it is after all a human institution. In the 1970s it was successfully prosecuted, under Anti-Trust law in California. Having been an exemplary employer when closing plants in small dependent communities in the southern States of America and around the world, the company badly upset employees and the city of San Antonio, Texas, when it closed four plants in one day. It only recently won a law suit with employees about the closures. The company is still the target for criticism from some activists over some of its sourcing practices. However, there is an overwhelming disposition among the company's stakeholders and the wider community to believe that, even when it gets things wrong, Levi's will have tried its best to get it right.

The strength of the company in the field of ethics and values is precisely that it has taken its heritage and updated it for a modern business in a global economy. It commits time and management resources to analyzing ethical and value issues, coming up with appropriate responses based on enduring shared principles. The company is no more *ad hoc* about its ethics and values work than it is about key commitments to production and marketing. It has invested in getting its values, and the processes to disseminate them, right. It consistently reaps the rewards of high performance and public recognition for its achievements. For Levi Strauss & Co, ethics and values are a core component of a successful global business strategy. Doing the right thing and doing well go together; there is no thought that the two principles are mutually exclusive.

Prior to establishing his own consultancy firm, Corporate Citizenship International, David Logan directed elements of Levi Strauss & Co's US community programmes and developed its European and international community programmes. He is a senior visiting fellow in corporate responsibility at Manchester Business School.

COMPANY, COMMUNITY AND COMPETITIVE ADVANTAGE

David Grayson

Companies once kept their distance from community involvement. The whim of the chairman was as likely to dictate policy as any strategy. Now, there is growing support from the business world for a wide range of community activities. These commitments go far beyond providing financial support, and often involve managers being seconded and expertise shared.

Corporate Community Involvement (CCI) is regarded by many organizations not only as sound business sense, but as an innovative and practically helpful means of achieving competitive advantage.

Many of us in our private lives, are involved in some form of community service – perhaps as a school governor, through our religious affiliations, or through a group such as Round Table or Civic Trust. Less well-established is the idea of community service through our companies. There is, though, a growing number of pioneering companies who are encouraging their employees to give some of their company and personal time to the community; and are instituting part-time community assignments as part of highly cost-effective management development.

Relatively few firms yet see that such community involvement can be beneficial for all sides – for the company, the community and the individual employee. Some are even suspicious of looking for business benefit from activities designed to help the community.

Corporate Community Involvement involves companies using some of their people, their expertise, their surplus products, premises, equipment, influence and, sometimes, their cash to help tackle problems such as urban deprivation, school-business links, job creation and environmental improvements.

Community Links in the East End of London is an excellent example of the kind of organization which companies are supporting. Community Links is an independent charity operating in one of the most deprived areas of the UK. It is run by a small group of full-time staff supported by over 320 volunteers who contribute help each week, encouraging and enabling people in difficult circumstances to tackle problems for themselves.

To refurnish its derelict offices the group raised donations, discounts and in-kind contributions from over 128 companies. It offers activities and facilities for younger people, as well as help for the elderly and disabled, and for other special needs groups. Community Links currently has two managers on secondment:

one for two years from Marks & Spencer to set up a café and leased office space. This secondee is accessing many skills from Marks & Spencer, plus equipment, such as borrowing Marks & Spencer training videos to train volunteers in customer care. The second secondee is a former food plant manager who is acting as site manager for the new Community Links' premises; and also as a surrogate personnel manager to help employees from different companies, who are volunteering to achieve their own objectives and those of their companies, as well as helping Community Links. Support has also come from a wide variety of companies – Tate & Lyle has been a long-established supporter of Community Links; W H Smith is making available surplus products for sale in the shop to generate revenue; Texaco donated 80 per cent of the furniture from its headquarters when it relocated; Ernst & Young helped Community Links to recover VAT on building repairs, which saved £95,000, and then subsequently helped with financial management disciplines.

The corporate support for Community Links illustrates three points:

- **Opportunities abound** – there are local and nationwide organizations through which businesses can make a contribution. Some of these may be traditional charities, like Help the Aged, while others may be newer, more activist organizations, such as the Terence Higgns Trust. Others may be partnerships between government, local authorities and business; or have been stimulated by government to provide a better delivery mechanism than direct government action such as the UK's Training and Enterprise Councils.
- **It is more than cheque-writing** – corporate assistance now takes many forms: opening up internal training courses; printing reports; giving marketing or financial management expertise; lending IT or quality management specialists; providing premises. Where companies provide cash, they are increasingly combining this with other forms of assistance in order to maximize the impact of their contribution. This can include secondment of managers, converting surplus premises into incubator units for small firms, launching low-interest loan funds and providing technical expertise.
- **Business can help itself as well as the community** – maximum, sustained corporate support is most likely to come when companies aim to achieve benefits for themselves as well as the community. These benefits will vary from firm to firm depending on their particular market circumstances, sector and history.

Among the most common benefits which companies themselves have quoted from their CCI are:

Building people
- making the company more attractive to new recruits;
- testing for and developing leadership potential;
- building team-spirit;
- improving self-confidence and communications skills;

- developing problem-solving abilities;
- establishing common, core values

Building business and reducing the costs of doing business
- reducing costs to business of insurance, security, crime caused by social exclusion;
- making business restructuring easier through using CCI to help deal with the problems caused and, as a result, reducing workforce/community resistance;
- CCI to help small firms expand the potential supplier and customer base supporting projects to reduce unemployment boosts purchasing power;
- a company with a positive track-record with consumers on CCI may find it easier to attract and retain customers.

Building the freedom to operate
- CCI helps the company to 'bank' goodwill with local communities, opinion-formers, regulators so that if the company ever needs friends, at least these external stakeholders will be prepared to listen to the company's side of the argument rather than condemning it unheard;
- meeting heightened societal expectations of the role which business will play.

There is a whole series of business arguments and the relative weight of those arguments is going to differ from company to company depending on the sector it is in and its particular circumstances – such as its profitability, the concerns of its employees, and the position or seniority of the key individuals who are going to drive CCI initiatives forward.

Starting points for individual managers

The very range of community issues and the organizations operating to tackle them, can be bewildering. Indeed, their profusion provides some organizations with a poor but readymade excuse for not involving themselves. They claim that it is difficult to identify the most worthy beneficiary. There are local opportunities, for example, working with schools, hospitals or other groups using managerial skills. There is, even so, an understandable tendency for the stretched line manager to throw up his or her hands and do nothing; there is the fear of being swamped with requests for help, and the whole thing getting out of control. So, how can individual managers begin to become involved and keep it manageable?

As an individual manager, you may be working in a company with a defined, well-publicized CCI strategy or, conversely (although nowadays much less likely), in a company with no tradition or experience in the field. Your starting point will depend on your personal and corporate situations.

Where are you starting from?

You:
- are taking the initiative yourself;
- are being asked by your senior management to act;
- are being pushed by your staff to pursue CCI.

The company:

- has no CCI activity nor has there been anything in your operation/plant/office;
- has a central CCI strategy but this has not involved your division;
- already has CCI activities running in your part of the business.

	Taking Initiative	Management Request	Employee Request
Nothing local or national	1	2	3
Nothing local but national	4	5	6
Existing local programme	7	8	9

1. The blank piece of paper
- what business objectives do you want to address?
- what do key local opinion-formers, community-leaders, etc, believe to be priority needs?
- how can these be married?

2. The trail-blazer
- does this programme have to be replicable across the organization?
- what national resources will be available?

3. By popular demand
- what are employees already doing in the community?
- what are their major concerns?
- will you match their personal endeavours with company time and cash?
- what other corporate resources, such as premises or in-house communications channels can be utilized?

4. The adapter
- what are the national priorities and guidelines?
- is there an in-house CCI specialist who can advise on techniques and good practice?

- is the company nationally a member of an organization, such as Business in the Community, so that you can obtain professional advice from their local representatives?

5. Follow my leader
- what are the CCI management performance targets?
- who are the best examples in other divisions who can be visited/studied?

6. Dual logic response
- how far do national CCI guidelines already reflect local employee concerns? How to resolve national/local conflicts? Do the guidelines give priority to organizations and issues in the community where there are opportunities for significant employee participation?
- are there national schemes to back up employees' involvement? For example, to share good practice and experience among employees who are school governors or who are mentors to young people starting their own business through organizations such as Livewire and the Prince's Youth Business Trust?

7. Catching up
- are there key community partners for the company's CCI programme and do they have a local presence?

8. Developing
- what are the main gaps in the local programme versus the national CCI strategy?
- are there internal/external training programmes which you can attend to improve your understanding of CCI?

9. Customizing
- what extra issues/contributions do employees want to tackle? How can these be aligned with national programmes?

Effective CCI

Effective involvement of organizations in the community has a number of characteristics:

- *It is professional:* a company needs to run its CCI just as professionally as any other aspect of its business activities, if it is to find and achieve mutually beneficial projects and to run them in ways which will maximize benefit both to the company and to the community.
- *Resources are packaged:* for example, cash is supplemented with management expertise in areas like marketing, IT, financial disciplines and personnel.

- *Resources are leveraged from others:* these may be other companies or public and charitable sources and there is an increasing number of government programmes.
- *The impact of any resources is maximized through effective support:* for example, companies like TSB and IBM have encouraged their staff to become business-nominated school governors and provide training courses to explain what is involved, what the likely issues will be for new governors, and where they can turn to for further advice and information.
- *Lateral thinking about potential partners:* such as, in the media – Birmingham Mid Shires Building Society has sponsored Merseyside Marvels – a competition to reward community activists who are doing something effective and practical to make a difference in their communities. This has been run in collaboration with the *Liverpool Echo* newspaper.
- Coherence between CCI and corporate values/activities.

Professionalizing business involvement

Effective corporate community involvement requires that companies should: Assess, Commit, Tell, Integrate, Organize, Nurture.

Assess existing community involvement, identify community needs and priorities, determine how long-term business needs can be met through such involvement and adopt a board policy for CCI which marries community and business objectives.

Commit the company at all levels through senior management leadership, employee involvement, and integration of community involvement into management development and appraisal.

Tell stakeholders (including shareholders, employees, customers and the wider community) about the company's community involvement activities and why it is involved.

Integrate community involvement with mainstream business functions such as marketing, purchasing and personnel.

Organize programmes professionally with measurable targets against which progress can be regularly monitored and reviewed.

Nurture long-term partnerships with organizations in the community just like successful companies now operate long-term, shared destiny relationships with suppliers and subcontractors.

Choosing partners

Like any other part of the business's activities, the choice of your community supplier or joint venture partner is critical to the success of any CCI programme. Particular criteria for choosing community partners include:

- Do customers and employees feel this organization is working on important issues (based on where they spend their own volunteering time and money)?
- Does the not-for-profit organization have a track-record? Does it convince you that it can deliver its side of the bargain?
- Does it have the ability to network with other similar organizations, or central/local government, etc?
- Are there any negative elements, such as poor relationships with one of your key customers?
- Does it offer the opportunity for a range of CCI involvements, for example, staff time, technical expertise, etc?
- Is it focused on an enduring issue? Also, is it sufficiently focused to deliver impact?

Pitfalls for CCI

The most common mistakes in corporate community involvement include:

- Responding *ad hoc* to external requests for help – without any clear objectives, priorities or guidelines.
- Being unclear about what you expect from your community partners, so that after the event, you feel that they have not delivered their side, and they are resentful because you appear to be changing the goalposts (or even worse – creating goalposts after the event).
- Allowing your community partner to build up unrealistic expectations of what you will be able to contribute/achieve.
- Becoming sucked in to too many different and disparate projects which drain energies and dissipate effort over too wide a field.
- Chopping and changing the organizations and issues you are supporting in the community. This creates an impression of dilettantism and you do not have the opportunity to build up knowledge of a sector and its effective players, nor is there the chance to establish a profile and track-record for your involvement.
- Conversely, carrying on with the same activity year-after-year without seeking to improve and innovate is potentially damaging. You can run the same broad themes, but still have a reputation for freshness and innovation. Shell, for example, has been a major supporter of small business activities for almost two decades – but it is constantly innovating and improving its programmes.
- Just providing cash, without otherwise being involved in the organization or the issue.

Myths and reality

CCI is not the preserve of indulgent organizations. It is not a conscience-salving luxury. Lord Sheppard, chairman of Grand Metropolitan recently commented: 'Grand Metropolitan often comes out as a leader in CCI, but I was also voted the toughest manager in Britain. Together, these things suggest a company with a sharp edge, that is professional, and has a sensible, realistic approach to people.'

All the available evidence suggests that CCI linked to the business is more sustainable if the company runs into a rough patch; and that it generates more resources for the community – and gets much wider involvement.

Recent research by a public relations company in the United States, together with the *Wall Street Journal International*, and with one of the main Japanese business magazines, asked chief executives of international companies how important they thought it was for corporate players to be good corporate citizens. Over half replied that it was 'extremely important'.

Similarly, a survey of 250 of the largest Canadian-headquartered companies asked chief executives and, separately, their CCI specialists, about the importance of their involvement in the community at present and how important it is compared with five years ago and in five years' time. Two important points came out of this: first, the expectation, both on the part of the CCI managers and the chief executives, that corporate community involvement is actually becoming very important, and it is expected to be even more important in the future. Second, the chief executives consistently ranked corporate community involvement as more important than the specialists in the companies to whom they have delegated the function.

Another frequent criticism is that CCI is a distraction to an organization's chief concern of actually running the business. Well-managed and, selectively and committedly undertaken, CCI should help managers do their jobs more effectively and advance the interests of the business.

A further lament is that an organization does not have any money available because it is experiencing business difficulties or is a partnership. CCI does not have to involve money. If you are a partnership, then you have much needed expertise – in law, accountancy, design, architecture or management consultancy – which could be invaluable to not-for-profit organizations. Even many small professional firms are now members of schemes like Lawyers for Enterprise or the Professional Firms Group, in which participating firms commit themselves to a certain amount of *pro-bono* time to the community.

Other organizations claim that they prefer to give any surpluses to their shareholders who can then decide what to do with the money. If they want to give it to charity that is their choice. It is not right for a company to make choices on behalf of shareholders. This argument too is flawed – do organizations say the same thing about *investments* in training or R&D or advertising, or public relations? If they organize CCI properly, it is about business benefit as well as community benefit – and it is irresponsible of management to abdicate their responsibilities to manage all the levers at their disposal to ensure that they can continue to achieve sustainable wealth-creation through meeting customer needs.

Equally unsustainable is the argument that it is wrong to claim credit for community involvement. If employees, customers and the wider community don't know about an organization's CCI, then it is going to be harder – sometimes even impossible – for it to achieve the desired business benefits. More importantly, if successful, respected companies, and achieving, high-flying business people, are known to be involved in community issues, this will be more persuasive than probably anything else, to encourage laggard companies to join in.

There is also a myth that CCI is the preserve of large organizations. In fact, CCI does not have to be complicated. It can be as simple as adopting your local school: helping with quality work experience placements, upgrading the information and contacts of the school's careers' service, encouraging staff to be mentors to at-risk children, providing space for an after-school hours homework/study centre. In Belfast, for example, the Ormeau Bakery with 50 employees, has worked closely with a local priest and the Short Strand community to help provide workspace and a shopping centre.

Consumers are increasingly expecting companies to be involved in community issues. MORI surveyed consumers in summer 1993, and asked: 'How would you feel about buying products or services from a company if you knew it has a strong record of community involvement?' A total of 31 per cent were strongly positive, and a further 26 per cent slightly positive. Research in 1994 in the US is even clearer. Carried out by Roper Starch Worldwide and Boston-based Cohn Associates, it found: 84 per cent believed cause-related-marketing creates a positive company image; 78 per cent of consumers are more likely to buy a product that is associated with a cause they care about; and 66 per cent would switch brands to support a cause they care about.

Dragon International's report, *Corporate Reputation – does the consumer care?*, researched the emergence of 'vigilante consumerism'. It was based on a series of focus groups around Britain in 1991. They came to the conclusion that 'consumers are interested in corporate reputation and are able to evaluate company behaviour'. Consumers do not expect companies to take responsibility for the world's problems, but they are willing to be favourably influenced by positive corporate behaviour. The report concluded that 'the link between consumer purchasing decisions and corporate reputation will increase significantly in the future with companies competing for opportunities to gain consumer approval.'

The Dragon research also showed that consumers were much more comfortable about business involvement in community issues where they could see a link between what the company was doing in the community and its business interests. For example, where National Westminster Bank is sponsoring a schools programme to promote financial literacy.

Consumers were also notably very suspicious of companies which seemed to be doing things in the community without any obvious business connection. This leads to two critical caveats. Companies need to be honest. If something is for marketing purposes rather than for community benefit, companies must not claim that their motivation is CCI.

They must also be consistent. CCI must fit in with a company's mainstream practices. It should not help small businesses while being a late-payer of its own small business suppliers, or support environmental organizations while remaining an inveterate polluter.

CCI is no longer a matter of following the sudden benevolent urges of the chairman. Most major companies now have clear board policies. Sometimes this may include small, discretionary funds for the individual priorities of directors – leaving the main programme to be managed against publicly stated objectives and guidelines.

Businesses get involved with a wide range of issues. However, among the most common subjects are: helping schools; assisting job creation and local economic development through small firms' growth; encouraging skilling/re-skilling, particularly for those who are outside the labour market; and giving support to turn around inner city housing estates. There are many different routes to becoming involved:

Helping schools

School reforms in recent years mean that companies can play a significant role:

- Through agreements with young people and schools – 'compacts' which set goals for students with incentives for course completion and achievement of qualifications and provide support to those at risk of failing or dropping out.
- By encouraging staff – especially parents – to become business governors of schools and by backing them up with information and training for their roles as governors.
- By helping teachers and students with curriculum development through opening up sites for visits and placements, providing materials, equipment and staff with expertise to work with teachers or to tutor young people.
- By encouraging staff to help with projects like Young Enterprise which give pupils the opportunity to develop entrepreneurial skills and competencies for employment.
- By providing challenging work experience placements and help with mock interviews etc.
- By opening up internal training courses or running specific programmes to help teachers to learn from business.
- By helping careers education and guidance programmes, and by making a point of asking to see young applicants' National Records of Achievement.
- By taking part as lecturers in colleges of further education.

Helping small firms

Companies can also directly help small and medium-sized companies by:

- Paying their bills on time.
- Developing long-term shared destiny relationships – known as partnership sourcing – to help subcontractors and suppliers constantly improve their quality and standards.
- By sharing their expertise with small firms in areas like environmental regulations and environmental business opportunities – for example, IBM is heavily involved in an exciting new project called Envirolink. This uses well-proven information technology to provide on-line information and intelligence on environmental legislation and its implications coming out of both Whitehall and Brussels.
- Opening up internal training courses to local companies.
- Being open to innovation: by being prepared to license technological innovations which they are not exploiting themselves; and being open to approaches from external innovators interested in joint venture projects.
- Joining schemes to provide venture finance for smaller companies.
- Making available surplus premises for small business start-up units.
- Providing cash, expertise and people to support the Business Links – the new one-stop-shops for small company support.

Promoting upskilling

Business itself must be flexible and creative in presenting work opportunities in such a way as to attract the best employees, and to support initiatives to retain their skills and commitment when not employed (family care policies, flexi-working, working from home, etc).

For example:

1. Review what skills a job really requires, rather than what skills it traditionally required and provide more appropriate training.
2. Promote Personal Development Plans for all staff.
3. Give credit for prior-job learning – which may not be formal qualifications but relevant experience.
4. Provide some accreditation for learning on the job – record and reward training undertaken.
5. Encourage mentoring in schools to promote science subjects for girls.
6. Set targets for employing and developing women in your workforce. Measure your performance.
7. Influence your supply chain.
8. Open up places on training programmes for people not currently in work – ethnic minority/disabled/women.
9. Recruitment – look for a broader range of achievement than just academic qualifications.
10. Undertake customized or pre-recruitment training programmes.

Helping local community groups

Established businesses can help local community groups and not-for-profit organizations by:

- mentoring community groups;
- providing technical expertise;
- seconding young managers on specific projects;
- social investment;
- providing premises for community use;
- networking across public/private sectors;
- permitting entry to internal training courses;
- giving help/endorsement for aid applications.

The range of options is wide and widening. Professional managers and other professionals possess skills which are highly valued in the community. Using them in new and completely different settings can benefit community groups and organizations and, equally, develop the skills of the manager.

David Grayson is an international authority on corporate community involvement. For the past 15 years he has worked the four sides of the table: advising companies, running a local community organization, leading a national charity, and, most recently, working for the UK's leading authority on CCI, Business in the Community (BITC), where he is currently managing director of the Business Strategy Group.

BITC exists to increase the quality and extent of business involvement in the community, and to make such involvement a natural part of successful business practice. David Grayson has lectured on and studied CCI in some 20 countries. He is also Director of The Prince of Wales Award for Innovation, and the Chairman of the National Assessment Panel for Business Links on behalf of the British Government.

MANAGING THE ENVIRONMENT

Kit Sadgrove

Environmental issues burst on to the management agenda in the 1980s. In the 1990s, however, political and business interest and action in improving environmental performance often appears to be less enthusiastic. By ignoring existing and emerging environmental issues, companies run the risk of missing out on a valuable source of competitive advantage and of eventually falling prey to more vigilantly enforced and more stringent regulations.

Is the environment still an important issue for management? Or was it merely a fad of the1980s? Going green has had several phases of development.

The first phase was that of *ignorance,* a stage that existed until the mid-1980s. Most companies paid little attention to the environment, and the consumer was unaware of green issues.

In the UK and elsewhere, this stage ended around 1990, a year when the environmental debate was at its height. It had ended some years earlier in the US, due to the zealous action of the Environmental Protection Agency, and the federal government's environmental laws.

The dawning of awareness brought an *immaturity* phase. This was characterized by corporate anxiety and even panic. Companies asked themselves: Will we be fined? Will the firm be closed down? How can we afford the alterations to the plant?

This phase was matched by growing consumer interest in green products. The customer was prepared to buy virtually any product marked 'environmentally friendly'.

By 1994, *reaction* was setting in. The consumer discovered that some green products did not work very well. Others did not deserve their 'environmentally friendly' label. Having risen strongly in the 1980s, the percentage of UK consumers prepared to 'pay more for environmentally friendly products' fell from 49 per cent to 40 per cent between 1990 and 1994.

Likewise, the proportion who disapproved of 'the effect of aerosols on the atmosphere' fell from 65 per cent to 49 per cent in the same period, reflecting a perhaps unjustified belief that the aerosol problem had been solved.

But it would be wrong to assume that the green movement has died. In 1993, at the height of the UK recession, the research company Nielsen found that only three per cent of consumers were unaffected by environmental considerations, and 68 per cent of consumers were still 'prepared to pay a little more for green products'.

Companies also went through a reaction phase. Many were surprised to find that their market had changed less than they had feared. In 1994 their world was still standing. They also found that regulators were less harsh than predicted.

The recession which hit many parts of the West in the early 1990s rein-forced the reaction against the environment. Companies became reluctant to spend money on anything that was not essential to their survival. Environmental initiatives were easily postponed. As a result, environmental progress in many companies was arrested in the reaction phase.

Many companies have now decided that they can afford either to ignore the environment, or to pay it lip service. They believe that the environment is a spent force. But this is a dangerous strategy.

Some businesses, though not many, have reached the fourth and final phase of environmental awareness, that of *maturity*. Companies in this phase have adopted good environmental practice, and regard the environment as just one of many issues which must be controlled. Mature companies take the environ-ment into account when planning new products and new premises; and they constantly monitor their emissions and discharges.

Their commitment is justified. Green issues may not command the head-lines they once did, but they remain a potent force. A tracking study by TGI found that the percentage of UK consumers who feel 'there is too much con-cern with the environment' has remained consistently low. Their numbers rose from 7 per cent to just 13 per cent in the year to 1990, and have remained level ever since.

Table 1: Phases of environmental awareness

Phase	Year	Business	Consumers	The law
Ignorance	To mid-1980s	Little attention paid to the environment	Unaware of green issues	Few environ-mental laws
Immaturity	1990	Companies panic at the extent of the new laws	Delight at new green products	Major new laws being introduced
Reaction	1994	The laws have less impact than feared	Rejection of 'green cons'	Laws and penalties modified
Maturity	1998	Environ-mental management systems are common	The consumer expects purchases to be green	Court action more common

While only a small number of companies have reached the maturity phase, it is often seen among petro-chemical companies and drug firms which, despite their poor history of pollution, or perhaps because of it, now take the issue seriously. But other large firms, such as regional electricity companies, have failed to do so, despite earnest statements in glossy brochures and annual reports.

Some industries have failed to reach environmental maturity despite an apparent green image. A hospital, for example, usually imagines itself as an oasis of well-being, in contrast to the grubby factories that surround it. In fact, hospital chimneys are often a town's most serious source of pollution. A survey of UK hospital chimneys found them to be well outside the government's pollution limits.

National ethos plays a part, too. The UK, the US and the Benelux countries rate the environment as the most important risk of all, as Table 2 shows. France, however, ranks it only sixth. The French see a smoking chimney as a sign of employment and economic prosperity, while other nations see it as a blot on the horizon.

The need to be green

So why do companies choose to go green? As Fig. 1 shows, the most basic reason is to stay within the law. To gain a permit to operate a polluting process, the company may have to reduce its emissions or keep them within certain limits.

Table 2: Ranking of the most critical risks

Category	UK	US	France	Benelux
Environment	1	1	6	1
Safety of employees	2	2	2	2
Product liability	3	3	5	4
Fire and explosion	7	6	1	5
Business interruption	3	5	3	10
Credit risk	6	12	4	3
Image impairment	8	8	7	7
Security of property	5	9	8	6
Directors' liability	9	4	9	11
Due diligence	11	7	11	8
Political risk	9	11	10	9
Pension fund integrity	12	9	12	11

In this survey, companies were asked to state which risks they considered to have the greatest impact on the business.

Environmental legislation can only become more stringent and, as a result, conforming to environmental legislation will affect an increasing number of companies. Companies need to assume that controls will become tighter.

In particular, legal conformance is the main reason why small companies go green. But not all small firms comply. A survey of small manufacturers in Scotland showed that they were aware of their legal obligations, but many had not taken action. Some were simply waiting for the regulatory authority to knock on the door. Lack of cash, as well as a lack of interest in environmental issues, was bringing them into conflict with the law.

A second group of companies realizes that environmental probity is good for profitability. The companies realize that by reducing waste they reduce their costs, while developing green products gives them a competitive advantage and increases their revenue.

One firm that has taken advantage of companies' need to be green is the Welsh firm Alchema. It recycles toxic waste from the UK's printed circuit board industry, recovering the key ingredients of ammonia and copper. The only waste product is salt, which it discharges into the sea under licence. Previously, the boards were dumped in landfill sites.

The profit motive also inspires publicly quoted companies which want to keep institutional shareholders happy. Pension fund managers believe that well-managed firms do not pollute. Polluters carry higher risks and are, therefore, less attractive to institutional investors.

A third group of companies manages its environmental impacts to avoid social criticism. These are the oil and gas companies, the electricity providers and the banks. These are the largest of companies, and those whose operations are most visible. They cannot afford an environmental scandal or a loss of reputation.

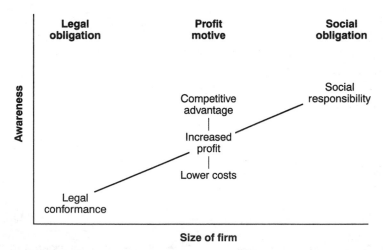

Fig. 1 Motives for going green

What does the future hold?

In the future, environmental issues will be more challenging still. Some of the potential changes are listed below:

Waste disposal will be substantially more expensive. Incineration with heat recovery will be the preferred solution, despite technical problems and its heavy cost; microwaving will grow in popularity.

Landfill will be increasingly restricted. This will result from the imposition of taxes on waste disposal. Some local authorities will ban the tipping of certain types of waste, especially pollutants.

Pressure to get BS 7750: Large companies will increasingly demand that their suppliers have BS 7750. They will do so in order to minimize their liability, and because BS 7750 will encourage them to choose environmentally responsible suppliers.

The CE mark will be required for more products which are sold within the EU. The CE mark may contain extra environmental requirements.

Energy and fuel from oil and gas will be more expensive. This will stem from many factors. The EU will want to reduce energy use for environmental reasons, and will therefore apply targets for energy reduction. As North Sea oil runs out, the UK government will seek to reduce fuel imports, using tax as a weapon.

Distribution will become more complex and more restricted. As traffic congestion grows in cities and motorways around the world, countries will start to restrict traffic, including lorries. Deliveries will take longer and be more costly, and rail use will grow.

Legal action for pollution will grow in frequency and fines will be heavier. Directors will be jailed more frequently. Communities and customers will be more ready to take action against firms.

Some raw materials now in common use will be banned, due to their toxicity.

Eco-labels will be common on all kinds of products. Customers will refuse to buy brands which do not carry the label.

Environmental performance will be more visible. Companies will be expected to reveal environmental risk in their annual reports. Publication of environmental data will be the norm in many markets.

These forecasts may seem pessimistic, but there will also be good news:

New markets will develop. They will include process control (such as monitoring devices), pollution control (such as filters), and waste management systems. There will be many others – though this requires that organizations develop the R&D capabilities to meet the emerging market needs.

Alternative fuels will be more common. Solar and other technologies will be more effective, as will battery storage. This will create new marketing opportunities.

Green companies will flourish. Because of these various changes, firms which take the environment seriously will succeed. They will have lower costs and more attractive products. They will produce less waste, and spend less time fire-fighting. In a pilot scheme, suppliers to the Rover car company each saved up to £100,000 in one year – through reduced waste and water, and through improved energy and process efficiency.

But just how green should the company go? In the following section, we look at the four different postures that companies can adopt, as defined in the Green Grid (Fig. 2).

The Green Grid

The Green Grid is a useful way of assessing a company's current environmental performance.

There are only four positions a company can adopt: that of leader, conformer, laggard and punished.

These positions reflect the amount of cost that the company commits to environmental management. They also show whether the company is seen as green or grey (that is, environmentally responsible or irresponsible).

The leader is a company which prides itself on its environmental advances. It publishes annual statistics about its declining output of waste, and its products use less energy than its competitors. The company has been working for many years to become green, and is at last seeing some payback. 3M is a typical leader. It looks for environmentally sound solutions to industrial problems. In doing so, it produces advanced products which satisfy the customer and which also have cost savings.

But leaders know that other companies in the industry are also trying hard. An innovation, such as a move from solvent-based paint spraying to water-based paint, is quickly adopted by competitors.

If the leader slackens its pace, it may slide back into the *conformer* quadrant. The Body Shop, the world's most outspoken corporate defender of green issues, was in danger of slipping from leader to conformer when criticisms surfaced about some of its policies. The critics alleged that the company's standards were not as high as it insisted. If the crown of such an undisputed leader can be challenged, no company is safe. It also demonstrates that leaders expose themselves to sniping from envious detractors. Other toiletries stores with poor environmental performance escape notice.

The conformer manages the environment, and does all that the law requires. But it does so with some reluctance. It asks stern questions about the financial benefits of any environmental investment, and will only commit money if there are good reasons for doing so. As a result, the conformer gets a green image without having to invest too heavily.

This is a logical position to adopt, and one where the majority of companies place themselves. It gives them the advantages of a green image without the risk that is associated with being a leader. It knows that a company which puts its head over the parapet is likely to get it shot off.

The laggard is a company which pays little attention to green issues. It has ignored many of the innovations which other companies have introduced (such as environmental committees). It produces lots of waste material, and has little understanding of environmental legislation. The laggard is not hostile to green issues; it simply fails to discuss them. One of Britain's biggest housebuilders, a company whose environmental impacts range from quarried products to the use of rainforest timber, has privately admitted complete ignorance of green issues.

Punished As we have seen, leaders which stop innovating become conformers. Similarly, conformers that grow complacent become laggards. And laggards which refuse to take action become punished.

	Green	Grey
High cost	**Leader** High risk high reward	**Punished** Failure
Low cost	**Conformer** No cost, low cost	**Laggard** Do nothing

Fig. 2 The green grid

A company becomes punished in two ways: by the market and by the courts. Customers start to buy from a greener competitor, and so the company's revenue declines. Or the company gets taken to court for pollution offences. It ends up paying to expensively retro-fit pollution control technology; or the court may even require it to cease production until it overcomes the pollution problem. Whatever form the punishment takes, the company faces high costs (or losses) and still retains its dirty image.

How to apply the Green Grid

It can be difficult to be objective, and companies often believe they are more advanced than they are. Laggards usually reckon they are conformers. The checklist below helps you determine your company's position on the grid.

The list contains a series of statements about the company's environmental performance. Tick all the statements which apply to your company. You will find that most of the ticks lie in one of the four quadrants. This is the company's true position.

Green Grid checklist

The leader

☐ The company is registered to BS 7750 or EMAS (the EU's Environmental Management and Audit Scheme).

☐ The company has had an environmental training programme for at least two years.

☐ Environmental impact is formally considered in new product development.

☐ The chief executive has talked publicly and favourably about green issues in the last six months.

The conformer

☐ The company has set a target for gaining BS 7750 or EMAS.

☐ The company has introduced environmental improvements into its main products or processes.

☐ Selected managers have attended seminars or conferences on green issues.

☐ The company has a written environmental policy statement.

☐ An environmental audit has taken place within the last three years.

The laggard

- ☐ The company lacks a written environmental policy.

- ☐ Much of the company's revenue is in markets threatened by green legislation (for example, foundries).

- ☐ The company believes that green issues are not important to its customers.

- ☐ The environment appears on the board's agenda, but time usually prevents a discussion.

The punished

- ☐ Sales have fallen due to competitors' innovations, which have included environmental improvements.

- ☐ The company has had a reportable pollution incident within the last two years.

- ☐ The company has been taken to court in the last 12 months for environmental offences.

A wide spread of ticks indicates a company in which different divisions are moving at different speeds, or a company in a dirty industry which is cleaning up its act.

Benchmarking the grid

Another way to determine whether the company is a leader, laggard, conformer or punished is to carry out a benchmarking exercise. It is fairly easy to discover whether competitors have:

- Been prosecuted for pollution offences
- Got an environmental policy
- Introduced green products
- Obtained BS 7750.

This information will help identify where major competitors are positioned on the grid. The company can then determine what steps it should take to either match or surpass them.

Becoming a conformer

Punished and laggard companies which want to become conformers will need to make changes. The company needs an environmental policy, an audit, performance standards and an action plan.

Writing an environmental policy

The company needs an environmental policy which will guide its employees. But the policy has to be honest and workable. It is dangerous to make statements about the environment if they are ignored as soon as a problem looms. The workforce will quickly learn that corporate policies are merely for show, and may apply this lesson to other policies, including the quality policy, with potentially disastrous results.

Commission an environmental audit

The audit is the traditional way of discovering the company's environmental problems. The same rules apply to environmental audits as to any other kind of audit. The audit should be comprehensive, independent, factual and objective. It should be properly planned, and should result in a written report. The audit should examine the entire lifecycle of the product, which means investigating the environmental probity of suppliers.

The audit can be undertaken in-house, providing the auditors have been trained for the job. But departmental managers may not audit their own department, because they are too close to the problems and are liable to overlook long-standing problems.

Set performance standards and targets

Corporate print-outs contain detailed data on sales, costs, stock levels and profits. But managers often have little idea about the scale of their firm's environmental impacts.

To manage its impacts, the company needs regular information. This applies especially to impacts which cost money, such as solid and liquid waste, and emissions to air.

It is important to measure only the significant impacts. In the early days of environmental action, companies tried to measure items whose effect on the business was slight, such as the weight of plastic cups used. Today for example, British Steel measures smoke density from coke ovens (a measure of air cleanliness), SO_2 emissions, and energy consumption. It also measures the concentration of dissolved metals in effluent (a measure of waste water cleanliness).

Companies should also set annual targets for reducing their environmental impacts. They should be attainable and be set in the context of long-term goals.

Develop a plan

Targets are not achieved without effort. The company needs a plan to bring about the desired result.

The plan needs to be no longer than one or two pages. It may set out changes that will be made in new plant or equipment, in training, or in methods. The company will lack answers to some of its environmental problems, and these may need to be investigated. For example, the company may instigate a search for environmentally superior raw materials, suppliers or processes. This kind of research should be identified in the plan. The green equivalent of quality circles may be established to solve the problems.

Becoming a leader

To move from being a conformer to a leader, the company will need a change of culture. It will also need to get BS 7750, provide training, and prepare reports for outsiders on its environmental progress.

Cultural change

The company should adopt a more positive attitude towards the environment. It means treating the environment as an opportunity rather than a threat. It also means being alive to the possibilities that environmental management can bring, including cost savings.

BS 7750

Environmental audits have one weakness. They are merely a report; and reports are easily shelved. This is why many organizations have sought a more rigorous and workable tool. They have found it in BS 7750 and EMAS.

To get BS 7750, you have to open your company to inspection by a certification body (such as BSI, BVQI or Yarsley). This exposure to a critical and independent inspector prevents the company from sweeping inconvenient facts under the carpet. Though environmental performance is difficult to assess objectively, BS 7750 makes that attempt.

Companies which are already certified to ISO 9000, the quality standard, will find BS 7750 relatively easy to understand, because the new standard is based on ISO 9000. Both BS 7750 and EMAS contain similar elements. They require the company to carry out an environmental audit, to set objectives and targets, and to set out a management plan. EMAS requires public disclosure of the information while BS 7750 does not.

Achieving BS 7750 is the acid test of environmental commitment. Without independent certification, detractors can dismiss any environmental action as mere corporate puffery. BS 7750 is incontrovertible proof that the company is actively managing its green affairs.

Management systems like ISO 9000 and BS 7750 are controversial. Critics claim that they reduce the company's flexibility, and increase bureaucracy. It is true that a poor implementation can be stultifying. But, providing the organization gets it right, the system will ensure that all staff know what is expected of them. It will turn best practice into normal practice. And it will provide a level of consistency that is often lacking.

Training

Environmental training is an integral part of BS 7750. In environmental management there is a widespread 'broom cupboard' syndrome. The firm allocates environmental responsibility to one manager, giving him or her few resources and little authority. Green issues are not promoted, and as a result, the firm fails to make advances.

If, instead, the firm trains *all* its employees to be aware of environmental issues, and links this awareness with the ideas of Total Quality Management, it can harness the intelligence and ingenuity of its entire workforce in solving environmental problems.

However, the training needs to be properly managed. Some businesses simply hand out thick ring binders containing environmental information. The staff then place the binder, unread, on a shelf next to all the other corporate manuals. This is not an approach which works. The best kind of training involves small groups examining their environmental impacts; and it is interactive, with management learning as much from the workforce as the other way around.

Environmental reporting

A leader will display its environmental awareness in its annual report. The report should identify any areas of environmental risk, and explain how they are managed. It should also demonstrate (by graphs) that its environmental impacts are being reduced. Some firms produce separate environmental reports which are useful for the media and other opinion formers. Others distribute information to local householders. Some companies go further: Sandoz has prepared an eco-balance sheet at its different plants in an effort to achieve sustainability.

Based in Bagley, Somerset, Kit Sadgrove is the author of several business books, including *The Green Guide to Profitable Management* (1994). As a consultant, he has conducted environmental audits for companies ranging from the National Health Service to National Power.

Further Reading

Fortlage, CA, *Environmental Assessment*, Gower, Aldershot, 1990.
Sadgrove, K, *The Green Guide to Profitable Management*, Gower, Aldershot, 1994.

Corporate Governance

'In the United States, the pressure of the quarterly corporate report has become one of the great weaknesses of their economy. Company directors always have to prove to their shareholders that things are going better. They are judged like politicians, only worse, because elections are held every three months. If they have two bad quarters in a row, the shareholders start complaining and looking round for another director.'

Andre Leysen, chairman Agfa-Gavaert[1]

4

---

[1] Quoted in Bloom, H, Calori, R and de Woot, P, *Euromanagement*, Kogan Page, London, 1994.

OVERVIEW

Nigel N Graham Maw

Corporate governance is a relatively new topic, but one which has gained public prominence, interest and importance as a result of well-publicized corporate disasters (Maxwell, Polly Peck and others) and, in the UK, through the setting-up of the Cadbury Committee on 'The Financial Aspects of Corporate Governance'.

Corporate governance – labelled 'stewardship' in the United States – is now well established and publicized, and is widely seen as of radical importance to the corporate life and future of major businesses. However, it remains ill-defined, and there are basic questions still to be addressed.

Fundamentally, it is unclear what the topic actually embraces. There is no accessible and commonly used workable definition as to the meaning of corporate governance. Its place in law is, so far, equally vague and there is continuing debate on how standards of corporate governance could be improved, evaluated and monitored, and who would be best qualified to do so. Finally, it is undecided what sanctions should be available against those who transgress, and who should impose those sanctions.

In the UK, for example, it is established in law that the duty of each company director is to act in good faith in the general interest of the company, but that is a trite and unclear expression of shareholders' expectations.

The law on directors' duties is historically founded, by analogy, on the duties of trustees to their beneficiaries. Such law is well furnished with examples of what should *not* be done, but conspicuously lacking in examples of what *should* (positively) be done and what standards of behaviour, diligence and ability are to be expected. Such standards can never be absolute and objective, or free from any risk of retrospective criticism. No one can be expected to be infallible about each and every business decision made today, and judged tomorrow with the gift of hindsight.

What, however, can and should be expected is that corporate structures, systems and procedures be put in place, and then strictly followed, so that decisions are made, implemented and appropriately publicized which are objective, free from self-interest, well-informed and thought-out, and rationally achievable in the light of best business judgment at the time.

Such expectations and their fulfilment lie at the very root of the concept of good corporate governance.

They go much further than the current requirements of statute or case law. Indeed, legal obligations must be sufficiently well defined to be enforced. Corporate governance is both *structural* (which, in theory, could be legislated for, but perhaps too inflexibly) and *behavioural* (which certainly could not be). Instead, we should look to the stock market, to investors (particularly the institutions) and to lenders for their potential sanctions and effective pressures.

Corporate governance, as it is now discussed and debated, need not cover all enterprises. One person and family-owned companies, for example, can be excluded. Instead, it should apply to companies listed on the Stock Exchange, public limited companies and unlisted companies with a significant (eg, 15 per cent or more) shareholding in the hands of banks or other financial institutions (such as venture capital houses) or with a wide spread of (non-family) shareholders. In addition, by way of exhortation and prior qualification, all companies contemplating a listing within the next three accounting periods should comply. It may also be appropriate for lenders to companies falling outside these criteria to make adherence to such prescribed standards a condition to their provision of finance, and its continuing availability.

In search of meaning

Corporate governance is a broad and as yet inchoate topic. 'Corporate governance is the system by which companies are directed and controlled,' observed Sir Adrian Cadbury. This, perhaps, is a little premature in its certainty. In practice, corporate governance covers the way the board should behave towards, and deal with, its shareholders, auditors, staff and financiers as well as its wider obligations, such as to regulatory and environmental issues. These various categories are sometimes (somewhat unsatisfactorily) referred to as 'stakeholders'.

Shareholders are the owners on whose behalf management should be working. This is stating the obvious, but it is too often ignored, forgotten, or delegated to the back of the mind, with directors referring to 'their' company, and behaving as if it was. It is when things go wrong that the focus of public (and press) attention turns to ask why, and to look for the culprits.

Management (and indeed the entire board of directors) is answerable to shareholders as to the custody and conduct of the company's business activities and the commercial exploitation and preservation of its assets. It is here that we find the vital element of accountability which lies at the root of the concept of corporate governance.

The other stakeholders all have an interest, in various ways, in the concept and in the resultant standards of structure, behavioural conduct and accountability.

Corporate governance and the law

Corporate governance should set behavioural standards, supported and promoted by structural systems, for them to be achieved under the full glare of public accountability.

Such behavioural standards cannot always be judicially measured in terms of the legal requirements of criminal guilt or actionable neglect. Instead, the task of measuring and assessing behaviour is more for the Stock Exchange, the investing public and also for the press, than for the judge in court.

Certainly the standards and supporting systems required must be clearly expressed, but they cannot, because of their very nature, be expressed in the black and white terms we should expect from legislation. Legislators have experienced great difficulties in forming clear-cut legislation to cover even extreme behavioural abuses – such as insider dealing.

By their very nature such subjects are usually beyond the scope of legislation. Behaviour in takeovers falls under a similar category – in the UK the Takeover Panel provides an example of how self-regulation can work to inhibit or sanction disobedience and quickly adapt to change.

The Stock Exchange must, if it is to behave responsibly, take the lead within its sphere of influence and play a leading role as self-regulator of standards of corporate governance. In the UK the Exchange has wide powers to criticize and sanction directors personally in addition to, or as a prelude to, its powers to suspend or cancel the listing of a company's securities. Those ultimate sanctions (of suspension or cancellation) hurt the general body of shareholders. In the area of non-compliance with structures and standards of corporate governance, shareholders are clearly blameless. It is the directors who should shoulder the blame and suffer the consequences, at least in the first place.

The Exchange's powers to criticize and sanction directors have been used little, if at all, but they should, I believe, be more readily used, and not only in the field of corporate governance. This requires a clearer and more mandatory Code of Practice. Otherwise, power to sanction simply will not work.

Despite such difficulties, there remains a need for clear stipulations as to an appropriate framework for the constitution of the board and of board committees, for the functioning of the board and its accountability, and for the matters to be disclosed to shareholders in the annual report and accounts.

Evaluation, and its effective monitoring, primarily depends on the quality and quantity of the information provided, and the reaction by the various stakeholders to such information. Of prime importance must be what the institutional shareholders ask, are told, say and do. Typically, their role is both insufficiently practised and (if necessary forcefully) brought to the attention of the board. (Legislation on inside information and the penalties of being accused of making market use of it have not been helpful in the quest for improvements.) The temptation to say nothing, ask nothing, and sell the shares remains strong.

But pressure for there to be a strong non-executive element on the board, for splitting the (distinct and different) roles of chairman and chief executive, for there to be mandatory standards of an independent non-executive corporate overview (eg, on financial accounting and executive remuneration) can be best and most effectively promoted by those with both financial and voting power. These are often a company's institutional shareholders.

The current emphasis appears to be on paying lip service to corporate governance. Voluntary requirements lack ultimate efficacy. In contrast, there is a tendency to impose extensive and inappropriate duties on auditors. The requirements of the Cadbury Code, for example, call upon auditors to certify matters of which they cannot have full knowledge, still less express a determinate view. Certain specific aspects of the Code could only be effectively reviewed by the auditors by their attending a number of board meetings and meetings of the board's Audit and Remuneration Committees (which would be both impracticable and an undesirable extravagance). There is also the risk that auditors take such a cautious approach to whether a business is a going concern that this might prejudice the survival of all but the most liquid and risk-free companies.

Having to express an audit opinion as to the accounts expressing a 'true and fair view' is exacting enough, without auditors being asked to stray so far from the traditional audit function.

In practice, the Cadbury Code has attracted some criticism and a degree of apathy. It, however, marks an important beginning.

The way forward

Sir Adrian Cadbury's Code is divided into four subheadings: the board of directors; non-executive directors; executive directors; reporting and controls. It suggests what *should* be done.

As an alternative, I have developed a more demanding and mandatory Code. This differentiates between what *shall* or *must be* done, and what *should* be done. It is also divided into four different subheadings: the constitution of the board; board committees; the functioning of the board; the board and its accountability.

The constitution of the board

Non-executive directors (NEDs) have an important role to play. The company board *shall* (mandatorily) consist of a minimum of one-third NEDs, the majority of whom should (preferably) be free of any other business, or financial connection, with the company, apart from their shareholdings.

This should not lead to a two-tier system (with a supervisory board and a management board, as found in Germany) since the formation of a two-tier board system cuts right across the flexible tradition of company law.

Neither should the NEDs be characterized as 'the checkers' of the executive director 'doers'. This ignores the fact that, in the eyes of the law, there is no distinction between NEDs and executive directors. It also denigrates the positive contribution NEDs can make towards helping in devising and assessing the company's planning, strategy and implementation; and displays an almost neurotic fear on the part of some executives of needing to be checked. Every corporate proposal needs to be evaluated and assessed, but for the executive proposer to see that process as a personal check, demonstrates a lack of confidence in both the proposal itself and in the proposer.

Further, the unitary board, in its deliberations, has the advantages of the (involved) executives sitting round the table and putting forward their views directly to the less involved (executive and non-executive) directors for probing, analysis, debate and decision.

How, then, should the board be constituted within this unitary system?

The chairman should, preferably, be a NED; he or she should not also be chief executive/managing director. The two jobs are wholly different. The chairman is not only there to supervise the proper and efficient conduct of board meetings; his or her task is also to encourage, question, evaluate and (sometimes) kick management. It is difficult to carry out these tasks adequately if a single person is performing two functions.

When appointing a new NED (a task often initiated and led by the chairman), boards should look for qualities of objectivity and a breadth of experience which enhances the composition of the board and the quality of its constructive planning and debate. The process of selection of NEDs should be a formal one, perhaps with the help of outside selection agencies. NEDs should be appointed initially for three years. The terms of their appointment should be set out in a letter. These should cover the NED's duties, predicted time involvement, fees, and the procedure for reimbursing expenses, including seeking independent professional advice where appropriate. NEDs should not get a company car, pension scheme, share options or bonus.

Service agreements with executive directors shall not exceed three years without prior shareholder approval. In the third year, the agreement can be renegotiated, so that continuity can be provided if appropriate. Rolling notice service agreements (providing for more than 12 months' notice of termination by the company) shall only be entered into with prior shareholder approval.

Each and every director (including NEDs) must maintain their own Directors' and Officers' (D&O) insurance policy to cover their position with the company (though the company should reimburse the cost of the premium).

Board committees

All company boards must set up Audit and Remuneration Committees, each composed entirely of NEDs (with executive directors attending by invitation only). Each committee should report to the board on decisions made and actions proposed, but not with details of the discussions.

The Audit Committee's responsibilities shall be to satisfy itself as to systems of internal financial control, the adoption of appropriate accounting principles, the appropriateness of adopting a going concern basis, compliance with accounting principles, liaison with the auditors as to their audit work, monitoring rotation of the audit partner, discussion with the auditors of all points of principle arising from their audit work, including points raised in their management letter, and recommending to the board a fair and appropriate level of audit fees.

The Audit Committee should additionally be aware of and keep under review the involvement of the audit firm in working for the company on any consultancy matters – evaluating the nature, extent and costs of other work (eg, consultancy, taxation). Additionally, the Audit Committee should periodically review the policy, performance, management and custodianship of the company's pension funds, unless a standing Pensions Committee or separate pension fund Trustee Board is set up.

The Remuneration Committee's responsibilities shall be to review the levels and bases for remuneration of the executive directors and the time periods for notice of termination, to negotiate the terms of their service agreements, to negotiate and approve the basis for any severance payments, to determine the levels of participation by executive directors in share option schemes and the like (including bonus schemes) and to co-ordinate and manage (sometimes even to initiate) the selection process for promotions, recruitment and retirement of directors.

The Remuneration Commission should also, at least every three years, commission independent reports from suitable management consultants on executive director appraisals, as to the level of executive director remuneration packages, and as to the rates of NED fees.

The functioning of the board

The primary initiative for this lies with the chairman and the company secretary.

The successful functioning of the board will, typically, depend on the regularity of its meetings; preparation for them; firm but sympathetic control from the chair; orderly but free-ranging board discussion; efficient minute-taking; and a clear understanding of reserved subjects which require board approval prior to action or implementation by the executives.

Crucial, therefore, to the proper functioning of the board is the provision, in advance of the meeting (ideally at least five days) of board papers and the agenda. The papers should include financial results to date (with prior year comparisons), cash flows (historical and projected), balance sheet figures (with comparatives), trading performance and prospects.

Additionally, over the course of each financial year, every major trading division or subsidiary should make a presentation to the board. This involves the attendance of divisional and subsidiary managers at board meetings so that their plans, and they themselves, can be evaluated.

The objective should be to ensure that all board members, including the NEDs, have an understanding of the operation and financing of the group and opportunities to evaluate and assess the effectiveness of those to whom management functions are delegated by the board.

What is clearly vital (particularly post-Maxwell) is that no one individual shall have delegated to him or her sole and unfettered powers of decision and implementation on any matter of a nature, or exceeding an amount, which shall be reserved for the board as a whole.

The board and its accountability

Accountability, here, is a much wider concept than the presentation to shareholders of the company's annual report and accounts, although the prime importance of that task cannot be doubted. It is, typically, through the report and accounts (and the ensuing annual general meeting) that the board tells the owners about the stewardship of the company's affairs.

While financial accountability and the clarity and formal presentation of the company's annual (and indeed interim) results are ultimately matters for the board as a whole, the work of the Audit Committee should be seen to be of great importance, and the board must be made fully aware of any critical comments emanating from that committee or from the auditors themselves.

Each director (whether or not on the Audit Committee, but particularly if so) must regard it as a primary duty to see that attention is drawn publicly to material information as to both past performance and future plans and prospects, highlighting matters which fall short of due and proper expectations which have not been corrected or are not being corrected and remedied. The existence of this primary duty (which goes further than current legal requirements) must be understood, shared, and respected around the board table. Failure to do so can, in extreme cases, lead to board resignations, and to the resigning director saying publicly (albeit, perhaps, in general terms) why he or she has left the board: it should be regarded as proper and standard practice for a resigning director to do so.

However, no director will (or should) rush into making a personal statement – whether or not he or she feels compelled to resign. He or she will need to be convinced not only that the issue is one of substantial importance (eg, to counter any risk of a false market being created or subsisting), but also that he or she has used every effort to persuade the board itself to do what is appropriate and has told the chairman what he or she feels and, therefore, has no alternative but to say so, and has taken appropriate independent advice.

The various legal obligations I advocate here may require legislation to counter the argument that, because of each director's duty to act in the best interests of the company, making any personal statement at all may be argued to constitute a breach of that duty.

There will, of course, be circumstances where it would be premature (and therefore even misleading or a breach of proper confidentiality obligations to third parties) to say anything about specific, future plans, but the overriding principle remains that an accurate and (reasonably) full public statement should be made as soon as possible so that the shareholders, the public and the market are aware of relevant information.

Timely public disclosure has become a particularly vital issue as a result of increased market and legislative neurosis as to insider dealing: while UK law is ingloriously vague but draconian, there remains the shining light of clarity and safety in one area: deal as you wish, provided everything you know has been publicized – don't if it hasn't.

A second limb to the issue of accountability is the Statement of Compliance with required standards of corporate governance.

Here, again, I follow the background ideas set out in Cadbury, but seek to make them (within the context of my suggested Code of Practice) clearer and more mandatory in nature. Therefore, within that context, I say that the Statement of Compliance with my Code must be obligatory for inclusion in the Directors' Report accompanying the annual report and accounts.

The Statement of Compliance must give details as to the extent of compliance with the mandatory requirements of the Code of Practice. If all the requirements have not been met, then details should be given, together with reasons for non-compliance. New legislation, again, may be necessary, for I would strongly suggest that there be a requirement for a shareholders' meeting to consider persistent (eg, for two successive years) non-compliance with the Code, and to determine whether any directorial removals should consequently follow.

A third (and topical) limb is full disclosure of the emoluments and terms of service or appointment of each and every director, details of remuneration being subdivided between salary and (for executive directors only) performance related pay (the basis on which performance is measured being summarized), together with details of share options and the like.

These proposals, again, require legislation for, currently, it is only required that directors pay be stated in 'bands' plus details given of the emoluments of the chairman and the highest paid director. Surely the shareholders should be told how much their company pays each and every director, and how such pay is computed. We again return to the basic point: the shareholders are the owners of the company and they should know how much they pay to those to whom they delegate the task of managing their business for them.

Finally, on the topic of the board and its accountability, brief mention must be made of pension schemes and of environmental issues.

As to pension schemes, the Directors' Report must include a statement of the board's policy, and its attitude towards funding and the adequacy thereof, who are the trustees, by whom the funds are administered, by whom those funds are held, and by whom the funds are invested.

As to environmental matters, I believe the board should, periodically and where appropriate (having regard to the nature of the company's business and assets) commission an environmental audit. Shareholders should be told that it is in the board's policy to do so, although the contents of the audit report will usually be kept confidential for obvious reasons.

The provision of a clear and mandatory Code of Practice gives directors both a behavioural and structural blueprint, and gives shareholders a greater yardstick for assessing their delegates. It cannot, however, itself ensure that improved standards of corporate governance will be universally accepted and adhered to. But the suggestions I have advanced would, I believe, provide such effective monitoring and available sanctions as to produce the range of improvements we should all be seeking within a self-regulating (rather than legislative) system for corporate governance.

Professor Nigel Graham Maw is a solicitor who has specialized in domestic and international corporate work, particularly mergers and acquisitions. He was a partner in Rowe & Maw from 1961 to 1993, serving as its senior partner for 17 years. Professor Maw has been a non-executive director, sometimes chairman, of a number of public and private companies operating in a wide range of businesses. He is a visiting special Professor to the Department of Law at Nottingham University and has written books on company directors and their duties, on public company takeovers and is prime author of *Maw on Corporate Governance* (1994).

Further Reading

Report of the Committee on The Financial Aspects of Corporate Governance, Gee/Profession Publishing Limited, London, 1992.

Maw, NNG, Lord Lane of Horsell, Craig-Cooper, Sir M, *Maw on Corporate Governance*, Dartmouth Publishing Company, Aldershot, 1994.

THE ROLE OF NON-EXECUTIVE DIRECTORS IN CORPORATE GOVERNANCE

Adrian Cadbury

Non-executive directors – or outside directors as they are more accurately labelled – are increasingly recognized as vital to the effective functioning of a company's board and in achieving high standards of corporate governance.

The influence of outside directors on the governance of companies is partly a matter of board structure and process, but ultimately it rests on the calibre and determination of those who take on these posts. To be an effective outside director requires commitment, experience and skill.

In any discussion of the role of non-executive directors in corporate governance, two points must be made at the outset. First, all directors are equally responsible for the supervisory aspects of the board's duties, and for the integrity of its financial reporting. They are not responsibilities which the executive directors can to an extent leave to the non-executive directors. As the report of the Committee on the Financial Aspects of Corporate Governance said: 'It is equally for chairmen to ensure that the executive directors look beyond their executive duties and accept their full share of the responsibilities of governance.'[1] In enlarging on the part which non-executive directors play in corporate governance, there should be no suggestion that executive directors are any less responsible for a company's performance in this area. There are differences in the roles of the two kinds of director, but not in their responsibilities.

The reverse is, of course, also true. Non-executive directors are as responsible for the forward march of the company and for its business success as their executive colleagues. If the executive directors concentrated on the direction of the company and the non-executive directors on its control, the special attribute of the unitary board, the bringing together of inside knowledge and outside experience would be vitiated.

The second point is that 'non-executive' is a misleading description. It refers to what these directors are not, as opposed to what they are, and it carries a suggestion of toothlessness. There are times when such directors have to take effective executive action. In addition, the description is largely meaningless in countries which do not have British-style boards. The more informative and accurate title is that used in the United States of 'outside director'.

The aim of a unitary board is to bring together two different types of director and to take advantage of their differences in outlook and experience. It is a basic error to suppose that if you sit competent people of goodwill round a boardroom table, they will function as a board. Effective boards do not simply happen; they are the result of hard work by their members and particularly by their chairmen. What chairmen are seeking on a board is the right degree of cohesion and of challenge, of collegiality and of individuality. The role of the outside directors has, therefore, to be seen within the context of the board as a whole.

The contribution of outside directors

In my experience, outside directors can play an important part in the formulation of a company's strategy and in ensuring that the board sets its sights high enough. Their contribution to strategy is often through asking well-directed questions, critically but constructively. Board colleagues who appraise the business from the outside see it through different eyes than those who have spent most of their working lives in it. They are, therefore, well-placed to question the conventional wisdom with which most enterprises are well-endowed. They also bring with them an external set of standards against which to assess the aims and targets which the executive directors have set for themselves.

Contributing to strategy and setting standards of performance are not primarily functions of corporate governance, they are, however, aspects of the outside directors' role. As such they are a reminder that in selecting outside directors their ability to add value to the board in such fields will be as relevant as their contribution to the supervisory side of a board's duties. Indeed, the more they play their full part in the board's work, the more effective they are likely to be over matters of governance, where their position as outsiders is especially relevant.

Independence

The Report of the Committee on the Financial Aspects of Corporate Governance specifically referred to the role of outside directors in terms both of board structure and board conduct. The Committee's Code of Best Practice, for example, recommends that where the chairman is also the chief executive, 'it is essential that there should be a strong and independent element on the board, with a recognized senior member'.

The reference to independence is important, because not all outside directors are independent. In the view of the Committee the majority of outside directors on a board should be independent of the company. This was defined as their being free from any business or other relationship which could materially interfere with the exercise of their independent judgement. Directors who are from the company's law firm or its bankers, or who are retired executives, may be valued board members but they are not independent of the company.

In particular, the Committee recommended that audit committees should have a minimum membership of three outside directors, the majority of whom should be independent. This sets the limit to the number both of outside directors and of independent outside directors on the boards of companies complying with the Code.

Conflicts of interest

Keeping in mind that all directors have broadly equal legal responsibilities, it is their independence of judgement which enables outside directors to play a particular role in the board's deliberations and decisions. There are, quite properly, issues where the interests of the executives and of the company (to which directors owe their duty) could diverge. In the search for a new chief executive, for example, it will be usual to look outside the company, as well as within it, for potential candidates and then to make a choice between them. Only the outside directors are able to weigh up impartially the merits of insiders against outsiders, although the final decision will be that of the board as a whole.

Takeovers and management buyouts are another field where a disinterested, independent judgement is essential in the interests of shareholders and employees. The danger for a bidding company is that is overpays, through being carried away or through being bid up by a rival. The hazard for a target company is that is a natural wish to remain independent will overly influence its assessment of the merits of a bid. The potential for conflicts of interest in a buyout need no elaboration. In all of these cases, independent outside directors have a key role to play, simply because they are in the best position to take an objective view of where the true interests of the company lie.

The most apparent field for conflicts of interest is pay. This is why the Committee recommended that boards should appoint remuneration committees, made up wholly or mainly of outside directors and chaired by an outside director. Setting the remuneration package for executive directors is a difficult and onerous task, which the outside directors alone are capable of discharging, with whatever external professional advice they require.

A misunderstanding which has, on occasions, arisen is that relying on the outside directors over issues, such as those just discussed, implies a lack of trust in the executive directors. This is as though trust was in finite supply and was, as a result, being vested in the outside directors at the expense of the executive directors. The reason why boards look particularly to their outside directors for a lead in these circumstances is that their interests are less directly at stake; it is not a question of trust.

Performance review

Another and different area of the board's work, where the outside directors have a key contribution to make, is in reviewing the performance of the board itself and that of the executives. Assessing how well the board is doing its job is a difficult but necessary task. Outside directors are likely to be able to draw on their experience of other boards in helping chairmen to undertake this kind of review. Their role in appraising the chief executive is of crucial importance when the chief executive is also the chairman.

Checks and balances

I have already referred to the recommendation in the Code of Best Practice that, where the chairman is also the chief executive, it is essential for there to be a strong and independent element on the board, with a recognized senior member. Recognition of the seniority of one of the outside directors strengthens the position of the outside directors in times of difficulty and enables them to act without delay.

Indeed, some boards have gone further and given their outside directors a formal role in the governance of their companies. The board of Guinness plc is required under its Articles to establish a Non-executive Committee made up of all board members, save those appointed as executive directors. The Committee has the sole power to elect or to remove the chairman. The issue here is how to ensure that the outside directors can exert an effective influence on the governance of the company without dividing the board into two camps. The outside directors provide some of the checks and balances which are needed, but they have to do so within the board framework, if the unity of the board is to be maintained.

Outside directors also have their part to play in the conduct of board meetings. All directors carry equal responsibilities, thus all directors should be encouraged to take a full part in the board's deliberations. When some board members are executively responsible to others around the board table, they may be chary of expressing views which are at odds with the generally held executive line. The board, however, needs to hear as wide a range of executive opinion as possible. The outside directors can help chairmen to create a climate which encourages freedom of expression and an understanding by the executive directors of their responsibility to speak out.

The last specific role of an outside director, I will mention, is as counsellor to the chairman. The chairman's job can be a lonely one, especially when facing difficult decisions over people – appointments, moves and dismissals – and over possible shifts in strategy with implications for the executive directors. It is invaluable for chairmen to be able to discuss such issues informally with outside board members, who are committed to the company, know something of its activities and people, but whose advice is basically disinterested.

Links with shareholders

In carrying out many of their board functions, the outside directors are acting as a bridge between the interests of the managers in running the business and those of the shareholders in seeing that it is run efficiently. The outside directors are in a position, if they play their full part, to strengthen the accountability of the executive to the shareholders, the lack of which has been a ground for criticism. Shareholders expect outside directors to guide their boards in holding an appropriate balance between the competing claims on the company's resources. They look to them to ask the questions of the executive which they would put if they had a voice at the board and to keep all board members continually in mind of their duty to further the interests of the enterprise.

The European Commission has gone further and allocated a separate governance role to outside directors. In the European Company Statute, it lays down that the main function of the non-executive members of a so-called administrative board is to supervise the executive members. This division of duties is not to my mind compatible with the concept of a unitary board.

Determinants of effectiveness

It is, however, necessary at this point to consider what enables outside directors to make the level of contribution to the governance of a company which has been discussed. First, there needs to be a board structure which provides outside directors with the opportunity to play their full part in the board's work. Attendance solely at meetings of the main board gives outside directors limited scope to get to know the company and the people in it. This is why the formation of committees of the board are an important means of making the most of the appointment of competent outside directors.

Audit committees, in particular, offer outside directors the chance to become involved with the working of a company below board level and in a field where their independence of judgement is of special value. Membership of remuneration and nomination committees also provides outside directors with insights into a company's values and systems and the opportunity to influence them. Assigning responsibilities to outside directors on such committees is entirely consistent with maintaining the unity of the board. The committees concerned are set up by the board, to whom they report and it is the board which determines their terms of reference. The outside directors' role on these committees is to help to prepare issues for the board, but the final decisions remain in the hands of the board as a whole.

While board committees buttress the position of the outside directors and give them the means to be effective, the key determinant of their ability to contribute to the governance and to the success of a company lies in the attitude of the chairman. It turns on chairmen appreciating the value which competent outside directors can add to a board and encouraging them to play their full part in its work. The problems which arise for outside directors, when chairmen are not doing their job, were graphically described in a *Harvard Business Review* article by Professor Louis W Cabot:

'I served for one fateful year on the board of Penn Central. The education was fast, brutal and highly practical. Even today the law suits are not all settled and that education has cost me several times more than the price of a Harvard Business School tuition. At each Penn Central directors' meeting, which only lasted one and a half hours, we were presented with long lists of relatively small capital expenditures to approve; we were shown sketchy financial reports which were rarely discussed in any detail. The reports were not designed to be revealing, and we were asked not to take them away from the meeting. We always had an oral report by the chief executive officer promising better results next month which never came true.'

Louis Cabot did all the right things as an outside director, including writing to the chairman to say that this was no way to run a railroad. But before any of his letters had even been answered, Penn Central had collapsed and Louis Cabot was sued along with the other directors.

What is clear from that vivid description of Penn Central board meetings is that the board simply failed to do its job. It exercised no real control over the chief executive, because it did not provide itself with the means of doing so. It spent relatively little time on its considerable responsibilities and part of that time was given to the discussion of irrelevant items of capital expenditure. The fault lay with the chairman and the outside directors, but primarily with the chairman. The chairman sets the agenda and it is for the chairman to ensure that board members receive the information which they need to carry out their duties conscientiously and that they receive it in time.

Board information

The outside directors were unable to contribute to Penn Central board meetings, because the meetings were short, the agenda misdirected and the information deficient. The all-important point made by that cautionary tale is that outside directors cannot do their job without adequate, relevant and timely information. This is true for all directors, but for the outside directors, who have no other means of finding out what is going on in a company, it is critical to their ability to fulfil their function.

The gap between the outside and the executive directors lies in their knowledge of the company. The effectiveness, therefore, of the outside directors depends crucially on their disadvantage in this regard being minimized. This may mean giving the outside directors additional background information and it certainly involves ensuring that board reports are succinct and intelligible to the outsider.

Thus two necessary conditions for outside directors to be effective are that their chairmen should wish to derive every possible benefit from their presence on the board, and that they have the information which they need for the proper discharge of their responsibilities.

A further condition is that the proportion of outside directors on a board should be such that their views will carry significant weight in the board's decisions and that, *in extremis*, their combined determination to resign will cause the board to think again. Three such directors, in my view, comprise the minimum outside presence which boards need to have to achieve a proper governance balance.

Board selection

Numbers alone, however, are not a sufficient guarantee of effectiveness; it is the calibre of the outside directors which counts above all. The selection of outside directors is, therefore, crucial. It is worth quoting the passage in the Committee's Report which deals with this point:

'Given the importance of their distinctive contribution, non-executive directors should be selected with the same impartiality and care as senior executives. We recommend that their appointment should be a matter for the board as a whole and that there should be a formal selection process, which will reinforce the independence of non-executive directors and make it evident that they have been appointed on merit and not through any form of patronage. We regard it as good practice for a nomination committee to carry out the selection process and to make proposals to the board.'

This recommendation has to be seen against the traditional way of appointing outside directors to public companies in Britain, which was on the advice of existing board members or of the company's professional advisers. It was done by word of mouth, drawing on the networks of those concerned. In addition, it was common for chairmen themselves to take personal responsibility for finding outside board candidates. If outside directors owe, or feel they owe, their position on the board to the good offices of the chairman, their independence is undermined from the outset.

The basic disadvantages of the word of mouth approach are that it draws candidates from too limited a pool – those that are within the relevant networks – and that the pool is largely made up of people whose experience and background is similar, with the likelihood that there will be insufficient challenge to accepted views.

There are a number of reasons why the Committee's stress on selecting outside directors through a formal process and involving all board members are important. The first advantage of a formal search process is that is forces chairmen to assess their existing board and to reflect on what kind of person – in terms of experience, background, competence, age and personality – would add most value to their board team. This means that the search is focused and purposeful. It is directed at finding the candidate who will best complement the existing board members, as opposed to the first name that finds general support. It ensure that selection starts with the task and not as it so often does – especially in the public sector – with names.

A second advantage is that, where the whole board has been involved, a new board member starts with their support. A candidate selected by the chairman has to spend time winning the confidence of the rest of the board, before becoming part of the team; quite apart from the dent to their independence which that form of selection entails.

Further advantages are that outside directors appointed through a formal process will be drawn from a wider pool than could be tapped by the traditional approach and that there will normally be a competitive element in the selection process. Boards will be presented with a number of potential board members to choose from. This enables them to appoint the best of the available candidates and it gives confidence to the individuals, who are eventually selected, that they have won their place on the board in open competition, and that they are there as a result of the considered choice of their fellow board members.

In the same way, the more that all board members are involved in the selection process and the more professionally it is carried out, the greater the mutual respect between executive and outside directors. Executive directors will have reached the board in manifest competition with their colleagues and they rightly expect their fellow-directors to have been similarly chosen, openly and on merit. Outside directors will only be seen to be independent, if the process by which they are chosen is as open and as thorough as it would be for any other senior appointment.

The independence of outside directors is also strengthened if they are appointed for fixed terms. This ensures that there is a natural break-point, when the chairman can review with the director concerned whether appointment for a further term makes sense on both sides. The increasing demands which are being made on outside directors argue for a degree of continuity. This is tempered by the need to bring about change on a board, as the challenges facing it change and for outside directors not to remain on a board so long as to become absorbed into the organization and to lose something of their independent edge.

The reason for laying this stress on how outside directors are chosen is that they can only be effective in governance terms, if the manner of their selection ensures their competence and reinforces their independence. It leads on to the understandable question, are there enough qualified people of the right calibre willing and able to fill these posts?

Supply and demand

More is undoubtedly being demanded of outside directors and this means that an individual can take on fewer of these posts than in the past. A modest further restriction on supply is that there is no longer a place for those directors whose main function on a board was ornamental. These constraints can, however, be met, provided that chairmen are prepared to look wider than main board directors of other plc's, and preferably their chief executives.

There are good reasons, in any case, for casting the net wider to meet the circumstances facing boards today. Boards have to take more account of the world outside their company than they had to do in less turbulent times. A good example is that major companies in the United States are being asked to sign up on the CERES Principles (an acronym for the Coalition for Environmentally Responsible Economies). Concern for the environment is just one of the outside pressures which boards nowadays have to take into account.

While, therefore, executives from other companies may well form the basis of the outside element on a board, they are from the same stock as the executive members of the board and are likely to share their mindset. Outside board members whose background and outlook is different from that of their executive colleagues have a particular contribution to make in respect of a company's relationship with the external world. More generally, they can broaden a board's viewpoint and add to board debates by providing a challenge to accepted executive thinking.

Although membership of board committees adds to the demands on the time of outside directors, it does not unduly restrict the pool from which they can be drawn. It is not necessary to be an accountant to be a useful member of an audit committee. The essential qualifications are diligence, coupled with knowing what questions to ask and how to interpret the answers. I do not believe, therefore, that there will be an insufficiency of potential, outside board members. Nor, at present, is there a shortage of candidates for these posts, thanks to the challenge and interest which they have to offer. It would only be if the risks, through litigation, began to outweigh the rewards, that the supply of outside directors might fail to meet demand.

The qualifications of an outside director were well summed up by Angus Murray, who followed his own advice admirably: 'A good non-executive director needs to have intellect, integrity and courage. Of these qualities courage is the most important, for without it the other two characteristics are useless.'

Sir Adrian Cadbury is chairman of PRO NED, an organization set up to encourage the appointment of outside directors and to help boards to find suitable candidates. He is chairman of the Committee on the Financial Aspects of Corporate Governance.

References

1 *Report of the Committee on The Financial Aspects of Corporate Governance*, Gee/Profession Publishing Limited, London, 1992.

CREATING AN EFFECTIVE BOARD

Colin J Coulson-Thomas

The importance of a company's board of directors is usually – and perhaps understandably – taken for granted. Few question the value the board adds to the organization or consider what would be lost if it ceased to exist. More surprisingly, very little time and energy are usually spent on considering what effect the board *should* have on the company's performance.

Growing interest in corporate governance has, among other things, created an interest in the actual and potential contribution of the board, as well as in how this vital element in the organization is undergoing rapid change. The dynamics of how boards work and the skills required of different sorts of directors are only now being examined in a new and objective commercial light.

Whether a company grows or declines depends upon the purpose and direction established by the board. It relies upon the values, the will to generate customer satisfaction, and the drive to achieve, develop and learn, that emanate from the board. Whether or not managers display leadership qualities depends in turn upon the extent to which they are motivated and empowered by the board. Some boards stifle initiative while others encourage it.

The vision articulated, communicated and shared by the board influences attitudes and behaviour to the extent that the board is visibly committed to its achievement. Members of the management team are likely to take their cue from the behaviour of directors. Directorial conduct can inspire and motivate, or sap the management spirit. A gulf between the directorial rhetoric of 'quality', 'transformation' and 'long-term relationships', and the corporate reality of 'downsizing' and 'short-termism' leads to cynicism and despair.

In recent years levels of cynicism and despair have been increased through allegations of malpractice in Europe, Japan and the US, and of excessive directorial compensation for inadequate performance. Investors are becoming restive and, within the boardroom, some boards appear less willing to act as rubber stamps. Boardroom coups, staged by independent directors, have led to the departure of such chairmen as John Akers at IBM and Kay Whitmore at Kodak.

Interest in corporate governance has focused attention upon the stewardship role of the board. But, the resulting concentration on the accountability of the board must not allow its business development and corporate renewal roles to be overlooked. It is dispiriting, if not perverse, to congratulate a board for having all the right committees in place while it meticulously reports mounting losses.

Confronting reality

Though the issues surrounding boardroom effectiveness are now regularly and openly discussed, fundamental processes often remain untouched. Basic questions go unasked. As a starting point in confronting reality, questions could include:

- Is the board proactive or reactive?
- Is it a learning board?
- Has it recently carried out a review of its function, composition and operations?
- Do the directors understand what is expected of them in the boardroom?
- Do they work well together as a team?

Surveys for *Creating Excellence in the Boardroom*[1] and *Developing Directors*[2] revealed that:

- Most chairmen believe the effectiveness of their company's board could be improved, but few boards undertake any form of periodic review of their structure, size, composition and operation.
- Few directors are prepared, either formally or informally, for their boardroom roles.
- The distinction between direction and management is generally confused, and routes to the boardroom are usually mysterious and hidden.
- Most boards fail to provide their organizations with a distinctive and compelling rationale for existence. People may work long hours and struggle to keep alive an entity that has no real purpose.
- Many boards craft excellent strategies without ensuring motivation, commitment, empowerment and other enablers are in place to turn aspiration into achievement. It might look good, and the numbers may add up, but outside of the boardroom nothing has happened, or is likely to happen.

In fact, many corporate transformation, re-engineering and TQM programmes are doomed to fail from the moment they leave the boardroom because crucial change elements are missing. Too few boards ensure all the pieces of the jig-saw puzzle needed for successful implementation are in place.

Given the small minority of boards that review their effectiveness and the lack of proper preparation, either formal or informal, among the great majority of directors, one should not expect directors to be competent or boards to be effective. Where they perform well, this is often by chance or good luck rather than by design.

Varieties of board

The reality is that a lack of vision cramps and stunts the growth of many companies. Crucial to any improvement is the recognition that there is no such thing as a standard board. There are subsidiary and holding company boards, and boards of private and public companies. There are one tier, or unitary, and two tier and supervisory boards. One country's conventions may be the exception elsewhere. The nature of every board, its structure, composition and how it operates, should reflect the situation and circumstances of the individual company.

A particular board may contain different types of director, for example, executive and non-executive directors, owner directors, or alternate directors. A particular individual could have multiple and distinct interests and responsibilities as a director, owner, and manager.

Given the various forms of board that are possible, it is surprising there has been so little experimentation with new ways of operating boards. Most of them function within self-imposed constraints that result from their own lack of imagination.

The diversity of the make-up of boards is, not surprisingly, matched by the diversity of their performance. Boards vary greatly in the value they add to the company. A board could be the source of a company's will and drive, or merely a rubber stamp. Some boards are positive instigators and enablers of change, while others are bystanders, or even obstacles to progress.

The role of the board

The board is accountable in various ways to a number of different stakeholders in a company, and the directors are required to achieve a balance between competing interests. In the US and UK, priority is generally given to the interests of shareholders. Directors' legal duties and responsibilities are onerous and have grown.

What is the board for? Seven out of ten chairmen describe the function of their board in terms of strategic direction, establishing objectives and strategy, and, subsequently, monitoring and reviewing their achievement. The role of the unitary board of a medium to large-sized company might be to:

- Determine a distinctive purpose for the company, a rationale for its continued existence, and articulate and share a compelling vision.
- Establish achievable and measurable objectives derived from the vision, and formulate a strategy for their achievement.
- Ensure the company has adequate finance, people, organization, supporting technology, and management and business processes to implement the agreed strategy.
- Appoint a management team and establish the framework of policies and values within which management operates.
- Agree and review plans, and monitor performance against agreed targets, taking corrective action where appropriate.
- Safeguard the physical, financial, and intellectual assets of the company, and ensure ethical conduct.

- Report performance to various stakeholders in the company, particularly to those with 'ownership rights' and a legal entitlement to certain information.

A strategy review process, such as that of Fig. 1, could be used to ensure both planning and implementation issues are addressed.

Some boards take great care to safeguard physical and financial assets, but are naive when it comes to intellectual property. When the best people walk off with promising ideas, and the corporation is intellectually asset stripped by consultants and business partners, a hollow shell may remain.

The distinction between direction and management

The role of the board, and the duties and responsibilities of the company director, are at the heart of the distinction between direction and management. They largely determine the qualities required by directors and those which distinguish them from managers.

Directors ought to have certain legal and financial knowledge, and their awareness and perspective should be strategic rather than departmental. They also need an awareness of boardroom issues and practice.

There are particular roles in the boardroom such as chairman, chief executive, or non-executive director that may require additional skills beyond those possessed by other directors. For example, independence and a willingness to probe and ask questions which executive directors may feel inhibited from raising are desirable qualities in non-executive directors.

Whether or not the head of a functional department such as personnel or information technology should be on a board depends upon both the individual and the corporate context. Challenges and opportunities facing the board rarely arrive pre-labelled as marketing or personnel issues. The general consensus

---

Strategy review process

- Determining what needs to be done
  - Creating the capability to do what needs to be done
- Ensuring that what needs to be done actually is done
- Ensuring that what is done satisfies legal and ethical requirements
  - Reporting to stakeholders on what has been achieved

Fig. 1 Plan of a board's strategy review

Source: C. Coulson-Thomas, *Transforming the Company*, Kogan Page, London, 1992; and *Creating Excellence in the Boardroom*, McGraw-Hill, Maidenhead, 1992

among chairmen is that an individual lacking in directorial qualities should not be put on a board simply to fill a particular slot. Even though they may be highly experienced, many professionals lack a balanced and holistic perspective, and have a distorted departmental view of corporate reality.

Certain successful women illustrate the distinction between direction and management, and that one does not necessarily need to be a good manager to become an effective director. There are women directors of large organizations who have circumvented the normal management career path as a result of raising families. In mid-life they become involved in voluntary work, or join a public sector committee, and subsequent commercial directorships result from the personal qualities they display.

Becoming a director

Apart from such routes as forming one's own company, or joining the board of a family company, there is no standard or automatic path to the board-room. It all depends upon the company, retirements, vacancies and the perceived requirements of a particular board.

Strategic awareness and personal qualities usually dominate the criteria for boardroom appointments. Loyalty, team spirit and generally 'fitting in' appear to be valued more highly by many chairmen than originality and creativity. People who go out of their way to appear bright and full of ideas can reduce rather than enhance their boardroom prospects.

The aspiring director might benefit from multi-functional experience, per-haps by participating in cross-functional teams which can help to provide an overview of the organization, and from joining international task forces and teams in order to develop an international perspective.

Many boards would benefit if the mystique and status associated with being a director were reduced. Where being a director is regarded as the peak of a career ladder, boards face pressures to include departmental heads and the most senior managers rather than those who might add the most value. It would be healthier if direction was perceived as a separate but complementary activity to management, and one that should not be taken to automatically suggest elevated status and higher earnings.

Many appointments of non-executive directors are also unimaginative. The safe options, those with long lists of past and current directorships, may be the people who just turn up to meetings and collect their fee. Paradoxically, the better directors may have spent less time on boards – as a result of taking their duties seriously, they may resign when faced with mat-ters they do not agree with.

The chairman who signs 'names' may end up with a room full of 'impor-tant' people who are impressive elsewhere without being an effective team.

The competent director

Competent directors require a combination of interrelated attributes. These include personal qualities such as integrity; drive and determination; balance; commitment; individuality; sensitivity and independence; strategic and ethical awareness; a sense of accountability and responsibility; and the ability to see a company as a whole and understand the context within which it operates. Formulating a differentiating vision and a realistic strategy requires objectivity, business acumen and the ability to look ahead.

Attempts to produce lists of specific directorial skills can encourage people to think about competence in the boardroom and how it might be improved. They tend, however, to be fatally flawed.

Such lists are limited in value because they fail to recognize the board as a team or take account of human interactions. In fact, if people do not think through the requirements of the particular board, they can do more harm than good. Lists of competences tend to grow in length as each person seeing a draft is tempted to add one or two more. As a result, the essence of what it is to be a good director may be overlooked.

Managerial promotion, through a succession of appraisal processes, can result from being quite good at lots of things rather than outstanding on certain criteria. Being below average in a particular area can deal a fatal blow to prospects for future advancement. However, the major deficiencies of a self-aware director can often be balanced by the compensating strengths of other members of the boardroom team; and may be more than made up for by strengths in some other dimension.

A group of outstanding individuals do not necessarily make an effective board. Directorial competence and contribution depends upon the interaction of a particular combination of people and personalities in the boardroom context. Hence, new directors tend to be selected to complement the qualities of existing board members, and improve the operating dynamics of the boardroom team. The person selected to be the financial director may be the individual who best balances the team, rather than the most technically proficient. Specialist expertise can be hired as and when required.

What characterizes a 'good' director also depends upon the corporate context. An individual who is appropriate in one situation may not be relevant or suitable in another.

The effective board

The effectiveness of a board can be constrained or enhanced by the limitations or strengths of its individual members. A confident board is open about the extent to which it adds value, and is willing to identify, discuss, and tackle barriers to its own contribution. For example, in relation to the formulation and communication of vision and strategy, it might ask the following questions:

- Do the members of the board share a common, clear and compelling vision?
- Has the board identified what represents value for customers, and the processes that deliver this value? Are there hidden barriers to improved customer satisfaction that fall between departmental responsibilities?
- Are the directors committed to an agreed and realistic strategy for the achievement of the vision? How effective are they at communicating with customers, employees and business partners?
- Have the necessary resources, capabilities, skills, motivations, empowerments, roles and responsibilities, and 'vital few' programmes for successful implementation been assembled? For example, is remuneration related to business goals and customer-related objectives?

A board should maintain a balance between short-term priorities and securing the longer-term future of the enterprise. Care needs to be taken to avoid a concentration upon the former at the expense of the latter. Short-term pressures should not be allowed to drive out longer-term considerations:

- A board could give certain directors special responsibilities for projects that stretch beyond a financial year, such as strategic business developments.
- 'Facilitating directors', responsible for reshaping an organization and establishing and supporting its process and systems requirements, could implement longer-term changes while colleagues tackle current issues.
- A more drastic solution might be a two tier board, the 'top' tier having a particular responsibility for looking into, and preparing for, the future.

The chairman of the board has a special responsibility for its effectiveness. Whether or not the roles of chairman and chief executive are combined, their differing requirements need to be understood:

- The chairman, elected by the board, chairs its meetings and should ensure that it concentrates upon determining and enabling the implementation of strategy.
- The chief executive, appointed by the board, should lead the management team in implementing the agreed strategy within the policy and enabling framework established by the board.

Where the two roles of chairman and chief executive are separated, there needs to be a high degree of mutual trust and respect if the individuals concerned are to support and complement each other's responsibilities and contributions.

Assessing effectiveness

While evaluations of individual and group performance at board level can be undertaken, they are sometimes difficult to assess. For example, a director with integrity and character could lose the opportunity to accumulate years of boardroom experience as a result of a resignation on principle. A more accommodating colleague may choose to ignore the principle and, as a result, build up what might appear to be a longer track record.

The challenges and circumstances facing any board are unique. For example, a winning product could lead to unexpected success in the marketplace. Another board might be wrestling with a combination of adverse factors that will inevitably lead to the demise of the company. However, as the result of its efforts the company might die with some dignity and in a way that enables more obligations to stakeholders to be discharged than would otherwise be the case. Which is the better board?

Both directorial competence and board effectiveness can be fleeting. At one moment a board can appear to be in command of the situation. Return six months later, and the company may be out of control. Perhaps the situation and circumstances have changed but the board hasn't.

What constitutes effectiveness depends very much upon the business environment, what a board is seeking to achieve, and the calibre of its management team. The relationship between the board and management team, and their respective roles and responsibilities, is of particular importance:

- A competent and self-motivated management team may resent, what it regards as, excessive interference from the directors. The board may need to exert a sensitive touch, keeping an eye on key factors, and only stepping in when the occasion demands it, or when there is a clear opportunity to add value.
- A board that has less confidence in the managerial team may need to become more involved. It will also need to take steps to strengthen the quality of management.

Introversion is the curse of busy people. Some boards become so engrossed in internal issues that they ignore the external business environment. The alert board monitors economic, political, social and technological developments and assesses both: their direct impact upon the company; and their indirect impact as a consequence of how they affect customers, suppliers and business partners. Impacts should be prioritized and appropriate responses determined.

Corporate transformation provides a demanding litmus test of board effectiveness and leadership. Most directors have limited experience of the fundamental transformation or re-design of an organization. Hence many boards would benefit from an objective and fundamental review of their approaches. Some boards are reluctant to recognize the reality of non-achievement. They seek refuge in a world of appearances, rhetoric and collective self-deception. Gaps between aspiration and achievement should be assumed rather than treated as an unwelcome surprise. If they do not exist, it may be that goals are too modest.

The development of the board team

Training and changing the composition of a board are the two most commonly cited means of improving the collective effectiveness of directors. The highest training priority is the development of strategic awareness and business understanding.

In the main, directors remain up-to-date by informal means such as discussion with colleagues. Meetings of the board also represent a learning opportunity, and a learning board regularly reviews what it has learned.

The chairman is generally in the best position to form an overview of the board and its operations. A chairman should ensure a company has an effective board composed of directors who work well together as a team. Poor teamwork limits the effectiveness of many boards. Improved communication, open discussion, regular meetings and a shared or common purpose are all ways of improving collective performance. Board workshops and reviews can also be used to develop directors, both individually and collectively. Those facilitating these sessions need to be aware of the distinct requirements of director and board development.

One survey, *Harnessing the Potential of Groups*, revealed that many team-building exercises at board level have harmful consequences.[3] They can emphasize being a team player at the expense of independent judgement. A sense of balance needs to be maintained, avoiding a board that is riven with factions at one extreme and one where individualism has been driven out at the other.

The board and management processes

Business processes are sequences and combinations of activities that deliver value to a customer, while management processes control and co-ordinate these business processes and ensure that business objectives are delivered. Most key management processes in the majority of companies will start in, end in, or at some point should pass throught the boardroom.

As a result of a growing focus upon processes, new requirements are emerging for facilitating and cross-functional roles in the boardroom. The key processes that deliver customer satisfaction are being identified, and 'process owners' with specific responsibilities for them appointed to boards. For example, the six main processes within Texas Instruments are all owned by a director, and process reports are given at board meetings.

Many boards find it difficult to add value to the organization because the management processes that would enable them to do so are not in place. Given the absence of policy-deployment processes and clear roles and responsibilities in many companies, it is not surprising that so many strategies remain as aspirations rather than value creating realities.

It is naïve for a board to think that if they get the processes right all else will follow. An obsession with processes can lead people to overlook the relevance of what passes along them and the quality of judgements at each stage. However, the 'right' processes, properly used, can focus the energies of what might otherwise be an erratic board and turn 'wish lists' into operational actions.

The point has already been made that a board's review process should monitor the business environment. It should also evaluate the requirements of stakeholders by such means as surveys of investor, customer and employee satisfaction. A board needs to understand the power of each group of stakeholders and the sanctions available to them.

Prioritization

A failure to undertake some form of prioritization can result in a board attempting to do too much. A preoccupation with activities and initiatives can lead to precious and expensive energy being devoted to matters of marginal importance.

For example, the members of one board proudly explained that over 8,800 quality improvement projects were under way in various parts of the world. Groups were even working on Saturdays and Sundays. When each director was asked to write down the key factors that would determine whether the corporation would live or die in the face of formidable competition, a fair degree of consensus emerged. However, not one of the company's quality improvement projects was focused on any of the ten top issues.

The future of boards

In the future, it is likely that boards will spend less time monitoring internal procedures, and will devote more time to building external relationships and establishing the conditions for ongoing adaptation and change. Boards will also need to devote greater effort to ensuring that measurable objectives are achieved rather than simply being set.

Governance needs to match the changing nature of organizations. For example, how should one govern a flexible and international network embracing customers, suppliers and business partners or a federal organization? New forms of board and new mechanisms of governance are required to direct and focus the network organizations and virtual corporations that are emerging.

Directing a network composed of various partners can require skills very different from those demanded in a 'single entity' environment. For example, one may need political skills to 'stand' and be 'elected' by network partners, or to articulate the values that distinguish the network from others, rather than the ability to climb to the top of a functional bureaucracy. In the case of many boards, few if any of the existing directors may make the necessary transition.

What is clear is that directors and boards face formidable challenges. Both will need to devote more effort to learning and adapting. New sorts of people and personalities are likely to enter the boardrooms of vibrant enterprises. While it has always been easy to be a bad director, remaining an effective director is likely to become progressively more difficult.

Dr Colin J Coulson-Thomas, chairman of Adaptation, is a counsellor to directors and boards, acts as a coach and mentor to individual directors, and has worked with over 50 boards on various activities to improve their performance. Dr Coulson-Thomas holds a portfolio of directorships, visiting appointments at a number of universities, and serves on the Professional Development Committee of the UK's Institute of Directors. He is the author of numerous books including *Creating Excellence in the Boardroom* (1993); *Developing Directors: Building an Effective Boardroom Team* (1993) and *Transforming the Company* (1992).

References

1 Coulson-Thomas, C, *Creating Excellence in the Boardroom*, McGraw-Hill, Maidenhead, 1993.
2 Coulson-Thomas, C, *Developing Directors: Building An Effective Boardroom Team*, McGraw-Hill, Maidenhead, 1993.
3 Coulson-Thomas, C, *Harnessing the Potential of Groups*, Adaptation, 1993.

PART

5

GLOSSARY
Richard Koch

A

ABC analysis, activity-based costing
This is a recent and important method of ensuring that all costs, and especially indirect costs and overheads, are properly allocated to particular products. Traditional costing methods allocated indirect costs via cost centres, which was an imprecise method. This did not matter so much when direct costs were the majority of the cost structure, but today many products comprise a greater amount of indirect than direct cost. Using the old methods tended to under-allocate cost to special products and services using a lot of indirect cost, resulting in average costing and average pricing, ie, pricing standard products too high and specials too low. ABC avoids this by allocating indirect costs better by identifying the cost drivers for each activity.

ABC works as follows:

1. The activities and objects (usually products, but sometimes customers or other relevant definitions of what is provided) are defined. This can be a lengthy and challenging process, overturning previous views of relevant categories for defining profit. For example, if a customer demands being supplied with two products, or special terms, it is more relevant to look at customer than individual product profitability.
2. The cost drivers (for example, what determines cost, the number of work orders) are defined in relation to each activity.
3. The costs are then allocated to each object and compared to price realization to determine profitability.

ABC can be turned into an accounting system, but it is really a way of analyzing product line profitability at a point in time. Since the cost drivers and activities can change, ABC analysis needs to be revised periodically to ensure that the previous data and insights are still valid. ABC should lead to changed decisions about pricing, product and customer focus, market share policy and other actions that can raise profitability.

ABM (Activity-Based Management)
An extension of ABC (activity-based costing) which makes it a whole philosophy of management by taking in consideration of customers' needs and working out where the extra cost of special products or services can be fully or more than fully recovered from customers. ABM has not yet achieved anything like the popularity of ABC, but it is a logical outgrowth of it and the focus on customer utility is very useful.

above-the-line promotion
Marketing spending, such as advertising, addressed to a mass audience (or segments thereof) rather than targeted at individuals, and always involving an advertising agency.

absorption

1. A method of cost accounting that makes each product absorb a certain amount of overhead to arrive at a full cost for each product. This method will understate the true costs if the budgeted quantity of the product is not sold. **2.** A cost which is not charged to clients but which is absorbed into overall overheads, as when a project overruns its cost but the excess cannot be charged. Used especially in professional service firms.

accelerated depreciation

A method of depreciation that makes higher charges to the profit and loss statement for an asset during the early years of its life. This results in lower stated profits (and lower immediate tax payable) than alternative methods; it is also usually more realistic.

action learning

An alternative to classroom-based management learning, action learning presents managers with real business issues from their own or another organization, and invites the best solutions. A good method to enhance problem-solving abilities.

adhocracy

Invented by Warren Bennis in 1968 and popularized by Alvin Toffler. Crudely the opposite of bureaucracy: an adhocracy is an organization that disregards the classical principles of management where everyone has a defined and permanent role.

adjacent segment

A product or product-customer combination that is close or similar to another one and that could be served by a company with relatively little extra effort.

appraisal

Process of assessing individuals and giving feedback on performance. A good appraisal system should work on a yearly or more frequent cycle and be a two-way process.

arbitrage

1. Technically, the process whereby someone buys in one market while simultaneously (or shortly thereafter) selling at a higher price in another market, thereby making a profit and also ironing out market imperfections. **2.** Used imprecisely to indicate any activity where a gain can be made through superior market knowledge or by bridging the gap between one person's perspective and another's. Arbitrage can also be a verb, used either technically or loosely, meaning to act as a middle-man or go-between.

articles of association
Document laying down rules for running a company, rights of shareholders and duties of directors.

asset cover
A firm's assets divided by its debt: hence the number of times debt is covered by assets.

asset management
1. The business of financial institutions in managing other people's money.
2. Getting the best return from assets owned, whether by individuals, commercial firms or financial institutions.

assets
Property, plant, buildings, raw materials, finished goods, cash or anything else of value owned by a business, and recorded on its balance sheet. Often classified into fixed assets which are for the firm's long-term use and current assets like raw materials that are of short-term use.

asset stripper
A generally pejorative term applied to an investor or manager who takes over a company and sells off assets, especially property, that are not essential for the business's core activities.

asset structure
The breakdown of assets in a balance sheet by category, which will help determine whether there is scope for further leverage (gearing).

asset turn
Also called *asset turnover*, *asset utilization* and *ratio of sales to capital employed*. The ratio of a firm's revenues to its assets and therefore a measure of efficiency if compared to other firms of a similar ilk. A high asset turn does not necessarily indicate that a firm is efficient; it is a useful diagnostic measure but not a sufficient proof of virtue.

asset value per share
The total net value of a firm's assets less its liabilities, divided by the number of shares. When compared with the share price, it can indicate the extent to which the company is being valued on its assets rather than its earnings.

associated company, associated undertaking, associate
Company where there is a significant cross-shareholding, either directly or via a parent. Generally applies to a shareholding of 20–49 per cent in the associate, which is enough to give the company holding the stake influence but not control.

audit
1. External inspection of a company's books by a firm of independent accountants (the auditors) to see that they give a true and fair view of the business. 2. By extension, any systematic inspection of a particular aspect of a firm's operations, even if carried out by internal staff: see for example internal audit, environmental audit and human resources audit.

authorized share capital
The total number of shares the directors of a company have been authorized by the shareholders to issue.

AVA (Activity Value Analysis)
A cost-cutting process that looks at the value being provided by any activity. A precursor of BPR (Business Process Re-engineering).

average costing
A term coined by the Boston Consulting Group to indicate inadequately accurate costing systems that average costs across products or services taking in reality quite different amounts of cost, especially indirect and overhead costs.

average pricing
Traditional costing systems understate the cost of producing special or one-off products. This *average costing* leads to average pricing which, as the name suggests, means failing to charge enough of a price premium for top-of-the-line or special products, and conversely charging too much for standard products (because the prices of the two types of product are averaged rather than sharply differentiated).

B

back-to-back loan
1. A loan issued in parallel with another, so that the identity of the seller is concealed from the buyer in a credit arrangement. 2. A loan where there is no real risk because another party is guaranteeing it.

backward integration
The process whereby a company competes with its suppliers by setting up as a producer earlier in the value chain than it had previously done: for example, a retailer deciding to manufacture some of the products he sells.

balanced management skills
The idea that management must ensure that all functions such as marketing, operations and finance are in balance to meet customer needs, and that one function is not relied on and the others neglected.

balanced product offering
Marketers and managers must ensure that a product package meets reasonable standards under three headings: (1) functional properties (performance/design/value); (2) availability (accessibility/presentation/pleasant environment); and (3) identity (brand presentation/recognition/ perception/meeting expectations).

balance sheet
Statement of a company's assets and the claims over those assets at a particular date. The balance sheet is the most important financial statement (even more important than the Profit & Loss Statement), although wreathed in mystery for many practising businessmen. The importance of understanding balance sheets cannot be overstated. It is actually not that difficult either, despite accountants' restrictive practices that make it appear so. A balance sheet is just a list of a firm's assets and liabilities together with their value.

barriers to entry
Obstacle making it difficult or impossible for competitors to enter a particular business segment. Barriers sometimes exist naturally but astute managers will try to raise these barriers and introduce new ones in order to restrict competition amongst their customers. It is worthwhile reflecting from time to time on what can be done to raise barriers, by examining a checklist of potential barriers.

barriers to exit
Exit barriers are undesirable forces that keep too many competitors in a market, and lead to over-capacity and low profitability, because it is thought too expensive for a firm to leave the business. Barriers to exit may be real or imagined, economic or illusory. In general, barriers to exit are given too much thought and barriers to entry too little.

barter
To exchange goods or services for others rather than for cash.

BCG (the Boston Consulting Group)
US-originated international consulting firm and the most important contributor to ideas on business strategy in the last 30 years. Founded in 1964 by Bruce Henderson, BCG went through its most creative period from about 1967 to 1973, when it invented the BCG Matrix (more properly, the Growth/Share Matrix) and the Experience Curve. More recently it has innovated with time-based competition and customer retention. BCG's ideas have been far more influential than any other consultancy and it has probably added more to our stock of useful knowledge about business than any business school or university.

BCG Matrix

The Boston Consulting Group BCG has invented several matrices, having consultants trained to think in terms of two-by-two displays, but the most famous and useful one is the Growth/Share matrix, invented in the late 1960s and still of great importance today. It measures market growth and relative market share for all the business a particular firm has. Many people have claimed that the importance of market share, and the value of the Growth/Share Matrix, have been greatly overstated, and produce examples of cases where larger businesses are less profitable than smaller businesses, or where there is no systematic difference in profitability according to scale. On detailed examination, however, there are few individual business segments where it is not or cannot be a real advantage to be larger, all other things being equal. The qualification in the last phrase is absolutely crucial: relative market share is not the only influence on profitability, and it may be overwhelmed by different competitors' operating skills or strategies or random influences on profitability.

One of the major causes of confusion is that businesses are often not defined properly, in a sufficiently disaggregated way, before measuring market share. The niche player who focuses on a limited product range or customer base is playing in just one segment from the broad line supplier, who may be playing in several segments and may actually not be very large in any one segment despite appearing to have a high overall market share.

If businesses are defined properly, the higher share competitor should have an advantage at least nine times out of ten. It therefore follows that the further to the left a business is on the BCG Matrix, the stronger it should be.

BCG superimposed on the Growth/Share Matrix a theory of cash management (sometimes confusingly called Portfolio Management) which is intriguing and makes some useful points, although it is also somewhat flawed. The theory looks at the cash characteristics of each of the quadrants. BCG's theory then came up with an hierarchy of uses of cash, numbered from 1 to 4 in their order of priority.

1. The best use of cash, we can agree, is to defend cash cows. They should not need to use cash very often, but if investment in a new factory or technology is required, it should be made unstintingly.
2. We can also agree that the next call on cash should normally be in stars. These will need a great deal of investment to hold (or gain) relative market share.
3. The trouble begins here, with BCG's third priority, to take money from cash cows and invest in question-marks. The bastardized version of the theory stressed this cash flow in particular. BCG countered by stressing that investment in question-marks should be selective, confined to those cases where there was a real chance of attaining market leadership. With this qualification, BCG's point is sensible.
4. The lowest priority was investment in dogs, which BCG said should be minimal or even negative, if they were run for cash. This may be a sensible prescription, but the problem is that the dog kennel may contain a large range of breeds with different qualities, and a differentiated cash strategy is generally required within the dog kennel.

One real weakness of the BCG cash management theory, however, as BCG came to realize, was the assumption that the portfolio had to be in balance in respect of cash on an annual or three-year basis. In fact, the cash invested in the overall business portfolio does not have to equal the cash generated. Surplus cash can be invested outside the existing portfolio, either by acquiring new businesses, by entering them from scratch, or by reducing debt or giving cash back to the shareholders. Conversely, if a business needs to invest more cash (for example, in an important and cash-guzzling star) than the business portfolio is generating, it should go out and raise the cash from bankers and/or shareholders to fund the cash gap. The business portfolio should not be thought of as a closed system.

The second major weakness of BCG views on cash, and one not fully realized until much later, was the implicit assumption that all businesses should be managed from the centre in a cashbox-plus-strategic-control way. BCG's theory was immensely attractive to chairmen and chief executives seeking a sensible role for the Centre, and probably did a great deal more good than harm, but it is only a small minority of businesses that are actually run in this way.

The BCG Matrix marked a major contribution to management thinking. From the mid- to late 1970s BCG tended to retreat too much under the weight of critical comment, and the matrix is not much used today. It is well overdue for a revival. Anyone who tries to apply it thoughtfully to his or her business will learn a lot during the process.

BDI (Brand Development Index)
BDI measures the penetration of a product in a particular region relative to its penetration in a (country) market as a whole.

below-the-line promotion
Activities such as PR, mail order, point-of-sale promotions, demonstrations or discounts targeted at individuals rather than a mass audience. May or may not involve an advertising or other specialist agency.

benchmark
Originally used in relation to computers to mean a standard set of computer programs used to measure computer output and speed. Now used much more widely to mean the product of benchmarking, that is, a measure of productivity of one department or activity compared to that achieved in other operating units or organizations.

benchmarking
One of the key management words of the 1990s, although relying on techniques developed over the past 30 years, benchmarking is the detailed study of productivity, quality and value in different departments and activities in relation to performance elsewhere. The basic idea is to take or build up a database

of relevant performance drawn up from looking at similar activities in other parts of the firm, and in other firms, and compare the performance of the unit being reviewed with the range of experience elsewhere. There are three different techniques that can be used in benchmarking:

1. Best Demonstrated Practice (BDP), a technique used successfully for the last 15 years, is the comparison of performance by units within one firm. For example, the sales per square foot of toothpaste in a chemists in Leeds can be compared with the same statistic for the Huddersfield store within the same chain, as can the unit cost of electricity, security, or any other cost item cut any way that is relevant. BDP usually throws up large variances, some of which can be explained by lack of comparability, but much of which is due to superior techniques or simply greater efficiency at one site. That site can then be used as a challenge to lever up all other sites' performance.
2. Relative Cost Position (see RCP): RCP analysis looks at each element of the cost structure (eg, manufacturing labour) per dollar of sales in firm X, compared to the same thing in competitor Y. Good RCP analysis is very hard to do but very valuable, as much for its insight into competitors' strategies as for cost reduction.
3. Best Related Practice is like BDP, but takes the comparisons into related (usually not competing) firms, where direct comparisons can often be made by co-operation between firms to collect and compare data.

book value
The value of an asset as recorded in a company's books. The book value is often different from the current market value.

bottom line
1. Profit, that is, the bottom line on the P&L statement, as in all the additional sales revenue, drops down to the bottom line. 2. By extension, what really matters, the heart of the matter.

BPR (Business Process Re-engineering)
A new way of rethinking what a company does and redesigning its processes from first principles in order to produce dramatic improvements in cost, quality, speed and service. BPR claims to reinvent the way that companies do business, from first principles, by throwing out the view that firms should be organized into functions and departments to perform tasks, and paying attention instead to processes. A process here is a set of activities that in total produce a result of value to a customer, for example, developing a new product. Who is in charge of this? In the non-BPRed company the answer is no one, despite the involvement of a large number of traditional functions.

brand
A visual design and/or name that is given to a product or service by an organization in order to differentiate it from competing products, and which assures consumers that the product will be of high and consistent quality.

1090

Branding goes back to the time when medieval guilds required tradesmen to put trademarks on their products to protect themselves and buyers against inferior imitations. Nowadays virtually everything has been branded. Consumers prefer brands because they dislike uncertainty and need quick reference points.

Brands have seven major advantages for suppliers:

1. They can help to build consumer loyalty and thus give a higher and more enduring market share.
2. Most brands involve a price premium which can be very substantial and which greatly exceeds the extra cost in terms of superior ingredients and marketing.
3. By virtue of their premium price (which widens margins for wholesalers and retailers as well as the manufacturer) and consumer pull, brands can make it easier for manufacturers to gain vital distribution. This is particularly crucial for new products and for smaller suppliers.
4. Brands can sometimes change the balance of power between different parts of an industry. The development of manufacturers' grocery brands between 1918 and 1960 helped to put manufacturers in the driving seat and give them higher margins than retailers. In the past 25 years consolidation in food retailing and the development of retailers' (own label) brands has handed higher margins to retailers and enabled them to introduce new products from smaller suppliers, including some high-margin innovations such as chilled ready meals.
5. Brands can make it easier to introduce new products and get consumers to try them, so that often a new product will use some of the brand equity in an existing brand by using it while adding a differentiating sub-brand, such as Miller Lite or Guinness Draught Bitter.
6. Closely associated with point 5, branding facilitates the creation of new market segments within an established product category: for instance, low-calorie or low-fat versions of almost any food or drink product, the creation of at least three classes of airline travel, or longer lasting products such as Duracell.
7. Finally, the combination of trust and razzmatazz that brands carry can enable whole industries to defy the market maturity stage of the alleged product life cycle, taking a fusty and declining market and injecting new growth into an industry. Besides the cider and stout examples, successful branding has helped to revive markets as diverse as shampoo, hand razors, bicycles and newspapers, all of which once seemed stuck in steady decline.

brand awareness
The proportion of consumers who spontaneously recognize a particular brand, the extent to which the brand is well known (regardless of how highly regarded it is).

brand equity
The value residing in a brand name. If brands are really valuable, why do almost no consumer companies have a person charged with protecting and

enhancing the brand equity, as opposed to exploiting it in the short term, which is what brand managers do?

brand extension, line extension
Introducing a new variant of a product in the same product category, for example, Tuna Whiskas or Pepsi Max.

brand premium
The extra price (most usefully expressed as a percentage) that a top brand can command, compared to a secondary brand or a retailer's own label.

brand stretching
The process whereby an existing well-known brand name is used on new products that compete in a different market from the brand's existing core product(s).

brand valuation
1. The process of putting a value on a brand so that this value can be put on the balance sheet of the company owning the brand.
2. The value of the brand thus established.

There are a number of rival ways of valuing brands, none of which is intellectually satisfactory, but all of which produce results enabling a finance director to strengthen ostensibly his company's balance sheet. Brand valuation somewhat resembles angels dancing on the end of a pin, but most consumer goods companies have put the value of their brands on the balance sheet.

brand vandalism
Destroying or reducing brand franchise by stretching the brand too far and/or by attaching the brand to a low-quality, new product.

break-even analysis
Shows when total sales turnover equals total cost, thus producing break-even, as well as showing the level of profit or loss at different volumes. One of the oldest, most basic, easiest-to-use and most useful tools for considering whether to go into business, launch a new product or for budgeting.

One of the greatest values of break-even analysis is its simplicity. Yet this renders it of limited value when modelling large, multi-product businesses, especially when several products share costs or where there is a once-for-all fixed cost (such as the launch of a new product) which will not be repeated in later years. Nor can it take account of long-term strategic variables such as penetration pricing or the lowering of costs through additional volume.

break-up value
The value put upon a firm by a stockbroking analyst or a predator in the event that the firm is split up into its component parts and sold off piecemeal to those who would pay the highest price for each piece.

brown goods
TVs, CD-players and other domestic electronic goods originally sold in wooden (*brown*) cabinets.

budget
The annual plan of sales and profits which must be met by a firm or part of a firm for satisfactory performance. Firms differ widely in their use of budgets. In some it is a stretching amount where attaining the budget is a sign of very good performance. In others the budget is deliberately set at a level which can almost definitely be attained, in order to avoid disappointing the owners, with perhaps a higher target set as well for motivational purposes. In some firms failure to meet budget does not attract penalties; in others the budget is sacrosanct and failure leads to resignation or firing.

Because budget alone does not denote a clear enough idea of its importance or function, executives setting or monitoring budgets should think very carefully about what the budget means and ensure that everyone involved has the same understanding. Different departments will have their own budgets which may simply be a name for the expenditure allowed (as in marketing budget) or may denote a more comprehensive plan, such as the production budget. In addition the finance department will prepare a number of specialist budgets, of which the most important are the capital expenditure budget and the cash budget.

bureaucracy
Commonly used to mean a large organization where rules and regulations are strangling entrepreneurial flair, imposing unnecessary cost and insulating managers from dealing directly and effectively with customers. Yet, bureaucracy, as originally invented by Max Weber, was not a pejorative term, and simply meant a rational organization where objectives and rules could lead to efficiency and avoid the evils of personal favouritism.

business plan
Simply a document describing where the business is going, usually over a 3–5 year period.

business segment
A defensible competitive arena within which market leadership is valuable. A business segment is an area within which a firm can specialize and gain competitive advantage.

business to business
The process of industrial marketing or providing a service to other businesses rather than to the consumer.

buy-in
1. See MBI (Management Buy-In).

2. Enthusiastic acceptance of a new plan, mission, behaviour standard or proposition, signifying that the executives involved really believe in it and take psychological ownership of it.

C

CAD-CAM (Computer Aided Design and Computer Aided Manufacture)
CAD enables designers and architects to change one aspect of a design and see on a computer screen the implications for all other aspects. CAM then makes it possible to go straight from the design phase to production, using computers. CAD/CAM should lower the cost and, even more importantly, the time required for practical new product development.

cannibalization
When a new product or service is introduced in the knowledge that it will eat into the market for an existing product or service already being provided by the supplier.

capacity
The amount of supply in an industry, or the quantity of goods that a machine or facility can produce. It is important to define the measure of capacity carefully to ensure comparability. The addition of capacity *by whom and when* will have the most decisive impact on market share, corporate and industry profitability. No industry is ever transformed except by pre-emptive investment. On the other hand, the profitability of many industries has been almost permanently blighted by mindless, copycat capacity additions. The most effective adders of capacity are those who plonk down huge investments while persuading their competitors not to follow suit. It is a game suited to visionaries and gamblers rather than to accountants with their DCF analyzes.

capital
Funding for business. Often used simply to mean equity or share capital, that is, the funds provided by shareholders and at risk if the business is not successful. But can also comprise loan capital, ie, amounts provided by banks and other lenders, which has a lower degree of risk than share capital since it ranks in front of it for payment.

capital and reserves
Also called equity, shareholders' equity and shareholders' funds. The share of a company's assets that are due to its shareholders, comprising share capital, share premium, retained profit and any other reserves.

capital employed
The total money tied up in a business to allow it to operate, comprising fixed assets and working capital. Also equals the sum of the equity, debt and tax

payable. The capital employed should be compared to the profits (returns) generated by the business. Net operating assets is a synonym for capital employed.

capital intensive
An industry or business continually requiring large investments of cash to prosper.

capitalization, capitalization
The market value of a company traded on the stock exchange, that is, the share price multiplied by the number of shares in issue.

capital structure
The relative proportions of a company's funding that are provided by debt and equity or, in a more detailed analysis, taking into account the amounts comprised in ordinary shares, preference shares, bonds and long-term debt. Capital structure is also called financial structure or funding structure.

captive demand
Demand that has no effective choice but to consume product from the supplier, because it is imprisoned within a wider business system.

career anchor
Ed Schein's term for the perceptions individuals have about themselves and their worth to, and role in, an organization, that encourage them to stay in it. Can also restrict a person's ambition if the role is perceived too narrowly.

career planning
Planning future steps in an individual's career, either by the individual or by the firm. Few organizations have organized career planning for any but a minority of identified high flyers. For the individual, career planning should include consideration of when to move firms or even professions.

cash cow
A business that is highly cash positive as a result of being a market leader in a low growth market. Such a business typically requires only moderate investment in physical assets or working capital, so that high profits result in high cash flow. Cash cows are one of the four positions on the BCG Matrix. In the BCG theory cash from cash cows can be used to support other businesses that are leaders or potential leaders in high-growth markets and that need cash to improve or maintain their market share positions.

The BCG theory has often been misinterpreted, partly as a result of the tag 'cash cow'. Cows need to be milked, so the natural (but incorrect) inference is that the main role of cash cows is to give cash to the rest of the portfolio. Yet the original BCG theory stressed the key point that cash cows should have the first call on their own cash: whatever investment was necessary to support and reinforce the cash cows' position should come first. This common-sense prescription is often overlooked. Cash cows are not glamorous, and generally require only moderate amounts of grass, but they should still be allowed to graze on the most verdant pastures. It would have saved us all a great deal of trouble if BCG had stuck to the alternative name for cash cows, namely *gold mines*. Nobody would dream of denying a gold mine its required share of the maintenance budget.

cash flow
The change in a company's cash balance over a period. Nothing is more important than cash flow, both short and long term.

cash trap
Useful jargon invented by the Boston Consulting Group to describe businesses that absorb cash but will never repay it fully or at all. BCG even went so far as to say in 1972 that 'the majority of the products in most companies are cash traps. They will absorb more money forever than they will generate. This is true even though they may show a profit in the books.'

cellular manufacturing
The arrangement of computer controlled equipment into groups of machines to process production.

centre
More positive name for headquarters, reflecting recently increased respectability of adding value from the centre.

chain of command
Hierarchical reporting relationships as seen on an *organization chart*. Best kept short, as in the Roman Catholic Church, which has only five levels.

chairman
Generally the most senior person in a company, although the title itself does not convey whether the chairman is part time or full time or whether he or she is effectively part of the executive team or a figurehead.

Chandler, Alfred (b. 1918)
Influential American economic historian whose book *Strategy and Structure* (1962) was based on studying major US corporations between 1850 and 1920. He is important for having made three points clearly:

1. He highlighted the close relationship between strategy and structure, and said that firms should first determine their strategy, then their structure. This was more unusual for the emphasis on strategy than the sequencing, because very few writers had paid attention to strategy: it is almost completely lacking in the earlier theorists.
2. He believed that the role of the salaried manager and technician was vital, and talked about the 'visible hand' of management co-ordinating the flow

of product to customers more efficiently than Adam Smith's 'invisible hand' of the market. This is an early recognition that corporations, in their internal dealings, favour a planned economy.

3. He was an advocate of decentralization in large corporations, contributing to the divisionalization and decentralization trend of the 1960s and 1970s. He praised Alfred Sloan's decentralization of General Motors in the 1920s and was influential in the transformation of AT&T in the 1980s from a production-based bureaucracy to a marketing organization.

change agent
Process consultant or other catalyst who helps to change the culture or direction of a company.

change management
The process whereby companies undergo a major change in their culture and performance. Fundamental change of this type is always difficult and risky; about three quarters of all serious attempts to change companies in Britain and America between 1970 and 1992 ended in failure. Yet it is apparent that many large companies will only survive and prosper as independent entities if they change their way of operating and lift performance to a new level. Many consultants offer change management services but most of them do not really understand the business realities; their skills are process related rather than strategic and operational. All successful transformations of companies have changed culture almost as a by-product of successful commercial changes; like happiness, culture change is a result of a frame of mind and taking decisive actions, not something that can be sensibly pursued as a goal in itself. And all successful transformations have depended on vigorous and visionary leadership from one person.

CIM (Computer Integrated Manufacturing)
The use of information technology to integrate all the processes involved in production: design, production engineering, production planning, production control and scheduling, materials procurement and flow planning, materials handling, stock control, all manufacturing operations, distribution, and cost accounting. A CIM system controls and integrates all the sub-systems, allowing each of the processes to 'talk' to each other via computer. CIM is the ultimate refinement of CAD-CAM.

cluster
1. A group of customers or other observations that have common characteristics and that are clearly differentiated from other customers/observations that belong in other clusters. 2. More recently, used to describe an employee grouping drawn from different functions who work together on a semi-permanent basis as a self-contained mini-firm. A cluster develops its own expertise and customers and shares accountability for action.

cluster analysis
Market research technique identifying clusters by computer analysis of a large number of variables. Useful because it often throws up non-obvious linkages.

cognitive dissonance
A useful concept from psychology, invented by the American psychologist Leon Festinger in 1951. The theory says that it is painful for there to be a discrepancy (*dissonance* in psycho-speak) between people's beliefs and their actions, so that they will move to bring either into line with the other.

competences
Skills that an organization has: what it is good at. Much recent thinking has stressed that an organization's operating skills relative to competition are at least as important to its success as the strategy it has. To be successful an organization must be at least as good as its competition in certain core competences. Assessing and improving competences (relative to competition) has rightly become the top priority for many managements.

competitive advantage
One of the most enduring and valuable catchwords of strategy. Competitive advantage obtains when one player has identified a market or market niche where it is possible to have a price advantage, or a cost advantage, or both, over competitors. Price advantage means that the product or service is thought sufficiently superior by its buyers to make a price premium (for equivalent quality and cost to produce) possible. Brand leaders usually command a price premium over secondary brands or own-label products, sometimes as much as 20 to 40 per cent, which far exceeds the additional cost of advertising and superior product formulation.

Cost advantage can come from superior scale (and therefore greater spreading of fixed costs), from having lower factor costs (for example, by using cheap labour), from superior technology, or simply having workers who perform their tasks more intelligently or quickly.

Competitive advantage is usually, although not invariably, related to superior market share in a defined segment. Even if not caused by competitive advantage, market leadership should be the result of competitive advantage: otherwise it is being under-exploited.

conglomerate
A firm that has many different divisions making a wide variety of different and unrelated products.

consolidated accounts
Accounts prepared for a parent company and its subsidiaries to summarize the total affairs of the group as though it were simply one company.

consolidation
1. The process of rationalizing an industry by acquisition in order to increase concentration. 2. A period of digestion in a company's history following rapid change and/or expansion. 3. The process of preparing consolidated accounts.

consortium
A group of companies that come together for a defined purpose, usually a one-off event relating to part of the business of each company and not implying a longer-term strategic alliance. Consortia are usually formed to bid for a large contract, often a public sector one, where each party brings different expertise.

consortium bid
A takeover bid where two or more parties are in alliance. Consortium bids are difficult to organize because of the different interests of the parties and the delay caused by debate between the parties.

constituency
Another name for stakeholder, that is, a collective group (such as customers, suppliers, employees, bankers or shareholders) to whom a firm has obligations.

contingency theory
Theory that says there is no universally right way to organize a firm: it all depends on the culture, the people, the degree of inter-dependence of activities within the firm, and the external environment. If this sounds vague and unhelpful, contingency theory goes on to say under what circumstances a matrix organization is desirable (when there is a great deal of cross-functional and cross-product interaction), when it is more appropriate to centralize and de-centralize, and so on. Contingency theory at least removed many of the simplistic notions and universal prescriptions that had previously held sway. Contingency theory is held in high esteem by most academics and has been applied outside the narrowly organizational arena, for example, in marketing and strategy. Managers, who still like to be told in simple, clear terms what to do on Monday morning, are not such great fans.

continuous improvement
A Japanese concept holding that competitive advantage of a company accrues from the persistent search for improvement and a series of tiny steps made continuously, rather than from great leaps forward. The latter are more consistent with Anglo-Saxon cultures, which helps to explain the popularity of re-engineering. The evidence is that the Japanese approach works very effectively for Asian cultures, while more revolutionary techniques are both more necessary and more acceptable for Anglo-Saxons.

contracting-out
Process of using outside suppliers of services to a corporation or public authority rather than using an internal department. There is a strong and

increasing trend towards contracting-out in both business and government, largely to cut cost, but partly also motivated by the belief that organizations should concentrate on their core competences and leave other specialists to fulfil other roles.

contractors
Those individuals and contracting firms that provide specialist services to larger firms.

contribution
Accounting term: the difference between the selling price and variable costs or, put another way, the contribution towards fixed overheads.

control systems
Any organized method of measuring and monitoring the attainment of objectives (such as customer quality levels or market share) or budgets, comparing actual results against plans, feeding back results and taking action to correct deviations from plan.

convertible bond/loan stock
A loan which the lender can choose to convert into shares of the company in lieu of repayment. Usually in unquoted companies.

convertible preference share
A long-term loan that may be converted into ordinary shares of the borrower at the option of the lender at certain times and share prices. Also called convertible shares, usually quoted on the stock market alongside the ordinary shares.

COO (Chief Operating Officer)
Role of US origin whereby the CEO (Chief Executive) has reporting to him the COO, who then controls the majority or all operating chiefs. It makes good sense in the USA where the CEO is usually also the chairman. In the UK and other countries where the Chairman and CEO are separate people, the need for a COO is less obvious. Yet the COO role is increasingly popular outside the USA. It usually indicates that the CEO is tired of the day-to-day running of the firm and wants to behave more like the chairman. This is not necessarily a bad thing, especially if the actual chairman is not active or if the CEO is trying to transform the company and needs to act as an agent provocateur, outside the normal constraints of the hierarchy. A good CEO with a good COO can usually achieve radical change much more easily.

co-op
A co-operative organization which aims to satisfy the needs of its workers or members rather than make a profit for shareholders.

core business
During the 1980s it became fashionable for diversified firms to categorize businesses as either *core* or *non-core*. A core business is one which the firm intends to keep and develop. Non-core businesses are candidates for sale if a good offer arrives.

core workers
Those people who are central to an organization's success and who need to be nurtured and rewarded accordingly. This professional core, increasingly made up of qualified professionals, technicians and managers, comprise the knowledge and skills that explain an organization's success (or lack thereof). Core workers are precious, hard to replace, expensive and increasingly footloose.

corporate governance
The rules and procedures to ensure that a company is properly run, that the right directors are in place with their roles defined, and that directors behave appropriately and in accordance with both the law and best practice. How companies are governed varies widely from country to country and even within countries, and there is no simple, universal model that can be followed.

corporate identity
The face a firm presents to the outside world, including but not confined to its name, logo, corporate advertising, and, if it has one, corporate catchphrase (such as Avis's 'We try harder'). Corporate identity has become big business to design firms and specialist advertising agencies and has been elevated by persuasive design gurus like Wally Olins on to the boardroom agenda. Olins and others stress that corporate identity should reflect the organization's strategy and core values: it is not just a matter of seductive logos and pretty stationery.

corporate planning
When corporate strategy became popular, in the 1970s, it was generally felt that every major corporate should have a large corporate planning staff to administer an annual cycle of corporate planning. This often involves operating units generating large amounts of paper, passing it to the next level up for review and consolidation with plans from other units, and so on until the corporate planning department and, eventually, the CEO and the Board could consider and approve the plans. Thereafter nothing much happened to change what would have happened anyway. Fortunately corporate planning as such is on its last legs. Strategy is recognized as too important to leave to the planners. Strategy is a line function, one for all executive leaders. Strategy should involve thinking and action, not planning, with its faintly Stalinist and strongly bureaucratic taint.

corporate raider
Rich individual or firm that buys a strategic stake in an underperforming company and tries to force it to improve performance.

corporate responsibility
The obligations a company owes to society and to its immediate environment such as the local community where it operates.

corporate strategy
1. The basis on which a company can beat its competitors, and the actions a company takes to strengthen its competitive advantage and maximize the value of the firm. Properly used, the word strategy is all about summoning up willpower and resources to beat competitors and then doing exactly that. Strategy derives from the Greek for generalship and means the marshalling and leadership of troops and weaponry in war against a particular enemy.
2. Corporate strategy is also used to mean the strategy of the top corporate level strategy, the Centre, as opposed to the strategy for individual business units (*business unit strategy*). Corporate strategy should include the major aspects of business unit strategy for the firm's most important businesses, but it also includes the deployment, inspiration and development of the firm's most important ammunition (in the form of people, knowledge and money) against the firm's most important competitors in order to build market share, earnings and corporate competences and to put competitors out of business altogether or at least persuade them to withdraw from markets which are the most profitable for and important to the firm. It is often said that corporate strategy is concerned with the allocation of resources (cash and people) between different businesses, and various tools have greatly helped resource allocation decisions, but more important than allocation of resources is the creation and magnification of the firm's skills, knowledge, self-confidence and fighting spirit.

It should be noted that corporate strategy is not a plan and it is certainly not a document, whatever the cover may say. A firm's strategy is what it does against competitors, not what it says it does or thinks it does. Every firm has a strategy, and some work better than others.

corporate venturing
Venture capital investment by a non-venture capitalist (ie, by a normal commercial firm). Often done to gain experience of a new technology and market without having to staff up for it inside the venturing firm.

corporate virtual workspace
Non-physical work environment, comprising links between members of a firm and/or outsiders provided by modern communications and information technology.

Cost-Benefit Analysis (CBA)
A monetary assessment of a project's worth which compares all its costs and benefits. Often used to assess public sector projects where an attempt is made

to quantify social benefits. Can also be used by private sector managers to take account of *soft* benefits of a major project. In CBA all the benefits and costs of the project are listed and quantified. For example, the benefits of an underground rail extension will include the social benefits of lower traffic congestion and pollution above ground, as well as avoidance of unemployment pay for those whom the project will put into employment. The benefits are quantified over time and then compared to the costs, usually via a DCF (Discounted Cash Flow). The project will be approved if the benefits exceed the costs by a certain margin.Capital will be rationed by only approving the highest Cost-to-Benefit ratio projects, up until the time that capital is exhausted.

CBA is not much used by the private sector, but is finding new favour with some executives. It can be used to evaluate projects that are thought to have major but indirect value, such as a corporate identity programme. Even approximate quantification of soft benefits can be useful, provided CBA is not used to justify decisions already taken.

cost drivers
The most important influences on the overall and relative costs of a firm or industry.

cost of capital
The cost to a firm of its capital: divided into the cost of equity (share) capital and the cost of debt. The latter is nearly always much lower, so the greater the proportion of debt (that is, the greater the gearing or leverage), the lower the weighted average cost of capital.

cost structure
The total cost elements of a company broken down into key elements and often shown in the form of a bar, which can then be compared to the cost structure of a competitor making the same product, or to the cost structure of other products in the same firm.

cost to switch, costs to switch
The psychological and/or financial cost to move from one supplier to another.

culture
The personality and character of a company, derived from generations of people and experience and leading people inside a firm to behave in certain characteristic ways without thinking about it. Different firms in the same country and industry may have radically different cultures, and the difference may be far more important in determining relative success than any other factor, including differences in strategy, which may themselves be partly explained by the culture. Increasing but still insufficient attention is being paid to creating and sustaining winning cultures within firms.

Current Cost Accounting (CCA)

Also called *inflation accounting*. Adjusting a firm's traditional (historical cost) accounts to take account of inflation, producing an additional profit and loss statement and balance sheet. In these accounts the cost of sales is based on their replacement cost, while depreciation is based on the replacement cost of the assets, not their actual historical cost. Not much used, especially now that inflation in most countries is back to moderate levels.

current liability

A liability on a balance sheet expected to be paid within a year.

current ratio

Current assets divided by current liabilities. Current assets should be greater than current liabilities (ie, the ratio should be more than 1.00); if not, a liquidity crisis may loom. The problem with the current ratio is that it is not a sufficiently short-term test. Liquidity crises normally have a much shorter time horizon than one year. If you have to pay the tax authorities at the end of the month, it is little comfort that a large customer must pay you in ten weeks' time. The trend in current ratio is worth watching (especially if it is deteriorating), but a current ratio above 1.00 is not a guarantee of safety.

customer proposition

A differentiating product or service of great appeal to a particular business segment. Each important product or service offered by a firm should have a clear customer proposition.

customer retention

The extent to which customers repeat-purchase. Customers defect at average rates of 10–30 per cent, and far more in some businesses like car dealing. Losing customers is expensive, because the marketing costs to win them over in the first place are so high.

customer value

The extent to which customers perceive a product or service as good value.

D

data

A much abused plural noun indicating the objective numerical and factual basis of analyzes and conclusions. Roughly equivalent to 'facts' but implying a body of supporting figures and/or documents.

databank

Collection of data, usually stored on computer.

database
Often used as synonym for databank but more correctly a computer software package for storing data.

database management systems (DBMS)
Interrelated software which makes multiple use of the same data in different applications possible. Comprises data description, data entry, data access, file creation and management applications generation.

data highway
The new electronic infrastructure vital to a nation's international competitiveness in the next century.

DCF (Discounted Cash Flow)
Calculation used in valuation and investment appraisal which involves listing all the cashflows from a particular business or investment, applies a discount rate to each of them to equalize their effective value today (on the grounds that £100 cash this year is worth more than £100 cash next year), and then adds them up to provide a total value or DCF, which can then be compared either with the value today, or the amount of investment required, or with the value of other businesses or investments.

debenture, debenture stock
Fixed-interest security issued by companies in return for long-term (usually 10–40 years) loans, secured either against specific company assets or by a floating charge on them.

debit
1. An accounting entry in double entry book-keeping of goods or services supplied by the company, thus either increasing its assets or decreasing its liabilities.
2. To enter the value of goods supplied to a customer in his account with the supplier.

debt service ratio
The value of a country's hard currency exports divided by its annual debt (interest and repayment) payments, and hence a crude way of assessing a country's credit-worthiness.

De Bono, Edward (b. 1933)
Inventor and apostle of lateral thinking – one big idea that has spawned 38 books and world-wide fame. Lateral thinking is not sequential, vertical or rational; it is discontinuous, turning ideas on their head or creating them 'from left field'. Uses analogy and random word association to break the tyranny of established ways of thinking.

debt
1. Funding that has a right to a known rate of interest and repayment terms and a first call on assets (ahead of the other form of funding, equity) in the event of liquidation. Debt should be, but rarely is, used as a strategic weapon by profitable market leaders. Because these do not require high levels of debt in the capital structure they do without it; but with more debt, they could be more aggressive, invest more, lower prices, provide better customer service, and still meet the required rate of return to shareholders while making life very difficult for marginal competitors. 2. Money, goods or services owed.

debt-to-equity ratio
Debt divided by equity. A measure of gearing. High gearing can mean high risk (or, more rarely, an aggressive and well thought strategy).

debt to total funding ratio
Debt divided by the sum of debt and equity. An alternative ratio to debt to equity, also mostly used to assess risk.

decentralization
Process of giving power to decentralized divisions or operating units. Popular trend from 1921 to 1993, but now the virtues of a small but powerful Centre are being rediscovered.

decision tree
A flow chart that sets out possible future events and highlights the effects of decisions or chance occurrences in a sequential order.

deferred revenue or income
Revenue (usually in the form of cash) already received but which cannot yet pass through the books (cannot be recognized) because the goods or services have not yet been provided.

deferred shares
Shares that do not yet have a right to a dividend (until and unless certain conditions, such as future profit targets, have been met).

deferred taxation
Tax that will not have to be paid in the next year (but which may be paid thereafter and for which provision has been made).

delayering
Removing whole layers of management, resulting in a more flat structure, lower costs, less bureaucracy, and greater accountability of executives.

delegation
Passing down responsibility for a task to a cheaper or less experienced executive. Rarely practised as much as it should be.

delivery system
The activities a firm performs in delivering a product and/or service to the customer. The concept of the delivery system far transcends physical distribution and can be used to think about new ways of delivering value to the customer.

Delphi technique
Forecasting technique using a number of experts (or managers) who each make estimates in round one, then receive everyone else's estimates and re-estimate in round two, and so on until consensus is reached.

de-merger
Split of one company into two (or, very rarely, more than two) separately quoted companies, each with a clear and distinct product and market identity. Most common where a company already has two divisions engaged in different businesses.

Deming, W Edwards (1900-1993)
American originator of the quality revolution.

denationalization
For international companies, this means deliberately throwing out vestiges of nationalism derived from the country of origin/domicile, and creating a system of values shared by executives in all countries.

depreciation
The amount by which an asset's book value is deemed to have fallen each year. Depreciation is then charged as an expense for that year, that is, it decreases profits. Since depreciation has no cash cost (the cash went in one fell swoop when the asset was bought), depreciation does not affect cash flow. One way of calculating cash flow is to add back the depreciation to the profit.

derivatives
Hugely important financial instruments which are derived from other, simpler financial instruments, such as shares or bonds, options, warrants and futures; they could not exist without the underlying shares, but they are becoming increasingly important in driving share prices. Derivatives are the financial instruments and investments of the future: volatile, increasingly technical, increasingly powerful. It is likely that within a decade or two more money will be traded in the US via derivatives than via shares or bonds.

design
Manufacturers and retailers are putting increasing muscle behind design as a way of differentiating their product offerings. Design is an under-rated dimension of branding but will become a much more important part of it.

development capital
Most so-called venture capital is in fact development capital – financing the expansion of small firms (rather than financing start-ups).

differentiation
Giving a product competitive edge by making it different, or making it appear so.

dilution
Event whereby a shareholder's share of a company is decreased if new money is required in a rights issue and he cannot or does not want to provide his share of the new money. Does not necessarily imply that the shareholder is worse off afterwards, but he will have less control over the company.

direct cost
The cost of labour and materials in a product, but not including any overhead costs.

direct labour
Production workers (or their cost) excluding indirect support functions and overhead.

direct mail
An attempt to sell through the mail, usually targeted via a mailing list at individuals thought most susceptible to respond. Direct mail is a cheap marketing method but whether it pays off depends on the response rate.

direct marketing
An attempt to sell direct to the customer without a salesforce calling on prospects. Includes direct mail, telesales and electronic shopping.

director
1. Member of the board of directors, the people legally responsible to shareholders and government for ensuring that a firm is run competently and that its obligations are fulfilled honestly. In most countries, including the USA and the UK, the law makes no distinction between the duties and obligations of the inside (executive) and the outside (non-executive) directors, thus requiring the latter to exercise effective control despite often having little knowledge of the details of the business and limited time to spend on the corporation's affairs.
2. Particularly in the USA, 'director' is often used to designate a senior executive, even if not a member of the board.

disclosure requirements
What must by law be revealed to shareholders or other interested parties (such as trade unions) by companies.

diseconomies of scale
Literally when larger scale in one product line leads to higher unit costs. This almost never happens. The term is generally used when a company grows too big, or enters too many product lines or markets, to make it possible to control and co-ordinate without adding another layer of overhead cost, which can make the firm's costs higher than those of smaller and simpler competitors; and/or when bigness makes the firm less flexible or responsive to customers. A better term for both of these frequent events would be 'diseconomies of scope', since the real problem is not scale in one product line, but having too many products.

distribution
1. Act of getting product to market. **2.** Accounting term meaning payment of profits to shareholders by way of a dividend.

distribution channel
Way of getting product from supplier to customer. Many firms will have several channels of distribution, including direct marketing, own direct salesforce to retailers, selling to wholesalers who then sell to retailers, and so on.

diversification
Being in, or moving towards being, a group of companies engaged in several different products and markets. Diversification is usually driven by the wish (or financial ability) to expand beyond the apparent limits of existing markets, and/or by the wish to reduce business risk by developing new 'legs'. Many forests have been destroyed by writers praising and damning diversification. The balance of recent opinion has been against diversification (as in 'stick to the knitting'), although this has not stopped conglomerates (diversified companies) gaining a larger and larger share of corporate activity throughout the world, and especially in Britain.

The main justifications behind diversification are:

1. *Financial*: the BCG Matrix developed a theory in the late 1960s/early 1970s that central management of successful firms can and should shovel cash around the corporation in order to move it away from businesses that would always consume cash and into those few businesses that have the potential for market leadership, thus for long-term cash generation. This was a rather selective theory of diversification, but Bruce Henderson became an apostle of conglomerates, convinced that the strategically directed conglomerate could continually compound its cash generation capability and expand the scope of its operations. Modern financial theorists counter that shareholders, not managers, should diversify their holdings and that it is better for shareholders to be offered a selection of 'pure plays' of non-diversified companies.

2. *Management skills:* several diversified companies such as Hanson and BTR are highly skilled at identifying under-performing companies and at changing management structures and behaviour in order to improve performance. Diversification of this type involves buying, fixing and, at the right time, selling, such companies.
3. *Core skills or competences:* a company's expertise may not really reside in knowing a particular market, but in certain skills that are applicable across several markets.

diversified company
1. One that has a large number of unrelated operations. **2.** Some writers, such as Kenichi Ohmae, distinguish between a diversified company and a conglomerate. For them, the diversified company actively tries to add value to its different divisions by (a) exploiting competences and functional synergies across several businesses; and (b) using specific knowledge about customers and competitors and the key factors for success in each business to beat conglomerate competitors.

divestment
Selling or, in extreme circumstances, closing one of a firm's business units.

dividend
Payment to shareholders out of a firm's after-tax profits (earnings). If current earnings do not exist or are insufficient to meet a dividend, one may still be paid if the firm has adequate reserves and the management is optimistic about future prospects: this is an uncovered dividend. Dividends are generally not increased in direct line with the progress of earnings; most managements try to 'smooth' dividend growth to avoid the possibility of having to cut the dividend from one year to the next.

dividend cover
The number of times a dividend is 'covered' by the after-tax earnings, ie, profit after tax for the year divided by the dividend payable. If dividend cover is less than 2, investors may get nervous about the possibility of a future dividend cut; if the dividend cover is less than 1, the dividend is 'uncovered' and very vulnerable unless profits rise sharply.

dividend yield
A firm's gross (pre-tax) dividend per share divided by the share price. Alternatively, the total gross dividends of the firm for the year divided by the market value of firm. The number will be the same, and will reflect the 'interest' being earned on the share at its current share price. If the dividend yield is less than elsewhere (on other shares, or bank interest) the rational investor must be expecting a compensating capital gain to justify continuing to hold the shares. And in practice, companies that are growing their earnings at above-average rates do tend to have below-average dividend yields.

divisionalization
The process of reorganizing a company into separate product divisions, usually away from a centralized or functionally controlled structure.

dominance
1. When a market leader is so much larger, lower cost or more profitable than its rivals that it dominates the market. As a rule of thumb this may happen once it is at least four times larger than its nearest rival. **2.** When one decision is better than another under any conceivable scenario.

dominant firm
One that has a relative market share well above that of competitors in a particular market. There is no accepted definition of how much larger a firm should be to be considered dominant, but it should be at least double the size of the next largest competitor (ie, have a relative market share of at least 2, and probably be at least four times as large. A dominant firm should be highly profitable.

double-entry book-keeping
The fundamental principle of accounting, whereby each transaction is recorded twice, as a debit and a credit.

downside
1. Risk of losses from a business or project. **2.** Extent of such losses. **3.** More generally, used to indicate what could go wrong with a decision. **4.** A scenario that estimates the returns if a number of things go wrong.

downsizing
Radical reduction in the size of an organization, usually by delayering. May also imply a re-focus on certain core businesses and disposal of peripheral ones.

downstream
Operations that are towards the market/consumer end of the value chain, as opposed to towards the start (upstream) like production. Companies can be classified as to whether the majority of their value added is downstream or upstream.

DPP (Direct Product Profitability)
System that has revolutionized many retail businesses by making it possible to calculate the profit from any given product in any given position within a store (in terms of money amount per facing per week) and even the effect that putting one product next to another will have on the sales and profitability of each product. Typically retailers make the best returns on leading brands and on their own-label products, but poor returns on secondary brands, many of which are being squeezed out as a result of DPP.

Peter Drucker (b. 1909)
The most original and prolific management guru of the twentieth century.

due diligence
Investigation by or on behalf of an intended buyer of a business to check that it has the desired assets, turnover, profits,market share positions, technology, customer franchise, patents and brand rights, contracts and other attributes required by the buyer or claimed by the seller.

E

earnings
Profit of a company for the year. In the UK, earnings generally implies after-tax earnings. In the USA, earnings is just a synonym for profit and may well mean pre-tax profits.

economies of scale
Reduction in unit costs through having greater scale. One of the main reasons why the high market share competitor has lower costs than the smaller player. Economies of scale can cease to operate (or more precisely, are thought incorrectly to exist) when additional revenue is not exactly of the same type, that is, requires additional cost.

economies of scope
Economies that come from having a broad product line that can utilize the same skills or cost infrastructure.

emoluments
Total pay or compensation: salary plus the money value of all perks.

empowerment
Giving individuals in a firm the power to act on their own initiative but in the interests of the team as a whole. One of the great management buzz-words of recent years, empowerment is meant to release latent energy of individuals and encourage them to use their talents to the full within flatter management structures and autonomous work groups. Empowerment as a concept and proselytizing force is largely the creation of Rosabeth Moss Kanter.

enabling technologies
Those that facilitated breakthroughs in a number of areas, being applicable to many different industries.

encounter group
Technique used by organizational psychologists and management developers whereby members of a work group say what they think of each other and come to terms with suppressed emotions. Intended to increase sensitivity and teamwork. Can be effective but requires openness on the part of participants, and, without this, may be more harm than good.

encounter points
The critical points at which a customer comes into contact with a service provider.

end-game strategy
Strategy for dealing with a declining industry, particularly when few competitors are left.

entrepreneur
Risk-taker who starts and runs a new business. More loosely used to describe any small businessman. Many entrepreneurs are brilliant at starting businesses but less good at managing them once they reach a certain size.

equity
Also known as capital and reserves, shareholders' equity and shareholders' funds. Funding by shareholders in the form of shares (in contrast to funding by bankers in the form of debt), in return for which shareholders are entitled to part of the company's assets; the latter is the technical meaning of equity.

equity method
Method of accounting for associated companies where the investment is shown on the investor's balance sheet as a share of the net assets of the associate.

ergonomics
The study of people and technology ('human engineering') to produce a better fit between man and machine.

ESOP (Employee Stock Ownership Plan)
American device which has now spread to other countries (including the UK) whereby employees gradually buy a company and assume ownership of it by making a series of stage payments. A very useful method but inhibited outside the USA to a large degree by more complex and less favourable tax treatment.

ethical investment
The practice of investing only in the shares of 'ethical' companies, which is usually defined by exclusion: not investing in companies making harmful goods (cigarettes, armaments, etc) or having harmful effects on the environment (eg, toxic chemicals).

exceptional item
An unusual item of income or expense that is part of a firm's normal activities, but is very large and cannot be relied upon to recur.

exception reporting
Practice within a system of management accountability whereby executives get on with fulfilling their objectives and only report back to their bosses when something unusual occurs.

exit route
The way in which venture capitalists and the managers in an MBO sell a business and realize the return on their investment and work. The two main exit routes are flotation (going public on the stock exchange) or a trade sale (selling to a larger firm in the same business).

expected value
The weighted average expectation as to what an investment will be worth or what any other outcome (revenues, profits, etc) will be. Usually calculated by constructing various scenarios and weighting them according to probability.

expense
An operating cost (as opposed to capital expenditure or prepayments) that relates to a particular accounting period.

experience curve
Along with the BCG Matrix, the greatest discovery of Bruce Henderson, although it started life in 1926 as the 'learning curve'. Briefly it states that when the accumulated production of any good or service doubles, unit costs in real terms (ie, adjusted for inflation) have the potential to fall by 20 per cent. Accumulated production is not a concept much used, nor is it usually very easy to calculate; it is the total number of units of a product that have ever been made by a firm, or the total number of units of a product ever made by all participants in the market. It is not related to time, because accumulated production can double within one year for a new or very fast-growth product, or take centuries for a very old or slow-growth one.

expert systems
A computer program that summarizes the opinions of experts and allows non-experts to make decisions that are likely to be correct.

external growth
The opposite of organic growth, although not used as much; it means relying on acquisitions and joint-ventures as the main source of growth.

externality
A negative or positive by-product that is not paid for by an individual, a firm, or society.

extraordinary item
Income or expense that is not part of a firm's ordinary activities and not expected to recur.

F

factor analysis
Statistical technique for analyzing customers or competitors (or any diverse group of people or firms) into clusters of variables ('factors') that sub-sets have in common.

federalism, organizational federalism
A potentially useful but confusing word that is given a different slant by its opponents and proponents. The root meaning is that a federal organization is decentralized into separate units (SBUs, countries, functions or divisions) that largely control their own destiny, but retaining an overall sense of identity and purpose.

feedback
Technical term from systems design now used widely to mean informal responses to people or what they have done. Feedback should come from all levels of an organization; without it people will be less effective.

field theory
Psychologist Kurt Lewin made a breakthrough (obvious in retrospect) when he hypothesized that people do not carry around a set of invariable traits that lead to consistent behaviour as individuals whatever the social context. Rather, a 'field' (like a magnetic field) of forces operates around a person, giving rise to quite different behaviour according to how they are treated, who is around them, and the culture of an organization.

final dividend
Not the last ever to be paid, but rather the dividend declared at the end of each financial year.

financial engineering
Clever use of financial instruments to facilitate transactions such as takeovers or to increase the market value of a firm without changing the underlying industrial performance; that is, financial rather than strategic or operational engineering.

first mover advantage
The (usually correct) idea that the first into a market, the innovator, has an opportunity to stay ahead of competition, provided that the first mover builds in as much customer value as possible, lowers costs aggressively, and pursues a low-price policy rather than maximizing short-term profits.

fishbone chart
A production flow chart with arrows and angles resembling (for the imaginative) a fishbone.

fixed asset
An asset used on a long-term continuous basis, as opposed to assets bought to sell on to customers or assets that will be consumed soon.

fixed costs
Costs that do not go up or down with volume. Typically overhead costs such as rent, depreciation and central services. In practice fixed costs have a tendency to go up in steps when volume increases beyond a certain point, as when larger premises are required. Increasingly, business people are asking whether the division of costs into fixed and variable is all that helpful.

flexible benefits
Also known as cafeteria perks (British) and packaged compensation (Australian), but originated in the USA. Very sensible personnel policy that allows employees a wide degree of choice in the fringe benefits that they take up to a certain monetary value, so that they only take the benefits they really value and they realize the full cost of the benefits to the employer.

flotation
Introduction of a company on to the stock exchange. Equivalent US term is IPO (Initial Public Offering).

fmcg (fast moving consumer goods)
Consumer products (usually branded) that are bought frequently, including all grocery products, confectionery, cosmetics, toiletries, newspapers and magazines, and even petrol, but excluding infrequent purchases such as white and brown goods. Fmcg are known as red goods.

FMS (Flexible Manufacturing System)
Modular manufacturing process using computers to produce a wide range of components and products, and able to switch at short notice to making other products; involves being able to make any one product on several different machines, so that demand can be satisfied quickly, despite large fluctuations.

Follett, Mary Parker (1868–1933)

American political scientist, active at the turn of the twentieth century, who was the first to extol management as the most important element in industry, above bankers and shareholders. Stressed the role of management in encouraging teamwork in reaction to Taylor's mechanistic and hierarchical principles. Largely neglected in the West, but honoured in Japan, where there is a Follett Society.

follower

Opposite of market leader, that is, someone who is smaller than a competitor in a particular business segment.

forward integration

Moving into the next stage of the value chain, as when a manufacturer buys a wholesaler, or a wholesaler buys a retailer.

four Os of purchasing

(1) *Objects:* what uses will the products, when supplied to customers, have?
(2) *Objectives:* why will the product be bought? what do customers want it to do?
(3) *Organization:* who, within an organization, is the actual buyer?
(4) *Operations:* how do they actually buy? what procedures do they follow?

four Ps of marketing

(1) *Product:* which product line variants to supply, how to brand them, how to design and package them? (2) *Price.* (3) *Promotion.* (4) *Place:* how to get the product to the customer.

fragmentation

The process (unusual today) whereby a market is served by an increasing number of small suppliers.

fragmented market

A market where there are many competitors and none has a large market share.

franchise

The right to sell branded products or services in an approved format and under tight rules designed to ensure consistency of product/service offering to the consumer.

full cost, full cost pricing

1. Pricing goods based on the full rather than marginal cost of production. **2.** Looser term indicating that a fat profit has been taken.

fully diluted EPS (Earnings Per Share)

EPS calculated after taking into account unissued shares which may have to be issued in future as a result of outstanding options or other obligations. The most reliable, and certainly the safest, way of thinking about EPS.

function
Usually means an area of organizational skill specialization such as Production, Finance, Marketing, Personnel, Research and Development, and so forth.

functional structure
Organization of a firm where the main hierarchy is drawn on functional lines. Once popular for large firms, now largely discredited. Even the existence of functions as powerful internal clusters of expertise is now being attacked, and will change over the next 25 years.

fundamental principle of accounting
That the assets of a firm must always exactly equal the claims over those assets.

funding
The process of procuring or providing money for business, in the form of debt and equity. Funding can take place at any stage in a company's history: either initially to start it, or later on to provide money for expansion or to replace earlier funding.

funding structure
The relative proportions of debt and equity in the money provided for a firm. Also known as capital structure and financial structure.

fund management
Taking and investing other people's money for a fee.

funds flow analysis
Comparison of two successive balance sheets to see where funds have come from and where they have gone.

futures
Contracts to buy or sell shares, bonds, currencies or commodities at some future date at a price now specified. Can be used by commercial firms to lower or hedge risk, but increasingly used to speculate on the future direction of markets. The direction of the world's largest stock markets is increasingly influenced, and very often driven, by activity in the futures markets. A very important type of derivatives.

G

Gantt chart
Chart used in production scheduling, showing work steps or customers on the left and weeks on the right.

gap analysis
1. Marketing technique for identifying 'empty niches': product or service opportunities not yet exploited by any competitor. **2.** Identification of gaps in a firm's own product line where competing products do exist. **3.** Analysis of where precisely and why budgets or plans have not been met.

gearing
1. Use of debt to increase return for equity shareholders (although at added risk). **2.** Used more specifically to describe the extent of debt usage relative to equity: see debt to equity ratio. Gearing is the English for the American term 'leverage'.

generative process planning
The more complex of the two forms of CAPP (Computer Aided Process Planning), in which a description of the parts, process and tooling are put into the computer system, which then devises the process plan. The simpler form is variant process planning.

generic strategy
Term used by Michael Porter who said there were three generic strategies: differentiated, undifferentiated, and concentrated.

gilts, gilt-edged securities
Stocks and bonds issued by the UK government and quoted on the stock exchange.

glass ceiling
Invisible barrier preventing women (or blacks, or low social status groups) from reaching the top in business.

global brand
American-originated term for a brand like Coca-Cola, Levis, Walt Disney or McDonalds that aims to be within arm's reach of consumers anywhere. The idea of a universal product is also generally implied; it is the same anywhere.

globalization, globalization
1. The process whereby global tastes and product offerings converge and are increasingly satisfied by global products rather than local ones. **2.** Also used to indicate something much more significant and far reaching. Few real global products exist, but globalization is a reality for most of the world's largest companies, in the sense that they think and operate with a global perspective on customers, technology, costs, sourcing, strategic alliances and competitors. The market for these firms' products is wherever there are affluent consumers or significant industrial customers; the firms must appeal to their customers wherever they are, regardless of borders, the firm's nationality (an increasingly tenuous concept) or where its factories are. Globalization is driven by hard

economics: to compete effectively firms have to incur high fixed costs (for R&D, development of technology, sales and distribution networks, brand building and so on), forcing executives to spread these costs over higher volumes, which means trying to gain market share in all important world economies. New technologies also get dispersed globally very quickly, so that innovators must exploit their property on a global scale, if necessary by means of strategic alliances, or see it adopted and adapted by competitors.

3. Ability to carry out financial transactions on an international basis (in London, New York, Tokyo, etc) around the clock.

global localization

Sony catch-phrase where a global product is adapted to local tastes by low-cost customization. Has the advantages of low cost but is a somewhat differentiated product. May also involve use or creation of a local distribution network peculiar to one country or region.

glocalization of organizations

Contraction of 'global localization' and a very useful word, describing an escalating process. Glocalization aims at making the organization everywhere responsive to customers, who may themselves be global, and insists that the organization be structured in the way that makes it as easy as possible for the global customer to deal with.

goodwill

Accounting term that arises when a firm buys another for more than its net book value: the excess amount is goodwill. There can also be negative goodwill, when the reverse applies. Goodwill is an intangible fixed asset that can be carried as an asset in the balance sheet; alternatively, it may be charged against profits and fully or partly written off in any year.

H

Hawthorne effect

Term derived from the Hawthorne Studies where output improved simply because experiments were taking place that persuaded workers that management cared about them. The term can imply either that output is improving because of higher morale, or that an experiment is not to be trusted because the very fact of the experiment is influencing the results.

Hawthorne studies

Early experiments into workers'attitudes and behaviour conducted in the late 1920s and early 1930s at the Western Electric Plant at Hawthorne, Chicago. Path-breaking research that showed the importance of workers' perceptions of management and of informal work groups and norms.

head office
What do you call the Centre of an organization? Head office is better than HQ or headquarters, with its faint military connotations, but it still suggests a degree of overlording that is inappropriate. Many firms simply refer to the head office by its location, thus avoiding the term altogether.

Herzberg, Frederick (b. 1923)
American clinical psychologist and perhaps the most influential of the Human Relations School: the *Harvard Business Review* sold well over a million reprints of his 1968 article 'One more time: how do you motivate employees?', by far their biggest hit. He held that business organizations could be an enormous force for good, provided they liberated both themselves and their people from the thrall of numbers, and got on with creative expansion of individuals' roles within them.

hierarchy of needs
Motivational construct invented by Abraham Maslow (1908–1970) that postulated an ascending series of human needs, starting with warmth, shelter and food and ending with 'self-actualization': achievement of personal potential. Once one need had been satisfied, it no longer motivated.

historic earnings
Profits (usually after tax) most recently reported, that is, those of the last year for which data are available. Contrast with prospective earnings, which are the estimated earnings for the current year or a designated future year.

historic PE
Also known as historic P/E, historic PER, or historic Price-Earnings Ratio. The price-earnings ratio calculated using historic earnings.

holding company
1. A company controlling another company or (more normally) several other companies. 2. A management style, where a company simply buys, sells and holds other companies without trying to add any value to them. In this sense, most conglomerates are not holding companies (because most conglomerates do seek to add value in one way or another to their holdings), although technically they are.

homeworking
Work done at home for a firm. Important in the early stages of the Industrial Revolution. Now increasingly important again, as phone, fax and computer links are more powerful and cheaper.

horizontal integration
Specialization of a firm in one stage of the value chain, and growth by undertaking more activities of the same type.

horizontal tracking
The idea that the career of individuals within an organization can progress and be tracked horizontally as well as vertically: that is, significant development can be marked by horizontal moves into a different area of the firm rather than just by vertical moves (promotion).

hot desking
When an executive (as in IBM) does not have a personal office, but uses any available desk in a general office to plug in his computer terminal, log on to the telephone system, and start working.

hub and spoke system, hub and spoke
Distribution system whereby one or several central depots has a number of other delivery points. The hub delivers to each delivery point, but they do not trans-ship between each other.

human asset accounting
Attempt, which has never really taken off, to look at people in an organization as assets (as well as costs) in which the firm invests via training and management development.

human relations school
Humanist industrial psychology that originated with Elton Mayo (1880–1949) and included Argyris, Herzberg, Likert, McGregeor and Maslow. Most influential between about 1930 and 1970. Now a new generation of industrial catalysts stressing the importance of the human side to corporate performance and the need to change culture to change performance has grown up, incorporating most of the new thinkers of the last 20 years. The new generation, which includes Rosabeth Moss Kanter, Ed Schein, Robert Waterman, Charles Hampden-Turner, Charles Handy, Andrew Campbell and, on good days, Tom Peters, is rather less starry-eyed and rather more hard-hitting, having realized the cultural influences behind the success of Japanese and Korean industry and the weakness in most Anglo-Saxon ways of doing business.

human resources
American-originated description for an organization's people and/or for its personnel function. Often adopted in order to sound more modern, but deeply unsatisfactory: puts people on the same level as machinery or money, as in the phrase 'human and financial resources'. It is much better to refer to 'people', 'members' or 'associates' if that is what is meant; the problem is that there is not an attractive alternative way of describing the personnel function.

human resources audit
Internal or external inspection of a firm's personnel policies and procedures to ensure that they comply with the law and represent corporate best practice.

hygiene factors
Also called 'maintenance factors'. Herzberg's name for basic economic needs, which he contrasted to motivation factors meeting deeper aspirations. The basic idea is that good hygiene is necessary but not enough.

I

ILE (Inter-Linked Economy)
Kenichi Ohame's phrase for the 'borderless' economy comprising the USA, Europe and Japan (the Triad), and increasingly taking in aggressive, outward-looking economies such as Korea, Taiwan, Hong Kong and Singapore.

industrial democracy
Power sharing within industry between management and workers, which may take the form of worker-directors and boards elected by workers.

industrial engineering
Application of science and technology to production and office management in order to increase efficiency.

industrial marketing
Marketing to other business firms rather than the consumer.

industrial relations
The handling of negotiations between management and trade unions or other representatives of employees.

inertia selling
1. Sending unsolicited goods by mail in the hope that they will be appreciated and paid for, as with charity Christmas cards. **2.** More broadly, putting the onus on someone else to reject your solution, as when a memo is sent saying 'I will assume everyone agrees unless I hear to the contrary within the next week'.

intangible asset, intangible fixed asset, intangbles
A fixed asset which is 'non-physical' (literally, cannot be touched), such as patents, brand names or goodwill.

internal audit
Inspection of a firm's accounts and operations by a small, high-level team of internal accountants to ensure that the accounts give a true record of its affairs and that operations have been carried out honestly and to required standards.

internal funds
Cash generated by a company's own operations.

investor relations (IR)
The serious branch of PR concerned with informing and capturing institutional investors: attracting them to and keeping them on the share register of particular quoted companies.

issued share capital
Also called allotted share capital: the amount of the authorized share capital that has actually been allotted to investors.

IT (Information Technology)
Collection, processing and dissemination of data via computers to provide an organization with information. Also means both the department that does this, and the associated hardware and software. In many organizations, sophisticated and expensive IT has not greatly improved the quality or speed of decision-making. This is not wholly the fault of IT or its providers, but more that careful thought has not been given to what information should be collected and how it should be used.

J

Jacques, Elliott (b. 1917)
Path-breaking Canadian psychologist and doctor who was a founder of the Tavistock Institute of Human Relations in London. Conducted a very long series of studies on the factory floor of the Glacier Metal Company between 1948 and 1965. Difficult to categorize because always eclectic and, some would say, at times confused. He is most famous for having developed a theory of the value of work based on the *time span of discretion*, which basically said that different levels of management should be based on how long it was before their decisions could be checked, and that people should be paid accordingly. The theory is developed at great length with a huge amount of supporting data and analysis. It encapsulates one important truth: that leaders of businesses should be concerned with the very long term. Apart from that, in my opinion, it is bizarre and unhelpful.

On the other hand, Jacques was well ahead of his time in many respects. He was one of the first to stress that organization charts do not tell the true story of who reports to whom, and that wise executives knew who their real managers and subordinates were, and acted accordingly. He was also one of the first to realize the importance of changing company culture and of employees feeling that the firm was run fairly.

j-curve
Term from economics, not much used by managers, indicating a small decrease in some variable (eg, revenues, profits) followed by a large, rapid increase.

joint venture
Term that can mean, precisely, a firm that is owned in some proportion by two parent firms; or more loosely, collaboration between two or more firms for specific purposes. The latter sense is sometimes called a strategic alliance.

junk bond
Loan stock carrying a high coupon used to finance small American companies and later large LBOs (Leveraged Buy Outs).

Juran, Joseph M (b. 1904)
Romanian-born American electrical engineer and quality guru, who was jointly responsible (with W Edwards Deming) for the quality revolution in Japan after 1950. He published his *Quality Control Handbook* in 1951 and began work in Tokyo in 1953. He developed Company-Wide Quality Management (CWQM), a systematic methodology for spreading the gospel of quality throughout a firm. He insisted that quality could not be delegated and was an early exponent of what has come to be known as empowerment; for him quality had to be the goal of each employee, individually and in teams, through self-supervision. He was less mechanistic than Deming and placed greater stress on human relations.

Just-In-Time (JIT)
Valuable system developed first in Japan for production management aimed at minimizing stock by having materials and work-in-progress delivered to the right place at the right time.

knowledge industry
One where know-how and expertise rather than low factor costs are the key to competitive advantage.

Knowledge Management Structure (KMS)
Concept put forward by Tom Peters as a development of the learning organization. The 'new' firm must destroy bureaucracy but needs to nurture knowledge and skill, building expertise in ways that enhance the power of market-scale units, and that encourage those units to contribute knowledge for the benefit of the firm as a whole.

L

LBO (Leveraged Buy Out)
American 1980s piece of financial engineering, whereby takeover bids are put together using a small amount of equity and a large amount of debt (hence: a high degree of leverage).

lead time
Time between placing an order and its delivery. Minimizing lead times is often the key to competitive advantage

lean enterprise
Catch-phrase describing re-engineered companies that have five attributes: (1) they embrace a cluster of cross-functional processes; (2) they include close relationships with suppliers, distributors and customers to enhance value continually; (3) they have a core of defined expertise; (4) functional areas like design, engineering, marketing, procurement, personnel and accounting should still exist, but be schools of learning and skill-bases that different teams in the firm can draw on; (5) careers should alternate between membership of multi-functional teams and time spent building up skill within particular functions or departments. Honda has used this alternating approach successfully both in Japan and the USA.

lean production
Techniques used to help companies attain low cost status (eg, Just-in-Time and TQM). The lean production system was pioneered by Toyota and involves three main points: (1) redesigning each process step so that it is part of a continuous flow; (2) setting up multi-functional teams; and (3) continually striving for improvement, both in terms of quality and cost reduction.

learning organization
Term first used by Chris Argyris to mean a firm that learns as it goes along, adjusting its way of doing business very responsively. The organization retains knowledge independently of its employees.

leverage
1. American word, increasingly used, for what the British call gearing. 2. bargaining power. 3. Operating leverage: the same as operational gearing, that is, the extent to which profits can be increased when revenues and capacity utilization rise.

Levitt, Theodore (b. 1925)
German-born American marketing guru, professor at Harvard Business School. Wrote the legendary *HBR* article on marketing myopia in 1960: it has since sold half a million reprints. The article said that firms and industries should be 'customer-satisfying' rather than 'goods-producing' in their orientation: marketing-led not production-led. He said that it was not good enough to meet customer demand with a new product, and then believe that the key to continued success was low-cost production. He criticized Fordism for giving the customer what was thought to be good for him, rather than continually being alert to what the customer wanted. Hence Ford's decline in the face of General Motors' policy of offering cars in any colour and later in the face of

the compact car from Japan and Europe. He also castigated the myopia of the US railroad industry in thinking that they were in the railroad business (a production-led view) rather than consumer transport; if they had had the latter view they would have diversified into airlines and not seen their business wither. Levitt was wholly right and partly wrong. He was well ahead of his time in telling firms to be customer-obsessed. But his railroads example and the other he gave (such as buggywhips) were simplistic and possibly wrong. What possible expertise or cost sharing did the railroads have for entering the airline business? Perhaps they should have been experts at marketing transport to passengers, expertise that would have been transferable. But they weren't, and if Penn Central had bought an airline it would have gone bust much quicker than it did. The criticism was right, the remedy wrong. More recently, Levitt has become a prophet of global brands.

Lewin, Kurt
German-born Jewish professor of psychology who fled to America from the Nazis in 1932. He originated the model of change that says that behaviour patterns need to be 'unfrozen' before they can be changed and then 'refrozen'. To help such change he designed the T-Group (see Encounter Group).

Likert, Rensis (1903-81)
American psychologist and researcher, who was a pioneer in studying leadership and management styles, and a great exponent of participation. He identified four types of management style, which he called System 1 through System 4: (1) Exploitative authoritarian: management by fear. (2) Benevolent autocracy: carrot more than stick, but top-down. (3) Consultative: communication is up and down, but decisions are still largely top-down. (4) Participative: decision-making in working groups which communicate with each other via individuals who are *linking pins*, team leaders or others who are also members of one or more other groups. Likert asserted that System 4 was better and more profitable. He also postulated a future System 5 in which all formal authority disappears.

limited company
A company with limited liability, where the most that shareholders can lose is what they have already put into the company.

limited partnership
Useful legal form, originally from Germany, where some partners (the limited partners) may have limited liability, while other partners (the general partners) still have unlimited liability. The general partners run the business, while the limited partners supply cash or assets or technology to the partnership, and can do so without suffering unlimited liability for something they cannot control.

line manager
Normal term for manager with subordinates. Generally implies that the manager is part of the 'line', that is, operational personnel, rather than 'staff',

which implies support or overhead functions. Confusingly, though, managers in staff functions can have line management responsibility for their own subordinates. In practice the distinction between line and staff is blurred; and perhaps it was never a very useful distinction in the first place.

liquidity
1. A firm's ability to pay its short-term liabilities. 2. The existence of cash available for investment and expenditure. 3. The amount of room to trade in a financial market: a liquid market is one able to absorb large sales or purchases because there is a good two-way market.

logistics
Very important process of moving goods and people to deliver product to customers by co-ordinating the whole delivery system. Includes raw material, work-in-progress and stock movement and scheduling, stock control, warehousing, packaging and physical distribution.

loss leader
Selling something at below cost to attract other business. The term is often used more loosely to include goods sold at below average profitability, even if not sold at a loss.

M

M&A
Universal abbreviation for mergers and acquisitions. Can describe the process of acquisition, but more normally the department of a merchant or investment bank that tries to stimulate acquisitions, or the whole concept of acquisition.

McGregor, Douglas (1906–64)
American social psychologist and central figure in the Human Relations School. He stressed the role of belief in management: everything stems from the mental models and beliefs held by managers. He pioneered two ways of describing managers' thinking: Theory X and Theory Y. Theory X was traditional carrot-and-stick thinking: workers were inherently lazy, needed to be supervised and motivated, and work was a necessary evil to provide money. Theory Y, on the other hand, posited that people wanted and needed to work, and what should be sought was the individual's commitment to the firm's objectives, and then the liberation of his or her abilities on behalf of those objectives. McGregor had great faith in what people could do if their potential was tapped.

make or buy decision
1. The decision on whether to make components or any other part of the product or service in-house, or whether to use outside suppliers. Make or buy has

long been a topic of debate, but it is becoming increasingly important. It can now determine relative profitability in an industry, as in computers. **2.** Igor Ansoff used make or buy to mean organic expansion versus expansion by acquisition.

management
From an Italian word meaning to handle horses, horsemanship. Generally held now to be achieving business objectives by mobilizing other people. But how, and with what mental model?

management accounting
The process of providing accounting information to management, as opposed to preparing accounts for external reporting purposes.

Management By Wandering Around (MBWA)
Open and participative style invented by Hewlett-Packard of face-to-face management that works well for them. The idea is to be aware of what is happening throughout the firm and in particular at lower levels. Not so much a technique as a value system.

management consulting
Covers a huge range of services and has an interesting industrial structure, with a few very large firms (the accounting consultancies, a few generalists like Booz Allen and PA, a few specialists like Proudfoot and Hay-MSL, and the leading strategy houses), many medium to small firms, and a massive tail of one-man-and-a-dog suppliers.

management development
Improving the skills, both technical and managerial, of managers.

margin
Usually means profit margin, the difference between price and cost.

marginal costing
1. Costing that does not include overheads. **2.** The practice of pricing some product at above marginal cost but below full cost, in order to produce a contribution. More properly called marginal-cost pricing or marginal pricing, but usually referred to as marginal costing. Dangerous if a significant proportion of revenues comes from this practice.

market capitalization
The total value of all the ordinary shares of a company. Sometimes also called market value.

Market Development Process (MDP)
An integrated approach to NPD and increasing sales, based on pooling efforts and understanding between sales, marketing, and other functions that have contact with customers.

marketing
Planning and carrying out all customer related activities except selling.

marketing-led
Until the late 1950s most Western firms were production-led. The focus was on making the product, expanding volume and driving down costs. In the early 1960s Theodore Levitt and others told managers to be marketing-led. The emphasis was now on winning the hearts and minds of customers and working out what new products to sell them. Marketing executives replaced those with production backgrounds as chief executives. More recently, in the 1980s and 1990s, customer obsession has become the watchword of the wise.

marketing mix
The Four Ps: *Product* (quality, branding, features, packaging); *Pricing*; *Promotion*; and *Place* (where sold and use of distributors). It is often instructive to compare the marketing mix used by your company compared with that of competitors, or to compare your marketing mix across different products.

market intelligence
Useful information about customer needs, perception of different competitors, and about what competitors are doing.

market leader
The firm with the greatest market share in a business segment. Leadership is usually very valuable.

market niche
A small business segment where leadership is valuable and attainable for small firms, where they are protected from competition from their larger brethren.

market penetration
1. The percentage of all potential customers (in a defined market) who have bought a company's product. 2. A similar meaning can be applied to the penetration of a product, from all competitors, in a market. Thus the penetration of colour TVs in the USA may be 99 per cent, regardless of which companies supply them.

market penetration pricing
Pricing in order to gain market share rapidly or establish a new product in the market place; that is, pricing lower than normal profit margins or even pricing at a loss.

market positioning
The relative position that a product has in a market, or the process of trying to attain a certain position.

market potential
How large a market might become with appropriate supply side actions.

market power
The ability to dictate terms to a market (eg, on pricing) as a result of market dominance (being much the largest supplier).

market research
Data collection and analysis to provide information about customers and competitors.

market saturation
When a product has reached as many new buyers as it is likely ever to reach, and is reduced to a lower level of replacement demand.

market segment
Part of a market where buyers have similar purchase criteria.

market skimming, market skimming pricing
Charging a high price for a new product so as to skim off what the first tranche of buyers are willing to pay, and then reducing the price after a time to capture the next tranche.

market structure
The characteristics of a market that will influence its profitability, including: the degree of concentration in the market, the behaviour of competitors in it; the bargaining power of suppliers; and the bargaining power of buyers.

market targeting
Usually refers to tactical market segmentation: trying to reach and raise market share of a particular type of buyer. Can also refer, more usefully, to business segmentation, that is, trying to increase share and obtain or reinforce leadership in a particular business segment.

Maslow, Abraham (1908–1970)
Inventor of the *hierarchy of needs* which stressed the progressive upgrading of needs as earlier needs were satisfied, culminating in 'self-actualization'. Not wholly correct as an observation of what was, or is, industrial reality; the theory under-estimates the propensity of people to want money and more money and continuously upgrade their standard of living.

mass manufacture, mass marketing
Selling a standard product in high volume around the world.

matrix, matrix management, matrix organization
An organization structure which is not based on a simple chain of command, but where individuals may report to two (or more) bosses.

Mayo, Elton (1880–1949)
Australian founder of the Human Relations School and propagandist of the Hawthorne Studies at Western Electric in 1927–32. Realized the importance of self-esteem and group consensus. Also one of the first to realize the importance of the informal organization and how it could be either destructive or harnessed. He pioneered proper communications between management and workforce, that helped ultimately to corrode the negative power of trade unions. Prophet of teamwork and securing the commitment of the individual and the group to corporate objectives.

MBI (Management Buy-In)
A takeover where a group of outside managers, backed by venture capitalists and banks, buys a firm, generally an under-performing quoted company.

MBO (Management Buy-Out)
A bid by the top managers of a firm to buy it, backed by providers of equity (venture capitalists) and debt (commercial bankers).

MbO (Management by Objectives)
Venerable Anglo-Saxon management tool originally conceived by Peter Drucker in the 1950s and introduced into the UK by John Humble, who defined it as 'the attempt to clarify the goals of management objectively, so that the responsibility for achieving the goals was reasonably distributed round the management team.' Basically MbO invites all managers to sit down and compile a list of objectives for which they were willing to be held accountable, and agree with their boss these objectives, together with how to measure them and the timetable involved.

mezzanine, mezzanine debt
Debt that carries a high rate of interest, that is the 'mezzanine floor', half-way between normal debt and equity.

middle manager
One between top management and the shop floor. Imprecise but still useful term. The death of the middle manager has been predicted by many management futurologists who claim that successful firms will have almost no middle managers.

minimum stock level
The level below which stock should not go. Can be precisely calculated.

minority interest, minority
Holding held by one firm in another, where there is a majority holding by another firm. There are laws protecting the rights of minority holders ('minorities'), but the holders of minority interests in private (unquoted) companies are very exposed to what the holders of the majority interest do. Unlike such holders in quoted companies, they cannot easily sell if they do not like what is happening. This has led some observers to claim (with not ungrounded hyperbole) that a minority interest in a private company is worthless.

Mintzberg, Henry (b. 1939)
Canadian strategy and management guru.

mission
What a company is for; why it exists; its role in the world.

mission statement
A document that often pays lip service to the idea that a company should have a flesh-and-blood purpose, but occasionally reflects what a company believes in.

Mittelstand
Germany's owner-managed, medium-sized firms, usually of a few hundred employees (up to a maximum of about 3,000).

N

5

net assets
The net worth of a business, that is, total assets minus liabilities. Also called NAV (Net Asset Value).

net book value
The value of an asset recorded in the company's books, after deducting (that is, net of) accumulated amortization and depreciation.

net operating assets
Synonym for capital employed. The total money tied up in a business in fixed assets and working capital. Also equal to the sum of the firm's equity, debt and any corporation tax payable.

network analysis
Also called PERT (Programme Evaluation and Review Techniques). Drawing charts for major engineering projects to plan the work.

networking
1. Linking of computers so they can communicate with each other. 2. Using a network of professional contacts to sell worth or exchange favours. 3. Part of

Charles Handy's Shamrock Organization. **4.** Linking a firm to others that can help it by a series of informal, mutually reinforcing contacts and contracts.

networks
To be successful, firms need to bring knowledge to bear quickly and effectively and compound that knowledge over time. Part of this must be done in-house, but the depth and breadth of network that a firm possesses with other firms will also be key.

non-executive director, non-exec
British name for outside director. Non-executives have been posited as the solution to many problems of corporate governance, and the Cadbury Report in the UK recommended that there be more, more highly qualified, more independent, more powerful and better paid non-executives. The idea is that qualified outsiders can give an additional perspective and exercise control over the executives, when this is important, and so protect shareholders and society against abuses of managerial power.

O

occupational testing
Psychological and psychometric tests used in the world of work intended to gain an objective assessment of personal attributes, such as aptitudes, interests or personality, and to provide information which is difficult to glean from interview impressions or past performance.

OD (Organization Development)
School of thought and practice of developing management groups in order to improve interpersonal and organizational effectiveness.

off-balance sheet financing
Using financial engineering to avoid having to put assets on the balance sheet; any form of finance that does require a liability to appear on a firm's balance sheet.

Ohmae, Kenichi (b. 1943)
Brilliant, un-Japanese, Japanese, whose book *The Mind of the Strategist* (published in Japan in 1975, but not in the USA until 1982) is one of the best books on strategy, and who contributed towards the development of Toyota's Just-In-Time system. An analyst who gives a higher place to intuition and insight, Ohmae was among the first to drive everything outward from the customer, and place the customer at the heart of the firm's value system. In recent years, notably in his landmark 1990 book, *The Borderless World*, Ohmae has turned his attention to the way that the world's largest companies are creating what he calls the ILE (Inter-Linked Economy) of the USA, Europe and Japan/Asia, based

largely on the need to meet the requirements of demanding consumers in all important economies. He argues persuasively the case for inevitable and beneficent globalization, albeit based on local globalization rather than universal products, a process being slowed down but not stopped by the rearguard actions of protectionists, bureaucrats and governments around the world. The companies forcing the change are becoming multilocals rather than multinationals.

operating cash flow
Cash that comes in (during an accounting period) as a result of the company's operations, not including any cash flows of a non-operational nature (such as payments of interest, tax or dividends, or cash received from issuing more equity or taking on more debt).

operating expense
Expense incurred by a firm's underlying operations, not including financial items such as interest or tax.

operating profit
Profit from a firm's underlying operations, before taking account of interest paid or received, or taxes.

operations management
The management of production. Should be closely integrated with all other functions, especially those related to serving customers.

option
The right to buy or sell shares (or other financial instruments) at a certain price (the exercise price) within a defined period. Some options in major corporations are traded options, that is, they can be bought or sold readily: traded options are more volatile than the underlying shares to which they relate, and therefore can make or lose large amounts of money quickly.

OR (Operations Research)
Also called Operational Research in the UK. OR began in the USA and boomed during the 1960s and 1970s. It involves applying mathematics and statistics to management issues, principally those related to production, logistics and forecasting.

organic growth
Growth from expanding market share, being in growth markets, and entering new markets from existing resources; not growth by acquisition, merger or joint venture. Also called internal growth.

organizational analysis
Using organization theory to define or restructure reporting relationships in an organization. Also called organization design.

organizational behaviour
General term for academic work on organizational effectiveness, drawing on the disciplines of psychology and sociology. Again, closely associated with the Human Relations School, many of whom were professors of organizational behaviour.

outsourcing
Buying components, goods or services from outside.

overcapacity
When industry supply exceeds industry demand. Can persist for long periods.

overheads
Costs (like top management, administration, finance, IT and personnel departments, R&D and distribution) that are not allocated directly to particular products. The term is somewhat imprecise, because product line profitability exercises often do allocate such costs, though they are still generally called overheads. Increasing product complexity and the increased factory efficiency (resulting in a decrease in non-overhead costs) has raised the importance of overheads. Firms that can organize themselves effectively around customers and their needs, and therefore have lower overhead costs than competitors, will be the winners in the future.

P

P&L account, P&L, profit and loss account
The second most important accounting statement, after the balance sheet. Explains how the retained profit as shown on the balance sheet got there: how and why it changed over the period, by starting with revenues and then deducting all costs including taxes.

parent company, parent
A company with two or more subsidiaries.

parenting advantage
A new term essential to the management of multi-business companies. These companies are being challenged because they are often worth more broken up or slimmed down than their current market capitalization.

Pareto rule
The 80/20 rule, that 80 per cent of sales or profits or any other variable may come from 20 per cent of the products.

Parkinson's law
C Northcote Parkinson's dictum that 'work expands to fill the time available for its completion'.

partnership
Legal structure which has many advantages in most countries but one major disadvantage: in nearly all cases it consigns the working partners to unlimited liability, that is, creditors can pursue the partners for all their personal assets in the event of default.

patent
Intellectual Property Rights (IPR) granted to inventors of new products, processes, etc. Rules are highly complex and differ from country to country.

payback, payback period
The time it takes for an investment to return its original capital.

pay systems
Also called in the US 'Compensation' systems. Methods of determining who should be paid what in an organization, by means of a systematic structure.

PBIT (Profit Before Interest & Tax)
Also called EBIT and operating profit.

PBT (Profit Before Tax)
Profit after all expenses including interest but before corporation tax.

PD, P/D Ratio, PDR (Price Dividend Ratio)
The current price of a share divided by the total dividends per share in the previous financial year.

PE, P/E, PER (Price Earnings Ratio)
The number of times that the stock market multiplies the after-tax earnings of a company in order to place a total value (the market capitalization or market value) on the company's shares.

performance-related pay (PRP)
Popular in some countries (such as the UK currently) because of pay breaks, but in any case a better way than basing pay on a job evaluation system.

personnel
1. The department or function concerned with recruitment, selection, induction, training, management development, manpower planning, appraisal, pay systems, and other matters related to people in an organization, and also dealing

with industrial relations, particularly when the workforce is unionized. Sometimes chillingly called human resources. **2.** Employees.

PERT (Programme Evaluation and Review Technique)
See Network Analysis. PERT was the very early (1958) forerunner of Just-In-Time (JIT).

Peter principle
Laurence Peter (b. 1919) said that people in an organization would rise to their level of incompetence, through being promoted until they failed to do well in their current job. Perverse, logical, generally untrue.

Peters, Tom (b. 1942)
Probably the world's foremost contemporary management guru.

PIMS (Profit Impact of Market Strategy)
A co-operative database originating from research by GE in the USA that collects data from member firms about market share, profitability, and a variety of other variables (like R&D spend) that might be expected to influence profits. The data is confidential but aggregate results are fed back to members so that they can see how to raise profits. Some of the research has been published and demonstrated beyond reasonable doubt that high market share correlates with high profits, though there are significant industry variations.

PLC, plc, (Public Limited Company)
British acronym corresponding to French SA, Dutch NV, etc. A common misperception is that PLCs have to be quoted companies: most PLCs are not. They just have slightly more onerous paid-up capital and reporting requirements than limited companies.

Porter, Michael (b. 1947)
Harvard Business School professor, consultant, and the star of corporate strategy worldwide.

portfolio
A very useful word, but confusing because it has so many different meanings, depending on the context. **1.** An investor's portfolio is his or her holdings of shares, the idea being that holding several shares (a portfolio) is lower risk than holding just one or two. **2.** A firm's portfolio is its relative market share positions in different business segments, or, more loosely, its spread of activities. **3.** An individual's work portfolio is all the different activities he or she has, particularly if self-employed and working with or for several clients. The idea comes from Charles Handy, who believes that knowledge workers will have shorter careers in more firms and will increasingly divide their time into two, three or more areas that they choose themselves.

portfolio management
How a portfolio in any of the senses above is managed. In sense 1, it refers to effective diversification of risk by holding about a dozen or 15 different shares. In sense 2, it refers to management of the firm's business portfolio along lines indicated by the BCG Matrix or any other way a firm decides to handle the transfer of cash and other scarce resources between its businesses.

positioning
Finding a marketing position for a product or a company that differentiates it from competitors and occupies a 'slot in the brain'.

PR (Public Relations)
1. A firm's activities designed to put it in the most favourable light with consumers, government, regulators, and the public at large. Means used include press releases, annual reports and other corporate literature, corporate lobbying, company videos and in-house magazines, as well as attempts to place favourable articles in the financial press, and fend off unwelcome ones. 2. The internal department and/or external consultants that provide the service.

pricing strategy
1. Setting prices in order to gain a long-term competitive advantage, rather than to maximize short-term profits. There are three main rules: (1) in introducing a product, price at or below cost in order to gain volume, cut costs, and deter competitors; (2) in fighting competition, especially when the market is still growing, consider sudden, startlingly short price cuts, so that the price is immediately perceived as low by the consumer, and as too low to match by competitors; and (3) ensure that the true costs of all products are known, including all overhead costs, and that the more complex, special products are not under-priced and the standard, high-volume products under-priced. 2. More broadly, the major decisions made on pricing.

process/product-based organization
The opposite of functional organizations and increasingly believed to be better. The benefits are better co-ordination and integration of work, faster response to customers and quicker time to market, simpler control systems, fewer people, and greater employee fulfilment and creativity.

production
Process of manufacturing. Must be integrated with the rest of the customer-satisfying process.

productivity
Any measure of output divided by a measure of input (eg, profit per pound of capital employed). Productivity is not a clear end in itself: it depends on the measure adopted and why.

product life cycle
Ludicrous but once well-respected theory that all products go through a life analogous to that of animals: birth/launch; youth/growth; maturity; decline and death.

profit centre
Unit of a firm where the manager in charge is responsible for meeting a profit budget. The preferred term nowadays is SBU (Strategic Business Unit): all SBUs are profit centres, though not all profit centres would pass the strict definition of SBU.

profitability
The amount of profit made for each pound or dollar of capital invested. Normally expressed as Return On Capital Employed (ROCE) and/or Return On Equity (ROE).

profit maximization, profit optimization
Words commonly used but woolly and unsatisfactory. There are three main issues: (1) which profits? Many would say EPS (earnings per share), as these drive share prices and hence shareholder wealth. But EPS can be manipulated, and need not turn into cash, which is all that matters ultimately; (2) which time period? The shareholders are a constantly changing body in a quoted company, so which shareholders should one be trying to satisfy? Does a high share price next year have a higher or lower priority than a high share price in 30 years' time? To increase profits and share price long term may require actions like market share gain or price cuts that will hurt in the short term: see short-termism; and (3) many argue that shareholders should not be the only, or even the main, constituency that managers should be trying to satisfy: customers, employees, or the long-term health of the firm itself may be other important constituencies. In practice, few firms and their top managers are really trying to maximize profits, whatever they say.

Profit Related Pay (PRP)
A particular form of Performance-Related Pay which in the UK has significant tax advantages to employees.

project management
Managing change in an organization by means of an ad hoc, temporary group (often called a taskforce) drawn from different areas and disciplines, in order to achieve specific objectives. Once these have been attained the project management team is disbanded.

psychological contract
Term invented by Ed Schein meaning the implicit agreement between an individual and his firm about his role and the way he is treated, and the extent of

his obligations to the firm. If the contract is to work long term, the implicit assumptions in the contract must be consistently observed by both sides.

psychological testing
Using tests drawn from psychology using standardized samples of behaviour to help appraise candidates for recruitment or promotion.

psychometric testing
Use of tests of aptitudes and abilities. Often used alone for applicants for junior level jobs, and in conjunction with psychological testing on applicants for middle and senior level jobs.

Q

Qualification (of accounts), qualified opinion, qualified auditors' report
When the auditors cannot say that the accounts represent a 'true and fair' picture without making a qualification, because of some reservations or lack of data about the business.

Quality
Along with low costs and high service, quality is the third member of the trilogy holding the key to customer satisfaction, competitive advantage, and long-term corporate success. Arguably, quality is the most important of the three. Without quality, a low-cost position will mean low prices and low margins; without quality, high service will not satisfy customers. Quality is more and more important the greater the value added and product complexity. Quality is also crucial when a product is part of a bigger product or business system, which is increasingly the case.

Quality was the great business revolution of the West in the 1980s, but of Japan in the 1950s and 1960s. Quality came from the West, but has found its most prolific breeding ground in Asia, and now not just in Japan. Quality is an integral part of a management approach, not a box on its own. Quality should not be inspected, it should be in-built; it should not be a department, but the loving responsibility of all employees. Quality should not be part of a process, or a step, or a function, or an area of expertise: it should be the inside and the outside of any product produced, the core that runs through everything, the glue that binds everything, the commitment to the customer that unites the whole firm and binds each individual to each group, each group to the firm, and the firm to the customer.

Quality cannot be practised properly in a firm that has a resented hierarchy, alienation, imperfect communications, sectional interests, or lack of commitment of people to the firm and its purpose. Quality cannot be practised without a passion for quality; conscientious, rational behaviour is not enough. Quality means constantly striving to do things better, to make current standards of excellence obsolete, to push oneself and one's colleagues to the edge of achievement. Quality is not easy and should not be viewed as a series of techniques, like quality circles of TQM (Total Quality Management), though these can start to change behaviour. Quality is in the hearts and minds of the workforce.

Quality Circle (QC)
System that became popular in Japan and has since spread extensively where groups of workers meet to discuss how to raise quality. A genuinely participative technique that requires full commitment from employees if it is to work well. Not all Western QCs have been a success, in some cases being seen as a manipulative attempt by management to extract more from its workers. QCs still exist but are now generally seen as part of TQM (Total Quality Management).

Quality Control (QC)
Refers both to the process of controlling quality and the department and people who do it. QC departments used to be popular, but were based on a false idea: that quality was external to production and the way to get higher quality was to inspect and reject poor quality items. People now realize that quality must be built into the product at the start and that quality is the responsibility of everyone in the firm. Quality control makes no more sense than 'service control'.

R

R&D (Research and Development)
Key department of firm in a knowledge industry like pharmaceuticals or any high-tech business, and many others. The quality of the R&D staff and its culture, and the degree to which it is keyed into marketing and customers, may be the most important competitive advantage in such a firm.

raider, corporate raider
Person or firm that is highly acquisitive and preys on under-performing companies.

range
Product range, or the extent to which a supplier 'covers the waterfront' or specializes.

range versus focus
The dilemma of whether to expand the number of products by line extension and/or entering adjacent segments, in order to realize economies of scope, or alternatively to focus very tightly in order to reduce or avoid the costs of complexity.

rate of return
1. The IRR (Internal Rate of Return) on an investment. **2.** Sometimes used loosely to mean either return on capital employed (ROCE) or return on equity (ROE).

rationalization
1. Cutting costs and delayering an organization by removing a large number of employees. **2.** Making something simpler and cleaner, like product line rationalization, which means cutting out slow-selling or unprofitable lines. **3.** Industry rationalization, which means removing capacity unilaterally or by agreement with other suppliers.

RCP (Relative Cost Position)
The cost position of a firm in a product relative to that of a competitor.

RCR (Relative Customer Retention)
How well a firm retains its customers relative to its competitors. A key influence on relative profitability.

realization
1. Selling something; turning an asset into cash. **2.** What is actually realized, as in price realization; price received, not list price or asking price.

real money
Money adjusted for inflation, so you can compare over time without this distortion.

relational database
A database which incorporates clever software, enabling it to be organized or recalled easily in any way desired, not just in the way it has been put in.

relationship marketing
Understanding your customers and their customers so that you can provide the most effective product or service and ensure that its role is properly appreciated.

reorganization
1. Changing reporting relationships and possibly the whole way the firm is organized. **2.** A euphemism for downsizing or redundancy.

repeat purchases, repeat purchase rate
The proportion of customers who, having made a purchase, buy from the same supplier. A key indicator of customer satisfaction.

replacement cost
The cost of replenishing stock or replacing a fixed asset. Replacement cost should be borne in mind when pricing.

repositioned, repositioning
Marketing term meaning the process of moving a product (or even a whole industry) from one consumer perception to another.

re-segment
To redefine a market to your firm's advantage, to create a new segment, based on a detailed understanding of why a particular group of consumers buys a product.

resource allocation
The way an organization allocates resources, principally money.

resources
1. Term used in ABC analysis, meaning things like people, machines or computer systems that perform work and cost money. **2.** Things available to central management which can be channelled to or taken from businesses. The 'things' are usually cash, people, technology, and other assets.

retained earnings, retained profit
1. Profit after tax in any year not distributed to shareholders in dividends, but retained in the business. **2.** The total amount of such profits that has accumulated over time.

retention ratio
The proportion of earnings in a year that is retained profit rather than distributed in dividends. If a firm makes £5 million after tax and £2 million is distributed in dividends, the retention ratio is 3/5 = 60 per cent.

return on assets (ROA)
Operating profit divided by net assets. Not a good measure of performance.

return on capital employed (ROCE)
Increasingly actually called 'ROCE', as though it were one Italian word. One of the best measures of profitability: operating profit divided by capital employed.

return on equity (ROE)
A good measure of corporate profitability: profit before tax (or sometimes profit after tax) divided by shareholders' equity. It thus takes into account the extent to which gearing (leverage) is used, and is the best measure of how productively the most scarce resource from shareholders' point of view, their money, is being used. Also called return on shareholders' funds.

return on sales
Operating profit (not profit before tax) divided by sales. Also called ROS.

revaluation
Process to increase (or, rarely, decrease) the value of an asset to reflect a change in its market value. The change in value is reflected on the balance sheet by a change in the firm's reserves.

Revans, Reg (b. 1907)
Obscure British educationalist and consultant who invented action learning, the title also of his 1974 book. The book was remaindered but Action Learning had a better fate as a movement. Well ahead of his time and unjustly neglected.

revenue
1. The amount that is paid or due to a firm for supplying goods or services, and recorded in its books. Revenue is usually stated net of sales taxes such as VAT, that is, after deducting (or before adding on) the tax. 2. The total annual amount of money received by a firm for its goods or services: a synonym for turnover. Note that revenue does not mean profit, though it is occasionally confused with it.

reverse engineering
Breaking down a competitor's product to see how it was made and analyze its costs.

reverse takeover
1. When a smaller company (usually measured by market capitalization) takes over a bigger one. 2. When the management of an acquired company emerges on top in the new entity.

right brain processes
The creative and intuitive part of the brain.

right first time
The idea that goods should not need to be inspected for quality, because the objective should be to build quality in and ensure that all product is of high quality the first (and only) time round. Not only increases quality, but decreases cost and speeds up time to market.

rights issue
When a firm issues new shares and the existing shareholders have the right to buy them before they are offered to new shareholders, thus avoiding dilution.

risk analysis
Systematic review of any business risk, for example of doing business with a new customer, or entering a new market, or of making a large investment.

risk capital
Another name for shareholders' equity investments, emphasizing the greater degree of risk attached to this class of instrument.

risk premium
The amount being paid or necessary to be paid over and above a riskless investment such as a government security.

RMS (Relative Market Share)
The share of a firm in a business segment divided by the share of the largest competitor that the firm has. Much more important than market share as an absolute number.

rollout
Implementation of a plan, or replication of a model in a large number of areas, as with the rollout of a fast-food chain.

ROI (Return On Investment)
US term used as a synonym for Return On Capital Employed (ROCE).

RONA (Return On Net Assets)
Operating profit divided by NET ASSETS, expressed as a percentage.

ROS (Return On Sales)
Operating profit over sales.

RPP (Relative Price Position)
A complement to RCP (Relative Cost Position). RPP looks at the price realization for two or more competitors in the same product or service. RPP shows how far there is a brand, quality or distribution advantage.

S

sales
1. The total revenues or turnover of a firm in a period. **2.** The sales department in a firm, or its selling activities.

sales force, salesforce
The total group conducting sales activities, including reps (representatives) covering a region, key account salesmen, telesales staff, demonstrators and merchandizers, sales management and general management.

SBU (Strategic Business Unit)
A profit centre within a firm that is organized as an autonomous unit and that corresponds roughly to one particular market.

scenario
Term made popular by Royal Dutch/Shell for an imagined future.

Schein, Edgar H
Ed Schein is a distinguished and commercially astute American social psychologist based at MIT. He is 'well networked', having worked with and been influenced by Doug McGregor, as well as having close links with Warren Bennis, Chris Argyris and Charles Handy, whom he taught. Schein was one of the first to focus on process consulting, the title of his 1969 book, which involves looking at how a firm operates and its culture and helping it be more effective, rather than supplying expert content-oriented consulting. Schein has been influential for the past 20 years, and has added three concepts to management language: besides process consulting, there are also the psychological contract and the career anchor.

Schonberger, Richard J (b. 1937)
Interesting and creative American industrial engineer and the author of the two best-selling books on manufacturing: *Japanese Manufacturing Techniques* (1982) and *World Class Manufacturing*(1986). Introduced Just-In-Time and other techniques used in Japan to the US market in the early 1980s. But his most interesting book is *Building a Chain of Customers* (1990), which argues boldly that world-class business can only be built if each function in a business is viewed as the customer of the preceding stage, all the way to the final customer. Schonberger laid the foundations for re-engineering and for the recent theories of Tom Peters and other prophets of customer obsession.

Schumacher, E F (1911–77)
Fritz Schumacher will be for ever associated with the phrase 'Small is Beautiful', actually coined for him by the publishers of his collection of essays *Small is Beautiful* in 1973; the subtitle was also intriguing: *A Study of Economics As If People Mattered*. He was a German economist who was a socialist and worked for the British National Coal Board between 1950 and 1970. Some have commented that his reputation rests on pretty slender foundations, since his writing was neither extensive nor detailed, and he himself was a pretty odd bird. On the other hand, he did come up with one-and-a-half Big Ideas, and if he was lucky to be influential, we too are fortunate that he was. *Small is Beautiful* was an interesting idea, not just because it ran counter to the prevailing corporatist mentality, but because Schumacher was the first explicitly to urge that big organizations should try to simulate smallness. He did not advocate breaking up the National Coal Board, for example, but claimed that it could be seen as a federation of semi-autonomous units, each with its own feel and culture.

Scientific Management
The body of knowledge and practice associated with F W Taylor (1856–1917) that was the first systematic attempt to make management a profession based on clear principles.

S-curve
The growth pattern resembling an S: slow to pick up, followed by a period of maximum growth, then a point of inflection leading to gradually slower growth.

segment
Part of a market identified by one or more firms as a target. A sharp distinction should be drawn between market segments, which are defined by marketeers and very often have at best tactical significance, and business segments, that are arenas within which a firm can establish a competitive advantage. A small, defensible business segment is sometimes called a niche.

segmentation
Most usefully, the process of analyzing customers, costs and competitors in order to decide where and how to wage the competitive battle; or a description of the competitive map according to the contours of the business segments. Sadly, segmentation is often used to describe a more limited (and often misleading) exercise in dividing up customer groups.

Seven S, 7S framework
A framework for thinking about a firm's personality; a diagnostic tool for describing any company, developed by Peters and Waterman and their then colleagues in McKinsey around 1980. Seven elements of an organization, all beginning with S – strategy, structure, systems, style, skills, staff and shared values – can be used as a checklist. Do the Ss fit well together, or are they inconsistent or unclear? When the Ss fit well together and reinforce each other, the organization is likely to be moving forward purposefully; where the Ss are in conflict, it is likely to lack unity and momentum.

shareholder value, shareholder wealth
Phrase often used to mean what is in shareholders' interests, as in 'create shareholder value'. Often means 'get the share price as high as sustainably possible', and includes a sense of medium- and long-term value creation rather than short-term share price maximization (or manipulation). Generally not a neutral term: the users tend to imply that the main or exclusive responsibility of top management is to maximize shareholder value rather than worry about other stakeholders.

Share options, executive share options
Rights granted to valuable employees to buy shares in the future at today's price and, thus, if the shares perform well, to make a potentially large capital gain sometimes amounting to millions of dollars or pounds for top executives.

share price index, share index
A basket of shares against which individual shares or the performance of a portfolio can be judged.

shell, shell company
A quoted company but one which has few or no trading activities and where much or all of the value of the company is in its quote.

short-term
Generally means something within a 1–2 year horizon.

short-termism
Tendency to think more about the short term (and especially this year, half-year or quarter's financial results) than about the long term. Generally recognized to be a major problem with Anglo-Saxon business.

Sloan, Alfred P (1875–1966)
One of the very few industrialists to be referred to as an authority on management; head of General Motors from 1923 to 1955; author of *My Years with General Motors* (1963) and notable for three reasons. First, he virtually invented the decentralized, divisionalized firm, establishing what he called *federal decentralization*, when he transformed General Motors in the early 1920s from a mass of untidy and overlapping entities, with sporadic but ineffective central control, into eight separate divisions (five car divisions and three component divisions) which were treated as though they were separate businesses, but which were subject to professional controls on finance and policy from the Centre.

Second, Sloan changed the structure of the car industry and its segmentation, and provided a model for how other firms could do the same. When he took over, there were just two car segments in the USA: the mass market, dominated by the black Ford Model T, which had 60 per cent of the total car market volume; and the very low-volume, high-class market. Sloan aimed to plug the gap between these two markets by creating five price and performance segments and aiming that the five markets so created should be dominated by one of the new five GM car ranges: the Chevrolet, Oldsmobile, Pontiac, Buick and Cadillac (this represented a range rationalization for GM from eight competing models). He turned Ford's no-choice policy on its head by introducing a range of colours and features so that cars could be customized at relatively little extra cost, as well as introducing new models each year to encourage trading up.

The segmentation fitted neatly with the divisionalization: each of the five car segments and models had its own division, thus inventing the idea of the SBU (Strategic Business Unit) about 50 years before GE actually articulated it.

Sloan's third innovation was to establish the three component divisions as separate profit centres that supplied not only the five car divisions but also outside customers.

slot in the brain
The effective *positioning* of a product or service can result in it coming to occupy a unique and memorable 'slot in the brain' as with the Avis slogan, 'we try harder'.

small firm

There is no accepted definition of what is a small firm. Nowadays the preferred terminology is *developing firm* or SME (Small and Medium-sized Enterprises).

sole trader

1. Individual businessman owning 100% of his concern. **2.** By extension, someone in a firm, especially a professional firm like a solicitor's, who behaves as though he or she is a one-person business, and tries to ignore responsibilities to partners or other colleagues.

SPU (Strategic Planning Unit)

A product-market segment that requires its own strategy, even though organizationally it may be part of a larger grouping, the SBU (Strategic Business Unit).

stakeholder

Loaded term now widely used to mean someone who has a real or psychological 'stake' in an organization: used to include anyone who has significant dealings with it, such as customers, employees, suppliers, distributors, joint venture partners, the local community, bankers and shareholders. It is generally a normative rather than a descriptive term, implying that the user believes that a number of stakeholders have a right to determine what happens within an organization, and more particularly in a firm, rather than just the owners.

stakeholder theory

The theory that a firm should be run in the interests of all its stakeholders rather than just the shareholders.

strategic alliance

A mutual commitment by two or more independent companies to co-operate together for specific commercial objectives, usually because the cost of development is too high for a single company, and/or because the companies have complementary technologies or competences. A strategic alliance is different from a joint venture in that no legal entity is set up, and the scope of co-operation can be both broader and deeper, despite (or perhaps because of) the absence of tight contractual definitions of the partners' obligations.

strategic fit

The extent to which a firm's strategy fits its capabilities.

strategic intent

The overall medium- to long-term strategic objective of a company.

strategic planning

One of three main management styles identified by Andrew Campbell and Michael Goold, and the one that gives the centre the greatest role in planning the firm's strategy and ensuring that it is carried through. Strategic Planning companies have relatively few core businesses, and seek to establish long-term competitive advantage in each of these by means of co-ordinated, global strategies. The Centre works with the divisional or SBU managers to develop strategy, and has a major influence both on business unit strategy and on the overall corporate strategy, which is usually much more than just the addition of the SBU strategies. The Centre often pays great attention to encouraging synergies between the divisions and developing and nurturing a common winning culture. Annual financial targets are less important than longer-term strategic objectives.

strategy

Over-used word, and one that commonly confuses what a company should be doing (and sometimes, indeed, what it says it is doing) with what it is actually doing: the word strategy can and is applied in both cases. To differentiate, the word is defined below in these two separate senses.

1. In the normative sense, a good strategy is the commercial logic of a business, that defines why a firm can have competitive advantage and a place in the sun. To be complete, a strategy must include a definition of the domain – the lines of business, types of customer and geographical reach – in which the firm competes. It must also include a definition of the firm's distinctive competences and the competitive advantage that gives the firm a special hold on the chosen business domain.
2. Strategy also means what a company does, how it actually positions itself commercially and conducts the competitive battle. You can always attempt to describe a competitor's strategy, whether or not you think it is sound. In this sense, a strategy is what a firm does, not what it says it does, or what its strategy documents propound.

stream

Business unit or product of one type. Cadbury Schweppes has two streams (of business): confectionery and soft drinks.

structure

1. Organization structure. The generally accepted view now (first propounded by Peter Drucker) is that 'structure should follow strategy', that is, first determine the strategy, and then ensure that the structure is fully aligned with it. In practice, structure and strategy may be determined simultaneously, as with Alfred Sloan and General Motors in the early 1920s: a new marketing strategy based on innovative segmentation was introduced alongside a new divisional structure to implement the strategy. Tom Peters takes a third view: that Chandler was 100 per cent wrong. Peters holds that the structure of a firm will determine a firm's strategy, and certainly will prevent it changing radically. 2. Market structure.

succession planning
The very important task of ensuring that there is a nominated or implicit successor for each key manager.

supervisory board
Top board of many large companies in Germany, Holland and Scandinavia that exercises general supervision over the firm's affairs and is responsible for appointing and removing members of the executive board. Supervisory boards are generally elected by a combination of shareholders and trade unions.

supply chain
The relationships between customers, distributors and suppliers.

supply side
1. Emphasis on what suppliers provide and initiatives they take, rather than on the demand side, what customers require. Many innovations take root not because of articulated consumer demand, but because of persistent faith on the part of the suppliers: the refrigerator and the Sony Walkman are two examples. **2.** A school of economics in favour of removing restrictions on business, in order to free up the supply side.

sustainable profits
The level of profits or profitability that can be reached and sustained indefinitely in steady state.

SWOT analysis
An overview of a company's prospects, generally undertaken in a loose and qualitative way by collecting management opinions about the company's Strengths, Weaknesses, Opportunities and Threats.

synergy
2 + 2 = 5 (or more), rather than 4, or 3 (negative synergy). Usually used in the context of an acquisition: if there is no synergy expected, it is difficult to justify paying a premium for an acquisition; and even if it is a merger with no premium, why bother unless there is some synergy? There is often a great deal of cynicism about the reality of claimed synergies, and the word is certainly overused, but it is a key concept.

There are really two different types of synergy: structural synergy, where the synergy derives from combining resources to lower costs or raise revenues; and management synergy, where the improvement is due to better management, without structural change. Some people only use synergy in the structural sense.

T

tall organization
One with many levels: opposite of flat organization. Tall organizations in the West are usually bureaucratic and inefficient; in Japan there are many examples of successful tall organizations.

tangible fixed asset
Property, plant or equipment that can be pointed to and touched.

task force, taskforce
A short-term team put together to solve a particular problem. The team is usually drawn from different parts of an organization, cutting across functional and national lines of command, and sometimes involves an outside catalyst as well.

Tavistock Institute
Much of the best early work on the sociology of industry was conducted by the Tavistock Institute of Human Relations in London in the years between 1945 and 1970.

team building
The practice of encouraging individuals to work productively in teams and of making particular groups of workers effective as a team. Good team building requires differentiation of roles within a team and a good fit of each individual to the particular role, as well as good communication within the team.

teamwork
Magical concept more talked about than practised: when individuals complement each other and demonstrate team synergy. Nearly all successful firms demonstrate a high degree of teamwork; nearly all unsuccessful ones do not, at least in their upper reaches. Increasingly, the team rather than the individual should be the basic unit that is accountable for achieving objectives. Some pioneering firms are experimenting with the idea of career teams, groups of individuals who move through an organization together and have a collective career. This substantially reduces learning costs and helps liberate talent and build commitment in a way that conventional organizations simply cannot do.

tear-down analysis
Graphic Japanese phrase for what used to be called *reverse engineering*. Companies such as Isuzu, Nissan or Honda systematically take apart competitors' products, analyzing the materials used, the way they have been moulded, the process used to assemble the product, and therefore the likely cost. The aim is to take any ideas that are lower cost and ensure that your firm is both lower cost and higher quality than the competitors.

technology transfer

Sharing knowledge of new technologies, whether across parts of the same firm, with a strategic partner, or more broadly in society. The speed of technology transfer differs widely and can be more important than invention.

telesales

Increasingly important practice of selling via the telephone rather than face to face, or using telesales staff to 'pre-qualify' prospects, that is, provide sales people with high quality leads. Telesales is a cheap and efficient way of selling any but the most expensive for personal items.

teleworker

Same as homeworker or telecommuter: executive or self-employed person who works from home making full use of telephone, fax and computer links to colleagues or business partners.

tertiary brand

An obscure manufacturer's brand sold on price, with the intention of taking spot market share away from both top brands, secondary brands, and retailers' own label.

T-group

Invented by Kurt Lewin: an early form of encounter group for encouraging colleagues to expose their true feelings about each other, in order to provide sensitivity training for individuals and encourage better teamwork. Can be dangerous stuff and not much used now.

Theory W

Humorous but seriously-barbed management theory invented in 1974 to provide an alternative to Theory X and Theory Y. Theory W (for Whiplash) is even more primitive than Theory X, preferring the stick to the carrot. Theory W is probably the one under which most people in history have lived, and even today it is unfortunately still widely practised, although mainly in goals, prison camps and the many gulags around the world that linger and even flourish under repressive regimes.

Theory X

Doug McGregor's management construct, used to characterize the prevailing management ethos when he wrote (c.1960). Theory X managers believe that people are inherently lazy and need to be energized and supervised through a combination of carrot and stick. McGregor thought this incorrect, and advocated instead Theory Y management.

Theory Y

McGregor's preferred management style: predicated on the belief that workers are inherently motivated, and that the manager's job is to encourage, channel and orchestrate that natural energy for the good of the firm and the individual alike.

Theory Z

When McGregor died in 1964 he was working on Theory Z, the ultimate synthesis between the good of the firm and the striving of the individual for self-realization. The term was later used as the title of a book by William Ouchi, which focused on what the West could learn from Japan about teamwork, training and generating employee commitment. The Theory Z organization has these Japanese characteristics: lifetime employment, concern for employees including their social life, informal control, decisions made by consensus, slow promotion, excellent transmittal of information from top to bottom and bottom to top with the help of middle management, commitment to the firm and high concern for Quality.

throughput time

The total time to process a customer's order, or to get a product from the drawing board to the customer.

time and motion, time and motion study

The old name for the stop-watch element in Scientific Management. Now a part of work study.

time-based competition

Concept invented by BCG which holds that the time it takes a firm to get a product from conception to the customer, or to complete its tasks and provide goods or services to market can be the key to competitive advantage. Time is a crucial factor in the internal and external chain of customers and suppliers. At each internal or external customer/supplier interface there is not just a risk, but a near certainty, that time will be wasted. And time really is money, as well as being service to boot. The total time taken through the chain throughput time determines not only the firm's costs, but is also a litmus test of the firm's responsiveness to customers.

Concentration of time to market therefore kills two birds with one concept: service and cost. If quality is free, reducing the time to market has negative costs as well as customer benefits. Notwithstanding its importance, time-based competition is basically a package of earlier discoveries, and it in turn has been repackaged as just a part of BPR (Business Process Re-engineering).

It has long been realized that most of the time taken to make a product or provide a service is generally not 'productive' time but the gaps between different stages of the process.

time elasticity of profitability

BCG's term for the relationship between a supplier's profit and the speed with which the product is supplied (the elapsed time between the customer's decision to buy and his receipt of the product or service). Short elapsed time equals high profit; long elapsed time equals low profit.

time management
The movement started in Denmark and is now much used in the West to record, monitor and improve how executives use time.

time to market
The time taken to get a new product introduced into the market, from conception to launch; or the time taken to process and deliver a customer order.

Toffler, Alvin
Popular and provocative futurologist whose three main books, *Future Shock*, *The Third Wave*, and *Power Shift*, are all worth reading or re-reading. The most prophetic and interesting is *The Third Wave*, published in 1980 and since broadly vindicated by events. In it Toffler argues that industrialization (the Second Wave) split apart consumer and producer, which had been integrated on the land under the First Wave. The Third Wave includes the arrival of the super-industrial society but is much more, making obsolete the nation-state, specialization, mass production, the concept of employment, the power of political parties, traditional family values and most other assumptions of Second Wave thinking. Not all Toffler trends are soundly based but one that is is the prosumer, Toffler's neologism for proactive consumers who participate in the product design process: one example Toffler gives is the prosumer who sits at a computer work station at a car dealer's and makes choices fed to him on car design and features by a CAD/CAM software programme. Toffler noted the impact of technology and information on industrial society, the rise of homeworking, the decline of the big organization, the secular rise in unemployment, and the need for new political and social mechanisms more appropriate to the new age: all themes taken up and made more specific by Charles Handy. The book also coined the phrase 'small-within-big is beautiful'.

top management
Vague expression meant to encompass all very senior executives, usually comprising all executive members of a firm's top board and any particularly influential executives not thus included. Top management is useful for pandering to status or obfuscation; but a more useful concept is 'those who run a company': that is, those executives (and occasionally non-executives) who have veto power over any important decision in the firm, whether or not the decision falls within 'their' area.

total assets
Gross assets of a firm, including all fixed and current assets, before deducting liabilities.

TQM (Total Quality Management)
Technique for building quality into products by training all employees in quality and motivating them to 'do it right first time'. Contrasts with and clearly superior to earlier attempts at Quality Control, that set up a separate department to monitor work after the fact. TQM is both a set of techniques, including Quality Circles, and an overall philosophy of management. As such it has been generally successful: and that cannot be said of too many major management movements. In the end, though, the Anglo-Saxon need for a cut-and-dried programme such as TQM can be self-defeating. What is needed is total obsession with Quality, and not a programme to 'take care' of it. To have this obsession requires being able to see the big picture of customers' needs and the total business system, and TQM is too much a technique and too narrowly based to be able to supply this.

trading account
1. The top of a P&L showing sales revenue, cost of sales and gross profit.
2. Term used by stockbrokers to mean the period during which credit is extended on sale or purchase of stock, to be paid on settlement day, a few days after the end of the account.

trading period
The period between two sets of accounts (eg, a month or a year).

trading profit
The same as PBIT (Profit Before Interest & Tax) or EBIT; the profit from trading before taking account of interest paid or received and before paying tax. Usually the best guide to the underlying performance of a business.

trading volume
The daily total of shares bought and sold on the stock market for individual shares and the market as a whole. Volume can be as important as the direction of the market in helping to divine future trends.

transaction
Anything a firm does that affects its financial position and balance sheet.

Transactional Analysis (TA)
The 'I'm OK, You're OK' school of thought, developed in the 1960s by Eric Berne, an American psychologist, which holds that people can only work together (as two people or a group) if each member of the group accepts and appreciates the other members.

transactional leadership
Style concerned more with immediate events and tactics than with long-term direction or mission.

transformation
Changing an organization's culture and behaviour, so that it ascends to a new level of financial and market performance. Not surprisingly, transformation is difficult: 75 per cent of all attempts fail. There do seem, however, to be six conditions of successful transformation, which are always present in successful transformations:

1. They are driven by demanding and inspiring leaders, and one person embodies the transformation ethic.
2. The top team (those who really run the company) are emotionally united; they are on the same side and want to help each other personally, as well as the firm.
3. There is a slogan used as a rallying cry: either a medium-term cause or a longer-term statement of strategic intent.
4. Baronies are absent or destroyed.
5. The change process focuses on real business issues, changing attitudes on the back of commercial success. There are simple performance measures so that everyone knows what is expected.
6. The firm has or builds at least one world class competence: a skill where it is as good as or better than any competitor.

transformational leadership
Leadership style oriented to making long-term changes in a firm, providing vision and inspiration to employees. Contrast transactional leadership.

transnational corporation
Term used by Fons Trompenaars and others to describe an ideal for the international corporation: polycentric, flattish in structure, drawing on a multiplicity of expertise centres, with each country within the corporation specializing in what it does best, but linked together in an unbeatable product or service.

turnaround
A company that has recovered from severe crisis and losses to sustainable profits, or one that is in the process of 'being turned around'.

turnaround time
Nothing to do with turnarounds in the sense above. Turnaround time is the time to get something completed, from arrival in the in-tray to delivery to customer, or the time taken to undertake one specific task (such as the time it takes a typist to complete a report).

turnkey project
A major public works or construction project where a single firm is responsible for co-ordinating all suppliers and activities.

turnover
1. Annual sales revenue. 2. Annual rate at which labour, stocks or anything else 'turns over' (see *labour turnover* and *stock turn* respectively). 3. The total value of stock exchange transactions.

U

undercapitalized
Where a firm has insufficient capital. May need to be recapitalized by the injection of new funds.

underwriting
When an investment bank or other financial institution guarantees a financing transaction by offering to buy shares that are not sold to others, or where an insurance company provides cover and assumes risks.

undistributed profit, undistributed earnings
Earnings retained in a business and not distributed to shareholders in dividends.

ungeared
Without debt. Ungeared companies are usually doing their shareholders no favours: the return on equity could be higher and the competitive strategy more aggressive if the firm took on some debt.

unissued capital
Share capital that is authorized but has not yet been sold or allocated.

unit cost
The cost of producing one unit of a good or service; the average cost per unit.

unlimited liability
Partnerships and a few other entities have unlimited liability, that is, liability is not limited to what is in the business; creditors can ask for the partners' houses if they are not paid.

unlisted shares, unlisted securities
Shares that are quoted but not on the official or main market.

unquoted shares, unquoted securities
Shares in a private company, not listed on any stock exchange.

USP (Unique Selling Point, Unique Selling Proposition)
The customer proposition – what the customer is being offered – that differenti-ates one firm's product or service from a competitor's. Many commodity products

do not have a USP. Unless a product has a USP, or is lower cost and lower price than competing products, its market share and profitability will be vulnerable.

V

valuation methods

Valuation of companies falls into two types: market-based approaches, which are used by the stock market; and intrinsic value methods, which are used to evaluate acquisitions. The market-based method relies upon placing a multiple on the firm's earnings. The intrinsic methods are based either on net assets, or more normally on a DCF (Discounted Cash Flow) model. There are flaws in all these approaches, but a consistent methodology at least allows a sensible ranking of different options. In considering acquisitions, the most important point to consider is the extent of the synergy.

value added

What a firm adds in value; the firm's turnover minus the cost of bought-in raw materials and services. The concept of value-added is becoming a little less useful, because sometimes a lot of the value accrues from good relationships with suppliers, and this falls outside the technical definition of value added.

value chain

A firm's co-ordinated set of activities to satisfy customer needs, starting with relationships with suppliers and procurement, going through production, selling and marketing, and delivery to the customer. Each stage of the value chain is linked with the next stage, and looks forward to the customer's needs, and backwards from the customer too. Each link in the value chain must seek competitive advantage: it must either be lower cost than the corresponding link in competing firms, or add more value by superior quality or differentiated features.

values

The set of cultural norms, ways of behaving, beliefs, objectives, relationships, methods of control, view of the outside world, style, character and business philosophy shared by those in a firm; what the executives believe in at the deepest level and what conditions their behaviour.

Venture capital (VC)

Provision of finance to new or small companies in the form of risk (equity) capital, in return for a high proportion of the shares. Venture capital is technically the highest risk part of this activity, financing start-ups; helping small firms grow and financing MBOs (Management Buy Outs) is technically development capital. This distinction is not always made, however, and *venture capital* is used to describe both activities.

vertical integration
Moving to cover a greater part of the total industry value chain, by buying or competing with suppliers (backward integration or upstream integration) or customers (forward integration or downstream integration).

W

Weber, Max (1864–1920)
The prophet of bureaucracy, which he saw as the best prototype for the modern organization. He saw the role-determined organization – where everyone knew what they were supposed to do, and reported upwards through a boss with greater responsibility, promotion was by merit and the whole thing could operate as a smooth machine – as indubitably the most efficient and even liberating model. He contrasted it with two other forms: the traditional, hereditary system, where authority was inherited and required deference, as in the family firm; and the charismatic, which relies upon an outstanding individual like Henry Ford, and was likely to disintegrate or transmute to another style when the charismatic leader retired. (Weber was the first writer to clearly define the charismatic leader and his type of company.) Weber was right: bureaucracy was best at that time, and was the engine of wealth creation. The idea led to the formation of big business empires and the multinational corporation, organized on bureaucratic lines. Even today, the role-type culture may be the most efficient in slow-changing markets such as insurance.

Since the Second World War it has become increasingly clear that bureaucracy is not enough, and even in its original sense is an albatross for any firm facing volatile markets, demanding customers and fearsome competitors. Fast response requires adhocracy, roughly the opposite of bureaucracy. Moreover, as the people in companies who comprise its knowledge have become increasingly central, and demanding, the role of the charismatic leader has become much more important, even in many cases necessary. Finally, Weber could not be expected to see the damaging effects of managerialism and the absentee landlords in the form of investing institutions. The divorce of ownership from management, and the short-term view of Western investors, has led the Anglo-Saxon corporation to be ill-equipped to deal with the Japanese challenge, where investors are more central and long term. Weber would have been the first to turn his ideas on their head in response to changed circumstances.

white goods
Consumer durables in a white cabinet like washing machines, tumbledriers, cookers, dishwashers and refrigerators.

work flow, workflow
The series of work sequences in producing a product or service.

work in progress
Goods or services being prepared for sale but not yet finished goods. Recorded on the balance sheet as an asset.

working capital
Funding required for day-to-day operations to cover the gap between payment for inputs (raw materials, labour, etc) and the time that customers pay. Working capital plus fixed assets equal capital employed.

X

x-inefficiency
The extent to which a plant or other part of a firm falls below the efficiency of the best comparable unit within the firm.

Y

yellow goods
A term covering both brown and white goods (brown + white = yellow): high ticket items bought infrequently. Contrast red goods (frequent purchases) and compare orange goods (bought moderately often).

yield
The return on shares, bank deposits or other financial instruments. It is the interest or dividend received annually divided by the current market price (not the cost paid by an investor) of the instrument. Some shares are bought principally for the yield: these are generally companies where earnings have declined, but where the dividend has not (yet) been cut. There are two dangers with such shares: (1) the yield may never be received, since it is always quoted on the basis of last year's dividend, which may be cut; and (2) the share price may fall if earnings continue to decline or the dividend is cut. Conversely, however, if the dividend is held and the earnings look like recovering, the investor may receive not only a large yield but also healthy capital appreciation through a share price increase. Some investors and investment trusts specialize in high yield shares, trying to pick the less risky ones and those with greatest recovery potential. All that can safely be generalized about high yield instruments is that they have above average risk.

yield curve
Graph showing the yield of fixed-interest securities according to the length of their maturity: normally slopes gently up to reflect premium expected for long-term funds. If it slopes down at some point, this indicates the expectation that medium-term interest rates will fall.

yield gap
The difference between the yield on risk-free government stock and the average yield on shares.

Z

Zero-Based Budgeting (ZBB)
Budgeting with a clean sheet of paper, disregarding historical costs, in order to remove any unnecessary costs. A useful discipline but not often done, except as a one-off exercise by consultants.

zero-based production
Design of a product from scratch to standards acceptable to consumers, combined with value analysis and value engineering and production analysis to ensure that the cost for this standard is as low as possible. The basis of success for many Japanese products, including the Honda Civic and Ricoh's copiers, as well as Toyota and Nissan cars.

zero defects
The idea that quality should be absolute: 99.9 per cent is not enough.

zero-sum game
The idea derived from game theory that if I gain you must lose: there is a finite amount of goodies in a market and if one competitor grabs some it must be at the expense of the other competitors. In general, in competitive markets (that is, in the absence of a cartel), it may be the best assumption that it is a zero-sum game in the short term. If Coke wins, Pepsi loses; if Canon wins in photocopiers, Xerox suffers. There are, however, two important qualifications to the zero-sum game concept. First, a sub-set of competitors may co-operate on some issues, such as market development or sharing technology, to their mutual advantage and to everyone else's detriment. This still represents a zero-sum game between the bloc of collaborators and all others, but a positive-sum game for competitors within the bloc. Groupings such as the EC and NAFTA may be seen in this way. The second qualification is that competitors within an industry may have a mutual interest in increasing the size of the market for their product, or in increasing the size and health of the economy as a whole. In practice, life and competition are never zero-sum games: competitors help each other by encouraging higher standards, which in turn enlarges the market and conduces towards a richer society. The concept of zero-sum competition is, nevertheless, of great value, and in the short-term broadly correct; and longer-term, the concept itself helps us create its opposite.

Zipf's law
G K Zipf's 'Principle of least effort': serious, mathematical 'proof' that mankind strives to produce any given outcome with the minimum amount of work.

Z-score
A single number, based on a number of accounting ratios, indicating the risk of a firm going bust. Useful as one input to risk assessment.

Richard Koch is an entrepreneur, consultant and author of numerous books. This Glossary is an abridged and edited version of Koch's *Management and Finance: An A-Z of Tools, Terms and Techniques* (FT/Pitman, 1994).

INDEX

ABB, *see* Asea Brown Boveri
ABC, *see* Activity Based Costing
Abrams, Frank, 1013
Aburdene, Patricia & Naisbitt, John, *Megatrends for Women,* 301
Accounting Rate of Return (ARR), 550–1
Activity Based Costing (ABC), 523–4, 533
Adair, John, 101
Adler, Nancy, 889, 898
Advanced Micro Devices, 874
advertising, 574
AEG, 682
Air France, 39, 935
Akai, 956
Aker, David, *Managing Brand Equity,* 597
Akers, John, 110, 1070
Alcatel, 46
Alcoa, 229
Allaire, Paul, 234, 235,1017
Allen, Louis, 66–7
Allied Dunbar, 367
Allied Lyons, 525
American Express, 219
American Management Association, 70, 887
American Medical Association, xi
Analogue Devices, 692
Andrews, Kenneth, *Ethics in Practice,* 1002
Anheuser-Busch, 594–7
Ansoff, H Igor, xxv, 125, 136–8
Antioch College, 106
Apple, 606, 643, 681
appraisal, 283–9
ARCO, 969
Argyris, Chris, 95,145, 676, 687–90
Armstrong, Geoff, 761
ARR, *see* Accounting Rate of Return
Asda, 716
Asea Brown Boveri (ABB), 10,13–20, 37, 45, 50, 802, 845, 863–4, 893, 896, 910–11, 914, 925

Ashridge Management College, xxiii, 103, 450, 891, 895; *Management for the Future*, 291–2
assessment centres, 280–1
Asset-Based Analysis, 533
Association of Independent Research and Technology Organizations, 414
AT&T, 57, 923
Athos, Anthony, 35, 269, 270
attribute listing, 171
Auton, Paul, 414

BA, *see* British Airways
BAA, *see* British Airports Authority
Bain & Co, 506, 912, 913
Baldrige Awards, 198, 215, 633, 639
Banque Indosuez, 459
Barclay's Property Holdings, 696, 698
Barclays Bank, 397, 470–1
Barnard, Chester, 3
Barnett, Theresa, 697
Barnevik, Percy, 13–20, 45, 102, 749, 802, 831, 863
Bartlett, Christopher, & Ghoshal, Sumantra, *Managing Across Borders*, 541, 843, 845–6, 921
Bartlett, Christopher, 4
Basis Risk, 556
BAT, 156, 326
Bateson, Gregory, *Steps to an Ecology of Mind*, 27
Bath University, 407
BAUM, 861
Bean, LL, 219
Beddowes, Peter, 450
Bell Atlantic, 236, 364
Bennis, Warren, 95, 99, 105–7; *On Becoming a Leader*, 1016
Bergman, David, *Disasters: Where the Law Fails*, 1007
Berry, Len, 223
Binney, George, 747
biodata, 277–8
Birmingham Midshires Building Society, 1032
Blanchard, Kenneth, *The One Minute Manager*, xxiv
Blankhart, Franz, 850
BMW, 260, 602
Body Shop, 37, 206
Boeing, 681
Bolton Report, 989
Bono, Edward de, 824
Boote, Alfred, 602–3

Borne, RW, 293
Bosch, 204
Boston Consulting Group, 20, 145
Boston University, 106; *Manufacturing Futures Survey*, 371 –2
Bouygues, 277
Boyatzis, Richard, 70; *The Competent Manager*, 472, 887
BP, *see* British Petroleum
BPR, *see* re-engineering
brand management, 442, 573, 581–93
  Europeanization of brands, 598–614
Branson, Richard, 100, 102, 676
British Aerospace, 682
British Airports Authority (BAA), 225, 434–41, 473
British Airways (BA), 206, 263, 406, 443, 634, 638, 692, 699
British Leyland, 261
British Petroleum (BP), 91, 120–4, 897
British Rail, 634
British Steel, xxvii
British Telecom (BT), 93, 101, 218, 263, 381, 397,
BT, *see* British Telecom
BTR, 910
Burgelman, Robert, 846
Burns, James McGregor, 103
Burton Group 260, 307
Business in the Community, 972
Business Process Re-engineering (BPR), *see* re-engineering
Business Round Table, 974, 1013
business schools, 463–9
Business Week, 129, 198
Buzan, Tony, 865

Cabot, Louis, 1965
CAD/CAM (Computer Aided Design/Computer Aided Manufacturing), 650
Cadbury Committee, 1052, 1062
Cadbury Schweppes, 442, 897, 969
Cadbury, George, 967
Cadbury, Sir Adrian, 470, 1053, 1055
Campbell, Andrew, 179, 1009
Canon, 51, 59, 844
careers, 78, 475–7, 927
  career management, 325–37
Carlzon, Jan, 112–3, 264
Cartier, 51
Cash Flow Return On Investment (CFROI), 160
Castrol, 443

Caterpillar, 860
Cattell 16 PF Personality Test, 293
CBI, *see* Confederation of British Industry
CBS, 698
Cedar International, 238
Center for Creative Leadership, 294–6, 305
CFROI, *see* Cash Flow Return On Investment
Champy, James, 1109, 229, 233–6
Chandler, Alfred, 41, 964, 974
change management, 25–33
Chaos Theory, 28
Chaplin, Charlie, 362
Chartered Institute of Purchasing & Supply, 387
Chicago Mercantile Exchange, 525
Christopher, Martin, Ballantyne, David & Payne, Adrian, *Relationship
    Marketing*, 763
Churchill, Winston, 102, 822
Cleaver, Sir Anthony, 328
Clinton, Bill, 129
CNN (Cable News Network), 8, 37, 698
Co-operative Bank, 398, 969
coaching, 47, 49, 684, 714–22
Coca Cola, 443, 570, 578, 595
Coe, Trudy, 331
Cohn Associates, 1035
Colgate Palmolive, 679
command and control, 5
communication, 349
  crisis management, 812–30
  government and parliamentary relations, 796–801
  internal marketing, 759–65
  international public relations, 785–95
  negotiating, 766–75
  networking, 776–84
  overview, 747–9
  teamworking, 802–11
  with employees, 750–8
community, relationships with, 1027–38
Compact Disc Interactive, 665
Compagnie Bancaire, 277
Compaq, 91
competencies, 70–3, 274–5, 329
  for international management, 887–99
Cone/Coughlin Communications, 1018
Confederation of British Industry (CBI), 633

consultants, using, 735–45
Coopers & Lybrand, 415–16, 419, 568, 633
Corning–Vitro, 380
corporate governance
  creating an effective board, 1070–81
  overview, 1052–60
  role of non-executive directors, 1061–9
corporate identity, 442–9
corporate responsibility
  company, community and competitive advantage, 1027–38
  managing the environment, 1039–50
  overview, 1002–10
  role of ethics, 1011–19
Cost Volume Profit Analysis, 529
Cott, 578
Cottin, Jean Francois, 257
Cottle, Tom, 881
Counter Party Risk, 556
Courage, 597
Cox, CJ, & Cooper, CL, *High Flyers,* 293
Crane, Dwight, 346
Cranfield School of Management, 621, 763
creativity
  role in strategy, 164–77
Crédit Lyonnais, 935
Creswick, Chris, 494
crisis management, 812–30
Crosby, Philip, 194
Cummings, Stephen, 146–7
Cunningham, Ian, *The Wisdom of Strategic Learning,* 676
customer retention, 217
customer service, 214–29

Daimler Benz, 39
Dana Corporation, 90
database marketing, 571–2, 623–31
Davidow, William, *Marketing High Tehcnology,* 616
Davies, John, 146–8
Davison, John, 423, 426
Day, Sir Graham, 693
DEC, *see* Digital Equipment Corporation
Deming Awards, 198, 639
Deming, W Edwards, 196–7, 201–4
Department of Trade & Industry, *UK R&D Scorecard,* 410–11
derivatives, 525

design
  corporate identity, 442–9
  design management, 434–41
Design Management Institute, 437
Deutsche Aerospace, 679, 682
Digital Equipment Corporation (DEC), 39, 578, 644, 678, 682
digitization, 645
Dior Cosmetics, 601
Direct Line, 218
Disneyworld, 214, 218, 221
Distribution Requirements Planning (DRP), 390
Domino's Pizzas, 221, 226
Donaldson, John, *Key Issues in Business Ethics,* 971
Dow Jones Industrial Index, xxvii
Doz, Yves, 466
Dragon International, *Corporate Reputation,* 1035
DRP, *see* Distribution Requirements Planning
Drucker, Peter F, xxi, xxix, 5, 183, 232, 242, 243, 299, 495, 567, 568, 642, 979–81; 1001; *The Age of Discontinuity,* 290; *The Practice of Management,* xxvi
Dukakis, Michael, 21
Duke University, 457
DuPont, 570, 928

Earnings Per Share (EPS), 151
Eccles, Robert, 346
Eccles, Tony, 746
Economist, The, 126
EDI, *see* Electronic Date Interchange
education, development and training
  business schools, 463–69
  evaluating training effectiveness, 482–93
  outdoor management development, 494–504
  overview, 451–62
  top management development, 470–81
Egan, Sir John, 434, 473
Einstein, Albert, 210
Electronic Data Interchange (EDI), 390
Elf Aquitaine, 878, 937
Elida Gibbs, 367
Elves, Dr Michael, 414
Emerson Electric, 844, 846
employees, communicating with, 750–8
empowerment, 74, 679
  empowerment, 345–57

Engels, Frederick, 966
entrepreneurial corporation, building the, 39–63
EPS, *see* Earnings Per Share
Ericsson, 152
Ernst & Young, 1028
Estée Lauder, 606
ethics, role of, 1011–19
Eurocopter, 686
European Foundation for Quality Management, 198–9
Evian, 606
executive derailment, 296–7
Exxon, 1004–5

Fast Moving Consumer Goods (FMCG), 415, 583
Fayol, Henri, 65–6, 85–6
Federal Express, 214, 221
Fl Group, 398
Fiat, 890, 935
Fife, Gene, 108
financial accounting, 528–9
finance function, 535–43
financial futures, 558–60
financial management
  management accounting, 527–34
  managing financial risk, 554–66
  managing long-term investment decisions, 544–53
  managing the finance function, 535–43
  overview, 520–6
financial risk, 554–66
Financial Times, The, 974
Financial World, 445
First Direct, 218
Fisher, George, 9
Floating Rate Note (FRN), 555
Florida Light & Power, 198
FMCG, *see* Fast Moving Consumer Goods
Follett, Mary Parker, 66, 299
Food, Drink & Tobacco Industry Training Board, 494
Ford Motor Corporation, 204, 246, 259, 444, 455, 490
Ford, Henry II, 972, 1014
Ford, Henry, 362, 1014
Foreign Direct Investment, 832
Fortune 500, xxvii, 6, 694
Forward Rate Agreements (FRA), 560
Foster, Richard, 145

Fournier, Bernard, 108, 116, 235
FRA, *see* Forward Rate Agreements
FRN, *see* Floating Rate Note
Fuji, 6
functional organization, 42, 233, 363–5

Gabett, Thomas, *How to Build the Corporation's Identity and Project its Image*, 813–14
Garfield, Charles, *Peak Performers*, 472–4
Gates, Bill, xxiv
Gateway Food Markets, 234
GE, *see* General Electric
GEC, 459
General Electric (GE), xxvii, 6, 40, 45, 224, 271, 459, 460, 643, 1013, 1016
General Motors, 39, 40, 41, 90, 678, 908
Gerstner, Lou, 11
Ghoshal, Sumantra, 4
Gilligan, Carol, *In a Different Voice*, 300
GKN, 716
Glaxo, 297, 412
globalization, 61, 576, 837–9
  achieving global competitiveness, 850–67
  managing the global company from the centre, 905–19
  managing the global company, 920–9
Gordon Group, 1017
government and parliamentary relations, 796–801
Grand Metropolitan, 581, 912, 1033–4
graphology, 275
Groupe ESC Lyon, 900
groupware, 667–8
Grove, Andy, 46, 58–9
GTE, 234, 246
Gulick, Luther, 65

Haas, Robert, xxviii, 1021, 1025
Hallmark Cards, 246
Hamel, Gary, & Pralahad, CK, *Competing for the Future*, 409, 414
Hamel, Gary, 6, 145, 396, 579
Hammer, Michael, 109, 229, 233
Hampton Inns, 227
Hanan, Mack, *Tomorrow's Competition*, 367
Handy, Charles, xxviii, 11, 64, 77, 95–8, 451, 577, 651, 963; *The Age of Unreason*, 723, 863, 864; *The Empty Raincoat*, 301
Hanover Insurance, 695
Hanson, 326, 910

Harley Davidson, 206
Harvard Business Review, 358
Harvard Business School, xxi, 349
Harvey-Jones, John, 3, 100, 519, 746
Hay McBer, 274
hedging methods, 577–8, 561–2
Heider, John, 104
Heller, Robert, 38, 201
Henderson, Rebecca, 6
Henley Management College, 82, 93, 678, 682
Hennig, Margaret, & Jardim, Ann, *The Managerial Woman,* 300
Herald of Free Enterprise, 1004
Herman Miller, 344
Herzberg, Frederick, 257, 264, 299, 311, 350
Hewlett Packard, 273, 277, 681, 928
hierarchies, xxviii, 5, 363
high-fliers, 290–8
high performance work organizations, 338–44
Hiram Walker, 685
Hitachi, 679
Hodgson, Phil, xxiii, 103
Hoechst, 901, 968
Hoffman-La Roche, 151
Holland, John, 332–3
Holway Report, 395
Home Depot, 152, 156
Honda, 6, 261, 269, 634, 694, 836, 928
Honey, Peter, 676, 729
Honeywell, 578
Horton, Bob, 110
Houghton, Jimmy, 46
Human Resource Management
  appraisal, 283–9
  career management, 325–37
  empowerment, 345–57
  high performance work organizations, 338–44
  managing high-fliers, 290–8
  overview, 258–67
  recruitment and selection, 273–82
  reward and remuneration, 309–24
  women in management, 299–308
Huthwaite Group, 772–4

IBM, xxvii, 6, 9, 11, 21, 39, 59, 215, 225, 234,326, 327, 328, 340, 381,
  409–10, 443, 570, 643, 644,1020, 1032, 1070

ICA Handlarnas, 235
ICI, 39, 260, 328, 412, 731–2
ICL, 335–336, 404–5, 423
Information Technology (IT), xxviii, 5, 54, 80, 89, 254–5, 395, 399
  IT management, 653–63
INSEAD, xxi, 460, 466, 467, 925
Institute of Directors, 460
Institute of Management, xxix, 302, 331, 677
Institute of Personnel & Development, 455, 681, 761
Integrated Services Digital Network (ISDN), 646, 667, 756
Intel, 57–61, 152
internal marketing, 759–65
Internal Rate of Return (IRR), 151, 550–1
International Harvester, 860
interviews, 278
IRR, *see* Internal Rate of Return
ISDN, *see* Integrated Services Digital Network
ISO 9000, 404
IT, *see* Information Technology

Jaeger Tailoring, 220
Jaguar, 444
Japan Airlines, 1006
Japanese management, 947–62
Jefferson, Thomas, 1012
JIT, *see* Just-In-Time
job evaluation, 313–5
Johnson & Johnson, 457
joint ventures, 939–46
Jones, Helen, 777
Juran, Joseph, 196, 197, 198, 232
Just–In–Time (JIT), 390, 403, 416

KAI, *see* Kirton Adaptor/Innovator Test
Kaizen, 196, 955
Kakabadse, Andrew, *The Wealth Creators*, 472–3
Kanban, 144, 955
Kant, Immanual, 1017
Kanter, Rosabeth Moss, xxx, 21 –4, 64, 1008; *The Challenge of
  Organizational Change*, 28; *When Giants Learn to Dance*, 472; *Men and
  Women of the Corporation*, 300
Kao, 52–6
Kinsman, Francis, 92
Kirton Adaptor/Innovator Test (KAI), 293
Kodak, 6, 9, 39, 444, 445, 639, 1070

Kolb, David, 478, 497
Kotler, Philip, *Marketing Management*, 583
Kotter, John, 103
KPMG Management Consulting, 10
Kuhn, Thomas, 964

L'Oreal, 279
Lancôme Cosmetics, 601
LANs, *see* Local Area Networks
Lauren, Ralph, 601
Laurie, Donald, 9
Lawler, Edward, xxviii
LeadershipTrust, 100
leadership, 9, 47
  overview, 100–4
  work of the leader, 108– 19
  at British Petroleum, 120
learning, 31–3
  coaching and mentoring, 714–22
  learning organization, 691–700
  overview, 676–86
  project-based, 723–34
  self-managed learning, 701–13
  using consultants, 735–45
Leers, David, 778–80
Leonard's, Stew, 214, 220
Leverhulme, Lord, 967, 969
Levi Strauss & Co, xxviii, 969, 1020–26
Levitt, Theodore, 81–2, 220, 567, 576, 600, 850
Lewin, Kurt, 27
Leysen, Andre, 1051
LIBOR, *see* London Interbank Offered Rate
Liquidity Risk, 556
Lloyd Masters Consulting, 681
Lloyds Bank, 157
Local Area Networks (LANs), 645
Lock, Edwin, 147
logistics management, 385–93
London Business School, 584
London Interbank Offered Rate (LIBOR), 555
Long-Term Credit Bank, 838
long-term investment decisions, 544–53
Lorange, Peter, 180
Lowell, Francis, 967, 969
Lucas Industries, 634

MacLaurin, Ian, 676
Macleod, Francis, 100
Magnet Joinery, 227
Major, John, 198
management accounting, 527–34
Management by Objectives (MBO), xxv
Management Charter Initiative, xxv, 70–1, 678, 679
Managerial Grid, xxv, 819
Managing By Walking About (MBWA), 269
managing internationally
  achieving global competitiveness, 850–67
  competencies, 887–99
  cultural factors, 871–86
  Japanese management, 947–62
  joint ventures, 939–46
  managing the global company, 920–9
  managing the global company from the centre, 905–19
  mergers and acquisitions, 930–8
  overview, 832–49
  training, 900–4
manufacturing strategy, 369–84
marketing
  competitor analysis and benchmarking, 632–41
  brand management, 581–93
  database marketing, 623–31
  Europeanization of brands, 598–614
  overview, 568–80
  relationship marketing, 615–22
Market Rate Risk, 556
Marks & Spencer, 583, 923, 1020, 1028
Marlboro, 445
Mars, 576, 604
Marshall, Judi, *Women Managers*, 300
Marshall, Sir Colin, 108, 111, 746
Maruta, Dr Yoshio, 52–6
Maslow, Abraham, 299
Massachusetts Institute of Technology (MIT), xxv, 6, 106, 643, 692
Master of Business Administration (MBA), xi, xxi, 453, 900
Materials Requirements Planning (MRP), 390
matrix structure, 16–17, 47, 922–4
Matsushita, 40, 50, 51, 59, 957
Matsushita, Konosuke, xxiv, 25
Maturana, Humberto, 28
Maxwell Communications, 970
Mayo, Elton, 299

Mazda, 955
MBA, *see* Master of Business Administration
MBNA, 217, 617
MBO, *see* Management By Objectives
MBWA, *see* Managing By Walking About
McCauley, Cynthia, 294–5
McClelland, David, 274
McDonald's, 143, 595, 596, 605
McGregor, Douglas, xxv, 101, 299
McKinsey & Co, 932
Mellon, Andrew, 969
Mercury, 181
MES, *see* Minimum Efficient Scale
Metallgesellschaft, 525
Michelin, 273, 973
Microsoft, 173, 578, 648, 756, 841
Midland Bank, 406, 407
Milka, 602
Mill, John Stuart, 1012
Miller, Danny, *The Icarus Paradox* 182
Milliken, 214
Mills, D Quinn, 361
Minimum Efficient Scale (MES), 994
Mintzberg, Henry, xxii, 125–6, 136, 184, 513–17, 900; *The Nature of Managerial Work*, xxiii, 68–9
Mische, Justus, 901
mission
  role in strategy development, 139–49
mission statements, 129–30, 146, 169–71
Mission, Objectives, Strategy & Tactics (MOST), 139, 146, 148
MIT, *see* Masschusetts Institute of Technology
Mitroff, Ian, 866
Moore, Gordon, 58, 61
MORI, 800, 1035
Morita, Akio, 850
MOST, *see* Mission, Objectives, Strategy & Tactics
Motorola, 6, 58,145, 271, 344, 459, 679
MRP, *see* Materials Requirements Planning
Mulholland, Mike, 696, 698
multidivision organization, 41
multimedia, 664–75
multinational organizations, xv
multiplexing, 533
Mumford, Alan, *Developing Top Managers*, 472–3, 477–8, 676, 729
Murata Manufacturing, 152
Murphy, John, *Brand Strategy*, 594

Nadler, David, 865
NAFTA, *see* North American Free Trade Area
Napoleon, 102
NASA, *see* National Aeronautics and Space Administration
National Aeronautics and Space Administration (NASA), 351
National Freight, 260
National Health Service, 303
National Industrial Conference Board, 66
National Training Laboratories, 106
National Vocational Qualifications (NVQ), 263
National Westminster Bank, 329, 1035
NEC, 459
negotiating, 766–75
Nestlé, 969
Net Present Value (NPV), 217, 541–2, 549–50
networking, 684, 776–84
New York Life, 91
Nikkei Business, 52
Nissan, 6, 836
Nomura, 963
non-executive directors, 1061–9
Nordstrom, 225, 271
Nordstrom, John, 108
North American Free Trade Area (NAFTA), 837, 920
Northern Telecom, 679
Novotel, 601
Noyce, Robert, 58
NPV, *see* Net Present Value
Nucor Steel, 344
Nuffield, Alfred, 969
NVQ, *see* National Vocational Qualifications

O'Brien, William, 695
O'Connell, Angela, 696, 698
O'Neil, Paul, 229
Objectives, Goals, Strategies & Measures (OGSM), 537–40, 543
OECD, 411
OGSM, *see* Objectives, Goals, Strategies & Measures
Ohmae, Kenichi, 125, 834
Ohno, Taichi, 954, 955
Olivetti, 39, 973
Opportunity 2000, 302, 306
OTC, *see* Over-the-Counter
outdoor management development, 494–504
outsourcing, 394–401

Over-the-Counter (OTC), 556–7
Owen, Robert, 963, 967, 969
Owners Abroad, 442

P&G, *see* Procter & Gamble
P&O, 1006
Pacific Bell, 246
Pacioli, Luca, xxiv
Pascale, Richard, xxvi, 6, 8, 35, 694; *Managing on the Edge*, xxv; 268–72
Payback Period (PP), 550
Pedler, Mike, *et al*, *The Learning Company*, 692, 695
Pennsylvania, University of, 453
Pepsi, 381
Perrier, 973
Peters, Tom & Waterman, Robert, *In Search of Excellence*, xxv, xxvii, 34–6, 214, 1016
Peters, Tom, 3, 34–8, 695, 870, 922; *Thriving on Chaos*, 36; *Liberation Management*, 36–7, 270, 358, 513
pharmaceuticals industry, 412–13
Philip Morris, 445
Philips, 46, 409, 612, 859, 921
Pilkington, Sir Anthony, 1001
PIMS, *see* Profit Impact of Marketing Strategy
Pinault–Printemps, 935
Pirelli, 906–7
Pirsig, Robert, *Lila: An Inquiry Into Morals*, 28
Planning Forum, 506
Playtex, 608
Polly Peck, 1052
Porter, Michael, 131, 145, 450, 920, 935, 999; *The Competitive Advantage of Nations*, 540
Post Office, The, 455
Prahalad, CK, 145
Price Waterhouse, 677
Procter & Gamble (P&G), 52, 535–43, 570, 582, 607, 612, 815, 841, 908
Profit Impact of Marketing Strategy (PIMS), 215, 609
project-based learning, 723–34
project management, 684
  role in implementing strategy, 178–93
ProNed, 973
Prowess (company), 306
psychological contract, 335
psychometric tests, 279
Public Policy Unit, 779
public relations, 785–98
public service management, 982–8

quality
  customer service, 214–29
  overview, 195–200
  total quality, 205–13
quality circles, 339–340
Queen's Moat Houses, 521
QVC (Quality Value Convenience), 670–1

rationalization, 56–7
recruitment and selection, 273–82
re-engineering, 25, 109, 144, 381
  overview, 231–41
  in practice, 245–56
Reed International, 152, 156
references, 279
Reich, Robert, 1017
Reichheld, Frederick, 617
Reiner, Gary, 643
relationship marketing, 615–22
Renault, 608
research and development, 409–14
Return on Capital Employed (ROCE), 92,151, 644
Return on Sales, 151
Revans, Reg, 726
reward and remuneration, 309–24
Ricardo, David, 1012
RJ Reynolds, 968
Robertson, Tom, 579, 569–71
ROCE, Return On Capital Employed
Roethlisberger, Fritz, 229
Roos, Johan, 940
Rosener, Judy, 300
Rothmans, 204
Rover Group, 198, 237–8, 260, 634, 692, 693, 696, 698
Ryder Rentals, 215–16

S Curve, 145
Saatchi & Saatchi, 524
Sadler, Philip, 869
Sainsbury, 91, 263, 578, 591
Sainsbury, David, 108, 111, 113, 116, 117
Saint Laurent, Yves, 601, 937
sales force, management of, 421–33
Sandoz, 1050
Sanofi, 937

Sarch, Yvonne, *How to be Head Hunted*, 475
SAS, 264, 699
Sasser, WE, & Reicheld, FF, 217
Sayles, Leonard, 102
scenario daydreaming, 168
Schien, Edgar, 95, 332–4
Schon, Donald, 688
Schonberger, Richard, 194
Schumacher, EF, *Small Is Beautiful*, 989
scientific management, xi
Securicor, 407
self-managed learning, 685, 701–13
Semco, 28, 29, 358–60
Semler, Ricardo, 29
Senge, Peter, 99, 145, 675, 692–3
Seven S Framework, 35, 270
Shamrock Organization, 11, 77, 651
Shapiro, Benson, 368
ShareholderValue, 141
Sharp Corporation, 858, 957
Sharrock, Robert, 102
Shell, 6, 328, 444, 605, 694, 815, 921, 924
Sheppard, Lord, 1033– 4
Shewhart, Walter, 201
Sieff, Lord, 257
Siemens, 40, 968
Siemens, Werner von, 969
Simon, Herbert, *Administrative Behaviour*, 366; 840
Singapore Institute of Management, 70
Skinner, Wickham, 369, 370, 373
Slater, Philip, 106
Slim, Field Marshall William, 100–1
Sloan, Alfred P, 39–41
small business management, 989–1000
SMH, 171
Smith, Adam, 1012
Smith, Adam, 362
Smith, Fred, 221
Smith, Robert, 568
SmithKline Beecham, 368
Sony, 409, 443, 575, 850
Southwest Airlines, 218
Stata, Ray, 692
Sterling, Jeffrey, 1006
Sternberg, Robert, *Intelligence Applied*, 474

Stewart, Rosemary, 72
Strangemore, Norman, 427
strategic management
  corporate value creation, 150–63
  mission, vision & strategy development, 139–49
  overview, 126–35
  role of creativity, 164–77
  role of project management, 178–93
Strategic Success Paradigm, 137
Sundridge Park Management Centre, 730
supply chain management, 385
Sykes, Richard, 297

Tanni, Akio, 46
TARP, 224
Tata Industries, 1020
Tate & Lyle, 1028
Taylor, Frederick Winslow, xi, xxx, 65, 66, 85, 242–4, 299, 362–3, 926, 954
Taylor, Martin, 470
teamworking, 685, 802–11
technology
  IT management, 653–63
  multimedia, 664–75
  overview, 643–52
Technology plc, 423
teleworking, 92–3
Tesco, 91, 591
Tetra Pak, 175
Texas Instruments, 405
Thank God It's Friday, 225
Thatcher, Margaret, 100
3M, 50, 681, 692, 695, 1044
Tiger, Lionel, *The Manufacture of Evil*, 1015
Time Manager International, 457
Time-Based Analysis, 533
Timmer, Jan, 46, 108, 111, 194
TNT Express, 198
Toshiba, 40,46
Total Quality, 205–13
Total Quality Management (TQM), xxv, 10, 25, 28, 128, 246, 247, 339, 376, 380, 416, 506, 633, 635, 1049
Total Shareholder Return (TSR), 151
Toyota, 6, 46, 52, 144, 444, 694, 836, 954
TQM, *see* Total Quality Management
trade unions, 259

Trafalgar House, 900
Trevor, Malcolm, 956
Truman, Harry, 99
TSB, 455, 461, 697, 699
TSR, *see* Total Shareholder Return
Tunnicliffe, Denis, 116
Turner, Paul, 699
Tzu, Hsun, *The Art of War*, 100

Unilever, 39, 368, 574, 581, 815, 910–11, 914, 928
Union Carbide, 1004
Union Pacific, 696
United Biscuits, 969
United Shareholders' Association, 973

Vallance, Sir Iain, 93
Value Based Management (VBM), 524
value chain, 385
value creation, 151–2
Varela, Francsico, 28
variance analysis, 530
VBM, *see* Value Based Management
Vincent, Sir Richard, 129
Viney, John, & Jones, Stephanie, *Career Turnaround*, 476
Virgin, 8
virtual organization, the, 87–94
vision, 351–2, 434
  role in strategy development, 139–49
Volcker, Paul, 555
Volkswagen, 612
Volvo, 730
Vries, Manfred Kets de, 102, 103

Wachem, Lo Van, 924
Wal-Mart, 570, 864
Wall Street Journal International, 1034
Wall Street, 965
Wallace, Ken, 423
Wang, 644
Waterman, Robert, 5, 34–8, 270
Watson, Thomas Jr, 1013
Welch, Jack, 6, 45, 102, 133
Wellcome, 330, 412, 413
Wendt, Henry, xxix
Western Electric, 197